JANE'S
FIGHTING SHIPS
OF WORLD WAR I

FOREWORD BY CAPTAIN JOHN MOORE RN

JANE'S
FIGHTING SHIPS
OF WORLD WAR I

FOREWORD BY CAPTAIN JOHN MOORE RN

STUDIO EDITIONS

LONDON

PUBLISHER'S NOTE

The editors and publishers of *Jane's Fighting Ships of World War I* wish to state that, in reproducing pictures and typematter from wartime editions of Jane's *All the World's Ships* they have done their best to ensure the retention of as much of the original detail of the material as possible. They are aware, however, that some of the original pictures are of poor quality, but since no others are available these have been included in the interests of completeness.

To provide readers with the most comprehensive record of the ships that fought in World War I the compiler of *Jane's Fighting Ships of World War I*, John Moore, has supplemented the 1919 material by extracting entries on significant ships from the 1914 edition.

Jane's Fighting Ships of World War I
Originally published by Jane's Publishing Company 1919

All rights reserved

This edition published 1990 by Studio Editions
an imprint of Studio Editions Ltd.
Princess House, 50 Eastcastle Street,
London W1N 7AP, England.

By arrangement with the proprietor

Copyright © for this edition Studio Editions, 1990

Printed and bound in Italy

ISBN 1 85170 378 0

CONTENTS.

ABBREVIATIONS, MAJORITY INTRODUCED
IN THIS EDITION

AA. . . . . Anti-Aircraft
C.M.B. . . . . . Coastal Motor Boat
D.A.M.S. . . Defensively Armed Merchant Ship
D.C. . . . . Depth Charge
Dir. Con. . . Director Controlled
M.L. . . . . Motor Launch
PV. . . . . Paravane
R.F. . . . . Range Finder
R.F.A. . . . . . . Royal Fleet Auxiliary
S.D.V. . . . . . . Submarine Decoy Vessel
SL. . . . . Searchlight
S/M . . . . Submarine

* Including Ships salved at Scapa Flow and those named for surrender in Peace Treaty.

FOREWORD

ONE hundred and one years separated the Battle of Malaga, an indecisive battering between the French and British fleets in 1704, and the Battle of Trafalgar. A study of the diagrams and paintings of these two encounters shows little difference in the form of the ships and the make-up of the fleets engaged in these two battles. One hundred years after Trafalgar the Japanese and Russian fleets met in the Battle of Tsushima. Any comparison between the pictures of these two actions is impossible for the Industrial Revolution had, by the beginning of the 20th Century, changed the shape of navies beyond recognition. Propulsion was by steam not sails, hulls were of steel not wood, guns were breech-loading rather than muzzle-loading with ranges in miles not hundreds of yards. In all this century of transformation there had been no major fleet action to guide peoples' minds in the search for effective ways of harnessing and directing this astounding increase in naval power – strategy and tactics lagged far behind the advances in material affairs.

By the time of Tsushima there was no excuse for any student of naval warfare being ignorant of the capabilities of the world's navies. In 1898 a British journalist published the first volume of what was to become the world's greatest naval reference book, accepted as a symbol of accuracy and authority from then until the present day. Fred T. Jane produced "All the World's Fighting Ships", a title which soon became "Jane's Fighting Ships" and, subsequently, just plain "Jane's". As is always the case, the more the book was used the more contributors it attracted and the wider became its coverage. Jane travelled widely in his search for information and by 1914, the starting point for this reprint, it had become, without breaching security or confidences, a necessary reference book amongst all concerned with naval affairs.

That 1914 edition is of enormous value in that it shows the diversity of naval thought, design and application which had taken place in Jane's life-time. Born during the American Civil War and dying in the second year of World War One, he had lived through an extraordinary period of upheaval in naval matters. Not only had fundamental changes in construction, propulsion and gunnery taken place but the first elements of what is now known as C3 (command, control and communications) were evident, and two totally new elements in the naval equation, the submarine and the aircraft, had appeared. Jane appreciated the importance of the flying machine and, with only half a dozen flights of more than a mile in the record books, he produced "All the World's Air-Ships (Flying Annual)" in 1909, the first comprehensive guide to the early aircraft.

The submarine had a longer history than the aeroplane but its potential was equally under-estimated by a high proportion of naval officers. During the American Civil War semi-submersibles were employed, some as monitors but, more importantly, some as attack craft. These last were armed with a charge mounted on a spar in the bows and rammed the target, an operation not dissimilar to Japanese suicide operations in World War Two. They had some successes but the true submersible with far greater potential was only a few years ahead. Intrepid inventors in France and Spain preceded the Irishman John Holland who built

his submarines in the USA using a petrol engine for surface propulsion and an electric motor when dived. A series of inventions and developments between 1880 and 1910 transformed the early submersibles into formidable, long-range boats. The diesel engine replaced the petrol and heavy oil engines, storage batteries were improved, a proper periscope was designed, wireless telegraphy was fitted, a gun was mounted on the casing and, most important of all, the torpedo was enabled to run a steady course under the control of its own gyroscope.

The whole concept was so much at variance with the centuries-old doctrine of the battle fleet being the hub of all naval power that it was left to a few enthusiasts, supported by a small group of imaginative senior officers, to devise tactics for submarine operations in war time. This blindness to the potential threat is even more incomprehensible when one sees in this book that there were well over 300 submarines in commission in 1914, a considerable proportion being of modern construction.

This lack of appreciation was evident in many other areas of naval affairs. In part this was due to the failure by most navies to provide a Naval Staff – what Winston Churchill later referred to as "a group of intelligent officers given time to think." What policies were made wer normally generated by senior officers relying on their experience. As this often stretched back to the days of sail and very few had any practical wartime experience, it is hardly surprising that the results were generally unsatisfactory. Arguments raged in public on the merits and demerits of various designs of ships but very rarely was there any informed discussion on such matters as the role of a navy, where it should fit into the country's overall strategy and what influence modern developments should have on the tactics and handling of a fleet.

Had any navy allowed their group of intelligent officers time to think, such matters as the increasing range of guns, the formidable effect of modern explosive shells, the danger from mines, the likelihood of a fleet being directed by wireless rather than signal flags, the necessity to provide means of fire control for the increasingly long ranged artillery, the threat from submarines and lastly, but of cardinal importance, the protection of merchant ships, might have been on their agenda.

This book gives a very clear picture of the manner in which naval affairs had been handled up to 1914, the results of this activity and the measures which had to be put in hand to redress the balance. At the outbreak of war on August 4 1914 there were eight major naval powers – Great Britain, Germany, USA, Japan, France, Italy, Austro-Hungary and Russia. Of these only Japan and Russia had any experience of major naval engagements in recent years, the battles of the Spanish-American war being somewhat static by comparison. The Battle of Tsushima in 1905 was the only action in which the opposing fleets had sufficient sea-room in which to manoeuvre.

Comparison of the fleets of the eight navies shows many similarities. The battleships were the centre of all plans and the change in the design of these huge ships which followed the arrival of HMS Dreadnought is 1906 is most marked. In that year both the USA and Germany laid down ships which incorporated certain of the major features of Dreadnought, in

particular the mounting of an increased battery of large calibre guns at the expense of the profusion of smaller weapons in previous designs. The aim was simple – to provide the heaviest broadside possible at the greatest range attainable. By 1909 the Japanese, Italians and Russians had followed suit with the French and Austrians a year behind – with building times of two and a half to three years the first three navies in the race had a clear numerical advantage. By the time the first French battleship to the new design was laid down, the USA had completed four, Germany five and Great Britain twelve. The race was on.

The second improvement which was included in HMS Dreadnought's design was the use of steam turbines in place of reciprocating machinery. This more efficient arrangement provided an increase of speed of some three knots in the battleships and nine knots in the battle-cruisers and both the USA and Germany were quick to follow.

Thus by the start of World War One there were 83 of this new type of ship in commission world-wide – 31 in Great Britain, 18 in Germany, 10 in the USA and France, 5 in Japan, 4 in Italy, 3 in Austria-Hungary and 2 in Russia. To provide the backing considered necessary for such battle-fleets, large squadrons of cruisers and numerous destroyer flotillas had been built. These are all laid out in the back of this book but extraordinary gaps exist in all the navies of 1914 – the war-time building and acquisition programmes of minesweepers point a need which was not appreciated pre-war; the range of destroyers and what few other escorts there were was inadequate for long distance convoy escort and this was a design failure which was to persist well on into World War Two. These are the most evident deficiences at a time when the range and effectiveness of submarines were increasing rapidly. Fortunately for the Allies, the German Naval Staff had been slow to appreciate the potential of their underwater fleet otherwise the crisis of 1917 might not have been surmounted by the Allied navies and the war would have been lost.

The 1919 edition illustrates the first steps towards the great carrier battles of the Pacific war of 1942-45. The three true aircraft carries Argus, Furious and Vindictive of the Royal Navy were adaptations while HMS Hermes, laid down in January 1918, was the first of this type to be designed from the keel up. Learning had been swift, frequently painful but naval warfare would never be the same again.

What followed World War One showed only too clearly how little had been learned by the politicians concerning naval affairs. The Washington Naval Conference of 1921-22 concerned itself chiefly with the limitation of battle-ship building. Where submarines were concerned, there was an unfruitful outcry to have them outlawed – an unlikely approach to those countries which had appreciated their value. As for aircraft-carriers, they were classified as auxiliaries. This conference and its successors were of no value in achieving their objectives because they concentrated on the wrong things. between the wars many naval officers were laggardly in appreciating the lessons of 1914-18 but one had to search diligently to find any politicians who gave the matter more than a passing thought. Had Fred T. Jane survived, his comments would have been of the greatest interest.

John Moore

PREFACE.

PREFACE.

WORK on the present Edition of "FIGHTING SHIPS" was begun in December, 1918, and was pushed on without intermission during the succeeding months. The results now presented, although a little delayed, will, we feel sure, be satisfactory to our readers.

The labour incurred in preparing this Edition has been exceptionally heavy; we doubt if any issue of our Annual has occasioned so much anxiety. The Editors have had to deal with large masses of information, withheld from publication by the belligerent Naval Powers since 1914. They have also had to investigate the demobilisation of the War Fleets to a peace footing. The indeterminate state of the late Enemy Navies, and the chaotic conditions of the Russian Fleet, have presented very perplexing problems.

Dealing, as is our custom, with the various sections of this book in sequence, we offer the following comments on the present Edition.

GLOSSARY.

The glossary of technical terms was overhauled thoroughly last year, and brought up-to-date. This year, our lists of foreign naval expressions have been completed by the addition of French and Swedish terms.

BRITISH NAVY.

Various new Maps have been added, and the Gunnery Tables have been renovated by Captain R V. Walling, R. G. A. (retired). Mr. E. L. King has kindly allowed us to make use of his " Silhouettes of Effective British Warships." These drawings depart very largely from the usual scale and form of " FIGHTING SHIPS " Silhouettes. We should be glad to have our readers' opinions, whether Mr. King's form of drawings should be generally adopted for all Navy sections. The British Ship Pages have been entirely renovated this year. Plans and illustrations of British Warship types have been prepared on a lavish scale. Since the signing of the Armistice, the Admiralty have been able to release much information which, undoubtedly, has raised the standard of accuracy in British Warship data. All textual details are founded on the latest and most reliable information that can be secured. One of the most interesting features added is Aircraft recognition views, presenting British Warships from a new angle of vision. We tender our grateful thanks to British Shipbuilders, for the very large amount of information they have kindly placed at our disposal. Exigencies of space have prevented us from using all the excellent photographs furnished to us by British Shipbuilders. The views which we could not use have been presented to the Imperial War Museum, where they will form a permanent record of the magnificent output of British shipyards during the war.

UNITED STATES.

This section has been revised from the latest official data, placed at our disposal by the U.S. Naval Headquarters in London. We are happy to say that we have, once more, the valuable services of Lieut. Henry Reuterdahl, U.S. N.R.F., the distinguished naval artist and critic. It is largely through his kind assistance that we are able to publish so many new and up-to-date illustrations of U.S. Warships.

JAPAN.

The Navy Department, Tokyo, has once again verified all the technical details of this section. A considerable number of Japanese Minelayers and Fleet Auxiliaries, hitherto unheard of, have been added. Some very valuable notes, received shortly before publication, are given on an Addenda page.

FRANCE.

During his attendance at the Versailles Peace Conference, Capt. R. V. Walling, R.G.A., approached Mons. Leygues (the Minister of Marine) and Admiral le Bon (then Chief of Staff) on our behalf, with a view to the French Navy Section being officially revised. M. Leygues and Admiral le Bon readily assented to the proposals made, and authoritative details of French warships are now given. We may add that very cordial relations have been established between " FIGHTING SHIPS " and Capitane le Marquis de Balincourt, Editor of our esteemed contemporary " Flottes de Combat." We are indebted to Capitane le Marquis de Balincourt for a large series of very useful notes, dealing with the World's Navies.

ITALY.

Pressure of work again prevents Mr. Charles de Grave Sells from preparing his Engineering Article, but it was largely through his kind interest that we secured an official revision of our Italian Navy Section. Attention is called to that extraordinary creation, the Monitor *Faa' de Bruno*—a vessel which approaches the future naval "hippopotami," as defined by Admiral of the Fleet, Lord Fisher of Kilverstone.

MINOR NAVIES.

During the war, the edicts of the Allied Censors debarred us from paying too close attention to the Allied Navies. The barriers erected by our late Enemies also made it very difficult—at times—to secure information regarding their Fleets. Attention was therefore concentrated on the field of the Neutral Navies and these were put in a satisfactory condition. This year the Minor Navies have not been neglected, but have been checked from the latest official information. Among the new Navy Sections will be found the Belgian and Esthonian Navies. Details were specially prepared for us by the Naval Staff at Reval at the request of Mr. John Piitka, the Marine Agent of Estonia in London. The Hellenic Naval Section has been revised by command of Admiral Condouriotis, the Minister of Marine. The Chinese and Siamese pages, although they occupy but a small space, have given a considerable amount of trouble during the past four years. It was found extremely difficult to secure reliable details of these Navies. Thanks to the kindness of Correspondents, they have both been brought up-to-date.

LATE ENEMY AND RUSSIAN NAVIES.

The treatment of these Sections has been the subject of much anxious thought. No steps have yet been taken to dispose of the German ships salved at Scapa Flow. Although the future establishment of the German Navy is strictly laid down in the Peace Treaty, Germany has (as yet) taken no steps to reduce her Navy to the status required by the Allies. The Austrian Fleet, the Hungarian Danube Flotilla, the Bulgarian and Turkish Fleets are all interned under Allied and U.S. supervision. The disposal of the warships belonging to these Powers is still a matter of pure speculation. The Russian Fleet is rent between contending factions, and various units of the Russian Navy have been temporarily added to the Allied Navies. All these Navies have been relegated to the end of this Edition, on the ground that they cannot be considered as effective fighting forces at the present moment.

SPECIAL ARTICLE.

Five years have elapsed since Illustrations of British Warships have been allowed to appear in "FIGHTING SHIPS." British Illustrations have been re-instated, but H.M. Ships appear in so altered a guise, compared with their 1914 build, that some lay and foreign readers may be perplexed by the changes carried out between 1914 and 1919. A short and non-technical article has been prepared by the Editors, dealing with the War's influence on British Naval Construction. It consists largely of notes, generally covering all British Warship types, which could not be accommodated in the British Navy section without an undue degree of repetition.

WAR LOSS SECTION.

Mr. Francis E. McMurtrie has prepared a Final Summary of the naval casualties of the late War, based on official and authoritative information. The lists given afford the most complete compendium of information on this subject ever presented; they are the outcome of the perseverance and care of Mr. McMurtrie in collecting information. The long tables detailing the circumstances and dates of destruction of German Submarines will be scanned with interest.

CONCLUSION.

It may be finally said that, in this Edition, there is only one page which was transferred in unaltered form from 1918 "FIGHTING SHIPS." Particulars of the world's warships now given are based on highly reliable information. The number of illustrations added or renovated this year runs to nearly eight hundred.

Shortly before his lamented death, the late Mr. Fred T. Jane made arrangements that this annual should be edited in conjunction by Dr. Oscar Parkes and Mr. Maurice Prendergast.

These plans have been held in abeyance. Dr. Oscar Parkes joined H.M. Navy in 1916, as Surgeon-Lieutenant. Being stationed in the Mediterranean, he was unable to give the degree of assistance planned by the late Mr Jane. Mr. Maurice Prendergast therefore carried on the work of Editorship up to the date of the Armistice. Surgeon-Lieut. Oscar Parkes, O.B.E., R.N. has now joined Mr. Prendergast as Joint Editor, and is largely responsible for the splendid series of British Warship Photographs added to this Edition. To them, our Editors, we offer our cordial thanks for their labours in preparing our present Edition—an Edition which we know has been anxiously awaited by our patrons. Under the control of Surgeon-Lieut. Parkes, R.N. and Mr. Prendergast —and through the assistance of our innumerable correspondents throughout the world — future Editions of " FIGHTING SHIPS " will not fall below the high standard of the Edition we now issue.

The copyright of all Plans, Silhouettes and Sketches appearing in this book is strictly reserved. Photographs may not be reproduced without express permission. We are compelled to lay emphasis on this, on account of the increasing infringements by foreign naval books and periodicals.

THE PUBLISHERS.

"OVERY HOUSE," 100, SOUTHWARK STREET, LONDON, S.E. 1.

GLOSSARY OF TECHNICAL TERMS.

ENGLISH.	GERMAN.	FRENCH.	ITALIAN.	RUSSIAN.	SPANISH.	SWEDISH.	DUTCH.
1 Abaft	1 Achtern (adv) hinter (prep); achterlicher als quer ab (abaft the beam)	1 Sur l'arrière	1 A poppa	1 Korma	1 A popa	1 Akterligt	1 Achterlijker dan dwars
2 Abeam	2 dwars ab, quer ab	2 Par le travers	2 Per traverso	2 Poperek	2 Por el través	2 Tvärs ut /direction/	2 Dwars
3 Above water	3 Ober wasser	3 Au dessus de l'eau	3 Sopracqua	3 Nadvodnie	3 Sobre el agua	3 Ofvervattens	3 Boven water
4 Accommodation hulk	4 Wohnschiff	4 Caserne flottant; 4 Ponton	4 Pontone d'accomodamento		4 Ponton de comodidad	4 Logementsfartyg	4 Accomodatie legger
5 Ahead	5 Vorwärts	5 Avant	5 A prora (davanti)	5 Vpered	5 A proa	5 Förut /direction/. Framat /movement/	5 Vooruit
6 Air lock	6 Luftverschluss (?)	6 Ecluse de chauffe/sas	6 Serratura d'aria		6 Cerradura de aire	6 Luftsluss	
7 Amidships	7 Mittschiffs	7 Au milieu	7 Al centro	7 Vseredinu	7 Al centro	7 Midskepps	7 Midscheeps
8 Ammunition ship	8 Munitionsschiff	8 Porte-munitions	8 Nave di munizioni	8 Soodno s ammunicziei; boevimi pripasami	8 Buque de municiónes	8 Ammunitionsfartyg	8 Ammunitie schip
9 Anti-aircraft (gun)	9 Fliegerabwehrgeschütz kanone (abbrev. Flak)	9 Canon contre-aeriens	9 Cannone anti-aeroplani	9 Protivo-aeroplanniya	9 Cañon antiaeroplanos	9 Luftförsvarskanon /generally "Luftkanon"/	9 Anti-luchtschip (kanon)
10 A.P. (projectile)	10 Panzersprenggranate	10 Projectil de rupture	10 Proiettile	10 Probivanshii-bronu	10 Proyectil	10 Halvpansargranat	
11 Armament	11 Armierung		11 Armamento	11 Vo-oroojenie	11 Armamento	11 Bestyckning	11 Bewapening
12 Armed liner, or Auxiliary cruiser	12 Hilfskreuzer	12 Croiseur auxiliaire	12 Nave armata/ incrociatore ausilare	12 Vo-oroojennii passajirskii-parokhod; Vspomogatelnii krieser	12 Buque armado/o crucero auxiliar	12 Hjälpkryssare	12 Gewapende lyner of hulp kruiser
13 Armour	13 Panzer	13 Cuirasse	13 Corazzato	13 Bronia	13 Coraza Blindage	13 Pansar	13 Pantser
14 Armoured cruiser	14 Panzerkreuzer	14 Croiseur cuirassé	14 Incrociatore corazzati	14 Bronenosnii-kreiser	14 Crucero acorazado	14 Pansarkryssare	14 Gepantserde Kruiser
15 Astern	15 Rückwärts	15 Arrière	15 A poppa	15 Nazad	15 A popa	15 Back	15 Achteruit
16 Athwartship	16 dwarsschiffs	16 Par le travers (d'un navire)	16 Atraverso il bastimento	16 Soodno-na-traverze	16 Por el través del buque	16 Tvärskepps	
17 Awash	17 im überflüten Zustand		17 A flor d'acqua	17 Vroven-s-vodoi	17 A flor de agua	17 I övervattensläge	
18 Barbettes	18 Barbetten	18 Barbettes	18 Barbette	18 Barbeti	18 Torres-barbetas	18 Barbettorn	18 Barbette
19 Bases (of barbettes)	19 Trunk (Schacht)	19 Au dessous la tourelle	19 Piattoforme	19 Vnizu	19 Plataformas	19 Fasta torn	19 Torenwal
20 Battery	20 Batterie	20 Batterie	20 Batteria	20 Battereya	20 Bateria	20 Batteri	20 Batterij
21 Battle-cruiser	21 Panzerkreuzer	21 Cuirassé rapide. 21 Croiseur de bataille.	21 Incrociatore di battaglia	21 Boevoi kreiser	21 Crucero de batalla	21 Slagkryssare	21 Slag kruiser
22 Battleship	22 Linienschiff	22 Cuirassé d'escadre	22 Nave da battaglia	22 Bronenosets	22 Acorazado	22 Slagskepp	22 Slagschip
23 Beam	23 Breite	23 Largeur	23 Larghezza	23 Shirina	23 Manga	23 Bredd	23 Breedte
24 Before	24 vorn; vor (prep.) vorlicher als quer ab (before the beam)	24 Avant.	24 Avanti	24 Pered; pred	24 A proa	24 Förut	24 Voor
25 Belt	25 Gürtel	25 Ceinture	25 Cintura	25 Poyass	25 Faja	25 Gördelpansar	25 Gordel
26 Bilge k.	26 Schlingerkiel	26 Quille de roulis	26 Chiglia di rollio	26 Bokovoi keel	26 Quilla de pantoque	26 Slingerköl	26 Kimkiel
27 Binnacle	27 Kompassgehäuse	27 Boussole	27 Abitacolo		27 Bitácora	27 Nakterhus	27 Nachthuis

JAPANESE (pronounce as French).

Term	Romanization	No.	Japanese
Fighting tops	Sento-Shorou	79	戰鬪檣樓
Ends	Hashi	77	両端
Draught	Kissui	70	吃水
Displacement	Hai-sui-Tonsu	65	排水噸數
Destroyer	Kuchiku-lei	62	驅逐艦
Deck	Kanpan	51	甲板
Cruiser	Junyo-Kan	50	巡洋艦
C. T. (Conning tower)	Shireito	46	司令塔
Complement	Teiin	45	定員
Coal	Shekitan	41	石炭
c/m (Centimetre)		38	センチメートー
Casemates	Kuku-Hoddi	36	穹窖砲臺
Capacity	Yorio	34	容量
Bunkers	Shekitanko	33	石炭庫
Bulkheads	Kakukeki	32	隔壁
Bridge	Kankio	29	艦橋
Boilers	Kikan	31	汽罐
Bow	Kanshu	25	艦首
Belt	Kotai	23	甲帶
Beam	Haba	22	巾
Battleship	Sento-Kan	20	戰鬪艦
Battery	Hoddi	19	砲臺
Bases (of Barbettes, etc.)	Hobo-no-Kibu	18	砲塔の基部
Barbettes	Roloto	15	露砲塔
Astern	Tomo	14	艦後
Armoured Cruiser	Koletsu-Junyo Kan	13	甲鐵巡洋艦
Armour	Kotetsu	7	甲鐵
Amidships	Chuo	5	中央
Ahead	Onote		艦前
Above water		3	水上

ENGLISH.	GERMAN.	FRENCH.	ITALIAN.	RUSSIAN.	SPANISH.	SWEDISH.	DUTCH.
28 B.L. (gun)	28 Hinterlader	28 Canon culasse	28 Cannone a retrocarica	28 Zaryajansheesyas kazennoi chasti	28 Cañón de retrocarga	28 Bakladdningskanon	
29 Boilers	29 Kessel	29 Generateurs	29 Caldaie	29 Kotli	29 Calderas	29 Angpannor	2 Ketels
30 Boom (port defence)	30 Hafensperre	30 Estacade	30 Asta da bome (per difesa portuale)		30 Cadena de troncos (para defensa de puerto)	30 Bomstängsel	30 Sluitboom
31 Bow	31 Bug	31 Avant	31 Prora	31 Noss	31 Proa	31 Bog	31 Boeg
32 Bridge	32 Kommando-Brücke	32 Pont	32 Ponte di comando	32 Most	32 Puente	32 Brygga	32 Brug
33 Bulkheads	33 Schötten	33 Traverses	33 Paratie	33 Pereborki	33 Manparos	33 Skott	33 Schot
34 Bunker (coal)	34 Kohlenbunker	34 Soute à charbon	34 Carbone per carboniere	34 Oogolnaya yama. To bunker, groozitsya ooglem	34 Carbón de las carboneras	34 Kolboxar	34 Bunker (Kolen)
35 Camouflage	35 Unsichtbarmalen	35 Camouflage	35 Camuffamento or "Camouflage"	35 Iskoostvennoe prikpitie	35 "Camouflage"	35 Maskering	35 Identiteits verberging
36 Capacity	36 Capacität	36 Enposant de charge	36 Capacita	36 Poinyestchenie	36 Capacidad	36 Kapacitet	36 Vermogen
37 Capstan	37 Ankerspill, Ankerwinde	37 Cabestan	37 Argano		37 Cabrestante	37 Ankarspel, Spel	37 Spil
38 Casemates	38 Casematten	38 Casemates	38 Casamette	38 Kazemat	38 Casamatas	38 Kasemater	38 Kazemat
39 Centre-, (keel-) line	39 Kiellinie	39 Quille centrale/mediane	39 Paramezzale centrale	39 Srednyaya liniya; diametralnaya ploskost	39 Sobrequilla central	39 Midskeppslinje	39 Midden (kiel) lijn
40 Chart house	40 Kartenhaus	40 Sala nautica	40 Sala nautica	40 Shtoormanskaya roobka	40 Caseta de derrota	40 Styrhytt	40 Kaarthuis
41 Coal	41 Kohlenvorrat	41 Charbon	41 Carbone	41 Ugol	41 Carbon	41 Kol	41 Steenkolen
42 Coast defence ship	42 Küstenpanzerschiff	42 Garde-côtes	42 Nave per difesa della costa	42 Soodno beregovoi oboroni	42 Buque para defensa de costas	42 Kustförsvarsfartyg	42 Kust verdedigings schip
43 Coastguard vessel	43 Küstenschutzschiff	43 Navire garde-côtes	43 Nave guarda costas	43 Soodno beregovoi okhrani	43 Buque guarda costa	43 Kustbevakningsfartyg	43 Kust bewakings schip
44 Compass	44 Kompass		44 Bussola		44 Brújula	44 Kompass	44 Kompass
45 Complement	45 Besatzung	45 Équipage	45 Equipaggio	45 Kompleki	45 Dotacion	45 Besättning	45 Bemanning
46 C.T. (conning tower)	46 Kommando Turm	46 Block-haus (C.T.)	46 Torre di comando	46 Roolevaia bashnia	46 Torre de mando	46 Stridstorn	46 Commando-toren
47 Crane	47 Kran	47 Grue	47 Grua	47 Kran	47 Grua	47 Kran	47 Kraan
48 "Creep" (anti-submarine)	48 U–drache (?)	48 Gerbe sousmarine	48 "Serpeggiare" (anti-sommergibile)	48 Tral	48 Arrastramiento (anti-submarino)		
49 Crow's nest	49 Krähennest	49 Nid de pie	49 Gabbia di crocetta		49 Garita para el vijía	49 Utkikskorg	49 Kraaie nest
50 Cruiser	50 Kreuzer	50 Croiseur	50 Incrociatore	50 Kreiser	50 Crucero	50 Kryssare	50 Kruiser
51 Deck	51 Deck	51 Pont	51 Ponte	51 Palooba	51 Cubierta	51 Däck	51 Dek
52 Depôt ship	52 Stammschiff, Mutterschiff	52 Soutien/Convoyeur de	52 Nave di deposito/Nave appoggio	52 Soodno sklad; soodno baza	52 Buque de depósito	52 Depotfartyg	52 Depot schips
53 ,, (torpedo craft)	53 ,, (für Torpedofahrzeuge)	53 ,, (Torpilleurs).	53 ,, Siluranti		53 ,, (torpederos)	53 ,, för torpedbåtar	53 Depot (torpedo vaartuig)
54 ,, (destroyers)	54 ,, (,, Zerstörer)	54 ,, (Destroyers).	54 ,, Cacciatorpediniere	54 Soodno-matka dlya kontr-minonosetzev	54 ,, (cazatorpederos)	54 ,, ,, jagare	54 ,, (torpedo jagers)

JAPANESE. (pronounce as French.)

Term	Romanization	No.	Japanese
Water line	Suihen	216	水線
Upper deck	Johanpan	213	上甲板
Turrets	Yihoto	212	圍砲塔
Trials	Shi Unten (Kohoromi Unten)	206	試運轉
Tons		194	噸
Torpedo tubes	Suirai Hatsushahuan	193	水雷發射管
Torpedo boat	Suirai-Tei	192	水雷艇
Torpedo	Suirai	191	水雷
Submerged	Suichu	182	水中
Submarine	Shen-sui	180	潛水
Stern	Kanbi	179	艦尾
Starboard (side)	Ugen	178	右舷
Speed	Sokuryoku	176	速力
Shields	Tate	173	楯
Screens	Kukusho	167	スクルー
Ram	Shoto	155	撞頭
Protection to vitals	Yobu-Bogio	150	要部防禦
Port (side)	Sagen	147	左舷
Normal displacement	Kilei	135	規定
m/m (Millimetre)			ミリメートー
M. (Metre)			メートー
Masts	Hobashira	123	檣
Main (-deck)	Chukan-pan	121	中甲板
Machinery		119	機械
Lower (-deck)	Gekan-pan	118	下甲板
Liquid fuel	Yakitai-Nenrio	117	液体燃料
L. (Length)	Nagasa	113	長
Kts. (Knots)		112	節
Hoods	Hogai	101	砲蓋
Guns	Hou	95	砲
Funnels	Yentotsu or Entotsu	92	烟突

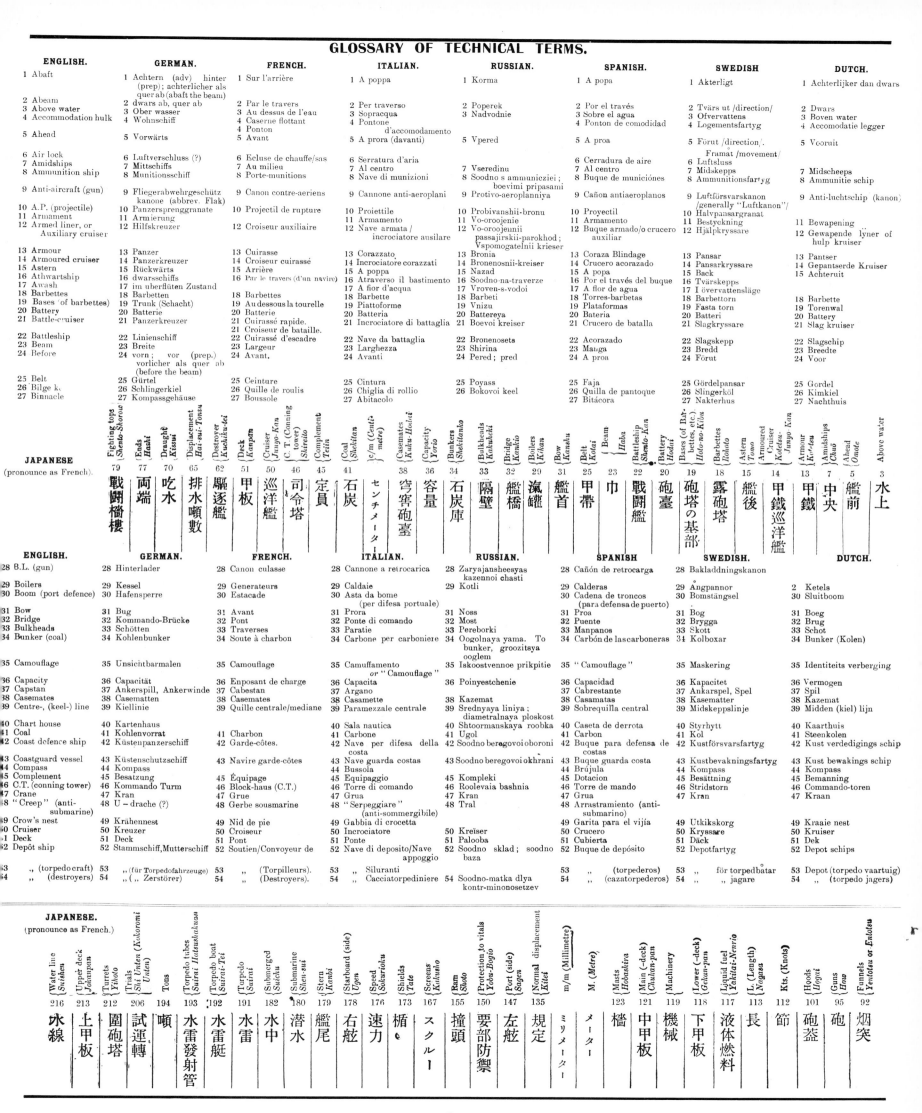

ENGLISH.	GERMAN.	FRENCH.	ITALIAN.	RUSSIAN.	SPANISH.	SWEDISH.	DUTCH.
55 Depôt ship (T.B.)	55 Stammschiff (für Torpedoboote)	55 Soutien de (Torpilleurs)	55 Nave appoggio (torpedine)		55 Buque de dépósito (torpederos)	55 Depotfartyg för torpedbåtar	55 Depôt (T.B.)
56 ,, (M.L.)	56 ,, (,, Motorboote)	56 ,, (Vedettes).	56 ,, (moto-scafo)		56 ,, (lancha de motor)	56 ,, ,, motorbåtar	56 ,, (M.L.)
57 ,, (submarines)	57 Mutterschiff (für Unterseeboote)	57 ,, (Sous-marins).	57 ,, (sommergibili)	57 Soodno-matka dlya podvodnikh lodok	57 ,, (submarinos)	57 ,, förundervattensbåtar	57 ,, (onderseeërs)
58 Depression (of guns)	58 Senkung	58 Angle negatif de pointage	58 Depressione (cannone)	58 Oogol snijeniya	58 Puntería baja (de las piezas)	58 Dumpning	
59 Depth charge	59 Wasserbombe	59 Charge de fond	59 Carica di fondo (esplosivo)	59 Bomba dlya vzriva pod vodoi	59 Carga de fondo (explosiva)	59 Vattenbomb	59 Diepte lading
60 Derrick	60 Ladebaum	60 Mât de charge	60 Albero da carico	60 Nod-emnaya strela	60 Pescante de carga	60 Bom	60 Laadboom
61 Despatch vessel	61 Aviso	61 Aviso	61 Nave per dispacci	61 Posilnoe soodno	61 Buque de aviso	61 Avisofartyg	61 Koerier schip
62 Destroyer	62 Zerstörer	62 Contre-torpilleur	62 Caccia-torpediniere	62 Kontr-minonosets	62 Cazatorpederos	62 Jagare	62 Torpedobootjager
63 Diesel engine	63 Dieselmaschine, Ölmaschine, Olmotor	63 Moteur Diesel	63 Macchina " Diesel "	63 Dizel-motor	63 Máquina " Diesel "	63 Dieselmotor	63 Diesel machine
64 Dirigible	64 Lenkbares Luftschiff	64 Dirigeable.	64 Dirigibile	64 Derijabl	64 Dirigible	64 Luftskepp	64 Bestuurbare
65 Displacement	65 Deplacement	65 Déplacement	65 Dislocamento	65 Vodoizmiestchenie	65 Desplazamiento	65 Deplacement	65 Waterverplaatsing
66 Division (of fleet)	66 Division	66 Division	66 Divisione (di una flotta)	66 Deviziya; devizion	66 División (de una flota)	66 Division	66 Eskader
67 Dock (floating)	67 Schwimmdock	67 Dock (flottant).	67 Bacino (galleggianto)	67 Dok (plavoochii)	67 Dique flotante	67 Flytdocka	67 Dok (drijvend)
68 ,, (graving)	68 Trockendock	68 Cale sèche	68 Bacino (di carenaggio)	68 Dok (sookhoi)	68 Dique seco	68 Torrdocka	68 ,, (droog)
69 Dockyard (D.Y.)	69 Werft	69 Arsenal	69 Arsenale	69 Shipyard, Verv.	69 Arsenal	69 Varv	69 ,, werf
70 Draught (mean)	70 mittlerer Tiefgang	70 Tirant d'eau	70 Immersione media		70 Calado medio	70 Djupgående, medel—	70 Diepang (gemiddeld)
71 ,, (max.)	71 grösster Tiefgang	71 Tirant d'eau maximum	71 Immersione massima		71 Calado máximo	71 ,, maximi—	71 ,, (grootste)
72 Dreadnought	72 Dreadnought	72 Dreadnought	72 Dreadnought	72 Drednaoot	72 Dreadnought	72 Dreadnought	
73 Drifter	73 Drifter, Dampflogger	73 Chalutier	73 Nave di pesca (" Drifter ")	73 Maloe soodno	73 Vapor de pesca ("Drifter")		73 Smak
74 Echelon	74 Staffellinie	74 Echelon. 74 En quinconce.	74 Linea in " Echelon "	74 Eshelon	74 Linea en escalones	74 Flankformering	
75 " Electric drive "	75 elektrische Antrieb	75 Commande electrique	75 Comando elettrico		75 Impulsión electrica	75 Elektrisk drift	
76 Elevation (of guns)	76 Höhewichtung,Elevation	76 Angle de pointage positif	76 Elevazione (cannone)	76 Oogol vozvosheniya	76 Elevación (tiro de cañón)	76 Elevation	
77 Ends	77 Ends	77 Extrémités	77 Estremita	77 Krai	77 Extremos	77 Stävar	77 Einden
78 Examination Vessel	78 Untersuchungschiff	78 Arraisonneur	78 Nave d'ispezione		78 Buque de inspección	78 Undersökningsfartyg	78 Onderzoekings schip
79 Fighting tops	79 Marsen	79 Hunes	79 Coffe militari	79 Poostchechnii mars	79 Cofas militares	79 Stridsmärsar	79 Gevechtsmars
80 Fire Control	80 Feuerleitung	80 Direction de tir	80 Controllo del tiro	80 Kontrol ognya	80 Regulator de tiro	80 Eldledning	80 Controle by het vuren
81 ,, ,, top	81 Artilleriestand im Topp	81 Hune télémètrique.	81 ,, ,, (coffa)		81 ,, ,, (cofa)	81 Eldledningsmärs	
82 Fire director	82 Zentralabfeuerung	82 Direction du feu	82 Direttore de tiro	82 Mekhanizm oopot reblyaemii pri strelbl zalpom	82 Director de tiro	82 Centralavfyining	
83 Fisheries vessel	83 Fischerieschutzboot	83 Garde-pêche. 84 Navire amiral	83 Nave peschiera	83 Maloe voennoe soodno dlya ohhrani ribnikh promislov	83 Buque de pesquería	83 Fiskeri-inspektionsfartyg	83 Controle schip (visschery)
84 Flagship	84 Flaggschiff		84 Nave ammiraglia	84 Flagmanskii korabl	84 Buque almirante	84 Flaggskepp	84 Vlagschip
85 Fleet	85 Flotte	85 Flotte.	85 Flotta		85 Flota	85 Flotta	85 Vloot
86 Flotilla	86 Flotille	86 Flotille.	86 Flottiglia	86 Flotiliya	86 Esquadrilla	86 Flottilj	86 Flotilje
87 ,, leader	87 Führerschiff	87 Conducteur de flotille.	87 Nave capofilo	87 Soodno vedooshii flotiliu	87 Buque cabo de fila	87 Flottiljchefsfartyg	87 ,, leider
88 Forecastle	88 Back	88 Gaillard d'avant.	86 Castello di prua	88 Bak	88 Castillo	88 Back	88 Logies
89 Foremast	89 Fockmast	89 Mât de nusaine	89 Albero di trinchetto		89 Palo trinquete	89 Fockmast, Förligmast	89 Fokkemast
90 Freeboard	90 Freibord	90 Franc-bord	90 Bordo libero	90 Zapas plavoochesti soodna	90 Obra muerta	90 Fribord	90 Uitwatering
91 Full load displ't	91 Gesamte Wasserverdrängung	91 Deplacement en plein charge	91 Carico completo (dislocamento)	91 Vodvizmeshenie v polnom groozoo	91 Cargamento completo (desplazamiento)	91 Deplacement, fullt rustad	91 Volle lading merk
92 Funnels	92 Schornsteine	92 Cheminées	92 Fumaioli	92 Trubi	92 Chimeneas	92 Skorstenar	92 Schoorsteen
93 Fuze	93 Zünder	93 Amorce	93 Spoletta	93 Vzrivatel	93 Espoleta	93 Tändrör	93 Grut
94 Gunboat	94 Kanonenboot	94 Cannonière	94 Cannoniera	94 Kanonerskaya lodka	94 Lancha cañonera	94 Kanonbåt	94 Kanonneerboot
95 Guns	95 Geschütze	95 Artillerie	95 Cannoni	95 Orudiia	95 Cañones	95 Kanoner	95 Kanonnen
96 Gyroscopic compass	96 Kreiselkompass	96 Compas gyroscopique	96 Busola giroscopica	96 Jiroskop	96 Brújula giroscópica	96 Gyroskopkompass	96 Gyroskoop kompas
97 Hawse	97 Klüse	97 Crussiere	97 " Hawse " (apertura per la catena dell 'ancora)	97 Kluz	97 Escobén	97 Klys	97 Slang
98 H.E.(bursting charge	98 Sprengladung	98 Haut explosif	98 Alto esplosivo	98 Silno-vzrivchatii	98 Fuerte explosivo	98 Sprängladdning	
99 H.E. (shell)	99 Sprenggeschoss, Sprenggranate	99 Obu à grande capacité	99 Granata di alto esplosivo	99 Silno-vzrivchatii snaryad	99 Granada de fuerte explosivo	99 Spränggranat	
100 Hoist (ammunition)	100 Munitionsaufzug	100 Monte-charges.	100 Elevatore di munizioni	100 Podem (in full, podemnaya mashina)	100 Ascensor para municiónes	100 Ammunitionshiss	100 Hysche (ammunitie)
101 Hoods	101 Kuppel	101 Carapaces	101 Scudi	101 Pokrishki	101 Carapachos	101 Kåpor	101 Pantserkoepel
102 " Horns " (of mine)	102 Kontakte, Fühlhörner (?)	102 Antennes	102 Corna (di una mina)		102 Conteras (de una mina)	102 Horn	102 " Hoorns " (van mijn
103 Hospital ship	103 Hospitalschiff, Lazarettschiff	103 Navire-hôpital	103 Nave ospedale	103 Gospitalnoe soodno	103 Buque-hospital	103 Lasarettsfartyg	103 Hospitaal schip
104 Hull	104 Rumpf	104 Coque	104 Scafo	104 Korpoos; koozov soodna	104 Casco	104 Skrov	104 Hol
105 Hulk	105 Hulk	105 Ponton	105 Pontone	105 Blokshiv	105 Pontón	105 Pråm	105 Legger
106 Hydroplane (boat)	106 Gleitboot	106 Hydroplane (bateau)	106 Idroplano (battello)	106 gidroplane	106 Hidroplane (buque)	106 Hydroplan	
107 ,, (in subs.)	107 Tiefenruder					107 Djuproder	
108 Ice-breaker	108 Eisbrecher	108 Brise-glace.	108 Rompighiaccio	108 Ledokol	108 Rompehielos	108 Isbrytare	108 Ysbreeker
109 Jumping wire	109 Minenabweiser, Minendraht	109 Orin.	109 Salto del filo (?)		109 Paso del alambre	109 Avledarewire	
110 Kite-balloon	110 Drache	110 Saucisse /" Captif "	110 Pallone a cervo-volante	110 Zmeikovii aerostat	110 Globo-cometa cautivo	110 Ballong	110 Kabel ballon
111 Kite-balloon ship	111 Drachenschiff	111 Navire porte ballon captif	111 ,, id (nave d'appoggio)	111 Soodno-matkadlya zmeikovikh aerostatov	111 ,, (buque portador)	111 Ballongfartyg	111 ,, ,, schip
112 Kts. (Knots)	112 See-meilen (or knotten)	112 Noeuds	112 Nodi	112 Uzell	112 Millas	112 Knop	112 Knoopen (mylen)
113 Length (*p.p*)	113 Länge zwischen den Perpendikeln	113 Longueur (entre perpendiculaires)	113 Lunghezza tra le perpendicolari		113 Eslora entre perpendiculares	113 Längd mellan perpendiklarne	113 Lengte (p.p)
114 ,, (*w.l.*)	114 Länge auf der Wasserlinie (?)	114 ,, (à la flottaison)	114 Lunghezza alla linea di carico		114 Eslora en la linen de ague, máxima	114 ,, i vattenlinjen	114 ,, (w.l.)
115 ,, (*o.a.*)	115 Länge uber alles	115 ,, (totale)	115 Lunghezza massima		115 Eslora de fuera a fuera de miembros	115 ,, överallt	115 ,, (grooste)
116 Light cruiser	116 kleiner Kreuzer	116 Croiseur léger	116 Incrociatore leggiera	116 Legdii kreiser	116 Crucero ligero	116 Lätt kryssare	
117 Liquid Fuel	117 Heizoil	117 Combustile liquide	117 Combustibile liquido	117 Jhidkoe toplivo	117 Combustibele liquido	117 Brännolja	117 Vloeibare brandstof
118 Lower deck	118 Zwischen-deck	118 Faux pont	118 Ponte inferiore	118 Nijhniaia paluba	118 Cubierta baja	118 Mellandäck, Trossdäck	118 Tusschendeks
119 Machinery	119 Maschinen	119 Machines	119 Machinaria	119 Mekhanizm	119 Máquinas	119 Maskineri	119 Werktuigen (machin
120 Magazine	120 Munitionskammer	120 Soute.	120 Magazino-deposito munizioni	120 Sklad; magazin	120 Pañol de municiónes	120 Ammunitionsdurk	120 Magazyn
121 Main-deck	121 Batterie deck	121 Pont de batterie	121 Ponte principale	121 Glavnaia paluba	121 Cubierta principal	121 Huvuddäck	121 Kuildek
122 Mainmast	122 Grossmast		122 Albero di maestra		122 Palo mayor	122 Stormast	122 Groote mast
123 Mast	123 Mast	123 Mât.	123 Albero		123 ,, macho	123 Mast	123 Mast
124 ,, (tripod)	124 Dreibein, Dreifussmast	124 ,, (tripode).	124 ,, (treppiedi)	124 Machta trepojnaya	124 ,, trípode	124 Tripodmast	
125 ,, (lattice)	125 Gittermast	125 ,, (en treillis)	125 ,, (graticcio)	125 Reshetchataya machta	125 ,, de celosía	125 Gallermast	
126 Microphone	126 Geräuschempfänger	126 Microphone	126 Microfono	126 Mikrofon	126 Micrófono	126 Mikrofon	126 Microphone
127 Mine	127 Mine	127 Mine	127 Mina	127 Mina	127 Mina	127 Mina	127 Mijn
128 Mine-layer	128 Minenleger	128 Mouilleurs de mines 128 Pose-mines	128 Posa-mina	128 Minnii zagraditel	128 Colocador de minas	128 Minutläggningsfartyg	128 Mijn legger
129 Mine-sweeper	129 Minensucher	129 Dragueurs de mines	129 Draga-mina	129 Minnii tralshik	129 Rastreador de minas	129 Minsvepningsfartyg	129 Mijn veeger
130 Mizzen-mast	130 Besanmast	130 Mât de artimon.	130 Albero di mezzana		130 Palo mesana	130 Mesanmast	130 Bezaans mast
131 M.L. (motor launch)	131 Motorboot	131 Vedette	131 Lancia a motore	131 Motornoe patrolnoe soodno (literally, motor patrol vessel)	131 Lancha de motor	131 Motorbåt	131 M.L. motor launch
132 M. S. (motor ship)	132 Motorschiff	132 Bateau automobile	132 Nave a motore	132 Motornoe soodna	132 Buque de motor	132 Motorfartyg	132 M.S. motor schip
133 Monitor	133 Monitor	133 Monitor	133 Monitor	133 Monitor	133 Monitor	133 Monitor	133 Monitor
134 Navy yard	134 Marinewerft	134 Arsenal	134 Cantiere dello stato	134 Admiralteistve	134 Arsenal del estado	134 Orlogsvarv	134 Marine werf
135 Normal displ't	135 Normale Wasserdrängung	135 Deplacement normal	135 Dislocamento normale	135 Normalnoe vodoizmeshenie	135 Desplazamiento normal	135 Normal deplacement	135 Normale water verplaatsi
136 Net Cutter	136 Netzschere	136 Coupe-filets	136 Taglia-rete		136 Cortador de redes	136 Nätsax	136 Net breeker
137 Net layer	137 Netzleger	137 Mouilleur de filets	137 Posa-rete		137 Colocador de redes	137 Nätutläggningsfartyg	137 Net legger
138 Oil tanker	138 Öldampfer, Tankdampfer	138 Pétrolier	138 Nave petroliera a cisterna	138 Nalivnoe soodno	138 Buque de cisterna petrolero	138 Oljetankfartyg	138 Olie tankship.
139 Paddle-wheel	139 Rad	139 Roue	139 Ruote a palette	139 Grebnoe parokhodnoe koleso	139 Rueda de paletas	139 Skovelhjul	139 Wiel (raderboot)
140 ,, steamer	140 Raddampfer	140 Navire à roues.	140 Piroscafo a ruote		140 Vapor de ruedas	140 Hjulångare	140 Raderboot

No.	ENGLISH	GERMAN	FRENCH	ITALIAN	RUSSIAN	SPANISH	SWEDISH	DUTCH
141	Patrol boat/vessel	Vorpostenboot, Fahrzeug	Patrouilleur	Battello / nave di pattuglia	Patrolnoe soodno	Buque de patrulla/ Lancha de patrulla	Bevakningsbat	Patrouille boot
142	Periscope	Sehrohr	Periscope.	Periscopio	Periskop	Periscopio	Periskop	Periskoop
143	Pilot vessel	Lotsenboot	Bateau pilote	Battello pilota		Bote de práctico	Lotsbat	Loods boot
144	Pinnace (steam)	Dampfpinasse	Chaloupe à vapeur	Canotto a vapore	Kater	Pinaza de vapor	Ångslup	Stoom barkes
145	Pole mast	Stangenmast	Mât gaule	Albero a palo		Palo enterizo ó tiple	Pålmast	
146	Poop	Poop, Hinterschiff	Dunette.	Cassero di poppa	Korma ; oot	Toldilla	Poop, Hytta	Poep
147	Port (side)	Backbord	Babord	Sinistra	Lievii	Babor	Babord	Bakboord
148	Powder (propellant)		Charge d'explosion	Polvere impellente	Porokhovoi	Pólvora impelente	Krut	Poeder
149	Propeller	Schraube, Propeller	Hélice	Elica	Grebnoi vint	Hélice	Propeller	Schroef
150	Protection to vitals	Schutz an vitalen stellen	Protection des machines	Protezione delle parti vitali	Zastchita	Protection de las partes vitales	Skydd för vitala delar	Bescherming der vitale deelen
151	Protective deck	Schutzdeck	Pont cuirassé.	Coperta protegente	Bronevaya palooba	Cubierta de protección	Pansardäck	Beschermings dek
152	Q.F. (= R.F. in U.S.)	Schnell Feuer Geschutz	à tir rapide.	Tiro rapido	Skorostrelnii	Tiro rápido	Snabbskjutande kanon	Snelvuur
153	Radius of action	Fahrbereich, Aktionsradius	Rayon d'action.	Raggio d'azione	Radius deistviya	Radio de acción	Aktionsradie	Straal van actie
154	Rake (of masts, &c.)	Rak	Incliné/e/s sur l'arriere	Inclinazione (di nu albero)	Ooklon	Inclinación (de un palo)	Fall /pa master. etc./	Hang (van masten)
155	Ram	Ramsporn	Eperon	Sperone	Tarann	Espolon	Ramm	Ram
156	Range yds./metres	Entfernung, Schlussweite	Portée	Portate—yarde/metri	Dalnost boya	Alcance yardas/metros	Avstånd	Afstand (yds./meters)
157	Range-finder	Entfernungsmesse	Télémètre.	Telemetro	Dalnomer	Telémetro	Avstandsmätare	Afstand zoeker
158	Repair ship	Reparaturschiff	Transport/Navire-atelier	Nave per riparazione	Plavoochaya masterskaija	Buque de reparaciones	Verkstadsfartyg	Reparatie schip
159	River gunboat	Flusskanonenboot	Cannonière de riviere	Cannoniera da fiume	Rechnaya kanonerskaya lodka	Lancha cañónera de río	Flodkanonbat	Rivier kanonneerboot
160	River monitor	Flussmonitor	Monitor de riviere	Monitor da fiume		Monitor de río	Flodmonitor	Rivier monitor
161	Royal yacht	Königliche Yacht	Yacht royal/impérial/présidentiel	Yacht reale	Korolevskaya yakhta	Yate real	Kunglig yacht	Koninklijk yacht
162	Rudder	Ruder, Steuerruder, Seitenruder, Ventikalruder	Gouvernail.	Timone	Rool	Timón	Roder	Roer
163	Salvage ship	Bergungsschiff	Navire releveur	Nave di salvataggio	Spasatelnoe soodno	Buque de salvamento	Bärgningsfartyg	Bergings schip
164	S. S. (steamship)	Dampfer	Navire à vapeur	Vapore		Buque de vapor	Ångfartyg	S.S. (stoomschip)
165	S. V. (sailing vessel)	Segler	Voilier	Bastimento a vela		Buque de vela	Segelfartyg	Z.S. (zeilschip)
166	Scout	Aufklärungskreuzer	Eclaireur/Estafette	Nave esploratrice	Raabedchik	Buque explorador	Spaningsfartyg	Verkenaer
167	Screens	Splitter-traversen	Écrans	Schermi	Shirmi	Pantallas	Splintskärmar	Splinterschilden Schermen
168	Seaplane	Wasserflugzeug	Hydravion.	Idrovolante	Gidroaeroplan	Hidrovolante	Hydroaeroplan	Water vliegtuig
169	Seaplane-carrier	Flugzeugmutterschiff	Porte-avions.	,, (nave appoggio)	Soodno-matka dlya gidroaeroplanov	,, (buque portador)	Flygmaskins—depotfartyg	Watervliegtuig drager
170	Searchlight	Scheinwerfer	Projecteur.	Proiettore	Projektor	Proyector	Stralkastare	Zoeklicht
171	Searchlight-top	Scheinwerfertopp	Hune à projecteurs	,, (coffa)		,, (cofa)	Stralkastaremast	Controle top zoeklicht
172	Sheer (of hull)	Sprung		Cervatura dello scafo		Arrufo del casco	Språng	Geer (van hol)
173	Shields	Schützschildern	Boucliers.	Scudi	Stchit	Mantelete	Sköldar	Schilden
174	Sloop	Sloop, U-bootsabwehrkreuzer	Aviso(?)	Scialuppa	Shlup	Balandra		Sloep
175	Sounding machine	Lotmaschine	Sonde/Appareil	Macchina da scandaglio		Aparato para sondar		Diepte peiling machine
176	Speed	Geschwindigkeit	Vitesse	Velocita	Skorost khoda	Velocidad	Fart	Vaart, Snelheid
177	Squadron (of fleet)	Geschwader	Escadre	Squadra (di una flotta)	Eskadra ; brigada	Escuadra de una flota	Eskader	Eskader (van vloot)
178	Starboard	Steuerbord	Tribord	Dritta	Pravaia storona	Estribor	Styrbord	Stuurboord
179	Stern	Heck	Arrière	Poppa	Korma	Popa	Akter	Hek
180	Submarine	Untersee-Boote	Sousmarin	Sottomarino	Podvodnaia lodka	Submarino	Undervattensbat	Onderzeetorpedoboot
181	Submarine-chaser	U-bootsjäger	Contre-sousmarins	Cacciasommergibili		Caza-submarino	U-batsjagare	Onderzeër jager
182	Submerged	Unterwasser	Submergé	Subacqueo	Podvodnii	Sumergido	Under vattnet	Onderwater
183	Submersible	Tauchboot	Submersible	Sommergibile	Opooskanshiisya pod vodoo ; mogooshii opooskatsya	Sumergible	Dykbat	Duikboot
184	Super-firing (guns)	Übereinandergestellt	Superposé/e/s (canons.)		Strelba s visshei pozitsii cherez nizshoon		Överhöjda kanoner	
185	Supply ship	Proviantschiff	Ravitailleur/Transport vivres	Nave di provviste		Buque de abastecimiento	Provianfartyg	Toever schip
186	Surveying ship	Vermessungsschiff	Navire pour Service Hydrographique	Nave idrografica	Opisnoe soodno	Buque hidrográfico	Sjömätningsfartyg	Controle schip
187	Tank vessel (for water)	Wasserfahrzeug	Citerne	Nave-cisterna (acqua)	Nalivnoe soodno	Buque de cisterna (agua)	Vattenbat	Tank schip (voor water)
188	Tender	Beiboot, Tender	Annexe	Battello d'avviso	Tender	Bote-aviso	Hjälpfartyg	Lichter
189	Topmast	Marsstänge	Mât de hune	Albero di freccia	Stenga	Mastelero de galope	Stang	Steng
190	Top gallant mast	Bramstänge	Mât de perroquet	Albero di velaccio	Bram-stenga	Mastelero de juanete	Bramstang	Bovenbram steng
191	Torpedo	Torpedo	Torpille	Siluro	Mina	Torpedo	Torped	Torpedo
192	Torpedo boat	Torpedo boot	Torpilleur	Torpediniera	Minonosets	Torpedero	Torpedbat	Torpedoboot
193	Torpedo tubes	Torpedo lancier-röhre	Tubes lance torpille	Tubi lancia siluri	Minnie aparati	Tubos lanza torpedos	Torpedtub	Lanceerinridiling (Cuis
194	Tons	Tonnen	Tonnes	Tonnelate	Tonni	Toneladas	Ton	Tonnen of Kanon)
195	Training ship	Schulschiff	Navire-École	Nave scuola di marina	Oochebnoe soodno	Buque escuela de marina	Övningsfartyg	Opleidings schip
196	,, (boys)	Schiffsjungen-schulschiff	,, mousses	,, (ragazzi)		,, (muchachos)	Skeppsgossefartyg	,, (jongens)
197	,, (engineers)	Maschinenschulschiff	,, mecaniciens	,, (macchinisti)		,, (máquinistas)	Maskinistkolfartyg	,, (machinisten)
198	,, (gunnery)	Artillerieschulschiff	,, de cannonage	,, (artiglieria)		,, (artilleria)	Artilleriskolfartyg	,, (kanonneers)
199	Training ship (midshipmen, &c.)	Kadettenschulschiff	,, d'application	,, (guardie-marine)		,, (guardia-marinas)	Kadettfartyg	,, (adelborsten, etc.)
200	Training ship (navigation)	Navigationsschulschiff	,, navigation	,, (navigazione)		,, (navegacion)	Skolfartyg	,, (navigatie)
201	,, (mine)	Minenschulschiff	,, de torpilles	,, (mina)		,, (minas)	Minskolfartyg	,, (mijn)
202	,, (stokers)	Heizerschulschiff	,, de chauffe	,, (fuochisti)		,, (fogoneros)	Eldareskolfartyg	,, (stokers)
203	,, (torpedo)	Torpedoschulschiff	,, de torpilles automobils	,, (siluri)		,, (torpedos)	Torpedskolfartyg	,, (torpedo)
204	Transport	Transporten, Transportdampfer	Transport	Trasporto	Transport ; transportnoe soodno	Buque transporte	Transport	Transport
205	Trawler	Fischdampfer	Chalutier	"Trawler"	Traooler	"Trawler" (Buque de pesca)	Trawlare, Fiskeångare	Stoom visscherman
206	Trials	Probefahrten	Essais	Prove	Ispitanii	Pruebas	Provturer	Proeftocht
207	Trimming tank	Trimmtank		"Trimming tank" (cisterna di assettamento)	Ooravnitelnaya sisterna	"Trimming tank" (cisterna de equilibración)	Trimtank	Ballast tank
208	Tug	Schleppdampfer	Remorqueur	Rimorchiatore	Booksir ; booksirnoe soodno	Remolcador	Bogserbat	Sleep boot
209	Turbo-generator	Turbogenerator	Turbo-moteur	Turbo generatore		Turbo-generador	Turbingenerator	
210	Turbine	Turbine	Turbine	Turbina	Turbina	Turbina	Turbin	Turbine
211	,, (geared)	Turbine mit Reduziervorrichtung, Turbine mit mehrfacher Übersetzung	Turbines à engrenages	Turbina ad ingranaggio		Turbina con engranaje	Utväxlad turbin	
212	Turrets	Türme	Tourelles	Torri	Bashnia	Torres	Torn	Torens
213	Upper deck	Oberdeck	Pont de gaillards	Ponte superiore	Verkhniaia paluba	Cubierta alta	Övre däck	Opperdek
214	Uptake (to funnels)	Rauchfang, Exhaustor	Base de cheminées	Cassa a fumo (nel fumaiolo)	Naroojnaya dimovaya trooba	Flus de reunion de chimenea	Rökupptag	
215	Ventilator	Ventilator, Lüfter	Ventilateur	Ventilatore	Ventilyator	Ventilador	Ventilator	Luchtkoker
216	Water line	Wasserlinie	Flottaison	Linea d'acqua	Vaterliniia	La linea de flotacion	Vattenlinje	Waterlyn
217	Wireless telegraphy (W/T)	Funkentelegraphie (F.T.) ; drachtlose Telegraphie	Telegraphie sans fils (T.S.F.)	Radiotelegrafia	Bezprovolornoe telegrafirovanie	Radio-telegrafia	Gnisttelegrafi, Radiotelegrafi	Telegraphie zonder draad
218	,, ,, aerials	Antennen, Luftdrähte	Antennes de T.S.F.	,, (antenne)	Anteni	,, (antenas)	Antenner, Luftnät	
219	,, ,, spreaders	Antennen spr (?)	Deflecteurs de T.S.F.	,, (Stendadori ærei)		,, (Extendedores aéreos)	Spröt för gnisttråd	
220	Watertight door	Wasserdichte Tür	Porte de cloison etanche	Porta stagna	Vodoneproniczaemaya dver	Puerta estanca	Vattentät dörr	Waterdichte deur
221	,, compartment	Wasserdichte Abteilung	Cloison etanche	Compartimento stagno	Vodoneproniczaemoe otdelenie	Compartimiento estanco	Vattentät avdelning	Waterdichte afdeeling
222	Yacht (steam)	Dampfyacht	Yacht (à vapeur)	Yacht a vapore	Yakhta (parovaya)	Yate de vapor	Ångyacht	Yacht (stoom)

BRITISH DOCKYARD—HOME WATERS.

(All maps divided into 2000 yard squares. Soundings in fathoms. Heights in feet.)

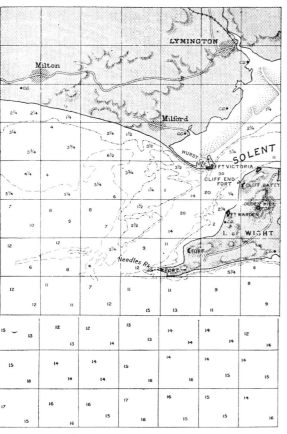

WESTERN ENTRANCE.

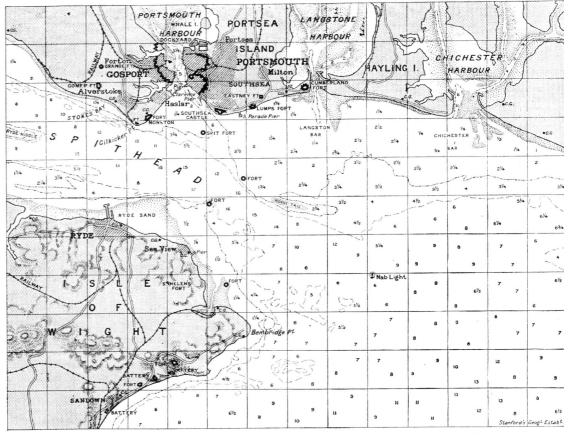

EASTERN ENTRANCE.

2. PORTSMOUTH. One slip for building battleships or cruisers up to 750 feet.
Three large and one small basins.
Dry docks :—No. 15, 563 × 94 × 33½ feet.
,, 14, 770 × 100 × 33½ ,,
,, 13, 560 × 82 × 33½ ,,
,, 12, 485 × 80 × 33½ ,,

Lock A. 461 × 80 × 33½ feet.
,, B, 461 × 81¾ × 34 ,,
,, C, 850 × 110 × 40 ,,
,, D, 850 × 110 × 40 ,,
and ten smaller docks. Total employees, about 8000 normally, probably 16,000 now.
Admiralty Chart No. 2631-2045. Rise of Spring Tide, 13½ feet (Dockyard).
Note.—Breakwater from Lumps Fort due south about 2 miles. Aircraft base at Calshot, Southampton, before the war. By the end of 1913, 17 oil fuel reservoirs were built.

BRITISH NAVAL PORTS AND HARBOURS—HOME WATERS.

DOVER. New harbour, 610 acres; depth of 30 feet at low water over half the area. E. entrance, 1 cable; W. entrance, 800 feet. Coaling station. Well fortified. Floating dock for Destroyers.

Moorings for 16 battleships, 5 large cruisers, 7 *Counties*, 4 small cruisers, and for destroyers.

(The tide at entrance is very strong, making ingress difficult).

Admiralty Chart No. 1698-1828.

Rise of Spring Tide, 18¾ feet.

PORTLAND. 1500 acres of enclosed harbour; minimum depth, 30 feet. Floating dock suitable for destroyers. Coaling station. N. and E. entrances 700 feet wide. Strongly fortified.
Admiralty Chart No. 2255. Rise of Spring Tide, 9 feet (Bill of Portland); 6¾ feet (Breakwater).

Other Naval Harbours and Stations in Home Waters.

BEREHAVEN. Good anchorage. **SCILLY.** The anchorage is moderately good. The entrance is very narrow, difficult and dangerous. **LOUGH SWILLY & BUNCRANA.** Very moderately fortified. Good anchorage. **KINGSTOWN** (DUBLIN), **TORBAY, FALMOUTH, CROMARTY FIRTH, MORAY FIRTH,** (SCOTLAND, E. COAST), **SCAPA FLOW, LOCH EWE, LAMLASH,** &c. **CAMPBELTOWN.** Submarine Training Station. **SHANDON, GARELOCH.** Anti-Submarine Station, for Experiments and Training.

West Coast (Wales).

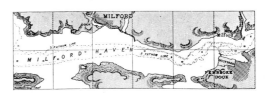

PEMBROKE. Building yard. Two large slips. Dry docks :—One, 404 × 75 × 24¾ feet (high water). About 2500 employees.

Admiralty Chart No. 915-2393.

Rise of Spring Tide, 22½ feet (Dockyard).

BRITISH DOCKYARDS AND NAVAL HARBOURS. (HOME STATIONS).

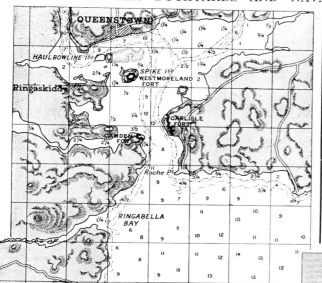

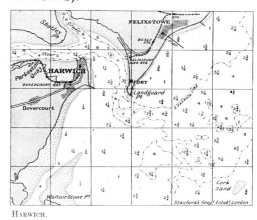

HARWICH. Base for Torpedo Craft, Submarines, &c. Admiralty Chart No. 2693.

IMMINGHAM. For Repairs.

OSEA ISLAND. River Blackwater. C.M.B. Base.

HARWICH.

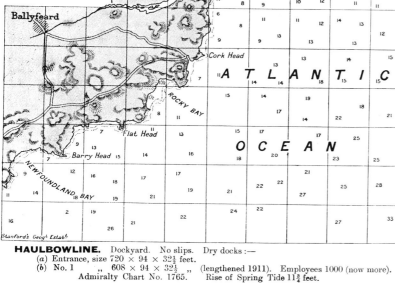

HAULBOWLINE. Dockyard. No slips. Dry docks :—
(a) Entrance, size 720 × 94 × 32½ feet.
(b) No. 1 „ 608 × 94 × 32½ „ (lengthened 1911). Employees 1000 (now more).
Admiralty Chart No. 1765. Rise of Spring Tide 11¾ feet.

ROSYTH (and **PORT EDGAR**). Three docks 850 × 110 × 36 feet. Entrance lock 850 × 110 × 36 feet. Also Floating Docks.
Admiralty Chart No. 114 B. Rise of Spring Tide, 16½ feet.
Aircraft Base at Carlinghouse before War.

BRITISH DOCKYARDS—THE NORE (Home Station).

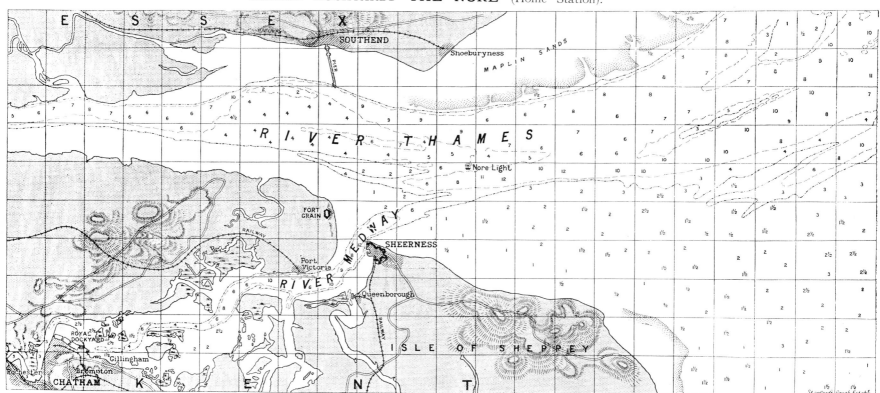

CHATHAM. Three building slips. Three large closed basins. Dry docks :—
No. 9, 650 × 84 × 33 feet.
„ 8, 456 × 82 × 33 „
„ 7, 456 × 82 × 32½ „ Also floating docks.
„ 6, 456 × 80 × 32½ „
„ 5, 460 × 80 × 32½ „
There are four other docks suitable only for small craft (Nos. 1, 2, 3, 4). Total employees, 12,000.
Admiralty Chart No. 1834-1607-1185. Rise of Spring Tide, 18¼ feet.

SHEERNESS. No slips. One small basin. Dry docks :—Five, all small, and able to take small craft only. Also floating docks. Destroyer base. Flying school and aircraft base at Isle of Grain, before the war. Floating dock, 680 × 113 × 36 feet (33,000 tons). Employees, 2,500.
Admiralty Chart No. 1833. Rise of Spring Tide 16 feet.

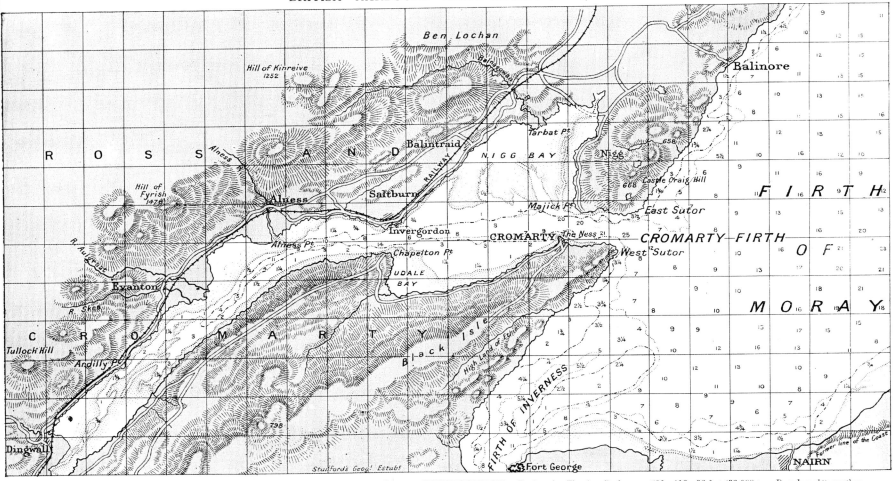

Errata : East Sutor now *North Sutor*.
West Sutor now *South Sutor*.

Cromarty Firth. Fleet Anchorage. **INVERGORDON.** Dockyard. Floating Docks, one, 680 × 113 × 36 feet (33,000 tons *Dreadnought*), another *Dreadnought* Floating Dock, third Floating Dock for Light Cruisers, T.B.D. and S/M.

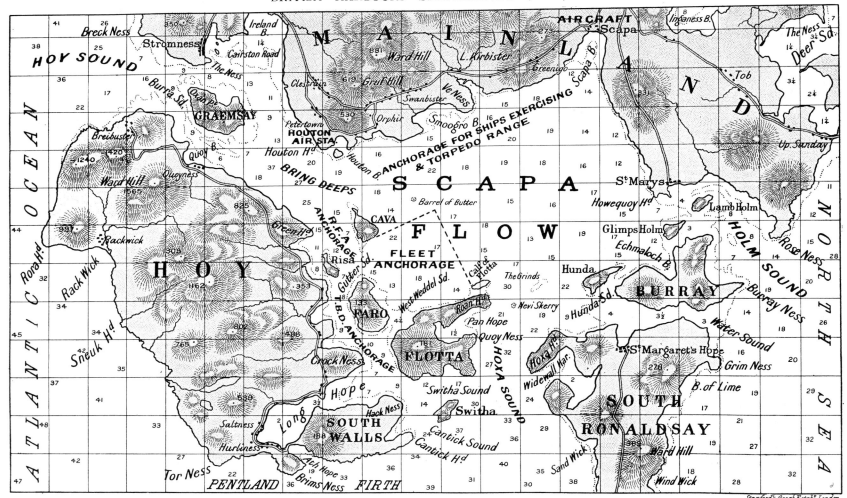

SCAPA FLOW. Fleet Anchorage only, 1919. Admiralty Chart Nos. 2180, 2581, 3729.

Stanford's Geog.ᴵ Estab.ᵗ London.

(To uniform scale.   Divided into 2000 yard squares.   Soundings in fathoms).

Note.

A Map of Salonika is published with Greek Navy.

GIBRALTAR.   *West Harbour*—No slips.   Dry docks:—

No. 1 (Prince of Wales), size, $850 \times 90 \times 35\frac{1}{2}$ feet.

,,   2 (Queen Alexandra)   ,, $550 \times 90 \times 35\frac{1}{2}$,,

,,   3 (King Edward)   ,, $450 \times 90 \times 35\frac{1}{2}$,,

There is another dock (No. 4) for torpedo craft.

Area of harbour, 450 acres, depth 30 feet at low water. Well fortified—guns mounted 1000 feet above water.

Admiralty Chart No. 144.   Rise of Spring Tide, $3\frac{1}{4}$ feet (New Mole).

Private Docks.

PORT SAID.   Floating Dock: $295 \times 61 \times 18$ feet.

ALEXANDRIA.   Naval and Military base during War:— Dry Dock: $553 \times 64 \times 23$ feet.

SUEZ CANAL.   90 miles long, 31 feet deep $\times$ 108 feet wide at bottom.

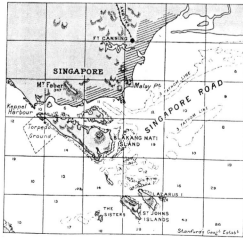

MEDITERRANEAN.

MALTA.   One small building slip.   Dry docks:—

No. 1 (double), $536\frac{1}{2} \times 73 \times 26$ feet.

,,   2 (Hamilton), $520 \times 94 \times 33\frac{1}{2}$,,

,,   3 (Somerset), $468 \times 80 \times 32\frac{1}{4}$,,   Also floating docks.

,,   4 (double), $770 \times 95 \times 34\frac{1}{2}$,,

,,   5 (single), $550 \times 95 \times 34\frac{1}{2}$,,

Employees, 4000 or more.

Area of war harbour, about 100 acres.   New works completed 1908. Well fortified.   Good anchorage.   Base for Mediterranean Fleet.   Large Aircraft Station being built here 1918—19.

Admiralty Chart No. 194.   Rise of Spring Tide 2 feet.

BRITISH DOCKYARDS AND HARBOURS: ASIATIC & PACIFIC.

(Divided into 2000 yard squares.   Uniform scale.   Soundings in fathoms.   Heights in feet.)

CHINA STATION.

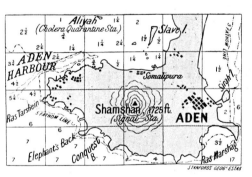 

EAST INDIES.

ADEN.   Well fortified.   Coaling.   Harbour 8 × 4 miles.   Admiralty Chart No. 7.

COLOMBO (CEYLON).   Fortified Coaling station.   Excellent and deep harbour, sheltered by breakwaters. Dry dock: 708 × 85 × 32 feet (*Dreadnought*.)   Admiralty Chart No. 3686.

MAURITIUS (PORT LOUIS).   Good harbour, with awkward entrance.   Coaling station.   Fortified.   One dry dock: 384 × 60 × 19½ feet, and one smaller.

Note.—For KARACHI, BOMBAY, CALCUTTA, see Royal Indian Marine Section.

HONG-KONG.   (China Station).

CHINA STATION.

PENANG (STRAITS SETTLEMENTS).   Good deep harbour.   Coaling.   Dry dock: 343 × 46 × 14½ ft.

SINGAPORE.   Coaling station.   Good roads.   Average anchorage, 10 fathoms.   Tanjong Pagar Docks: (1) Victoria, 467 × 65 × 20; (2) Albert, 478 × 60 × 21.   Keppel Harbour: (1) 400 × 47 × 16; (2) 450 × 52 × 19; (3) King's, 846 × 100 × 34, (*Dreadnought* and to take any warship.)

HONG KONG.   Repairing yard.   No slips.   Dry docks:—Admiralty No. 1, 555 × 95 × 39 feet (*Dreadnought*.)   New dock: Quarry Bay, (Butterfield & Swire) 750 × 88 × 34½ feet (*Dreadnought*.) At Kau-Lung (see map): No. 1, 700 × 86 × 30 feet (*Dreadnought*.)   Hope Dock, 432½ × 84 × 24 feet. Cosmopolitan, 466 × 85½ × 20 feet.   Also three smaller, able to take torpedo craft, etc.

N.B.—All the foregoing, except the two first, are the property of the Hong Kong & Whampoa Dock Co., Ltd.   Area of basin (tidal), 9¼ acres.   Average depth of harbour, 40 feet.   Admiralty Charts No. 1180-1459.   Rise of Spring Tide, 8 feet.

WEI-HAI-WEI (CHINA).   Anchorage.   Unfortified base.   Coaling station.

SINGAPORE.   (China Station).

(Maps to Uniform Scale. Divided in 2000 yard squares. Soundings in fathoms).

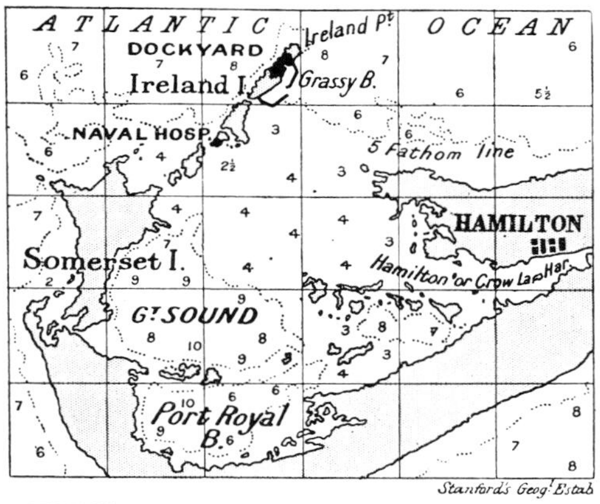

BERMUDA.

N. America and West Indies.

BERMUDA. Naval Dockyard. Fortified. Large floating dock, 545 × 92¾ × 33 feet (*Dreadnought*, 17,500 tons). Shallow harbour. Admiralty Chart No. 360.

BRIDGETOWN (Barbados). Coaling. Open roadstead. There is a small dock here, able to take vessels drawing up to 14 feet.

ST. JOHN'S (Newfoundland). There is a private dock here, 569½ × 85 × 24 feet. (*Dreadnought, if lightened.*)

TRINIDAD. 4,000 tons floating dock, 365 × 65 × 18 feet.

Note: ESQUIMAULT and Docks in the Dominion of Canada transferred to Royal Canadian Navy Section.

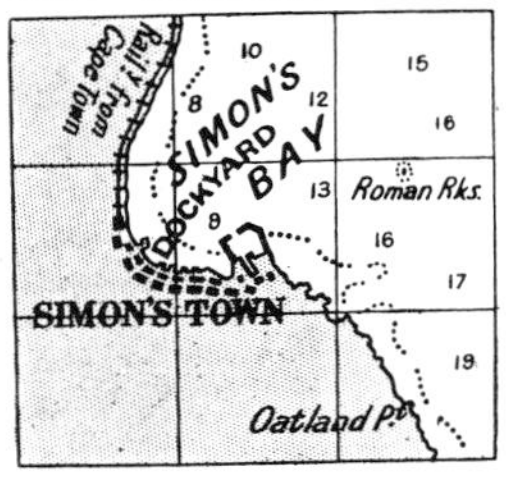

Cape Station.

CAPE COAST CASTLE (British Gold Coast, W. Africa). Fortified coaling station. Anchorage average 28 feet.

PORT STANLEY (Falkland Is.) Good deep harbour. Fortified coaling station.

ST. HELENA. Fortified coaling station. 10-fathom harbour.

SIERRA LEONE (W. Africa). Fortified coaling station. Anchorage, 6-16 fathoms.

SIMON'S BAY (Cape of Good Hope). Naval dockyard. Selborne Dock, 750 × 95 × 36 feet. (*Dreadnought.*) Tidal basin, 28 acres, 30 feet deep. Fortified moderately. Admiralty Chart No. 1849. There is a dock at Capetown, 500 × 66 × 24½ feet, and a floating one at Durban, 425 × 70 × 23 feet.

Australia.

(See Royal Australian Navy Section).

New Zealand.

(See New Zealand Section).

BRITISH COMMERCIAL HARBOURS AND IMPORTANT SHIPPING PORTS.

British Private Docks, at Home, able to take Dreadnoughts.

There are 235 dry docks of considerable size in U.K outside Royal Yards.

HEBBURN (Graving)	size, 700 × 90 × 28½ feet.
BRISTOL (Avonmouth)	„ 855 × 100 × 34 „
SOUTHAMPTON (No. 5)	„ 745 × 91 × 28½ „
„ (No. 6)	„ 782 × 100 × 31 „
LIVERPOOL (Canada Graving)	„ 925 × 94 × 32 „
„ (Brocklebank Graving) ...	„ 800 × 93 × 31½ „
„ (Gladstone)	„ 1020 × 120 × 47 „
BIRKENHEAD (No. 3)	„ 750 × 85¼ × 26 „
„ (No. 6)	„ 730 × 82 × 30 „
„ (No. 7)	„ 880 × 92 × 33 „
GLASGOW (No. 4)	„ 1020 × 110 × 40 „
RENFREW	„ 1020 × 100 × 36 „
BELFAST (No. 1)	„ 850 × 96 × 35¼ „
„ (No. 2)	„ 750 × 96 × 33 „

Principal Commercial Harbours (*1914*).

(In order of importance, with approximate tons of shipping clearing annually).

London (9 million); Liverpool (7 million); Cardiff (6¾ million); Newcastle and district (4½ million); Hull (2¼ million); Glasgow (2 million); Southampton (1½ million); and Newport, Blyth, Swansea, Sunderland, Leith, Dover, Kirkcaldy, Grimsby, Middlesbrough, Grangemouth (all doing about 1 million); Harwich, Manchester, Bristol, Goole, Hartlepool, Belfast, and Folkestone (all doing from ¾ to ¼ million).

Mercantile Marine (British and Colonial).

Lloyds Return, June 1919, as follows:—

	Tons *Gross.*
United Kingdom	16,345,000
British Dominions	1,863,000
Total	18,208,000

BRITISH WARSHIP BUILDERS.

Note.—The headings give the abbreviated titles by which builders are mentioned on later Ship Pages. With a few exceptions, all details given below were kindly approved or furnished in 1919 by the firms mentioned.

Armstrong.

Note.—Hitherto it has been the custom to refer to this firm as "Elswick." The Elswick Shipyard has practically ceased naval construction. From now onwards, the firm will be mentioned as "Armstrongs" or "Armstrong Whitworth."

SIR W. G. ARMSTRONG, WHITWORTH & CO., Ltd. (Newcastle-on-Tyne). *Armstrong Naval Yard.* 70 acres. Frontage about a mile. Nine slips, 1000 to 500 ft. long. *Walker Shipyard.* Area 30 acres. Frontage 317 yards. Six slips from 650 to 450 ft. long. Total employees, including ordnance, armour plate, marine engine and steel works, about 31,000.

Beardmore.

WM. BEARDMORE & CO., Ltd. (Naval Construction Works, Dalmuir, nr. Glasgow). All classes of ships, naval and mercantile, up to largest size and highest speed. Engines of all types and sizes. Six big slips, four smaller. Employees *circa* 10,000. This yard is designed for vessels up to 900 ft. long. 220-ton crane. Fitting basin of 8 acres, 28 ft. at low water. Patent slip 460 ft. long.

U. S. NAVY YARDS—ATLANTIC—NEW YORK DISTRICT.

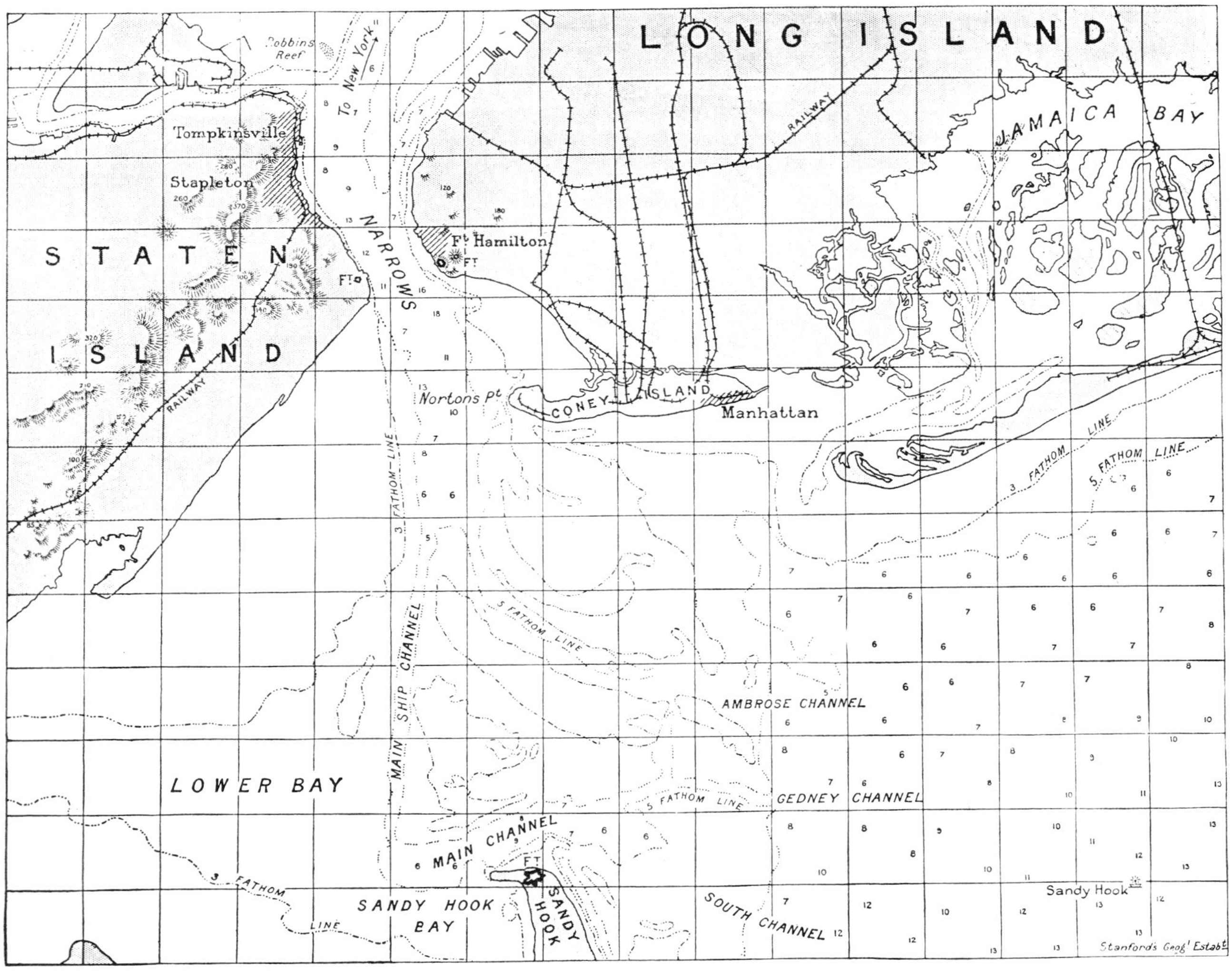

General Note to all Navy Yards on Atlantic and Pacific Coasts.

In 1919 U.S. Government placed orders for two 20,000 ton floating docks and eight 10,000 ton floating docks. When delivered, these will be assigned to the most suitable ports.

Navy Yards.

NEW YORK (& **BROOKLYN**).—3rd Naval District. Depot and shipbuilding yard. Two slips before war. Two new slips suitable for building largest types of Dreadnoughts and Battle-Cruisers begun 1917, when new plant was also installed, workshops re-arranged and renovated, new offices and general stores built, and magazine stores greatly enlarged.

Dry docks:
(1) granite, 330 × 66 × 25 feet.
(2) concrete, 440 × 90 × 26 feet.
(3) wood 613 × 105¾ × 29½ feet.
(4) granite and concrete, 700 × 120 × 35 feet.

Naval hospital here. Admiralty Chart No. 3204, 2491. Rise of Spring Tide, 4¾ feet. On Long Island: Naval Diving School, Bay Shore and Rockaway Aviation Stations.

Note.—Private docks. The Erie Co. at Brooklyn has two timber docks: (1) 485 × 100 × 20 feet; (2) 620 × 85 × 25 feet.

Private Floating Docks and Patent Slips.

Situation	Docks No.	Docks Capacity—tons.	Slips No.	Slips Capacity—tons.
BROOKLYN ...	12	1100—15000*	4	1000—2000
NEW YORK ...	4	2000— 3500†		...
HOBOKEN ...	5	1000—10000‡		...
STATEN I. ...	4	1800— 4200	2	1000—4500
JERSEY CITY ...	3	1800— 4200		...
PERTH AMBOY .	3	1500— 2500	1	1000
WEEHAWKEN .	1	1800		...
NEWBURGH ...		...	1	1000

* 15,000-ton Floating Dock, property of Morse Iron Works, 478 × 110 × 28 feet.

† In 1919 there were 15 docks up to 350 ft. long in the New York district.

‡ 10,000-ton Floating Dock, property of Tietjen and Lang D.D. Co., 168 × 98 × 22 feet.

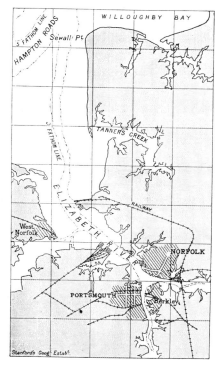

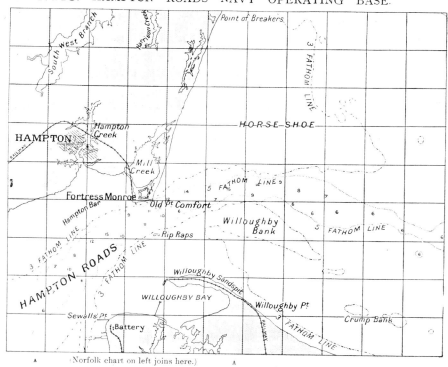

(Norfolk chart on left joins here.)

(HAMPTON ROADS AS ABOVE MAP.)

NORFOLK, VA.—5th Naval District. To be the dockyard section of the Hampton Roads Navy Operating Base. Depôt and shipbuilding yard. Naval hospital here. One or more slips for bu'lding Dreadnoughts or Battle-Cruisers begun 1917. (1) Wood dock, 460×85×25½ feet ; (2) granite, 303×60×25½ feet; (3) granite dock, 550 ×112×34 feet. New 1917-18 dock, over 1000 ft. long×110×43½ feet, divisible into 2 sections, about 650 and 350 feet long ; to have electric towing gear, 50-ton electric crane, and hydraulic lifts for rapid handling of repair materials, &c. Capable of being emptied in 30 mins. ; floating pontoon crane 150 tons, and auxiliary 25 tons on hoist. In 1917 new foundry, workshops, and plant for making mines begun, new plant installed and old renovated. Three patent slips here each 1500 tons. Admiralty Chart No. 2818,2843a.

HAMPTON ROADS NAVY OPERATING BASE (continuation to N. and N.W. of Norfolk Chart).—5th Naval District. Site on ground of Jamestown Exposition was purchased here in 1917, where it is intended that in conjunction with the Norfolk N.Y., a great Naval Base shall be established which will be developed into the principal warship port on the Atlantic coast. Plans as laid down during 1917 by the Navy Department, contemplated the following works : Submarine and Aviation Bases; Training Station for 10,000 men ; Fuel Station (for coal and oil) ; Depots for fleet stores, mines, torpedoes and anti-submarine nets, &c.

U. S. YARDS, HARBOURS, ETC.—**ATLANTIC.**

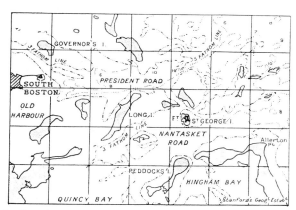

Admiralty Chart No. 1227,2482. Rise of Spring Tide, 5 feet (Charlestown Naval Yard).

Navy Yards (ATLANTIC COAST).

BOSTON, MASS.—1st Naval District. Depôt. One granite dock, 389 × 46 × 26 feet ; one granite and concrete dock, 729 × 101½ × 30½ feet. Naval hospital here. Also two wooden private docks and four patent slips 1000–2300 tons.

LEAGUE ISLAND, PHILADELPHIA PA.— 4th Naval District. Depôt. Two new slips to build Dreadnoughts or Battle-Cruisers. New workshops, foundry and Marine Barracks, 1917-18. One wooden dock, 420 × 89 × 25½ feet ; second dock, granite and concrete, 707 × 104 × 30 feet. New dock, 1022 × 144 × 43½ feet, divisible into two sections, viz.— 684 feet outer section and 338 feet inner section. Pier 1000 feet long, with 350-ton crane. Aircraft base and flying ground ; also Government seaplane factory. Naval hospital here.

WASHINGTON. No docks. Yard devoted to ordnance construction. Naval hospital here.

PORTSMOUTH, N.H.—1st Naval District. One granite and concrete, 720 × 101½ × 30½ feet. Naval hospital here.

CHARLESTON, S.C.—6th Naval District. 2nd class Navy yard. Dry dock, 503×113×34½ feet.

Naval Stations.

NARRAGANSET BAY, R.I.

NEWPORT, R.I.—2nd Naval District. Chief torpedo station. Manufactory of torpedoes, etc. Naval war college and apprentice-training station. Naval hospital and coal depôt.

CAPE MAY, N.J.—4th Naval District. Base for Submarines and Navy Airships. 349 acres bought 1919 for developing this Station.

NEW LONDON, CONN.—2nd Naval District. Submarine Training Station.

Note.—Charleston, Norfolk, and Bradford, R.I., are stations for petrol and oil fuel. A large number of Naval Stations and Training Camps, Aviation Schools, &c., created during the war have been abolished. 9th, 10th and 11th Naval Districts are on the Great Lakes. Doubtful if any stations are maintained there now.

PRIVATE DOCKS, &c.

(exclusive of those in New York and Brooklyn districts, previously listed).

NEW LONDON (CONN.), three patent slips, 1000–2000 tons. PHILADELPHIA, one floating dock (3500 tons) and two patent slips (1000 and 2300 tons). CAMDEN (N.J.), three patent slips, 1200–1500 tons. BALTIMORE (MD.), Wm. Skinner & Sons dry dock, 600×80×22½ feet. Columbian Iron-works Dock (wood), 437×80×21 feet. Maryland Steel Co., Sparrow Point, wood and steel floating dock, 20,000 tons. Also one 3000 ton floating dock and two patent slips (2000 and 1500 tons). At Portland (Me.), Savannah (Ga.), Jacksonville (Fla.), small patent slips of 1200 tons (Jacksonville, one 4500 ton floating dock).

Mercantile Ports (ATLANTIC COAST *).

(In order of importance, with approximate tons of shipping cleared per year in brackets).

New York, N.Y. (13½ million ?); Boston, Mass. (1¾ million); Philadelphia, Pa. (2⅓ million); Baltimore, Md. (1½ million); Hampton Roads, Va. (¾ million); Portland, Me. (⅓ million).

* Figures compiled 1913-14. Post-war statistics not available yet.

LEAGUE ISLAND. Admiralty Chart No. 2564.

PORTSMOUTH N.H. Admiralty Chart No. 2482,2487. Rise of Spring Tide, 8½ feet.

U. S. PRIVATE SHIPYARDS.—ATLANTIC.

(Warship builders *only*. Revised from details furnished by firms named, 1919.)

Bath I.W.

BATH IRONWORKS (BATH, ME.). Build battleships, scout cruisers, destroyers and torpedo vessels, mercantile vessels of fast passenger types and large steam yachts of very fast design. Slips: one 600 ft., one 500 ft., three 350 ft. Cranes: one 100-ton stiff leg derrick (electric), one 35-ton floating sheer-legs (steam), three 15-ton electric locomotive cranes for steel runways. Yard covers 13 acres. Water-front 1000 feet. Plant up-to-date. Yard builds boilers, engines, equipment for ships, &c. Employees: 1300 (peace), 2000 (war).

Bethlehem Fore River.

FORE RIVER PLANT, BETHLEHEM SHIPBUILDING CORPORATION (QUINCY, MASS.). 21 launching slips, 41 building slips, 20 building slips for submarines and four for 300 ft. destroyers. One 20-ton lift hammer-head crane, one 75-ton lift gantry crane, 16 overhead cranes over slips, capacity 5 and 10 tons and one 50-ton lift overhead crane. Yard covers 85 acres and water-front $1\frac{1}{4}$ miles. Yard builds boilers, machinery and equipment. Plant thoroughly modern. Employees, 14,356.

Bethlehem Squantum.

NAVAL DESTROYER PLANT, BETHLEHEM SHIPBUILDING CORPORATION (SQUANTUM, MASS.). 10 building slips with electric bridge cranes and three wet slips. Maximum length of slips 310 ft. (*p.p.*). One 20-ton stiff leg derrick; one 10-ton guy derrick; wet slips have one 25-ton and two 10-ton bridge cranes. Yard covers 60 acres approximately. Water-front about 3600 feet. Boilers, engines, &c., supplied by other Bethlehem Plants. Employees, about 9000.

Cramps.

MESSRS. THE WM. CRAMP & SONS SHIP & ENGINE-BUILDING CO. (PHILADELPHIA, PA.). Build dreadnoughts, battle cruisers, scout cruisers, destroyers and mercantile vessels of all types. 8 slips. Longest ship which can be built, 850 feet. One 100-ton floating derrick with 25-tons auxiliary lift; one 70-ton lift revolving hammer-head crane; numerous other cranes to lift 5—25 tons. Graving dock 433 ft. *over all*; width at entrance 69 ft. (top), 48 ft. (bottom); depth of water $20\frac{1}{2}$ ft. H.W.O.S. and $15\frac{1}{2}$ ft. L.W.O.S. Patent slips: one 3000-ton and one 1000-ton railways. Area of yard 175 acres. Water-front 6300 ft. Yard builds boilers, machinery and naval equipment. Plant is up-to-date. Employees, 7000 (peace), 11 500 (war).

Fore River.

FORE RIVER CO. (QUINCY, MASS.). Nine big slips. Area, 40 acres. Yard railway of 4 miles. Depth of water in channel, 33 feet. Employees, about 12,000 now. New Yard, 1917-18.

Note.—This firm has made no return of its shipyard, plant, &c., for several years past. Above details may not be correct now.

Harlan, Wilmington.

(LATE HARLAN & HOLLINGSWORTH CO.)

HARLAN SHIPBUILDING PLANT (WILMINGTON, DELAWARE). 35 acres. Water frontage, 1800 feet. Depth at low tide, 22 feet. 5 slips, able to build up to 15,000 tons. Dry dock, $330 \times 90 \times 13\frac{1}{2}$ feet. Equipment thoroughly up-to-date. Employees, 1000.

Note.—Above details are not up-to-date.

Hollands.

ELECTRIC BOAT CO. (GROTON, CONN.) Submarines of the "Holland" type, which are chiefly built at the Fore River Co.'s Yard.

Lake CO.

LAKE TORPEDO BOAT CO. (BRIDGEPORT, CON.). Submarines of the "Lake" type.

Newport News.

NEWPORT NEWS SHIPBUILDING & DRY DOCK COMPANY (NEWPORT, VA.). 125 acres. Deep water alongside. Water-front, $\frac{3}{4}$ mile. One 140-ton revolving derrick, one 100-ton sheer-leg, one 50-ton floating derrick, one 10-ton ditto. Very large modern shops. Total employees 11,500. Eight big slips. Dry docks: (2) $804 \times 80 \times 30$ feet; (3) $537\frac{1}{2} \times 79 \times 24\frac{1}{2}$ feet; (1) $593 \times 50 \times 24\frac{1}{2}$ feet.

New York S.B. Co.

NEW YORK SHIPBUILDING CO. (CAMDEN, N.J.). Can build dreadnoughts, cruisers, destroyers, mine-layers and sweepers, naval tenders and all classes of mercantile vessels, with boilers, machinery, and all equipment. 9 big slips, 4 smaller and 10 for destroyers. Yard can build ships up to 1000 ft. long, and covers 190.6 acres. Water-front about $\frac{4}{5}$ths of a mile. Plant up-to-date. All machine tools and cranes electrically driven. Hydraulic and compressed air plant. Employees about 7000 (peace), 19,000 (war).

Todd, Brooklyn.

TODD SHIPYARDS CORPORATION (TEBO YACHT BASIN YARD, BROOKLYN, N.Y.). Three slips, 250 ft. long. Two 30-ton floating cranes. Two floating docks: (1) 105×23 ft. to lift 600 tons *d.w.* (2) 150×64 ft. to lift 1100 tons *d.w.* Yard covers 25 acres. Plant is modern. Employees, 1000. Associated firms:—Robin D.D. & Repair Co., Brooklyn, N.Y.; Tietjen & Lang D.D. Co., Hoboken (10,000-ton floating dock); Clinton Plant, Brooklyn; Quintard Iron Works, N.Y. (build engines, &c., for ships built by Todd Co.); White Fuel Oil Engineering Co., N.Y. Also see Pacific Coast for Tacoma Yard.

Also a very large number of other shipyards solely engaged on mercantile construction.

U. S. NAVY YARDS, STATIONS, &c.—GULF COAST, CARIBBEAN, &c.

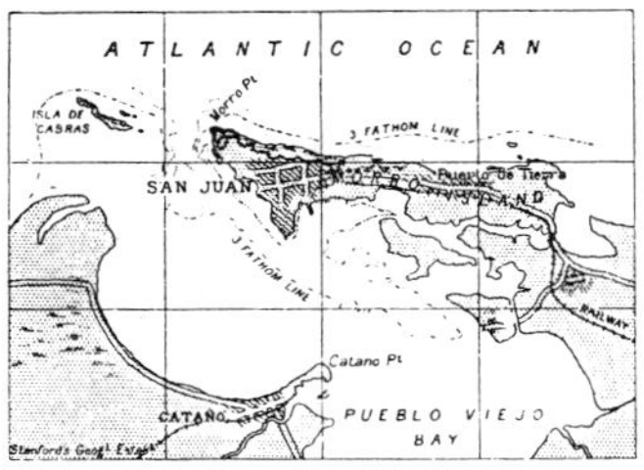

SAN JUAN, PUERTO RICO.

Admiralty Chart No. 478,3408. Rise of Spring Tide, 1 foot.

NEW ORLEANS, LA.—8th Naval District. Floating dock, $525 \times 100 \times 28\frac{1}{4}$ feet.

PENSACOLA, FLA.—8th Naval District. 2nd class yard. 8th Naval District. Big new Aviation Station for seaplanes, dirigibles, kite-balloons, &c. Floating dock, $450 \times 82 \times 27$ feet (12000 tons).

KEY WEST.—7th Naval District. No docks. Submarine and Aircraft Station.

Small Naval Stations may also exist at San Juan (Porto Rico) and St. Thomas (Virgin Islands).

Private Docks.

NEW ORLEANS: Government dock, $525 \times 100 \times 28$ feet, and two floating docks, 2000 and 2500 tons.
MOBILE (ALA.): Pinto Dry Dock, $232 \times 86 \times 17$ feet, and two floating docks, 1000 and 1400 tons.

Private Shipyards.

Various New Yards established 1917-18. Do not undertake Naval construction, all being devoted to mercantile contracts.

Mercantile Ports.*

(In order of importance and approximate tons of shipping cleared annually).

New Orleans ($2\frac{1}{4}$ million); Galveston, Texas ($\frac{1}{2}$ million); Mobile, Ala. ($\frac{3}{4}$ million); Pensacola, Fla. ($\frac{1}{2}$ million); Savannah, Ga. ($\frac{1}{3}$ million); Key West ($\frac{1}{2}$ million).

* 1911 figures: post-war statistics not available.

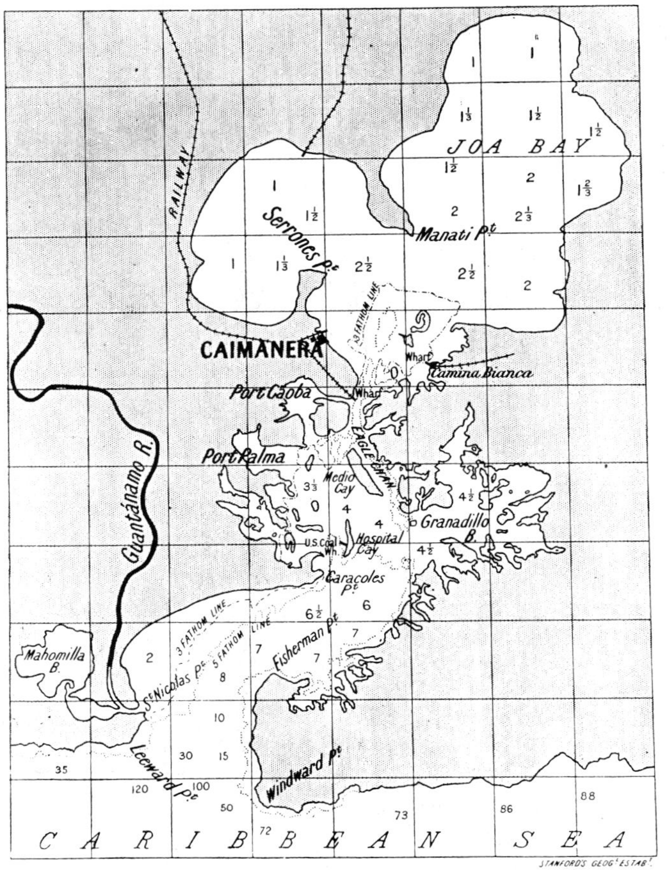

GUANTANAMO BAY (CUBA). Fleet Anchorage and Exercising Grounds. Small repairs undertaken here. Fuel Depôt. Admiralty Chart No. 904.

U. S. A.—PANAMA CANAL ZONE.

Canal about 50 miles long.   Channel 300–1000 feet wide at bottom; depth 41–85 feet.   Time of passage about 10 hours.

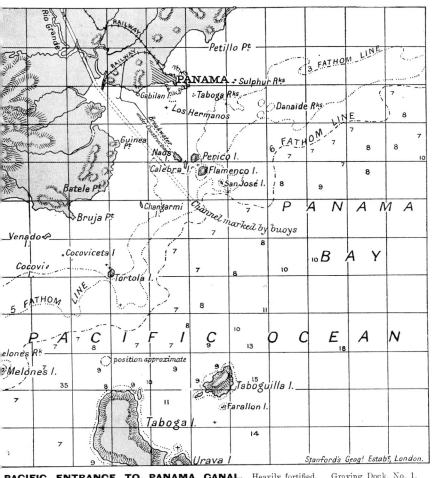

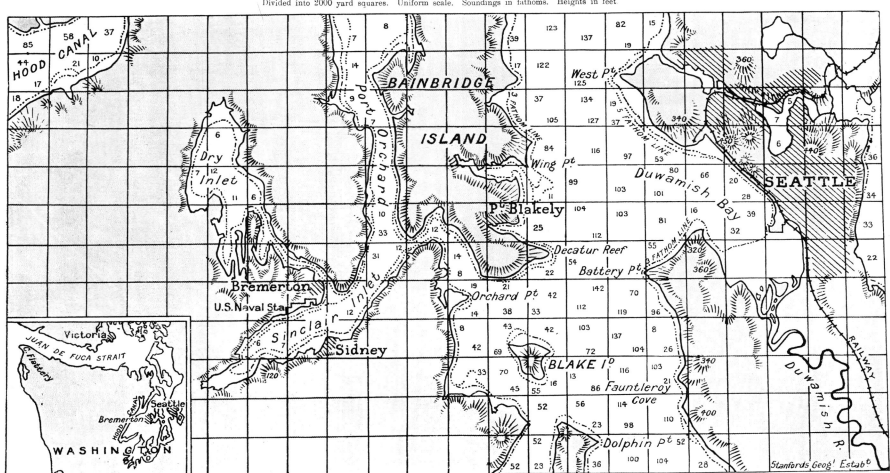

PACIFIC ENTRANCE TO PANAMA CANAL. Heavily fortified.   Graving Dock, No. 1, Balboa, 1110×110×41½ feet.   Also fuel depot for 300,000 to 350,000 tons of coal at Balboa. 2—250 ton floating cranes.

ATLANTIC ENTRANCE TO PANAMA CANAL. Heavily fortified.   Dock and Coal Depot at Cristobal same size as Balboa (see opposite).   In the Canal, Gatun and Miraflores Locks (over 1000×110×41½ feet) can be used as docks.

U. S. NAVY YARDS AND STATIONS—PACIFIC.

Divided into 2000 yard squares.   Uniform scale.   Soundings in fathoms.   Heights in feet

Sketch map of district.

BREMERTON, PUGET SOUND.— 13th Naval District.   Naval Station.   Slips for building Scout Cruisers or Auxiliaries begun here during 1917.

Dry docks : (1) Wood   ...   ...   618×73×27½ feet.
            (2) Granite and concrete ...   801⅔×113×35½ feet.

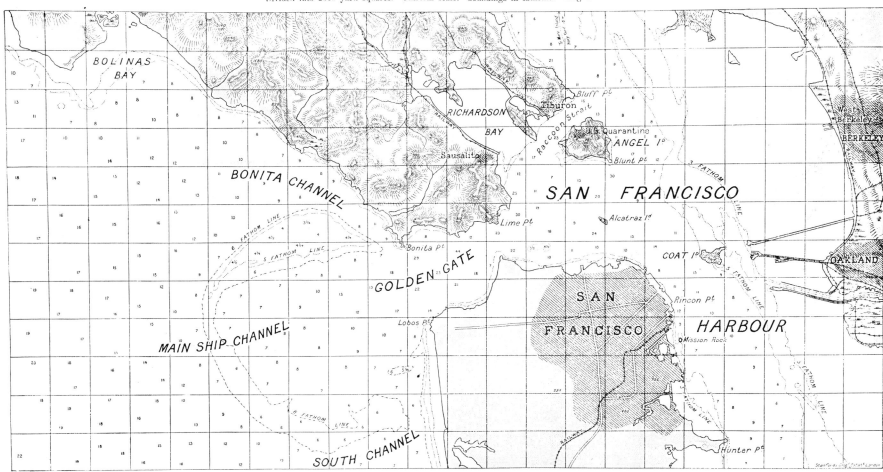

SAN FRANCISCO HARBOUR. **MARE ISLAND.**—12th Naval District. Depôt and Navy Yard (22 miles N. of San Francisco), of which small Map is given on next page. Slip to build Dreadnoughts of 600 feet length, or above, begun at Mare Island in 1916 or 1917. Destroyers also built. Dry Docks: (1) Granite ... 418×88×27½ feet.
(2) Concrete ... 883×102×31½ „

U. S. HARBOURS, Etc.—PACIFIC & ASIATIC.

Principal Private Yards.—PACIFIC COAST.

Note : No Pacific Coast Shipyards have made returns for several years past.

BETHLEHEM SHIPBUILDING CORPORATION (SAN FRANCISCO). Large new yard and engine shops at Alameda, new yard projected at Risdon. Builds Destroyers.

CALIFORNIA SHIPBUILDING CO. (LONG BEACH, CAL.), Submarine builders.

MORAN & CO. (SEATTLE, PUGET SOUND). One big slip. Floating dock 468×85×27½ feet (12,000 tons) and another *smaller*.

SEATTLE DRY DOCK AND CONSTRUCTION CO. (SEATTLE, WASHINGTON). Now controlled by Skinner & Eddy, Seattle. Floating dock, 325×100 (extreme) × 25 feet, for 6000 tons; one floating dock for 2500 tons; one patent slip, 3000 tons.

TODD DRY DOCKS & CONSTRUCTION CO. (TACOMA, WASHINGTON). No details available. Is building Cruisers. 12,000 ton floating dock completing at end of 1918.

⊙ UNION IRON WORKS CO. (SAN FRANCISCO). (Affiliated to the Bethlehem Shipbuilding Co.) 38 acres. Three dry docks (Hunters Point): (1) 750×103×30 feet (28,000 tons), (2) 485 × 97 × 24 feet (10,000 tons), (3) 1110 × 110 × 41½ feet. Three small floating docks of 2500 and 1800 tons and a third of unknown capacity. Six slips of 600 feet long, fully equipped with electric cranes, etc., and 4 smaller. Five wharves 585×50 feet, berthing for 15 average sized vessels. One sheer leg 100 tons, one 40 tons. 2 marine railways. All plant dates from 1910 or later. *Employees*: Average 2300. Enlarged 1917.

* Details not revised since 1914. Title may have been altered to BETHLEHEM UNION PLANT.

Also 30–40 new shipyards on Pacific coast, but these are engaged in mercantile construction only.

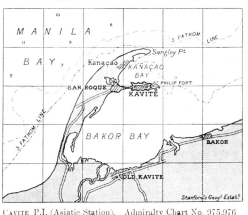

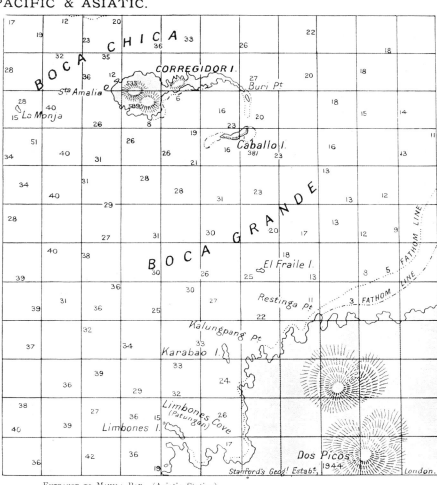

MARE ISLAND. Admiralty Chart No. 2887. CAVITE P.I. (Asiatic Station). Admiralty Chart No. 975,976 ENTRANCE TO MANILA BAY. (Asiatic Station).

Divided into 2000 yard squares.   Uniform scale.   Soundings in fathoms.   Heights in feet.

OLONGAPO & PORT SUBIC.

Naval Hospital.

LAS ANIMAS, Cal.

Naval Stations.—2ND CLASS, PACIFIC.

PEARL HARBOUR (1) Honolulu. (2) Pearl Harbour, on S. side of Island of Oahu, about 10–15 miles west of Honolulu. Large dock here. $1001 \times 114 \times 34\frac{2}{3}$ feet.

TUTUILA (SAMOA).

Asiatic Naval Stations.

CAVITE (P.I.) Small dry dock at Manila. Maps on preceding page.

OLONGAPO (P.I.) Dewey Floating dock, 18,500 tons, $501' \ 0\frac{3}{4}'' \times 100' \times 37' \ 0''$?

Chief Mercantile Ports.—PACIFIC COAST.*

Seattle ($2\frac{1}{4}$ million) ; San Francisco ($1\frac{1}{4}$ million).

* These figures were compiled before 1914, and can no longer be regarded as really trustworthy.

TUTUILA (SAMOA).
Admiralty Chart No. 1730.

JAPANESE DOCKYARDS.

Divided into 2000 yard squares.   Uniform scale.   Soundings in fathoms.   Heights in feet.

YOKOSUKA

KURE

MAIDZURU.

RYOJUN (PORT ARTHUR).

Imperial Dockyards.   Principal Naval Harbours (Ching-ju-fu).

YOKOSUKA (in Sagami). Fleet Base, Dockyard, T.B.D., Submarine and Aircraft Stations. Fortified. Six slips, one for battle-cruisers, two for Dreadnoughts, three smaller. Docks No. 5, $747 \times 115 \times 41$ feet, able to take any ship, and No. 4, $538 \times 98\frac{1}{2} \times 32$. Also one dock (No. 2) $447 \times 94\frac{1}{2} \times 29$ feet; two others : No. 1, $298 \times 82 \times 21$ feet ; No. 3, $265 \times 45 \times 18$ feet. Employees (in 1914) 8000. Naval Engineering Academy here. Naval Aviation Station at Oihama. Admiralty Chart No. 997.

KURE (in Aki). Fleet Base, Dockyard, T.B.D., and Aircraft Base. Three slips. Docks No. 1, $413 \times 58\frac{1}{2} \times 28$ feet ; No. 2, $485\frac{1}{2} \times 81 \times 35\frac{1}{2}$ feet. No. 3, $666 \times 100 \times 34$ feet. Perhaps a fourth big dock. Ordnance and Armour Plate built here. Cadets Academy at Etajima. Admiralty Chart No. 3469.

*SASEBO (in Hizen). Fleet Base, Dockyard, T.B.D. and Aircraft Base. One slip. There are four docks here : (1) $435 \times 94 \times 29$; (2) $475 \times 85 \times 32$; (3) $538 \times 93\frac{1}{2} \times 33$ feet, (4) $777 \times 111 \times 38$ feet. Perhaps a fifth big dock. There is also a floating dock for torpedo craft here (1500 tons). Admiralty Chart No. 359.

MAIDZURU (or MAIZURU) (in Tango). Admiralty Chart No. 2174. One dock 450 feet long, one small for t.b. (completed 1908). a third dock 540 feet long completed 1913. Perhaps a fourth dock.

RYOJUN (PORT ARTHUR). Dry docks : No. 1, $370 \times 72 \times 30$ feet ; No. 2, $500 \times 92\frac{1}{2} \times 32$ feet. Admiralty Chart No. 1236-1798.

DAIREN (Dalny). Naval dock, $381 \times 43 \times 19\frac{3}{4}$ feet.

CHINKAI (Korea), previously known as Masampo.

* See next page for Map.

JAPANESE DOCKYARDS.

Divided into 2000 yard squares. Uniform scale. Soundings in fathoms. Heights in feet.

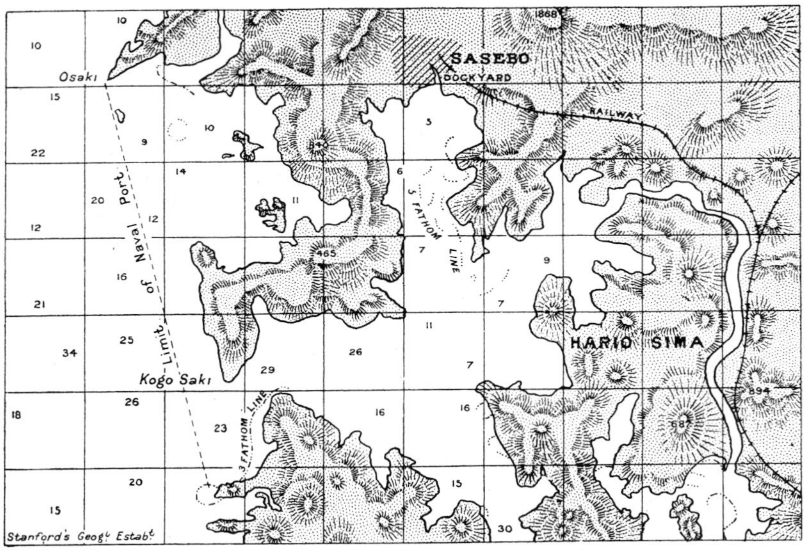

SASEBO.

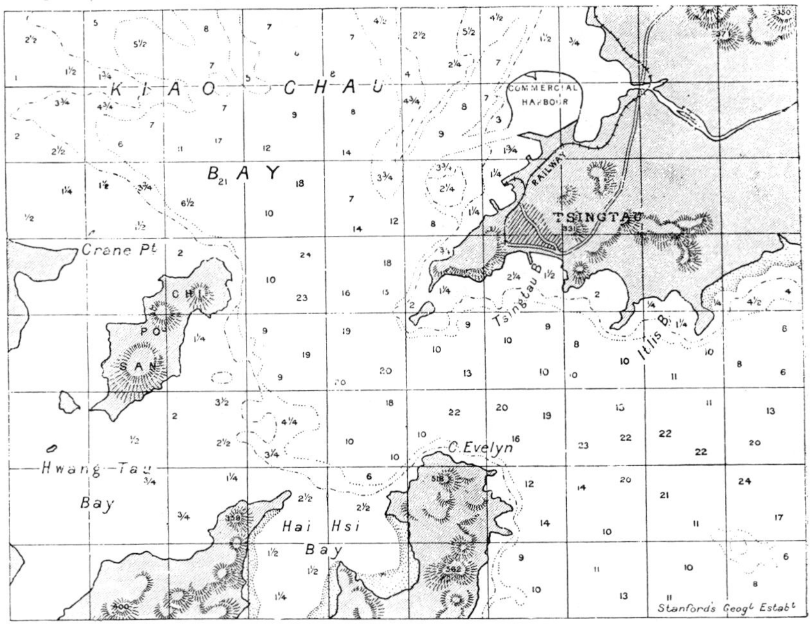

KIAO-CHAU and TSINGTAO (China). German naval base in the Far East, occupied by the Anglo-Japanese Expeditionary Army, 1914. There used to be a floating dock here, $410 \times 100 \times 30$ feet (12,000 tons), but it was probably destroyed by the Germans before surrender. Tsingtao is only being used as a commercial harbour, but the naval base facilities, created during German occupation, are at the disposal of Japanese warships in any emergency.

Lesser Naval Harbours (*Yoko*).

OMINATO. Torpedo base.
BAKO (Pescadores).
} Repair Stations for T.B.D., &c. Small 1500 ton Floating Dock at each.

Mercantile Marine.

June, 1919, 2,325,000 tons *gross*. A considerable amount of new mercantile tonnage is being built.

Coinage.

Yen (100 sen) = 2s. $0\frac{1}{2}$d. British, \$0.50 U.S.A., *about*.

Principal Mercantile Ports.

Yokohama, Hakodate, Nagasaki, Moji, Kobé, Dairen (Dalny).

Overseas Possessions.

Formosa, Karafuto (Saghalien), Pescadores. Protectorate in Chosen (Korea). Kiaochau Peninsula and Tsingtao leased from China.

Private Docks.

Details of Private Docks will be found on a later page (after the Silhouettes), with a full description of the Private Japanese Shipbuilding Yards.

FRENCH NAVAL BASES.

CHANNEL.

For Charts, **see preceding page.**

DUNKIRK. Fine harbour. Breakwater. Torpedo, Submarine and Aircraft base. There are five docks here—one $622 \times 69 \times 26\frac{1}{4}$, two $357\frac{1}{4} \times 46 \times 26$ or 21 feet, and one smaller.

CALAIS. Torpedo and submarine base. Dock, $426\frac{1}{4} \times 69 \times 28\frac{1}{2}$.

Private Docks.

BOULOGNE. Floating Dock, $236\frac{1}{4} \times 62\frac{1}{4}$ feet (1000 tons).
DIEPPE. Dry Dock, $361 \times 59 \times 27$ feet.
HAVRE. (No. 4). $674\frac{1}{4} \times 98\frac{3}{4} \times 28\frac{1}{2}$ feet ; also 2 large and 3 small docks.
GRANVILLE. Dry Dock, $225 \times 46\frac{1}{2} \times 23$ feet.
PAIMPOL. Dry Dock, $229\frac{1}{2} \times 36 \times$ feet.

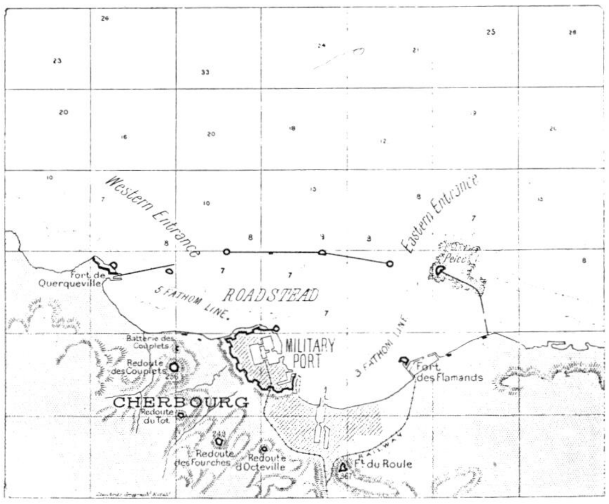

CHERBOURG. Admiralty Chart No. 2602. Rise of Spring Tide, $17\frac{3}{4}$ feet.

CHERBOURG. Protected by a breakwater about two miles long. Heavily fortified.

Dry Docks.

No. 1	$360 \times 62\frac{1}{3} \times 32\frac{1}{2}$ feet.	No. 5	$656 \times 93\frac{1}{4} \times 39\frac{1}{2}$ feet
,, 2	$393 \times 62\frac{1}{3} \times 32\frac{1}{2}$,,	,, 6	$606 \times 69\frac{1}{2} \times 29\frac{1}{4}$,,
,, 3	$390\frac{1}{2} \times 62\frac{1}{3} \times 32\frac{1}{2}$,,	,, 7	$265 \times 59 \times 20\frac{1}{2}$,,
,, 4	$360 \times 62\frac{1}{3} \times 32\frac{1}{2}$,,	,, 8	$257 \times 59\frac{1}{2} \times 20\frac{1}{2}$,,

Floating Submarine Salvage Dock, about 200×28 feet.

T.B.D., T.B., and S/M. built here.

ATLANTIC COAST.

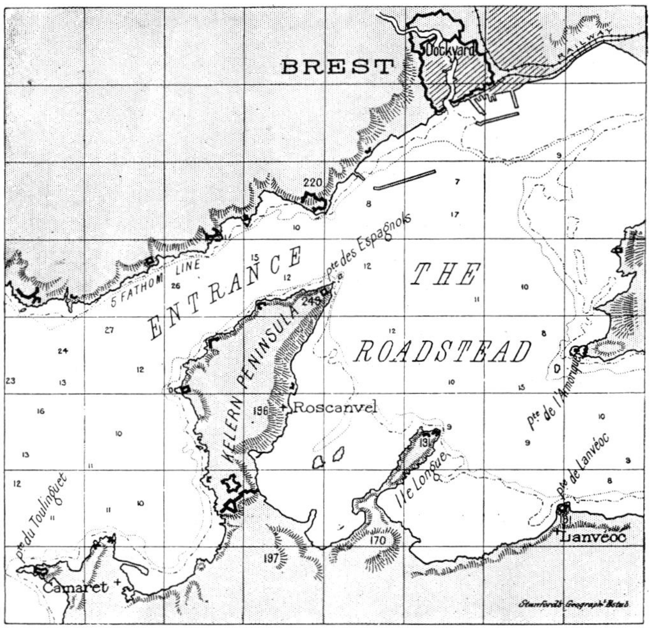

BREST. Admiralty Chart No. 3427. Rise of Spring Tide, $19\frac{1}{2}$ feet.

BREST. There is only one dock able to take big modern warships. There are eight smaller docks unable to take any modern warship of importance. Forts, very numerous and powerful. Very big dock in town, $737 \times 114 \times 34$. Particulars of naval docks here :

Nos. 1 & 3	$574\frac{1}{4} \times 70\frac{1}{4} \times 35\frac{1}{2}$	No. 7	$410 \times 87\frac{3}{4} \times 35\frac{1}{2}$ } Can be used
,, 2 & 4	$518\frac{1}{4} \times 91\frac{3}{4} \times 35\frac{1}{2}$	,, 8	$354 \times 66\frac{1}{4} \times 35\frac{1}{2}$ } as one dock.
No. 5	$377\frac{1}{4} \times 66\frac{1}{4} \times 35\frac{1}{2}$	,, 9	$387 \times 66\frac{1}{4} \times 35\frac{1}{2}$
,, 6	$223 \times 47\frac{3}{4} \times 16$		

Docks Nos. 7 and 8 are being united with a view to being used as a building yard.
Two Naval docks, 656×144 feet are under construction.

LORIENT. Dockyard and Base for Torpedo Craft and Submarines. No. 1, $380\frac{1}{2} \times 56\frac{1}{3} \times 20\frac{1}{2}$ feet ; No. 2, $620 \times 86\frac{1}{2} \times 29\frac{1}{3}$ feet ; No. 3, *proj.* $620 \times 92 \times 32$ feet.

ROCHEFORT. The three docks here cannot accommodate modern big ships. The largest is $489 \times 67\frac{1}{2} \times 25\frac{1}{4}$.

There is a Government dock at LA PALLICE (ROCHELLE), $553 \times 72 \times 30\frac{1}{2}$ feet, and another smaller.

Note.—During the war, various minor naval and aircraft stations were established along Atlantic Coast, principally for anti-submarine duties.

Big Private Docks.

BREST. (Town) $737 \times 114 \times 34$ feet.
ST. NAZAIRE. (C.G.T.) $731\frac{1}{2} \times 98\frac{1}{4} \times 29$ feet (enlarged).
BORDEAUX. $591 \times 108\frac{1}{4} \times 33$ feet ; $505 \times 72 \times 23$ feet.
LA ROCHELLE. $590 \times 72 \times 30$ feet.

FRENCH NAVAL BASES—MEDITERRANEAN.

(To uniform scale. Divided into 2000 yard squares. Soundings in fathoms. Heights in feet.) **Dockyards named in heavy type.**

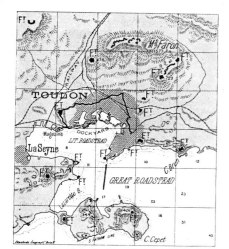

TOULON. Admiralty Chart No. 151-2608

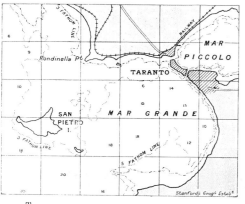

AJACCIO. Admiralty Chart No. 429.

Large Private Docks (*Mediterranean*).

MARSEILLES.—(No. 1) $595\frac{1}{2} \times 61 \times 22\frac{1}{2}$ feet, and No. 7, $669\frac{1}{4} \times 82 \times 29\frac{1}{2}$ feet.

TOULON. Very strongly fortified. Aircraft and Submarine base. Destroyers, T.B. and Submarines built here in Dockyard.

Dry Docks.

MISSIESSY.	No. 1	$427 \times 93\frac{1}{2} \times 30\frac{1}{2}$	CASTIGNEAU.	No. 1	$325 \times 70\frac{1}{2} \times 25\frac{1}{2}$
,,	,, 2	$427 \times 93\frac{1}{2} \times 30\frac{1}{2}$	,,	,, 2	$385\frac{1}{2} \times 70\frac{1}{4} \times 27\frac{1}{2}$
,,	,, 3	$585 \times 93\frac{1}{2} \times 30\frac{1}{2}$	,,	,, 3	$535 \times 75\frac{1}{2} \times 27\frac{1}{2}$
,,	,, 4	$600 \times 92 \times 32\frac{1}{2}$			

Floating dock for torpedo craft. Submarine Floating Salvage Dock, "Atlas" $300 \times 42\frac{2}{3}$ feet, 1000 tons lift. Also 3 small docks in the Arsenal Principal.

Naval Aviation Centres.

Very large establishment at Fréjus, St. Raphael, near Toulon. Also Training School at Berre, near Marseilles.

Naval Bases.—(*Continued*).

AJACCIO. } Fortified harbours used by the French fleet. No docks.
BONIFACIO. }

ALGIERS. Coaling Station. Two dry docks (No. 1) $455 \times 74 \times 28$ feet; (No. 2) $268 \times 54 \times 19$ feet. Average depth of harbour, 8 fathoms.

ORAN. Torpedo base. Excellent harbour, with an average depth of five fathoms. Two breakwaters. Fortified. Floating Submarine Salvage Dock 210×64 feet.

BIZERTA. Submarine and Aircraft base. Lies inside a narrow channel. One large dock suitable for any warship, one small one. Floating dock for torpedo craft. (No. 1) $656 \times 90\frac{1}{2} \times 33\frac{1}{2}$; (No. 3) $295 \times 46\frac{1}{2} \times 17\frac{1}{4}$; (No. 4) $656\frac{1}{4} \times 90\frac{1}{2} \times 33\frac{1}{2}$. Submarine Salvage Ship *Vulcain* stationed here.

Note.—Temporary Naval Base established at Beyrout. During the War the French Fleet was first based at Malta, but was transferred to Corfu. Milo, Mudros, Salonika, Salamina, Gulf of Patras, were netted for use as anchorages for French Warships.

ORAN. Admiralty Chart No. 812.

BIZERTA.
Admiralty Chart No 1569.

FRENCH **COLONIAL** NAVAL BASES.

DAKAR (Senegal).
Admiralty Chart No. 1001.

African W. Coast.

DAKAR (Senegal). Naval dry dock here, $629\frac{3}{4} \times 92\frac{2}{3} \times 30\frac{1}{2}$ feet.

African E. Coast.

Also one or two small Naval Stations in Madagascar; location not known.

In the Far East.

SAIGON. Situated 42 miles up the Donnoi River, Anchorage average, 9 fathoms. One large dry dock $518 \times 72 \times 30$ feet, and two small ones. Floating Dock 400 $\times 66$ feet, 10,000 tons lift. Slip for building ships up to 300 feet long.

ITALIAN DOCKYARDS, WEST & SOUTH COAST.

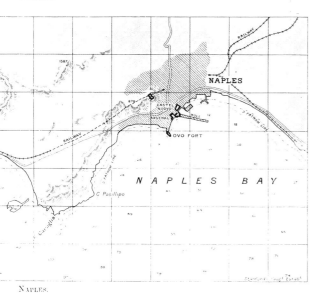

TARANTO.

SPEZIA.

TABLE OF DISTANCES.

MADDALENA		
	to	knots.
Ajaccio	...	60
Bonafacio	...	20
Naples	...	210

SPEZIA		
	to	knots.
Ajaccio	...	160
Bizerta	...	430
Genoa	...	50
Leghorn	...	40
Maddalena	...	175
Malta	...	580
Naples	...	290
Taranto	...	630
Toulon	...	195
Venice	...	1000

NAPLES		
	to	knots.
Ajaccio	...	265
Bizerta	...	315
Bonafacio	...	225
Maddalena	...	210

TARANTO			VENICE		
	to	knots.		to	knots.
Bizerta	...	550	Pola	...	75
Malta	...	310	*Taranto*	...	575
Messina	...	220	Toulon	...	1197
Naples	...	380			
Venice	...	575			

TRIESTE to

		MILES.			MILES.
Brindisi	...	372	*Pola*	...	61
Cattaro	...	337	Smyrna⊙	...	902
Constantinople⊙	...	1050	,, †	...	1000
,, †	...	1152	Salonika⊙	...	950
Corfu	...	480	,, †	...	1049
Fiume	...	110	Toulon	...	1169
Gibraltar	...	1648	Wilhelmshaven§	...	3207
Malta	...	730	,, ‡	...	3744
Piraeus⊙	...	708	Zeebrugge§	...	3050
,, †	...	839	,, ‡	...	3756

⊙ By Canal of Corinth.
† By Cape Matapan.
§ By English Channel.
‡ By North of Scotland and West of Ireland.

Royal Dockyards.

SPEZIA. Docks: No. 5, $702 \times 105\frac{1}{2} \times 33$ feet; No. 6, $508 \times 90 \times 33$ feet; No. 4, $354\frac{1}{4} \times 71\frac{1}{2} \times 29$ feet; Nos. 3 and 2, $430 \times 77 \times 30$ feet; No. 1, $358 \times 71 \times 30$ feet. Two large slips. (At Muggiano, there is a special testing dock for submarines belonging to Fiat-San-Giorgio Co.) Total employees about 5300. Admiralty Chart No. 155.

NAPLES (NAPOLI). One small Government dock, $247 \times 62 \times 19\frac{1}{2}$ feet. New large dock, *projected*, 1918. One small slip. Total employees 3029. Good anchorage. Commercial harbour and various new harbour works *projected*. There are two municipal docks (*v.* preceding page). Admiralty Chart No. 1728.

CASTELLAMARE. No docks. Building yard. Two large slips, two small. Total employees 1920.

TARANTO. One dock, "Principe do Napoli," $709 \times 108 \times 32\frac{1}{2}$ feet (2 sections). Floating dock, $365 \times 61 \times 25$ feet (4800 tons), and another smaller (2900 tons). One large slip. Total employees 1561. Admiralty Chart No. 1643. Two 130 ton old Krupps are mounted in a turret on San Pietro.

MADDALENA (Sardinia). No docks. Total employees 113. **MESSINA** (Sicily): Government Dock $343 \times 71\frac{1}{2} \times 26$ feet.

Torpedo Craft, Submarine and Naval Aircraft Stations: Spezia, Naples, Taranto. Also minor Naval Stations at Genoa, Maddalena, Gaeta, Messina.

ITALIAN DOCKYARDS.—ADRIATIC.
(To Uniform Scale. Divided into 2000-yard squares. Soundings in fathoms. Heights in feet.)

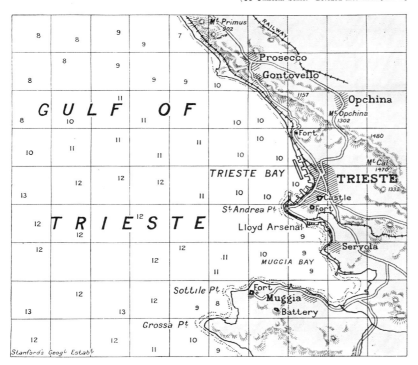

Arsenals.

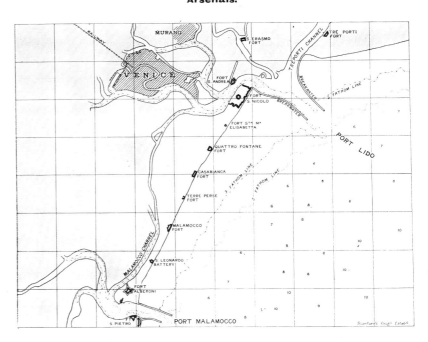

Royal Dockyards.

VENICE (VENEZIA). One dock, No. 4, 656×106×38½ feet; one dock for long cruisers, No. 1, 525×78×25½ feet; one small dock No. 2, for third-class cruisers, 295×59×19½ feet. Two large slips, one small slip. Submarines built in this yard. Employees 2797. Depth of Port Lido, 29 feet. Malamocco, 28 feet at low water. Commercial harbours at both. Admiralty Chart No. 1483.

TRIESTE. No Government docks. One slip. Two Private docks here, 456×73×19 feet and 360×54×18¾ feet; there is a dock at San Rocco, across the bay, 414×66×21 feet. Two floating of 2,000 and 1,500 tons. Admiralty Chart No. 1434. Rise of Spring Tide, 2 feet.

POLA (Late Austro-Hungarian Naval Base). Heavily fortified. Slips: One 690 feet long and two smaller. Two dry docks: (a) 467×85×27¾ feet and (b) 397×86×31½ feet. Floating docks: (c) 585×111×37 feet (22,500 tons); (d) 459½×90×32¼ feet (15,000 tons); (e) 300×82½×20 feet; (f) small, only used for torpedo craft, 1,000 tons lift, completed June, 1914. Employés 4500. 3 slips. Naval hospital. Admiralty Chart No. 202. Rise of Spring Tide, 3½ feet.

Torpedo Craft, Submarine & Naval Aircraft Stations: Venice, Brindisi. Also minor Naval Station at Ancona.

(For BRINDISI, see next page).

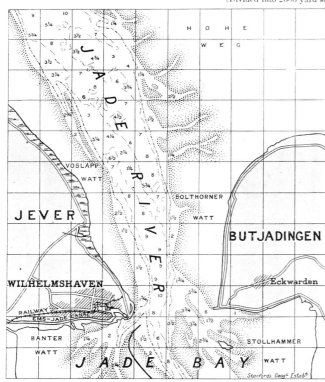

GERMAN DOCKYARDS.—NORTH SEA.
(Divided into 2000 yard squares. Uniform scale. Soundings in fathoms. Heights in feet).

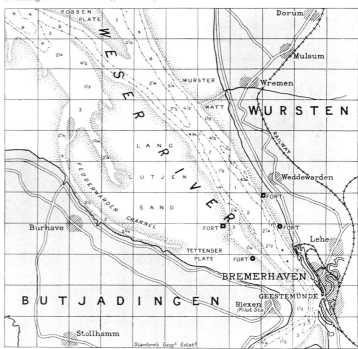

WILHELMSHAVEN. Fleet base; also base for torpedo craft, and seaplanes. Two large basins. Harbour for torpedo craft inside yard.

Docks (Graving): Nos. (1), (2) and (3), 625×99½×36 feet; No. (4), 584×101×35 feet; No. (5), 584×101×35 feet; No. (6), 584×94×35 feet; No. (7), 822×131×34 feet; No. (8), 822×114¾×34 feet. Five floating docks and 4 pontoons for torpedo boats. One 35,000 ton floating dock. Four building slips, (1) 600 feet, (2) 345 feet, (3) 300 feet, (4) about 600 feet. Men employed, about 11,500. Machinery: 38 of 9300 H.P. Admiralty Chart No. 3346. Rise of Spring Tide, 11½ feet. Harbour has to be dredged continually on account of the sand which silts up very badly. Wangeroog (at mouth of Jade) is a minor Naval Station.

BREMERHAVEN. Port for Bremen, which is 50 miles inland of river mouth, and about 28 miles from Bremerhaven. At Bremen are the headquarters of the N. Deutscher Lloyd, and the big shipbuilding firm, Weser Act-Gesellschaft. Trade of the district (Bremerhaven, Vegesack, etc. included) was 2,750,000 tons of shipping cleared annually before the war. Kaiser Dry Dock No. 1, 741×98×35 feet, can take ships up to 50,000 tons. Another (N.D.L. floating) 450×58×19½ feet. At Bremerhaven, Seebeck Co. has one dock (No. 1) 550×65×21 feet, and three smaller. At Geestemünde, the same firm has two docks, each 547×80×18 feet. Also at Geestemünde, two smaller dry docks; and at Hammelwarden, one small dry dock. At Bremen, one floating dock, 490×90×23 feet (12,000 tons), and another smaller (3000 tons). Geestemünde, Bremen, and Bremerhaven are minor Naval Stations. Naval Hospital, Barracks, &c., at Lehe, near Bremerhaven.

Admiralty Chart No. 3346. Rise of Spring Tide, 10¾ feet.

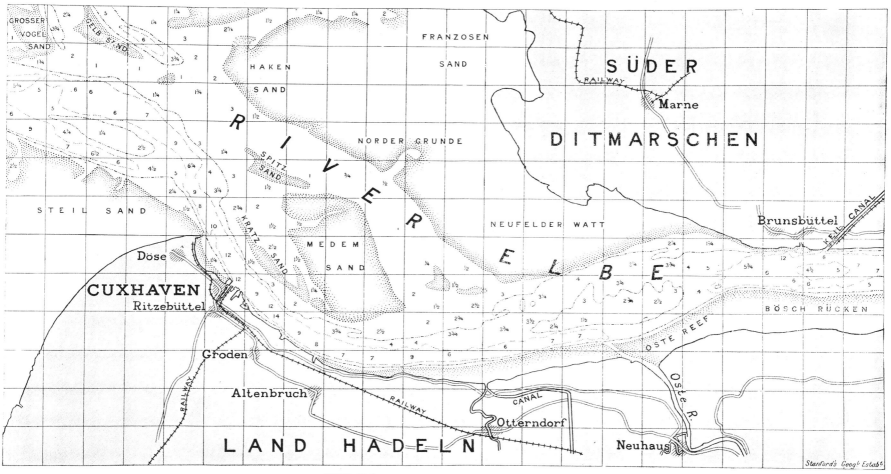

CUXHAVEN (and North Sea entrance to Kiel Canal).

CUXHAVEN. Port for Hamburg, which is 65 miles from the sea, and headquarters of the H.A.P.A.G. (Hamburg-American Line). Mine and Torpedo Station at Groden. Ammunition Stores; Naval Airship and Seaplane Base; Naval Hospital and Barracks; W/T. Station. Before the war, trade of Hamburg and Cuxhaven amounted to about 9,500,000 tons of shipping cleared per. annum. Very strongly fortified. A dredged channel for Destroyers is believed to exist north of Medem Sand. Brunsbüttel coaling basin 1700×680 feet area. Naval Airship Station at Fuhlsbüttel, near Hamburg. Admiralty Chart No. 3261.   Rise of Spring Tide, 10¼ feet.

Map is to Special Scale : see Note inset.

EMDEN. New and large W/T. Station. One floating dock (Inner Harbour) 284½ × 59½ × 17¾ feet (3500 tons). 1 smaller (2500 tons). Lock between Inner Harbour and Ems River 853 × 131 × 43 feet. Inner and Outer Harbours 37 feet deep connected by dredged channel 40 feet deep. There is a small canal (Ems-Jade) between this port and Wilhelmshaven, which was only suitable for small vessels of shallow draught in 1914. The Borkum is fortified. Big Naval W/T. Station at Norddeich. Admiralty Chart No. 3761.

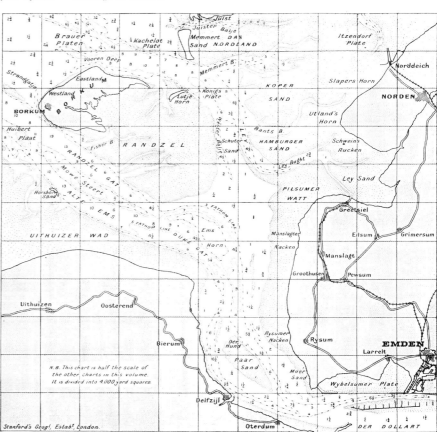

Note.—Channel along Wybelsumer Plate from Ems River into Port said to be dredged now to 5 fathoms. Channel out to Borkum may also be dredged.

GERMAN NAVY.

KIEL CANAL.

Length : 61¾ miles. Width at surface : 394 feet and 144 feet at bottom. New double locks : 1082 × 147 × 36 feet. Old locks (at Holtenau and Brunsbüttel) : 482 × 82 × 29½ feet. Sidings : 4 of 3600 × 540 feet. 11 other bays of 984 feet for turning. Speed of ships : 10 kts. for large, 15 kts. for small. Time of passage : 7 to 10 hours, according to size of ships ; but 16 battleships can, in emergency, pass in 6 hours.

Naval Airship Stations.

AHLHORN	NORDHOLZ
FRIEDRICHSHAVEN	STOLP (in Pommern)
KÖNIGSBERG (Seerappen)	WITTMUNDHAFEN
NIEDERGORSDORF	

NORTH SEA Seaplane Bases.

BORKUM	NORDENEY
HELIGOLAND	WILHELMSHAVEN
LIST	

BALTIC—Seaplane Bases.

APENRADE	KIEL
BUG (Rügen Island)	PUTZIG
DANZIG	SEERAPPEN
FLENSBURG	SEDDIN
HOLTENAU	WIEK (Rügen Island)
NEST	WARNEMÜNDE

Note.

The following details of Principal Private Yards in North Sea and Baltic relate to conditions up to August, 1914.

NORTH SEA (*Nordsee*).

Principal Private Yards :

BLOHM & VOSS (HAMBURG). Ten *Slips* (four 600 feet long, five each about 500 feet long, and one slip 328 feet). Five *Docks* (floating). (1) 320 × 52 × 18. (2) 355 × 52 × 18. (3) 558 × 88 × 25. (4) 595 × 88 × 25. (5) 728 × 123 × 36 feet (46,000 tons). Possibly a sixth (40,000 tons) intended originally for Pola D.Y. (Austria-Hungary). Probably build submarines and destroyers now. *Employees*, 10,000. *Machinery*, 10,000 H.P. Bought Janssen & Schmilinsky Yard for extensions, 1917, with dock 400 × 50 × 16 feet.

A. G. WESER (BREMEN). Five *Slips* (one of 650 feet, one of 490 feet, two of 328 feet, one small). Three *Docks* (floating) of small size. Build submarines. *Employees*, 6000. *Machinery*, 4220 H.P.

BREMER-VULKAN (VEGESACK). Six *Slips* (one of 650 feet, two about 500 feet, three smaller). *Docks*, one floating. Probably build submarines and destroyers now. *Employees*, about 3100. *Machinery*, 2800 H.P.

VULCAN (HAMBURG). Two *Slips*, 650 feet or so. Four floating docks : No. 4, 605 × 85 × 28 feet (17,500 tons) ; No. 3, 610 × 106 × 28 feet (27,000 tons). Another dock, 723¾ × 108½ × 32¾ feet (32,000 tons) may exist. Two smaller floating docks, 433 × 70 × feet (6000 tons) and 510 × 82 × feet (11,000 tons). *Employees*, about 9000. H.P. 6500.

JOHANN C. TECKLENBORG (GEESTEMÜNDE). Six *Slips* (two of 600 feet, two about 500 feet, two smaller). 2600 men. H.P. 2600. Two dry docks.

REIHERSTIEG SCHIFFSWERFTE (HAMBURG). One *Slip* about 550 feet, one about 400, five small. *Docks* : one (floating) 511½ × 97 × 26 feet (20,000 tons), three smaller. *Employees*, about 2000. H.P. about 4000. Bought J. & N. Wichorst Yard, 1917, for extensions.

BALTIC (*Ostsee*).

(A)—Principal Private Yards.

HOWALDT (KIEL). Nine *Slips* (two over 700 feet, one about 500 feet, six smaller). *Docs* : one floating (11,000 tons). *Employees*, about 3500. *Machinery* :

KRUPP'S GERMANIA (KIEL). Nine *Slips* (five of 700 to 520 feet, the rest smaller). Submarines built here for which 10-12 slips were available in 1914. *Employees*, 6400. *Machinery*, 4000 H.P. *Docks* : None.

SCHICHAU (ELBING). Twenty-seven *Slips* (six over 650 feet long, the others all small). Two *Docks* (floating) for torpedo craft. *Employees*, about 10,000. *Machinery*, 5000 H.P.

VULCAN (BREDOW-STETTIN). Seven *Slips* (two over 650 feet, two about 500 feet, three about 350 feet or so). Two *Docks* (floating). (1) 416 × 58 × 17 feet. (2) 300 × 37 × 14½ feet. *Employees*, 7000.

GERMAN HARBOURS—BALTIC.

(Uniform Scale.   Divided into 2000 yard squares.   Soundings in fathoms).

KIEL (and Baltic entrance to Kiel Canal). Fleet, torpedo craft, and seaplane bases and training stations. Two large basins. Docks : (1) 423 × 71 × 28. (2) 382 × 70 × 25½ (3) 362 × 64½ × 22½ (4) 344 × 67 × 16 (5) 570 × 94 × 30 (6) 570 × 94 × 30. Also one floating dock (40,000 tons), 660 × 96 × 32 feet, and five small floating. Another 36,000 ton floating, and 1 small private floating dock (Swentine). Two building slips. (1) 427 feet. (2) 427 feet. Men employed, *about* 10,500. Machinery : 109 of 23,240 H.P. Admiralty Chart, No. 33.

GERMAN DOCKYARDS.—BALTIC—(Continued).

(Divided into 2000 yard squares. Uniform Scale. Soundings in fathoms).

Other smaller Naval Stations in 1914 in Baltic, were :—

FRIEDRICHSORT (see Kiel Map). Torpedo manufactory and range ; munitions and mine depots ; naval hospital and barracks.

DIETRICHSDORF : Ammunition depot.

WARNEMÜNDE : Seaplane base 1914–19.

NEUMÜNSTER 1 H : Big naval W/T. station.

SONDERBURG : Naval hospital and barracks.

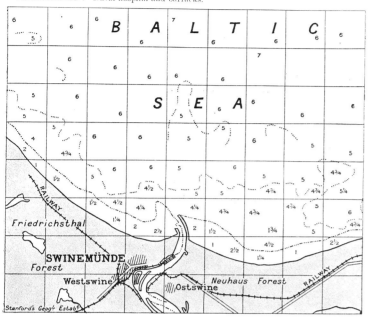

SWINEMÜNDE. Port for Stettin, a smaller naval station, which is 36 miles up the river. Trade of Stettin and Swinemunde is about 1,300,000 tons of shipping cleared annually, but is much greater at present. No docks here suitable for large warships.

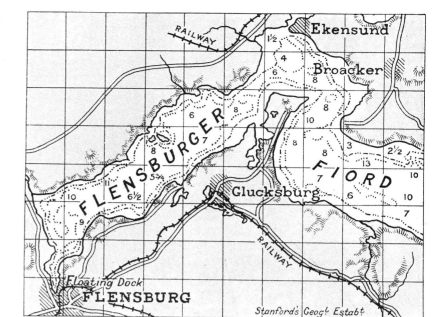

FLENSBURG - MURWICK. Seaplane Station. Smaller Naval Station in 1914, with Gunnery and Torpedo Schools, Naval Hospital and Barracks. Floating Pontoon Dock, 280 × 49 × 19 feet. 2,800 tons.

Note.

By plebiscite of the population of Slesvig, Flensburg may become a Danish Port in the near future.

ROYAL DOCKYARDS—HOME WATERS.

SEAPLANES.

ENSIGN

JACK

ADMIRAL

VICE ADMIRAL

REAR ADMIRAL

ROYAL STANDARD

NAVAL RESERVE (BLUE ENSIGN)

MERCANTILE ENSIGN (RED ENSIGN)

Red	▥
White	□
Blue	▦
Yellow	▨

ROSYTH to	knots.
Aberdeen	95
Dover	473
Helder	360
Hull	260
Kronstadt ...	1345
Newcastle ...	130
Portsmouth ...	570
Sheerness... ...	458
Wilhelmshaven	445

SHEERNESS to	knots.
Dover	45
Dunkirk	70
Helder	190
Hull	200
Kronstadt ...	1200
Newcastle ...	328
Portsmouth ...	150
Wilhelmshaven	270

PORTSMOUTH to	knots.
Barbados ...	3600
Berehaven ...	375
Brest	226
Cherbourg ...	72
Devonport ...	155
Gibraltar... ...	1200
Lorient	331
New York ...	3080
Pernambuco ...	3900

Portland	55
Wilhelmshaven	620

DEVONPORT to	knots.
Berehaven ...	375
Brest	140
Cape of Good Hope ...	5890
Cherbourg ...	110
Gibraltar... ...	1050
Lorient	233
New York ...	2905
Portland	100
Queenstown ...	292
Rochefort ...	370
Toulon	1764

GIBRALTAR to	knots.
Ajaccio	1000
Algiers ...	420
Berehaven ...	1170
Bizerta	875
Brest	953
Devonport ...	1050
Malta	980
Oran	225
Toulon	713

MALTA to	knots.
Aden	2320
Ajaccio	450
Bizerta	240

Constantinople...	702
Port Said... ...	920
Sevastopol ...	1000
Spezia	580
Suda Bay ...	575
Suez	1010
Toulon	612

ADEN to	knots.
Batavia	3950
Beira	2824
Bombay	1652
Cape Town ...	4450
Colombo	2100
Delagoa Bay ...	3340
Devonport... ...	4350
Durban	3650
Karachi	1470
Mauritius... ...	2600
Suez	1310
Tamatave ...	2290
Zanzibar	1770

COLOMBO to	knots.
Bombay	900
Calcutta	1240
Devonport... ...	6450
Fremantle (W.A.) ...	3105
Karachi	1400
Penang	1280
Rangoon	1207

Singapore... ...	1600
Sydney(N.S.W.)	5450

SINGAPORE to	knots.
Bangkok	820
Batavia	500
Devonport... ...	8020
Hong Kong ...	1430
Manila	1320
Saigon	648

HONG-KONG to	knots.
Devonport... ...	9450
Kiao-chau ...	1270
Manila	650
Nagasaki	1067
Port Arthur ...	1415
Saigon	930
Shanghai	870
Ta-kau(Formosa)	340
Vladivostock ...	1927
Wei-hai-wei ...	1470
Yokosuka... ...	1620

CAPE OF GOOD HOPE to	knots.
Ascension	2395
Durban	812
Falkland Isles	4800
Fremantle (W.A.) ...	4850
Hobart	5527

Madagascar ...	1800
Port Elizabeth	428
Portsmouth ...	5960
St. Helena ...	1710
Teneriffe	4470

ESQUIMAULT to	knots.
Honolulu	2410
San Francisco...	750
Seattle	76
Yokosuka... ...	4300

SYDNEY (N.S.W.) to	knots.
Adelaide	1076
Auckland... ...	1280
Batavia	4476
Brisbane	510
Cape of Good Hope	6157
Colombo	5450
Devonport (via Cape)...	12,047
Hobart	630
Melbourne ...	570
Singapore ...	4980
Wellington, (N.Z.)	1234

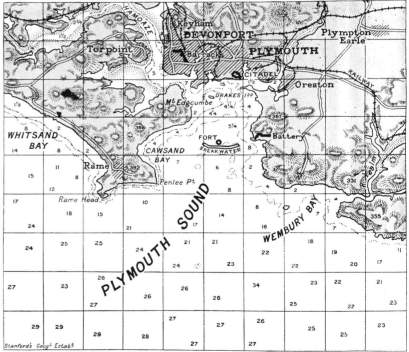

(In 2000 yard squares. Soundings in fathoms. Heights in feet.)

1. DEVONPORT and KEYHAM. At *Devonport* (South Yard)—two big slips, three small. Dry docks :—No. 3, could just take *Duncan* class, size 430 × 93 × 34¾ feet, and three others, of which one (No. 2 Dock) can take a second class cruiser ; other two suitable for small craft only. At *Keyham* (North Yard)—No slips. New basin, 35½ acres, depth, 32½ft. Tidal basin, 10 acres, depth, 32ft.

Dry Docks in New Extension :—

Entrance lock, 730° × 95 × 44 feet.

No. 9 (double) 745 × 95 × 32 ,,

Keyham (North Yard) No. 10 (double) 741 × 95 × 44 feet.

,, 8 659 × 95 × 32 ,,

* Can be lengthened 86 feet.

In the old part of the yard there are three docks, of which one (No. 7) can take a second class cruiser ; the others small craft only. Total employees for the two yards, 14,000–15,000.

Admiralty Chart No. 1267. Rise of Spring Tide 15½ feet (Dockyard).

(ROYAL) BRITISH NAVY.

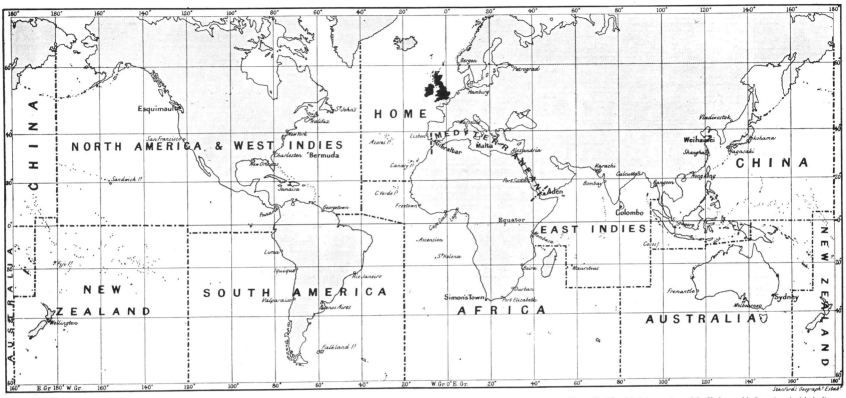

LIMITS OF BRITISH NAVAL STATIONS, 1919.

From Chart furnished by courtesy of the Hydrographic Department, Admiralty.

BRITISH NAVY.

Diesel Engine Builders.

(From "The Motorship," New York.)

	Type of Engine.
Cammell Laird & Co., Birkenhead	Fullagar (2-cycle)
North British Diesel Engine Co., Glasgow	———? —— (4-cycle)
Clyde Shipbuilding & Engineering Co., Govan, Glasgow ..	Carels (2-cycle)
Harland & Wolff Diesel Dept., Glasgow	Burmeister & Wain (4-cycle)
Wm. Doxford & Sons (Northumberland Shipbuilding Co., Ltd.), Sunderland	Junkers (2-cycle, Solid-injection)
Wallsend Slipway, Wallsend-on-Tyne ..	———?———?——
North Eastern Marine Engineering Co., Wallsend-on-Tyne	Werkspoor (4-cycle)
John I. Thornycroft & Co., London	Carels (2-cycle)
Wm. Denny Bros. & Co., Ltd., Dumbarton	Sulzer (2-cycle)
J. Samuel White & Co., East Cowes	White M.A.N. (2-cycle)
⊙Vickers Limited, Barrow-in-Furness	Vickers (4-cycle)
Mirrlees, Bickerton & Day, Stockton-on-Tees ..	Mirrlees (4-cycle)
Willans, Robinson & Co., Rugby	Willans (4-cycle)
Yarrows Limited, Scotstoun	M .A .N. (2-cycle)
Fairfield Shipbuilding & Engineering Co., Port Glasgow ..	M. A. N. (2-cycle)
Scotts Shipbuilding & Engineering Co., Greenock ..	Ansaldo-Fiat (2-cycle)
Alex. Stephen & Sons, Linthouse (Glasgow)	———?———?——
Sir W. G. Armstrong, Whitworth & Co., Newcastle-on-Tyne	Armstrong-Whitworth (2 & 4-cycle)
Richardsons Westgarth, Middlesborough	Carels (2-cycle)
Wm. Beardmore & Co., Ltd., Dalmuir	Beardmore & Tosi (4-cycle)
Swan, Hunter & Wigham Richardsons Ltd., Newcastle-on-Tyne	Neptune & Polar (2-cycle)
Palmers Shipbuilding & Engineering Co., Jarrow-on-Tyne	———?———?——
Barclay, Curle & Co., Glasgow	Burmeister & Wain (4-cycle)
Norris, Henty & Gardners Ltd., Patricroft	Gardner (4-cycle)
Union Ship Engineering Co. Ltd., Montrose	———?—— (4-cycle)
Ruston & Hornsby, Lincoln	Nelseco† (4-cycle)

* Also building engines in association with Messrs. Petters, Yeovil.

† Several other British engineering companies also built the Nelseco (American) marine Diesel engine during the war.

Uniforms.

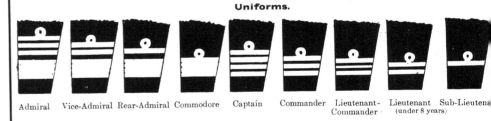

| Admiral | Vice-Admiral | Rear-Admiral | Commodore | Captain | Commander | Lieutenant-Commander | Lieutenant (under 8 years) | Sub-Lieutenant |

Admiral of the fleet one stripe more than a full Admiral.

In relative ranks, Engineers have the same *with the curl*, and with purple between the stripes (1915 change).

" "	Surgeons	"	"	"	red	"	" (1918 change).
" "	Paymasters	"	"	"	white	"	" (" ").
" "	Naval Instructors	"	"	"	blue	"	" (" ").

Note.—On the right sleeve only, inverted chevrons are worn for every year of War Service since August 5th, 1914. The first and lowest chevron in silver is for War Service up to Dec. 31st, 1914. The upper gold chevrons are for each year's service from Jan. 1st, 1915. Also worn by the Royal Marines, R.A.N., R.C.N., R.N.R., R.F.R., R.N.V.R., R.N. Sick Berth Reserve and officers of the Mercantile Marine serving in H.M. Ships and Auxiliaries.

Personnel and Navy Estimates. 1919-20.

Provisional Estimates have only been presented to Parliament, for the sum of £149,200,000, but it is noted that revised and detailed Estimates will be presented at a later date in the Financial Year. Personnel is estimated at 280,000 officers, seamen, boys, coastguards and Royal Marines, but this total is being rapidly decreased by demobilisation and discharges. It was 180,000 in August, 1919, and will be about 147,000 in Jan., 1920.

Admiralty (October, 1919).

First Lord	..	The Right Hon. Walter Long, M.P.
First Lord and Chief of Staff ..	..	Admiral Earl Beatty, G.C.B., D.S.O., &c.
Deputy First Sea Lord	..	
Deputy Chief of Staff	..	
Assistant Chief of Staff	..	
Second Sea Lord	..	
Third Sea Lord and Controller ..	..	
Fourth Sea Lord	..	
Civil Lord	..	
Chief Constructor	..	Sir Eustace H. Tennyson D'Eyncourt, K.C.B.

(left margin: Operations / Maintenance)

BRITISH NAVAL ORDNANCE, HEAVY, B.L. (Capt. R. V. WALLING, R.G.A., retired).

NOTE.—All details are unofficial, but believed to be approximately correct. Particulars given, for reference purposes, of some older marks of guns, now dismounted from H.M. Ships.

Designation, Calibre, ins.	Mark.	Length.	Weight of piece without B.M.	Weight of Projectile.	M.V.	M.E.	Weight of Charge.	Max. R.P.M.	REMARKS.
		cals.	tons cwts. qrs.	lbs.	f. s.	f. t.	lbs.		
18	I	35 ?	150 0 0 ?	3,600 ?	?	?	?	?	Monitors and "Furious" originally mounted these pieces, but they have been removed.
15	"B"	45	96 0 0	1950	2500	84,500	450	1.2	Particulars doubtful. Mk. I also reported to be 42 cals. long.
15	I	45	96 0 0	1920	2655	84,070	428	1.2	
13.5	V	45	74 18 1	1250	2700	63,190	296	1.5	With tapered inner "A" tube, without forward step, weighs I cwt. more. Obsolete Marks: I; II; III; IIIa, b, c, d, e, and f; IV.
12	XII	50	65 13 1	850	3010	53,400	307	2	} Dreadnoughts and Battle Cruisers.
	XI	50	65 13 1	850	3010	53,046	307	2	
	XI*								
	X	45	56 16 1	850	2800	47,800	258	2	
	X*	45	56 12 1						
	IX	40	50 0 0	850	2650	39,200	246	2	Mk. IX guns in "King Edward" class only:—Wt. of Charge, 254 lbs. Marks: VI, IV, V, Vw, VIII, VIIIe, VIIIv, IX, IXe, IXv, IXw, X, X*, XI, XI* and XII have been introduced into the Naval Service.
10	VII	45	30 4 2	500	2850	26,945	146 2/3	3	Only mounted in "Triumph," now sunk.
	VI	45	36 10 0	500	2800	27,181	146 2/3	3	Only mounted in "Swiftsure." Mk. VI*, land guns. Wt. given is that without "Ring, connecting hydraulic buffer."
	VI*								A Mk. V pattern was sealed, but the gun was never made.
9.2	XI	50	28 0 0	380	3000	23,700	128 1/2	4	
	XI*	50	27 15 2	380	3000	22,930	128 1/2	4	
	Xv	46	27 19 0	380	2800	20,685	120	4	Only two Mk. Xv guns in the Service.
	X	46	27 19 0	380	2800	20,685	120	4	There is one Mk. X/IX gun for Naval Service.
	VIII	40	24 6 3	380	2347	14,520	66	4	"Terrible" only; two guns from "Powerful" mounted in R.G.A. Battery at Scapa Flow. Twenty different Marks have been made and fourteen introduced in Naval Service.
14	I	45	85 0 0	1400	2700	70,770	324	2	Elswick Ordnance Co., "Armstrong" design. H.M.S. "Canada" only.
	?	45	70 6 0	1400	2600	65,700	?	?	Bethlehem guns, mounted in monitors only ("Abercrombie" class).

MEDIUM, B.L.

Designation, Calibre, ins.	Mark.	Length.	Weight of piece without B.M.	Weight of Projectile.	M.V.	M.E.	Weight of Charge.	Max. R.P.M.	REMARKS.
7.5	III	50	15 9 3	200	3000	12,481	54 1/4	5	Monitors, removed from "Swiftsure." Mks. IV and IV* were for "Triumph," sunk.
	III*								
	II**	50	14 16 2	200	2800	12,500	61	5	New Mark in "Hawkins" and "Raleigh," of which no details available.
	V								
	I	45	13 9 2	200	2600	9340	61	5	"Devonshire" class only. Other Marks in Naval Service: 1* and 1** of 45 cal./L; II and II* of 50 cal./L.
6	XVIII	50	?	100	?	?	?	7	New ships.
	XIV	50	?	100	3100	6665	?	7	"Cleopatra" class.
	XI*	50	8 8 2	100	3000	6240	32 1/2	7	
	XI								
	VIII	45	7 7 2	100	2750	5250	23	7	Mk. VIII left hand guns for "T" mounting in "County" class.
	VII								Many new Marks of 6 in. introduced during the War, including a short Mk. XIX for L.S. (Travelling Carriage.)
5.5	I	50	3 10 0	115	2870	6000 (?)	?	8	Woolwich Arsenal. Details doubtful. Mounted in "Furious" and "Hood," "Birkenhead" and "Chester" 5.5 guns and mountings by Coventry Ordnance Co.
4.7	I	50	3 14 0	45	3000	2800	14	12	Woolwich Arsenal. Modified 4.7 inch Q.F. V (L.S.). New T.B.D's.

Also :—
Q.F. 6 in., many marks } quite obsolete, but were mounted in D.A.M.S. and S.D.V.
Q.F.C. 6 in., " " } during the War.
Q.F. 4.7 in. Mk. V, Land Service only.

Mk. IV, three-motion B.M., Mk. IV "B," same, converted to single-motion.
Mk. III, " Mk. III "B" " "
Mk. II, " Mk. II "B" " "
Mk. I, " Mk. I "B" " "

BRITISH NAVAL ORDNANCE, TORPEDOES, MINES, &c.

Torpedoes.

No official details available. Various Marks of 21 inch, 18 inch and 14 inch torpedoes said to be in service; the first two with heaters, the third without. Also a specially light 14 inch mark for use by "Cuckoo" type Torpedo-dropping Seaplanes and C.M.B.

Mines.

No official figures available. Among the various Marks of mines produced during the War, the following are said to exist: (a) Spherical types with swinging-bar contact, either above or below mine; (b) "British Elia" type—may be the same as (a) just described; (c) Pear-shaped and spherical types with horn contacts; reported to be very like German mines; (d) Special types for laying by Destroyers, Submarines and C.M.B.

Aircraft Bombs.

There are only vague and unofficial references to these types: Experimental 3300 lb. type; 1650 lb. type (with bursting charge of 1100 lbs. T.N.T.), 530 lb., 230 lb. (with A.P. nose?), 112 lb. and 100 lb. Fuzes said to be impact, delay action and special types for use against submarines.

Depth Charges.

Only mark reported is 300 lb. type.

Searchlights.

36 inch, 24 inch, 20 inch (all controlled in latest ships). About 8—36 inch and 2—24 inch (Signalling) in Dreadnoughts and Battle Cruisers; 4—36 inch in Light Cruisers; 1—24 inch or 20 inch in T.B.D. Twin 24 inch mountings were used in *Iron Duke, King George, Orion, Colossus, Neptune, Lion* and *New Zealand* Classes, but these are said to have been replaced by single 36 inch controlled S.L.

Paravanes (PVs.)

No official details available. Reported that there are about twenty marks, roughly divided into "M," "B" and "C" patterns. "M" type said to be "otter gear" of simple design for use by mercantile craft up to 18 kts. speed, keeping depth by ordinary form of hydrostatic valve. "B" type said to be for Battleships and older Cruisers up to 22 kts. speed; "C" pattern for Light Cruisers, &c., up to 28 kts. speed. Depth kept in these by hydrostatic valves, plus "mercury oscillators," the hydrostatic valve by itself being too sluggish to prevent the PVs. "porpoising." Length about 12 feet, breadth about 7 feet across spread of 'planes. Destroyers reported to use special types of PVs., viz., H.S.S.S. and H.S.M.S. PVs. towed in large ships by chains from skeg (or PV. plate) attached to forefoot, under stem; also by sliding bar shoes at stem. Destroyers and vessels of light draught can tow their PVs. from stern.

Naval Ordnance.—*continued.*

Also (for Anti-Submarine purposes) :—

11 inch howitzer mounted in some ships of "Devonshire" and "County Classes."
200 lb. stick bomb howitzer in some Special Service Vessels.
Thornycroft Depth Charge Thrower in Destroyers, P-boats, some Sloops and Special Service Vessels.

Also :—

Q.F., 12 pr. 12 cwt. Mk. I.
" " 12 pr. 18 cwt. Mk. II (war model): mostly for merchantmen.
" 12 pr. 18 cwt. Mk. I, for "G," "H" and "I" classes of T.B.D.
" 12 pr. 8 cwt. Mk. I (boat gun).
" 14 pr. Mk. I (H.M.S. "Swiftsure"—now removed).
" 6 pr.
" 3 pr. } have been used as AA. guns.
" 3 pr. (semi-automatic, Vickers design) } Saluting guns in big ships.
" 2½ pdr. (automatic) modified "pom-pom" for AA. work.
" 77 mm.—captured German field guns, adapted for use in some submarines.

Machine Guns :—
.303 inch Vickers.
.303 inch Maxim.
.303 inch Lewis.

Rifles :—
.303 inch Lee-Enfield (Long).

Pistols :—
.45 inch Webley automatic (H.V.).

BRITISH WARSHIPS: RECOGNITION SILHOUETTES.
By E. L. KING.

Strictly Copyright : limited to Effective Ships in Commission.

ONE FUNNEL.

O & ONE FUNNEL.

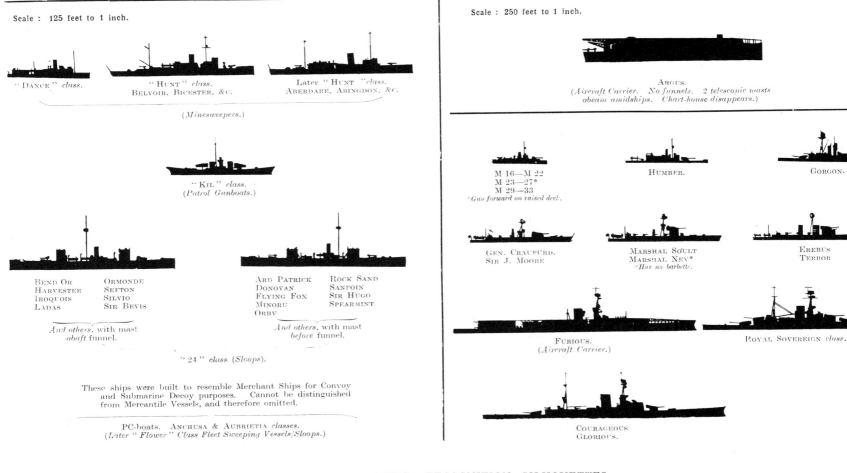

Scale : 125 feet to 1 inch.

"DANCE" class.

"HUNT" class.
BELVOIR, BICESTER, &c.

Later "HUNT" class.
ABERDARE, ABINGDON, &c.

(Minesweepers.)

"KIL" class.
(Patrol Gunboats.)

BEND OR	ORMONDE	ARD PATRICK	ROCK SAND
HARVESTER	SEFTON	DONOVAN	SANFOIN
IROQUOIS	SILVIO	FLYING FOX	SIR HUGO
LADAS	SIR BEVIS	MINORU	SPEARMINT
		ORBY	

And others, with mast abaft funnel.

And others, with mast before funnel.

"24" class (Sloops).

These ships were built to resemble Merchant Ships for Convoy and Submarine Decoy purposes. Cannot be distinguished from Mercantile Vessels, and therefore omitted.

PC-boats. ANCHUSA & AUBRIETIA classes.
(Later "Flower" Class Fleet Sweeping Vessels/Sloops.)

Scale : 250 feet to 1 inch.

ARGUS.
(Aircraft Carrier. No funnels. 2 telescopic masts abeam amidships. Chart-house disappears.)

M 16—M 22
M 23—27*
M 29—33
*Gun forward on raised deck.

HUMBER.

GORGON.

GEN. CRAUFURD.
SIR J. MOORE

MARSHAL SOULT
MARSHAL NEY*
*Has no barbette.

EREBUS
TERROR

FURIOUS.
(Aircraft Carrier.)

ROYAL SOVEREIGN class.

COURAGEOUS
GLORIOUS.

BRITISH WARSHIPS.—RECOGNITION SILHOUETTES.
(E. L. KING.)

Note.—All Ships on this page of Mercantile Build.

TWO FUNNELS.

ONE & TWO FUNNELS.

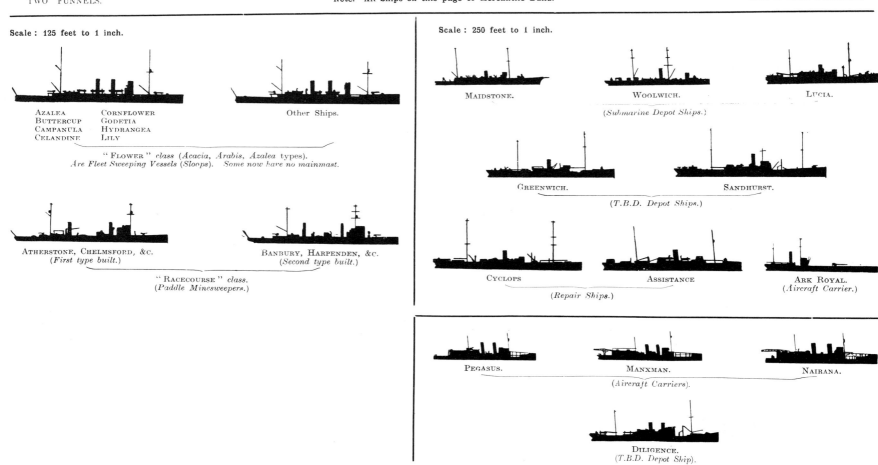

Scale : 125 feet to 1 inch.

AZALEA	CORNFLOWER
BUTTERCUP	GODETIA
CAMPANULA	HYDRANGEA
CELANDINE	LILY

Other Ships.

"FLOWER" class (Acacia, Arabis, Azalea types).
Are Fleet Sweeping Vessels (Sloops). Some now have no mainmast.

ATHERSTONE, CHELMSFORD, &c.
(First type built.)

BANBURY, HARPENDEN, &c.
(Second type built.)

"RACECOURSE" class.
(Paddle Minesweepers.)

Scale : 250 feet to 1 inch.

MAIDSTONE.

WOOLWICH.

LUCIA.

(Submarine Depot Ships.)

GREENWICH.

SANDHURST.

(T.B.D. Depot Ships.)

CYCLOPS

ASSISTANCE

ARK ROYAL.
(Aircraft Carrier.)

(Repair Ships.)

PEGASUS.

MANXMAN.

NAIRANA.

(Aircraft Carriers).

DILIGENCE.
(T.B.D. Depot Ship).

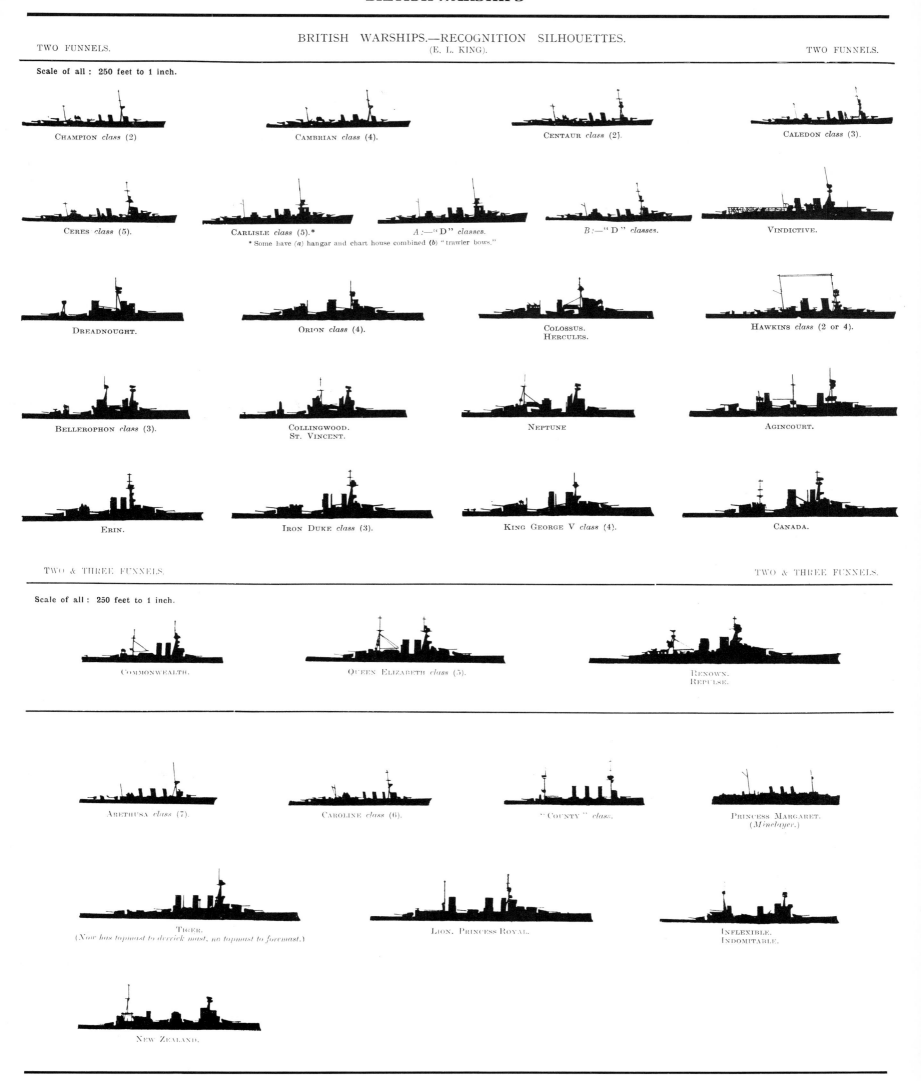

BRITISH WARSHIPS.—RECOGNITION SILHOUETTES.
(E. L. KING).

TWO FUNNELS.   TWO FUNNELS.

Scale of all : 250 feet to 1 inch.

CHAMPION *class* (2).   CAMBRIAN *class* (4).   CENTAUR *class* (2).   CALEDON *class* (3).

CERES *class* (5).   CARLISLE *class* (5).*   A:—"D" *classes*.   B:—"D" *classes*.   VINDICTIVE.
* Some have (*a*) hangar and chart house combined (*b*) "trawler bows."

DREADNOUGHT.   ORION *class* (4).   COLOSSUS. HERCULES.   HAWKINS *class* (2 or 4).

BELLEROPHON *class* (3).   COLLINGWOOD. ST. VINCENT.   NEPTUNE   AGINCOURT.

ERIN.   IRON DUKE *class* (3).   KING GEORGE V *class* (4).   CANADA.

TWO & THREE FUNNELS.   TWO & THREE FUNNELS.

Scale of all : 250 feet to 1 inch.

COMMONWEALTH.   QUEEN ELIZABETH *class* (5).   RENOWN. REPULSE.

ARETHUSA *class* (7).   CAROLINE *class* (6).   "COUNTY" *class*.   PRINCESS MARGARET. (*Minelayer.*)

TIGER.
(*Now has topmast to derrick mast, no topmast to foremast.*)   LION. PRINCESS ROYAL.   INFLEXIBLE. INDOMITABLE.

NEW ZEALAND.

BRITISH WARSHIPS.—RECOGNITION SILHOUETTES.

(E. L. KING).

FOUR FUNNELS.   FOUR FUNNELS.

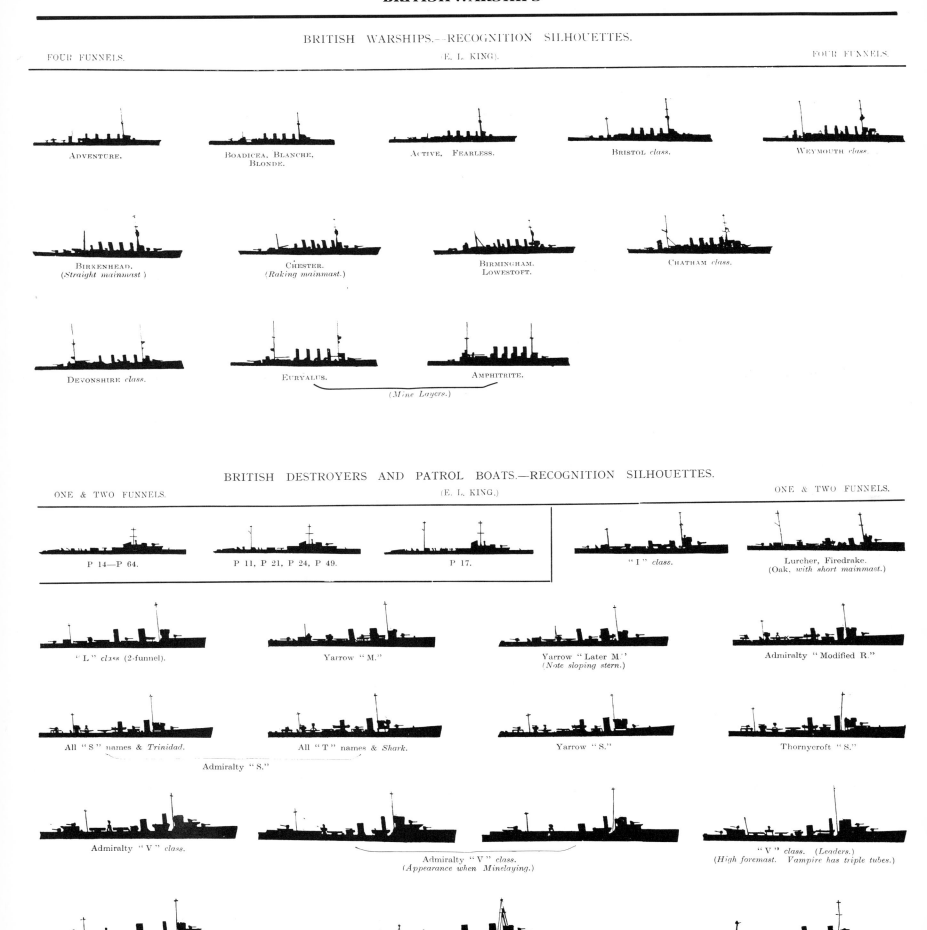

ADVENTURE.

BOADICEA, BLANCHE, BLONDE.

ACTIVE, FEARLESS.

BRISTOL class.

WEYMOUTH class.

BIRKENHEAD. (Straight mainmast)

CHESTER. (Raking mainmast.)

BIRMINGHAM. LOWESTOFT.

CHATHAM class.

DEVONSHIRE class.

EURYALUS.

AMPHITRITE.

(Mine Layers.)

BRITISH DESTROYERS AND PATROL BOATS.—RECOGNITION SILHOUETTES.

(E. L. KING.)

ONE & TWO FUNNELS.   ONE & TWO FUNNELS.

P 14—P 64.

P 11, P 21, P 24, P 49.

P 17.

"I" class.

Lurcher, Firedrake. (Oak, with short mainmast.)

"L" class (2-funnel).

Yarrow "M."

Yarrow "Later M" (Note sloping stern.)

Admiralty "Modified R."

All "S" names & Trinidad.

All "T" names & Shark.

Yarrow "S."

Thornycroft "S."

Admiralty "S."

Admiralty "V" class.

Admiralty "V" class. (Appearance when Minelaying.)

"V" class. (Leaders.) (High foremast. Vampire has triple tubes.)

Thornycroft "V" class.

Spencer, Shakespeare, Wallace. (Leaders.)

Bruce, Douglas, &c. "Large Admiralty type." (Leaders.)

BRITISH DESTROYERS.—RECOGNITION SILHOUETTES.

(E. L. KING.)

THREE & FOUR FUNNELS.

THREE & FOUR FUNNELS.

Scale of all : 125 feet to 1 inch.

"G" *class.*

SWIFT. (*Leader.*)

"L" *class* (3 funnels).
(*Legion :* Minelaying screens.)

Thornycroft "M"* & "R" *classes.*
* After gun *not* on platform.

Admiralty "M's"

Admiralty "R's" (A).
(*Tarpon, Telemachus :* Minelaying screens)

Admiralty "R's" (B).

Talisman, Termagant, Trident.

· "H" *class.*

"K" *class.*

Medea, Melampus, Melpomene.

Grenville, Parker, Seymour, Saumarez.
(*Leaders.*)

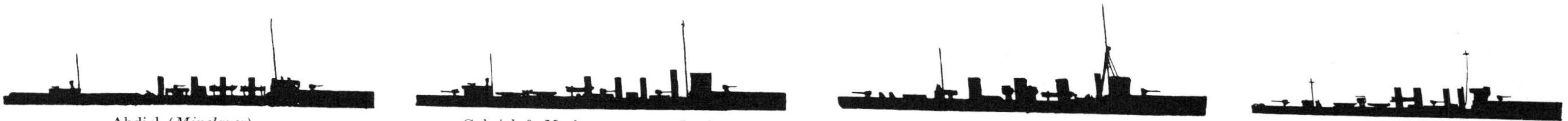

Abdiel (*Minelayer*).

Gabriel & Marksman type (*Leaders*).

Botha, Broke, Faulknor. (*Leaders.*)

Mansfield, Mentor.

BRITISH SUBMARINES.—RECOGNITION SILHOUETTES.

(E. L. KING.)

Scale of all : 125 feet to 1 inch.

"F" *class.*

"H 21—32 & Later" *class.*

"E 7—20 & Later" *class.*

"G" *class.*

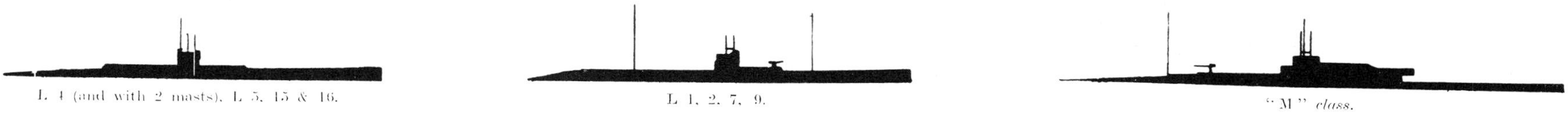

L 4 (and with 2 masts), L 5, 15 & 16.

L 1, 2, 7, 9.

"M" *class.*

L 3.

L 6, 10, 12, 14, 17.

"K" *class.*

"R" *class.*

BRITISH NAVY.

ADDENDA AND CORRECTIONS :—1.

NAVAL ORDNANCE : MEDIUM B.L. Following are correct details of 5.5 inch. Length, 50 cals. Weight of gun, 6 tons 4 cwt. Weight of projectile, 82 lbs. M. V., 2950 ft.-secs. M. E., 4520 ft.-tons. Weight of charge, 23½ lbs. Rounds per minute : 12. *Remarks.*— Mounted in *Hood.* Range, at 30° elevation : 12,000 yards.

The Russian (Black Sea) Dreadnought, **VOLYA** was temporarily taken over by the British Navy during 1919 : reported to have joined Gen. Denikin's Naval Forces in the Black Sea and to have been re-named **GENERAL ALEXEIEFF.**

INDOMITABLE to be sold.

CAPETOWN to be towed to Pembroke D.Y. for completion.

Unofficially reported that *EFFINGHAM* will be built as an Aircraft carrier.

CALLIOPE (and other Light Cruisers) no longer have searchlight and control tower amidships.

FOX for disposal.

Monitors.

MARSHAL SOULT.

Monitors—*continued.*

ROBERTS.   *Official R.A.F. Photo.*

Note.—*Roberts* is not included in the Post-War Fleet Organization. The above photograph has, however, been selected as an illustration, because it gives, by far, the best impression of the box-like hull and huge beam of the big Monitors. The projection of the " bulges " is also very clear in the above view. The formation and throwing-off of the coarse bow-wave are also worth noting.

BRITISH NAVY.

ADDENDA & CORRECTIONS :—2.

Monitors—*Continued.*

HUMBER, M 33 for sale. **M 31** to be converted for Minelaying.

M 19 (of M 19—27 class).   **M 23** for sale.

M 16 (of M 16—18 class).

Destroyers.

Russian (Black Sea) Destroyer **Derski** has been temporarily taken over by British Navy.

Tryphon (Yarrow "S" Type) did not go aground on Danish Coast, as stated. She went aground at Tenedos about last June and lay there on her beam-ends for three weeks. She was salved and brought to Pera for temporary repairs. She was then towed to Malta but nearly sank on passage. She is said to be too badly damaged for any further use, but an H.M.S. *Triton*—perhaps *Tryphon*—was recently reported as repairing by Yarrows.

Illustration of **Taurus** (Thornycroft " R ") is really **Patriot** (Thornycroft " M ").

TRIDENT.   *Photo. Cribb, Southsea.*

Nizam to be sold.

D.C.B. (*Depth Charge Boats*).

These are a modified type of C.M.B. without torpedoes in troughs but carrying Thornycroft Depth Charge Throwers or U.S. type Y-guns and special load of Depth Charges.

About 100 M.L. (Motor Launches) have been sold.

Submarines.

Delete: **F** Class Submarines and **E 54** : all are for sale.   *Delete:* **L 55,** lost 1919.

Aircraft Carriers.

VINDICTIVE reported very badly damaged by grounding in the Baltic. **NAIRANA** re-conditioned for mercantile service. **EAGLE** to be towed to Portsmouth D.Y. for completion.

Minesweepers.

Delete: **KINROSS** (of later " Hunt " Class), lost in Ægean, 1919. **FANDANGO** (not listed) of " Dance " Class, armed with 1—6 pdr. A.A. gun, lost 1919.

Salvage Vessel.

MELITA for sale.

1913-14 BRITISH DREADNOUGHTS.

(Royal Sovereign Class.)

SOVEREIGN (29th April, 1915), **ROYAL OAK** (17th Nov., 1914), **RESOLUTION** (14th Jan., 1916), **RAMILLIES** (12th Sept., 1916), **REVENGE** (29th May, 1915).

Normal displacement, 25,750 tons (about 31,250-33,500 tons *full load*). Complement, 937-997.

Length (*over all*), $624\frac{1}{4}$ feet. Beam, $88\frac{1}{2}$ feet.* *Mean* draught, 27 feet. Length (*p.p.*), 580 feet.

*For *R.S.* and *R.O.* With bulge protection, *Revenge* and *Resolution* 101′ 5″, *Ramillies* $102\frac{1}{2}$ feet.

Guns:
- 8—15 inch, 42 cal. } **Dir. Con.**
- 14—6 inch, 50 cal. } **Dir. Con.**
- 2—3 inch (anti-aircraft)
- 4—3 pdr.
- 5 M.G.

Torpedo tubes (21 inch):
- 4 *submerged*

Armour (K.C.):

Vertical.
- 13″ Belt
- 6″—4″ Belt (ends)
- 1″ Belt (bow)
- 6″, 4″ Bulkheads(f. & a.)
- 6″ Battery
- 10″—7″ Barbettes
- 13″— ″ Gunhouses
- $1\frac{1}{2}$″ Funnel uptakes
- 6″—3″ C.T. Base
- 11″ C.T. (6″—3″ Hood)
- 6″ Fore Com. Tube
- 6″ Torp. Con. Tower
- 4″ Tube (T.C. Tower)

Armour (H.T.):

Deck.
- 1″ Fo'xle over Battery
- $1\frac{1}{4}$″—$1\frac{1}{2}$″ Upper
- 2″, $1\frac{1}{2}$″, 1″ Main
- $2\frac{1}{2}$″, 1″ (forw'd) } Lower
- 4″, 3″, $2\frac{1}{2}$″ (aft) } Lower

Special Protection:
$1\frac{1}{2}$″—1″ Internal citadel between end barbettes

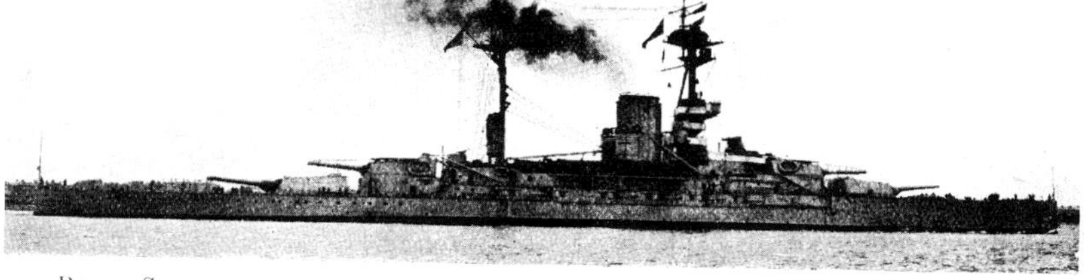

Royal Sovereign. *Photo, Cribb, Southsea.*

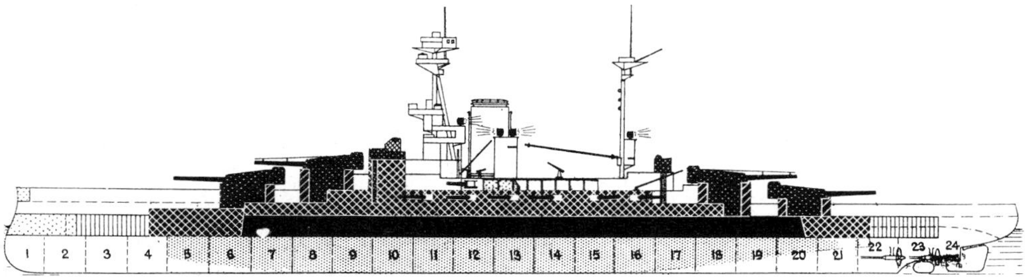

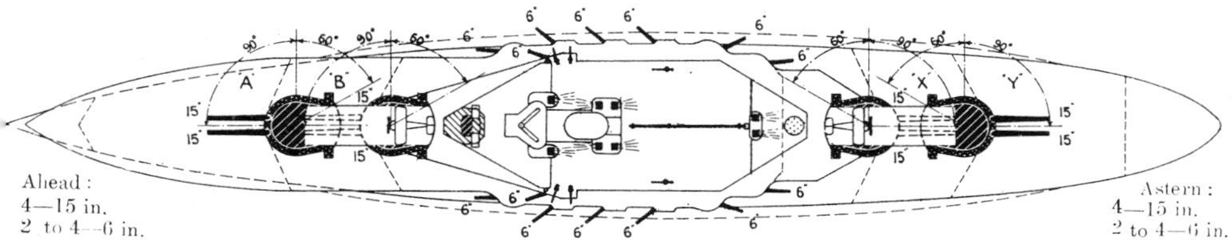

Ahead:
4—15 in.
2 to 4—6 in.

Astern:
4—15 in.
2 to 4—6 in.

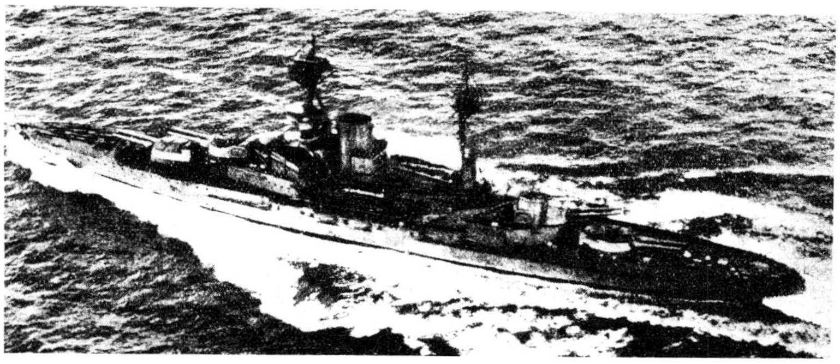

Ramillies. Aircraft View. *Official R.A.F. Photo.*

Broadside: 8—15 in., 7—6 in., 2—21 in. tubes.

Machinery: Turbine, Parsons. Boilers: (see *Notes*). 4 screws. Designed H.P. 40,000 = 23 kts. *without* bulges, about $21\frac{1}{2}$-22 *with* bulges. Fuel: Oil only, *normal*, 900 tons; *maximum*, about 3400 tons. Coal: 140 tons (only for "domestic" use).

Name	*Builder*	*Machinery*	*Laid down*	*Completed*	*Trials:*	*Boilers*	*Best recent speed*
Royal Sovereign	Portsmouth Y.	Parsons	Jan.'11	May, '16	41,115 = 21·6	18 Babcock	
Royal Oak	Devonport Y.	Hawthorn	Jan.'11	May, '16	40,360 =	18 Yarrow	
Resolution	Palmer	Palmer	Nov.'13	Dec., '16	41,106 =	18 Yarrow	
Ramillies	Beardmore	Beardmore	Nov.'13	Sept. '17	42,356 = 21·5	18 Babcock	
Revenge	Vickers	Vickers	Dec.'13	Mar., '16	42,962 = 21·9	18 Babcock	

Gunnery Notes.—Much as *Queen Elizabeth* class. Battery differently disposed in these ships. 6 inch batteries are wet in head seas, but dwarf walls in battery retain water and it is rapidly drained away.

Armour Notes.—Thicknesses much as *Queen Elizabeth* class, but armour differently distributed. Barbettes 6″—4″ as they descend behind belt. Gunhouses, 13″ face, 11″ sides and rear; crowns specially heavy. In these ships 2″ protective deck has a high 2″ slope behind belt, so that flat part of protection can be put on main deck and at top of belt, instead of a deck lower. Internal protection is very good, and with bulge protection, these ships are heavily defended against underwater attack. *Royal Sovereign* and *Royal Oak* have yet to be fitted with bulges.

Engineering Notes.—Designed to burn coal, but while building "all oil fuel" was adopted, and it was hoped that 23 kts. would be secured without increase of H.P. Addition of bulges has brought speed down again to about 21 kts. On deep load, the bulge protected ships cannot get much above 19.5 kts. till they have burnt off fuel.

General Notes.—Begun under 1914-15 Estimates. *Revenge* first named *Renown*. *Ramillies* injured herself at launch and was delayed in completion. They are fine ships, but suffer rather from reduced freeboard. They are steady ships, those with bulge protection being splendid gun platforms. With bulges, *normal* displacement is really about 29,350 tons (33,500 *full load*).

1912-13 BRITISH DREADNOUGHTS. ("Fast Division.")

(Queen Elizabeth Class.)

QUEEN ELIZABETH (Oct., 1913), **WARSPITE** (Nov., 1913), **VALIANT** (4th Nov., 1914), **BARHAM** (31st Dec., 1914), **MALAYA** (18th Mar., 1915).

Normal displacement, 27,500 tons (about 31,000-33,000 *full load*). Complement, 955-1016.

Length (*p.p.*), 600 feet. Beam, $90\frac{1}{2}$ feet. { *Mean* draught, $30\frac{2}{3}$ feet. / *Max.* „ $33\frac{1}{2}$ „ } Length (*over all*) { *Q.E.* $643\frac{3}{4}$ ft. / Rest $639\frac{3}{4}$ „ }

Guns:
- 8—15 inch 42 cal. } **Dir. Con.**
- 12—6 inch, 50 cal. } **Dir. Con.**
- 2—3 inch (anti-aircraft)
- 4—3 pdr.
- 5 M.G.

Torpedo tubes (21 inch):
- 4 *submerged* (broadside).

Armour (K.C.):

Vertical.
- 13″ Lower belt
- 6″—4″ Upper belt
- 6″—4″ Belt (ends)
- 6″, 4″ Bulkheads(f. & a.)
- 6″ Battery
- 10″—7″ Barbettes
- 11″ Gunhouses
- $1\frac{1}{2}$″ Funnel uptakes
- 6″—3″ C.T. base
- 11″ C.T. (6″—2″ Hood)
- 4″ Fore com. tube
- 6″ Torpedo C.T.
- 4″ Tube (T.C. tower)

Armour (H.T.):

Deck.
- 1″ Fo'xle (over battery)
- 2″—$1\frac{1}{4}$″ Upper
- $1\frac{1}{4}$″ Main
- 1″ Middle
- 3″ (ends) } Lower
- 1″ (amidships) } Lower

Special Protec.:
2″—1″ Internal citadel between end barbettes

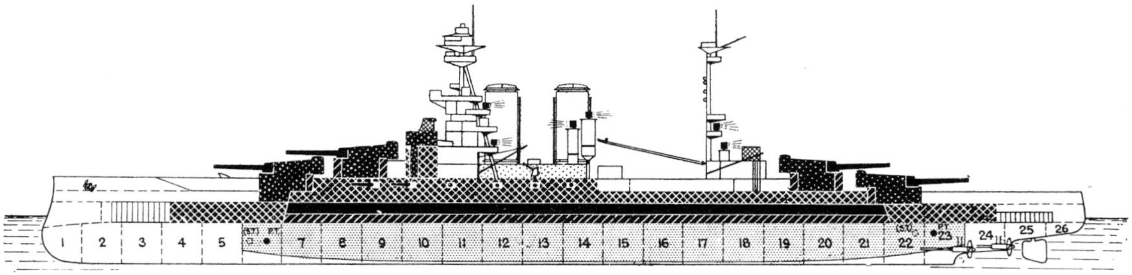

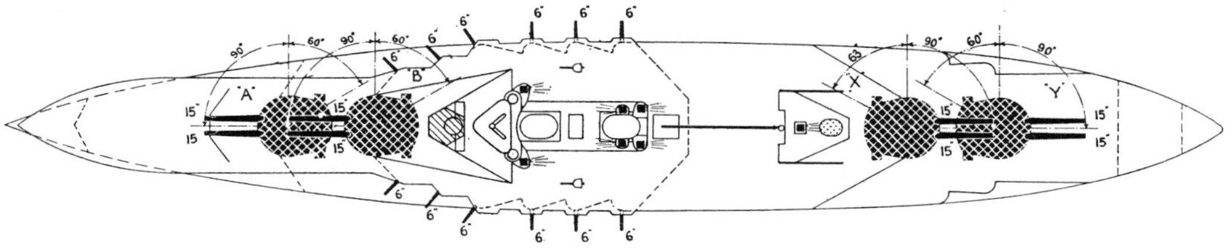

Ahead:
4—15 in.
3 to 6—6 in.

Astern:
4—15 in.

Broadside: 8—15 in., 6—6 in., 2—21 in. tubes.

Machinery: Parsons turbine, but *Barham* has Brown-Curtis. Geared cruising turbines in all ships. Boilers: 24 (see *Notes*). Designed H.P. 75,000 = 25 kts. Fuel: Only oil, 550 tons *normal*, 3400 tons *max*. Coal: 100 tons. for starting boilers and "domestic" purposes.

Gunnery Notes.—Range of 15 inch only limited by *max.* visibility. Elevation of these guns has been enlarged. 6-inch controlled in two groups from director towers on middle bridges. *Queen Elizabeth* completed with four extra 6-inch at stern; these were found useless, guns removed and ports plated over. *Barham* came into service with 2—6 inch in shields on fo'xle deck amidships; these, too, have been removed, but in a head sea they were said to have been equal to whole main deck battery.

Armour Notes.—Belt is 13″ at w.l. only, 6″ on upper edge, 8″ on lower, and applied in vertical strakes. Barbettes, 6″ and 4″ within belt. $1\frac{1}{2}$″ traverses to battery, but no rear screens—only dwarf walls to retain and drain away water admitted to battery. Rear bulkhead to battery is 6″ diagonal and 4″ where it crosses centre line. Internal protection of these ships is very fine.

Engineering Notes.—"All oil" installation very successful. These ships steam splendidly, and can maintain a high average speed for long periods. H.P. turbines on wing shafts, with cruising turbines geared at forward end; L.P. turbines on inner shafts.

1912-13 BRITISH DREADNOUGHTS. ("Fast Division.")

QUEEN ELIZABETH.*   *Photo, Graphic Union.*

*Other ships without fore topmast, as *Warspite* view.

WARSPITE.   *Photo, Cribb, Southsea.*

Name.	Builder.	Machinery.	Laid down.	Completed.	Trials.	Boilers.	Best recent speed.
Queen Elizabeth	Portsmouth	Wallsend	Oct. '12	Jan. '15	57,130=	24 Babcock	
Warspite	Devonport	Hawthorn	Oct. '12	Mar. '15	77,510=	24 Yarrow	
Valiant	Fairfield	Fairfield	Jan.'13	Feb.,'16	71,112=	24 Yarrow	
Barham	Clydebank	Clydebank	Feb.'13	Oct., '15	76,575=	24 Yarrow	
Malaya	Elswick	Wallsend	Oct. '13	Feb.,'16	76,074=	24 Babcock	

Note.—First four begun under 1912 Estimates. *Malaya*, extra ship, gift of Federated Malay States. Estimated cost (average) £2,500,000 per ship = £90 per ton. At the Battle of Jutland, *Warspite*, *Valiant*, *Barham* and *Malaya* supported the First Battle-Cruiser Squadron. *Queen Elizabeth*, Flagship, C.-in-C., Grand Fleet, 1917-18. *Barham* grounded on May Island during War and badly injured herself, but was salved and repaired. In appearance and general design, these five ships are the finest in the British Navy. Their decks are remarkably clear, and internal arrangements are very spacious. Taken all round, they present the most successful type of capital ship yet designed.

MALAYA (Aircraft view).   *Official R.A.F. Photo.*

1912 BRITISH DREADNOUGHTS.

(IRON DUKE CLASS.)

BENBOW (Nov., 1913), **EMPEROR OF INDIA** (ex-*Delhi*, Nov., 1913), **IRON DUKE** (Oct., 1912), **MARLBOROUGH** (Nov., 1912).

Normal displacement, 25,000 tons. *Full load*, 28,800 tons. Complement, 995 to 1022.

Length (o.a.), 622¾ feet. Beam, 89½ feet. { Mean draught, 28½ feet. Max. ,, 32¾ ,, } Length (p.p.), 580 feet

Guns :
10—13·5 inch (M.V.) } **Dir. Con.**
12—6 inch, 50 cal.
2—3 inch (anti-aircraft)
4—3 pdr.
5 M.G.
(1 landing)
Torpedo tubes (21 inch) :
4 submerged (broadside)

Armour (K.C.) : *(Vertical.)*
12"-8" Lower belt ....
9" Middle belt ....
8" Upper belt ....
6"—4" Belt (ends) ....
8", 6", 4" Bulkheads (f. & a.) ....
6" Battery* ....
10"—7" Barbettes .....
11"— " Gunhouses ....
1½" Funnel uptakes ....
6"—3" C.T. base .....
11" C.T. (4"—3" hood)..
6" Fore com. tube ....
6" Torpedo C.T. ......
4" After com. tube ...
* See Notes.

Armour (H.T.) : *(Deck.)*
1" Fo'xle (over battery)
2"—1½" Upper .... } middle
1" (amidships)
2½"—1½" (aft)
2½"—1" Lower ....
Special Protection :
1½"—1" Screens to Mags, shell and engine rooms.

IRON DUKE.

Gunnery Notes.—Originally had 2—6 inch in casemates at stern, but these were found utterly useless. Ports were sealed up and guns re-mounted on forecastle deck. Forward 6-inch battery used to be swamped out in head seas. Rubber sealing joints for gun-ports were designed and added at Scapa Flow.

Armour Notes.—Belt is 12" at w.l. only and 8" on lower edge. Barbettes, 6" and 3" as they descend through decks behind belt. Battery has 1" traverses and 4" bulkhead completely athwartships, just before fore funnel. Internal protection more complete than in *King George V* class, but, all the same, screens do not completely extend between end barbettes. At Jutland, *Marlborough* was torpedoed over boiler rooms, where there is *no* internal protection. Lord Jellicoe is therefore in error when he says that the torpedo struck " at about one of the most favourable spots for the ship."

Name.	Builder.	Machinery.	Laid down.	Completed.	Trials. 30 hrs.	Full power.	Boilers.	Best recent speed.
Benbow	Beardmore	Beardmore	May '12	Oct. '14		32530=21·5	18 Babcock	
E. of India	Vickers	Vickers	May '12	Nov '14		29654=		Yarrow
Iron Duke	Portsmouth Y	Laird	Jan.'12	Mar.'14		30040=21·6	18 Babcock	
Marlborough	Devonport Y	Hawthorn	Jan.'12	June'14	20,875=19	32015=21·6		Yarrow

Note.—Begun under the 1911 Estimates. Derived from *Orion* class through *King George* type. Average cost about £1,891,600. *Emperor of India* was originally named *Delhi*. *Iron Duke*, Flagship, C.-in-C., Grand Fleet, 1914-16

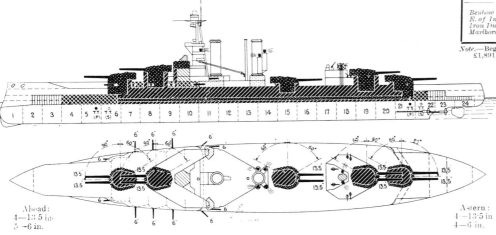

Broadside : 10—13.5 in., 6—6 in., 2—21 in. tubes.

Ahead:
4—13.5 in.
5 —6 in.

Astern :
4—13.5 in
4—6 in.

Machinery : Turbine (Parsons). Boilers : (see *Notes*). Designed H.P. 29,000 = 21 kts.
Coal : *normal*, 1000 tons ; *maximum*, 3250 tons. Oil : *normal*, 1050 tons ; *max.*, 1600 tons.

1911 BRITISH DREADNOUGHT *(purchased 1914).*

CANADA (ex *Almirante Latorre*), (Nov., 1913.)

Displacement, 28,000 tons (about 32,000 *full load*). Complement (1176).

Length (*p.p.*), 625 feet. Beam, 92½ feet. {Mean draught, 29 feet. / Max. ,, 32 ,, } Length (*over all*), 661 feet.

Guns (Elswick) :
- 10—14 inch, 45 cal. } **Dir. Con.**
- 12—6 inch 50 cal. }
- 2—3 inch (anti-aircraft)
- 4—3 pdr.
- (2 landing)
- 4 M.G.

Torpedo tubes (21 inch) :
- 4 *submerged*

Armour :
Vertical.
- 9" Lower belt . . . .
- 7" Middle belt . . . .
- 4½" Upper belt . . . .
- 6"—4" Belt (ends) . . . .
- 4½", 4" B'lkh'ds (f. & a.)
- 6" Batteries . . . .
- 10" Barbettes . . . .
- 10"—" Gunhouses . . . .
- 3" C.T. base* . . . .
- 11" C.T. (6"—3" hood) . .
- 6" Fore com. tube . . . . .
- 6" Torpedo C.T. . . . . . .
- 6" Aft com. tube . . . . .

*Not shown on plans.

Armour :
Decks.
- 1" Shelter (over case- mates) . . . .
- 1" Fo'xle (over battery)
- 1½" Upper (outside battery) . . . .
- 1½" Main (aft) . . . . . .
- 1" Protective . . . .
- 2" (forward) } lower
- 4" (aft) . . . }

Special Protec. :
- 2"—1½" Internal screens (mags.. &c.) . . . . . .

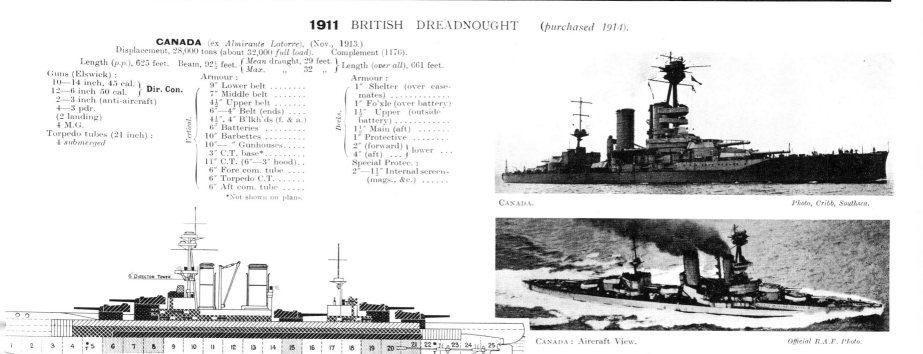

CANADA.   *Photo, Cribb, Southsea.*

CANADA : Aircraft View.   *Official R.A.F. Photo.*

Ahead :
4—14 in.
4 to 8-4 in.

Astern :
4—14 in.
3 to 6-4 in.

Broadside : 10—14 in., 6 or 7—6 in., 2—2 in. tubes.

Machinery : Turbine, 4-shaft : (L.P.) Parsons ; (H.P.) Brown-Curtis. Boilers : 21 Yarrow.
Designed H.P. 37,000 = 22.75 kts. Coal : *normal*, 1150 tons ; *maximum*, 3300 tons. Oil : 520 tons.

Gunnery Notes.—14-inch have a range only limited by *max.* visibility. Originally had 16—6 inch, but the 2—6 inch on upper deck, abeam of after funnel, were removed and ports plated over. Reason for removal was because guns were only a few feet from muzzle of "Q" turret 14-inch guns on extreme bearing and were damaged by blast. Fourteen 6-inch are shown on plans ; two more 6-inch have been removed, but from which positions is not yet known.
Armour Notes.—Barbettes, 6" and 4" as they descend behind belts.

Engineering Notes.—Reported that the Chilean Ministry of Marine stipulated, at the last moment, that full speed should be attained without using forced draught. Funnels were accordingly raised to increase natural draught. Reported to have made 23-24 kts. in service.
Torpedo Notes.—Tubes are 21 inch Elswick side-loading, worked by hydraulic power.

Name	Builder	Machinery	Laid down	Com- pleted	Trials	Boilers	Best recent speed
Canada	Elswick	Clydebank	Nov.'11	Sep.'15	39247	Yarrow	

General Notes.—Laid down for Chile as the *Valparaiso*, her name being altered afterwards to *Almirante Latorre*. Purchased for British Navy on outbreak of War. Additional protection, &c, added during War is said to have raised her *normal* displacement to over 30,000 tons. First designed with secondary battery of 22—4.7 inch, and 2 stump masts abeam aft. Her sister ship, *Almirante Cochrane*, also taken over for British Navy, re-named *Eagle* and modified for service as an Aircraft Carrier.

1911 BRITISH DREADNOUGHT. (Purchased 1914).

ERIN (ex *Reshadieh*), (Sept., 1913.)

Normal displacement, 23,000 tons ; 25,250 *full load*. Complement, 1130.

Length (*o.a.,*) 559½ feet. Beam, 91 ft. 7¼ in. {Max. draught, 30 ft. 11 in. / Mean ,, 28 ft. 5 in. } Length (*p.p.*), 525 feet.

Guns (Vickers) :
- 10—13.5 inch, 45 cal. } **Dir. Con.**
- 16—6 inch, 50 cal. }
- 2—3 inch (anti-aircraft)

Torpedo tubes (21 inch) :
- 4 *submerged*

Armour (K.C.) :
Vertical.
- 12"—9" Lower belt . . . .
- 8" Upper belt . . . .
- 8"—5", 4" B'lkh'ds (f.&a.)
- 5" Battery . . . .
- 1" Battery traverses . .
- 10"—8" Barbettes . . . . .
- 11" Gunhouses . . . .
- 1" Funnel uptakes . . . .
- 12" C.T. (6" tube) . . . .
- 4" Torpedo C.T. (3" tube)

Armour (H.T.) :
Decks.
- 1½" Fo'xle (over battery)
- 1½" Upper (beyond battery)
- 1½" Main . . . .
- 3" (ends) } middle
- 1" (amidships) }

Special Protection :
- 1½" internal citadel . . .

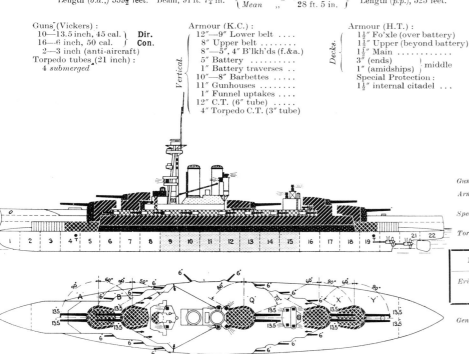

ERIN.   *Photo, Topical.*

Gunnery Notes.—On plan 6—6 pdr. of original design shown ; these guns not mounted now.

Armour Notes.—12" belt at w.l. with very narrow strap of 9" over. Barbettes 5" and 3" within belt. 1" battery traverses divide 6-inch guns by pairs.

Special Protection (correction to plans).—Internal screens (shown by dot shading in sections 9-15 on profile) should really extend to end barbettes over sections 6-18.

Torpedo Notes.—Elswick side-loading tubes. Stern tube removed during War.

Name.	Builder.	Machinery.	Laid down.	Com- pleted.	Trials.	Boilers.	Turbines.	Best recent speed.
Erin	Vickers	Vickers	Feb.'11	Aug.'14		Babcock	Parsons	

General Notes.—Designed by Armstrong, Vickers and Brown, in conjunction with Turkish Ministry of Marine. Purchased for British Navy, August, 1914. Designed with after tripod mast ; had tall pole mast stepped when completing, but this was cut down when ship was taken over for British Navy. The design forms an interesting comparison with *King George V* class of same displacement. *Erin* has, in comparison, 16—6 inch guns in 5" battery added and better internal protection. But her scantlings are lighter than those ruling in British Navy : her fuel supply is about 1000 tons less than in British Dreadnoughts, and her ammunition supply is below the average. Steams well, is a good sea-boat, and remarkably handy. Internal accommodation is rather cramped.

Broadside : 10—13.5 in., 8—6 in., 2—21 in. tubes.

Machinery : Parsons turbines. 4 screws. Designed H.P. 26,500 = 21 kts. Boilers : 15 Babcock. Coal : *normal*, 900 tons ; *maximum*, 2120 tons + 710 tons oil.

1911 BRITISH DREADNOUGHT. (*Purchased 1914*).

AGINCOURT (ex *Sultan Osman I*, ex *Rio de Janeiro*), (January, 1913).

Normal displacement, 27,500 tons (30,250 tons *full load*). Complement, 1267.

Length *over all*, 671½ feet. Beam, 89 feet. { Mean draught, 27 feet. / Max. „ 30½ ft. } Length, (p.p.) 632 feet, (*waterline*) 668 feet.

Guns (Elswick) :
14—12 inch, 50 cal. } Dir. Con.
20—6 inch, 50 cal.
8—3 inch
2—3 inch (anti-aircraft)
4—3 pdr.
1—3 pdr. (anti-aircraft)
Torpedo tubes (21 inch) :
2 *submerged* (Elswick side-loading)

Armour :
9″ Lower belt . . . .
6″ Upper belt . . . .
6″—4″ Ends . . . .
6″—3″ Bulkh'ds (f. & a.)
6″ Battery . . . .
6″ Battery bulkheads
1″ Battery traverses .
9″ Barbettes . . . .
12″—8″ Gunhouses . . . .
12″ C.T. (6″—4″ hoods)
8″ Fore com. tube . . . . .
9″ Torpedo C.T. . . . . . .
6″ After com. tube . . .

Armour :
Decks {
1½″ Fo'xle (over battery)
1½″ Upper (outside battery) . . . .
1½″—1″ Main . . . .
2½″ Lower cover rudder
Special Protection :
1½″ & 1″ double screens (end barbettes).
1½″ single screens ('midships barbettes).

AGINCOURT.

Ahead :
4—12 in.
6—6 in.

Astern :
4—12 in.
6—6 in.

Broadside : 14—12 in., 10—6 in., 1—21 in. tube.

Name	Builder	Machinery	Begun	Completed	Trials. H.P.	kts.
Agincourt	Armstrong	Vickers	Sept.,1911	Aug.,1914	40,279	22.42

Machinery : Parsons 4-shaft turbine. Boilers : 22 Babcock. Designed H.P. 34,000 = 22 kts. Coal : *normal*, 1500 tons ; *maximum*, 3200 tons + 620 tons oil.

Gunnery Notes.—Barbettes are a special Elswick design, all operations of loading and firing being controlled by a single lever, working in a quadrant very like the change-speed "gate" of a motor car.

Armour Notes.—Internal protection as stipple shading on numbered sections in profile. Barbettes 3″ within belt.

Torpedo Notes.—Stern tube removed during War. Owing to limited space athwartships, 21-inch torpedoes have small war heads. Water from tubes pumped out into flat, to re-load ; when rapid firing of torpedoes is required, there is 3 feet of water in flat.

General Notes.—The history of this ship merits recording with some detail. Four designs were drafted at first for her. That accepted was for a battleship of 32,000 tons, armed with 12—14 inch, 16—6 inch and 14—4 inch guns. The Brazilian Government then considered her too large and expensive a unit, and her construction was stopped. A special mission was went by Armstrongs to Rio de Janeiro, and new outline scheme was prepared in one night. This was the Elswick "Design 690A," as given on this page. In January, 1914, she was sold to Turkey by Brazil for £2,725,000, and became the *Sultan Osman I*. In July, 1914, she docked at Devonport for trials, and, on the outbreak of war, was appropriated by the British Navy, being named *Agincourt*. Alterations were begun, including the removal of the big flying-boat deck joining the two superstructures. She joined the Grand Fleet in 1915. In 1916, the after tripod mast was removed and replaced by a pole mast. In 1918, the pole mainmast was removed, and she attained present rig. With extra protection and other war additions, she displaces about 29,500 tons now. A good steamer, a good sea-boat, and a steady gun platform. Handles very well, considering her length. In Reserve, 1919. Proposed to give her bulge protection, but nothing has been done in this matter. A full and interesting history of this ship appeared in "The Marine Engineer," May, 1919.

(KING GEORGE V. CLASS.)

KING GEORGE V (Oct., 1911), **CENTURION** (Nov., 1911), **AJAX** (March, 1912). **AUDACIOUS** (Sept., 1912).

Normal displacement, 23,000 tons (about 25,500 *full load*). Complement, 812 to 849.

Length *over all*, 597⅔ feet. Beam, 89 feet. { Mean draught, 27½ ft. / Max. „ 30 ft. 10 in. } Length (p.p.) 555 feet.

Guns :
10—13.5 inch (M.V.) } Dir. Con.
16—4 inch
2—4 inch (anti-aircraft *Cent.*)
2—3 inch (anti-aircraft K.G.V.)
4—3 pdr
5 M.G.
(1 landing)
Torpedo tubes (21 inch) :
2 *submerged* (broadside)

Armour (K.C.) :
12″ Lower belt . . . .
9″ Middle belt . . . . . .
8″ Upper belt . . . .
4″, 6″, 8″ B'lkh'ds (fore)
2″ 10″ 8″ B'lkh'ds (aft)
6″—4″ Belt (bow) . . . .
2½″ Belt (stern) . . . . .
10″—7″ Barbettes . . . .
11″—″ Gunhouses . . . .
1½″ Funnel uptakes . . .
3½″—1″ Battery (4 inch guns) . . . .
1″ C.T. base (5″ tube within) . . . .
11″ C.T. (4″ hood) . . . . .
6″ Torpedo C.T. (4″ tube)

Armour (H.T.) :
Deck {
1¾″. 1½″ Upper . . . .
1½″ Main . . . .
1″ Middle . . . .
2¼″—1″ (bow) . . }
3″ (stern) . . . . . . lower
4″ (over rudder))
Special Protec. . . . . . .
—″ Internal screens to magazines, &c. . . . . . .

Note to Plans.—These require revision, but new plans cannot be put in hand until definite information is secured, describing present positions of 4 inch guns, AA. guns and searchlights. "Coffee box" S.L. towers added to after funnel and extra tops to mast.

AUDACIOUS ; also AJAX & CENTURION. *Photo, Cribb.*

KING GEORGE V. *Photo, Topical.*

Gunnery Notes.—Heavier projectile said to be fired by 13.5 inch in these ships.

Armour Notes.—As *Orion* class ; internal protection is more extensive in these ships, but internal screens are continuous between end barbettes. Battery for 4-inch guns on forecastle, 3″ face, 3½″ ports, 1″ rear screen towards ships. Deck armour more extensive in these ships.

Torpedo Notes.—Stern tube removed during War.

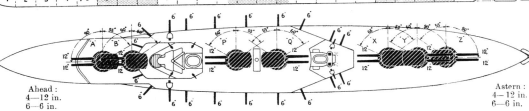

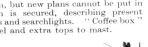

KING GEORGE V

Ahead :
4—13.5 in.

Astern :
4—13.5 in.

Broadside : 10—13.5 in., 1—21 in. tube.

Machinery : Turbine (Parsons). Boilers : 18 Babcock or Yarrow. Designed H.P. 27,000 = 21 kts. Coal : *normal*, 900 tons ; *maximum* (A. & C.) 3150 tons, (K. G. V.) 2870 tons + 850 tons oil in all three.

Name	Builder.	Machinery.	Laid down	Completed.	Trials.		Boilers	Best recent speed
George V	Portsmouth Y.	Hawthorn	Jan.'11	Jan.'13	19,808	28,005=22·13	Babcock	22·47
Centurion	Devonport Y.	Hawthorn	Jan.'11	Jan.'13		=21·88	Yarrow	...
Ajax	Scotts	Scotts	Feb.'11	'13	19,830	28,200=21·06	Babcock	...
Audacious	Laird	Laird	Feb.'11	'13		=	Yarrow	...

General Notes.—Begun under 1910 Estimates. Are generally similar to *Orion* class. Average cost, £1,945,200 about £85 per ton. On first commission, *Centurion* had experimental form of fire-control for 4-inch guns and searchlights, centrally controlled.* *King George V*, also an experimental form of coaling gear. *Audacious* lost during the War. *King George V* has anti-rolling tanks.

NOTE.

*These remarks re *Centurion* have appeared in previous editions, but their importance is not realised. The additions made to *Centurion* in 1913 show that the need for controlled secondary guns and searchlights for night action was realised three years before Jutland.

1909 BRITISH DREADNOUGHTS.

(ORION CLASS.)

ORION (Aug., 1910). **THUNDERER** (Jan., 1911), **MONARCH** (March, 1911), **CONQUEROR** (May, 1911).

Normal displacement, 22,500 tons (about 25,000 *full load*.) Complement, 806 to 828.

Length (*p.p.*), 545 feet. Beam, 88½ feet. { *Mean* draught, 26⅝ feet } Length *over all*, 581 feet. { *Max.* „ 30¾ feet. }

Guns :
10—13.5 inch (M.V.) **Dir.**
16—4 inch   **Con.**
1—4 inch (anti-aircraft)
1—3 inch (anti-aircraft)
4—3 pdr.
5 M.G.
(1 landing)
Torpedo tubes (21 inch) :
  2 submerged (broadside)

Armour (K.C.) :
  12″ Lower belt ....
  9″ Middle belt ....
  8″ Upper belt ....
  4″, 6″, 8″ B'lkh'ds (fore)
  6″—4″ Belt (bow) .....
  2½″ Belt (stern) .....
  2½″, 8″, 10″ B'lkh'ds (aft.)
  10″—7″ Barbettes ....
  11″ Gunhouses ....
  1½″ Funnel uptakes ...
  11″ C.T. (6″, 3″ hoods) .
  5″ Fore com. tube ....
  3″ Torpedo C.T. & tube

Armour (Nickel) :
  1½″ Upper ....
  1½″ Main ....
  1″ Middle ....
  2½″ Lower ......
  4″ over rudder ....
Special protection :
  —″ Internal screens to
  magazines, &c. .....

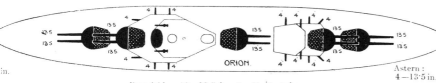

Ahead :
—13·5 in.

Broadside : 10—13.5 in., 1—21 in. tube.

Astern :
4—13·5 in.

ORION

THUNDERER.   *Photo, Abrahams & Sons*

ORION.   *Photo, C. N.*

Name	Builder	Machinery	Laid down	Completed	Trials :— 30 hrs.	Trials :— 8 hrs. full power (mean)	Boilers	Best recent speed
Orion	Portsmouth Y.	Wallsend	Nov.'09	Jan.'12	18,966=19·5	29,108=21·02	Babcock	22·3
Conqueror	Beardmore	Beardmore	Apl. '10	Nov.'12	19,100=19·5	28,400=22·13	Babcock	23·1
Thunderer	Thames I.W.	Thames I.W.	Apl. '10	June'12	18,927=18·8	27,416=20·8	Babcock	21·45
Monarch	Elswick	Hawthorn	Apl. '10	Apl. '12	19,128=	28,555=21·88	Yarrow	...

Machinery : Parsons turbine. Designed H.P. 27,000 = 21 kts. 4 screws. Boilers : 18 (see *Notes*). Coal : *normal*, 900 tons ; *maximum*, 3300 tons coal + 800 tons oil.

Armour Notes.—12″ belt very narrow and submerged at deep load. Barbette bases, 6″—3″ within belt. Internal vertical screens to magazines, &c., not continuous between end barbettes.

Torpedo Notes.—Stern tube removed during War.

General Notes.—*Orion* begun under 1909 Estimates : the others are ships which were known as "Conditional Dreadnoughts," laid down under the same Estimates. Average cost, £1,887,870. In these ships, protection is given to the boats for the first time. On her first cruise the *Orion* in the Bay of Biscay rolled 21°. This rolling was attributed to her small bilge keels, 6 feet only. During 1912, improved bilge keels were fitted and the ships roll far less. On trials, *Conqueror* made a *maximum* of over 23 kts. *Monarch* was originally named *King George V.* The general design for these ships was considered for the *Dreadnought*, but rejected on the score of size and cost.

Note to Plans.—Require revision, but new plans cannot be drafted until reliable information is secured describing present positions of 4-inch guns, AA. guns and searchlights. "Coffee-box" S.L. towers added to second funnel. 4-inch on shelter deck now housed in.

(COLOSSUS CLASS.)

COLOSSUS (April, 1910) & **HERCULES** (May, 1910).

Normal displacement, 20,000 tons (about 22,250 *full load*). Complement, 831 and 845.

Length (*waterline*), 540 feet. Beam, 85 feet. Draught { (*normal*), 27 feet. } Length *over all*, 546 feet. { (*max.*), 31 feet. }
Length, (*p.p.*) 510 feet.

Guns :
10—12 inch, 50 cal. } **Dir. Con.**
12—4 inch }
1—4 inch (anti-aircraft) (*Col.*)
1—3 inch (anti-aircraft) (*Herc.*)
4—3 pdr.
5 M.G.
(1 landing)
Torpedo tubes (21 inch) :
  2 submerged

Armour (K.C.) :
  11″ Lower belt ....
  8″ Upper belt ....
  1½″, 2″, 5″ & 8″ Bulkheads ......
  7″—2½″ Belt (bow) ...
  2½″ Belt (stern) .....
  10″—7″ Barbettes ....
  11″ Gunhouses ....
  1″ Funnel uptakes ....
  11″ C.T. (6″ & 3″ hoods) .
  5″ Fore com. tube ....
  3″ Torpedo C.T. ....
  3″ Tube, T.C.T. .....

Armour (Nickel) :
  1½″ Main ....
  1¾″ Middle ....
  2½″—1¾″ (bow) ....
  3″ (stern) .....
  4″ (over rudder) ...
Special Protection :
  —″ Screens to magazines &c. ...

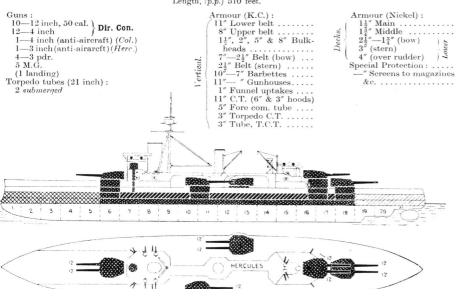

HERCULES

COLOSSUS.   *Photo, Topical.*

Ahead :
4 to 6—12 in.

Broadside : 8 to 10—12 in., 1—21 in. tube.

Astern :
6 to 8—12 in.

Machinery : Parsons turbine. Designed H.P. 25,000 = 21 kts. Boilers : Yarrow or Babcock.
Coal : *normal*, 900 tons ; *maximum*, 2900 tons + 800 tons oil.

Gunnery Notes.—Broadside of 10—12 inch not often used, as decks are badly stressed by firing over them.

Armour Notes.—Armouring different to *Neptune*. These ships are "soft enders." On plan, belt forward should stop at Section 2, and belt at stern at Section 20. Beam barbettes, 11″ on exposed faces, 6″ within belt ; other barbettes, 4″ inside belt. *Neptune's* internal protection not used in these ships, internal screens not being continuous between end barbettes. Weights of armour : 4560 tons vertical + 2010 tons decks = 6570 tons.

Torpedo Notes.—Stern tube removed during War. 21-inch tubes introduced in these ships.

Engineering Notes.—Much as *Neptune*.

Name	Builder	Machinery	Laid down	Completed	Trials 30 hours.	Trials 8 hours f.p.	Boilers	Best recent speed
Colossus	Scott S.& E. Co.	Scott	July,'09	July '11	18,000=19·6	27,334=21·3	18 Babcock	
Hercules	Palmer	Palmer	July,'09	Aug.'11	18,000=19·6	26,559=21·5	Yarrow	

HERCULES.

General Notes.—These ships are similar to the *Neptune*, differing mainly in disposition of anti-torpedo armaments, size of tubes, armouring and internal protection. Begun under the 1909 Estimates. Average cost, £1,730,000 = about £87 per ton. Placed in Reserve, 1919.

Note to Plans.—These require revision, but new plans cannot be prepared till definite information is secured describing present positions of 4-inch guns, AA. guns, and searchlights. After half of flying boat deck removed 1914-15. "Coffee-box" S.L. towers round 2nd funnel. All 4-inch guns decked in.

1909 BRITISH DREADNOUGHTS.

NEPTUNE (Sept., 1909).

Normal displacement, 19,900 tons (about 22,000 *full load*). Complement, 813.

Length (*waterline*), 540 feet. Beam, 85 feet. { Draught (*normal*), 27 feet. } Length *over all*, 546 feet (p.p. 510 feet).
{ „ (*max.*) 30 „ }

Guns :
10—12 inch, 50 cal. } **Dir.**
12—4 inch } **Con.**
2—3 inch (anti-aircraft)
4—3 pdr.
5 M.G.
(1 landing)
Torpedo tubes (18 inch) :
2 *submerged*

Armour (K.C.) :
Vertical {
10″ Lower belt . . . .
8″ Upper belt . . . .
5″ & 8″ Bulkheads . . . .
7″—2½″ Belt (bow) . . .
2½″ Belt (stern) . . . .
9″ Barbettes . . . .
11″— ″ Gunhouses . . .
11″ C.T. (5″ tube) . . . . .
1½″ Torpedo C.T. . . . .
1″ Funnel uptakes . . . .

Armour (Nickel) :
Decks {
1½″ Main . . . .
1¾″ Middle . . . .
1½″ (bow)
3″ (stern) } lower
Special protection :
″— ″ Internal screens
over magazines and
machinery spaces . . .
″ Bulkheads to keel. . . .

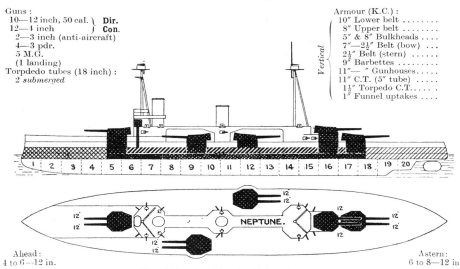

Ahead :
4 to 6—12 in.

Astern :
6 to 8—12 in.

Broadside : 8—12 in., 1—18 in. tube.

NEPTUNE.   *Photo, Sadler & Renouf.*

Machinery : Parsons turbine. Designed H.P. 25,000 = 21 kts. Boilers : Yarrow. Coal : *normal*
900 tons ; *maximum* 2710 tons + 790 tons oil fuel.

Armour Notes.—Armouring generally as *St. Vincent* class, but further internal sub-division. Internal screens are continuous between end barbettes and well inboard. Beam barbettes 10″ on exposed faces. On plan, Sections 1-3, 2½″ belt should be shown rising nearly to upper deck.

Gunnery Notes.—Firing of beam barbettes over decks (to get 10—12 inch broadside) not often resorted to, as decks get badly stressed by blast.

Torpedo Notes.—Submerged tube removed during War.

Engineering Notes.—Consumption on trial was 1.46 lbs. per h.p. at full power. Turbines : H.P. rotor diameter, 82 inch ; L.P. rotor diameter, 109 inch. R.P.M. 332. Boiler pressure : 235 lbs. per square inch. Heating surface : 63,630 square feet. Total weight of machinery with auxiliaries : 1109 tons + water to working level, 2036½ tons. Engine room complement, 231.

Name	Builder	Machinery	Laid down	Completed	First Trials :		Boilers	Best recent speed
					30 hrs.	8 hrs f.p.		
Neptune	Portsmouth	Clydebank	Jan. '09	Jan. '11	18,373 = 19	27,721 = 21	Yarrow	22·7

General Notes.—Begun under 1908 Estimates. Cost to build, £86.8 per ton. Cost of machinery, £258,000. Fore funnel heightened 1912. Forward half of flying decks removed, 1914-15. Has the best internal protection of all the 12-inch Dreadnoughts—in fact her internal protection was not equalled in later Battleships till the *Queen Elizabeth* and *Royal Sovereign* classes came into service. Placed in Reserve, 1919.

Note to Plans.—These require revision, but new plans cannot be prepared till definite information is secured regarding present positions of 4-inch guns, AA. guns and searchlights. Fore half of flying boat deck removed, 1914-15. " Coffee-box " S.L. towers added to 2nd funnel and mainmast, director top to foremast and " clinker screen " to fore funnel. All 4-inch guns decked in.

(St. Vincent Class).
ST. VINCENT (Sept., 1908), COLLINGWOOD (Nov., 1908), & VANGUARD (March, 1909).

Normal displacement, 19,250 tons. *Full load*, about 22,900 tons. Complement, 813 and 823.

Length (*waterline*), 530 feet. Beam, 84 feet. { Mean draught, 27 feet. } Length *over all*, 536 feet (p.p. 500 feet).
{ Max. „ 31¼ feet. }

Guns :
10—12 inch.— cal. } **Dir. Con.**
12—4 inch }
2—3 inch (anti-aircraft)
4—3 pdr.
5 M.G.
(1 landing)
Torpedo tubes (18 inch) :
2 *submerged* (broadside)

Armour (K.C.) :
Vertical {
10″ Lower belt . . . .
8″ Upper belt . . . .
7″ & 2″ Belt (bow) . . . .
2″ Belt (stern) . . . .
8″—5″ Bulkheads . . . .
9″ Barbettes . . . .
11″— ″ Gunhouses . . . .
11″ Fore C.T. (5″ tube)
8″ After C.T. (4″ tube)

Armour (K.N.C.) :
Decks {
1½″, ¾″ Main . . . .
1¾″ Middle . . . .
1½″, 3″ Lower
Special Protec. . . . . . .
— ″ Internal screens to
magazines, boilers and
engine rooms . . . .
— ″ Bulkheads to keel . .

ST. VINCENT (1). °

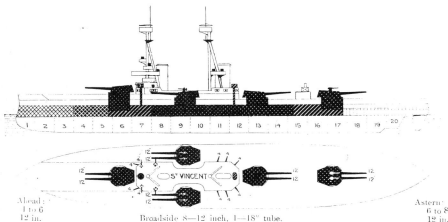

Ahead :
4 to 6
12 in.

Astern :
6 to 8
12 in.

Broadside 8—12 inch, 1—18″ tube.

ST. VINCENT (2). *

* After Control Top removed since above photographs were taken.

Machinery : Parsons turbine (as *Dreadnought*). 4 screws. Boilers : Yarrow or Babcock. Designed H.P. 24,500 = 21 kts. Coal : *normal*, 900 tons ; *maximum*, 2,800 tons + 940 tons oil + 190 tons patent fuel.

Torpedo Notes.—Stern tube removed during War.

Armour Notes.—Armour generally as *Bellerophon* class, but thinner belt at bow and stern. On plans, bow belt in Sections 1-3 should be shown rising almost to upper deck. Internal screens are continuous between end barbettes and set well inboard. Barbette bases, 10″.

Engineering Notes.—In this class (and all later Dreadnoughts up to *Iron Duke* class) no cruising turbines. An extra stage at forward end of H.P. turbine is used when running at cruising speed. For full speed, bye-pass valves used. H.P. rotor diameter, 68 inch. L.P. rotor diameter, 92 inch. 324 R.P.M. Pressure, 235 lbs. Heating surface : 63,414 square feet. Weight of main and auxiliary engines : 1072½ tons + water to working level = 1983½ tons. Average consumption on trials : 1.8 lbs. per H.P.

Note to Plans.—These require revision, but new plans cannot be prepared till definite information is secured describing present positions of 4-inch guns, AA. guns and searchlights.

Name.	Builder	Machinery and Boilers by.	Laid down.	Completed.	Last refit	Trials.	Boilers.	Best recent speed.
St. Vincent	Portsmouth	Scott Eng. & S. Co.	Dec. '07	Jan., '10		= 21·9	Babcock	22·5
Collingwood	Devonport	Hawthorn L.	Feb. '08	Jan., '10		26,319 = 21·5	Yarrow	22
Vanguard	Vickers	Vickers	April '08	Feb., '10		= 22·1	Babcock	22·4

General Notes.—Begun under 1907 Estimates. These ships are simply enlarged *Bellerophons* and second improvements on original *Dreadnought* design. *Collingwood* did not reach designed speed on first trials. Internal protection is very complete. Underwent large refit in 1912-13. *Vanguard* lost by explosion during the War. *St. Vincent* and *Collingwood* in Reserve or employed as Gunnery Training Ships in 1919.

1907 BRITISH DREADNOUGHTS.

(BELLEROPHON CLASS).

BELLEROPHON (July, 1907), **TÉMÉRAIRE** (Aug., 1907), **SUPERB** (Nov., 1907).

Normal displacement, 18,600 tons (about 22,000 *full load*). Complement, 733 to 793.

Length (*waterline*), 520 feet. Beam, $82\frac{1}{2}$ feet. { *Max.* draught, 30′ 11″ / *Mean* ,, $27\frac{1}{4}$ feet. } Length *over all*, 526 feet (*p.p.* 490 feet).

Guns:
- 10—12 inch, 45 cal. } **Dir. Con.**
- 11—4 inch (*Tem. & Superb*)
- 10—4 inch (*Bell'n*)
- 2—4 inch (anti-aircraft *B. & T.*)
- 2—3 inch (anti-aircraft *Sup.*)
- 4—3 pdr.
- 5 M.G.
- 1 (landing)

Torpedo tubes (18 inch, M. '04):
- 2 *submerged* (broadside)

Armour (K.C.):
Vertical
- 10″—9″ Lower belt ....
- 8″ Upper belt ....
- 7″—6″ Lower & upper belts (bow) ....
- 5″ Belt (stern) ....
- 8″ After bulkhead ....
- 10″—9″ Barbettes .....
- 11″— ″ Gunhouses.....
- 11″ Fore C.T. (4″ tube)
- 8″ After C.T. (4″ tube)

Armour (K.N.C.):
Decks.
- $1\frac{3}{4}$″—$\frac{3}{4}$″ Main.........
- 3″—$1\frac{3}{4}$″ Middle ....
- 4″—$1\frac{1}{2}$″ Lower ....
- Special protec. ....
- —″ Screens to magazines, boiler and engine rooms

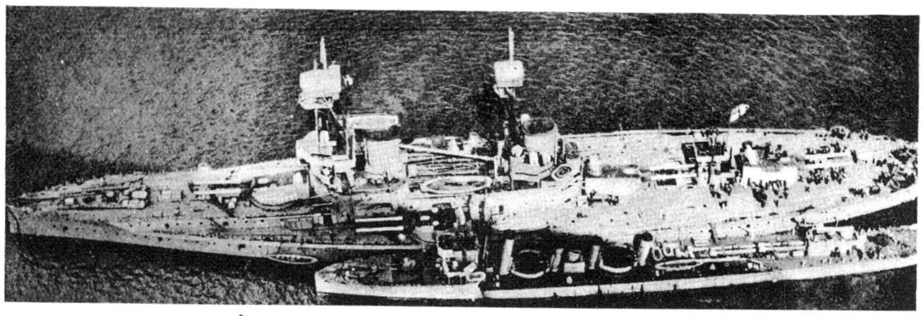

BELLEROPHON. (Marksman Type Leader alongside). *Official R.A.F. Photo.*

Name.	*Built at.*	*Machinery by.*	*Laid down.*	*Completed.*	*Trials. 8 hrs. full power.*	*Boilers.*	*Best recent speed.*
Bellerophon	Portsmouth	Fairfield	Dec., '06	Feb., '09	24090=21	Babcock	
Téméraire	Devonport	Hawthorn Leslie	Jan., '07	May, '09	24619=21	Yarrow	
Superb	Elswick	Wallsend Co.	Feb., '07	May, '09	25375=21	Babcock	

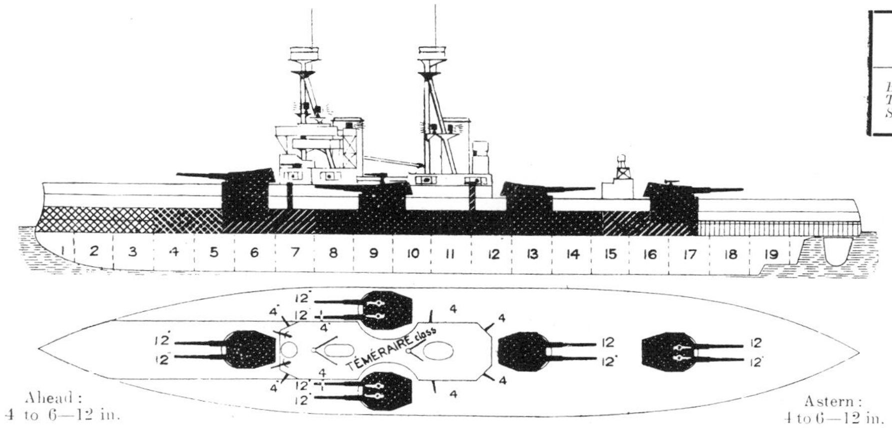

Ahead: 4 to 6—12 in.

Astern: 4 to 6—12 in.

Broadside: 8—12 in., 2—18 in. tubes.

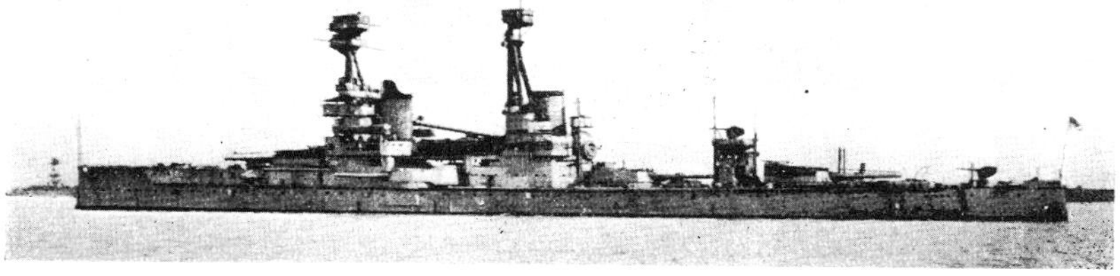

BELLEROPHON.

Machinery: Parsons turbine. 4 screws. Details as *Dreadnought*. Boilers: 18 Babcock or Yarrow. Designed H.P. 23,000 = 20.75 kts. Coal: *normal*, 900 tons; *maximum*, 2648 tons + 842 tons oil + 170 tons patent fuel.

Armour Notes.—Armouring is well planned. Internal screens in these ships run between end turrets and are set well inboard. Exposed faces of beam barbettes, 10″.

Engineereing Notes.—H.P. rotor diameter, 68 inch. L.P. rotor diameter, 92 inch. 324 R.P.M. Pressure: 235 lbs. Heating surface: 55,530 square feet. Weight of main and auxiliary engines: $1014\frac{1}{2}$ tons. Water to working level, total weight = *about* 1936 tons. Trial consumption averaged 1.55 lbs.

Torpedo Notes.—Stern tube removed during War.

Note to Plans.—These require revision, but new plans cannot be prepared till definite information is secured describing present positions of 4-inch guns, AA. guns and searchlights.

General Notes.—Begun under 1906 Estimates. Average cost of machinery, about £285,000. Underwent large refit in 1913-14. Design is generally as *Dreadnought*, but with larger degree of internal sub-division and protection against torpedo attack: also better anti-torpedo attack battery. All largely refitted in 1912-14, before outbreak of war. The internal protection of these ships is very complete. *Bellerophon* and *Superb* used as Gunnery Schools (Turret Drill), 1919. *Téméraire*, Cadets' Training Ship (sea-going).

1906 BRITISH DREADNOUGHT.

DREADNOUGHT (February, 1906).

Normal displacement, 17,900 tons. *Full load, about* 20,700 tons. Complement, 862.

Length (*w.l.*), 520 feet. Beam, 82 feet. { *Maximum* draught, 31 feet. / *Mean* ,, $26\frac{1}{2}$,, } Length, (*o.a.*) 526 feet (*p.p.* 490 feet).

Guns:
- 10—12 inch, 45 cal. } **Dir. Con.**
- 10—12 pdr.
- 2—3 inch (anti-aircraft, 13 pdr.)
- 2—12 pdr. (anti-aircraft)
- 4—3 pdr.
- 5 M.G.
- (1 landing)

Torpedo tubes (18 inch):
- 4 *submerged* (broadside)

Armour (K.C.):
Vertical.
- 11″—9″ Lower belt ....
- 8″ Upper belt ....
- 11″ Bulkhead (aft) ....
- 6″ Belt (bow) ....
- 4″ Belt (stern) ....
- 11″—8″ Barbettes .....
- 12″ Gunhouses ....
- 11″ Fore C.T. ....
- 5″ Fore com. tube ....
- 8″ After C.T. ....
- 4″ After com. tube ...

Armour (K.N.C.):
Decks.
- $\frac{3}{4}$″ Main (forward).....
- $1\frac{3}{4}$″ (flat) Middle .....
- $2\frac{3}{4}$″ (slope) (amidships)
- 4″ at ends (Middle) ...
- 3″—1″ Lower ....
- Special protection.....
- ″ Screens to Mags., &c.

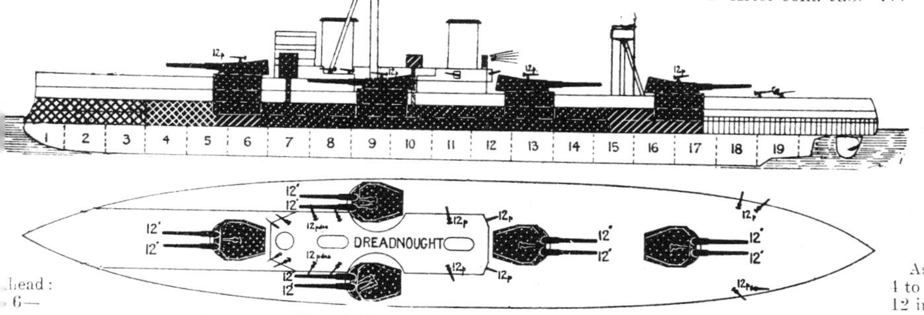

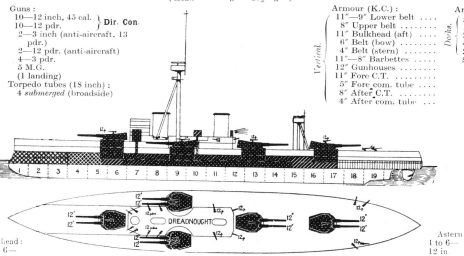

Ahead: 4 to 6—12 in.

Astern: 4 to 6—12 in.

Broadside: 8—12 in., 1—18 in. tube.

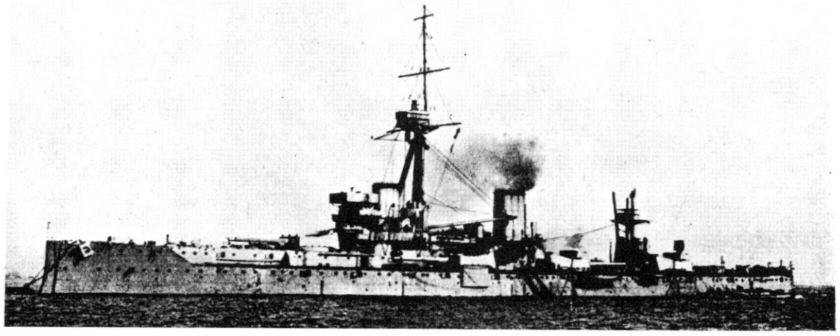

DREADNOUGHT. *Photo, Cribb.*

Machinery: Parsons turbine. 4 screws. Boilers: 18 Babcock & Wilcox in 3 groups. Designed H.P. 23,000 = 21 kts. Coal: *normal*, 900 tons; *maximum*, 2900 tons + 1120 tons oil + 120 tons patent fuel. *Nominal* radius: 6600 at 10 kts.: 5000 at 19 kts.

Torpedo Notes.—Stern tube removed during War.

Engineering Notes.—Full power, 400 revolutions. One H.P. ahead, one H.P. astern turbine on each wing shaft: inner shafts, 3 turbines each (cruising L.P. ahead: L.P. astern). 1 astern turbine on each. Boiler pressure: 250 lbs., reduced slightly at the turbines. Each turbine has 39,600 blades. Main condensers: 26,000 square feet; auxiliary: 6000. Grate surface: 1599 square feet. Heating surface: 55,400 square feet. On trials she exceeded her speed for short spurts (best mile at 21.78), but barely averaged it on her eight hours' run. Very free from vibration. Weight of machinery: main and auxiliary, $973\frac{1}{2}$ tons + water = $1897\frac{3}{4}$ tons.

Coal consumption.—Very economical at full speed, *about* 340 tons per day for full power. At slow speed consumption is heavy. At 4600 H.P. (13 kts.) it averages nearly 160 tons a day. At 10,000 H.P., *about* 250 tons per day.

Armour Notes.—Base of amidships barbettes is 8″ only and all barbette bases 3″ behind belt. Protective deck aft is 2″ flat, 3″ on slopes and over steering gear. Internal screens to magazines, &c., are not continuous between end barbettes.

Name.	*Built at*	*Machinery by*	*Laid down*	*Com. pleted*	*Trials (mean). 30 hrs. at 16,250.*	*8 hrs. full.*	*Boilers.*	*Best recent speed*
Dreadnought	Portsmouth	Vickers	Dec., '05	*Oct. '06	16,930=19·3	24,712=20·9†	Babcock	...

*Was not really complete at this date. First commission began Dec., 1906. £262,500 was spent in finishing her and £60,400 of this sum was voted in 1907-8. †Maximum attained, 27,518 = 21.6 kts.

Note to Plans.—These require revision, but new plans cannot be prepared till information is received giving present positions of 12-pdr. and AA. guns and searchlights.

General Notes.—Freeboard forward: 28 feet. Cost £1,797,497. Begun under 1905 Estimates. In this ship the officers' quarters are forward, crew aft. The ship is very steady, and consequently extremely wet and uncomfortable. She has a remarkably steady gun platform. Draws $2\frac{1}{2}$ feet more than designed, with normal coal. She was very quickly built. All material used is extremely strong. Tactical diameter, extreme helm: 865 yards at 19 kts.; 825 yards at 12 kts. The ship can stop in 1025 yards at 20 kts. (3 minutes), in 725 yards at 12 kts. Re-fitted 1916. Rammed and sank *U 29*, commanded by Kap. Leut. Otto Weddigen. Placed in Reserve, 1919.

Historical Notes.—When Lord Fisher went to the Admiralty, as First Sea Lord, in October, 1904, he brought with him, from the Mediterranean, plans for various new types of warships. Among these was a design for a battleship with 12—12 inch guns arranged in pairs along centre line: three pairs of guns at bows, three at stern, the inner barbettes rising in tiers, so that six guns could fire ahead, six astern, and all twelve on broadside. The Special Commission on Designs very much liked this plan, but it had to be rejected on the score of size and cost, and the risk of the superfiring system, on which no practical experience was then available. Lord Fisher's design was modified to an *Orion* plan, but this too had to be rejected on the score of cost and size. The penultimate design with 8—12 inch (two forward, two aft, two on each beam) turned out to be akin to a plan, evolved by Sir Philip Watts and Lord Fisher in the 'eighties, for combining the gun plans of the old *Inflexible* and *Devastation*. The fifth amidship turret of the final Dreadnought design was added, because it happened to fit in.

1915 BRITISH BATTLE CRUISERS

(Renown Class.)

REPULSE (8th January, 1916). **RENOWN** (4th March, 1916).

Normal displacement, 26,500 tons (about 32,000-32,700 *full load*). Complement, Renown, 999 ; Repulse 1016.

Length (p.p.), 750 feet. { *o.a.* 794 feet *Repulse* / *o.a.* 794 feet 1½in. *Renown* } Beam { *Repulse* 90 feet* / *Renown* 90 feet 2 in.* } Draught { *Repulse* 26¼ feet (*mean*), 30½ feet (*max.*) / *Renown* 26⅔ feet (*mean*), 30 feet (*max.*) }

Outside bulges:

Guns :
  6—15 inch, 42 cal. } **Dir.**
  17—4 inch, 50 cal. } **Con.**
  2—3 inch (anti-aircraft)
  4—3 pdr.
  5 M.G.
    (1 landing)
Torpedo tubes (21 inch) :
  2 *submerged*
    See Torpedo Notes.

Armour (K.C.) :
  6" (amidships) ....
  4" (within bow) ...... } Lower
  3" (stern) .... } belt
  4" Fore b'lkhead ....
  3" After b'lkh'd ....
  1½" Upper belt ......
  7"—4" Barbettes ......
  11"—7" Gunhouses......
  1½" Funnel uptakes ...
  2" C.T. base (3" tube within) ....
  10" C.T. ....
  6" Sighting hood over C.T. ....
  3" Torpedo C.T. ......

Armour (H.T.) :
  1½"—½" Fo'xle .....
  1⅕"—1¼" Upper ....
  3"—¾" Main (2" slopes)
  2½" Bow ....
  3½"—3" Stern } Lower
  Barbettes .....
  3" C.T. and hood .....
  1½" Torpedo C.T. .....
  Special protection :
    Modified bulges about 20 ft. deep, filled with oil ....

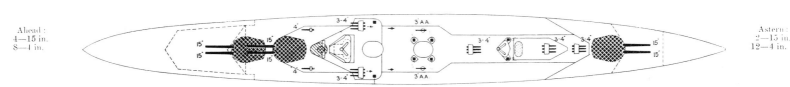

Ahead :
  4—15 in.
  8—4 in.

Astern :
  2—15 in.
  12—4 in.

Broadside : 6—15 in., 13—4 in., 1—21 in. tube.

Machinery : Brown-Curtis (direct drive) turbines. 4 screws. Boilers : 42 Babcock & Wilcox. Designed H.P. not exactly specified, but expected to be 110,000 to 120,000 S.H.P. for 30 kts. In service, S.H.P. 112,000 = about 31.5 kts. Fuel (oil only) : 1000 tons normal ; *Repulse* 4243 tons *maximum* ; *Renown* 4289 tons *maximum*.

Gunnery Notes.—15-inch have range only limited by maximum visibility. Director tower under control tower on foremast. 4-inch triples have 2 director towers, and all guns can be worked from either tower or half the 4-inch from one tower. If towers are destroyed, 4-inch can work independently. 4-inch triples are clumsy and not liked. They are not mounted in one sleeve ; have separate breech mechanism ; gun crew of 23 to each triple. First salvo fired by forward 15-inch of *Renown* did considerable damage forward, and she had to be docked for repairs.

Torpedo Notes.—Submerged tubes a failure. *Renown*, on 1919 re-fit, reported to have had *submerged* tubes removed and replaced by 8 *above water* tubes in 4 twin mountings on main deck.

Armour Notes.—Armouring adapted from *Invincible* and *Indefatigable* classes. Belt *about* 9½ ft. deep. *Special Protection.*—Projected that bulges be deepened. *Renown* may have had bulges enlarged on her 1919 re-fit, and her beam may be larger now.

Engineering Notes.—Turbines similar to *Tiger*. For full description, *v.* "Engineering," April 11th, 1919. Boilers : 250 lbs. per sq. in. Heating surface : 157,206 sq. ft. Consumption at full speed : *about* 1400 tons oil fuel per day.

Aircraft Notes.—Two aeroplanes carried on flying-off platforms on crowns of "B" and "Y" turrets.

Name	Builder	Machinery	Begun*	Completed	Trials H.P.	kts.	Where run
Repulse	Clydebank	Clydebank	Jan.25,'15	Aug.,1916	119,025	31.7	Skelmorlie (deep load)
Renown	Fairfield	Fairfield	Jan.25,'15	Sept.,1916	126,300	32.68	Arran (normal load)

*To Battle Cruiser design.

General Notes.—Provided for by 1914-15 Navy Estimates : first designed as slightly modified *Royal Sovereigns*, contracted for on that basis, and begun 1914, but building was not pushed on actively after the outbreak of War. After the Falklands Battle it was decided that these two ships should be re-designed as Battle Cruisers. Outline design was prepared in ten days, and builders received sufficient details by January 21st 1915, to begin building, but full designs were not finished and approved till April, 1915. Intended that they should be completely built in fifteen months, but this time was somewhat exceeded. Both ships have turned out remarkably well and reflect great credit on their designers and builders. Internally, they are most spacious, but they are lightly built, and their guns "shake them up" considerably. Remarkable speeds have been claimed for these ships. When attempting to intercept enemy warships in November, 1917, *Renown* is said to have touched 41 kts. Be this as it may, they have certainly done 33-34 kts. in service. Reported to have cost about three to four millions each.

1915 BRITISH BATTLE CRUISERS. (Illustrations.)

(For Plan and Description, v. opposite page.)

RENOWN.

RENOWN. REPULSE.

Photo, Sub-Lieut. Vickers, R.N.

1911 BRITISH BATTLE-CRUISERS. No. 22 & 27 (Dreadnoughts).

QUEEN MARY (March, 1912), & **TIGER** (1913).

Normal displacement, 27,000 tons. *Full load,* tons. Complement

Length (*waterline*), 720 feet. Beam, 87 feet. *Maximum* draught, 30 feet. Length *over all,* 725 feet.

Guns : *(see note).*
8—13·5 inch (A⁷)
16—4 inch
Torpedo tubes (21 inch) :
2 *submerged* (broadside)
1 *submerged* (stern)

Armour (Krupp) :
9″ Belt (amidships) .. *aa*
4″ Belt (ends) ....

QUEEN MARY.

Photo, Abrahams & Sons.

TIGER (present appearance).

Photo, Renouf.

Note.—*Tiger* tripod forward. Rumoured that her secondary battery may possibly consist of 12—6 inch guns instead of 16—4 inch as *Queen Mary.*

Machinery: Turbine (Brown-Curtis). Boilers: Babcock. Designed H.P. 75,000=27 kts. Coal: *normal,* 1000 tons ; *maximum* 3500 tons + oil, 1000 tons.

Name	Builder	Machinery	Laid down	Com-pleted	Trials	Boilers	Best recent speed
Queen Mary Tiger	Palmer Clydebank	Clydebank Clydebank	Mar. '11 June '12	1913 May '14		Yarrow Babcock	33

Tiger, 1911-12 estimates. *Queen Mary,* 1910-11 estimates.

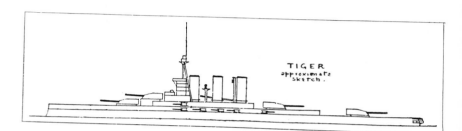

TIGER
approximate sketch.

1912 BRITISH BATTLE CRUISER.

TIGER (Dec., 1913).

Normal displacement, 28,500 tons. *Full load,* about 35,000 tons. Complement 1185.

Length (*waterline*), 675 feet. Beam, 90½ feet. { *Mean* draught, 28⅓ feet. { Length (o.a.) 704 feet.
{ Max. .. 34 ,, { Length (p.p.) 660 feet.

Guns :
8—13·5 inch (M.V.) } **Dir.**
12—6 inch (M. XII) } **Con.**
2—3 inch (anti-aircraft)
4—3 pdr.
5 M.G.
(1 landing)
Torpedo tubes (21 inch) :
4 *submerged* (broadside)

Armour (K.C.) :
9″ Lower belt ....
6″ Upper belt ....
3″ Under lower belt ..
4″ Bulkheads..........
6″ Battery (1″ traverses)
5″, 4″ Battery Bulk'ds)
6″ Casemates (2″ rear)
9″—8″ Barbettes .....
9″ Gunhouses ....
2″ C.T. base ....
4″ Com tube ....
10″ C.T. ....
6″—3″ hood over C.T.
6″ Torpedo C.T. (4″ tube)..............

Armour (H.T.) :
1½″—1″ Fo'xle........
1½″—1″ Upper ......
1″ Amidships } Lower
3″ Bow }
Special protection :
2½″—1″ H.T. magazine screens ....

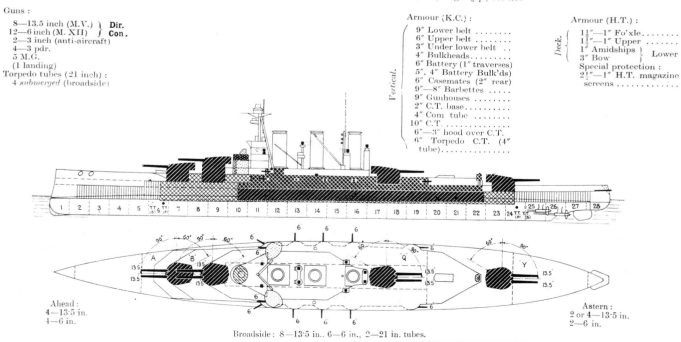

Ahead :
4—13·5 in.
4—6 in.

Astern :
2 or 4—13·5 in.
2—6 in.

Broadside : 8—13·5 in., 6—6 in., 2—21 in. tubes.

Machinery : Turbines (Brown-Curtis direct drive). 4 screws. Boilers : 39 Babcock. Designed H.P. 85,000 = 28 kts. (108,000 = 30 attained). Coal : *normal* 1000 tons, *maximum* 3320 tons coal and 3480 tons oil fuel.

Armour Notes.—Armour as *Lion* Class, but 6″ battery and extra H.T. decks added. Barbettes, 4″, 3″, 1″, as they descend through decks behind belts. 1″ rear screen to 6″ battery. Internal magazine protection is not continuous between barbettes.

Engineering Notes.—4-shaft turbines in 2 sets, each set has H.P. ahead and H.P. astern turbine on wing shaft, one L.P. ahead and one L.P. astern, in same casing on inner shaft. Boilers in 5 rooms. The enormous fuel capacity (6800 tons coal and oil) does not give this ship any exceptional radius of action, for she burns about 1200 tons of fuel per day at 60,000 S.H.P.

Name	Builder	Machinery	Begun	Completed	Trials : H.P.	kts.
Tiger	Clydebank	Clydebank	June, 1912	Oct., 1914	87,500 = 104,635 =	28 29

General Notes.—Begun under 1911 Estimates by J. Brown & Co., Clydebank ; machinery by builders. Completed October, 1914. Estimated cost was £2,593,095, but this was exceeded. As first designed, this ship was to have been very much like the *Lion* class. A year after the *Tiger* was laid down the Japanese battle-cruiser *Kongo* was completed and passed her trials. Comparison between the *Lion* and *Kongo* designs showed the Japanese ship to be superior in armament and protection. Work was suspended on the *Tiger,* and her design was altered to embody certain improvements displayed by the *Kongo.* These alterations resulted in the *Tiger* being one and a half years on the stocks before launching. Until *Hood* was launched in 1918, *Tiger* was the largest ship in H.M. Navy. She was also a remarkably handsome ship until the present hideous rig was adopted in 1918.

1909 BRITISH BATTLECRUISERS.

(LION CLASS.)

LION (August, 1910), **PRINCESS ROYAL** (April, 1911).

Normal displacement, 26,350 tons. *Full load*, 29,700 tons. Complement, 1085 & 1061.

Length (*w.l.*), 675 feet. Beam, 88½ feet. { *Mean* draught, 27⅔ feet. } { Length *over all*. 700 feet.
{ *Max.* draught, 31¾ feet. } { Length *p.p.*, 660 feet.

Guns :
8—13.5 inch (M.V.) } **Dir. Con.**
16—4 inch, 50 cal. }
2—3 inch (anti-aircraft)
4—3 pdr.
(*P.R.* 2—2 pdr. pom-pom)
5 M.G.
(1 landing)
Torpedo tubes (21 inch) :
2 *submerged* (broadside)

Armour :
Decks { 1″ Upper ....
{ 1½″—1″ Amidships } Lower
{ 2¼″ Ends }
Special protection :
—″ Magazine screens

PRINCESS ROYAL. (Aircraft Recognition View). *Official R.A.F. photo.*

Armour (K.C.) :
Vertical { 9″, 6″, 5″ Lower belt ..
{ 6″, 5″, 4″ Upper belt ..
{ 4″ Bulkheads ....
{ 9″—8″ Barbettes .....
{ 9″ Gunhouses ....
{ 1½″ Funnel uptakes ..
{ 10″ C.T. (4″ tube K.N.C.)
{ 6″—2″ Sighting hood .
{ 1″ Torpedo C.T. ......

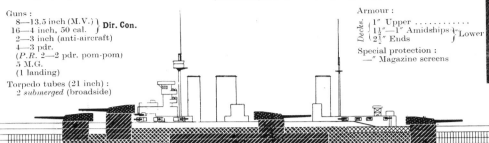

Ahead:
4—13.5 in.

LION.

Astern:
2—13.5 in.

Broadside : 8—13·5 in., 1—21 in. tube.

Machinery : Parsons turbine. 4 screws. Boilers : 42 Yarrow. Designed H.P. 70,000 = 28 kts. Coal : *normal* 1,000 tons ; *maximum*, 3500 tons + 1135 tons oil.

Armour Notes.—Barbettes are 3″ and 1″ below upper and main deck. Magazine screens not continuous between end barbettes. 2,900 tons vertical + 2,300 tons deck armour=5,200 tons.

Engineering Notes.—*Lion* on trials used coal only. No attempt was made on builders' trials to force these ships up to a phenomenal speed. In service, they have attained 30 kts., developing rather more than 100,000 H.P. Coal consumption : 950 tons a day at full power. *P. Royal* on 2/3 trial burned only 1·16 lbs. per h.p. per hour.

| Name | Builder | Machinery | Laid down | Completed | Trials (mean) | | Boilers | Best recent speed |
					At 3/4 power	Full power		
Lion	Devonport Y.	Vickers	Nov.'09	Jun. '12	54,763 = 24·5	73,802 = 27	Yarrow	
Princess Royal	Vickers	Vickers	May, '10	Nov. '12	53,315 = 27	76,510 = 28·52	Yarrow	

General Notes.—The *Lion* begun under the 1909 Estimates ; the *Princess Royal* is one of the "contingent Dreadnoughts" of the same year's estimates. On trials, flames from the fore funnel rendered the fire control station then over fore funnel on tripod, almost untenable. Alterations were consequently made. Average cost per ship, £2,087,000=about £73¾ per ton. About £60,000 was spent on altering each. *Lion* was disabled in the Dogger Bank action. A similar but slightly larger ship of this type, *Queen Mary*, was sunk in the Battle of Jutland.

LION. *Photo, Topical.*

Note to Plans.—These require revision, but new plans cannot be prepared till information is received giving position of 4 inch and AA. guns and searchlights.

1910 BRITISH BATTLE CRUISERS.

(Presented to the British Navy by the Dominion of New Zealand.)

(INDEFATIGABLE TYPE.)

INDEFATIGABLE (Oct., 1909), & **NEW ZEALAND** (1911).

Note.—For AUSTRALIA, a sister ship, see Royal Australian Navy Section.

Normal displacement, 18,800 tons ; about 20,000 tons, *full load.* Complement, 853.

Length (*waterline*), - feet. Beam, 80 feet. { *Mean* draught, 26½ feet. } Length *over all*, 590 feet (*p.p.*, 555 feet).
{ *Max.* „ 30 feet. }

Guns :
8—12 inch, 50 cal. } **Dir. Con.**
10—4 inch }
1—4 inch (anti-aircraft)
4—3 pdr.
2—2 pdr. pom-pom
5 M.G.
(1 landing)
Torpedo tubes (18 inch) :
2 *submerged* (broadside)

Armour (K.C.) :
Vertical { 6″ Belt (amidships) ...
{ 5″—4″ Belt (forward)
{ 4″ Bulkheads ....
{ 7″, 4″, 3″ Barbettes ...
{ 7″ Gunhouses ....
{ 1½″—1″ Funnel uptakes
{ (Nickel) ....
{ 10″ C.T. ....
{ 6″—3″ Hood over C.T.
{ 4″ Com. tube ....
{ 1″ Torpedo Director
{ Tower ....

Armour—*continued.*
Decks { 1″ Main ....
{ 2″—1″ Amidships } Lower
{ 2½″ Fore and aft } Deck
Special protection :
—″ Screens to Magazines

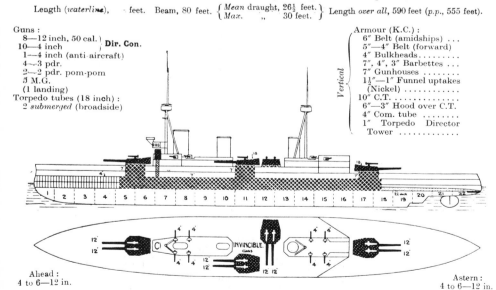

Ahead:
4 to 6—12 in.

INVINCIBLE CLASS.

Astern:
4 to 6—12 in.

Broadside : 8—12 in., 2—18 in. tubes.

Machinery : Parsons turbine. 4 screws. Designed H.P. 44,000 = 25 kts. Boilers : Babcock.
Coal : *normal*, 1000 tons ; *maximum*, 3170 tons coal + 840 tons oil.

Armour Notes.—On plans, belt should not extend to stem or stern. 6″ belt from lower to middle deck, Sections 7-17. 5″ belt, Sections 5, 6 and 18, 19 ; 4″ belt, Sections 3, 4 and 20-21 ; 2½″ belt, Sections 1, 2 and 22, 23. Armour for funnel uptakes not shown. Magazine screens not continuous between end barbettes.

Torpedo Notes.—Stern tube removed during War.

| Name | Builder | Machinery | Laid down | Completed | Trials (mean) | | Boilers | Best recent speed |
					30 hours 3/4	8 hours full		
Indefatigable	Devonport	Clydebank	Feb.'09	Feb '11	32,000 = 24·6	= 26·7	Babcock	
New Zealand	Fairfield	Fairfield	1910	Jan. '12	= 24·8	29,000 = 27	Babcock	29·13

Photo, Symonds & Co.

*General Notes—*Design is generally an enlarged *Invincible.* Special feature is that the amidships guns are further apart in order to permit of fairly free use on either broadside. Better sea-boats than the *Invincibles. New Zealand* was originally laid down for the Dominion of New Zealand, but finally presented to the Royal Navy. *Indefatigable,* the original ship of this type, was sunk in the Battle of Jutland.

Note to Plans.—These require revision, but new plans cannot be prepared till information is received giving present disposition of 4-inch guns, AA. guns and searchlights. Chart-house and forebridges have been moved back to leave C.T. unobstructed. For other corrections, see *Armour Notes.*

1906 BRITISH BATTLE CRUISERS.

(INVINCIBLE CLASS).

INVINCIBLE (April, 1907), **INFLEXIBLE** (June, 1907), & **INDOMITABLE** (March, 1907).

Normal Displacement, 17,250 tons (about 20,000 *full load*). Complement, 837.

Length (*waterline*), 560 feet. Beam, 78ft. 10 in. { Mean draught, 26 feet. } Length *over all*, 567 feet (*p.p.* 530). { Max. ,, 29¾ feet. }

Guns :
- 8—12 inch, XI, 45 cal. **Dir.**
- 12—4 inch **Con.**
- 1—4 inch (anti-aircraft)
- 1—3 inch (anti-aircraft)
- 4—3 pdr.
- 5 M.G.
- (1 landing)

Torpedo tubes (18 inch) :
- 4 submerged

Armour (K.C.) :
Vertical {
- 6″ Belt (amidships) ...
- 4″ Belt (bow) ......
- 7″—6″ Bulkheads ...
- 7″ Barbettes ......
- 7″ Gunhouses ......
- 10″ C.T. (fore) ......
- 4″ Tube (fore) ......
- 6″ C.T. (aft) ....
- 3″ Com. tube (aft) ....
}

Armour—continued.
Decks {
- 1″—¾″ Main.........
- 1½″ Middle ......
- 2½″ Lower (aft) .....
- 2″ Slopes }
- 1½″ Flat } Lower (amidships)
}
Special protection :
- —″ Screens to magazines

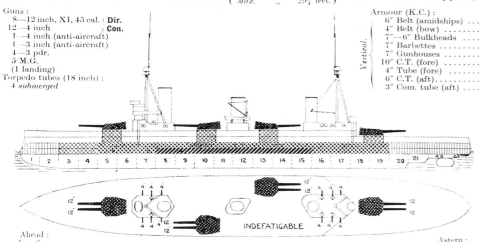

INDEFATIGABLE

Ahead :
4 or 6—
12 in.

Broadside : 6—12 in., 2—18 in. tubes.

Astern :
4 to 6—
12 in.

INDOMITABLE

Photo, Topical.

Machinery : Parsons turbines. 4 screw. Boilers : Yarrow or Babcock. Designed H.P. 41,000 = 25 kts. Coal : *normal*, 1000 tons ; *maximum*, 3080 tons + 710-725 tons oil fuel.

Gunnery Notes.—Amidship turrets are very cramped together, and broadside of 8—12 inch can only be rarely fired.
Armour Notes.—Internal magazine screens not continuous between end barbettes.
Torpedo Notes.—Stern tube removed during War.

Name	Builder.	Machinery, etc.	Laid down.	Completed.	Trials (mean).	Boilers.	Best recent speed.
Invincible	Elswick	Humphrys & T.	April, '06	'08	46,000 = 26·6	Yarrow	28·6
Inflexible	Clydebank	Clydebank	Feb., '06	'08	= 26·5	Yarrow	28·4
Indomitable	Fairfield	Fairfield	March, '06	'08	= 26·1	Babcock	28·7

General Notes.—Begun under 1905-6 Estimates. Average cost of each, *about £1,752,000 = £101·6 per ton.* These ships at full speed burn *about 500 tons of coal a day,* plus *about 125 tons of oil.* They are not very steady gun platforms. Average cost of machinery, *about £472,000. Invincible* of this class lost in Battle of Jutland. *Inflexible* severely damaged by a mine in the bombardment of the Dardanelles, March 18th, 1915. Placed in Reserve, 1919.

Notes to Plans.—These require revision, but new plans cannot be prepared till information is received giving present distribution of 4-inch guns, AA. guns and searchlights. Stern tube removed. Chart-house and forebridges re-built to leave C.T. clear. 4-inch guns now in unarmoured casemates.

AIRCRAFT VIEW.

Official R.A.F. photo.

1904 BRITISH BATTLESHIPS (18½ knot). (Pre-Dreadnoughts.)

(LORD NELSON CLASS—2 Ships).

LORD NELSON (September, 1906), & **AGAMEMNON** (June, 1906).

Normal displacement, 16,500 tons. Complement, 865.

Length (*waterline*), 435 feet. Beam, 79½ feet. *Mean draught,* 27 feet. *Length over all,* 445 feet.

Guns :
- 4—12 inch, XI., 45 cal. (A⁵)
- 10—9·2 inch, XI., 50 cal. (A³)
- 15—12 pdr.
- 16—3 pdr.
- 2 Maxims.

Torpedo tubes (18 in.) ('04 M) :
- 4 submerged (broadside).
- 1 submerged (stern).

Armour (Krupp) :
- 12″ Belt (amidships) ...... *aaa*
- 6″ Belt (forward) (N.C.) *b*
- 4″ Belt (aft) (N.C.) ...... *d*
- 2″ Deck (slopes) ....
- Protection to vitals ...= *aaaa*
- 14″ Barbettes (N.C.) ...*aaaa*
- 8″ Turrets to these (K.C.) = *aaa*
- 8″ Lower deck side ...... *aa*
- 7″ Secondary turrets (N.C.) *a*
- 12″ Conning tower (N.C.) *aaa*

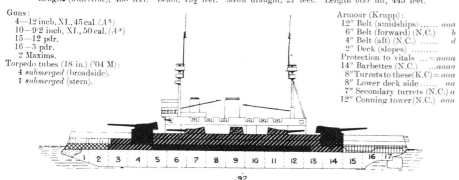

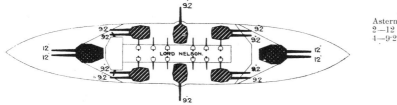

LORD NELSON.

Ahead
2—12
4—9·2

Broadside : 4—12 in., 5—9·2 in.

Astern
2—12
4—9·2

Machinery : 2 sets 4 cylinder vertical triple expansion. 2 screws. Boilers : 15 Yarrow or Babcock. Designed H.P. 16,750 = 18·5 kts. Coal : *normal* 900 tons ; *maximum* 2000 tons : also 400 tons oil.

Gunnery Notes.—Big guns, central pivot mountings. Hoists, electric or hand all guns. Guns manœuvred hydraulic and hand gear. The 9·2 inch double turrets are not regarded as being anything like so satisfactory a design as the single 9·2 inch single turrets in earlier types.
Arcs of fire : 12 inch, 240°.
Torpedo Notes.—1904 model torpedoes. Complete electrical installation. 8 search-lights.
Engineering Notes.—Average cost of machinery, £213,000.

Name.	Builder	Machinery	Laid down	Completed	Last refit	Trials	Boilers	Best recent speed
Lord Nelson	Palmer	Palmer	Nov., '04	1908	...	... 17,115 = 18·9	Babcock	19
Agamemnon	Beardmore	Hawthorn Leslie	Oct., '04	1907	...	17,285 = 18·8	Yarrow	18·9

General Notes.—Estimates 1904-05. Estimated cost about £1,500,000 per ship. Designed by Sir P. Watts. These ships have an abnormally small tactical diameter and can practically spin round on their sterns. They heel considerably in doing so. In appearance they are quite unlike other British ships and have a distinctly French look.

LORD NELSON.

Photo, Symonds.

Photo, Oscar Parkes, Esq.

LORD NELSON

AGAMEMNON

1902 BRITISH BATTLESHIPS (18-19 knot).

(KING EDWARD CLASS—8 SHIPS).

COMMONWEALTH (May, 1903), **KING EDWARD** (July, 1903), **DOMINION** (August, 1903), **HINDUSTAN** (December, 1903), **ZEALANDIA** (ex *New Zealand*), (February, 1904). **HIBERNIA** (June, 1905), **AFRICA** (May, 1905) and **BRITANNIA** (December, 1904).

Normal displacement, 16350 tons. *Full load,* 17,500 tons. Complement, 777.
Length (*waterline*), 439 feet. *Beam,* 78 feet. *Mean draught,* 26¾ feet. *Length over all,* 453¾ feet.

Guns :
4—12 in. IX, 40 cal. (*AAAA*)
4—9·2 in. IX, 45 cal. (*AA*)
10—6 in., VII.
12—12 pdr.
14—3 pdr.
2 Maxims.
Torpedo tubes
(18 inch) :
4 *submerged*
(*broadside*).
1 *submerged* (stern)

Armour (Krupp) :
9″ Belt (amidships) .... *aa*
6—2″ Belt (forward) ....*a-f*
2″ Deck (slopes) ....
Protection to vitals ......=*aaa*
12″ Barbettes (N.C.) ....*aaa*
8″ Turrets to these (K.C.) = *aaa*
8″ Lower deck side .... *aa*
7″ Battery .... *a*
7″ Secondary turrets .... *a*
12″ Conning tower .... *aaa*

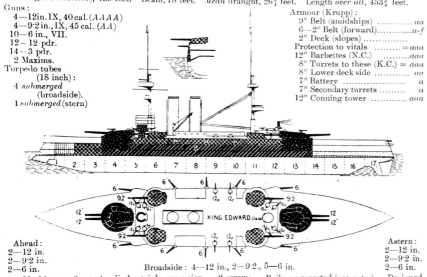

Ahead :
2—12 in.
2—9·2 in.
2—6 in.

Astern :
2—12 in.
2—9·2 in.
2—6 in.

Broadside : 4—12 in., 2—9·2, 5—6 in.

Machinery : 2 sets 4 cylinder triple expansion. 2 screws. Boilers : assorted (*see notes*). Designed H.P. 18000=18·9 kts. Coal : *normal* 950 tons ; *maximum* 2150 tons ; *also* 400 tons oil (except *New Zealand*).
Armour Notes.—Main Belt is 7¼ feet wide by about 285 feet long ; lower edge 9″ thick amidships. Main deck 1″ thick ; upper deck ditto amidships.
Gunnery Notes.—Loading positions, big guns : all round. Hoists, electric for all guns. Big guns manœuvred by hydraulic and hand gear. 6 inch guns : 13 feet about l.w.l.
Arcs of fire : 12 in., 240° ; 9·2 in., about 135° ; 6 in., 120°.
Torpedo Notes.—1904 model torpedoes carried. Nearly all round net defence. 8 searchlights. Stern tube not actually fitted in some.
Engineering Notes.— 120 revolutions=full power. Pressure : 200 lbs. Heating surface varies from 43,940 square feet in the earlier ships to 47,360 square feet in the later. Grate area from 1306 to 1402 square feet. Superheaters to all Babcock boilered ships except first three.

Name.	Builder.	Machinery	Laid down.	Completed.	Last refit	30 hours ½ power.	8 hours full power.	Boilers.	Best recent speed.
Commonwealth	Fairfield	Fairfield	June '02	1905	1907	12,769=17·9	18,538=19·01	16 Babcock	18·7
King Edward	Devonport	Harland & W.	Mar. '02	1905	1907	12,884=17·5	18,138=19·04	10 Babcock, 6 Cyl.	19·1
Dominion	Vickers	Vickers	May '02	1905	1907	12,843=18·3	18,439=19·35	16 Babcock	18·2
Hindustan	Clydebank	Clydebank	Oct. '02	1905	1907	12,926=17·9	18,521=19·08	18 Babcock, 3 Cyl.	18·9
Zealandia	Portsmouth	Humphrys & T.	Feb. '03	1905	1907	12,981=16·9	18,440=18·6	12 Niclausse, 3 Cyl.	18·9
Africa	Chatham	Clydebank	Jan. '04	1906	1907	12,860=17·9	18,621=18·95°	Babcock	18·2
Britannia	Portsmouth	Humphrys & T.	Feb. '04	1906	1907	13,087=16·8	18,725=18·74	Babcock & Cyl.	17·5
Hibernia	Devonport	Harland & W.	Jan. '04	1906	1907	12,700=15·5	18,112=18·12°	Babcock	18·8

All were light on first trials.

HINDUSTAN. All alike except last three, which have a double top on foremast and top mast abaft. *Photo, Cribb.*

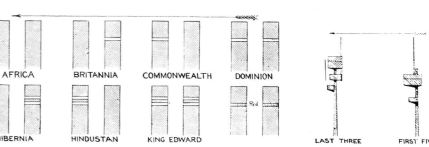

AFRICA. BRITANNIA. COMMONWEALTH. DOMINION.

HIBERNIA. HINDUSTAN. KING EDWARD.

LAST THREE. FIRST FIVE.

HIBERNIA, AFRICA and BRITANNIA. All alike except that *Africa* has his standard compass.

Class distinction.—To be recognised at once by rig and by the enormous funnels. No after-bridge.

General Notes.—Tactical diameter very small, about 310 yards at 15 knots. Extremely handy. Cost per ship about £1,500,0 The last British battleships designed by Sir William White. Estimates '01-'02, (3 ships), '02-'03, (2 ships), and '05-'04, (3 ships).

Coal consumption : Averages 11 tons an hour at 12,000 H.P., and from 15½-18 tons at full power. The Babcock boilered sh fitted with superheaters are considerably more economical than those not to be fitted. Economical speed : about 16 kts.

The ships cost about £120,000 per annum each to maintain with full crews ; and £60,000 with two-thirds crews.

General Notes—King Edward VII mined off N. Scotland coast Jan. 1916 and *Britannia* torpedoed by U-boat off Cape Trafalgar 9 Nov. 1918.

1902 BRITISH BATTLESHIPS (20 knot).

SWIFTSURE & TRIUMPH (January, 1903).
(Purchased from Chili, 1903).
Normal displacement, 11,800 tons. Complement, 700.
Length (*waterline*) 458 feet ; *Beam,* 71 feet ; *Maximum draught,* 24⅝ feet ; Length (*over all*) 470 feet.

Guns :
4—10 inch, 45 cal. (*AAA*).
14—7·5 inch, II, 50 cal. (*A*).
14—14 pdr.
1—12 pdr., 8 cwt.
4—6 pdr.
4 Maxims.
Torpedo tubes (Elswick, 18 in.) :
2 *submerged.*

Armour (Krupp) :
7″ Belt (amidships) ... *a*
3″ Belt (ends) .... *ϵ*
10″ Bulkheads .... *aaa*
1½″ Deck (amidships) ...
Protection to vitals ......=*aa*
3″ Deck (outside citadel)
10″ Barbettes .... *aa*
8″—6″ Turrets(K.C)=*aaa-aa*
6″ Lower deck........... *a*
7″ Battery................. *a*
7″ Casemates (4) (N.C.) ... *a*
10″ Conning tower ...... *aa*
(Total weight : *about* 3200 tons).

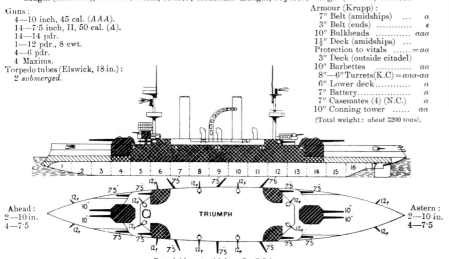

Ahead :
2—10 in.
4—7·5

Astern :
2—10 in.
4—7·5

Broadside : 4—10 in., 7—7·5 in.

Machinery : 2 sets triple expansion. 2 screws. Boilers : 12 Yarrow large tube. Designed H.P. 14,000=20 kts. Coal : *normal* 800 tons ; *maximum* 2000 tons.
Armour Notes.—Belt is 15 feet wide, 7″ tapering to 3″, Citadel 260 feet long. 1″ screens in battery. 1″ main deck. Flat sided K.C. turrets.
Gunnery Notes.—Loading positions, big guns : all round, load in any position. Hoists, electric, all guns. Big guns manœuvred hydraulically. 7·5's run in and out hydraulically, otherwise hand worked. Spotting platforms low. *Swiftsure's* 7·5 loading arrangements are inferior to those of *Triumph* and cannot maintain the same rate of fire. In both the arcs of training of 7·5's are small. Ammunition carried : 10 in., 86 per gun ; 7·5 in., 150 per gun.
Torpedo Notes.—Main deck shelf for nets. Amidship defence only.
Engineering Notes.—These ships are very fast for short spurts, but cannot maintain speed well in a sea way. At full power the vibration is great. *Actual* full speed radius about 3,000 miles.
Trials.—

Name.	Builders.	Engines and Boilers.	Laid down.	Completed.	30 hours 3/5. 130 revs.	6 hours full. 152 revs.	Boilers.	Present speed.
Swiftsure	Elswick	Humphrys and T.	March, '02	1904	8700=17	14,018=20	Yarrow	19·1
Triumph	Vickers	Vickers	March, '02	1904		14,090=20·17	Yarrow	19·3

Coal consumption averages at 10,000 H.P. 9 tons per hour ; at 14,000 H.P. 12—13 tons per hour. Both ships tended to be "coal eaters" originally, but in service have proved very fairly economical as a rule. In 1907 manœuvres both ships averaged about 18 kts.
General Notes.—Purchased from Chili for £949,900 each. Scantlings much lighter than in normal British ships. Designed by Sir E. J. Reed.
"Triumph torpedoed off Gallipoli, May 1915."

SWIFTSURE. *Photo, Symonds.*

Differences.—

SWIFTSURE.
Higher cowls.
Bow scroll.
Very conspicuous fire controls.

TRIUMPH.
Low cowls.
No bow scroll.

1901 BRITISH BATTLESHIPS
(QUEEN CLASS—2 SHIPS).
QUEEN (March, 1902) & **PRINCE OF WALES** (March, 1902).

Displacement, 15,000 tons. Complement, 750 (flagship, 789).
Length *(waterline)*, 411 feet. Beam, 75 feet. *Maximum* draught, 29 feet. Length *over all*, 430 feet.

Guns:
- 4—12 inch, IX, 40 cal. (AAAA)
- 12—6 inch, VII, 45 cal.
- 16—12 pdr., 12 cwt.
- 2—12 pdr., 8 cwt.
- 6—3 pdr.
- 2 Maxims.

Torpedo tubes (18 inch):
- 4 submerged.
(Total weight with ammunition 1200 tons.)

Armour (Krupp):
- 9″ Belt (amidships) ....aa
- 6″—2″ Belt (bow) ....a-f
- 12″ After bulkhead ....aaa
- 3″ Armour deck....................
- Protection to vitals ....=aaa
- 12″ Barbettes ....aaa
- 10″—8″ Turrets (K.C) ... aaa-aa
- 6″ Casemates (12) (N.C.) ...... b
- 12″ Conning tower (N.C.) ...aaa
(Total weight 4295 tons.)

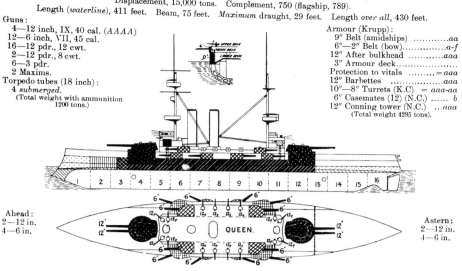

QUEEN. *Photo, Symonds.*

Ahead:
2—12 in.
4—6 in.

Astern:
2—12 in.
4—6 in.

Broadside : 4—12 in., 6—6 in.

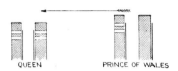

QUEEN   PRINCE OF WALES

Machinery : 2 sets 3 cylinder vertical inverted triple expansion. 2 screws. Boilers : *Queen*, 15 Babcock, *Prince of Wales*, 20 Belleville. Designed H.P. 15,000 = 18 kts. Coal : *normal* 900 tons ; *maximum* 2100 tons.
Armour Notes.—Belt is 15 feet wide by 300 feet long, from bow. Flat-sided turrets, K.C.
Gunnery Notes.—Loading positions, big guns : all round. Hoist, for 6 inch, electric. Big guns manœuvred by hydraulic gear. Arcs of fire : Big guns, 260° ; secondary guns, 120°. Fire control fitted or fitting as plan. Ammunition carried : 12 in., 80 rounds per gun ; 6 in., 200 per gun.
Torpedo Notes.—Main deck shelf for nets. Defence almost all round. 2 torpedo launches carried. 8 searchlights.
Engineering Notes.—Pressure 300 lbs. at boilers, reduced to 250 at engines. Heating surface, *Queen*, 38,400 sq. feet ; *Prince of Wales* 37,000 sq. feet.

Name.	Built at	Engines & Boilers by	Laid down	Completed	30 hours 4/5 power. 101 revs.	8 hours full power. 110 revs.	Speed last Boilers. sea trial.
Queen	Devonport	Harland & Wolff	March, '01	1904	11,670 = 16·97	15,556 = 18·39	Babcock 18
Prince of Wales	Chatham	Greenock Foundry	March, '01	1904	11,669 = 17·04	15,364 = 18·45	Belleville 18

Coal consumption in service : Averages 9 tons an hour at 10,000 H.P. (15 kts.), 12—14 at 15,000 H.P. (18 kts.)
On first trials the *Queen* was the more economical of the two especially at mean powers.
General Notes.—Very handy ships. Slightly improved *Londons*. Open 12 pdr. batteries and kidney-shaped fighting tops. Cost per ship averaged just over £1,000,000.

Class distinctions.—Kidney-shape lower tops. Open 12 pdr. battery. Flat-sided turrets. No scuttles to lower deck forward.

1898 BRITISH BATTLESHIPS (19 knot).
(DUNCAN CLASS—5 SHIPS.)
RUSSELL (February, 1901), **ALBEMARLE** (March, 1901), **DUNCAN** (March, 1901), **CORNWALLIS** (July, 1901), **EXMOUTH** (August, 1901).

Normal displacement, 14,000 tons. Complement, 750 (flagships 778).
Length *(waterline)*, 418 feet. Beam, 75½ feet. *Maximum* draught, 27¼ feet. Length *over all*, 429 feet.

Guns:
- 4—12 inch, IX. (AAAA).
- 12—6 inch, VII.
- 12—12 pdr.
- 6—3 pdr.
- 2 Maxims.

Torpedo tubes (18 inch) :
- 4 submerged.

Armour (Krupp):
- 7″ Belt (amidships) ...... a
- 5″—3″ Belt (bow).........b-c
- 1½″ Belt (aft) ....
- 2½″ Deck (on slopes) ...
- Protection to vitals ...=aa
- 11″ Barbettes (N.C.) ... aa
- 6″ Turrets (K.C.)........= aa
- 6″ Casemates (12) ...... b
- 12″ Conning tower ...... aaa
(Total weight *about* 3500 tons.)

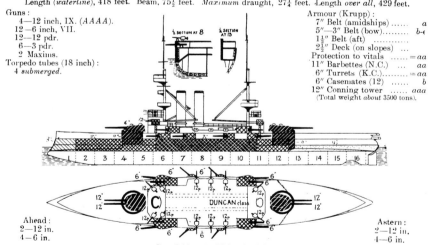

ALBEMARLE. *Photo, Symonds.*

Ahead:
2—12 in.
4—6 in.

Astern:
2—12 in.
4—6 in.

Broadside : 4—12 in., 6—6 in.

Machinery : 2 sets 4 cylinder vertical inverted triple expansion. 2 screws. Boilers : 24 Belleville.
Coal : *normal* 900 tons ; *maximum* 2000 tons. Designed H.P. 18,000 = 19 kts. *Nominal* radius 7,200 at 10 kts.
Armour Notes.—Main belt is 14 feet wide by 285 feet long ; lower edge is full thickness. Flat-sided turrets (K.C.).
Gunnery Notes.—Loading positions, big guns : all round. Hoists, for 6 inch, electric and hand. Big guns manœuvred by hydraulic gear. Fire control stations fitted 1905-6.
Arcs of fire : 12 in., 240° ; 6 in., 120°.
Engineering Notes.—Machinery, etc., weighs 1580 tons.

Distinctions.—All identical with each other. They are to be distinguished from other battleships by their large round funnels. Open upper deck. They are lower in the water than the *Londons* and *Formidables*. No cowls. *Russell* and *Exmouth* have very large funnel tops and the former has conspicuous steampipes. *Cornwallis* has smaller fire controls than the others.

Albemarle (only) has stockless anchors of *Duncan* class.

Name.	Builder.	Engines by	Laid down	Completed	Last big Refit.	First trials :— 30 hours at 4/5.	8 hours full.	Boilers.	Last recorded best speed.
Russell	Palmer	Palmer	March, '99	1903	—	13,695 = 17·95	18,922 = 19·3	Belleville	19·8
Duncan	Thames I.W.	Thames I.W.	July, '99	1903	—	13,717 = 18·1	18,232 = 19·11	Belleville	20·1
Cornwallis	Thames I.W.	Thames I.W.	July, '99	1904	—	13,694 = 17·91	18,238 = 18·98*	Belleville	19·56
Exmouth	Laird	Laird	Aug., '99	1903	—	13,774 = 18	18,346 = 19·03	Belleville	20·0
Albemarle	Chatham	Thames I.W.	Jan., '00	1903	'09	13,587 = 17·2*	*18,296 = 18·6	Belleville	19·8

*Run in bad weather.

Coal consumption averages 2¾ tons an hour at 10 kts. ; at 13,000 H.P. (17 kts.) about 10¾ tons an hour ; at 18,000 H.P. (19 kts.) about 15 tons an hour or less. All these ships are excellent steamers, and make or exceed their speeds in almost any weather. Boilers are of 1900 pattern.
General Notes.—The ships are proving very passable sea boats. Hull without armour weighs 9055 tons. Cost per ship, *complete*, just over £1,000,000. Very handy. *Montagu*, of this class, wrecked on Lundy, 1906.

Russell mined off Malta May 1916.
Cornwallis sunk by U-boat off Malta Jan. 1917.

1898 BRITISH BATTLESHIPS.—(18 knot)

(LONDON CLASS—3 SHIPS).

LONDON (Sept., 1899), **BULWARK** (Oct., 1899), **VENERABLE** (Nov., 1899).

Displacement, 15,000 tons. Complement, 750 (flagship, 789).

Length (waterline), 411 feet. Beam, 75 feet. Maximum draught, 29 feet. Length over all, 430 feet.

Guns :
1 —12 inch, IX., 40 cal. (AAAA).
12 —6 inch, VII., 45 cal.
16 —12 pdr., 12 cwt.
2 —12 pdr., 8 cwt.
6 —3 pdr.
2 Maxims.
Torpedo tubes (18 inch) :
4 submerged.
(Total weight with ammunition, 1200 tons.)

Armour (Krupp)
9″ Belt (amidships) .... aa
6″—2″ Belt (bow) .... a-f
12″ After bulkhead .... aaa
3″ Armour deck.............
Protection to vitals .... = aaa
12″ Barbettes .... aaa
10″—8″ Turrets (K.C.) = aaa-aa
6″ Casemates (12) (N.C.) ... b
12″ Conning tower (N.C.) ... aaa
(Total weight 4295 tons).

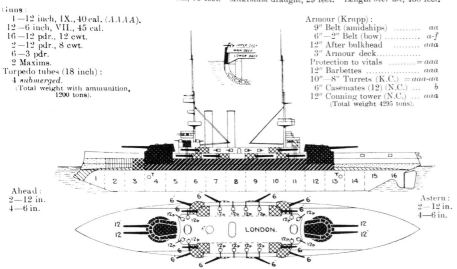

Ahead :
2—12 in.
4—6 in.

LONDON.

Astern :
2—12 in.
4—6 in.

Broadside : 4—12 in., 6—6 in.

Machinery : 2 sets 3 cylinder vertical inverted triple expansion. 2 screws. Boilers : 20 Belleville. Designed H.P. 15,000 = 18 kts. Coal : normal 900 tons ; maximum 2100 tons.

Armour Notes.—Belt is 15 feet wide by 300 feet long, from bow. Flat sided K.C. turrets.

Gunnery Notes.—Loading positions, big guns : all round. Hoist, for 6 inch, electric. Big guns manœuvred, hydraulic gear. Arcs of fire : Big guns, 260° ; secondary guns, 120°. Ammunition carried : 12 in., 80 rounds per gun ; 6 in. 200 per gun.

Torpedo Notes.—Main deck shelf for nets. Defence almost all round. 2 torpedo launches carried. 6 searchlights.

Engineering Notes.—Pressure, 300 lbs. at boilers, reduced to 250 at engines. Heating surface, 37,000 square feet.

LONDON.   Photo, Symonds.

Differences.—

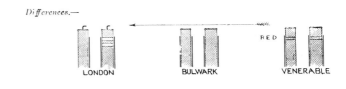

LONDON   BULWARK   RED   VENERABLE

Name.	Built at	Engines by	Laid down.	Completed.	Last Refit.	30 hours 4/5 power. 161 revs.	8 hours full power. 116 revs.	Boilers.	Speed last sea trial.
London	Portsmouth	Earle	Dec. '98	1902	'08–'09	11,718 = 16·4	15,261 = 18·10	Belleville	17·75
Bulwark	Devonport	Hawthorn Leslie	March, '99	1902	nil	11,755 = 16·8	15,355 = 18·15	Belleville	18·5
Venerable	Chatham	Maudslay	Nov. '99	1902	'08–'09	11,364 = 16·8	15,345 = 18·40	Belleville	18·5

Coal consumption in service : Averages 8¼ tons an hour at 10,000 H.P. (15 kts.), 11¾ at 15,000 H.P. (18 kts.).

General Notes.—Very handy ships Cost per ship averaged just over £1,000,000.

"Bulwark sunk by internal explosion Nov. 1914."

1898 BRITISH BATTLESHIPS (18 knot).

(FORMIDABLE CLASS—3 SHIPS).

FORMIDABLE (Nov. 1898), **IRRESISTIBLE** (Dec. 1898), & **IMPLACABLE** (March, 1899).

Displacement, 15,000 tons. Complement, 780 (flagship 810).

Length (waterline), 411 feet. Beam, 75 feet. Maximum draught, 29 feet. Length over all, 430 feet.

Guns :
4—12 in., IX., 40 cal. (AAAA)
12—6 in., VII., 45 cal.
16—12 pdr., 12 cwt.
2—12 pdr., 8 cwt.
6—3 pdr.
2 Maxims.
Torpedo tubes (18 inch) :
4 submerged.
(Total weight with ammunition, 1200 tons).

Armour (Krupp) :
9″ Belt (amidships) .... aa
2″ Belt (bow) .... f
1½″ Belt (aft) .... f
12″ Bulkheads .... aaa
3″ Deck (on slopes) ....
Protection to vitals ...... = aaa
12″ Barbettes (N.C.) .... aaa
10″—8″ Turrets (N.C.) = aaa-aa
6″ Casemates (12) (N.C.) ... b
12″ Conning tower (N.C.) ... aaa
(Total weight about 4300 tons)

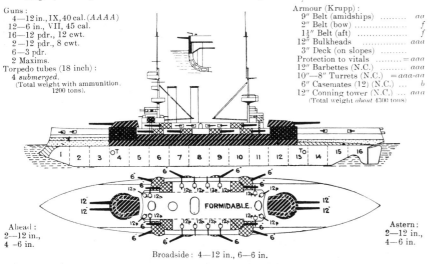

Ahead :
2—12 in.,
4 –6 in.

FORMIDABLE.

Astern :
2—12 in.,
4—6 in.

Broadside : 4—12 in., 6—6 in.

Machinery : 2 sets 3 cylinder vertical inverted triple expansion. 2 screws. Boilers : 20 Belleville. Designed H.P. 15,000 = 18 kts. Coal : normal 900 tons ; maximum 2200 tons.

Armour Notes.—Belt is 15 feet wide by 216 feet long ; 2″ continuation to bow ; lower edge is normal thickness. Curved turrets of K.N.C.

Gunnery Notes and Torpedo Notes.—As for later Formidables, previous page.

Engineering Notes.—(See also later Formidables.)

IMPLACABLE.   Photo, Symonds.

Differences—

FORMIDABLE   IMPLACABLE   IRRESISTABLE

Name.	Built at	Engines & Boilers by	Laid down.	Completed	Refit.	30 hours 4/5 power.	8 hours full power.	Boilers.	Speed last sea trial.
Formidable	Portsmouth	Earle	March, '98	1901	'08–'09	11,618 = 17·15	15,511 = 18·13	Belleville	18·4
Irresistible	Chatham	Maudslay	April, '98	1902	nil	11,626 = 17·5	15,603 = 18·20	Belleville	18·5
Implacable	Devonport	Laird	July., '98	1902	'08–'09	11,618 = 16·81	15,244 = 18·22	Belleville	18·7

Coal consumption in service averages 8 tons an hour, at 10,000 H.P. (15 kts.), 11½ tons at 15,000 H.P. (18 kts.)

General Notes.—Very handy ships, answer the least touch of helm. Average cost just over £1,000,000 per ship.

Formidable sunk by U-boat off Portland Jan. 1915.
Irristible sunk by U-boat off Gallipoli Mar. 1915.

Class distinctions :—

Formidable ⎫
London ⎬ Fore funnel close to foremast and smaller than after.
Queen ⎭

Oval turrets.
No scuttles lower deck forward. Flat-sided turrets.
Open upper deck. Flat-sided turrets.

Duncan — Funnels as in Formidable, but equal sized and big.

Slightly smaller ship. Open upper deck. Flat-sided turrets.

Canopus — Funnels close together, and more amidships.

Shorter masts, closer together, ship lower in water, and generally smaller. Oval turrets.

1896 BRITISH BATTLESHIPS (18¼ knot).

(CANOPUS CLASS—6 SHIPS).

CANOPUS (October, 1897), **GOLIATH** (March, 1898), **ALBION** (June, 1898), **OCEAN** (July, 1898), **GLORY** (March, 1899), *also* **VENGEANCE** (July, 1899).

Displacement, 12,950 tons. Complement, 750 (flagship 780).

Length (*waterline*), 400 feet. Beam, 74 feet. *Maximum* draught, 26½ feet. Length *over all*, 418 feet.

Guns:
4—12 inch, VIII, 35 cal. (*AAA*)
12—6 inch, *wire*, 40 cal.
10—12 pdr., 12 cwt.
2—12 pdr., 8 cwt. boat.
6—3 pdr.
2 Maxims.
Torpedo tubes (18 inch):
4 *submerged*.
(Total weight, with ammunition, 1000 tons).

Armour (Harvey-nickel):
6″ Belt (amidships) ... *b*
2″ Belt (bow) .... *f*
1½″ Belt (aft) .... *f*
12″ Bulkheads ...... *aaa*
2½″ Deck (on slopes).
Protection to vitals ... = *a*
12″ Barbettes...... *aaa-aa*
8″ Turrets to these...
5″ Casemates (12) ... *c*
12″ Conning tower ... *aaa*
(Total weight, *about* 3600 tons).

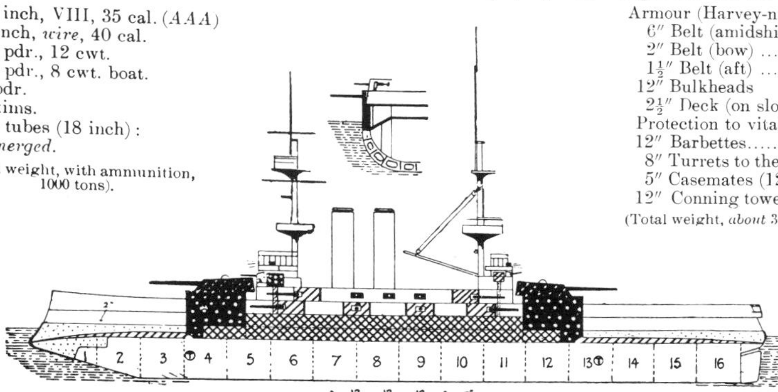

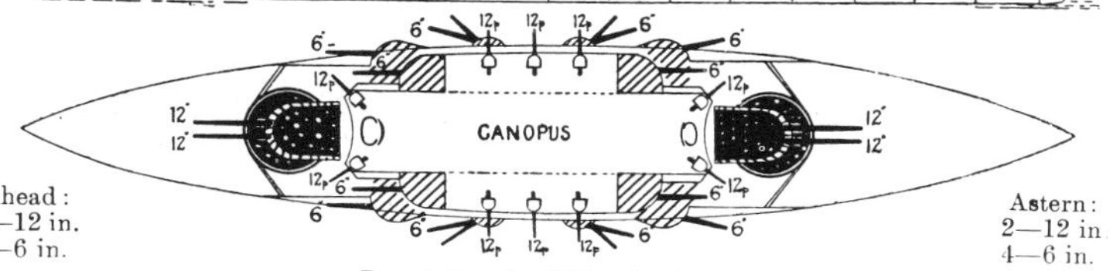

Ahead:
2—12 in.
4—6 in.

Astern:
2—12 in.
4—6 in.

Broadside: 4—12 in., 6—6 in.

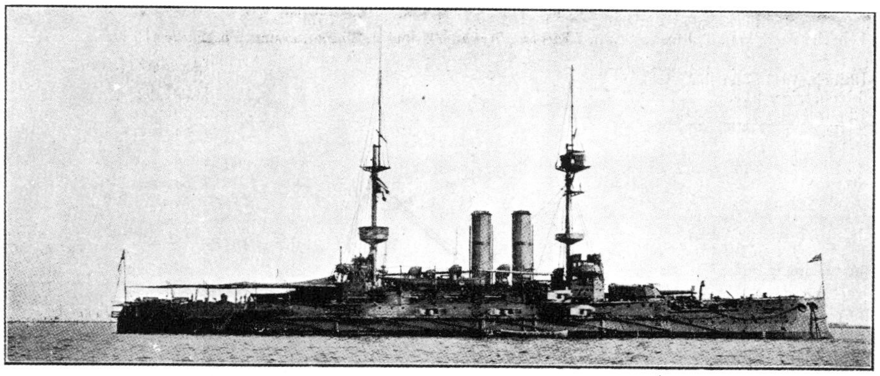

VENGEANCE.

Differences.—

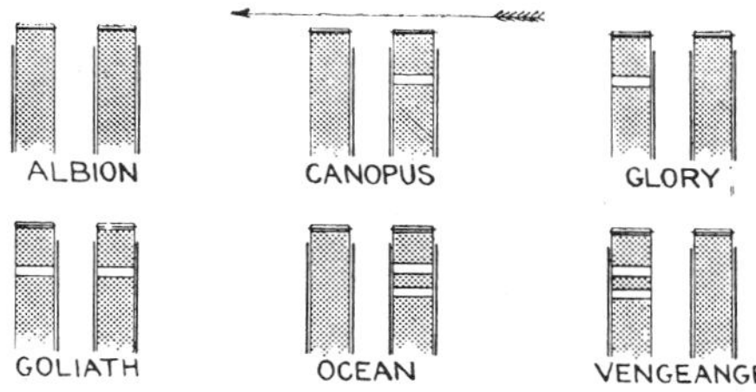

For identifications of class from *Formidables* and *Duncans* see *Formidable* class.
Albion has specially large fire control on fore.

Machinery: 2 sets 3 cylinder vertical inverted triple expansion. 2 screws. Boilers: 20 Belleville. Designed H.P. 13,500 = 18·25 kts. Coal: *normal* 1000 tons; *maximum* 2300 tons.

Armour Notes.—Belt is 14 feet wide by 210 feet long. Barbettes circular, the thickness given being the maximum. Belt is normal thickness at lower edge. Weight of side armour only, 1740 tons. Main deck 1″ steel. Barbettes 37 feet in diameter. Circular turrets (H.N.)

Gunnery Notes.—Loading positions, big guns: all round. *Vengeance's* load in any position also. Big guns manœuvred: hydraulic and hand gear, Hoists, for 6 inch, electric and hand. Fitting with fire control stations as plan.
Arcs of fire: Big guns, 260°; casemates, 120°.

Torpedo Notes.—Net defence amidships; stowage on shelf at main deck level. Electric machinery: 3 dynamos, 8 electric fans for ventilation.

Name	Built at	Engines and boilers by	Laid down	Completed	Last Refit	30 hours 4/5. 99-102 revs.	8 hours full power. 107-110 revs.	Boilers.	Best recent speed.
Canopus	Portsmouth	Greenock Fdy.	Jan., '97	1900	'07	10,454 = 17·2	13,763 = 18·5	Belleville	16·5
Goliath	Chatham	Penn	Jan., '97	1900	'07	10,413 = 17·3	13,918 = 18·4	Belleville	
Albion	Thames I.W.	Maudslay	Dec., '96	1902	'06	10,809 = 16·8*	13,885 = 17·8*	Belleville	18·2
Ocean	Devonport	Hawthorn Leslie	Feb., '97	1900	'10	10,314 = 16·2	13,728 = 18·5	Belleville	17·8
Glory	Laird	Laird	Dec., '96	1901	'07	10,587 = 16·8	13,745 = 18·1	Belleville	17·6
Vengeance	Vickers	Vickers	Aug., '97	1901	'05	10,387 = 17·2	13,852 = 18·5	Belleville	18

* Run in a gale.

Coal consumption averages: 9 tons an hour at 10,000 H.P. (16·5 kts.), 12½ tons at 13,500 H.P. (18·25 kts.)

In 1907 manœuvres *Vengeance* and *Ocean*, in the chase, beat all the *King Edward* class except *King Edward*; but the ships are getting worn out, and few can now steam well except for short spurts.

Engineering Notes.—70 revolutions = 12½ kts. Boilers: 15—9 element generators, and 5—8 element generators. Total heating surface (including economisers), 33,700 square feet. Grate area 1055 feet. Pressure, 300 lbs., reduced to 250 lbs. at engines. Distilling machinery: 2 evaporators, capacity 68 tons per 24 hours. Distillers produce 40 tons per day. Auxiliary engines: 4 air compressing, 2 boat hoists, 2 refrigerating, 2 coal hoists, 5 blowing, 2 steam fans. Funnels 11 feet in diameter. Height above furnace bars, 90 feet. Screws: 4 bladed. Diameter of cylinders 30 in., 49 in., and 80 in. Stroke 51 in.

General Notes.—Tactical diameter, extreme helm at 15 kts. 450 yards; with the engines, 350 yards. Cost, *complete*, about £900,000 per ship. Maintenance cost, in full commission, about £94,000 per annum per ship.

1894 BRITISH BATTLESHIPS (16½ knot).

(MAJESTIC CLASS—9 SHIPS).

MAGNIFICENT (December, 1894), **MAJESTIC** (January, 1895), **HANNIBAL** (April, 1895), **PRINCE GEORGE** (August, 1895), **VICTORIOUS** (October, 1895), **JUPITER** (November, 1895), **MARS** (March, 1896), *also* **CÆSAR** (September, 1896), & **ILLUSTRIOUS** (September, 1896).

Displacement, 14,900 tons. Complement, 757.

Length (*waterline*), 399 feet. Beam, 75 feet. *Maximum* draught, 30 feet. Length *over all*, 413 feet.

Guns:
4—12 inch, VIII., 35 cal. (*AAA*)
12—6 inch, *wire*, 40 cal.
16—12 pdr.
12—3 pdr.
2 Maxims.
2—12 pdr. boat guns.
Torpedo tubes (18 inch):
4 *submerged*.
1 *above water* (stern).
(Total weight with ammunition, 1500 tons).
(Ammunition only, 355 tons).

Armour (Harvey):
9″ Belt (amidships) *a*
14″ Bulkheads ...... *aa*
4″ Deck (on slopes)
Protection to vitals = *aaa*
14″ Barbettes .... *aa*
10″ Turrets to these = *aa*
6″ Casemates (12) ... *c*
14″ Conning tower *aa*
(Total weight 4260 tons).

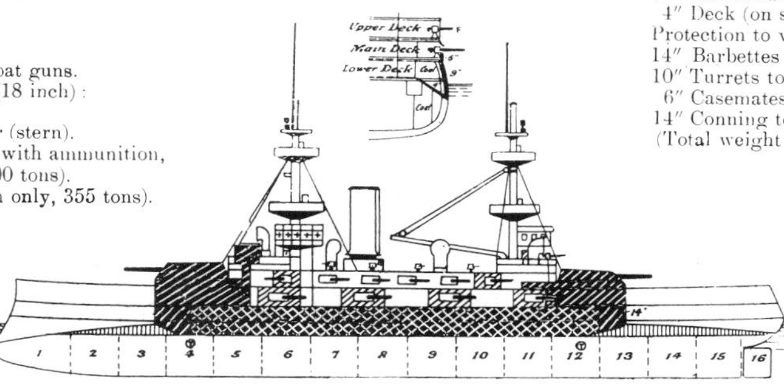

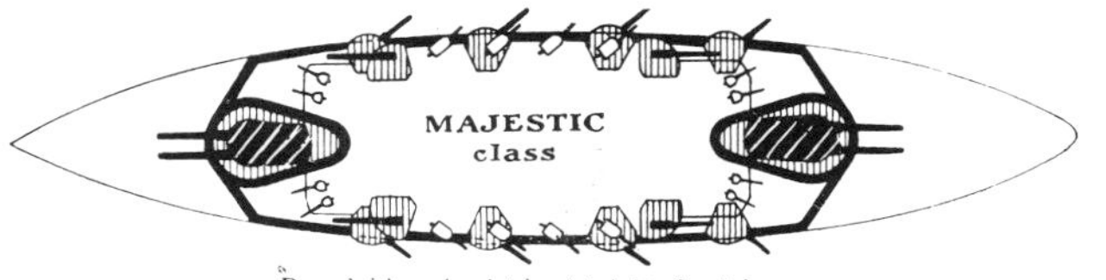

Ahead:
2—12 in.
2—6 in.

Astern:
2—12 in.
2—6 in.

Broadside: 4—12 in. (AAA), 6—6 in.

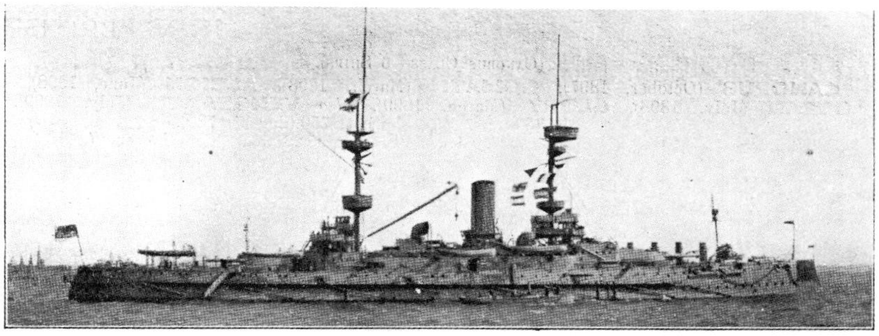

MAGNIFICENT *only*. (Note different rig.) *Photo, Cousens.*

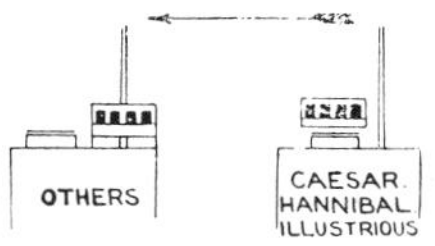

Mars has smaller fire controls than the others.

Cæsar, *Hannibal* and *Illustrious* have the fore-bridge before foremast—the others round about it (*see plan*).

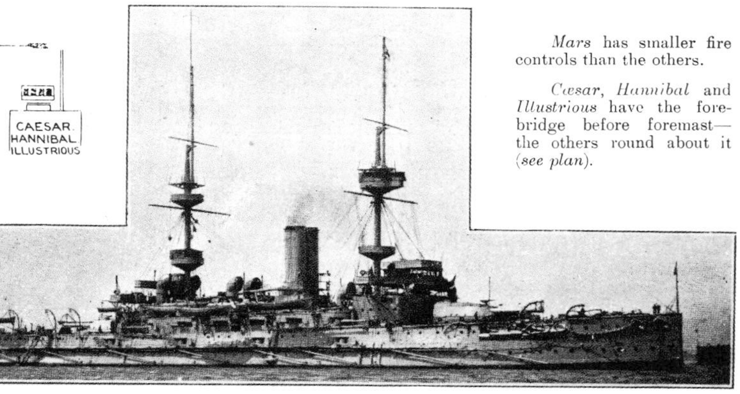

ILLUSTRIOUS. *Photo, Symonds.*

Machinery: 2 sets 3 cylinder vertical inverted triple expansion. 2 screws. Boilers: 8 cylindrical, with 4 furnaces each. Designed H.P. *natural* 10,000 = 16·5 kts.; *forced* 12,000 = 17·5 kts. Coal: *normal* 1200 tons; *maximum* 2,000 tons (always carried). Oil, 400 tons.

Armour Notes.—Belt is 16 feet wide by 220 feet long. *Cæsar* and *Illustrious* have circular barbettes.

Gunnery Notes.—Loading positions, big guns: all round (end on in first two and all round for a few rounds). Hoists, electric and hand. Big guns manœuvred, hydraulic and hand.
Arcs of fire: Big guns, 260°; Casemates, 120°.

Torpedo Notes.—Midship net defence. Nets stow on main deck shelf in most of the class (all are being so fitted). Two torpedo launches. 6 searchlights.

Engineering Notes.—Machinery and boilers weigh 1,600 tons. 32 furnaces. Heating surface, 24,400 square feet. All fitting or fitted for oil fuel. Screws: 17 feet in diameter, 19¾ feet pitch, 4 bladed. Cylinders: 40, 59 and 88 ins. diameter. Stroke: 51 ins. Pressure: 155 lbs.

Name.	Builder.	Engines by	Laid down	Completed	First trials:— 8 hours nat.	8 hours f. d.	Best recent speed
Magnificent	Chatham	Penn	Dec., '93	1895	10,301 = 16·50	12,157 = 18·4	15·9
Majestic	Portsmouth	Vickers	Feb., '94	1895	10,418 = 16·99	12,097 = 17·9	16·8
Hannibal	Pembroke	Harland & Wolff	April, '94	1897	10,357 = 16·30	12,138 = 18·0	16·2
Prince George	Portsmouth	Humphrys & T.	Sept., '94	1896	10,464 = 16·52	12,253 = 18·3	—
Victorious	Chatham	Hawthorn, L.	May, '94	1897	10,319 = 16·92	12,201 = 18·7	16·4
Jupiter	Clydebank	Clydebank	Oct., '94	1897	10,258 = 15·80	12,475 = 18·4	—
Mars	Laird	Laird	June, '94	1897	10,159 = 15·96	12,434 = 17·7	16·6
Cæsar	Portsmouth	Maudslay	March, '95	1897	10,630 = 16·70	12,652 = 18·7	17
Illustrious	Chatham	Penn	March, '95	1898	10,241 = 15·96	12,112 = 16·5•	16·1

•Bad weather.

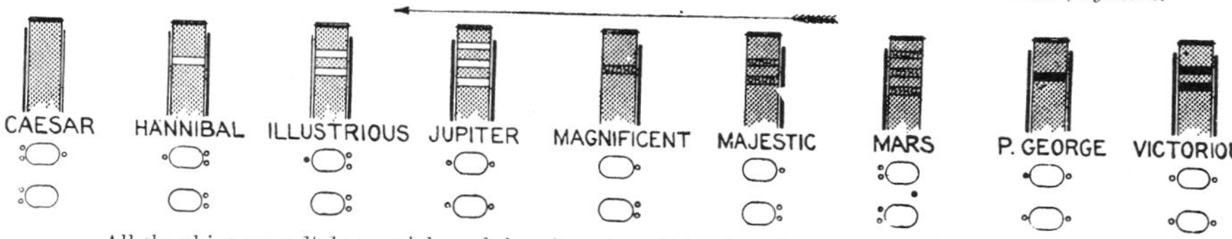

All the ships were *light* on trials and drawing about 2 feet less than the normal. Sea trials run with full coal and stores aboard.

Coal consumption for the class averages: at 8 kts., 1¼ ton an hour; at 8,000 H.P. (15 kts.), 8½ tons; at 10,000 H.P. (16·5 kts.), 10¼ tons. The *Hannibal*, which is the most economical ship, burns somewhat less.

General Notes.—150 w. t. compartments. 208 w. t. doors. Tactical diameter: at 15 kts., 450 yards; with one engine, 350 yards. Ships answer helm very well. Cost nearly £1,000,000 per ship *complete*.

Majestic sunk by U-boat off Gallipoli May 1915

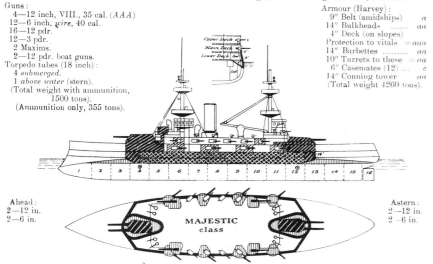

1916 BRITISH CRUISERS.

(COURAGEOUS CLASS—2 Ships).

COURAGEOUS (5th February, 1916), **GLORIOUS** (20th April, 1916).

Normal displacement, *about* 18,600 tons (*about* 22,700 tons *full load*). Complements C. 842. G. 829.

Length $\begin{Bmatrix} p.p. \ 735 \ \text{ft.} \\ o.a. \ 786\frac{1}{2} \ \text{ft.} \end{Bmatrix}$ Beam (outside bulges), 81 ft.   Draughts $\begin{Bmatrix} mean \ 22\frac{1}{4} \ \text{ft.} \\ max. \ 26 \ \text{ft.} \end{Bmatrix}$

Guns :
- 4—15 inch, 42 cal. } **Dir. Con.**
- 18—4 inch
- 2—3 inch (anti-aircraft)
- 4—3 pdr.
- 5 M.G.
- (1 landing)

Torpedo tubes (21 in.) :
- 2 *submerged*
- 12 *above water* (4 triple deck)

Armour :
Vertical:
- 3″ Belt (amidships) ...
- 2″ Belt (within bow) ..
- 2″ (H.T.) Fore bulkhead
- 3″—1″ (H.T.) After Bulkhead ....
- 1½″ Side over belt.....
- 7″—3″ Barbettes .....
- 9″—7″ Gunhouses ...
- 1″—1½″ Funnel uptakes
- 2″ C.T. base.........
- 3″ Tube ....
- 10″ C.T. ....
- 6″ Sighting hood ...
- 3″ Torpedo C.T. (2″ tube)

Armour—*continued*.
Decks (H.T.):
- 1″ Forecastle ...
- 1″ Upper ....
- 1¾″—¾″ Main (between barbettes) ....
- 1½″ Lower (stern, flat)
- 3½″ Lower (stern, over rudder) ....
- 2″ Lower (on slopes) ..
Crowns:
- 4¼″ Barbettes (since increased) ....
- 3″ C.T. and sighting hd.
- 1¾″—¾″ Torpedo C.T.
Torpedo protection (H.T.):
- Modified bulges 25 ft. deep filled with oil fuel ....
- 1½″—1″ Outer internal screens between barbettes ....
- ¾″ Inner screen to boiler and engine room vents

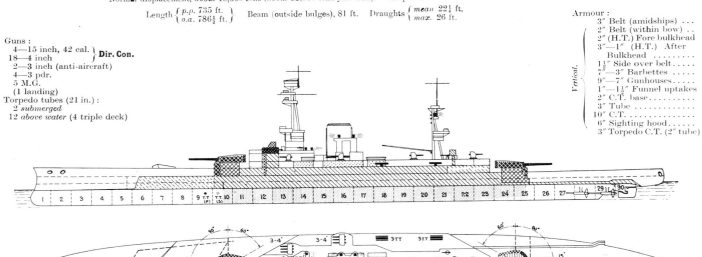

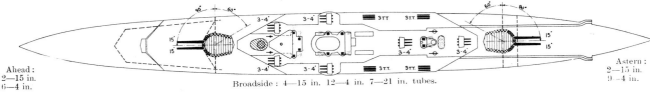

Ahead :
2—15 in.
6—4 in.

Broadside : 4—15 in. 12—4 in. 7—21 in. tubes.

Astern :
2—15 in.
9—4 in.

Machinery : Parsons (all-geared) turbines. 4 screws. Boilers : 18 Yarrow (small tube).
Designed H.P. 90,000 = *about* 31 kts. Fuel (oil only) : *normal*, 750 tons : *maximum*, 3160 tons.

Gunnery Notes.—Range of 15-inch only limited by maximum visibility. 15-inch director tower on foremast under control tower. Arcs as plans : 20° elevation, 5° depression. 4-inch director tower on each mast, all 4-inch can be controlled from either tower, or half of 4-inch from one tower. Triple 4-inch guns are reported to be an indifferent type of mounting and rate of fire, singly or in salvo, is not good, as loaders are liable to obstruct one another. Arcs for 4-inch : 155° fore guns, 180° amidships guns, 120° for forward centre-line triple, 150° after C.L. triple.

Torpedo Notes.—Submerged tubes not successful, as bars bend when attempting to fire torpedoes at speeds over 22-23 kts.

Armour Notes.—General scheme of armouring on Light Cruiser lines, the 3″ belt being built up of 2″ plating on 1″ shell plating. Decks round magazines thickened during completion. Gunhouses : 13″ face, 7″ sides, 11″ rear, 4½″ roof (now thicker), 5″ overhang. Barbettes : 7″—6″ above upper deck, 6″—4″ above main deck, 3″ below main deck.

Engineering Notes.—General arrangement of machinery as in Light Cruiser *Champion*. 4-shaft geared turbines and double helical gearing. Have done 32-33 kts. in service. A rather singular point is that these ships are 1½ kts. faster on *deep load* draught than when in normal trim.

Aircraft Notes.—Flying-off platforms on barbette crowns ; 2 aeroplanes carried.

GLORIOUS. Aircraft Recognition View.   *Official R.A.F. Photo.*

1916 BRITISH CRUISERS. (Illustration and Notes.)

For Plans and Description, see opposite page.

GLORIOUS.   *Photo, Cribb, Southsea.*

Name	Builder	Machinery	Begun	Completed	Trials
Courageous	Armstrong	Parsons	May, 1915	Dec., 1916	93,780 = 31·58
Glorious	Harland & Wolff, Belfast	Harland & Wolff	Mar., 1915	Nov., 1916	91,165 = 31·6

General Notes.—Emergency War Programme ships. Design of these ships is said to have been formulated by Admiral of the Fleet Lord Fisher, when First Sea Lord, 1914-15. Their shallow draught is said to have been planned with a view to future operations in the Baltic. In 1915, credits could not be secured for commencing extra Battle Cruisers, taking two years to build. But additional Light Cruisers had been approved, and the opportunity was taken to design these two ships as "Large Light Cruisers." They were designed about January, 1915, and it was intended that they should be finished in a year. Accordingly, the number of big guns and mountings available had to be taken into consideration in planning armament. The twelve months' projected building time was exceeded by six months, as these ships were not commissioned till October, 1916.

The intended Baltic operations having been negatived, a tactical role as "Light Cruiser Destroyers" was assigned to these vessels. The objection is, their end-on fire of two 15-inch guns (when in chase), is too heavy and slow-firing. Against a small and rapidly-moving target, like an enemy Light Cruiser (continually altering her course), two 15-inch guns have only a fair chance of securing hits—but one salvo on the target would probably be decisive.

The lines of these vessels are remarkably fine, the beam at fore barbette being only 71 feet. On her acceptance trials, *Courageous* met heavy weather and was driven hard into a head sea. Her hull became badly strained just before the fore barbette. She was docked and doubling plates added here ; subsequent trials showing that the defect had been overcome. *Glorious* did not develop this weakness, but after twelve months' service she was strengthened in the same way, as a precautionary measure. When running into a head sea, these two ships can easily outstrip destroyers. They are said to have done 35 kts. in service.

These vessels are abnormal in type—so abnormal, they have been dubbed the "Outrageous Class." In 1919, they were laid up in reserve, as their cost of maintenance is very high. It does not appear that they will have a very long life. No figures are available for cost, but they are said to have run to three millions each. A third unit, *Furious*, of slightly modified *Courageous* design, was converted for service as an Aircraft Carrier.

1905 BRITISH CRUISERS (23 knot).

(MINOTAUR CLASS—3 Ships.)

MINOTAUR (June, 1906), **DEFENCE** (April, 1907), **SHANNON** (—1906).

Normal displacement, 14,600 tons. Complement, 755.

Length (waterline), 520 feet. Beam, 74½ feet. Maximum draught, 28 feet. Length over all, 525 feet (p.p. 490).

(But Shannon has 75½ feet beam and a foot less draught.)

Guns :
4—9·2 inch, XI., 50 cal. (A³)
10—7·5 inch, II., 50 cal. (A)
14—12 pdr.
2—12 pdr. Field.
Torpedo tubes (18 inch) :
  5 submerged.

Armour (Krupp) :
6″ Belt (amidships) .... a
4″ Belt (bow) .... d
3″ Belt (stern)..................... e
1½″—¾″ Deck
Protection to vitals .... = aa
7″ Barbettes .... a
8″—6″ Turrets to these (K.C.) .. aa-a
8″—6″ Secondary turrets ......aa-a

SHANNON.   Photo, Symonds & Co.

Ahead :
2—9·2 in.
2—7·5 in.

Astern :
2—9·2 in.
2—7·5 in.

Broadside : 4—9·2 in., 5—7·5 in.

Differences.—Minotaur and Defence have signal bridge on level with the fore shelter deck, between fore mast and fore funnel ; Shannon not. Defence has steam pipes either side of funnels : Minotaur has them in pairs abaft.

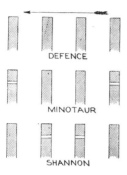

DEFENCE

MINOTAUR

SHANNON

Machinery : 2 sets 4 cylinder. 2 screws. Boilers : Yarrow or Babcock. Designed H.P. 27,000 = 23 kts. Coal normal 1000 tons (only 950 in Shannon) ; maximum 2000 tons. Oil : 400 tons.

Gunnery Notes.—Loading positions, big guns : central pivot. Hoists, electric all guns. Guns hydraulically manoeuvred. Weight of 9·2 guns, mountings and armour, 500 tons. Weight of 7·5 guns, mountings and armour, 1,573 tons.

Torpedo Notes.—1904 model torpedoes. Stern submerged tube.

Engineering Notes.—n.d. in Minotaur, f.d. in other two. 120 revolutions = about 21 kts.

Name	Builder	Machinery	Laid down	Com-pleted	Trials	Boilers	Best recent speed
Minotaur	Devonport	Harland & Wolff	Jan. 2, '05	Mar. '08	19,500 = 22·9	Babcock	23·1
Defence	Pembroke	Scotts S. & E. Co.	Feb. 22, '05	1908	27,853 = 23	Yarrow	
Shannon	Chatham	Humphrys & T.	Jan. 2, '05	Mar. '08	28,128 = 22·41	Yarrow	21·5

General Notes.—Cost: Minotaur, £1,410,356 ; Defence, £1,362,970 ; Shannon, £1,415,535. Designed by Sir P. Watts. Built under 1904-5 Estimates. As designed, these ships had short funnels. The uptakes were heightened 15 feet in 1909. These ships are on the whole not so successful as the Warrior class.

Note.—The Minotaur has not, at present, got any funnel markings, these having been removed for her commission on the China Station.

Defence sunk at Jutland May 1916.

1904 BRITISH CRUISERS (22⅓ knot).

(WARRIOR CLASS—4 Ships.)

ACHILLES (June, 1905), **COCHRANE** (May, 1905), **NATAL** (Sept., 1905) & **WARRIOR** (Nov., 1905).

Displacement, 13,550 tons. Complement, 704.

Length (p.p.) 480 feet. Beam, 73½ feet. Maximum draught, 27½ feet.

Guns :
6—9·2 inch, IX., 45 cal. (A³)
4—7·5 inch, II., 50 cal. (A)
24—3 pdr. (semi-automatic)
4 Maxims.
1—12 pdr. Field.
Torpedo tubes (18 inch) :
  3 submerged.

Armour (Krupp) :
6″ Belt (amidships) .... a
4″ Belt (bow) .... d
3″ Belt (aft.) .... e
1½″—¾″ Deck ....
Protection to vitals .... = a
7″ Barbettes (6)................... d
8″—6″ Turrets to these (K.C.) = aa-a
8″—6″ Secondary turrets (4) = aa-a

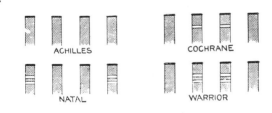

ACHILLES   COCHRANE

NATAL   WARRIOR

Natal sunk by internal explosion Dec., 1915.
Cochrane wrecked in Mersey Nov. 1918.
Warrior sunk at Jutland June 1916.

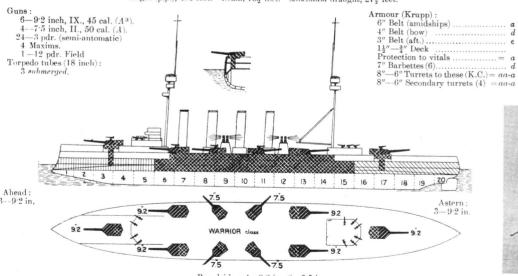

Ahead :
3—9·2 in.

Astern :
3—9·2 in.

Broadside : 4—9·2 in., 2—7·5 in.

COCHRANE.   Photo, Symonds & Co.

Machinery : 2 sets 4 cylinder triple expansion. 2 screws. Boilers : 19 Yarrow large tube and 6 cylindrical. Designed H.P. 23,500 = 22·33 kts. (but 24 kts. hoped for). Coal, normal 1,000 tons ; maximum 2,000 tons. Also 400 tons of oil.

Armour Notes.—Thick part of belt 300 feet long. Armour deck made of two thicknesses of ⅜″ steel.

Gunnery Notes.—Loading positions, big guns : central pivot. Hoists, hydraulic and hand. 9·2 and 7·5 manoeuvred, hydraulically and hand. Arcs of fire : End 9·2 in.—285° ; Broadside 9·2 in.—120° ; 7·5 in.—about 110°.

Torpedo Notes.—1904 model torpedoes. Submerged stern tubes.

Engineering Notes.—Machinery all standardized. Weight complete, 2250 tons. These ships burn about 23½ tons an hour at full power, about 15 tons an hour at 21 knots.

Name.	Builders	Machinery and Boilers made by	Laid down.	Com-pleted	Trials : 4/5 P. (126 R.)	Full p. (139 R.)	Boilers.	Present best speed.
Achilles	Elswick	Hawthorn Leslie	22 Feb., '04	1907	16,009 = 21·5 (max.)	23,968 = 23·27 (max.)	Yarrow & Cyl.	23
Cochrane	Fairfield	Fairfield	24 Mar., '04	1907			″	22·8
Natal	Vickers	Vickers	6 Jan., '04	1907	15,937 = 21·35	23,344 = 22·4	″	23·1
Warrior	Pembroke	Wallsend Co.	5 Nov., '03	1907-08		= 22·9	″	22·9

General Notes.—Design altered since first conception. These were originally to have been sisters to the Duke of Edinburgh. Average cost per ship about £1,180,000. Designer : Sir P. Watts. Built under 1903-4 estimates. These ships are singularly successful sea boats, and are held by all who have served in them to be the best cruisers ever turned out.

Differences—

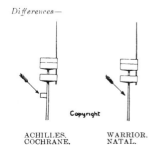

Copyright

ACHILLES.   WARRIOR.
COCHRANE.   NATAL.

1903 BRITISH CRUISERS

(DUKE OF EDINBURGH CLASS—2 SHIPS).

DUKE OF EDINBURGH (June 1904), & **BLACK PRINCE** (November, 1904).

Normal displacement, 13,550 tons. Complement, 704.

Length (*p.p.*), 480 feet. Beam, 73½ feet. *Maximum* draught, 27½ feet.

Guns:
6—9·2 inch, IX., 45 cal. (A³).
10—6 inch, XI., 50 cal.
20—3 pdr. (semi-automatic)
Torpedo tubes (18 inch):
  3 *submerged*.

Armour (Krupp):
6″ Belt (amidships) .... *a*
4″ Belt (bow) .... *d*
3″ Belt (aft) .... *e*
1½″—¾″ Armour deck ....
Protection to vitals .... = *a*
7″ Barbettes (6) (N.C.) .... *a*
8″—4″ Turrets to them (K.C.) = *aaa*-*a*
6″ Battery (N.C.) .... *b*

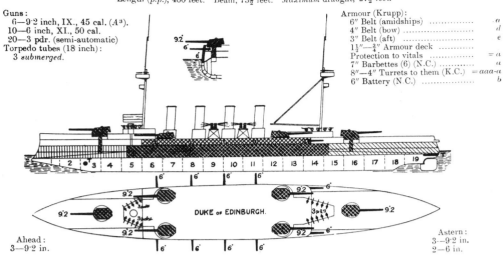

Photo, Symonds & Co.

Ahead:
3—9·2 in.

Astern:
3—9·2 in.
2—6 in.

Broadside: 4—9·2 in., 5—6 in.

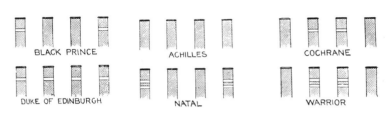

BLACK PRINCE   ACHILLES   COCHRANE

DUKE OF EDINBURGH   NATAL   WARRIOR

Machinery: 2 sets 4 cylinder triple expansion. 2 screws. Boilers: 20 Babcock and Wilcox + 6 cylindrical. Designed H.P. 23,500 = 22·33 kts. Coal: *normal* 1000 tons; *maximum* 2000 tons; also 600 tons oil.
Gunnery Notes.—Loading positions, big guns: central pivot. Hoists: hydraulic for 9·2 inch; electric for 6 inch guns.
  Big guns manœuvred hydraulically and hand.
  Arcs of fire: End, 9·2, 235°; Beam, 9·2, 120°; Battery guns, about 120°.
Torpedo Notes.—1904 model torpedoes. *Submerged* stern tube. Nets to be fitted.
Engineering Notes.—Standardised machinery. Weight 2250 tons complete. The *Duke of Edinburgh* is usually the better steamer of the two.

Name	Builder	Engines and boilers	Laid down	Completed	Trials:— 30 hours at 4/5 8 hours full		Boilers	Last recorded best speed
Duke of Edinburgh	Pembroke	Hawthorne Leslie Thames I.W.	Feb., '03	Dec., '05	16,908 = 21·1	23,685 = 22·84	Babcock & Cyl.	23·1
Black Prince	Thames I.W.	Thames I.W.	June,'03	Jan., '06	16,699 = 21·6	23,939 = 23·66*ᵃ	Babcock & Cyl.	20·5

*ᵃBad weather.

Black Prince sunk at Jutland May 1916.

General Notes.—Estimates, 1902-3. Cost, per ship, about £1,150,000. Designed by Sir P. Watts. Not very good sea boats. The 6 inch guns cannot be fought in a sea-way.

1898 BRITISH CRUISERS (22 knot).

(CRESSY CLASS.—6 SHIPS.)

SUTLEJ (November, 1899), **CRESSY** (December, 1899), **ABOUKIR** (May, 1900), **HOGUE** (August, 1900),
BACCHANTE (February, 1901), & **EURYALUS** (May, 1901).

Displacement, 12,000 tons. Complement, 700 (flagship 745).

Length (*waterline*), 454 feet. Beam, 69½ feet. *Maximum* draught, 28 feet.

Guns:
2—9·2 inch, VIII., 40 cal. (A)
12—6 inch, VII., 45 cal.
12—12 pdr., 12 cwt.
1—12 pdr., 8 cwt.
3—3 pdr.
Torpedo tubes (18 inch):
  2 *submerged*.

Armour (Krupp):
6″ Belt (amidships) ...... *a*
2″ Belt (bow) (N.) ..... *f*
5″ Bulkheads .... *b*
3″ Deck....................
Protection to vitals ...... = *aa*
6″ Barbettes (H.N.) ...... *b*
6″ Turrets to these ...... *b*
5″ Casemates (12) (K.N.C.) *c*
12″ Conning tower ...... *aaa*
(Total weight 2100 tons).

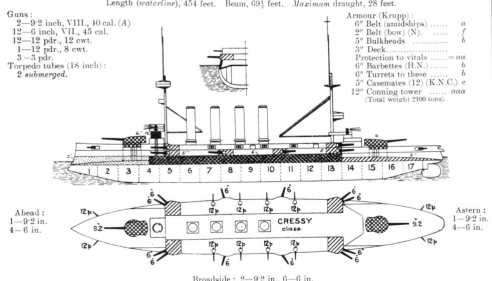

Photo, Symonds & Co.

Ahead:
1—9·2 in.
4—6 in.

Astern:
1—9·2 in.
4—6 in.

Broadside: 2—9·2 in., 6—6 in.

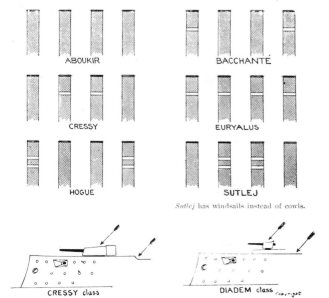

ABOUKIR   BACCHANTE

CRESSY   EURYALUS

HOGUE   SUTLEJ

Sutlej has windsails instead of cowls.

CRESSY class   DIADEM class

Machinery: 2 sets 4 cylinder vertical inverted triple expansion. 2 screws. Boilers: 30 Belleville. Designed H.P. 21,000 = 21 kts. Coal: *normal* 800 tons; *maximum* 1600 tons.
Armour Notes.—Belt is 11½ feet wide by 230 feet long, 5 feet of it below water.
Gunnery Notes.—Loading positions, big guns: all round (central pivot). Hoists: Electric for 6 inch guns. Big guns manœuvred by hydraulic gear. Fire control platforms fitted 1905-06.
Engineering Notes.—Used to be very good steamers, but now getting worn out, and only good for short spurts. Machinery weighs 1800 tons. Boiler space 130 feet.

Name	Builder	Machinery and Boilers by	Laid down	Completed	First Trials. 30 hours at 4/5 114 revs.	8 hours full power 122 revs.	Boilers	Best recent speed.
Sutlej	Clydebank	Clydebank	Aug., '98	1902	16,604 = 20·62	21,261 = 21·77	Belleville	17·9
Cressy	Fairfield	Fairfield	Oct., '98	1901	16,800 = 20·50	21,200 = 20·79	Belleville	19·2
Aboukir	Fairfield	Fairfield	Nov., '98	1902	16,274 = 20·40	21,352 = 21·6	Belleville	18·6
Hogue	Vickers	Vickers	July, '98	1902	16,456 = 20·15	22,065 = 22·1*	Belleville	17
Bacchante	Clydebank	Clydebank	Dec., '99	1902	16,416 = 20·60	21,520 = 21·75	Belleville	19·5
Euryalus	Vickers	Vickers	July, '99	1903		21,318 = 21·63	Belleville	20·3

* Run in bad weather.

Coal consumption: at 21,000 H.P. is now about 18-19 tons an hour; at 16,000 H.P. about 13 tons an hour.
General Notes.—Tactical diameter about 700 yards. Non-flammable wood fittings. Hull with armour weighs 7840 tons. Cost complete just under £800,000.

Hogue, Aboukir and *Cressy* sunk on 22 Sept., 1914 off Holland.

OLD BRITISH CRUISERS.

CARNARVON.

SUFFOLK.

HAMPSHIRE (Sept., 1903) **ROXBURGH** (Jan., 1904) **ARGYLL** (Mar., 1904)
CARNARVON (Oct., 1903), **ANTRIM** (Oct., 1903), **DEVONSHIRE** (April, 1904).

Displacement, 10,850 tons. Complement, 653.

Length (over all), 473½ feet. Beam, 68½ feet. Maximum draught, 25½ feet.

Guns (2—11 inch anti-submarine howitzers may still be mounted in some ships): 4—7·5 inch I, 6—6 inch VII, 8—3 pdr., 5 machine, (1 landing). Torpedo tubes (18 inch): 2 submerged. Armour (Krupp): 6"—4½" Belt (amidships), 2⅝" Belt (forward), 2" Deck (aft), 4½" Bulkheads (aft), 6" Barbettes, 7¾"—4½" Hoods to these, 6" Casemates, 10" Conning tower (fore). Machinery: 2 sets vertical triple expansion. 2 screws. Boilers, various: 17-15 water-tube and 6 cylindrical. Designed H.P. 20,500 (n.d.), 21,000 (f.d.)=22·25 kts. Coal: normal 800 tons; maximum 1,750 tons (Carnarvon + 250 tons oil).

Name.	Built at	Laid down.	Completed	Trials :—		Boilers 4/5.	Last best speed.
				30 hours at 4/5.	8 hrs. full power		
Devonshire	Chatham	March, '02	Aug., '05	14,830 = 21·0	21,475 = 23·17	15 Niclausse	23·1
Antrim	Clydebank	Aug., '02	July, '05	14,628 = 21·21	21,604 = 23·20	17 Yarrow	22·4
Carnarvon	Beardmore,	Oct., '02	May, '05	15,212 = 21·45	21,460 = 23·1	17 Niclausse	22·1

(Engines by builders, except for Devonshire, which are by Thames Ironworks.)

General Notes.—Cost, per ship, about £850,000. Built under 1901 Estimates. Argyll and Hampshire of this class lost during the war. 1919: Devonshire in Reserve; Antrim for Signals and W/T. experiments. Some of these three ships partially dismantled. Carnarvon, sea-going Training Ship for Cadets. Roxburgh for sale.

Argyll wrecked off Scotland October 1915. Hampshire mined off Orkneys June 1916.

KENT (Mar 1901), **ESSEX** (Aug., 1901), **MONMOUTH** (Nov., 1901).
LANCASTER (Mar., 1902), **BERWICK** (Sept., 1902), **DONEGAL** (Sept., 1902), **CORNWALL** (Oct., 1902), **CUMBERLAND** (Dec., 1902), and **SUFFOLK** (Jan., 1903). Normal displacement, 9,800 tons. Complement, 690. Length over all, 463½ feet. Beam, 66 feet. Max. draught, 25½ feet. Guns (2—11 inch howitzers may still be in some ships): 6 in., 45 cal., as follows : 4 in Cornwall and Cumberland, 8 in Donegal and Berwick, 10 in Lancaster, 14 in Suffolk, and (in all ships) 4—12 pdr., 2—3 pdr. (anti-aircraft), 2 or 1 machine, (1 landing). Torpedo tubes (18 inch) : 2 submerged. Armour (Krupp): 4" Belt (amidships), 2" Belt (bow), 5" Bulkhead (aft), 2" Deck (aft), 4" Barbettes (H.N.), 5" Turrets to these (H.N.), 4" Casemates (10), 10" Conning tower. Machinery : 2 sets 4 cylinder vertical triple expansion. 2 screws. Boilers : Various—see Notes. Designed H.P. 22,000=23 kts. Coal : normal 800 tons; maximum 1,730 tons.

Name.	Built at	Machinery	Laid down.	Completed	30 hrs. 4/5.	8 hours full power.	Boilers.	Last recorded best speed
Essex	Pembroke	Clydebank	Jan., '00	1904	16,132 = 19·6	22,219 = 22·8	Belleville	22
Lancaster	Elswick	Hawthorn L.	Mar., '01	1904	16,004 = 22·0	22,881 = 24	Belleville	24·1
Berwick	Beardmore	Humphrys	Apl., '01	1903	16,554 = 21·7	22,680 = 23·7	Niclausse	24·4
Donegal	Fairfield	Fairfield	Feb., '01	1903	16,333 = 22·5	22,154 = 23·7	Belleville	24·3
Cornwall	Pembroke	Hawthorn	Mar., '01	1904	16,487 = 21·8	22,694 = 23·6	Babcock	24·0
Cumberland	L. & Glasgow	L. & Glasgow	Feb., '01	1904	16,472 = 22·1	22,784 = 23·7	Belleville	24·4
Suffolk	Portsmouth	Humphrys & T.	Mar., '02	1904	16,350 = 21·2	22,645 = 23·7	Niclausse	23·7

General Notes.—1900 Estimates. Cost about £775,000 each. Bedford, of this class, was wrecked 1910 on the China Station, Monmouth sunk in battle, off Chile, Essex, in 1919, only Harbour Depot and Accommodation Ship for Destroyers in Reserve.

Note.

Following old Cruisers for disposal (will not be required for War Fleet) : Leviathan, Edgar.* Following assigned to Special Service (Harbour Duties only) : Sutlej, Diadem, Europa, Terrible, Theseus,* Grafton,* Crescent. For sale : King Alfred, Kent, Argonaut, Bacchante, Endymion.⊙ Both Amphitrite and Euryalus converted to Minelayers.
* Fitted with bulge protection.

1898 BRITISH CRUISERS (24 knot).

(DRAKE CLASS—4 SHIPS.)

GOOD HOPE (February, 1901), **DRAKE** (March, 1901), **LEVIATHAN** (July, 1901) and **KING ALFRED** (Oct., 1901).

Displacement, 14,100 tons. Complement, 900.

Length (waterline), 515 feet. Beam, 71 feet. Maximum draught, 28 feet. Length over all, 529½ feet.

Guns :
2—9·2 inch, IX., 45 cal. (A²)
16—6 inch, VII., 45 cal.
12—12 pdr.
3—3 pdr.
Torpedo tubes (18 inch) :
2 submerged

Armour (Krupp) :
6" Belt (amidships) ...... a
3 Belt (bow) .... e
8" Bulkheads (aft) (H.N.) ... a
3"—2" Deck slopes ......
Protection to vitals ...... aa
6" Barbettes (N.C.) ...... b
5" Turrets to these ......
6" Casemates (16) (N.C.) b
12" Conning tower (H.N.) aaa
(Total weight about 2700 tons).

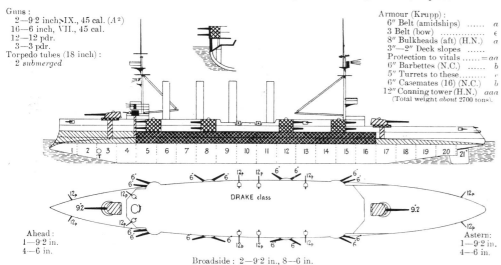

DRAKE class

Ahead :
1—9·2 in.
4—6 in.

Astern:
1—9·2 in.
4—6 in.

Broadside : 2—9·2 in., 8—6 in.

DRAKE.

Good Hope sunk at Battle of Coronel 1 Nov. 1914.
Drake torpedoed by U-boat 2 Oct. 1917.

Differences :—

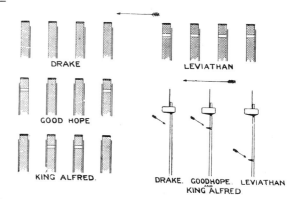

DRAKE   LEVIATHAN
GOOD HOPE
KING ALFRED.   DRAKE. GOODHOPE LEVIATHAN AND KING ALFRED

Drake has Admiral's bridge forward. No after-bridge. All have now no yards on main mast.

Machinery : 2 sets 4 cylinder vertical inverted triple expansion. 2 screws. Boilers : 43 Belleville. Designed H.P. 30,000 = 23 kts. Coal : normal 1250 tons : maximum 2500 tons.
Armour Notes— Belt is 11½ feet wide by 400 feet long.
Gunnery Notes—Loading positions, big guns: all round. Hoists, electric for 6 inch guns. Big guns manœuvred by hydraulic gear. Fire controls fitted 1905-06.
Engineering Notes—Machinery, boilers with water, &c., weigh 2,500 tons. Boiler rooms 185 feet long. All the class are excellent steamers. Heating surface, 72,000 square feet. Grate area, 2313 square feet.

Name	Builder	Machinery	Laid down	Completed	First Trials :—		Boilers	Last recorded best speed
					30 hrs. at 4/5	Full power		
Good Hope	Fairfield	Fairfield	Sept., '99	1902	22,705 = 22·7	31,071 = 23·05	Belleville	23·54
Drake	Pembroke	Humphrys & T.	Apl., '99	1902	23,105 = 22·08	30,849 = 23·05	Belleville	24·6
King Alfred	Clydebank	Clydebank	Nov., '99	1903	22,540 = 21·98	30,893 = 23·46	Belleville	25·1*
Leviathan	Vickers	Vickers	Aug., '99	1903	22,990 = 21·96	31,203 = 23·25	Belleville	23·7

* 1907. Mean for best hour. Mean of 8 hours was 24·8

Coal consumption averages 11 tons an hour at 19 kts. ; and 19-24 tons an hour at 30,000 H.P. (24 kts).
General Notes—Tactical diameter about 750 yards, extreme helm. Cost complete per ship averaged just over £1,000,000.

1895 BRITISH CRUISERS (21 knot.)

(DIADEM CLASS).

DIADEM (October, 1896), **EUROPA** (March, 1897), **ARGONAUT** (January, 1898),
ARIADNE (April, 1898), **AMPHITRITE** (July, 1898), **SPARTIATE** (October, 1898).

(*Niobe* of this class, see CANADA).

Displacement, 11,000 tons. Complement, 677.

Length (*waterline*), 450 feet. Beam, 69 feet. *Maximum draught*, 27½ feet. Length *over all*, 462½ feet.

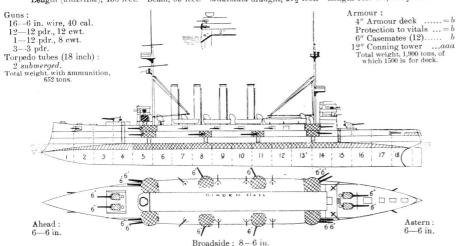

Photo, Symonds.

Guns :
16—6 in. wire, 40 cal.
12—12 pdr., 12 cwt.
1—12 pdr., 8 cwt.
3—3 pdr.
Torpedo tubes (18 inch) :
2 submerged.
Total weight, with ammunition,
652 tons.

Armour :
4″ Armour deck ......= b
Protection to vitals ... = b
6″ Casemates (12)...... b
12″ Conning tower ...aaa
Total weight, 1,900 tons, of
which 1500 is for deck.

Ahead :
6—6 in.

Astern :
6—6 in.

Broadside : 8—6 in.

Machinery: 2 sets 4 cylinder vertical inverted triple expansion. 2 screws. Boilers: 30 Bellevilles. Designed H.P. 16,500=20·25 in earlier three; 18,000=20·75 in later four. Coal: *normal* 1000 tons; *maximum* 2000 tons; 400 tons oil also to be carried.

Gunnery Notes.—Each gun has its own hoist. Electric hoists. Ammunition carried : 200 rounds per gun.

Engineering Notes.—Machinery weighs 1525 tons. Boiler space 132 feet. Heating surface 47,282 square feet. Grate area 1390 feet. Boilers of last four ships are of an improved pattern to those in the three earlier.

Differences.—

LATER DIADEMS.   EARLY DIADEMS.

Distinction.— From *Cressy* class by being generally "lighter" in appearance, and the absence of large fore and aft turrets.

Ariadne sunk by U-boat off beachy Head 26 July 1917 when in service as a minelayer.

Name	Builder	Machinery and Boilers by	Laid down	Completed	Trials :—		Boilers	Best recent speed
					30 hours at 4/5.	8 hours full.		kts.
Argonaut	Fairfield	Fairfield	Nov.'96	1900	13,815=19·86	18,894=21·17	Belleville	
Ariadne	Clydebank	Clydebank	Oct.'96	1900	14,046=20·1	19,156=21·50	Belleville	about
Amphitrite	Vickers	Vickers	Dec.'96	1900	13,695=19·5	18,229=20·78	Belleville	18-19
Spartiate	Pembroke	Maudslay	May'97	1902		18,658=21	Belleville	
Diadem	Fairfield	Fairfield	Jan.'96	1899	12,791=19·8	17,262=20·65	Belleville	about
Europa	Clydebank	Clydebank	Jan.'96	1899	12,739=19·3	17,137=20·4	Belleville	18-17

Coal consumption is now heavy in all this class. All are getting worn out.

General Notes.––Hull with armour weighs 6975 tons. Tactical diameter about 1000 yards. Average cost per ship, about £600,000. *Niobe* of this class sold to Canada. *Andromeda* struck off effective list. *Argonaut* is used for training stokers.

1893-91 OLD BRITISH CRUISERS.

ROYAL ARTHUR (1891) and **CRESCENT** (1892). 7700 tons. Armament: 1—9·2 inch, 30 cal., 12—6 inch, VII (of which four are in 6″ casemates on main deck, others shields), 12—6 pdr., 5—3 pdr., 2 boat, 2—18 inch *submerged* tubes. Designed H.P. 12,000=19·5 kts. Coal: *maximum* 1250 tons. Still steam very well.

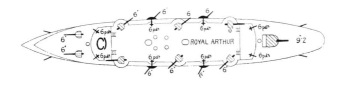

EDGAR (1890), **HAWKE** (1891), **ENDYMION** (1891), **THESEUS** (1892), **GRAFTON** (1892) and **GIBRALTAR** (1892). 7350 tons (except *Gibraltar*, which is sheathed and coppered, 7700 tons). Armament: 2—9·2 inch, 30 cal., 10—6 inch VII (four in 6″ main deck casemates, others shields), 12—6 pdr., 5—3 pdr., 2—18 inch *submerged* tubes. Armour: 5″—3″ deck. Designed H.P. 12,000= 19·5 kts. Coal: *maximum* 1250 tons. Excellent steamers.

St. George, of this class, is a torpedo depôt ship. The *Hawke* lost her ram in collision with the S.S. *Olympic* in 1911 and has now a straight stem.

Hawke sunk by U-boat 15 Oct., 1914.

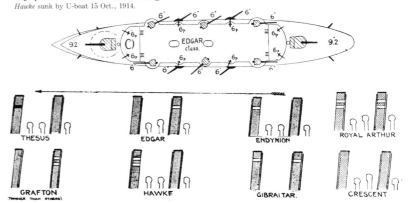

1917-18 BRITISH LIGHT CRUISERS.

(CARLISLE CLASS—5 SHIPS.)

CAIRO (19th Nov., 1918), **CALCUTTA** (——, 1919), **CARLISLE** (9th July, 1918), **CAPETOWN** (28th June, 1919) **COLOMBO** (18th Dec., 1918).

Displacement; 4190 tons. Complement, about 330-350.

Length $\begin{cases} p.p. & 425 \text{ feet} \\ o.a. & 451\frac{1}{2} \text{ ,,} \end{cases}$ Beam, $43\frac{1}{2}$ feet. Draught $\begin{cases} mean & 14 \text{ feet} \\ max. & 16\frac{1}{2} \text{ ,,} \end{cases}$

Guns:
5—6 inch, 50 cal. (**Dir. Con.**)
2—3 inch AA.
4—3 pdr.
2—2 pdr. pom-pom
1 M.G.
Torpedo tubes (21 inch):
 8 above water, in 4 double
 mountings

Armour (H.T.):
3″ Side (amidships) . . .
$2\frac{1}{4}$″—$1\frac{1}{2}$″ Side (bow) . .
2″ Side (stern) . . . . . .
1″ Upper deck (amids.)
1″ Deck over rudder . .
(No C.T. or tube)

CARLISLE. (*Capetown* same.)

Ahead: 2—6 inch.

Broadside: 5—6 in., 4—21 in. tubes.

Astern: 2—6 inch.

Machinery: Turbines (all-geared), Brown-Curtis or Parsons types. Designed S.H.P. 40,000 = 29 kts. 2 screws. Boilers: — Yarrow. Fuel (oil only): *normal*, 300 tons; *maximum*, 950 tons.

Name	Builder	Machinery	Begun	Completed	Trials: H.P. kts.	Turbines
Cairo	Cammell Laird	Cammell Laird	Nov.28,'17	Sep.23,'19		
Calcutta	Vickers	Vickers	1917 ?			
Carlisle	Fairfield	Fairfield	1917	Nov.11,'18	40,930 = 28·45	
Capetown	Cammell Laird	Cammell Laird	Feb.23,'18	1919		
Colombo	Fairfield	Fairfield	1917 ?	June, '19		

General Notes.—Emergency War Programme ships, ordered June-July, 1917, that is, *after* the first three units of " D Class " (*Danae, Dragon, Dauntless*) were ordered. In these ships, " trawler bows " were added, to remedy defects shown by *Ceres* and *Calypso* classes. Conning tower also abolished, and hangar for aeroplanes combined with chart-house. Unofficially referred to as " Repeat C Class."

To distinguish.—From *Danae* and other D Cruisers—*no* 6-inch gun between foremast and first funnel. From *Ceres* class, by " trawler bows " and aeroplane hangar before tripod mast.

" Trawler bow," large forebridges, but *no* hangar.

CAIRO.

1916-18. BRITISH LIGHT CRUISERS.

(" D CLASS," THIRD GROUP— SHIPS.)

DESPATCH (24th Sept., 1919), **DIOMEDE** (29th April, 1919)—For others see *Cancelled Ships*.

Length $\begin{cases} p.p. & \text{feet} \\ o.a. & \text{,,} \end{cases}$ Beam, feet. Draught $\begin{cases} mean & \text{feet.} \\ max. & \text{,,} \end{cases}$

(" D CLASS," SECOND GROUP—3 SHIPS.)

DELHI (23rd Aug., 1918), **DUNEDIN** (1919), **DURBAN** (29th May, 1919).

Length $\begin{cases} p.p. & 445 \text{ feet} \\ o.a. & 472\frac{1}{2} \text{ ,,} \end{cases}$ Beam, $46\frac{1}{2}$ feet. Draught $\begin{cases} mean & 14 \text{ feet} \\ max. & 16\frac{1}{4} \text{ ,,} \end{cases}$

(" D CLASS," FIRST GROUP—3 SHIPS.)

DANAE (26th Jan., 1918), **DAUNTLESS** (10th April, 1918), **DRAGON** (29th Dec., 1917).

Length $\begin{cases} p.p. & 445 \text{ feet} \\ o.a. & 471 \text{ ,,} \end{cases}$ Beam, 46 feet. Draught $\begin{cases} mean & 14\frac{1}{4} \text{ feet.} \\ max. & 16\frac{1}{4} \text{ ,,} \end{cases}$

Displacement (of all above), 4,650 tons. Complement, *about* 350.

Guns:
6—6 inch, 50 cal. (**Dir. Con.**)
2—3 inch AA.
4—3 pdr.
2—2 pdr. pom-pom.
1 M.G.
Torpedo tubes (21 inch):
12 in 4 triple deck mountings.

Armour (H.T.):
3″ Side (amidships) . . .
2″, $1\frac{3}{4}$″, $1\frac{1}{2}$″ Side (bow and stern) . . . .
1″ Upper deck (amids.)
1″ Deck over rudder . .

DANAE.

Photo, Seward, Weymouth.

Hangar forward, as *Carlisle*. Bows as *Danae* above.

DRAGON, DAUNTLESS.

Ahead: 2—6 in.

Broadside: 6—6 in., 6—21 in. tubes.

Astern: 2—6 in.

Machinery: Turbines (all-geared), Brown-Curtis or Parsons types. Designed S.H.P. 40,000 = 29 kts. 2 screws. Boilers: Yarrow (small tube). Oil fuel only: *normal*, 300 tons; *maximum*, 1050 tons.

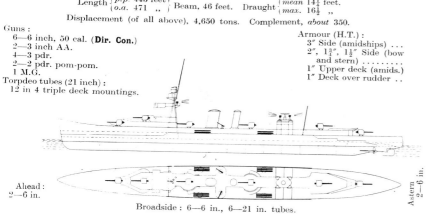

Name	Builder	Machinery	Ordered	Begun	Completed	Trials H.P. kts.	Turbines
Despatch	Fairfield*	Fairfield	Mar., 1918	1918			
Diomede	Vickers*	Vickers	Mar., 1918	1918			
Delhi	Armstrong		Sept., 1917	29 Oct., '17	June, 1919	41,000 = 28·5†	
Dunedin	Armstrong	Scotts	Sept., 1917				
Durban	Scotts*		Sept., 1917				Brown-Curtis
Danae	Palmer	Wallsend	Sept., 1916	Dec., 1916	July, 1918	40,463 =	
Dauntless	Palmer	Scott	Sept., 1916		Dec., 1918		
Dragon	Scott		Sept., 1916	Jan., 1917	Aug., 1918	40,035 =	Brown-Curtis

*Towed to following Dockyards for completion: *Diomede* to Portsmouth, *Despatch* to Chatham, *Durban* to Devonport.
† With PVs. out, and on deep draught.

No hangar, " trawler " bows, high bridges, revolving launching platform for aeroplane abaft fourth 6-inch gun.

DELHI.

General Notes.—Emergency War Programme ships. Note that first three were ordered *before Carlisle* class. Design generally as *Ceres* class, but lengthened *about* 20 feet, to add a sixth 6-inch between foremast and first funnel; also triple tubes. Completion of *Despatch* and *Diomede* may be indefinitely postponed.

Cancelled Ships (Third Group).—*Daedalus* (Armstrong), *Daring* (Beardmore), *Desperate* (——), *Dryad* (Vickers). All ordered March, 1918, with *Diomede* and *Despatch*. Cancelled 1918. Possible that *Desperate* may proceed, so as to complete three ships in third group, as in other two groups. Contractor for *Desperate* not known; may be Palmer.

1916 BRITISH LIGHT CRUISERS.

(CERES CLASS—5 SHIPS.)

CARDIFF (ex *Caprice*, 12th May, 1917), **CERES** (24th March, 1917), **COVENTRY** (ex *Corsair*, 6th July, 1917), **CURACOA** (5th May, 1917), **CURLEW** (5th July, 1917).

Displacement, 4190 tons. Complement, 327.

Length $\begin{cases} p.p. \ 425 \text{ feet} \\ o.a. \ 450 \quad ,, \end{cases}$ Beam, 43½ feet. Draught $\begin{cases} mean \ 14 \text{ feet.} \\ max. \ 16¼ \quad ,, \end{cases}$

Guns :
5—6 inch, 50 cal. (**Dir. Con.**)
2—3 inch AA.
4—3 pdr.
1 M.G.
Torpedo tubes (21 inch) :
8 above water, in 4 *double* mountings

Armour (H.T.) :
3″ Side (amidships) . . .
2½″—1½″ Side (bow) . .
2″ Side (stern) . . . . .
1″ Upper deck (amids.)
1″ Deck over rudder
(Harvey or Hadfield)
3″ C.T. . . . .
— Tube . . . .

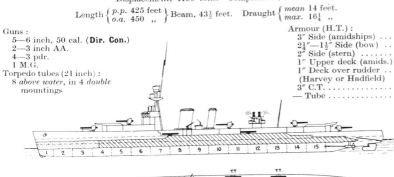

Ahead :
2—6 in.

Broadside : 5—6 in., 4—21 in. tubes.

Astern :
2—6 in.

Machinery : Turbines (all-geared), see Table. 2 screws in all. Designed S.H.P. 40,000 = 29 kts. Boilers : Yarrow. Fuel (oil only) : 300 tons, *normal* ; *maximum*, 950 tons.

Name	Builder	Machinery	Begun	Completed	Trials H.P. kts.	Turbines
Cardiff	Fairfield	Fairfield	July, 1916	July, 1917	41,450 = 28·96	B.-Curtis A.G.
Ceres	Clydebank	Clydebank	Apl.26,'16	June, 1917	39,425 = 29·1	B.-Curtis A.G.
Coventry	Swan Hunter	Wallsend	Aug., 1916	Feb., 1918	39,967	B.-Curtis A.G.
Curacoa	Pembroke D.Y.	Harland & Wolff	July,1916	Feb., 1918	40,428	B.-Curtis A.G.
Curlew	Vickers	Vickers	Aug., 1916	Dec., 1917	40,240 = 28·07	Parsons A.G.

CURLEW.   *Photo, Seward, Weymouth.*

COVENTRY   *Photo, Messrs. Swan Hunter & Wigham Richardson, Builders.*

General Notes.—All Emergency War Programme ships, ordered April, 1916. Very wet forward, to remedy which defect the later *Carlisle* and *Dragon* classes were given " trawler " bows.

To distinguish : From *Dragon* and " D " Cruisers.—No 6 inch between foremast and first funnel. The same point separates this class from the *Caledon* class.

(IMPROVED BIRMINGHAM CLASS—2 or 4 SHIPS.)

EFFINGHAM (building), *FROBISHER* **HAWKINS** (Oct., 1917), **RALEIGH** (29th Aug., 1919).

Displacement, 9750 tons. Complement, —

Length $\begin{cases} p.p. \ 565 \text{ feet} \\ o.a. \ 605 \quad ,, \end{cases}$ Beam $\begin{cases} w.l. \quad\quad\quad 58^* \text{ feet.} \\ outside \ bulges \ 65 \quad ,, \end{cases}$ Draught $\begin{cases} mean \ 17¼ \text{ feet.} \\ max. \ 20½ \quad ,, \end{cases}$

*Approximate.

Guns :
7—7·5 inch, 50 cal. (**Dir. Con.**)
8—12 pdr.
4—3 inch AA.
4—3 pdr.
2—2 pdr. pom-pom
— M.G.
Torpedo tubes (21 inch) :
4 above water
2 submerged

Armour (H.T. or Nickel) :
3″—2″ Side (amidships)
2½″—1½″ Side (bow) . .
2½″—2½″ Side (stern) . .
1″ Upper deck (amids.)
1½″—1″ Deck over rudder (Hadfield) . .
3″ C.T. . . . .
Anti-Torpedo Protection :
Bulges, 10 ft. deep . . .
Unpierced Bulkheads, below lower deck . . .

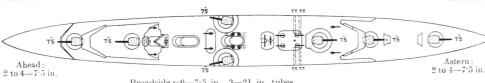

Ahead :
2 to 4—7·5 in.

Broadside :—6—7·5 in., 3—21 in. tubes.

Astern :
2 to 4—7·5 in.

Machinery : Turbines, Brown-Curtis or Parsons (geared cruising). Designed S.H.P. in *Hawkins*, 60,000 = 30 kts. (other 3 ships, with oil fuel only, expected to develop 70,000 S.H.P. and about 31 kts.). 4 screws. Boilers : 12 Yarrow (small tube). Fuel : *As originally designed.* Coal : *normal*, 800 tons ; *maximum*, 1000 tons + 1600 tons oil. *Hawkins* reported to have these proportions of fuel, but other three ships may be modified to take about 3000 tons oil only, *max.* capacity.

Gunnery Notes.—7·5's are a new semi-auto. B.L. mark on centre-pivot mountings and with H.A. elevation. Unofficially stated that projectile is light and muzzle velocity high, so that guns have practically a range only limited by *maximum* visibility. Armaments originally projected for this class were (*a*) mixed battery of 9·2 inch and 6 inch, (*b*) 14—6 inch.

Torpedo Notes.—*Above water* tubes are single (side-loading ?), mounted athwartships on upper deck below mainmast. In *Repulse* class, *Glorious* class and *Centaur* class, *submerged* tubes have proved very satisfactory, as bars bend when attempting to fire torpedoes over 20 kts. Possible that *submerged* tubes have not been mounted in *Hawkins*.

Armour and Protection Notes.—Armour on Light Cruiser lines. Estimated that bulges and sub-division will keep ship afloat, even if all three boiler-rooms and both engine-rooms are flooded.

Name	Builder	Machinery	Begun	Completed	Trials H.P. kts.	Turbines
Effingham	Portsmouth D.Y.		1916 ?	No.		
Frobisher	Devonport D.Y.		1916 ?	No.		
Hawkins	Chatham D.Y.		1916 ?	July25,'19		
Raleigh	Beardmore	Beardmore	Dec.9,'15	No.		Brown-Curtis

Cancelled Ships.—Building of *Effingham* and *Frobisher* has been proceeding intermittently for the past three years, and, in the spring of 1919, *Effingham* was only in frame, and *Frobisher* little advanced. Possible that these two ships may be stopped. *Raleigh* is launched, but her completion is being delayed indefinitely.

HAWKINS. Port quarter view.   *Photo, Cribb, Southsea.*

General Notes.—Begun under Emergency War Programme. These ships were designed in the summer of 1915 and ordered December, 1915. They were planned to meet possible improvements in German Light Cruiser types, and also for hunting enemy commerce raiders in the Atlantic—hence their big fuel capacities. Since oil fuel might not be obtainable at distant naval stations and ports, they were given some coal and 4 small coal-burning boilers arranged to provide sufficient steam for cruising speeds. In the post-war era, they will prove excellent Flagships to Light Cruiser Squadrons. Internally, design is very spacious, and *Hawkins* has proved a very good sea-boat. One unit of this class, *Cavendish* (Harland & Wolff), was accelerated in building, and completed as the Aircraft Carrier *Vindictive* (q.v.).

HAWKINS. Port bow view.   *Photo, Cribb, Southsea.*

1916 BRITISH LIGHT CRUISERS.

(Caledon Class—3 Ships.)

CALEDON (25th Nov., 1916), **CALYPSO** (24th Jan., 1917), **CARADOC** (23rd Dec., 1916).

Displacement, 4120 tons. Complement, 344.

Length { *p.p.* 425 feet / *o.a.* 450 ,, } Beam, 42¾ feet. Draught { *mean* 14¼ feet. / *max.* 16¼ ,,

Guns :
5—6 inch, 50 cal. (**Dir. Con.**)
2—3 inch AA.
4—3 pdr.
1 M.G.
Torpedo tube (21 inch) :
8 *above water*, in 4 double mountings

Armour (H.T.) :
3″ Side (amidships) . . .
2¼″—1¼″ Side (bow) . .
2½″—2″ Side (stern) . .
1″ Upper deck (amids.)
1″ Deck over rudder . .
(Harvey or Hadfield)
6″ C.T. } probably
4″ Tube } removed

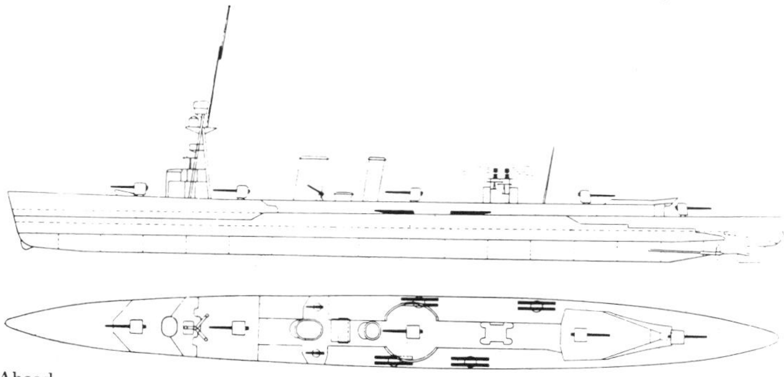

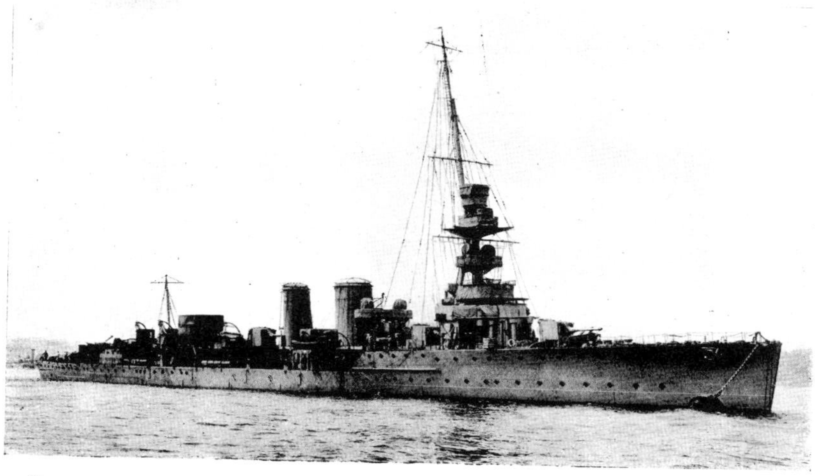

Calypso. *Photo, by courtesy of Messrs. Hawthorn Leslie & Co. (Builders).*

Ahead :
1—6 in.

Broadside : 5—6 in., 4—21 in. tubes.

Astern :
2—6 in.

Machinery : Turbines (all-geared), Parsons. 2 screws. Designed S.H.P. 40,000 = 29 kts. Boilers : 8 Yarrow. Fuel (oil only) : *normal*, 300 tons ; *maximum*, 935 tons.

Gunnery Notes.—Mark of 6-inch gun introduced in this class and mounted in later Light Cruisers has about 40 elevation.

Name	*Builder*	*Machinery*	*Begun*	*Completed*	*Trials: H.P. kts.*
Caledon	Cammell Laird	Cammell Laird	Mar.17,'16	Mar., '17	47,887 =
Calypso	Hawthorn Leslie	Hawthorn Leslie	Feb.7,'16	June 21,'17	43,312 =
Caradoc	Scott S.B. Co.	Scotts	Feb., '16	June, '17	41,196 =

General Notes.—Emergency War Programme. Were known as "Tyrwhitt's Dreadnoughts," as they were units of Harwich Force, under Vice-Admiral Sir Reginald Tyrwhitt. When new, they could make 29-30 kts. Are very wet forward, the fo'xle 6-inch being almost unfightable in a head sea. *Cassandra*, of this class, built by Messrs. Vickers Ltd., lost in Baltic by mine, soon after Armistice was signed.

To distinguish

Caledon class
1. *Three* yards on foremast.
2. AA. guns abeam *between* funnels.
3. *Deck* tubes.
4. *Raking* stem.

Note.—Searchlight bridge before forefunnel not fitted in *Caledon*.

from

Centaur class
1. *Two* yards on foremast.
2. AA. guns on centre line *before and abaft* S.L. tower.
3. Tubes *submerged*.
4. "*Yacht*" stems.

Note.—S.L. bridge before forefunnel not fitted in *Centaur*.

1915 BRITISH LIGHT CRUISERS **1914-15**

Very like *Calypso* above.

(Centaur Class—2 Ships.)

CENTAUR (6th Jan., 1916), **CONCORD** (1st April, 1916).

Displacement, 3750 tons. Complement, 336-329.

Length, (*p.p.*) 420, (*o.a.*) 446 feet. Beam, 42 feet. Draught { *mean* 14½ feet. / *max.* 16⅓ ,,

Guns :
5—6 inch, 50 cal. (**Dir. Con.**)
2—3 inch AA.
2—2 pdr. pom-pom
1 M.G.
Torpedo tubes (21 inch) :
2 *submerged*

Plans :—Generally same as *Caledon* class.

Armour (H.T.) :
3″ Side (amidships) . . .
2¼″—1¼″ Side (bow) . .
2½″—2″ Side (stern) . .
1″ Deck (amidships). . .
1″ Deck over rudder . .

Ahead :
1—6 in.

Astern :
2—6 in.

Broadside : 5—6 in., 1—21 in. tube.

Machinery : Parsons I. R. turbines. 4 screws. Boilers : 8 Yarrow. Designed S.H.P. 40,000 = 28·5 kts. Fuel (oil only) : *normal*, 300 tons ; *full load*, 824 tons.

Name	*Builder*	*Machinery*	*Begun*	*Completed*	*Trials: H.P. kts.*
Centaur	Armstrong	Vickers	Jan., 1915	Aug., 1916	31,679 = 26·8
Concord	Armstrong	Vickers	Feb., 1915	Dec., 1916	40,908 =

General Notes.—Emergency War Programme ships. When new, could make 30-32 kts. Specially well sub-divided. *Submerged* tubes unsatisfactory; may be replaced by twin or triple deck tubes in the future. *Centaur* had her bow and stern blown off by mines during War.

Very like *Champion* and *Calliope*, *v.* illustration of *Calliope* on page 58.

(Cambrian Class—Later 4 Ships.)

CAMBRIAN (3rd March, 1916), **CANTERBURY** (21st Dec., 1915), **CASTOR** (28th July, 1915), **CONSTANCE** 12th Sept., 1915).

Displacement, 3750 tons. Complement, 323.

Length, (*p.p.*) 420, (*o.a.*) 446 feet. Beam, 41½ feet. Draught, 16¼ feet *max*, 14⅚ *mean*.

Guns :
4—6 inch, 50 cal. (**Dir. Con.**)
1—4 inch AA. (*Canterbury*)
2—3 inch AA. (other ships)
2—2 pdr. pom-poms
Torpedo tubes (21 inch) :
6 *above water* (*Canterbury*)
4 *above water* (other ships)

Armour (H.T. and Harvey) :
3″ side (amidships) . . .
2¼″—1½″ Side (bow) . .
2½″—2″ Side (aft) . . . .
1″ Deck (amidships). . .
1″ Deck over rudder . .
6″ C.T. } Removed
4″ Tube } from some

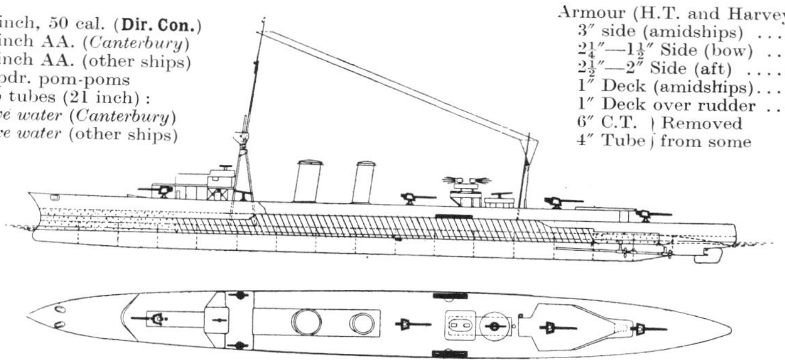

Ahead :
1—6 in.

Broadside : 4—6 in. (2 or 3—21 in T.T. ?).

Astern :
2—6 in.

Machinery : Turbines, as *Notes*. 4 screws. Boilers : 8 Yarrow in all. Designed S.H.P. 40,000 = 28.5 kts. Fuel (oil only) : *normal*, 420 tons ; *maximum*, 841 tons.

Name	*Builder*	*Machinery*	*Begun*	*Completed*	*Trials: H.P. kts.*	*Turbines*
Cambrian	Pembroke	Cammell Laird	Dec., 1914	May, 1916		Parsons I.R.
Canterbury	Clydebank	Clydebank	Oct.14,'14	May, 1916	40,100=	Brown-Curtis
Castor	Cammell Laird	Cammell Laird	Oct.28,'14	Nov., 1915	42,337=	Parsons I.R.
Constance	Cammell Laird	Cammell Laird	Jan.25,'15	Jan., 1916	41,892=	Parsons I.R.

General Notes.—Begun under 1914-15 Estimates. Design generally same as *Champion* and *Calliope*. *Castor* flies broad pennant of Commodore (*D*).

1914 BRITISH LIGHT CRUISERS (Purchased 1915).

BIRKENHEAD (ex *Antinauarkos Condouriotis*, 18th Jan., 1915). **CHESTER** (8th Dec., 1915).

	Length (feet).		Beam (ft.)	Draught (feet).		Displacement (tons).	Complement.
	(p.p.)	(o.a.)		mean	max.		
Birkenhead	430	446	49⅝	15½	17	5235	452
Chester	430	456½	49⅝	15¼	17¼	5185	402

Guns :
- 10—5·5 inch (**Dir. Con.**)
- 1—3 inch A.A.
- 2 or 1—3 pdr. A.A.
- 1 M.G.

Torpedo tubes (21 inch) :
- 2 *submerged*

Armour :
- " Belt ....
- " Ends ....
- " Deck ....
- " Shields ....
- " C.T. ....

No plans available.

BIRKENHEAD.

Ahead :
3—5·5 inch.

Astern :
5—5·5 inch.

Broadside : 6—5·5 in., 1—21 in. tube.

Machinery : Turbines : Parsons (compound re-action). 4 screws. Boilers : 12 Yarrow. Designed S.H.P. : *Birkenhead*, 25,000 = 25 kts. ; *Chester*, 31,000 = 26·5 kts. Fuel : *Birkenhead*, 1070 tons coal + 352 tons oil, both *max.* ; *Chester*, 1172 tons *max.* oil only.

Gunnery Notes.—5·5 inch guns and mountings by Coventry Ordnance Co. They are said to have proved so successful that it was decided to introduce this calibre into the Navy as an official mark of gun.

To distinguish.—Birkenhead has *straight* pole mainmast, as above view ; Chester's pole mainmast is *raked aft*.

Name	Builder	Machinery	Begun	Completed	Trials*	
					H.P.	kts.
Birkenhead	Cammell Laird	Cammell Laird	Mar.21,'14	May, 1915	26,767	=
Chester	Cammell Laird	Cammell Laird	Oct. ,7,'14	May, 1916	31,423	=

*S.H.P. only ; no speeds taken.

General Notes.—Begun for Greek Navy ; purchased for British Navy under the War Emergency Programme. These ships have been very well reported on. They are good sea-boats, and the majority of their guns are mounted well above waterline. Steam well and are good for 23 kts. continuous, except in bad head seas. Designed by Messrs. Cammell Laird & Co. as an improvement on the British *Chatham* and Australian *Melbourne* classes.

1914 BRITISH LIGHT CRUISERS.

(CAMBRIAN CLASS—FIRST TWO SHIPS.)

CALLIOPE (Dec. 17th, 1914), **CHAMPION** (May 29th, 1915).

Displacement, 3750 tons. Complement, 324.

Length, 420 (p.p.), 446 (o.a.) feet. Beam, 41½ feet. Draught { mean 14½ feet. / max. 16 „.'

Guns :
Calliope
- 4—6 inch (**Dir Con.**)
- 2—3 inch A.A.
- 1 M.G.
Torpedo tubes (2—21 inch*):
- *submerged*
- *4—2! inch *above water* reported added 1919.

Champion
- 4—6 inch (**Dir Con.**)
- 1—4 inch A.A.
- 1—3 pdr. A.A.
Torpedo tubes (6—21 inch):
- *above water*

Armour (H.T.) :
- 4" Side (amidships) ...
- 2½"—1½" Forward ....
- 2½"—2" Aft ....
- 1" Deck (amidships)...
- 1" Deck over rudder hd. (Hadfield)
- 6" C.T. } removed ? ..
- 2" Tube }

CALLIOPE.

Photo, Topical.

Plans generally same as *Cambrian* class on page 57.

Note.

Calliope very badly damaged by oil fuel fire at sea, November, 1919. If not scrapped, she will require extensive re-construction before she can return to service.

Ahead :
1—6 inch.

Astern :
2—6 inch.

Broadside : 4—6 in., —21 in. tubes.

Machinery : Turbines (all-geared), Parsons. Screws : 4 in *Calliope*, 2 in *Champion*. Designed S.H.P. in *Calliope*, 37,500 ; in *Champion*, 40,000 = 28·5 kts. in both ships. Boilers : 8 Yarrow. Fuel (oil only) : 405 tons, *normal* ; *maximum*, 772 tons.

Name	Builder	Machinery	Laid down	Completed	First trials :	Turbines	Boilers	Best recent speed
Calliope	Chatham	Parsons	Jan.'14	June'15	30,917 = 28	Parsons A.G.	Yarrow	
Champion	Hawthorn	Hawthorn	Mar., 9 '14	Dec. 20, '15	30,290 = / 41,000 = 29			

General Notes.—Begun under 1913-14 Estimates, with 6 *Caroline* class, on next page. Same hull, &c., but all-geared turbines adopted. Also carry less oil fuel, have thicker side plating, and—of course—one funnel less.

1913-14 BRITISH LIGHT CRUISERS.

(CAROLINE CLASS—6 SHIPS.)

CAROLINE (Sept. 29th, 1914), **CARYSFORT** (Nov. 14th, 1914), **CLEOPATRA** (Jan. 14th, 1915),
COMUS (16th Dec., 1914), also **CONQUEST** (20th Jan., 1915). **CORDELIA** (Feb. 23rd, 1914).

Displacement, 3750 tons. Complement, 325.

Length (p.p.), 420 feet. Beam, 41½ feet. Draught, (max.) 16, (mean) 14½ feet. Length over all, 446 feet.

CAROLINE (and *Carysfort, Comus*). Photo, Topical.

Caroline, Carysfort, Comus — Guns :
4—6 inch (**Dir. Con.**)
2—3 inch AA.
1 M.G.
Tubes :
4—21 inch *above water* in 2 pairs

Conquest — Guns :
4—6 inch (**Dir. Con.**)
1—4 inch AA.
2—2 pdr. pom-poms
1 M.G.
Tubes :
As *Cleopatra*

Cleopatra —
4—6 inch (**Dir. Con.**)
2—4 inch AA.
2—2 pdr. pom-poms
1 M.G.
Tubes :
8—21 inch *above water* in 4 pairs

Cordelia —
4—6 inch (**Dir. Con.**)
1—4 inch AA.
1 M.G.
Tubes :
As *Cleopatra*

Armour (H.T.) :
3″ Side (amidships), 2½″—1½″ forward, 2½″—2″ aft. 1″ Deck (amidships), 1″ Deck over rudder head. (Hadfield), 6″ C.T. and 4″ tube, but removed from some.

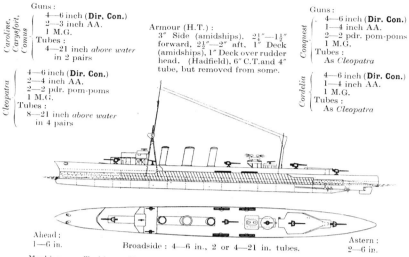

Ahead : 1—6 in.

Broadside : 4—6 in., 2 or 4—21 in. tubes.

Astern : 2—6 in.

CLEOPATRA.

CONQUEST.

CORDELIA.

Machinery : Turbine : Parsons or Brown-Curtis. Boilers : 8 Yarrow. Designed H.P. 40,000 = 28·5 kts. Fuel (oil only) : normal, 482 tons , maximum, 917 tons.

Name	Builder	Machinery	Laid down	Completed	Trials	Turbines	Boilers	Best recent speed
Caroline	Cammell-Laird	Cammell-Laird	Jan. '14	Dec. '14	30,735 = 27	Parsons I. R.		
Carysfort	Pembroke	Hawthorn	Feb.'14	June,'15	32,573 = 28·4	Brown-Curtis		
Cleopatra	Devonport	Cammell-Laird	Feb.'14	June,'15	31,280 =	Parsons	Yarrow in all.	
Comus	Swan, Hunter	Wallsend	Nov.'13	May, '15	32,736 =	Parsons I R		
Conquest	Chatham	Scotts	Mar '14	June,'15	31,825 =	Parsons I.R.		
Cordelia	Pembroke	Hawthorn	July,'13	Jan. '15	30,716 =	Parsons I.R.		

General Notes.—Caroline of this class was built within twelve months. Belong to the 1913-14 Estimates. Originally had 2—6 inch and 8—4 inch : re-armed during War.

1912-13 BRITISH LIGHT CRUISERS.

(ARETHUSA CLASS—7 Ships.)

AURORA (30th Sept., 1913), **GALATEA** (May 14th, 1914), **INCONSTANT** (July 6th, 1914),
ROYALIST (Jan. 14th, 1915), **PENELOPE** (Aug. 25th, 1915), **PHAETON** (Oct. 21st, 1914),
ARETHUSA (Oct. 1913) **UNDAUNTED** (April 28th, 1914).

Displacement, 3500 tons. Complement, 318.

Length (p.p.), 410 feet. Beam, 39 feet. { Mean Draught, 13½ feet. / Max. ,, 15½ ,, } Length over all, 436 feet.

Guns :
Galatea, Inconstant, Phaeton, Royalist :—
3—6 inch) **Dir.**
4—4 inch) **Con.**
2—3 inch AA.
Penelope as above, but 1—4 inch AA. in place of 2—3 inch AA.

Guns :
Undaunted, Aurora :—
2—6 inch) **Dir.**
6—4 inch) **Con.**
1—4 inch AA.) *Undaunted*
2—2 pdr. AA.)
2—3 inch AA.—*Aurora*

Armour (H.T.) :
3″ Amidships.........
2½—1½″ Forward .....
2½—2″ Aft ....
1″ Deck (amidships)...
1″ Deck over rudder hd. (Hadfield)
6″ C.T.) Removed from
4″ Tube) some ships

and —in all—
Torpedo tubes : 8—21 inch *above water*

UNDAUNTED (and *Aurora*). Photo, Topical.

Ahead : 1—6 inch.

Broadside : 2 or 3—6 in., 3 or 2—4 in., 4—21 in. tubes.

Astern : 1—6 inch. 2—4 inch.

Machinery : Turbine (see *Notes*). Boilers : 8 Yarrow in all. Designed H.P. 40,000 = 28.5 kts. Fuel : Oil only, 482 tons *normal* ; 810 tons *maximum.*

Armour Notes.—C.T. removed and replaced by revolving launching platform for a seaplane or aeroplane. Side armour serves dual purpose of providing protection and giving skin plating.

Gunnery Notes.—Beam 4-inch forward very wet and cannot be fought in a head sea. Accordingly, 2—4 inch right forward have been taken out of five ships and a third 6-inch mounted on centre-line between 3rd funnel and S.L. tower.

Note :—Ships fitted to tow Kite Balloons have aftermast *before* S. L. tower.

Arethusa sunk 11 Feb 1916 off Felixstowe by mine.

Name	Builder	Machinery	Laid down	Completed	Trials	Turbines	Boilers	Best recent speed
Aurora	Devonport	Parsons	Oct. '12	Oct. '14	30,417 = 27·4	Parsons I. R.		
Galatea	Beardmore	Beardmore	Jan. '13	Dec. '14	30,796 =	Parsons I. R.		
Inconstant	Beardmore	Beardmore	April '13	Jan. '15	30,357 =	Parsons I. R.	Yarrow small tube in all	
Royalist	Beardmore	Beardmore	June '13	Mar. '15	31,034 =	Parsons I. R.		
Penelope	Vickers	Vickers	Feb.'13	Dec. '14	32,052 =	Parsons I. R.		
Phaeton	Vickers	Vickers	Mar.'13	Feb. '15	34,595 =	Parsons I. R.		
Undaunted	Fairfield	Fairfield	Dec '12	Sep.'14	32,161 = 27·5	Brown-Curtis		

General Notes.—Built under 1912 Estimates. Arethusa of this class lost in the War. All have tripod masts. Very cramped internally.

1912. BRITISH LIGHT CRUISERS

(Chatham Class—Later Ships.)

NOTTINGHAM (April, 1913), **BIRMINGHAM** (May, 1913), **LOWESTOFT** (April, 1913).

Displacement, 5440 tons. Complement, 433.

Length (p.p.), 430 feet. Beam, 49⅔ feet. { Mean draught, 15¾ feet. } { Max. ,, 17½ ,, } Length over all, 457 feet.

Guns:
9—6 inch (**Dir. Con.**)
1—3 inch anti-aircraft
4—3 pdr.
2 machine
Torpedo tubes (21 inch):
2 submerged

Armour (Nickel and H.T.):
3″ Side (amidships) ....
1½″ Side (forward) ....
1¾″ Side (aft) ....

(C.T. removed).

BIRMINGHAM.　　　　　　　Photo, Dr. B. H. Pitcock.

Ahead:
2 to 4—6 in.

Broadside, 5—6 in., 1—21 in. tube.

Astern:
3 to 5—6 in.

Machinery: Parsons turbine. Boilers: 12 Yarrow. Designed H.P. 25,000 = 25·5 kts.
Coal: normal, tons; maximum, 1165 tons + 235 tons oil = 4680 miles at 10 kts.

Name	Builder	Machinery	Laid down	Completed	Trials	Boilers	Best recent speed
Nottingham	Pembroke Y.	Hawthorn	June '12	'14		Yarrow	...
Birmingham	Elswick	....	'12	'11		Yarrow	...
Lowestoft	Chatham Y.	....	July, '12	'11		Yarrow	...

Belong to 1911 Estimates. Average cost of above two ships £356,768. Nottingham sunk by U-boat 19 Aug. 1916.

LOWESTOFT.

Following Notes also for Southampton, Dublin and Chatham (next page):—
Armour Notes.—Vertical side plating from 2 ft. 7 in. below w.l. to (a) upper deck amidships, (b) 3 ft. below upper deck fore and aft. Armour is really 2″ nickel amidships, 1″ forward and aft, but side plating is added for total thicknesses given.
Machinery Notes.—Impulse reaction turbines, viz., on each shaft, one ahead impulse turbine plus an ahead reaction turbine, an impulse astern turbine and an astern reaction turbine.

1911 BRITISH LIGHT CRUISERS. 1909

(Chatham Class—Earlier Ships.)

SOUTHAMPTON (May, 1912), **DUBLIN** (April, 1912), **CHATHAM** (Nov., 1911).
Displacement, 5400 tons. Complement, 429-440.

Length (p.p.), 430 feet. Beam, 49⅔ feet. { Mean draught, 15¾ feet. } { Max. ,, 17′ 8″ } Length over all, 457 feet.

Guns:
8—6 inch (M. XI)
1—3 inch anti-aircraft
4—3 pdr.
4 or 2 machine
(1 landing).
Torpedo tubes (21 inch):
2 submerged

Armour:
2″ Deck on slopes ....
3″ Side (amidships).........

C.T. may have been replaced by aeroplane platform.

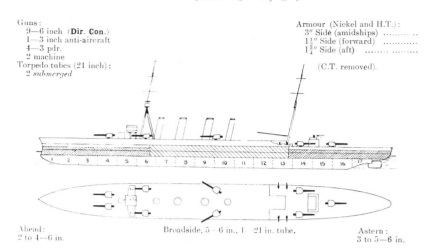

Ahead:
3—6 in.

Broadside: 5—6 inch, 1—21 inch tube.

Astern:
3—6 in.

Machinery: Curtis turbine in Southampton, 2 screws; others Parsons, 4 screws. Boilers: Yarrow.
Designed H.P. 25,000 = 25·5 kts. Coal: normal 750 tons; maximum 1240 tons + 260 tons oil.

Name	Builder	Machinery	Laid down	Completed	Trials ½ power	Trials Full power	Boilers	Best recent speed
Southampton	Clydebank	Clydebank	Apl. '11	Feb. '13	23,607 =	26,006 = 26·5	Yarrow in all.	
Dublin	Beardmore	Beardmore	Apl. '11	Mar. '13	22,606 =	26,011 = 25·7		24
Chatham	Chatham	Thames I.W.	Jan.'11	Dec. '12	23,127 =	25,901 = 25·7		

Belong to 1910 Estimates. Average cost £334,953. Tripod masts fitted to all. Australian Melbourne, Sydney, Brisbane and Adelaide are similar ships.

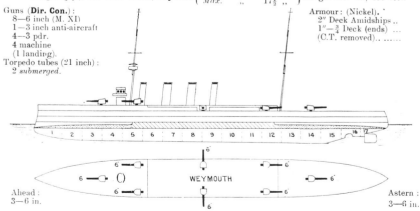

WEYMOUTH.　　　　　(Weymouth Class.)

WEYMOUTH (1910), **YARMOUTH** (1911), **FALMOUTH** (1910), **DARTMOUTH** (1911).
Displacement, 5250 tons. Complement, 433.

Length (p.p.), 430 feet. Beam, 48½ feet. { Mean draught, 15 feet. } { Max. ,, 17½ ,, } Length over all, 453 feet.

Guns (**Dir. Con.**):
8—6 inch (M. XI)
1—3 inch anti-aircraft
4—3 pdr.
4 machine
(1 landing).
Torpedo tubes (21 inch):
2 submerged.

Armour: (Nickel).
2″ Deck Amidships ..
1″—¾″ Deck (ends) ...
(C.T. removed).. ......

Ahead:
3—6 in.

Broadside: 5—6 inch, 1—21 inch tube.

Astern:
3—6 in.

Machinery: Parsons turbine (compound re-action), 4 screws, except Yarmouth, Curtis, 2 screws.
Boilers: 12 Yarrow. Designed H.P. 22,000 = 25 kts. Coal: normal 750 tons; maximum 1290 tons + 260 tons oil = 5600 miles at 10 kts.

Name	Builder	Machinery	Laid down	Completed	Trials 30 hrs. at 3/4	Trials 8 hrs. full power	Boilers	Best recent speed
Dartmouth	Vickers	Vickers	Nov.'09	To be	18,839 = 24·95	23,467 = 25·90		
Falmouth	Beardmore	Beardmore	Nov.'09	1911	18,374 =	26,311 = 27·01	Yarrow	
Weymouth	Elswick	Parsons Tur.Co.	Nov.'09		18,076 =	23,532 = 25·60		
Yarmouth	London & Glas. Co.	L. & G. Co.	Nov.'09	'12	=	24,000 = 26·00		

General Notes.—These three belong to the 1909 Estimates. Average cost £393,363. Falmouth sunk 20 Aug 1916.

1908 BRITISH LIGHT CRUISERS.

LIVERPOOL. (Pre-War Photo, but shows S.L. on Foremast.)   *Photo, Symonds & Co.*

NEWCASTLE. (No topmast to mainmast.)

(BRISTOL or "TOWN" CLASS.)

BRISTOL (Feb., 1910), **GLASGOW** (Sept., 1909), **GLOUCESTER** (Oct., 1909),
LIVERPOOL (Oct., 1909), and **NEWCASTLE** (Nov., 1909).

Displacement, 4800 tons. Complement, 411.

Length (*p.p.*), 430 feet. Beam, 47 feet. { *Mean* draught, 15¼ feet. } Length *over all*, 453 feet.
{ *Max.* ,, 17¾ ,, }

Guns (**Dir. Con.**):
2—6 inch (M. XI)
10—4 inch (M. VIII)
1—3 inch (anti-aircraft)
4—3 pdr.
4 (or 2) machine
(1 landing).
Torpedo tubes (18 inch):
2 submerged.

Armour (Cast or Nickel):
2" 1¾" 3" Deck............
6" Conning tower ....
4" Tube ....

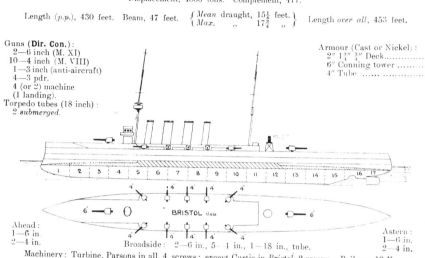

Ahead:
1—6 in.
2—4 in.

BRISTOL *class*

Astern:
1—6 in.
2—4 in.

Broadside: 2—6 in., 5—4 in., 1—18 in., tube.

Machinery: Turbine, Parsons in all, 4 screws; except Curtis in *Bristol*, 2 screws. Boilers: 12 Yarrow, small tube. Designed H.P. 22,000=25 kts. Coal: *normal* 600 tons; *maximum* 1353 tons+260 tons oil. Built under 1908 Estimates.

BRISTOL. (Big top to foremast.)

Name	Builder	Machinery	Laid down	Completed	Trials: ¾ power.	Full power.	Boilers
Bristol	Brown	Brown	Mar.'09	Feb.'11	11,300=24·06	21,227=26·84	Yarrow in all.
Glasgow	Fairfield	Fairfield	Mar.'09	Jan.'11	11,055=23·7	22,472=25·8	
Gloucester	Beardmore	Beardmore	Ap.'09	Jan.'11	13,968=23·447	21,335=26·296	
Liverpool	Vickers	Vickers	Feb.'09	Oct.'10	13,970=23·883	24,718=26·171	
Newcastle	Elswick	Wallsend Co.	Mar.'09	Oct.'10	11,038=23·342	24,669=26·266	

1910-11 BRITISH LIGHT CRUISERS. 1909

FEARLESS.

BLANCHE.

(BOADICEA TYPE—LAST TWO.)

ACTIVE (Feb., 1911), **AMPHION** (Dec., 1911), **FEARLESS** (June, 1912).

Displacement, 3440 tons. Complement, 325-321.

Length, (*p.p.*) 385, (*o.a.*) 406 feet. Beam, 41½ feet. *Max.* draught, 15 feet 7 ins.

Guns:
Fearless 8— } 4 inch M. VII.
Active 10— }
1—3 inch anti-aircraft
4—3 pdr.
1 machine gun
Torpedo tubes (21 inch):
2 above water

Armour (Hadfield):
1" Deck ....
4" Conning tower.......
2½" Tube ....

"Fearless" attached to Submarines.

(Plan as *Blanche* and *Blonde*).

Machinery: Parsons turbine. Boilers: 12 Yarrow (small tube). Designed H.P. 18,000=25 kts. Coal: *normal* 350 tons; *maximum* 780 tons. Also 190 tons oil. Built under 1911 Estimates. *Amphion* of this class sunk, August, 1914.

Name	Builder	Machinery	Laid down	Completed	Trials	Boilers	Best recent speed
Active	Pembroke	Hawthorn	July.'10	1912	=25·1	} Yarrow	—
Amphion	Pembroke	Hawthorn	Mar.'11	1912		} in	27
Fearless	Pembroke	Hawthorn	Nov.,'11	1913	=	} all	—

(BOADICEA TYPE).

BLANCHE (November, 1909), **BLONDE** (July, 1910).

Normal displacement, 3350 tons. Complement, 314.

Length, (*p.p.*) 385, (*o.a.*) 405 feet. Beam, 41½ feet. *Max.* draught, 15½ feet.

Guns:
8—4 inch (M. VII)
1—4 inch anti-aircraft
4—3 pdr.
1 machine.
Torpedo tubes (18 inch):
2 above water

Armour (Hadfield):
1½" Deck ....
4" Conning tower
2½" Tube..... ......

BLANCHE.

Machinery: Parsons turbine. Boilers: 12 Yarrow. Designed H.P. 18,000=24-25 kts. Coal: *normal*, 450 tons; *maximum*, 780 tons coal+190 tons oil. Both built under 1909 Estimates.

Name	Builder	Machinery	Laid down	Completed	Trials 30 hrs.	8 hrs.	Boilers	Best recent speed
Blanche	Pembroke, Y.	Hawthorn	Ap.'09	1910	15,000=22·3	18,542=25·67	} Yarrow	26·1
Blonde	Pembroke, Y.	Laird	Dec.,'09	1911		18,772=25·3	} small tube	

Note to Plans.—2—4 inch removed, but from which positions is not yet known.

1907-9 BRITISH LIGHT CRUISERS. 1903.

(Boadicea Type.)

BOADICEA (May, 1908). **BELLONA** (March, 1909).

Normal displacement, 3300 tons. Complement, 317.

Length (*p.p.*), 385 feet. (*o.a.* 405). Beam, 41 feet. *Mean* draught, $13\frac{1}{2}$ feet ($14\frac{5}{6}$ *max.*).

Guns:
10—4 inch (M. VII.)
1—4 inch anti-aircraft
4—3 pdr.
1 machine.
Torpedo tubes (18 inch):
2 *above water*

Armour: (Hadfield).
1″ Deck ....
4″ C.T. ....
$2\frac{1}{2}$″ Tube ......

Machinery: Parsons turbine Boilers: 12 Yarrow. Designed H.P. 18,000 = 25 kts. Coal: *normal*, 450 tons; *maximum*, 855 tons coal + 200 tons oil.

Name	*Builder*	*Machinery*	*Laid down*	*Com-pleted*	*Trials (mean) Full power.*	*Boilers*	*Best recent speed*
Boadicea	Pembroke Y	Clydebank	July'07	1909	18,536 = 25·5	Yarrow	27·9

1907 Estimates: *Bellona*, (1908 Estimates.) for sale 1919.

HERMES (April 1898), **HYACINTH** (October, 1898).
HIGHFLYER (June, 1898). Large re-fit, 1919. 5600 tons. Complement, 450. Dimensions: 350 (*p.p.*) × 54 × 22 feet (*max.* draught). Guns: 11—6 inch wire (M. VII, VIII), 6—12 pdr., 4—3 pdr., 4 Maxims, 1 landing. Torpedo tubes (18 inch): 2 *submerged*. Armour: 3″ Armour deck, Protection to vitals, 5″ Engine hatches, 6″ Conning tower. Machinery: 2 sets 4 cylinder triple expansion. 2 screws. Boilers: Belleville. Designed H.P. 10,000 = 19·5 kts. Coal: *normal*, 500 tons; *maximum*, 1120 tons. Complement, 481.

Hermes sunk by U-boat 31 Oct 1914 in Straits of Dover while acting as seaplane carrier.

(Astræa Class.)

Photo, N. O'Toole, Esq.

ASTRÆA, CHARYBDIS, FORTE, FOX, HERMIONE (—1893). 4360 tons (sheathed and coppered). Complement, 318. Dimensions: (*p.p.*) 320 × $49\frac{1}{2}$ × $21\frac{1}{2}$ feet (*max.* draught). Armament: 2—6 inch, 8—4·7 inch, 1—12 pdr., 2—6 pdr., 1—3 pdr., 4 M.G., 1 landing. Torpedo tubes (18 inch): 3 *above water* (*may be removed*). Armour: 2″ Deck, 5″ Engine hatches, 3″ Conning tower. Designed H.P. (*f.d.*) 9000 = 19·5 kts. Coal: *maximum*, 1000 tons. Built under Naval Defence Act, 1889. *Hermione*, Depot Ship at Southampton.

NOTE.—All the old Light Cruisers of "Sentinel" type given below will not be used again for Fleet Service except in emergency.

ATTENTIVE (24th November, 1904).

ADVENTURE (Sept., 1904). By Elswick. Displacement, 2670 tons. Dimensions: 374 × $38\frac{1}{4}$ × $13\frac{1}{2}$ feet (*maximum* draught). Complement, 301. Guns: 2—6 inch, 6—4 inch, 1—3 inch AA., 1—6 pdr., 2—2 pdr. AA. Torpedo tubes (14 inch): 2 *above water*. Armour: 2″ Deck. Machinery: 2 sets 6 cylinder. 2 screws. Boilers: $\frac{4}{5}$ Yarrow curved, $\frac{1}{5}$ cylindrical. *About* H.P. 16,000 = 25·5 kts. Coal: *normal*, 150 tons; *maximum*, 455 tons. *Attentive* for Sale.

FORWARD (29th August, 1904),

FORESIGHT (Oct., 1904). By Fairfield. Displacement, 2850 tons. Dimensions: 360 × $39\frac{1}{4}$ × $15\frac{1}{3}$ feet (*maximum* draught). Complement, 298. Guns: 9—4 inch (M. VII), 1—3 inch AA. Torpedo tubes (14 inch): 2 *above water*. Armour: 2″ Belt amidships, $1\frac{1}{2}$″—$\frac{5}{8}$″ Deck. Machinery: 2 sets 6 cylinder. 2 screws. *About* H.P. 15,000 = $25\frac{1}{4}$ kts. Coal: *normal*, 150 tons; *maximum*, 500 tons. *Forward* for Sale.

PATHFINDER (16th July, 1904), & **PATROL** (13th October, 1904).
Pathfinder sunk by U-boat 5 Sept., 1914.

SENTINEL (April, 1904) and **SKIRMISHER** (Feb., 1905). Both by Vickers, Ltd. Displacement, 2895 tons. Dimensions: 360 × 40 × $14\frac{3}{4}$ feet (*maximum* draught). Complement, 298. Guns (M. VII): 9—4 inch and (in *Sentinel*) 1—3 inch AA., 1—6 pdr. AA., 1—3 pdr. AA., (in *Skirmisher*) 1—3 inch AA., 1—6 pdr. Torpedo tubes (14 inch): 2 *above water*. Armour: $1\frac{1}{2}$″—$\frac{5}{8}$″ Deck. Machinery: 2 sets 4 cylinder. 2 screws. H.P. *about* 17,000 = 25 kts. Coal: *normal*, 160 tons; *maximum*, 410 tons.

VINDICTIVE (December, 1897).
Displacement, 5750 tons. Complement, 480.
Length, 320 feet. Beam, $57\frac{1}{2}$ feet. *Maximum* draught, 24 feet
Sunk as blockship at Ostend May 10 1918.

(Topaze Class.)

DIAMOND (Jan., 1904), **SAPPHIRE** (March, 1904).

TOPAZE (July, 1903), **AMETHYST** (Nov., 1903). Displacement, 3000 tons. Complement, 290-300. Dimensions: 360 × 40 × $14\frac{1}{2}$ feet (*mean* draught). Guns: *Topaze*, 12—4 inch, 1—6 pdr. AA., 2—3 pdr. AA., 1—6 pdr., 3 M.G.; *Amethyst*, 2—6 inch, 8—4 inch, 2—3 pdr., 3 M.G. Torpedo tubes (18 inch): 2 *above water*. Armour (steel): 2″ Deck. Machinery: 2 sets triple expansion, except *Amethyst*, Parsons turbine. 2 screws. Boilers: Normand-Laird in *Topaze*, Yarrow in *Amethyst*. *Max.* H.P. *Topaze*, 9800 = 22·2 kts.; *Amethyst*, 12,000 = 23·4 kts. *nominal*. Coal: *normal*, 300 tons; *maximum*, 750 tons. Built under 1902-3 Estimates.

(Eclipse Class.)

ECLIPSE (July, 1894), **TALBOT** (April, 1895), **MINERVA** (Sept., 1895), **VENUS** (Sept., 1895)
JUNO (Nov., 1895), **DIANA** (Dec., 1895), **DIDO** (March, 1896),
DORIS (March, 1896), & **ISIS** (June, 1896) Displacement, 5600 tons. Complement, 393. Dimensions: 364 (*w.l.*) × 54 × 23 feet (*max.* draught). Length *over all*, $370\frac{1}{3}$ feet. Guns: 9—6 inch, 45 cal. M. VII, 4—12 pdr., 12 cwt., 1—3 pdr., 2 M.G. Torpedo tubes (18 inch): 2 *submerged*, 1 *above water* (stern). Armour: $2\frac{1}{2}$″ Armour deck, Protection to vitals, 6″ Engine hatches, 6″ Conning tower (Harvey). Machinery: 2 sets inverted triple expansion. 2 screws. Boilers: 8 single-ended cylindrical. Designed H.P. *natural* 8000 = 18·5 kts.; *forced* 9600 = 19·5 kts. Coal: *normal*, 550 tons; *maximum*, 1065 tons.

(Pelorus Class)

PELORUS (Feb., 1896), **PEGASUS** (March, 1897),
PYRAMUS (May, 1897), **PERSEUS** (July, 1897), **PSYCHE** (July, 1898)
PIONEER (June, 1899), **PROSERPINE** (1896).

Displacement, 2,135 tons, *except* last 2, which are 2,200 tons. Complement, 224.
Length, 300 feet. Beam, $36\frac{1}{2}$ feet. Draught (*max.*), 17 feet; *Pandora*, *Pioneer*, and *Psyche*, $19\frac{1}{2}$ feet.
Psyche and *Pioneer* to Australia.
Pegasus sunk by Königsberg off Zanzibar 20 Sept. 1914.

(Apollo Class.)

APOLLO, THETIS, INTREPID, IPHIGENIA, SIRIUS, SAPPHO, MELPOMENE, BRILLIANT

ANDROMACHE (1890), **LATONA** (1890), **NAIAD** (1890). 3400 tons. Complement, 273. Dimensions: (*p.p.*) 300 × $43\frac{2}{3}$ × 18 feet. Guns: 1 small. Armour: 2″ Deck. Designed H.P. 7000 = 18·5 kts. (*nat.*); 9000 = 20 kts. (*f.d.*). Coal: *maximum*, 560 tons. Built under Naval Defence Act, 1889. Converted to Minelayers about 1910, but not so used now.

Thetis, Intrepid, Iphigenia, Brilliant and *Sirius* sunk as blockships at Zeebrugge 23 April 1918.

BRITISH NAVY.

Coast Defence Vessel.

Photo, Cribb, Southsea.

GORGON (ex *Nidaros*, 9th June, 1914).

Displacement, 5700 tons. Complement, 303.

Length (*o.a.*), 310 feet. Beam, 73⅔ feet. *Max.* Draught, 16½ feet.

Guns (Elswick):
2—9·2 inch
6—6 inch
2—3 inch anti-aircraft.
4—2 pdr. pom-poms.

Armour:
*7" Belt
*4" Ends
2" Deck
4" Citadel
8" Turrets
6" Secondary guns
8" Fore C.T.
6" Aft C.T.
* Not fitted ?

Machinery: Triple expansion. 2 screws. Boilers: Yarrow. Designed H.P. 4000=13 kts. Coal: *maximum* 364 tons + 170 tons oil.

Name	*Builder*	*Machinery*	*Begun*	*Completed*	*Trials.*
Gorgon	Armstrong	H. Leslie	June, 1913	June, 1918	

Notes.—There were originally two ships in this class, begun at Elswick in May-June, 1913, for the Norwegian Navy, as the Coast Service Battleships *Bjoergvin* and *Nidaros*. Construction was stopped when war began, and they lay in the Tyne in an incomplete condition until 1915, when they were taken over for the British Navy and named *Glatton* (ex *Bjoergvin*) and *Gorgon* (ex *Nidaros*). *Glatton* blew up at Dover during September, 1918. As originally designed, this ship had a beam of 55¾ feet and a speed of 15 kts. Beam has been increased and speed reduced by the addition of "blisters" to the hull. The belt may never have been fitted.

Monitors

EREBUS.

EREBUS (19th June, 1916), **TERROR** (18th May, 1916).

Displacement, 8000 tons. Complements, 226 and 223.

Length, (*p.p.*) 380, (*o.a.*) 405 feet. Beam, 88 feet. *Mean* Draught, 11 feet.

Guns:
2—15 inch, 42 cal. (**Dir. Con.**)
8—4 inch
2—12 pdr.
2—3 inch (anti aircraft)
2—2 pdr. (anti-aircraft)
4 M G.

Armour:
4" Bulkheads, F. & A.
8" Barbettes
13"-4¼" Gunhouses
4" Box Citadel (over magazines)
6" C.T.
1" Fo'xle & Upper D'ks
4" Main Deck (Slopes)
2" Main Deck
1½"-¾" Lower Deck
Anti-torpedo Pro.
Bulges

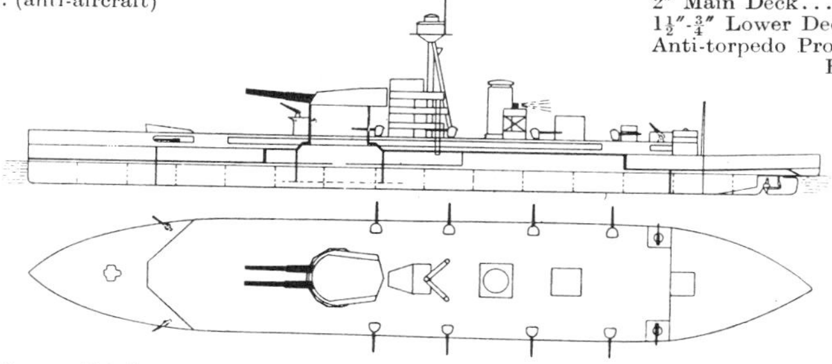

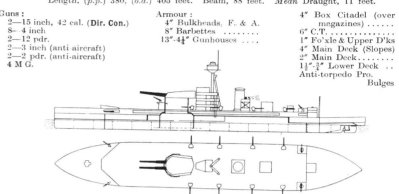

Machinery: Triple expansion. 2 screws. Boilers: Babcock. Designed H.P. 6000=12 kts. Fuel: 650 tons *normal*, 750 tons, *maximum*, oil only.

Gunnery Notes.—15 inch are high angle and can range up to 40,000 yards. Smoke screen apparatus fitted. *Erebus* has 15 inch removed from *M. Ney.*

Special Protection.—Bulges about 15 feet deep, sub-divided into 50 w.t.c. *Erebus* hit full amidships by distance-controlled boat, carrying heavy charge. Was repaired in a fortnight and rails were fitted to "blisters" of both ships to prevent distance-controlled boats riding up blisters. *Terror* hit by three torpedoes in succession—2 right forward beyond bulge protection inflicted heavy damage. The third torpedo hit the bulge and did no harm at all.

Name	*Builder and Machinery*	*Begun*	*Completed*	*Trials*
Erebus *Terror*	Harland & Wolff (Govan) Harland & Wolff (Belfast)	Oct., 1915 Oct., 1915	Sept., 1916 Aug., 1916	7244 H.P. = 14·1 kts. 6235 H.P. = 13·1 kts.

General Notes.—Both Emergency War Programme. Designed as an improved "Abercrombie" type to outrange the 15 and 11 inch guns mounted by Germans on Belgian Coast. Their speed, considering their great beam, is remarkable. Were the "crack" monitors of the famous Dover Patrol.

Cancelled 1918.—Large monitor (unnamed) by Messrs. Wm. Hamilton.

BRITISH NAVY—MONITORS.

M. NEY.

Guns: Has only 6—6 inch, 2—3 inch AA., 2—3 pdr. AA.

See Addenda pages

M. SOULT.

Guns: 2—15 inch (DIR. CON., H. A. elevation), 8—4 inch, 2—12 pdr., 2—3 inch AA., 2—2 pdr. AA.

MARSHAL NEY (24th August, 1915), **MARSHAL SOULT** (17th June, 1915).

Displacement, 6670 tons. Complements, *M. Ney* 186, *M. Soult*, 228.

Length, 340 (*p.p.*), 355⅔ (*o.a.*) feet. Beam, 90¼ feet. Draught, 10½ feet.

Armour: in *Soult* only, 8" Barbette, 13"—4¼" Gunhouse: in both, 4" Bulkheads fore and aft, 6" C.T., 4"—1" Box Citadel over Magazine, 1" Fo'xle Deck, 2"—1½" Upper Deck, Lower Deck 3" at bow, 1½" at stern, 1" Navig. Position. Deep Bulge Protection.

Machinery: 2 sets Diesel. 2 screws. Designed H.P 1500 = 6-7 kts. Fuel: 235 tons, *maximum* oil only.

Name	*Builder*	*Machinery*	*Begun*	*Completed*	*Trials*
M. Ney *M. Soult*	Palmer Palmer	White Vickers	Jan., 1915 Jan., 1915	Aug., 1915 Nov., 1915	2309 H.P. = 6·3 kts. 1898 H.P. = 6·6 kts.

General Notes.—Emergency War Programme. *M. Ney* practically a failure, on account of her engines being highly unreliable. 15 inch guns and barbette removed from her about 1917, and she was moored as Guard-Ship in the Downs.

ABERCROMBIE, HAVELOCK, RAGLAN, ROBERTS.
Raglan sunk off Imbros 20 Jan. 1918.

SIR JOHN MOORE.

GENERAL CRAUFURD (8th July, 1915), **SIR JOHN MOORE** (31st May, 1915).

Displacement, 5900 tons. Complements, 237.

Length, 320 (*p.p.*), 335½ (*o.a.*) feet. Beam, 87¼ feet. Draught, 10½ feet.

Guns:
2—12 inch, M. VIII, 25 cal.
4 to 2—6 inch
2—12 pdr.
2—3 inch AA.
2—2 pdr. anti-aircraft.
4 M.G.

Armour (Krupp):
6" Bulkheads F. & A.
8"—2" Barbettes
10½"—2" Gunhouse
6" Conning tower
1" Foxle deck
6" Upper deck (slopes)
2" Upper deck
1½" Main deck
Anti-torpedo protection:
Deep bulges.

Machinery: Triple expansion. 2 screws. Boilers: Babcock & Wilcox. Designed H.P. 2310 (?) = 6-7 kts. 2 screws. Coal: 350 tons, *maximum*.

General Notes.—Emergency War Programme. Armed with 12 inch from old *Majestics*. These Monitors are extremely slow and unwieldy—in fact against a strong head wind and sea, they can only make 1 or 2 kts. But most remarkably steady gun platforms, on account of their huge beam and bulges.

Name	*Builder and Machinery*	*Begun*	*Completed*	*Trials*
Gen. Craufurd *Sir Jno. Moore*	Harland & Wolff (Belfast) Scotts S.B. Co.	Jan., 1915 Jan., 1915	Aug., 1915 July, 1915	2523 H.P. = 7·4 kts. 2500 H.P. = 7·75 kts.

Special Note.—All other Monitors of *Abercrombie* (14 inch) type and *Earl of Peterborough* (12 inch) type on Disposal List, 1919—not required for War Fleet and will be broken up soon.

BRITISH NAVY—MONITORS & ARMOURED GUNBOAT.

Monitors.

M 29, M 31 (Workman Clark), **M 32, M 33** (Harland & Wolff, Belfast). All launched and completed during 1915. 535 tons. Complement, 75. Dimensions : 170 × 31 × 6¾ feet. Guns : 2—6 inch (1—3 inch AA. in *M 31, M 33*), 1—6 pdr. AA., 4 or 2 M.G. Designed H.P. 400 = 10 kts. Machinery : Triple expansion. 2 screws. Boilers : Yarrow. Oil fuel : 45 tons. *M 30* lost during the War.

Notes.—All Emergency War Programme.

M 23 (with 7·5 inch gun).

For description, v. next column.

Monitors—continued.

For photo, see Addenda pages.

M 19, M 20, M 22, M 23, M 24, M 25, M 26, M 27. All built by Sir Raylton Dixon & Co. Launched May-September, 1915. Completed May-October, 1915. 540 tons. Complement, 67-82. Dimensions : 170 × 31 × 6 feet. Guns : *M 19—20* as *M 16—18* below, *M 22* also as those below, but 1—12 pdr. and 1—3 pdr. extra. *M 23—26*, 1—7·5 inch, 1 or 2—3 inch AA., 1—12 pdr. and (in some) 1—6 pdr. or 2—2 pdr. AA., or pom-pom, 2 M.G. *M 27*, 1—4·7 inch, 2—3 inch AA., 2—2 pdr. pom-pom, 2 M.G. Machinery : *M 19—20, 23—27*, Bolinders oil engines, 640 B.H.P. *M 22*, triple expansion engines and White-Forster boilers. I.H.P. 650. 4 screws in *M 24, 26, 27*, 2 in others. Speed : 12 kts. in all. Oil : 25-28 tons. *M 15, 21, 25, 27* and *M 28* of this class lost during the War.

For photo, see Addenda pages.

M 16, M 17, M 18. Built by Messrs. Gray & Co. Launched April-May, 1915, completed June-July, 1915. Guns : 1—9·2 inch, 1—3 inch AA., 2 M.G. I.H.P. 800 = 12 kts. Triple expansion engines. 2 screws. Boilers : Loco. Oil : 32 tons. All other details as *M 19—27* above, from which they differ in appearance. *M 15* lost during the War.

General Notes.—All Emergency War Programme.

Armoured Gunboat.

Photo, Abrahams, Devonport.

HUMBER (ex *Jarary*, Vickers, 1913). 1260 tons. Dimensions : 261 (*p.p.*), 266¾ (*o.a.*) × 49 × 5¾ feet. Guns : 3—6 inch, 2—4·7 inch howitzers, 4—3 pdr., 1—3 pdr. AA. Armour : 2″ sides, ″ Barbette, ″ C.T. Upper deck is protective. H.P. 1450 = 12 kts. Boilers : Yarrow. Coal : 187 tons + 90 tons oil fuel.

General Notes.—Brazilian River Monitor *Jarary*. Purchased 1914. 1—6 inch gun (salved from old wrecked *Montagu*) was added, mounted on quarter deck. Purchased for British Navy on outbreak of war. Designed for service on the Amazon, S. America, but has actually taken part in several coastal bombardments and other operations entailing long sea voyages. Sister ships, *Mersey* (ex *Madera*), *Severn* (ex *Solimoes*), on Sale List, 1919.

BRITISH NAVY.

Large China Gunboats.

LADYBIRD.   (INSECT CLASS—12 BOATS.)

APHIS (1915), **BEE** (1916), **CICALA** (December, 1915), **COCKCHAFER** (December, 1915), **CRICKET** (December, 1915), **GLOWWORM** (February, 1916). All by Barclay Curle.

GNAT (1915), **LADYBIRD** (1915). Both by Messrs. Lobnitz.

MANTIS (1915), **MOTH** (1915). Both by Sunderland S.B. Co.

SCARAB (1915), **TARANTULA** (1915). Both by Wood, Skinner & Co.

645 tons. Complement, 53. Dimensions : 230 (*p.p.*), 237½ (*o.a.*) × 36 × 4 feet. Guns : 2—6 inch, 2—12 pdr., 6 M.G.; also 2—3 inch AA. in a few. Machinery : Triple expansion. Twin screws in tunnels fitted with Messrs. Yarrow's patent balanced flap. Boilers : Yarrow. Designed H.P. 2000 = 14 kts. Fuel (coal or oil) : 35 tons coal + 65 tons oil.

Notes.—Emergency War Programme. Ordered February, 1915. Completed November, 1915-April, 1916. Built to Yarrow design under Messrs. Yarrow's supervision. Originally intended that these boats should proceed to Salonika, be dismantled, transported in sections overland and be re-erected and re-floated on a tributary of the Danube, to fight the Austro-Hungarian Danube Flotilla. To conceal their objective, they were ordered as River Gunboats for the Chinese Rivers—hence their name of "China Gunboats." Several were towed out to Malta, but the great "drive" by the enemy armies through Serbia stopped these plans. These ships then proceeded to the Tigris and Euphrates. *Glowworm* badly injured by explosion, 1919, on Dvina River.

Small China Gunboats.

SEDGEFLY.   (FLY CLASS—16 BOATS.)

BLACKFLY, BUTTERFLY, CADDISFLY, CRANEFLY, DRAGONFLY, FIREFLY, GADFLY, GRAYFLY, GREENFLY, HOVERFLY, MAYFLY, SAWFLY, SEDGEFLY, SNAKEFLY, STONEFLY, WATERFLY. Built by Messrs. Yarrow, Ltd., in sections, shipped out to Mesopotamia and erected at Abadan, 1915-6—See *Notes* below. 98 tons. Complement, 22. Dimensions : 120 (*p.p.*), 126 (*o.a.*) × 20 × 2 feet. Guns : 1—4 inch, 1—12 pdr., 1—6 pdr. (not in all), 1—3 pdr. AA., 1—2 pdr. pom-pom, 5 or 4 M.G. Machinery : 1 set triple expansion engines. Single screw in tunnel fitted with Messrs. Yarrow's patent balanced flap. Boilers : 1 Yarrow, burning coal or oil. Designed H.P. 175 = 9·5 kts. Fuel : 5 tons coal + 10 tons oil.

Notes.—Twelve of these craft are said to have been ordered by the Admiralty in February, 1915, from Messrs. Yarrow, Ltd. They were intended to police the Tigris against Arab guerillas. After capture of *Firefly* by Turks, the number was increased to 16. *Firefly* was re-captured in the British advance from Kut-el-Amara to Bagdad. They were built in sections and shipped out, the port and starboard sections being numbered and painted red and green, to facilitate erection by native labour at Abadan. *Firefly* began to be erected August, 1915, and entered service in November of the same year. The last of the original twelve were shipped out in August, 1915, and were in service by March, 1916, the extra four (*Blackfly, Caddisfly, Hoverfly, Sedgefly*) following them later. All Emergency War Programme. Eight of these transferred to War Office.

	Begun.	Sent out.		Begun.	Sent out.
Blackfly	12/15	4/16	Greenfly	2/15	9/15
Butterfly	2/15	7/15	Hoverfly	11/15	4/16
Caddisfly	12/15	4/16	Mayfly	2/15	8/15
Cranefly		7/15	Sawfly	2/15	8/15
Dragonfly		7/15	Sedgefly	11/15	9/16
Firefly	2/15	7/15	Snakefly		
Gadfly		8/15	Stonefly	2/15	9/15
Grayfly		8/15	Waterfly		

BRITISH TORPEDO GUNBOATS.

Note.—Most of these are adapted as Mine Sweepers. The others are mostly on Fishery protection duties.

HALCYON *class.* Class feature. a poop.

HUSSAR *only.*

DRYAD, HALCYON, HARRIER, HAZARD, & HUSSAR.

(All launched 1893-94.)

Displacement, 1070 tons. Complement, 120.

Length, 250 feet. Beam, 30½ feet. *Maximum* draught, 13 feet.

Guns: 2—4·7 inch, 4—6 pdr. Tubes: 5—18 inch. *Hussar* has one 4 inch: forward only.

Machinery: 2 sets vertical triple expansion. 2 screws. Boilers: *Harrier*, locomotive; *Halcyon*, Express; *Hussar*, Thornycroft.

Designed H.P. 3500 = 18·5 kts. Only *Halcyon* can get anywhere near this now.

Coal: *normal* 100 tons; *maximum* 160 tons.

DRYAD class

SPEEDY *only.*   *Photo, Symonds.*

CIRCE (1892), **HEBE** (1892), **JASON** (1892), **LEDA** (1892), **NIGER** (1892), **SPEEDY** (1893), & **ANTELOPE** (1893).

Displacement, 810 tons. Complement, 85.

Length, 230 feet. Beam, 27 feet. *Maximum* draught, 12½ feet.

Guns: 2—4·7 inch, 4—3 pdr. Tubes: *Speedy, Jason* and *Niger*, 3—18 inch; others, 5—14 inch.

Machinery: 2 sets vertical triple expansion. 2 screws. Boilers: 4 locomotive, except *Speedy*, Thornycroft; *Niger*, Reed.

Designed H.P. 3500 = 19 kts., but few of them can get near it now.

Coal: *normal* 100 tons; *maximum* 160 tons.

ALARM class

CIRCE.

The majority are like this, *except*

SEAGULL *only.*

SPEEDWELL *only.*

GOSSAMER (1890), **SEAGULL** (1889), **SHELDRAKE** (1889), **SKIPJACK** (1889), **SPANKER** (1889), & **SPEEDWELL** (1889)

Displacement, 735 tons. Complement, 90.

Length, 230 feet. Beam, 27 feet. *Maximum* draught, 12 feet.

Guns: 2—4·7 inch, 4—3 pdr. Tubes: 5—14 inch.

Machinery: 2 sets vertical triple expansion. 2 screws. Boilers: *Gossamer*, Reed (1902); *Seagull*, Niclausse (1898); *Skipjack*, Reed (1900); *Spanker*, Du Temple (1897); *Speedwell*, Reed (1903); *Sheldrake*, Babcock.

Designed H.P. 3500 = 19 kts. Coal: *normal* 100 tons; *maximum* 160 tons.

ANTELOPE. CIRCE. DRYAD. GOSSAMER. HALCYON. HARRIER. HAZARD. HEBE. JASON. LEDA. NIGER. SEAGULL. SKIPJACK. SPANKER. SPEEDWELL

White   Red   Black

River Gunboats.

WIDGEON (1904). 180 tons. Dimensions: 165 × 24½ × 2½ feet. Also **TEAL** (1901) & **MOORHEN** (1901). 180 tons. Dimensions: 165 × 24½ × 2½ feet. Armament: 2—6 pdr. and 4 M.G. Bullet-proof hull, &c. H.P. 670 = 13 kts. Complement, 37–31. Coal: 39—36 tons.

KINSHA (bought 1900). 616 tons. 192¼ × 30 × 6¾ feet. Guns: 2—12 pdr., 7 Maxims. H.P. 1200 = 14 kts. Coal: 65 tons. Complement, 58.

WOODCOCK (1897) & **WOODLARK** (1897). 150 tons. Dimensions: 148½ × 24 × 2 feet. Armament: 2—6 pdr., 4 M.G. Bullet-proof hull, etc. H.P. 550 = 13 kts. Coal: 28 tons. Complement, 26.

Photo by favour of Lt. Com. Hutton.

NIGHTINGALE, ROBIN, SANDPIPER, SNIPE (all 1897). 85 tons. 107¾ × 20 × 2 feet. Guns: 2—6 pdr., 4 M.G. H.P. 240 = 9 kts. Coal: 11 tons. Complement, 25.

Gunboats: 1st Class.

HUSSAR (1894), ex-Torpedo Gunboat. Serves as Yacht and Despatch Vessel, C-in-C., Mediterranean. 1070 tons. Guns: 1—4·7 inch, 2—12 pdr., 1—6 pdr. AA. I.H.P. 2500 = 17·5 kts. Coal: 190 tons. Complement, 190.

Note.— Similar vessels, *Circe, Gossamer, Speedwell, Skipjack, Spanker, Seda,* are on Disposal List, 1919. *Halcyon* on Sale List.

BRAMBLE, BRITOMART, DWARF, THISTLE (1898-99). 710 tons. Complement, 90. Dimensions: 187½ × 33 × 9¾ feet. Guns: 2—4 inch, 4—12 pdr., 4 or 6 machine. Designed H.P. 1300 = 13·9 kts. Yarrow boilers. Coal: 145 tons.

Gunboat **SPHINX** given as Despatch Vessel among miscellaneous pages at end of British Navy Section.

Gunboats: 3rd Class.

Old *Blazer, Bloodhound, Banterer* (ex *Plucky*), *Bustard, Kite,* &c., still exist, but are only used for subsidiary duties.

Old Sloops.

Note.—Fleet Sweeping Vessels (Sloops are listed after the Submarine Section on later pages).

Photo, G. M. Carter, Esq.

CADMUS, CLIO, ESPIEGLE, ODIN (1900-03). 1070 tons. Complement, 121–112. 6—4 inch, 4—3 pdr. (*Espiegle* and *Odin* 4—4 inch *only*), 2 or 3 M.G. I.H.P. 1400 = 13¾ kts. Boilers: first two, Niclausse; other two, Babcock. Coal: 195—225 tons.

Photo, Symonds.

VESTAL & RINALDO (1890-1898). 980 tons. 4—4 inch, 4—3 pdr., 1 M.G. I.H.P. 1400 = 13·5 kts. Belleville boilers. Coal: 160 tons. Complement, 40.

ALERT (1893-95). 960 tons. 4—4 inch, 4—3 pdr., 3 M.G. I.H.P. 1400 = 13·5 kts. Coal: 156 tons. Complement, 107.

BRITISH NAVY—PATROL GUNBOATS.

(KIL CLASS—81 BOATS.)

4 *G. Brown & Co.*: **KILBERRY** (July, 1918), **KILBEGGAN** (September, 1918), **KILBIRNIE** (——), **KILBRACHAN.**

21 *Cochrane*: **KILDALKEY** (March, 1918), **KILDARE** (April, 1918), **KILDANGAN** (March, 1918), **KILDONAN** (April, 1918), **KILDRESS** (April, 1918), **KILDWICK** (April, 1918), **KILFINNY** May, (1918), **KILFREE** (——), **KILGOWAN** (——), **KILKEE** (——), **KILKENNY** (——), **KILKENZIE** (——), **KILKERRIN** (——), **KILHAMPTON** (——), **KILLADOON** (——), **KILLIGAN** (——), **KILLALOO** (——), **KILLANE** (——), **KILLARNEY** (——), **KILLARY** (——), **KILLEGAN** (——).

14 *Cook, Welton & Gemmell*: **KILCHATTAN** (April, 1918), **KILCHVAN** (——), **KILCLIEF** (May, 1919), **KILCLOGHER** (——), **KILCOLGAN** (——), **KILCOMMON** (——), **KILCONNELL** (——), **KILCOOLE** (——), **KILCORNEY** (——), **KILCOT** (——), **KILCREGGAN** (——), **KILCULLEN** (——), **KILCURRIG** (——), **KILDALE** (——).

4 *Hall Russell*: **KILBRIDE** (May, 1918), **KILBURN** (May, 1918), **KILBY** (——), **KILCAVAN** (——),

30 *Smith's Dock Co.*: **KILCHRENAN** (January, 1918), **KILCHREEST** (June, 1918), **KILCLARE** (January, 1918), **KILCOCK** (April, 1918), **KILDARY** (November, 1917), **KILDAVIN** (February, 1918), **KILDIMO** (April, 1918), **KILDORRY** (February, 1918), **KILDOROUGH** (November, 1917), **KILDYSART** (May, 1918), **KILFENORA** (December, 1917), **KILFULLERT** (March, 1918), **KILGARVAN** (May, 1918), **KILGOBNET** (December, 1917), **KILHAM** (June, 1918), **KILKEEL** (March, 1918), **KILLERIG** (July, 1918), **KILLINEY** (July, 1918), **KILLOUR** (August, 1918), **KILMALLOCK** (December, 1918), **KILMANAHAN** (December, 1918), **KILMARNOCK** (March, 1919), **KILMARTEN** (March, 1919), **KILMEAD** (May, 1919), **KILMELFORD** (——, 1919), **KILMERSDON** (——, 1919), **KILMINGTON** (——), **KILMORE** (——), **KILMUCKRIDGE** (——, 1919), **KILMUN** (——, 1919).

8 (*Builders unknown*): **KILDPART** (——), **KILLENA** (July, 1918), **KILLOWEN** (September, 1918), **KILLYBEGS** (September, 1918), **KILLYGORDON** (——), **KILMACRENNAN** (November, 1918), **KILMAINE** (November, 1918), **KILMALCOLM** (October, 1918).

KILDWICK.   *Photo by courtesy of Messrs. Cochrane & Co. (Builders).*

890-893 tons. Complements, 39. Dimensions : 170 (*p.p.*), 182 (*o.a.*) × 30-30½ × 11¼ feet. Guns : 1—4 inch (1—4·7 inch in a few). Designed H.P. 1400 = 13 kts. Machinery : 1 set inverted triple expansion. 1 screw. Boilers : Cylindrical return tube. Coal : 330 tons.

General Notes.—All Emergency War Programme. Many completed after end of War without armament. Some now serving as Tenders to Training Ships, Schools, &c. ; others laid up.

Cancelled boats.—*Kilglass* (Brown), *Kilbrittan, Kilcar, Kilbane, Kilbarchan* (all Hall Russell). Others listed above may have been stopped, September, 1918, but no list available.

BRITISH NAVY—FLOTILLA LEADERS.

7 Admiralty Large Design.

DOUGLAS.

5 *Cammell Laird* : **Bruce, Campbell, Douglas, Mackay** (ex *Claverhouse*), **Malcolm.**

2 *Hawthorn Leslie* : **Montrose, Stuart.**

Displacement : 1801 tons. Dimensions : 320 (*p.p.*), 332½ (*o.a.*) × 31⅗ × 10½ feet (*mean*) draught. Guns : 5—4·7 inch (DIR. CON.), 1—3 inch AA. (*Stuart*, also 2—2 pdr. AA). Tubes : 6—21 inch in two triple mountings. Machinery : Parsons (all-geared) turbines. Designed S.H.P. 40,000 = 36·5 kts. Boilers : Yarrow. Oil : *about* 505/480 tons. Complement, 164.

General Notes.—Emergency War programme boats. War Losses: *Scott* (Cammell Laird) 15 Aug. 1918. Cancelled 1918: *Barrington, Hughes* (both Cammell laird).

		Begun.	Launch.	Comp.			Begun.	Launch.	Comp
Bruce ..	..	12/5/17	26/2/18	30/5/18	Mackay	..	5/3/18	21/12/18	6/19
Campbell	..	10/11/17	21/9/18	21/12/18	Malcolm	..	27/3/18	29/5/18	20/5/19
Douglas	..	30/6/17	8/6/18	2/9/18	Montrose	..	4/10/17	10/6/18	14/9/18
					Stuart ..	..	18/10/17	22/8/18	21/12/18

3 + *2?* Thornycroft Type.

As *Douglas*, but Thornycroft funnels.

5 or 3 *Thornycroft*: *Keppel, Rooke* (both building 1919, but may be stopped), **Shakespeare, Spencer, Wallace.** 1740 tons. Dimensions : 318¼ (*p.p.*), 329 (*o.a.*) × 31½ × 19½ feet (*mean*) draught. Guns : 5—4·7 inch (DIR. CON.),* 1—3 inch AA., 1—2 pdr. pom-pom. Tubes : 6—21 inch in 2 triple deck mountings.

Machinery : Brown-Curtis all-geared turbines. Designed S.H.P. 40,000 = 36 kts. 2 screws. Boilers : Yarrow. Oil : *about* 550/400 tons.

General Notes.—Built under War Emergency Programme. Appearance almost exactly same as *Bruce, Campbell, &c.,* but these boats have the usual big, flat-sided Thornycroft funnels with caged caps. Complement, 164. No War Losses. *Cancelled* 1918 : *Saunders, Spragge* (*Keppel* and *Rooke* may have been stopped in Sept., 1919).

*Unofficial and unverified reports credit *Keppel* and *Rooke* with 4—5·5 inch (DIR.CON.), 1—3 inch AA. or 2—2 pdr. AA.

		Begun.	Launch.	Comp.	Trials.
Keppel ..	..	10/18	....	....	....
Rooke ..	..	11/18	....	....	....
Shakespeare	..	10/16	7/7/17	10/17	38.74
Spencer ..	..	10/16	22/9/17	12/17	37.76
Wallace ..	..	8/17	26/10/18	2/19	37.72

BRITISH NAVY—FLOTILLA LEADERS.

5 "Admiralty V" Leaders.

VALENTINE.

Photo, Seward, Weymouth.

2 *Cammell Laird* : **Valentine, Valhalla** : 1339 tons.
2 *Denny* : **Valkyrie, Valorous :** 1325 tons.
1 *White* : **Vampire :** 1316 tons.

Dimensions : 300 (*p.p.*), 312 (*o.a.*) × 29½ × 9 feet (*mean*), 11⅞ (*max.*) draught. Guns : 4—4 inch (Mk. V. DIR. CON.), 1—3 inch AA. Tubes : 4—21 inch in pairs, but *Vampire* only has 6—21 inch in two triples. Machinery : Turbines, all geared-types. *Valentine* and *Valhalla* Parsons, others Brown-Curtis. Designed S.H.P. 27,000 = 34 kts. 2 screws. Boilers : Yarrow, except *Vampire* with White-Forster. Oil : *about* 370/320 tons. Complement, 115.

General Notes.—Emergency War Programme boats. Are exactly the same as the Admiralty V Destroyers, but specially fitted as Leaders. No War Losses.

To distinguish : From Admiralty and Thornycroft V's : *high* foremast, bridges rather larger, more boats carried abeam of 2nd funnel ; searchlight platform between tubes extended to take standard compass. After mast stands *against* after superstructure.

	Begun.	Launch.	Comp.			Begun.	Launch.	Comp.
Valentine	7/8/16	24/3/17	27/6/17		Valorous	25/5/16	8/5/17	21/8/17
Valhalla	8/8/16	22/5/17	31/7/17		Vampire	10/10/16	21/5/17	22/9/17
Valkyrie	25/5/16	19/3/17	16/6/17					

4 Marksman (later) Type.

SEYMOUR.

Photo, C.N.

4 *Cammell-Laird :* **Grenville, Parker** (ex *Frobisher*), **Saumarez, Seymour.** First two 1,666 tons, last two 1673 tons. Dimensions : 315 (*p.p.*), 325 (*o.a.*) × 31¼ × 10 feet (*mean*), 12½ (*max.*) draught. Guns : 4—4 inch (DIR. CON.), 2—2 pdr. pom-pom, 1 M.G. Tubes : 4—21 inch in pairs. Machinery : Parsons turbines. 3 screws. Designed S.H.P. 36,000 = 34 kts. Boilers : Yarrow. Oil : *about* 510/420 tons. Complement, 116.

General Notes.—All Emergency War Programme. Same design as *Gabriel, Marksman*, &c., but have only three funnels.

War Losses.—*Hoste* (Cammell Laird). 21 Dec 1916. *Removals.*—*Anzac* (Denny) presented to Australia, 1919.

	Begun.	Launch.	Comp.		Begun.	Launch.	Comp.
Grenville	19/6/15	17/6/15	11/10/16	Saumarez	2/3/16	14/10/16	21/12/16
Parker	19/6/15	16/8/16	13/11/16	Seymour	23/11/15	31/8/16	30/11/16

BRITISH NAVY—FLOTILLA LEADERS.

7 Marksman Type.

LIGHTFOOT.

Cammell Laird : **Abdiel.** 1687 tons. Parsons turbines. Armament : 3—4 inch, 2—2 pdr. Tubes : None. This boat is a Minelayer carrying *about* 60-70 mines behind screens from fourth funnel to stern. Complement, 110. Dimensions, H.P., speed, etc., as *Gabriel*, &c., below.

LIGHTFOOT.

3 *Cammell Laird :* **Gabriel, Ithuriel,** 1655 tons, **Kempenfelt,** 1607 tons.
1 *White :* **Lightfoot,** 1607 tons.
1 *Hawthorn Leslie :* **Marksman,** 1604 tons.
1 *Denny :* **Nimrod,** 1608 tons.

Dimensions : 325 × 31¼ × 11½ feet. Armament : 4—4 inch (DIR. CON.), 2—2 pdr. AA.* 4—21 inch tubes in pairs. Machinery : Turbines.* Brown-Curtis in *Marksman* and *Nimrod*, Parsons in rest. All 3 screws. Boilers : White-Forster in *Lightfoot*, Yarrow in others. Designed H.P. 36,000 = 34 kts. Fuel : 510/413 tons oil. Complements, 106-116.
Nimrod 1—3 inch AA., 1—2 pdr. pom-pom, *Kempenfelt* 1—3 inch AA., 2—2 pdr. pom-poms.
Notes.—*Abdiel, Gabriel,* and *Ithuriel,* Emergency War Programme. *Nimrod* and *Kempenfelt*, 1914-15 Programme. *Marksman* and *Lightfoot,* 1913-14 Programme.

	Begun.	Launch.	Comp.		Begun.	Launch.	Comp.
Abdiel	6/5/15	12/10/15	26/3/16	Lightfoot	9/6/14	28/5/15	29/5/15
Gabriel	12/1/15	23/12/15	1/7/16	Marksman	20/7/14	28/4/15	18/11/15
Ithuriel	14/1/15	18/3/16	2/8/16	Nimrod	9/10/14	12/4/15	25/8/15
Kempenfelt	2/10/14	1/5/15	20/8/15				

3 White Boats (ex-Chilean).

FAULKNOR.

3 *White :* **Botha** (ex *Almirante Williams Rebolledo*, 1911), 1742 tons : **Broke** (ex *Almirante Goni*, 1913), 1704 tons : **Faulknor** (ex *Almirante Simpson*, 1913), 1694 tons. Dimensions : 331½ × 32½ × 11 ft. 7 in. Armament : 2—4·7 inch, 2—4 inch, 2—2 pdr. pom-poms. 4—21 inch tubes.* Designed H.P. 30,000 = 31 kts. in *Botha*, = 32 kts. in *Broke* and *Faulknor.* Machinery : Turbines. Boilers : White-Forster. 3 screws. Fuel : (*max.*) 403 coal + 83 oil. Complement, 205.

Note.—Another of the class, *Tipperary,* ex *Almirante Riveros,* sunk in battle of Jutland 1 June 1916. Purchased, August 1914, on outbreak of war, from Chile. re-armed 1918-19.

*Tubes singly mounted in *Botha*, in pairs in *Broke* and *Faulknor.*

1 Special Boat.

1 *Cammell Laird :* **Swift** (1907). 2207 tons. Dimensions : 353 × 34½ × 13 feet. Oil : 385/280 tons. H.P. 30,000 = 35 kts. Parsons turbines. 4 screws. Yarrow boilers. Armament : 1—6 inch, 2—4 inch, 1—2 pdr. pom-pom. 2—18 inch tubes. Complement, 138. Cost about £280,500.

Notes.—Although 12 years old, still the biggest Leader in British Navy. Extensively rebuilt after action in Dover Straits, 1918.

BRITISH NAVY.—DESTROYERS.

4 + 17? "Admiralty V" (with 4·7 inch guns).

WHITSHED.

Photo, Messrs. Swan Hunter (Builders).

		Begun.	Launch.	Comp.			Begun.	Launch.	Comp.
Vansittart	..	1/7/18	17/4/19	....	Whitehall	..	6/18	1919	....
Vimy	..	16/9/18	1919	....	Whitshed	..	6/18	1/19	7/19
Warren*	..	....	....	....	Wild Swan	..	7/18	10/5/18	....
Venomous	..	31/5/18	21/12/18	6/19	Werewolf*	..	1918	17/7/19	....
Verity	..	17/5/18	19/3/19	....	Witherington	..	27/9/18	16/1/19	10/19
Veteran	..	30/8/18	26/4/19	....	Wivern	..	19/8/18	15/4/19	....
Volunteer	..	16/4/18	17/4/19	6/19	Wolverine	..	8/10/18	17/7/19	....
Watson*	..	....	....	....	Worcester*	..	20/12/18		
Wanderer	..	1918	1/5/19	1919	Wrangler*	..	3/2/19		
Whelp*	..	....	1/18	....	Wren*	..	1/18		
					Wye*	..	1/18		

*Probably cancelled with some other boats (names unknown) on above List.

Boats cancelled 1918.—Vashon, Vengeful (Beardmore), Vigo, Vigorous, Virulent, Volage, Volcano, Wistful (Clydebank), Votary, Wager, Wake, Waldegrave, Walton, Whitaker (Denny), Ware, Weazel, White Bear (Fairfield), Welcome, Welfare, Wellesley (Hawthorn Leslie), Wheler, Whip, Whippet (Scott), Whitehead, Willoughby, Winter (Swan Hunter), Wishart, Witch (Thornycroft), Westphal, Westward Ho! (White), Wayfarer, Woodpecker, Yeoman, Zealous, Zebra, Zodiac (Yarrow).

2 Beardmore : **Vansittart, Vimy** (ex Vantage).
1 Chatham D.Y. : Warren.*
3 Clydebank : **Venomous** (ex Venom), **Verity, Veteran.**
1 Denny : **Volunteer.**
1 Devonport D.Y. : Watson.*
1 Fairfield : **Wanderer.**
1 Pembroke D.Y. : Whelp.*
3 Swan Hunter : **Whitehall, Whitshed, Wild Swan.**
6 White : **Werewolf,* Witherington, Wivern, Wolverine,*** Worcester,* Wrangler.*
2 Yarrow : Wren,* Wye.*

*Probably cancelled, Sept., 1919.

Displacement : 1300 tons *average*. Dimensions : 300 (*p.p.*), 312 (*o.a.*) × 29¼ × 9 feet (*mean*) draught. Guns : 4—4·7 inch (*Dir. Con.*), 2—2 pdr. pom-poms. Tubes : 6, in two triple mountings. Machinery : Turbines (all-geared type)—all above probably Brown-Curtis, but *Whitehall* (and perhaps one or two others) Parsons. Designed S.H.P. 27,000 = 34 kts. 2 screws. Boilers : Yarrow, except *White* boats with White-Forster. Oil : *about* 350/320 tons. Complement, 127.

General Notes.—Begun under War Emergency Programme, but cost of completion of many may come under post-war Estimates. The position regarding these boats is as follows :—56 were ordered, out of which 35 were stopped in Nov.-Dec., 1918, as list opposite. 21 were proceeding up to Sept., 1919, when further boats (number uncertain) were stopped. Completion of boats launched may be postponed indefinitely. Differ from preceding V's in armament. Sometimes—but unofficially—referred to as "Repeat W Class." No War Losses, none of these boats being finished till 1919.

To distinguish.—Proportions of funnels reversed compared with other V's. These boats have *thick* fore funnel and *thin* after funnel. No 3 inch A.A. abaft 2nd funnel. 2 pdr. pom-poms abeam between funnels.

BRITISH NAVY—DESTROYERS.

7 "Yarrow S."

7 *Yarrow* : **Tomahawk, Torch, Tumult, Tryphon,* Turquoise, Tuscan, Tyrian.** Displacement, 930 tons. Dimensions : 260¼ (*p.p.*), 269½ (*o.a.*) × 25¼ × 9 feet (*mean*) draught. Guns : 3—4 inch (Mk. IV with 30° elevation), 1—2 pdr. pom-pom. Tubes : 4—21 inch in pairs. Machinery : Brown-Curtis (direct drive) turbines. Designed S.H.P. 23,000 = 36 kts. Boilers : Yarrow. Oil : *about* 255/215 tons. Complement, 90.

General Notes.—Emergency War Programme boats. Otherwise as "General Notes" to "Admiralty S boats.

To distinguish.—From Admiralty and Yarrow S : shorter fo'xle, sloping Yarrow stern. From other types : as Distinction Notes for Admiralty S boats. No War Losses.

		Begun.	Launch.	Comp.	Trials.			Begun.	Launch.	Comp.	Trials.
Tomahawk	..	4/17	16/5/18	7/18	35.15	Turquoise	..	6/17	9/11/18	3/19	39.6
Torch	..	4/17	16/3/18	5/18	39.19	Tuscan	..	6/17	1/3/19	6/19	
Tryphon	..	4/17	22/6/19	9/18	35.37	Tyrian	..	6/17	5/19	1919	
Tumult	..	6/17	17/9/18	12/18	35.70						

*Tryphon injured by grounding on Danish Coast. Salved and reported to be re-fitting, 1919.

5 "Thornycroft S."

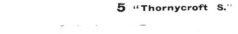

SPEEDY.

Photo, Messrs, Thornycroft (Builders).

5 *Thornycroft* : **Speedy, Tobago, Torbay, Toreador, Tourmaline.** 1087 tons. Length : 266¾ (*p.p.*), 275¾ (*o.a.*) × 27¼ × 9 feet (*mean*) draught. Guns : 3—4 inch (Mk. IV with 30° elevation), 1—2 pdr. pom-pom. Tubes : 4—21 inch in pairs. Machinery : Brown-Curtis (all-geared) turbines. 2 screws. Designed S.H.P. 29,000 = 36 kts. Boilers : Yarrow. Oil : *about* 300/250 tons. Complement, 90.

General Notes.—Emergency War Programme boats ; otherwise as "General Notes" to Admiralty S Class. No War Losses.

To distinguish.—From Admiralty S and Yarrow S : note that fo'xle 4 inch is *raised* ; big funnels ; stand higher out of water. From other classes, distinction notes as for Admiralty S boats.

		Begun.	Launch.	Comp.	Trials.			Begun.	Launch.	Comp.	Trials.
Speedy	..	5/17	1/6/18	8/18	38.51	Toreador	..	11/17	7/12/18	4/19	36.40
Tobago	..	7/17	15/7/18	10/18	38.21	Tourmaline	1/18		4/19	1919	....
Torbay	..	11/17	6/3/19	7/19	......						

BRITISH NAVY—DESTROYERS.

50 "Admiralty S."

TILBURY.
Photo, Messrs. Swan Hunter (Builders).

2 *Beardmore* : **Tactician, Tara.**

9 *Clydebank* : **Scimitar, Scotsman, Scout, Scythe, Seabear, Seafire, Searcher, Seawolf, Simoom.**

6 *Denny* : **Senator, Sepoy, Seraph, Serapis, Serene, Sesame.**

2 *Doxford* : **Shamrock, Shikari.**

5 *Fairfield* : **Sikh, Sirdar, Somme, Spear, Spindrift.**

4 *Hawthorn Leslie* : **Tenedos, Thanet, Thracian, Turbulent.**

4 *Palmer* : **Steadfast, Sterling, Stonehenge, Stormcloud.**

4 *Scott* : **Strenuous, Stronghold, Sturdy, Swallow.**

3 *Stephen* : **Sabre, Saladin, Sardonyx.**

6 *Swan Hunter* : **Shark, Sparrowhawk, Splendid, Sportive, Tilbury, Tintagel.**

5 *White* : **Tribune, Trinidad, Trojan, Truant, Trusty.**

1075 tons. Dimensions : 265 (*p.p.*), 275-277 (*o.a.*) × 26⅔ × 9 feet (*mean*) draught. Guns : 3—4 inch (Mk. IV with 30° elevation), 1—2 pdr. pom-pom. Tubes : 4—21 inch in pairs. Machinery : Turbines (all-geared type). Brown-Curtis (A.G.) in all except following :—Palmer boats, Parsons (A.G.) ; *Tilbury, Tintagel,* Parsons (A.G.). Designed S.H.P. 27,000 = 36 kts. 2 screws. Yarrow boilers in all, except White boats with White-Forster. Oil : *about* 300/250 tons. Complement, 90.

General Notes.—Emergency War Programme boats, but cost of completion of about 40 boats may come under post-war Estimates. Design derived from "Admiralty Modified R" boats. Came into service with a single 14 inch tube on each beam (mounted on turntables or racks) at break of fo'xle, making six tubes in all. These 14 inch have now been removed. Reported to be not quite so successful as the Admiralty M's and R's. No War Losses. *Saturn, Sycamore* (both Stephen) cancelled. *Stalwart, Success, Swordsman, Tattoo, Tasmania,* presented to Royal Australian Navy, 1918.

To distinguish.—Long fo'xle, sheered and slightly turtle-backed. Funnels about equal in size, the extra height of fore funnel not being very prominent. Wedge-shaped bridges built off fo'xle, and open underneath. Features in these boats which also appear in the R and Modified R types are :—Mounting of searchlight on after pair of tubes ; pom-pom on platform just before mainmast ; after 4 inch in bandstand ; boats abeam of 2nd funnel.

		Begun.	Launch.	Comp.			Begun.	Launch.	Comp.
2 *B'more*	Tactician	21/11/17	7/8/18	23/10/18	4 H. L.	Tenedos	6/12/17	21/10/18	6/19
	Tara	21/11/17	12/10/18	9/12/18		Thanet	13/12/17	5/11/18	1919
						Thracian	17/1/18	....	....
9 *Clydebank*	Scimitar	30/5/17	27/2/18	4/18		Turbulent	14/11/17	....	....
	Scotsman	10/12/17	30/3/18	6/18	4 *Palmer*	Steadfast	....	8/8/18	3/19
	Scout	25/10/17	27/4/18	6/18		Sterling	....	8/10/18	3/19
	Scythe	14/1/18	25/5/18	7/18		Stonehenge	....	1919	9/19
	Seabear	13/12/17	6/7/18	9/18		Stormcloud	....	30/5/19	....
	Seafire	27/2/18	10/8/18	11/18					
	Searcher	30/3/18	11/9/18	11/18	4 *Scott*	Strenuous	....	9/11/18	1/19
	Seawolf	4/10/17	2/11/18	1/19		Stronghold	....	5/18	1919
	Simoom	30/5/17	26/1/18	3/18		Sturdy	....	....	....
						Swallow	....	1/8/18	1/18
6 *Denny*	Senator	10/7/17	2/4/18	7/6/18					
	Sepoy	6/8/17	22/5/18	6/8/18	3 *Stephen*	Sabre	10/9/17	23/9/18	9/11/18
	Seraph	4/10/17	8/7/18	25/12/18		Saladin	10/9/17	17/2/19	11/4/19
	Serapis	4/12/17	17/9/18	21/3/19		Sardonyx	25/3/18	27/5/19	1919
	Serene	2/2/18	30/11/18	30/4/19					
	Sesame	13/3/18	30/12/18	28/3/19	6 *S. H.*	Shark	....	9/4/18	7/18
						Sparrowhawk	....	14/5/18	9/18
2 *Dox'f'd*	Shamrock	....	8/18	1919		Splendid	....	10/7/18	10/18
	Shikari	....	14/7/19	1919		Sportive	....	19/9/18	12/18
						Tilbury	....	13/6/18	9/18
5 *Fairf'd*	Sikh	....	7/5/18	29/6/18		Tintagel	....	9/8/18	11/18
	Sirdar	....	6/7/18	6/9/18					
	Somme	....	10/9/18	4/11/18	5 *White*	Tribune	21/8/17	28/3/18	16/7/18
	Spear	....	9/11/18	17/12/18		Trinidad	15/9/17	20/5/18	9/9/18
	Spindrift	....	30/12/18	2/4/19		Trojan	3/1/18	20/7/18	6/12/18
						Truant	14/2/18	18/9/18	17/3/19
						Trusty	11/4/18	6/11/18	9/5/19

BRITISH NAVY—DESTROYERS.

2 Thornycroft "V" (Later Six-tube Boats).

WOOLSTON.
Photo, Messrs. Thornycroft (Builders).

2 *Thornycroft* : **Wolsey, Woolston.** 1315 tons. Dimensions : 300 (*p.p.*), 312 (*o.a.*) × 29½ × 9 feet (*mean* draught). Guns : 3—4 inch (Mk. V. DIR. CON.), 1—3 inch AA. Tubes : 6—21 inch in two triple deck mountings. Machinery : Brown Curtis turbines (all-geared type). 2 screws. Designed S.H.P. 30,000 = 35 kts. Yarrow boilers. Oil : *about* 370/320 tons. Complement, 127.

General Notes.—Emergency War Programme. Differ from other Admiralty Later V's in H.P., speed, and a few other particulars. No War Losses.

To distinguish.—Big flat-sided funnels with caged caps. Divide from *Viceroy* and *Viscount* by the triple tubes in these boats.

	Begun.	Launch.	Comp.	Trials.			Begun.	Launch.	Comp.	Trials.
Wolsey	3/17	16/3/18	14/5/18	36.64		Woolston	4/17	27/14/18	28/6/18	37.11

18 Admiralty "V" (Later Six-tube Boats).

Appearance generally same as *Woolston*, but funnels as Admiralty "V" boats.

2 *Beardmore* : **Wakeful, Watchman.**

2 *Denny* : **Walker, Westcott.**

2 *Doxford* : **Walpole, Whitley.**

2 *Fairfield* : **Walrus, Wolfhound.**

2 *Hawthorn Leslie* : **Warwick, Wessex.**

2 *Palmer* : **Waterhen, Wryneck.**

2 *Scott* : **Westminster, Windsor.**

2 *Swan Hunter* : **Whirlwind, Wrestler.**

2 *White* : **Winchester, Winchelsea.**

Displacement : 1280-1316 tons (1300 *average*). Dimensions : 300 (*p.p.*), 312 (*o.a.*) × 29 × 9 feet (*mean*), 11¼ (*max.*) draught. Guns : 3—4 inch (Mk V DIR. CON.), 1—3 inch AA. Torpedo tubes : 6—21 inch in two triple deck mountings. Machinery : "All-Geared" turbines, Brown-Curtis in all except Palmer boats with Parsons. 2 screws. Designed S.H.P. 27,000 = 34 kts. Boilers : Yarrow, except White boats with White-Forster. Oil : *about* 370/320 tons. Complement, 127.

General Notes.—All Emergency War Programme. The Notes to the Admiralty V's also apply to these boats, the only difference being in the increased number of tubes in above. The triple tubes are actually lighter than the "Admiralty M" Mark of twin tubes mounted in all preceding classes back to the M's. No War Losses.

To distinguish.— From Modified V's : 3 inch AA. gun in bandstand abaft second funnel ; from first V's : by shorter mainmast ; from *Vampire* : by shorter foremast, no extension to S.L. platform for standard compass, after mast stands away from after superstructure.

		Begun.	Launch.	Comp.			Begun.	Launch.	Comp.
Wakeful		17/1/17	6/10/17	11/17	Wessex	23/5/17	12/3/18	11/5/18
Watchman		17/1/17	2/12/17	1/18	Waterhen		26/3/18	17/7/18
Walker		26/3/17	29/11/17	12/2/18	Wryneck		13/5/18	11/18
Westcott		30/3/17	14/2/18	12/4/18	Westminster		24/2/18	18/4/18
Walpole		....	12/2/18	7/8/18	Windsor		21/6/18	28/8/18
Whitley		....	....	10/18	Whirlwind		21/6/18	28/8/18
Walrus		....	27/12/17	8/3/18	Wrestler		15/12/17	3/18
Wolfhound		....	14/3/18	27/3/18	Winchester	24/5/17	15/12/17	15/3/18
Warwick		10/3/17	28/12/17	18/3/18	Winchelsea	12/6/17	1/2/18	20/4/18

BRITISH NAVY—DESTROYERS.

2 "Thornycroft V."

VICEROY.   *Photo. Messrs. Thornycroft (Builders).*

2 Thornycroft : **Viceroy, Viscount.** 1325 tons. Dimensions : 300 (p.p.), 312 (o.a.) × 30' 7" × 9½ feet (mean) 11½ feet (max.) draught. Guns : 3—4 inch (Mk. V Dir. Con.), 1—3 inch AA. Tubes : 4—21 inch in pairs. Machinery : Brown Curtis (all-geared) turbines. 2 screws. Designed S.H.P. 30,000 = 35 kts. Boilers : Yarrow. Oil fuel : about 375/320 tons. Complement, 110.

General Notes—Emergency War Programme boats. Differ from Admiralty V design in dimensions, H.P. and speed. No War Losses.

To distinguish.—Have big, flat-sided funnels with caged caps. The fore funnel not being so prominently raised as in other " V " boats. Other distinctive features as Admiralty V's.

	Begun.	Launch.	Comp.	Trials.
Viscount	12/16	29/12/17	3/18	37.69
Viceroy	12/16	17/11/17	1/18	36.5

21 "Admiralty V."

——————as Minelayer.

F.21

3 *Beardmore* : **Vancouver, Vanessa, Vanity.**
2 *Clydebank* : **Vanoc,* Vanquisher.***
1 *Denny* : **Venturous.***
2 *Doxford* : **Vega, Velox.**
2 *Fairfield* : **Vendetta, Venetia.**
2 *Hawthorn Leslie* : **Verdun, Versatile.**
3 *Stephen* : **Vesper, Vidette, Voyager.**
2 *Swan Hunter* : **Violent, Vimiera.**
2 *White* : **Vectis, Vortigern.**
2 *Yarrow* : **Vivacious, Vivien.**

* Minelayers.

Displacements : 1272-1339 tons (1300 average). Dimensions : 300 (p.p.), 312 (o.a.) × 29½ × 9 feet (mean), 11½ (max.) draught. Guns : 4—4 inch (Mk. V. Dir. Con.), 1—3 inch AA. Torpedo tubes : 4—21 inch in pairs. Machinery : " All-Geared " turbines : Brown-Curtis in all, except Doxford and Swan Hunter boats with Parsons. 2 screws. Designed S.H.P. 27,000 = 34 kts. Boilers : Yarrow in all, except White boats with White-Forster. Oil : about 370/320 tons. Complement, 110. Trials : Viracious 33·01, Vivien 36.79.

General Notes.—All Emergency War Programme. These boats are of remarkable size and power for Destroyers ; in fact, five of them, with slight modifications, have been converted to Flotilla Leaders.

To distinguish.—From " W " type, *no triple tubes* ; mainmast *short*. From " V Leaders," foremast shorter, forebridges different, no extension to S.L. platform for standard compass, mainmast *away* from after superstructure, fewer boats.

	Begun.	Launch.	Comp.		Begun.	Launch.	Comp.
Vancouver	15/3/17	28/12/17	10/3/18	Vendetta	....	3/9/17	17/10/17
Vanessa	16/5/17	16/3/18	27/4/18	Venetia	....	29/10/17	19/12/17
Vanity	28/7/18	3/5/18	21/6/18	Verdun	13/1/17	21/8/17	3/11/17
Vanoc	20/9/16	14/6/17	8/17	Versatile	31/1/17	31/10/17	11/2/18
Vanquisher	27/9/16	18/8/17	9/17	Vesper	27/12/16	15/12/17	20/2/18
Venturous	9/10/16	21/9/17	29/11/17	Vidette	1/2/17	28/2/18	27/4/18
Vega	....	1/9/17	12/17	Voyager	17/5/17	24/6/18	24/6/18
Velox	....	17/11/17	1/4/18	Violent	11/16	1/9/17	11/17
				Vimiera	10/16	22/6/17	9/17
				Vectis	7/12/17	4/9/17	5/12/17
				Vortigern	17/1/16	15/10/17	25/1/18
				Vivacious	7/16	3/11/17	12/17
				Vivien	7/16	16/2/18	28/5/18

War Losses.—Vehement (Denny) 2 August 1918, *Verulam* (Hawthorn Leslie) and *Vittoria* (Swan Hunter) lost 1919 in Baltic operations.

BRITISH NAVY—DESTROYERS.

4 Yarrow "Later M."

As illustration of *Mounsey* on page 72 but with sloping stern.

4 Yarrow : **Sabrina, Sybille, Truculent, Tyrant.** Displacements : 897-923 tons. Dimensions : 269½ (p.p.), 271½ (o.a.) × 25¾ × 8½ feet (mean), 10½ (max.) draught. Guns : 3—4 inch, 1—2 pdr. pom-pom, 1 M.G. Torpedo tubes : 4—21 inch in pairs. Machinery : Brown-Curtis turbines. 2 screws. Designed S.H.P. 23,000 = 36 kts. Boilers : 3 Yarrow. Oil fuel : 256-213/215-200 tons. Complement, 82.

General Notes.—All Emergency War Programme. Generally same as the first group of " Yarrow M's " (*Miranda, Mounsey, Nerissa, Rival,* &c.), but the above boats have the Yarrow form of strongly sloping stern. Note that these have *no geared turbines*, nor is the after 4 inch in a bandstand. Accordingly, there is *no* ,Yarrow " R " design.

War Losses.—*Strongbow* 17 Oct. 1917, *Surprise* 22 Dec. 1917, *Ulleswater* 15 Aug. 1918 (all Yarrow).

	Begun.	Launch.	Comp.	Trials.		Begun.	Launch.	Comp.	Trials.
Sabrina	8/15	24.7.16	9/16	36.96	Truculent	3/16	24/3/17	5/17	38.27
Sybille	8/15	5.2.17	2/17	39.11	Tyrant	3/16	19.5/17	7/17	37.37

5 "Thornycroft R."

TAURUS.   *Photo, Messrs. Thornycroft (Builders).*

5 Thornycroft : **Radiant, Retriever, Rosalind.** 1034-7 tons. Dimensions : 274 (o.a.) × 27½ × 11 feet (max.) draught. Also **Taurus, Teaser.** 1064 tons. Dimensions : 274½ (o.a.) × 27 × 11 feet (max.) draught. Following details for all six boats : Length (p.p.), 265 feet. Mean draught, 8½ feet. Guns : 3—4 inch, 1—2 pdr. pom-pom, 1 M.G. Tubes : 4—21 inch in pairs. Machinery : Brown-Curtis (all-geared) turbines. 2 screws. Designed S.H.P. 29,000 = 35 kts. Boilers : 3 Yarrow. Oil fuel : about 285/220 tons. Complement, 82.

General Notes.—All War Emergency Programme. Are separated from the " Thornycroft M's " in the same way as the " Admiralty R's " are divided from the " Admiralty M's," viz., by after 4 inch guns being in bandstand and machinery being " all-geared " turbines. No War Losses.

	Begun.	Launch.	Comp.	Trials.		Begun.	Launch.	Comp.	Trials.
Radiant	12/15	5/11/16	2/17	39.67	Taurus	3/16	10/3/17	5/17	39.27
Retriever	1/16	15/1/17	3/17	36.8	Teazer	3/16	21/4/17	7/17	40.22
Rosalind	10/15	14/10/16	12/16	37.09					

BRITISH NAVY—DESTROYERS.

10 "Admiralty Modified R."

1 *Beardmore :* **Ulster.** 1086 tons. Brown-Curtis A.G. turbines.
1 *Doxford :* **Umpire.** 1091 tons. Brown-Curtis A.G. turbines.
1 *Fairfield :* **Undine.** 1090 tons. Brown-Curtis A.G. turbines.
2 *Palmer :* **Urchin, Ursa.** 1085 tons. Parsons A.G. turbines.
2 *Scott :* **Tirade, Ursula.** 1076 tons. Brown-Curtis A.G. turbines.
1 *Swan Hunter :* **Tower.** 1087 tons. Brown-Curtis A.G. turbines.
2 *White :* **Trenchant, Tristrum.** 1085 tons. Brown-Curtis A.G. turbines.

TOWER. *Photo by courtesy of Messrs. Swan Hunter (Builders).*

Dimensions : 265 (*p.p.*). 275½-276 (*o.a.*) × about 26⅜ × 10½ feet (*mean*), 11¾ (*max.*) draught. Guns : 3—4 inch (Mk. IV with 30° elevation in *Ulster* and *Ursa*), 1—2 pdr. pom-pom. Tubes : 4—21 inch in pairs. Machinery : "All-Geared " (A.G.) turbines as noted above. 2 screws. Designed S.H.P. 27,000 = 36 kts. Boilers : 3 Yarrow in all except *Trenchant* and *Tristram* by White with 3 White-Forster. Oil : *about* 300/250 tons. Complement. 82.

General Notes.—All Emergency War Programme. These boats are said to be an attempt by the Admiralty to combine the " Admiralty R" design with that of the Yarrow " Later M's." They are said to be not quite so satisfactory as the Admiralty M's and R's, but good sea-boats.

To distinguish.—Very long and high fo'xle, which is *not* sheered or turtle-backed as in " S " boats. Charthouse built on fo'xle. Fore funnel *very close* to foremast. Funnels nearly equal in size with boats in davits abeam of after funnel. Quarter-deck abaft of mainmast is shorter than in " Yarrow M " boats, and has 4 inch in bandstand.

War Losses.—Ulysses (Doxford) 29 Oct 1918.

	Begun.	Launch.	Comp.			Begun.	Launch.	Comp.
Ulster	19/9/16	10/10/17	21/11/17	Tirade		....	21/4/17	6/17
Umpire	....	9/6/17	8/17	Ursula		....	8/17	9/17
Undine	....	22/3/17	26/5/17	Tower		9/16	5/4/17	8/17
Urchin	....	7/6/17	8/17	Trenchant		17/7/16	23/12/16	30/4/17
Ursa	....	23/7/17	10/17	Tristram		23/9/16	24/2/17	30/6/17

URCHIN. Some boats have platform on after pair of tubes, as above. *Photo, Topical.*

BRITISH NAVY—DESTROYERS.

34 "Admiralty R."

THISBE. *Photo by courtesy of Messrs. Hawthorn Leslie (Builders).*

3 *Beardmore :* **Satyr, Sharpshooter,** Parsons A.G. turbines, **Tancred,** Brown-Curtis A.G. turbines.
7 *Clydebank :* **Restless, Rigorous, Romola, Rowena, Skate Tarpon,* Telemachus.***
3 *Denny :* **Rob Roy, Rocket, Redgauntlet.**
1 *Doxford :* **Redoubt.**
1 *Fairfield :* **Tempest.**
6 *Harland & Wolff (Goran) :* **Salmon, Skilful, Springbok, Sylph, Tenacious, Tetrarch.**
5 *Hawthorn Leslie :* **Sarpedon, Stork, Starfish, Thisbe, Thruster.**
3 *Stephen :* **Sceptre, Sturgeon, Tormentor.**
4 *Swan Hunter :* **Radstock, Raider, Sorceress, Torrid.**
1 *White :* **Sable.**

*Tarpon, Telemachus, Minelayers.

TELEMACHUS as Minelayer. After-pair of tubes and 4 inch gun are dummies painted on screens. *Photo, Lt. C. de Brock, R.N.*

Displacements vary from 1096 to 1036 tons (1065 *average*). Length, (*p.p.*) 265 feet (*o.a.* varies from 274 to 276 feet). Beam, 26⅜ feet. *Mean* draught, 9 feet. *Max.* draughts, 11½ to 12 feet. Guns : 3—4 inch, 1—2 pdr. pom-pom (1 M.G., but not in all). Torpedo tubes : 4—21 inch in pairs. Machinery : Turbines—"all-geared " types. Clydebank, Denny, Fairfield, Harland & Wolff, Stephen, Swan Hunter and White boats, Brown-Curtis A.G. turbines ; Doxford and Hawthorn Leslie boats, Parsons A.G. turbines. Beardmore boats as separately noted. Designed S.H.P. 27,000 = 36 kts. 2 screws in all. Boilers : 3 Yarrow or Modified Yarrow, except *Sable* by White, with White-Forster boilers. Oil fuel : 295-285/250-243 tons. Complement, 82.

		Begun.	Launch.	Comp.			Begun.	Launch.	Comp.
3 B'd'more,	Satyr	15/4/16	27/12/16	2/2/17	6 H. & W.	Salmon	27/8/15	7/10/16	20/12/16
	Sharpshooter	23/5/16	27/2/17	2/4/17		Skilful	20/1/16	3/2/17	26/3/17
	Tancred	6/7/16	30/6/17	1/9/17		Springbok	27/1/16	9/3/17	30/4/17
	Restless	22/9/15	12/8/16	10/16		Sylph	30/8/16	15/11/16	10/2/17
7 Clydebank	Rigorous	22/9/15	30/9/16	11/16		Tenacious	25/7/16	21/5/17	12/8/17
	Romola	25/8/15	14/5/16	8/16		Tetrarch	26/7/16	20/4/17	2/6/17
	Rowena	25/8/15	1/7/16	3/16	6 H.L.	Sarpedon	27/9/15	1/6/16	2/9/16
	Skate	12/1/16	11/1/17	2/17		Stork	10/4/16	25/11/16	1/2/17
	Tarpon	12/4/16	10/3/17	4/17		Starfish	26/1/16	27/9/16	16/12/16
	Telemachus	12/4/16	21/1/17	6/17		Thisbe	13/6/16	8/3/17	6/6/17
3 D'y	Rob Roy	15/10/15	29/8/16	15/12/16		Thruster	2/6/16	10/1/17	3/3/17
	Rocket	28/9/15	2/7/16	7/10/16	3 Stn.	Sceptre	10/11/15	18/4/17	26/5/17
	Redgauntlet	30/9/15	23/11/16	7/2/17		Sturgeon	10/11/15	11/1/17	26/2/17
(Doxf'd) Redoubt		....	28/10/16	3/17		Tormentor	1/5/16	22/5/17	22/8/17
(F'field) Tempest		....	26/1/17	20/3/17	4 S.H.	Radstock	9/15	3/6/16	9/16
						Raider	9/15	17/7/16	10/16
						Sorceress	11/15	29/8/16	12/16
						Torrid	7/16	10/2/17	5/17
					(White)				
						Sable	20/12/15	18/6/16	30/11/16

STARFISH. *Note.—Satyr, Skate, Sharpshooter, Starfish, Stork* only, have mainmast as above illustration.

General Notes.—All Emergency War Programme boats. General design is as the " Admiralty M's " but these boats have geared turbines and 2 screws, and are rather faster than the " Admiralty M's."

To distinguish.—Note that the after 4 inch is mounted in a bandstand.

War Losses.—Simoon (Clydebank) 23 Jan 1917, *Recruit* (Doxford) 9 Aug 1917, *Tornado* (Stephen) 22 Dec 1917, *Torrent* (Swan Hunter) 22 Dec 1917, *Setter* (White) 17 may 1917.

BRITISH NAVY—DESTROYERS.

74 "Admiralty M."

(23 "Repeat M" + 45 "M" + 6 "Pre-War M.")

PYLADES ("Repeat M").

2 *Beardmore:* * **Pelican, Pellew.** (Repeat M.)

10 *Clydebank:* **Napier, Penn, Peregrine.** (Repeat M.) **Ossory, Mameluke, Marne, Mons**—also **Milne, Morris, Moorsom.** (Pre-War.)

7 *Denny:* **Petard, Peyton.** (Repeat M.) **Maenad, Marvel, Mystic, Narwhal, Nicator.**

9 *Doxford:* **Norseman, Oberon.** (Repeat M.) **Octavia, Ophelia, Opportune, Oracle, Orestes, Orford, Orpheus.**

11 *Fairfield:* **Observer. Offa, Phœbe.** (Repeat M.) **Mandate, Manners, Mindful, Mischief, Onslaught, Onslow, Orcadia, Oriana.**

3 *Hawthorn Leslie:* **Pigeon, Plover.** (Repeat M.)

8 *Palmer:* **Oriole, Osiris.** (Repeat M.) **Nonsuch, Norman, Northesk, Nugent**—also **Murray, Myngs.** (Pre-War).

6 *Scott:* **Plucky, Portia.** (Repeat M.) **Obdurate, Obedient, Paladin, Parthian.**

5 *Stephen:* **Prince, Pylades.*** (Repeat M.) **Nizam,* Noble** (ex *Nisus*), **Nonpariel.**

4 *Swan Hunter:* **Pasley.** (Repeat M.) Brown-Curtis turbines. **Martial,** Parsons turbines, **Menace,** Brown-Curtis turbines—also **Matchless.** (Pre-War) Parsons turbines.

6 *Thornycroft:* **Michael, Milbrook, Minion, Munster, Nepean, Nereus.**

4 *White:* **Medina** (ex-*Redmill*). **Medway** (ex*Redwing*), (both Repeat M). **Magic, Moresby.**

**Nizam* and *Pylades* were launched by Messrs. Stephen and completed by Messrs. Beardmore.

Displacements vary from 994 to 1042 tons (1025 *average*). Length: 265 feet (*p.p.*) (*o.a.* varies from $271\frac{1}{2}$ to $276\frac{1}{4}$ feet). Beam: $26\frac{2}{3}$ to $26\frac{3}{4}$ feet. *Mean* draught: $8\frac{2}{3}$ feet. *Max.* draught: *about* $10\frac{1}{4}$ feet. Guns: 3—4 inch, 1—2 pdr. pom-pom., 1 M.G. Tubes: 4—21 inch in pairs. Machinery: Clydebank, Fairfield and Stephen boats, Brown-Curtis turbines; Beardmore, Denny, Doxford, Hawthorn Leslie, Palmer, Scott, Thornycroft, White boats, all Parsons turbines; Swan Hunter boats as specially noted above. Designed S.H.P. 25,000 = 34 kts. 3 screws in all. Boilers: 3 Yarrow in all, except White boats with White-Forster. Oil fuel: 298-237/243-202 tons. Complement, 80.

General Notes.—Boats with "N," "O" and "P" names, all Emergency War Programme: the War boats with "M" names, Emergency War Programme, but part of their cost was met by the provision in 1914-15 Navy Estimates for ten destroyers. The Pre-War M's, 1913-14 Programme. Proved a remarkably successful type of Destroyer, although not so fast as the Thornycroft and Yarrow "M's."

To distinguish.—Easily distinguished by their three, small round funnels, with 4 inch mounted between second and third funnels. Can be separated from the Admiralty R's by the after 4 inch *not* being mounted in "bandstand." The Repeat M's have *raking* stems; the Pre-War M's have rather shorter funnels.

War Losses.—Repeat M's: *Pheasant* (Fairfield), *Partridge* (Swan Hunter). War M's: *Narborough* (Clydebank), *Opal* (Doxford), *Mary Rose, Negro, North Star* (all Palmer), *Nomad* (Stephen). *Marmion, Nessus, Nestor* (all Swan Hunter). Pre-War M's: No losses.

		Begun.	Launch.	Comp.
2 B'dmore.	*Pelican*	25/6/15	18/3/16	1/5/16
	Pellew	28/6/15	18/5/16	30/6/16
10 Clydebank.	*Napier*	24/3/15	27/11/16	1/16
	Penn	9/6/15	8/4/16	5/16
	Peregine	9/6/15	29/5/16	7/16
	Ossory	23/12/14	9/10/16	11/15
	Mameluke	23/12/14	14/8/15	10/15
	Marne	30/9/14	29/5/15	8/15
	Mons	30/9/14	1/5/15	7/15
	Milne	1914	5/10/14	12/14
	Morris	1914	19/11/14	12/14
	Moorsom	1914	21/12/14	2/15
7 Denny.	*Petard*	5/7/15	24/3/16	23/5/16
	Peyton	12/7/15	2/5/16	29/6/16
	Maenad	10/11/14	10/8/15	12/11/15
	Marvel	11/1/15	7/10/15	28/12/15
	Mystic	27/10/14	26/6/16	11/11/15
	Narwhal	21/4/15	3/12/15	3/3/16
	Nicator	21/4/15	3/2/16	15/4/16
9 Doxford.	*Norseman*	....	15/8/16	11/16
	Oberon	....	29/9/16	12/16
	Octavia	....	21/6/16	11/16
	Ophelia	....	13/10/15	5/16
	Opportune	....	20/11/16	6/16
	Oracle	....	23/12/15	8/16
	Orestes	....	21/3/16	6/16
	Orford	....	19/4/16	12/16
	Orpheus	....	17/6/16	9/16
11 Fairfield.	*Observer*	....	1/5/16	15/6/16
	Offa	....	7/6/16	31/7/16
	Phoebe	....	20/11/16	28/12/16
	Mandate	....	27/4/15	13/8/15
	Manners	....	15/6/15	21/9/15
	Mindful	....	24/8/15	10/11/15
	Mischief	....	12/10/15	16/12/15
	Onslaught	....	4/12/15	3/3/16
	Onslow	....	15/2/16	15/4/16
	Orcadia	....	26/7/16	29/9/16
	Oriana	....	23/9/16	4/11/16

		Begun.	Launch.	Comp.
2 H. Leslie	*Pigeon*	14/7/15	3/3/16	2/6/16
	Plover	30/7/15	3/3/16	30/6/16
8 Palmer.	*Oriole*	....	31/7/16	11/16
	Osiris	....	26/9/16	12/16
	Nonsuch	....	8/12/15	2/16
	Norman	....	20/3/16	8/16
	Northesk	....	5/7/16	10/16
	Nugent	....	23/1/17	4/17
	Murray	....	6/8/14	12/14
	Myngs	....	24/9/14	2/15
6 Scott.	*Plucky*	....	21/4/16	7/16
	Portia	....	10/8/16	10/16
	Obdurate	....	21/1/16	3/16
	Obedient	....	16/11/16	2/16
	Paladin	....	27/3/16	5/16
	Parthian	....	3/7/16	9/16
5 Stephen.	*Prince*	27/7/15	26/7/16	21/9/16
	*Pylades**	27/7/15	28/9/16	30/12/16*
	*Nizam**	11/2/15	6/4/16	29/6/16*
	Noble	6/2/15	25/11/15	15/2/16
	Nonpareil	24/2/15	16/5/16	28/6/15

*Completed by Messrs. Beardmore.

		Begun.	Launch.	Comp.
4 Swan Hunter.	*Pasley*	7/15	15/4/16	7/16
	Martial	10/14	1/7/15	10/15
	Menace	9/14	9/11/15	4/16
	Matchless	11/13	5/10/14	12/14
6 Thornycroft.	*Michael*	10/14	19/5/15	8/15
	Milbrook	11/14	12/7/15	10/15
	Minion	11/14	11/9/15	11/15
	Munster	11/14	24/11/15	1/16
	Nepean	2/15	21/1/16	3/16
	Nereus	3/15	24/2/16	5/16
4 White.	*Medina*	22/9/15	8/3/16	30/6/16
	Medway	2/11/15	19/4/16	2/8/16
	Magic	1/1/15	10/9/15	8/1/16
	Moresby	14/1/15	20/11/15	7/4/16

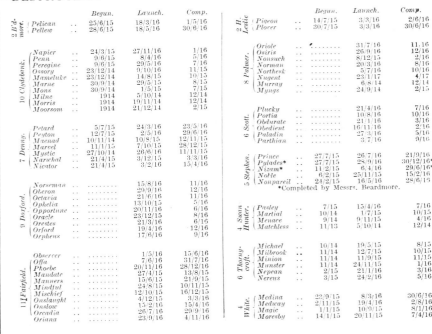

OBDURATE (War M's). *Official R.A.F. Photo.*

BRITISH NAVY—DESTROYERS.

6 "Thornycroft M."

READY. *Photo. Messrs. Thornycroft.*

6 *Thornycroft:* **Rapid, Ready,** 1033 tons. **Patriot, Patrician,** 1004 tons. **Meteor,** 1070 tons. **Mastiff,** 985 tons. Dimensions: 265 (*p.p.*), 271-274 (*o.a.*) × $27\frac{1}{2}$ × $10\frac{1}{2}$-11 feet. Guns: 3—4 inch, 1—2 pdr. pom-pom, 1 M.G. Tubes: 4—21 inch in pairs. Machinery: *Meteor* and *Mastiff*, Parsons turbines, 26,500 S.H.P. = 35 kts.; other Brown-Curtis turbines, 27,500 S.H.P. = 35 kts. 3 Yarrow boilers. Oil: *about* 285-250/220-200 tons. Complement, 82.

Note.—Meteor and *Mastiff* 1913-14 Programme; rest Emergency War Programme. Proved very successful boats.

6 THORNYCROFT.

	Begun.	Launch.	Comp.	Trials.
Rapid	8/15	7/16	8/16	35.45
Ready	9/15	8/16	10/16	34.36
Patriot	7/15	4/16	6/16	37.34
Patrician	6/15	6/16	7/16	35.6
Meteor	5/13	7/14	9/14	34.85
Mastiff	7/13	10/14	11/14	37.52

10 YARROW.

	Begun.	Launch.	Comp.	Trials.
Relentless	....	4/16	5/16	37.69
Rival	5/15	6/16	9/16	36.83
Nerissa	11/14	2/16	3/16	36.74
Moon	9/14	4/15	6/15	37.86
Morning Star	9/14	6/15	8/15	36.92
Mounsey	9/14	9/15	11/15	39.02
Musketeer	9/14	11/15	12/15	35.6
Miranda	10/12	5/14	8/14	33.53
Minos	10/12	8/14	10/14	36.73
Manley	10/12	10/14	11/14	33.88

10 "Yarrow M."

MOUNSEY. *Photo, Messrs. Yarrow, Ltd.*

10 *Yarrow:* **Relentless, Rival, Nerissa, Moon, Morning Star, Mounsey, Musketeer, Miranda, Minos, Manley.** Displace 879-898 tons. Dimensions: $260\frac{1}{4}$ (*p.p.*), $269\frac{1}{2}$-$271\frac{1}{2}$ (*o.a.*) × $25\frac{2}{3}$ - 27 × $10\frac{1}{3}$ feet. Guns: 3—4 inch, 1—2 pdr. pom-pom. Torpedo tubes: 4—21 inch in pairs. Brown-Curtis turbines. 3 Yarrow boilers. Designed S.H.P. 23,000 = 35-36 kts. Oil fuel: 228/202 tons. Complement, 79.

Notes.—Miranda, Minos, Manley, 1913-14 Programme; *Morning Star, Mounsey, Musketeer,* part Emergency War Programme, plus sum voted for ten boats in 1914-15 Estimates; *Relentless, Rival, Nerissa,* Emergency War Programme. Very successful boats. Design by Messrs. Yarrow, Ltd. These boats have *straight* sterns.

2 "Hawthorn M."

MANSFIELD. *Photo, Sub-Lt. H. Lawrence, R.N.R.*

2 *Hawthorn:* **Mansfield, Mentor.** Launched 1914. 1057 and 1053 tons. Dimensions: 265 (*p.p.*), 271 (*o.a.*) × 27 × $10\frac{3}{4}$ feet. Guns: 3—4 inch, 1—2 pdr. AA., 1 M.G. Tubes: 4—21 inch in pairs. Parsons turbines. 3 screws. Yarrow boilers. Designed S.H.P. 27 000 = 35 kts. Oil: 290/220 tons. Complement, 76.

Notes.—1913-14 Programme boats.

BRITISH NAVY—DESTROYERS

3 ex-Turkish.

TRIDENT.   *Photo by courtesy of Messrs. H. Leslie.*

3 *Hawthorn Leslie:* **Talisman, Termagant, Trident.** 1098 tons. Complement, 102. Dimensions : 309 ft. × 28 ft. 7 in. × 9 ft. 6 in. Guns : 5—4 inch. Torpedo tubes : 4—21 inch in pairs (very light type). Carry D.C. Machinery : Parsons turbines and Yarrow boilers. 3 screws. Designed H.P. 25,000 = 32 kts. Fuel : 237 tons oil. *Turbulent* lost during War. All begun for Turkish Navy, but taken over by Admiralty. Proved so successful, their design formed basis for the later Admiralty V's and W's.

	Begun.	Launch.	Comp.		Begun.	Launch.	Comp.
Talisman	7/12/14	15/7/15	19/1/16	Trident	7/1/15	20/11/15	24/3/16
Termagant ..	17/12/14	26/8/15	18/3/16				

3 ex-Greek.

MEDEA.

1 *Clydebank:* **Medea** (ex *Kriti*). 1007 tons.
2 *Fairfield:* **Melpomene** (ex *Samos*), **Melampus** (ex *Chios*). 1040 tons. Complement, 80.
Dimensions: 273½ × 26½ × 10½ feet. Guns : 3—4 inch, 1—2 pdr. pom-pom, 1 M.G. Torpedo tubes : 4—21 inch in twin deck mountings. Also usual D.C. Machinery : Brown-Curtis turbines and Yarrow boilers. 3 screws. Designed H.P. 25,000 = 32 kts. Fuel : 276/225 tons.
Notes.—Ordered for Greek Navy, and taken over for British Navy, 1914. *Medusa* (ex Greek *Lesvos*), built by Clydebank, lost 25 March 1916.

	Begun.	Launch.	Comp.		Begun.	Launch.	Comp.
Medea	8/4/14	30/1/15	5/15	Melampus ..	....	16/12/14	29/6/15
Melpomene ..	....	1/2/15	16/8/15				

17 L Class (16 Pre-War + 1 War).

LEGION, as Minelayer. After 4 inch and tubes are dummies painted on screens.

(ALL 3 FUNNELS.)

1 *Beardmore:* **Lochinvar** (Oct., 1915). 1010 tons. Brown-Curtis turbines.
2 *Beardmore:* **Llewellyn** (1913), **Lennox** (1914). 996 tons. Parsons turbines.
2 *Fairfield:* **Lawford** (1913). **Lydiard** (1914). 1003 tons. *Trials : Lydiard* 29·9 kts.
2 *Parsons* (*Hawthorn*): **Leonidas** (1913), **Lucifer** (1913). 987 tons.
2 *Swan, Hunter & W. Richardson:* **Laertes** (1913). 982 tons. **Lysander** (1913). 976 tons. *Trials : Laertes* 31·2, *Lysander* 29·9.
2 *Thornycroft:* **Lance** (1914). 997 tons. **Lookout** (1914). 1002 tons.
2 *Denny:* **Loyal** (1913). 995 tons, **Legion** (1914), 1072 tons.
War Losses in above: *Laforey, Louis, Lassoo.*

LAUREL.   (ALL 2 FUNNELS.)   *Photo, Symonds.*

2 *White:* **Laurel** (1913), **Liberty** (1913). 965-975 tons.
4 *Yarrow:* **Lark** (1913), 968 tons. **Landrail** (1914), 983 tons. **Laverock** (1914). 994 tons. **Linnet** (1913), 970 tons. All Brown-Curtis turbines.
All to Admiralty design. Armament : 3—4 inch, 1—2 pdr. pom-pom, 1 M.G. 4—21 inch tubes in pairs. Machinery : Parsons turbines in all, except where otherwise noted. Designed H.P. 24,500 = 29 kts. ; *Leonidas* and *Lucifer* only, 22,500 = 29 kts. Dimensions : 269 × 27½ × 10½ feet. Fuel : 290-270,230-200 tons oil. Complement, 77.
Lochinvar (and lost *Lassoo*), Emergency War Programme ; rest 1912-13 Programme.

1911 BRITISH DESTROYERS. 1911

13 K Class.

" K CLASS" SPECIAL BOATS. Amidships 4 inch *abaft* funnel and *before* after tube. After S.L. or A.A. gun platform *before* mainmast. *Garland* has cut-away stern.

" K CLASS" ADMIRALTY BOATS. S.L. or A.A. gun platform *abaft* 3rd funnel, amidships 4 inch *between* after tubes and mainmast. Forefunnel close to foremast.

Special Boats.

3 *Thornycroft:* **Porpoise,** 934 tons, **Unity, Victor,** 954 tons (1913). Designed H.P. 22,500 = 31 kts. All made about 30.3 on trials.
1 *Thornycroft:* **Hardy** (1912). 898 tons. H.P. 21,000 = 32 kts.
1 *Parsons* (hull sub-contracted to Cammell Laird): **Garland** (1913). 984 tons. Dimensions as Admiralty boats. Designed H.P. 24,500 = 30 kts. *Trials,* 31 kts.
Notes to above.—Dimensions (except *Garland*) : 265½ × 26½ × 9¼-10¼ feet. All Parsons turbines, 2 screws. Yarrow boilers. Oil : 250-260/200-220 tons. *Hardy* said to have Diesel engine for cruising speeds ; she was so designed, but it is uncertain if this Diesel engine was ever installed or not.
War Losses.—*Paragon, Fortune.*

Admiralty Design Boats.

3 *Clydebank:* **Acasta,** 996 tons, **Achates,** 982 tons (1912), **Ambuscade,** 935 tons (1913). *Trials : Acasta* 29 kts. *Achates* 32·3 kts. *Ambuscade* 30·4 kts. *Acasta* practically destroyed at Jutland and rebuilt. Brown-Curtis turbines in these boats.
2 *Hawthorn Leslie:* **Christopher,** 938 tons, **Cockatrice,** 951 tons (1912). *Trials : Christopher* 30.9 kts. *Cockatrice* 29·7 kts.
2 *London and Glasgow:* **Midge, Owl,** 936 tons. (1913). *Trials : Midge* 32·9 kts, *Owl* 32·7 kts.
1 *Swan Hunter:* **Spitfire** (1913). 935 tons. *Trials :* 30·3 kts.
Notes to above boats.—Dimensions : 267½ × 27 × 10½ feet. Designed H.P. 24,500 = 29 kts. All Parsons turbines, except Clydebank boats. 2 screws. Yarrow boilers. Oil : 260/200 tons.
War Losses.—*Ardent, Contest, Lynx, Sparrowhead, Shark.*
General Notes.—All 1911-12 Programme. Guns : 3—4 inch (1—4 inch on A.A. mounting in some boats), 1—2 pdr. pom-pom in nearly all, 1 M.G. Tubes : 2—21 inch single. The single tube between 2nd and 3rd funnels is a distinctive feature of this class. Complement, 75-77.

23 I Class (3 this page, 18 next page).

OAK. (LURCHER and FIREDRAKE high mainmasts.)

Special Boats.

3 *Yarrow:* **Lurcher, Firedrake, Oak** (all 1912). 765 tons. *Firedrake* 767 tons. Dimensions : 262 × 25¾ × 9½ feet. Guns : 2—4 inch, 2—12 pdr., 1—3 pdr. A.A., 1 M.G. Tubes : 2—21 inch. Designed H.P. 20,000 = 32 kts. On trials *Firedrake* made 33·1, *Lurcher* 35·34 mean of 8 hrs. *Oak* : 32·4. Turbines : Parsons, 2 screws. Boilers : special Yarrow oil burning ; oil, *about* 170/155 tons. Built to replace three boats of this class, transferred to Royal Australian Navy, and now H.M.A.S. *Parramatta, Yarra* and *Warrego.* Complement, 70.

(" I " Class continued on next page.)

1911 BRITISH NAVY—DESTROYERS. 1910

23 I Class (18 this page, 3 preceding page).

General Notes to all below.

Built under 1910-11 Programme. Armament of all: 2—4 inch, 2—12 pdr., 1—3 pdr. AA., 1 M G., 2—21 inch tubes. Complement, 70.

JACKAL. *Photo, Ellis, Malta.*

To Builders' Designs.

2 *Parsons:* **Badger** (1911), 799 tons, **Beaver** (1911), 810 tons. Designed H.P. 16,500 = 30 kts. Hull, etc., contracted for by Hawthorn. *Trials: Badger* 30.7. Parsons turbines.

1 *Thornycroft:* **Acheron** (1911) 773 tons. Designed H.P. 15,500 = 29 kts. On trial, 29.4. Parsons turbines.

1 *Yarrow:* **Archer** (1911). 775 tons. Designed H.P. 16,000 = 28 kts. Brown-Curtis turbines. *Trials: Archer* 30.9.

Notes.—Dimensions: *Acheron*, 252¼ × 26⅓ × 9¼ feet; others about 246 × 25¼ × 9⅓ feet. 2 screws in all. Oil fuel: 182-170/158-150 tons. All Yarrow boilers.

War Losses.—Ariel (Minelayer), *Attack*

Admiralty Design Boats.

1 *Beardmore:* **Goshawk** (1911). 760 tons. Parsons turbines.

3 *Clydebank:* **Hind, Hornet** 1911), **Hydra** (1912). 770-5 tons. *Trials: Hind* 28.1, *Hornet* 28.7, *Hydra* 28.1. Brown-Curtis turbines.

2 *Denny:* **Defender, Druid** (1911). 762-770 tons. *Trials: Defender* 28.3, *Druid* 28.2. Parsons turbines.

2 *Hawthorn:* **Jackal, Tigress** (1911). 745 tons. *Trials: Jackal* 26.9, *Tigress* 28.1. Parsons turbines.

2 *Laird:* **Lapwing, Lizard** (1911). 745 tons. *Trials: Lapwing* 27.2 *Lizard* 27.5. Parsons turbines.

1 *Swan Hunter:* **Sandfly** (1911). 750 tons. *Trials:* 27.7. Parsons turbines.

2 *White:* **Ferret, Forester** (1911). 750 and 760 tons. *Trials: Ferret* 30.2, *Forester* 29.8. Parsons turbines.

Notes.—Dimensions: 246¼ × 25⅝ × 8¾-9 feet. All 3 screws, except the Clydebank boats with Brown-Curtis turbines, which have 2 screws. All Yarrow boilers, except White boats with White-Forster. Oil: *about* 180/148 tons.

War Losses: Phœnix.

20 H Class.

SHELDRAKE.

3 *Clydebank:* **Acorn, Alarm, Brisk** (1910). 760-780 tons. *Acorn* and *Alarm*, Parsons turbines; *Brisk*, Curtis turbines. *Trials: Acorn* 27.2, *Alarm* 27.2, *Brisk* 27.6.

1 *Denny:* **Sheldrake** (1911). 748 tons. Parsons turbines. *Trials: Sheldrake* 28.3.

1 *Fairfield:* **Cameleon** (1910). 747 tons. Parsons turbines. *Trials: Cameleon* 28.03.

3 *Hawthorn:* **Nemesis,* Nereide** (1910), **Nymphe** (1911). All 740 tons. Parsons turbines. *Trials: Nemesis* 27, *Nereide* 27 8, *Nymphe* 27.5.

1 *Inglis:* **Fury** (1911). 760 tons. Parsons turbines. *Trials:* 27.3.

1 *Swan Hunter:* **Hope** (1910). 745 tons. Parsons turbine. *Trials:* 27.1.

4 *Thornycroft:* **Larne, Lyra, Martin** (all 1910), **Minstrel*** (1911). All 730 tons. Parsons turbine. *Trials: Larne* 27.9, *Lyra* 28.7, *Martin* 28.9, *Minstrel* 28.9.

3 *White:* **Redpole, Rifleman, Ruby** (1910). All 720 tons. Parsons turbine. White-Forster boilers. *Trials: Redpole* 29.8, *Rifleman* 28.6, *Ruby* 29.3.

**Minstrel* and *Nemesis* loaned to Japanese Navy, 1917-18, and commissioned as Japanese *Sendan* (*Minstrel*) and *Kanran* (*Nemesis*). Returned to British Navy, 1919.

Notes.—Formerly *Acorn* class. Belong to 1909-10 Programme, laid down end of 1909. About 800 tons. Dimensions: *about* 246½ x 24⅓ x 8⅔ feet. Armament: 2—4 inch, 2—12 pdr., 1—3 pdr. A.A.*. 1 M.G., 2—21 inch tubes. Designed H.P. 13,500 = 27 kts. 3 screws. Yarrow boilers in all, except *Redpole, Rifleman* and *Ruby,* with White-Forster. Fuel: *about* 170/140 tons oil. Complement, 72.

*In a few boats only.

To distinguish.—High bridges, thick middle funnel, no gun or tubes between 2nd and 3rd funnels. 12 pdrs. at break of fo'xle. Big ventilators between funnels.

War Losses.— Comet, Goldfinch, Staunch.

BRITISH NAVY—DESTROYERS AND P. C. BOATS.

16 G Class.

SCOURGE. *Photo, Lieut.-Com. Holberton, R.N.*

3 *Clydebank:* **Beagle, Bulldog, Foxhound** (1909). 950, 952, 995 tons. Parsons turbine. H.P. 12,500.

3 *Fairfield:* **Grasshopper** (1909), **Mosquito** (1910), **Scorpion** (1910). 923, 983, 987 tons. Parsons turbines. H.P. 12,000.

1 *Hawthorn:* **Scourge** (1910). 922 tons. Parsons turbine. H.P. 12,500.

1 *Cammell Laird:* **Renard** (1909). 918 tons. Parsons turbine. H.P. 12,500.

1 *London & Glasgow:* **Rattlesnake** (1910). 946 tons. Parsons turbine. H.P. 12,000.

1 *Thames Ironworks:* **Grampus** (ex *Nautilus*), (1910). 975 tons. Parsons turbine. H.P. 12,000.

1 *Thornycroft:* **Savage** (1910). 897 tons. Parsons turbine. H.P. 12,500.

2 *White:* **Basilisk** (1910). **Harpy** (1909). 972, 976 tons. Parsons turbine. White-Forster boilers. H.P. 12,600.

General Notes.—These boats belong to the 1909-18 Programme, and were formerly known as the *Basilisk* class, or "The Mediterranean *Beagles.*" *Displace 860 to 995 tons. Dimensions: average* 274⅛ x 28 x 10 feet. Armament: 1—4 inch, 3—12 pdr.,* 1—3 pdr. AA.,† 1 M.G., 2—22 inch tubes. *Average* H.P. 12,500 = 27 kts. 3 screws. Boilers: Yarrow in all, except *Basilisk* and *Harpy,* with White-Forster. Coal: 200-241 tons. Complements for all, 96. All made 27 or a little over on *trials,* except *Grampus* 28.1, *Basilisk* 27.9, *Harpy* and *Foxhound* 27.7. Are the only coal-burning Destroyers now in British Navy, and will probably be scrapped within the next two years.

War Losses.—Pincher, Racoon, Wolverine.

**Scorpion* 2—12 pdr.

†3 pdr. AA. not in *Basilisk, Grasshopper, Savage, Scourge.*

19 PC Boats (Converted Patrol Boats).

PC 68. *Photo, Messrs. J. S. White & Sons (Builders).*

Note.—Above illustration is typical only: these vessels have varying mercantile disguises as small coasting steamers, tugs, &c. Some have only one mast forward.

2 *Barclay Curle:* **PC 55, PC 56** (both 1917). 682 tons.

2 *Caird:* **PC 42, PC 43** (both 1917). 682 tons.

1 *Connell:* **PC 63** (1917). 682 tons.

2 *Eltringham:* **PC 44.** (682 tons. **PC 65** (both 1917). 694 tons.

1 *Harland & Wolff (Govan):* **PC 62** (1917). 682 tons.

1 *Harkness:* **PC 66** (1918). 694 tons.

1 *Tyne Iron Co.:* **PC 51** (1917). 682 tons.

6 *White:* **PC 67, PC 68** (both 1917). **PC 71–PC 74** (1918). All 694 tons.

2 *Workman Clark:* **PC 60, PC 61** (both 1917). 682 tons. **PC 69, PC 70** (both 1918). 694 tons.

Dimensions: 682 ton boats: 233 (*p.p.*), 247 (*o.a.*) × 25½ × 8-8½ feet. 694 ton boats: 233 (*p.p.*). 247 (*o.a.*) × 26¾ × 8 feet. 682 and 694 ton boats reported to have shallow bulge protection. Guns: 1—4 inch. 2—12 pdr. Torpedo tubes: removed. Carry 24-30 D.C. Machinery: Parsons or Brown-Curtis turbines. Yarrow boilers. 2 screws. Designed S.H.P. 3,500 = 20 kts. Oil: 134 tons in 682 ton boats; 164 tons in 694 ton boats: all *max.* These two types carry extra fuel in bulges. Complement, *about* 50-55.

General Notes.—All built under Emergency War Programme. Design as P-boats, but these craft were converted or modified while building, to act as Submarine Decoy Vessels or "Q-boats." The after 4 inch gun was hidden behind various forms of dummy deck loads, *e.g.*, bales or packing cases of merchandise, trusses of hay: in a few boats it was located within a collapsible pantechnicon furniture van, or under a dummy boat built in folding sections. It was expected that, on account of shallow draught, torpedoes fired by U-boats would under-run these *PC*-boats, while, if hit by torpedo, bulge protection and special fillings would keep them afloat long enough to destroy the *U*-boat.

1909 BRITISH DESTROYERS **1908** and earlier.

12 F Class.

These boats belong (first five) to the 1907-08 programme, the two next to the 1906-07 programme, the remaining five to the 1905-06 programme. They were formerly known as "Ocean-going Destroyers," also as the "Tribal class."

As no two are alike, details are given separately under each boat.

All destroyers from this class to the "A" class had been deleted by mid-1919.

Photo, Cribb.

1 *White :—***Crusader.** 945 tons. Armament : 2—4 inch (25 pdr.), 2—18 inch tubes. Parsons turbine. White-Foster boilers. Oil fuel. (Fore funnel heightened, 1912).

1 *Denny :—***Maori** (1909). 980 tons. Armament : 2—4 inch (25 pdr.), 2—18 inch tubes. Parsons turbine. Yarrow boilers. (Fore funnel now heightened, 1912).
Mined off Zeebrugge 7 May 1915.

F Class—*(Continued).*

Photo, Oscar Parkes, Esq.

1 *Thornycroft :—***Nubian.** 990 tons. Armament : 2—4 inch (25 pdr.), 2—18 inch tubes. Parsons turbine. Thornycroft boilers. Oil fuel.
Torpedoed off Folkstone 27 October 1916 (see Zula).

1 *Palmer :—***Viking** (1909). 1000 tons. Armament : 2—4 inch (25 pdr.), 2—18 inch tubes. Parsons turbine. Yarrow boilers.

Photo, Oscar Parkes, Esq.

1 *Hawthorn :—***Zulu** (1909). 1000 tons. Armament : 2—4 inch (25 pdr.), 2—18 inch tubes. Parsons turbine. Yarrow boilers. (Fore funnel heightened 1911.)

Mined off Dover 27 October 1916. The undamaged portions of *Zula* and *Nubian* were united to form one destroyer, known as *Zubian.*

BRITISH DESTROYERS.

F Class—*(Continued).* (2 of 1906-07 programme).

1 *Thornycroft :—***Amazon** (1908). 966 tons. Dimensions : 280×26½×8½ feet. H.P. 15,500. Parsons turbine. Thornycroft boilers. Oil : 86 tons *normal* ; *maximum*, 185 tons. Armament, 2—4 inch (25 pdrs.), 2—18 inch tubes.

Photo, Oscar Parkes, Esq.

1 *White :—***Saracen.** 970 tons. Dimensions : 272×26×8½ feet. H.P. 15,500. Parsons turbine. White-Foster boilers. Oil : 84 tons *normal* ; *maximum* 185 tons. Armament, 2—4 inch (25 pdrs.) 2—18 inch tubes. (Fore funnel heightened 1911.)

BRITISH DESTROYERS (ordered 1906). 1907

Parsons turbine, and oil fuel in all. *Maximum* radius, 1500—1700 miles.

Unclassed boat of equal date.

1 Cammell-Laird :— **Swift** (1907). 1825 tons. Dimensions : 345 × 34½ × 10½ feet. Oil : 180 tons. H.P. 30,000 = 36 kts. Yarrow boilers. Armament : 4—4 inch (25 pdr.), 2—18 inch tubes. Cost about £280,500.
(This boat has reached 39 knots).

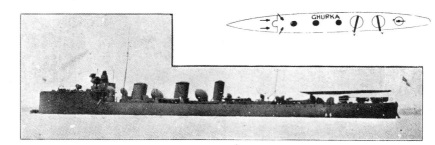

1 Hawthorn :— **Ghurka.** 870 tons. Dimensions : 255 × 25½ × 8 feet. H.P. 14,250. Oil : 95 tons ; *maximum*, 185 tons. Armament : 5—12 pdr., 2—18 inch tubes. Yarrow boilers. Mined off Dungeness 8 February 1917.

F Class—*(Continued)*.

1 Elswick :— **Afridi** (1907). 855 tons. Dimensions : 250 × 25 × 7½ feet. H.P. 14,250 = 32·75. Oil : 92½ tons. Armament : 5—12 pdr., 2—18 inch tubes. Yarrow boilers.

1 White :— **Mohawk** (1907). 865 tons. Dimensions : 270 × 25 × 8 feet. H.P. 14,500. Oil : 95 tons ; *maximum*, 185 tons. Armament : 5—12 pdr., 2—18 inch tubes. White-Foster boilers. *Photo, Symonds.*

1 Cammell-Laird :— **Cossack** (1907). 885 tons. Dimensions : 270 × 26 × 8 feet. H.P. 14,000. Oil : 76 tons ; *maximum* 185 tons. Armament : 5—12 pdr., 2—18 inch tubes. Yarrow boilers. *Cossack* has proved to be a remarkably good sea boat. (*Now carries a small mast aft*).

1 Thornycroft :— **Tartar** (1907). 870 tons. Dimensions : 270 × 26 × 8 feet. H.P. 14,500. Oil : 74 tons ; *maximum*, 185 tons. Trial : *maximum*, 37·4 kts. ; *mean*, 35·36. Armament : 5—12 pdr., 2—18 inch tubes. Thornycroft boilers.

34 BRITISH "E Class" DESTROYERS (1903-05). 1904-06 (ex *River* Class).

(*Two short funnels*).
6 *Hawthorn :—* **Boyne, Derwent, Doon, Kale, Waveney, Eden** (turbine).
Derwent mined off Havre 2 May 1917. *Kale* mined in North Sea 27 March 1918.
Eden sunk in collision in the Channel 17 June 1916.

(*Two high funnels*).
4 *Thornycroft :—* **Chelmer, Colne, Jed, Kennet.**

2 White :— **Nith, Ness** (1905).

(*Four funnels closely paired*).
9 *Palmer :* **Cherwell, Dee, Erne, Ettrick, Exe, Swale, Ure, Wear** (1904), **Rother** 1905).

(*Two medium funnels*).
8 *Cammell-Laird :—* **Arun, Foyle, Itchen, Liffey, Moy, Ouse;** also replace boats **Stour, Test.**

Foyle mined off Dover 15 March 1917. *Itchen* torpedoed by U-boat in North Sea 6 July 1917. *Erne* wrecked off Aberdeen 6 February 1915.

(*Four funnels openly paired, and no raised piece in the eyes*).
5 *Yarrow :—* **Ribble, Teviot, Usk, Welland** (1904), **Garry** (1905).

Note.—Average displacement, 550 tons. Average dimensions, 225 × 23½ × 12 feet (*maximum draught*).
Armament : 1—12 pdr., 12 cwt., 3—12 pdr., 8 cwt., 2—18 inch tubes.
Average H.P. 7000 = 25½ kts. Machinery : Reciprocating. Boilers : *Hawthorn* boats, Yarrow ; *Palmer*, Reed ; others, makers' types. Coal : about 130 tons. Complements : 70.
All these are good sea-boats, and are good for a steady 24 kts. Their endurance at full power is about 12—15 hours. At low speeds they are extremely economical, and their actual radius something like 2000 miles.

BRITISH DESTROYERS. *about* **1897**

8 Class D.

Average 335 tons. Armament of all, 1—12 pdr. *(forward)*, 5—6 pdr., 2—18 inch tubes. Designed H.P., *average* 5,700 = 30 kts. Boilers: Thornycroft in all. Coal, 80 tons. Complement, 60.

Special feature : *all boats of D class have only 2 funnels.*

(Cut-away bow, big round stern, both tubes abaft funnels).

3 *Thornycroft* :— **Angler, Desperate, Fame.** Trials: *Angler*, 30·4 ; *Desperate*, 30·3 ; *Fame*, 30·1.

(Cut-away bow, rudder showing (instead of Thornycroft stern), tubes both aft).

5 *Thornycroft* :— **Cygnet, Cynthia, Coquette, Mallard, Stag.** Trials: *Cygnet*, 30·3 ; *Cynthia*, 30·2 ; *Coquette*, 30·3 ; *Mallard*, 30·1 ; *Stag*, 30·5.
Coquette mined off E. Coast UK, 7 March 1916.

BRITISH DESTROYERS.

35 Class C.

Average 335 tons. Armament of all, 1—12 pdr. *(forward)*, 5—6 pdr., 2—18 inch tubes. Designed H.P., *average* 5,700 = 30 kts. Boilers: Thornycroft in all. Coal : 80 tons. Complement : 60.

Special feature : *all boats of C class have 3 funnels.* Turtleback bow, big bridge.

6 *Fairfield* : **Falcon, Fairy, Gipsy, Leven, Ostrich, Osprey** (tube between 2 and 3 funnels and abaft).
Falcon lost in collision 1 April 1918. Fairy sunk after ramming UC75 31 May 1918.

(High funnels.)

5 *Hawthorn* :— **Cheerful, Mermaid, Racehorse, Roebuck, Greyhound.** 5 *Vickers* :— **Avon, Bittern, Leopard, Otter, Vixen.** 2 *Earle* :— **Dove, Bullfinch.**
Cheerful mined off Shetlands 30 June 1917. Bittern sunk in collision 4 April 1918.

6 *Palmer* :— **Bat, Crane, Star, Fawn, Flying Fish,** and (with different funnel tops and searchlight on platform abaft bridge) **Flirt.** 2 *Clydebank* :— **Vigilant, Thorn.** 2 *Doxford* :— **Sylvia, Violet.**
Flirt torpedoed off Dover 27 October 1916.

5 *Clydebank* :— **Brazen, Electra, Kestrel, Recruit, Vulture.**
Recruit torpedoed by U-boat off the Galloper LV 1 May 1915.

(Three equal funnels).

1 *Thornycroft* :— **Albatross** (both tubes abaft).

1 *Hawthorn* :— **Velox** (tubes as Albatross, s.l. platform abaft bridge, after funnel much smaller than other two).
Mined off Nab, 25 October 1915.

BRITISH DESTROYERS 1901—1895.

21 Class B.

General details as below. Armament of all except first two is 1—12 pdr. (forward), 5—6 pdrs., 2—18 inch tubes. Were originally classed as 30-knot destroyers.

Special feature of these is the big fore-bridge, and turtleback bow. *All boats of B class have four funnels.*

1 *Clydebank:*—**Arab** (1901). 470 tons. Dimensions: 218×20×5 (*mean*). H.P. 8,600=31 kts. Coal, 90 tons. Comp., 60.

1 *Laird:*—**Wolf** (details as per *Earnest*, etc.)

(*Funnels very wide apart*).

10 *Laird:*—**Earnest, Griffon, Locust, Quail, Thrasher, Panther, Seal, Orwell, Lively, Sprightly.** Vary from 395–355 tons. H.P. in all, 6,300=30 kts. Coal, 80 tons. Complement, 60.

2 *Palmer:*—**Albacore** & **Bonetta** (1909). 410 tons. Armament: 3—12 pdr, 2—18 inch tubes. Parsons turbine. Coal fuel. (*Replace boats.*)

1 *Laird:*—**Express** (stern somewhat depressed aft) (1897). 465 tons. Dimensions: 235×22×9 feet. H.P. 9,250=30·1 kts, (*first trials*). Coal, 80 tons. Complement, 60.

(*Middle funnels extremely close together*).

5 *Palmer:*—**Kangaroo, Myrmidon, Peterel, Spiteful, Syren.** 1 *Doxford:*—**Success** (*middle funnels still closer together and without the bands which the Palmer boats have*). These average 380 tons. Coal, 85 tons. Complement, 62.

Success wrecked off Fife Ness 27 December 1914, *Myrmidon* lost in collision 26 March 1917.

BRITISH DESTROYERS. 1895-93

12 Class A

Old boats dating from 1893-95. Average displacement: 290 tons. Average dimensions: 200×19 × about 9 feet (*max.*) Armament in all: 1—12 pdr. (forward), 5—6 pdr., 2—18 inch tubes. Original H.P. about 4000 = 27 kts.

Special feature of these, originally classed as 27 kt. t.b.d., is turtleback bow and *small* fore bridge.

2 *Palmer:*—**Lightning, Porcupine.** 1 *Clydebank:*—**Surly.**

Lightning sunk by mine 30 June 1915.

(*Ram bow, round Thornycroft stern, small bridge, tubes both aft*).

2 *Thornycroft:*—**Boxer, Bruiser.**

Boxer sunk in collision in English Channel 8 February 1918.

(*Irregular funnels*).

2 *White:*—**Conflict, Wizard** (*very low in water, and with cut-away sterns*).

3 *Hawthorn:*—**Ranger, Opossum, Sunfish.**

2 *Hanna-Donald:*—**Fervent, Zephyr.**

BRITISH NAVY—P-BOATS & TORPEDO BOATS.

43 P-Boats (Patrol Boats.)

P 21. *Photo, Robertson, Gourock, N.B.*

Note.—*P 11, P 21, P 24, P 29*, now have mainmast. *P 17* has mainmast and funnel 4 feet higher. Remainder as above photo.

3 *Barclay Curle*: **P34** (1916), **P53, P54** (1917).
2 *Bartram*: **P23, P41** (both 1916).
2 *Caird*: **P22, P35** (both 1916).
1 *Connell*: **P14** (1916).
2 *Eltringham*: **P27** (1915), **P36** (1916).
4 *Gray*: **P29, P30, P37** (all 1916), **P45** (1917).
4 *Hamilton*: **P75** (ex *P13*, 1916), **P38, P57, P58** (all 1917).
2 *Harland & Wolff (Govan)*: **P24** (1915), **P25** (1916).
2 *Harkess*: **P32** (1916), **P46** (1917).
3 *Inglis*: **P18** (1916), **P39, P64** (both 1917).
1 *Napier & Miller*: **P33** (1916).
2 *Northumberland S.B. Co.*: **P19, P20** (both 1916).
3 *Readhead*: **P31** (1916), **P47, P48** (1917).
1 *Russell*: **P21** (1916).
1 *Tyne Iron Co.*: **P50** (1916).
2 *R. Thompson*: **P28** (1916), **P49** (1917).
4 *White (Cowes)*: **P11** (1915), **P40, P52** (both 1916), **P59** (1917).
3 *Workman Clerk*: **P15, P16** (both 1916), **P17** (1915).

Displacement: 613 tons. Dimensions: 230 (*p.p.*), $244\frac{1}{2}$ (*o.a.*) × $23\frac{3}{4}$ × 7 feet 7 inch. Guns: Designed to mount 2—4 inch but only *P 52* has this armament: others, 1—4 inch and (in all) 1—2 pdr. pom-pom. Tubes: 2 single 14 inch, removed from old Torpedo Boats. Two depth charge throwers and D.C. Machinery: Brown-Curtis or Parsons turbines. 2 screws. Yarrow boilers. Designed S.H.P. 3500 = 20 kts. Oil fuel: *normal* 50 tons, *max.* 93 tons. Complement, 50-54.

General Notes.—All built under Emergency War Programme. Were designed to relieve destroyers of patrol and escort work and submarine hunting. Outline scheme for these boats stipulated; minimum size consistent with sea-keeping qualities, simplicity of construction, and adequate speed to run down submarines: also shallow draught; low upperworks to reduce visibility: and economy of fuel. Built of mild steel, but with hard steel stem for ramming submarines. Large rudder area and hull strongly cut up aft to give rapid turning. Proved very useful boats and an excellent anti-submarine type in all weathers. Those converted to Decoy Ships or "Q-boats" listed as *PC* boats on the preceding page.

War Losses.—*P 12, P 26.*

P-boat (aircraft view). *Official R.A.F. photo.*

No. 30. *Photo, Ellis, Malta.*

4 *Denny* boats: ***30, 29,*** also ***18, 17.*** 272 tons. Dimensions: 183 × 18 × 6 feet. Armament: 2—12 pdr., 3—18 inch tubes. H.P. 4000 = 26 kts. Oil: 51/43 tons.

Note.—All "oily wad" T.B. *1–36* now have pole mainmast and openings under fore bridge screened in, as above illustration.

7 *White* boats: ***28, 27, 26, 25*** (1908), 283 tons: also ***16, 15, 14*** (1907), 270 tons. Dimensions: $185\frac{1}{4}$ × 18 × $6\frac{3}{4}$ feet. Armament: 2—12 pdr., 3—18 inch tubes. H.P. 4000 = 26 kts. Parsons turbine. 3 screws. Oil: 50-53/42-45 tons. No. 13 lost during War.

1 *Yarrow* boat: ***23*** (1907). 282 tons. Dimensions: 181 × 18 × *mean* $6\frac{1}{4}$ feet. Armament: 2—12 pdr., 3—18 inch tubes. H.P. 4000 = 26 kts. Parsons turbine. 3 screws. Oil: *normal* 49/41 tons.

To distinguish all above.—One tube *before* first funnel. Funnels fairly close together. Eyes set back from stem.

32 Torpedo Boats.

At the outbreak of war there were 106 Torpedo Boats in service.
Of these eleven were sunk (046, 064, 9, 10, 11, 12, 13, 24, 90, 96 and 117).
Of the remainder a large proportion was paid off at the end of the war and those listed below were in service in 1919.

No.	Builders.	Numbers.	Launched.	Displacement.	H.P.	*Max.* speed.	Tubes.	Coal or oil.	Complement.
				tons. *average.*		kts.		tons	
12	*Various*	36—25 ('07—8 Ests.)	1908—9	290	4000	26	3	53–41*	39
10	*Various*	23—14 ('06—7 Ests.)	1907—8	290	4000	26	3	51–40*	39
9	*Various*	8—1 ('05—6 Ests.)	1906	250	3750—3600	26	3	43–36*	35
1	White	116	1903	197	2900	25	0	44†	38

* Oil only. † Coal.

2 *Palmer* boats: ***36, 35*** (1909). 313-5 tons. Dimensions: $181\frac{3}{4}$ × $17\frac{3}{4}$ × $7\frac{1}{4}$ feet. Armament: 2—12 pdr., 3—18 inch tubes. H.P. 4000 = 26 kts. Parsons turbine. Oil: 46/41 tons *No. 24* lost during War.

4 *Hawthorn* boats: ***34, 33*** (1909); also ***22; 21.*** (1907-8). 325-8 tons. Dimensions: $189\frac{1}{4}$ × $18\frac{1}{2}$ × 7 feet. Armament: 2—12 pdr., 3—18 inch tubes. H.P. 4000=26 kts. 3 screws. Parsons turbine. Oil fuel: 48/41 tons.

4 *Thornycroft* boats: ***32, 31*** (1908), 278 tons; also ***20*** (1908), 291 tons, ***19*** (1907), 312 tons. Dimensions: $183\frac{1}{4}$ × $18\frac{1}{4}$-$18\frac{3}{4}$ × $6\frac{1}{2}$ feet. Armament: 2—12 pdr., 3—18 inch tubes. H.P. 4000 = 26 kts. 3 screws. Parsons turbine. Oil: 48/41 tons.

To distinguish all above.—One tube *before* funnel, *big* ventilators between funnels. Eyes set back from stem. Funnels fairly wide apart.

3 *Thornycroft*: ***8, 7, 6*** (1906). 244-7 tons. Dimensions: $171\frac{1}{2}$ × $17\frac{1}{2}$ × $6\frac{3}{4}$ feet. Armament: 2—12 pdr., 3—18 inch tubes. H.P. 3750 = 26 kts. Parsons turbine. 3 screws. Oil: 42/35 tons. Were originally named in order given: *Gnat, Glow-worm*, and *Gadfly*. *No.* 9 (ex *Grasshopper*), *No.* 10 (ex *Greenfly*), *No.* 11 (ex *Moth*), *No.* 12 (ex *Mayfly*), have been lost during the War.

To distinguish.—One tube *between* funnels: funnels wide apart.

5 *White* boats: ***5, 4, 3, 2, 1*** (1906). 261 tons. Dimensions: 178 × $17\frac{1}{2}$ × $6\frac{1}{2}$ feet. Armament: 2—12 pdr., 3—18 inch tubes. H.P. 3600 = 26 kts. Parsons turbine. Oil fuel: 44/37 tons. Were originally named in order given: *Spider, Sandfly, Firefly, Dragonfly, Cricket.*

To distinguish.—Tubes *before and abaft* first funnel. *No* tube before after 12 pdr. position. Funnels wide apart.

1 *White* boat: ***116*** (1903). 197 tons. Dimensions: 165 × $17\frac{1}{2}$ × 7 feet. Armament: *Nil.* H.P. 2900 = 25 kts. 44 tons.

BRITISH NAVY—M. L., C. M. B., AND D. C. B.

M. L. (Motor Launches).

M.L. 381. Some boats have mainmast right at stern for spreading W/T. aerials.

Third type: 30 originally built: ***M.L. 551—580.*** Built 1918. No details known, but similar to first and second types below.

Second type: 500 originally built: ***M.L. 51—550.*** Built 1915. 37 tons. Dimensions: 80-88 × 12$\frac{1}{6}$ feet × 3′ 10″. Guns: 1—3 inch AA. or lesser calibre of AA. and other types. B.H.P. 440-450 = 19 kts. Machinery: 2 sets of Standard petrol motors. Petrol: *about* 1850 gallons. Complement, 9.

First type: 50 originally built: ***M.L. 1—50.*** Built 1915. 34 tons. Dimensions: 75 × 12 × 3$\frac{3}{4}$ feet. Guns: 1—3 pdr. or 2 pdr. AA. and/or 1 or 2 M.G. or Lewis guns. B.H.P. 440-450 = 19 kts. Petrol: *about* 1650 gallons. Complement, 8.

General Notes.—Present boats in service can be ascertained by reference to current Navy List. Others now scrapped, being worn out. Mostly built in U.S. and Canadian Yards and shipped across the Atlantic. During War, fitted with D.C., smoke boxes, hydrophones, &c., but special gear now removed from nearly all. Petrol consumption heavy.

War Losses: Twenty-nine boats, detailed in War Losses Section. *M.L. 229,* one of the eleven British M.L. on the Rhine, was almost destroyed by a petrol explosion and fire during 1919. May not be repaired.

C. M. B. (Coastal Motor Boats.

Third Type: (from p 117 bottom left)

Second type: 55-ft. Series numbers, ***a, b, bd, c*** and ***e,*** from about ***13a*** up to ***87 b*** or above. 10 tons. Dimensions: 55 × 11 × 3 feet. Armament: Some had 2 Lewis guns on a paired mounting, others 4 Lewis guns in pairs, with 2—18 inch torpedoes in troughs at stern. Some modified to take 4 Lewis guns in pairs, with only 1—18 inch torpedo and 4 D.C. Other boats, when used for low speed work could carry 4 torpedoes in dropping gears over beams. 1 Thornycroft 375 H.P. "Y" type motor = 35 kts., but have done 41 kts. and over in service. Also Green, F.I.A.T. and Sunbeam motors. W/T. fitted in these. Complement, 3.

C, M. B. 27 = 40-FT. TYPE. *Photo, Cribb, Southsea.*

First type: 40-ft. Original boats ***3—12,*** and later boats numbered up to ***61*** or above. Dimensions: 40 × 8$\frac{1}{2}$ × 3 feet. 350 H.P. Thornycroft motor = over 30 kts. 1 torpedo carried in central trough over stern. Harwich Light Cruisers used to each take a pair of these boats to sea, slung from davits, while, in the Mediterranean, light cruiser *Diamond* served as a special C.M.B. Carrier.

General Notes.—Above types designed by Messrs. Thornycrofts Ltd. Full descriptions have appeared in technical press. It need only be remarked that they discharge their torpedoes tail first from troughs over stern, then swerve on their course and allow torpedoes to run past to target. All stepped hydroplane type hulls with chine to damp down bow wave. Considering their small size, they have exeellent nautical qualities. First boats were secretly built in 1916, and ran trials by night. 13 lost during War and 4 or more in Baltic operations. Boats now in commission can be ascertained from current Navy List. It is little use stating totals and numbers here, as these craft can be laid up and placed out of commission at very short notice. For full description *v.* "Engineer," April 18th, 1919, and Messrs. Thornycroft's own descriptive brochure.

D. C. B.

Are modified C.M.B. No details for publication. A few were finished about August, 1918, and good results were expected from them. The War ended before they could be put into operation.

BRITISH NAVY—SUBMARINES.

127 Submarines (100 Completed, *27 Building*).

No.	Type	First begun.	Last completed.	Displacement	H.P.	*Max.* speed	Fuel	Complement	T. Tubes	*Max.* draug't
				tons		kts.	tons			ft.
12	*R 1—12.*	1917	1918	420/500	250/1000	10/15	...	20	4-6	12
4	*M 1—4.*	1917	'20 ?	1600/1950	...	15/9	...	60	...	10
37	*L 1—71.*	1917	20	890/1070	2400/1600	17·3/10·5	76	36	4-6	13$\frac{1}{2}$
13	*K 2—16, K 22.*	1916	1918	1880/2650	10000/1400	24/9·5	200	55	6	16
32	*H 21—52.*	1917	1919	440/500	180/320	13/10·5	16	22	4	11$\frac{1}{4}$
7	*G 3—13.*	1915	1916	700/975	1600/810	14/10	44	30	5	13$\frac{1}{4}$
(3)	*F 1—3.*	1915	1917	353/525	900/100	14·5/8·8	17$\frac{1}{2}$	20	3	10$\frac{3}{4}$
22	*E 21—E 55.*	1915	1917	662/807	1600/840	15/10	45	30	3-5	12$\frac{1}{2}$

Notes to above Table.

Excepting *H 21-52* of "Holland" type, all above types are to Admiralty design. Above Table and description by classes on later pages, arranged alphabetically by Class Letters. Rough division by types and building dates is thus:—

61 *Ocean-going* boats: *L 1—71, M 1—4* (Monitors), *K 2—16* and *K 22, G 3—13.*
54 *Sea-going* boats: *H 21—52, E 21—55.*
12 *Coastal* boats: *R 1—12* (*F 1—3* not included).
— *Minelayers:* Various units of *L, H* and *E* types; exact total not known.

As regards the totals given over Table for boats finished and building: These are approximate only, some of the 27 boats given as building may not be finished. Six "Later K" boats not mentioned in Table or included in total, as they seem to be stopped. Coastal *F 1—3* not included in total of completed boats, as they will be sold very soon. The *E* and *G* Classes will probably be sold off within the next eighteen months.

With reference to missing Class Letters in alphabetical order, the following brief notes may be of service. All *A, B, C* and *D* boats sold off or for sale. *J* Class presented to Australia. *N 1* (late *Nautilus*) for sale 1919, having proved more or less a failure. *S 1* (late *Swordfish*) converted into surface patrol boat. *V 1—4* for sale 1919. *W 1—4* presented to Italy during the War. No I, O, P, Q, T, U, X, Y, Z Classes.

Various surrendered German Submarines are in service under the White Ensign, but only for experiments. By agreement with all the Allies, such ex-German boats will not be added to the British Navy, but must be broken up when trials are finished.

12 R Class.

R—. *Photo, Cribb, Southsea.*

R 1—4 by Chatham D.Y., ***R 5, R 6*** by Pembroke D.Y., ***R 7, R 8*** by Vickers, ***R 9, R 10*** by Armstrong Whitworth, ***R 11, R 12*** by Cammell Laird. All launched and finished 1918.

Single hull type to Admiralty designs. Approximate dimensions: 160 × 15-16 × 12 feet. Guns: 1—3 inch or 4 inch in some. Tubes: Unofficially reported to have 4 or 6—18 inch bow. Machinery: No exact details, but said to have 1 set of hot-bulb or heavy oil motors. Oil capacity small, but have an abnormal submerged endurance. Other details as Table.

Notes.—Built under Emergency War Programme. These boats (sometimes called the "Little Arthurs") were produced as a "submarine destroyer of submarines." Their outstanding feature is that—unlike nearly all other submarines in the world—they are faster below water than on the surface. They are short in length, have large rudder and hydroplane areas and small reserve of buoyancy for quick diving and rapid handling. It was intended that they should submerge and chase U-boats, and use their four bow tubes by salvo, specially big torpedo-compensating tanks with rapid flooding gear being placed in bows. Also said to have hydrophones for tracking hostile submarines.

BRITISH NAVY—SUBMARINES.

L 55.

L Classes. (Totals and Description next page).

M Class Submarine Monitors = { **1** Completed. / **3** Completing ? } = 4?

M 1. *Photo, M. Davidson, Esq.*

M 1 ex K 18 (1918), **M 2** ex K 19 (——), both by Vickers. **M 3** ex K 20 (——). **M 4** ex K 21 (——), both by Armstrong Whitworth. Launching dates of M 2—4 not reported : these three boats may not be finished.

Few details available. Designed by Admiralty ; reported to be double-hulled type. Dimensions : about 200 × 20 × 10 feet. Guns : 1—12 inch, 35 cal., 1—3 inch AA. Machinery : Type not known, but reported to be Diesel engines. Oil fuel : tons. Other details as Table.

Gunnery Notes.—12 inch believed to be one of those removed from old *Majestic* Class of Battleships, firing a 520 lb. projectile. No turntable, but high-angle elevation. Reported that gun is loaded and laid to high angle elevation : then boat is dived to about 12-20 feet, leaving muzzle of 12 inch gun above water. There is a bead sight on gun-muzzle, so that gun can be sighted by periscope and fired when running at shallow submersion. To re-load, it is necessary to return to surface.

General Notes.—Begun under War Emergency Programme. These "Submarine Monitors" are a unique design, but reports are not available of M 1's performance during War, so that their practical worth is a matter of conjecture.

L 29. *Photo, Cribb.*

L Classes { About **23*** Completed ? / About *14* Building ? } = 37*?

19* *Vickers* : **L 1** ex E 57, **L 2** ex E 58, **L 3** (all 1917), **L 4. L 11. L 12. L 14. L 17—20** (all 1918). **L 21 - L 23** (1919), **L 24—27. L 32** (completing 1919 ?).
2* *Swan Hunter* : **L 5** (1918), **L 33** (1919).
2* *Beardmore* : **L 6** (1918), **L 69** (1918).
2* *Cammell Laird* : **L 7. L 8** (both 1917).
2* *Denny* : **L 9** (1918), **L 54** (1919).
5* *Fairfield* : **L 15** (1917), **L 16** (1918), **L 36. L 55. L 56** (all 1919).
2* *Pembroke D.Y.* : **L 34. L 66** (1919-20 ?).
2* *Armstrong Whitworth* : **L 52. L 53** (both 1919).
1 *Scotts* : **L 71** (1919).

*All totals liable to revision. Some of the boats launched 1919 may be abandoned.

Following boats reported stopped 1918 :—

21* boats stopped : L 28—31 (Vickers), L 35 (Pembroke D.Y.), L 50, 51, 63, 64, 65 (Cammell Laird), L 67, 68 (Armstrong), L 37—62 (Fairfield), L 70 (Beardmore), L 72 (Scotts), L 73 (Denny).

14 boats never ordered : L 13, L 37—49.

†Liable to revision. Some may be completed.

Design and type of hull not known ; reported to be a wing-tank type designed by Admiralty. Dimensions : 222 (p.p.), 231 (o. a.) × 23½ × 13½ feet. Guns : 1—3 inch AA. or 4 inch, but minelayers may have no guns. Torpedo tubes : in earlier boats, up to (about) L 9, 6, viz., four bow, two beam, all 21 inch ; boats above L 9, 6—21 inch, all in bows. Mine-laying boats numbered under L 9 have no beam tubes—only four bow—21 inch. Machinery : 2 sets 12-cylinder solid injection Vickers type, but others may have Cammellaird-Fullager, Armstrong, and other types. Oil : 76 tons. Other details as Table.

Notes.—The "L Class" is in a highly complex state, owing to the variations in build, giving ten or more types by appearance. Further uncertainty is introduced by inadequate information regarding boats whose construction has been stopped. All built under Emergency War Programme, but funds for completion of some boats will fall within post-war Navy Estimates. In dimensions, H.P., speed, &c., these boats have a marked resemblance to the 1914-18 German ocean-going Submarines. Minelaying boats not known exactly, but unverified reports say L 2, 14, 17 are equipped for sowing mines.

War Losses.—L 10.

13 K Class (+ 6 *Building ?*)

K 10. K 12 & K 16 have gun on high fairwater *before* C.T. *Photo, Cribb, Southsea.*

K 15 (higher funnels). *Photo, Topical.*

K 2, K 5 (both by Portsmouth D.Y., 1916). **K 6** (Devonport D.Y., 1916). **K 3, K 8, K 9, K 10** (all by Vickers, 1916). **K 11, K 12** (both by Armstrong Whitworth, 1916-17). **K 14, K 22,** ex K 13 (both by Fairfield, 1916). **K 15** (Scott, 1917). **K 16** (Beardmore, 1917).

(K 23—K 28 : See General Notes.)

All double-hulled type, designed by Admiralty for service as "Fleet Submarines" with Grand Fleet. Dimensions : 334 (p.p.), 337 (o.a.) × 26½ × 16 feet. Guns : see Notes below. Oil fuel : 170 tons. Other details as Table. Torpedo tubes : 8—18 inch, viz., 4 bow, 4 beam. Machinery : see Notes below. Oil fuel : 170 tons. Other details as Table.

Engineering Notes.—These are not the first steam-driven boats in British Navy, having been preceded by *Swordfish* (S 1), now scrapped. Surface machinery consists of combined steam turbines and Diesel engine. 2 sets of single reduction turbines, one H.P. and one L.P. in each set, with double helical gearing. 2 screws. 2 Yarrow small-tube type boilers with forced draught, boilers, turbines, funnels being lagged with incombustible non-conducting materials. Small electric motors are fitted for lowering funnels and closing w.t. hatches over funnel wells. Boiler room air vents closed by hydraulic power. To assist in diving quickly, or getting away after breaking surface (while steam motors are being started up), an 800 B.H.P. 8-cylinder Diesel motor is fitted, which can also be used for surface cruising. Drive from Diesel engine is through electric motors, so that these boats have three systems of transmission, (a) geared turbines for steam drive, (b) Diesel and electric transmission, (c) electric battery drive when submerged. 2 high-power compressors to charge 2500 lbs. air bottles : 2 low-power compressors to blow main ballast tanks after breaking surface. 2 electric-power bilge pumps. Hydraulic rams for raising periscopes and telescopic masts. Hydro-electric controlling gear to hydroplanes, forward hydroplanes being of housing type.

Gunnery and Torpedo Notes.—Were first completed with 2 guns before and below C.T. and 1 abaft C.T. on superstructure deck, but these were removed. For a time, these boats had only 1—3 inch, but K 17 at time of her loss mounted 1—5.5 inch. There were also 2—18 inch tubes in superstructure, above water when in surface trim, making eight tubes in all. The original three guns and superstructure tubes were removed to D.A.M.S. and S.D. Vessels (Q-boats).

General Notes.—All built under Emergency War Programme. Were first completed with flush level bows, but showed a tendency to trim by the head and dive "on their own." To remedy this, bows were raised, as shown in above illustrations. Accommodation for officers and men is remarkably spacious for submarines. Are said to be rather hot on account of steam system of propulsion, but in the North Sea this proved rather an advantage than otherwise. Considering that these boats were of a highly experimental type, they have turned out most remarkably well. Further boats, K 23—28 reported ordered in 1918, which were to have 6—21 inch bow tubes. Nothing further has been heard of these later boats ; they may be cancelled.

War Losses.—K 1, 4, 17. K 13 also foundered, but was salved and re-numbered K 22.

Removals.—K 7 on Sale List, 1919.

J Class.)

All presented in 1919 to Royal Australian Navy, q. v. for details. *War Loss.—J 6.*

H Class { about **20** delivered / about *8 building* } = 32.*
*Some adapted for Minelaying.

12 *Vickers* : **H 21 - H 32** (launched 1917-18).
8 *Cammell Laird* : **H 33—H 40** (launched 1918-19).
6 *Armstrong Whitworth* : **H 41—H 46** (launched 1918-19).
4 *Beardmore* : **H 47—H 50** (launched 1918-19).
2 *Pembroke D.Y.* : **H 51** (1918), **H 52** (1919).

Single-hull "Holland" (Electric Boat Co.) type modified by Admiralty. Dimensions : 164½ (p p.), 171 (o.a.) × 15¾ feet. Guns : Majority have 1—3 inch AA. Tubes : 4—21 inch bow, but minelaying boats may have only two or none. Machinery : 2 sets of Diesel engines of various types. Oil : 16 tons. Other details as Table.

Notes.—Not known how many of these boats are Minelayers. All built under War Emergency Programme. Not yet certain that all of these will be finished ; some may be cancelled. During the War, H 1—10 type were assembled by the Canadian Vickers Co., Montreal, and crossed Atlantic under their own power. On war service, these boats proved very successful, and were about the most popular type with the British Submarine Service. H 11—20 were assembled by the Bethlehem Steel Co. and Fore River Co., U.S.A., but were interned by the U.S. Government. On the entry of the U.S. into the War, the boats were released, but were not taken over by British Navy. Six boats (H 15, H 16—20) were presented to Chile, H 14, H 15 presented to Canada, H 11, H 12 put on Sale List. 1919. H 21—52 were designed as an improvement on the original H 1—10 boats, having 21 inch tubes instead of 18 inch.

War Losses.—None in above H 21—52 Class. Of the H 1—10 Class, H 3, 5, 6, 10 lost during War.

Removals.—H 1, 2, 4, 7, 8, 9, (H 1—10 Class), H 11, H 12 (H 11—20 Class), all on Sale List, 1919.

BRITISH NAVY—SUBMARINES.

7 G Class.

Photo, Dr. J. A. Prendergast.

G3, G4, G5 (all Chatham D.Y., 1916). **G6** (Armstrongs, 1916), **G10, G13** (Vickers, 1916). Admiralty double-hull type. Dimensions: 185 (*p.p.*), 187 (*o.a.*) × 22½ × 13¼ feet. Guns: 1—3 inch AA. Torpedo tubes: 5, viz., 2—18 inch bow, 2—18 inch beam, 1—21 inch stern. Diesel engines: Vickers, Armstrong (2 sets). Oil: 44 tons. Other details as Table.

Notes.—All Emergency War Programme. Built as "Bight and North Sea Patrols," being the first genuine ocean-going boats in British Navy. Had their bows raised during War. The above boats will probably be brought home from Mediterranean during the next twelve months and placed on Sale List, except *G 3* which is in home waters and may already be for sale. *G 1, 2, 12, 11,* on Sale List, 1914.

War Losses.—G 7, 8, 9, 11.

3 F Class.

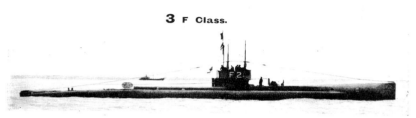

F 2 (and F 3. F 1 slightly different).   *Photo, Messrs J. S. White & Sons.*

F 1 (Chatham D.Y., 1915). **F 2** (White, 1917). **F 3** (Thornycroft, 1916). Admiralty double-hull type. F 1, 1913-14 Programme, F 2, F 3, 1914-15 Programme. Dimensions: 150 (*p.p.*), 151 (*o.a.*) × 16 × 10¾ feet. Guns: *Nil,* but were designed to mount a 2 pdr. pom-pom. Tubes: 3—18 inch, 2 bow or beam, 1 stern. Diesel engines, 2 sets. Oil: 17½ tons. Other details as Table.

Note.—Will probably be put on Sale List at an early date.

D 8—2. Diesel motors. Radius: 4000 miles. Armament: 2—12 pdr., 3 tubes.   *Photo, Symonds & Co.*

D 1. Diesel motor. Armament: 1—12 pdr., 3 tubes.   *Photo, Symonds & Co.*

C 38—C 19. 12 cylinder petrol motors. Radius: $\frac{2000}{150}$.   *Photo, Symonds & Co.*

C 18—C 1. Dimensions: 135 × 13½ × 11¼ feet. 1 screw. Surface radius, 1500 miles. Engine: 16 cyl. horizontal opposed.

B 11—B 1. Dimensions: 135 × 13½ × 11¼ feet. 1 screw. Surface radius, 1500 miles. Engine: 16 cyl. horizontal opposed.

22 E Class.—18 boats + 4 Minelayers.

Now have steel bridge screen.

E 7—20 & LATER CLASS :— 22 boats.

E 21, E 23 (Vickers, 1915), **E 25** (Beardmore, 1915), **E 27** (Yarrow, 1917), **E 31** (Scott, 1915), **E 32** (White, 1916), **E 33** (Thornycroft, 1916), **E 35** (J. Brown, 1916), **E 38** (Fairfield, 1916), **E 39, E 40** (launched by Palmers, 1916-17 and completed by Armstrongs), **E 41,* E 42** (Cammell Laird, 1915), **E 44** (Swan Hunter, 1916), **E 45,* E 46*** (Cammell Laird, 1916), **E 48** (launched by Fairfield 1916, completed by Beardmore), **E 51 *** (Scotts, 1916), **E 52** (Denny, 1916), **E 53, E 54** (Beardmore, 1915-16), **E 55** (Denny, 1916).

*These are Minelayers.

All Admiralty wing-tank type. Built under Emergency War Programme. First British type of submarine with internal sub-division by w.t. bulkheads and with beam tubes. Dimensions: 180 (*p.p.*), 181 (*o.a.*) × 22½ × 12½ feet. Tubes: 3 to 5—18 inch, viz., 2 bow, 0, 1, or 2 beam, 1 stern. Minelayers marked * have no beam tubes, and carry about 20 mines. Diesel engines: 2 sets of Vickers, Sulzer, Carels, M.A.N., or other types. Oil: 45 tons. Other details as Table.

Notes.—Performed splendid work during War, and proved most satisfactory. Heavy losses sustained by this class are an index to the arduous work they performed, 1915-18. E 2, 4 (of *E 1—6* type), 11, 12, 29, 43, 56 (all *E 7—20* and later type), put on Sale List, 1919 ; the others detailed above will be sold off as new *L* boats come into service.

War Losses.—E 1,* 3, 5, 6 (E 1—6 type), E 7, 8,* 9,* 10, 13, 14, 15, 16, 17, 18, 19,* 20, 22, 24, 26, 28, 30, 34, 36, 37, 47, 49, 50 (all E 7—20 and later type).

AE1 and AE2, see Australian section.   *Scuttled in Baltic.

A 14—A 5. Dimensions: 100 × 12½ × 11¼ feet. 1 screw. Surface radius, 1000 miles. Engine: 16 cyl. horizontal.

No.	Type	Date	Displacement	H.P.	Max. speed	Fuel	Complement	T. Tubes	Max. draug't
1	"S" *Fiat* S.G. type	1913	$\frac{300}{345}$	...	$\frac{13}{8\cdot5}$	...	...	2	...
11	E 11—1	1912	$\frac{725}{810}$	$\frac{1750}{600}$	$\frac{16}{00}$	...	...	4	...
7	D 8—D 3	1911}	$\frac{550}{600}$	$\frac{1750}{550}$	$\frac{16}{10}$	...	...	3	...
1	D 2	1910}							
8	C 38—C 31	1909}	$\frac{280}{313}$	$\frac{600}{200}$	$\frac{14}{10}$	15	16	2	12
12	C 30—C 19	1908}							
1	D 1	1907	$\frac{550}{600}$	$\frac{1200}{550}$	$\frac{16}{9}$	...	...	3	...
7	C 18—C 12	1907}	$\frac{280}{313}$	$\frac{600}{200}$	$\frac{13}{8}$	15	16	2	12
10	C 10—C 1	1906}							
10	B 11—B 1	1905	$\frac{280}{313}$	$\frac{600}{200}$	$\frac{13}{8}$	15	16	2	12
8	A 13—A 5	1904	$\frac{180}{207}$	$\frac{550}{150}$	$\frac{11\cdot5}{7}$	7	11	2	11½

C 11, B 4, A 7 and *A 3* have been lost.

Note.—By 1919 all A, B, C and D classes with the exception of C4 on trials had been paid off.

War losses:
"D" Class—D2, 3, 5 and 6
"C" Class—C3, 16, 26, 27, 29, 31, 32, 33, 34, 35
"B" Class—B10

BRITISH NAVY—AIRCRAFT CARRIERS.

VINDICTIVE (17th Jan., 1918.) Late Light Cruiser *Cavendish.*

Displacement, 9750 tons. Complement $\left\{ \begin{array}{l} \text{R.N.} \\ \text{R.A.F.} \end{array} \right\}$ = -

Length 565 feet (p.p.). 605 feet (o.a.). Beam, 65 feet. Draught $\left\{ \begin{array}{l} Mean\ 17\frac{1}{4}\ \text{feet.} \\ Max.\ 20\frac{3}{4}\ \text{feet.} \end{array} \right.$

Guns :
  4—7·5 inch, cal.
  4—12 pdr.
  4—3 inch A.A.
  4 M.G.
  (1 landing).
Torpedo tubes (21 inch) :
  2 *submerged.*
  4 *above water.*

Armour :
  3″—2″ Side (amidships)..
  2½″—1½″ Side (f. & a.) ...
  1″ Upper Deck (amid.) ...
  1½″ Lower Deck (aft) ...

VINDICTIVE.

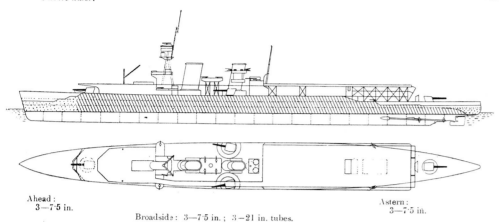

Ahead :
3—7·5 in.

Astern :
3—7·5 in.

Broadside : 3—7·5 in. ; 3—21 in. tubes.

Machinery : Parsons (all geared) turbines. 4 screws. Boilers : Yarrow. Designed S.H.P. 60,000 = 29·75 (*cf.* trials). Fuel : 1000 tons coal and oil *normal,* 800 tons coal + 1500 tons oil *maximum.*

Gunnery Notes ⎫
Armour Notes ⎬ As *Hawkins, Raleigh,* &c., on a previous page.
Engineering Notes ⎭

Name	Builder	Machinery	Begun	Completed	Trials : H.P. = kts.
Vindictive	Harland & Wolff, Belfast	Harland & Wolff, Belfast	July, 1918	Oct., 1918	63,000 = 29.12

Aircraft Notes.—No reliable details available. Reported to carry six aeroplanes.

General Notes.—Built under Emergency War Programme. Commenced under name of *Cavendish,* as a unit of the "Improved *Birmingham*" type of Light Cruisers. Modified by builders before delivery as an Aircraft Carrier.

FURIOUS (15 August, 1916). Late Cruiser.

Normal Displacement, *about* 19,100 tons, about 22,900 tons *full load.* Complement, $\left\{ \begin{array}{l} \text{R.N.} \\ \text{R.A.F.} \end{array} \right\}$ = 737.

Length, (p.p.) 750 feet, (o.a.) 786¼ feet. Beam, 88 feet. Draught $\left\{ \begin{array}{l} mean\ 21\frac{1}{2}\ \text{feet.} \\ max.\ 25\ \text{feet.} \end{array} \right.$

Guns (**Dir. Con.**) :
  10—5·5 inch, — cal.
  5 3 inch A.A.
  4—3 pdr.
  5 M.G.
  (1 landing.)
Torpedo tubes (21 inch) :
  16 *above water.*
  2 *submerged.*

Armour :
  3″ Belt (amidships)................
  2″ Belt (bow). ....
  3″-2″ Bulkheads F. & A. ....
  7″-3″ Barbettes. ....
  1″ Decks (H.T. at stern).........
  3″-1½″ Decks (H.T. at stern)....
  10″ C.T. ....
  6″-3″ Sighting hood. ....
  3″ C.T. tube ....
  2″ C.T. base. ....
Anti-Torp. Pro.
  Shallow bulge ....
  1″ H.T. vertical. ....
  ¾″ Funnel and vent screen. ...

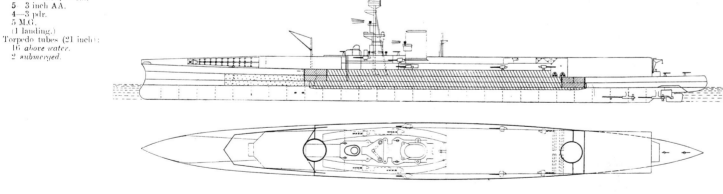

Ahead :
6—5·5 in.

Broadside : 5—5·5 in., 8(?)—21 inch tubes.

Astern :
2—5·5 in.

Machinery : Brown-Curtis (all geared) Turbines. 4 screws. Boilers : Yarrow. Designed S.H.P. 90,000 = 31 kts. Fuel (oil only) : 750 tons *normal,* 3,393 tons *maximum.*

Armour Notes.—3″ Belt consists of 2″ plating over 1″ shell plating, as in Light Cruisers. Belt forward is set inboard, as plans. Barbettes are still in, though no large guns are mounted in them. Fo'xle. Upper Decks, 1″ H.T. Main Deck, 1¼″—1″. Lower deck at stern, 1½″—1″ flat, 2″ slopes, 3″ over rudder head—all H.T.

Internal Protection.—Bulge deeper than that of *Glorious* and *Courageous,* but *not* filled with oil fuel. There is a complete internal citadel of 1″ vertical plating from barbette to barbette, well inboard and covering magazines, shell and boiler rooms. Outside and below this citadel and on each beam, are 1″ screens, 250-300 ft. long, covering boiler and engine rooms. From within the citadel rise the ¾″ screens protecting funnel and boiler room vents.

Gunnery Notes.—Originally designed to mount 2—18 inch and 11—5·5 inch guns, provision being made to mount 4—15 inch if the 18 inch guns proved unsatisfactory. The fore 18 inch gun was never mounted, being replaced by flying-off deck and hangar. When in service in 1917-18, she fired the after 18 inch a few times, and it is said "it shook her up considerably." In 1918, the after 18 inch was also taken out, flying-on deck and after hangar added. At the same time, 1—5·5 inch was removed and other 10—5·5 inch re-distributed. The after tripod mast, with gunnery controls was also removed.

Torpedo Notes.—Submerged tubes are not satisfactory, and may be removed. There are four sets of triple 21 inch tubes on upper deck aft, and one pair of 21 inch tubes on each beam forward on upper deck. On re-construction, the 3″ (after) Torpedo Control Tower was removed and controls re-located.

Name	Builder	Machinery	Begun	Completed	Trials H.P. = kts.
Furious	Armstrong Whitworth	Wallsend Co.	June, 1915	July, 1917	90,820 =

General Notes.—Built under Emergency War Programme. Designed as a modified *Courageous,* but altered to Aircraft Carrier (see Gunnery and Aircraft Notes). Since conversion, she is said to be rather light, and is good now for 32-33 kts. Including cost of alterations, this ship is said to have absorbed nearly six million pounds. Flagship, Vice-Admiral Commanding Aircraft.

Aircraft Notes and Illustrations on opposite page.

BRITISH NAVY: AIRCRAFT CARRIERS. FURIOUS—*Continued.*

FURIOUS. (**For details, v. oppposite page.**)

Aircraft Notes.—When first completed, she carried about four Short seaplanes and six Sopwith "Pups." These were easily flown off bows, but there was difficulty in getting seaplanes shipped inboard by derricks. Experiments were made to use the forward flying-off deck for landing also, but it was found too dangerous. Later, the big after flying-on deck was added, and proved satisfactory. Forward flying-off deck is about 160 feet long, tapers to bows, has collapsible wind-breaking pallisades. There is also a power-operated lift before C. T. to hoist seaplanes from forward hangar to flying-off deck. The after flying-on deck is about 300 feet long by 100 feet wide, with stopping net just abaft funnel. There is also another lift aft for raising seaplanes from after hangar. Narrow decks on each side of the funnel connect the flying-off deck with flying-on deck, small trolleys on rails being used to move seaplanes forward or aft. No seaplanes are now carried, but only aeroplanes of "Cuckoo" (torpedo dropping) and other types.

FURIOUS. Aircraft View.　　　　　*Official R.A.F. Photo.*

ARGUS (2nd Dec., 1917). Late Liner.

Normal displacement, 15,775 tons. Complement $\left\{ \begin{array}{c} \text{R.N.} \\ \text{R.A.F.} \end{array} \right\}$ = 495.

Length (*p.p.*), 535 feet (*w.l.*) 560 feet (*o.a.*) 565 feet. Beam, 68 feet. Draught, 22¾ feet, *mean.*

Guns :
2—4 inch, 50 cal.
2—4 inch AA.
Torpedo tubes :
Nil.

Armour :
Nil.

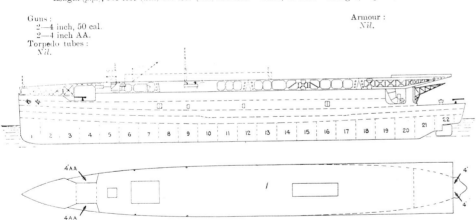

ARGUS (port view).

Machinery : Parsons turbines. 4 screws. Designed S.H.P. 22,000 = 20·5 kts. Can make 20·75 kts. for short periods, but 20 kts. is usually best speed under ordinary conditions. Boilers : 12 cylindrical (6 D.E. and 6 S.E.), with Howdens forced draught. Fuel : 2000 tons oil.

Capacity, &c.—Hangar is 350 ft. long by 68 ft. wide (*over all*) and 48 ft. clear width, 20 ft. clear height. It is divided into four sections by fire-proof screens, and can accommodate 20 seaplanes.

Stores, &c.—Torpedoes are carried for Sopwith "Cuckoo" type torpedo-dropping aeroplanes ; aero-bombs, spare parts, wings, propellers, &c. Full equipment is carried for maintenance and repair of aircraft. There are large carpenters' and engineers' workshops, for executing rapid repairs.

Handling Gear.—Two electrically controlled lifts for raising aircraft from hangar to flying deck. Forward lift, 30 ft. × 36 ft. After lift, 60 ft. × 18 ft. When forward lift is at flying deck level, two roller platforms slide to the sides and uncover well opening. When lift descends, the platforms are closed together and give a 20-ft. platform for flying off. When a deck load of aeroplanes is carried, wind-breaking pallisades can be raised simultaneously to 14 ft. above flying deck. Two derricks with electric winches amidships on flying deck, and two electric cranes at stern on hangar deck level ; all to pick up aeroplanes from the water.

Flying-off.—Flying deck is 68 ft. wide and 550 ft. long. Chart-house is on hydraulic lift ; masts, jackstaff, &c., all fold down to give perfectly level flying-off space.

Landing.—Wind safety mattress (or landing net) fitted. Steam jet indicators fitted for day use and special illumination for night landings. There is a wide safety net all round flying deck.

Engineering Notes.—At the time designs were got out, a ¼-inch scale model was prepared for testing in the air tunnel at the National Physical Laboratory, Teddington, to solve various structural problems and to test eddy-making effects of hull. It was found that the emission of hot furnace gases from the usual type of funnels created such serious air disturbances, safe landings would be very difficult. Accordingly, horizontal smoke-ducts with big expelling fans were fitted, to deliver all furnace gases and smoke out over stern. Designed for 18 kts., but modifications during conversion raised speed by 2 kts.

*For all details in these notes, we are indebted to "Engineering," which published a full description of H.M.S. *Argus*, in its issue of March 28th, 1919.

ARGUS (starboard view.)　　　　　*Photo, C N.*

Note to Illustrations.—Two views are given, as *Argus* exemplifies dazzle-painting excellently. Note the reversed direction of diagonal striping on one beam, compared with the other.

Name	Builder	Machinery	Begun	Completed	Trials : H.P. = kts.
Argus	Beardmore	Beardmore	1914	Sept., 1918	

General Notes.—Begun 1914, for Italian Lloyd Sabaudo Line, as S.S. *Conte Rosso*. All work on her ceased in 1914. She was purchased in 1916 and converted to Aircraft Carrier. In appearance, she is quite unique, and she is sometimes called "THE FLOATING ISLAND." As a mobile hangar and floating aerodrome, she has proved very successful.

BRITISH NAVY: AIRCRAFT CARRIERS.

PEGASUS (ex G. E. Railway Co. s.s. *Stockholm,* built by J. Brown & Co., ——, purchased 1917). 3300 tons. Dimensions: 330 (*p.p.*), 332 (*o.a.*) × 43 × 15 (*mean*), 15⅔ (*max.*) feet. Guns: 2—12 pdr. and 2—12 pdr. AA. S.H.P. 9500 = 20.25 kts. (20.8 trials). Machinery: Brown-Curtis turbines (all-geared). 2 screws. Boilers: Cylindrical. Oil fuel: 360 tons. Complement, 258 R.N. and R.A.F.

May be re-conditioned for mercantile service. Photo, Topical.

NARIANA (Denny Bros., ——, chartered 1917). 3070 tons. Dimensions: 315 (*p.p.*), 352 (*o.a*), including projection of stern gantry) × 45½ × 13¼ feet (*mean*), 13⅚ (*max.*). Guns 2—12 pdr. and 2—12 pdr. AA. S.H.P. 6700 = 19 kts. (20.32 trials). Machinery: Parsons turbines (all-geared). Boilers: Babcock & Wilcox. 2 screws. Coal: 448 tons. Complement, 278 R.N. and R.A.F.

ARK ROYAL (Blyth S.B. Co., 1914, purchased 1914). 7450 tons. Dimensions: 352½ (*p.p.*), 366 (*o.a.*) × 50⅚ × 18 feet (*mean*). Guns: 4—12 pdr., 2 M.G. I.H.P. 3000 = 11 kts. Machinery: Vertical triple expansion. 1 screw. Boilers: Cylindrical. Oil: 500 tons. Complement, 180 R.N. and R.A.F.

Photo, Messrs. Lobnitz.

SLINGER (——). Experimental Aeroplane Catapult Ship, built by Messrs. Lobnitz. I H P. 1030 = 10 kts. No other details received.

BRITISH NAVY—MINELAYERS.

PRINCESS MARGARET (built 1913-14, chartered and converted during War, purchased 1919). 5440 tons. Complement, 215. Dimensions: 395½ (*o.a.*) × 54 × 16⅚ feet (*max.* draught). Guns: 2—4.7 inch, 2—12 pdr., 2—6 pdr. AA., 1—2 pdr. pom-pom. S.H.P. 15,000 = 22.5 kts. (23.15 on *trials*). Oil fuel: 585 tons.

LONDON (Sept., 1899). Old Battleship of 15,000 tons, converted 1918. Complement, 481. Dimensions: 431¾ (*o.a.*) × 75 × 27⅔ feet (*max.* draught). Guns: 3—6 inch, 1—4 inch AA., 2 M.G., 1 landing. Torpedo tubes (18 inch): 4 *submerged.* Armour: 9″, 6″ and 2″ belt, 6″ casemates, 3″ deck. Old 10″—8″ turrets also left in, though 12 inch guns, shields, etc., are removed. I.H.P. 15,000 = 18 kts. Machinery: 2 sets 3-cylinder vertical triple expansion. 2 screws. Boilers: 20 Belleville. Coal: 2000 tons *max.*

AMPHITRITE (1898). Ex-Cruiser, converted 1917. 11,000 tons. Complement, 409. Dimensions: 466 (*o.a.*) × 69 × 27 feet (*max.* draught). Guns: 4—6 inch, 1—12 pdr. Armour: 4″ deck, 6″ casemates. Machinery: 2 sets 4-cylinder vertical inverted triple expansion. Boilers: 30 Belleville. I.H.P. 18,000 = 21 kts. 2 screws. Coal: 1730 tons.

7 Mine Layers.

IPHIGENIA, THETIS, APOLLO, ANDROMACHE, INTREPID, LATONA, NAIAD (all about 1891) of the *Apollo* class 3400 to 3600 tons. Armament: 6—6 pdrs. *Note*—See Apollo class under Light Cruisers.

EURYALUS (1901). Old Cruiser of 12,000 tons, partially converted to a Minelayer at Hong Kong D.Y., 1918-19, but now laid up in Reserve. Dimensions: 472 (*o.a.*) × 69½ × 27¾ feet *max* draught. Guns: 2—9·2 inch (probably removed), 2—6 inch, 2—6 pdr. AA., 2—3 pdr. Machinery: 2 sets vertical triple expansion. 2 screws. Boilers: Belleville. I.H.P. 21,000 = 21 kts. Coal: 1600 tons *max.*

Note.

The 20th Destroyer Flotilla (Minelayers) consists of *Abdiel, Gabriel* (Leaders), *Vanoc, Vanquisher, Venturous* (Admiralty "V" type), *Tarpon, Telemachus* (Admiralty "R" Class), *Meteor* ("M" Class), used for experiments. Other "V" and "W" Destroyers were fitted as Minelayers during the War.

Submarine Minelayers are units of "L" Classes (numbers not known), *E 41, E 45, E 46, E 51*, carrying about 20 mines.

C.M.B. also used as Minelayers during War. If necessity arises, Warships of nearly all types can be quickly fitted out as Minelayers.

BRITISH NAVY—FLEET SWEEPING VESSELS (SLOOPS).

SIR BEVIS. *Photo, by courtesy of Messrs. Osbourne Graham.*

ARD PATRICK, DONOVAN, FLYING FOX, MINORU, ROCK SAND (*and others*) — As above view. Mast *before* funnel

ORMONDE. *Photo by courtesy of Blyth S.B. Co.*

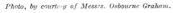

IROQUOIS, SEFTON, SILVIO, SIR BEVIS (*and others*) — As above illustration. Mast *abaft* funnel.

("24 CLASS"—24 SHIPS.)

ARD PATRICK (June, 1918), **CICERO** (July, 1918), **FLYING FOX** (March, 1918), **MINORU** (———, 1919), **ORBY** (October, 1918), **ROCK SAND** (July, 1918), **SPEARMINT** (September, 1918), **SUNSTAR** (*building?*), all eight by Swan Hunter. **BEND OR** (September, 1918), **HARVESTER** (November, 1918), **IROQUOIS** (August, 1918), **SEFTON** (July, 1918), **SILVIO** (April, 1918), **SIR BEVIS** (May, 1918), all six by Barclay, Curle. **DONOVAN** (April, 1918), **ISINGLASS** (———, 1919), **SANFOIN** (June, 1918), **SIR HUGO** (September, 1918), all by Greenock & Grangemouth Co. **GALITEE MORE** (———, 1919), **LADAS** (September, 1918), **PERSIMMON** (March, 1918), **SIR VISTO** (Dec., 1918), all by Osbourne, Graham. **ORMONDE** (June, 1918), **MERRY HAMPTON** (December, 1918), both by Blyth S.B. Co.

All 1320 tons. First delivered April, 1918, three or four not finished by September, 1919. *Sunstar* not launched and may be stopped. Dimensions: $267\frac{1}{2}$ (*p.p.*), $276\frac{1}{2}$ (*o.a.*) × $34\frac{5}{6}$ × 12 feet. Guns: 2—4 inch, as designed; those completed in 1919 may have only 3 pdr. guns or none at all. Machinery: Inverted 4-cylinder triple expansion. Boilers: Cylindrical return smoke tube. 1 screw. Designed H.P. 2500 = 17 kts. Coal: 260 tons. Complement, 82.

General Notes.—All officially rated as "Fleet Sweeping Vessels (Sloops)" and built under Emergency War Programme. Although not built as Submarine Decoy Vessels (or "Q-boats"), they have a resemblance to the Standard Cargo Ships. It is extremely difficult to distinguish bows from stern when these ships are dazzle-painted, or to separate the *Silvio* group (mast *abaft* funnel) from the *Flying Fox* group (mast *before* funnel). The *Silvio* group have rather higher bridges, mast is close to and *abaft* funnel and ventilators between bridges are rather higher. *Flying Fox* group have mast further away from and *before* funnel. *Minoru* and others completed in the summer of 1919, had after bridge cut down, the higher fore bridge indicating position of bows. Are said to be indifferent sea-boats, and roll a lot: not so successful as the "Flowers." None lost during War. Officially classified as the "24 Class," and not as "Racehorse Class," as this might lead to confusion with the Paddle Minesweepers named after racecourses. The whole 24 ships may not be completed finally.

BRITISH NAVY—FLEET SWEEPING VESSELS (CONVOY SLOOPS).

"Q" Boat—Flower Type—30 Ships.

POLYANTHUS. *Photo, Messrs. Lobnitz & Co. (Builders).*

COREOPSIS.

(ANCHUSA TYPE—26 SHIPS.)

CONVOLVULUS (May, 1917), **COREOPSIS** (Sept., 1917), **DIANTHUS** (Nov., 1917), **EGLANTINE** (June, 1917), **GARDENIA** (Dec., 1917), **GILIA** (Feb., 1918), **HAREBELL** May, 1918), all by Barclay, Curle. **AURICULA** (Oct., 1917), **BRYONY** (Oct., 1917), **CEANOTHUS** June, 1917), **CHRYSANTHEMUM** (Nov., 1917), all by Armstrong, Whitworth. **HIBISCUS** (Nov., 1917), **MARJORAM** (Dec., 1917), **MISTLETOE** (Nov., 1917), all by Greenock & Grangemouth Co. **LYCHNIS** (Aug., 1917), **PELARGONIUM** (March, 1918), both by Hamilton. **POLYANTHUS** (Sept., 1917), **SAXIFRAGE** (Jan., 1918), both by Lobnitz. **SILENE** (March, 1918), **SPIRAEA** (Nov., 1917), both by Simons. **SWEETBRIAR** (Oct., 1917), **TUBEROSE** (Nov., 1917), both by Swan Hunter. **SYRINGA** (Sept., 1917), **WINDFLOWER** (April, 1918), both by Workman, Clark. **IVY** (Blyth S.B. Co., Oct., 1917), **MONTBRETIA** (Irvine S.B. Co., Sept., 1917).

All 1290 tons. Completed Aug., 1917-June, 1918. Dimensions: 250 (*p.p.*), $262\frac{1}{4}$ (*o.a.*) × 35 × $11\frac{1}{2}$-12 (*mean*), $12\frac{1}{2}$-$13\frac{2}{3}$ (*max.*) feet draught. Designed to mount 2—12 pdr., 1—7.5 howitzer or 1—200 lb. stick-bomb howitzer, 4 Depth Charge Throwers, but actually armed with 2—4 inch, 1 or 2—12 pdr. and D.C. Throwers. Machinery: 4-cylinder triple expansion. Boilers: 2 cylindrical. 1 screw. Designed H.P. 2500 = 17 kts., but some only about 16 kts. on this power; about 2800 = 17 kts. actually. Coal: 260 tons. Complement, 93. Also see *General Notes.*

(AUBRIETIA TYPE—4 SHIPS.)

AUBRIETIA (Blyth S.B. Co., June, 1916), **HEATHER** (Greenock & Grangemouth Co., June, 1916), **TAMARISK** (Lobintz, June, 1916), **VIOLA** (Ropner, July, 1916).

All 1250 tons. Completed Aug.-Oct., 1916. Dimensions: $255\frac{1}{4}$ (*p.p.*), $267\frac{3}{4}$ (*o.a.*) × $33\frac{1}{2}$ × $11\frac{1}{2}$ (*mean*), $12\frac{1}{2}$ (*max.*) feet draught. Designed to mount 3—12 pdr., 2—3 pdr. AA., but have 2—4 inch, 1—3 pdr. AA. and D.C. throwers. Machinery, boilers, as "Anchusa Class," opposite. 1 screw. Designed H.P. 2500 = 17.5 kts., but actually can only make 15-$16\frac{1}{2}$ kts. with this power, and require 3000 I.H.P. for $17\frac{1}{2}$ kts. Coal: 255 tons. Complement, 80.

General Notes to Anchusa and Aubrietia types.—All are Fleet Sweeping Vessels (Sloops) of the "Flower Classes," modified in external build for service as Convoy Sloops. Disguised as mercantile vessels, these ships accompanied Convoys, and acted as Submarine Decoy Vessels, or "Q-boats"—hence their popular name of the "Q-boat Flowers." Each builder was allowed to adopt a form of mercantile disguise, with the result that, by appearance, these ships are divided into 15-20 types. All were built under Emergency War Programme.

War Losses.—Owing to the nature of the service these ships were engaged on, war losses were heavy. *Anchusa, Arbutus, Bergamot, Candytuft* (all by Armstrong Whitworth), *Cowslip* (Barclay Curle), *Gaillardia* (Blyth S.B. Co.), *Rhododendron, Salvia* (both by Irvine S.B. Co.), *Tulip* (Richardson, Duck), were all lost during the War. In all, 39 vessels of *Anchusa* and *Aubrietia* types were built. Although nominally rated as "Fleet Sweeping Vessels," they have no gallows at stern, and it is doubtful if they carry sweeping gear, unless of "otter" types.

BRITISH NAVY: FLEET-SWEEPING VESSELS (SLOOPS).
"Flower" Classes—56 Ships.

VALERIAN.

Appearance Notes for all Types.—Majority as *Valerian*, but *Azalea, Buttercup, Campanula, Celandine, Cornflower, Godetia, Hydrangea,* completed with topmasts 40 feet higher ; *Lily* completed with topmasts about 20 feet higher. Illustration for *Primrose* shows alterations to ships employed for duty on Mediterranean Convoys, Patrols, &c., mainmast, after gun and gallows, being removed to permit towing of Kite Balloons.

(ARABIS TYPE—26 SHIPS.)

BUTTERCUP (Nov., 1915), **CAMPANULA** (Dec., 1915), **CELANDINE** (Feb., 1916), **CORNFLOWER** (Mar., 1916), all four by Barclay, Curle. **GLADIOLUS** (Oct., 1915), **GODETIA** (Jan., 1916), **HYDRANGEA** (Mar., 1916), all three by Connell. **NIGELLA** (Dec., 1915), **PANSY** (Feb., 1916), both by Hamilton. **ASPHODEL** (Dec., 1915), **BERBERIS** (Feb., 1916), both by Henderson. **WALLFLOWER** (Nov., 1915), **WISTARIA** Dec., 1915), both by Irvine S.B. Co. **CROCUS** (Dec., 1915), **CYCLAMEN** (Feb., 1916), both by Lobnitz. **LOBELIA** (Mar., 1916), **LUPIN** (May, 1916), both by Simons. **MYOSOTIS** (Bow, McLachlan, April, 1916), **VERBENA** (Blyth S.B. Co., Nov., 1915), **AMARYLLIS** (Earle S.B. Co., Dec., 1915), **DELPHINIUM** (Napier & Miller, Dec., 1915), **VALERIAN** (C. Rennoldson, Feb., 1916), **ROSEMARY** (Richardson, Duck, Nov., 1915), **SNAPDRAGON** (Ropner, Dec., 1915), **POPPY** (Swan, Hunter, Nov.,1915), **PENTSTEMON** (Workman, Clark, Feb., 1916).

All 1250 tons. Completed, Dec., 1915-June, 1916. Dimensions : 255¼ (p.p.), 267¾ (o.a.) × 33½ × 11 (*mean*), 11½-11¾ feet (*max.* draught). *Designed* armament : 2—4.7 inch or 4 inch. 2—3 pdr. AA., but some have only 1—4.7 or 4 inch, with or without the 2—3 pdr. AA. A few are only armed with 2—3 pdr. AA. Designed I.H.P. 1400 = 17 kts., but for this speed they really have to develop about 2400 I.H.P. Machinery : 1 set 4-cylinder triple expansion. Boilers : 2 cylindrical. 1 screw. Coal : 130 tons *normal*, 260 tons *max.* = about 2000 miles at 15 kts. Complement, 79. Also see *General Notes.*

General Notes to "Arabis," "Azalea," and "Acacia" Types.—Single-screw Fleet Sweeping Vessels (Sloops), all built under Emergency War Programme. Popularly known as the "Flower Class," but are also referred to as the "Cabbage Class," or "Herbaceous Borders." Have triple hulls at bows to give extra protection against loss when working up mines. Very successful ships, but can only make designed speed with difficulty. Good sea-boats. Copies of this class were built in British yards for the French Navy. The last series of "Flowers" converted to Convoy Sloops (*q.v.*). Several mined during War and extensively re-built.

War Losses, Removals, &c.—*Alyssum, Aster* (both Earle S.B. Co.), *Arabis* (Henderson), *Begonia* (Barclay, Curle), *Genista* (Napier & Miller), *Mignonette* (Dunlop & Bremner), *Lavender, Nasturtium* (both McMillan), *Primula* (Swan Hunter), all lost during War. *Gentian* (Greenock & Grangemouth Co.) and *Myrtle* (Lobnitz), sunk in Baltic, 1919, during anti-Bolshevist operations. *Geranium, Marguerite, Mallow,* presented to Australian Navy. *Peony* (McMillan), sold out. *Petunia* (Workman, Clark), has also gone ; not certain if she has been lost or sold out. In all, 72 of these ships were built.

PRIMROSE.

(AZALEA TYPE—9 SHIPS.)

CARNATION (Sept., 1915). **CLEMATIS** (July, 1915), both by Greenock & Grangemouth Co. **JESSAMINE** (Sept., 1915), **ZINNIA** (Aug., 1915), both by Swan Hunter. **AZALEA** (Barclay, Curle, Sept., 1915). **CAMELLIA** (Bow, McLachlan, Sept., 1915). **HELIOTROPE** (Lobnitz, Sept., 1915). **SNOWDROP** (McMillan, Oct., 1915). **NARCISSUS** (Napier & Miller, Sept., 1915).

All details as "Acacia Type" below, but these ships were designed to mount 2—4.7 inch or 4 inch and 2—3 pdr. AA. Nearly all so armed, but one or two have no 3 pdrs. Complement, 79. Also see *General Notes.*

(ACACIA TYPE—21 SHIPS.)

DAHLIA (April, 1915), **DAPHNE** (May, 1915), **FOXGLOVE** (Mar., 1915), **HOLLYHOCK** (May, 1915), **LILY** (June, 1915), all five by Barclay, Curle. **BLUEBELL** (July, 1915), **DAFFODIL** (Aug., 1915), **MAGNOLIA** (June, 1915), all three by Scotts S. B. Co. **MARIGOLD** (May, 1915), **MIMOSA** (July, 1915), both by Bow, McLachlan, **JONQUIL** (May, 1915), **LABURNUM** (June, 1915), both by Connell & Co. **HONEYSUCKLE** (April, 1915), **IRIS** (June, 1915), both by Lobnitz. **ACACIA** (April, 1915), **ANEMONE** (May, 1915), both by Swan Hunter. **VERONICA** (Dunlop, Bremner, May, 1915), **LILAC** (Greenock & Grangemouth Co., April, 1915), **SUNFLOWER** (Henderson, May, 1915), **LARKSPUR** (Napier & Miller, 1915), **PRIMROSE** (Simons, June, 1915).

All 1200 tons. Completed, May-Sept., 1915. Dimensions : 250 (p.p.), 262½ (o.a.) × 33 × 11 (*mean*), 11½-12 feet (*max.* draught). Designed to mount 2—12 pdr. and 2—3 pdr. AA. Some still armed in this way ; others have (a) 2—4 inch, (b) 1—4 inch, (c) 1—4 inch and 1—12 pdr., (d) 2—12 pdr., with or without the 2—3 pdr. One or two armed *only* with 1 or 2—3 pdr. Designed H.P. 1400 or 1800 = 17 kts., but actually require about 2200 I.H.P. for this speed. Machinery : 1 set 4-cylinder triple expansion. Boilers : 2 cylindrical. 1 screw. Coal : 130 tons *normal*, 250 tons *max.* = about 2000 miles at 15 kts. Complement, 77. Also see *General Notes.*

BRITISH NAVY—TUNNEL MINE-SWEEPERS.

(DANCE CLASS—12 BOATS.)

QUADRILLE.

Photo, McClure, Macdonald.

MORRIS DANCE (——), **STEP DANCE** (——), builders not known, **GAVOTTE** (Mar., 1918), and **SARABANDE** (April, 1918), both by Goole Co., **TARANTELLA** (Hamilton, Oct., 1917), **PIROUETTE** (Rennie Forrest, Sept., 1917). These displace 265 tons. I.H.P. 512 = 10.4 kts., *except Gavotte* and *Tarantella*, I.H.P. 450 = 10.4 kts. **COTILLION** (——) and **MINUET** (——), both by Day, Summers, **COVERLEY** (——), and **QUADRILLE** (——), both by Ferguson Bros., **HORNPIPE** (——) and **MAZURKA** (——), both by Murdoch & Murray. All displace 290 tons. I.H.P. 450 = 9¼-10 kts. Twin screw (shallow-draught) Minesweepers with screws working in tunnels. Dimensions : 130 (o.a.) × 26-27 × 3½ feet. Guns : *Gavotte*, 1—12 pdr., 1—6 pdr. ; *Step Dance*, 1—6 pdr. AA. ; rest, 1—3 pdr. Machinery : Vertical compound. Boilers : Cylindrical. Fuel : 37-41½ tons oil. Complement, 22-26. Completed Nov., 1917-Sept., 1918.

Notes.—All built Emergency War programme. *Sword Dance* and *Fandango,* sunk by Bolshevist mines in River Dvina. Further units of this Class may be completing and others cancelled, but no details arew available of these extra boats.

BRITISH NAVY—TWIN-SCREW MINESWEEPERS.

CRAIGIE.

Photo, Robertson, Gourock, N.B.

CAMBERLEY (Tender, Navigation School).

Photo, Robertson, Gourock, N.B.

(TWIN SCREW "HUNT" CLASS—LATER TYPE—87 Ships.)

ABERDARE (April, 1918), **ABINGDON** (June, 1918), **ALBURY** (Nov., 1918), **ALRESFORD** (Jan., 1919), **APPLEDORE** (1919), **LEAMINGTON** (ex *Aldeburgh*, Aug., 1918), all six by Ailsa S.B. Co., **BADMINTON** (Mar., 1918), **BAGSHOT** (May, 1918), **BARNSTAPLE** (Mar., 1919), **SWINDON** (ex *Bantry*, 1919), all four by Ardrossan Co., **BANCHORY** (May, 1918), **BLOXHAM** (ex *Brixham*, 1919), **BRADFIELD** (May, 1918), **BURSLEM** (ex *Blakeney*, Mar., 1918), **GOOLE** (ex *Bridlington*, 1919), all five by Ayrshire Co., **BLACKBURN** (ex *Burnham*, Aug., 1918), **BOOTLE** (ex *Buckie*, June, 1918), **CAERLEON** (Dec., 1918), **CAMBERLEY** (Dec., 1918), **CARSTAIRS** (ex *Cawsand*, 1919), **CATERHAM** (Mar., 1919), all six by Bow, McLachlan, **CRAIGIE** (May, 1918), **DERBY** (ex *Dawlish*, Aug., 1918), **FAIRFIELD** (1919), *****FORRES** (ex *Fowey*, Nov., 1918), **DORKING** (Sept., 1918), **DUNDALK** (Jan., 1919), **DUNOON** (Mar., 1919), all seven by Clyde S.B. Co.), **BATTLE** (1919), **FERMOY** (1919), **FORFAR** (Nov., 1918), all three by Dundee S.B. Co., **FAREHAM** (June, 1918), **FEVERSHAM** (July, 1918), **FORD** (ex *Fleetwood*, Oct., 1918), **RUGBY** (ex *Filey*, Sept., 1918), all four by Dunlop & Bremner, **BURY** (May, 1919), **CHEAM** (July, 1919), **GADDESDEN** (Nov., 1917), **GAINSBOROUGH** (ex *Gorleston*, Feb., 1918), **GRETNA** (April, 1919), **HARROW** (July, 1918), **HAVANT** (Nov., 1919), **HUNTLEY** (ex *Helmsdale*, Jan., 1919), **INSTOW** (ex *Ilfracombe*, April, 1919), **NORTHOLT** (June, 1918), all ten by Jos. R. Eltringham, **IRVINE** (Dec., 1917), **KENDAL** (Feb., 1918), **LYDD** (ex *Lydney*, Dec., 1918), all four by Fairfield Co., **MALLAIG** (Oct., 1918), **MALVERN** (Feb., 1919), **MARAZION** (1919), **MUNLOCHY** (ex *Macduff*, June, 1918), all four by Fleming & Ferguson, **LONGFORD** (ex *Minehead*, Mar., 1919), **MARLOW** (Aug., 1918), **MISTLEY** (ex *Maryport*, Oct., 1918), **MONAGHAN** (ex *Mullion*, May, 1919), all four by W. Harkness. **NAILSEA** (ex *Newquay*, Aug., 1918), **NEWARK** (ex *Newlyn*, June, 1918), **REPTON** (ex *Wicklow*, 1919), **WEYBOURNE** (Feb., 1919), all four by A. & J. Inglis, **PANGBOURNE** (ex *Padstow*, Mar., 1918), **PETERSFIELD** (ex *Portmadoc*, Mar., 1919), **PONTYPOOL** (ex *Polperro*, June, 1918), **PRESTATYN** (ex *Porlock*, Nov., 1918), **ROSS** (ex *Ramsey*, 1919), all five by Messrs. Lobnitz, **SUTTON** (ex *Salcombe*, May, 1918), by Messrs. McMillan, **SALFORD** (ex *Shoreham*, April, 1918), **SALTASH** (July, 1918), **SALTBURN** (Oct., 1918), **SELKIRK** (Dec., 1918), all four by Messrs. Murdoch & Murray, **SHREWSBURY** (Feb., 1918), **SLIGO** (Mar., 1918), **WIDNES** (ex *Withernsea*, June, 1918), **YEOVIL** (Aug., 1918), all four by Messrs. Napier & Miller, **STAFFORD** (ex *Staithes*, Sept., 1918), **STOKE** (ex *Southwold*, July, 1918), both by Chas. Rennoldson, **CLONMEL** (ex *Stranraer*, May, 1918), **ELGIN** (ex *Troon*, Mar., 1919), **SHERBORNE** (ex *Tarbert*, June, 1918), **TIVERTON** (Sept., 1918), **TONBRIDGE** (Nov., 1918), **TRALEE** (Dec., 1918), **TRING** (ex *Teignmouth*, Aug., 1919), **TRURO** (April, 1919), **WEM** (ex *Walmer*, 1919), **WEXFORD** (1919), all ten by Messrs. Simons.

* *Forres* contracted for by Messrs. Dunlop Bremner, but contract and materials transferred to Clyde S.B. Co.

All Emergency War Programme. First ship delivered Feb., 1918; all deliveries not completed by Oct., 1919. Displacement, 800 tons. Dimensions : 220 (*p.p.*), 231 (*o.a.*) × 28 ft. 6⅝ in. × 7½ (*mean*), — feet (*max.* draught). Guns : A few have 1—4 inch and 1—12 pdr. AA. or 2—3 pdr., but majority have only 1—6 or 3 pdr. Several not armed now. Machinery : Vertical triple expansion. 2 screws. Designed I.H.P. 2200 = 16 kts. Boilers : Yarrow. Coal : 185 tons. Complement, 74.

General Notes.—Much the same as original Ailsa Co. design of Twin-Screw Sweepers (*Belvoir, Bicester, &c.*), but slight modifications introduced in these ships by Admiralty. In 1919, several had been assigned to Special Service, *e.g., Marazion, &c.* (Tenders to Submarine Depot Ships), *Salford, Camberley, Caterham* (Tenders to Navigation School), *Petersfield* (Admiral's Yacht and for service on South American Rivers), and so on. Six have been re-named and completed as Surveying Ships (*q.v.*). But on the demobilisation of the Mine Clearance Force, the majority of these ships will be laid up. Those originally named after coastal towns, watering places, fishing ports, &c., were all re-named after inland towns and villages, to obviate misunderstanding of signals and orders.

To distinguish from original "Hunt Class."—Look rather bigger and heavier. Thicker funnel, foremast higher and stepped *through* Chart House. Searchlight on forward extension of bridge. Superstructure runs well towards mainmast and has 4 ventilators arranged in a square. Hull level, *not* broken between mainmast and gallows.

Losses (after-Armistice).—*Cupar* (ex *Rosslare*, built by McMillan), *Kinross* (Fairfield), *Penarth* (Lobnitz). No War Losses.

Cancelled Ships.—*Alton* (ex *Arbroath*), *Ashburton*, both by Ailsa S.B. Co.; *Bideford, Bolton* (ex *Beaumaris*), both by Ardrossan D.D. & S.B. Co.; *Atheleney, Bathgate*, both by Clyde S.B. Co.; *Beccles, Blickling*, both by Dundee S.B. Co.; *Northepps*, by Messrs. Lobnitz; *Tain, Wembdon, Yealmpton*, all three by Messrs. Simons. Also the following ships (contractors not known) :—*Clifton, Crediton* (ex *Colyton*), *Curragh, Frome, Kew, Kingussie, Knowle, Okehampton, Oundle, Radnor, Reading, Retford, Ringwood, Runcorn, Shifnal.* Also *Fairburn, Clovelly*, either cancelled or re-named ; if latter, present names wanted.

BRITISH NAVY—P. W. & T. S. MINESWEEPERS.

(PADDLE SWEEPERS—7 OF LATER GROUP.)

HEXHAM.

Photo, Robertson, Gourock, N.B.

(TWIN SCREW "HUNT CLASS"—19 OF EARLIER GROUP.)

CATTISTOCK.

Photo, Robertson, Gourock, N.B.

BANBURY (Dec., 1917) and **HARPENDEN** (Feb., 1918), both by Ailsa S.B. Co. **HEXHAM** (Clyde S.B. Co., Dec., 1917). **LANARK** (Dec., 1917) and **LEWES** (Mar., 1918), both by Fleming & Ferguson. **SHINCLIFFE** (Dunlop, Bremner, Jan., 1918), **WETHERBY** (Murdoch & Murray, Mar., 1918).

Paddle minesweepers, design by Admiralty, adapted from Ailsa Co. design for *Atherstone, &c.* (*v.* next page). Completed Jan.-June, 1918. Displacement, 820 tons. Complement, 50-52. Dimensions : 235 (*p.p.*), 249¾ (*o.a.*) × 29 ft. 0¼ in. (58 feet outside paddle boxes) × 6¾-7 feet. Guns : 1—12 pdr. (12 cwt.), 1—3 inch AA. Designed I.H.P. 1400 = 15 kts. (actually 1500 = about 14½ kts.). Machinery : Diagonal compound. Boilers : Cylindrical return tube. Coal : 156 tons.

Notes.—All built under Emergency War Programme. Suffer from same defects as *Atherstone, &c.* (next page). To distinguish, note that foremast is stepped *through* chart house ; two *high* ventilators abaft fore funnel ; *no* derricks abeam of second stack. Commonly known as the "Improved Racecourse" type.

War Losses.—Nil. *Shirley* (Dunlop, Bremner) sold out for commercial service as a ferry boat, 1919.

BELVOIR (Mar., 1917) and **BICESTER** (June, 1917), both by Ailsa S.B. Co. **CATTISTOCK** (Clyde S.B Co., Feb., 1917), **COTSWOLD** (Nov., 1916) and **COTTESMORE** (Feb., 1917), both by Bow, McLachlan. **CROOME** (Clyde S.B. Co., May, 1917), **DARTMOOR** (Mar., 1917) and **GARTH** (May, 1917), both by Dunlop, Bremner. **HAMBLEDON** (Mar., 1917), and **HEYTHROP** (June, 1917), both by Fleming & Ferguson. **HOLDERNESS** (Nov., 1916) and **MEYNELL** (Feb., 1917), both by D. & W. Henderson. **MUSKERRY** (Nov., 1916) and **OAKLEY** (Jan., 1917). **PYTCHLEY** (Mar., 1917), and **QUORN** (June, 1917), both by Napier & Miller. **SOUTHDOWN** (1917) and **TEDWORTH** (June, 1917), both by Simons. **ZETLAND** (Murdoch & Murray, 1917).

Twin Screw Minesweepers, built to design by Ailsa Co. Completed Mar.-Oct., 1917. Displacement, 750 tons. Complement, 71. Dimensions : 220 (*p.p.*), 231 (*o.a.*) × 28 × 7 feet (*mean* draught.) Guns : 2—12 pdr., and 2—2 pdr., but some have temporary armament of 1—12 pdr. and 1—6 pdr. Designed I.H.P. 1800 = 16 kts. Machinery : 3-cylinder triple expansion. Boilers : Yarrow. Coal : 140 tons.

Notes.—All built under Emergency War Programme, and proved very successful. To distinguish from *Aberdare, Abingdon, &c.*, note that searchlight is on tower separated from fore bridges ; foremast is stepped *abaft* chart house ; superstructure round funnel runs out to beam and does not extend far towards stern ; hull at stern breaks level between mainmast and gallows. Generally known as the "Hunt" Class.

War Losses.—*Blackmorevale* (Ardrossan D.D. Co.).

BRITISH NAVY—PADDLE MINE SWEEPERS.

(PADDLE SWEEPERS—19 OF EARLIER GROUP.)

ERIDGE.

Photo, Robertson, Gourock, N.B.

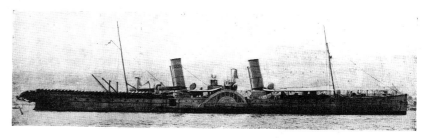

QUEEN VICTORIA.

* **QUEEN VICTORIA.** Purchased 1915. Used as Net Layer and later as Paddle Mine Sweeper. No details known.

* **PRINCE EDWARD** (ex *Prince of Wales*). Purchased 1915. No details known.

* **DUCHESS OF BUCCLEUCH.** Purchased 1916. No details known.

*Note.—Although these three ships were purchased outright for H.M. Navy, it is very likely they will be re-conditioned and sold out for mercantile use in the near future.

ATHERSTONE (Jan., 1916) and **CHELMSFORD** (April, 1916), [both by Ailsa S.B. Co., **CHELTENHAM** (Ardrossan Co., June, 1916), **CHEPSTOW** (April, 1916), **CROXTON** (April, 1916), **DONCASTER** (June, 1916) and **EGLINTON** (Sept., 1916), all by Ayrshire D.Y. Co., **EPSOM** (G. Brown, May, 1916), **ERIDGE** (Clyde S.B. Co., Feb., 1916), **GATWICK** (April, 1916) and **GOODWOOD** (June, 1916), both by Dundee S.B. Co., **HALDON** (Mar., 1916), **HURST** (May, 1916) and **SANDOWN** (July, 1916), all by Dunlop, Bremner, **LINGFIELD** (Fleming & Ferguson, April, 1916), **MELTON** (Hamilton, Mar., 1916), **NEWBURY** (A. & J. Inglis, July, 1916), **PONTEFRACT** (Murdoch & Murray, June, 1916), **TOTNES** (McMillan, May, 1916).

Paddle Mine Sweepers, built to designs by Ailsa Co. Completed, April-Oct., 1916. Displacement, 810 tons. Complement, 50. Dimensions : 235 (*p.p.*), 245¾ (*o.a.*) × 29 (58 feet over paddles) × 6¾ feet (*mean draught*). Guns : 2—12 pdr. Designed H.P. 1400 = 15 kts. Machinery : Inclined compound. Boilers : Cylindrical return tube. Coal : 156 tons.

Notes.—All built under Emergency War Programme. Fairly good sea-boats, but lose speed badly in a seaway, through paddle boxes getting choked with water. *Eridge* and *Melton* were originally fitted to carry seaplanes. To differentiate from *Banbury, Hexham*, &c., note that foremast is stepped *before* fore bridges : also these boats have derricks abeam of second funnel. Unofficially known as the "Racecourse" Class.

War Losses.—*Ascot* (Ailsa Co.), *Redcar* (Ayrshire D.Y. Co.), *Kempton* (Ferguson Bros.), *Ludlow* (Goole Co.) *Plumpton* (McMillan).

Patrol Gunboats *Kildonan, Kilmallock, Kilmanahan, Kilmarnock, Kilmarten, Kilmead, Kilmelford*, all described on an earlier page—are fitted as Mine Sweepers.

In addition to those listed above the following appear in "British Vessels Lost at Sea 1914-18" HMSO. Screw sweepers: *Roedean, Newmarket, Clacton.* Paddle sweepers. St. *Seiriol, Ericks Isle, Queen of the North, Brighton Queen, Duchess of Hamilton, Hythe, Lady Ismay, Fair Maid, Nepaulin, Duchess of Montrose, Marsa, Princess Mary II* lost in Aegean August 1919.

BRITISH NAVY—DEPOT SHIPS.

Depot Ships.

Note—The following old warships have been allocated for service as Depot Ships, but will serve only as Accommodation Ships, Hulks for overflow purposes, &c. Since they will not be required for War Fleet and have no fighting value, details and illustrations are not given for them.

Battleships :—

Implacable	*Cæsar*	*Mars*
Venerable	*Hannibal*	*Victorious*
Glory		

Cruisers and Light Cruisers :—

Crescent	*Imperieuse*	*Naiad*

The following vessels have been assigned to duty as Depot Ships. They will not serve in a sea-going capacity any longer, but only as Depot Ships to Local Defence Flotillas and Destroyers, Submarines, &c., in Reserve. No illustrations or details given of these ships.

For T.B.D. :—*Prince George, Essex, Europa, Dido, Apollo,*

For Patrol Gunboats :—*Hermione.*

For Anti-Submarine Service :—*Gibraltar.*

For Submarines :—*Rosario, Pactolus, Onyx, Dolphin.*

Destroyer Depot Ships.

Photo wanted.

SANDHURST (ex s.s. *Manipur*, Harland & Wolff, purchased 1915 and converted by Workman, Clerk.) 11,500 tons. Dimensions : 470 (*p.p.*) × 58 × 20 feet (*max. draught*). Guns : 4—4 inch, 2—6 pdr. AA. I.H.P. 4000 = 10.5 kts. Coal : 1475 tons. Complement, 269. Cyl. boilers.
Tenders : 2 Drifters.

Destroyer Depot Ships—(*Continued*).

Photo, Dr. J. A. Prendergast.

GREENWICH (Dobson & Co., completed by Swan Hunter. Purchased 1915). 8600 tons. Dimensions : 390 (*p.p.*) × 52 × 19¾ feet (*max. draught*). Guns : 4—4 inch, 2—6 pdr. AA. I.H.P. 2500 = 11 kts. Coal : 960 tons. Complement, 261. Cyl. boilers.
Tenders : 2 Drifters.

WOOLWICH (Scotts. S. & E. Co., 1912). 3380 tons. Dimensions: 320 × 40 × 14¼ feet. Guns : 2—4 inch. H.P. 2600 = 13.5 kts. Coal : 370 tons. Complement, 263.
Tenders : 2 Drifters.

Destroyer Depot Ships—(*Continued*).

DILIGENCE (ex *Tabaristan*, 1907. Purchased 1913). 7400 tons. Dimensions : 390 (*p.p.*) × 46 × — feet. Guns : 4—4 inch. H.P. 5000 = 14.2 kts. Coal : 780 tons. Complement, 258.
Tenders : 2 Drifters.

BLENHEIM.

BLAKE (1889) & **BLENHEIM** (1890.) Both converted 1907. 9000 tons. Dimensions : 375 (*p.p.*) × 65 × 25¾ feet (*max. draught*). Guns : 4—old 6 inch, and 2—4 inch in *Blake*; 1—4 inch and 7—12 pdr. in *Blenheim*. Designed H.P. 20,000 = 21.1 kts. Coal : *normal*, 624 tons ; also 650 tons carried in small bags (1 cwt. each) for destroyers.
Tenders : 2 Drifters *each*.

Destroyer Depot Ships—(Continued).

LEANDER (1882). 4380 tons. Dimensions : 300 (p.p.) × 46 × 21¼ feet. (max. draught). Guns : 2—12 pdr., 2—6 pdr., 1 M.G. Armour : 1½″ deck amidships. H.P. 5000 = 16.5 kts. Coal : 813 tons.
Tender : 1 Drifter.

TYNE (purchased 1878). 3590 tons. Dimensions : 320 (p.p.) × 34 × 20 feet (mean draught). Guns : 1—12 pdr., 2—6 pdr. Designed H.P. 1200 = 11.7 kts. Coal : 510 tons. Complement, 172.

HECLA (purchased 1878). 5600 tons. Dimensions : 391½ (p.p.) × 38¾ × 21¾ feet (mean draught). Guns : 4—4 inch. 1 M.G. Designed H.P. 2400 = 13.4 kts. Coal : 572 tons. Complement, 266.
Tenders : 2 Drifters.

BRITISH NAVY—DEPOT SHIPS—Continued.

Torpedo Sub-Depot Ships (R.F.A.)

* **SOBO** 4163 tons. Speed : 9 kts. Coal : 413 tons.

* **SOKOTO** 3870 tons. Speed : 9 kts. Coal : 380 tons.

*Purchased 1914. As it is very probable that these ships will be sold out of H.M. Navy in the near future, they are not illustrated

Submarine Depot Ships.

Note.—Light Cruiser, **FEARLESS** and Flotilla Leader **ITHURIEL,** are attached to 1st and 2nd Submarine Flotillas

Photo, Abrahams, Devonport.

AMBROSE (Clyde S.B. Co., 1915. Purchased 1915). 6480 tons. Dimensions : 387¾ (o.a.) × 47½ × 20½ feet. Guns : 2—12 pdr. I.H.P. 6350 = 14½ kts. Complement, 240.
Tenders : *Marazion* and 1 Drifter. (Also serve for *Pandora*.)

TITANIA (Clyde S.B. Co., 1915, purchased 1915). 5200 tons. Dimensions : 335 (p.p.) × 46¼ × 18¼ feet. I.H.P. 3200 = 14.5 kts. Torpedo tubes : 2. Coal : 498 tons. Complement, 245. Cyl. boilers.
Tenders : *Adamant*, 1 Drifter.

Photo, Dr. J. A. Prendergast.

LUCIA (Furness Withy Co., ex German Prize, *Spreewald*, converted by Clyde S.B. Co., 1916). 6005 tons. Dimensions : 366 (o.a.) × 45¼ × 19¾ feet. Guns : 2—3 pdr. AA. I.H.P. 2700 × kts. Coal : 700 tons. Cyl. boilers. Complement, 245.
Tenders : *Repton*, 1 Trawler.

Submarine Depot Ships—Continued.

PANDORA (ex *Seti*, purchased from Russia, 1914). 4350 tons. Dimensions : 330 × 43 × 16 feet. Guns : Nil. H.P. 2200 = 11 kts. Coal : 580 tons. Complement, 70.
Tenders : *Marazion* and 1 Drifter (also serve for *Ambrose*).

Photo, Cribb.

MAIDSTONE (Scott's S. & E. Co., 1912). 3600 tons. Dimensions : 355 × 45 × 17¾ feet. Guns : Nil. H.P. 2800 = 14·3 kts. Coal : 465 tons. Complement, 159.
Tenders : *Salford*, 1 Drifter.

ADAMANT and **ALECTO** (both Laird, 1911). 935 tons. Dimensions : 190 × 32½ × 11 feet (mean draught). Guns : *Adamant*, 1—4 inch. Designed H.P. 1400 = 14 kts. Coal : 180 tons. Complement, 63.

No photo available.
Similar to St. George below.

ROYAL ARTHUR (ex *Centaur*) (1891). 7700 tons. Dimensions : 360 (p.p.) × 60¾ × 26⅓ feet. Guns : Nil. I.H.P. 12,000 = 20 kts., but 7000 = 15-16 kts. may be present maximum. Coal : 1230 tons. Complement, —.
Tenders to *Royal Arthur* : 2 Drifters.

Submarine Depot Ships—Continued.

ST. GEORGE (1890). Cruiser of *Edgar* type ; converted 1911. 7700 tons. Dimensions : 360 (p.p.) × 60¾ × 23⅓ feet (mean draught). Guns : 2—6 inch, 2—12 pdr. AA., 2—3 pdr. AA. Designed H.P. 12,000 = 19.5 kts. (present maximum H.P. 7000 for about 15-16 kts.). Coal : normal, 850 tons ; maximum, 1120 tons. Complement, 301.
Tenders to *St. George* : 2 Drifters.

Submarine Depot Ships—Continued.

VULCAN (1889). Rebuilt 1908. 6620 tons. Dimensions : 350 × 58 × 23½ feet (max. draught). Guns : 2—8.7 inch. Armour : 5″ deck (amidships), 6″ conning tower, 5″ engine hatches. Designed H.P. 12,000 = 20 kts. Can do now about 16 kts. Coal : maximum 1347 tons. Dürr boilers (1909). Complement, 255.
Tenders to *Vulcan* : *Alecto* and 1 Drifter.

THAMES (1885) & **FORTH** (1886). 4050 tons. Dimensions : 300 (p.p.) × 46 × 19¾ feet (max. draught). No guns. Designed H.P. 5700 = 17.2 kts. originally. Coal : 740 tons maximum. Fitted as Floating Workshops. Complement, 187.

Tenders to *Thames* : *Fermoy*, 1 Drifter.
Tenders to *Forth* : *Elgin*, *Forres*, 4 Trawlers.

ARROGANT (1896). 5750 tons. Designed H.P. 10,000 = 19 kts. Belleville boilers. Coal : normal, 500 tons ; maximum 1175 tons. (Converted 1911-12.)

BONAVENTURE (1892), of the *Astræa* class. 4360 tons. Armament : 2—6 inch, 8—6 pdrs. Deck 2 on slope. Designed H.P. 9000 = 19·5 kts. Cylindrical boilers. Coal : normal, 400 tons ; maximum, 1000 tons.

BRITISH NAVY—REPAIR & SALVAGE SHIPS.

Repair Ships—(R.F.A.).

SCOTSTOUN Begun, February, 1916. Launched, Completed, July, 1916. Built by Yarrows, as Repair Ship for "Insect", and "Fly" Classes of Gunboats. 300 tons. Dimensions: 132 (*p.p.*), 150 (*o.a.*) × 31 × 3¼ feet draught. I.H.P. 200 = 7.7 kts. Compound surface condensing engines. Loco. boiler. Oil: 20/36 tons.

BACCHUS (Hamilton & Co., 1915, purchased 1915). About 3500 tons. Dimensions: 295 × 44 × 12½ feet. Guns: Not known. I.H.P. = kts. Coal: 873 tons.

RELIANCE (ex *Knight-Companion*, 1910, bought 1913). 3250 tons. Dimensions: 470 × 57¾ × — feet. H.P. 3250 = 11 kts. Coal: 1700 tons.

CYCLOPS (ex *Indrabarah*, 1905). 11,300 tons. Dimensions: 460 (*p.p.*) × 55 × 21 feet. Guns: 6—4 inch. Machinery: Triple expansion. Designed H.P. 3500 = 11.75 kts. Coal capacity: 1595 tons. Fitted as Floating Workshop and Distilling Ship. Complement, 294.

Repair Ships—(*Continued*).

ASSISTANCE (1901). 9600 tons. Dimensions: 436 (*p.p.*) × 53 × 20 feet. Guns: 10—3 pdr. Machinery: Triple expansion. Boilers: Cylindrical. Fitted with Howden's forced draught. Designed H.P. (*f.d.*) 4000 = 12 kts. Coal: 2180 tons. Fitted as Floating Workshop and Distilling Ship. Complement, 283.

AQUARIUS (*ex Hampstead*) (1902). 2800 tons. Length (*p.p.*), 268 feet. Beam, 37¾ feet. Draught, 16 feet. Speed, 10·5 kts.

Salvage Vessels.

REINDEER (1884). 970 tons. Re-engined by Fairfield Co., 1918. I.H.P. 1200 = kts.

RACER (1884, rebuilt 1916-17) 970 tons. I.H.P. 1100 = 11 kts. Re-engined with starboard machinery of old T.B. 8 submersible electric, steam centrifugal and compressed air pumps throwing 3000 tons per hour. 2—17 ton derricks.

MELITA (ex *Ringdove*, 1889). Ex-gunboat. 820 tons. H.P. 750 = 11 kts. Coal: 80 tons. Complement, 74.

MARINER (1883). Ex-Sloop and Boom Defence Vessel. 970 tons.

Also *Moonfleet*, *Hippopotamus* and *Rhinoceros*, built 1917. Are probably only chartered vessels which may no longer be in H.M. Navy.

BRITISH NAVY—OIL TANKERS (R.F.A.).

Oil Tankers (R.F.A.).

Oil Tankers *Birchleaf*, *Appleleaf* (ex *Texol*), *Plumleaf* (ex *Trinol*), *Erivan*, &c., are understood to have been disposed of, or returned to owners. It is possible that some of the "*Ol*" Tankers detailed hereafter may have taken up commercial service.

1 funnel with 1 mast just before, both raking and aft of amidships.

PETROBUS, PETRELLA, PETRONEL (Dunlop, Bremner, 1918). 1024 tons. Dimensions: 164 × 28 × 11½ feet. I.H.P. 500 = 9-10 kts. Own oil: 50 tons. Cylindrical boilers. Complement, 16.

Appearance unknown.

DREDGOL (Simons, 1918). About 7000 tons. Dimensions: 326 × 54½ × 18¾ feet. I.H.P. 2400 = 11 kts. Own oil: 360 tons. Cylindrical boilers.

1 funnel with 1 mast before, close together, as in Standard Cargo Ships.

FRANCOL (Earle S.B. Co.), **MONTENOL** (W. Gray), **SERBOL** (Caledon S.B. Co.). All details as *Belgol* below, but of different appearance. All launched 1917.

Oil Tankers (R.F.A.)—*Continued.*

2 masts fore and aft: 1 funnel between. *Rapidol* a little different to other ships.

BELGOL (Irvine D.D. Co.), **CELEROL** (Short Bros.), **FORTOL** (McMillan), **PRESTOL** (Napier & Miller), **RAPIDOL** (W. Gray), **SLAVOL, VITOL** (Greenock and Grangemouth Co.). All launched 1917. 4900 tons. Dimensions: 335 × 41½ × 20¼ feet. I.H.P. 3375 = 14 kts. Own oil: 300 tons. Cylindrical boilers. Complement, 39.

1 mast forward.
1 funnel aft.

BIRCHOL, BOXOL (Barclay, Curle), **EBONOL** (Clyde S.B. Co.), **ELDEROL, ELMOL** (Swan Hunter), **LARCHOL, LIMOL,** (Lobnitz). All launched 1917. As *Sprucol*, *Teakol*, below, but these have triple expansion engines and cylindrical boilers. I.H.P. 700 = 12 kts.

1 mast forward.
1 funnel aft.

SPRUCOL, TEAKOL (Short Bros.), **OAKOL, PALMOL** (W. Gray & Co.). All launched 1917. 1925 tons. Dimensions: 220 × 34 × 12 feet. Bolinders oil engines. B.H.P. 640 = 8-10 kts. Own oil: 40 tons. Complement, 19.

Oil Tankers (R.F.A.)—*Continued.*

1 mast forward.
1 funnel aft.

CREOSOL (Short Bros.), **DISTOL, PHILOL, SCOTOL** (Tyne Iron S.B. Co.), **KIMMEROL, VISCOL** (Craig, Taylor). All launched 1916. 1920 tons. Dimensions: 220 × 34⅔ × 12¼ feet. I.H.P. 700 = 9 kts. Own oil: 40 tons. Cylindrical boilers. Complement, 19.

2 masts, 1 funnel at stern.

MIXOL (Greenock & Grangemouth Co., 1916). **THERMOL** (Caledonian S.B. Co., 1916). 4145 tons. Dimensions: 270 × 38½ × 20¼ feet. I.H.P. 1200 = 11 kts. Oil: 150 tons.

TREFOIL (Pembroke, 1913). 4060 tons. Dimensions: 280 × 39 × 18¼ feet. 2 sets 6-cylinder 2-cycle Diesel engines. H.P. 1500 = 12 kts. Deadweight capacity: 2000 tons. Own oil: 200 tons.

"*Ferol*," "*Servitor*," "*Attendant*," *Carol*" *one mast forward, one funnel aft.*

FEROL (Devonport, 1914). **SERVITOR** (Chatham, 1914). 2007 tons. Dimensions: 200 × 34 × 13 feet. 2 sets 4-cylinder 2-cycle Diesel engines. B.H.P. 450 = 8 kts. Deadweight capacity: 1000 tons. Own oil fuel: 29 tons.

ATTENDANT (Chatham, 1913), **CAROL** (Devonport, 1913). 1935 tons. Dimensions: 200 × 34 × 13 feet. I.H.P. 450 = 8 kts. Coal: 60 tons.

(*Continued on next page.*)

BRITISH MISCELLANEOUS.

Special Service.

Photo, Abrahams & Sons.

FORTITUDE (*ex Neptune*) (1896). 400 tons. H.P. 1200.

MAGNET (1883). 430 tons. Guns: 4—3 pdr. H.P. 650 = 12 kts.

Photo, Abrahams & Sons.

TRAVELLER (1883). 700 tons. Guns: 4—3 pdr. H.P. 1100 = 12 kts.

> 1 funnel, 2 masts.

IMOGENE (1882). 460 tons. H.P. 390 = 11 kts.

SPHINX (1882). 1130 tons. Guns: 1—old 6 in., 6—old 4 in. H.P. 1100—12·5 kts.

SEAHORSE (1880). 670 tons. Guns: 1—12 pdr. howitzer. H.P. 1100—12·5 kts.

Photo, Abrahams & Sons.

UNDINE (*ex Wildfire, ex Hiawatha*) (1880). 453 tons. Speed 9 kts.

VESUVIUS (1874). 245 tons. 2 torpedo tubes.

Miscellaneous Special Service.

RAVEN (1882). (*ex gunboat*). 465 tons. *Diving School.*

Special Petrol or Oil Ships.

PETROLEUM, KHAKI, ISLA (1903). 4521 tons. Length 370 feet. Beam, 49 feet. *Depth*, 39 feet. Also **BURMA.** 394? tons.

Also *TREFOIL & TURMOIL building.*

Special Collier.

MERCEDES (1902). 9900 tons. Dimensions: 351'×50×28 feet. H.P. 2350 = kts.

Oil Tankers (R.F.A.)

BURMA (Greenock, 1911). 3945 tons. H.P. 1200 = 11 kts. Cargo capacity: 2500 tons oil fuel. Own fuel: 210 tons.

PETROLEUM (Wallsend, 1901). 9900 tons. Dimensions: 370 × 48¾ × 24 feet. H.P. 2000 = 13 kts. Oil: 426 tons.

KHARKI (1899, bought 1900). 1430 tons. H.P. 775 = 13 kts. Fuel: 90 tons.

ISLA (1903, purchased 1907). 1010 tons. Dimensions: 170 × 26 × 12 feet. H.P. 650 = 10 kts. Petrol-carrying vessel for submarines. Fuel: 75 tons.

INDUSTRY (1901). 1460 tons. H.P. 750 = 10 kts. Fuel: 180 tons.

Collier (R.F.A.)

MERCEDES (1901, purchased 1908). 9930 tons. Dimensions: 350 × 50¼ × 28 feet. H.P. 2350 = 9 kts. Coal: 750/1603 tons.

Hospital Ships.

"*Soudan* Type."—One ship assigned for duty with Atlantic Fleet, and another for duty with Mediterranean Fleet. Names not known, but one believed to be **ST. MARGARET OF SCOTLAND** of which no photographs or details are available.

Ice Breakers (R.F.A.)

> "Ermiak type."
> 2 funnels, 2 masts

SVIATOGOR (ex-Russian *Sviatogor*, Clyde, 1915-16). No details available.

ALEXANDER (ex-Russian *Aleksandr Nevski*). Built by Armstrongs. Begun June, 1916 (for Russian Government), launched December, 1916, completed December, 1917. 3 screws (2 aft, 1 forward). Cylindrical boilers. No other details known.

Tugs.

ST. ANNE,   **ST. COLUMB,**   **ST. FINBARR,**
ST. ARVANS,   **ST. CYRUS,**   **ST. ISSEY,**
ST. BLAZEY,   **ST. FERGUS,**   **ST. SAMPSON.**

No details available. For Target Work and General Fleet or Squadron duties.
Also many other Tugs, Tanks, &c., but as these are not attached to Fleets or Squadrons, they are not listed.

Despatch Vessels.

WATERWITCH Begun, May 6th, 1914. Launched, October 17th, 1914. Completed, June 7th, 1915. Late Turkish *Rechid Pasha*, purchased 1915. Built by Fairfield. 400 tons. Dimensions: 165 × 26 × 6½ feet (*mean draught*). Designed H.P. 625 = kts. *Trials:* 615 = 13.1. Triple expansion engines and cylindrical boilers. 2 screws. Coal 34 tons. Complement, 14.

SPHINX (1882). 1130 tons. Guns: 4—4 inch, 2 M.G. H.P. 1100 = 12.5 kts. Coal: 220 tons.

Royal Yachts.

ALEXANDRA (1907). 2050 tons. Dimensions: 275 (p.p.) × 40 × 12¼ feet (*mean* draught). Guns: 2—7 pdr. (bronze). Parsons turbines. H.P. 4500 = 18.25 kts. (19.1 on first trials). Yarrow boilers. Coal: 270 tons. Complement, 17?.
(*Continued on next page.*)

Royal Yachts—Continued.

VICTORIA AND ALBERT (1899). 4700 tons. Dimensions: 380 (p.p.) × 40 × 18 feet (mean draught). Guns: 2—6 pdr. (bronze). H.P. 11,800 = 20 kts. Belleville boilers. Coal: normal, 350 tons; maximum, 2000 tons. Comp. 336.

Admiralty Yacht.

ENCHANTRESS (1903). 3470 tons. Dimensions: 320 × 40 × 15 feet. Guns: 4—3 pdr. H.P. 6400 = 18 kts. Yarrow boilers. Coal: 350 tons.

Yachts.

TRIAD Yacht, S. N. O. Persian Gulf. (Caledonian S.B. Co., 1909, purchased 1915). 2354 tons. Dimensions: 264 × 35 × 15¾ feet. Guns: Not known. I.H.P. 2235 = 14 kts. Coal: 480 tons.

BRITISH NAVY—MISCELLANEOUS.

Yachts—Continued.

ALACRITY (ex Russian Mlada, taken over 1919). No details known. Yacht and Despatch Vessel, C.-in-C., China.
Note.—Gunboat Hussar is Despatch Vessel, C.-in-C., Mediterranean. Convoy Sloop Bryony has served as Yacht, Rear-Admiral, Ægean. Hunt Class T. S. Minesweeper Petersfield may also serve as Yacht on South American Station.

ROSITA (Leith, 1900). 93 tons gross. Dimensions: 100 × 16 × feet. I.H.P. 250.

DOTTER. No details known.

Admiralty Whalers.

ZEDWHALE.   Photo, Parry & Sons.

ARCTIC WHALE,	CACHALOT,	PILOTWHALE,
BALAENA,	COWWHALE,	RIGHTWHALE,
BELUGA,	FINWHALE,	RORQUAL,
BOWHEAD,	HUMPBACK,	ZEDWHALE,
BULLWHALE,	ICEWHALE,	(ex Meg.)

Emergency War Programme. Built 1915, by Smiths Dock Co. 336 tons. Dimensions: 139¾ × 25 × 6½ feet. Guns: 1—12 pdr., but Zedwhale has also 1—6 pdr. AA. and 1—3 pdr. H.P. 1000 = 12-13 kts. Coal: 60 tons. Complement, 26.

Admiralty Trawlers.

JAMES CATON.   Builders' Photo, Messrs Lobnitz & Co.

Nine assigned to Fleet Target Service, Atlantic and Mediterranean Fleets; about 40 to Training and Experimental Establishments, as detailed on a later page. Disposal of rest not known.

Belong to "Castle," "Mersey," and "Strath" types. Usually as follows:—(a) 665 tons, 11 kts. speed, 204 tons coal; (b) 547 tons, 10½ kts., 164 tons coal; (c) 429 tons, 10 kts., 95 tons coal. Guns: Usually 1—12 pdr., but a few have 1—4 inch. Above illustrations typical of appearance.

Admiralty Drifters.

In addition to those detailed on next page as Tenders to Training Establishments, about 60 other Drifters are assigned as Tenders to the Atlantic, Home and Mediterranean Fleets. Displace 199 tons. Speed: 9 kts. Gun: Usually 1—6 pdr. Coal: 34-39 tons.

Surveying Service.

BEAUFORT (ex Ambleside, 1919), **COLLINSON** (ex Amersham, 1919), by Ailsa S.B. Co. **FITZROY** (ex Pinner, ex Portreath, 1919), **FLINDERS** (ex Radley, 1919), by Lobnitz & Co. **KELLET** (ex Uppingham, 1919), **CROZIER** (ex Verwood, ex Ventnor, 1919), by Simons & Co. Converted Twin Screw Minesweepers of "Hunt Class." 800 tons. Dimensions: 231 (o.a.) × 28½ × 7½ feet. Guns: 1—3 pdr. I.H.P. 2200 = 16 kts. Machinery: Vertical triple expansion. 2 screws. Boilers: Babcock or Yarrow. Coal: 185 tons.

ENDEAVOUR.

ENDEAVOUR (Fairfield, 1912). 1280 tons. Dimensions: 200 × 34 × 10 feet. Guns: 1—3 pdr., 2 Maxims. H.P. 1100 = 13 kts. Coal: 221 tons. Complement, 44. Specially built for survey.

RESEARCH (1888). 520 tons. Guns: 1—old 7 pdr. M.L. Speed about 9½ kts.

SEALARK (1878). 900 tons. Speed about 9-10 kts.

TRITON (1882). 410 tons. Guns: 1—old 7 pdr. M.L. Speed, 9 kts.

Surveying Service—Continued.

DAISY (1911) & **ESTHER** (1912). 600 tons. (On surveying service at present.)

MERLIN (1901). 1070 tons. **MUTINE** (1900). 980 tons. Guns: 2—3 pdr., 2 M.G. All about 13¼ kts. Belleville boilers. Coal: about 160-203 tons.

HEARTY (1885). 1300 tons. Guns: 4—3 pdr. H.P. 2100 = 14 kts.
For Sloop Fantome, on Surveying Service, see Australian Navy Section.

Fishery Protection Vessels.

Kilbeggan	Kilclogher
Kilfree	Kilmalcolm
Kilclief	

Above Patrol Gunboats for Fisheries Protection Service. All are described on an earlier page.

Coastguard Cruisers.

SAFEGUARD (Day, Summers, 1914). 875 tons. Dimensions: 160 × 29 × 10⅔ feet. H.P. 1350 = 15 kts. Guns: 2—3 pdr. Coal: 170 tons. Complement, 39.

Builders' photo, Messrs. Hall Russell & Co.

WATCHFUL (Hall, Russell, 1912). 612 tons. Dimensions: 154 × 25 × 11¾ feet. H.P. 800 = 11.5 kts. Guns: 2—3 pdr. Coal: 150 tons. Complement, 32.

ARGON.

ARGON (ex Argus, 1905). 380 tons. H.P. 650 = 12.25 kts. Guns: 2—6 pdr. Coal: 55 tons.
SQUIRREL (1905). 230 tons. H.P. 300 = 10 kts. Guns: 2—3 pdr. Coal: 44 tons.
JULIA (ex Maretanza, 1897). 310 tons. H.P. 650 = kts. Guns: 2 old 7 pdr. M.L. Coal: 53 tons.

ROYAL INDIAN MARINE.

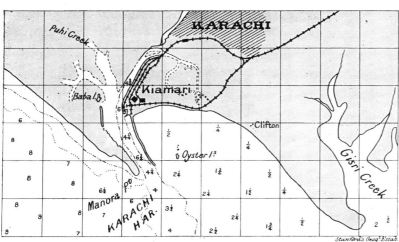

KARACHI (Indian Ocean). Graving Dock (Port Trust), $263\frac{1}{4} \times 50 \times 12\frac{3}{4}$ feet. Admiralty Chart No. 40.

Docks.

CALCUTTA.—Eleven, 535–202 feet long, 76–41 feet at entrance, 23–8 feet over sill H.W.O.S.

BOMBAY.—One dock, $1000 \times 100 \times 34$ feet; Merewether, $525 \times 65 \times 28\frac{1}{2}$ feet; Ritchie, $495 \times 66 + 18$ feet; five others.

Troopships.

NORTHBROOK (Clydebank, 1907). 5820 tons. Dimensions: $360 \times 51\frac{3}{4} \times 18$ feet. H.P. 7000 = 16 kts. Armament: 6—4 inch, 6—3 pdrs.

RECOGNITION SILHOUETTES.

Scale : 1 inch = 160 feet.

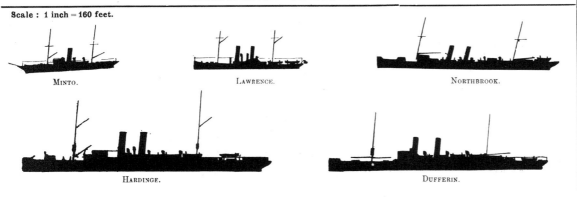

MINTO.   LAWRENCE.   NORTHBROOK.

HARDINGE.   DUFFERIN.

DUFFERIN (Vickers, 1904). 7457 tons. Dimensions: $437 \times 53 \times 19$ ft. H.P. 9800 = 19 kts. Coal: 1200 tons. Armament: 8—4 inch, 8—3 pdrs.

Troopships—(continued).

HARDINGE (Fairfield, 1900). 6520 tons. Dimensions: $407 \times 51 \times 19$ feet. H.P. 9366 = 18 kts. Fitted with Howden's forced draught. Armament: 6—4·7 inch, 6—3 pdrs., 4 Maxims.

MINTO.   *Photo, W. Ewart Williams, Esq., R.I.M.*

MINTO (Birkenhead, 1893). 930 tons gross. Dimensions: $205\frac{1}{2} \times 31\frac{1}{2} \times$ — feet. H.P. 2028 = 14 kts.

ELPHINSTONE (Newcastle, 1887). 950 tons. Dimensions: $205\frac{1}{2} \times 28\frac{1}{4} \times 14\frac{1}{2}$ feet. H.P. 1670 = 14 kts.

DALHOUSIE (Greenock, 1886). 1960 tons. H.P. 1500 = 13 kts. Coal: 300 tons. Armament: 6—6 pdrs.

CLIVE (Glasgow, 1882). 3570 tons. Dimensions: $300 \times 45\frac{1}{2} \times 16\frac{1}{2}$ feet. H.P. 2300 = 12 kts.

Steamers.

NEARCHUS (Beardmore. Begun Oct., 1913; launched 15th Nov., 1914; completed 7th Dec., 1914.) 925 tons. Dimensions: 180 $(p.p.) \times 29 \times 11$ feet. S.H.P. 550 = 11 kts. (trials 650 = 11·75). Parsons geared turbines. 1 Yarrow boiler. Oil: 120 tons.

MAYO 1125 tons *gross*.

GUIDE 817 tons *gross*.

Despatch Vessel.

Photo by favour of N. O'Toole, Esq.

LAWRENCE (1886). Paddle wheel steamer. 1154 tons. Dimensions: $212 \times 32\frac{1}{4} \times 18\frac{3}{4}$ feet. Guns: 4—6 pdr., 4 machine. H.P. 1200 = 13·5 kts. Coal: 270 tons.

Hospital Ships.

HP I—HP II. Paddle-wheel Hospital Ships. Built by Beardmore, Caird & Co., Bow, McLachlan, Lobnitz, Ailsa S.B. Co., Blyth S.B. Co., 1916–17, for Mesopotamia.

Yachts.

2 small Viceregal Yachts, *Maud* and *Lytton*.

Surveying Ships.

Photo, W. Ewart Williams, Esq., R.I.M.

INVESTIGATOR (Vickers, 1907). Gross tonnage 1015, net 515. I.H.P. 1500.

Also *Nancowry* of 70 tons gross and 7 kts. speed.

Pilot Vessel.

LADY FRASER (1908). 2062 tons. Dimensions: $270 \times 38 \times 13\frac{1}{2}$ feet. Speed: 13·7 kts.

River Craft.

P 51, 51 (Beardmore). **P 52—57** (Caird & Co.). **P 58, 59.** (————). **P 60, 61** (Lobnitz). Paddle-wheel Vessels, built 1916–17 for Tigris and Euphrates. H.P. 1200 = 15 kts. Guns: 1—3 pdr.

PALINURUS (1907). Screw River Steamer. 298 tons.

BHAMO. Composite Stern-wheel Vessel. 255 tons. Guns: 2 machine.

IRRAWADY. Paddle-wheel River Steamer. 338 tons *gross*. Guns: 2 machine.

SLADEN. Paddle-wheel River Steamer. 260 tons. Guns: 5 machine.

There are also about 24 yard craft, launches and small submarine mining vessels. Also various stern wheel and tunnel screw craft built during War by British Shipyards for service on Tigris and Euphrates.

Federated Malay States.

Bore expense of building the battleship **MALAYA.**

COMMONWEALTH OF AUSTRALIA.

ROYAL AUSTRALIAN NAVY.

Personnel :   *Minister of the Navy.*—The Rt. Hon. Sir Joseph Cook, P.C.

Navy Yards.

COCKATOO ISLAND (SYDNEY), with one completed slip, for building Light Cruisers and another large slip building. Employees about 1500–2000. May be closed down owing to labour troubles.
GARDEN ISLAND. Repairs only.
Also a Government yard at Walsh Island, N.S.W., devoted to mercantile construction.

Private Docks, &c.

ADELAIDE (S. AUSTRALIA). Commercial harbour, 7 miles from the town.
BRISBANE (QUEENSLAND, AUSTRALIA). 25 miles up river. Navigable for ships drawing 20 feet. Coaling station. Dry dock : 431½ × 55 × 19 feet.
FREMANTLE (W. AUSTRALIA). Dry dock, originally designed as 594 feet long, but enlarged to 694 feet and may now be 910 × 100 × 34 feet (L.W.O.S.), divisible into two sections (*Dreadnought*).
HOBART (TASMANIA). Coaling station. Anchorage average, 10 fathoms.
KING GEORGE SOUND (W. AUSTRALIA). Coaling station. Fortified.
SYDNEY (N.S.W., AUSTRALIA). Fortified coaling station and base for R.A.N. Harbour excellent. Bar 27 feet at low water. Dry docks : (Sutherland) 638 × 84 × 32 feet (*Dreadnought*), (Fitzroy) 477 × 59 × 21½ feet. Woolwich dock (private) 675 × 83 × 28 feet (*Dreadnought*), and four smaller.
MELBOURNE. Commercial harbour. One dry dock : 470 × 80 × 27 feet, and three smaller. Port Phillip has an area of 800 square miles.
NEWCASTLE (N.S.W., AUSTRALIA). Government floating dock, 426 × 64 × 25 feet. (9500 tons.)

T.B.D. & SUBMARINE SILHOUETTES (E. L. KING).

Scale : 125 feet to 1 inch.

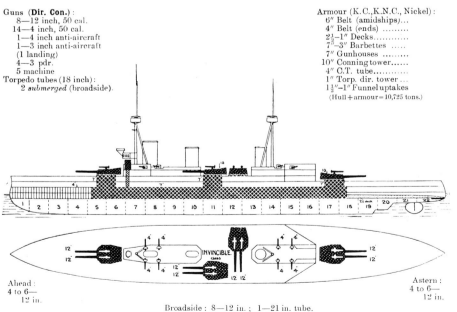

Anzac (*Leader*).   Parramatta *class* t.b.d.

J 1—J 5 (*Submarines*).

J 7 (*Submarine*).

Scale : 1 inch = 160 feet.

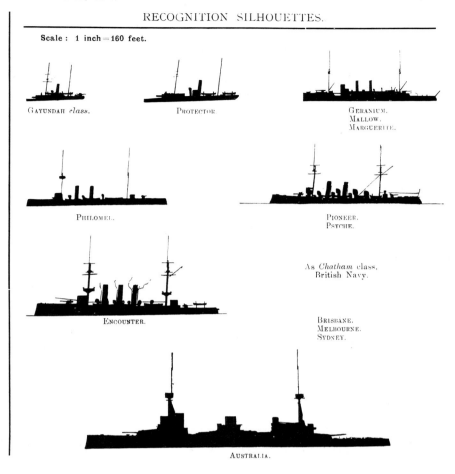

GAYUNDAH *class.*   PROTECTOR   GERANIUM. MALLOW. MARGUERITE.

PHILOMEL.   PIONEER. PSYCHE.

As *Chatham* class, British Navy.

ENCOUNTER.

BRISBANE. MELBOURNE. SYDNEY.

AUSTRALIA.

1910 BATTLE-CRUISER (25 kts.)

(INDEFATIGABLE TYPE—1 ship.)

AUSTRALIA (Oct. 25th, 1911).

Normal displacement, 18,800 tons (about 21,300 *full load.*) Complement, 820. (Flagship.)

Length (*waterline*),   feet. Beam, 80 feet. { Mean draught, 26¼ feet. / Max. draught, 30 feet. } Length, (*p.p.*) 555 feet, (*over all*) 590 feet.

Guns (Dir. Con.) :
  8—12 inch, 50 cal.
  14—4 inch, 50 cal.
  1—4 inch anti-aircraft
  1—3 inch anti-aircraft
  (1 landing)
  4—3 pdr.
  5 machine
Torpedo tubes (18 inch) :
  2 *submerged* (broadside).

Armour (K.C.,K.N.C., Nickel) :
  6″ Belt (amidships)...
  4″ Belt (ends) ....
  2½–1″ Decks...........
  7″–3″ Barbettes .....
  7″ Gunhouses ....
  10″ Conning tower......
  4″ C.T. tube...........
  1″ Torp. dir. tower ...
  1½″–1″ Funnel uptakes
  (Hull+armour=10,725 tons.)

Ahead :
4 to 6—
12 in.

Astern :
4 to 6—
12 in.

Broadside : 8—12 in. ; 1—21 in. tube.

Machinery : Parsons turbines by builders. 4 screws. Boilers : Babcock. Designed H.P. 44,000= 25 kts. Coal : *normal* 1000 tons, *maximum* 3170+840 tons oil fuel. Endurance : about 6,300 miles at 10 kts.

Armour Notes.—Main belt 12 feet deep, closed by 4″ bulkheads and with 1″ deck above. Lower deck 1″ amidships, 2½″ at ends outside belt. For more detailed particulars, *v. New Zealand*, British Navy Section.

Internal Protection.

AUSTRALIA. (Topmasts and topgallant masts as Silhouette).

| Name | Builder | Machinery | Laid down | Completed | Trials (mean) : | | Boilers | Best recent speed |
					30 hrs. at ⅔	8 hrs. full power		
Australia	J. Brown, Clydebank	J. Brown, Clydebank	June '10	June '13	30,800=23·5	48,422=26·89	Babcock	

General Notes.—An improved *Indefatigable*, and a sister-ship to *New Zealand*, described on a previous page.

AUSTRALIAN LIGHT CRUISERS.

(CHATHAM CLASS—4 SHIPS.)

MELBOURNE (May, 1912), **SYDNEY** (Aug., 1912), **BRISBANE** (Sept., 1915), and **ADELAIDE** (July, 1918).

Displacement, 5400 tons. Complement, 390–392.

Length (*p.p.*), 430 feet. Beam, 49⅚ feet. ⎰ *Mean* draught, 15¾ feet. ⎱ Length (*over all*), 457 feet.
⎱ *Max.* „ 17¾–18½ feet. ⎰

Guns (**Dir. Con.**) :
8—6 inch, 50 cal.
1—3 inch anti-aircraft
4—3 pdr.
4 machine
Torpedo tubes (21 inch) :
2 broadside (*submerged*)

Armour (Hadfield :
2″ Deck (on slopes)

MELBOURNE. Can be distinguished from *Sydney* by director tower placed over control top on foremast.

Ahead :
3—6 in.

Astern :
3—6 in.

CHATHAM

Broadside : 5—6 in., 1—21 in. torpedo tube.

Machinery : Parsons turbine. 4 screws. Boilers : Yarrow. Designed H.P. (*n.d.*) 22,000, 25,000 *f.d.*=25 kts. Coal : *normal* 750 tons, *maximum* about 1240 tons + about 260 tons oil fuel. *Brisbane*, 1196 coal + 260 oil.

Gunnery Notes.—Electric ammunition hoists.

Torpedo Notes.—7 torpedoes carried. 4 or more searchlights.

Armour Notes.—Internal protection by longitudinal and transverse bulkheads. Double bottom extends over magazine and machinery spaces. Conning Tower in *Sydney* (and others) replaced by revolving platform carrying a small aeroplane or seaplane.

Engineering Notes.—500 r.p.m.=full power. Boilers : 3 drum small tube type. Uniflux condensers.

Name	Builder	Machinery	Laid down	Completed	Trials : 30 hrs. at ⅔	8 hrs. full power	Boilers	Best recent speed
Melbourne	Cammell-Laird	Cammell-Laird	Apl. '11	Jan. '13		25,800 = 25·7	Yarrow	
Sydney	L. & Glasgow	L. & Glasgow	Feb. '11	Jun. '13	22,400 =	25,572 = 25·7	„	
Brisbane	Sydney	Vickers	Jan. '13	…			„	
Adelaide	Sydney		1915	…				

General Notes.—Practically same design as British *Chatham* class. Served during War in North Sea.

Photo, Symonds & Co.

PSYCHE (1897), 2135 tons and **PIONEER** (1899), 2200 tons. Complement, 234. Armament : *Psyche*, 8—4 inch, 3 M.G. *Pioneer* has only 4—3 pdr. Tubes : 2—14 inch *above water.* Designed H.P. 7000 (*f.d.*)=20 kts. (not over 16 kts. at present). Coal : 520—540 tons.

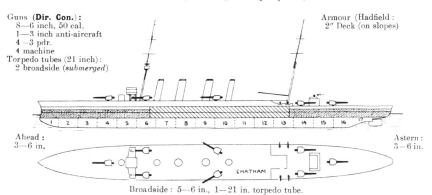

(Obsolete Light Cruisers.)

Obsolete Light Cruisers.

PHILOMEL (Jan., 1890). 2575 tons. Complement, 222. Dimensions (*o.a.*) : 278 × 41 × 16⅜ (*max.*) feet. Armament : 1—3 pdr. Torpedo Tubes : 3—14 inch *above water.* Armour : 2½″ Deck. Designed H.P. 7500=19 kts. (*f.d.*) Coal : 450 tons.

ENCOUNTER (1902, *transferred* 1912). 5880 tons. Complement, 457. Dimensions : 376 (*o.a.*) × 56 × 20⅝ feet (*max* draught). Armament : 11—6 inch, 4—12 pdr., 4—3 pdr., 3 M.G., 1 landing. 2—18 inch tubes, *sub.* Designed H.P. 12,500 = 21 kts. 12 Dürr boilers. Coal : 1300 tons *max.*

AUSTRALIAN NAVY.

12 Destroyers.

No.	Type	Date	Displacement	H.P.	Speed	Oil	Complement	Tubes	Max. draug't
1	Anzac	'16–'17	tons 1666	36,000	kts. 34	tons 416/515	116	4	12
5	Admiralty "S"	'17–'19	1075	27,000	36	254/301	90	4	12?
3	Swan	'15–'16	⎱ 700	⎰ 11,300 t	26	173 189/157	69	3	8½–9
3	Parramatta	'09–'12	⎰	⎱ 10,600 t					

Flotilla Leader.

1 Marksman (later) Type.

1 Denny. **Anzac.** 1,666 tons. Dimensions : 315 ft. (*p.p.*), 325 ft. (*o.a.*) × 31 ft. 10 in. × 12 ft. 1½ in. (*max.* draught aft). Guns : 4—4 inch, 2—2 pdr. pom-poms, 1 M.G. Torpedo tubes : 4—21 inch in 2 rev. deck mountings. Machinery : Brown-Curtis turbines. 3 screws. Boilers : Yarrow small tube. Designed S.H.P. 36,000 = 34 kts. *Trials :* Oil, 416/515 tons = *about* 2500 miles at 15 kts. Complement, 116. Begun January 31st, 1916. Launched January 11th, 1917. Completed April 24th, 1917. Begun under Emergency War Programme and presented to Australia, 1919. Sister to *Parker*, *Seymour*, &c., of British Navy, but fo'xle of *Anzac* is 2½ feet higher, and she has a few other small differences.

AUSTRALIAN NAVY.—DESTROYERS & TORPEDO BOATS.

Destroyers—*Continued.*

5 "Admiralty S" type.

2 *Beardmore*: **Tasmania, Tattoo.**

1 *Doxford*: **Success.**

1 *Scott*: **Swordsman.**

1 *Swan Hunter*: **Stalwart.**

1075 tons. Dimensions: 265 (*p.p.*), 276 (*o.a.*, *Success* 277) × 26¾ × 9 feet (*mean*) draught. Armament: 3—4 inch (Mk. IV with 30° elevation), 1—2 pdr. pom-pom, 4—21 inch tubes in two deck mountings, 1—24 inch search-light controlled in unison with guns. May have D.C. Thrower and High Speed type of P.Vs. Machinery: Brown-Curtis all-geared turbines. 2 screws. Boilers: 3 Yarrow small tube. Designed S.H.P. 27000. = 36 kts. Fuel (oil only): 254/301 tons = *about* 2000 miles at 15 kts. Complement, 90.

	Begun.	Launch.	Comp.			Begun.	Launch.	Comp.
Tasmania ..	18/12/17	22/11/18	29/1/19	Swordsman ..		....	28/12/18	3/19
Tattoo ..	21/12/17	28/12/18	7/4/19	Stalwart ..	..	4/18	23/10/18	4/19
Success ..	....	29/6/18	4/19					

Notes.—Built under Emergency War Programme and presented to Australian Navy, 1919. For any further notes, refer to description of "S Class" in British Navy Section.

Destroyers—*Continued.*

WARREGO.

Parramatta, Yarra (1910, **Warrego** (1911), **Huon** (ex *Derwent*, 1914), **Swan** (Dec., 1915), **Torrens** (Aug., 1915). Dimensions: Length (*o.a.*) 250¾ Huon, Swan, Torrens, 245¾ Yarra, 246 Parramatta, Warrego × 24½ × 8 feet. Armaments: 1—4 inch, 3—12 pdrs., 3—18 inch tubes. Parsons turbines. Yarrow boilers. Radius: 2500 kts. Oil fuel. *Yarra* by Denny, Dumbarton; *Parramatta* and *Warrego* by London & Glasgow Engineering Co., *Warrego* being re-erected at Cockatoo N.Y., Sydney. *Swan, Huon* and *Torrens* built at Cockatoo N.Y., Sydney. Are modified British "I" Class boats.

AUSTRALIAN NAVY.—SUBMARINES.

6 Submarines.

Note: *AE1* and *AE2* were transferred to RAN at beginning of the war. Both of British "E" class and both lost – *AE1* off Bismarck Achipelago in September 1914 and *AE2* in Sea of Marmara April 1915.

No.	Class	Begun	Comp.	Displacement Tons.	B.H.P. E.H.P.	Speed kts.	Endurance	Tubes	Comp't.
6	J 7	1916	1917	1200 1760	3600 1400	19 9·5	4,000 miles at 12 kts.	6	44
	J 1—5	1915	1916	1260 1820					

"J Class"—6 Boats.

6 *Admiralty type*: **J 7** (Feb., 1917), **J 5** (Sept., 1915), both by Devonport D.Y. **J 4** (Feb., 1916), **J 3** (Dec., 1915), both by Pembroke D.Y. **J 2** (Nov., 1915), **J 1** (Nov., 1915), both by Portsmouth D.Y. *J 1—5*, 1916; *J 7*, Nov., 1917. Dimensions: 270 (*p.p.*), 274½ (*o.a.*) × 23½ × 14 feet. Armament: 1—4 inch gun and 6 —18 inch tubes (4 bow, 2 beam). Surface machinery: 3 sets of Vickers 12 cylinder solid injection, direct reversing 4 cycle 1200 B.H.P. Diesel engines (14½ in. bore × 15 in. stroke, 380 r.p.m.). Oil: 80/91 tons. Built under Emergency Programme as "Bight Patrols." *J 6* lost during War. Presented to Australia, 1918. Other details as Table.

Fleet Sweeping Vessels (Sloops).

See illustration of *Valerian* and *Primrose*—British Navy Section.

GERANIUM (Greenock & Grangemouth Co. Begun Aug., 1915; launched 8th Nov., 1915; completed March, 1916). **MARGUERITE** (Dunlop Bremner. Begun July, 1915; launched 23rd Nov., 1915; completed Jan., 1916). Fleet Sweeping Vessels (Sloops) of *Arabis* type. 1250 tons. Dimensions: 255¼ (*p.p.*), 267¾ (*o.a.*) × 33½ × 10½ feet (*mean*), 11¾ (*max.* draught). Guns: 1—4·7 inch, 2—3 pdr. (AA. in *Geranium*). Designed I.H.P. 2000=17 kts. Trials: *Geranium*, 2312=17; *Marguerite*, 2309=16·1. Machinery: boilers, screws, as *Mallow*, opposite. Coal: 260 tons=2050 miles at 15 kts. Complement, 79. Built under Emergency War Programme; presented to Australian Navy, 1919.

Fleet Sweeping Vessel (Sloop).

See illustration for *Valerian*—British Navy Section.

MALLOW (Barclay Curle. Launched 13th July, 1915; completed Sept., 1916.) Fleet Sweeping Vessel (Sloop) of *Acacia* type. 1200 tons. Dimensions: 250 (*p.p.*), 262½ (*o.a.*) × 33 × 10¼ feet (*mean*), 11¼ (*max.* load). Guns: 1—12 pdr. (12 cwt.), 2—3 pdr. AA. I.H.P. 1800=17 kts. Trials: 2328=16·3 kts. Machinery: 1 set triple expansion inverted and 2 cylindrical boilers. Coal: 250 tons=2000 miles at 15 kts. Complement, 77. Built under Emergency War Programme; presented to the Australian Navy, 1919.

Sloop (Surveying Ship).

UNA (ex-German Surveying Ship *Komet*, built about 1911, captured 1914). 1438 tons. Dimensions: 210½ × 31 × 15¾ feet. Guns: 3 —4 inch, 2—12 pdr. H.P. 1300 = 16 kts. Coal: 270 tons. Complement, 114.

FANTOME (1901, lent from Royal Navy, 1915). 1070 tons. Guns: 2—4 inch, 1—3 pdr., 2 M.G. Speed, 13½ kts. Coal: 195 tons. For Surveying Service. Complement, 135.

AUSTRALIAN NAVY.—*Continued.*

Obsolete Gunboats.

PROTECTOR (Elswick, 1884). 920 tons. Guns: 3—4 inch, 2—12 pdr., 4—3 pdr. H.P. 1600 = 14 kts. originally. Re-boiled 1910-11. Tender to Williamstown Gunnery School. (*South Australia*).

GAYUNDAH (Elswick, 1884, reported to have been re-built at Cockatoo N.Y., Sydney, 1914). **PALUMA** (Elswick 1884) 360 tons. Guns: 1—4.7, 2—12 pdr. Speed originally: 10.5 kts.

Also *Cerberus*, now Naval Depot at Williamstown, with Cruiser *Psyche* and 1st Class T.B. *Countess of Hopetoun* and *Coogee, Gannet, Gayundah, Protector* as tenders.

Submarine Depot Ship.

PLATYPUS (J. Brown, Clydebank. Begun Sept. 2nd, 1914; launched Oct. 28th, 1916; completed Mar., 1917.) 2,460 tons. Dimensions: 310 (*w.l.*), 325 (*o.a.*) × 44 × 15$\frac{2}{3}$ feet. (*max.* draught). Guns: *nil?* I.H.P. 3600 = 15$\frac{1}{2}$ kts. Reciprocating engines and cylindrical boilers. 2 screws. Coal: 450 tons. Complement, 357.

Fuel Ships (R.F.A.)

BILOELA. Fleet Collier, built at Cockatoo Island D.Y. Completed 1919. No details known.

KURUMBA (Swan Hunter. Begun Sept., 1915; launched Sept., 1916; completed Jan., 1917; machinery by Wallsend.) Oil Tanker. 8350 tons. Dimensions: 365 (*p.p.*), 377$\frac{1}{4}$ (*o.a.*) × 45$\frac{1}{2}$ × 23$\frac{1}{4}$ feet *max.* load draught. Guns: 3 (calibre not known). I.H.P. 2000 = 10 kts. Triple expansion engines and S.E. cylindrical boilers. 2 screws. Fuel: *max.*, 688 tons coal + 257 tons oil, exclusive of cargo. Complement, 65–100.

Armed Patrol Vessels.

COOGEE (————). 762 tons *gross.* H.P. = 16 kts. Guns: 1—4.7 inch, 2—3 pdr. Coal: 210 tons.

GANNET (ex *Penguin*, ————). 208 tons *gross.* H.P. 420 = 10 kts. Guns: 1—12 pdr. Coal: 87 tons.

MOORILYAN (——·———). 1349 tons *gross.* H.P. 2330 = 14.4 kts. Guns 1—4.7 inch Q.F., 2—3 pdr. Hotchkiss. Coal: 280 tons.

SLEUTH (ex *Ena*). 108 tons. H.P. 160 = , kts. Guns: 1—3 pdr.

Miscellaneous.

NUSA. 64 tons. Ex-German ship seized at Kawieng, 1914.
SUMATRA. No details known.
FRANKLIN (ex-*Adele*). 288 tons. Training Ship for Cadets. Tender to R.A.N. College, Jervis Bay.
TINGIRA. Training Ship.

DOMINION OF NEW ZEALAND.

Battle Cruiser **NEW ZEALAND** was built at the expense of the Dominion. The annual subvention of £100,000 paid by the Dominion is to be devoted to the maintenance of the Light Cruiser **CANTERBURY** and a Training Ship of 3000 tons.

Docks.

AUCKLAND. Coaling station. Excellent harbour; average 40 feet deep. Dry dock (Calliope): 521 × 66 × 33 feet. Also one smaller, able to take torpedo craft.
PORT CHALMERS (S. ISLAND). Otago dry dock, 500 × 70 × 21 feet, *and another smaller.*

Sloop.

FIREBRAND (ex *Torch*, 1894). Transferred from British Navy, 1917. 960 tons. Armament: 4—4 inch, 4—3 pdr., 2 M.G. Speed, 13.4 kts. Coal, 130 tons.

Gunboat.

(*Training Service.*)

AMOKURA (Greenock, 1889). 805 tons. Guns: 6—4 inch, 3—3 pdr. H.P. 1200 = 13 kts. Coal: 105 tons.

Miscellaneous.

A yacht, **HINEMOA**, and two small mining vessels. Also cable ship, **TUTANEKAI.**

DOMINION OF CANADA.

Minister of Marine: Hon. Col. C. C. Ballantyne.
Personnel: *Uniforms:* As British Navy.

Pacific:—

ESQUIMAULT.—Naval Dockyard. Admiralty Chart No. 576. (For Docks, see below.)

Atlantic:—

HALIFAX (NOVA SCOTIA).—Formerly Dockyard. Coaling Station. Anchorage averages 13 fathoms. Examination Base during War. (For Docks, see below.)

Private Shipyards.

CANADIAN VICKERS CO. (MONTREAL).—Affiliated to Messrs. Vickers, Ltd., Barrow-in-Furness. No details available of this establishment. "H" class Submarines built here during the War. For large Floating Dock, see Docks below.
MESSRS. YARROW, LTD. (LANG'S COVE, ESQUIMAULT).—Branch of Messrs. Yarrow, Ltd., Scotstoun, N.B. Can build ships up to 2000 tons. Slipway 315 × 30 feet (3000 tons capacity). Fitting-out Wharf 500 feet long. Repair shops; one 60-ton sheer legs; one 10-ton floating derrick. Yard covers eight acres, with Government Dock adjoining.

Docks.

COLLINGWOOD. Collingwood Dry Dock Co. 524 × 60 × 15$\frac{1}{2}$ feet.
ESQUIMAULT. Government Dock 450–180 × 65 × 26$\frac{1}{4}$ feet. Also 2400 tons patent slip.
ST. JOHNS (NEW BRUNSWICK). At Courtenay Bay, new dock *projected*, 1150 × 125 × 40 feet (*over sills*).
HALIFAX (NOVA SCOTIA). Dry dock: Halifax Graving Dock Co., 572 × 89 × 29 feet (*Dreadnought*).
KINGSTON (ONTARIO). Government dock, 290 × 55 × 18 feet.
MONTREAL. Duke of Connaught floating dock (Proprietors, Canadian Vickers Co.), 600 × 100 × 28$\frac{1}{2}$ feet. (*Dreadnought*.) Two other private docks, 400 × 45 × 10 feet.
PORT ARTHUR. Dry dock, 700 × 74$\frac{1}{4}$ × 15$\frac{1}{2}$ feet.
PORT DALHOUSIE. Muir Bros'. dock, 260 × 16 × 10 feet.
OWEN SOUND. Dock, 300 × 60 × 12 feet.
QUEBEC: Canadian Government dry dock, 1150 × 120 × 30 feet, divisible into two docks, 650 and 500 feet long respectively. (*Dreadnought.*) Levis dock, 600 × 63 × 20$\frac{1}{4}$ feet. Three floating docks, 1600, 2200, and 2500 tons lift.

A: ROYAL CANADIAN NAVY.

RECOGNITION SILHOUETTES.

Scale : 1 inch = 160 feet.

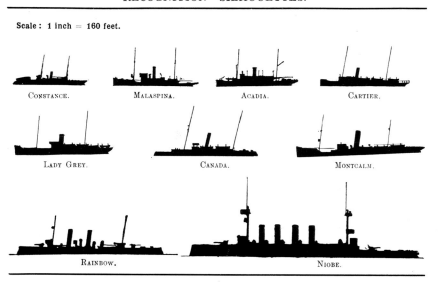

CONSTANCE. MALASPINA. ACADIA. CARTIER.

LADY GREY. CANADA. MONTCALM.

RAINBOW. NIOBE.

Scale : 1 inch = 80 feet.

SUBMARINES.

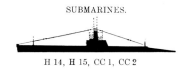

H 14, H 15, CC 1, CC 2

TORPEDO BOATS AND SUBMARINES.

Grilse (1913). 225 tons. Dimensions : 207 × 18½ × 6 feet. Guns : 2—12 pdr. 1 torpedo tube. Designed H.P. 6000 = 30 kts. Oil : 53 tons.

Tuna (1902). 150 tons. Dimensions : 153 × 15 × 5 feet. Guns : 1—3 pdr. Torpedo tubes : 2. Designed H.P. 2000 = 24 kts. Coal : 27 tons.

4 Submarines.

2 *Holland* type : **H 14, H 15** (1918). Displacements : 364 tons *surface*, 435 tons *submerged*. Dimensions : 150 × 15¼ × 12¼ feet. Torpedo tubes : 4—18 inch (bow). B.H.P. 480 = 13 kts. *on surface* ; H.P. 320 = 11 kts. *submerged* (for about one hour continuous running). Complement 20—22. Built under Emergency War Programme and presented to Canadian Navy, 1919.

1 *Holland* type : **CC 2** (Seattle Con. & D.D. Co., 1914). Displacements : 310 tons *on surface*, 373 tons *submerged*. Dimensions : 157 ft. 6½ in. × 14 ft. 11½ in. × feet. Torpedo tubes : 3—18 inch. H.P. 600 *on surface* = 13 kts. ; 260 *submerged* = 10½ kts.

1 *Holland* type : **CC 1** (Seattle Con. & D.D. Co., 1911). Displacements : 313 tons *on surface*, 373 tons *submerged*. Dimensions : 111 ft. 3½ in. × 14 ft. × 11 ft. 6 in. Torpedo tubes : 5—18 inch. H.P. 600 *on surface* = 13 kts. ; 260 *submerged* = 10½ kts.

Note.—Above two boats were begun for Chilean Navy as *Antofagasta* and *Iquique*. They were purchased by Canada just before outbreak of war.

Submarine Depot Ship.

SHEARWATER (1900). Sloop. 980 tons. Guns : 4—4 inch, 4—3 pdr., 2 machine. H.P. 1400 (*f.d.*) = 13¼ kts. Coal : 160 tons. Lent from Royal Navy, 1914.

Sloop.

ALGERINE (1895). 1050 tons. Guns : 4—3 pdr., 3 M.G. H.P. 1400 = 13½ kts. Boilers : cylindrical. Coal 160 tons. Lent from Royal Navy.

Armed Patrol Vessels.

Belongs to the Department of Naval Service.

CANADA (1904). 780 tons. Guns : 2—12 pdr., 2—3 pdr. H.P. 1600 = 14 kts. Coal : 110 tons. (F.)

FLORENCE (——). Guns : 1—3 pdr. Q.F. Speed, 12 kts.

Cruiser.

(Depot Ship—is dismantled.)

NIOBE (1897, transferred 1913). 11,000 tons. Complement —. Guns and torpedo tubes : *Is disarmed.* Armour : Deck, 4″ ; Casemates, 6″. Designed H.P. 16,500 = 20·25 kts. Present speed : somewhere about 18 kts. or less, owing to damage received by stranding in 1914. Coal : 2000 tons.

Light Cruiser.

(Training Ship for Pacific Coast.)

RAINBOW (1891, bought 1909). 3600 tons. Complement —. Guns and torpedo tubes : *Is disarmed.* Deck : 2″. Designed H.P. 9000 = 19·75 kts. Present speed : about 12 kts. Coal : 560 tons.

HOCHELAGA (——). Guns : 1—12 pdr. Speed, 12 kts.

Belongs to Department of Customs.

MARGARET (1913). 950 tons. Guns : 2—6 pdr. Designed H.P. 2000 = 15½ kts, *max.* speed. Coal : 200 tons.

PREMIER (——). 374 tons *gross*. Guns : 1—6 pdr. Speed, 13 kts.

SEAGULL. Patrol Depot Ship. No details known.

STADACONA (——). Guns : 1—4 inch Q.F. Speed, 12 kts.

STARLING (——). Guns : 1—3 pdr. Speed, 12 kts.

Trawlers and Drifters.

Twenty-seven of these were loaned to U.S. Navy for war duties ; others served with H.M. Navy during the war. No other details available.

B: CANADIAN GOVERNMENT VESSELS.

(From Official List. Arranged *alphabetically*. All speeds are *maximum*.)

Department of the Naval Service.

Note.

Vessels marked (H) were engaged in 1915 on Hydrographic Survey duty, and those marked (F) on Fishery Protection.

ACADIA.

ACADIA (1913). 1050 tons. H.P. 1200 = 12 kts. Coal : 260 tons. (H.)

BAYFIELD (1889). 550 tons. Speed, 12 kts. Coal : 100 tons. (H.)

CARTIER (1910). 850 tons. H.P. 830 = 12 kts. Coal : 150 tons. (H.)

Department of Marine and Fisheries (continued) :—

EARL GREY (ex-Russian *Kanada*, ex-Canadian *Earl Grey*). (Vickers, 1909). 3400 tons. 250 × 47½ × 17¾ feet. H.P. 6000 = 17 kts. (did 18 on trial). Boilers : cylindrical Is specially built for ice-breaking.

LADY GREY.

LADY GREY (1906). 1080 tons. H.P. 2300 = 14 kts. Coal : 200 tons.

LADY LAURIER (1902). 1970 tons. H.P. 1800 = 13 kts. Coal : 175 tons.

LAMBTON (1906). 510 tons. Speed, 11 kts. Coal : 92 tons.

Photo, Lieut. Com. Saul, R.C.N.

MINTO (1899). 2070 tons. H.P. 2900 = 15½ kts. Coal : 290 tons.

Department of the Naval Service—Continued.

CONSTANCE.

CONSTANCE (1891). **CURLEW** (1892). 400 tons. Speed 10kts. Coal : 46 tons. (F).

GAUSS (1901).

GULNARE (1893). 500 tons. Speed, 10 kts. Coal : 65 tons. (F.)

LILLOOET (1908). 760 tons. Speed, 11¾ kts. Coal : 140 tons. (H.)

Department of Marine and Fisheries (continued) :—

MONTCALM (1904) & **CHAMPLAIN** (1904). 1432 tons. 243 × 40 × 18 feet. H.P. 3600 = 14 kts.

NEWINGTON (1889). 475 tons. Speed, 10 kts. Coal : 85 tons.

PRINCESS (1896). 850 tons. Speed, 11 kts. Coal : 124 tons.

QUADRA (1891). 1260 tons. Speed, 11 kts. Coal : 200 tons.

SIMCOE (1909). 1630 tons. Speed, 12½ kts. Coal : 100 tons.

STANLEY (1888). 1890 tons. Speed, 15½ kts. Coal : 250 tons.

Photo, "Syren and Shipping."

VIGILANT (Polson I.W., 1918). No details available.

Also 4 other ships, 1 steel-built and 3 wooden-built. *Wilfrid* (ex S.S. *Wilfrid C.*, 1897), 90 tons *gross*, purchased 1918.

Department of the Naval Service—Continued.

MALASPINA.

MALASPINA (1913). 850 tons. Guns : 1—6 pdr. H.P. 1350 = 14¼ kts. Coal : 200 tons. (F.)

PETREL (1902). 400 tons. Speed, 11 kts. Coal : 65 tons. (F.)

Also 4 other vessels under 500 tons, 1 iron-built, 1 composite-built, and 2 wooden-built.

Department of Marine and Fisheries.

ABERDEEN (1894). 1330 tons. H.P. 1510 = 13 kts. Coal : 125 tons.

ARANMORE (1890). 500 tons (net registered). Speed, 13 kts. Coal : 200 tons.

BELLECHASSE (1912). 576 tons. H.P. 900 = 11¼ kts. Coal : 24 tons.

CHAMPLAIN (1904). 800 tons. Speed, 11 kts. Coal : 60 tons.

DOLLARD (1913). 323 tons (net registered). Speed, . Oil fuel.

DRUID (1902). 1000 tons. Speed, 13 kts. Coal : 100 tons.

ESTEVAN (1912). 2100 tons. H.P. 1500 = 12½ kts. Coal : 350 tons.

GRENVILLE (1914). tons. H.P. 900 = kts. Coal : 100 tons.

J. D. HAZEN (1916). Ice breaker. 4900 tons. Dimensions : 275 × 57½ × 19 feet (*max* draught). Designed H.P. 8000 = kts. Coal : 1300 tons. Was transferred to Russia, 1915 or 1916, but is reported to have returned to Canada from the White Sea in 1918.

(Continued on next page.)

Department of Militia and Defence :—

Three small vessels *Alfreda* (1904), 270 tons ; *Armstrong* (1903), 230 tons ; and *Beryl* (1903), 45 tons. All 9½—8 kts. speed.

Department of Public Works.

TYRIAN (1869). 1300 tons. Speed, 10 kts. Coal : 340 tons.

Also *Speedy* (1896). 420 tons. 12 kts. speed.

Department of Railways and Canals :—

DURLEY CHINE (1913). 5173 tons. Speed, 10½ kts. Coal : 457 tons.

MULGRAVE (1892). 925 tons. Speed, 14 kts. Coal : 40 tons.

SCOTIA (1901). 2550 tons. Speed, 12 kts. Coal : 120 tons.

SHEEBA (1912). 5668 tons. Speed, 10½ kts. Coal : 340 tons.

(Also 13 other smaller vessels.)

Department of the Post Office :—

LADY EVELYN (1901). 680 tons. Speed, 14 kts.

Department of Agriculture :—

ALICE (1907). 550 tons. Speed, 11½ kts.

And 4 smaller vessels.

NEWFOUNDLAND.

PETREL. Armed Patrol Vessel. Speed about 10 kts. Guns : 1—3 pdr. Q.F.

Also old *Briton* (ex-*Calypso*) as Training Ship.

EGYPT.

ENSIGN & JACK.	SULTAN'S STANDARD.

Red ▥ White ☐

River Gunboats.

MELIK, SHEIK, SULTAN (1897). 140 tons. Speed, 11 kts. 2 screws in tunnels. Guns : 1—12 pdr. + 1—24 pdr. howitzer, 3 machine.

FATEH, NASIR, ZAFIR (1896). 128 tons. Stern-wheel Steamers. Speed, 12 kts. Guns : 1—12 pdr. + 1—24 pdr. howitzer, 4 machine.

ABU KLEA, HAFIR, METEMMEH, TAMAI. Stern-wheel Steamers. Guns : 1—22 pdr. in first ; 1—9 pdr. in others.

Also 24 other River Steamers, built 1908-1885.

Transport, &c.

GHARBIEH. 3700 tons. Also another steamer, **MUKBIR**, of 420 tons.

There are also 5 Paddle-wheel Steamers and about 15 Tugs.

Yacht.

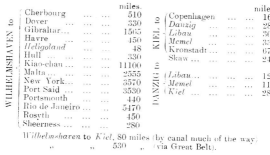

MAHROUSSA (1865, rebuilt 1906). 3417 tons. Parsons turbine. H.P. 5500 = 17.5 kts.

Also 2 other small Yachts, and 3 Despatch Vessels.

MINOR AFRICAN NAVIES.

Customs Cruisers.

ABDUL MONEIM (Clydebank, 1902). 598 tons. Guns : 1—3 pdr. H.P. 1000 = 13 kts.

ABBAS (1891). 298 tons. Guns : 1—3 pdr. H.P. 650 = 13 kts.

NOUR-EL-BAHR (1884). 450 tons. Guns : 1—3 pdr. H.P. 870 = 13.5 kts.

RESHID. About 650 tons. Guns : 2—6 pdr.

Ports and Lights Administration.

AIDA. 723 tons. 1 gun. H.P. 130 = ?

Also about 25 launches and miscellaneous craft.

NYASALAND.

Gunboat.

GWENDOLEN (1897). 350 tons. Guns : 4—6 pdr., 4 machine. Speed 11½ kts.

Adventure, Pioneer. (1892). 30 tons. Speed, 12 kts.

Dove, Paddle Gunboat of 20 tons. Speed, 8 kts. Armed with 1 M.G.

NORTHERN RHODESIA.

Two Thornycroft motor patrol boats, **Mimi** & **Tou-tou**, originally intended to act as tenders to Greek seaplanes. They were requisitioned and shipped out to Lake Tanganyika in 1915, where they sank the German gunboat *Hedwig von Wissmann* and captured the *Kingani*, now British **Fi-fi**.

BRITISH EAST AFRICA.

Rose (1901). Speed, 8 kts.

M'Vita, Patrol Boat.

NATAL.

Before the war, only possessed a Tug, **Sir John** (1897), and a Surveying Ship, **Churchill.**

NIGERIA.

Empire, Kapelli, Kampala, Sarota, Valiant. Stern-wheel Gunboats, built about 1902. Speed, 10 kts.

Sultan (1907), *Etobe, Egori.* (1909). Stern-wheel Steamers. Speed, 8-10 kts.

Raven (1904). Stern-wheel Steamer. 260 tons. Speed, about 9 kts.

Corona (——). 320 tons. Speed, 9 kts. Governor's Yacht.

Ivy (1896). Yacht.

Also a Stern-wheel Tug of 428 tons. There are also about 18 other small launches and miscellaneous craft.

GERMAN FLEET.

INCLUDING SHIPS SALVED AT SCAPA FLOW AND THOSE TO BE SURRENDERED UNDER PEACE TREATY.

		miles.			miles.
WILHELMSHAVEN to	Cherbourg	510	KIEL to	Copenhagen	160
	Dover	330		Danzig	280
	Gibraltar	1565		Libau	360
	Havre	450		Memel	330
	Heligoland	48		Kronstadt	670
	Hull	330		Skaw	240
	Kiao-chau	11100			
	Malta	2555	DANZIG to	Libau	120
	New York	3570		Memel	113
	Port Said	3530		Kiel	280
	Portsmouth	440			
	Rio de Janeiro	5470			
	Rosyth	450			
	Sheerness	280			

Wilhelmshaven to Kiel, 80 miles (by canal much of the way).
    ,,   530 ,, (via Great Belt).

MAP OF GERMAN COAST, SHOWING NAVAL AND PRIVATE YARDS, &c.

Fortifications to be Dismantled.

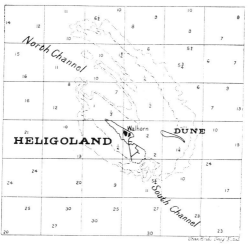

HELIGOLAND.— West Mole, 1950 feet long ; East Mole, 1290 feet long. Of very little worth for large ships, owing to insufficient depth of water. Harbour can be used by torpedo craft, gunboats and small light cruisers. Naval hospital, barracks, and W/T. station. Admiralty Chart No. 126.

	Miles
To Cuxhaven	40
,, Wilhelmshaven	48
,, Yarmouth	260

Flags.

Reported new National Ensign has black, gold and red horizontal and equal stripes. Naval flags not known.

Mercantile Marine.

June, 1919, 3,427,000 tons *gross* but a large amount must be handed over to the Allies and United States.

Coinage.

Mark (100 pfennige *nominal* value = 11¾d. British, 24 cents U.S.A.) but rate of exchange has depreciated.

Colour of Ships.

Big ships : light grey all over.

Torpedo craft : varies from black to dull brown.

Active Naval *Personnel.*

Floating Docks.

Note :—Several of these have been sold, though such sales are reported to be contrary to the Treaty of Peace.

GERMAN WARSHIPS

Scale : 1 inch = 160 eet

ONE FUNNEL.

DELPHIN.

FUCHS

M 1—60 (and 61—138 ?)
(*Mine Sweepers.*)

' Wachtschiffen."
(*Trawler Mine Sweeper.*)

HAI

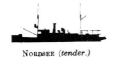

NORDSEE (*tender.*)

ZIETEN (D).

TWO FUNNELS. (D = Disarmed.)

DRACHE (*tender*).

BLITZ *class* (D).

PANTHER.

NAUTILUS (*minelayer*). (D)

LORELEY.
(*Surrendered to Allies.*)

ALBATROSS (*mine layer*) (D).

NYMPHE *class* (D) also NIOBE (D).
(*Conning tower and bridge against fore-funnel*
"Arkona," "Medusa," has slightly thicker funnels).

ODIN (D).
BEOWULF—*Icebreaker.*

HOHENZOLLERN.
(*Paid Off*).

NOTE.—(D) **Signifies disarmed ships used as Depot and Training Ships, Hulks, &c.**

TWO FUNNELS—*continued.*

KAISER FRIEDRICH *class.* (D)
" K. Barbarossa " has cranes between funnels like " Hertha "
class. " K Karl der Grosse." resembles " Wittlesbach "
class. (*Mostly Hulks.*)

HERTHA *class.* (D)
(*Depot and Training Ships.*)

BADEN.
At Scapa Flow, under salvage.

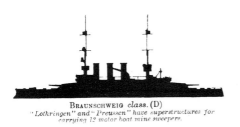

PRINZ HEINRICH. (D)

WITTELSBACH *class.*
Turrets removed from 2 ships—others disarmed.

TO BE SURRENDERED ?

NASSAU *class. Guns dismounted.*
" Rhineland " dismantled and armour removed.

THREE FUNNELS.

DEUTSCHLAND *class.* (D)

BRAUNSCHWEIG *class.* (D)
" Lothringen " and " Preussen " have superstructures for
carrying 12 motor boat mine sweepers.

TO BE SURRENDERED.

OSTFRIESLAND *class. Guns dismounted.*

1911 GERMAN DREADNOUGHTS. Nos. 18, 19, 20 & 22.

KRON PRINZ (1913), **GROSSER KURFÜRST** (May, 1913), & **KÖNIG** (March, 1913),
MARKGRAF (June, 1913).

Displacement, *about* 25,500 tons. Complement, *about* 1100.

Length, *about* 580 feet *over all.* Beam, *about* 96 feet. *Mean* draught, *about* 27½ feet.

Guns:
10—12 inch, 45 cal.
14—6 inch.
12—24 pdr.
4—14 pdr. anti-aerial

Torpedo tubes (20 inch):
4 (broadside) *submerged.*
1 (stern) *submerged.*

Armour (Krupp):
14″ Belt (amidships)...aaaaa
″ Belt (bow) ....
″ Belt (stern) ....
Protection to vitals (*see notes*):
12″ Turrets ... .
8″ Battery ....

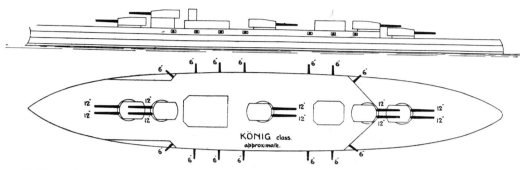

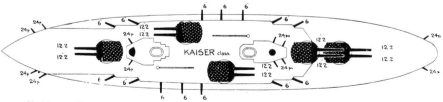

KÖNIG class.
approximate.

Machinery: 3 sets turbine (see table). Boilers: Schulz-Thornycroft. Designed H.P. 34,000 = 21·5 kts.
Coal: *normal,* 1000 tons; *maximum,* 4400 tons. Also 700 tons oil. 3 screws.

Gunnery Notes.—There are 2 conning towers, 4 special armoured fire control towers, one torpedo control tower.

Armour Notes.—Funnels, 6 inch armour to height of 20 feet above upper deck. Special under water 3 inch plating for length of 350 feet amidships. Internal protection as for *Kaiser* class.

Name	Builder	Machinery	Laid down	Completed	Trials	Turbines	Best recent speed
Markgraf	Weser, Bremen	Weser	Oct. '11	Oct. '14	=		...
G. Kurfürst	Vulkan, H'b'g	Vulkan	May '11	Oct. '14		Bergmann	...
Koenig	W'l'mshav'n Y.	...	Sept. '11	Oct. '14	=	A.E.G. (Curtis)	...
K. Prinz / E. Weissenburg	Krupp	Krupp	Ap'l '12	July '15		Parsons (mod.)	...

First three belong to the 1911 programme, *Markgraf* to the 1912.

General Notes.—It was originally intended to fit Diesel motors to the centre engine; but this was subsequently abandoned.

1909-10 GERMAN DREADNOUGHTS. Nos. 11, 12, *also* 14, 15, 16

(KAISER CLASS—5 SHIPS.)

KAISER (March, 1911), **FRIEDRICH DER GROSSE** (June, 1911), **KAISERIN** (Nov., 1911),
PRINZ REGENT LUITPOLD (Feb., 1913) & **KONIG ALBERT** (April, 1912).

Displacement, 24,700 tons. Complement, 1088.

Length (*waterline*), 564 feet. Beam, 95¼ feet. *Maximum* draught, 27¼ feet.

Guns:
10—12 inch, 50 cal. (A^6)
14—6 inch
12—24 pdr.
4—14 pdr. anti-aerial

Torpedo tubes (20 inch):
4 *submerged* (broadside)
1 *submerged* (stern)

Armour (Krupp):
14″ Belt (amidships) ...... aaaa
6″ Belt (bow) .... b
5″ Belt (aft) ....
Protection to vitals ......=
12″ Turrets .... aaaa
7″ Battery .... a
(Total weight: 6000 tons).

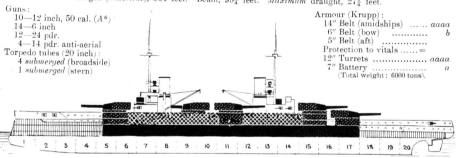

KAISER class.

Machinery: Turbine (Parsons). 3 screws. Boilers: Schulz-Thornycroft. Designed H.P. 25,000 = 20 kts. Coal: *normal* 1000 tons; *maximum* 3600 tons. Oil: *about* 200 tons.

Gunnery Notes.—Fire controls on turret tops; also towers. Special improved mountings for big guns. Hoists to the 6 inch deliver 9 rounds a minute.

Torpedo Notes.—Bullivant net defence fitted.

Armour Notes.—Under water protection consists of double longitudinal bulkheads: the outer one 2⅜ inch, the inner 1¼ inch. The outer bulkhead is 9 feet away from ships side. Minute sub-division: all bulkheads solid. The upper deck is possibly armoured against attacks from aircraft, but no details are available.

Name.	Builder	Machinery	Laid down	Completed	Trials 6 hrs. mean	1 hr.	Boilers	Best recent speed
Kaiser	Kiel Yard		Oct. '09	Oct. '12	31,516 = 22·3	35,100 = 23·46		23·6
Friedrich der G.	Vulkan, H'b'g	Vulkan Co.	Oct. '09	Oct. '12	31,721 = 21·4	42,113 = 23·8		
Kaiserin	Howalt	Howalt	July '10	Aug. '13			Schulz-T. in all.	
K. Albert	Schichau	Schichau	July '10	Aug. '13				
P. R. Luitpold	Krupp	Krupp	Apl. '10	Aug. '13				

General Notes.—First two, 1909 programme; the others, 1910 programme. They have *four* bilge keels. The *Kaiser's* 23·6 was for one hour. Average cost, £2,400,000 per ship.

Note.—This class consists of five ships instead of the usual four. Usual anti-rolling tanks.

1908 GERMAN DREADNOUGHTS.

(OSTFRIESLAND CLASS).

THÜRINGEN (Nov., 1909), **HELGOLAND** (Sept., 1909), **OSTFRIESLAND** (Sept., 1909),
OLDENBURG (June, 1910).

Normal displacement, 22,800 tons. Complement, 1097 to 1106.

Length (waterline), 546¼ feet. Beam, 93¼ feet. { Maximum draught, 29¼ feet.
{ Mean „ 27 „ feet.

Guns :
12—12 in., 50 cal. (A⁶)
14—5·9 in., 45 cal.
4—22 pdr. anti-aircraft
2 machine.
Torpedo tubes (19·7 inch) :
1 submerged (bow)
1 submerged (stern)
4 submerged (broadside)

Armour (Krupp) :
11¾" Belt ....
8" Belt (bow) ....
4" Belt (aft) ....
1½" Deck on slopes ..
12" Turrets ....
12" Turret bases .....
6¼" Battery ....
12" Conning tower
(fore)
8" C. T. (aft) ....
(Total weight: 5100 tons.)

HELGOLAND.

Appearance.

Funnels have been raised by about 6 feet.

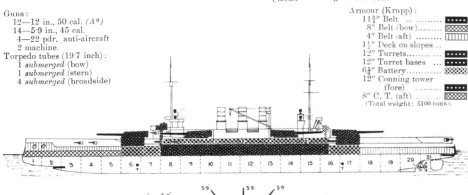

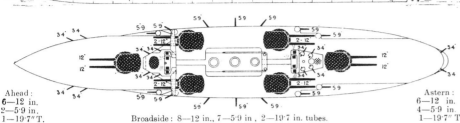

Ahead :
6—12 in.
2—5·9 in.
1—19·7" T.

Broadside : 8—12 in., 7—5·9 in., 2—19·7 in. tubes.

Astern :
6—12 in.
4—5·9 in.
1—19·7" T.

Machinery : Reciprocating. 3 screws. Boilers : 15 Schulz-Thornycroft. Designed H.P. 25,000 = 20·5 kts.
Coal : normal 900 tons; maximum 3,000 tons, including oil (200 tons, may be more now).

Engineering Notes.—125 r.p.m. = 21 kts. about. Have double (athwartship) rudders.

Name	Builder	Machinery	Ordered	Laid down	Began trials	Trials (full power). Mean	Best speed	Finished trials
Thüringen	Weser, Bremen	Weser	June.'08	Jan. '09	July, '11	34,944 = 21·075	21·2	Sept. '11
Helgoland	Howaldt, Kiel	Howaldt	May. '08	Dec.,'08	Aug. '11	31,258 = 20·81	22	Dec. '11
Ostfriesland	W'l'mshaven Y		May. '08	Oct., '08	Aug. '11	34,944 = 21·10	21·39	Sept. '11
Oldenburg	Schichau, Danzig	Schichau	Apl. '09	Mar., '09	July, '12	34,394 = 21·3	22·2	July, '12

General Notes.—All four ships are extremely good sea boats. Thüringen (Ers. Beowulf), Helgoland (Ers. Siegfried), and Ostfriesland (Ers. Oldenburg), 1908 Programme. Oldenburg (Ers. Frithjof), 1909 Programme.

1907 GERMAN DREADNOUGHTS (Linienschiffe).

(NASSAU CLASS).

WESTFALEN (July, 1908), **NASSAU** (March, 1908), **POSEN** (Dec., 1908) & **RHEINLAND** (Sept., 1908).

Normal displacement, 18,900 tons. Complement, 957 to 966.

Length (waterline), 478 feet. Beam, 88¼ feet. { Mean draught, 26¼ feet. } Length (p.p.), 451½ feet.
{ Max. „ 27½ feet. }

Guns (M '04) :
12—11 inch, 45 cal. (A⁵).
12—5·9 inch, 45 cal.
22 pdr. anti-aircraft.
2 machine.
Torpedo tubes (17·7 inch) :
6 submerged (one bow, one stern,
and four broadside).

Armour (Krupp) :
11¾" Belt (amidships) ......
8" Belt (bow) ....
4" Belt (aft) ....
" Deck on slopes ......
11" Barbettes ....
11" Turrets to these ......
8" Lower deck redoubt ...
7" Battery ....
12" Conning tower ....
(Total weight: — tons)

Reported that surrender of all is demanded under Peace Treaty

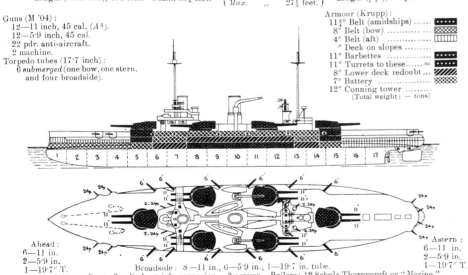

Ahead :
6—11 in.
2—5·9 in.
1—19·7" T.

Broadside : 8—11 in., 6—5·9 in., 1—19·7 in. tube.

Astern :
6—11 in.
2—5·9 in.
1—19·7" T.

Machinery : 3 sets 3 cylinder triple expansion. 3 screws. Boilers : 12 Schulz Thornycroft or "Marine."
Designed H.P. 20,000 = 19·9 kts. Coal : normal, 950 tons; maximum, 2700 tons, also 200 tons oil.

Armour Notes.—Underwater lateral bulkheads, 2" thick amidships.

Gunnery Notes.—All round loading positions to big guns, but fixed elevation. Electric, hydraulic and hand gear. Electric hoists to all guns. Ammunition supply to 6 inch reported unsatisfactory. Spotting stations aloft. Controls in each turret. 22—pdr. AA. guns in aft superstructure ; all other 3·4 inch removed.

Torpedo Notes.—Net defence fitted to all. Specially large searchlights.

Engineering Notes.—Excellent steamers. Nominal radius 5700 miles at economical speed.

Name	Builder	Machinery	Ordered	Laid down	Began trials	Trials : (full power) mean	Best speed	Finished trials
Westfalen	Weser, Bremen	Weser	Oct., '06	July, '07	Nov., '09	27,104 = 20·3	20·4	May, '10
Nassau	Wilhelmshaven		May., '06	July, '06	Oct., '09	25,508 = 20	20·8	May, '10
Posen	Germania, Kiel	Krupp	Apl., '07	July, '07	May, '10	27,745 = 20	21·39	Sept., '10
Rheinland	Vulkan, Stettin	Vulkan	Apl., '07	Aug.,'07	Apl., '10	26,100 = 20·3		Sept., '10

General Notes.—Cost of Nassaus £1,838,000 per ship. Keel of Nassau laid 1906, but no further progress was made on her till July, 1907. As originally designed she was to have carried only eight big guns. These ships steam well, but they draw more than the designed draught by at least a foot. They are very cramped internally and it is difficult to accommodate the crews. Some cabins have to accommodate 4 officers. Ventilation is very poor. They are only moderately successful, being overgunned for their displacement, but they are extremely steady gun platforms. The shooting from these ships always averages better than from any others. Nassau (Ers. Bayern) and Westfalen (Ers. Sachsen), 1906 Programme ; Rheinland (Ers. Württemburg) and Posen (Ers. Baden), 1907 Programme.

OSTFRIESLAND.

WESTFALEN.

1912 GERMAN BATTLE-CRUISERS (*Linienschiff Kreuzer*). Nos. **23, 24** (Dreadnoughts).

DERFFLINGER (June, 1913), LÜTZOW (Nov., 1913), ~~ERSATZ HERTHA~~ (1914). HINDENBURG

Displacement. 28,000 tons. Complement,

Length,   feet. Beam,   feet. Draught,   feet.

Guns (see *Note*):
  8—12 inch, 50 cal.
  12—6 inch, 45 cal.
  12—24 pdr.
  — anti-aerial.
Torpedo tubes (22 inch):
  4 *submerged* (broadside)
  1 *submerged* (stern)

Armour:
  About 13" Belt (amidships) ... aaa
  4" Belt (ends) .... d
  4" Deck (flat) amidships ......
  3" Deck (slopes) below it.

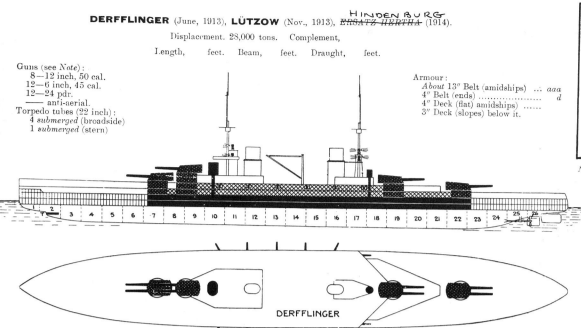

No photo procurable.

Note—Lützow sunk at Jutland. May 31 1916.

DERFFLINGER

*Armour Notes.—*There is a flat 4" upper protective deck amidships against aerial attack.

Name	Builder	Machinery	Laid down	Com-pleted	Trials	Turbines	Best recent speed
Derfflinger	Blohm & Voss	Blohm & Voss	Mar. '12	July '14			
Lützow	Schichau, Dan'g	Schichau	Sept. '12	'15			
~~E. Hertha~~	Wilhelmsh'n Y.	...	July '13	'16			

1911 GERMAN BATTLE-CRUISERS. Nos. **17** *and* **21** (Dreadnoughts)

SEYDLITZ (April, 1912).

Displacement, 25,000 tons. Complement,

Length (*over all*), 656 feet (*waterline* 648). Beam, 93⅓ feet. *Maximum* draught, 28 feet *or less* (*mean* 26¼).

Guns:
  10—11 inch, 50 cal. (A⁶)
  12—6 inch
  12—24 pdr.
  4—14 pdr. anti-aerial.
Torpedo tubes (20 inch):
  1 *submerged* (bow)
  2 *submerged* (broadside)
  1 *submerged* (stern)

Armour (Krupp):
  11" Belt (amidships)......... aaa
  4" Belt (ends) .... d
  3" Deck (2) (amidships) ...
  8" Turrets ....
  10½" Barbettes ....
  6" Mantlets to funnels ...=aa
  4" Battery .... d

Note raised forecastle.

SEYDLITZ

Machinery: Parsons turbine (2 stage). 3 screws. Boilers: 27 Schulz-Thornycroft. Designed H.P. 63,000=26·5 kts.

*Armour Notes.—*Generally as *Moltke*, but higher forward. The mantlet of fore funnel is 20 feet high, after funnel 12 feet. Main belt is about 400 feet long from turret to turret, of uniform thickness at waterline, reduced at upper and lower edges. Its height is about 15 feet. The double 3" protective deck is amidships only; Upper flat, lower curved.

*Gunnery Notes.—*One of the turrets is electrically and hand manoeuvred; all the others are hydraulic and hand.

*Torpedo Notes.—*Net defence fitted. Also special internal protection more or less similar to that of the Argentine *Rividaria*.

Name	Builder	Machinery	Laid down	Com-pleted	Trials	Turbines	Best recent speed
Seydlitz	Blohm & Voss	Blohm & Voss	Feb.'11	May '13	=	Parsons	29

General Note.—Seydlitz 1910 programme. Immensely strong construction is the special feature of this type; they are specially designed to withstand attack by high explosives. Freeboard forward about 33 feet, aft 18 feet. Except for the high forecastle forward this ship closely resembles the *Moltke* class in appearance.

1909 GERMAN BATTLE-CRUISERS (*Linienschiff Kreuzer*). 9, 13 (Dreadnoughts).

MOLTKE (April, 1910) & **GOEBEN** (March, 1911).
Displacement, 23,000 tons. Complement, 1107.
Length (*waterline*), 590½ feet. Beam, 96¾ feet. *Max.* draught, 28 feet. Length *over all*, 610 feet.

Guns:
10—11 inch, 50 cal. (A⁶)
12—6 inch.
12—24 pdr.
Torpedo tubes (20 inch):
 2 submerged (broadside)
 1 „ (bow)
 1 „ (stern)

Armour (Krupp).
11″ Belt (amidships) ....aaa
4″ Belt (ends) .... d
3″ Decks (2) (amidships) ...
8″ Turrets ....=aa
10½″ Turret bases ...
6″ Mantlets to funnels ......=aa
4″ Battery.................... d

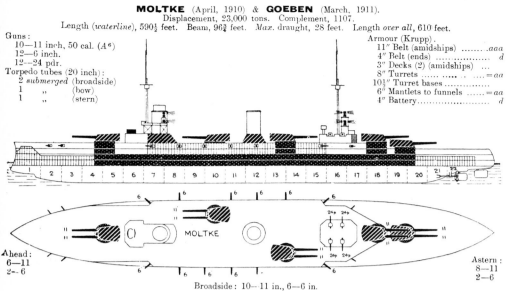

Ahead:
6—11
2—6

Astern:
8—11
2—6

Broadside: 10—11 in., 6—6 in.

Extra Gunnery Notes.—Big guns controlled from two armoured towers amidships. Unprotected spotting pos
each masthead connected by voice-pipe with the towers. Big guns hand loaded with wooden rammers wh
spring coils on head to allow of uniformly seating projectiles. Large holes cut in the back of turret in rea
gun to allow the rammers to come out. Turrets are very roomy: no partition between guns. Guns can be
at any arc, but at only one fixed elevation. Crew of each turret, including magazine parties, is 70 men. T
electric and hand. Loading, hydraulic and hand. Projectiles have 2 copper bands at ends, one for seating
rotating. Come up between guns delivered on a rocking tray. Charges come up in brass cylinders, in tw
(each 140 lbs.) which are loaded into the guns separately. Breech opens by hand by means of a coarse t
screw and small fly wheel. At drill using a single dummy charge, loading time has been timed 5 seconds
turret has a range finder and rate instrument, connected with a transmitting station below. The 6 inch gu
their own control towers. Crew of each 6 inch gun, six men.

Details of *Moltke*.

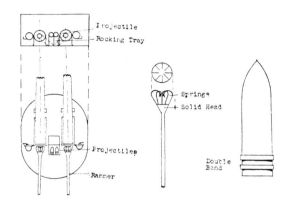

Fire controls of *Moltke* are not amidships as in *Goeben*; but 3 on top of each other at base of each mast.

Machinery: Parsons turbine. 4 screws. Boilers: 24 Schulz Thornycroft. Designed H.P. 70,000 = 27 kts.
Coal: *normal* 1000 tons; *maximum* 3300 tons. Also oil, *about* 200 tons. Also 600 extra tons can be
carried on deck.
Armour Notes.—The protection deck, the lower curved, the upper flat on top of main deck are amidships only. Protection decks at end are slight or non-existent. The funnel mantlets rise 12 feet above the upper deck, no special
protection below upper deck. Belt about 390 feet long by 15 feet wide, uniform thickness at w.l.; tapering at upper
and lower edges.
Gunnery Notes.—Hydraulic and hand gear to big guns; but superposed turret aft has special electrical gear which
admits of one round every 7 or 8 seconds. Each turret stows 16 shell and charges for same in brass cases.
Torpedo Notes.—Net defence: 400 feet. 8—60″ searchlights in two groups of 4 each. No special control. 3 torpedoes
per tube carried. 8 tubes have been reported, but this is doubtful.
Engineering Notes.—The nominal h.p. of these ships is 50,000 only, but this is obviously merely a fancy figure. The
actual contract h.p. was 70,000. This was easily exceeded on trial with the *Moltke*, but her normal maximum speed
is not much over 27 kts a the outside, and 25 may be nearer actuality. 320 r.p.m.=about 27·75 kts. 428=29·5 kts.
At full power consumption is 48 tons per hour, at 15 kts it is 16 tons

Name	Builder	Machinery	Laid down	Completed	Trials 6 hrs. mean. runs.	Turbines	Best recent speed
Moltke	Blohm & Voss	Blohm & Voss	Apr.'09	To do '11 Oct. '11	76,795=27·25 85,782=28·4	Parsons	28·4
Goeben	Blohm & Voss	Blohm & Voss	July,'09	Oct. '12	71,275=27·2 85·661=28	Parsons	28

General Notes.—Moltke, 1908 programme; Goeben belongs to the 1909 programme. Designed by Prof. Kretsschner.
Meta centric height: 22¼ feet. Cost *about* £2,200,000 per ship. Fitted with Frahm anti-rolling tanks. All cupboards,
shelves, etc., are of light sheet iron, the only wood being the tables and chairs. There are no pictures, arm chairs,
settees or sofas in the wardroom. There are no ventilators on deck other than the erections around the fore funnel,
and mainmast. Freeboard forward 26 feet, aft 18 feet. There are 2 steering engines in separate compartments in
tandem. Officers' quarters, aft.

1907 GERMAN BATTLE-CRUISER (*Linien-Kreuzer*). No. 5.

VON DER TANN (20th March, 1909).
Normal displacement, 19,400; *full load*, 21,000 tons. Complement, 910.
Length (*waterline*), 558 feet. Beam, 85 feet. *Max.* draught, 27½ feet. Length *over all*, 561 feet.

Guns (M. '04) (see Notes):
8—11 inch, 45 cal. (AAAAA).
10—6 inch.
16—24 pdr.
Torpedo tubes: (18 inch)
 1 submerged (bow)
 1 submerged (stern)
 2 submerged (broadside)

Armour (Krupp):
10—7″ Belt (amidships) ...aaa-a
4″ Belt (bow) N.C............ d
4″ Belt (stern) N.C. .... d
″ Deck ...
8″ Turrets .... =aa
6″ Turret bases (N.C.) ...... b
? 4½″ Battery .... d
Protection to vitals .... =aa

Torpedo nets now fitted.

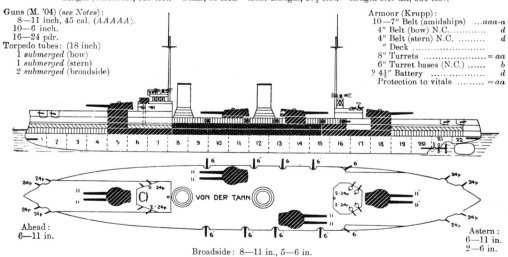

Ahead:
6—11 in.

Astern:
6—11 in.
2—6 in.

Broadside: 8—11 in., 5—6 in.

Machinery: Turbine (Parsons). 4 screws. Boilers: 18 Schulz-Thornycroft. Designed H.P. 50,000 =
25 kts. Coal: *normal* 1000 tons; *maximum* 2800 tons. Also 300 tons oil.
Armour Notes.—Main belt is 14½ feet wide amidships. About 10 feet is above waterline and 4½ below l.w.l.
There is a flat armour deck on top of this belt: usual sloping deck from bottom edge. The
armour thicknesses given are approximately correct to about an inch. *Exact* thicknesses cannot
be ascertained. Belt at ends is about 11½ feet wide, the upper strake being considerably thinner
than the lower. Except amidships the belt does not rise to the main deck, though always so
represented in plans of German origin.
Gunnery Notes.—
Torpedo Notes.—The stern submerged tube is on the starboard side of the stern post.

Name	Builder	Machinery	Laid down	Completed	Trials	Boilers	Best recent speed
Von der Tann	Blohm & Voss	Blohm & Voss	Oct '08	Sept., '10	= 79,802=27·4	Schulz-T.	28·1

General Notes.—Cost, £1,833,000. Belongs to 1907 programme, but there was considerable delay in commencing her.
The *Von der Tann* is an excellent steamer; but not a particularly good sea-boat. The guns are very well
placed, and there is practically no interference at all. All the work in this ship is extremely good, and all
details of her internal fittings are most carefully thought out. Frahm tanks. Designed by Prof. Kresschner.

1904 GERMAN BATTLESHIPS (18 knot). PRE-DREADNOUGHTS.

(Deutschland Class—5 Ships).

DEUTSCHLAND (Nov., 1904), **HANNOVER** (Sept., 1905), **POMMERN** (Dec., 1905), **SCHLESWIG-HOLSTEIN** (Dec., 1906), and **SCHLESIEN** (May, 1906).

Displacement, 13,200 tons. Complement, 729.

Length (*waterline*), 410 feet. Beam, 72 feet. *Mean* draught, 25 feet. Length *over all*, 430 feet.

Guns (M. '01):
4—11 inch, 40 cal. (*AAA*).
14—6·7 inch, 40 cal. (*B*).
20—24 pdr.
4—1 pdr.
4 Machine.
Torpedo tubes (17·7 inch):
6 *submerged* (bow, stern, and broadside).

Armour (Krupp) *see Notes*:
9¾" Belt (amidships) ... *aaa*
4" Belt (ends) .... *d*
3" Deck on slopes ......
Protection to vitals... = *aaaa*
11" Barbettes .... *aaa*
11" Turrets to these ...... *aaa*
8" Lower deck (side) ... *aa*
6¾" Battery .... *a*
6¾" Casemates (4) ...... *a*
12" Conning tower (fore) *aaa*
5½" After C.T. .... *b*
(Total weight, 430 tons.)

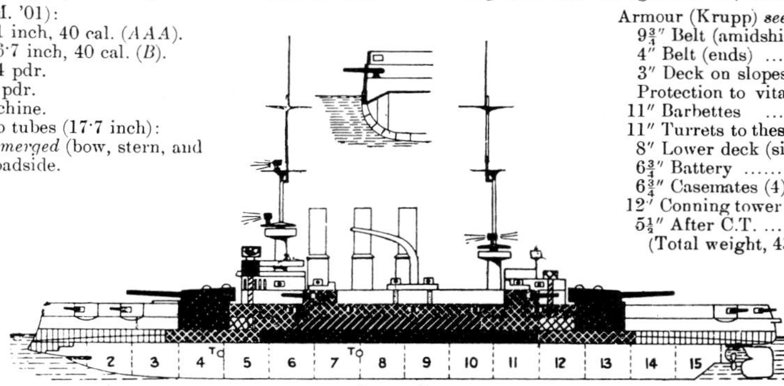
2 3 4 TO 5 6 7 TO 8 9 10 11 12 13 14 15

Ahead:
2—11 in.
4—6·7 in.

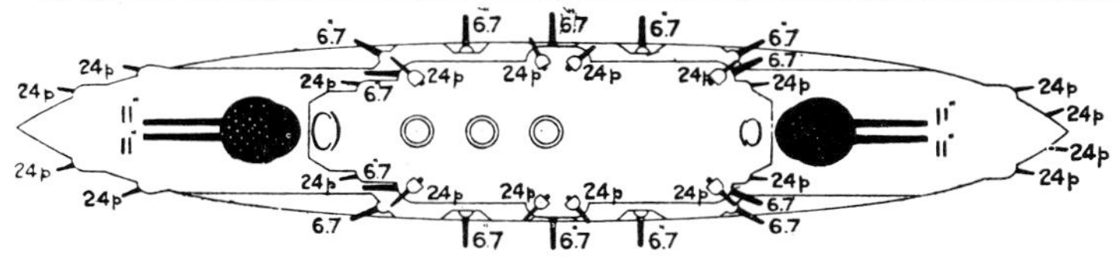
6.7
24p
11
6.7
24p

Astern:
2—11 in.
4—6·7 in.

Broadside: 4—11 in., 7—6·7 in.

Machinery: 3 sets 3 cylinder vertical triple expansion. 3 screws. Boilers: 12 Schulz Thornycroft. Designed H.P. 16,000 = 18 kts. Coal: *normal* 800 tons; *maximum* 1800 tons. Also 200 tons liquid fuel (in double bottom). *Nominal* radius 5500 kts. at 10 kts.

Armour Notes.—*Deutschland's* belt is only 9 inch, and battery is ½ inch thicker than in the other 4.

Gunnery Notes.—Loading positions, big guns: all round. Hoists: electric, all guns. Big guns manœuvred by electric and hand gear; secondary guns, electric and hand gear.

Arcs of fire: Big guns, 270°; casemates and end battery guns 135° from axial line; other battery guns, 110°.

Engineering Notes.—Coal consumption: *normal* 8½ tons an hour at 17 kts.; about 13 tons at 18 kts. Can steam about 3500 miles at 17 kts. and 2500 at full speed.

Name.	*Builder.*	*Machinery.*	*Laid down.*	*Com pleted*	*Trials: 22 hrs. at ¾.*	*6 hrs. full p.*	*Boilers.*	*Best recent speed.*
Deutschland	Krupp	Krupp	1903	1906	11,377 = 17·1	16,935 = 15·53	Schulz in all.	18·9
Hannover	Wilhelmsh'vn	...	1904	1907	12,153 = 16·9	17,768 = 18·7		19·16
Pommern	Vulkan Co.	Vulkan	1904	1907		17,696 = 18·5		19·21
Schleswig-Holstein	Schichau	Schichau	1905	1908		19,868 = 19		
Schlesien	Krupp	Krupp	1905	1908		19,465 = 18·5		19·03

General Notes.—Cost per ship complete about £1,200,000. These ships of the *Deutschland* class are over-gunned. The secondary guns fire too heavy a projectile for man-handling, and the actual value of the class is well below their paper value. They are very good steamers; but otherwise hardly equal to British, U.S.A., and French ships of equal date.

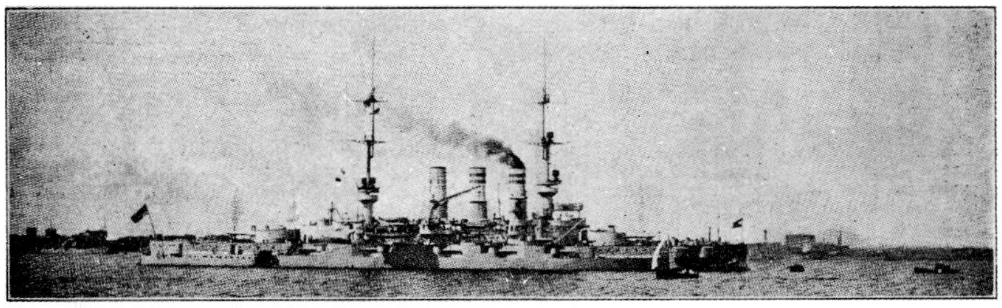

Note.—In *Deutschland* and *Hannover* the searchlight forward instead of being carried on the fighting top is on a platform just above it.

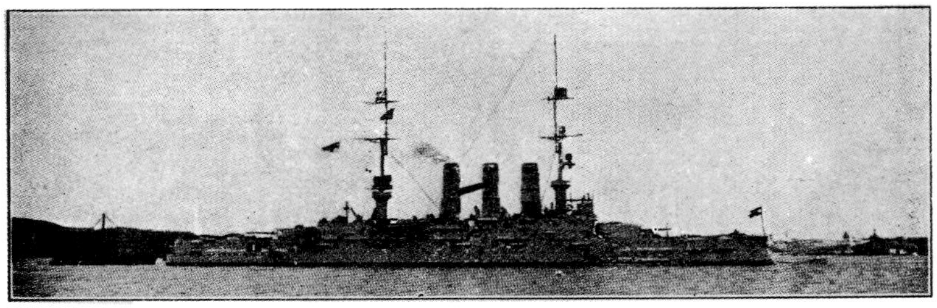

Pommern sunk at Jutland 1st June 1916.

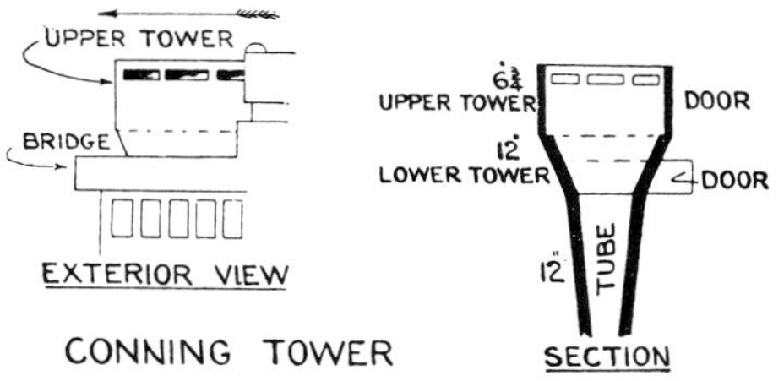
UPPER TOWER
BRIDGE
EXTERIOR VIEW
6¾
UPPER TOWER
DOOR
12
LOWER TOWER
DOOR
12
TUBE
SECTION

CONNING TOWER

(Braunschweig Class—5 Ships).

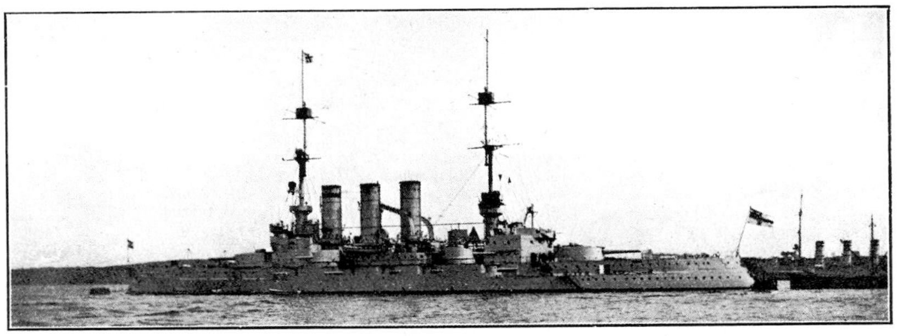

BRAUNSCHWEIG (Dec., 1902), **ELSASS** (May, 1903), **LOTHRINGEN** (May, 1904), **HESSEN** (Sept., 1903), & **PREUSSEN** (Oct., 1903). Displacement, 13,200 tons. Complement, (743?). Length (*waterline*), 413⅓ feet. Beam, 72⅘ feet. *Mean* draught, 25¾ feet. Length *over all*, 430 feet. *Guns (M. '01.): 4—11 inch, 40 cal, (A^3), 14—6·7 inch, 40 cal., 18—3·4 inch (22 pdr.)?, 2 Machine. Torpedo tubes (17·7 inch): 5 *submerged* (bow and broadside), 1 *above water* (stern). Armour (Krupp): 8¾" Belt (amidships), 4" Belt (ends), 3" Deck on slopes, 11" Barbettes to these, 11" Turrets (side). 5" Lower deck, 6" Battery, 6¾" Small turrets, 12" Conning tower, 6" Conning tower (aft). Machinery: 3 sets 3 cylinder vertical inverted triple expansion. 3 screws. Boilers: 8 Schulz-Thornycroft + 6 cylindrical. Designed H.P. 16,000 = 18 kts. Coal: *normal* 700 tons; *maximum* 1670 tons. Also 200 tons of oil (in double bottom). *Nominal* radius: 5500 miles at 10 kts.

**Note.*—Guns and tubes given, those originally mounted. Present guns and disposal of ships as follows:—

Name	*Guns*	*Service.*
Braunschweig	Disarmed; guns removed.	Accommodation Ship.
Elsass	,, ,,	Accommodation Ship.
Lothringen	,, ,,	Sea-going Parent Ship for Motor Boat Minesweepers.*
Hessen	,, ,,	Accommodation Ship.
Preussen	,, ,,	Sea-going Parent Ship for Motor Boat Minesweepers.*

Name.	*Builder.*	*Machinery.*	*Laid down.*	*Com-pleted.*	*Full power trials: 24 hrs.*	*6 hrs.*	*Boilers.*	*Best recent speed.*
Braunschweig	Germania, Kiel	By Builders	1901	1904	11,382 = 16·3	17,312 = 18·6	8 Schulz-T. and 6 cyl. in all.	18·1
Hessen	Germania, Kiel		1902	1905	11.384 = 16·4	16,900 = 18·23		
Preussen	Vulkan, Stettin		1902	1905	11.304 = 16·2	18,374 = 18·69		
Elsass	Schichau, D'zig		1901	1904	11,554 = 16·7	16,812 = 18·7		18·6
Lothringen	Schichau, D'zig		1902	1906	11,573 = 16·5	16,950 = 18·54		

* Each has superstructures for carrying 12 Motor Boat Minesweepers.

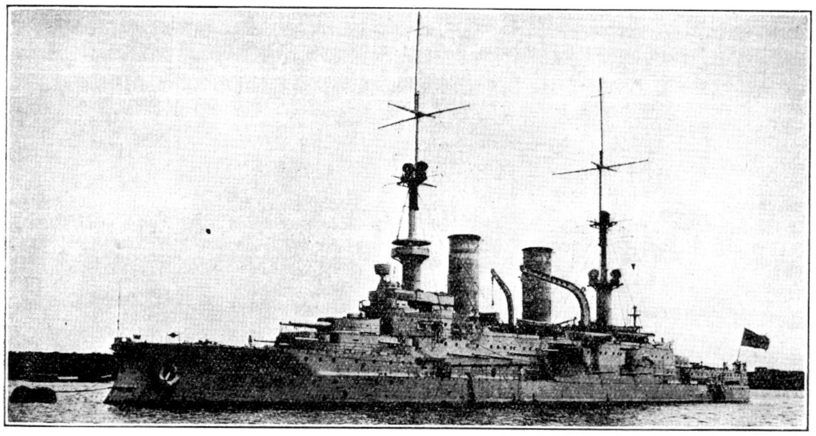

WITTELSBACH (1900), **WETTIN** (1901), **ZÄHRINGEN** (1901), **MECKLENBURG** (1901), **SCHWABEN** (1901). Displacement, 11,800 tons. Complement was 683. Dimensions: 410¾ (*w.l.*), 416½ (*o.a.*) × 68¼ × 28 feet (*maximum* draught). *Guns (M. '99): 4—9.4 inch, 40 cal., 18—5·9 inch, 40 cal., 12—3·4 inch (15 pdr.), 2 M.G. *Torpedo tubes (17·7 inch): 6 *submerged* (bow, stern and broadside). Armour (Krupp): 9" Belt (ends), 3" Deck on slopes, 10" Barbettes, 10" Turrets to them, 5½" Lower deck (redoubt), 5½" Battery, 6" Casemates (4 bow), 6" Small turrets, 10" Conning tower. Machinery: 3 sets vertical triple expansion. 3 screws. Boilers: 6 Schulz-Thornycroft and 6 cylindrical. Designed H.P. 15,000 = 18 kts. Coal: *normal*, 653 tons; *maximum*, 1800 tons. Oil: 200 tons.

*Guns and tubes given, those originally mounted. Present armament and disposal of ships as follows:—

Name	*Guns*	*Service*
Wittelsbach, *Wettin*	Disarmed.	Parent Ships for Minesweepers, Wilhelmshaven.
Zahringen	Turrets removed. 7—5·9 inch.* 4—15 pdr.*	Training Ship, Danzig.
Mecklenburg	Disarmed.	Accommodation Ship, Kiel.
Schwaben	Turrets removed. 6—5·9 inch.* 4—15 pdr.*	Sea-going Parent Ship for Motor Boat Minesweepers, Wilhelmshaven.

*Guns on board, but ships are disarmed.

1890 OLD GERMAN BATTLESHIPS. 1887

BRANDENBURG (1891) & WÖRTH (1892).

Displacement, 10,060 tons. Complement, 568.

Length (waterline), 354¼ feet. Beam, 64 feet. Maximum draught, 26 feet. Length over all, 380½ feet.

Guns—(old models):
4—11 inch, 40 cal. (A).
2—11 inch, 35 cal. (B).
8—4·1 inch, 30 cal.
8—15½ pdr.
12—1 pdr.
4 Machine.
Torpedo tubes (17·7 inch):
2 submerged.
1 above water (stern).

Armour (compound):
15″ Belt (amidships) ... *aa*
12″ Belt (ends)............ *a*
2½″ Deck (flat on belt)
Protection to vitals is... *aa*
12″ Barbettes .... *a*
5″ Turrets (may be less) *d*
3″ Battery   ,,   *e*
12″ Conning tower ...... *a*
(Total weight 2800 tons).

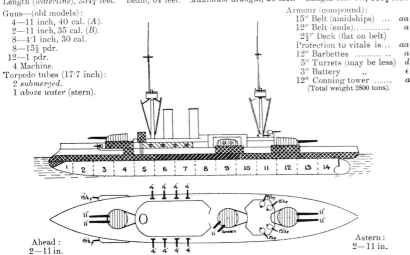

Ahead:
2—11 in.

Astern:
2—11 in.

Broadside: 4—11 in., 2—11 in., 4—4·1 in.

Machinery: 2 sets vertical triple expansion. 2 screws. Boilers: 12 cylindrical, return flame.
Designed H.P. *forced* 10,000=17 kts. Coal: *normal* 600 tons; *maximum* 1050 tons.
Gunnery Notes.—Loading positions, big guns: end on. Big guns manœuvred: hydraulic and hand
gear. Continuous firing slow, but they have special arrangements for firing a few rounds quickly.

KAISER FRIEDRICH III. (1896), K. WILHELM II. (1897), K. BARBAROSSA (1900),
K. WILHELM DER GROSSE (1899), K. KARL DER GROSSE (1899),

Displacement, (reconstructed) 10,790 tons. Complement, 658.

Length (waterline), 384 feet. Beam, 65½ feet. Maximum draught, 27 feet.

Guns—(M. '95):
4—9·4 inch, 40 cal. (A).
14—6 inch, 40 cal. (K. Karl 18).
12—15½ pdr.
12—1 pdr.
8 Machine.
Torpedo tubes (17·7 inch):
5 submerged
(bow and broadside).
1 above water (stern).

Armour (Krupp):
12″ Belt (amidships) ... *aaa*
4″ Belt (bow) .... *d*
8″ Bulkheads (aft) ...... *aa*
3″ Deck (flat on belt) ...
Protection to vitals is... *aaa*
10″ Barbettes .... *aa*
10″ Turrets to these ... *aa*
6″ on secondary guns ... *b*
10″ Conning tower (N.C.) *aa*
(Total weight 3,800 tons).

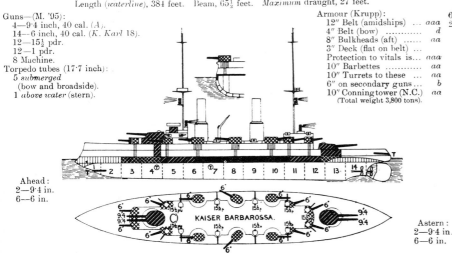

KAISER BARBAROSSA.

Ahead:
2—9·4 in.
6—6 in.

Astern:
2—9·4 in.
6—6 in.

Machinery: 3 sets vertical 3 cylinder triple expansion. 3 screws. Boilers: 8 cylindrical, 4
Schultz; (in K. Karl der Grosse and K. Barbarossa 6). Designed H.P. 14,000=18 knots. Coal:
normal 650 tons; *maximum* 1,050 tons; also 200 tons liquid fuel (double bottom).

Name	Builder	Machinery	Laid down	Completed	Refit	Trials	Boilers	Best recent speed
K. Friedrich III.	Wilhelmsh'vn	...	1895	1898	1908			
K. Wilhelm II.	Wilhelmsh'vn	...	1896	1900	1908			
K. W. der Grosse	Krupp	Krupp	1898	1901	1908			
K. Karl der Grosse	Blohm & Voss	Blohm & Voss	1898	1901	1907	7360=15·5	13,940=18	
K. Barbarossa	Schichau	Schichau	1898	1901	1907			17·5

ODIN (1894) & ÆGIR (1895), 4150 tons.
and
SIEGFRIED (1889), BEOWULF (1890), FRITHJOF (1891), HEIMDALL (1892),
HILDEBRAND (1892), HAGEN (1893). 4100 tons.

Guns (in all): 3—old 9·4 inch, 35 cal. (C); 10—15½ pdr.; 6—1 pdr.; 4 machine. Torpedo tubes: 3—17·7
inch, *submerged*. Armour: In first two, nickel, belt (amidships only) 8½″; in others, compound,
complete belt 9½″—6″, barbettes (2 guns forward, 1 aft) 8″. Speeds: about 15 kts. (Fuller details
see 1910 and previous editions.)

(Employed on coast defence in the Baltic.)

1906 GERMAN ARMOURED CRUISER (*Panzer-Kreuzer*).

BLUCHER (April, 1908).

Normal displacement, 15,500 tons. Complement, 847.

Length (waterline), 489 feet. Beam, 80⅓ feet. Maximum draught, 27 feet. Length over all, 493 feet.

Guns (M. '04):
12—8·2 inch, 45 cal. (A).
8—6 inch, 45 cal.
16—24 pdr., 40 cal.
Torpedo tubes:
3 submerged.

Armour (Krupp):
6″ Belt (amidships) ....
4″ Belt (ends)................
″ Armour deck...........
Protection to vitals ....
6″ Turrets ....

BLUCHER.

Ahead:
6—8·2 in.
2—6 in.

Astern:
6—8·2 in.
2—6 in.

Broadside: 8—8·2 in., 4—6 in.

Machinery: 3 sets vertical inverted triple expansion. 3 screws. Boilers: 18 Schulz-Thornycroft.
Designed H.P. 32,000=24·5 kts. Coal: *normal* 900 tons; *maximum* 2300; and 200 tons oil.
Gunnery Notes.—Most of big guns replaced, 1912. Fire control in each turret. Masthead spotting stations.
Torpedo Notes.—Nets fitted, 1911.

Name	Builder	Machinery	Laid down	Completed	Trials	Boilers	Best recent speed
Blucher	Kiel Yard		Oct '06	Sep '09	mean. 43,886 = 25·86	Schulz Thornycroft	26·4

General Notes.—Total cost, £1,349,000. On her trials this ship touched 26·4 kts. She is a very successful ship
in all respects.
Note—Sunk at Battle of Doger Bank 24 February 1915.

BLUECHER, 1914, new rig.

1904 GERMAN ARMOURED CRUISERS (*Panzer-Kreuzer*) (22½ knot).

(SCHARNHORST CLASS—2 Ships)

SCHARNHORST (March, 1906) & **GNEISENAU** (June, 1906).

Displacement, 11,600 tons. Complement, 765.

Length (*waterline*), 449¾ feet. Beam, 71 feet. Mean draught, 25 feet. Length *over all*, feet.

Note—Both sunk at Battle of the Falkands 8 December 1914.

Guns :
- 8—8·2 inch, 40 cal. (A).
- 6—6 inch, 40 cal.
- 20—24 pdr., 35 cals.
- 4 Machine.

Torpedo tubes (18 inch) :
- 4 *submerged* (bow, stern, and broadside).

Armour (Krupp) :
6″ Belt (amidships)	a
4¾″ Belt (bow)	c
4″ Belt (aft)	d
2″ Armour deck	
Protection to vitals ... ═	aa
5″ Bulkheads	b
6″ Barbettes	b
6¾″ Turret hoods	a
6″ Lower deck side	a
6″ Battery (N.C.)	b
6″ Upper battery (N.C.)	b
5″ Battery bulkheads (K.C.)	b
8″ Conning tower.........	a

Ahead :
4—8·2 in.
2—6 in.

Astern :
4—8·2 in.
2—6 in.

Broadside : 6—8·2 in., 3—6 in.

Machinery : 2 sets vertical inverted triple expansion. 3 cylinder : one set, central, 4 cylinder. 3 screws. Boilers : 18 Schulz Thornycroft. Designed H.P. 26,000 =22·5 kts. Coal : *normal* 800 tons ; *maximum* 2000 tons (also 200 tons oil).

Armour Notes.—

*Gunnery Notes.—*Hoists, electric and hand (one serving two or three guns). Masthead fire controls fitted 1912.

*Torpedo Notes.—*6 searchlights. Electrical installation at 115 volts. Two turbo generators each 4000 r.p.m.—load, 850 amperes.

*Engineering Notes.—*Full speed 120 revs. 95 = 20·5 kts. *about.* The three engine rooms separated by solid bulkheads. Boiler rooms ditto.

Name.	Builders.	Machinery.	Laid down.	Completed.	Refit.	Trials, full power.		Boilers.	Best recent speed.
Gneisenau	Weser, Bremen.		1904	1907			=24·8	S. Th'nyc'ft.	24·8
Scharnhorst	Blohm & Voss,Hamburg		1905	1907		18,052 =20·7	27,759 =22·7	S. Th'nyc'ft.	21

*General Notes.—*Scharnhorst grounded badly in 1909 and since then has never been able to steam as well as before. These carry two 200 h.p. 48 feet motor launches (16 kts.), 1—8 kt. motor barge, 2 steam boats.

1902 GERMAN ARMOURED CRUISERS (21 knots).

(ROON CLASS.—2 Ships).

ROON (June, 1903) & **YORCK** (May, 1904).

Displacement, 9050 tons. Complement, 557.

Length (*waterline*), 403¼ feet. Beam, 65½ feet. *Maximum* draught, 25¾ feet.

Guns :
- 4—8·2 inch, 40 cal. (A).
- 10—6 inch, 40 cal.
- 14—24 pdr.
- 4 Machine.

Torpedo tubes (18 inch) :
- 4 *submerged* (bow, stern, and broadside).

Armour (Krupp) :
4″ Belt (amidships)	
3″ Belt (ends)	e
2¾″ Deck (slopes).........	
Protection to vitals	═c
6″ Turrets...................	b
4″ Turret bases	d
4″ Lower deck redoubt	d
4″ Battery	d
4″ Small turrets	d
6″ Conning tower (fore)	b
3″ ″ ″ (aft)	e

Roon (solid cranes).

Ahead :
2—8·2 in.
4—6 in.

Astern :
2—8·2 in.
4—6 in.

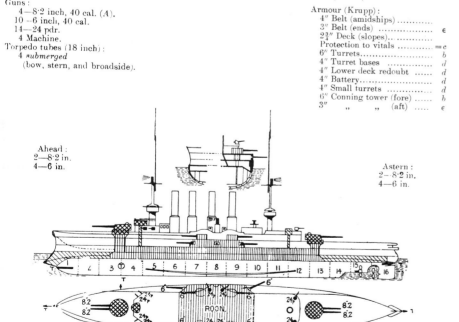

Broadside : 4—8·2 in., 5—6 in.

Machinery : 3 sets vertical triple expansion. 3 screws. Boilers : 16 Dürr. Designed H.P. 19,000 = 21 kts. Coal : *normal* 750 tons ; *maximum* 1600 tons ; also 200 tons of oil. 118 revs. = full speed.

*General Notes.—*Except for some minor details and slightly increased H.P., these ships are identical with the P. Adalbert class (*q.v.*).

Name.	Built at	Laid down.	Completed.	Trials.			Boilers.
				24 hours.			
Yorck	Blohm & Voss	April, '03	May, '06	13,711 = 19 kts.	20,295 = 21·4 kts.		Dürr
Roon	Kiel Dockyard	Aug., '02	Oct., '05		20,625 = 21·17 kts.		Dürr

YORCK (pierced cranes).

1900 GERMAN ARMOURED CRUISERS. 1899

PRINZ ADALBERT (June, 1901) & **FRIEDRICH KARL** (June, 1902).
Displacement, 9050 tons. Complement, 557.
Length (*waterline*), 394 feet. Beam, 65 feet. *Maximum* draught, 25¾ feet.

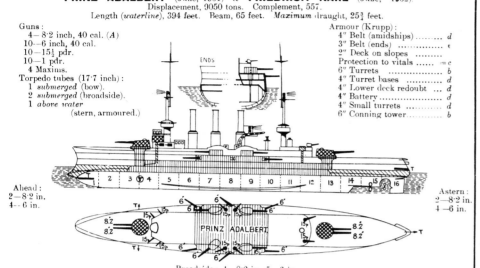

Guns :
4—8·2 inch, 40 cal. (A)
10—6 inch, 40 cal.
10—15½ pdr.
10—1 pdr.
4 Maxims.
Torpedo tubes (17·7 inch) :
1 *submerged* (bow).
2 *submerged* (broadside).
1 *above water*
(stern, armoured.)

Armour (Krupp) :
4″ Belt (amidships) .... d
3″ Belt (ends) .... e
2″ Deck on slopes ....
Protection to vitals ...... =c
6″ Turrets .... b
4″ Turret bases .... d
4″ Lower deck redoubt .... d
4″ Battery .... d
4″ Small turrets .... d
6″ Conning tower .... b

Ahead :
2—8·2 in.
4—6 in.

Astern :
2—8·2 in.
4—6 in.

Broadside : 4—8·2 in., 5—6 in.

Machinery : 3 sets 4 cylinder vertical inverted triple expansion. 3 screws. Boilers : P. A., 14 Dürr ; F. K.
(1908) Schulz-Thornycroft. Designed H.P. 18500 = 21 kts. Coal : *normal* 750 tons ; *max.* 1500 tons. Oil : 200 tons.

Name	Builder	Machinery	Laid down	Completed	Refit	Trials	Boilers	Best recent speed
P. Adalbert	Kiel Y.		Apl., '00	Oct.,'03		17,600 = 20·3	Dürr	21
F. Karl	Blohm & Voss		Aug.,'01	Oct.,'03	1908	17,700 = 29·5		...

Note—Friedrich Karl sunk by mine in Baltic 26 November 1914. Prinz Adalbert torpedoed by British submarine 23 November 1915.

1896 GERMAN ARMOURED CRUISER.

(*Seagoing torpedo school ship*) **FÜRST BISMARCK** (1897). (*Reconstructing.*)
Displacement, 10,700 tons (Sheathed). Complement, 529.

Length (*waterline*), 399 feet. Beam, 65½ feet. *Maximum* draught, 27 feet. Length *over all*, 410 feet.

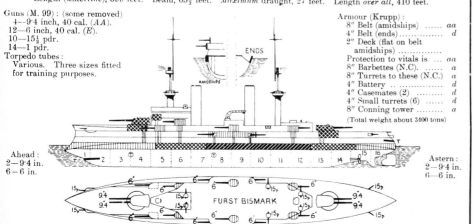

Guns (M. 99) : (some removed)
4—9·4 inch, 40 cal. (AA)
12—6 inch, 40 cal. (E)
10—15½ pdr.
14—1 pdr.
Torpedo tubes :
Various. Three sizes fitted
for training purposes.

Armour (Krupp) :
8″ Belt (amidships) ...... aa
4″ Belt (ends) .... d
2″ Deck (flat on belt
amidships) ....
Protection to vitals is ... aa
8″ Barbettes (N.C.) .... a
8″ Turrets to these (N.C.) a
4″ Battery .... d
4″ Casemates (2) .... d
4″ Small turrets (6) ...... d
8″ Conning tower .... a
(Total weight about 3400 tons)

Ahead :
2—9·4 in.
6—6 in.

Astern :
2—9·4 in.
6—6 in.

Machinery : 3 sets vertical triple expansion. 3 screws. Boilers : 8 Schulz Thornycroft and 8 cylindrical.
Designed H.P. 13,600 = 19 kts. Coal : *normal* 1000 tons ; *maximum* 1200 tons.

GERMAN BIG PROTECTED CRUISERS. 1895

(*Training service*) **FREYA** (1897), **HERTHA** (1897), **VICTORIA LUISE** (1897), **HANSA** (18—
and **VINETA** (1897).
Displacement, 5660, but last two 5885 tons. Complement, 465.
Length, 344½ feet. Beam, 57 feet. *Maximum* draught, 23 feet.

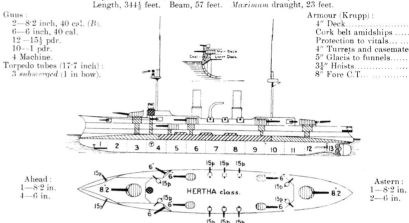

Guns :
2—8·2 inch, 40 cal. (B).
6—6 inch, 40 cal.
12—15½ pdr.
10—1 pdr.
4 Machine.
Torpedo tubes (17·7 inch) :
3 *submerged* (1 in bow).

Armour (Krupp) :
4″ Deck ....
Cork belt amidships .....
Protection to vitals .....
4″ Turrets and casemate
5″ Glacis to funnels......
3½″ Hoists ....
8″ Fore C.T........

Ahead :
1—8·2 in.
4—6 in.

Astern :
1—8·2 in.
2—6 in.

Broadside : 2—8·2 in., 3—6 in.

Machinery : 3 sets 4 cylinder triple expansion. 3 screws. Designed H.P. 10,500 = 19 kts. C°
normal 900 tons ; *maximum* 1,000 tons.

Name	Builder	Machinery	Laid down	Completed	Reconstructed			Boilers	R
Freya	Danzig Y.	Krupp	Oct. '95	1898	1908				
Hertha	Vulk. Stettin	Vulkan Co.	Sep. '95	1898	1907			8 Schulz Thornycroft except Freya 12 Niclausse	
V. Luise	Weser, Bremen	Weser, Bremen	Sep. '95	1898	1907				
Hansa	Vulkan Co.	Vulkan Co.	Mar.'96	1898	1907				
Vineta	Vulkan Co.	Vulkan Co.	Jun.'96	1898	1910				

(*Stokers' Training Ship.*)
PRINZ HEINRICH (March, 1900). Displacement, 8900 tons. Complement (was 567).
Dimensions : 409¾ × 64¼ × 25½ feet (*maximum* draught). Guns : None. Torpedo tubes
18 inch) : 1 *submerged* (bow), 2 *submerged* (broadside), 1 *above water* (stern), all probably
removed. Armour (Krupp) : 4″ Belt (amidships), 3″ Belt (ends), 2″ Deck, 6″ Turrets, 4″
Turret bases, 4″ Lower deck side, 4″ Battery. Machinery : 3 sets triple expansion 4-cylinder.
3 screws. Boilers : 14 Dürr. Designed H.P. 15,000 = 20·5 kts. Coal : *normal*, 750 tons ;
maximum, 1500 tons. Also 200 tons liquid fuel.
Note: Fürst Bismark sold 1919.

(*Gunnery School Ship.*)
KAISERIN AUGUSTA (1892). Displacement, 6060 tons. Complement (was 439). Dimensions : 401 × 51 × 25½ feet. Guns : 1—5·9 inch, 4—4·1 inch, 10—3·4 inch (22 and 15 pdr.). Torpedo tubes (13·8 inch) : 1 *submerged* (bow), 2 *above water* (broadside). Armour : 3½″ Deck (amidships), 1½″ at ends. Machinery : 3 sets vertical triple expansion. 3 screws. Boilers : 8 two-ended cylindrical. Designed H.P. *forced draught* 12,000 = 21·5 kts. (much less now). Coal : 810 tons.

GERMAN LIGHT CRUISERS.

(All are officially rated as "Kleine Geschützte Kreuzer" or "Small Protected Cruisers.")

KÖNIGSBERG CLASS.

EMDEN (February, 1916).   **NÜRNBERG** (January, 1916).

KÖNIGSBERG (December, 1915).

Displacement, about 4,200 tons.   Complement, —.

Length, 450 feet.   Beam, 43½ feet.   Draught, 16 feet.

Guns :
8—5·9 inch, 50 cal. (semi-auto)
2 or 3—22 pdr. anti-aircraft
Torpedo tubes (19·7 inch) :
2 *above water*
2 *submerged.*

Armour :
" Belt (amidships) ....
" Belt (ends) ....
" Deck (amidships) ....
" Gun Shields ....
" Conning Tower (fore) ....
" Conning Tower (aft) ...

Photo by courtesy of Dr. J. A. Prendergast.

Photo, C.N.

Ahead :
4—5·9 in.

Broadside : 5—5·9 in.

Astern :
4—5·9 in.

Machinery : "Marine type," but some may have geared turbines.   screws.   Boilers : Schulz-Thornycroft.   Designed H.P.   = 28·5 kts.   Coal : *normal,*   tons ; *maximum,* 1240 tons (+500 tons oil fuel).

Gunnery Notes.—In Karlsruhe class, the 5·9 inch guns under fore bridges are a deck higher than in *Frankfurt* ; that is, on same level as the forecastle 5·9's.

Name	Builder	Machinery	Laid down	Completed	Trials	Turbines
Emden	Weser, Bremen	Weser, Bremen	1915	Aug.'15		
Nürnberg	Howaldt, Kiel	Howaldt	1915	Nov.'16		
Königsberg	Weser Co., Bremen	Weser Co.	1914	Aug.'16		

General Notes.—Emden begun as *Ersatz Nymphe,* Nurnberg as *Ersatz Thetis,* both under 1915-16 Programme.   Königsberg begun as *Ersatz Gazelle,* 1914-15 Programme.—*Dresden (Ersatz Amazone,* of 1916-17 Programme), launched by Howaldt, Kiel, November, 1916, and delivered 1918 ; *Koln (Ersatz Ariadne,* of 1916-17 Programme), launched by Blohm & Voss, Hamburg, October, 1916, and finished 1917 : *Karlsruhe (Ersatz Niobe,* of 1914-15 Programme), launched at Kiel D.Y., February, 1916, and completed November, 1916.   Two Minelaying Cruisers, *Bremse* and *Brummer* (not of *Königsberg* class), also scuttled at Scapa Flow.

1913 GERMAN LIGHT CRUISERS.

FRANKFURT.

Salved at Scapa Flow.
FRANKFURT (March, 1915).

Displacement, 5120 tons.   Complement,

Length, 465 feet.   Beam, 45½ feet.   Draught, 17 feet.

Note to Plans.—Delete 5·9 inch as dotted ; above water tube are in these positions, and *not* guns.

Guns :
8—5·9 inch, 50 cal., S.A.
2—22 pdr. anti-aircraft.
Torpedo tubes (19·7 inch) :
2 *above water.*
2 *submerged.*
Can carry 120 mines.

Armour :
6" Belt ....
4—3" Ends ....
1½" Deck ....
" Gun shields.........
" C.T. (fore) ....
" C.T. (aft) ....

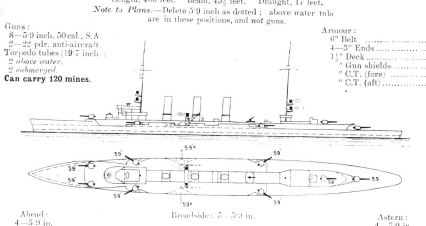

Ahead :
4—5·9 in.

Broadside : 5—5·9 in.

Astern :
4—5·9 in.

Machinery.—"Marine type" turbines, but may have geared turbines.   Boilers : Schulz-Thornycroft.   Designed H.P.   = 28 kts.   Coal : *normal,*   tons ; *maximum,* 1,500 tons (+oil fuel ?).

Name.	Builder.	Machinery.	Laid down.	Completed.	First trials.	Turbines.	Best recent speed.
Frankfurt	Kiel D.Y.		Dec.'13	Aug.'15			

Notes.—Begun under 1913-14 Programme as *Ersatz Hela.*   Note that her second funnel is plain and wholly cased up to top, instead of being half-cased like first and third funnels.   The half-casing to second funnel in above view is not correct.

No photo available—see Silhouettes.

Plans show design with original Russian armament of 8—5·1 inch guns. Now has raised fore funnel.   Only has 2—22 pdr. anti-aircraft guns mounted now ; armour belt and tubes removed.

PILLAU (ex-Russian *Muraviev Amurski,* April, 1914).

Displacement, 4350 tons.   Complement, 372.

Length (p.p.), 403 feet.   Beam, 46 feet.   { Mean draught, 16 feet.   { Max.   "   19 feet. }   Length (o.a.), 441 feet.

Guns :
8—5·9 inch, 50 cal., S.A.
2—22 pdr. anti-aircraft
Torpedo tubes (19·7 inch) :
2 *above water.*

Armour :
1½" Deck (on slopes).........
¾" Deck (bow) ....
3" Deck (over rudder) ...
3" Conning tower ....

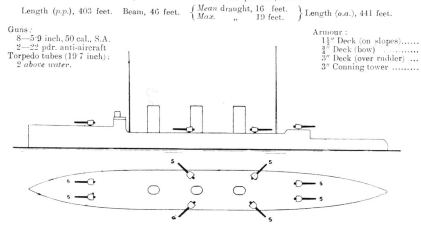

Machinery : Schichau (Melms & Pfenninger) turbines.   3 screws.   Designed H.P. 27,400 = 27½ kts.   Boilers : Yarrow (may be altered to Schulz Thornycroft).   Coal : *normal* 500 tons ; *maximum* 1000 tons, and 250 tons oil fuel.

Name	Builder	Machinery	Laid down	Completed	Trials F.P.	Boilers	Best recent speed
Pillau	Schichau, Danzig	Schichau	Apl., '13	Dec.'15			

General Notes.—Design is based on *Kolberg* class.   A sister ship, *Elbing,* sunk in the Battle of Jutland.   Both vessels were seized by Germany on outbreak of war with Russia, for whom they were originally laid down.

Differ in build : REGENSBURG has thick funnels.

REGENSBURG (April, 1914), GRAUDENZ (October, 1913).

Normal displacement 4900 tons.   Complement 364.

Length (waterline) 456 feet.   *Beam* 45 feet.   *Mean draught* 16 feet.   (*Max.* 17 feet).

Plans as before being re-armed.

Guns :
  7—5·9 inch, 50 cal.
  2—22 pdr. anti-aircraft
  2 machine
Torpedo tubes (19·7 inch):
  2 *submerged*

Carry 120 mines each.

Armour :
  4″ Belt (amidships)
  2½″ Belt (ends) ..
  2″ Deck (amidships)
  4″ Conning tower

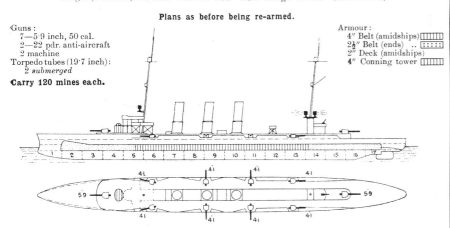

Machinery : "Marine Type" Turbine.   4 screws.   Boilers : 14 Schulz-Thornycroft.   Designed H.P. 26,000 = 27·25 kts.   Coal : *normal* 470 tons ; *maximum* 1300 tons.   Oil : 220 tons.

Gunnery Notes.—Originally had 2—5·9 inch and 8—4·1 inch, as plans above.

Armour Notes.—Belt is rather deeper than in *Stralsund* and *Strassburg.*

General Notes.—Belong to 1912 Programme.   *Regensburg* built and engined by Weser, Bremen ; *Graudenz* built by Kiel D.Y.   Both laid down 1912 and completed 1914.   Radius of action about 5,500 to 6,000 miles at cruising speed.   Most of the notes for *Breslau* class apply to these ships.   Two other light cruisers (*Karlsruhe* and *Rostock*) intermediate between this class and *Stralsund* and *Strassburg* have been lost during the war.

STRALSUND (Nov., 1911), STRASSBURG (Aug., 1911).

Normal displacement, 4550 tons ; 5100 tons, *full load.*   Complement, 370-373.
Length (w.l.), 446½ feet.   *Beam,* 43·6 feet.   *Mean draught,* 16⅜ feet.

Plans as before being re-armed.   "Stralsund" to be surrendered ?   "Strassburg" Leader, Baltic Sweepers ; has only 1 gun.

Guns :
  7—5·9 inch, 50 cal.
  2—22 pdr. anti-aircraft
  2 machine
Torpedo tubes (19·7 in.) :
  2 *submerged.*
  2 *above water.*

Carry 120 mines.

Armour :
  3½″ Belt (amidships)
  2¼″ Belt (ends)......
  2″ Deck (amidships)
  4″ Conning tower...

Machinery : Turbine.   4 screws.   Boilers : 16 Schulz-Thornycroft.   Designed H.P. : *Stralsund* 24,200, 26·75 kts.   *Strassburg* 26,000, 27 kts.   Coal : *normal* 750 tons ; *maximum* 1200 tons.   Oil : 130 tons.

Armour Notes.—Belt is very narrow, and at full load practically submerged.
Engineering Notes.—4 boilers are oil burning.

Name	Builder	Machinery	Laid down	Completed	Trials (mean) 6 hours	Best hour	Turbines	Best speed
Stralsund	Weser, Bremen	Weser	Ap. '10	June '12	27,032 = 26·9	35,515 = 28·7	Bergmann	...
Strassburg	W'l'mshaven Y.	...	Ap. '10	Dec. '12	25,647 = 26·9	33,742 = 28·28	Parsons	...

Belong to the 1910 Programme.   *Magdeburg* of this class sunk 1914 in the Baltic.   *Breslau* mined and sunk off Imbros, 1918.   They are very fast ships, but vibrate greatly over 22 kts.   Proved bad sea boats on first trials, and large bilge-keels were fitted to lessen rolling.   All were heavily forced on trials.   Very lightly built, extensive use being made of steel castings and aluminium.   Engine-rooms very cramped.   Double-bottom shallow, and only carried up amidships to under side of protective deck.   Above protective deck are coal-bunkers, about 12 feet wide.

Both to be surrendered ?   Both disarmed.

(KOLBERG CLASS).

KOLBERG (Nov. 1908), & AUGSBURG (July, 1909).

Normal displacement, 4350 tons.   Complement, 379.

Length (waterline), 426½ feet.   *Beam* 46 feet.   *Maximum draught,* 17¾ feet.

Guns :
  6—5·9 inch.
  2—22 pdr. anti-aircraft
  2 Machine.
Torpedo tubes (17·7 in.)
  2 *submerged.*

Carry 120 Mines.

Armour (Krupp) :
  2″ Deck (amidships)
  ¾″ Deck (ends) ......
  4″ Conning tower...

Plans as before being re-armed.

Machinery : Turbines : *Kolberg,* Melms & Pfenninger ; *Augsburg,* Parsons.   4 screws.   Boilers : 15 Schulz-Thornycroft.   Designed H.P. 19,600 = 25 kts.   Coal : *normal* 400 tons ; *maximum* 900 tons, and some oil fuel.

Name	Builder	Machinery	Laid down	Completed	Trials	Turbines	Best recent speed
Kolberg	Schichau	Schichau	Mar.'07	Dec. '09	30,100 = 26·3	Melms & P.	...
Augsburg	Kiel Yard.	...	Sept.'08	Oct. '10	31,340 = 27	Parsons	...

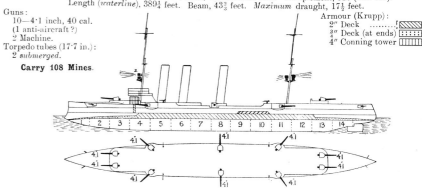

**Appearance probably altered as both Seaplane carriers now.   Are disarmed.
To be surrendered ?**

(STETTIN CLASS.)

STUTTGART (Sept., 1906), STETTIN (March, 1907).

Normal Displacement, *Stuttgart* 3470 tons ; *Stettin* 3550 tons.   Complement, 328 (350 war).
Length (waterline), 389¼ feet.   *Beam,* 43¾ feet.   *Maximum draught,* 17½ feet.

Guns :
  10—4·1 inch, 40 cal.
  (1 anti-aircraft ?)
  2 Machine.
Torpedo tubes (17·7 in.) :
  2 *submerged.*

Carry 108 Mines.

Armour (Krupp) :
  2″ Deck ....
  ¾″ Deck (at ends)
  4″ Conning tower

Machinery : *Stuttgart* 2 sets 4 cylinder triple expansion, 2 screws.   *Stettin,* Turbine (Parsons), 4 screws.   Boilers : 10 Schulz-Thornycroft.   Designed H.P. 13,000 *Stuttgart* and 13,400 *Stettin* = 23 kts.   Coal : *normal* 400 tons ; *maximum* 880 tons.

Name	Builder	Machinery	Laid down	Completed	Refit	Trial on sea course of 170 miles.	Boilers	Best speed
Stuttgart (r)	Danzig Yard	Vulcan Co.	1905	1908		13,745 = 23·7	Schulz-Thornycroft	...
Stettin (t)	Vulcan	Vulcan Co.	1905	1908		15,448 = 24*		...

*Maximum was 19,768 = 24·9.   She once touched 21,400 = 25·7.

OLD GERMAN LIGHT CRUISERS.

DANZIG. Has bridges round foremast.

HAMBURG, &c., as above.

DANZIG (September, 1905), **HAMBURG** (July, 1903), **BERLIN** (September, 1903), **LÜBECK** (March, 1904), and **MÜNCHEN** (April, 1904). *Normal* displacement, 3250 tons. Complement, 303. Dimensions : 362.9 × 43.3 × 17½ feet (*maximum* draught). Guns : As noted below. Torpedo tubes (17.7 inch) : 2 *submerged*. Armour (Krupp) : 2″ Deck, ¾″ Deck (at ends), 4″ C.T. Machinery : 2 sets 4-cylinder triple expansion. 2 screws. *Lubeck*, turbine (Parsons), 8 screws on 4 shafts. Boilers : 10 Shulz-Thornycroft. Designed H.P. 10,000 (*Lubeck* 11,200 S.H.P.) = 22 kts. Coal : *normal*, 400 tons ; *maximum*, 860 tons. *Nominal* radius, 5900 at 10 kts. *Danzig* begun 1904, completed 1907 ; others begun 1902-3, completed 1904-5.

Notes.

Reported that DANZIG, MÜNCHEN and LÜBECK are named for surrender in Peace Treaty.

Name	Armament	Mines	Present Service	Station
Danzig	10—4.1 inch, 2 M.G.	108	Paid off.	Danzig.
Hamburg	,, ,,	,,	,,	Wilhelmshaven
Berlin	,, ,,	,,	Headquarters S.N.O. Baltic.	Kiel.
München	,, ,,	,,	Paid off.	Kiel.
Lübeck	2—5.9 inch, 6—4.1 inch, 2 M.G.	,,	,,	Kiel.

OBSOLETE GERMAN LIGHT CRUISERS.

ARKONA (April, 1902). Displacement, 2700 tons (sheathed). Complement, 281. Dimensions : 342.4 × 40.3 × 17¼ feet (*maximum* draught). Guns : 10—4.1 inch, 2 M.G. Torpedo tubes (17.7 inch) : 2 *submerged*. Can carry 400 mines. Armour (Krupp) : 2″ Deck, 4″ C.T. Machinery : 2 sets 4-cylinder triple expansion. 2 screws. Designed H.P. 8000 = 21.5 kts. Coal : *normal*, 450 tons ; *maximum*, 710 tons. Boilers : 9 Schulz-Thornycroft.

Condition of all Ships named on this page.

Arkona :—Guns on board. Sea-going Parent Ship for Motor Boat Minesweepers (UZ boats), North Sea.

Nymphe :—Disarmed. Depot Ship.

Thetis :—Disarmed.

Amazone :—Disarmed.

Medusa :—Guns on board. Sea-going Parent Ship for North Sea Motor Boat Minesweepers (UZ boats).

Niobe :—Disarmed and paid off.

(*Gazelle :*—Only Mine Hulk. Is deleted.)

(*Gefion :*—Hulk. Is deleted.)

MEDUSA.　　　　　　　　　　　*Photo, Abrahams, Devonport.*

NYMPHE (1899), **THETIS** (1900), **AMAZONE** (1900), & **MEDUSA** (1900). *Normal* displacement, 2650 tons. (Sheathed and Muntz metalled.) Complement, 275. Dimensions : 324.4 × 38.7 × 17¼ feet (*maximum* draught). Guns : 6—4.1 inch, 2 M.G. Torpedo tubes (17.7 inch) : 2 *submerged*. Armour (Krupp) : 2″ Deck (amidships), ¾″ Deck (at ends), 3½″ Glacis to engine room hatches, 3″ C.T. Cofferdam and cellulose amidships. Machinery : 2 sets 4-cylinder triple expansion. 2 screws. Boilers : 9 Schulz-Thornycroft. Designed H.P. 8000 = 21 kts. Coal : *normal*, 380 tons ; *maximum*, 580 tons.

As *Medusa.*

NIOBE (1899). *Normal* displacement, 2600 tons. (Sheathed and Muntz metalled.) Complement, 268. Dimensions : 342.5 × 38.7 × 17¼ feet (*maximum* draught). Guns : 10—4.1 inch, 40 cal., 2 M.G. Torpedo tubes (17.7 inch) : 2 *submerged*. Armour (Krupp) : 2″ Deck (amidships), ¾″ Deck (at ends), 3½″ Glacis to hatches, &c., 3″ C.T., Cofferdam and cellulose amidships. Machinery : 2 sets 4-cylinder triple expansion. 2 screws. Boilers : 5 Thornycroft in *Niobe*. Designed H.P. 8000 = 21.5 kts. Coal : *normal*, 300 tons ; *maximum*, 600 tons.

GERMAN DESTROYERS (Grosse Torpedoboote).

90 (a) Modern }
88 (b) Older   } Destroyers = 178.

(a) About 45 of these unfinished.   *(b) About 12—15 of these quite useless.*

Totals.	Class.	Begun.	Completed.	Displacement.	Nominal H.P.	Nominal Speed.	T. Tubes.	Coal/Oil.†	Complement.
				tons		kts.		tons	
35	G 148—H 190	1917	..	..	..	..	..	..	..
10	S 115—B 124	1916	1919 ?	1400	..	35—38	4	..	..
13	V 125—H 147	1916	1918 }		..	34—35	4 or 6	..	..
9	S 53—G 95	1915	1916 }	750—800	..				
1	V 100	1915	1916	1300	..	34	6	..	..
2	B 97, 98								
4	V 43—S 51	1914	1915	700—750	23,000t	34	6	300	..
1	G 102	1913	1915	1250	24,000t	32	6	345	9½
2	V 26, V 28	1913	1915	650	20,000t	32·5	6	290	..
4	S 18—24	1912	1914	570	15,000t	32·5	4	135/55	..
9	{ G 11—7 } { V 6—1 }	1911	1912	564	15,000t	32·5	4	140/60	73
8	{ T 197—192 } { T 191—186 }	1910	1911	648—656	16,000t	32·5	4*	165/55	83—93
11	{ T 185—180 } { T 179—176 } { T 175—174 }	1909	1910	636—654	16,000t	31·5—32.5	4*	170/45	83
7	{ T 173—169 } { T 168—165 } { T 164—163 }	1908	1909	613—636	14,000t	30—32	3*	160/40	83
11	T 161—151	1907	1908	554	10,250	30	3*	160	83
11	T 149—139	1906	1907	530	10,000	30	3*	190	72
1	T 137	1905	1907	572	10,800t	32	3*	170	80
6	T 136—132	1905	1907	487	6500	27	3*	135	60
10	{ T 131—125 } { T 122—120 } { T 114	1904 / 1903 / 1902	1906 / 1905 / 1904	485 / 470 / 420	6500 / 6500 / 6200	27 / 27 / 26	}	116	60—56
6	T 113—108	1901	1903	400	5600	27	}		
6	T 107—102	1900	1902	400	5400	26	3*	92-116	56
11	T 101—91	1899	1900	400	5400	26			

*Tubes removed from nearly all these boats.
†An additional deck load of coal can be carried as follows :—+ 10 tons up to T 114, + 15 tons from T 120 up to T 149, about 20 tons up to V 28, about 25 tons in later boats.

1915-16.

From the " Illustrirte Zeitung."

6 Schichau : **S49, S50, S52, S53,* S60,* S63** |
6 Vulkan : **V69, V71, V73, V79, V80,* V81*** | Launched 1915-16.

*Salved at Scapa Flow.

(Raised fore funnel now).
1 Krupp-Germania : **G 95** (1916).

Displacement **about** 750 tons. **Approximate** dimensions : 270 to 272 × 27 × feet. S.H.P. 23,000 Designed speed : 34 kts. Armament : 3—4·1 inch, 2 machine, may also have a small automatic (or semi-auto.) anti-aircraft gun. Torpedo tubes : 6—19·7 inch, in 2 single and 2 twin deck mountings. Complement, 96 to 100. Oil only 330 tons.

Photo, Newspaper Illustrations Co.

V 84-67, S 66-58, S 57-49.

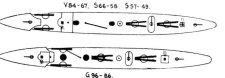

G 96—86.

1917-19 (majority unfinished).

2 Krupp-Germania : **G 148, G 149.**
6 Howaldt : **H 166—H 169, H 188—H 190.**
15 Schichau : **S 152—S 157, S 179—S 187.**
12 Vulkan : **V 158—V 165, V 140—V 144.**

Launched 1918-19, but all work now stopped. No details available, but said to be about 750 to 800 tons. Believed that G150 and 151 were never begun, and boats numbered 170 to 178 were never contracted for.

1917-19 (majority unfinished).

3 Blohm & Voss : **B 122—B 124.**
1 Krupp-Germania : **G 119.**
3 Schichau : **S 113—S 115.**
3 Vulkan : **V 116—118.**

Launched 1917-18, but only a few finished. G 120, G 121 abandoned. About 1400 tons. Armed with 4—5.9 inch and 4—23.6 inch tubes. Speed : 35-38 kts. No other details known.

1917-18.

2 Howaldt : **H 146, H 147.**
6 Schichau : **S 132—S 135, S 137, S 139.**
5 Vulkan : **V 125—V 128, V 130.**

Launched 1917-18. About 750-800 tons. Dimensions : about 270 × 27 × 10½ feet. Armament : 3—4.1 inch, 2 M.G., 4 or 6 tubes (size unknown). Speed : about 35 kts.
Notes.—All above H, S and V boats believed to be same in build as boats numbered S 51 to G 95.
Scuttled at Scapa Flow.—H 145, S 131, S 132 (salved), S 136, S 137 (salved), S 138, V 125—127 (all salved).
War Losses.—None.

Notes.

Under the Peace Treaty, Germany may not keep more than 12 Destroyers in commission, and, excepting accidental losses, no boat may be replaced until 15 years old. Any future Destroyers built by Germany must not exceed 800 metric tons in displacement.

Reported that Germany has still to surrender 42 modern Destroyers. Not yet known which boats Germany will retain and which she will hand over.

With the exception of boats engaged in Minesweeping, Germany has only the " Iron Flotilla " in effective condition now. The "Iron Flotilla" consists of H 147, H 146, S 139, S 135, S 134, S 133, V 130, S 116, S 113, B 97

Majority of boats with " T " index letter have had armament removed and are fitted for Minesweeping.

General Notes to Table.

B boats built by Blohm & Voss (Hamburg), G boats at Krupp's Germania Yard, H boats by Howaldt (Kiel), S boats by Schichau, V boats by Vulkan (Stettin). All are officially rated as " Grosse Torpedoboote," or " Big Torpedo Boats." and not as Destroyers (" Torpedoboote-Zerstörer "). Unless otherwise noted, all boats have Schulz-Thornycroft (or " Marine Type ") boilers. The details tabulated are generally simplified to the average design of each group.

Note to boats in preceding column :—
War Losses.— S 57, S 58, S 59, S 61, S 62, S 64, S 66, V 67, V 72, V 74, V 76, V 77, V 81, V 84, G 85, G 87, G 88, G 90, G 93, G 94, G 96.
Scuttled at Scapa Flow (not salved).—S 55, S 56, S 65, V 70, V 78, V 82, V 83, G 86, G 89, G 91, G 92.

1915.

Appearance as B 98 below, but derrick is before second funnel with boom slung forward. Very big ventilator between 2nd and 3rd funnels. Searchlight on aft bridge is not raised on tower.

Under salvage at Scapa Flow.

1 Vulkan : **V 100** (probably built 1915-16). Displacement : About 1300 tons. Dimensions : about 328 × 32 × 10 feet (mean draught). Designed speed : 34 kts. A.E.G.-Curtis or " Marine type " turbines. Armament : 4—4.1 inch, 2 M.G. May also have an automatic (or semi-auto.) AA. gun. May carry some mines. Torpedo tubes : 6—19.7 inch. Complement, about 140-160. Oil fuel only. V 99 lost during War.

1915.

2 Blohm & Voss : **B 98** and **B 97.** Launched, 1915.

Displacement about 1300 tons. Approximate dimensions 325×32×10 feet (mean draught). Designed speed : 31 kts. Turbine engines. Armament : 4—4·1 inch, 2 machine—may also have a small automatic or semi-auto. anti-aircraft gun and carry mines. Torpedo tubes : 6—19·7 inch. Complement, about 140-160. Oil fuel only.
Note.—B 98 arrived at Scapa Flow with German Fleet mails just after German Fleet (and B 109—112) had been scuttled. She was seized at once. Probably boats begun in 1914 for Chinese Navy.

GERMAN DESTROYERS.

1915.

As illustration of *S* & *V* types on preceding page.

1 *Schichau* : **S 51***
3 *Vulkan* : **V 43,* V 44,* V 46*** , Launched 1915.

About 700-750 tons. Dimensions : 262-270 × 26-27 × 10-11 feet. Guns : 3—3·4 inch (22 pdr.), 2 M.G. Torpedo tubes : 6—19·7 inch (2 twin, 2 single mountings). Designed S.H.P. *about* 23,000 = 34 kts. Oil fuel only : *about* 300 tons. *V 46* last of pre-war (1914-15) Programme boats.

*Salved at Scapa Flow. *S 50, S 52, V 43* not salved.

V 47, V 48 (special type), both War Losses.

G 37, G 41, G 42 War Loss. *G 38, G 39, G 40*, not salved at Scapa Flow. *G 37—40* class therefore extinct.

1913—14.

S 31—36 class has been totally destroyed, viz.:—*S 31, 33, 35*, War Losses ; *S 32, 36*, scuttled at Scapa Flow and not salved.

2 *Vulkan* : **V 26, V 28.** Launched 1914. *About* 650 tons. Armament : 3—3·4 inch (22 pdr.), 2 M.G. Torpedo tubes : 6—19·7 inch. S.H.P. 20,000 = 32·5 kts. Oil only : *about* 290 tons. Complement, 90.

War Losses.—*V 25, V 27, V 29. V 30* sunk November 20th, 1918.

1912—13.

4 *Schichau* : **S 18, S 19, S 23, S 24.** Launched 1913. *About* 570 tons. Dimensions : 234⅔ × 24½ × 10 feet. Armament : 2—4·1 inch, 1—3·4 inch (22 pdr.). Torpedo tubes : 4—19·7 inch. Designed S.H.P. 15,000 = 32·5 kts. Melms-Pfenninger turbines. Fuel : 135 tons coal + 55 tons oil. Complement, 75.

War Losses.—*S 13, S 14, S 15, S 16, S 17, S 20, S 21, S 22.*

1914 (*ex-Argentine*).

1 ex-*Argentine* boat : **G 102** (Krupp-Germania, 1914). Displacement : *normal,* 1250 tons ; *full load,* 1460 tons. Dimensions : 312¼ × 30 × 8⅝ feet (*mean* draught). *Max.* draught, 9½ feet. Armament : 4—4·1 inch guns, 2 M.G. ; may also have a small automatic (or semi-auto.) AA. gun. Torpedo tubes : 6—19·7 inch. Machinery : Turbines and 5 double-ended boilers. Designed H.P. 24,000 = 32 kts. Fuel : (oil only) 345 tons.

Note.—*G 102* salved at Scapa Flow. *G 101, G 103, G 104*, not salved. These were originally the destroyers *San Luis, Santa Fé, Santiago*, and *Tucuman*, laid down for the Argentine in 1913-14 and appropriated for German Navy after outbreak of war.

1911-1912 (and 2 **1913** Replace Boats).

G 7, 9, 8, 10.

Photo by courtesy of S. Anderson, Esq.

Note.— All have raised fore funnels now.

G 9.

4 *Krupp-Germania* : **G 7, G 8, G 9, G 10, G 11** (launched 1911-12).

5 *Vulkan* : **V 1—V 3** (1911), **V 5, V 6** (1913).

Displacement 564 to 570 tons *normal* ; 700 tons *full load* ? Dimensions : 233 × 25 × 9⅝ feet (*mean* draught). Armament : 2—4·1 inch (22 pdr.) 39 cal., 2 machine. Torpedo tubes : 4—19·7 inch. Machinery : turbines, Parsons in Germania boats, A.E.G.-Curtis in Vulkan boats. Designed H.P. 15,000 = 32·5 kts. *S 27* made 37 kts. on trials, other boats all exceeded designed speeds. Fuel : 110 tons coal, 60 tons oil. 4 Schulz-Thornycroft boilers (1 oil burning). Complement, 75.

Appearance Notes.—Raking stem. Rise of turtle-back strongly marked. Gun on forecastle, large ventilator between bow tubes. W/T. cabin immediately abaft fore-funnel. Mainmast well aft of 2nd funnel.

Notes.—*V 5* and *V 6* built to replace original *V 5* and *V 6* sold to Greece, and now Greek *Keravnos* and *Neagenea*. *V 4, G 12*, lost during war. *V 2, V 3, V 5*, non-effective.

S—
S 21.   *S 22.*

S 19.   *S 20.*

From the "Illustrirte Zeitung."

For description of above T.B.D. see previous page.

GERMAN DESTROYERS

Notes.

Nearly all the Destroyers listed on this and succeeding pages have had their tubes removed and fitted for minesweeping.

About a dozen of them have been mined or otherwise injured during the War and not repaired ; they are entirely non-effective for fighting purposes. Boilers and engines of many are in a very poor condition, and the *maximum* speeds given must be taken with reserve.

All these boats were built with the usual *G*, *S* and *V* builders' index letters, but were given letter *T* to avoid duplication of numbers, with the later boats numbered from *V 1* up to *H 190*, described on preceding pages. In description of *T* boats, *G* refers to Krupp-Germania boats, *S* to Schichau boats, and *V* to Vulkan boats.

1910.

Note :— All have raised fore funnel now.

V Boats (V 186). Ventilator between bow tubes *low*.

V186-191
G192-197
650 TONS.

G Boats (G 196). Ventilator between bow tubes *high*.
5 *Krupp Germania*, **T 192, T 193, T 195—T 197.**
3 *Vulkan*, **T 190, T 189** and **T 186.** } launched 1910-11.

Displacements : *G* boats 648 tons, *V* boats 656 tons *normal* (750 tons *full load ?*). Dimensions : 213×26×10½ feet. Armament : 2—3·4 inch (22 pdr.) 30 cal., 2 machine guns. Torpedo tubes : 4—19·7 inch. Machinery : Parsons turbines in *G* boats, A. E. G.—Curtis in *V* boats. Designed H.P. 16,000=32·5 kts. Fuel : 160-170 tons coal, 55 tons oil. 4 Schulz-Thornycroft boilers (1 oil burning). Complement 83 (93 War Complement).

Appearance Notes.—Break between forecastle and bridges small, the space for working bow (beam) tubes being extremely cramped. Heights of bow ventilators vary, see note to illustrations above. Gun on forecastle, W/T. cabin immediately abaft forefunnel. Mainmast well aft of funnels in *G* boats, but not so far in *V* boats.

War Losses : V 187, V 188, V 191, G 194. At present *T 190* and *T 196* are quite useless.

1909-10.

G174-175
S176-179
V180-185
640-670 TONS

Now have tall foremasts.
6 *Vulkan*, **T 185—180**
3 *Schichau*, **T 179, T 178,*** **T 176** } launched 1909-10.
2 *Krupp-Germania*, **G 175** and **G 174**

Displacements : *V* boats 637 tons, *S* boats 636 tons, *G* boats 651 tons *normal* (760 tons *full load ?*). Dimensions *about* 213 × 26 × 10 feet. Armament : 2—3·4 inch (22 pdr.) 30 cal., 1 or 2 machine guns. Torpedo tubes : 1—19·7 inch. Machinery : A. E. G-Curtis turbines in *V* boats, Schichau (Melms and Pfenninger) in *S* boats, Parsons in *G* boats. Designed H.P. 16,000=31·5 to 32·5 kts. Fuel : *S* and *V* boats, 150 tons coal and 10 tons oil ; *G* boats, 190 tons coal and 50 tons oil. Complement 83.

Appearance Notes.—Break between forecastle and bridges very small. In *G* and *S* boats forecastle is *short*, with big, tall ventilator just abaft. In *V* boats forecastle is *long*, and *small* ventilator (*or none ?*) abaft of same. *G* and *S* boats *very big and tall* funnels, standard compass is *on* after bridge, and derrick *abaft* of mast. Note that beam torpedo tubes are *not* between forecastle and bridges but *abaft* of bridges and forefunnel. In this type, ventilators between funnels are near to second funnel. Gun mounted on forecastle. *G* boats have big ventilator close to and abeam of mainmast on *port* side only. Boat in davits on port beam and abeam of after funnel may also be a distinguishing feature.
* *S 178* sunk by *Yorck* in 1913. She was salved. *S 177* War Loss. *T 174, T 185,* both useless.

1908-9.

Fore funnels of all now raised.
3 *Krupp Germania*, **T 169, T 170, T 173.**
4 *Schichau*, **T 168—165.**
2 *Vulkan*, **T 164, T 163.**

V162-164
S165-168
G169-173
615-640 TONS

All launched 1908—9. Displacements : *G* boats, 636 tons, *S* boats 615 tons, *V* boats 613 tons *normal* (750 tons *full load ?*) Dimensions : *about* 243 × 26 × 10 feet. Armament : 2—3·4 inch (22 pdr.) 30 cal., 4 or 2 machine guns. Torpedo tubes, 3—17·7 inch. Machinery : Turbines ; Parsons in *G* boats (*G 173* Zoelly turbines), Schichau (Melms & Pfenninger) in *S* boats and A. E. G.-Curtis in *V* boats. Designed H.P. 11,000=30 to 32 kts. Fuel : 160 tons coal, 40 tons oil. Complement 83.

Appearance Notes.—*G 169—173* almost same as *G 192—197* Class. *V* and *S* boats have slightly longer forecastles, higher funnels and derrick *abaft* mast. Ventilators differently arranged (see Silhouettes).
G 171 lost by collision in 1912. *V 162, T 172,* War Losses. *T 168- 170,* quite useless. Original *S 165- 168* sold to Turkey. War loss *T 138.*

1907-08.

554 TONS.

T 156- T 161 as above photo, and plan.

T 151- T 155.

Two tubes between funnels, with ventilator between same. Ventilator in space between 2nd funnel and mainmast, closer to funnel than to mainmast.

11 *Vulkan*, **T 161 151,** launched 1907-8. Displacement : 551 tons, *normal* (670 tons *full load ?*). Dimensions : 236½ × 25¾ × 10 feet *mean* draught. Guns : 2—3·4 inch (15 pdr.) 35 cal., 2 machine guns. Torpedo tubes : 3—17·7 inch. Machinery : *T 161* has A.E.G.-Curtis turbines, the remainder reciprocating engines. Designed H.P. 10,250=30 kts. Coal : 160 tons ; *T 161,* 170 tons. Complement, 83.

Appearance Notes. Very big funnels ; short and high forecastle, with gun mounted on same. Derrick abaft mainmast. Standard compass not on after bridge, but just before it.

War Losses : V 150.

GERMAN DESTROYERS (*Grosse Torpedoboote*).

1906.

T 138. *T 146.* *T 147.* *T 141.* *T 144.*

S138-149
530 TONS

Note: Fore bridges and chart house, now raised.

War Loss: T 138.

T 144. (Now has gun on fo'xle).

11 *Schichau* : **T 149—139,** launched 1906-7. Displacement : 530 tons. Dimensions : 231 × 25⅜ × 8⅝ feet (*mean draught.*) Armament : 1—3·4 inch (15 pdr.), 35 cal., 3—1 pdr., 55 cal., 2 machine. Torpedo tubes : 3—17·7 inch. Machinery, reciprocating. Designed H.P. 10,000 = 30 kts. Coal : 190 tons. Complement, 80.

Appearance Notes.—Break between forecastle and bridges fairly long. Bridges run well aft of forefunnel. Funnels large and *tall*. Mainmast well aft of second funnel with single large ventilator centrally in space between second funnel and mainmast. 1 pdr. gun between mainmast and this ventilator. Compass on raised platform immediately abaft mainmast.

1904-2.

T 130. Note rudder under forefoot, which is fitted to all German Destroyers.

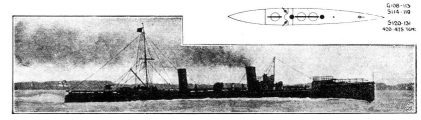

T 121 OFF THE MOUTH OF THE EMS.   1917 War Photo.

9 *Schichau* : { **T 131, T 130,** * **T 128—125** (launched 1901-5). 185 tons. } Plans as given in next column with 1901-1898 boats.
{ **T 121—120** (launched 1901). 170 tons. }
{ **T 114*** (launched 1902). 120 tons. }

Armament : 3—1 pdr., 10 cal., 2 machine, 3—17·7 inch tubes. Designed H.P. 6500 = 27 kts. (T 111, 6200 = 26 kts.) Coal : 116 tons. Complement, 60.

Appearance Notes.—Low in water. Long forecastle without any gun, long space between forecastle and bridges. Tall funnels, with raised steam pipe to fore funnel.

* T 129, T 121, T 123, T 122, 119, 118, 117, 116 and 115 have been sunk. T 125 useless.

1905-6.

G 137
570 TONS

1 *Krupp-Germania* special boat : **T 137** (launched 1907). Displacement : 565 tons. Dimensions : 231½ × 25 × 9⅝ feet. Armament : 1—3·4 inch (15 pdr.), 35 cal., 3—1 pdr., 55 cal., 2 machine. Torpedo tubes : 3—17·7 inch. Machinery : Parsons turbine. Designed H.P. 10,000 = 32 kts, made 33·9 on trials. Coal : 170 tons. Complement, 80.

Appearance Notes.—Raised forecastle short. Raised steam-pipe to fore funnel. Ventilators between funnels close to fore funnel and mast well aft of second funnel—compare these details with boats below. Distinctive features are the guns on raised platforms, between second funnel and aft as shown in above photo. Steam-pipe to fore funnel *raised*, as boats below.

G 132-136
490 TONS

6 *Krupp-Germania* : **T 136—132** (launched 1905-06).

Displacement : 487 tons. Dimensions : 207 × 23 × 7½ feet. Armament : 4—1 pdr., 55 cal., 2 machine. But T 135 (illustrated above) has special armament of 1—3·4 inch (15 pdr.), 35 cal., 2—4 pdr., 55 cal., 2 machine. Torpedo tubes : 3—17·7 inch. Machinery, reciprocating. Designed H.P. 6500 = 27 kts. Coal : 135 tons. Complement, 68.

Appearance Notes.—Raised forecastle very short, no gun mounted on same. Space between forecastle and bridges long. Steam-pipe raised above forefunnel. Funnels spaced wide apart. Mainmast close to second funnel, with derrick on after side. *Two guns abaft mainmast.*

1901-1898.

G 108-113
S 114-119
S 120-131
420-475 TONS

6 *Krupp-Germania* : **T 113—108** (1901-2). 400 tons. Armament : 3—4 pdr., 2 machine. 3—17·7 inch tubes. H.P. 6000 = 26 kts. Coal : about 110 tons. Complement, 56.

Appearance Notes.—Much the same as T 131—114 class, but shorter forecastle, no raised steam pipe to forefunnel, mainmast rather more aft.

Plan as given above for T 113—108 boats, but only *one* tube midway between funnels, the third tube being *abaft mainmast.*

6 *Schichau* : **T 107—102** (1900-01). As T 113-108 above, but coal 95 tons and H.P. 5100 = 26 kts. T 107 useless.

Appearance Notes.— Long fo'xle, funnels and mainmast set well towards stern. Big after funnel.

No Photo available.

See Silhouettes : Also Appearance Notes below.

8 *Schichau* : **T 98—91*** (1899-1900). 400 tons. Armament : 3—4 pdr., 2 M.G. 3—17.7 inch tubes (probably removed from majority). H.P. 5400 = 26 kts. Coal : 95 tons.

2 *Schichau* : **T 101, T 99.** As above boats, but tubes removed and perhaps guns. Both were Submarine Tenders before war.

Appearance Notes.— Much as T 131—114 boats on this page, but have *large and tall* funnels. Single and fairly large ventilator midway between funnels ; a similar ventilator before and at foot of mainmast. *High* sterns.

* T 97 bears name **Sleipner.**

War losses: T 100, T 90 and Taku of separate Single class.

GERMAN TORPEDO BOATS (*Torpedoboote*).

74* Modern } **Torpedo Boats = 134§**
60† Old

*11 of these interned.   †Majority are useless.

§Peace Treaty limits Germany to 12 Torpedo Boats. Not to be replaced unless 15 years old or lost by accident.
New boats not to be over 200 tons.

Totals.	Name or Number.	Date.	Displacement.	I.H.P.	Max. Speed.	* Torpedo Tubes.	Coal.	Complement.
			tons.		kts.		tons.	
3	V 105—108	1914–15	320	5300t	32	4	..	..
1	D 10	1897–99	355	5500	28	2	80	60
1	D 9	1893–94	380	4040	24½		105	59
2	D 8, D 7	1890–92	350	4000	23	3	75	49
2	D 6, D 5	1888–90	320	3600	23		90	49
2	D 4, D 3	1887–89	300	2500	21		65	49
30	A 59—95	1916–17			24	1	35	..
27	A 26—55	1915–16	200	..				
14	A 1—25	1915	80	..	15	2	29	..
2	T 88 & 89	1898	160	1800	25	2	36	24
6	T 87—82							
7	T 81—74	1889—	180—150	1500	25—22	3	30	24—16
5	T 73—69	1897						
6	T 63—55							
2	T 53, T 49	1889—	150	1500	25—22	3	30	16
2	T 45, T 42	1897		1350				
22	T 40—T 3	1885-7	85	1000	20	3	30	16

*Note.—Many have been converted into Mine Sweepers and have no tubes now.

1914 Appropriated Boats.

No Photo available : for appearance as originally designed, r. Silhouettes.

3 *ex-Dutch* boats: **V 108, V 106, V 105** (Vulkan, 1913-14). 320 tons. Dimensions: 201 × 20½ × 6 feet (**mean** draught).
Armed with 2—13 pdr. guns and 4—17·7 inch tubes. Designed H.P. 5,300 = 27 kts. Turbines.

Note.—The above were originally the Dutch *Z 1—Z 4*, and were appropriated for German Navy after the outbreak of war.
War Loss.—V 107.

"Divisional Boats."

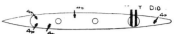

1 *Thornycroft* : **D 10** (1895). 355 tons. Armament: 5—4 pdr., 2—17·7 inch tubes. Speed (originally) 28 kts. Boilers:
Yarrow.

D 7, with guns and tubes removed, used for Subsidiary Service.   *Photo, Seward, Weymouth.*

7 *Schichau*. **D 9** (1891), **D 8, D 7** (1891), **D 6, D 5** (1888-89), **D 4, D 3** (1887). For details, see Destroyer Tables on
a preceding page. Armament: 3—4 pdrs., 3—17·7 inch tubes, one *submerged* in bow. Tubes probably removed
from all now. Reconstructed and given two funnels 1907-09.
Note.—D 5 had tubes removed and was used for Fisheries Protection before war, being armed with 4—4 pdr. guns.
D 3 also had tubes removed and was Tender to Submarine Depot Ships. *D 1 and D 2 still exist, but are quite
useless.

GERMAN FIRST-CLASS TORPEDO BOATS.

1915-17

A 26—36 (later boats similar, but longer fo'xle).   *From the "Illustrirte Zeitung."*

30 boats, by various yards: **A 59, A 61—A 66, A 68—A 70, A 74—A 76, A 78, A 80—A 95.** Built about 1916-17.

27* boats, by various yards: **A 26—A 31,* A 33—A 36, A 37—A 44, A 46—A 49,* A 52—A 55.** Built about 1915-16.

**A 30, A 40, A 42, A 43, A 47,* interned in Holland on German evacuation of Belgium. Present disposal not known.
If deducted, total is 22 boats.

General Notes.—Displace *about* 200-250 tons. Dimensions : *about* 170 × 16¾ × 5·7 feet. Guns : 2—3.4 inch (22 pdr.),
1 M.G. Torpedo tubes (17.7 inch) : 1 (removed from sweeping boats). Speed : 24 kts. Fuel : Oil only. Complement, 35.

War losses.— *A 32, A 50, A 56, A 57, A 58, A 60, A 71, A 72, A 73, A 77, A 79. A 67* does not seem to exist now, but is not
reported as War Loss. *A 45* destroyed on German evacuation of Flanders.

1915

A 1—25 TYPE.   *Photo, L. N. A.*

14* boats, by various yards (several sent in sections to Antwerp and assembled there): **A 1, A 5,* A 8,* A 9,* A 11,***
A 16,* A 17, A 18, A 20,* A 21—25. Built about 1915.

* Interned in Holland after German evacuation of Belgium. Present disposal not known. If deducted, total is 12 boats.

About 80 tons. Dimensions : 140 × 19½ × 8¼ feet. Guns : 1—4 pdr., 1 M.G. Torpedo tubes (17.7 inch) : 1 or 2
(removed from sweepers). Speed : 15 kts. Coal: *about* 30 tons. Complement, 29.

War Losses.—*A 2, A 3, A 6, A 7, A 10, A 13, A 15, A 19. A 4, A 12, A 14,* abandoned in Flanders and now units of
Belgian Navy.

OLD GERMAN TORPEDO BOATS (Kleine Torpedoboote).

Above-water tubes probably removed. Now used as Minesweepers, Tenders, &c.

2 *Krupp-Germania*, **T 89** and **T 88** (1897-8). 1—4 pdr., 2—17·7 inch tubes.

6 *Schichau*: **T 87—T 82** (1898). 1—4 pdr., 3—17·7 inch tubes (1 bow *submerged*, 2 deck).

5 *Schichau*: **T 81—74**° (1893-4). Armed as *T 87—T 82* above.
° Less *T 78* War Loss.

Motor Launches.

49 boats: **F...—F...** (built 1917-18). 23 tons. About 55 feet long.

Total Number uncertain: **UZ 1—50** (built 1916-17). About 60 tons. Length, 85 feet. Speed, 15 kts.
Note.—UZ = *Unterseeboote-Zerstorer* (Submarine Destroyer). All *UZ* and *F* boats fitted as Anti-Submarine craft and Minesweepers.

"Controlled Torpedoes."

These craft were used off the Belgian Coast, and are simply a modern development of the old Brennan and Lay torpedoes. The "controlled torpedo" is a small boat with twin petrol motors, partly covered in. The crew leave after it has been started. About 30-50 miles of single-core insulated electric cable connect the boat's steering and control gears with the shore directing station. A seaplane, escorted by a strong escort of fighting 'planes, "spots" for the "controlled torpedo," sending instructions by W.T. on course, speed, etc., to the shore controlling station. About 300-500 lbs. of high-explosive are contained in the bows of the "torpedo," being exploded on impact with the target.

Mine Layers (are disarmed).

T 42 (1887). Appearance after being re-boilered and re-engined.
16 *Schichau*: **T 73—69, T 63—59, T 55, T 53, T 49, T 45, T 42** (1889-1897). 1—4 pdr., 3—13·8 inch tub
(1 bow *submerged*, 2 deck).
War Losses: T 45, 46, 47, 50, 51, 52, 54, 56, 58, 58, 61, 65, 66, 68.

2nd & 3rd CLASS.

Like *T 81—74* but shorter and with big funnel.

22 old boats: **T 40—33, T 31—27, T 25, T 24, T 21—20, T 16, T 15—13, T 11, T 3** (1885-1889). 85 tons.
Speed: 17 kts. (probably much less now). Guns and tubes (2 deck and 1 *submerged* bow).
Guns and tubes may have been removed from some. Complement, 16.
Appearance: Similar to *T 81—74* opposite, but much shorter in length.
Notes.—T 36, 35, 31—27 and 25 converted to Mine sweepers, tubes being removed; some (or all) of the other boats may also have been altered for this service. *T 25 War Loss.*

ALBATROSS after naval action of 1/7/15; foremast partly shot away.
(*Was Mining School Ship before the war.*)
ALBATROSS (October, 1907). 2200 tons. Complement, 197. Length, 295 feet. Beam, 42⅔ feet. *Maximum* draught, *about* 13 feet. Armament: 8—3·4 inch (15 pdr.), 35 cal. Boilers: Schulz-Thornycroft. Designed H.P. 6000 = 20 kts. Coal, 450 tons. **Carries 600 mines.**
Note.—Was disabled and driven ashore near Ostergarm Lighthouse, Gothland Island (Baltic), by Russian Cruisers on July 1st, 1915. Above illustration shows her being towed to internment at Viborg. Released from internment by Sweden in 1918.

S.M.S. "Nautilus," Minenleger.

NAUTILUS (1906). 1950 tons. Complement, 198. Length, 305 feet. Beam, 42⅔ feet. Draught, 13⅓ feet. Armament: 8—3·4 inch, 15 pdr. Boilers: Schulz-Thornycroft. Machinery: reciprocating. Designed H.P. 6000 = 20 kts. Coal, 115 tons. **Carries 200 mines.**

SMALL GERMAN MINE LAYERS AND SWEEPERS.

F.M. 1—36 (Built 1917-18.) 175 tons. *About* $139\frac{1}{2} \times 19\frac{3}{4} \times 4\frac{1}{2}$ feet. Guns : 1—3.4 inch 22 pdr. I.H.P. 600 = 13.5 kts. Coal, 33 tons. Fitted to carry mines.

Notes.—Shallow draught sweepers. Proved of little worth owing to inadequate fuel supply and dangerous instability.

M 19, M 20, M 21, M 25. (Built 1915.) *About* 400 tons. *About* 164×20×9 feet. Guns: see below. I.H.P. 1500 = 16 kts. Complement, 40. Can carry 30 mines.

War Losses : M 22, M 23, M 24, M 26, M 27.

M 28—30, M 32—35, M 37, M 38, M 42—46, M 48, M 50—54, M 57—62, M 65, M 66, M 68—82, M 84—90, M 93—94, M 96—122, M 125, M 129, M 137, M 138. (Built 1915-18.) *About* 480 tons. *About* 192×24×8½ feet. Guns : see next column. I.H.P. 1600 = 17 kts. 2 screws. Coal : 150 tons and 12 tons oil. Complement 40. Can carry 30 mines.

War Losses : M 31, M 36, M 39, M 40, M 41, M 47, M 49, M 55, M 56, M 63, M 64, M 67, M 83, M 91, M 92, M 95.

Not finished ?—M 123, M 124, 126—128, 130—136.

M 1—5, M 7, M 8, M 10, M 13, M 17, M 18. (Built 1915.) *About* 350 tons. *About* 106×23×9 feet. Guns: see below. I.H.P. 1500 = 16 kts. Complement, 40. Carry 30 mines.

War Losses : M 6, M 9, M 11, M 12, M 14, M 15, M 16.

Armaments for all "M" Types.

(*a*) 3—4.1 inch, *or* (*b*) 2—4.1 inch, *or* (*c*) 1—4.1 inch, *or* (*d*) 2—3.4 inch, 22 pdr. Also 2 machine.

GERMAN GUNBOATS (*Kanonenboote*).

Perhaps never begun.

METEOR ? (Danzig Yard, 1914 or 1915 ?). 1150 tons. Dimensions : $219\frac{3}{4} \times 33\frac{1}{2} \times 10\frac{1}{2}$ feet. Guns : 4—4.1 inch, 2—1 pdr., 2 machine. Machinery : 2 sets triple expansion. 2 screws. Boilers : 4 Schulz-Thornycroft. Designed H.P. 1550 = 14 kts. Coal : tons. Was intended for "surveying service" on East African Coast.

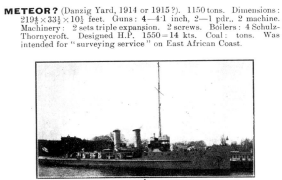

DRACHE (Germania, 1908). 790 tons. Complement 64. Guns : 4—3.4 inch (22 pdr.), 4—4 pdr. Speed : 15 kts. Coal : 150 tons.

HAI (Geestemünde, 1907). 640 tons. Complement 51. Armament : 8—4 pdr. Speed : 12.5 kts. Coal : 75 tons.

DELPHIN (Meyer, Papenburg, 1906). 450 tons. Complement 41. Armament : 4—3.4 inch (22 pdr.), 2—4 pdr., 4 M.G. Speed : 9.5 kts. Coal : 55 tons.

FUCHS (Meyer, Papenburg, 1905). 640 tons. Complement 51. Armament : 2—4.1 inch, 2—3.4 inch (15 pdr.). Speed : 12.5 kts. Coal : 75 tons.

PANTHER (April, 1901). Displacement, 1000 tons. Dimensions : 210.3 × 31.8 × 10.2 feet. Complement, 130. Guns : 2—4.1 inch, 40 cal., 6—1 pdr., 2 Machine. Machinery : Triple expansion. 2 screws. Boilers : 4 Schulz-Thornycroft. Designed H.P. 1300 = 14 kts. Coal : 275 tons.

Photo, S. Anderson, Esq.

BLITZ & PFEIL (1882). 1388 tons. Dimensions : 246 × 34½ × 13¼ feet. Complement, 134. Guns : 6—3.4 inch (15 pdr.), 4 machine. Tubes : 2 *above water* (probably removed), 1 *submerged.* Designed H.P. 2700 = 15 kts. Coal : 250 tons.

(*Continued on next page*)

GERMAN MISCELLANEOUS.

Gunboats—(continued).

ZIETEN (1876). 1006 tons. Complement, 108. Guns : 6—4 pdr. Tubes (13·8 inch) : 2 *submerged* (bow and stern). Speed : under 13 kts. Coal : 140 tons.

GREIF. No details known.

PRIMULA. Sea-going Parent Ship, 5th Minesweeping Flotilla.

SPERBER. No details known.

Also :

Grille (1857). 350 tons. Speed : 13 kts. Guns : 2—3·4 inch.

Condor (Mine Hulk), *Schwalbe* (Target Hulk).

Admiralty Trawlers.

("Wachtschiffen.")

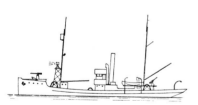

About 250 tons *gross*. H.P. 450 = 10 kts. Guns : 1 or 2 small.

These are Trawler Mine-Sweepers, of which a large number were built by the smaller German Shipyards during the War. The majority have been sold to private owners for fisheries purposes, but a few may still remain for Mine Clearance duties. About 100 were built during the War and 30 were sunk.

Fleet Auxiliaries.

Various Oilers, Colliers, &c., including a few ships used as Auxiliary Mine Layers. Believed that all have reverted to mercantile service, including German Mercantile and Fishing Vessels used as Submarine Decoy Ships ("Q-boats").

River Gunboats.

(*All on Vistula.*)

MÖWE. Ex Shallow Draught River Steamer, armed with 1— 1 pdr. and 1 M.G.

LIEBE. Ex Shallow Draught Tug. Guns : 1—3·4 inch (22 pdr.) 1—1 pdr.

GARDENGO. Ex Shallow Draught Tug. Guns : 1—3·4 inch (22 pdr.), 1 M.G.

Submarine Depot and Salvage Ship.

(*Surrendered.*)

CYCLOP (Danzig, 1914). Dock and Salvage Ship for Submarines, designed for raising 1200 tons deadweight. 2800 tons. Dimensions : 295 × 64 × 13 feet. Guns : None. Machinery : Reported to be Diesel engines. Speed : 9 kts.

Fleet Tender.

NORDSEE (Atlas Werfte, Bremen, 1914). 790 tons. Dimensions : 175¾ × 30¾ × feet. Armed with 2—3·4 inch (22 pdr.) guns. H.P. 1700 = kts. Serves as Leader of North Sea Patrols.

Surveying Ships (*Vermessungsfahrzuge*).

HYÄNE (1878). 493 tons. Complement, 85. Guns : 1—3·4 inch (15 pdr.), 1—4 pdr., 3—1 pdr. H.P. 340 = 8 kts. Coal : 110 tons.

TRITON. No details known. May be the ex-Russian Surveying Ship, launched at and during German occupation of Reval, 1918. If so, her details are :—270 tons. Dimensions : 127¾ × 20 × 10 feet.

Surveying.

PLANET (1905) & **MÖWE** (1906). tons. Speed : 10 kts.

Yachts (*Jachten*).

Not finished.

—— (ex *Ersatz Hohenzollern*, Vulkan, Stettin, 1915). 7300 tons. Complement, 455. Dimensions : 528¼ × 62⅓ × 20 feet. (Guns : Not known, but is capable of mounting about 12—5·9 inch. Machinery : Turbines. 3 screws. Boilers : 10 Schulz-Thornycroft (2 oil burning). Designed H.P. 25,000 = 24 kts. Coal : 1000 tons + 500 tons oil.

Royal Yacht.

HOHENZOLLERN. (Vulkan, Stettin, 1892 ; re-constructed 1907). 4200 tons. Complement, 348. Dimensions : 380½ × 46 × 19⅓ feet. Armament : 2—4 pdr. Boilers (1907) : Schulz-Thornycroft. Designed H.P. 9500 = 21·5 kts. Coal : 510 tons.

(*Surrendered.*)

LORELEY (ex *Mohican*, Henderson, Glasgow, 1885). 925 tons. Dimensions : 207·4 × 27·1 × 13½ feet. Guns : 2—4 pdr. Speed : Made 13.4 kts. on trials ; now about 12 kts. Coal : 165 tons. Complement, 60.

Training Ships.

For Gunnery :—

KAISERIN AUGUSTA. Old Cruiser, previously described on an earlier page.

Sea-going Torpedo School Ship :—

WÜRTTEMBERG, (*old*) (1878). 7300 tons. I.H.P. 6000 = 15 kts. Guns : 2—3·4 inch (22 pdr.), 8—1 pdr., 4 M.G. Torpedo tubes : 2—19·7 inch, *submerged* ; 2—13·7 inch, *submerged* ; 1—13.7 inch, *above water*. Coal : 650 tons. Is serving temporarily as Sea-going Tender to Minesweepers.

2 M

(Submarines).

Under the Peace Treaty, Germany is absolutely prohibited from building (or maintaining in service) any Submarines, whether of Naval or Mercantile types.

All unfinished German Submarines—of which there were a considerable number at the end of 1918—have been dismantled, broken up, scuttled outside German ports or otherwise disposed of.

German Submarines, divided among the Allied Navies for investigation and trials noted in each Allied (and U.S.) Navy Section.

Type: Coastal Submarines (1+1+2+4)
Class: "U1", "U2", "U3", "U5"
Displacement, tons: U1, 238/283; U2 341/430; U3-4 421/510; U5-8 506/636
Dimensions, feet: Varying from U1 139 x 12.3 x 10.5 to U5 188 x 18.3 x 11.3
Torpedo armament: U1 1 x 18in (bow). Remainder 4 x 18in (2 bow, 2 stern)
Guns: 1 x 37mm in U3 and U5 classes. (1 x 4pdr added in U6 and U8 in 1915)
Main machinery: 2 heavy oil engines of (U1) 400bhp, (U2 and U3) 600bhp, (U5) 900bhp; 2 main motors, (U1) 400bhp, (U2) 630bhp, (U3 and U5-8) 1,040bhp; 2 shafts
Speed: knots: Surfaced U1 – 10.8, U2 13.2, U3 11.8, U5-8 13.4, Dived 9-10 knots
Complement: 22 (29 in U5 class)

Dates: 1906-1911

Notes: Germaniawerft Kiel: U1, U5-8; Danzig DY: U2, U3,4
Although three "Karp" class were ordered in Germany by Russia in 1904, U1 completed in December 1906, was the first U boat built for the German navy. From the start double hulls and twin screws were incorporated. The Germans very sensibly abjured the petrol engine and used Körting heavy oil engines. These, although they emitted clouds of exhaust and sparks through an upper deck exhaust, were much safer than the contemporary engines in British submarines. By 1908 suitable diesels had been evolved, to be used from the U19 class onwards
The incorporation of stern torpedo tubes in these early submarines gave the Commanding Officers an advantage not achieved in the RN until the "D" class of 1910.

Note: torpedo tube diameters listed as 18in and 20in in earlier classes. Technically these were 17.7in and 19.7in respectively.

U1 (Drüppel)

Type: Patrol Submarines (4+4+4+11+8+6)
Class: "U19", "U23", "U27", "U31", "U43", "U51"
Displacement, tons: U19 650/837; U23 669/864; U27 675/867; U31 685/878; U43 725/940; U51 712/902
Dimensions, feet: U19 210.5 (U23 & U27 & U31 212.5; U43 213.3; U51 214) x 20.5 x 11.7
Torpedo armament: 4 x 20in (2 bow, 2 stern)
Mines: U43 and U44 acted as minelayers from 1916
Guns: 1 x 3.4in in U19, U23, U31, U43 and 2 x 3.4in in U27 and U51. (Some boats also mounted 4.1in guns during the war)
Main machinery: 2 diesel engines of 1,700bhp (U19) – 2,400bhp (U51); 2 main motors of 1,200bhp; 2 shafts
Speed, knots: 15 surfaced (U19 & U43); 17 (remainder) 9-10 dived
Complement: 35
Dates: 1912-1916

Notes: Danzig DY: U19-22, U27-30, U43-50
Germaniawerft Kiel: U23-26, U31-41, U51-56 (U42 unallocated)
These were the first classes to be engined with diesels. With the aim of attacking merchant ships the calibre of the guns was increased to allow the saving of torpedoes by surface action. A number of these guns were designed to fold sideways thus disappearing into the casing.
From U19 onwards net-cutters were provided as well as jumping-wires.

"U 19-51"

Type: Patrol Submarines (3+3+3+5)
Class: "U57", "U60", "U63", "U66"
Displacement, tons: U57 786/954; U60 768/956; U63 810/927; U66 791/933
Dimensions, feet: U57 & U60 219.7 (U63 224.3; U66 228) x 20.6 x 12.5
Torpedo armament: 4 x 20in (2 bow, 2 stern). 5 x 18in 4 bow, 1 stern in U66
Guns: 1 (or 2) x 3.4in (or 4.1in)
Main machinery: 2 diesels of 1,800bhp (U57 & U60) 2,200bhp (U63) and 2,300 (U66) and 2 main motors 1,200bhp
Speed, knots: Surfaced 14.7 (U57 & U60); 16.5 (U63 & U66); dived 8.4 (U57 & U60); 9-10 (U63 & U66)
Complement: 39
Dates: 1915-1916

Notes: A.G. Weser, Bremen: U57-59, U60-62
Germaniawerft, Kiel: U63-65, U66-70
The U66 class, completed in 1915, was built for the Austro-Hungarian Navy as U8-U12 but taken over by the Germans.

Type: Patrol Submarines (4+3+1+2)
Class: "U9", "U13", "U16", "U17"
Displacement, tons: U9 493/611; U13 516/644; U16 489/627; U17 564/691
Dimensions, feet: U9 188 (U13 190, U16 200, U17 204.5) x 19.7 x 11.5
Torpedo armament: 4 x 18in (2 bow, 2 stern)
Guns: 1 x 37mm in U9 and U17; 1 x 4pdr in U13 and U16
Main machinery: 2 heavy oil engines of (U9) 1,000bhp; (U13 and U16) 1,200bhp; (U17) 1,400bhp; 2 main motors of 1,150bhp; 2 shafts
Speed, knots: 14/15 surfaced; 8/10.7 dived
Complement: 29
Dates: 1910-1912

Notes: Danzig DY.: U9-15, U17 & 18; Germaniawerft Kiel: U16
These were the last classes with heavy oil engines. U9 sank the British cruisers *Hogue*, *Cressy* and *Aboukir* on 22nd September 1914 resulting in an appreciation by many hitherto unconvinced people of the capabilities of submarines.

U13 (Drüppel)

Type: Submarine Minelayers (2+2+5)
Class: "U71" (UE-1), "U73" & "U75"
Displacement, tons: U71 755/830; U73 745/829; U75 755/832
Dimensions, feet: 186.3 x 19.3 x 15.7
Torpedo armament: 2 x 20in (external)
Mines: 32 in 2 tubes
Guns: 1 x 3.4in or 4.1in
Main machinery: 2 diesels of 8-900hp; 2 main motors of 8-900hp; 2 shafts
Speed, knots: 10.5 surfaced; 8 dived
Complement: 32-39
Dates: 1915-1916

Notes: AG Vulkan, Stettin: U71-72, U75-80
Danzig DY: U73-74
These were two classes of long-range submarine minelayers to complement the large class of smaller UC boats. It is rumoured that HMS *Hampshire* with Lord Kitchener aboard was lost on a mine laid by U75. The second group, the UE-II, comprised U117-126.

U71

Type: Patrol Submarines (6)
Class: "U81"
Displacement, tons: 808 surfaced; 946 dived
Dimensions, feet: 230 x 20.6 x 13
Torpedo armament: 4 x 20in (2 bow, 2 stern)
Guns: 1 x 4.1in (U81-83); 2 x 3.4in (U84-86)
Main machinery: 2 diesels of 2,400hp; 2 main motors of 1,200hp; 2 shafts
Speed, knots: 17 surfaced; 9 dived
Complement: 38
Dates: 1916

Notes: U81-86 built by Germaniawerft, Kiel. No reason can be found for the reduction of the bow salvo to two but, apart from the "U99" class and the "U151", (Merchant) class this was the end of a plan which must have been both disconcerting for the CO and inefficient in its results."

U81 (Drüppel)

Type: Patrol Submarines (6)
Class: "U87"
Displacement, tons: 757 surfaced; 998 dived
Dimensions, feet: 215.7 x 20.5 x 12.7
Torpedo armament: 6 x 20in (4 bow, 2 stern)
Guns: 1 x 4in (plus 1 x 3.4in in U87-89)
Main machinery: 2 diesels of 2,400hp; 2 main motors of 1,200hp; 2 shafts
Speed, knots: 15.6 surfaced; 8.6 dived
Complement: 38
Dates: 1917

Notes: U87-92 all built by Danzig DY.

Type: Patrol Submarines (6)
Class: "U93" and "U96"
Displacement, tons: 838 surfaced; 1,000 dived
Dimensions, feet: 235.5 x 20.6 x 12.7
Torpedo armament: 6 x 20in (4 bow, 2 stern)
Guns: 1 x 3.4in ("U93" class); 1 x 4.1in ("U96" class)
Main machinery: 2 diesels of 2,400hp; 2 main motors of 1,200hp; 2 shafts
Speed, knots: 16.8 surfaced; 8.6 dived
Complement: 38
Dates: 1917

Notes: U93-98 all built by Germaniawerft, Kiel.

U93

Type: Patrol Submarines (6)
Class: "U99"
Displacement, tons: 750 surfaced; 952 dived
Dimensions, feet: 221.7 x 20.7 x 11.7
Torpedo armament: 4 x 20in (2 bow, 2 stern)
Guns: 2 x 3.4in (U100 1 x 4.1in)
Main machinery: 2 diesels of 2,400hp; 2 main motors of 1,200hp; 2 shafts
Speed, knots: 16.5 surfaced; 8.5 dived
Complement: 39
Dates: 1917

Notes: U99-104, all built by A.G. Weser (Bremen). Except for "U151" (Merchant) class, the last of the U-boats with only two bow tubes. Otherwise a handy and popular class.

U99 (Drüppel)

Type: Patrol Submarines (6 + 4)
Class: "U105" and "U111"
Displacement, tons: 798 surfaced; 1,000 dived
Dimensions, feet: 235.5 x 20.7 x 12.7
Torpedo armament: 6 x 20in (4 bow, 2 stern)
Guns: 1 x 4.1in; 1 x 3.4in
Main machinery: 2 diesels of 2,400/2,300hp; 2 main motors of 1,200hp; 2 shafts
Speed, knots: 16.4 surfaced; 8.4 dived
Complement: 36
Dates: 1917-1918

Notes: U105-110 and U111-114 all built by Germaniawerft Kiel, although the hulls of U111-114 were built by Bremer-Vulkan (Vegesack).
U115-116 were cancelled whilst building by Schichau, Danzig. These were to have been boats of 1,250 tons dived displacement.

U105 as French submarine (Drüppel)

Type: Minelaying Submarines (5 + 5)
Class: "U117" and "U122" (UE-II)
Displacement, tons: 1,164 surface; 1,612 dived (U122 1,470)
Dimensions, feet: 267.5 x 24.5 x 13.7
Torpedo armament: 4 x 20in. (bow)
Mines: 2 tubes for 42 mines
Guns: 1 x 5.9in (2 guns in some)
Main machinery: 2 diesels of 2,400hp; 2 main motors of 1,200hp; 2 screws
Speed, knots: 14.7 surface; 7 dived
Complement: 40
Dates: 1918

Notes: U117-121 built by A.G. Vulkan, Hamburg and U122-126 by Blohm and Voss, Hamburg. This was the second group of long-range minelayers, designed for operations off the US Atlantic coast and the first to carry the very large 5.9in gun.

U117 (Drüppel)

Type: Coastal Submarines (17 + 30 + 88)
Class: "UB"
Displacement, tons: UBI 127/142; UBII 263/292; UBIII 520/650 (508/639)
Dimensions, feet: UBI 92.3 x 9.7 x 10; UBII 118.5 x 14.3 x 12; UBIII 182 x 19 x 12
Torpedo armament: 2 x 18in (bow) UBI; 2 x 20in (bow) UBII; 5 x 20in (4 bow, 1 stern) UBIII
Guns: 1 x 2in or 3.4in (UBII); 1 x 3.4in or 4.1in (UBIII)
Main machinery: UBI: 1 heavy oil engine of 60hp; 1 main motor 120hp; 1 shaft; UBII: 2 diesels of 284hp; 1 main motor of 280hp; 2 shafts; UBIII: 2 diesels of 1,100hp; 2 main motors of 788hp; 2 shafts
Speed, knots: UBI 6.5/5.5; UBII 9/5.7; UBIII 13.5/8
Complement: 14-23-34
Dates: 1915-1919
Notes: UBI Series: "UBI" Class (UB1-8) Germaniawerft, Kiel; "UB9" class (UB9-17) A.G. Weser (10, 12, 16 and 17 converted for minelaying with 8 mines in 4 chutes length 105ft).
UBII Series: "UB18" Class (UB18-23) Blohm and Voss; "UB24" Class (UB24-29) A.G. Weser; "UB30" Class (UB30-41) Blohm and Voss, (121ft, 274/305 tons); "UB42" Class (UB42-47) A.G. Weser (as "UB30" class).
UBIII Series: "UB48" Class (UB48-132) 48-53 Blohm & Voss, 54-59 A.G. Weser, 60-65 A.G. Vulkan, 66-71 Germaniawerft, 72-74 A.G. Vulkan, 75-79 Blohm & Voss, 80-87 A.G. Weser, 88-102 A.G. Vulkan, 103-117 Blohm & Voss, 118-132 A.G. Weser; "UB133" Class (133-141) surrendered or scrapped before completion; "UB142" Class UB142, 143, 148, 149 A.G. Weser; UB144, 145, 146, 147, 150-153, 155, 170, 178; 196 surrendered or scrapped before completion.
A busy and useful series of boats much employed in the Mediterranean and patrolling as far as the Irish Sea. The UBI Series and "UCI" Class were the only single screw submarines Germany built.

Type: Patrol Submarines (3 + 1)
Class: "U139", "U142"
Displacement, tons: 1,930 surfaced; 2,483 dived
Dimensions, feet: 311 x 29.7 x 17.3
Torpedo armament: 6 x 20in (4 bow, 2 stern)
Guns: 2 x 5.9in
Main machinery: 2 diesels of 3,500hp and 1 auxiliary charging unit of 450hp; 2 main motors of 1,780hp; 2 shafts
Speed, knots: 16 surface; 8 dived
Complement: 62
Dates: 1918
Notes: U139-141 built by Germaniawerft, Kiel. These were very large boats with a formidable gun armament and long range. They were also the first to bear names (U139 *Schwieger* and U140 *Weddigen* (of U9 fame)). U139 was retained in commission by the French Navy to whom she surrendered in November 1918, until 1935 being renamed *Halbronn*.
The subsequent class, "U142", was composed of U142-150 of which only U142 herself was completed one day before the Armistice. In many ways this class was similar to the "U139" although of 300 tons more dived displacement.

U139 (Drüppel)

Type: Patrol Submarines (8)
Class: "U160"
Displacement, tons: 821 surface; 1,002 dived
Dimensions, feet: 235.5 x 20.5 x 13.5
Torpedo armament: 6 x 20in (4 bow, 2 stern)
Guns: 1 or 2 x 4.1in
Main machinery: 2 diesels of 2,400hp; 2 main motors of 1,200hp; 2 shafts
Speed, knots: 16.2 surface; 8.2 dived
Complement: 38
Dates: 1918-1919
Notes: All (U160-167) built by Bremer-Vulkan (Vegesack), being the last class of U boats completed at the war's end. Two (U162 as *Pierre Marrast* and U166 as *Jean Roulier*) were transferred to the French Navy, remaining in commission until 1935. U168-172 were broken up before completion. These boats are interesting because they show a return to the smaller type of submarine with a more reasonable gun-armament. The twelve boats of the "U201" class (U201-212) were similar to the "U160", whilst the "U229" class (U229-246), the "U247" class (U247-262) and the "U263" class (U263-276) were slightly smaller. None of these was completed. The "U173" class (U173-176) and the "U177" class (U177-200) of 2,790 tons dived displacement showed a return to the big boat idea, mounting 2 x 5.9in guns, whilst the "U213" class (U213-218) and "U219" class (U219-228) were of an intermediate size – 1,900 tons dived displacement – mounting four bow and four stern tubes in the "U219" with a single 5.9in gun. Again none of these were completed.

Type: Patrol Submarines (2)
Class: "U135"
Displacement, tons: 1,175 surface; 1,534 dived
Dimensions, feet: 274 x 24.7 x 13.7
Torpedo armament: 6 x 20in (4 bow, 2 stern)
Guns: 1 x 5.9in
Main machinery: 2 diesels of 3,500hp; 2 main motors of 1,690hp; 2 shafts
Speed, knots: 17.5 surface; 8.1 dived
Complement: 46
Dates: 1918
Notes: U135 and U136 built by Danzig DY. U137-138 of same class and the same builders were broken up in 1919 before completion.

U135 (Drüppel)

Type: Ex-Merchant Cruisers (7)
Class: "U151"
Displacement, tons: 1,512 surface; 1,875 dived
Dimensions, feet: 213.3 x 29.3 x 18.5
Torpedo armament: 2 x 20in (bow)
Guns: 2 x 5.9in or 4.1in
Main machinery: 2 diesel engines of 800hp; 2 main motors of 800hp; 2 shafts
Speed, knots: 12.4 surfaced; 5.2 dived
Complement: 56
Dates: 1916-1918
Notes: Built (U151-157) by Germaniawerft, Kiel with hulls built at Flensburg, Hamburg and Bremen. The original design was to provide cargo-carrying submarines to penetrate the British blockade – in fact *Deutschland* (later U155) made two such trips to the USA. *Oldenburg* (later U151) was converted for naval operations. *Bremen* was damaged on her first voyage and converted into a surface ship, whilst U152, 153, 154, 156 and 157 were completed for naval service, two being sunk. Despite the need for maximum numbers for "unrestricted warfare" these must have been brutal boats to take on patrol with their slow speed and minimal torpedo armament.

Type: Coastal Minelaying Submarines (104)
Class: "UC"
Displacement, tons: UCI 168/183; UCII 400/434 to 480/511; UCIII 491/571
Dimensions, feet: UCI 111.5 x 10.3 x 10; UCII 162-173 x 17 x 12; UCIII 185.3 x 18.3 x 12.5
Torpedo armament: UCI nil; UCII 3 x 20in (2 bow external, 1 stern); UCIII 3 x 20in (2 beam external, 1 stern)
Mines: UCI 12 in 6 vertical tubes; UCII 18 in 6 vertical tubes; UCIII 14 in 6 vertical tubes
Guns: UCI 1 MG; UCII 1 x 3.4in; UCIII 1 x 4.1in
Main machinery: UCI 1 heavy oil engine of 90hp; 1 main motor of 175hp; 1 shaft; UCII 2 diesels of 500/600hp; 2 main motors of 460/620hp; 2 shafts (UCIII same, 600/770hp)
Complement: 15-28-32
Dates: 1915-1919
Notes: UCI Series: UC1-8 A.G. Vulkan; UC9-15 A.G. Weser.
UCII series: UC16-24 Blohm and Voss; UC25-33 A.G. Vulkan; UC34-39 Blohm and Voss; UC40-45 A.G. Vulkan; UC46-48 A.G. Weser; UC49-43 Germaniawerft; UC53-60 Danzig DY; UC61-64 A.G. Weser; UC65-73 Blohm & Voss; UC74-79 A.G. Vulkan.
UCIII series: UC90-114 Blohm & Voss. (UC106-114 surrendered incomplete, 115-118 scrapped before completion).
In addition to these minelaying submarines UA (building for Norway) was taken over by Germany August 1914. The "UDI" class of large boats and UF series of small submarines were both cancelled.

U151 (Drüppel)

UC1

***Note:* For U-boat losses see pages 327-329.**

UNITED STATES FLEET.

Revised from 1918-19 Edition of official handbook, "Ships' Data, U.S. Naval Vessels."

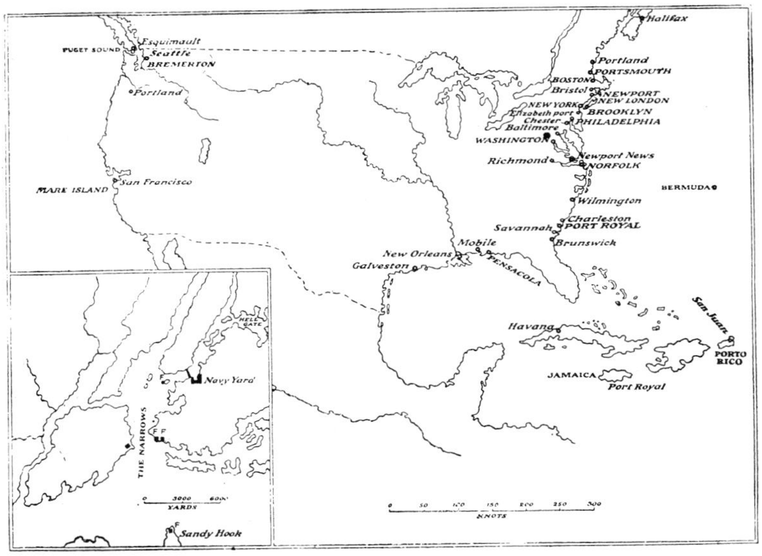

NEW YORK. to	miles
Bermuda	680
Boston (Mass.)	315
Brest	2954
Cherbourg	3066
Colon	1985
Galveston	1910
Gibraltar	3670
Havana	1320
Havre	3125
Jamaica	1495
Key West	1180
La Guayra	1840
Liverpool	3062
New Orleans	1710
Norfolk Navy Yard	300
Pernambuco	3690
Philadelphia (Pa.)	240
Portsmouth Navy Yard	330
Portsmouth (England)	3060
Wilhelmshaven	3570

NEW YORK (*via* Panama Canal) to	miles
Callao	3328
Colon	1981
Hong Kong	11,684
Iquique	3837
Manila	11,585
Puget Sound	6074
San Francisco	5299
Shanghai	10,885
Sydney	9811
Valparaiso	4630
Yokohama	9835

PORT ROYAL to	miles
Bermuda	810
Key West	450
New York	650
Pensacola	785

KEY WEST to	miles
Bermuda	1100
Boston (Mass.)	1387
Galveston	730
Jamaica (Port Royal Harbour)	850
New York	1180
Pensacola	235
Philadelphia	1020
Port Royal Naval Station	450
Portsmouth Navy Yard	1400

MARE ISLAND to	miles
Auckland (N. Zealand)	5965
Esquimault	750
Honolulu	2095
Kiao-chau	5600
Manila	7500
Panama	3424
Puget Sound	800
Yokosuka	4500

KAVITE to	miles
Amoy	700
Hong Kong	650
Kiao-chau	1325
Nagasaki	1300
Saigon	875
Singapore	1320
Vladivostock	2080
Yokosuka	1720

FLAGS.

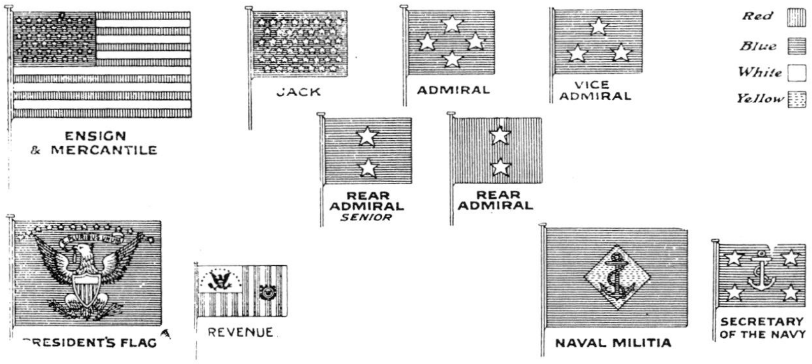

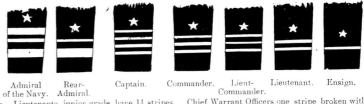

Senior officer when of or below rank of captain flies a blue triangular flag. Assistant-Secretary of Navy has a flag same as Secretary's with colours reversed, *i.e.*, white ground and blue anchor and stars.

Secretary of the Navy: Hon. J. Daniels. *Chief Constructor*: Rear-Admiral D. W. Taylor.

Uniforms.

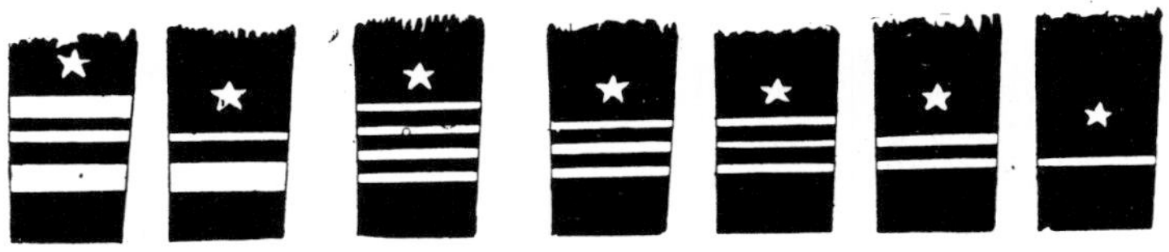

Admiral of the Navy. Rear-Admiral. Captain. Commander. Lieut-Commander. Lieutenant. Ensign.

Note.—Lieutenants, junior grade, have 1½ stripes. Chief Warrant Officers one stripe broken with blue. Line Warrant Officers star without any stripe. Staff Warrant Officers under Chiefs have no sleeve mark. Engineers same as Line Officers (interchangeable). Other branches than executive wear no sleeve star, but have distinctive colours between the sleeve stripes.

Colour of significance (between the sleeve stripes): *Medical*, dark maroon; *Pay*, white; *Constructors*, purple; *Civil Engineers*, light blue: *Professors of Mathematics*, olive green. In 1919 the undress uniform of U.S. Naval officers was altered to a pattern resembling that of the British Navy.

Personnel.—War, 450,000. Post-war establishment not known yet.

Mercantile Marine.—Lloyds Return, 1919, gives 9,773,000 tons sea-going and 2,160,000 on the Great Lakes.

Coinage.—Dollar (100 cents) = approximately 4*s.* 2*d.* British at pre-war rate of exchange.

Overseas Possessions.—Panama Canal Zone, Porto Rico, Virgin Islands, Alaska and Aleutian Islands, Guam, Tutuila, Wake and Johnston Islands, Philippine Islands.

U. S. NAVAL ORDNANCE, TORPEDOES, &c.

Principal Guns in the U. S. Fleet.

(Corrected from the official figures, 1913.)

Built at Washington Gun Factory, proved at Indian Head, Ind., and Potomac Range.

Notation.	Nominal Calibre.	Mark or Model.	Length in Calibres.	Weight of Gun.	Weight of A.P. Shot.	*Service* Initial Velocity.	*Maximum* penetration firing *capped* A.P. direct impact against K.C. armour. 9000	6000	3000	Approximate Danger Space average ship, at 10,000	5000	3000	Muzzle Energy
	inch.			tons.	lbs.	ft. secs.	in.	in.	in.	yards.	yards.	yards.	
A^8	16	...	45-50	128 ?	2100 ?	...	...	...	...	...	...	...	...
A^7	14	...	45	63⅓	1400	2600	18	...	...	...	...	...	...
A^3	13	I. & II	35	61½	1130	2000	8	9¾	12	110	310	550	31,333
A^6	12	VII	50	56·1	870	2950	11·0	13·9	17·5	...	...	...	52,483
A^6	12	VI	45	53·6	870	2850	10·6	13·3	16·6	...	...	...	48,984
A^5	12	V	45	52·9	870	2700	9·8	12·3	15·5	...	...	...	43,964
A^4	12	III & IV	40	52·1	870	2600	9·3	11·7	14·8	...	...	...	40,768
A^3	12	III & IV	40	52·1	870	2400	8·3	10·5	13·3	39†	126	264	34,738
A^2	12	I & II	35	45·3	870	2100	7·2	8·8	11·2	100	390	580	26,596
A^2	10	III	40	34·6	510	2700	6·9	9·0	11·9	140	460	700	25,772
..	10	I & II	30	25·1	510	2000	5·0	6·1	8·0	...	...	...	14,141
A	8	VI	45	18·7	260	2750	4·4	6·1	8·6	15†	...	...	13,630
B	8	V	40	18·1	260	2500	4·0	5·3	7·5	45	...	...	11,264
C	8	III & IV	35	13·1	260	2100	3·6	4·2	6·0	...	...	...	7,948
C	6	...	52	...	...	...	...	...	...	...	...	...	...
C	6	VIII	50	8·6	105	2800	2·3	3·2	5·2	...	...	...	5,707
D	6	VI	50	8·3	105	2600	2·2	2·9	4·7	75	250	470	4,920
*D**	6	IX	45	7·0	105	2250	2·1	2·5	3·8	...	..	..	3,685
*E**	6	IV, VII	40	6·0	105	2150	2·1	2·4	3·6	35	150	355	3,365
*E**	5	VII	51	5·0	50	3150	1·4	1·8	3·4	...	...	...	3,439
	5	VI	50	4·6	50	3000	1·4	1·7	3·2	...	...	...	3,122
	5	V & VI	50	4·6	60	2700	1·6	2·0	3·5	...	...	...	3,032
*F**	5	II, III, IV	40	3·1	50	2300	1·4	1·7	2·6	...	...	...	1,834
*F**	4	VIII	50	2·9	33	2800	1·2	1·5	2·6	...	...	...	1,794
*F**	4	VII	50	2·6	33	2500	1·2	1·4	2·2	...	..	...	1,430
*F**	4	III,IV,V,VI	40	1·5	33	2000	...	1·2	1·7	...	...	..	915
F	3	V, VI, *S-A*	50	1·0	13	2700	...	0·8	1·2	...	...	...	658
*F**	3	II, III	50	0·9	13	2700	...	0·8	1·2	...	...	...	658

* = Brass cartridge case. † = Calculated for a 20 ft. target.
Guns of 1899 and later have Vickers breech, etc. All guns use nitro-cellulose.
Anti-aircraft guns are 3 inch (13 pdr.) and 1 pdr.

16 inch, 50 cal. in *Massachusetts* class (6) and *Constellation* class (6).

16 inch, 45 cal. in *Colorado* class.

14 inch, 50 cal. mounted in *California* (2), and *New Mexico* (3) classes.

14 inch, 45 cal. mounted in *Texas* (2), *Nevada* (2) and *Pennsylvania* (2) classes.

12 inch, 50 cal. mounted in *Arkansas* (2) and *Utah* (2) classes.

12 inch, 45 cal. mounted in *Delaware* (2), *Idaho* (2), *Louisiana* (2), *Kansas* (4), and *S. Carolina* (2) classes.

12 inch, 40 cal. mounted in *Maine* (3), *New Jersey* (5), and *Ozark* (4) classes.

"Director" fire-controls have been installed in all the Dreadnoughts and Battleships back to the *New Jersey* type. Dreadnoughts have enlarged elevation to main guns, and directors for 5 inch guns. *Star shell* for 3, 4 and 5 inch guns. Range: 3-6 land miles. Time fuze ignites lamp and expels parachute and burner through base of shell. Shell usually detonates at 1000 feet, and 800,000 candle-power burner burns for 30 seconds, lighting up sea over ½ mile radius. *Non-ricochet shell* (flat-nosed) for 3, 4, 5 and 6 inch guns. Fired at elevation over 2° and delay action fuze begins on impact with water. *Y-gun* has two barrels set at 90° with powder chamber common to both barrels. Range: *about* 30 yards. *Davis non-recoil gun* (9 pdr.) consists of 2 guns placed breech to breech. Recoil absorbed by expulsion of powder charge case from after gun; aimed by tracer bullets from Lewis gun fixed on barrel. 8 inch Trench Mortar Howitzer under test.

Aircraft Bombs.—20 lb. Cooper, 112, 163, 230, 270, 520 lbs. Mark VI is 10 inch diameter and 6 feet long.

Paravanes.

Generally as British Navy types, with minor modifications in inhaul gear.

Depth Charges.

18 inch diameter, 28 inches long. 300 lb. T.N.T. or Amatol charge. Detonation controlled by hydrostatic valve, with safety device to 20 feet depth. Effective up to 100 feet.

Torpedoes.

Built at the Torpedo Station, Newport (Rhode Island), and the Naval Gun Factory, Washington, D.C. No exact details are available. Ranges of torpedoes were improved by experiments in 1914, and a new type of net-cutter, which gave excellent results on trials, has been adopted. A new torpedo model is said to have been adopted recently of a simplified pattern, possessing few Bliss-Leavitt features. New 24 inch non-gyro model said to be under test. Nearly all ships are now equipped with submarine signalling and receiving sets.

NEW U. S. FLEET ORGANISATION, 1919.

(Exclusive of Ships on Asiatic Station and in European Waters.)

ATLANTIC FLEET.

Fleet Flagship : *Pennsylvania.*

BATTLESHIP FORCE :—

2nd Battleship Squadron.

3rd Division :—
Connecticut (Flag)
Louisiana
New Hampshire
Kansas

4th Division :—
Minnesota (Flag)
South Carolina
Michigan

3rd Battleship Squadron.

5th Division :—
Utah (Flag)
Florida
Delaware
North Dakota

7th Division :—
Pennsylvania
(Force Flag)
Oklahoma
Nevada
Arizona

CRUISER FORCE :—

1st Cruiser Squadron, 1st Division : *Huntington* (Flag), *Wheeling, Topeka, Castine.*

DESTROYER FORCE :—

3rd DESTROYER SQUADRON (ACTIVE).

Flagship (D) : *Rochester.*

First Flotilla. Tender : *Dixie.* 5th, 6th, 7th Divisions, each composed of six " flush-deck " type T.B.D.

Second Flotilla. Tender : *Bridgeport.* 8th, 9th and 28th Divisions, each composed of six " flush-deck " type T.B.D.

Third Flotilla. Tender : *Panther.* 19th, 20th and 22nd Divisions, each composed of six " flush-deck " type T.B.D.

1st DESTROYER SQUADRON (RESERVE).

Flagship (D) : *Chester.*

Seventh Flotilla. Tender : Not yet selected. 1st Division composed of 7 *Aylwin* class T.B.D. ; 2nd Division composed of 6 *Cushing* class T.B.D. ; 3rd Division composed of 5 *Conyngham* Class T.B.D. and *Cummings.*

Eighth Flotilla. Tender : Not yet selected. 4th and 26th Divisions, each composed of six " flush-deck " type T.B.D., and 26th Division composed of five " flush-deck " type T.B.D.

Ninth Flotilla. Tender : Not yet selected. 24th, 27th and 36th Divisions, each composed of six " flush-deck " type T.B.D.

SUBMARINE FORCE :—

7th Division. Tender : *Camden.* Eight " S " type submarines.
12th Division. Tender : *Rainbow.* Five " S " type submarines.
15th Division. Tender : *Bushnell.* Three " AA " type submarines.

MINE FORCE :—

First Squadron (Planters) : *San Francisco* (Flag), *Shawmut.*
Second Squadron (Sweepers) : 1st and 2nd Divisions, each composed of six " Bird " class Sweepers.

TRAIN FORCE :—

Flagship (Train) : *Columbia.*

Repair Ship : *Prometheus.* Hospital Ships : *Solace* (to be placed on reserve shortly). *Mercy.* Supply Ships : *Bridge, Culgoa.* Fuel Ships : *Nereus, Mars, Nero, Cæsar, Proteus, Arethusa, Maumee, Pecos.* Target Repair Ship : *Lebanon.* Tugs : Thirteen in number.

IN RESERVE AND/OR OUT OF COMMISSION :—

8 Battleships, 6 Cruisers, *about* 40 Destroyers, Coast Torpedo Vessels, &c. Total of Submarines not known. Also various Monitors, Gunboats, Auxiliaries, &c.

PACIFIC FLEET.

Fleet Flagship : *New Mexico.*

BATTLESHIP FORCE :—

1st Battleship Squadron.

1st Division :—
Virginia (Flag)
New Jersey
Rhode Island

2nd Division :—
Georgia (Flag)
Nebraska
Vermont

4th Battleship Squadron.

6th Division :—
Wyoming (Flag)
Arkansas
New York
Texas

8th Division :—
New Mexico
(Force Flag)
Tennessee
Idaho
Mississippi

CRUISER FORCE :—

2nd Cruiser Squadron. 2nd Division : *Seattle* (Flag), *Cleveland, Denver, Tacoma, Marblehead, Machias, Vicksburg.*

DESTROYER FORCE :—

4th DESTROYER SQUADRON (ACTIVE).

Flagship (D) : *Birmingham.*

Fourth Flotilla. Tender : *Melville.* 10th, 11th and 12th Divisions, each composed of six " flush-deck " type T.B.D.

Fifth Flotilla. Tender : *Prairie.* 13th, 14th and 15th Divisions, each composed of six " flush-deck " type T.B.D.

Sixth Flotilla. Tender : *Buffalo.* 16th, 17th and 18th Divisions, each composed of six " flush-deck " type T.B.D.

2nd DESTROYER SQUADRON (RESERVE).

Flagship (D) : *Salem.*

Tenth Flotilla. Tender : *Black Hawk.* 29th and 31st Divisions, each composed of six " flush-deck " type T.B.D.; and 20th Division, five " flush-deck " type T.B.D.

Eleventh Flotilla. Tender : Not yet selected. 22nd, 23rd and 35th Divisions, each consisting of six " flush-deck " type T.B.D.

Twelfth Flotilla. Tender : Not yet selected. 32nd, 33rd and 34th Divisions, each comprising six " flush-deck " type T.B.D.

SUBMARINE FORCE :—

11th Division. Tender : *Savannah.* Eight " S " type Submarines.
16th Division. Tender : *Beaver.* Six " S " type Submarines.

MINE FORCE :—

Third Squadron (Planters) : *Baltimore* (Flag), *Aroostook.*
Fourth Squadron (Sweepers) : 3rd and 4th Divisions, each composed of six " Bird " class Sweepers.

TRAIN FORCE :—

Flagship (Train) : *Minneapolis.*

Repair Ship : *Vestal.* Hospital Ship : *Mercy.* Supply Ships : *Rappahannock, Glacier, Celtic.* Fuel Ships : *Orion, Vulcan, Neptune, Brutus, Jupiter, Jason, Neches, Kanawha, Cuyama, Brazos.* Target Repair Ship : *Nanshan.* Radio Repair Ship : *Saturn.* Tugs : Eleven in number.

Also various craft attached to the 12th Naval District (Mare Island), 13th Naval District (Bremerton), 14th Naval District (Hawaii), and Canal Zone.

Scale : 1 inch = 160 feet.

U. S. NAVY RECOGNITION SILHOUETTES.

ONE FUNNEL.

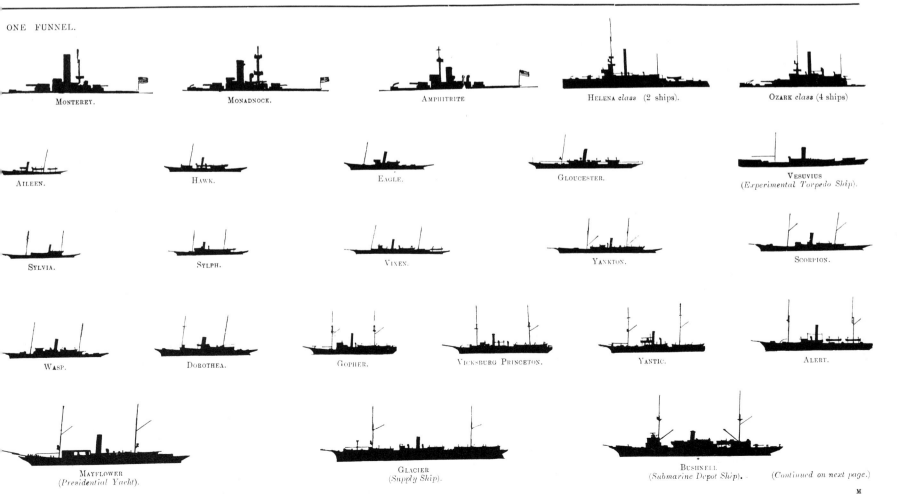

MONTEREY.

MONADNOCK.

AMPHITRITE

HELENA *class* (2 ships).

OZARK *class* (4 ships)

AILEEN.

HAWK.

EAGLE.

GLOUCESTER.

VESUVIUS
(*Experimental Torpedo Ship*).

SYLVIA.

STLPH.

VIXEN.

YANKTON.

SCORPION.

WASP.

DOROTHEA.

GOPHER.

VICKSBURG PRINCETON.

YANTIC.

ALERT.

MAYFLOWER
(*Presidential Yacht*).

GLACIER
(*Supply Ship*).

BUSHNELL.
(*Submarine Depot Ship*). (*Continued on next page*).

M

Scale : 1 inch = 160 feet.

U. S. NAVY RECOGNITION SILHOUETTES.

ONE FUNNEL—*continued.*

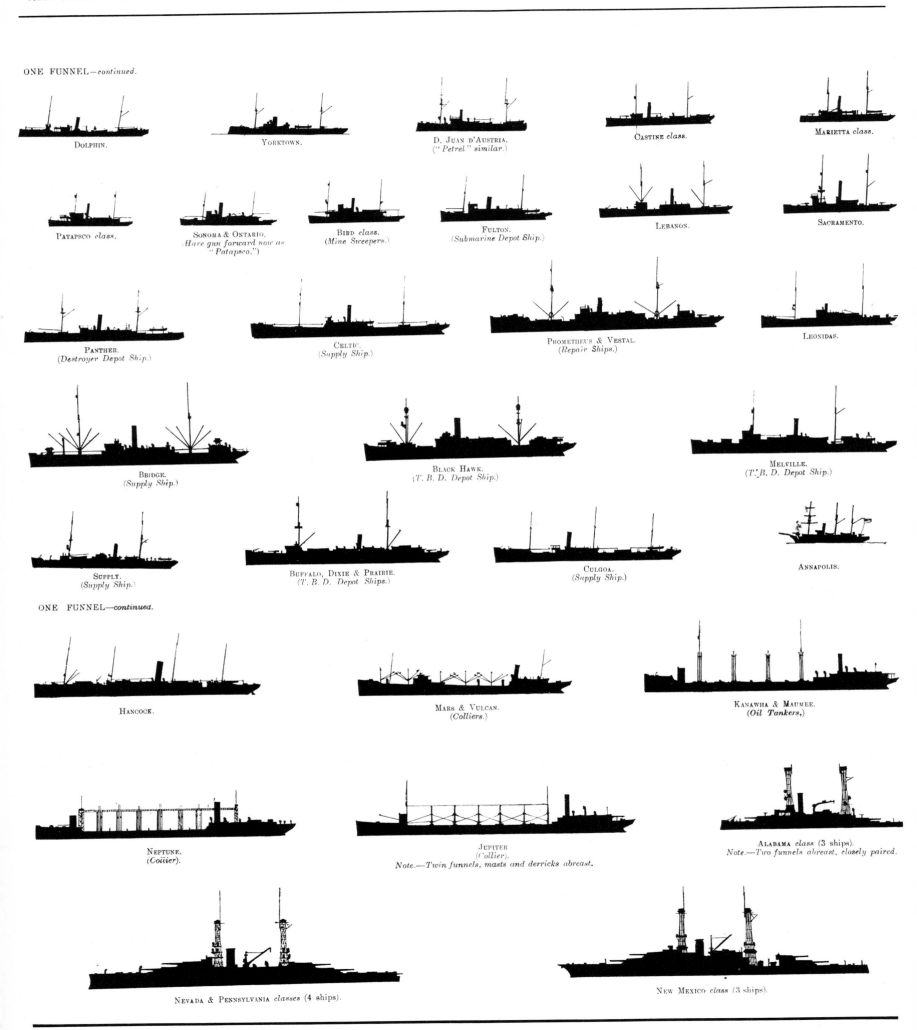

DOLPHIN.

YORKTOWN.

D. JUAN D'AUSTRIA.
("*Petrel*" similar.)

CASTINE *class.*

MARIETTA *class.*

PATAPSCO *class.*

SONOMA & ONTARIO.
(Have gun forward now as
"*Patapsco.*")

BIRD *class.*
(Mine Sweepers.)

FULTON.
(Submarine Depot Ship.)

LEBANON.

SACRAMENTO.

PANTHER.
(*Destroyer Depot Ship.*)

CELTIC.
(*Supply Ship.*)

PROMETHEUS & VESTAL.
(*Repair Ships.*)

LEONIDAS.

BRIDGE.
(*Supply Ship.*)

BLACK HAWK.
(*T. B. D. Depot Ship.*)

MELVILLE.
(*T. B. D. Depot Ship.*)

SUPPLY.
(*Supply Ship.*)

BUFFALO, DIXIE & PRAIRIE.
(*T. B. D. Depot Ships.*)

CULGOA.
(*Supply Ship.*)

ANNAPOLIS.

ONE FUNNEL—*continued.*

HANCOCK.

MARS & VULCAN.
(*Colliers.*)

KANAWHA & MAUMEE.
(*Oil Tankers,*)

NEPTUNE.
(*Collier.*)

JUPITER
(*Collier.*)
Note.—*Twin funnels, masts and derricks abreast.*

ALABAMA *class* (3 ships).
Note.—*Two funnels abreast, closely paired.*

NEVADA & PENNSYLVANIA *classes* (4 ships).

NEW MEXICO *class* (3 ships).

Scale : 1 inch = 160 feet. U. S. NAVY RECOGNITION SILHOUETTES.

TWO FUNNELS.

CINCINNATI.

ISLA DE LUZON.

ANNISTON.
MARBLEHEAD.

RALEIGH.

SAN FRANCISCO.
(Mine Layer.)

NEW ORLEANS class (6).

BALTIMORE
(Mine Layer).

OLYMPIA.

CHICAGO.

AROOSTOOK
SHAWMUT
(Mine Layers).

MINNEAPOLIS.

NASHVILLE.

DENVER class (6 ships).

MONOCACY
PALOS
(River Gunboats).

PADUCAH class (2 ships).

TWO FUNNELS—Continued.

KEARSARGE class (2 ships).

S. CAROLINA class (2 ships).
Half-cased funnels. Appearance distinctive.

DELAWARE class (2 ships).
Distinguish from "Utah" class by both cage masts being before funnels.

UTAH class (2 ships).

ARKANSAS class (2 ships).

TEXAS class (2 ships).

Can be distinguished by number and arrangement of after turrets; also by spacing of funnels and cage masts.

THREE FUNNELS.

MAINE class (3 ships).
Low freeboard aft; "Ohio" shorter funnels.

NEW JERSEY class (5 ships).
Note.—Some ships have mainmast close to third funnel.
Identify by two-tier turrets.

KANSAS class and LOUISIANA class (6 ships).
Note.—"New Hampshire" has half-cased funnels.

(Continued on next page.)

Scale: 1 inch = 160 feet.

U. S. NAVY RECOGNITION SILHOUETTES.

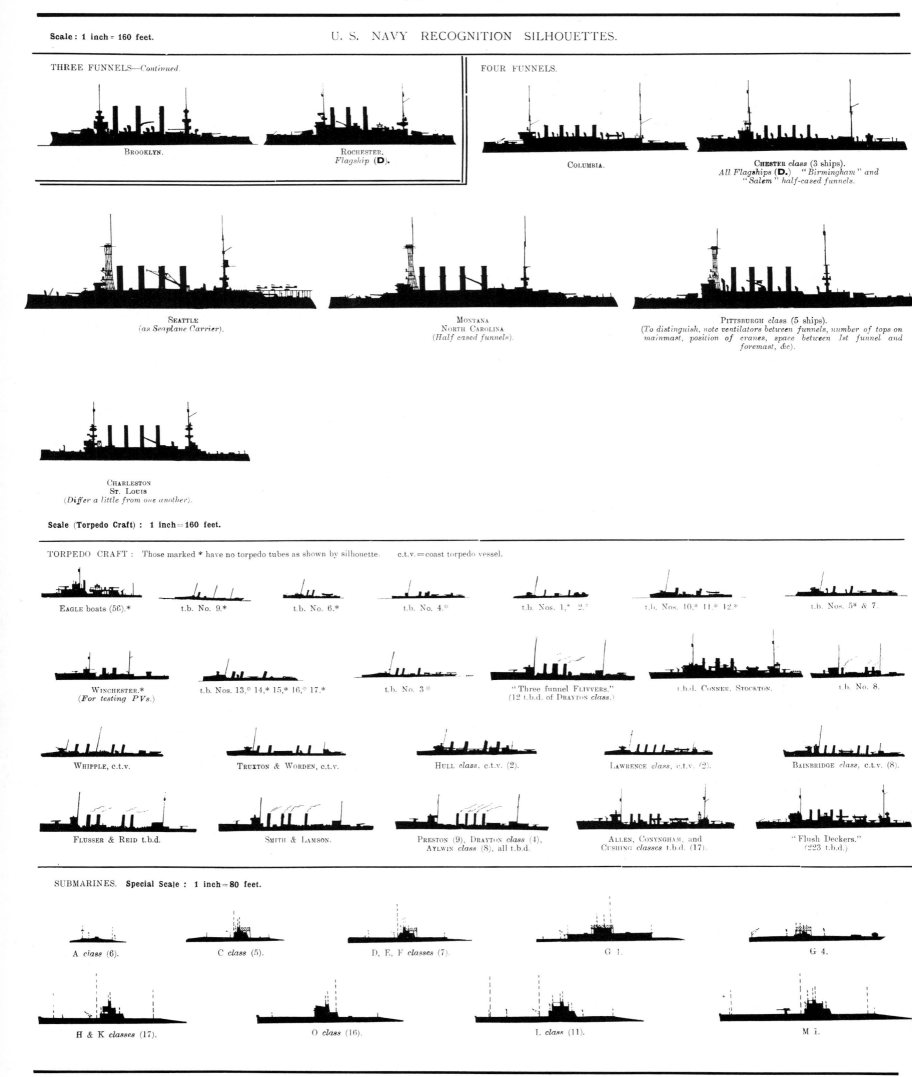

THREE FUNNELS—*Continued.*

BROOKLYN.

ROCHESTER.
Flagship (**D**).

FOUR FUNNELS.

COLUMBIA.

CHESTER *class* (3 ships).
All Flagships (**D.**) "Birmingham" and
"Salem" half-cased funnels.

SEATTLE
(as Seaplane Carrier).

MONTANA
NORTH CAROLINA
(Half cased funnels).

PITTSBURGH *class* (5 ships).
(To distinguish, note ventilators between funnels, number of tops on
mainmast, position of cranes, space between 1st funnel and
foremast, &c).

CHARLESTON
ST. LOUIS
(Differ a little from one another).

Scale (Torpedo Craft) : 1 inch = 160 feet.

TORPEDO CRAFT : Those marked * have no torpedo tubes as shown by silhouette.   c.t.v. = coast torpedo vessel.

EAGLE boats (50).*

t.b. No. 9.*

t.b. No. 6.*

t.b. No. 4.

t.b. Nos. 1,* 2.

t.b. Nos. 10,* 11,* 12.*

t.b. Nos. 5* & 7.

WINCHESTER.*
(*For testing PVs.*)

t.b. Nos. 13, 14,* 15,* 16, 17.*

t.b. No. 3

"Three funnel FLIVVERS."
(12 t.b.d. of DRAYTON *class.*)

t.b.d. CONNER, STOCKTON.

t.b. No. 8.

WHIPPLE, c.t.v.

TRUXTON & WORDEN, c.t.v.

HULL *class*, c.t.v. (2).

LAWRENCE *class*, c.t.v. (2).

BAINBRIDGE *class*, c.t.v. (8).

FLUSSER & REID t.b.d.

SMITH & LAMSON.

PRESTON (9), DRAYTON *class* (4),
AYLWIN *class* (8), all t.b.d.

ALLEN, CONYNGHAM, and
CUSHING *classes* t.b.d. (17).

"Flush Deckers."
(223 t.b.d.)

SUBMARINES.   **Special Scale : 1 inch = 80 feet.**

A *class* (6).

C *class* (5).

D, E, F *classes* (7).

G 1.

G 4.

H & K *classes* (17).

O *class* (16).

L *class* (11).

M 1.

1915 U. S. DREADNOUGHTS. (Battleships—*Single Calibre.*)

New Mexico *class* (3 ships).

NEW MEXICO (April, 1917), **IDAHO** (June, 1917) and **MISSISSIPPI** (January, 1917).

Normal displacement, 32,000 tons. Full load, 33,000 tons. Complement, 1117.

Length (*waterline*), 600 feet. Beam, 97½ feet 4½ in. {Mean draught, 30 feet. / Max. „ 31 „} Length *over all*, 624 feet.

Guns (Dir. Con.) :
12—14 inch, 50 cal. (A⁷).
14—5 inch, 51 cal.
4—3 inch (anti-aircraft)
4—6 pdr. (saluting)
2—1 pdr.
2 machine
1 landing
Torpedo tubes (21 inch):
2 submerged

*War; N.M. 1560, I. & M. 1600.

Armour :
14" Belt (amidships) ......
8" Belt (aft) ....
„ Deck ends ....
15"—9" Funnel base ......
18"—9" Turrets
16" Conning tower & tube

IDAHO. *Photo, New York Shipbuilding Co.*

Ahead:
6—14 in.
—5 in.

Broadside: 12—14 in., 7—5 in., 1—21 in. torpedo tube.

Astern :
6—14 in.
—5 in.

Machinery : *New Mexico*: G.E. turbines with electric reduction gear (see *Notes*). *Idaho* : Parsons 4-shaft (geared cruising) turbines. *Mississippi* : Curtis 4-shaft (geared cruising) turbines. 4 screws in all three ships. Boilers ; 9 Babcock & Wilcox. Designed H.P., *New Mexico* 27,500, others 32,000 = 21 knots. Fuel: Oil only, normal 2200 tons, maximum 3271 tons.

Armour and Gunnery Notes.—Generally as *Pennsylvania* and *Nevada* classes, but have still greater degree of internal protection. It is unofficially reported that they have *triple* bottoms and double longitudinal bulkheads, the space between outer bulkhead and inner skin being filled up with shock-absorbing materials. As designed, it was intended they should mount 45 calibre 14 inch guns, but while building, the more powerful 50 calibre model of the 14 inch gun was adopted.

Engineering Notes.—New Mexico has 2 turbine-driven generating units and 4 propelling motors. Generators are bipolar alternators. For economical cruising speeds of 15—18 knots and under, one generator is used on 36-pole connection. For higher speeds, 24-pole connection will be employed. One generator can drive ship at 19 kts. in emergency. 175 propeller r.p.m. = full speed. Estimated weight of machinery, *New Mexico* 2351 tons, *Idaho* 2408 tons, *Mississippi* 2298 tons. Estimated heating surface, 55,458 sq. feet (+ 4476 feet superheaters in *New Mexico*). 250 lbs. pressure at steam chest. Electric installation, 6—300 k.w., 120—240 volt turbo-generators in *New Mexico*, 4 in other ships. Oil on trials 1467 tons and 209 feed water.

Note to Plans.—These are not uniform in scale with other plans in this book. Delete (*a*) the 4—5 inch guns before and abeam of first barbette ; (*b*) the 4—5 inch guns abaft fourth barbette : thus reducing the 22—5 inch shown on plans to the present armament of 14—5 inch.

MISSISSIPPI. *Copyright photo, O. W. Waterman.*

Name.	Built at.	Machinery.	Laid down.	Completed	Trials. (4 hrs.)	Boilers.	Best recent speed.
New Mexico	New York Yard	New York Yard	Oct., '15	May, '18	31,000 = 21·3	Babcock	
Idaho	N. York S.B. Co.	N. York S.B.Co.	Jan., '15	Mar., '19		Babcock	
Mississippi	Newport News	Newport News	Apl., '15	Dec., '17		Babcock	

General Notes.—Authorised 1914, as No. 40 (*New Mexico*), 41 (*Mississippi*) and 42 (*Idaho*). *New Mexico* fitted with Division Flag Officer's quarters. Originally, only two ships were to have been built, but the sale of the old *Idaho* and *Mississippi* to Greece contributed two-thirds of the cost for a third unit. *New Mexico* was first named *California*. The type is derived from the *Nevada* design through the *Pennsylvania* class, upon which all the above are improvements. The electrical transmission of *New Mexico* was adopted through the excellent results given by the Melville-Macalpine electric-drive system in the Fleet Collier *Jupiter*. She is expected to be very economical in fuel and steam consumption.
*Unofficial Notes.

1913 U. S. DREADNOUGHTS. (Battleships—*Single Calibre.*)

(Pennsylvania Class—2 Ships).

PENNSYLVANIA (March, 1915) & **ARIZONA** (June, 1915).

*Normal displacement, 31,400 tons. Full load, 32,567 tons. Complement, 1117.**

Length (*waterline*), 600 feet. Beam, 97 feet. {Mean draught, 28⅔ feet. / Max. „ 29⅚ „} Length *over all*, 608 feet (p p. 596 ft.).

Guns (Dir. Con.) :
12—14 inch, 45 cal. (A⁷).
14—5 inch, 51 cal.
4—3 in (anti-aircraft)
4—3 pdr. (saluting)
2—1 pdr.
2 M.G.
2 landing
Torpedo tubes (21 inch) :
2 submerged

* War :—
Penn. 1574. *Ariz.* 1620.

Armour :
14" Belt (amidships) ....
8" Belt (aft) ....
3" Deck (ends) ....
15"—9" Funnel base ......
18"—9" Turrets
6" Conning tower & tube ...
(Total, 8072 tons.)

head:
6—14 in.
—5 in.

Astern :
6—14 in.
—5 in.

Broadside: 12—14 in., 7— 5 in., 1—21 in. torpedo tube.

Machinery : *Pennsylvania*, Curtis (geared cruising) turbines. 4 screws. *Arizona* Parsons, (geared cruising) turbines. 4 screws. Boilers : 12 Babcock. Designed H.P. (*Pennsylvania*), 31,500 (*Arizona*) 34,000 = 21 kts. Fuel : oil only, normal 2,322 tons (694,830 gallons).

* *Armour Notes.*— Generally as for *Nevada* class on next page. Increase of armour weight due to increased internal protection against submarine explosions and greater length of belt. Armour for each triple barbette, 226½ tons. *Arizona* has cement backing to belt, instead of teak, and armoured fire-control tops.

* *Gunnery and Fire Control Notes.*—14 inch guns mounted in single sleeve, and can be fired as one piece. Maximum elevation enlarged to 30 in 1917. Triple positions weigh about 650 tons each (guns, mountings and armour). Hoists deliver 1 round per 40 secs., which may be improved to 2 rounds per minute, but three rounds fired per turret per minute probably represents actual rate of fire in service. Breech blocks worked by hand power. Interior of the shields to 14 inch guns very roomy and well arranged.
Each barbette has a built-in R.F. to rear of shield, with ports projecting beyond sides and protected by armoured hoods. Large R.F. in central control station in upper storey of conning tower, where the director is also located probably. Small-base R.F. on roof of super-firing barbette shields and in fire-control tops.

Engineering Notes.—Oil fuel carried for trials, 1548 tons. Heating surface, 53,322 sq. feet. *Arizona*, not yet ascertained (2250 tons estimated). 4—300 k.w. Weight of Machinery : *Pennsylvania*, 2396 tons. ; *Arizona*, not yet ascertained (2250 tons estimated). 4—300 k.w. 125-volt turbo-generators in *Pennsylvania* ; *Arizona* same, but 120-240 volts. In *Pennsylvania*, 240 r.p.m. = full power ; in *Arizona*, 220 r.p.m. = full power.

PENNSYLVANIA. *Copyright Photo, O. W. Waterman.*

Note to Plans.—8—5 inch guns removed during War, but from which positions not known, beyond the fact that they were taken from main and upper decks. These guns may now be remounted in new positions.

Name	Builder	Machinery	Laid down	Completed	Trials Full Power : 12 hrs.	Boilers	Best recent speed
Pennsylvania	Newport News	Newport News	Oct.'13	June,'16	29,366 = 21·05	Babcock	
Arizona	New York Yard	New York Yard	Mar.'14	Oct. '16		Babcock	

General Notes.—*Pennsylvania* authorized 1912, as No. 38, *Arizona* 1913, as No. 39. Both ships are enlarged and improved *Nevadas*. They have proved excellent sea boats, very steady gun platforms, and have proved to be very economical ships. Their general design is marked by great simplicity and a very high standard of excellence. Living quarters are very roomy and well ventilated. Taken all round, these two ships represent one of the most successful, if not the most successful, of all Dreadnought designs up to the present time.
* Unofficial Notes.

(NEVADA CLASS—2 SHIPS).

OKLAHOMA (March, 1914) & **NEVADA** (July, 1914).

Normal displacement, 27,500 tons. *Full load*, 28,400 tons. Complement, 1049.*

Length (*waterline*), 575 feet. Beam, 95¼ feet. { *Mean* draught 28½ feet. / *Max.* ,, 29⅔ ,, } Length *over all*, 583 feet.

Guns (**Dir. Con.**):
10—14 inch, 45 cal. (A7)
12—5 inch, 51 cal.
4—3 inch (anti-aircraft)
4—3 pdr. (saluting)
2—1 pdr.
2 machine.
1 landing.
Torpedo tubes (21 inch):
2 *submerged*

*War: *Nevada*, 1598, *Oklahoma*, 1628.

Armour:
13½" Belt (amidships) ....
8" Belt (aft) ....
13½" Bulkheads ....
13½" Funnel base ....
3" Deck ....
18"—9" Triple Turrets..
16"—9" Double turrets ..
16" Conning tower and tube .....
(Total weight, 7661 tons.)

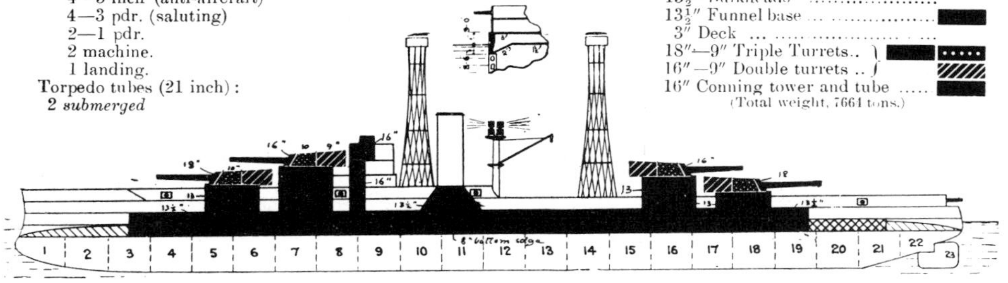

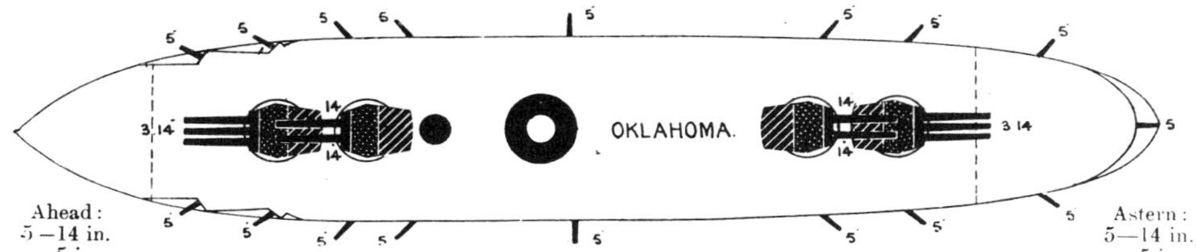

Ahead:
5—14 in.
—5 in.

Astern:
5—14 in.
—5 in.

Broadside: 10—14 in., 6—5 in., 1—21 in. torpedo tube.

Machinery: *Oklahoma*, Triple expansion; *Nevada*, Curtis (geared cruising) turbines. 2 screws in both. Boilers: *O*, 12 Babcock; *N*, 12 Yarrow. Designed H.P. 24,800 = 20·5 kts. Coal: none. Oil, 598,400 gallons (2000 tons), *maximum capacity*. Radius of action: 4000 miles at full speed, 10,000 miles at 10 kts.

**Armour Notes*.—Main belt is 400 feet long by 17½ feet wide; 8½ feet of it being below *l.w.l.* Lower edge is 8". The ends are unarmoured; the battery also. Plates are applied in vertical strakes. Two protective decks, upper 3" flat, lower 1½" flat, 2" on slopes. Barbette bases are 13½" thick, but turrets are only 4½" where below protective deck and behind belt. Barbette shields: 18" port plate for triple positions, 16" port plate for twin positions, 10" sides, 9" back 5" roof. Sighting slits in conning tower closed by splinter-proof shutters. There is a signalling station protected by 16" armour behind conning tower. These ships mark a new era in naval construction, being the first to embody the "everything or nothing" idea in the matter of protection.

**Gunnery Notes*.—Guns in the triple turrets in one sleeve, can be fired as one piece. Maximum elevation of 14-inch guns enlarged to 30° in 1917.

Engineering Notes.—*Nevada* has 2 H.P. and 2 L.P. Curtis turbines. Cylinders of *Oklahoma* are H.P. 35", I.P. 59", L.P. (2) 78". Stroke, 48". Total heating surface, 48,000 sq. feet. Weight of machinery, *Nevada*, 1880 tons: *Oklahoma*, 1998 tons. Electric installation in both is 4 generating sets of 300 k.w., 125 volts, 2400 amp. each. Boilers are in 6 compartments and occupy less than 70 feet of length. Boilers are large tube "Express" type, those specially designed by Messrs. Babcock & Wilcox for *Oklahoma* proving most satisfactory. No superheaters. Electric-driven f.d. blowers proved too unreliable, and were replaced by steam turbine-driven blowers. All oil fuel carried in double bottom; no wing tanks.

Note to Plans.—9—5 inch guns removed from upper and main decks during War and ports plated up. Plans cannot be revised at present, because positions so dealt with have not been described. The 5 inch gun over stern has been suppressed. These 9—5 inch may now be re-mounted in new positions

OKLAHOMA. *Copyright Photo. O. W. Waterman.*

NEVADA. *Photo, U.S. Navy Recruiting Bureau.*

Name	*Builder*	*Machinery*	*Laid down*	*Completed*	*Trials (Full Power—12 hrs.)*	*Boilers*	*Best recent speed*
Oklahoma	N. York Shipb'g	N.Y. Shipb'ld'g	Oct. '12	May, '16	21,703 = 20·58	Babcock	22
Nevada	Fore River Co.	Fore River	Nov. '12	Mar. '16	23,312 = 20·53	Yarrow	

General Notes.—Authorized 1911 as *No. 36* (*Nevada*), *37* (*Oklahoma*).

* Unofficial Notes.

1911 U.S. DREADNOUGHTS. (Battleships—*Single Calibre*.)

TEXAS CLASS—2 SHIPS.

NEW YORK (Oct., 1912) & **TEXAS** (May, 1912).

Normal Displacement, 27,000 tons. *Full load*, 28,367 tons. Complement, 1026.*

Length (*waterline*), 565 feet. Beam 95¼ feet. { *Mean* draught, 28½ feet. / *Max.* ,, 29⅔ ,, } Length *over all*, 573 feet.

Guns (**Dir. Con.**):
10—14 inch, 45 cal. (A7)
16—5 inch, 51 cal.
2—3 inch anti-aircraft
4—3 pdr. (saluting)
2—1 pdr.
2 M.G.
2 landing.
Torpedo tubes (21 inch):
4 *submerged*

*War: *N.Y.*, 1554 (Flag-C-in-C., 1538); *Texas*, 1612.

Armour (Midvale):
12" Belt (amidships)......
" Belt (bow) ....
" Belt (aft) ....
" Deck..........
" Upper Belt ..
14"—8" Turrets...
" Barbettes..........
" Battery ....

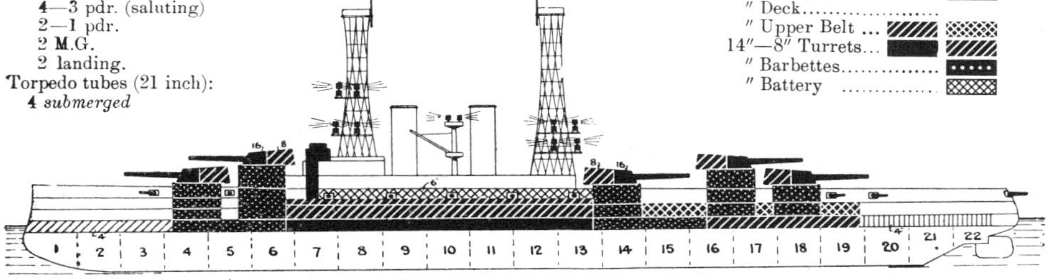

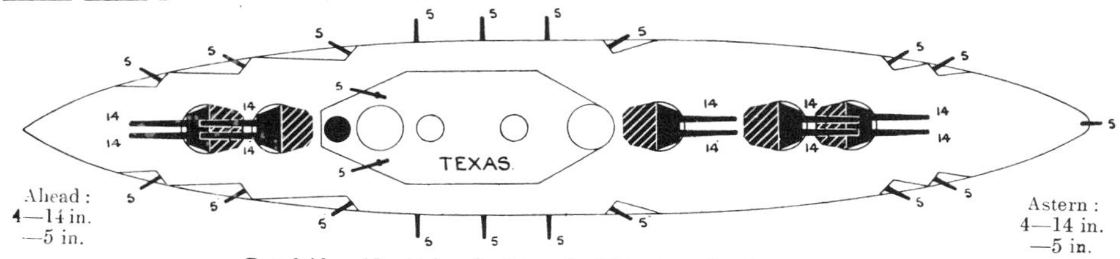

Ahead:
4—14 in.
—5 in.

Astern:
4—14 in.
—5 in.

Broadside: 10—14 in., 8—5 in.; 2—21 in. torpedo tubes.

Machinery: Vertical triple expansion, 4 cylinder. 2 screws. Boilers: 14 Babcock (8 with superheaters). Designed H.P. 28,100 = 21 kts. Coal: *normal* tons; *maximum*, 2918 tons in *New York*; 2960 tons in *Texas*. Oil: 400 tons.

Engineering Notes.—Builders of turbine engines in the U.S. refused to adopt the standards laid down by the Navy Department. Accordingly, in these ships, reciprocating engines were reverted to, to show the turbine builders that the Navy Department was determined to have turbines built to official specification, or else the older type of engines would be taken up again. Cylinders: H.P. 39", I.P. 63", L.P. (2) 83". Stroke: 48". Grate area: 1554 sq feet. Heating surface: 62,213 + 3267 sq. feet (superheaters). Weight of machinery: 2375 tons. Electrical installation: 4 sets each of 300 k.w., 125 volts, 2400 amps., by General Electric Co.

Name	*Builder*	*Machinery*	*Laid down*	*Completed*	*Trials:* Full Power.*	*Boilers*	*Best recent speed*
Texas	Newport News	Newport News	Apl. '11	Mar. '14	28,373 = 21·05	Babcock	22
New York	New York Yard	New York Yard	Sept. '11	Apl. '14	29,687 = 21·47	Babcock	...

* Both ships were light on trials—about 750 tons under normal displacement.

General Notes.—Authorised 1910 as *No. 34* (*N.Y.*) and *35* (*Texas*). Both ships fitted as flagships. First design for these ships is said to have included 15—12-inch guns in five triple turrets. Are very economical ships.

Note to Plans.—Delete (*a*) the foremost pair of 5 inch guns, (*b*) the fifth 5 inch gun from bows on each beam, (*c*) the 5 inch gun over stern, thus reducing 21—5 inch on plans to present armament of 16—5 inch. But the 5—5 inch removed during War may be re-mounted in new positions.

TEXAS. *Photo, U.S. Navy Recruiting Bureau.*

Note that all U.S. Dreadnoughts are now as above photo, viz., (*a*) aeroplanes and flying-off platforms on barbette crowns; (*b*) deflection scales painted on gun-houses; (*c*) large charthouse at foot of fore cage mast; (*d*) range clocks on cage masts—all these being features adopted from British Navy,

NEW YORK *Copyright photo, O. W. Waterman.*

Note.—These ships are distinguishable from the *Arkansas* class owing to the funnels being smaller and fore funnel nearer foremast.

1910 U. S. DREADNOUGHTS. (Battleships—*Single Calibre.*)

(ARKANSAS CLASS—2 SHIPS.)

ARKANSAS (Jan., 1911), & WYOMING (May, 1911).

Normal displacement, 26,000 tons. Full load, 27,243 tons. Complements, 1056 and 1041.

Length (*waterline*), 554 feet. Beam, 93¼ feet. {Mean draught, 28½ feet. Max. ,, 29⅔ feet.} Length *over all*, 562 feet.

*War: 1591 (flag 1663).

Guns (Dir. Con.):
12—12 inch, 50 cal.
16—5 inch, 51 cal.
2—3 inch (anti-aircraft)
4—3 pdr. (saluting)
2—1 pdr.
2 machine
2 landing
Torpedo tubes (21 inch):
  2 submerged

Armour (Midvale):
11″ Belt amidships ...... ▪▪▪▪▪
5″ Belt (ends) ....
12″—9″ Turrets ...
11″ Turret bases ...... ▪▪▪▪▪
6½″ Casemates (*see Notes*)
12″ Conning tower........ ▪▪▪▪

ARKANSAS.   *Copyright photo, O. W. Waterman.*

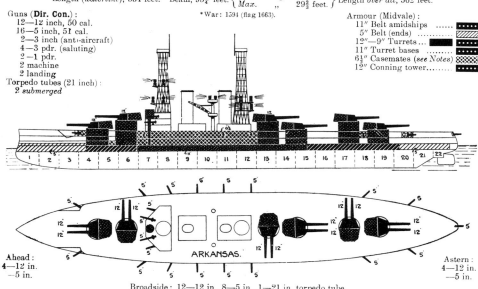

Ahead:
4—12 in.
—5 in.

Astern:
4—12 in.
—5 in.

Broadside: 12—12 in., 8—5 in., 1—21 in. torpedo tube.

Machinery: Parsons turbine. 4 screws. Boilers: 12 Babcock. Designed H.P. 28,000 = 20·5 kts. Coal: *normal* 1669 tons; *maximum,* 2754 tons in *Arkansas* ; 2704 tons in *Wyoming.* Oil, 400 tons. Radius of action, about 8000 miles at 10 kts.

Gunnery Notes.—Height of guns above water: No. 1 turret, 28¼ feet; No. 2, 36¼ feet; No. 3, 33 feet; No. 4, 25 feet; No. 5, 31¼ feet; No. 6, 23¼ feet. Arcs of training: (1) 300°, (2) 270°, (3) 280°, (4) 260°, (5) 330°, (6) 300°.

Armour Notes.—Main belt 400 feet long, 9″ on bottom edge, 11″ on upper edge. Upper belt is same, but is 11″ on bottom edge and 9″ on upper. Internal protection is by 1¾″ high-tensile longitudinal bulkheads. Two protective decks over all machinery and magazine spaces, one deck at ends. 6½″ armour and 1½″ splinter bulkheads to funnel uptakes, up to main deck.

Engineering Notes.—Approximately 148 r.p.m.= 10·5 kts., 215 = 15 kts., 300 = 20 kts., 320 = 22 kts. Grate area: 1428 sq. feet. Heating surface: 64,234 sq. feet. Weight of machinery: 2178 tons in *Arkansas,* 2095 tons in *Wyoming.* Electrical installation: 4 sets each 300 k.w., 125 volts, 2400 amps.. by General Electric Co. Searchlights: 16. It was intended that these ships should have combined turbines and reciprocating engines, but the plan was dropped in favour of complete turbine propulsion.

General Notes.—Authorised 1909, as No. 32 (*Wyoming*). 33 (*Arkansas*). Contracts awarded Sept. & Oct., 1909. Both fitted as flagships, and when so serving. complements are 1116 for *Arkansas,* and 1117 for *Wyoming.* Freeboard: Forward, 25′: amidships, 19′ 2″; at No. 6 turret, 18′; at stern, 16′ 3″.

*Unofficial Notes.

WYOMING.   *Official photo, U.S. Naval Air Service.*

Note to Plans. 5—5 inch removed from upper and main decks during War and ports plated up. Positions so dealt with not known, except that stern 5 inch shown on plans is removed. These guns may be re-mounted in new positions.

Name	Builder	Machinery	Laid down	Completed	Trials (mean) 24 hrs. at 19	4 hrs. f.p.	Boilers	Best recent speed
Arkansas	N.Y.Shipbld. Co Cramp	N.Y. Shipbld. Co. Cramp	Jan.,'10 Feb.,'10	Sept.,'12 Sept.,'12	= 20,784 = 19·21	28,533 = 21·05 31,437 = 21·22	Babcock Babcock	21·15 22·45
Wyoming								

1909 U. S. DREADNOUGHTS. (Battleships—*Single Calibre.*)

(UTAH CLASS—2 SHIPS.)

UTAH (Dec. 1909) & FLORIDA (May, 1910).

Normal displacement 21,825 tons. Full load, 23,033 tons. Complement, 944 (as flagship, 980).

Length (*waterline*), 510 feet. Beam, 88¼ feet. {Mean draught, 28¼ feet. Max. ,, 30 ,, } Length *over all*, 521½ feet

*War: 1381 (flag 1122).

Guns (Dir. Con.):
10—12 inch, 45 cal. (A⁵)
12—5 inch, 51 cal.
2—3 inch anti-aircraft
4—6 pdr. (saluting)
4 machine
2 landing
Torpedo tubes (21 inch):
  2 submerged

Armour (Midvale):
11″ Belt (amidships) ....
3″ Belt (ends) ....
,, Deck (slopes) ....
10″ Upper belt (amidships)
12″—8″ Turrets (N.C.)
,, Turret bases ....
6½″ Battery amidships
6½″ Casemates ....
,, Conning tower ....

FLORIDA.   *Copyright photo, O. W. Waterman.*

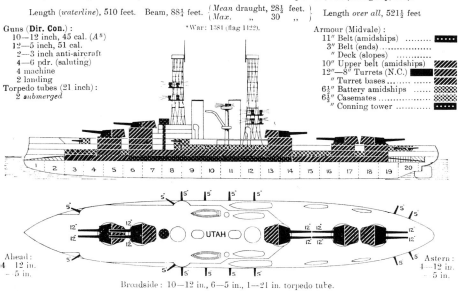

Ahead:
4—12 in.
—5 in.

Astern:
4—12 in.
—5 in.

Broadside: 10—12 in., 6—5 in., 1—21 in. torpedo tube.

Machinery: Parsons turbine. 4 screws. Boilers: 12 Babcock. Designed H.P. 28,000 = 20·75 kts. Coal: *normal* 1667 tons; *maximum,* 2581 tons in *Utah* ; 2560 tons in *Florida.* Oil, 400 tons. *Nominal* radius, 6720 miles at 10 kts., about 4600 at 19 kts. and 3000 at full speed.

Armour Notes.—Main belt 8¼ feet wide ; upper belt 8 feet wide. 2″ splinter bulkheads between all 5 inch battery guns. ¾″ wall in rear. Special sub-division and powerful pumping system against damage by mines or torpedoes.

Gunnery Notes.—Height of guns above water: in fore fore-turret, 33 feet; after fore-turret, 40 feet; amidship turret, 32 feet; in after pair of turrets, 25 feet.

Engineering Notes.—Although turbines are adapted for superheated steam, no superheaters are installed. Have new type feed heaters. Grate area: 1128 sq. feet. Heating surface: 64,234 sq. feet. Weight of Machinery: *Florida,* 2152 tons; *Utah,* 2064 tons. Electrical installation: 4 sets, each 300 k.w., 125 volts, 2400 amps., by General Electric Co. *Florida* on trials developed 41,810 shaft h.p. inclusive of main engines and all auxiliaries. In *Utah* 192 r.p.m.= 21 kts.; 313 = 21 kts. Searchlights: 16.

Name	Builders	Machinery	Laid down	Completed	Trials Full Power.	Turbines	Boilers	Best recent speed
Florida	New York Y.	New York Yard	Mar.,'09	Sep., '11	40511 = 22·08	Parsons	Babcock	
Utah	N.Y.Shipbld.Co.	N.Y. Shipbld. Co.	Mar.,'09	Aug.,'11	27026 = 21·01	Parsons	Babcock	

General Notes.—Authorised 1908, as No. 30 (*Florida*), 31 (*Utah*). *Florida* fitted as flagship.

*Unofficial Notes.

UTAH.   *Copyright photo, O. W. Waterman.*

Note to Plans.—Delete foremost pair of 5 inch guns on *upper* deck ; also the foremost pair of 5 inch on *main* deck ; thus reducing 16—5 inch shown to present armament of 12—5 inch. The 4—5 inch removed during War may be re-mounted in new positions.

1907 U. S. DREADNOUGHTS. (Battleships *Single Calibre*.)

(DELAWARE CLASS—2 SHIPS).

DELAWARE (February, 1909), & **NORTH DAKOTA** (November, 1908).

Normal displacement, 20,000 tons. Full load. 22,060 tons. Complement, 946.*

Length (*waterline*), 510 feet. Beam, 85¼ feet. { Mean draught, 27 feet. } Length *over all*, 518¾ feet.
{ Max. " 28⅚ " }

° War : *Delaware*, 1384 ; *N. Dakota*, 1284.

Guns (Dir. Con.) :
  10—12 inch, 45 cal. (A⁵).
  14—5 inch, 51 cal.
  2—3 inch (anti-aircraft)
  4—3 pdr. (saluting).
  2 machine.
  2 landing.
Torpedo tubes (21 inch).
  2 *submerged*.

Armour (Krupp and Midvale) :
  11″ Belt (amidships) .....
  3″ Belt (ends) ....
  ″ Deck (slopes) ....
  10″ Upper belt (amidships)
  12″–8″ Turrets (N.C.)
  Turret bases (N.C.) ......
  5″ Battery (amidships) (N.C.)

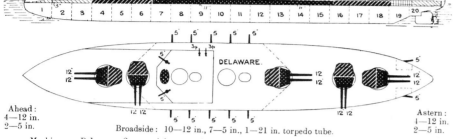

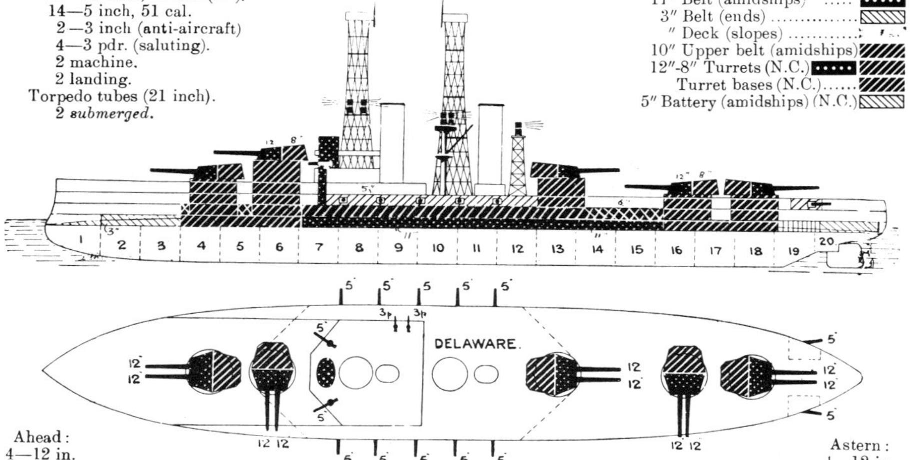

DELAWARE.

Ahead :
4—12 in.
2—5 in.

Astern :
4—12 in.
2—5 in.

Broadside: 10—12 in., 7—5 in., 1—21 in. torpedo tube.

DELAWARE. *Photo, U.S. Navy Recruiting Bureau.*

Machinery : *Delaware*, 2 sets triple expansion. 2 screws. *N. Dakota*, originally Curtis turbines but re-engined 1916-17 with Parsons turbines and reduction gear. 2 screws. Boilers : 14 Babcock. Designed H.P. 25,000 = 21 kts. Coal : *normal*, 1016 tons ; *maximum*, 2732 tons in *Delaware*, 2740 tons in *N. Dakota*. Also 380 tons oil.

Gunnery Notes.—*Delaware* fitted 1917 with new ammunition hoists and latest type of fire-controls.

Armour Notes.—Main belt 8 feet wide, 6¾ feet of it below waterline at full load displacement, 11″ thick amidships, upper belt, 7⅔ feet wide. Splinter-proof armour on uptakes and ventilators within citadel and in battery and upper deck.

Engineering Notes.—Cylinders of *Delaware* are 38½″ (H.P.) 57″ (I.P.) 2–76″ (L.P.)×48″ stroke. Full speed, *Delaware* = 128 revs. *N. Dakota*, 263 r.p.m. for 21 kts., 229 for 19 kts., 142½ for 12 kts.* Trial consumption : 1·83 lbs. per H.P. all purposes. At 12 kts. *Delaware* burned 100 tons per 24 hours, *N. Dakota* 140 tons.* Grate area : 1439 sq. feet. Heating surface : 61,943 sq. feet. Weight of machinery : D. 2036 tons, *N.D.* 2047 tons.* 4—300 k.w. 125-volt turbo-generators. *Delaware* was the first U.S. ship to have forced lubrication which proved so successful, it was afterwards fitted to all the older battleships with reciprocating engines.

Nominal Radii : About 6500 at 12 kts., 4600 at 18 kts., 3000 at 21·5 kts. for *N. Dakota*.* Somewhat more for *Delaware*.

Name.	Builder.	Laid down	Completed	Trials : Full power.		Boilers	Best recent speed
Delaware	Newport News	Nov., 1907	Feb., '10	=19·74	24,578 = 21·56*	Babcock	21·98
North Dakota	Fore River Co.	Dec., 1907	Apl., '10	=	31,300 = 21·01	Babcock	22·25

Delaware, after steaming 19,000 miles, did 21·86 *max*. and averaged 21·32 for 24 hours.

NORTH DAKOTA (1919). *Photo, U.S. Navy Recruiting Bureau.*
New R.F. station, Director Tower of fore cage mast, "coffee-box" S.L. tower to after funnel.
These ships have especially large boilers. The grates are 7ft. long by 14¾ft. wide = about 100 sq. ft. per boiler.
General Notes.—*N. Dakota* has a torpedo defence control platform under s.l. platform, abaft after funnel. Authorised 1906, as *No. 28* (D) and *29* (N.D.) Cost, without armament, £789,200. *N. Dakota*, large refit, 1916.
* These particulars relate to first trials of *North Dakota*, when originally engined with Curtis turbines. No details available of any trials run with new Parsons turbines and reduction gear.

1906 U. S. DREADNOUGHTS. (Battleships—*Single Calibre*.)

(S. CAROLINA CLASS—2 SHIPS).

SOUTH CAROLINA (1908) & **MICHIGAN** (May, 1908).

Normal displacement, 16,000 tons. *Full load* displacement, 17,617 tons. Complement, 813.°

Length (*waterline*), 450 feet. Beam, 80¼ feet. { Mean draught, 24½ feet. } Length *over all*, 452¾ feet.
{ Max " 27 feet. }

Guns (**Dir. Con.**) :
  8—12 inch, 45 cal. (A⁵).
  14—3 inch, 13 pdr.
  2—3 inch anti-aircraft
  (a) 2–3 pdr. } S.C.
      2–1 pdr. }
  (b) 4–3 pdr. Mich.
  2 M.G. } both
  2 landing }
Torpedo tubes (21 inch) :
  2 *submerged*.
    (Total about 1150 tons).

° War Complements : *Michigan* 1154 ; *S. Carolina* 1351, flagship 1368.

Armour (S.C. Krupp ; M. Midvale) :
  11″–9″ Belt (amidships) ......
  1½″ Belt (ends) ....
  3″ Armour deck (slopes) (*see notes*)
  10″ Bulkheads ....
  12″–8″ Turrets (N.C.).....
  10″–8″ Turret bases (N.C.)
  10″–8″ Lower deck, redoubt
  12″ Conning tower (N.C.)
  9″ Tube ....
    (About 4000 tons).

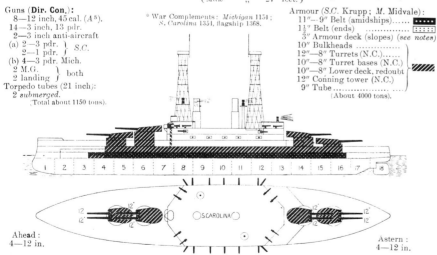

S. CAROLINA.

Ahead :
4—12 in.

Astern :
4—12 in.

Broadside : 8—12 in., 7—3 in. ; 1—21 in. torpedo tube.

Machinery : 2 sets vertical 4 cylinder triple expansion. 2 screws (outward turning). Boilers : 12 Babcock (1906 model) in 3 compartments. Designed H.P. 16,500 = 18·5 kts. Coal : *normal* 900 tons ; *maximum* 2437 tons in *Michigan*, 2433 tons in *S. Carolina*.

Armour Notes.—Main belt, 8 feet wide ; 6¾ feet of it below waterline ; top and bottom, 9″ ; waterline, 11″–10¼″. Redoubt belt 8″ at upper edge, 10″ lower. Low turrets with small bases. Fronts of turrets, 12″ ; sides, 8″. Redoubt, 300 ft. long. Armour deck forward and amidships is 1½″ on slopes, aft it is 3″.

Gunnery Notes.—Hoists, electric. Big guns manœuvred electrically. Arcs of fire, 270° each turret. Fore turret guns 24 ft. above water, "after fore turret" guns 32 feet. Barbette of this rises 12 feet above the deck. Twelve hoists for 3 inch guns. *South Carolina* fitted with new ammunition hoists and latest type of fire-control system, 1917.

SOUTH CAROLINA. *Photo, O. W. Waterman.*

Engineering Notes.—Cylinders are 32″ (H.P.), 52″ (I.P.), 2—72″ (L.P.)×48″ stroke. Pressure, 265 lbs. Revolutions full power = 121. Machinery, etc., weighs 1555 tons in *Michigan* and 1533 tons in *S. Carolina*. Grate area, 1050 sq. feet. Heating surface, 47,220 sq. feet. 4 sets 200 k.w. 125-volt turbo-generators. The first large U.S. ships to be fitted for burning oil fuel, though they do not appear to carry oil. Electric-driven f.d. blowers.

Name	Builder	Laid down	Completed	Trials (mean)		Boilers	Best recent speed
S. Carolina	Cramp	Dec., '06	Mar., '10		17,607 = 18·86	Babcock	19·68
Michigan	N.Y. Ship Bldg. Co.	Dec., '06	Jan., '10	13,253 = 17·95	16,016 = 18·79	Babcock	20·01

General Notes.—Authorised 1905 as *Nos. 26* (*Michigan*) and *27* (*S. Carolina*). These ships, though laid down after, were projected *before* the British *Dreadnought* and so may be considered as the first "Dreadnoughts" (*i.e.*, all big gun ships). They are good sea-boats, but roll heavily In January, 1918, *Michigan's* lattice foremast fell during a gale. She has been re-equipped with a new lattice foremast of the latest type. ° Unofficial Notes.

Note to Plan.—8—3 inch, 14 pdr., either temporarily or permanently dismounted during War. Positions from which these guns were removed are not known, and guns cannot be deleted from plans. They were probably taken from the upper deck battery.

1904-3 U. S. BATTLESHIPS (19-18 knot). *Mixed Calibre* 1902-1899

VERMONT. (Note to photo : Main deck battery now removed.) *Photo, U.S. Naval Air Service.*

KANSAS (Sept., 1905), **VERMONT** (Aug., 1905), **MINNESOTA** (April, 1905), **NEW HAMPSHIRE** (—1906). *Normal displacement,* 16,000 tons. *Full load displacement,* 17,650 tons (*N. H.* 17,784 tons). Complement, 963. Length (*waterline*), 450 feet. Beam, 76⅝ feet. *Max.* draught, 26⅔ feet. Length *over all,* 456½ feet. Guns (**Dir. Con.**): 4—12 inch, 45 cal., 8—8 inch, 45 cal., 12—3 inch, 13 pdr., 2—3 inch anti-aircraft. Torpedo tubes (21 inch): 4 *submerged.* Armour (Krupp): 9″ Belt (amidships), 4″ Belt (ends), 3″ Deck (slopes), 7″ Lower deck side, 10″ Barbettes, 12-8″ Turrets to these, 7″ Battery, 2″ Casemates (for 14 pdrs.), 6½″—6″ Small turrets, 9″ Conning tower, 5″ Director station (near C.T.). Machinery: 2 sets vertical 4 cylinder triple expansion. 2 screws (outward turning). Boilers: 12 Babcock. Designed H.P. 16,500 = 18 kts. Coal: *normal* 900 tons; *maximum,* 2455 tons in *Kansas,* 2486 in *Vermont,* 2420 in *Minnesota,* 2592 in *N. Hampshire.* Built 1904-8.

LOUISIANA (Aug., 1904) & **CONNECTICUT** (Sept., 1904). As *Kansas, &c.,* above, but differ as follows :—Displacement : *Full load,* 17,666 tons. Armour (Krupp): 11″—9″ Belt (amidships), 3″ Deck (flat on belt), 12″—8″ Turrets (N.S.), 10″—7½″ Turret bases (N.C.), 7″ Lower deck redoubt, 7″ Battery, 2″ Casemates (14 pdr.), 6″ Secondary turrets (N.C.). Designed H.P. 20,525 = 18 kts. Coal: *maximum* 2446 tons, *Louisiana;* 2510 tons, *Connecticut.* Built 1903-6.

(Illustration in preceding column.)

VIRGINIA (April, 1904), **NEW JERSEY** (Nov., 1904), **GEORGIA** (Oct., 1904), **NEBRASKA** (Oct., 1904), **RHODE ISLAND** (May, 1904). *Normal displacement,* 14,948 tons. *Full load displacement,* 16,094 tons. Complements (nucleus.) Length (*waterline*), 435 feet. Beam, 76¼ feet. *Max.* draught, 52⅝ feet. Length *over all,* 441¼ feet. Guns (Model, '99): 4—12 inch, 40 cal. (A⁴), 8—8 inch, 45 cal., 8—3 inch, 13 pdr., 2—3 inch AA. Torpedo tubes (21 inch): 4 *submerged.* Armour (Krupp and H.N.): 11″—8″ Belt (amidships), 4″ Belt (ends), 3″ Deck (flat on belt amidships), 10″—7½″ Barbettes (H.N.), 12″—8″ Turrets (H.N.), 6″ Secondary turrets, 6″ Lower deck side (H.N.), 6″ Battery (H.N.), 9″ Conning tower (K.N.C.) Machinery: 2 sets 4 cylinder vertical inverted triple expansion. 2 screws. Boilers: 12 Babcock. Designed H.P. 25,463 = 19 kts. Coal: *normal* 900 tons; *maximum* 1961 to 2031 tons (average 1995). Built 1901-7.

MISSOURI. *Photo : U. S. Navy Recruiting Bureau.*

OHIO (May, 1901), **MAINE** (July, 1901), **MISSOURI** (Dec., 1901). *Normal displacement,* 12,500 tons. *Full load displacement,* 13,500 tons. Complement (nucleus.) Length (*waterline*), 388 feet. Beam, 72½ feet. *Max.* draught, 25½ feet. Length *over all,* 393⅝ feet. Guns (M. '99): 4—12 in., 40 cal. (A⁴) (Mk. III, mod. 3), 8—6 inch, 50 cal., 2—3 inch AA. Torpedo tubes (18 inch): 2 submerged. Armour (Krupp): 11″—7½″ Belt (amidships), 4″ Belt (bow), 10″ Bulkhead (aft), 2½″ Deck (on slopes), 4″ Deck (aft), 12″ Turrets (H.N.), 12″—8″ Turret bases (H.N.), 6″ Lower deck side, 6″ Battery, 6″ Casemates (forward), 10″ Conning tower. Machinery: 2 sets vertical inverted triple expansion 4 cylinder, except *Missouri,* which is 3 cylinder. 2 screws. Boilers: 12 Thornycroft, except *Maine,* 12 Babcock. Designed H.P. 16,000 = 18 kts. Coal: *normal* 1000 tons; *maximum* 2331 tons, *Ohio;* 1904 tons, *Maine;* 1933 tons, *Missouri.* Built 1900-1904.

(INDIANA CLASS—3 SHIPS.) *Photo, Abrahams & Sons.*

OLD U. S. BATTLESHIPS. *Second line.*

IOWA (March, 1896). *Photo, Abrahams & Sons.*

Displacement, 11,346 tons. Complement, 683.

Length (*waterline*), 360 feet. Beam, 72¼ feet. *Maximum* draught, 28 feet. Length *over all,* 362½ feet.

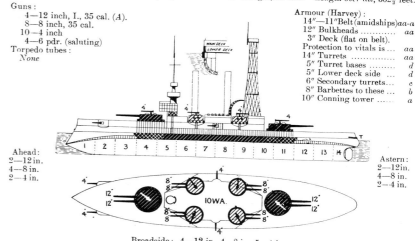

Guns:
4—12 inch, I., 35 cal. (A).
8—8 inch, 35 cal.
10—4 inch
4—6 pdr. (saluting)
Torpedo tubes :
None

Armour (Harvey):
14″—11″ Belt (amidships) *aa-a*
12″ Bulkheads .... *aa*
3″ Deck (flat on belt).
Protection to vitals is ... *aa*
14″ Turrets .... *aa*
5″ Turret bases .... *d*
5″ Lower deck side ...... *d*
6″ Secondary turrets... *c*
8″ Barbettes to these ... *b*
10″ Conning tower ...... *a*

Ahead:
2—12 in.
4—8 in.
2—4 in.

Astern:
2—12 in.
4—8 in.
2—4 in.

Broadside: 4—12 in., 4—8 in., 5—4 in.

Machinery: 2 sets vertical inverted triple expansion. 2 screws. Boilers: cylindrical. Trial H.P. *forced* 11,933 = 17·09 kts. Coal: *normal* 625 tons; *maximum* 1643 tons.

Armour Notes : Belt is 7½ feet wide by 200 feet long; 5 feet of it below waterline; lower edge is 9½″ thick amidships. Main belt is reinforced by coal bunkers 10 feet thick. 12″ turrets have trunked-in hoists.

General Notes : Laid down at Cramp's, August, 1893; completed 1897. Cost *complete,* nearly £1,000,000.

INDIANA (February, 1893), **MASSACHUSETTS** (June, 1893). **OREGON** (October, 1893). Displacement, 10288 tons. Complement, 678.

Length (*waterline*), 348 feet. Beam, 69¼ feet. *Maximum* draught, 28 feet. Length *over all,* 351 feet.

Guns:
4—13 inch, I, (AAA).
8—8 inch, 35 cal.
12—3 inch, 14 pdr., 50 cal.
4—6 pdr. (saluting)
Torpedo tubes :
None

Armour (Harvey):
18″-15″ Belt (amidships) *aaaa-aaa*
17″ Bulkheads .... *aaaa*
3″ Deck (flat on belt)
Protection to vitals is *aaaa*
17″ Barbettes .... *aaaa*
8½″ Turrets............... *a*
5″ Turret bases .... *d*
5″ Lower deck side .... *d*
6″ Secondary turrets ... *c*
8″ Barbettes to these ... *b*
3″ Hoist .... *e*
5″ Sponsons to 6″ guns *d*
10″ Conning tower ...... *a*

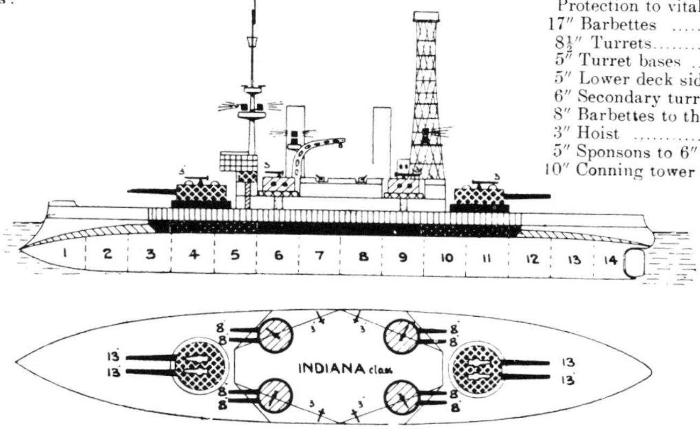

Ahead:
2—13 in.
4—8 in.

Astern:
2—13 in.
4—8 in.

Broadside: 4—13 in., 4—8 in., 2—6 in.

Machinery: 2 sets vertical inverted triple expansion 3 cylinder. 2 screws. Boilers: Original cylindrical. Replaced by 8 Babcocks on refit. Designed H.P. 9000 = 17 kts. Coal: *normal* 400 tons; *maximum* 1475 tons.
Armour Notes.—Belt is 7½ feet wide by 200 feet long.

Name.	Builder	Machinery.	Laid down.	Completed.	Refit.	Trials.	Boilers.	Present best speed.
Indiana	Cramps		1891	1895	1905	= 15·55		
Massachusetts	Cramps		1891	1895	1907	= 16·21	} Babcock in all.	
Oregon	Union Co., Fris.		1891	1896	1908	= 16·79		

OLD U. S. BATTLESHIPS. *Mixed Calibre.*

WISCONSIN.   *Photo, O. W. Waterman.*

ALABAMA (May, 1898), **ILLINOIS** (October, 1898), **WISCONSIN** (November, 1898). *Normal* displacement, 11,552 tons. Complement (nucleus). Guns : 4—13 inch, 35 cal. (A³), 8—6 inch, 40 cal., 2—3 inch AA. No torpedo tubes. Armour (Harvey-nickel) : 16½—9½″ Belt, 4″ Belt (bow), 4″ Deck (aft), 12″ Bulkheads, 14″ Turrets, 15″—10″ Turret bases, 5¼″ Upper belt and battery, 6″ Casemates, 10″ Conning tower. Machinery : 2 sets vertical triple expansion. 3 cylinders. 2 screws. Boilers : 8 single-ended cylindrical, except *Illinois*, 8 Mosher. Designed H.P. *forced* 11,207＝16 kts. Coal : *normal* 850 tons ; *maximum*, 1481 tons *Alabama* ; 1522 tons *Illinois* ; 1447 tons *Wisconsin*. Built 1896-1901.

KEARSARGE.   *Photo, U. S. Navy Recruiting Bureau.*

KEARSARGE & **KENTUCKY** (both March, 1898). *Normal* displacement, 11,520 tons. Complement (nucleus). Guns : 4—13 inch, 35 cal. (A³), 4—8 inch, IV, 35 cal., 8—5 inch, 40 cal., 2—3 inch AA. Torpedo tubes : none. Armour (Harvey-nickel) : 16½″—9½″ Belt, 4″ Belt (bow), 5″ Deck (aft), 2¾″ Deck (flat on belt) 4″ aft, 10″ Fore bulkhead, 12″ After bulkhead, 17″-9″ Turrets (for 13in.), 9″ Turrets (for 8 inch). 15½″—12½″ Barbettes, 5¼″ Lower deck side, 5½″ Battery, 7″ & 6″ Battery (bulkheads), 10″ Conning tower. Machinery : 2 sets vertical triple expansion 3 cylinder. 2 screws. Boilers : 8 Mosher (fitted 1910-11). Designed H.P. 10,500＝16 kts. Coal : *normal* 410 tons ; *maximum* 1679 tons in *Kearsarge*, 1658 tons in *Kentucky*.

U. S. COAST DEFENCE MONITORS

TONOPAH (1901).
CHEYENNE (1900).
OZARK (1901).
TALLAHASSEE (1901).

TONOPAH.   *Photo, O. W. Waterman.*

3235 tons. Complements, 237. Dimensions : 252×50×12½ feet (*mean draught*). Guns : 2—12 inch (40 cal.) 4—4 inch, 1—3 inch AA, 2—6 or 3 pdr., 2—1 pdr. Armour : Krupp, 11″ belt and turret H.P. 2400＝12 kts. Coal : *maximum*, *Ozark* 304 tons, *Tallahassee* 344 tons, *Tonopah* 346 tons. *Cheyenne* 132 tons coal＋60,816 gallons of oil fuel.

MONTEREY (1891). 4084 tons. Guns : 2—12 inch, 35 cal., in fore turret ; 2—10 inch, 30 cal., in after turret ; 6—6 pdr., 1—1 pdr. Armour (Harvey) : 13″—5″ belt, 8″ turrets. Base of fore turret 13″, of after turret 11½″. Designed H.P. 5000＝14 kts. Babcock boilers. Coal, 211 tons. Complement, 228.

AMPHITRITE (1883). 3990 tons. Guns : 4—10 inch, 30 cal., 2—4 inch, 40 cal., 2—3 pdr., 2—1 pdr. Armour : Iron belt 9″, steel turrets 11½″—7½″. H.P. 1600＝10·5 kts. Coal : 271 tons.

Note.

MONADNOCK listed as a Submarine Depot Ship, but will probably be withdrawn from this duty in the near future and placed out of commission.

AMPHITRITE (see *Naval Militia*).

MIANTONOMOH (1876). 3990 tons. Guns : 4—10 inch, 2—6 pdr. Armour : iron belt 7″, turrets 11½″ steel. Designed H.P. 1600＝12 kts. Coal, 250 tons. Complement, 183.

TERROR (1883). All details as for *Miantonomoh* except Coal, 276 tons and Complement, 229.

1903 U. S. ARMOURED & FIRST CLASS CRUISERS. 1902--1

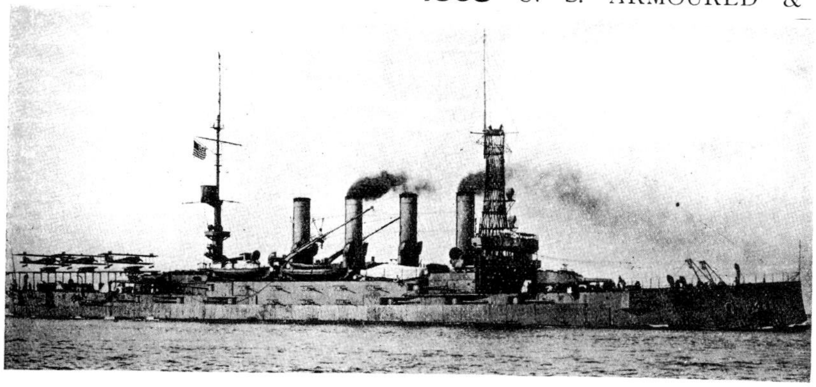

SEATTLE (as Seaplane Carrier—main deck battery now removed). *Photo, O. W. Waterman.*

NORTH CAROLINA* (October 1906), **MONTANA*** (December, 1906), **WASHINGTON** (March 1905). **TENNESSEE** (December 1904).
1905). *Normal* displacement, 14,500 tons. *Full load*, 15,981 tons. *Seattle*, 15,712 tons. Complement (nucleus). Length (*waterline*), 502 feet. Beam, 72⅚ feet. *Maximum* draught, 27 feet. Length *over all*, 504½ feet. Guns (M. '99): 4—10 inch. 40 cal., 4—6 inch, 50 cal., 12—3 inch, 14 pdr., 2—3 inch anti-aircraft, 4—6 or 3 pdr. (saluting). Torpedo tubes (21 inch): 4 *submerged*. Armour (Krupp; but part Midvale in *N.C.* and *M.*): 5"—3" Belt, 3" Deck (ends), 5" Lower deck side, 6" Lower deck bulkheads, 8"—4" Barbettes (N.C.), 9"--5" Turrets, 5" Battery, 2" Battery for 14 pdrs., 9" Conning tower (fore), 5" Tube (N.C.), 5" After C. T. (N.C.). Machinery: 2 sets 4 cylinder triple expansion. 2 screws, outward turning. Boilers: 16 Babcock. Designed H.P. 23,000 = 22 kts. Coal: *normal* 900 tons; *maximum*, *N. Carolina* and *Montana*, 2164 tons; *Seattle*, 2062 tons. Built 1903-8. Fitted with Seaplane Catapults. *Memphis* of this class wrecked 1916.
Renamed Charlotte (ex-*North Carolina), Missoula* (ex-*Montana), Seattle* (ex-*Washington*), *Memphis* (ex-*Tennesse), Memphis* wrecked 1916.

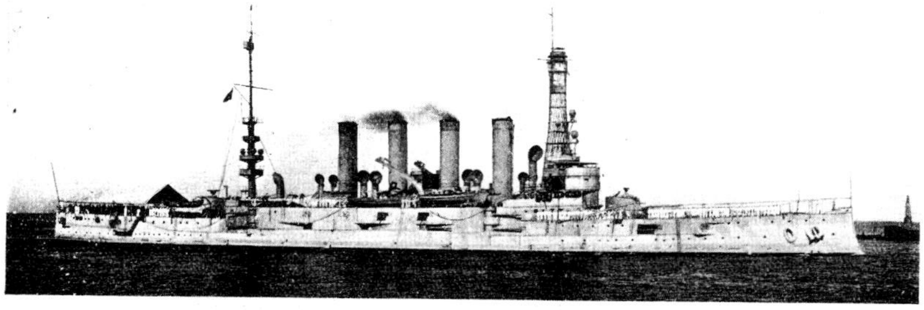

PITTSBURGH.

(Illustration in preceding column.)

HUNTINGTON (April, 1903), **PUEBLO** (April, 1903), **PITTSBURGH** (Aug., 1903), **FREDERICK** (Sept., 1903) & **SOUTH DAKOTA*** (July, 1904). Displacement, *normal*, 13,680 tons, *full load*, 15,138. Complement (nucleus). Length (*waterline*), 502 feet. Beam, 69½ feet. *Maximum* draught, 26 feet at *full load* displacement. Length (*over all*), 504 feet Guns (model 1899): 4—8 inch, 45 cal. (*A*), 4—6 inch, 50 cal., 10—3 inch, 14 pdr., 50 cal., 2—3 inc anti-aircraft. Torpedo tubes (18 in.): 2 *submerged*. Armour (Krupp): 6" Belt, 3½" Belt (ends), 4" Deck (on slopes), 5" Upper belt, 4" Bulkheads, 6" Turrets (N.C.), 5" Battery, 6" Casemates (N.C.), 9" Conning tower (N.C.). Machinery: 2 sets 4 cylinder vertical triple expansion. 2 screws. Boilers: 16 or 20 Babcock & Wilcox. Designed H.P. 23,000 = 22 kts. Coal: *normal* 900 tons; *maximum*, *S. Dakota* 2233 tons; *Frederick* and *Huntington*, 2098 tons; *Pittsburgh*, 1992 tons; and *Pueblo*, 1976 tons. Built 1901-8.

**South Dakota* to be re-named.

Names changed in this period to *Huntinton* (ex *West Virginia, Pueblo* (ex *Colorado), Pittsburgh* (ex *Pennsylvania, Frederick* (ex *Maryland), Huron* (ex *South Dakota), San Diego (ex California), San Diego* sunk by mine off New York 19 July 1918.

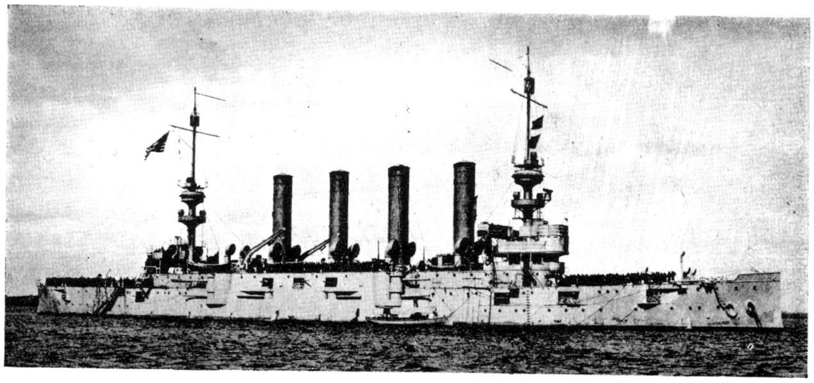

ST. LOUIS. *Photo, O. W. Waterman.*

(Officially rated as First Class Cruisers.)

CHARLESTON (Jan., 1904), **ST. LOUIS** (May, 1905). Displacement, *normal*, 9700 tons, *full load*, 10,839 tons. Complement (nucleus). Length (*waterline*), 424 feet. Beam, 66 feet. *Maximum* draught, 24⅚ feet. Length *over all*, 426½ feet. Guns: 12—6 inch, 50 cal., 4—3 inch, 14 pdr., 2—3 inch AA., and in *Charleston* only, 4—3 pdr. (saluting). Torpedo tubes: *nil*. Armour (Krupp): 4" Belt, 3" Deck, 4" Lower deck redoubt, 4" Battery, 5" Conning tower. Machinery: 2 sets vertical 4 cylinder triple expansion. 2 screws. Boilers: 16 Babcock. Designed H.P. 21,000 = 21·5 kts. Coal: *normal* 650 tons; *maximum* 1818 and 1793 tons. Begun 1902, completed 1905-6. *Milwaukee* of this class wrecked 1917.

1901 U. S. ARMOURED CRUISERS (22 knot).

(CALIFORNIA CLASS—6 SHIPS).

WEST VIRGINIA (April, 1903), **COLORADO** (April, 1903), **PITTSBURG** (Aug., 1903), **MARYLAND** (Sept., 1903), **CALIFORNIA** (April, 1904) & **SOUTH DAKOTA** (July, 1904).

Displacement, *normal*, 13,680 tons, *full load*, 15,138. Complement, 878 (as flagship 921).

Length (*w.l.*), 502 feet. Beam, 69½ feet. *Maximum* draught, 26½ feet at normal displacement. Length (*o.a.*), 504 feet.

—(model 1899):
–8 inch, 45 cal. (*A*).
–6 inch, 50 cal.
–3 inch, 14 pdr., 50 cal.
–3 pdr.
do tubes (18 in.):
ubmerged.
0 tons with two-thirds ammunition).

Armour (Krupp):

6" Belt	*a*
3½" Belt (ends)	*de*
4" Deck (on slopes) ...	
Protection to vitals	= *aa*
5" Upper belt	*b*
4" Bulkheads	*d*
6" Turrets (N.C.)	*b*
6½" fronts to these	= *aa*
4" Hoists to these.........	*d*
5" Battery	*b*
2½" Screens in battery ...	
6" Casemates (N.C.)	*b*
9" Conning tower (N.C.)	*aa*
5" Signal tower (aft) ...	*c*

(Total 2219 tons).

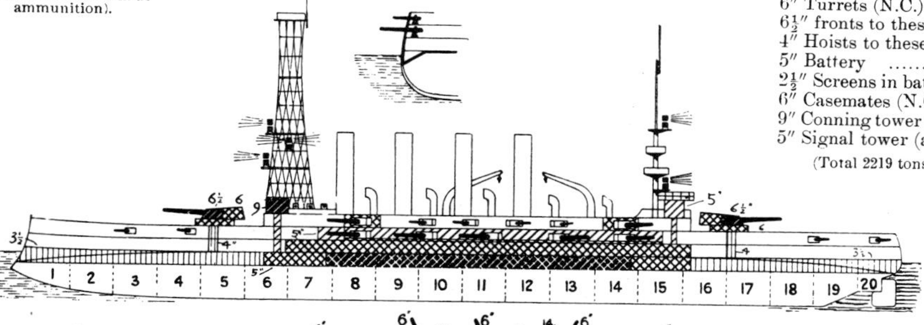

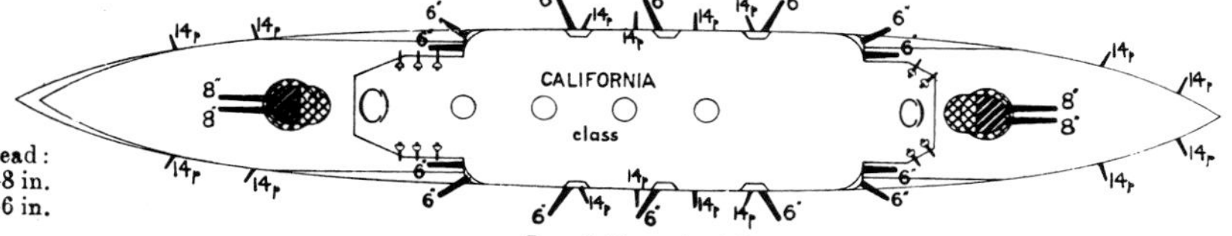

head:
–8 in.
–6 in.

Astern:
2—8 in.
4—6 in.

Broadside: 4—8 in., 7—6 in.

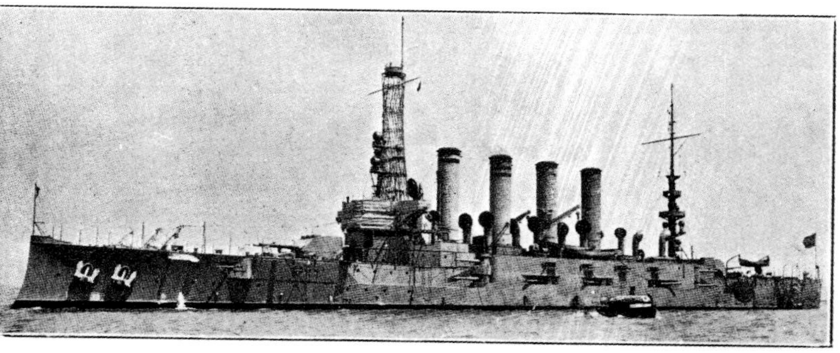

Photo, Müller.

California and *S. Dakota* are without the big cowl abaft foremast.

Class distinction.—Smaller turrets than *Washingtons*.

Machinery: 2 sets 4 cylinder triple expansion. 2 screws. Boilers: See *Engineering Notes*. Designed H.P. 23,000 = 22 kts. Coal: *normal* 900 tons; *maximum* 1929 tons.

Gunnery Notes.—8 inch manœuvred electrically and by hand; electric hoists supply 1 round per 50 seconds.
6 " " by hand; " " " 3 " " minute.

Rounds per gun: 8 inch, 125; 6 inch, 200; 14 pdr., 250; lesser guns, 500 per gun.

Arcs of fire: 8 inch, 270°; casemate and angles of battery, 6 inch, 150°; remaining *starboard*, 6 inch, 75° before the beam and 55° abaft; remaining *port* guns, 55° before only, and 75° abaft; 3 inch, all about 135°.

Armour Notes.—Main belt amidships 244 feet long by 7½ feet wide, 6½ feet below water, 1 foot above. Lowest strake of it is 5" thick. Deck behind belt amidships is only about 2½" on slopes. Cellulose belt. Upper belt, 232 feet long and 7½ feet wide, forming redoubt with 4" bulkheads.

Engineering Notes.—Grate area 1,600 square feet. Heating surface 70,944 square feet. Weight of machinery and boilers, with water, 2,100 tons. The Niclausse boilers of *Pittsburg* and *Colorado* are being gradually replaced by Babcocks. Cylinders: 38½, 63½, 74 and 74 inch. Stroke 48.

General Notes.—Authorised 1899 and 1900. Average cost, *complete*, about £1,200,000 per ship. *Pittsburg* was formerly named *Pennsylvania.*

Name	*Where built*	*Machinery*	*Laid down*	*Completed*	*4 hours full power trial. I.H.P. Kts.*	*Boilers*	*Present best speed*
California	Union Ironw'k.	By builders in each case.	1902	1907	29,381 = 22·20	Babcock	
Pittsburg	Cramp's		1901	1905	28,600 = 22·44	Bab. & Nic.	
West Virginia	Newport News		1901	1905	26,135 = 22·14	Babcock	
Colorado	Cramp's		1901	1905	26,837 = 22·24	Bab. & Nic.	
Maryland	Newport News		1901	1906	28,059 = 22·41	Babcock	22·5
South Dakota	Union Ironw'k.		1902	1907	28,543 = 22·24	Babcock	22·4

1902 U. S. FIRST CLASS CRUISERS (21½ knot).

(ST. LOUIS CLASS.—3 SHIPS.)

CHARLESTON (Jan., 1904), **MILWAUKEE** (Sept., 1904), **ST. LOUIS** (May, 1905).

Sheathed and coppered.

Displacement, *normal*, 9700 tons, *full load*, 10,839 tons. Complement, 727.

Length (*waterline*), 424 feet. Beam, 66 feet. *Maximum* draught, 23¼ feet. Length *over all*, 426½ feet.

Guns :
14—6 inch, 50 cal.
18—3 inch, 14 pdr.
4—3 pdr.
Torpedo tubes :
nil

Armour (Krupp) :
4″ Belt .... *d*
3″ Deck ....
Protection to vitals... = *b*
4″ Lower deck redoubt *d*
4″ Battery .... *d*
4″ Casemates .... *d*
5″ Conning tower ...... *d*
3″ Tube ....
(Total 854 tons, including cellulose.)

Ahead :
5—6 in.

St. Louis.

Astern :
5—6 in.

Broadside fire : 8 —6 in.

Machinery : 2 sets vertical 4 cylinder triple expansion. 2 screws. Boilers : 16 Babcock and Wilcox. Designed H.P. 21,000 = 21·5 kts. Coal : *normal* 650 tons ; *maximum* 1776 tons.

Armour Notes—The belt is partial ; 197 feet long, by 7½ feet wide. Armour weighs 854 tons.

Gunnery Notes—All guns fitted with electric hoists, which will serve 6 rounds per minute to 6 inch guns, and 15 per minute to the 3 inch 14-pounder guns.

Arcs of fire : Fore and aft 6 inch, 270° ; upper casemate guns 145° from axial line ; end guns main deck 130° (85° ahead and 55° astern for fore ones, *vice versâ* for after) : other guns 110°.

Weight of ammunition *normal* 519 tons.

Engineering Notes.—Heating surface 64,000 sq. ft., grate area, 1,400 sq. ft., working pressure 265, cylinders 36, 59½, 69 and 69 inches diameter. Stroke 45 inches. Average weight 1,800 tons. Electric plant 2 sets 100 k.w., 125 v. and 3 sets 50 k w., 125 v.

ST. LOUIS.   *Photo, Müller.*

Name.	Builders.	Machinery.	Laid down.	Completed	Refit.	Trials, 5 runs mile f.p. at 143 revs.	Boilers.	Present best speed
Charleston	Newport News		1902	1905		27,200 = 22·04	Babcock	
Milwaukee	Union I.W., 'Frisco		1902	1906		24,166 = 22·22	Babcock	
St. Louis	Neafie & Levy		1902	1906		27,264 = 22·13	Babcock	22·4

Consumption : Burn about 19¼—20 tons an hour at 21,000 H.P.

General Notes—Hull and armour deck weigh 5346 tons. Although armoured amidships these ships are officially rated as armoured cruisers.

Milwaukee wrecked 1917.

OLD U.S. FIRST CLASS CRUISERS.

New photo wanted.   *Photo, Rau.*

BROOKLYN (1895). *Normal* displacement, 9215 tons ; *full load*, 10,068 tons. Complement, 729. Length (*waterline*), 400½ feet. Beam, 64⅔ feet. *Maximum* draught, 26¼ feet. Guns : 8—8 inch, 35 cal. (E), 8—5 inch, 40 cal., 2—3 inch (anti-aircraft), 4—6 pdr. (saluting). Torpedo tubes : *Nil.* Armour (Harvey): 3″ Belt, 6″ Deck (amidships), 3″ Deck (ends), 8″ Barbettes, 5½″ Hoods to barbettes, 6″ Hoists, 4″ Shields (fixed), 5″ guns, 7½″ Conning tower. Machinery : 4 sets vertical triple expansion. 2 screws. Boilers : 7 cylindrical (5 double-ended and 2 single-ended). Designed H.P. *forced* 18,000 = 21 kts. Coal : *normal* 900 tons ; *maximum* 1449 tons. Laid down 1893. Completed 1896. Reconstructed 1909.

Photo, Lieut. H. Reuterdahl, U.S.N./R.F.

(*Flagship, Destroyer Force, Atlantic Fleet.*)

ROCHESTER (ex *Saratoga*, ex *New York*). (December, 1891.) (Reconstructed 1907-08.) *Normal* displacement, 8150 tons ; *full load*, 8900 tons. Complement, 630. Length (*waterline*), 380½ feet. Beam, 64⅔ feet. *Maximum* draught, 24⅝ feet. Guns : 4—8 inch, 45 cal. (A), 8—5 inch, 50 cal., 8—3 inch AA. Torpedo tubes : *Nil.* Armour (Harvey nickel) : 4″ Belt, 6″ Deck (amidships) ; (Krupp) 6″—4″ Barbettes, 6½″ Turrets ; 5″ Hoists, 7″ Conning tower. Machinery : 4 sets vertical triple expansion. 2 screws. Boilers (1907) : 12 Babcock. Designed H.P. *forced* 16,500 = 21 kts. Coal : *normal* 750 tons ; *maximum* 1100 tons. Laid down at Philadelphia, Sept., 1890. Completed 1893. Re-named *Saratoga*, 1911, and again re-named *Rochester*, 1917. Large refit in 1917.

OLD U. S. SECOND CLASS CRUISERS.

New photo wanted, as re-armed 1917-18.

OLYMPIA (November, 1892). *Normal* displacement, 5865 tons (*full load* 6588 tons). Complement, 439. Length (*waterline*) 340 feet. Beam 53 feet. *Maximum* draught, 25 feet. Guns: 10—5 inch (51 cal.), 2—1 pdr. Armour: 4¾″ deck on slopes, 2″ flat.

Machinery: 2 sets vertical inverted triple expansion. 2 screws. Boilers: 4 double-ended and 2 single-ended. Designed H.P. *forced* 17,000 = 21·69 kts. Coal: *normal* 500 tons ; *maximum* 1169 tons.

General Notes.—Laid down at San Francisco, June, 1891. Completed 1895. Cost, *complete*, about £550,000. Flagship of the late Admiral Dewey, at battle of Manila. Reconstructed partially 1901-03, re-armed 1917-18.

BALTIMORE (1888). Displacement, 4413 tons. Complement, 374. Dimensions: 327 (*w.l.*) × 48¼ × 19½ (*mean*) feet. Guns: 12—6 inch, 40 cal., 4—6 pdr. Armour: 4″ deck. Designed H.P. 8500 = 20 kts. Boilers: 8 Babcock. Coal: *maximum* 1075 tons.

(*Flagship, Train, Atlantic Fleet.*)

COLUMBIA (see next column for details). *Photo, O. W. Waterman.*

MINNEAPOLIS. *Photo, Geiser.*

(*Flagship, Train, Pacific Fleet.*)

COLUMBIA (July, 1892), & **MINNEAPOLIS** (August, 1893). Displacement, 7,350 tons. Complement, 480 and 489. Length (*waterline*), 411½ feet. Beam, 58¼ feet. *Maximum* draught, 24½ feet. Guns: 3—6 inch, 45 cal., 4—4 inch, 40 cal., 2—3 inch AA. (and 2—1 pdr. in *Minneapolis*).

Machinery: 3 sets vertical inverted triple expansion. 3 screws. Boilers: 8 double-ended, 2 single-ended cylindrical. Designed H.P. *forced* 18,500 = 22·80 kts. Coal: *normal* 750 tons ; *maximum* 1561 tons in *Columbia*, 1433 tons in *Minneapolis*.

CHICAGO (1885). Displacement, 4500 tons. Complement, 333. Armament: 4—5 inch, 51 cal., 1—3 pdr., 2—1 pdr., 2 M.G. Designed H.P. 9000 = 18 kts. Boilers: 6 Babcock + 4 S.E. Coal, 870 tons.

1905 U. S. THIRD CLASS CRUISERS. **1900**

BIRMINGHAM. (CHESTER CLASS—3 SHIPS.) *Photo, O. W Waterman.*

SALEM (July, 1907), **BIRMINGHAM** (May, 1907), **CHESTER** (June, 1907).

Normal Displacement, 3750 tons ; *full load*, 4687 tons. Complement, 392 (B'ham 410, flag 451).

Length (*waterline*), 420 feet. Beam, 47 feet. { *Maximum* draught, 18¾ feet. } Length *over all*, 423 feet. { Mean ,, 16¾ }

(Dir. Con.)   Armour :
5 inch, 51 cal.   2″ Nickel on w.l.........
3 inch, 50 cal.   2″—1″ Steering gear
3 inch AA   protection............
do tubes (21 inch):   2″—1″ Protection to
ove water.   **Note.**   engines............
. Re-armed 1917-18. No plans available of new gun positions.   No conning tower.

Machinery: *Salem*, G. E. turbines with reduction gear (new 1916-17). *Chester*, Parsons' turbine. 4 screws. ingham, 2 sets 4 cylinder triple expansion. 2 screws. Boilers: various (*see Notes*). Designed H.P. a (with new turbines) 20,000, *Birmingham* and *Chester*, 16,000 = 24 kts.

normal 475 tons ; *maximum*, *Salem* and *Birmingham* 1433 tons ; *Chester*, 1408 tons.

Name.	Builder.	Laid down.	Completed.	Refit.	Trials :—4 hours full p.	Boilers.	Best recent speed.
m (t)	Fore River Co.	Aug., '05	July, '08	1916-17	15,273 = 25·95*	12 Fore River	
ningham	Fore River Co.	Aug., '05	Apl., '08		15,476 = 24·32	12 Fore River	
ster (t)	Bath Ironworks	Sept., '05	Apl., '08		25,400 = 26·52†	12 Normand	

* With original Curtis turbines.   † Light on trials, 3673 tons.

al Notes:—Authorised 1904, re-armed 1917-18. Average cost, *exclusive* of armament, £325,000 each. hese ships are good sea boats, but roll heavily. All now serve as Flagships to Destroyer Forces, Atlantic nd Pacific Fleet. Are very lightly built, and cannot maintain full power for any length of time.

CLEVELAND. (Foremost pair of 5 inch guns on main deck now removed.) *Photo, O. W Waterman.*

(DENVER CLASS—6 SHIPS.)

CHATTANOOGA (March, 1903), **CLEVELAND** (September, 1901), **DENVER** (June, 1902), **DES MOINES** (September, 1902), **GALVESTON** (July, 1903), & **TACOMA** (June, 1903). (Wood sheathed and coppered). *Normal* displacement, 3,200 tons. Complement, 299 to 338. Length (*waterline*), 292 feet. Beam, 44 feet. *Maximum* draught, 17 feet. Guns (model 1899): 8— 5 inch, 50 cal., 6—6 pdr., 2 landing. No torpedo tubes. Armour (Harvey-nickel): 2½″ Deck (on slopes), ¼″ (flat) Machinery: 2 sets 4 cylinder triple expansion. 2 screws. Boilers: 6 Babcock & Wilcox. Designed H.P. 5,398 = 16·5 kts. Coal: *normal* 467 tons ; *maximum* 705 to 741 tons = 7,000 miles at 10 kts. *nominal*.

Notes.—15 " Long arm " doors to the first four. Length *over all* varies from 308′-6″ to 309′-10″. Are remarkably good sea boats.

Name.	Builder	Machinery	Laid down	Completed	Refit	Trials full p.	Boilers	Present best speed
Chattanooga	Crescent Co. P.		1900	1904		5227 = 16·65		
Cleveland	Bath Ironw'rks		1900	1903		4586 = 16·45		...
Denver	Neafie & Levy		1900	1904		6073 = 16·75	Babcock	
Des Moines	Fore River Co		1900	1904		5059 = 16·65	in all.	15·7
Galveston	W. R. Trigg		1901	1905		4984 = 16·41		...
Tacoma	Union Ironw'k		1900	1904		5235 = 16·58		16

OLD U.S. THIRD CLASS CRUISERS.

(NEW ORLEANS CLASS—2 SHIPS.)

ALBANY.
Photo, O. W. Waterman.

(RALEIGH CLASS—2 SHIPS.)

RALEIGH.
Photo, U. S. Recruiting Bureau.

NEW ORLEANS (Dec., 1896) & **ALBANY** (Jan., 1899). *Normal* displacement, 3430 tons (*full load*, 3954). Complement, 326. Length (*w.l.*), 326 feet. Beam, 43¾ feet. *Maximum* draught, 19 feet. Length *over all*, 354⅚ feet. Guns (U.S. models) : 8—5 inch, 50 cal., 2—3 or 1 pdr. No torpedo tubes. Armour (Harvey-nickel) : 3½″ Deck (slopes) and Cofferdam amidships, no gun shields, 1¼″ Deck (flat). Machinery : 2 sets 3 cylinder triple expansion. 2 screws. Boilers : 4 double-ended. Designed H.P. forced 7500 = 20 kts. Coal : *normal* 450 tons ; *maximum* 782 tons in *Albany*, 693 tons in *New Orleans*.

General Notes.—Laid down at Elswick (for Brazil) as the *Amazonas* (*New Orleans*) and *Abreu* (*Albany*). Purchased by U. S. (1898) just before war with Spain. *Albany* completed 1900, *New Orleans* 1898. Re-armed with U. S. guns, 1907.

MARBLEHEAD.
U.S. Navy photo.

ANNISTON (ex *Montgomery*, 1891), **MARBLEHEAD** (1892) 2072 tons. Complement, 260—263. Dimensions : 257 *w.l.* × 37 × 14½ feet, *mean* draught. Guns : 8 - 4 inch. Designed H.P. 5400 = 17 kts. Machinery : 2 sets inverted triple expansion. Boilers : *Anniston* 6 Almy ; *Marblehead* 3 D.E. and 2 S.E. Coal : 346 tons.

Gunboats.

SACRAMENTO (Feb., 1914). *Normal* displacement, 1425 tons. Complement, 163. Length (*waterline*), 210 feet. Beam, 50⅚ feet. *Mean* draught, 11½ feet. Guns : 3—4 inch, 50 cal. ; 2—1 pdr. Machinery : 1 set triple expansion. Boilers : 2 Babcock. H.P. (on trials), 1022 = 12·78 kts. Coal : *maximum*, 428 tons. Built by Cramps. Completed, 1914.

WILMETTE (ex s.s. *Eastland*, 1903, taken over 1918). 2,600 tons. Complement, 181. Length (*waterline*), 265 feet. Beam, 38½ feet. Draught, feet. Guns : 4—4 inch, 2—3 inch AA., 2—1 pdr. Machinery : 2 sets triple expansion. 2 screws. Boilers : Designed I.H.P. 4000 = 16·5 kts. Fuel, tons.

CINCINNATI.
Photo, U. S. Navy Recruiting Bureau.

RALEIGH (Norfolk N.Y., March, 1892) & **CINCINNATI** (New York N.Y., Nov., 1892). *Normal* displacement, 3183 tons (*full load* 3339 tons). Complement : 282 and 317. Length (*w.l.*), 300 feet. Beam, 42 feet. *Maximum* draught, 19½ feet. Length *over all*, 306 feet. Guns (M. '99) : 9—5 inch, 40 cal., 4—6 pdr. S.A. No torpedo tubes. Armour (steel) : 2½″ Armour deck, 2″ Conning tower. Machinery : 2 sets 4 cylinder vertical triple expansion (new 1900-2). 2 screws. Boilers : 8 Babcock and Wilcox. Designed H.P. 8,000 = 18 kts. Coal : *normal* 396 tons ; *maximum* 720 tons. Laid down 1892, completed 1894, re-built and re-armed 1901-3.

(Continued on next page.)

SAMOA (ex German s.s. *Staatssekretaer Solf*) (1913, seized 1917 550 tons. Complement, 32. Dimension : 131 (*waterline*) × 25 × feet. Guns : 4—3 pdr., 2 M.G. Machinery : 1 set ver compound. H.P., Speed and Fuel not known.

DUBUQUE.
Photo, Navy Dept.

DUBUQUE (1904), **PADUCAH** (1904). *Normal* displacement, 1085 tons. Complement, 190 and 176. Length (*waterline*), 174 feet. Beam, 35 feet. *Mean* draught, 12¼ feet. Guns : *Dubuque*, 2—4 inch, *Paducah*, 4—4 inch, and in both, 4—6 pdr., 2—1 pdr. Machinery : 2 sets triple expansion. 2 screws. Boilers : 2 Babcock. Designed H.P. 1000 = 12·9 kts. Coal : *maximum* 252 tons.

WHEELING.
Photo, Fons.

MARIETTA & **WHEELING** (1897). *Normal* displacement, 99 tons. Complements, 182 and 163. Length (*waterline*), 174 feet. Beam, 34 feet. *Mean* draught, 12 feet. Guns : 4—4 inch, 40 cal. 2—3 pdr. ; 2—1 pdr. (+1-Y in *Wheeling*). Machinery : 2 set vertical triple expansion. 2 screws. Boilers : *Marietta*, 2 Babcock *Wheeling*, 2 single-ended. Designed H.P. 1250 = 13 kts. Coal *maximum*, 234 and 256 tons. *Nominal radius* : 4000 at 10 kts.

U. S. GUNBOATS.—(Continued).

(Mainmast of *Princeton* removed). *Photo, Abraham & Sons.*

ANNAPOLIS (1896). **NEWPORT** (1896). **PRINCETON.**
Normal displacement, 1010 tons. Complement, 165—147. Length (*waterline*), 168 feet. Beam, 36 feet. *Mean* draught, 12 feet. Guns : *Annapolis*, 6—4 inch, 4—6 pdr., 1 Y-gun. *Newport*, 1—4 inch, 2—3 inch, 2—6 pdr. *Princeton*, none. Machinery : 1 set vertical triple expansion. 1 screw. Boilers : 2 Babcock. Designed H.P. 800 = 12 kts. Coal : 235 tons.

Notes.—Vicksburg now Fisheries Protection Gunboat, Alaska.

HELENA (1896) & **WILMINGTON** (1895). Displacement, 1392 tons. Complement, 207 *average*. Length (*waterline*), 250¾ feet. Beam, 39¾ feet. *Mean* draught, 9 feet. Guns : 8—4 inch, 40 cal. ; 4—3 pdr. Machinery : 2 sets vertical triple expansion. 2 screws. Designed H.P. 1988 = 13 kts. Coal : *maximum*, 258 tons in *Wilmington* ; 307 tons in *Helena*. Nominal radius : 2200 miles at 10 kts.

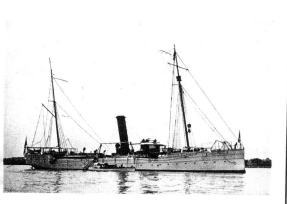

Photo, Navy Dept.
(*Used as Yacht by the Secretary of the Navy*.)

DOLPHIN (1884). 1486 tons. Complement, 156. Guns : 2—3 inch, 4—6 pdr. Speed, 15·5 kts. Coal : 255 tons.

NANTUCKET (ex *Rockport*, ex *Ranger*, 1876). 1261 tons. Guns : 1—4 inch, 2—3 inch. I.H.P. 500 = 10 kts. Coal, 182 tons.

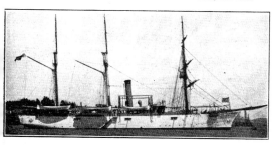

Mainmast now removed.
ALERT (1875). 1100 tons. Complement : 137. Dimensions : 177⅓ × 32 × 13 feet (*mean* draught). Guns : 1—6 pdr. H.P. 500 = 10 kts. 2 Babcock boilers. Coal : 202 tons.

ESSEX (1874). 1375 tons. Guns : 6—3 pdr. H.P. 800 = 10 kts. Coal : 155 tons.

Photo, copyright, Rau.
NASHVILLE (1895). 1371 tons. Guns : 8—4 inch, 4—6 pdr., 2—1 pdr., 2 machine. 2¼″ sponsons to 4 inch guns. H.P. 2500 = 16 kts. Coal : 381 tons. Complement 188.

MACHIAS. *Photo, U.S. Navy.*
CASTINE (1892), **MACHIAS** (1891). 1177 tons. Complement, 182—177. Guns : *Castine*, 2—4 inch, 6—6 pdr., 2—1 pdr., 1 Y-gun ; *Machias*, 4—4 inch, 2—3 pdr., 2—1 pdr. Speed, 15½ to 16 kts. Coal : *Castine*, 246 tons ; *Machias*, 267 tons.

YORKTOWN (1888). 1710 tons. Complement, 219. Guns : 6—5 inch, (40 cal.), 4—6 pdr., 2—1 pdr. Original speed, 17 kts. Coal : 336 tons.

GOPHER (1871). 840 tons. 5—3 pdr., 4—1 pdr. Speed, 9 kts. Coal : 80 tons.

WOLVERINE (1842). 685 tons. H.P. 365 = 10·5 kts. Paddle wheel. Coal : 115 tons. Guns : 6—3 pdr.

YANTIC (1864). 900 tons. 4—3 pdr., 2—1 pdr. H.P. 310 = 8·3 kts. Coal : 130 tons.

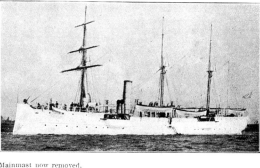

Mainmast now removed.
PETREL (1888). Displacement, 890 tons. Complement, 135. Guns : 4—4 inch, (40 cal.), 2—3 pdr., 2—1 pdr. Designed H.P. 1000 = 11·5 kts. Coal : 198 tons.

DON JUAN DE AUSTRIA (1887). 1130 tons. Guns : 4—4 inch. 2—1 pdr. H.P. 941 = 12·2 kts. Coal : 201 tons.

Small Gunboats for Service in the Philippines.

MONOCACY. *Photo, Leslie's Weekly.*
MONOCACY (1914), **PALOS** (1914). 190 tons. Complement, 47. Guns : 2—6 pdr., 6 machine. Machinery : 2 sets vertical compound. Boilers : 2 Babcock. Designed H.P. 800 = 13¼ kts. Coal : 34 tons. Built at Mare Island Navy Yard and re-erected by Shanghai Dock and Engineering Co.

QUIROS (1895), **VILLALOBOS** (1896). 360 tons. Complement, 56. Guns : 4—3 pdr. Designed H.P. 550 = 11 kts. Coal : 70 tons.

CALLAO (1888), **PAMPANGA** (1888), **SAMAR** (1888). 243 tons. Guns : *Callao* none ; others 4—3 pdr. Speed, 10 to 10½ kts. Coal : 33 tons. Old gunboats captured in Spanish War.

No photo available.
ECLANO (1885). 620 tons. Complement, 99. Guns : 4—4 inch, 4—3 pdr. Speed, 11 kts. Coal : 98 tons. Old gunboat captured in Spanish War.

Note.

Romblon, Bobol, Cebu, Jolo, Marie Duque, (Uraga Dock Co., 1902-3), are small gunboats belonging to the War Department, Philippines. 350 tons. Guns : 3 small Q. F. Designed H.P. 450 = 10 kts.

U. S. DESTROYERS—Continued.

68 Boats by various Yards. (Flush Deckers.)

12 boats (not contracted for): Nos. 348—359. Construction of these boats may not be proceeded with.

3 *Bath I. W.*: Nos. 345, 346, 347. Designed S.H.P. 26,000 = 35 kts. Parsons turbines and reduction gears. 2 screws. 4 Normand boilers—27,000 sq. ft. heating surface. Other details as "General Notes."

39 *Bethlehem S. B. Co.* (San Francisco): **Chase, Farquhar, Farragut, Fuller, John Francis Burns, Kennedy, Kidder, La Valette, Marcus, Mervine, Mullany, Nicholas, Paul Hamilton, Percival, Reno, Robert Smith, Selfridge, Shirk, Sloat, S. P. Lee, Somers, Stoddert, Thompson, William Jones, Wood, Woodbury, Yarborough, Young, Zeilin,** Nos. 320—355. Designed H.P. 27,000 = 35 kts. Machinery: in *Farragut, Fuller, J. F. Burns* and *Percival*, Curtis turbines with reduction gear; in others, G. E. turbines and reduction gear. 2 screws. 4 Yarrow boilers—27,540 sq. ft. heating surface. Other details as "General Notes."

6 *Mare Island N. Y.*: **Lichfield, Trever, Wasmuth, Lane,** Nos. 340—341. S.H.P., speed, turbines, boilers, as Bath I. W. boats above. Other details as "General Notes."

3 *Norfolk N. Y.*: **Hulbert, Noa, William B. Preston.** S.H.P., speed, turbines, boilers, as Bath I. W. boats above. Other details as "General Notes."

5 *New York S. B. Co.*: **Brooks, Fox, Gilmer, Humphreys, Kane.** Designed S.H.P. 27,000 = 35 kts. Westinghouse turbines with reduction gear. 4 White-Forster boilers—27,500 sq. ft. heating surface. Other details as "General Notes."

General Notes.—Normal displacement, 1215 tons (1308 *full load*). Dimensions: 310 (*w.l.*) × 30' 11½" × 9½ feet *mean* draught (9' 9¾" *full load*). Armament: 4—5 inch, 51 cal., 1—3 inch, 23 cal. AA., 12—21 inch tubes in 4 triple deck mountings. (S.H.P., speed, machinery and boilers are separately noted under builders.) Oil fuel: tons. Complement, . Are same as boats described immediately hereafter, but are more powerfully armed.

Bethlehem, San Francisco

	Begun.	Launch.	Comp.
Chase ..	Yes	....	....
Farquhar ..	13/8/18	18/1/19	....
Farragut ..	4/7/18	21/11/18	....
Fuller ..	4/7/18	5/12/18	....
J. F. Burns ..	4/7/18	10/11/18	....
Kennedy ..	25/9/18	15/2/19	....
Kidder ..	5/3/19	Yes	....
La Valette ..	Yes	....	....
Marcus ..	....	22/8/19	....
Mervine ..	....	11/8/19	....
Mullany ..	....	....	....
Nicholas ..	11/1/19	....	....
P. Hamilton ..	25/9/18	21/2/19	....
Percival ..	4/7/18	5/12/18	....
Reno ..	4/7/18	22/1/19	....
R. Smith ..	Yes	....	....
Selfridge ..	Yes	....	....
Shirk ..	13/2/19	....	....
Sloat ..	18/1/19	....	....
S. P. Lee ..	31/12/18	22/3/19	....
Somers ..	4/7/18	28/12/18	....
Stoddert ..	4/7/18	8/1/19	....
Thompson ..	14/8/18	15/1/19	....
Wm. Jones ..	2/10/18	....	....
Wood ..	23/1/19	....	....
Woodbury ..	3/10/18	8/2/19	....
Yarborough ..	27/2/19	....	....
Young ..	20/1/19	....	....
Zeilin ..	20/1/19	....	....

Navy Yards

	Begun.	Launch.	Comp.
Hulbert ..	18/11/18	....	....
Litchfield ..	15/1/19	5/7/19	....
Noa ..	18/11/18	....	....
Trever ..	Yes	....	....
Wasmuth ..	Yes	....	....
W. B. Preston ..	18/11/18	....	....
Zane ..	15/1/19	5/7/19	....

N.Y.S.B. Co.

	Begun.	Launch.	Comp.
Brooks ..	11/6/18	24/4/19	....
Fox ..	25/6/18	12/6/19	....
Gilmer ..	25/6/18	24/5/19	....
Humphreys ..	31/7/18	18/7/19	....
Kane ..	3/7/18	....	....

100 boats, by various yards, (Flush Deckers).

10 *Bethlehem S. B. Co.* (Quincy): **Aulick, Bancroft, Belknap, Gillis, Ingram, McCalla, McCook, Rodgers,** (ex *Kalk*), **Turner, Welles.** Designed S.H.P. 27,000=35 kts. Curtis turbines and reduction gear. 2 screws. 4 Yarrow boilers—27,540 sq. ft. heating surface. Other details as "General Notes."

35 *Bethlehem Destroyer Plant* (Squantum): **Bailey, Ballard, Breck, Delphy, Doyen, Edwards, Greene, Henshaw, Laub, McCawley, McDermut, McLanahan, Meade, Meyer, Moody, Morris, Sharkey, Shubrick, Sinclair, Swasey, Thornton, Tingey, Toucey,** Nos. 284—288 (begun), Nos. 289—295 (contracted for). Designed S.H.P. 2700 = 25 kts. Curtis turbines with reduction gear. 4 Yarrow boilers—27,540 sq. ft. heating surface. Other details as "General Notes."

25 *Cramp* (Philadelphia): **Alden, Barker, Borie, Broome, Chandler, Hovey, Long, Smith Thompson, Southard, Tracy,** Nos. 216, 217 (begun), Nos. 218—230 (contracted for). Designed S.H.P. 27,500 = 35 kts. Parsons turbines with reduction gear, 2 screws. 4 White-Forster boilers—27,500 sq. ft. heating surface in *Chandler, Hovey* and *Southard*, 27,000 in remainder. Other details as "General Notes."

14 *Newport News*: **Abel P. Upshur, Branch, Clemson, Dahlgren, Dallas, George E. Badger, Goldsborough, Graham, Herndon, Hunt, Mason, Satterlee, Semmes, Welborn C. Wood.** (Contract for Nos. 200—205 has been cancelled). Designed S.H.P. 27,000 = 35 kts. Westinghouse turbines with reduction gear. 2 screws. 4 White-Forster boilers—27,500 sq. ft. heating surface. Other details as "General Notes."

15 *New York S. B. Co.*: **Childs, Hatfield, James L. Paulding, King, McFarland, Overton, Sturtevant,** Nos. 244—250. Designed S.H.P. 27,000 = 35 kts. Machinery: *Hatfield* has Parsons turbines and reduction gear; remainder Westinghouse turbines and reduction gear. 2 screws in all; also 4 White-Forster boilers—27,500 sq. ft. heating surface. Other details as "General Notes."

1 *Union I. W.*: **Chauncey,** Designed S.H.P. 27,500 = 35 kts. Curtis turbines with reduction gear. 2 screws. 4 White-Forster boilers—27,500 sq. ft. heating surface.

General Notes.—Normal displacement, 1215 tons (1308 *full load*). Dimensions: 310 (*w.l.*) × 30' 11½" × 9½ feet *mean* draught (9' 9¾" *full load*). Armament: 4—4 inch, 50 cal., 1—3 inch, 23 cal. AA., 12—21 inch tubes in 4 triple deck mountings. (S.H.P., speed, machinery, boilers, as separately noted to each class). Oil fuel: —— tons. Complement, 139 (War).

Bethlehem (Quincy).

	Begun.	Launch.	Comp.
Aulick ..	Yes	11/4/19	....
Bancroft ..	4/11/18	21/3/19	....
Belknap ..	3/10/18	14/1/19	28/4/19
Gillis ..	27/12/18	....	....
Ingram ..	15/10/18	28/2/19	....
McCalla ..	25/9/18	18/2/19	30/4/19
McCook ..	10/9/18	31/2/19	19/5/19
Rodgers ..	5/10/18	26/4/19	....
Turner ..	21/12/18	17/5/19	....
Welles ..	18/11/18	8/5/19	....

Bethlehem (Squantum).

	Begun.	Launch.	Comp.
Bailey ..	3/6/18	5/2/19	Yes
Ballard ..	3/6/18	7/12/18	5/6/19
Breck ..	24/5/19	....	....
Delphy ..	20/4/18	18/7/18	30/11/18
Doyen ..	24/3/19	26/7/19	....
Edwards ..	20/4/18	10/10/18	24/4/19
Greene ..	3/6/18	2/11/18	9/5/19
Henshaw ..	31/12/18	28/6/19	....
Laub ..	20/4/18	25/8/18	17/3/19
McCawley ..	4/11/18	14/6/19	....
McDermut ..	20/4/18	6/8/18	27/3/19
Mc Lanahan ..	20/4/18	22/9/18	5/4/19
Meade ..	24/9/18	24/5/19	....
Meyer ..	6/2/19	....	....
Moody ..	10/12/18	28/6/19	....
Morris ..	20/7/18	12/4/19	Yes
Sharkey ..	14/4/19	....	....
Shubrick ..	3/6/18	31/12/19	3/7/19
Sinclair ..	10/10/18	2/6/19	....
Swasey ..	27/8/18	7/5/19	Yes
Thornton ..	3/6/18	22/3/19	Yes
Tingey ..	8/8/18	24/4/19	Yes
Toucey ..	26/4/19	....	....
(283) ..	8/5/19		
(285) ..	3/6/19		
(286) ..	16/6/19		Not launched.
(287) ..	30/6/19		Not completed.
(288) ..	30/6/19		

Cramp.

	Begun.	Launch.	Comp.
Alden ..	24/10/18	7/6/19	....
Barker ..	30/4/19	....	....
Borie ..	30/4/19	....	....
Broome ..	8/10/18	14/5/19	....
Chandler ..	19/3/19	19/3/19	....
Hovey ..	7/9/18	26/4/19	....
Long ..	23/9/18	26/4/19	....
S. Thompson ..	24/3/19	....	....
Southard ..	18/8/18	31/3/19	....
Tracy ..	3/4/19	....	....
(216) ..	21/5/19	....	....
(217) ..	12/6/19	....	....

Newport News.

	Begun.	Launch.	Comp.
A. P. Upshur ..	20/8/18	....	....
Clemson ..	11/5/18	5/9/18	Yes
Dahlgren ..	8/6/18	20/11/18	Yes
Dallas ..	25/11/18	....	....
G. E. Badger ..	24/9/18	....	....
Goldsboro' ..	8/6/18	20/11/18	....
Graham ..	7/9/18	....	....
Herndon ..	25/11/18	....	....
Hunt ..	20/8/18	....	....
Mason ..	10/7/18	....	....
Satterlee ..	10/7/18	21/12/18	....
Semmes ..	10/7/18	21/12/18	....
W. C. Wood ..	24/9/18	....	....

N.Y.S.B. Co.

	Begun.	Launch.	Comp.
Childs ..	19/3/19	....	....
Hatfield ..	10/6/18	17/3/19	....
J. L. Paulding ..	31/7/18	....	....
King ..	28/4/19	....	....
McFarland ..	31/7/18	....	....
Overton ..	30/10/18	....	....
Sands ..	22/3/19	....	....
Sturtevant ..	23/11/18	....	....
(244) ..	27/3/19	....	....
(245) ..	2/4/19	....	....
(246) ..	27/5/19	....	....
(247) ..	16/6/19	....	....
(248) ..	26/7/19	....	....
(249) ..	30/7/19	....	....
(250) ..	Yes	....	....

U.I.W.

	Begun.	Launch.	Comp.
Chauncey ..	17/6/18	29/8/18	....

U. S. DESTROYERS—*Continued.*

11 Newport News boats. (Flush Deckers.)

LAMBERTON.   *Photo by courtesy of Navy Dept. (Bureau C. & R.).*

11 *Newport News*: **Abbott, Bagley, Breese, Gamble, Haraden, Hopewell, Lamberton, Montgomery, Radford, Ramsay, Thomas.**

General Notes.—*Normal* displacement 1213 tons, 1306 *full load*). Dimensions : 310 (*w.l.*) × 30′ 11¼″ × 9′ 3⅜″ *mean* draught (9′ 9¾″ *full load*). Armament : 4—4 inch, 50 cal., 2—3 inch, 23 cal. AA. Designed S.H.P. 25,000 = 35 kts. 2 screws. Machinery : Parsons (geared cruising) turbines. Boilers : 4 Thornycroft—28,000 sq. ft. heating surface. Oil : —— tons. Complement, 139 (War).

		Begun.	Launch.	Comp.			Begun.	Launch.	Comp.
Abbot ..	..	5/4/18	4/7/18	Yes	Lamberton	..	1/10/17	30/3/18	Yes
Bagley	..	11/5/18	19/10/18	Yes	Montgomery ..		2/10/17	23/3/18	26/7/18
Breese	..	10/11/17	11/5/18	23/10/18	Radford		2/10/17	5/4/18	30/9/18
Gamble	..	12/11/17	11/5/18	29/11/18	Ramsay	..	21/12/17	8/6/18	Yes
Haraden	..	30/3/18	4/7/18	6/6/19	Thomas	..	23/3/18	4/7/18	Yes
Hopewell	..	19/1/18	8/6/18	Yes					

10 New York S. B. boats. (Flush Deckers.)

10 *New York S. B. Co.*: **Babbitt, Badger, De Long, Dickerson, Herbert; Jacob Jones, Leary, Schenck, Tattnall, Twiggs.**

General Notes.—Displacements, 1211 tons *normal* (1304 or 1306 *full load*). Dimensions : 310 (*w.l.*) × 30′ 11¼″ × 9¼ feet *mean* draught (9′ 9½″ *full load*). Armament : 4—4 inch, 50 cal. 2—3 inch, 23 cal. AA. Torpedo tubes : 12—21 inch, in 4 triple deck mountings. Designed S.H.P. 36,000 = 35 kts. 2 screws. Machinery : Parsons turbines with reduction gear. 4 Thornycroft boilers—27,048 sq. ft. heating surface. Oil only : —— tons. Complement, 139 (War).

		Begun.	Launch.	Comp.			Begun.	Launch.	Comp.
Babbitt	..	19/2/18	30/9/18	....	Jacob Jones	..	21/2/18	20/11/18	....
Badger	..	9/1/18	24/8/18	29/5/19	Leary	..	5/3/18	21/12/18	....
De Long	..	21/2/18	29/10/18	....	Schenck	..	26/3/18	23/4/19	....
Dickerson	..	25/5/18	12/3/19	....	Tattnall	..	1/12/17	5/9/18	26/6/19
Herbert	..	9/4/18	18/5/19	....	Twiggs	..	23/1/18	28/9/18	28/7/19

52 Fore River & Union I. W. boats. (Flush Deckers.)

LUCE (& Fore River boats).

26 *Fore River*: **Bell, Bush, Colhoun, Cowell, Foote, Crosby, Dyer, Gregory, Israel, Kalk** (ex *Rodgers*) **Kimberley, Lansdale, Little, Luce, Maddox, Mahan, Maury, Meredith, Murray, Palmer, Sigourney, Stevens, Stribling, Stringham, Thatcher, Walker.**

Trials : Bell, 34·76. Colhoun, 34·65. Dyer, 34·75. Gregory, 34·75. Israel, 34·34. Kimberley, 34·8. Luce, 34·81. Maury, 34·59. Murray, 34·84. Sigourney, 34·7. Stevens, 34·53. Stringham, 34·8.

26 *Union I.W.*: **Anthony, Burns, Champlin, Chew, Crane, Gridley, Harding, Hart, Hazlewood, Hogan, Howard, Ingraham, Ludlow, Mackenzie, McKean, McKee, Mugford, O'Bannon, Renshaw, Ringgold, Rizal, Robinson, Schley, Sproston, Stansbury, Williams.**

Trials : Robinson, 34·2. Schley, 35·2.

Displacement, 1185 tons *normal* (1278 tons *full load*). Dimensions : 310 (*w.l.*) × 30′ 11¼″ × 9′ 1¼″ (*mean*) draught (9¾ feet *full load*). †Armament : 4—4 inch, 50 cal, and (*a*) 2—3 inch, 23 cal. AA., or (*b*) 2—1 pdr. AA. Tubes : 12—21 inch in 4 triple deck mountings. Designed S.H.P. 27,000 = 35 kts. Machinery : *Gridley, Harding, McKee, McKean, Ringgold, Robinson*, G. E. turbines with reduction gear. all other boats, Curtis with reduction gear. 2 screws (*Gridley* only, 3). 4 Yarrow boilers—27,549 sq. ft. heating surface. Oil fuel: —— tons. Complement, 139 (*Ludlow* and *Mackenzie*, 114). *Rizal* built at expense of Philippines Government, and to be manned by Filipino crew.

RINGGOLD (& Union I. W boats).   *Photo, Lieut. H. Reuterdahl, U.S.N./R.F.*

FORE RIVER BOATS :—

		Begun.	Launch.	Comp.			Begun.	Launch.	Comp.
Bell	..	15/11/17	20/4/18	1/8/18	Luce	..	9/2/18	29/6/18	11/9/18
Bush	..	4/7/18	27/10/18	19/2/19	Maddox	..	27/7/18	27/10/18	10/3/19
Colhoun	..	19/9/17	21/2/18	12/6/18	Mahan	..	4/5/18	4/8/18	24/10/18
Cowell	..	15/7/18	23/11/18	17/3/19	Maury	..	25/2/18	4/7/18	23/9/18
Crosby	..	23/6/18	28/9/18	24/1/19	Meredith	..	29/6/18	22/9/18	29/1/19
Dyer	..	26/9/17	13/4/18	2/7/18	Murray	..	22/12/17	3/6/18	20/8/18
Foote	..	7/8/18	14/12/18	21/3/19	Palmer	..	29/5/18	18/8/18	22/11/18
Gregory	..	25/8/17	25/1/18	31/5/18	Sigourney	..	25/7/18	16/12/17	14/5/18
Israel	..	26/1/18	22/6/18	20/8/18	Stevens	..	20/10/17	13/1/18	23/5/18
Kalk	..	19/8/18	21/12/18	29/3/19	Stribling	..	14/12/17	29/5/18	10/8/18
Kimberley	..	21/6/17	4/12/17	27/4/18	Stringham	..	19/10/17	30/3/18	2/7/18
Lansdale	..	20/4/18	21/7/18	26/10/18	Thatcher	..	8/6/18	31/8/18	14/1/19
Little	..	18/5/17	11/11/17	5/4/18	Walker	..	18/6/18	14/9/18	31/1/19

UNION I. W. BOATS :—

		Begun.	Launch.	Comp.			Begun.	Launch.	Comp.
Anthony	..	18/4/18	10/8/18	Yes	Mackenzie	..	4/7/18	29/7/18	
Burns	..	15/4/18	4/7/18	Yes	McKean	..	12/2/18	4/7/18	Yes
Champlin	..	31/10/17	7/4/18	11/11/18	McKee	..	29/10/17	3/3/18	7/9
Chew	..	2/1/18	26/5/18	12/12/18	Mugford	..	20/7/18		
Crane	..	7/1/18	4/7/18	Yes	O'Bannon	..			
Gridley	..	1/4/18	4/7/18	Yes	Renshaw	..	8/5/18	21/9/18	
Harding	..	12/2/18	4/7/18	24/1/19	Ringgold	..	20/10/17	14/4/18	11/1
Hart	..	8/1/18	7/7/18	Yes	Rizal	..	26/6/18	21/9/18	
Hazlewood	..	24/12/17	22/6/18	Yes	Robinson	..	31/10/17	28/3/18	19/10
Hogan	..	....	....	....	Schley	..	29/10/17	28/3/18	16/8
Howard	..	....	....	....	Sproston	..	20/4/18	18/8/18	
Ingraham	..	12/1/18	7/7/18	Yes	Stansbury	..	....	....	Y
Ludlow	..	7/1/18	9/6/18	23/12/18	Williams	..	25/3/18	4/7/18	

U. S. DESTROYERS—*continued.*

21 Cramp boats (Flush Deckers).

DENT. *Photo by courtesy of Navy Dept. (Bureau C. & R.)*

21 *Cramp:* **Barney, Bernadou, Biddle, Blakely, Breckinridge, Cole, Dent, Dorsey, Du Pont, Elliott, Ellis, Greer, J. Fred Talbott, Lea, Rathburne, Roper, Talbot, Tarbell, Upshur, Waters, Yarnall.**

Displacements: 1165 tons *normal* (1247 tons *full load*). Dimensions: 310 (*w.l.*) × 30′ 11¼″ × 9 feet *mean* draught. *Full load* draught, 9½ feet. Armament: 4—4 inch, 50 cal., 2—3 inch, 23 cal. AA., 12—21 inch tubes in 4 triple deck mountings. Designed S.H.P. 26,000 = 35 kts. Machinery: Parsons turbines with reduction gear. Boilers: 4 White-Forster—27,500 sq. ft. heating surface. Oil: tons. Complement, 103/139 (War). *Trials: Cole* 41·1 (unofficial), *Dent* 35·11, *Dorsey* 35·16, *Talbot* 35·3, *Upshur* 35·2.

	Begun.	Launch.	Comp.
Barney	26/3/18	5/9/18	14/3/19
Bernadou ..	4/6/18	7/11/18	19/5/19
Biddle	22/4/18	3/10/18	22/4/19
Blakely	26/3/18	19/9/18	8/3/19
Breckinridge ..	11/3/18	17/8/18	27/2/19
Cole	25/6/18	11/1/19	19/6/19
Dent	30/8/17	23/3/18	9/9/18
Dorsey	18/9/17	9/4/18	16/9/18
Du Pont ..	2/5/18	22/10/18	30/4/19
Elliott	24/2/18	4/7/18	25/1/19
Ellis	8/7/18	30/11/18	7/6/19
Greer	24/2/18	1/8/18	31/12/18
J. F. Talbott ..	8/7/18	14/12/18	30/6/19
Lea	18/9/17	29/4/18	21/10/18
Rathburne ..	12/7/17	27/12/17	24/6/18
Roper	31/2/18	17/8/18	15/2/19
Talbot	12/7/17	20/2/18	20/7/18
Tarbell	31/12/17	28/5/18	27/11/18
Upshur	19/2/18	4/7/18	20/12/18
Waters	26/7/17	9/3/18	8/8/18
Yarnall	12/2/18	19/6/18	29/11/18

17 Bath I.W. & Navy Yard boats (Flush Deckers).

EVANS. *U.S. Navy photo.*

4 *Bath I. W.:* **Aaron Ward, Buchanan, Crowninshield, Hale.** These boats have 2—3 inch, 23 cal. AA. guns. Designed S.H.P. 24,200 = 35 kts. Otherwise as "General Notes" below.

4 *Bath I. W.:* **Evans, Philip, Wickes, Woolsey.** These boats have 2—1 pdr. auto. AA. Designed S.H.P. 24,610 = 35 kts. *Trials: Philip* 35.53, *Wickes* 35.34. *Woolsey* 24,575 S.H.P. = — kts. Otherwise as "General Notes" below.

6 *Mare Island N. Y.:* **Boggs, Claxton, Hamilton, Kennison, Kilty, Ward.** These boats have 2—3 inch, 23 cal. AA. guns. Designed S.H.P. 26,000 = 35 kts. Otherwise as "General Notes" below.

2 *Mare Island N. Y.:* **Fairfax, Taylor.** These boats have 2—1 pdr. AA. guns. Designed S.H.P. 24,200 = 35 kts. Otherwise as "General Notes" below.

1 *Charleston N. Y.:* **Tillman.** As *Boggs, Claxton,* &c., above.

General Notes.—Displacements: 1154 tons *normal* (1247 *full load*). Dimensions: 310 (*w.l.*) × 30′ 11¼″ × 9 feet *normal* draught (*full load* draught, 9½ feet). Armament: 4—4 inch, 50 cal. (AA. guns are separately noted), 12—21 inch tubes in 4 triple deck mountings. Designed S.H.P. and speed as separately noted. Machinery: Parsons turbines with reduction gear. 2 screws. 4 Normand boilers—27,000 sq. ft. heating surface. Oil fuel only: —— tons. Complement, 139 (War).

	Begun.	Launch.	Comp.
A. Ward ..	1/8/18	....	....
Buchanan ..	29/6/18	2/1/19	....
Crowninshield ..	5/11/18	Yes	24/7/19
Hale	7/10/18	Yes	12/6/19
Evans	28/12/17	30/10/18	11/11/18
Philip	1/9/17	25/7/18	24/8/18
Wickes	26/6/17	25/6/18	31/7/18
Woolsey	1/11/17	17/9/18	30/9/18
Boggs	15/11/17	25/4/18	23/9/18
Claxton	25/4/18	15/1/19	......
Hamilton ..	8/6/18	15/1/19	......
Kennison ..	14/2/18	8/6/18	......
Kilty	15/12/17	25/4/18	Yes
*Ward**	15/5/18	1/6/18	24/7/18
Fairfax	10/7/17	15/12/17	6/4/18
Taylor	15/10/17	14/2/18	Yes
Tillman	29/7/18	......	......

*Note rate of building.

6 Caldwell class.

STOCKTON (& CONNER). *Photo, Lieut. H. Reuterdahl, U.S.N/R.F.*

2 *Cramp:* **Conner, Stockton.** *Conner,* 1225 tons *full load*; *Stockton,* 1238 tons *full load.* Designed H.P. 20,000 = 30 kts. Parsons (geared cruising) turbines. 3 screws. Boilers: 4 White-Forster—22,520 sq. ft. heating surface. *Trials: Conner* 30·17, *Stockton* 30.12.

Note.—These two boats have 5—4 inch, 2—4 inch being paired on the fo'xle mounting. Otherwise as "General Notes" below.

"Manley," flush deck type; appearance of "Craven," "Caldwell, "Gwin," not known,

1 *Norfolk N. Y.:* **Craven.** 1187 tons *full load.* Desgined H.P. 20 000 = kts. Parsons turbines, with reduction gear. 2 screws. Boilers: 4 Thornycroft—21,500 sq. ft. heating surface.

1 *Mare Island N. Y.:* **Caldwell.** As *Craven,* above, but engined with G. E. Curtis turbines and reduction gear. *Trials:* 31.7.

1 *Seattle Con. & D. D. Co.:* **Gwin.** 1228 tons *full load.* Designed H.P. 18,750 = 30 kts. Parsons turbines with reduction gear. 2 screws. Boilers: 4 Yarrow—22,252 sq. ft. heating surface.

1 *Bath I. W.:* **Manley** (1917). As *Craven,* above, but boilers 4 Normand—21,500 sq. ft. heating surface. *Trials:* 32·23.

General Notes.—*Normal* displacement: 1125 tons, *full load* as separately noted. Dimensions: 310 (*w.l.*) × 30⅔ × 8 feet (*mean* draught). *Full load* draught: 9 feet 5¼ inches. Armament: *Conner* and *Stockton* 5—4 inch (50 cal.), others 4—4 inch (50 cal.), (and in all) 2—1 pdr. auto. anti-aircraft, 12—21 inch tubes in 4 triple deck mountings. 260 tons oil fuel. Complement 103/139 War *Conner* and *Stockton* 134.

CALDWELL CLASS:—

	Begun.	Launch.	Comp.
Conner	16/10/16	21/8/17	10/2/18
Stockton ..	13/10/16	17/7/17	26/11/17
Craven	29/11/17	29/6/18	19/10/18
Caldwell	9/12/16	19/7/17	1/12/17
Gwin	21/6/17	22/12/17	19/10/18
Manley	22/8/16	23/8/17	15/10/17

6 Allen class.

SAMPSON. *Davis* has after S.L. *before* mainmast on high lattice tower. *Photo, O. W. Waterman.*

2 *Bath I.W.:* **Allen** (1916), **Davis** (1916). 1071 tons (1185 *full load*). Designed H.P. 17,500 = 30 kts. Parsons (geared cruising) turbines. Machinery weighs 350 tons. Boilers: 4 Normand—22,500 sq. ft. heating surface. Trials: *Allen,* 30·29; *Davis,* 30·36 kts.

2 *Fore River:* **Rowan** (1916), **Sampson** (1916). 1110 tons (1125 *full load.*) Designed H.P. 17,000 = 29·5 kts. Curtis (geared cruising) turbines. Machinery averages 385 tons. Boilers: 4 Yarrow—21,500 sq. ft. heating surface. Trials: *Rowan,* 29·57 kts.; *Sampson,* 29·52 kts.

1 *Mare Island Navy Yard:* **Shaw** (1916). Displacement, H.P. and speed as *Rowan.* Parsons (geared cruising) turbines. Boilers: 4 Thornycroft.

1 *Cramp:* **Wilkes** (1916). 1110 tons (1124 *full load*). Designed H.P. 17,000 = 29·5 kts. Parsons (geared cruising) turbines. Machinery weighs 367 tons. Boilers: 4 White-Forster. Trials: 29·58 kts.

General Notes.—Dimensions: 310 (*w.l.*) × 29⅚ × 9¼ to 9½ feet *mean* draught. *Full load* draught of first two: 9 ft. 9¼ in. Others, 10 ft. 8¼ in. Armament: 4—4 inch (50 cal.), 2—1 pdr. auto. anti-aircraft, 12—21 inch deck tubes in 4 triple deck mountings. Designed H.P. 17,000 = 29·5 kts. Oil fuel: 290 tons (estimated). Complement: 103/136 war,

U. S. DESTROYERS—(Continued.)

(All on this page unofficially known as "Thousand Tonners.")

5 Conyngham Class.

CONYNGHAM.

Photo, U.S. Navy Recruiting Bureau.

TUCKER (of *Conyngham* class).   *Copyright Photo, O. W. Waterman.*

2 *Cramp :* **Conyngham** (1915). **Porter** (1915). 1090 tons (1205 *full load.*) Designed H.P. 18,000 = 29½ kts. Parsons (geared cruising) turbines. Machinery weighs 375 tons. Boilers : 2 White-Forster—24,000 sq. ft. heating surface. Trials : *Conyngham*, 29·63 kts. ; *Porter*, 29·58 kts.

1 *New York S.B. Co. :* **Wainwright** (1915). 1050 tons (1265 *full load.*) Designed H.P. 17,000 = 29½ kts. Parsons (geared cruising) turbines. Machinery averages 369 tons. Boilers : 4 Normand—21,500 sq. ft. heating surface. Trials : 29·67 kts. (*Jacob Jones* of this type lost during war.)

1 *Fore River :* **Tucker** (1915). Displacements as *Conyngham*. Designed H.P. 17,000 = 29½ kts. Curtis (geared cruising) turbines. Machinery weighs 369 tons. Boilers : 4 Yarrow—21,500 sq. ft. heating surface. Trials : 29·56 kts.

1 *Bath I.W. :* **Wadsworth** (1915). 1060 tons (1174 *full load*). Designed H.P. 17,000 = 29½ kts. Parsons turbines with reduction gear. Machinery weighs 323 tons. Boilers : 4 Normand—21,500 sq. ft. heating surface. Trials : 30·67 kts.

General Notes.—Dimensions : 310 (*w.l.*) × 29⅝ × 9⅜ to 9⅝ feet (*mean draught*). *Full load* draught 10 feet 1¼ inches to 10 feet 8¼ inches. Armament : 4—4 inch (50 cal.). 8—21 inch tubes in 4 twin-deck mountings. Designed H.P. 17,000 = 29·5 kts. 290 tons oil fuel. Complement : 101, (132 war.)

War loss : Jacob-Jones torpedoed off Scilly Isles by U-boat 6 December 1917.

8 Aylwin Class.

(Unofficially known as " Thousand Tonners.")

DUNCAN.

Copyright photo, O. W. Waterman.

4 *Cramp :* **Aylwin, Balch, Benham, Parker** (1913). 1036 tons (1156 *full load*). Cramp-Zoelly turbines. Machinery : 347 tons. Boilers : 4 White-Forster—21,600 sq. feet heating surface. Oil fuel : *Aylwin*, 287 tons ; *Balch*, 306 tons ; *Benham*, 295 tons ; *Parker*, 317 tons. Trials : *Aylwin* 29·6, *Balch* 29·62, *Benham* 29·59, *Parker* 29·55 kts.

2 *Bath I.W. :* **Cassin, Cummings** (1913). 1020 tons (1139 *full load*). Parsons turbines and reciprocating engines. Machinery : 329 tons. Boilers : 4 Normand—21,509 sq. feet heating surface. Oil fuel : 312 tons. Trials : *Cassin* 30·14, *Cummings* 30·57 kts.

1 *New York S. B. Co. :* **Downes** (1913). 1072 tons (1190 *full load*). Turbines and reciprocating engines. Machinery : 386 tons. Boilers : 4 Thornycroft—26,456 sq. feet heating surface. Oil fuel : 306 tons. Trials : 29·07 kts.

1 *Fore River :* **Duncan** (1913). 1011 tons (1133 *full load*). Turbines and reciprocating engines. Weight : 348 tons. Boilers : 4 Yarrow—21,500 sq. feet heating surface. Oil fuel : 290 tons. Trials : 29·14 kts.

Note.— Dimensions about 300 (*w.l.*) × 30¼ × 9¼ to 9⅝ (*mean*). *Full load* draught 10¼ to 10⅜ feet. *Designed* H.P. : 16,000 = 29 kts. Armament : 4—4 in. (50 cal.). 8—21 in. tubes in four twin-mountings. Complement 101, war 134. Built to specified radius at 15 kts. Reciprocating engines not used over 15 kts. Very economical steamers. *Benham* reported to have had 4″ guns in twin mountings, installed during 1917 for experimental purposes.

6 Cushing Class.

NICHOLSON.

Copyright Photo, O. W. Waterman.

1 *Fore River :* **Cushing** (1912). 1050 tons (1071 *full load*). Parsons (geared cruising) turbines. Machinery weighs 360 tons. Boilers : 4 Yarrow—21,500 sq. feet heating surface. Trials : 29·18 kts.

1 *New York S.B. Co. :* **Ericsson*** (1914). 1090 tons (1211 *full load*). 3 sets Parsons turbines with reciprocating machinery weighs 364 tons. Boilers : 4 Thornycroft—26,936 sq. ft. heating surface. Trials : 29·29 kts.

1 *Bath I.W. :* **McDougal** (1914). 1025 tons (1139 *full load*). Two sets Parsons turbines and two reciprocating. Machinery weighs 325 tons. Boilers : 4 Normand—21,509 sq. feet heating surface. Trials : 30·7 kts.

3 *Cramp :* **Nicholson** (1914), **O'Brien*** (1914), **Winslow** (1915). 1050 tons (1171 *full load*). 2 Cramp-Zoelly turbines with 2 reciprocating. Machinery weighs 351 tons. Boilers : 4 White-Forster—21,600 sq. feet heating surface. Trials : *Nicholson* 29·08 kts., *O'Brien* 29·17 kts., *Winslow* 29·05 kts.

General Notes.—Dimensions are about 300 (*w.l.*) × 30½ × 9 feet 4 inches to 9 feet 9 inches (*mean*). *Full load* draught : 9 feet 8 inches to 10 feet 9 inches. Armament : 4—4 inch (50 cal.). 8—21 inch tubes in 4 twin-deck mountings. Designed H.P. 16,000 = 29 kts. Oil fuel : 309 tons, but *McDougal* carries 327 tons. Complement : 101, (war 132.) Built to guaranteed radius at 15 kts.

* Have very low mainmasts.

21 Drayton Class.

(Unofficially known as " Flivver Type.")

All 742 tons (883 *full load*). Dimensions : 289 (*w.l.*) × 26½ × 8½ (*mean*). Armament : 5—3 inch, 50 cal. 6—18 inch tubes (in pairs). Designed H.P. 12,000 = 29½ kts. Oil capacity varies from 186 to 269 tons. *Full load* draught from 9½ to 11 feet. Complement 91 ; war 107.

TRIPPE.

Photo, U.S. Navy Recruiting Bureau.

5 *Bath I.W. :* **Drayton** (1910), **Jenkins** (1912), **Jouett** (1912), **Trippe** (1910), **Paulding** (1910). Machinery : Parsons turbines. Weight of machinery : 263 tons in first three, 250 tons in *Trippe*, 269 tons in *Paulding*. Boilers : 4 Normand. Oil fuel : *Drayton*, 191 tons ; *Jenkins*, 222 tons ; *Jouett*, 225 tons ; *Trippe*, 233 tons ; *Paulding*, 269 tons. Trials : *Drayton*, 30·83 ; *Jouett*, 32·27 ; *Jenkins*, 31·27 ; *Paulding*, 32·80 ; *Trippe*, 30·89.

4 *New York S. B. Co. :* **Ammen** (1910), **Burrows** (1910), **Jarvis** (1912), **McCall** (1910). Parsons turbine. 3 screws. Machinery : 269 tons in *Jarvis*, 288 tons in others. Boilers : 4 Thornycroft. Oil fuel : 188 tons in *McCall*, 223 in *Jarvis*, 227 in *Ammen* and *Burrows*. Trials : *Ammen*, 30·48 ; *Burrows*, 30·67 ; *Jarvis*, 30·01 ; *McCall*, 30·66 kts.

(Continued on next page.)

U. S. DESTROYERS ("Flivver" Type)—*Continued.*

21 Drayton class—*Continued.*

(General details given on preceding page.)

BEALE.
Copyright photo, O. W. Waterman.

4 *Cramp:* **Beale** (1912), **Mayrant** (1910), **Patterson** (1911), **Warrington** (1910). *Mayrant* re-engined **1916-17** with Westinghouse turbines and mechanical reduction gear (284 tons). *Warrington* has Cramp-Zoelly turbines. 2 screws. Weight of machinery, 284 tons. Oil, 200 tons. Boilers: 4 White-Forster. *Beale* and *Patterson* have Parsons turbines. 3 screws. Machinery: 273 tons. Oil fuel: 227 tons. Boilers: 4 White-Forster. Trials: *Beale,* 29·65; *Mayrant,* 30·22; *Patterson,* 29·69; *Warrington,* 30·12 kts.

4 *Fore River:* **Henley** (1912), **Perkins** (1910), **Sterett** (1910), **Walke** (1911). *Henley* re-engined **1916-17** with Westinghouse turbines and mechanical reduction gear (305 tons). Other three Curtis turbines only (300 tons). 2 screws. Boilers: 4 Yarrow. Oil fuel: *Perkins* and *Sterett,* 193 tons; *Walke,* 201 tons; *Henley,* 250 tons. Trials: *Henley,* 30·32; *Perkins,* 29·76; *Sterett,* 30·37; *Walke,* 29·78 kts.

ROE.
Photo, Lieut. H. Reuterdahl, U.S.N./R.F.

4 *Newport News:* **Fanning** (1912), **Monaghan** (1911), **Roe** (1909), **Terry** (1909). Parsons turbines. 3 screws. Machinery: 276 tons. Boilers: 4 Thornycroft. Oil fuel: 225 in *Fanning,* 186 to 190 in other three. Trials: *Fanning,* 29·99; *Monaghan,* 30·45; *Roe,* 29·60; *Terry,* 30·24 kts.

1 *New York Shipbuilding:* **Preston** (1909). *Full load* draught, 11 feet. Parsons turbines. 3 screws Machinery: 255 tons. Boilers: 4 Thornycroft. Coal: 290 tons. Trials: 29·18 kts.

U. S. COAST TORPEDO VESSELS.

15 Coast Torpedo Vessels.

(Are Old Destroyers not serviceable for duty with Fleet. Are unofficially known as "*Tinclads.*")

No.	Class	Date	Displacement	H.P.	Max. speed	Coal	Complement	T. tubes	Max draug't
			tons		kts.	tons			feet.
8	*Bainbridge*†	'00-'02	420	8000	28	184-209	76/91	2	6½
3	*Truxtun*†	'00-'02	433	8300	28*	177-187	76/91	2—4	6
2	*Hull*†	'00-'02	414	8000	28*	158	76/91	2	6
2	*Lawrence*†	'99-'01	400	8400	28*	108-119	76/91	2	6¼

* Only just reached this speed on first trials. Present *max.* speed 25 kts. *or less.*
† May be re-numbered as *CTB 1—16.*

8 Bainbridge class.

1 *Gas Engine Co.* **Stewart*** (1902). Machinery, 205 tons. Boilers: 4 Seabury. Coal, 194 tons. Trial speed: 29·69 kts.

2 *Neafie and Levy.* **Bainbridge*** (1901), **Barry*** (1902). Machinery, 209 tons. Boilers: 4 Thornycroft. Coal: 183 tons. Trials: *Bainbridge,* 28·45; *Barry,* 28·13. *Chauncey,* of this class, lost during the War.

2 *Trigg.* **Dale*** (1900), **Decatur*** (1900). Machinery, 204 tons. Boilers: 4 Thornycroft. Coal: 186 tons. Trials: *Dale,* 28; *Decatur,* 28·10 kts.

3 *Union Iron Works.* **Paul Jones*** (1902), **Perry*** (1900), **Preble*** (1901). Machinery, 206 tons. Boilers: 4 Thornycroft. Coal: 184 tons. Trials: *Paul Jones,* 28·91; *Perry,* 28·32; *Preble,* 28·03 kts.

War loss: *Chauncey* lost in collision 19 November 1917.

General Notes.—All 420 tons (*full load* 592 tons). Dimensions: *about* 245 (*w.l.*) × 23 × 6¼ feet (*mean*). Designed H.P. 8000 = 28 kts., but none of them can get anywhere near this now. Armament: 2—3 inch, 4—6 pdr., 2—18 inch tubes. (1 twin mounting in *Paul Jones,* *Perry* and *Preble,* 2 single in other ships.) Complement, 76. (91 war.)

5 Flusser class. "Flivver" type.

All 700 tons (*full load,* 902 tons). Dimensions: 289 (*w.l.*) × 26 × 8 feet (*mean*). Armament: 5—3 inch, 50 cal., 6—18 inch tubes, in 3 twin deck mountings. Designed H.P. 10,000 = 28 kts. Complement: 88 (113, War).

REID.
Copyright photo, O. W. Waterman.

2 *Bath I.W.:* **Flusser** (1909), **Reid** (1909). *Full load* draught 10 feet. Parsons turbines. 3 screws Machinery, 228 tons. Boilers: 4 Normand. Coal: 321 tons. Trials: *Flusser,* 30·41; *Reid,* 31·82 kts.

2 *Cramp:* **Lamson** (1909), **Smith** (1909). *Full load* draught, 10 feet 7 inches. Parsons turbine. 3 screws. Machinery: 250 tons. Boilers: 4 Mosher. Coal: *Lamson,* 291 tons; *Smith,* 305. Trials: *Lamson,* 28·61; *Smith,* 28·35 kts.

**Note.*—May be re-numbered thus :—*CTB 1* (Bainbridge), *CTB 2* (Barry), *CTB 5* (Dale). *CTB 4* (Decatur), *CTB 10* (Paul Jones), *CTB 11* (Perry), *CTB 12* (Preble), *CTB 15* (Stewart). and names transferred to new T.B.D. building.

7 Other Boats.

("*Whipple*" *differs in appearance : see Silhouettes*).

3 *Truxtun class:*—**Truxtun*** (1901), **Whipple*** (1902), **Worden*** (1902). 433 tons. H.P. 8300 = 28 kts. Armament: 2—3 inch (fore and aft), 4—6 pdr. Tubes: in *Truxtun* and *Worden,* 4—18 inch in 2 twin mountings: in *Whipple,* 2—18 inch in 1 twin mounting. Coal: 177, 179 and 188 tons. Complement 76. (91 war.)

**Note.*—May be re-numbered *CTB 14, CTB 15, CTB 16* respectively, and names transferred to new T.B.D. building.

(*4 funnels—like Truxton's, but higher*).

2 *Hull class:*—**Hopkins*** (1902), 420 tons, and **Hull*** (1902), 408 tons. H.P. 8000 = 28 kts. Armament: 2—3 inch, 6—6 pdrs. 4—18 inch tubes (in twin mountings). Coal: 158 tons. Complement 76. (91 war.)

**Note.*—May be re-numbered *CTB 6* and *CTB 7* respectively, and names transferred to new T.B.D. building.

2 *Lawrence class:*—**Lawrence*** (1900), **Macdonough*** (1900). 400 tons. H.P. 8400 = 28 to 29 kts. Armament 7—6 pdr. 2—18 inch tubes. Coal: 108 and 119 tons. Complement 76. (91 war.)

**Note.*—May be re-numbered as *CTB 8* and *CTB 9* respectively, and names transferred to new T.B.D. building.

OLD U. S. TORPEDO BOATS.

7 *Shubrick class*:— **Shubrick** ('99), **Thornton** ('00) **Stockton** ('99) (Built by Trigg), **De Long** ('00), **Blakely** ('00) (Built by Lawley, Boston), **Wilkes** ('01) (Gas Engine Co. and Seabury), and **Tingey** ('02) (Columbian Ironworks). 196 tons. H.P. 3000=26 kts. (*Shubrick* did 28 on trial). Thornycroft boilers (except *Wilkes*, which has Seabury). Armament: 3—1 pdr. 3—18 inch tubes (two of them between funnels, the other right aft). Coal: *max.* 72 tons. Complement, 29. *Max.* draught: about 6 feet.

3 *ex-Barney class*:—**No. 11** (ex *Barney*, 1900), **No. 12** (ex *Biddle*, 1901), **No. 10** (ex *Bagley*, 1900). 175 tons. Designed H.P. 3920=28·5 kts. Normand boilers. Armament: No. 11 has 3—1 pdr., No. 12 has 3—1 pdr., 1 Y-gun, No. 10 has 2—1 pdr., 1 Y gun. No tubes in any of these boats. Coal: 44 tons. Complement 12–36.

1 *Stringham* ('99) (Built by Harland & Hollingsworth). 340 tons. Designed H.P. 7200=30 kts. (*nominal*). Boilers: Thornycroft. Armament: 4—6 pdrs. S.A. 2—18 inch tubes (aft). Coal: 96 tons; *max.* 120 tons. *Max.* draught: 8 feet. *Mean* draught: 6 feet. Complement, 55. Never made designed speed. Best actual 25.33.

No. 8 (ex *Bailey*, 1899) (Built by Gas Engine Co. and Seabury). 280 tons. H.P. 5600=30 kts. Normand boilers. Armament: 4—6 pdr. S.A., 1 Y-gun. 2—18 inch tubes. Coal: 101 tons. Complement, 75.

1 *Wolff & Zwicken*: **No. 7** (ex *Goldsborough*, 1899). 255 tons. Guns: 4—3 pdr. Torpedo tubes: 2—18 inch. I.H.P. 5850=27·4 kts. on first trials. 3 Thornycroft boilers. Coal: 91 tons. Complement, 65.

5 *ex Shubrick class*:— **No. 15** (ex *Shubrick*, 1899) and **No. 16** (ex *Thornton*, 1900), 200 tons. **No. 14** (ex *De Long*, 1900) and **No. 13** (ex *Blakely*, 1900), 196 tons. **No. 17** (ex *Tingey*, 1901), 165 tons. H.P. 3000=26 kts. (*Shubrick* did 28 on trial). Thornycroft or Normand boilers. Armament: No. 13 has 3—3 pdr., 1 M.G.; Nos. 14, 15 and 17, 2—1 pdr., 1-Y gun. No. 16 disarmed. No tubes in any of these boats. Coal: *max.* 74 to 87 tons. Complement, 13–21.

2 *Dahlgren class*:—**Dahlgren** ('96) (T.A.M.), **Craven** ('96) (Built at Bath Ironworks). 146 tons. Designed H.P. 4200=22·5 kts. Normand boilers. Armament: 4—1 pdr., 2—18 inch tubes (single) aft. Coal: 32 tons. Complement, 26.

1 *Union I. W.*: **No. 5** (ex-*Farragut*, 1898). 279 tons. Guns: 4—3 pdr., 1 Y. No tubes. Designed H.P. 5600 = 30 kts. 3 Thornycroft boilers. Coal: 97 tons. Complement, 65.

1 *Schichau* type: **No. 9** (ex-*Somers*, Elbing, Germany, 1895). 150 tons. Guns: 3—1 pdr., 1 M. G., 1 Y. No tubes. Designed H.P. 1900 = 17.5 kts. 1 Loco. boiler. Coal: *max.* 38 tons. Complement, 34.

DAVIS.

Morris type:— **Morris** ('96). 105 tons. (Herreshoff Co.). **Davis** ('98). 154 tons. Designed H.P. 1750=22·5 kts. (23·54 trial). Boilers: 2 Thornycroft, except *Morris*, 2 Normand. Armament: 3—1 pdr., 3—18 inch tubes. Coal: *max.* 40 tons. Complement, 27.

1 *Herreshoff Co.*: **No. 3** (ex-*Dupont*, 1897). 105 tons. Guns: 3—3 pdr., 1 M. G. and 1 Y. No tubes. Designed H.P. 3800=30 kts. 3 Normand (modified) boilers. Coal: 42 tons. Complement, 78.

2 *Columbian I. W.*: **No. 2** (ex-*Rodgers*, 1896), **No. 1** (ex-*Foote*, 1896). 142 tons. Guns: No. 2, 3—3 pdr., 1—1 pdr.; No. 1, 3—1 pdr. No tubes. Designed H.P. 2000—2400=24.5 kts. 2 Mosher boilers. Coal: 45 tons. Complements 37 and 36.

U. S. SUBMARINES: COASTAL & SEA-GOING TYPES.
90 (+ 8 or 9 old Holland) = 98 or 99 boats.

Note.—" Number 108 " a small experimental boat, will not be built.

6 *Holland* type : **H 4—H9** (1918), built by Bremerton D. Y., Puget Sound.   No details known, but probably of same type as British *H Class Submarines*.

6 *Lake* type : **O 11—O 16** (1917-18), viz., *O 11—O 13* by Lake T. B. Co., *O 11—O 16* by California S. B. Co.   Dimensions : about 172 × 18 × — feet.   1—3 inch A.A. gun.   4 torpedo tubes.   Machinery : 2 sets Sulzer Diesel engines.   Radius of action as *O 1—O 10* below.   Completed 1918.

O3.   *Photo, N. G. Moser.*

10 *Holland* type : **O 1—O 10** (1917-18), viz., *O 1* by Portsmouth N.Y., *O 2* by Bremerton, Pugent Sound, N.Y., *O 3—O 10* by Electric Boat Co. and Fore River Co.   Dimensions : about 175 × 17 × feet.   1—3 inch A.A. gun.   4 torpedo tubes.   Machinery : 2 sets of 4-cycle Nlesco Diesel engines.   Electric batteries weigh 65 tons.   Radius of action : 5000-6000 miles, at 11-12 kts. *on surface*.   Completed 1918.

4 *Lake* type : **N 4, N 5, N 6, N 7,** (launched 1916-17) by Lake T. B. Co.   Dimensions : about 155 × 14½ × feet.   1—3 inch A.A. gun.   4 torpedo tubes.   Machinery : 2 sets Sulzer Diesel engines.   Radius of action : about 2500 miles at cruising speed *on surface*;   100-120 miles at 5 kts. *submerged*.   Completed 1918.

3 *Holland* type : **N1—N3** (1916-17) viz., *N 1—N 3* by Electric Boat Co., and Seattle Con. and D. D. Co.   Dimensions : about 147 × 16 × 12 feet.   1—3 inch A.A. gun.   4 torpedo tubes.   Machinery : 2 sets 450 H.P. Nlesco Diesel engines.   Radius of action : 2500 miles at cruising speed *on surface*, and 100-120 miles at 5 kts. *submerged*.

Photo, copyright by E. Muller, Junr.

1 *Holland* type : **M 1.** (Electric Boat Co., 1915.)   Dimensions : 165 × 16 × 13½ feet.   Armament : 1—3 inch, 50 cal. gun (high angle anti-aircraft model) and 4 torpedo tubes.   Machinery : 2 sets of 8 cylinder 900 H.P. Nlesco Diesel engines.   Radius of action : 3000 miles at 14 kts. *on surface*.   Has three periscopes.

K 5.   *Photo, U.S. Navy Recruiting Bureau.*

Photo (copyright) by E. Muller, Junr.

1 *Laurenti-Cramp* type : **G 4** (ex-*Thrasher*) (1912).   Fiat-Laurenti type built by Cramp.   Dimensions : 157½ × 17½ × 9½ feet.   4 torpedo tubes.   Radius of action : *about* 1700 miles at 8 kts. *on surface*, 40 miles at 5 kts. *submerged*.

---

4 *Lake* type : **L 5** (Lake T. B. Co., 1915).   *L 6, L 7* (Craig S. B. Co., Long Beach, Cal., 1916).   *L 8* (Portsmouth N. Y., 1917).   Dimensions : about 165 × 14½ feet.   1—3 inch A.A. gun.   4 torpedo tubes.   Machinery : 2 sets of 600 B.H.P. Busch Sulzer Diesel engines.   Radius of action : about 4500 miles *on surface* at cruising speed, 150 miles at 5 kts. *submerged*.

L 3.   *Photo, U. S. Navy Recruiting Bureau.*

7 *Holland* type : **L 1—4, L 9—11** (1914-15), viz., Electric Boat Co.   Dimensions : about 169 × 17½ × feet.   1—3 inch A.A. gun.   4 torpedo tubes.   Machinery : 2 sets of 650 H.P. Nlesco Diesel engines in *L 1—4* and *9—11*.   Radius of action : about 4500 miles *on surface* at cruising speed, and 150 miles at 5 kts. *submerged*.   Cost £650,000

Note.—*L 6* and *L 7* contracted for by Lake Co., but were built by the California S. B. Co., Long Beach, Cal.

8 *Holland* type : **K 1** (ex-*Haddock*), **K 2** (ex-*Cachalot*), **K 3** (ex-*Orca*), **K 4** (ex *Walrus*), and **K5—K8.** (1913-14.)   K 1, 2, 3, 6, by Fore River, K 5, 7, 8, by Union I. W., K 4 by Moran Co.   Dimensions : about 153 × 16¾ × 12 feet.   4 bow torpedo tubes.   8 torpedoes carried.   Machinery : 2 sets 6-cylinder 500 B.H.P. Nlesco Diesel engines.   Radii of action : 4500 miles at 10 kts. *on surface*, 120 miles at 5 kts. *submerged*.

H 1, H 2.   *Photo, Navy Dept. (Bureau C. & R.)*

3 *Holland* type : **H1** (ex-*Seawolf*), **H2** (ex-*Nautilus*), and **H3** (ex-*Garfish*).   (1913.)   H 1, H 2 by Union I. W., H 3 by Moran Co.   Dimensions : about 150 × 16 × feet.   4 torpedo tubes.   Radii of action : about 2300 miles at 11 kts. *on surface*, 100 miles at 5 kts. *submerged*.

G 1.   *Photo wanted of G 3.*   *Photo (copyright), by E. Muller, Jr.*

2 *Lake* type : **G 1** (ex-*Seal*); and **G 3** (ex-*Turbot*) (1912-13).   *G 1* built by Newport News, *G 2, G 3,* by Lake T. B. Co.   Dimensions : *about* 161 × 13 × feet.   2 or 1 torpedo tubes.   Radii of action : 3500 at 8 kts. *on surface* ; 70 miles at 5 kts. *submerged*.   *G 2* foundered 1919.

U. S. SUBMARINES—COASTAL TYPES—*continued.*

3 Holland type: **D1** (ex-*Narwhal*), **D2** (ex-*Grayling*), and **D3** (ex-*Salmon*). (1909-10). Built by Fore River Co. Dimensions: 134½×11× feet. 4 torpedo tubes. Radius of action *on surface*, 1210 miles at cruising speed of 9-10 kts.

Photo, Boston News Co.

2 Holland type: **E1** (ex-*Skipjack*), and **E2** (ex-*Sturgeon*), (1911). Built by Fore River Co. 4 torpedo tubes. Radii, 2100 at 11 kts. *surface*, 100 at 5 kts. *submerged.* E 2 experimentally equipped with Edison nickel batteries.

Photo, H. Reuterdahl, Esq.

2 Holland type: **F2** (ex-*Barracuda*), and **F3** (ex-*Pickerel*), (1911). F 2 by Union Ironworks, F 3 by Moran Co., Seattle. Dimensions about 140×15× feet. 4 torpedo tubes. Radii 2300 at 11 kts. *surface*, 100 at 5 kts. *submerged.* Reported to have been re-engined during 1915-16 with Nlesco & Craig Diesel engines. F 4 (ex-*Skate*) foundered before the war, was salved and stricken from the Navy Register. F 1 (ex-*Carp*) lost during the war.

(Canal Zone). *Photo, Copyright, E. Muller, Jr.*

5 Holland type: **C1** (ex-*Octopus*), **C2** (ex-*Stingray*), **C3** (ex-*Tarpon*), **C4** (ex-*Bonita*), **C5** (ex-*Snapper*). (1906-9). Built by Fore River Co. Dimensions, *about* 105¼×15× feet. 2 torpedo tubes. Nominal radius, 800 at 8 kts. *surface*, 80 at 5 kts. *submerged.*

U. S. SUBMARINES & EAGLE BOATS.

8 or 9 Old Holland Boats.

Will probably be stricken from the Navy Register within next twelve months. Are on Asiatic Station.

3 Holland type: **B1** (ex-*Cuttlefish*), **B2** (ex-*Viper*), **B3** (ex-*Tarantula*). (1906-7). Built by Fore River Co., Quincy, Mass. Dimensions, about 82½×12⅜× feet. 2 torpedo tubes in bows. Radii of action: 540 miles at 9 kts. *on surface;* 12 miles at 4 kts. *submerged.* Possess very little practical worth now.

5 or 6 Holland type: **A2** (ex-*Plunger*), **A3** (ex-*Adder*), **A4** (ex-*Grampus*), **A5** (ex-*Mocassin*), **A6** (ex-*Pike*) or **A7** (ex-*Porpoise*). (1901-3). A 2, 4, 6, by Crescent Shipyard, Elizabeth Port, N.J.; A 3, A 5, by Union Ironworks, San Francisco. Dimensions: 61×11½×12 feet. 1 torpedo tube in bows. Single benzine motors. Radii 300 at 8.5 kts. *surface;* 12 miles at 1 kts. *submerged.* Practically non-effective now. A7 was badly damaged at Cavite, P.I., during July, 1917, through a fuel explosion. Considering her age, she is hardly worth repairing and has probably been scrapped.

Mine Laying Boats.

No Submarines of this type reported building or in service, but it is not impossible that some of the R and S types may be adapted for this duty.

Fabricated Patrol Vessels.

EAGLE 17. *Photo by courtesy of the Ford Motor Co., Detroit.*

53 "EAGLE BOATS" :—

Eagle 1—4	Eagle 27—34	Eagle 46—54
Eagle 6—14	Eagle 36—44	Eagle 56—60
Eagle 16—24		

Missing Numbers :—Twelve boats were allotted to Italian Government, viz., 5, 15, 25, 35, 45, 55, 65, 75, 85, 95, 105, 112. In December, 1918, contracts for 61—112 (inclusive of both numbers) were cancelled, but boats over 61 for Italian Navy are reported as proceeding to completion.

Down to *Eagle* 12, launched 1918, remainder 1919.

45 boats building and completing July 1st, 1919.

Displacement, *normal* 500 tons, *full load* 615 tons.

Dimensions : Length, 200 feet (*p.p.* and *o.a.*). Beam, 25½ feet. *Mean draught,* 7¼ feet ; *full load,* 8½ feet.

Armament : 2—4 inch (50 cal.), 2—3 inch AA., 2 M.G., 1 Y-gun (depth charge projector). Carry depth charges.

Machinery : Ljungstrom turbine with planetary reduction gear. 2 Sterling w.t. boilers. 1 screw. Designed H.P. 2500 = 18 kts. Fuel : 105 tons coal + 45 tons oil. Endurance : 3500 miles at 10 kts. Machinery weighs 77.73 tons. Heating surface, 3000 sq. feet.

Complement, 72.

Notes.—Complement, 73. Assembled by Ford Eagle Boat Plant, River Rouge ; machinery and fittings by Ford Plant, Highland Park, Detroit. Estimated cost, £275,000 per vessel, but this has been largely exceeded. Are the American equivalent of the British " P-boats." The first British P-boat was commissioned on January 1st, 1916 ; the first Eagle Boat on October 28th, 1918. A very large sum of money was spent on erecting the fabricating plant for the Eagle Boats. British shipbuilders, without any extraordinary preparations, additional plant or slips, produced the larger British P-boats in about the same time as the Ford Eagle Boats are built.

U. S. SUBMARINE CHASERS.

SC 200. *Photo, Navy Dept. (Bureau C. & R.)*

331 110-FOOT BOATS :—

SC 1–4
SC 6
SC 17—27
SC 34—59
SC 61—64
SC 68—74
SC 77—116
SC 118—131
SC 133—138
SC 143–145
SC 147—159
SC 164—169
SC 178—186
SC 188—208
SC 210—218
SC 220—242
SC 244 -248
SC 250—273
SC 275—301
SC 303—310
SC 320—346
SC 349
SC 351—356
SC 405
SC 407—409
SC 411—441
SC 443
SC 444.

Missing Numbers :—Transferred to French Government—*SC 5, SC 7—16, SC 28—33, SC 65—67, SC 75—76, SC 140—142, SC 146, SC 160—163, SC 170—177, SC 243, SC 249, SC 313—319, SC 347—348, SC 350* (all of first contract), *SC 357—404, SC 406* (all second contract). Transferred to Cuba : *SC 274, 302, 311, 312* (all first contract). Never built : *SC 139.* Contracts cancelled : *SC 410, 442, 445—448* (third contract). War losses : *SC 60, 117, 132, 187, 209, 219* (all first contract).

Built 1917-19. *Designed* displacement, 54 tons ; *actual* displacement, owing to heavier guns and other alterations, 77 tons *normal*, 85 tons *full load*. Wooden hulls. Length, 105 feet (*p.p.*), 110 feet (*o.a.*). Beam, 14 feet $8\frac{3}{4}$ ins. *Mean* hull draught, 5 feet $5\frac{1}{2}$ ins., *full load* aft, 5 feet $8\frac{1}{2}$ ins. Machinery : three sets of 220 B.H.P. Standard petrol motors = 18 kts. *designed* speed. Owing to added weights, 16·85 kts. is reported to be actual full speed. 2400 gallons petrol = 900 miles at 10 kts. Complement, 27. Have small radius W/T.

Armaments : Designed for 1—6 pdr. and 2 M.G., but these were only mounted in a few boats. Majority have 1—3 inch (23 cal.), 2 Colt M.G. and 1 Y-gun. Some boats have an extra 6 pdr. Carry depth charges.

Hydrophone Gear : Boats fitted out in this way have either (*a*) K-tube fish hydrophones of 30 miles acoustic radius, or (*b*) SC and MB hydrophone tubes built into (and insulated from) hull of 3 miles acoustic radius. All boats with hydrophones carry extra load of depth charges.

Notes.—Quick rollers with period of about 5 secs. A very full description of these craft was given in the "Journal of the U.S. Naval Institute" in an article contributed by Comm. J. A. Furer, Construction Corps, U.S.N. To this article we are indebted for the majority of foregoing details and following Table.

TABLE OF BUILDERS :—

(Boats transferred to France and Cuba and War Losses not deleted.)

Builders.		Boats and numbers.		
Name.	Address.	First contract.	Second contract (for French government)	Third contract.
New Orleans Naval Station ..	New Orleans, La. ..	1–4	....	443–444
		114–115	....	....
New York Navy Yard ..	Brooklyn, N. Y. ..	5–64	....	....
Mathis Yacht Bldg. Co. ..	Camden, N. J. ..	65–74	(381–385)	426–430
		209–213	....	....
Hiltebrant D. D. Co.	Kingston, N. Y. ..	75–89	(371–375)	421–425
Elco Co.	Bayonne, N. J. ..	90–105	(361–364)	....
Charleston Navy Yard ..	Charleston, S. C. ..	106–113	....	....
Norfolk Navy Yard	Norfolk, Va. ..	116–136	....	....
Hodgdon Bros.	E. Boothbay, Me.	137–138	....	....
Hartman-Greiling Co.	Green Bay, Wis. ..	140–141	....	....
Rocky River D. D. Co. ..	Rocky River, Ohio	142–143	(403–406)	437–438
Vinyard S. B. Co.	Milford, Del. ..	144–146	....	....
L. E. Fry & Co. (E. J. Wright)	Clayton, N.Y. ..	147–148	....	....
		337–338	....	....
Dubuque Boat & Boiler Wks.	Dubuque, Iowa ..	149–150	....	....
Gibbs Gas Engine Co.	Jacksonville, Fla. ..	151–155	(365–370)	....
		204–208	....	....
F. M. Blount	Pensacola, Fla. ..	156–159	....	....
Howard E. Wheeler	Brooklyn, N. Y. ..	160–168	....	339–441
Matthews Boat Co.	Port Clinton, Ohio	169–178	(386–392)	431–433
International S. B. & Marine Eng. Co.	Upper Nyack, N. Y.	179–188	....	....
General S. B. & Aero Co. ..	Washington, D. C.	189–203	....	....
Alexander McDonald	Mariner's Harbor, L. I., N. Y. ..	214–217	....	434–436
Newcomb Life Boat Co. ..	Hampton, Va. ..	218–222	....	....
N. Y. Yacht, Launch & Engine Co.	Morris Heights, N. Y.	223–242	(393–242)	....
Eastern Shipyard Co.	Greenport, N. Y. ..	243–247	....	....
Camden Anchor-Rockland Machine Co.	Camden, Me. ..	251–252	....	407–408
Geo. Lawley & Son	Neponset, Mass. ..	253–272	....	....
Mare Island Navy Yard ..	Mare Island, Cal. ..	273–287	....	....
Puget Sound Navy Yard ..	Bremerton, Wash.	288–312	....	....
Robert Jacob	City Island, N. Y.	313–317	....	....
Luders Marine Const. Co. ..	Stamford, Conn. ..	318–322	....	....
Kyle & Purdy	City Island, N. Y.	323–327	(376–380)	....
Great Lakes B. B. Corp. ..	Milwaukee, Wis. ..	328–329	....	419–420
Burger Boat Co.	Manitowoc, Wis. ..	330	....	....
Smith & Williams Co.	Salisbury, Md. ..	331–332	....	....
Barrett S. B. Co.	Mobile, Ala. ..	333–336	....	....
American Car & Found. Co. ..	Wilmington, Del. ..	339–346	....	....
College Point Boat Corp. ..	College Point, N. Y.	347–356	(357–360)	413–418
Clayton S. & B. Bldg. Co. ..	Clayton, N. Y. ..	....	....	411–412
Chance Marine Const. Co. ..	Annapolis, Md. ..	248–250	409	....

U. S. TENDERS TO TORPEDO CRAFT (AND MOTOR PATROL BOATS).

Motor Patrol Boats.

464 of these craft were purchased, chartered or loaned by private owners, for War Duty. The multiplicity of their types renders any description impossible. The majority have gone back to their owners, and it is doubtful if any will be retained by the Regular Navy.

Tenders to Torpedo Craft.

Third class cruiser, **BIRMINGHAM,** is fitted for and serves as flagship to T.B.D. in full commission, Pacific Fleet. She is described on a previous page.

Third class cruiser, **SALEM,** serves as flagship to T.B.D. in reserve, Pacific Fleet. Is described on a previous page.

First class cruiser, **ROCHESTER,** is flagship to T.B.D. in full commission, Atlantic Fleet. Third class cruiser, **CHESTER,** is flagship to T.B.D. in Reserve, Atlantic. Both ships described on preceding pages.

Two Tenders to Torpedo Craft, Pacific Fleet, and three Tenders to Torpedo Craft, Atlantic Fleet, not selected at the time these pages were prepared ; accordingly, they cannot be listed.

WHITNEY, DOBBIN. Both ships authorized but not yet under contract or construction. 10,600 tons. Dimensions : 460 (*w.l.*) $483\frac{5}{6}$ (*o.a.*) × 61 × 21 feet (*mean* draught). Guns : 8—5 inch, 4—3 inch AA. Torpedo tubes : 2—21 inch. Geared turbines. 1 screw. Designed S.H.P. 7000 = 16 kts. Coal : 1107 tons. Complement, —. Generally sister ships to *Holland*, Tender to Submarines.

Photo, C. E. Waterman.

(*Pacific Fleet.*)

MELVILLE (1915) 7150 tons. Complement, 397. Dimensions : 400 × $54\frac{1}{2}$ × 20 feet (*mean* draught). Guns : 8—5 inch (51 cal.), 1—3 inch AA., 2—3 pdr. Torpedo tubes : 1—18 inch. Machinery : Parsons turbines and Westinghouse reduction gear. 2 Babcock and Wilcox boilers. H.P. (*on trials*) 4006 = 15.09 kts. Fuel : 900 tons *oil*.

Copyright photo (see Note).

(*Pacific Fleet Reserve Flotillas.*)

BLACK HAWK (Cramp, 1913, ex-Grace Steamship Co. S.S. *Santa Catalina*, taken over 1917). 13,500 tons. Dimensions : $404\frac{1}{2}$ × $53\frac{3}{4}$ × $28\frac{1}{2}$ feet. Guns : 4—5 inch, 2 M.G. I.H.P. 3400 = 13 kts. Oil : 2108 tons. Complement, 442. Served 1917-18 as Repair Ship to Mine Force.

Note.—Above illustration from "The Northern Barrage," prepared by U.S. Mine Force, and published by U.S. Naval Institute, Annapolis.

Photo, Müller.

IRIS (1885). 6100 tons. No guns. Speed : 10 kts. Coal : 300 tons.

(*Atlantic Fleet.*)

BRIDGEPORT (Vegesack, Germany, 1901, ex-North German Lloyd S.S. ***Breslau***, seized 1917). 8600 tons. Dimensions : $429\frac{1}{3}$ × $54\frac{1}{3}$ × $28\frac{1}{4}$ feet. Guns : 8—5 inch, 2 M.G. I.H.P., 3600 = 12.5 kts. Coal : 1060 tons. Complement, 386.

(*Atlantic Fleet.*)

DIXIE (ex *El Sud*), (1893). 6114 tons. Complement, 448. Dimensions : 391 × $48\frac{1}{4}$ × 20 feet (*mean* draught). Armament : 10—3 inch, 2—6 pdr., 2—1 pdr., 2 M.G. H.P. 3800 = 14.5 kts. Coal : 1100 tons.

(*Continued on next page.*)

U.S. TENDERS TO TORPEDO CRAFT AND SUBMARINES.

Tenders to Torpedo Craft.

(Pacific Fleet.)

BUFFALO (*ex El Cid*), (1892). 6000 tons. Complement: 424. Dimensions: $391 \times 48\frac{1}{4} \times 19\frac{1}{4}$ feet. Armament: 6—4 inch, 4—3 pdr., 2—1 pdr., 2 M.G. H.P. 3600 = 14·5 kts. Coal: 1408 tons.

PRAIRIE. *Official Photo, U.S. Naval Air Service.*

(Pacific Fleet).

PRAIRIE (*ex El Sol*), (1890). 6620 tons. Complement: 350. Dimensions: $401\frac{3}{4} \times 48\frac{1}{4} \times 20\frac{3}{4}$ feet (*mean draught*). Armament: 10—3 inch, 2—1 pdr., 2 M.G. H.P. 3800 = 14·5 kts. Coal: 1331 tons.

(Atlantic Fleet).

PANTHER (1889). 3380 tons. Complement: 242. Dimensions: $304\frac{3}{4} \times 40\frac{3}{4} \times 15\frac{3}{4}$ feet (*mean draught*). Guns: 4—3 inch. H.P. 3200 = 13·5 kts. Coal, 691 tons.

GENERAL ALAVA (1895). 1115 tons. Guns: 2—6 pdr. Speed: 10·5 kts. Coal: 240 tons.

U.S. TENDERS TO SUBMARINES, SEAPLANES, SUBMARINE CHASERS.

Tenders to Submarines—*continued.*

(Pacific Fleet.)

SAVANNAH (Flensburg, Germany, 1899, ex-Hamburg-American S.S. *Saxonia*, seized 1917). 10,800 tons. Dimensions: $414 \times 46 \times 26\frac{1}{2}$ feet. Guns: 1—5 inch, 2 M.G. I.H.P. 2000 = 10·5 kts. Coal: 743 tons + 531 tons additional stowage = 1274 tons. Complement, 412.

(Atlantic Fleet.)

RAINBOW (1890, purchased 1898). 4300 tons. Dimensions: $351\frac{1}{3} \times 41 \times 17\frac{1}{4}$ feet. Guns: 4—5 inch, 2 M.G. I.H.P. 1800 = 12 kts. Coal: 1166 tons. Complement, 274.

MONADNOCK (1883). 3990 tons. Guns: 4—10 inch, 2—4 inch, 4—6 pdr., 2—1 pdr. Armour: Iron belt 9″, steel turrets $11\frac{1}{2}″$—$7\frac{1}{2}″$. H.P. (on trials) 2163 = 11·63 kts. Coal: 395 tons. Complement, 228.

Note.—Above Old Monitor Submarine Depot Ship, Asiatic Fleet, with *Mohican* as Tender. She is to be withdrawn from service and placed out of commission.

Tenders to Torpedo Craft—*Continued.*

(Asiatic Fleet.)

POMPEY (1888). Ex-Collier, 3085 tons. Complement: 121. Dimensions: $234 \times 33\frac{1}{2} \times 15\frac{5}{8}$ feet (*mean draught*). Guns: 4—6 pdr. Speed: 10·5 kts. Coal: 205 tons.

Tenders to Submarine.

HOLLAND. Authorized; not yet under contract or construction. 10,600 tons. Dimensions: 460 (*w.l.*), $483\frac{5}{6}$ (*o.a.*) × 61 (*extreme*) × 21 feet (*mean draught*). Guns: 4—5 inch, 2—3 inch AA. Geared turbines. 1 screw. Designed S H P. 7000 = 16 kts. Oil: 1107 tons. Complement. Generally sister ship to *Whitney* and *Dobbin*, Tenders to Torpedo Craft.

BUSHNELL. *U.S. Navy Photo.*

(Atlantic Fleet).

BUSHNELL (1915). 3580 tons. Complement: 194. Dimensions $300 \times 45\frac{3}{4} \times 15$ feet (*mean draught*). Guns: 4—5 inch (51 cal.), 2—3 pdr. (saluting). Machinery: Turbines with reducing gear. H.P. (on trials) 2617 = 14·15 kts. Fuel: 660 tons *oil.*

(Atlantic Fleet.)

CAMDEN (Flensburg, Germany, 1900, ex-German-Australian ss. *Kiel*, seized 1917). 9000 tons (estimated). Dimensions: $403\frac{3}{4}$ (*o.a.*) × 48 × feet. Guns: 4—4 inch, 2—3 inch AA., 2—1 pdr., 4 M.G. I.H.P. 2550 = 12 kts. Coal: 975 tons. Complement, 345.

A:—Aircraft Carriers.
B:—Tenders to Seaplanes.
C:—Kite Balloon Ships.

U.S. Dreadnoughts now carry and fly off small aeroplanes from barbette crowns, in the same way as British Ships.

Armoured Cruisers, **NORTH CAROLINA** and **SEATTLE** were specially equipped to serve as Seaplane Carriers and Depot Ships. See illustration of *Seattle* on an earlier page. Doubtful if these Armoured Cruisers are still on this duty.

Mine Layers, **AROOSTOOK** and **SHAWMUT,** acted as Tenders to the *NC* Flying Boats on Cross-Atlantic Flight.

Kite Balloons worked by nearly all classes of warships.

Up to the present, no special Aircraft Carriers, like British *Argus*, *Furious*, *Nairana*, etc., have been added to U.S. Navy.

Tenders to Submarine Chasers.

Cruisers, **SALEM** and **CHICAGO**, Auxiliary **PRAIRIE**, Coastguard Cruiser **SNOHOMISH**, Armed Yacht *Yacona* and various Tugs have been used for convoying Submarine Chasers across the Atlantic. They will be released from this duty when all *SC*-boats have been withdrawn from European waters.

Gunboat, **VICKSBURG,** listed as Fisheries Protection Vessel, Alaska, also serves as Parent Ship to four Submarine Chasers.

Tenders to Submarines—*Continued.*

Photo, Copyright, E. Muller. Jr.

FULTON (*ex-Niagara*) (1914). 1408 tons. Complement: 173. Dimensions: $216 \times 35 \times 13$ feet (*mean draught*). Guns: 2—3 inch (50 cal.), 1—1 pdr. auto. anti-aircraft. Torpedo tubes: None officially listed, but from published plans and photos 4 tubes appear to be mounted on foc'sle in two twin deck-mountings. Machinery: 1100 B.H.P. 6-cyl. 2-cycle Nlseco Diesel engine. 1 screw. Designed speed: 12·25 kts.; 12·34 *on trials.* Fuel: 234 tons *oil.*

(Pacific Fleet.)

BEAVER (Newport News, 1910, purchased 1918). 5970 tons. Dimensions: 380 (*o.a.*) × 47 × 21 feet (*max. draught*). Guns: 4—5 inch, 2—3 inch AA., 2—1 pdr, 2 M.G. 1 screw. I.H.P. 4500 = 16·5 kts. Fuel: 2350 barrels oil fuel. Complement, 373.

CASTINE (1891). 1177 tons. Guns: 2—6 pdr. R.F. Speed: 16 kts. Coal: 210 tons.

SEVERN (1899). 1175 tons. No guns. Coal: 13 tons.

ALERT (1875). 1100 tons. Guns: 6—4 inch, 40 cal., 4—6 pdr. Speed: 10 kts. Coal: 197 tons.

Photo, Lieut. H. Reuterdahl, U.S.N./R.F.

LEONIDAS (1898). Ex-Fuel Ship. 4023 tons. Dimensions: $274 \times 39\frac{1}{4} \times 17\frac{3}{4}$ feet. Complement, 167. Guns: 1—6 inch, 2—3 inch, 2 M.G. H.P. 1100 = $8\frac{1}{2}$ kts. Coal: 205 tons.

Similar to "Leonidas" above.

HANNIBAL (1898). Ex-Fuel Ship. 4000 tons. Dimensions: $274 \times 39\frac{1}{4} \times 17\frac{3}{4}$ feet. Complement, 295. Guns: 1—4 inch, 2—3 inch, 2 M.G. H.P. 1100 = 9 kts. Coal: 491 tons.

Ammunition Ships.

Building.

NITRO, PYRO (both building by Puget Sound, N.Y.). 10,600 tons. Dimensions: $460 \times 61 \times 21$ feet. Guns: 4—5 inch, 4—3 inch AA. Designed S.H.P. 5300. Speed, 16 kts. Parsons (geared) turbines, 2 screws. Fitted with plant for powder testing and cooling, also large cold storage capacity for meat, in addition to ammunition carrying spaces.

U. S. MINE PLANTERS AND SWEEPERS.

Mine Planters.

Note.—The Mine Planting Force during the War consisted of the ex-Cruisers *San Francisco* and *Baltimore*, and Converted Liners *Aroostook*, *Canandaigua*, *Canonicus*, *Housatonic*, *Quinnebaug*, *Roanoke*, *Shawmut*, with *Blackhawk* as Tender. *Aroostook* and *Shawmut* are retained, and *Black Hawk* assigned to new duties; the other vessels have been reconditioned for Mercantile Service. These ships laid the Northern Barrage from Scotland to Norway.

Same as "Shawmut" below

(*Pacific Fleet.*)

AROOSTOOK (Cramps, 1907. Ex-S.S. *Bunker Hill*, of Eastern Steamship Co., purchased 1917 and converted into Mine Planter). All details as *Shawmut*, below. Served as Tender to *NC* Flying Boats during Cross Atlantic Flight.

SHAWMUT (AROOSTOOK same). *Photo, O. W. Waterman.*

(*Atlantic Fleet.*)

SHAWMUT (Cramps, 1907. Ex-S.S. *Massachusetts*, of Eastern Steamship Co., purchased 1917 and converted into Mine Planter). 3800 tons. Complement, 314. Dimensions: 395 (*o.a.*) × $52\frac{1}{4}$ × 16 feet (*mean*). Guns: 1—5 inch, 2—3 inch AA., 2 M.G. Reciprocating engines and 8 S. E. boilers. 2 screws. H.P. 7000 = 20 kts. Fuel: 400 tons coal + 160 tons oil. Served as Tender to *NC* Flying Boats during Cross-Atlantic Flight.

Mine Planters—*continued.*

Photo, U. S. Navy.

(*Atlantic Fleet.*)

SAN FRANCISCO (1889). Displacement, 4083 tons. Complement, 315. Dimensions: 410 (*w.l.*) × $49\frac{1}{6}$ × $18\frac{3}{4}$ (*mean*) feet. Armament: 4—5 inch, 2—1 pdr., 2 M.G. Carries 300 Mark II mines. 4 searchlights. Designed H.P. 8500 = 19 kts. 8 Babcock boilers. Coal: 663 tons.

Photo, U. S. Navy

(*Pacific Fleet.*)

BALTIMORE (1888). Displacement, 4413 tons. Complement, 345. Dimensions: $327\frac{1}{2}$ (*w.l.*) × $48\frac{2}{3}$ × $19\frac{1}{2}$ (*mean*) feet. Guns: 4—5 inch, 51 cal., 2—3 inch AA., 2 M.G. Armour: 4″ deck. Designed H.P. 8500 = 20 kts. Boilers: 8 Babcock. Coal: *maximum* 1092 tons.

Mine-Sweepers.

In addition to the vessels described below, about 100 other ships (such as Trawlers, Tugs, etc.) were chartered or purchased for War Duty. It is not definitely known yet how many of these vessels will be retained in the Post-War Fleet Organisation, and so no attempt is made to describe them this year. For Tugs, fitted as Mine Sweepers, see a subsequent page.

Photo wanted.
2 masts. 1 funnel.

("BIRD" CLASS—54 BOATS.)

LAPWING, OWL, ROBIN, SWALLOW, SANDERLING, AUK, CHEWINK, CORMORANT, GANNET (all built by Todd S. B. Co., Tebo Yacht Basin, Brooklyn, N. Y.).

TANAGER, CARDINAL, ORIOLE, CURLEW, GREBE, MALLARD, ORTOLAN, PEACOCK (all built by Staten Id. S. B. Co., N. Y.).

AVOCET, BOBOLINK, LARK, REDWING, RAVEN, SHRIKE (all built by Baltimore D. D. & S. B. Co.).

PELICAN, FALCON, OSPREY, SEAGULL, TERN (all built by Gas Engine & Power Co., Morris Heights, N. Y.).

TURKEY, WOODCOCK, QUAIL PARTRIDGE (all built by Chester S. B. Co.)

SANDPIPER, WARBLER, VIREO, WILLET (all built by Philadelphia Navy Yard).

SWAN, WHIPPOORWILL, BITTERN (all built by Alabama S. B. & D. D. Co., Mobile).

WIDGEON, TEAL, BRANT (all built by Sun S. B. Co., Chester).

KINGFISHER, RAIL (both built by Puget Sound Navy Yard).

EIDER, THRUSH (both built by Pusey & Jones, Wilmington).

FINCH, HERON (both built by Standard S. B. Co., N. Y.).

FLAMINGO, PENGUIN (both built by New Jersey D. D. & T. Co., Elizabeth Port).

PIGEON. Builder not known. Built 1918-19. 950 tons *normal*, 1009 *full load* at $10\frac{1}{4}$ feet aft. Dimensions: $187\frac{3}{4}$ (*o.a.*) × $35\frac{1}{2}$ × $9\frac{3}{4}$ feet (*mean* draught). Guns: 2—3 inch AA., 2 M.G. Machinery: 1 set triple expansion and 2 B. & W. boilers. Designed I.H.P. 1400 = 14 kts. Oil fuel only

Note.—Condor, Plover, Goshawk and *Nos. 55, 56, 57* stopped. Nine boats still unfinished on July 1st, 1919. These craft may also serve as Mine Layers, Tugs, Coastguard Cutters and Salvage Ships.

Fuel Ships.

(*Oil Carriers.*)

TWELVE OIL TANKERS are listed in the monthly returns of U.S. naval construction, but are not included in the official Handbook, "Ships' Data." They are believed to be vessels, ordered by the Government from the Emergency Fleet Corporation and transferred to Navy. No details known.

("*Pecos*" *Atlantic Fleet*, "*Neches*" & "*Brazos*" *Pacific Fleet*).

BRAZOS (1919), *NECHES, PECOS*: all three building by Boston N.Y. 14,800 tons. Dimensions: $475\frac{3}{4}$ (*o.a.*) × 56 × $26\frac{2}{3}$ feet *mean*. Recipro. engines and 4 B. & W. boilers. Designed I.H.P. 5200 = 14 kts. Deadweight capacity 9600 tons. Guns: 4—5 inch.

KANAWHA (& CUYAMA). *Photo, O. W. Waterman.*

("*Kanawha*," "*Cuyama*" *Pacific Fleet.* "*Maumee*" *Atlantic Fleet*).

CUYAMA (1916) **MAUMEE** (1915), **KANAWHA** (1914). Oil Tankers. 14,500 tons. Dimensions: $475\frac{1}{2}$ × 56 × $26\frac{1}{4}$ (*mean*). *Cuyama* and *Kanawha* reciprocating engines, 5200 H.P. *Maumee* 2-cycle Diesel motors 5000 H.P. Speed: 14 kts. Fuel capacity: 7500 tons cargo oil, 1575 tons own bunker oil. Guns: *Cuyama* 4—5 inch; *Maumee* 4—4 inch; *Kanawha* 4—4 inch, 2 M.G.

(*Pacific Fleet*).

JASON (1912), **ORION** (1912). 19,250 tons. Dimensions: 536 × 65 × $27\frac{3}{4}$ (*mean*). Speed: 14 kts. Fuel capacity (deadweight to designed draft): 10,500 tons cargo fuel + 2000 tons own bunker fuel. *Maximum* cargo capacity (close stowage): 11,500 tons coal + 2575 tons oil. Guns: 4—4 inch.

Fuel Ships.—*Continued.*

(*Colliers and Oil Carriers.*)

(*Atlantic Fleet*).

NEREUS (1913), **PROTEUS** (1912). 19,080 tons. Dimensions: 522 × 62 × $27\frac{2}{3}$ (*mean*). Speed: 13 kts. Fuel capacity (deadweight to designed draft): 10,500 tons cargo fuel + 2000 own bunker fuel. *Maximum* cargo capacity (close stowage): 11,800 tons coal + 1125 tons oil *or* 10,100 tons coal + 3050 tons oil. Guns: 4—4 inch.

(*Pacific Fleet*). *Photo, O. W. Waterman.*

NEPTUNE (1911). 19,480 tons. Dimensions: 542 × 65 × $27\frac{2}{3}$ (*mean*). Speed: 13 kts. Fuel capacity (deadweight to designed draft): 10,500 tons cargo fuel + 2000 tons own bunker fuel. *Maximum* cargo capacity (close stowage): 10,200 tons coal + 2925 tons oil *or* 11,700 tons coal + 1250 tons oil. Guns: 4—4 inch.

(*Pacific Fleet*). *Photo, O. W. Waterman.*

JUPITER (1912). 19,360 tons. Dimensions: 542 × 65 × 27 (*mean*). Speed: 14 kts. Fuel capacity (deadweight to designed draft); 10,500 tons cargo fuel + 2000 tons own bunker fuel *Max.* cargo capacity (close stowage); 11,600 tons coal + 127 tons oil *or* 10,100 tons coal + 3075 tons oil. Guns: 4—4 inch.

War loss: *Cyclops* foundered March 1918.

(*Colliers and Oil Carriers*).

(*Colliers—"Mars" Atlantic Fleet. "Vulcan" Pacific Fleet*).

HECTOR (1909)
MARS (1909), **VULCAN** (1909). 11,250 tons. Dimensions: 403 × 53 × $24\frac{2}{3}$ (*mean*). Speeds about 12 knots. Fuel capacity (deadweight to designed draft), 7200 tons cargo fuel + 300 tons own bunker fuel. *Max.* capacity (close stowage); 7600 tons cargo fuel + 825 tons own bunker fuel. Guns: 4—4 inch.

(*Colliers bought during Spanish-American War.* (As) = *Asiatic Fleet.* (A) = *Atlantic Fleet.* (P) = *Pacific Fleet*).

(As) **ABARENDA** (1892). Ex-Collier, 6680 tons. Dimensions: $325\frac{1}{2}$ × 42 × $22\frac{5}{6}$ (*Plimsoll mark*). Guns: 4—6 pdr. H.P. 1050 = 9 kts. *Max.* fuel capacity: 3500 tons cargo + 825 own bunkers.

(As) **AJAX.** 9250 tons *approx.* Dimensions: $387\frac{1}{2}$ × $46\frac{1}{2}$ × H.P. 3000 = 10 kts. *Max.* fuel capacity; 4800 tons cargo + 500 own bunkers. Guns: 4—6 pdr.

(A) **ARETHUSA.** 6160 tons. Dimensions: $343\frac{1}{2}$ × $42\frac{1}{4}$ × $22\frac{3}{4}$ (*Plimsoll mark*). H.P., 1700 = 10 kts. *Max.* fuel capacity, 4450 tons *oil*. Guns: 4—3 inch, 2 M.G.

(P) **BRUTUS.** 6550 tons. $332\frac{1}{2}$ × $41\frac{1}{2}$ × 23. (*Plimsoll mark*). H.P. 1200 = 10 kts. *Max.* fuel capacity; 4850 tons cargo + 450 tons own bunkers. Guns: 4—6 pdr.

(A) **CÆSAR.** 5940 tons. Dimensions: 322 × 44 × $19\frac{3}{4}$. (*Plimsoll mark*). H.P., 1500 = 10 kts. *Max.* fuel capacity: 3250 tons cargo + 800 tons own bunkers. Guns: 4—6 pdr.

(A) **NERO.** 6100 tons. Dimensions: $323\frac{1}{2}$ × 41 × $21\frac{1}{2}$. (*Plimsoll mark*). H.P., 1000 = 9 kts. *Max.* fuel capacity: 4300 tons cargo + 30 tons own bunkers. Guns: 1—3 inch, 4—6 pdr.

STERLING. (*Out of commission*). 5660 tons *approx.* Dimensions: 284 × 37 × . H.P.: 1000 = 11 kts. *Max.* full capacity: 2750 tons cargo + 475 tons own bunkers. Guns: 4—6 pdr.

U.S. SUPPLY AND REPAIR SHIPS.

Supply Ships.

(*Atlantic Fleet.*) *Photo, U.S. Navy.*

BRIDGE (1916). 8500 tons. Complement, 238. Dimensions: 423 × $55\frac{1}{4}$ × $20\frac{2}{3}$ feet (*mean* draught.) Guns: 4—5 inch, 50 cal., 1 M.G. H.P. 4000 = 14 kts. Reciprocating engines. 2 screws. Fuel: 1000 tons *oil.*

(*Pacific Fleet.*)

RAPPAHANNOCK (Vegesack, Germany, 1913, ex-North German Lloyd s.s. *Pommern*, seized 1917). 17,000 tons. Complement, Dimensions: $471\frac{1}{4}$ × $59\frac{1}{4}$ × $26\frac{3}{4}$ feet. Guns: 1—5 inch, 1—3 inch. I.H.P. 4850 = 11·5 kts. Coal: 3060 tons.

(*Refrigerator and Supply Ship, Pacific Fleet.*)

GLACIER (1891). 8325 tons. Complement, 149. Dimensions: $355\frac{2}{3}$ × 46 × $25\frac{1}{3}$ feet (*mean* draught). Guns: 1—5 inch, 2—3 inch. H.P. (*on trials*) 2127 = 12·3 kts. Coal: 939 tons.

Supply Ships—*Continued.*

(*Refrigerator and Supply Ship, Pacific Fleet.*)

CELTIC (1891) 6750 tons. Complement, 152. Dimensions: 383 × $44\frac{1}{2}$ × 21 feet (*mean* draught). Guns: 4—3 inch, 50 cal., 1—3 inch AA. H.P. 2200 = 10·5 kts. Coal: 757 tons.

(*Supply Ship, Atlantic Fleet.*)

CULGOA (1889). 6000 tons. Complement, 142. Dimensions: $346\frac{1}{3}$ × 43 × $21\frac{3}{4}$ feet (*mean* draught). Guns: 4—3 inch, 50 cal., 1—3 inch AA. H.P. 2350 = 13·25 kts. Coal: 980 tons.

(*Atlantic Fleet.*)

SUPPLY (1873). 4325 tons. Complement, 128. Dimensions: $355\frac{2}{3}$ × $43\frac{1}{3}$ × $19\frac{1}{2}$ feet (*mean* draught) Armament: 4—6 pdr., 2—1 pdr. H.P. (*on trials*) 1009 = 9·66 kts. Coal: 1053 tons.

Repair Ships.

Projected.

MEDUSA (authorized; not yet begun). 10,000 tons. 460 × 70 × 19 feet. Guns: 4—5 inch, 4—3 inch AA. Geared turbines. Designed S.H.P. 7000 = 16 kts.

(“*Prometheus*,” *Atlantic Fleet;* “*Vestal*,” *Pacific Fleet.*) *U.S. Navy Photo.*

PROMETHEUS (1908). **VESTAL** (1908). 12,585 tons. Guns: 4—5 inch, 50 cal. (+ 1—3 inch AA. in *Vestal* only). H.P. 7500 = 16 kts. Coal, *Prometheus*: 1614 tons; *Vestal*: 1422 tons. Babcock boilers.

(*For Target Repairs: Pacific Fleet.*)

NANSHAN. 5140 tons. Dimensions: $295\frac{2}{3}$ × 39 × feet. H.P., 1400 = $10\frac{1}{2}$ kts. *Max.* fuel capacity; 425 tons. Guns: 4—6 pdr.

Photo, U.S. Navy.

(*For Target Repairs: Atlantic Fleet*)

LEBANON (1897). 3285 tons. Dimensions: 249 (*o.a.*) × $37\frac{1}{3}$ × $17\frac{1}{4}$ feet. Guns: 1—6 inch, 2—3 inch, 2 M.G. H.P. 1000 = 10 kts. Coal: 192 tons. Complement, 61.

(*For Radio Repairs: Pacific Fleet.*)

SATURN. 4840 tons. Dimensions: 297 × $40\frac{1}{2}$ × feet. H.P., 1500 = 11 kts. *Max.* fuel capacity: 400 tons. Guns: 1—6 inch, 2—3 inch.

Salvage Department.

Following ships in European waters: **CHESAPEAKE** (1900), 2000 tons; 1—3 inch gun; speed 11 kts. **FAVORITE** (1907), 950 tons; guns: 2—3 inch, 1—3 inch AA., 2 M.G.; speed 14 kts. **MANNA HATA. UTOWONA:** No details known. This unit may be demobolised in the near future.

U. S. TRANSPORTS, HOSPITAL SHIPS, TUGS.

Navy Transports.

HEYWOOD. (*Authorized: not yet begun*). 10,000 tons. Complement 258. Dimensions: 460 × 64 × 19 feet. Guns: 4—5 inch, 2—3 inch AA., 2—6 pdr., 2—1 pdr. Turbines and B. and W. boilers. Designed S.H.P. 5400 = 10 kts. Fuel, 1200 tons. Assigned to Philadelphia N.Y. for building.

HENDERSON (1916). 10,000 tons. Complement: 214. Dimensions: $482\frac{3}{4}$ × 61 × 20 feet (*mean* draught). Guns: 8—5 inch, 50 cal., 2—3 inch, 2—1 pdr. H.P. 4000 = 14 kts. Reciprocating engines. 2 screws. Fuel: 1200 tons *oil*. Has Sperry gyro. stabilisers. To take 2000 men and 32 horses.

Photo, Capt. F. C. Bowen, R.M.L.I.

HANCOCK (1879). 8500 tons. Complement: 227. Dimensions: $465\frac{1}{2}$ × $45\frac{1}{4}$ × $24\frac{1}{3}$ feet. (*mean* draught). Guns: 4—3 inch, 2—3 inch AA., 2—3 pdr., 6—1 pdr., 2 M.G. H.P. 3100 = 13 kts. Coal: 1423 tons.

RELIEF (1903). 3300 tons. Speed: 15 kts. Armament: *Nil.*
Hospital Ship.

Hospital Ships.

(*Pacific Fleet*).

COMFORT (ex-Ward Liner *Havana*, built by Cramp, 1906), 10,102 tons, and **MERCY** (ex-Ward Liner *Saratoga*, built by Cramp, 1907), 10,112 tons. Complement 322. Dimensions: 430 × $50\frac{1}{6}$ × 24 to 26 feet. I.H.P. 8500 = 18 kts. Coal: 1010/1060 tons. Purchased 1918.

Photo, U.S. Navy.

(*Atlantic Fleet*).

SOLACE (1896). 5700 tons. Complement: 153, out of which 59 only are U. S. naval ratings. Dimensions: 377 × 44 × 22 feet (*mean* draught). H.P. 3200 = 15 kts. Armament: *Nil.*

Tugs.

Note: For **BRANT, CARDINAL, SANDPIPER** (Tugs, Pacific Fleet) and **PEACOCK, WARBLER, WILLETT** (Tugs, Atlantic Fleet), see “Bird Class Mine-Sweepers” on a preceding page.

NUMBER 21—39, building and completing. **ALLEGHENY*** (1917), **SAGAMORE*** (1917). Ocean-going Tugs of 1000 tons. $149\frac{1}{3}$ × 30 × $14\frac{3}{4}$ feet. Guns: 2—3 inch AA., 2 M.G. I.H.P. 1800 = 13 to 14 kts. Oil, 279 tons.

* Both Atlantic Fleet.

NUMBER 48—85. Building. Tugs of 215 tons. $82\frac{1}{4}$ × 20 × $8\frac{3}{4}$ feet. Guns: 2—1 pdr., 1 M.G. H.P. 300 = 10 kts. Oil fuel only.

(*Pacific Fleet*).

DREADNAUGHT (1917), **UNDAUNTED** (1917). 450 tons. Guns: 1—3 pdr., 2 M.G. I.H.P. 1000 = 11·5 kts. Oil fuel only.

(*Atlantic Fleet*).

CHEMUNG (ex-*Pocahontas*, 1916). **WANDO** (1916). 575 tons. Dimensions: $123\frac{1}{2}$ × $26\frac{3}{4}$ × $11\frac{1}{2}$ feet. 2—3 pdr., 1 M.G. H.P. 800 = 11 kts. Oil fuel only.

(*“Arapaho” Atlantic Fleet. “Mohave” Pacific Fleet*).

ARAPAHO (1914), **MOHAVE** (1914). 575 tons. 2—3 pdr. H.P. 800 = 10 to 11 kts. Oil: 149 tons.

(*Atlantic Fleet*).

LYKENS (1913). 625 tons *gross*. Dimensions: 157 × 29 × 15 feet. Guns: 1—3 inch. 2 M.G. H.P. 1000 = kts.

ONTARIO. *Photo, U.S. Navy.*

(*Pacific Fleet.*)

SONOMA (1912) and **ONTARIO** (1912). 1120 tons. Dimensions 175 (*p.p.*) × 34 × $12\frac{1}{2}$ feet (*mean*). Guns: 1—3 inch AA., 2 M.G. Speed: 13 kts. Coal: 440 tons (*average*). These two tugs are ocean-going, and available as repair ships.

(*Continued on next page*).

U. S. TUGS AND CONVERTED YACHTS.

Tugs—*Continued.*

(Atlantic Fleet.)

PATAPSCO (1908), **PATUXENT** (1908). 755 tons. Dimensions: 148 × 29 × 12¼ feet. Guns: 1—3 inch AA., 2 M.G. H.P. 1160 = 13 kts. Coal: 324 tons.

(Pacific Fleet.)

SEA ROVER (1902). tons. Guns: 1—3 inch, 2 M.G. I.H.P. 700 = 10 kts. Fuel: 1200 barrels oil fuel.

(Atlantic Fleet.)

POTOMAC (1897). 785 tons. Guns: 2—3 pdr. H.P. 2000 = 16 kts. Coal: 200 tons.

(Asiatic Fleet.)

PISCATAQUA (1897). 854 tons. Guns: 2—3 pdr., 2 M.G. H.P. 2000 = 16 kts. Coal: 236 tons.

(Asiatic Fleet.)

WOMPATUCK (1896). 462 tons. Guns: 2—1 pdr., 1 M.G. H.P. 650 = 13 kts. Coal: 130 tons.

(Pacific Fleet.)

IROQUOIS (1892). 702 tons. Guns: 2—3 pdr. H.P. 1000 = 13¼ kts. Oil fuel.

(Pacific Fleet.)

ASPINET (ex-*Apache*, 1889). 650 tons. Guns: 2—1 pdr., 2 M.G. I.H.P. 550 = 10 kts. Coal: 123 tons.

Also many other Tugs not assigned to fleet duties.

Converted Yachts.

(See next page for Table of Yachts purchased during War.)

WASP (1898). 630 tons. Guns: 2—3 pdr., 2—1 pdr. H.P. 1800 = 16½ kts. Coal: 79 tons.

SYLPH (1898). 152 tons. Armament: 2 M.G. H.P. 550 = 15 kts. Coal: 48 tons. Complement, 31.

DOROTHEA (1897). 594 tons. Guns: 3—3 inch, 2 M.G., 1 Y-gun. H.P. 1560 = 14 kts. Coal: 80 tons. Boilers: Yarrow.

Photo, H. Reuterdahl, Esq.

AILEEN (1896). 192 tons. Guns: 1—3 pdr., 2—1 pdr. H.P. 500 = 14 kts. Coal: 46 tons.

YANKTON (1893). 975 tons. Armament: 2—3 inch, 2—3 pdr., 2 M.G. H.P. 750 = 14 kts. Coal: 174 tons. Complement, 86. 1″ deck amidships.

Photo: favour of Commodore R. P. Forekew, N.Y.N.M.

GLOUCESTER (1891). 786 tons. Guns: 5—3 pdr., 2—1 pdr. H.P. 2000 = 17 kts. Coal: 120 tons. Boilers: Babcock.

Converted Yachts—*Continued.*

Photo, Lieut F. S. Dowell, U.S.N.

(Presidential Yacht.)

MAYFLOWER (1896). 2690 tons. Armament: 2—3 inch, 1—3 inch AA., 4—6 pdr. H.P. 2400 = 14½ kts. Coal: 537 tons. Complement, 180.

SCORPION (1896). 775 tons. Armament: 4—6 pdr. H.P. 2800 = 17·8 kts. Coal: 136 tons. Complement, 87. Station Ship at Constantinople; interned during War. Reported relieved by *Galveston*, 1919.

VIXEN (1896). 806 tons. Guns: 4—3 pdr., 2—1 pdr. H.P. 1250 = 16 kts. Coal: 190 tons.

Photo, H. Reuterdahl, Esq.

HAWK (1891). 375 tons. Guns: 1—3 pdr., 2—1 pdr. H.P. 900 = 14½ kts. Coal: 70 tons.

EAGLE (1890). 434 tons. Armament: 2—6 pdr. H.P. 850 = 12·5 kts. Coal: 68 tons. Complement, 69.

SYLVIA (1882). 302 tons. Guns: 3—1 pdr. 2 M.G. H.P. 165 = 9 kts. Coal: 60 tons.

The following Table gives the names and brief details of Yachts purchased and armed for War Service. Material (S) = Steel; (I) = Iron; (C) = Composite; (W) = Wood. Where two building dates are given, second date is of reconstruction. Tonnages are *gross* unless otherwise stated.

Present disposal of these vessels not known. Large Yachts, like *Aphrodite*, *Corsair*, *Kwasind* may be retained by the Navy and the other craft sold out. *Isabel* rated as a Destroyer during the War.

A very large number of other Yachts acquired for the war by Charter and free lease omitted, as all these vessels have been (or will be) returned to their owners.

Winchester listed on next page with experimental vessels.

War losses: Alcedo, Guinevere, Wakiva II.

Converted Yachts.—continued.

Name (Material).	Built.	Tons. Gross.	Kts.	Guns.
Niagra (S)	1898	703	13	4—4 inch, 2—M. G., 1 Y
Nokomis (S)	1917	872	16	4—3 inch, 2 M. G.
Onward (S)	1906	157	13.8	2—6 pdr., 2 M. G.
Parthenia (W)	1903	144	12½	1—3 pdr., 1 M. G.
Phalarope (W)	1881	55	12	1—1 inch, 1 M. G.
Piqua (S)	1899	575*	20	4—3 inch, 1—6 pdr., 2 M. G.
Remlik (S)	1903	600*	14	2—3 inch, 2 M. G.
Reposo II (W)	1882 1892	157	14	1—3 inch, 2 M. G., 1 Y
Sachsen (S)	1902	217	13	1—6 pdr., 2—3 pdr., 2 M. G.
Saivla (W)	1902	106	10.4	1—3 pdr., 1 M. G.
Sialia (S)	1914	558	14¼	2—3 inch (Davis), 2 M. G.
SP 237 (S)	1910	219	13	4—6 pdr.
SP 427 (W)	1888	157	18	2—6 pdr.
SP 507 (S)	1909	195	14	3—3 pdr., 2 M. G., 1 Y
SP 524 (S)	1913	161	14	1—3 pdr.
SP 582 (S)	1907	161	15	2—2 pdr., 2 M. G.
SP 852 (C)	1899	74	10	1—3 pdr., 1 M. G.
Stinger (—)	1917	47	14¾	1—1 inch, 1 M. G.
Thetis (W)	1917	98*	12	2—3 inch, 2 M. G.
Vega (S)	1907	276	15	1—3 inch, 1—6 pdr., 2 M. G.
Wacondah (S)	1901	190	18	2—6 pdr., 2 M. G.
Wanderer (S)	1897	362	12	2—3 inch, 2 M. G.
Wenonah (S)	1915	200	12	2—3 inch, 2 M. G.
Yacona (S)	1898	527	12	2—3 inch, 2 M. G.
Zara (S)	1891	184	10	2—6 pdr., 2 M. G.
Zoraya (W)	1901	129	12	2—3 pdr.

*Displacement.

Note.

During the War, vessels of the Naval Militia formed part of the Regular Navy, but were manned by the Naval Volunteer Reserve.

California.

Marblehead

Columbia (District of)

Ozark   Oneida

Connecticut.

Machias

Florida.

Mackenzie

Illinois.

Dubuque

Indiana.

Louisiana.

Amphitrite   Stranger

Maine.

Massachusetts.

Chicago   Rodgers

U. S. MISCELLAEOUS.

Surveying Service.

Vessels withdrawn from this Service during War. Present allocation of ships not known.

Non-Naval Vessels belonging to Coast and Geodetic Survey and Lighthouse Service served with Regular Navy during War on Patrol and Distant Service, but have now returned to their normal duties.

For Fisheries Duties (Alaska.)

Has no mainmast now.

(Gunboat.)

VICKSBURG (1896). 1010 tons. Guns : 6—4 inch, 4—3 pdr., 2—1 pdr. H.P. 800 = 12 kts. Boilers : 2 single-ended. Coal : 243 tons.

(Tenders, four SC boats : SC 309, SC 310, SC—, SC —.)

U. S. NAVAL MILITIA (in 1914).

Maryland.

Somers

Michigan.

Don Jaun de Austria   Yantic

Minnesota.

Gopher

Missouri.

Isla de Luzon   Huntress

New Jersey.

Marietta   Vixen

New York.

Gloucester   Haiok

Sandoval   Wasp

Ships reserved for Experimental Services .

MONTGOMERY Torpedo Experimental
SAN FRANCISCO
RESTLESS. Mining Experimental.

(Yacht converted for Testing PVs.)

WINCHESTER (Bath I. W., 1916). 437 tons. Dimensions : 225 × 21 × 7½ feet. Guns : 1—3 inch, 1—6 pdr., 2 M.G., 1 Y-gun. Parsons turbines and Normand boilers. S.H.P. 7000. Trial speed : 31.65 kts. Fuel : Oil only. 35,000 gallons = 1632 miles at 17.3 kts. Purchased for $300,000, 1917.

(Experimental Torpedo Ship.)

VESUVIUS (1888). Ex-" Dynamite Cruiser." 930 tons. Armament : 1—3 pdr. signalling. Original speed : about 21½ kts., much less now. Torpedo tubes : 1—21 inch sub., 1—18 inch sub., 2—18 inch above water.

North Carolina.

Elfrida   Foote

Oregon.

Boston

Ohio.

Dorathea   Essex

Pennsylvania.

Sylvia   Wolverine

Rhode Island.

Aileen

Washington.

Cheyenne   Concord

U. S. COASTGUARD SERVICE. (Alphabetically arranged.)

Revised 1919 from "Ships' Data," U.S. Naval Vessels. Armaments listed those mounted during War, when ships served on Patrol and Distant Service with the Regular Navy.

War losses: McCulloch, Tampa, Mohawk.

5 CUTTERS building and completing by Norway Con. Co., Everett, Wash. 1600 tons. 240 × 39 × 14 feet. S.H.P. 2600 = 16 kts. (These details unofficial.)

ACUSHNET. Steel, 1 screw. 800 tons. Dimensions: 152 × 29 × 13¾ feet. Speed, 12·5 kts. Guns: 2—1 pdr., 1 Y-gun.

ALGONQUIN (1898). Steel, 1 screw. 1181 tons. Dimensions: 205 × 32 × 13½ feet. Speed, 16 kts. Guns: 4—3 inch, 2 M.G.

ANDROSCOGGIN (1908). Wood, 1 screw. 1605 tons. Dimensions: 210 × 35 × 17½ feet. Speed, 13·2 kts. Guns: 3—3 inch, 1—6 pdr., 2 M.G., 1 Y-gun. Usually on Grand Banks for Fisheries Duty.

ONONDAGA (1898). Steel, 1 screw. 1192 tons. Dimensions: 205 × 32 × 13 feet. Speed, 14·5 kts. Guns: 4—6 pdr.

OSSIPEE (1915). Steel, 1 screw. 908 tons. Dimensions: 165¾ × 32 × 11¾ feet. Speed, 12·6 kts. Oil fuel only. Guns: 2—3 inch, 2 M.G.

PAMLICO (1907). Steel, twin screw. 451 tons. Dimensions: 158 × 30 × 5 ft. Speed: 11·2 kts. Guns: 2—6 pdr.

SENECA (1908). Steel, 1 screw. 1445 tons. Dimensions: 204 × 34 × 17 feet. Speed: 13·2 kts. Guns: 4—4 inch, 2 M.G., 1 Y-gun.

APACHE (1891). Iron, 1 screw. 708 tons. Dimensions: 175 × 29 × 9½ feet. Speed, 12 kts. Guns: 3—3 inch, 2 M.G., 1 Y-gun.

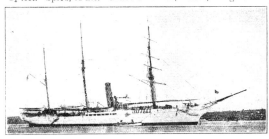

BEAR (1874). Wood, 1 screw. 1700 tons. Dimensions: 198 × 28¼ × 18¼ feet. Speed not known. Guns: 3—6 pdr.

(Depot Ship.)

COLFAX (1871). Iron, 610 tons. Dimensions: 179¼ × 25 × 9 feet. No other details known.

COMANCHE (1896). Steel, 2 screw. 670 tons. Dimensions: 169 × 27 × 9 feet. Guns: 1—3 inch, 2—6 pdr.

GRESHAM (1897). Steel, 1 screw. 1090 tons. Dimensions: 205 × 32 × 11 feet. Speed, 13 kts. Guns: 4—3 inch, 2 M.G.

Cruising Cutters—*Continued.*

SEMINOLE (1900). Steel, 1 screw. 860 tons. Dimensions: 188 × 29 × 11 feet. Speed, 14·7 kts. Guns: 4—3 inch, 2 M.G., 1 Y-gun.

SNOHOMISH. Steel, 1 screw. 879 tons. Dimensions: 152 × 29 × 15 feet. Speed: 12·5 kts. Guns: 1—3 inch, 2—6 pdr., 2 M.G.

TALLAPOOSA (1915). Steel, 1 screw. 912 tons. Dimensions: 165¼ × 32 × 11¾ feet. Speed: 12·7 kts. Oil fuel only. Guns: 1—4 inch, 2—6 pdr., 2 M.G., 1 Y-gun. Derelict Destroyer for Gulf of Mexico.

TAHOMA (1909). Steel, 1 screw. 1050 tons. Dimensions: 191 × 32 × 14 feet. 4—6 pdr. *Sig.*: GVHQ. *Headquarters*: Seattle, Wash.

Photo, Seward, Weymouth.

ITASCA (ex *Bancroft*, 1893). Steel, 2 screws. 980 tons. Dimensions: 189 × 32 × 13 feet. Speed, 14·37 kts. Guns: 2—3 inch, 2—6 pdr., 1 Y-gun.

MANNING (1897). Composite, 1 screw. 1155 tons. Dimensions: 205 × 32 × 13 ft. Speed, 14 kts. Guns: 4—4 inch, 2 M.G.

MIAMI (1912). Steel, 1 screw. 1180 tons. Dimensions: 190 × 32 × 13 ft. 3—6 pdr. *Headquarters*: Key West, Fla.

MORRILL (1889). Iron, 1 screw. 420 tons. Dimensions: 145 × 24 × 9 ft. Speed: 13·2 kts. Guns: 1—3 inch, 2—6 pdr., 2 M.G.

Cruising Cutters—*Continued.*

THETIS (1891). Wood, 1 screw. 1200 tons. Dimensions: 188 × 29 × 18 ft. 3—3 pdr. *Sig.*: GVFQ. *Headquarters*: Honolulu, Hawaii.

TUSCARORA (1902). Steel, 1 screw. 739 tons. Speed: 14·2 kts. Dimensions: 178 × 30 × 11 feet. Guns: 1—3 inch, 2—6 pdr., 1 Y-gun.

U. S. COASTGUARD SERVICE—(continued).

Cruising Cutters.—*Continued.*

Photo, U.S. Navy Publicity Bureau.

UNALGA (1912). Steel, 1 screw. 1180 tons. Dimensions: 190×32 ×13 feet. Speed 13 kts. 3—6 pdr.

WINDOM (1896). Steel, twin screw. 670 tons. Dimensions: 170×27×9 ft. Speed 12 kts.

WINONA (1890). Iron, twin screw. 340 tons. Dimensions: 148×26×6 ft. 1—3 pdr. S.A. *Sig.*: GVDP. *Headquarters*: Gulfport, Miss.

Harbour Cutters—*continued.*

GUTHRIE (1895). Iron, 1 screw. 126 tons. Dimensions: 88×17× 9 feet.

HARTLEY (1875). Wood, 1 screw. 48 tons. Dimensions: 64× 11×6 feet.

HUDSON (1893). Iron, 1 screw. 174 tons. Dimensions: 96× 20×9 feet. Guns: 1—1 pdr.

YAMACRAW (1909). Steel, 1 screw. 1082 tons. Dimensions: 191×32×14 feet. Speed, 13 kts. 2—4 inch, 2—3 inch, 2 M.G.

Harbour Cutters.

ARCATA (1903). Wood, 1 screw. 130 tons. Dimensions: 85×17×10ft.

ARUNDEL (ex *Manhattan*) (1873). Iron, 1 screw. 174 tons. Dimensions: 102×20×8 feet.

Harbour Cutters—*continued.*

MACKINAC (1903). Steel, 1 screw. 220 tons. Dimensions: 110×20×10 feet. *Sig.*: GVHB. Guns: 1—6 pdr., 1 M.G.

Photo, "Syren & Shipping."

MANHATTAN (1918). Steel, 1 screw. Ice Breaker, Salvage Vessel, Tug and Fire Float. 379 tons. 120½×24×10¾ feet. 12 kts.

VERGANA (——). 128 tons. No other details.

Harbour Cutters—*continued.*

CALUMET (1894). Iron, 1 screw. 169 tons. Dimensions: 94×20×8 feet. 2—6 pdr., 2 M.G.

DAVEY (1908). Steel, 1 screw. 153 tons. Dimensions: 92×19×10ft. 1—1 pdr.

EMMA KATE ROSS (1882). Iron, 1 screw. 350 tons. Dimensions: 104×20×10 feet.

GOLDEN GATE (1896). Steel, 1 screw. 220 tons. Dimensions: 110×20×9 feet.

Harbour Cutters—*continued.*

WINNISIMMET (1903). Steel, 1 screw. 174 tons. Dimensions: 96×20×9 feet. Guns: 2—1 pdr.

WISSAHICKON (1904). Steel, 1 screw. 174 tons. Dimensions: 96×20×8 feet. Guns: 1—1 pdr.

WOODBURY (1864). Wood, 1 screw. 500 tons. Dimensions: 146×28×11 feet. 1 gun.
Note.—Above probably re-named or scrapped as there is a new T.B.D. *Woodbury.*

12 Launches

ACTIVE (——) tons. ADVANCE (1917), 11 tons. ALERT (1907), 17 tons. GUARD (1913), 52 tons. GUIDE (1907), 32 tons. MAGOTHY (1895), 83 tons. PATROL (1899), 15 tons. PENROSE (1883), 30 tons. SCOUT (1896), 30 tons. SEARCH (1907). — tons. TYBEE (1895), 40 tons. VIGILANT (1910) 12 tons.

IMPERIAL JAPANESE NAVY.

Revised, 1919, by the Navy Department, Tokyo, by courtesy of H. E. The Minister of Marine.

(The Acting-Editor has also to acknowledge the use of many useful notes and sketches, kindly furnished to "Fighting Ships" by Mr. K. Shimada in 1918.)

MINISTER OF THE NAVY

Errata.

On Map :—
For **KOREA** read **CHOSEN**.
For **YEZO** read **HOKKAIDO**.
For **MASANPHO** read **CHINKAI**.

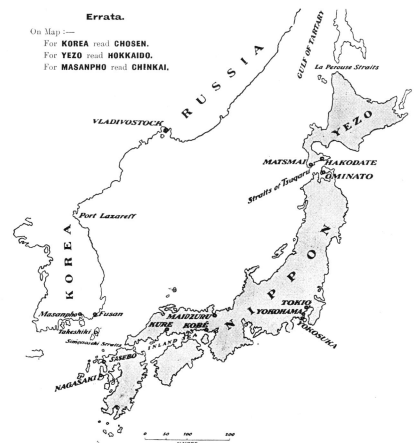

 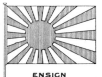 

ENSIGN   JACK & MERCANTILE ENSIGN   IMPERIAL STANDARD   TRANSPORT

Red
White
Gold
Blue

ADMIRAL   VICE ADMIRAL   REAR ADMIRAL   COMMODORE

SENIOR OFFICER

OFFICER COMMANDING TORPEDO DIVISION

YOKOSUKA	to	knots.
Hakodate	… … …	450
Hong Kong	… …	1580
Honolulu	… … …	3400
Kobe	… … …	300
Kure	… … …	400
Manila	… … …	1720
Nagasaki	… … …	760
Ryojun (Port Arthur) …		1350
Saigon	… … …	2400
Shanghai	… … …	1050

NAGASAKI	to	knots.
Chemulpo	… … …	446
Foo-chau	… … …	650
Hong Kong	… …	1067
Keilung (Formosa)	…	630
Kiao-chau	… …	450
Kure	… … …	240
Kobe	… … …	340
Maidzuru	… … …	400
Manila	… … …	1300
Chinkai	… … …	170
Matsumai	… … …	750
Pescadores	… … …	820
Ryojun (Port Arthur) …		585
Takeshiki	… … …	120
Saigon	… … …	1990
Shanghai	… … …	330
Vladivostock	… …	620
Wei-hai-wei	… … …	480

TAKESHIKI	to	knots.
Kiao-chau	… … …	420
Maidzuru	… … …	340
Chinkai	… … …	70
Matsumai	… … …	600
Nagasaki	… … …	120
Ryojun (Port Arthur) …		500
Vladivostock	… …	520
Wei-hai-wei	… … …	430

MATSUMAI	to	knots.
Maidzuru	… … …	440
Nagasaki	… … …	750
Ryojun (Port Arthur) …		1150
Takeshiki	… … …	600
Vladivostock	… …	380
Yokosuka	… … …	560
Nearest Russian coast (150 English miles N.E. by E. of Vladivostock)		250

MAIDZURU	to	knots.
Matsumai	… … …	440
Nagasaki	… … …	400
Ominato	… … …	465
Takeshiki	… … …	340
Vladivostock	… …	620

(RYOJUN) PORT ARTHUR	to	knots.
Hong Kong	… …	1275
Kiao-chau	… … …	280
Nagasaki	… … …	585
Vladivostock	… …	1170
Wei-hai-wei	… … …	100

JAPANESE NAVY.
Official Classification of Ships.

The official classification, instituted in 1912, is as follows :—

Battleships.	Battle-Cruisers.	1st class Cruisers (over 7000 tons).	2nd class Cruisers (under 7000 tons).	1st class Coast Defence Ships (over 7000 tons).	2nd class Coast Defence Ships (under 7000 tons).	1st Class Gunboats (over 800 tons).	2nd Class Gunboats (under 800 tons).
Kaga	Akagi	Nisshin	Oh-i	Iwami	Okinoshima	Mogami	Saga
Tosa	Amagi	Kasuga	Kitakami	Fuji	Mishima	Yodo	Uji
Mutsu	Kirishima	Aso	Kiso	Suwo	Chiyoda	Chihaya	Fushimi
Nagato	Haruna	Idzumo	Kuma		Akitsushima		Toba
Hiuga	Hi-yei	Iwate	Tama		Manshu		Sumida
Ise	Kongo	Yakumo	Tatsuta		Matsue		
Yamashiro	Kurama	Adzuma	Tenriu		Hashidate		
Fu-so	Ibuki	Asama	Hirado		Karasaki		
Settsu	Ikoma	Tokiwa	Chikuma		Komahasni		
Aki			Yahagi		Wakamiya		
Satsuma			Tone		Musashi		
Kashima			Niitaka		Yamato		
Katori			Tsushima				
Mikasa			Tsugaru				
Asahi			Chitose				
Shikishima			Suma				
Hizen			Akashi				

Destroyers:—1st class, over 1000 tons; 2nd class, 1000-600 tons; 3rd class, under 600 tons.
Torpedo boats:—1st class, over 120 tons; 2nd class, under 120 tons.

Present System of Nomenclature : Battleships named after Provinces ; Light Cruisers after Rivers ; 1st Class Destroyers after Winds ; 2nd Class Destroyers after Trees.

Personnel and Uniforms.

Minister of Marine : Admiral Tomasaburo Kato, G.C.M.G.

Personnel : Active, in 1916, 63,225 all ranks—more than this now. Yearly entries about 5,000—6,000 conscripts and 5,000—6,000 volunteers. Serve 4 years on active list and 7 years in reserve.

Reserves :—25,000 or more.

INSIGNIA OF RANK—EXECUTIVE OFFICERS—SLEEVES. (Changed to this ; 1908).

Sho-i Ko-hoshei.
Midshipman.

Executive Branch:	Tai-sho.	Chu-sho.	Sho-sho.	Tai-sa.	Chu-sa.	Sho-sa.	Tai-i.	Chu-i.	Sho-i Acting Sub-Lieut.	Has a stripe half the width of a Sho-i.
Corresponding British or U.S.:	*Admiral*	*Vice-Ad.*	*Rear-Ad.*	*Captain.*	*Commander.*	*Lieut. Com.*	*Lieutenant.*	*Sub-Lieut.*		

BAND between stripes. (BRANCHES, with but after Executive).

Violet   Kikwan (*Engineer*) (with executive rank and curl. Titles as above with the prefix Kikan).
Red   Gun-i (*Doctor*).
White   Shukei (*Paymaster*).
Brown   Zosen (*Constructor*).
,,   Zoki (*Engineer-Constructor*). -without curl.
Purple   Zohei (*Gun Constructor*).
Blue   Suiro (*Hydrographer*).

CAP.

The cap is the same as the British (but without gold embroidery in the senior ranks).

CAP BADGE.

Small anchor, surrounded by cherry leaves.

The senior officer of any branch on board the ship always carries the affix "cho." Thus : Ho-jitsu-cho (*Gunnery*), Sui-rai-cho (*Torpedo*), Ko-kai-cho (*Navigator*), Guni-i-cho (*Senior Doctor*), Shukei-cho (*Senior Paymaster*).

Undress is a military tunic (dark blue) with the sleeve insignia of rank in black braid only, with curl for executives and engineers. Other branches cannot be distinguished from each other in this tunic.

JAPANESE NAVAL ORDNANCE, TORPEDOES, &c.

Principal Naval Guns.

* = Q.F. with brass cartridge case.

Notation.	Calibre.	Length in calibres.	Model.	Weight of Gun.	Weight of A.P. shot.	*Maximum* Initial Velocity.	*Maximum* penetration firing A.P. capped at K.C. 5000 yards.	3000 yards.	Danger space against average ship, at 10,000 yards.	5000 yards.	3000 yards.	*Service* rate of Fire. Rounds per minute.
	inches.			tons.	lbs.	F. S.	inches.	inches.				
A[8]	14	45	V	82	1400	...	...	...	...	...	...	...
A[3]	12·6	40	C	66	990	2306	12	15	...	...	...	0·2
A[5]	12	45	('04)	58½	850	2800	16	20	185	500	780	...
A[3]	12	40	E	49	850	2423	12	15½	120	450	720	1
A[3]	10	45	E	32½	500	2710	10½	13½	150	480	720	3
A[3]	10	45	O	32	490	2500	9¾	12½	130	450	700	...
B	9	35	O	19½	268	2400	5½	7¼	...	...	...	...
*A**	8	45	O	15½	188	2800	7½	10½	105	430	625	1
A	8	45	E	17⅓	250	2740	7	10	110	425	600	1·2
*B**	8	40	E	15½	250	2580	5½	7½	100	400	580	1·2
C	6	45	('04)	8½	100	3000	4½	6½	75	250	475	...
C	6	50	V	8	100	3000	4½	6½	75	250	475	6
*E**	6	40	E	6½	100	2500	3	4½	65	210	435	7
*F**	6	40	E	6	100	2220	2½	4	35	150	360	8
*E**	5·5	...	...	...	...	...	...	...	...	...	...	...
*F**	4·7	45	...	...	...	...	...	...	...	...	...	...
*F**	4·7	40	E	2	45	2150	...	2½	...	...	...	8
*F**	4·7	32	E	1⅔	36	1938	...	...	...	...	...	8-6
*F**	3	...	...	...	14	...	...	...	...	...	...	...
*F**	3	40	...	2	12	2200	...	...	...	...	...	...

In the Model column C = Schneider-Canet; E, Elswick; O, Obukhoff (Russian); V, Vickers.

16 inch in *Kaga, Tosa, Nagato* and *Mutsu* ?
14 inch, 45 cal. in *Ise* class (2), *Fuso* class (2), *Kongo* class (4).
12 inch, 50 cal. in *Settsu.*
12 inch, 45 cal. in *Settsu, Satsuma, Aki, Kurama, Ibuki, Ikoma, Katori, Kashima, Iwami, Mikasa.*
12 inch, 40 cal. in *Asahi, Shikishima, Fuji.*
10 inch, 45 cal. in *Satsuma, Aki, Kashima, Katori, Suwo, Okinoshima,* Mishima.**
8 inch, 40-45 cal. in 1st Class Cruisers, *Kurama, Ibuki.*
6 inch, 50 cal. in *Fuso* class (2), *Kongo* class (4), *Settsu.*
6 inch, 40-45 cal. in *Aki* and older Battleships, 1st and 2nd Class Cruisers, &c.
5·5 inch in *Ise* class (2), *Tatsuta* class (2).

* May have been removed from these ships.

Note.

Kure Naval Arsenal has concluded experiments with anti-aircraft guns. Large numbers of these guns are now being manufactured for all classes of warships and defences of naval harbours.

(All details tabulated above are unofficial.)

Ordnance Factories.

Guns manufactured at Kure, N.Y. Also by Muroran Steel Works, Hokkaido, owned by Hokkaido Colliery & S.S. Co., Messrs. Vickers Ltd. and Sir W. G. Armstrong-Whitworth & Co., and licensed to build Armstrong and Vickers' types of guns. There are also Japanese "Yamanouchi" types of small types of guns.

Shells manufactured by Muroran Steel Works, Kobe Iron & Steel Works, Kawasaki Zosen Kaisha, Mitsubshi Zosen Kaisha, Nippon Heiki Kaisha, and other firms.

Armour Plates.

From Imperial Iron Works, Yawata, Kyushu and Kure D.Y.

Torpedoes.

Size	*Name or Mark*	*Air Pressure lbs.*	*Charge lbs.*	*Max. Range at*	*kts.*	*Type of Heater*
21″	...	...	...	...	...	...
18″	...	...	...	...	...	...
15″	...	...	...	...	...	...
14″	...	...	...	...	...	...

Torpedoes built by Mitsubishi Zosen Kaisha, Kobé Steel Works (output, 250 torpedoes p.a.), and by Navy Yards which also construct tubes.

Mines.—No details known.

Searchlights.—No details known.

Scale : 1 inch = 160 feet.

JAPANESE WARSHIPS RECOGNITION SILHOUETTES. (*Re-arranged 1919*).

ONE FUNNEL.

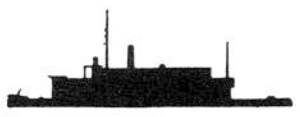

SUMIDA
(*River Gunboat*).

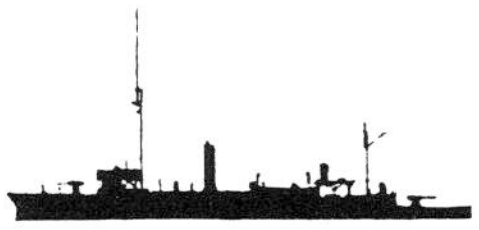

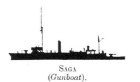

SAGA
(*Gunboat*).

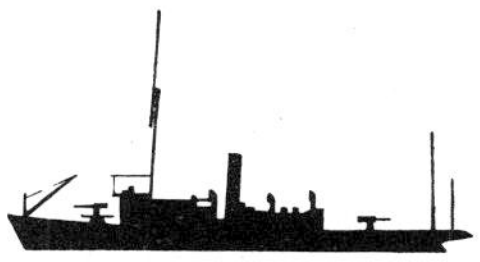

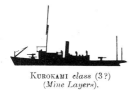

KUROKAMI *class* (3?)
(*Mine Layers*).

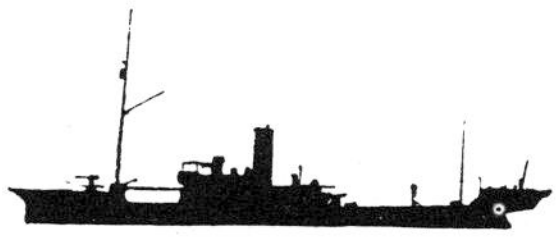

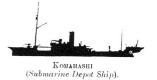

KOMAHASHI
(*Submarine Depot Ship*).

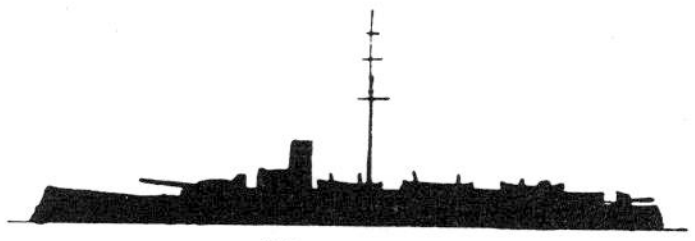

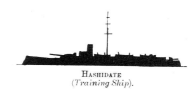

HASHIDATE
(*Training Ship*).

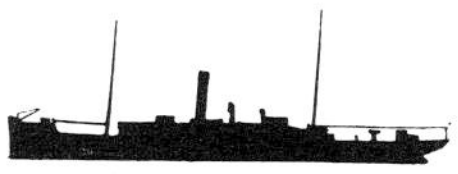

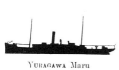

YURAGAWA MARU
(*Training Ship*).

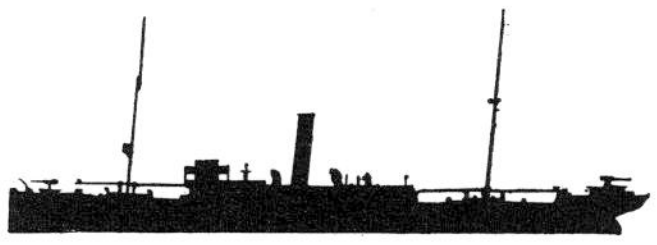

MANSHU
(*Naval Transport*).

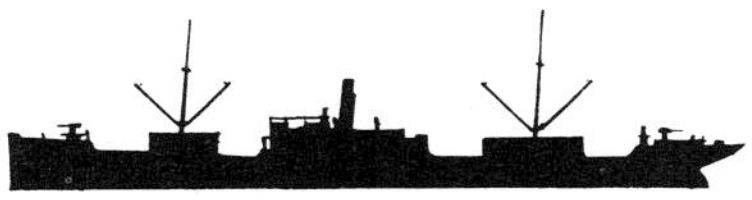

WAKAMIYA
(*Seaplane Carrier*).

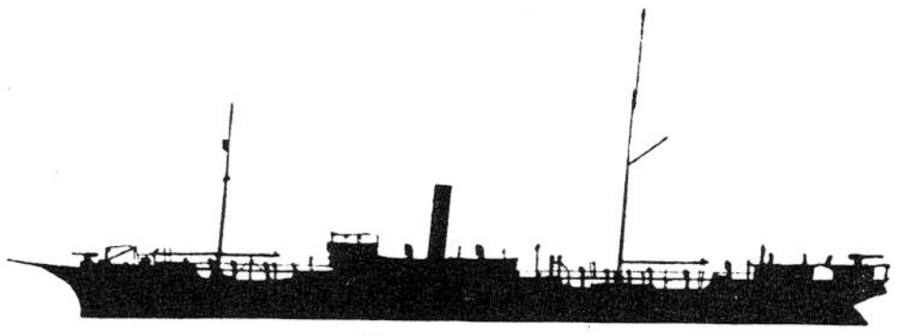

KARASAKI
(*Submarine Depot Ships*).

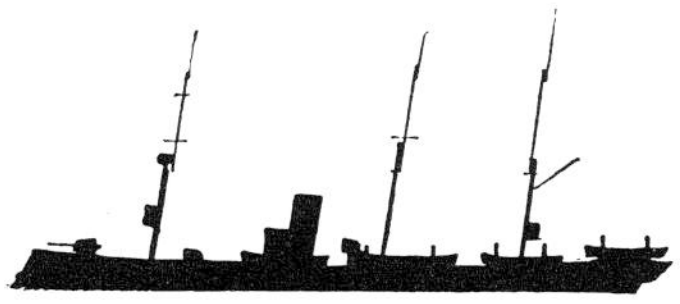

CHIYODA

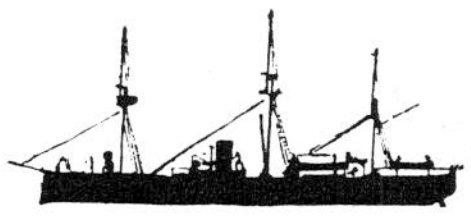

MUSASHI *class* (2)
(*Surveying Ships*).

Note.

Appearance of following Special Service Ships not known. Information regarding their appearance would assist in preparation of their Recognition Silhouettes.

T.B.D. Depot Ships :—ISUSAN, KENKAI, REKISAN, (Marus), SHIROGANE.
Mine Layers :—NINOSHIMA, YENOSHIMA, KUROSHIMA, TOSHIMA, NATSUSHIMA, ASHIZAKI, KATOKU, SOKUTEN (all Marus), KATSURIKI.
Oilers and Tankers :—ERIMO, NOTORO, SHIRETOKO, SUNOSAKI (Maru), TSURUGIZAKI, SHIJIKI.
Fleet Collier :—MUROTO.
Supply Ship :—NOSHIMA.
Transport :—TAKASAKI (*and Auxiliaries*) KOSHU, ROZAN, SEITO.
Repair Ship :—KWANTO (Maru).
Salvage Ships :—KURIHASHI, YODOHASHI, SARUHASHI, ITAHASHI.

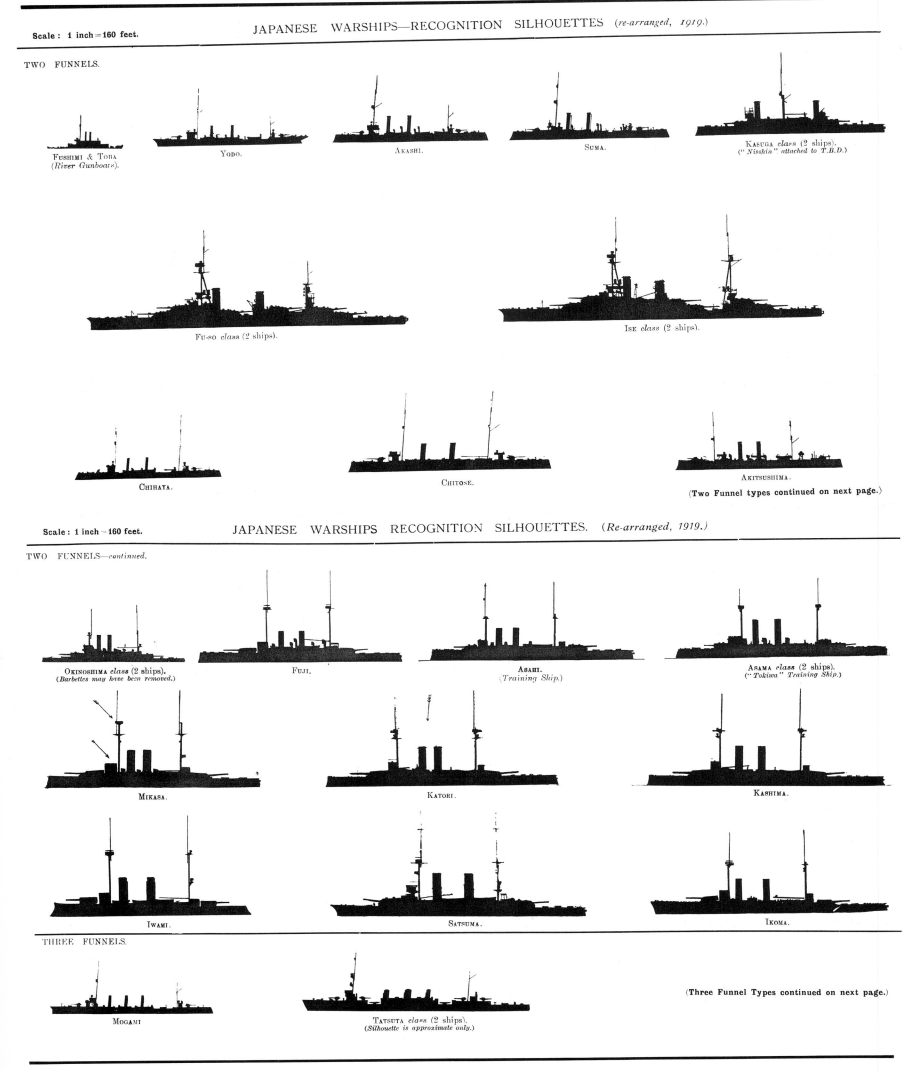

JAPANESE WARSHIPS—RECOGNITION SILHOUETTES (re-arranged, 1919.)

Scale : 1 inch = 160 feet.

TWO FUNNELS.

FUSHIMI & TOBA
(River Gunboats).

YODO.

AKASHI.

SUMA.

KASUGA class (2 ships).
("Nisshin" attached to T.B.D.)

FU-SO class (2 ships).

ISE class (2 ships).

CHIHAYA.

CHITOSE.

AKITSUSHIMA.

(Two Funnel types continued on next page.)

Scale : 1 inch = 160 feet.

JAPANESE WARSHIPS RECOGNITION SILHOUETTES. (Re-arranged, 1919.)

TWO FUNNELS—continued.

OKINOSHIMA class (2 ships).
(Barbettes may have been removed.)

FUJI.

ASAHI.
(Training Ship.)

ASAMA class (2 ships).
("Tokiwa" Training Ship.)

MIKASA.

KATORI.

KASHIMA.

IWAMI.

SATSUMA.

IKOMA.

THREE FUNNELS.

MOGAMI

TATSUTA class (2 ships).
(Silhouette is approximate only.)

(Three Funnel Types continued on next page.)

Scale : 1 inch = 160 feet.

JAPANESE WARSHIPS RECOGNITION SILHOUETTES (*Re-arranged, 1919.*)

THREE FUNNELS—*continued.*

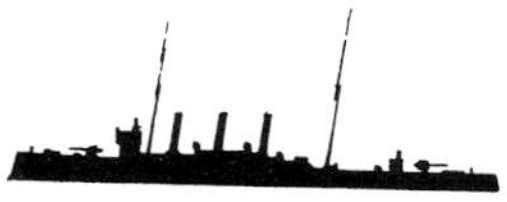

NAGAURA Maru.
(*Submarine Depot Ship.*)

NIITAKA *class* (2 ships).

TONE.

YAKUMO.
(*Training Ship.*)

SUWO.
(*Training Ship.*)

SHIKISHIMA.

IDZUMO *class* (2 ships).
"*Idzumo*" attached to T.B.D. Flotillas.

TSUGARU.
(*Training Ship.*)

HIZEN.

KURAMA
(*Ibuki* same without tripods).

SETTSU.

ADZUMA.
(*Training Ship.*)

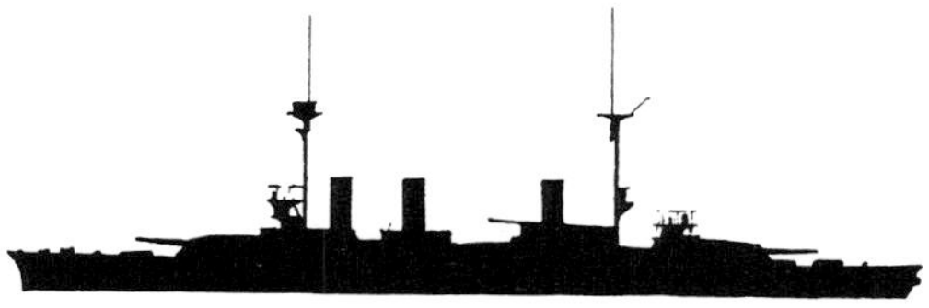

AKI.

KONGO *class* (4 ships).
("*Kongo*" has fore-funnel further forward.)

Scale: 1 inch = 160 feet.

JAPANESE WARSHIPS RECOGNITION SILHOUETTES. (*Re-arranged, 1919.*)

FOUR FUNNELS.

ASO.
(*Tender to Submarines.*)

HIRADO *class* (3 ships).

TORPEDO CRAFT.

Scale : 1 inch = 160 feet.

SUBMARINES.

Scale : 1 inch = 80 feet.

(These Silhouettes are only approximate.)

Shiritaka t.b.

Nos. 68—75 t.b.
(8 Schichau *type*.)

(1)

(2)

Hayabusa *class* t.b. (11)

Nos. 1—5.

No. 6.

No. 7.

Kagero *class* t.b.d. (3).

Urakaze t.b.d.

Momo *class* t.b.d (10).

No. 13.

(1)

(2)

Nos. 8—12, 16 & 17.

Sakura *class* t.b.d. (2).
(May now have raised fore funnels.)

Kaba *class* t.b.d. (10).

Amatsukaze *class* t.b.d. (4).

Akebona *class* t.b.d. (2).
Asashiho *class* t.b.d. (2).

Later Arare *class* t.b.d. (33).
Earlier Arare *class* t.b.d. (2).
(*Vary a little in details.*)

Yamakaze *class* t.b.d. (2).

No. 15 (& No. 14?).

1915 JAPANESE DREADNOUGHTS. Nos. **8** and **9.** (23 knot.)

せい ISE (Nov., 1916), か ろ ひ HIUGA (Jan., 1917).

Normal Displacement, 31,260 tons. Complement, 1,360. Length (p.p.) 640 feet.

Beam, 94 feet. *Max.* draught, 28⅓ feet. Length (o.a.), 683 feet.

Guns (Japanese) :
12—14 inch, 45 cal. (A⁸)
20—5·5 inch, — cal.
16—12 pdr.
4—12 pdr. (anti-aircraft).
Torpedo tubes (21 inch) :
6 *submerged*.

Armour (Japanese) :
12″—9″ Belt ....
4″ Belt (Ends)........
2—1⅟″ Decks ....
12″ Turrets............
6″ Battery ....
12″ C.T.

HIUGA.*   *Photo by courtesy of the Navy Department, Tok*

Ahead :
4—14 in.
6 to 8—5·5 in.

Broadside : 12—14 in., 10—5·5 in.

Astern :
4—14 in.
6—5·5 in.

ISE   *Photo by courtesy of the Navy Department, Tok*

Machinery : Brown-Curtis turbines in *Ise* ; Parsons turbines in *Hiuga*. 4 screws. Boilers : 24 Kansei. Designed H.P. 45,000 = 23 kts. Fuel : *normal* 1000 tons ; *maximum* 4000 tons coal + 1000 tons oil.

Armour Notes.—As *Fuso* class (next page).

Name	Built by	Machinery	Laid down	Completed	Trials. H.P. – kts.	Boilers	Turbines
Ise	Kawasaki Co.	Kawasaki Co.	May '15	Dec. '17	= 23·3.	Kansei.	Curtis-
Hiuga	Mitsu Bishi Co.	Mitsu Bishi Co.	May '15	Mar. '18		Kansei.	Parsons

Note.—In above illustrations of *Ise* and *Hiuga* running trials, chart-house and bridges are not fully built, an searchlights are not in position. The large tanks at base of after-tripod mast, in view of *Ise*, are temporari shipped for trial purposes.

General Notes.—Built under the 1914 Naval Programme. These ships are an improved and slightly faster *Fu* type. It is unofficially reported that they are strongly protected against aerial attack by three special thick protective decks over vital parts of the hull. They may not have the 16—12 pdr. listed. Spec attention is reported to have been paid to the rapid replenishment of fuel, stores, ammunition, &c. Usin internal protection against mine and torpedo explosions by minute sub-divisions, wing bulkheads ov machinery magazine spaces, &c.

1912-13 JAPANESE DREADNOUGHTS. Nos. **6** & **7.** (22½—22 kts.)

ふさ FU-SO (March, 1914), ろしまや YAMASHIRO (Nov. 1915),

Normal Displacement 30,600 tons. Complement, 1243 and 1272.
Length (p p) 630 feet. Beam, 94 feet. *Max.* draught, 28½ feet. Length *over all*, 673 feet.

Guns (Japanese) :
12—14 inch, 45 cal. (A⁸)
16—6 inch, 50 cal.
12—12 pdr.
4—12 pdr. (anti-aircraft).
4 machine.
4 landing.
Torpedo tubes (21 inch) :
6 *submerged*

Armour :
12″—9″ Belt (amidships)
4″ Belt (ends) ......
2″ and 1⅟″ Decks...
12″ Turrets............
6″ Battery ....
12″ Conning tower....

YAMASHIRO   *Photo by courtesy of the Navy Department, Tokyo*

FU-SO.

Ahead :
4—14 in.
4—6 in.

Broadside : 12—14 in., 8—6 in.

Astern :
4—14 in.,
4—6 in.

Armour Notes : (unofficial). 12 inch belt over amidships barbettes, boiler and engine rooms ; 9 inch belt between end pairs of superfiring barbettes. 6 inch battery closed by bulkheads at first and fifth barbettes.

Gunnery Notes : (unofficial). R.F. in roof of each gun-house, over C.T. and Torpedo control tower (aft) and in fire-control top.

Torpedo Notes : 10 searchlights. Net defence right up to stern.

Machinery : Brown-Curtis turbines. 4 screws. Boilers : 24 Miyabara ; *Yamashiro* may have Kansei. Designed H.P. 40,000 = 22·5 kts. in *Yamashiro*, 22 kts. in *Fuso*. Fuel : *normal*, 1000 tons *maximum* 4000 tons coal + 1000 tons oil fuel.

Name.	Builder.	Machinery.	Laid down.	Completed.	Trials. H.P. kts.	Turbine	Boilers	Best recent speed
Fu-So	Kure	Kawasaki	Mar.'12	Nov.'15	46,500 23.	Curtis	Miyabara	
Yamashiro	Yokosuka	Kawasaki	Dec.'13	Apl.'17	....	Curtis	Miyabara	

General Notes.—*Fu-so* 1911 Naval Programme, *Yamashiro* 1913 Programme. *Fu-so* built in dry dock and floated out March, 1914.

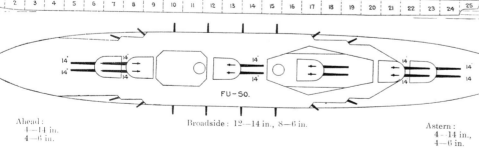

Fu-So.   *Photo by courtesy of the Imperial Japanese Embass*

1909 JAPANESE DREADNOUGHT. No. 1 (20·5 knot).

つつせ SETTSU (March, 1911).

Normal displacement, 21,420 tons. Complement, 1000.

Length (*p.p.*), 500 feet. Beam, $84\frac{1}{6}$ feet. { *Maximum* draught, $28\frac{1}{4}$ feet. *Mean* " $27\frac{1}{2}$ " } Length *over all*, 533 ft.

Guns (M. '04) (*See Notes*):
12—12 inch, 45 and 50 cal. (*A*5)
10—6 inch, 50 cal.
8—4·7 inch, 50 cal.
12—12 pdr.
4 Machine.
4 Landing.
Torpedo tubes (18 inch):
4 *submerged* (broadside).
1 " (stern).
(4458 tons.)

Armour (Krupp):
12″ Belt (amidships) ......
4″ Belt (ends) (N.C.) ......
3″ and $1\frac{1}{8}$″ Armour decks
7″-4″ Lower deck side
11″ Turrets ....
11″ Turret bases ......
6″ Battery ....
10″ Conning tower.........
(4960 tons.)

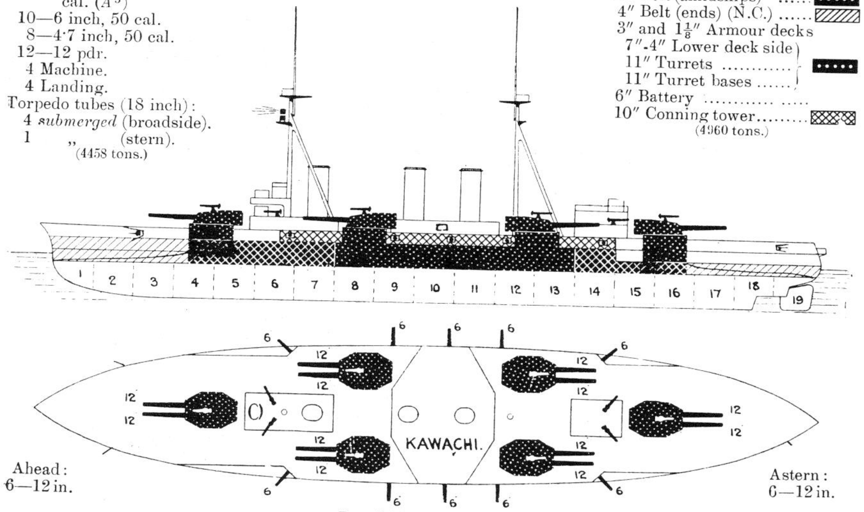

Ahead: 6—12 in.

Broadside: 8—12 in.

Astern: 6—12 in.

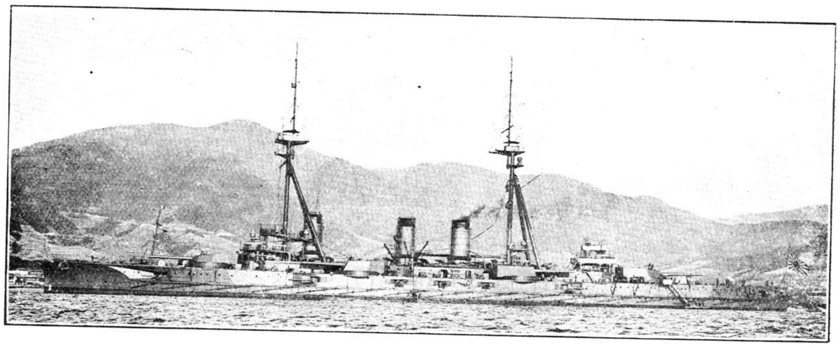

SETTSU. *Photo by courtesy of the Navy Department, Tokyo.*

Machinery: Curtis turbine; 2 screws. Boilers: 16 Miyabara. Designed H.P. 25,000 = 20.5 kts. Coal: *normal*, 1100 tons; *maximum*, 2300 tons + 400 tons oil fuel.

Gunnery Notes.—The 12 inch guns in end barbettes are 50 calibres long; those in the four beam barbettes are only 45 calibres long. With the exception of 12 pdrs. (make unknown), all calibres are Elswick models.

Engineering Notes.—Weight of machinery, 2146 tons.

Name.	*Built at*	*Machinery.*	*Laid down.*	*Completed.*	*Trials. H.P.*		*kts.*		*Turbines*	*Boilers.*	*Best recen speed.*
Settsu	Kure D.y.	Kure D.y.	Jan., '09	1912	15 000	=	18.3	=	Curtis	Miyabara	

Notes.—*Kawachi*, a sister ship to *Settsu*, destroyed by explosion in Tokuyama Bay, July, 1918

1911 JAPANESE BATTLE-CRUISERS. (Dreadnoughts Nos. 2, 3, 4, 5.)

うかんこ KONGO (May, 1912), HI-YEI (Nov., 1912),
なるは HARUNA (Dec., 1913), ましりき KIRISHIMA (Dec., 1913).

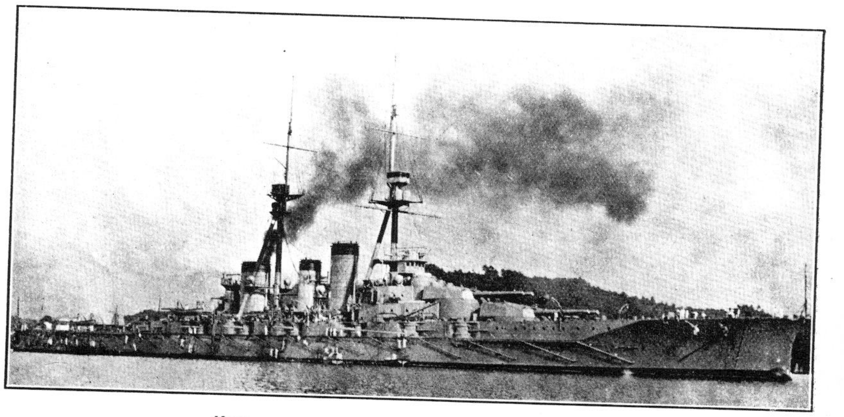

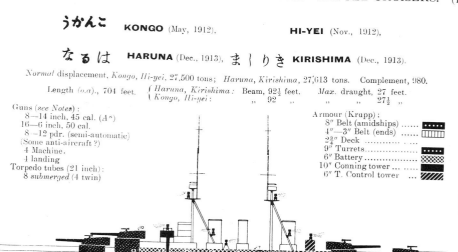

HIYEI. *Photo by courtesy of The Imperial Japanese Embassy.*

Normal displacement, *Kongo, Hi-yei*, 27,500 tons; *Haruna, Kirishima*, 27,613 tons. Complement, 980.

Length (*o.a.*), 704 feet. { *Haruna, Kirishima*: Beam, $92\frac{1}{2}$ feet. *Max.* draught, 27 feet. *Kongo, Hi-yei*: " 92 " " " $27\frac{1}{2}$ " }

Guns (*see Notes*):
8—14 inch, 45 cal. (*A*⁺)
16—6 inch, 50 cal.
8—12 pdr. (semi-automatic)
(Some anti-aircraft?)
4 Machine.
4 landing
Torpedo tubes (21 inch):
8 *submerged* (4 twin)

Armour (Krupp):
8″ Belt (amidships) ......
4″—3″ Belt (ends) ......
$2\frac{3}{4}$″ Deck ....
9″ Turrets............
6″ Battery..................
10″ Conning tower ... .
6″ T. Control tower ...

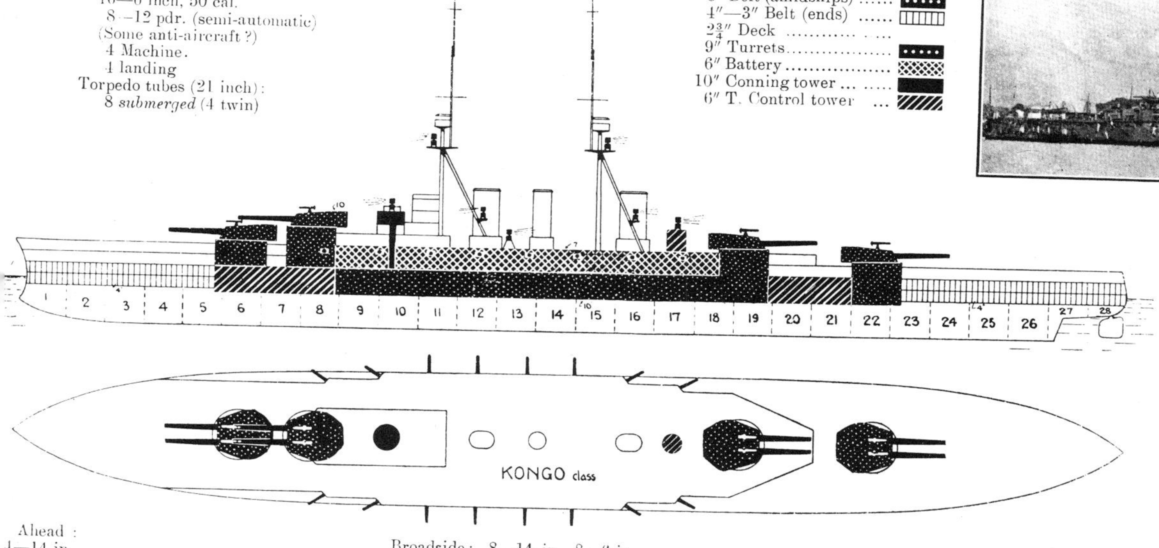

Ahead: 4—14 in. 2 to 4—6 in.

Broadside: 8—14 in., 8—6 in.

Astern: 4—14 in. 4—6 in.

Machinery: Parsons 4-shaft (in *Haruna* only Curtis 4-shaft) turbines. Designed H.P. 64,000 = 27·5 kts. Boilers: See *Notes*. Fuel: *normal*, 1,200 tons; *maximum*, 4,000 tons + 1,000 tons oil.

Name	*Builder*	*Machinery*	*Laid down*	*Completed*	*Trials*	*F.P.*	*Turbine*	*Boilers*	*Re-fit*
Kongo	Vickers	Vickers	Jan.'11	Aug.'13	41,800 = 25	78,000 = 27·3	Parsons	Yarrow	1916
Hi-yei	Yokosuka	Mitsu Bishi	Nov.'11	Mar.'14			Parsons	Kansei	
Haruna	Kawasaki	Kawasaki	Mar.'12	Mar.'15		82,000 = 27·77	Curtis	Yarrow	
Kirishima	Mitsu Bishi	Mitsu Bishi	Mar.'12	Apr.'15		80,000 = 27·54	Parsons	Yarrow	

General Notes. *Kongo* 1910-11 Programme, others 1911-12 Programme.

These Notes are not from any official data.

Appearance Notes.—All four ships now have raised fore-funnels, as *Hiyei* above, but *Kongo* has her fore funnel further forward and well away from the second funnel.

Gunnery Notes.—In *Kongo* guns are Vickers models; but in other three ships all calibres are of Japanese manufacture. *Kongo* has combined Vickers (hydraulic) and Janney-Williams (electric) manœuvring systems for her barbettes; there is also a small auxiliary hydraulic installation, generally used for cleaning purposes, which can be used in emergency for working the 14-inch guns. In the three Japanese-built ships no 12 pdrs. are mounted on the barbette crowns. *Kongo's* 12 pdr. as plans. *Kongo* is reported to be armed with a special 14 pdr. Vickers model, instead of 12 pdrs. but this is very questionable.

Armour Notes.—Plans not correct: Belt stops about 40 feet from bows and 33 feet from stern. The 6″ Battery and lower deck side extend to fore barbette.

Anti-Torpedo Protection Notes.—Internal sub-division by longitudinal and cross bulkheads. Extra protection given by armour to all magazine spaces. Port and starboard engine rooms are divided by an unpierced longitudinal bulkhead along keel-line. It is said contract for *Kongo* stipulated she should float with 50 feet of her side blown away, should not heel more than 11°, and *automatically* regain the vertical in a specified length of time, though at an increased draught.

Aircraft Notes.—Experiments with launching of seaplanes from *Kongo's* decks took place during September, 1917. Anti-aircraft guns mounted now in these ships.

Torpedo Notes.—Tubes are twin submerged type, at varying levels, some being only 6 feet below waterline. *Kongo* has combined hydraulic and electrically-operated tubes. In *Haruna*, tubes are Elswick 21-inch side-loading, hydraulically operated.

Engineering Notes.—In *Kongo, Hiyei* and *Kirishima* Parsons turbines have H.P. rotors on outboard shafts and L.P. on inner shafts, with astern turbines aft and in same casing. *Kongo's* 36 Yarrow boilers are in five compartments. Pressure: 205 lbs. per sq. inch.

1905 JAPANESE SEMI-DREADNOUGHT. (First-class Battleship.) (20 knot.)

AKI (April, 1907).

Displacement, 19,800 tons.   Complement, 937.

Length (o.a.), 492 feet; (p.p.), 460 feet.   Beam, 83¾ feet.   Maximum draught, 28 feet.

Guns (Elswick M. '04):
4—12 inch, 45 cal. (A⁵).
12—10 inch, 45 cal. (A³).
8—6 inch, 45 cal.
8—12 pdr.
4 Machine.
4 Landing.
Torpedo tubes (18 inch):
4 submerged (broadside).
1 submerged (stern).
(4040 tons.)

Armour (Krupp):
9″ Belt (amidships) ...
6″ Belt (bow) (N.C.) ...
4″ Belt (aft) ....
2″ Deck ....
7″ Upper belt............
8″ Turrets ....
9¾″ Turret bases ......
7″ Bases to 10 in. turrets
7″ Battery for Q.F.(N.C.)
(4812 tons.)

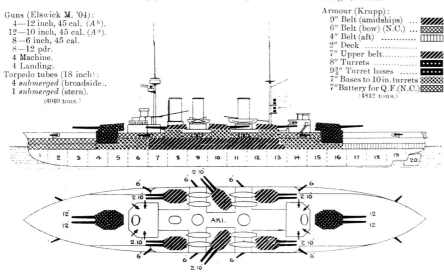

Ahead:
2—12 in.
4—10 in.
2—6 in.

Astern:
2—12 in.
4—10 in.
2—6 in.

Broadside: 4—12 in., 6—10 in., 4—6 in.

Machinery: Curtis turbine. 2 screws. Boilers: 15 Miyabara. Designed H.P. 24,000 = 20 kts. Coal: normal, 900 tons; max., 2000 tons, + 170 tons oil fuel.
⁹Gunnery Notes.—Turrets worked both electrically and hydraulically.
⁹Torpedo Notes.—Bullivant net defence; main deck shelf.
⁹Engineering Notes.—Weight of machinery, 2146 tons. R.P.M. 100 = 8½ kts., 160 = 14 kts., 210 = 18½ kts., 250 = 20¼ kts.

Name.	Builder.	Machinery.	Laid down.	Com-pleted.	Trials. Full power.		Turbines.	Boilers.
Aki	Kure	Fore River Co., U.S.A.	Mar. '05	1910	16,115 = 18·6	28,710 = 20·25	Curtis	Miyabara

General Notes.—Hull and fittings, 6764 tons. Equipment 754 tons. Refitted 1915.
    * These notes are unofficial.

SATSUMA まつ゛ま (November, 1906).

Normal displacement, 19,350 tons.   Complement, 937.

Length (waterline), 479 ft.   Beam, 83½ ft.   Maximum draught, 28 ft.   Length over all, 482 ft.; p.p., 450 ft.

Guns (Elswick M. '04):
4—12 inch, 45 cal. (A⁵).
12—10 inch, 45 cal. (A³).
12—4·7 inch, 45 cal.
4 Machine.
4 Landing.
Torpedo tubes (18 inch):
4 submerged (broadside).
1 submerged (stern).

Armour (Krupp):
9″ Belt (amidships) ...
6″ Belt (bow) (N.C.) ...
4″ Belt (aft) ....
2″ Deck ....
7″ Upper belt............
7″—9″ Turrets ....
9″ Turret bases.........
5″ Battery for Q.F.(N.C.)

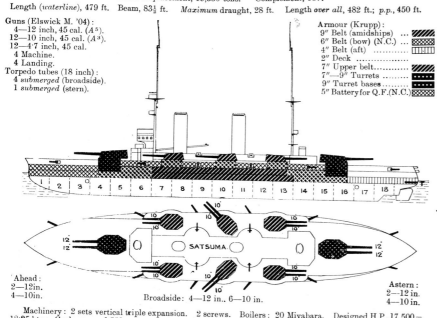

Ahead:
2—12 in.
4—10 in.

Astern:
2—12 in.
4—10 in.

Broadside: 4—12 in., 6—10 in.

Machinery: 2 sets vertical triple expansion. 2 screws. Boilers: 20 Miyabara. Designed H.P. 17,500 = 18·25 kts. Coal: normal 750 tons; maximum 2000 tons, + 300 tons oil fuel.
⁹Gunnery Notes.—Turrets worked both electrically and hydraulically.
⁹Torpedo Notes.—Net defence; main deck shelf.
⁹Engineering Notes.—

Name.	Builder.	Machinery.	Laid down.	Com-pleted.	Refit.	Trials. H.P. kts.		Boilers.	Best recent speed.
Satsuma	Yokosuka	Yokosuka	May, '05	Apl. '10	1916	18,507	= 18.95	Miyabara	

    * These notes are unofficial.

FORE TOP.   FORE TURRET.

1905 JAPANESE "BATTLE CRUISERS" (22-21¼ knot).

まらく **KURAMA** (Oct., 1907) & **IBUKI** (Nov., 1907). きふい

Normal displacement, 14,600 tons. Complement, 845.

Length (p.p.), 450 feet. Beam, 75½ feet. *Max.* draught, 26⅔ feet. Length *over all*, 485 feet.

Guns (Japanese):
4—12 inch, 45 cal. (A⁵)
8—8 inch, 45 cal. (A)
14—4·7 inch, 50 cal.
4 Machine
4 landing.
Torpedo tubes (18 inch):
3 *submerged*
(4158 tons.)

Armour (Krupp):
7″ Belt (amidships) ....
4″ Belt (ends) (N.C.) ....
2″ Armour deck ....
5″ Lower deck redoubt......
7″ Turrets (N.C.) ....
7″ Turret bases (N.C.) ....
5″ Battery ....
6″ Secondary turrets (N.C.)
8″ Conning tower (fore) ..
6″ „ „ (aft) ......
(4960 tons.)

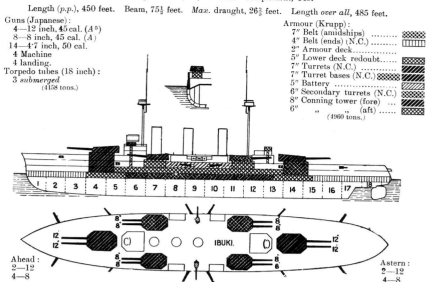

Broadside: 4—12 in., 4—8 in.

Ahead:
2—12
4—8

Astern:
2—12
4—8

Machinery: *Kurama*, 2 sets reciprocating. 2 screws. *Ibuki*, Curtis turbine. Boilers: Miyabara. Designed H.P., *Kurama*, 22,500 = 21·25 kts.; *Ibuki*, 27,000 = 22 kts. Coal: *normal*, 600 tons; *maximum*, 2000 tons + about 250 tons oil.
Armour Notes—Main belt is 7½ feet wide, thinning at ends.
Gunnery Notes—Loading positions, big guns: all round. Hoists: electric. Big guns: hydraulic and electric gears; secondary turrets, electric gear. Arcs of fire: 12 inch, 270°; secondary turrets, about 130°.
Torpedo Notes—Bullivant net defence to both ships.
Engineering Notes—Weight of machinery, 2078 tons.

Name.	Builder	Machinery	Laid down	Completed	Trials.		Boilers.	Best recent speed
					at 4/5.	6 hrs. f.p.		
Kurama	Yokosuka	Yokosuka	Aug.,'05	Oct.,'09	20,978 = 21.	27,353 = 20·87	Miyabara in both.	
Ibuki	Kure	Fore River Co., U.S.A.	May,'06	1910				

General Notes.—Weights: hull and fittings, 6105 tons; equipment 731 tons. *Ibuki* launched six months after laying down.
These notes are unofficial

(New photo of this ship wanted.)
IKOMA (April, 1906). まこい
(*Training Ship*:
Gunnery and Torpedoes.)

Photo, Symonds.

Displacement, *normal* 13750 tons; *full load* 15,150 tons. Complement, 817.
Length (p.p.), 440 feet; (o.a.), 475 feet. Beam, 75 feet. Mean draught, 26 feet.

Guns (see Notes):
4—12 inch, 45 cal. (A⁵)
10—6 inch, 45 cal.
8—4·7 inch.
6—12 pdr.
Torpedo tubes (18 inch):
2 *submerged*.
1 *above water* (stern).
(1719 tons.)

Armour (Krupp C. & N.C.):
7″ Belt (amidships) ....
4″ Belt (ends) ....
2″ Armour deck ....
5″ Lower deck redoubt ....
9-7″ Turrets ....
7″ Turret bases ....
5″ Lower deck side ....
5″ Casemates (N.C.) ....
8″ Conning tower (fore) ....
6″ „ „ (aft) ....
(3547 tons.)

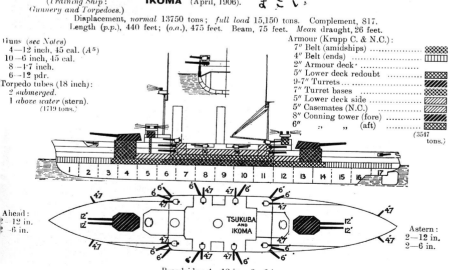

Broadside: 4—12 in., 6—6 in.

Ahead:
2—12 in.
2—6 in.

TSUKUBA and IKOMA

Astern:
2—12 in.
2—6 in.

Machinery: 2 sets reciprocating. 2 screws. Boilers: Miyabara. Designed H.P. 19,000 = 20·5 kts. Coal: *normal*, 600 tons; *maximum*, 2000 tons + 150 tons oil fuel. Weight of machinery, 2132 tons. Built and engined by Kure D.Y. 1905-7. On first trials made 21·9 kts. with 22,670 I.H.P. Refitted 1918-19. *Tsukuba*, of this class, destroyed by explosion, Jan., 1917.
1919 Corrections to Plans.—Main deck 6 inch battery removed and ports plated up. 4—4·7 inch over old two-tier sponsons removed. 6—6 inch now mounted on shelter deck, viz.: 4 over old two-tier sponsons (in old 4·7 inch positions) and 2 abeam of second funnel.

KURAMA. *Photo, Symonds.*

IBUKI.

Differences.—*Kurama* has tripod masts, and slightly taller funnels. Yard on foremast is high up with searchlight top *under*. In *Ibuki*, yard is lower down, with searchlight top *above* yard.

(Is second unit of the "KATORI" CLASS.)

まlか **KASHIMA** (March, 1905). Displacement, 16,400 tons. Complement, 946. Length (o.a.), 470 feet. Beam, 78 ft. 1¼ in. *Max.* draught, 26 ft. 7½ in. Guns: 4—12 inch, 45 cal. (A⁵), 4—10 inch, 45 cal. (A³). 12—6 inch, 45 cal., 10—12 pdr., 3—3 pdr., 4 M.G., 2 field. Torpedo tubes (18 inch): 5 *submerged*. Armour (Krupp): 9″ Belt (amidships), 6½″ Belt (ends), 3″ Deck on slopes, 9″ Turrets (K.C.), 9″—5″ Turret bases, 8″—6″ Secondary turrets (K.C.), 6″ Lower deck (side), 6″ Battery, 9″ Conning tower, 4″ Upper deck battery. Machinery: 2 sets 4 cylinder vertical quadruple expansion. 2 screws. Boilers: 20 Kansei. Designed H.P. 16,000 = 18·5 kts. Coal: *normal*, 750 tons; *maximum*, 2,150 tons. Built at Elswick 1904-6. Refitted 1916.

りとか

りとか **KATORI** (July, 1905). Displacement, 15,950 tons. Complement, 946. Length (o.a.), 455¾ feet. Beam, 78 feet. *Max.* draught, 27 feet. All other details as *Kashima* above, except *max.* coal, 1860 tons. Built by Vickers 1904-6. Refitted 1916. To *distinguish*: Funnels closer together than *Kashima*; fore topmast is *before* mast.

1899-8 OLD JAPANESE BATTLESHIPS 1897

MIKASA さかみ (November, 1900). (Reconstructed 1907-08.) Displacement, 15,362 tons. Complement, 830. Length (*waterline*), 415 feet. Beam, $76\frac{1}{4}$ feet. *Maximum* draught, 26 feet. Length *over all*, 432 feet. Guns: 4—12 inch, (45) cal. (A^5), 14—6 inch, 45 cal., 20—12 pdr., 2—3 pdr., 2—$2\frac{1}{2}$ pdr., 2 Maxims. Torpedo tubes (18 inch): 4 *submerged*. Armour (Krupp): 9″ Belt (amidships), 4″ Belt (ends), 12″ Bulkheads, 3″ Deck (slopes), 14″—10″ Barbettes, 10″—8″ Turrets to these, 6″ Lower deck redoubt, 6″ Battery (K.C.), 6″ Casemates (N.C.). Machinery: 2 sets 3 cylinder vertical triple expansion. 2 screws. Boilers: 25 Belleville. Designed H P. 15,000 = 18 kts. Coal: *normal* 700 tons; *maximum* 1500 tons. Built by Vickers, Barrow., 1899-1901. Sunk 1905. Salved and rebuilt 1906.

From "The Navy," Tokyo.

HIZEN (ex-Russian *Retvizan*) (October, 1900). (Reconstructed 1907-08.) Displacement, 12,700 tons. Complement, 791. Length (*waterline*), 376 feet. Beam $72\frac{1}{4}$ feet. *Maximum* draught, 26 feet. Guns: 4—12 inch, 40 cal. (A^4) (Obukhoff), 12—6 inch, 45 cal. (Japanese), 14—12 pdr., 4—$2\frac{1}{2}$ pdr., 2 M.G. Torpedo tubes (18 inch): 2 *submerged* (25° abaft). Armour (Krupp): 9″—6″ Belt (amidships), 4″ Belt (bow), 9″ Bulkhead, 3″ Deck (slopes), 6″ Lower deck redoubt, 10″ Turrets (N.C.), 9″ Turret bases (N.C.), 5″ Battery (N.C.), 10″ Conning tower (N.C.) Machinery: 2 sets, 3 cylinder triple expansion. 2 screws. Boilers: 24 Niclausse. Designed H.P. 16,000 = 18 kts. Coal: *normal* 1016 tons; *maximum* 2000 tons. Built by Cramp, Philadelphia. Scuttled at Port Arthur, 1904, and captured on fall of fortress. Salved and repaired, 1905-6

IWAMI みはい (July, 1902). (ex-Russian *Orel* reconstructed, 1907). *Normal* displacement, 13,516 tons. Complement, 806. Length (*p.p.*), $376\frac{1}{2}$ feet. Beam, 76 feet. *Mean* draught, 26 feet. Length *over all*, 397 feet. Guns (Japanese): 4—12 inch, 45 cal. (A^4), 6—8 inch, 45 cal., 16—12 pdr., 4—$2\frac{1}{2}$ pdr., 4 M.G. Torpedo tubes (15 inch): 2 *submerged* (broadside), 1 above water (*bow*). Armour (Krupp): $7\frac{1}{2}$″—6″ Belt (amidships), 4″ Belt (ends), 3″ Armour deck (slopes), 10″ Turrets (N.C.), 10″ Turret bases (N.C.), 6″—4″ Upper belt, 10″ Conning tower. Machinery: 2 sets vertical 4 cylinder triple expansion. 2 screws. Boilers: 20 Belleville. Designed H.P. 16000 = 18 kts. Coal: *normal* 750 tons; *maximum* 1520 tons. Laid down at Galernii Island, June, 1900, and completed for sea in September, 1904. Captured in Battle of Tsushima, 1905.

(*Cadets' Training Ship*).

うはす **SUWO** (ex-Russian *Pobieda*. May, 1900). *Normal* displacement (after reconstruction), 13,500 tons. Complement, 787. Length (*waterline*), 424 feet. Beam, $71\frac{1}{2}$ feet. *Maximum* draught, $25\frac{1}{4}$ feet. Length *over all*, 435 feet. Guns (Obukhoff): 4—10 inch, 45 cal. (A^5), 10—6 inch, 45 cal., 16—12 pdrs., 4 machine, 2 field. Torpedo tubes (15 inch): 2 *submerged* (at 20° abaft). Armour (*See Notes*): 9″—6″ Belt; $2\frac{3}{4}$″ Deck (on slopes); 10″ Turrets; 8″ Turret bases; 5″ Lower deck side; 5″ Casements (10); 10″ Conning tower (K.N.C.) Machinery: 3 sets vertical 3 cylinder triple expansion. 3 screws. Boilers: 30 Bellevilles, placed fore and aft. Designed H.P. 14,500 = 18 kts. Coal: *normal* 1063 tons; *maximum* 2100 tons. **Also** 250 tons liquid fuel. Scuttled at Port Arthur, 1904, and captured on fall of fortress. Salved and re-fitted 1905-6.

Note: near sister *Sagami* (ex. *Peresviet*) deleted during the war.

Asahi is something like *Mikasa*, but easily distinguished from her because her fore funnel is much nearer fore mast than *Mikasa's*. (*Gunnery Training Ship.*)

ひさあ **ASAHI** (March, 1899). *Normal* displacement, 14,765 tons. Complement, 836. Length *over all*, $425\frac{1}{4}$ feet. Beam, $75\frac{1}{4}$ feet. *Maximum* draught, $27\frac{1}{4}$ feet. Guns: 4—12 inch, 40 cal. (A^4), 14—6 inch, 40 cal., 20—12 pdr., 2—3 pdr., 2—$2\frac{1}{2}$ pdr. Torpedo tubes (18 inch): 4 *submerged*. Armour (Harvey Nickel): 9″ Belt (amidships), 4″ Belt (ends), 14″ Bulkheads, 3″ Deck (amidships slopes), 14″—10″ Barbettes, 10″—8″ Turrets to these, 6″ Lower deck redoubt, 6″ Casemates (14), 14″ Conning tower, 4″ After tower. Machinery: 2 sets vertical triple expansion. 2 screws. Boilers: 25 Belleville. Designed H.P. 16,000 = 18 kts. Coal: *normal* 700 tons; *maximum* 1690 tons. Built by Thomson, Clydebank, 1897-1900.

ましき志 **SHIKISHIMA** (November, 1898). 14,580 tons. Complement, 836. Length (*o.a.*), 438 feet. Beam, $75\frac{1}{2}$ feet. *Max.* draught, $27\frac{1}{4}$ feet. Guns: As *Asahi* above. Torpedo tubes: As *Asahi* above, but has an additional 18 inch tube *above water*. Armour, machinery, screws and boilers also as *Asahi*. Designed H.P. 14,500 = 18 kts. Coal (*max.*): 1590 tons. Built by Thames Ironworks, 1897-1900.

1899-98 OLD JAPANESE COAST DEFENCE BATTLESHIPS. 1894

(*Seamanship Training Ship*).

じふ **FUJI** (March, 1896). 12,649 tons. Complement, 741. Length (*waterline*), 390 feet. Beam, 73 feet. *Maximum* draught, 27 feet. Guns: 4—12 inch, 40 cal., 10—6 inch, 40 cal., 16—12 pdr. 4—3 pdr. 4—$2\frac{1}{2}$ pdr. Torpedo tubes (18 inch): 4 *submerged*, 1 *above water* (bow). Armour (Harvey): 18″ Belt (amidships). 14″ Bulkheads. $2\frac{1}{2}$″ Deck (flat on belt), 4″ Lower deck redoubt. 14″ Barbettes. 6″ Casemates. 14″ Conning tower. Machinery: 2 sets 4 cylinder vertical triple expansion. 2 screws. Boilers: 10 Miyabara. Designed H.P. *forced* 13,500 = 18 kts. Coal: *normal* 700 tons; *maximum* 1200 tons.

***OKINOSHIMA** (ex-Russian *General Admiral Graf Apraxin*, 1896) 4126 tons, & ましみ **MISHIMA** (ex-Russian *Admiral Senyavin*. 1894). 4460 tons 3—10 inch, 45 cal. (*AAA*). (*Mishima* has 4—10 inch) with, in both 4—4·7 inch, 10—3 pdrs., 2—$2\frac{1}{2}$ pdr. Armour: 10″—8″ belt amidships. 8″ turrets. Designed H.P. 5000 = 16 kts. Boilers: 8 Belleville. Coal: *maximum* 450 tons. Both captured in Battle of Tsushima, 1905.

* *Note.*—Reported 1919 that 10-inch guns had been removed and that both ships were serving as Ice Breakers. Previously these ships were Barracks for Boys.

1893—1887 OLD JAPANESE COAST DEFENCE BATTLESHIPS.

(Present appearance).

TANGO (Nov., 1894). Displacement 11,000 tons. Complement, 750. Length, 367 feet. Beam, 69 feet. *Maximum* draught, 28 feet. Guns (Obuchoff): 4—12 inch, 35 cal. (A.A.), 12—6 inch, 45 cal., and many 3 and 1 pdr. Armour (compound): Belt 15″ (partial). Turrets (steel) 10″, small turrets 5″. Designed H.P. 10,600 = 17 kts. Coal : *maximum* 1050 tons. Sunk at Port Arthur in the War 1904, salved in 1905. Deleted during the war.

きい **IKI** (Oct., 1889). Displacement 9670 tons. Sheathed. Armament : 2—old 12 inch (C), 4 old 9 inch, 7—6 inch, 45 cal., 20 light guns, 6—14 inch tubes (*above water*). Designed H.P. 8000 = 15·9 kts. Belleville boilers. Coal : 1200 tons. Deleted during the war.

1902 JAPANESE FIRST CLASS CRUISERS (20 knot). (Junjokan.) 1898

NISSHIN. (KASUGA also has plain funnels now). *Photo, Seward, Weymouth.*
"Nisshin" attached to T.B.D. Flotillas.

んしつに **NISSHIN** (Feb., 1903) & **KASUGA** (Oct., 1902). かすか
Displacement 7,750 tons. Complement 610 and 595.
Length (*waterline*), 357 feet. Beam, 61 feet 11 ins. *Maximum* draught, 25¼ feet.

Guns (Elswick) : Armour (Terni) :
4—8 inch, 45 cal. (A). 6″ Belt (amidships) ......
14—6 inch, 45 cal. 4½″ Belt (ends) ....
10—12 pdr. 1½″ Deck (on slopes) ......
4—2½ pdrs. 5½″ Turrets ....
2 Maxims. 5½″ Turret bases (N.C.)...
2 Field guns. 6″ Lower deck side ......
Torpedo tubes (18 inch) : 4½″ Lower deck bulkheads
4 *above water* (in casemates). 6″ Battery (N.C.) ....
4½″ Battery (bulkheads)...
4¾″ Conning tower ......

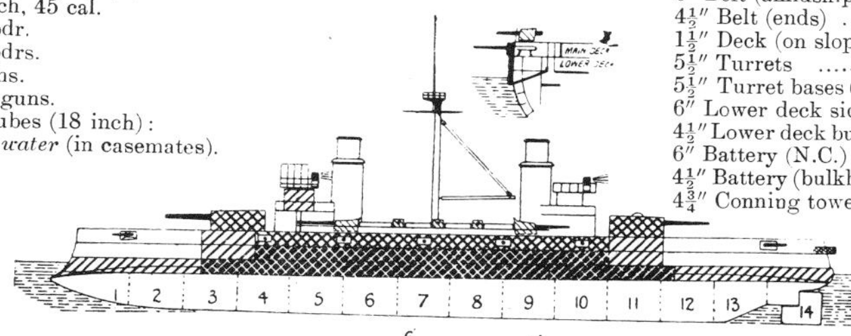

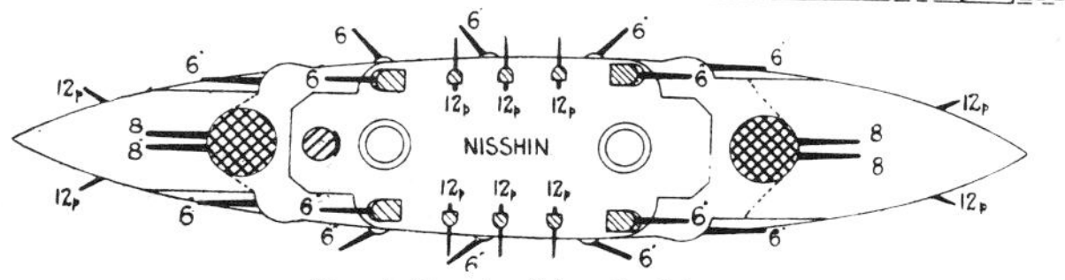

Ahead : Astern :
2—8 in. 2—8 in.
4—6 in. 4—6 in.

Broadside : 4—8 in., 7—6 in.

Machinery : 2 sets 3 cylinder vertical triple expansion. 2 screws. Boilers : 12 Kansei. Designed H.P. 13,500 = 20 kts. Coal : *normal*, 650 tons ; *maximum* 1,200 tons.
General Notes.—Laid down for Argentina by Ansaldo, Genoa, in 1902, as the *Moreno* and *Rivadavia*. Purchased end of 1903 by Japan for £760,000, just before outbreak of Russo-Japanese War. Both had large refits 1914. *Kasuga* stranded at N.W. entrance to Banka Straits, Dutch East Indies, during January, 1918, and was not refloated till May. She has undergone extensive repairs in a Japanese dockyard.

(Tender to Submarines). *Photo, His Honour Mr. Justice Ballon.*

そあ **ASO** (ex-Russian *Bayan*). (La Seyne, 1900). Displacement, 7800 tons. Complement, 791. Length (*waterline*), 443 feet. Beam 57½ feet. *Max.* draught, 22 feet. Length *over all*, 450 feet. Guns : 2—8 inch, 45 cal. (A), 8—6 inch, 45 cal., 16—12 pdr., 4—2½ pdr. Torpedo tubes (at 20° abaft) : 2 *submerged*. Tubes are 15 inch. Armour (Krupp) : 8″ Belt (amidships), 4″ Belt (forward), 8″ Bulkhead (aft), 2″ Deck, 3½″—2½″ Upper belt, 7″ Big gun turrets, Hoists, &c., 3½″ Battery redoubts, 6½″ Conning tower. (Total about 1500 tons.) Machinery : 2 sets vertical triple expansion. 2 screws. Boilers : 24 Belleville. Designed H.P. 16,500 = 21 kts. Coal : *normal* 550 tons ; *maximum* 1100 tons. Scuttled at Port Arthur, 1905, and captured on fall of fortress. Re-floated and re-fitted in Japan, 1905–6.

IDZUMO. "Idzumo" attached to T.B.D. Flotillas. *Photo, Seward, Weymouth.*

しつい **IDZUMO** (Elswick, 1899) & てばい **IWATE** (Elswick, 1900).
Displacement, 9750 tons. Complement, 658. Length (*p.p.*), 400 feet. Beam, 68½ feet. *Maximum* draught, 24¼ feet. Length *over all*, 434 feet. Guns (Elswick) : 4—8 inch, 40 cal. (B). 14—6 inch, 40 cal., 12—12 pdr., 4—2½ pdr., 2 M.G. Torpedo tubes : 4 *submerged*. Armour (Krupp) : 7″ Belt (amidship), 3½″ Belt (ends), 2½″ Deck (slopes), 5″ Turrets and bases, 6″ Casemates. 14″ Conning tower. (Total 2100 tons.) Machinery by Humphry and Tennant : 2 sets 4 cylinder triple expansion. 2 screws. Boilers : Belleville. Designed H.P. 16,000 = 20·75 kts. Coal : *normal* 550 tons ; *maximum* 1400 tons. Begun at Elswick 1898–99, and completed 1901. *Idzumo* made 22·04 kts. on acceptance trials and *Iwate* 21·74.

(Cadets' Training Ship). *Photo by favour of G. Blackaby, Esq.*

まつあ **ADZUMA** (St. Nazaire, 1899). Displacement, 9426 tons. Complement, 644. Length (*waterline*), 430 feet. Beam, 59½ feet. *Maximum* draught, 25 feet. Length *over all*, 452½ feet. Guns (Elswick) : 4—8 inch, 40 cal. (A). 14—6 inch, 40 cal., 16—12 pdr., 4—2½ pdr. Torpedo tubes : 4 *submerged*. Armour (Krupp mostly) : 7″ Belt (amidships), 3½″ Belt (ends), 2½″ Deck (on slopes), 6″ Turrets and bases (H.N.), 6″ Casemates (H.N.), 5″ Side above belt. (Total weight, 2000 tons). Machinery : 2 sets vertical triple expansion. 2 screws. Boilers : 24 Belleville. Designed H.P. 17,000 = 21 kts. Coal : *normal* 600 tons ; *maximum* 1200 tons.

TOKIWA (Cadet Training Ship). *Photo by favour of G. Blackaby, Esq.*

まさあ **ASAMA** (March, 1898). はきと **TOKIWA** (July, 1898). Displacement 9700 tons. Complement 648. Length (*o.a.*), 442 feet. Beam, 67⅓ feet. *Maximum* draught, 24¼ feet. Guns (Elswick) : 4—8 inch, 40 cal. (B), 14—6 inch, 40 cal., 12—12 pdr., 4—2½ pdr. Torpedo tubes (18 inch) : 4 *submerged*. Armour (Harvey-nickel) : 7″ Belt (amidships), 3½″ Belt (ends), 2″ Deck (slopes), 5″ Upper belt (amidships), 3½″ Bulkheads to it, 6″ Turrets and bases, 6″ Casemates (10), 14″ Conning tower. (Total, 2100 tons.) Machinery : 2 sets 4 cylinder triple expansion. 2 screws. Boilers : 12 Miyabara. Designed H.P. *forced* 18,000 = 21½ kts. Coal : *normal* 550 tons ; *maximum* 1400 tons. Both built at Elswick. Very 'handy' ships. *Asama* was badly damaged by grounding on Pacific Coast of Central America, in December of 1914. Was salved and has been repaired and re-fitted.

もくや

YAKUMO (Vulcan Co., 1899). Displacement, 9,735 tons. Complement, 698. Length (*p.p.*), 390 feet. Beam, 64¼ feet. *Mean draught*, 23¾ feet. *Length over all*, 434 feet. Guns: 4—8 inch, 40 cal. (*B.*), 12—6 inch, 40 cal., 16—12 pdr., 4—2½ pdr. Torpedo tubes (18 inch): 4 *submerged*. Armour (Krupp): 7″ Belt (amidships), 3½″ Belt (ends), 2½″ Deck (slopes), 6″ Turrets (N.C.), 6″ Turret bases (N.C.), 5″ Lower deck side, 6″ Casemates (8), 10″ Conning tower. (Total weight, 2040 tons.) Machinery: 2 sets vertical triple expansion. 2 screws. Boilers: 24 Belleville. Designed H.P. 15,500 = 20¾ kts. Coal: *normal* 550 tons; *maximum* 1200 tons. Armour Notes: Belt is 7 feet wide.

(Cadets' Training Ship.)

たよち

CHIYODA (June, 1890). Displacement 2439 tons. Complement 324. Length, 308 feet. Beam, 41¾ feet. *Maximum draught*, 15½ feet. Guns (Elswick): 10—4·7 inch, 40 cal., 15—3 pdr. Torpedo tubes: 2 *above water*. Armour (chrome steel): 4½″ Belt, 1″ Deck at ends [Deck flat on belt.] Machinery: 2 sets triple expansion. 2 screws. Boilers (1898): 12 Belleville without economisers. Designed H.P. 7000 = 19 kts. Coal: *normal* 330 tons; *maximum* 420 tons.

JAPANESE SECOND CLASS CRUISERS (23 knot).

CHIKUMA.   *Photo by courtesy of the Imperial Japanese Embassy.*

とらひ **HIRADO** (June, 1911). きはや **YAHAGI** (Oct., 1911).

まくち **CHIKUMA** (April, 1911).

Normal displacement 4950 tons. Complement 403.

Length (*p.p.*), 410 feet; *o.a.*, 475 feet. Beam, 46½ feet. *Max.* draught, 16½ feet.

Guns:
8—6 inch, 50 cal.
4—12 pdr.
2 M.G.
Torpedo tubes (18 inch)
3 *above water*.
(365 tons.)

Armour:
3″ Deck (amidships)
2″ Deck (ends) ......
4″ Conning tower...
(439 tons.)

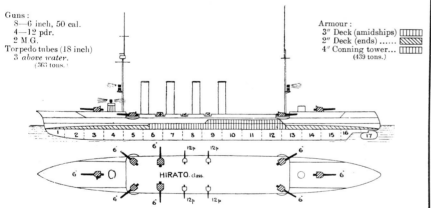

HIRATO. class.

Machinery: Curtis turbines; (2 screws), except *Yahagi*, Parsons turbines (4 screws). Boilers: 16 Kansei. Designed H.P. 22,500 = 26 kts. Coal: *normal* 500 tons; *maximum* 900 tons + 300 oil.

Name	Builder	Machinery	Laid down	Completed	Trials H.P. = kts.	Boilers	Best recent speed
Hirado	Kawasaki Co.	Kawasaki Co.	Aug.,'10	Oct., '12			
Yahagi	Mitsu Bishi	Mitsu Bishi	June,'10	July, '12	27,408 = 26.8	Kansei in all.	
Chikuma	Sasebo Yard	Kawasaki Co.	May, '10	May, '12	24,974 = 26.8		

Weight of hull, etc., 2278 tons. *Hirado* returned to Japan early in 1918 after having steamed 26,000 miles in nine months on active service.

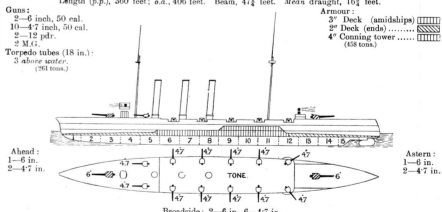

ねと **TONE** (Oct., 1907).

Normal displacement 4105 tons. Complement 401.

Length (*p.p.*), 360 feet; *o.a.*, 406 feet. Beam, 47¼ feet. *Mean draught*, 16¾ feet.

Guns:
2—6 inch, 50 cal.
10—4·7 inch, 50 cal.
2—12 pdr.
2 M.G.
Torpedo tubes (18 in.):
3 *above water*.
(261 tons.)

Armour:
3″ Deck (amidships)
2″ Deck (ends) ....
4″ Conning tower ......
(458 tons.)

Ahead:
1—6 in.
2—4·7 in.

Astern:
1—6 in.
2—4·7 in.

TONE.

Broadside: 2—6 in., 6—4·7 in.

Machinery: 2 sets triple expansion. 2 screws. Boilers: 16 Miyabara. Designed H.P. 15,000 = 23 kts. Coal: *normal* 300 tons; *maximum* 890 tons + 125 tons oil.

Name.	Builder	Machinery	Laid down	Completed	Refit	Trials	Boilers	Best recent speed
Tone	Sasebo	Mitsu Bishi Co.	1906	1909			Miyabara	

Correction to plans: Two 17 inch guns removed, positions unknown.

1918-19 JAPANESE SECOND

Building:—

Details unofficial.

KUMA (July, 1919). *TAMA* (building), *OH-1* (building), *KITAKAMI* (building), *KISO* (building).

Normal displacement: 5500 tons. Complement,

Length (*o.a.*), 500 feet. Beam, 49·6 feet. *Mean draught*, 15·6 feet.

Guns:
7—5.5 inch, — cal.
— Anti-aircraft.
— M.G.
Torpedo tubes: 4.

Armour:
(Not known.)

No plans available.

Machinery: Turbines. Boilers: screws. Designed H.P. =
33 kts. Fuel: *normal*,   tons; *maximum*,   tons.

Name.	Builder.	Machinery	Laid down.	Completed.	Refit.	First Trials.	Boilers.	Best recent speed.
Oh-i	Kawasaki	Kawasaki	} 1919					
Kitakami	Sasebo D.Y.							
Kiso	Mitsubishi Nagasaki	Mitsubishi						
Kuma	Sasebo D.Y.		Aug. '18					
Tama	Nagasaki D.Y.		Aug. '18					

General Notes.—*Kuma* and *Tama* begun under the 1917 Naval Programme; *Oh-i, Kitakami, Kiso* under 1918 Programme.

はとを **OTOWA** (Nov., 1903).

Displacement, 3000 tons. Complement, 312.

Length, (o.a.) 341 feet; p.p., 321½ feet. Beam, 41⅓ feet. *Mean draught*, 15⅜ feet.

Guns (Japanese):
2—6 inch, 50 cal.
6—4·7 inch.
4—12 pdr.
2 Machine.
Torpedo tubes :
Nil.
(199 tons.)

Armour :
3″ Deck (amidships) = ϵ
2″ Deck (ends) ...... = ϵ
1½″ Gunshields ......
4″ Conning tower (K.N.C.)
(204 tons.)

Ahead :
1—6 in.
2—4·7 in.

Astern :
1—6 in.
2—4·7 in.

Broadside : 2— 6 in., 3—4·7 in.

Machinery : 2 sets triple expansion. 2 screws. Boilers : Miyabara. Designed H.P. 10,000 = 21 kts. Coal : *normal* 600 tons ; *maximum* 850 tons. Laid down at Yokosuka, 1903.
Weights: hull and fittings, 1399 tons ; machinery, 803 tons. *Note.*—Wrecked 1 August 1917.

Niitaka has foremast aft of fore bridges ; Tsushima has foremast stepped through charthouse.

かたいに **NIITAKA.** ましつ **TSUSHIMA.**

NIITAKA (1902) & **TSUSHIMA** (Dec., 1902).

Displacement, 3420 tons. Complement, 307.

Length, 334½ feet. Beam, 44 feet. *Maximum draught*, 16 feet.

Guns (Elswick):
6—6 inch, 40 cal.
10—12 pdr.
4—2½ pdr.
Torpedo tubes :
None.

Armour (steel) :
2½″ Deck ....
[Cellulose belt.]
4″ Conning tower (K.N.C.) ....

Ahead :
3—6 in.

Astern :
3—6 in.

Broadside : 4—6 in.

Machinery : 2 sets triple expansion. 2 screws. Boilers : 16 Niclausse. Designed H.P. 9400 = 20 kts. Coal : *normal* tons ; *maximum* 600 tons. Laid down 1900 at Yokosuka and Kure.
A similar ship, *Otowa*, wrecked 1917. *Niitaka*, on patrol service during war, has steamed 50,000 miles in two years.

るか一 **TSUGARU** (ex Russian *Pallada*). (Aug., 1899.) Displacement 6630 tons. Complement 532. Length (*waterline*), 410 feet. Beam, 55 feet. *Maximum* draught, 21¼ feet. Length *over all*, 415¾ feet. Guns (Russian) : 10—6 inch, 45 cal., 12—12 pdr., 4—M.G. Torpedo tubes (18 inch) : 2 *above water*. Armour : 2½″ Deck, 4″ Hoists, 6″ C. T. (Harvey), 4½″ Engine hatches. Machinery : 3 sets horizontal 3 cylinder triple expansion. 3 screws. Boilers : 24 Belleville. Designed H.P. 11,600 = 20 kts. Coal : *normal* 900 tons ; *maximum* 1430 tons. Sunk at Port Arthur, October, 1904. Salved August, 1905. Used as a Training Ship.

せとち **CHITOSE** (January, 1898). Displacement 4992 tons. Complement 434. Length (*waterline*), 396 feet. Beam, 49¼ feet. *Maximum* draught, 18 feet. Guns : 2—8 inch, 40 cal. (B)., 10—4·7 inch, 12—12 pdr., 2—2½ pdr. Torpedo tubes (18 inch) : 4 *above water*. Armour : 4½″ Deck (amidships). Machinery : 2 sets vertical triple expansion. 2 screws. Boilers : 12 Miyabara. Designed H.P. : *forced* 15,500 = 22·5 kts. Coal : *normal* 350 tons ; *maximum capacity* 1000 tons. Built and engined by Union Ironworks, San Francisco. Laid down 1896, completed 1899. Made 22·87 kts. on first trials with 12,500 H.P. A sister ship, *Kasagi*, wrecked in Tsugaru Straits, 1916.

Now has fire-control top on foremast and a very small mainmast.

かあ **AKASHI** (1897). Displacement 2800 tons. Complement, 310. Length, 295¼ feet. Beam, 41¼ feet. *Maximum* draught, 16¼ feet. Guns (Elswick) : 2—6 inch, 40 cal., 6—4·7 inch, 40 cal. 12—3 pdr. Torpedo tubes (14 inch) : 2 *above water*. Armour : 2″ Deck, 4½″ Shields to 6 inch guns. Machinery : 2 sets vertical triple expansion. 2 screws. Boilers : 8 cylindrical (probably replaced now by Kansei or Miyabara). Designed H.P. 7600 = 19·5 kts. Coal : *normal* 200 tons ; *maximum* 600 tons.
Note.—Was intended to be a sister ship to *Suma* (given below), but as *Suma* proved a poor sea boat, *Akashi* was built up amidships.

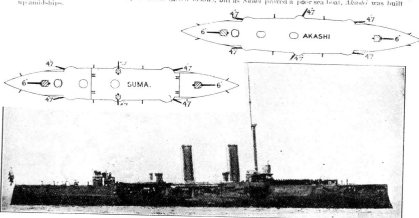

ます **SUMA** (1895). 2700 tons. Comp. 310. Dimensions : 305½ × 39½ × (*max.*) 16½ feet. Armament (Elswick) : 2—6 inch, 40 cal., 6—4·7 inch, 40 cal., 12—3 pdr. 2 tubes. 2″ Deck. 4½″ Shields to 6 inch guns. Machinery : 2 sets vertical triple expansion. 2 screws. Boilers : 4 Miyabara. Designed H.P. *forced* draught 8500 = 20 kts. Coal : *normal* 200 tons ; *maximum* 600 tons. (See *Note* to *Akashi* above.)

OLD JAPANESE CRUISERS.

まきつしあ **AKITSUSHIMA** (1892). 3172 tons. Comp. 314. Dimensions:—302×43×(Max.) 18½ feet. Armament: 4—6 inch, 6—4·7, 10—3 pdr. 2—14 inch tubes. 3″ Deck. Machinery: 2 sets vertical triple expansion. 2 screws. Boilers : 8 Miyabara. Designed H.P. *natural* 8500=19 kts. Coal : 550 tons.

(Conscripts' Training Ship.)

てたしは **HASHIDATE** (1891). 4277 tons. Comp. 360. Dimensions : 295×51×(max.) 21¼ feet. Armament : 1—12·6 inch Canet, 11—4·7 inch, 6—12 pdrs., 2—3 pdrs., 2 M., 2—14 in. tubes. Armour (steel) : 12″ Barbette with 4″ shield, 1½″ deck. Machinery : 2 sets triple expansion. 2 screws. Boilers : 8 Miyabara (1903). Designed H.P. 5400=16 kts. Coal : 680 tons.
(Above ship still in service as Training Cruiser).
Sister ship *Itsukushima* deleted during the war

JAPANESE GUNBOATS.

やろそ **SOYA** (Oct., 1899).
Displacement, 6500 tons. Complement, 571.
Length (*waterline*), 416 feet. Beam, 52 feet. *Maximum* draught, 21 feet.

Guns (Russian) :
  12—6 inch, 45 cal.
  12—12 pdr.
  6—3 pdr.
Torpedo tubes (18 inch)
  2 *submerged* (at 20° abaft)
  2 *above water.*

Armour :
  3″ Deck .... = d
  Engine hatches
  6″ Conning tower (H) ... c

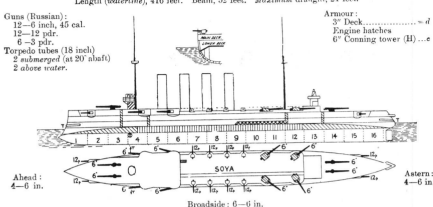

Ahead : 4—6 in.   SOYA   Astern : 4—6 in.

Broadside : 6—6 in.

Machinery : 2 sets 4 cylinder vertical inverted triple expansion. 2 screws. Boilers : ('07) Miyabara. Designed H.P. 20,000=23 kts. Coal : *normal* 770 tons ; *maximum* 1250 tons.
Engineering Notes.—Funnels 90 feet high above bars. Heating surface, 62,229 square feet.
  First *trials* : 100 revs.=16 kts. 120 revs.=19 kts. 140 revs. = 22 kts. 154=23 kts.
  12 hours, 149 revs., H.P. 16,270=23·25 kts. 8 hours, 160 revs., H.P. 20,000=24·6 kts.
Actual radius about 950 miles at full speed ; 4500 miles at 10 kts.
General Notes.—Sunk at Chemulpo during the Russo-Japanese War, February, 1904. Salved, August, 1905. Laid down at Cramp's, Philadelphia, May, 1898. Completed for sea early in 1901.

1st Class Gunboats *(Itto Hokan).*
(Over 800 tons).

みかも **MOGAMI** (Nagasaki, 1907). 1350 tons. Comp. 178. 316×31½×11½ feet. Guns : 2—4·7 inch (50 cal.), 4—12 pdr. Armour : 2½″ deck. Torpedo tubes : 2—18 inch. Machinery : Parsons turbine. 3 screws. No cruising turbines. Designed H.P. 8000=23 kts. Boilers : 6 Miyabara. Coal : *normal,*   tons ; *maximum,* 350 tons + 70 tons oil. First turbine-engined ship of Japanese Navy.

とめよ **YODO** (Kobe, 1907). 1250 tons. Comp. 193. 305½× 32×11 feet. Guns : 2—4·7 inch, 50 cal., 4—12 pdr. Armour : 2½″ deck. Torpedo tubes : 2—18 inch. Machinery : 2 sets 4 cyl. triple expansion. Designed H.P. 6500=22 kts. Boilers : 4 Miyabara. Ccal : *normal,*   tons ; *maximum* 340 tons+80 tons oil.

やはち **CHIHAYA** (1901). 1263 tons. Comp. 167. Guns : 2—4·7 inch, 4—12 pdr. 2—18 inch tubes. Designed H.P. 6000= 21 kts. Boilers : Thornycroft. Coal : *normal* 200 tons ; *maximum* 450 tons.

CHIHAYA.

2nd Class Gunboats *(Nito Hokan).*
(Under 800 tons).

たつた **TATSUTA** (1894). 875 tons. Comp. 100. Guns : 2—4·7 inch, 4—3 pdr. 2—14 inch tubes. Machinery : 2 sets triple expansion. 2 screws. Boilers (1904) : Miyabara. Designed H.P. 5500=21 kts. Coal : *normal*   tons ; *maximum* 188 tons.

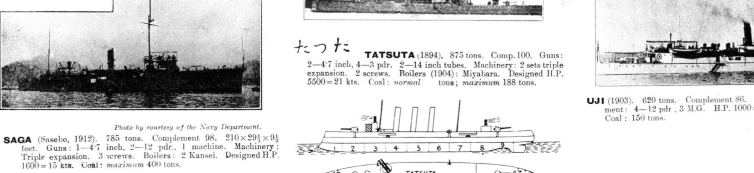

TATSUTA

UJI (1903). 620 tons. Complement 86. 180½×27¼×7 feet. Armament : 4—12 pdr. 3 M.G. H.P. 1000=13 kts. Belleville boilers. Coal : 150 tons.

Photo by courtesy of the Navy Department.

SAGA (Sasebo, 1912). 785 tons. Complement 98. 210×29½×9½ feet. Guns : 1—4·7 inch, 2—12 pdrs., 1 machine. Machinery : Triple expansion. 3 screws. Boilers : 2 Kansei. Designed H.P. 1600=15 kts. Coal : *maximum* 400 tons.

River Gunboats.

FUSHIMI (1906). 180 tons. Complement 45. $160 \times 24\frac{1}{2} \times 2\frac{1}{4}$ fe
Guns: 2—6 pdr., 4 M. 800 H P. = 14 kts. Yarrow boilers. Coa
25 tons.

Also **TOBA** (1911). 250 tons. Complement 59. $180 \times 27\frac{1}{4} \times 2\frac{1}{2}$ fe
Guns: 2—12 pdr., 6 M. 1400 H.P. = 15 kts. Coal: 80 tons.

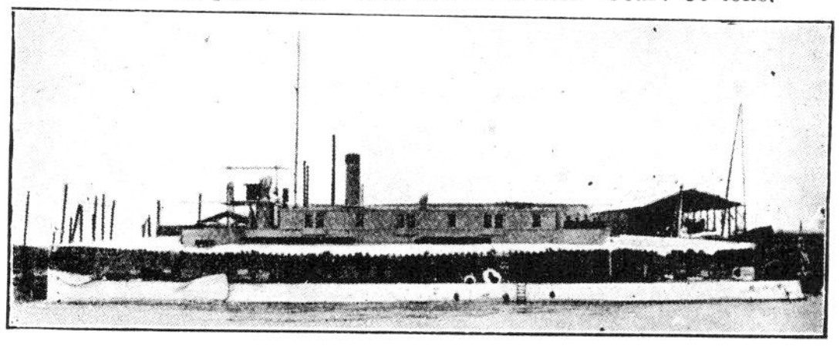

SUMIDA (1903). 126 tons. Complement 40. $145 \times 24 \times 2$ f
Guns: 2—6 pdr., 4 M. 550 H.P. = 13 kts. Thornycroft boil
Coal: 40 tons.

JAPANESE DESTROYERS (*Kuchikukan*).

81 Destroyers.

Boats over 1000 tons are officially rated first class: 1000—600, second class; and under 600 tons, third class.

Totals.	Class.	Date.	Displacement.	H.P.	*Max.* Speed.	Fuel.	Complement.	Tubes.	*Max.* Draught.
	First Class:—		tons.		kts.	tons.			feet.
4	*Okikaze*	'18—'20	1345	...*t*	...*t*	...	...	...	...
2	*Minekaze*	'17—'19				...	...	..	...
2	*Tanikaze*	'16—'18	1300	28,000 *t*	34	...	128	6	$10\frac{1}{2}$
4	*Amatsukaze*	'15—'17	1227	27,000 *t*	34	145+*195*	145	6	$10\frac{1}{2}$
2	*Umikaze*	'08—'11	1150	19,500 *t*	31·5	250+*180*	139	3 4	$9\frac{1}{4}$
	Second Class:—								
8	*Momi*	'18—'19	850	...*t*	...	...	...	...	...
6	*Tsubaki*	'17—'18	835	16,000 *t*	31·5	90+*210*	109	6	$7\frac{3}{4}$
4	*Momo*	'15—'16							
10	*Kaba*	'14—'15	665	9,500	30	90+*125*	92	4	$8\frac{1}{2}$
1	*Urakaze*	'13—'15	955	22,000 *t*	28	*248*	117	4	$10\frac{1}{2}$
2	*Sakura*	'11—'13	605	9,500 *t*	30	125+*30*	92	4	$7\frac{1}{4}$
	Third Class:—								
33	*Arare*	'05—'08	375–381	6,000	29	100 or 95+*15*	61	2	$8\frac{1}{4}$—9
2	*Asagiri*	'02—'04							
2	*Asashiho* (T)	'01—'04	333	7,000	31	96	60	2	$8\frac{1}{2}$
2	*Akebono* (Y)	'97—'00	306	6,000	31	90-95	55	2	8
3	*Kagero* (T)	'97—'00	326	5,400	30	81	61	2	$7\frac{1}{4}$

(T) Thornycroft. (Y) = Yarrow type. *t* = Turbine.

8 + *7* 1st class Destroyers—*continued.*

2 Umikaze class.

Fore-funnel now raised.

2 *Umikaze* class: ***Umikaze*** (Maidzuru, 1910) and ***Yamakaze*** (Nagasaki, 1911). 1150 tons. Dimensions: 310 (*p.p.*) $323\frac{1}{4}$ (*o.a.*) × $27\frac{3}{4}$ × 9 feet (*mean* draught) Armament: 2—4·7 inch (40 cal.), 5—12 pdr. Torpedo tubes: in *Umikaze*, 4—18 inch into two twin deck mountings; in *Yamakaze*, 3—18 inch in single deck mountings. One searchlight. Machinery: 3 sets Parsons turbine and Kansei boilers. Designed H.P. 19,500 = 31·5 kts. Fuel: 250 tons coal + 180 tons oil = 2700 miles at 15 kts. Complement, 139. Trials: *Umikaze* 33·46 kts.

Note.—During 1918, the British Destroyers *Minstrel* and *Nemesis* were loaned to the Japanese Navy and commissioned under the Japanese Flag as H.I.M. Ships *Kenran* and *Sendan*. Both boats have been returned to the British Navy.

8 Momi class.

8 + *7* 1st Class Destroyers (*continued.*)

2 Tanikaze class.

2 *Tanikaze* class: ***Tanikaze*** (Maidzuru D.Y., 1918) and ***Kawakaze*** (Yokosuka D.Y., 1917). 1300 tons. Dimensions: 320 × $29\frac{1}{4}$ × $9\frac{1}{2}$ feet. Armament: 3—4.7 inch, 6 tubes in three twin deck mountings. Two searchlights. Designed H.P. 28,000 = 34 kts. Machinery: Parsons turbines. Boilers: Kansei. Complement, 128. *Kawakaze* belongs to the 1917 Programme, *Tanikaze* to the 1916 Programme.

4 Amatsukaze class.

AMATSUKAZE. *Photo by courtesy of the Navy Department, Tokyo.*

4 *Amatsukaze* class: ***Amatsukaze*** and ***Isokaze*** (both launched at Kure, Oct., 1916). ***Hamakaze*** (Nagasaki, Oct., 1916), and ***Tokitsukaze*** (Kobe, Dec., 1916).* 1227 tons. Dimensions: 310 (*p.p.*), $326\frac{1}{2}$ (*o.a.*) × 2 × $9\frac{1}{4}$ feet. Armament: 4—4.7 inch (40 cal.), 2 M.G., and 6—18 inch tubes in 3 twin deck mountings. 1 searchlight. Machinery: 3 sets Parsons turbines and Kansei boilers. Designed H.P. 27,000 = 34 kts. Fuel: 145 tons coal + 195 tons oil. Complement, 145. Built under the 1915 Naval Programme.

**Note.*—*Tokitsukaze* wrecked; salved in three sections, March, 1918, and practically rebuilt at Kure D.Y.

10 Momo class (4 Momo + 6 Tsubaki).

Photo, Seward, Weymouth.

10 *Momo* class: ***Maki*** and ***Keyaki*** (Sasebo D.Y., 1918), ***Kuwa*** and ***Tsubaki*** (Kure D.Y., 1918), ***Enoki*** (Maidzuru D.Y., 1918), and ***Nara*** (Yokosuka D.Y., 1918). ***Yanagi*** (1917) and ***Momo*** (1916), both built at Sasebo; ***Kashi*** (1916) and ***Hinoki*** (1916), both built at Maidzuru. 835 tons. Dimensions: 275 (*o.a.*) × 25 × $7\frac{3}{4}$ feet. Armament: 3—4·7 inch, 2 M.G., and 6—18 inch tubes in two twin and two single deck mountings. One searchlight. Machinery: 3 sets Curtis turbines and 4 Kansei boilers. Designed H.P. 16,000 = 31·5 kts. Fuel: 90 tons coal + 210 tons oil. Complement, 109. The first six provided for by Special 1917 Programme. The last four built under the 1915 Naval Programme.

10 Kaba class.

10 *Kaba* class:—***Kaba*** (Yokosuka), ***Kaede*** (Maidzuru), ***Kashiwa*** and ***Matsu*** (Nagasaki), ***Katsura*** (Kure), ***Kiri*** (Uraga), ***Kusunoki*** and ***Ume*** (Kobe), ***Sakaki*** (Sasebo), and ***Sugi*** (Osaka). All launched February–March, 1915. 665 tons. Dimensions: 260 (*p.p.*) 274 (*o.a.*) × 24 × 7·9 feet. Armament: 1—4·7 inch, 4—12 pdr., (2 anti-aircraft model) and 4—18 inch tubes. Machinery: 3 sets, 4-cylinder triple expansion and 4 Kansei boilers. Designed H.P. 9,500 = 30 kts. Fuel: 90 tons coal + 135 tons oil. Complement, 92. These boats are said to have been built in seven months. Built under 1914 Naval Programme, and served in Mediterranean during war. 12 Replicas built in Japanese Yards for French Navy—see French *Tribal* class, *Algerien*, *Arabe*, &c.

(*Continued on next page.*)

JAPANESE DESTROYERS

23 + 8 2nd Class Destroyers—*Continued.*

1 Special Boat.

1 *Yarrow* type: **Urakaze** (Yarrow, Scotstoun, 1915). 955 tons. Dimensions: 275 (*p.p.*) 283 (*o.a.*) × 27·5 × 9·5 feet. Armament: 1—4·7 in., 4—12 pdr., 4—21 inch tubes in two twin deck mountings. Machinery: 22,000 H.P. turbines = 28 kts. Yarrow large tube boilers. Fuel: 248 tons oil only. Endurance about 1800 miles at 15 kts. Complement, 117.

Note.—It was intended that this boat should have a Diesel engine for cruising speed, combined by Föttinger hydraulic transmission to the turbines. Owing to the War, the Föttinger gear and Diesel engine were never delivered. They were replaced by a big oil tank. *Kawakaze* (sister-boat) ceded to Italy, and now Italian *Audace*.

The 37 *Arare* type are named :—**Arare, Ariake, Asakase, Asatsuyu, Fubuki, Fumitzuki, Hayakase, Hatsuharu, Hatsushimo, Hibiki, Hatsuyuki, Harukaze, Kisaragi, Kamikaze, Kikutsuki, Minatsuki, Mikazuki, Matsukase, Nagatsuki, Nowake, Oite, Shiratsuyu, Shirayuki, Shirōtaye, Satsuki, Shigure, Utsuki, Ushio, Wakaba, Yugure, Yayoi, Yudachi, Yunagi.** Also **Ajanami, Iranami, Uranami** ('08.)

Dimensions : 227 to 234½ (*o.a.*) × 21¼ × 6 feet. Armament : 6—12 pdr., and 2—18 inch tubes. 1 searchlight. Designed H.P. 6,000 = 29 kts. Coal : 100 tons, but *Ajanami, Isonami,* and *Uranami* have 95 tons coal + 15 oil. Endurance about 1,200 miles at 15 kts. Complement 61.

Note: Shirotaye sunk by German gun-boat Kiao-Chau Bay 4 September 1914. *Satsuki, Asatsuyu* and *Fumitzuki* deleted during the war.

2 Sakura Class.

Fore funnel may now be raised.

2 *Sakura* class:— **Sakura** (1911), **Tachibana** (1912). Both built at Maidzuru. 605 tons. Fuel : 125 tons coal + 30 tons oil ; otherwise as 10 *Kaba* class, on preceding page.

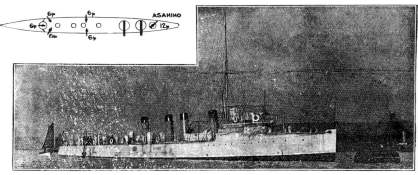

The 4 *Asashiho* (Thornycroft) type :—**Asashiho, Asagiri, Murasame, Shirakumo.** Armament : 1—12 pdr. (*aft*), 5—6 pdr. 335 tons. Guns : 2—12 pdr., 4—6 pdr. Torpedo tubes : 2—18 inch. H.P. 7000 = 30 to 31 kts. Boilers : Thornycroft. Coal : 96 tons. Complement, 60.

Note: *Asagiri* and *Murasame* deleted during the war.

JAPANESE DESTROYERS AND TORPEDO BOATS.

Note.

All T.B.D. listed below now used only as Tenders to Torpedo Schools. Will probably be removed from the Navy in the near future.

Note to Plans.—The 6 pdr. on forebridge has been replaced by a 12 pdr.

2 *Yarrow* type:—**Akebono, Oboro** (both 1899). 306 tons. Dimensions : 220 × 20½ × 5 feet. Guns : 2—12 pdr., 4—6 pdr. Torpedo tubes : 2—18 inch. H.P. 6000 = 31 kts. Coal : 90–95 tons. Complement, 51.

Note to Plans.—The 6 pdr. on forebridge has been replaced by a 12 pdr.

The 6 *Kagero* (Thornycroft) type :— **Kagero, Murakumo, Shinonome, Shiranui, Usugumo, Yugiri.** Armament : 1—12 pdr. (*aft*), 5—6 pdr.

Note: *Murakumo, Shinonome* and *Yugiri* deleted during the war.

Yamahiko. Armament : 1—12 pdr. (*aft*), 5—3 pdr. 2—18 inch tubes

1st Class Torpedo Boats

(*Itto Suiratei*).

(A) *Hayabusa* class (Normand type). Note position of mast and bridge, and compare with *Aotaka* class named **Aotaka, Hato, Hibari, Kari, Kiji, Tsubame, Sagi, Uzura, Kamome Hashitaka,** and **Otori**, all built in Japan. Armament : 1—6 pdr., 2—3 pdr. 3—18 inch tubes. Normand type.

Note—All deleted during the war.

JAPANESE TORPEDO BOATS AND SUBMARINES.

1st Class Torpedo Boats—*Continued.*

(B) *Hayabusa* class: Compare with (A) on preceding page.
11 *Aotaka* class (*Normand* type), viz.:—9 *Kure D.Y.*: **Aotaka, Hato, Hibari, Kari, Kiji, Sagi, Tsubame** (all 1903), **Kamome** and **Udzura** (1904): 2 *Kawasaki Co., Kobe*; **Hashitaka** (1903), and **Otori** (1904). 150 to 152 tons. Dimensions : 147 × 16 × 4½ feet. Armament : 1—6 pdr., 2—3 pdr., 3—14 inch tubes. Machinery : 2 sets triple expansion. Designed H.P. 4200=28·5 to 29 kts. Coal : 26 tons.

2nd Class Torpedo Boats.
(*2tô Suiratei*)
Are only used now for Harbour Duty.

8 *Schichau* type: **Nos. 70—75, 67—68** (built at Yokosuka, Sasebo and Kure, 1902-3). 87 to 89 tons. Dimensions : 128 × 16¼ × 3½ feet. Armament : 2—6 pdr., (Yamanouchi) and 3—14 inch tubes. Designed H.P. 1200=23¾ to 24 kts. Coal : 26¼ tons.

14 *Yarrow* type: **Nos. 62-75.** (built at Yokosuka, sasebo and Kure, 1902-3). 87 to 89 tons. Dimensions: 128 x 16¼ x 3½ feet. Armament: 2—6 pdr., (Yamanouchi) and 3—14 inch tubes. Designed H.P. 1200 = 23½ to 24 kts. Coal: 26½ tons. Note: *62-66* and *69* deleted during the war.

11 boats: **49, 47—44, 38—36, 33—31.** Armament: 1–3 pdr., 3 tubes. Schichau type.

Note—33 mined off Kiao-Chau Bay 11 November 1914.

Ex-German Submarines.

The following ex-German Submarines were taken over at British Naval Ports in 1919, and have proceeded to Japan:—
6 *Ocean-going* boats : *U 43, U 46, U 55, U 125, UB 125, UB 143.*
2 *Mine-Laying* boats : *UC 90, UC 99.*
These boats are only allowed to be used for experiments, and must be broken up. They are not to be incorporated in the Imperial Navy, and accordingly, they are not included in above Table, or described in the following pages.

12 Coastal Boats.

5 *Vickers-Japanese* type: **No. 12—10** (Kure D.Y. and Kawasaki Co., Kobe, 1910-11), **Nos. 9** & **8** (Vickers, Barrow, 1908). Displacements vary a little, but are generally similar to British "C" class submarines. Dimensions about 135 × 13½ × 12 feet. 2 bow tubes. Radius of action about 1000 miles *on surface* at 10 kts.

1 *type unknown* : **No. 7** (Kawasaki Co., 1906-7). Displacement : 79 tons *on surface*, 86 tons *submerged*. Dimensions : 85 × 8 × feet. 1 bow torpedo tube. 1 set petrol motors. Nothing else known about this boat. Considering her size and age, she may be almost worthless now.

1 *type unknown* : **No. 6** (Kawasaki Co., Kobe, 1906-7). Details as for No. 7 but is of different appearance. Doubtfully reported that this boat was rebuilt 1918-19 as an experimental Minelayer.

5 *early Holland* type: **Nos. 5—1** (1905-6, imported from U.S.A. about time of Russo-Japanese War). Dimensions : 66 × 11½ × feet. 1 bow torpedo tube. Petrol engine of 160 H.P. for surface running. 1 screw. Probably of little effective value now.

---

20 + *23 ?* **Submarines** (*Sensuikan*).

JAPANESE DEPOT SHIPS.

Destroyer Depot Ships.

1st Class Cruisers, **NISSHIN** and **IDZUMO,** attached to T.B.D. Flotillas.

ISUSAN (Maru). (——) 217 tons. No other details known.

KENKAI (Maru). (——) 315 tons. No other details known.

REKISAN (Maru). (——). 450 tons. 129½ × 22½ × 8¾ feet. Guns : Not known. I.H.P. 202 = 8.7 kts. No other details known.

SHIROGANE. (——). 413 tons. No other details known.

Submarine Depot Ships.

1st Class Cruiser **ASO** is Tender to Submarines.

Photo by courtesy of the Navy Department, Tokyo.
KOMAHASHI. (Sasebo, 1913). 1230 tons. 227 × 35 × 17? feet. Guns : 3—12 pdr. H.P. 1824 = 13.9 kts. Was originally built as a Naval Transport.

JAPANESE MISCELLANEOUS.

Submarine Depot Ships—*continued.*

KARASAKI (ex *Ekaterinoslav*, 1896, captured 1904). 6,710 tons. Dimensions : 440 × 49½ × 15¾ feet (*max.* draught). Armament : 1—12 pdr. H.P. 3200 = 13 kts.

NAGAURA (**Maru**) (ex-Gunboat *Tatsuta*, Elswick, 1894). 850 tons. 240 × 27½ × 9½ feet. Guns : Not known. I.H.P. 5000 = 21 kts. Coal : 155 tons.

Seaplane Depot Ship.

Photo by courtesy of the Navy Department.

WAKAMIYA (1901). 7600 tons. Dimensions : 365 × 48½ × 19 feet. Armament : 2—12 pdr. H.P. 1600 = 9½ kts. Carries 4 seaplanes. Was originally built as a Naval Transport.

Note.—Now has hangars at foot of each mast, as shown by Silhouette.

Mine Layers.

TAKACHIHO (1885). Light cruiser. Torpedoed by German destroyer in Kiao Chau Bay October 1914.

NINOSHIMA (**Maru**). Building or completing at Kure D.Y. No details known. 1918-19 Programme.

YENOSHIMA (**Maru**). Built under 1917 Special Programme, at Maidzuru D.Y. No details known.

KUROKAMI. *Photo, Navy Dept., Tokyo.*

YENTO (**Maru**,) Mar., 1917 ; **KATASHIMA** (**Maru**) Feb., 1917), both built at Maidzuru D.Y., and **KUROKAMI** (**Maru**) Kure D.Y., Feb., 1917. 800 tons. Built under 1916-17 Programme. No other details known.

KUROSHIMA (**Maru**) and **TOSHIMA** (**Maru**). Both built at Sasebo D.Y. about 1915-17. 433 tons. 150 × 25 × 7½ feet. Guns : Not known. H.P. 600 = 12 kts.

Note.—May be sister ships to *Ashizaki Maru* and *Katoku Maru*, given below.

KATSURIKI. (Kure D.Y., Oct., 1916). 2000 tons. Built under 1915-16 Programme. No other details known.

ASHIZAKI (**Maru**) 433 tons, and **KATOKU** (**Maru**). 300 tons. Both launched at Maidzuru D.Y., Oct., 1915. Guns : Not known. H.P. 700 = 12 kts. Built under 1915-16 Programme.

NATSUSHIMA (**Maru**). (Yokosuka D.Y., March, 1911). 421 tons. 200 × 22½ × 5½ feet. Guns : Not known. H.P. 500 = 12 kts.

SOKUTEN (**Maru**). No details known.

Mine-Sweepers.

Some of the Mine Layers, detailed above, probably equipped also as Sweepers. No exact details known.

Oilers & Tank Vessels.

ERIMO (——), **NOTORO** (——) and **SHIRETOKO.** All building or completing by Kawasaki Co., Kobé. 8,000 tons. Belong to 1918-19 Programme. No other details known.

SUNOSAKI (**Maru**) (Yokosuka D.Y., June, 1915). 9800 tons. Guns : Some small Q.F. H.P. 6000 = 14 kts. Carries 5000 tons oil. Built under 1916-17 Programme.

TSURUGIZAKI (Kure D.Y., June, 1917). 1970 tons. 220½ × 31 × 14 feet. H.P. 900 = 9 kts. Cargo : 1,100 tons oil. Built under 1916-17 Programme.

SHIJIKI (Kure D.Y., March, 1916). 5300 tons. 300 × 42 × 20¼ feet. H.P. 2500 = 12 kts. Own fuel : 540 tons oil., Cargo : 3000 tons oil. Built under 1915-16 Programme. Lost in typhoon 16 August 1919.

Also 10 (or more) other small Tank Vessels ; names and details not known.

Fleet Colliers.

MUROTO (1918). 8750 tons. Other details as Noshima below.

NOSHIMA (Mitsubishi Co., Kobé, Feb., 1919). 6000 tons. I.H.P. 2640 = 12.5 kts. Coal : 877 tons. Built under Special 1918-19 Programme.

Naval Auxiliaries and Transports.

KOMAHASHI (Submarine Depot Ship) and **WAKAMIYA** (Seaplane Carrier), both listed on preceding page. Were both originally built as Naval Transports, and can be so used if necessary.

ROZAN (ex-German S.S. *Ellen Rickmers*, built at Geestemünde 1906, and captured 1914). 4117 tons *gross*. Dimensions : 367.7 × 47.7 × 27.4 feet (*depth of hold*). H.P. 1600 = 11 kts.

SEITO (ex-German S.S. *Durendart*, built at Flensburg, 1906, and captured 1914). 3844 tons *gross*. Dimensions : 340.5 × 49.2 × feet. H.P. 1525 = 10 kts.

KOSHU (ex-German S.S. *Michael Jebsen*, built by Howaldt, Kiel, 1904, and captured 1914). 1521 tons *gross*. Dimensions : 251.1 × 36.1 × 18.9 feet (*depth of hold*). H.P. 800 = 9.5 kts. Now has fore topmast.

MANSHU (ex-*Manchuria*, 1901). 3916 tons. Complement, 193. Guns : 2—12 pdr., 2—3 pdr. I.H.P. 5000 × 17.6 kts. Coal : 400 tons.

MATSUE (ex-*Sungari*, 1898). 2550 tons. Complement, 126. Guns : 2—12 pdr., 2—3 pdr. I.H.P. 1500 = 13 kts. Coal : 130 tons and some oil fuel.

TAKASAKI (——). 4746 tons. No other details known.

Despatch Vessels, Yachts, &c.
None ?

Repair Ship.

KWANTO (**Maru**) (1898). 10,000 tons. 410 × 49½ × feet. I.H.P. 2500 = 10 kts. speed.

Salvage Ships.

KURIHASHI (**Maru**) (——). 1040 tons. 182 × 80¼ × 11¾ feet. I.H.P. 1200 = kts.

SARUHASHI (**Maru**) (——). 600 tons. 140 × 26½ × 10½ feet. I.H.P. 885 = kts.

ITAHASHI (**Maru**) (——). 333 tons. No other details known.

Surveying Ships.

Photo by courtesy of the Ministry of Marine

MUSASHI (Yokosuka, 1886, **YAMATO** (Kobe, 1885). Composite built. 1502 tons. Guns : 4—12 pdr., 4—3 pdr. H.P. 1622. Original speed was 13½ kts. Coal : 145 tons.

Training Ships.
(All described on preceding pages :)—
For Gunnery :
ASAHI. Battleship.
For Torpedoes (at Yokosuka) :
TSUGARU. 2nd Class Cruiser.
For Gunnery and Torpedoes :—
IKOMA. 1st Class Cruiser.
For Seamanship :
FUJI. Battleship.
For Engineer Branch : ?

YURAGAWA (**Maru**). No details known. Doubtful if this ship is still in service.
For Cadets :
SUWO. Coast Defence Battleship.
ADZUMA.
TOKIWA. 1st Class Cruisers.
YAKUMO.
For Conscripts :
HASHIDATE. 2nd Class Coast Defence Ship.
For Boys :
Old 2nd Class Coast Defence Ships, **OKINOSHIMA** and **MISHIMA**, are reported to be used for this service as Barracks, but may now be serving as Ice Breakers.

FRENCH FLEET.

(Officially Revised, 1919, by order of H.E. The Minister of Marine.

CHERBOURG to		knots.
Bermuda	... ...	2933
Brest	... ...	210
Copenhagen	... ...	834
Devonport	... ...	111
Dunkirk	... ...	180
Lorient	... ...	300
Kronstadt	... ...	1500
Portsmouth	... ...	72
Rochefort	... ...	410
Stockholm	... ...	1258
Toulon	... ...	1817
Wilhelmshaven	... ...	476

TOULON to		knots.
Aden	... ...	2882
Ajaccio	... ...	160
Algiers	... ...	405
Bizerta	... ...	450
Brest	... ...	1659
Constantinople	...	1356
Genoa	... ...	164
Gibraltar	... ...	713
Kronstadt	... ...	3289
Lorient	... ...	1656
Port Mahon	... ...	207
Malta	... ...	612
Naples	... ...	407
Oran	... ...	542
Port Said	... ...	1485
Portsmouth	... ...	1864
Saigon	... ...	7150
Sevastopol	... ...	1654
Spezia	... ...	195
Tangiers	... ...	738
Taranto	... ...	766

BREST to		knots.
Algiers	... ...	1360
Bermuda	... ...	2811
Cherbourg	... ...	210
Devonport	... ...	139
Gibraltar	... ...	953
Liverpool	... ...	407
Malta	... ...	1934
Kronstadt	... ...	1672
New York	... ...	2954
Oran	... ...	1876
Portsmouth	... ...	226
Rio de Janeiro	...	4837
Rochefort	... ...	260
Toulon	... ...	1659
Wilhelmshaven	... ...	686

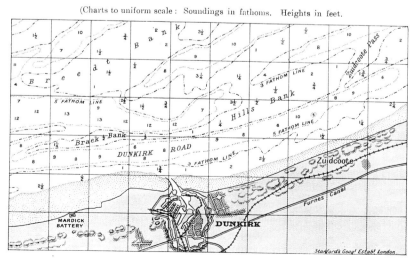

ORAN (Torpedo Station) to	knots.
Algiers ...	400
Bizerta ...	650
Gibraltar ...	225
Toulon ...	542

BIZERTA to	knots.
Algiers	400
Gibraltar ...	875
Malta	240
Oran	650
Spezia	430
Toulon	450

SAIGON to	knots.
Hong Kong ...	930
Manila	875
Port Arthur ...	2065
Singapore ...	640

MERCANTILE MARINE : 1051 steamers of 1,842,108 tons *gross.*
998 sailing ships of 466,348 tons *gross.*

COINAGE : 1 franc (100 centimes) = 9½d. British, 19 cents American.

TRADE PORTS (in order of importance) : Marseilles, Havre, Dunkirk, Bordeaux, Boulogne, Calais, Dieppe, Rouen.

OVERSEA POSSESSIONS : Corsica, Algeria, Tunis, Senegal, etc. Madagascar, Guiana, Martinique, S. Pierre, New Caledonia, Pondicherry, Annam, Cochin China, Tonquin.

FRENCH UNIFORMS AND NAVAL BASES—(Channel).

Vice-Amiral. Contre-Amiral. Capitaine de vaisseau. Capitaine de fregate. Lieutenant de vaisseau. Enseigne. Enseigne 2º classe and Aspirant

Corresponding British or U.S. Navies.

„ Rear-Ad. Captain. Commander. Lieut. Lieut. (junior). Sub-Lieut. and Midshipman. (U.S. Ensign.)

Note.—New rank of Capitane de corvette, introduced June, 1917, with four gold stripes on sleeve, and intermediate between ranks of Capitane de fregate and Lieutenant de vaisseau. Equivalent to British or U.S.A. rank of Lieut.-Commander.

Only one of the Capitaine de fregate's upper stripes is gold : the other is white.

Epaulettes with parade uniform are of the usual sort, *except that*—

A Vice-Admiral's epaulettes have the usual anchor and 3 stars.

A Rear-Admiral's „ „ „ „ „ „ 2 „

Caps are the usual shape, but have gold bands round. The cocked hat carries the tri-colour.

Before the war, personnel was about 65,000 including reserves.

Minister of Marine—Mons. Georges Leygues.

(Charts to uniform scale : Soundings in fathoms. Heights in feet.

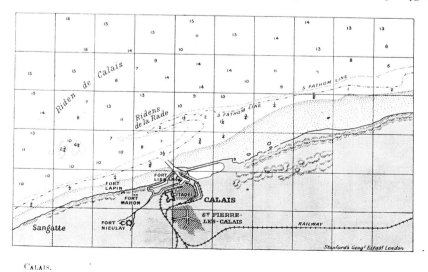

CALAIS.

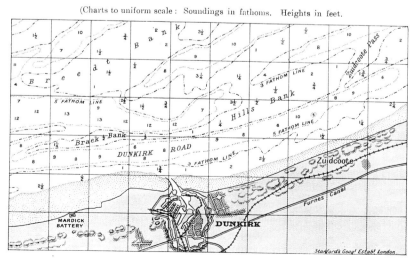

DUNKIRK.

FRENCH FLEET.

ADDENDA AND CORRECTIONS:—3.

Naval Ordnance (converted from official 1919 Table furnished by courtesy of the Ministry of Marine).

Calibre (ins.)	13.4		12						10.6	
Do. (c/m)	34		30						27	
Mark	1912		1906-10	1906	'93-96'M	1893-96	1893		1893–6	1893
Length (calibres)	45		45	45	40	40	40		40	45
Weight of Gun (English tons)	65.33		54.7	54.7	47.3	47.3	43.4		34.5	34.9
Weight of Shell (capped) in lbs.	A.P. 1190.5	Ogival 1256.6	922.3	960.4	770.3	770.3	770.3		579.1	579.1
Weight of Charge (lbs.)	330.7	337.3	267.4	282.2	284.4	244.7	217.2		197.4	148.8
Max. Pressure (lbs.)	59,525	57,320	57,320	57,320	61,729	63,934	51,808		62,831	47,619
Muzzle-Velocity (ft.-secs.)	2624.7	2605	2559	2559	2839	2674	2559		2674	2559
Remaining Velocity at 21,872 yds. 20,000 m.	..	1309	..	..	..	..	..		..	..
16,404 yds. 15,000 m.	1178	1462	..	..	..	..	..		..	..
10,936 yds. 10,000 m.	1473	1762	1529	1529	1411	1325	1260		1203	1188
5468 yds. 5000 m.	1640	2162	1992	1992	2028	1893	1801		1798	1739
Angle of descent at 20,000 m.	...	25° 10″	..	..	..	..	..		..	..
15,000 m.	21° 10″	14° 50″	..	..	..	..	..		..	..
10,000 m.	9° 30″	7° 35″	9° 25″	9° 25″	9° 50″	11° 20″	12° 40″		13° 10″	13° 50″
5000 m.	3° 10″	2° 53″	3° 14″	3° 14″	3° 0″	3° 20″	3° 40″		3° 30″	13° 50″

Calibre (ins.)	9.4			7.6			6.5				5.5		3.9
Do. (c/m)	24			19			16				14		10
Mark	1902–6	1893–6	1893	1902	1893–6	1893	'93-'96M	1893–6	1893	'91 (II)	1910	1893	'91 &'93
Length (calibres)	49.5	40	40	50	40	40	45	45	45	45	55	45	45
Weight of Gun (English tons)	29.1	23.6	20.4	14.9	12.5	10.2	7.96	7.96	6.52	6.94	5.17	4.01	1.67
Weight of Shell (capped) in lbs.	487.2	374.8	374.8	199	199	199	121	121	121	121	80.5	84	35.5
Weight of Charge (lbs.)	148.1	147.4	127.9	84	74.5	49.2	45.6	43.7	28.9	28.9	22.7	16	8.16
Max. Pressure (lbs.)	57,320	63,934	52,910	59,083	61,739	47,400	47,400	61,739	44,092	44,092	55,155	53,706	52,911
Muzzle-Velocity (ft.-secs.)	2625	2723	2625	3117	2756	2526	2953	2838	2527	2527	2723	2395	2329
Remaining Velocity at 21,872 yds. 20,000 m.	..	..	..	..	..	..	..	..	..	..	..	..	..
16,404 yds. 15,000 m.	1102	..	..	..	..	..	..	..	..	..	..	..	..
10,936 yds. 10,000 m.	1348	1135	1112	1106	1010	992	928	918	922	922	860	905	856
5468 yds. 5000 m.	1896	1755	1654	1860	1571	1447	1417	1351	1257	1257	1230	1168	1033
Angle of descent at 20,000 m.	..	..	..	..	..	..	..	..	..	..	..	..	..
15,000 m.	25° 50″	..	..	..	..	..	..	..	..	..	..	..	..
10,000 m.	11° 10″	14° 40″	16° 10″	14° 10″	18° 10″	20° 50″	23° 20″	24° 30″	26° 30″	26° 30″	27° 30″	28° 40″	34° 10″
5000 m.	3° 20″	3° 40″	4° 0″	3° 10″	4° 10″	5°	4° 20″	5° 10″	6° 20″	6° 20″	6° 10″	7° 20″	9° 20″

FRENCH FLEET.—GUNS, TORPEDOES AND NOTES.

Modern Naval Guns. *(All details unofficial.)*

Notation.	Calibre.		Length.	Model.	Weight of gun.	Weight of A.P. shot.	Initial velocity.	Penetration against K.C.			*Approximate* Danger Space for *average ship* at		
	m/m.	inches.	cals.		tons.	lbs.	f. s.	9000 in.	6000 in.	3000 in.	10,000 yards.	5000 yards.	3000 yards.
A[8]	*340*	13·4	...	1911	67	1433	2657	12	16	20	...	...	...
A[6]	*305*	12	50	1906	57	970	3005	11	14	18	200	640	
A[5]	*305*	12	45	1902	50	731	3000	8	13	17	160	610	
A[4]	*305*	12	45	1896	46½	644	2870	7	12	15	150	570	1080
AA	*305*	12	40 & 45	'93, '91	46½	644	2700	4½	9	12	150	510	1050
AAA	*274*	10·8	45	1896	35½	476	2870	5	10	13½	150	540	1020
AA	*274*	10·8	45 & 40	1893	35	476	2625	3	7	11¼			
A[2]	*240*	9·4	50	'02-'06	24	375	2969	4	9	14			
A	*240*	9·4	40	1893	22¾	317½	2625	3	6	9	144	540	1080
A	*194*	7·6	45 & 50	1902	15	185	3117	...	6	9	144	...	...
B	*194*	7·6	40	1896	12½	185	2870	...	5	8¼	120	525	1080
C	*194*	7·6	40 & 45	'93 & '91	10½	165	2625	...	3½	6	96	435	1020
C	*164*	6·5	45	1902	9¼	114½	3002		4¼	7		330	750
D	*164*	6·5	45	1896	9	114½	2870		4	6		285	630
E	*164*	6·5	45	1891	7	99¼	2625		...	4½	...	240	585
F	*164*	6·5	45	1887	6½	99¼	2297		...	3	...	150	360
F	*138*	5·5	55	1910	...	81	...	...	...	...	...	...	...
F	*138*	5·5	45	'93-'87	6½	{81½ / 77}	2395	...	...	3	...	120	300
F	*100*	3.9	55	'92 & '93	2¼	31	2494		...	2½	...	...	...
F	*100*	3·9	45	1891	1½	31	2428		...	2	...	...	...

NOTES ON GUNS.

In addition to the above guns, there are various models of 65 m/m (9 pdr.) and 47 m/m (3 pdr.) guns, some types being semi-automatic; also usual anti-aircraft models, 1 pdr. and machine guns.

Projectiles.—Capped A.P. for all calibres. Melinite shell for all guns.

Funnel Marking System, etc.

Big Ships:—1st squadron, 1 white band; 2nd squadron, 2 white bands. Ships in division distinguished by funnel on which bands are painted: *i.e.* flagship on foremast funnel, 2nd on 2nd, etc. Ships different to others, no marks.

Destroyers:—Coloured bands. 1st flotilla *blue*, 2nd *white*, 3rd *red*, 4th *green*, 5th *black*. Also initials of names on bows, and flotilla colour on name scroll on stern.

Torpedoes. *(Details unofficial.)*

Whitehead pattern, made at Toulon Torpedo Factory; also Schneider pattern at Schneider & Cie's works.

French Designation.	Diameter.	Length.	Charge.	Pressure in chamber.	*Maximum* range.
	inches.	feet.	lbs.	lbs. per sq. in.	
1904 model	18	19½	198	2150	6000
45 c/m *long*	18	16½	198	1270	2000
45 c/m *short*	18	13¾	185	1000	1500
38 c/m *long*	15	18¾	100		1000
38 c/m *short*	15	16½	85		1000

Notes.—All fitted with gyros. Mines are Sautter-Harlé type.

General Notes.

COLOUR OF SHIPS.

Big ships.—Grey all over, but some have grey-green or greenish-brown turrets, or black barbette shields.

Destroyers, etc.—Light grey; have identity letters, taken from their names, painted on bows—*e.g.*, CL = *Claymore*. FF = *Fanfare*, EH = *Enseigne Henry*.

Submarines.—Sea green or light grey; have identity letters painted on bows or "air rudders" on the same system as destroyers. Camouflage schemes also used.

Guns.

13·4 inch, M. '11, in *Bretagne* class (3).

12 inch, M. '02-'06, 45 cal., in *Danton* class (5), 50 cal., in *J. Bart* class (4).
M. '02, 45 cal., in *Verité* class (3).
M. '96, 45 cal., in *Republique* and *Patrie*.
M. '93, 40 cal., in *St. Louis*.

10·8 inch, M. '96, 45 cal., in *Henry IV*.

9·4 inch, M. '06, 50 cal., in *Danton* class (5).

9·4 inch, M. '93, 40 cal., in *D'Entrecasteaux*.

7·6 inch, 50 cal., in *Verité class* (3), *W. Rousseau* class (2), *E. Renan*, *Jules Michelet*.

7·6 inch, 45 cal., in *V. Hugo* class (2), and 40 cal. in older armoured cruisers.

6·4 inch, 50 cal., in *Patrie* class (2), and 45 cal., in cruisers.

5·5 inch, 55 cal., in *J. Bart* class (4), *Bretagne* class (3), and *Normandie* class (5).

FRENCH PRIVATE YARDS.

Principal Private Yards (arranged alphabetically).

CHANTIERS DE BRETAGNE (formerly De la Brosse & Fouché), NANTES. Destroyers, t. b., etc.

CHANTIERS DE LA GIRONDE, BORDEAUX. All kinds of warships. Water front: 623 yards. Area of works: about 48 acres. Four slips: (1) 597 feet, (2) 515 feet, (3) 436 feet, (4) 590½ feet. Titan cranes to first two. One dock, which can be used for building: 594×121½×32½ feet, with 140 ton electric crane. Special submarine workshop: 141×49 feet. Firm allied to Schneider et Cie.

CHANTIERS DE LA LOIRE. Works at St. Nazaire (all kinds of warships) and NANTES. Machinery works at SAINT DENIS.

CHANTIERS DE PROVENCE. Yard at Port de Bouc.

CHANTIERS DE ST. NAZAIRE (Penhoet). Principal yard ST. NAZAIRE. Works also at ROUEN. All kinds of warships.

CHANTIERS NAVALS FRANÇAIS, CAEN. 10 slips, 400-500 feet; 4 slips, 300 feet. Covers 1250 acres.

DYLE & BACALAN, BORDEAUX. Destroyers, t.b., etc. Five slips, longest of which is 394 feet. Served with two 40 ton cranes. Machinery: 7000 h.p.

FORGES ET CHANTIERS DE LA MEDITERRANÉE. Principal yard LA SEYNE, near TOULON. Other yards at HAVRE, GRANVILLE and MARSEILLES. 3 slips, (a) 492 feet, (b) 590 feet, (c) 656 feet. All kinds of warships built at La Seyne, smaller craft at other yards. Total employes circa 6500.

AUGUSTIN NORMAND & Cie. Destroyer, torpedo boat and submarine works at HAVRE. Build ships up to 4000 tons. Yard covers 4 hectares. Large water front. Employees: 1500. Build submarine mine-layers, Diesel engines, Normand and Normand-Sigaudy boilers, etc.

SCHNEIDER & Cie. (formerly Schneider-Canet). LE CREUSOT WORKS: Ordnance, Munitions, Armour Plate. HAVRE, HONFLEUR AND HOC WORKS: Aviation and Diesel engines, proving range. CHALON-SUR-SAONE YARD: Destroyers, torpedo boats and submarines. CHAMPAGNE-SUR-SEINE WORKS: Electric equipment for submarines. LA LONDES-LES-MAURES WORKS (VAR): Torpedoes. STATION DE CREUX ST. GEORGES (near Toulon): For testing submarines.

SOCIÉTÉ PROVENCALE DE CONSTRUCTIONS NAVALES, MARSEILLES.*

SOCIÉTÉ NORMANDE DE CONSTRUCTIONS NAVALES, HAVRE and CHERBOURG.*

*Firms allied to Schneider & Cie.

Scale : 1 inch = 160 feet.

FRENCH WARSHIPS RECOGNITION SILHOUETTES.

NO FUNNELS.

ONE FUNNEL.

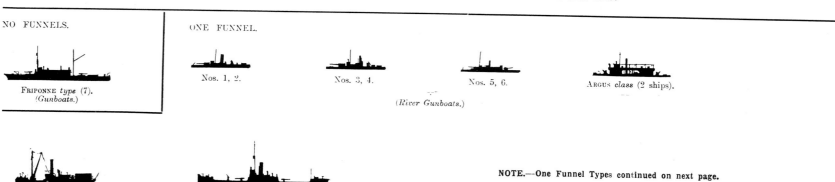

Friponne type (7). (Gunboats.)

Nos. 1, 2.

Nos. 3, 4.

Nos. 5, 6.

ARGUS class (2 ships).

(River Gunboats.)

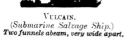

VULCAIN. (Submarine Salvage Ship.) Two funnels abeam, very wide apart.

NANCY type (31?) (Convoy Despatch Vessels.) Silhouette approximate only

NOTE.—One Funnel Types continued on next page.

Scale : 1 inch = 160 feet.

FRENCH WARSHIPS RECOGNITION SILHOUETTES.

ONE FUNNEL.—(continued from preceding page).

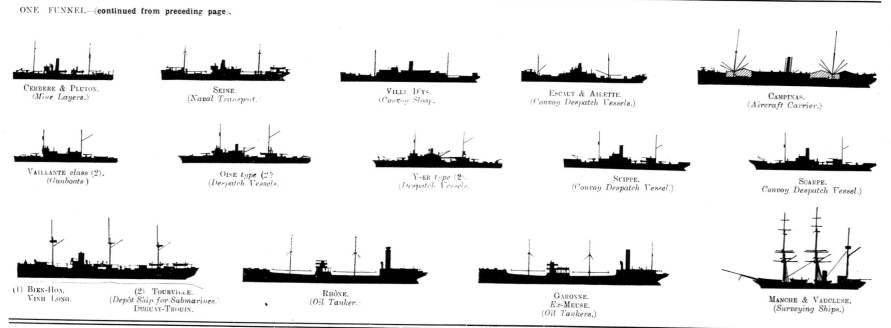

CERBERE & PLUTON. (Mine Layers.)

SEINE. (Naval Transport.)

VILLE D'YS. (Convoy Sloop.)

ESCAUT & AILETTE. (Convoy Despatch Vessels.)

CAMPINAS. (Aircraft Carrier.)

VAILLANTE class (2). (Gunboats.)

OISE type (2?) (Despatch Vessels.)

YSER type (2?) (Despatch Vessels.)

SUIPPE. (Convoy Despatch Vessel.)

SCARPE. Convoy Despatch Vessel.)

(1) BIEN-HOA, VINH LONG. (2) TOURVILLE. (Depôt Ship for Submarines.) DUGUAY-TROUIN.

RHÔNE. (Oil Tanker.)

GARONNE. Ex-MEUSE. (Oil Tankers.)

MANCHE & VAUCLUSE. (Surveying Ships.)

TWO FUNNELS—(continued on next page).

ARDENT type (27) (Gunboats.—Vary a little in details.)

MARNE type (2?) (Despatch Vessels.)

ALTAIR type (5).

CASSIOPÉE, REGULUS.

"Star Class" (7). (Sloops.)

Scale: 1 inch = 160 feet.

TWO FUNNELS—(continued).

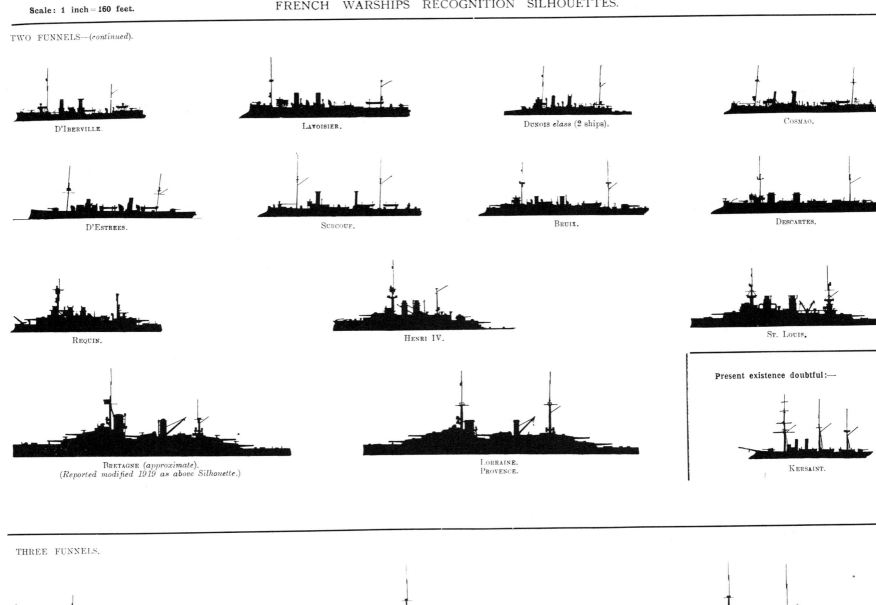

D'IBERVILLE.

LAVOISIER.

DUNOIS *class* (2 ships).

COSMAO.

D'ESTREES.

SURCOUF.

BRUIX.

DESCARTES.

REQUIN.

HENRI IV.

ST. LOUIS.

BRETAGNE *(approximate)*.
(Reported modified 1919 as above Silhouette.)

LORRAINE.
PROVENCE.

Present existence doubtful:—

KERSAINT.

THREE FUNNELS.

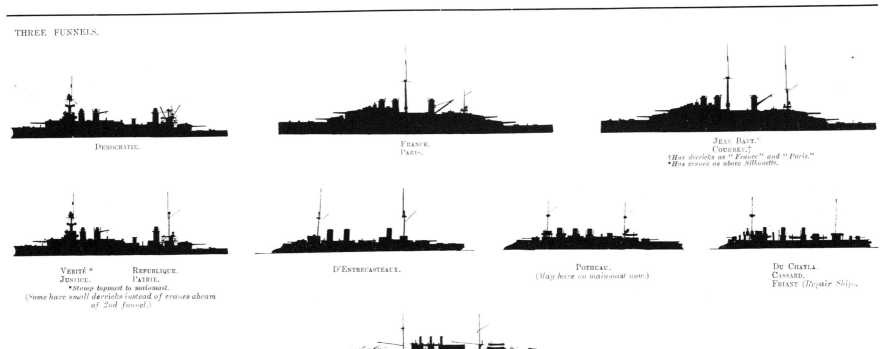

DEMOCRATIE.

FRANCE.
PARIS.

JEAN BART.*
COURBET.†
†*Has derricks as " France" and " Paris."*
Has cranes as above Silhouette.

VERITÉ *   REPUBLIQUE.
JUSTICE.   PATRIE.
Stump topmast to mainmast.
(Some have small derricks instead of cranes abeam of 2nd funnel.)

D'ENTRECASTEAUX.

POTHUAU.
(May have no mainmast now.)

DU CHAYLA.
CASSARD.
FRIANT *(Repair Ship).*

FOUDRE.
(Aircraft Carrier).

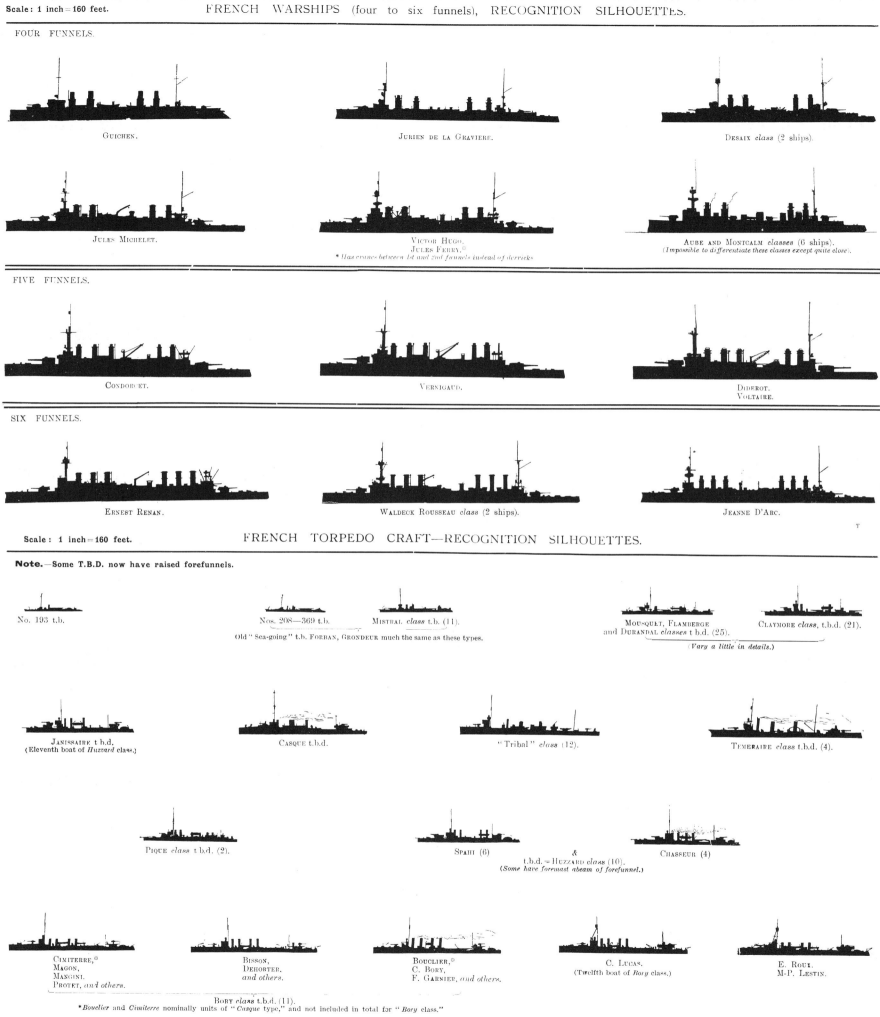

Scale: 1 inch = 160 feet.

FRENCH WARSHIPS (four to six funnels), RECOGNITION SILHOUETTES.

FOUR FUNNELS.

GUICHEN.

JURIEN DE LA GRAVIÈRE.

DESAIX *class* (2 ships).

JULES MICHELET.

VICTOR HUGO.
JULES FERRY.◎
* *Has cranes between 1st and 2nd funnels instead of derricks*

AUBE AND MONTCALM *classes* (6 ships).
(*Impossible to differentiate these classes except quite close*).

FIVE FUNNELS.

CONDORCET.

VERNIGAUD.

DIDEROT.
VOLTAIRE.

SIX FUNNELS.

ERNEST RENAN.

WALDECK ROUSSEAU *class* (2 ships).

JEANNE D'ARC.

Scale : 1 inch = 160 feet.

FRENCH TORPEDO CRAFT—RECOGNITION SILHOUETTES.

Note.—Some T.B.D. now have raised forefunnels.

No. 193 t.b.

Nos. 208—369 t.b.

MISTRAL. *class* t.b. (11).

Old "Sea-going" t.b. FORBAN, GRONDEUR much the same as these types.

MOUSQUET, FLAMBERGE
and DURANDAL *classes* t b.d. (25).

CLAYMORE *class*, t.b.d. (21).

(*Vary a little in details.*)

JANISSAIRE t b.d.
(Eleventh boat of *Huzzard* class.)

CASQUE t.b.d.

"Tribal" *class* (12).

TEMERAIRE *class* t.b.d. (4).

PIQUE *class* t b.d. (2).

SPAHI (6)

t.b.d. = HUZZARD *class* (10).
(*Some have foremast abeam of forefunnel.*)

CHASSEUR (4)

CIMITERRE,◎
MAGON,
MANGINI,
PROTET, *and others.*

BISSON,
DEHORTER.
and others.

BOUCLIER,◎
C. BORY,
F. GARNIER, *and others.*

C. LUCAS.
(Twelfth boat of *Bory* class.)

E. ROUX.
M-P. LESTIN.

BORY *class* t.b.d. (11).
Bouclier and *Cimiterre* nominally units of "*Casque* type," and not included in total for "*Bory* class."

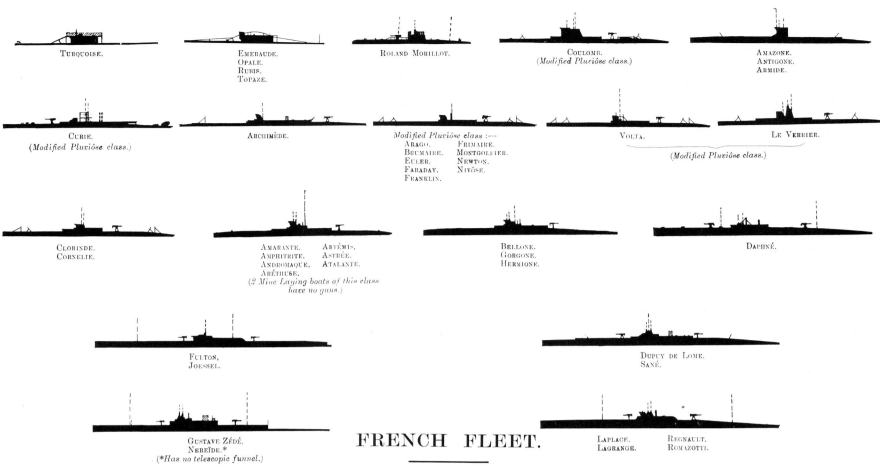

TURQUOISE.

EMERAUDE.
OPALE.
RUBIS.
TOPAZE.

ROLAND MORILLOT.

COULOMB.
(Modified Pluviôse class.)

AMAZONE.
ANTIGONE.
ARMIDE.

CURIE.
(Modified Pluviôse class.)

ARCHIMÈDE.

Modified Pluviôse class :—
ARAGO.   FRIMAIRE.
BRUMAIRE.   MONTGOLFIER.
EULER.   NEWTON.
FARADAY.   NIVÔSE.
FRANKLIN.

VOLTA.

LE VERRIER.

(Modified Pluviôse class.)

CLORINDE.
CORNELIE.

AMARANTE.   ARTÉMIS.
AMPHITRITE.   ASTRÉE.
ANDROMAQUE.   ATALANTE.
ARÉTHUSE.
(2 Mine Laying boats of this class
have no guns.)

BELLONE.
GORGONE.
HERMIONE.

DAPHNÉ.

FULTON,
JOESSEL.

DUPUY DE LOME.
SANÉ.

GUSTAVE ZÉDÉ.
NEREÏDE.*
(*Has no telescopic funnel.)

FRENCH FLEET.

LAPLACE.   REGNAULT.
LAGRANGE.   ROMAZOTTI.

ADDENDA AND CORRECTIONS:—1.

Flags (1919).

Drawings prepared from information furnished by courtesy of the Ministry of Marine, Paris.

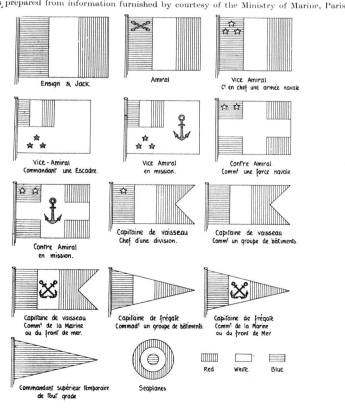

Ensign & Jack.

Amiral

Vice Amiral
Ct en chef une armée navale.

Vice-Amiral
Commandant une Escadre.

Vice Amiral
en mission.

Contre Amiral
Commt une force navale.

Contre Amiral
en mission.

Capitaine de vaisseau
Chef d'une division.

Capitaine de vaisseau
Commt un groupe de bâtiments.

Capitaine de vaisseau
Commt de la Marine
ou du front de mer.

Capitaine de frégate
Commdt un groupe de bâtiments.

Capitaine de frégate
Commt de la Marine
ou du front de Mer.

Commandant supérieur temporaire
de leur grade.

Seaplanes.

Red   White   Blue.

NORMANDIE class Dreadnoughts.—Reported that, if these ships are completed, their equipment will be brought up-to-date by the installation of director fire controls, "quadripod" masts, flying-off platforms, and aeroplanes on barbette crowns, &c. Unofficial statements have been published, saying that schemes have been considered for completing *BÉARN* as a Battle-Cruiser, armed with 6—17 inch guns. It must be added that, owing to the high costs of material and labour, it is doubtful if all or any of the *Normandie* class will be finished. *Béarn* may be launched to clear her slip and be left uncompleted.

The main turrets of **PATRIE, REPUBLIQUE,** and **POTHUAU** have been removed to Gunnery Schools ashore, but the below-deck portions of the turrets are left in these ships. They now have deck houses on fox'le and quarter decks. **PATRIE** has one *above water* tube over stern.

SIX NEW LIGHT CRUISERS, of a "*Modified Lamotte-Picquet*" type, projected under the 1919 Naval Programme. 4750 tons. Guns: 8—5·5 inch. Armour: 2" Side amidships, 1" Deck. Speed, 30 kts.

Regarding deletion of *Lamotte-Picquet* from this Edition of "Fighting Ships": this ship was actually begun, but never got beyond a very elementary stage of construction. Building may be resumed to above design, and this ship may be built under 1919 Programme.

BRUIX may be removed from the Effective List soon, with all Protected Cruisers.

Add the following to Lists of

Gunboats.

DUBOURDIEU, DU CHAUFFAULT, DUPERRÉ, DUMONT-D'URVILLE, DE CONEDIC, DECRES. These are Diesel-engined Gunboats of a modified *Vaillante* type, launched by Lorient and Rochefort Dockyards, 1918. *Dubourdieu* completed about June, 1919. Further Gunboats of this and other new types reported to be cancelled.

River Gunboat **STYX** (not listed), removed from Effective List.

SIX NEW DESTROYERS, of 2000 tons displacement, projected under the 1919 Naval Programme. Guns: 3—5·5 inch. Speed, 35 kts.

Opiniâtre (of *Temeraire* class) has been re-boilered and given four funnels, as Silhouette opposite.

Following Torpedo Boats reported removed from Effective List:
Chasseur, Arc, Flamberge, Epée.

Torpedo Boats: Nos. *195, 208—229* to be sold out.

Scale: 1 inch = 160 feet. SILHOUETTES.

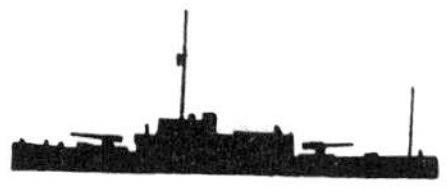

ARA ("*Aviso.*")

OPINIÂTRE *t.b.d.*

1912 FRENCH DREADNOUGHTS. Nos. **7, 6, 5** (*Cuirassés de 1er rang*) (20 knots).

(BRETAGNE CLASS—3 SHIPS.)

BRETAGNE (April, 1913), **LORRAINE** (September, 1913), **PROVENCE** (April, 1913).

Normal displacement, 23,230 tons. Complement, 1109.

Length (*waterline*), 541⅓ feet. Beam, 88½ feet. *Maximum* draught, 29 feet. Length *over all*, 544½ feet

Guns (M. '11):
- 10—13·4 inch, 45 cal. (A⁷)
- 22—5·5 inch, 55 cal. (M. '10)
- 4—3 pdr.
- 2—1 pdr.
- 2 landing.

Torpedo tubes (18 inch) M. '12:
- 4 *submerged*

Armour:
- 10¾" Belt (amidships) ..
- 7" Belt (ends) ....
- Deck (*see Notes*) ....
- 10"—6" Lower deck side
- 17"—10" Turrets.........
- 11" Turret bases (N.C.)
- 7" Secondary battery ...
- 12½" Conning tower ......

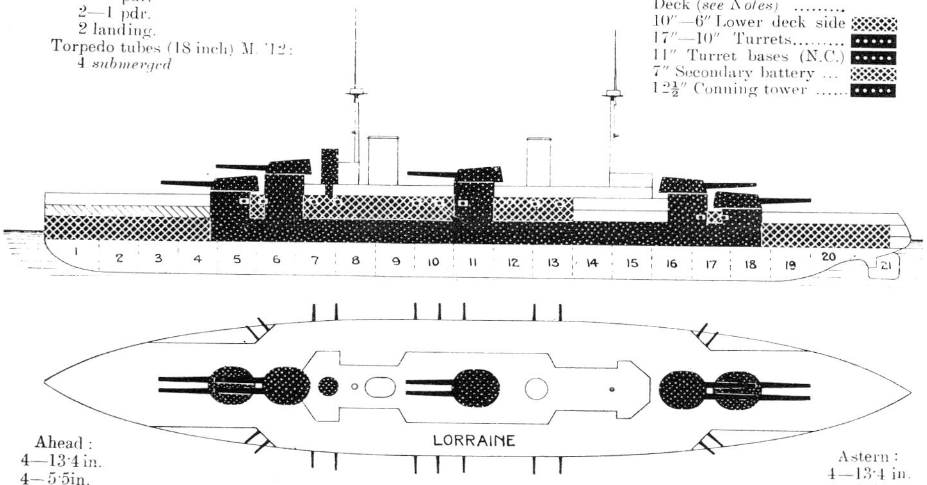

Ahead:
4—13·4 in.
4—5·5 in.

Astern:
4—13·4 in.
4—5·5 in.

Broadside: 10—13·4 in., 11—5·5 in.

Machinery: Parsons turbine. 4 screws. Boilers: see *Notes*. Designed H.P. 29,000 = 20 kts.
Coal: *normal* 900 tons; *maximum* 2680 tons. Also 300 tons oil.

**Gunnery Notes.*—Carry 100 rounds per gun for 13·4 inch and 275 per gun for the 5·5 inch. Janney electro-hydraulic mountings to big guns. Special cooling for magazines—temperature 77° Fahr. Magazines can be completely flooded inside ten minutes. Height of guns above l.w.l.: 1st turret, 30½ feet; 2nd, 37¾ feet; 3rd, 33½ feet; 4th, 28½ feet; 5th, 21⅓ feet. Arcs of training: Nos. 1 and 5, 270°; Nos. 2 & 4, 280°; No. 3, 120° either beam. Arcs of secondary guns: 120°.

**Torpedo Notes.*—Bullivant net defence. 8—36" and 2—30" searchlights. 4—200 k.w. dynamos. Torpedoes: 1912 Schneider, 6000 yards range. 24 carried. Also 30 blockade mines.

**Armour Notes.*—Turrets of maximum thickness at ports, instead of uniform thickness as in *J. Barts.* (See Addenda Notes.) The double bottom is carried to the under side of protective deck. Main belt is 13⅓ feet wide, 5 7/12 feet below and 7¾ above l.w.l. Battery 197 feet long with 7 in. bulkheads. Protective decks: lower 2" slopes, 1¾" flat. Upper, 1¾" flat on top of belt.

**Engineering Notes.*—Boilers: *Bretagne*, 24 Niclausse; *Lorraine*, 24 Belleville; *Provence*, 18 Guyot du Temple. Grate area: *Bretagne*, 2,090 sq. feet; *Lorraine*, 2,030 sq. feet; *Provence*, 1,492 sq. feet. Heating surface: *Bretagne*, 64,660 sq. feet; *Lorraine*, 63,700 sq. feet; *Provence*, 62,585 sq. feet. Pressure, 256 lbs. per sq. in. 300 turbine r.p.m. 2,700 tons coal in 13 bunkers, 250 tons oil in 4 tanks. Endurance: 1,790 miles at 10 kts. 2,800 at 18¾ kts.

Name	*Builder*	*Machinery*	*Laid down*	*Completed*	*Trials*	*Turbines*	*Boilers*	*Best recent speed*
Bretagne	Brest	La Seyne	July '12	Sept. '15		Parsons	Niclausse	
Lorraine	S.Nazaire (Pen.)	S.Nazaire (Pen.)	Nov, '12	1916		Parsons	Belleville	
Provence	Lorient	La Seyne	June '12	June '15		Parsons	D.T.Guyot	

General Notes.—*B.*, *L.* and *P.* belong to the 1912 programme, one of them being a replace ship for the *Liberté*, blown up September, 1911. Estimated cost, £2,908,000 per ship = £126 per ton. Bilge keels: 213 × 2¾ feet. Bulkheads are longitudinal and transverse; latter solid amidships.

*Unofficial.

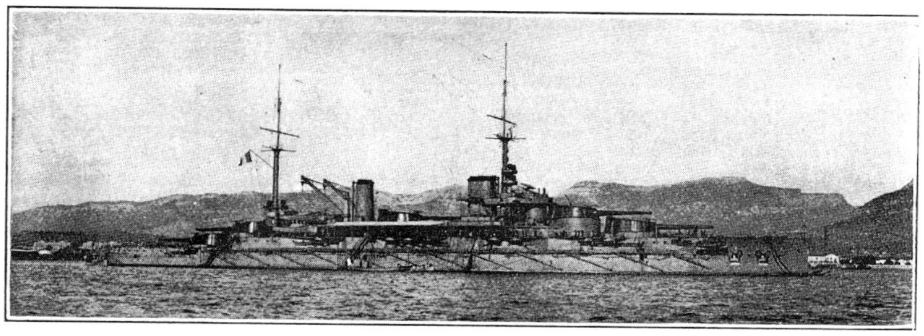

PROVENCE (1). *Copyright Photo, M. Bar, Toulon.*

Note.

Bretagne reported re-built 1918-1919 with fore tripod mast (with big fire control top), raised fore funnel and mainmast, cut down to stump. No photo available but approximate change in appearance shown by Silhouette.

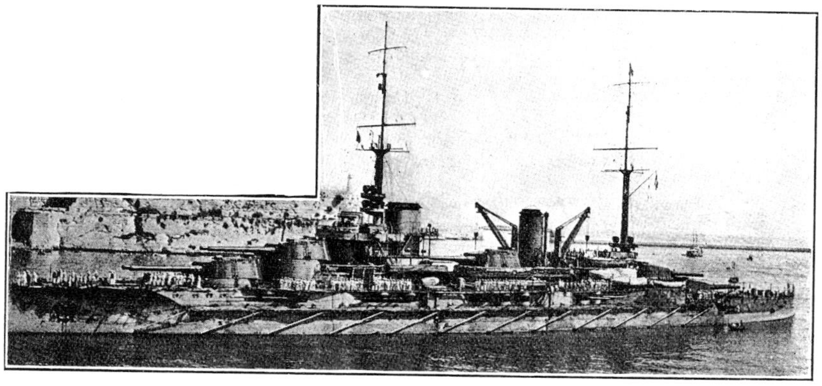

PROVENCE (2).

Addenda Notes.—According to the 1917 Edition of "Flottes de Combat," the barbette shields are not of uniform design. Those for the end barbettes are 13·4" thick, for the super-firing barbettes 9¾" thick and for the central barbette 15¾" thick.

1910 FRENCH DREADNOUGHTS. Nos. 4—1 (*Cuirassés de 1er rang*) (20 knots).

COURBET (Sept., 1911), **JEAN BART** (Sept., 1911), **PARIS** (Sept., 1912) & **FRANCE** (Nov., 1912).
Normal displacement, 23,120 tons. *Full load*, 25,850 tons. Complement, 1108.
Length (*p.p.*), 541⅓ feet. Beam, 88½ feet. *Maximum* draught, 29 feet. Length *over all*, 544½ feet.

Guns (M. '06) :
12—12 inch, 50 cal. (A^6).
22—5·5 inch, 55 cal. (M. '10).
4—3 pdr.
2—1 pdr.
2—landing.
Torpedo tubes (18 inch) :
4 *submerged*.

Armour :
11¾" Belt (amidships)......
7" Belt (bow) (N.C.) ...
7" Belt (aft) (N.C.) ......
2¾" Deck ....
10"—6" Lower deck side
12½" Turrets (N.C.) ......
11" Turret bases (N.C.) ..
7" Secondary battery ...
11¾" Conning tower (N.C.)

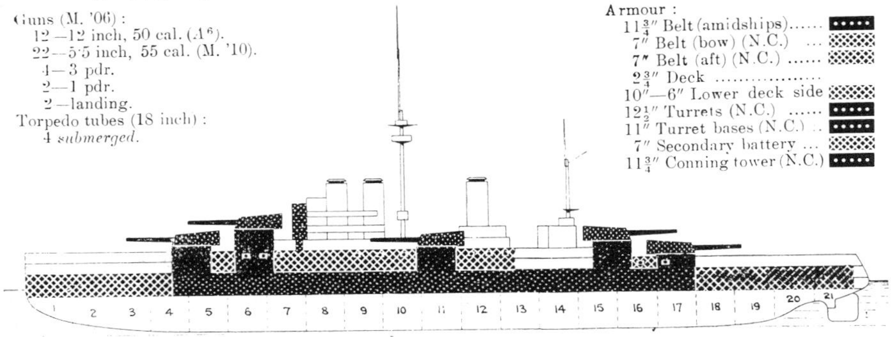

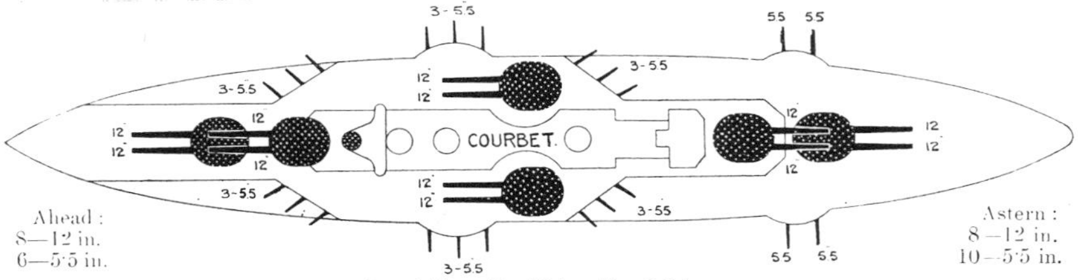

Ahead :
8—12 in.
6—5·5 in.

Astern :
8—12 in.
10—5·5 in.

Broadside : 10—12 in., 11—5·5 in.

Machinery: Parsons turbine. 4 screws. Boilers: 24 Belleville or Niclausse. Designed H.P. 28,000=20 kts. Coal: *normal* 906 tons; *maximum* 2452 tons.; also 250 tons oil. Endurance at 10 kts., 2700 at 18¾ kts.

**Armour Notes*—Belt, 13¼ feet wide; 7¾ feet of it above water, 5½ feet of it below. For about 325 feet it is 10¾". Upper belt 7" thick forms redoubt for secondary battery. The 4—5·5 inch aft. are in casemates. Prot. decks: 2¾" curved from lower edge of belt to l.w.l. level. Above that a flat 1¾" deck from end to end on top of main belt. Above again is a 1⅕" splinter deck against aerial attack. Conning tower is in three stories. 10¾" communication tube. Two armoured fire control stations on top.

**Gunnery Notes.*—Amidship 12 inch 180°, the centre line turrets 270° each. The 5·5 inch 120°. Height of guns above water: Turrets (1) 30½ feet, (2) 37¾ (amidships) 25 feet, (5) 28½ feet, (6) 21⅓ feet; upper deck battery, 5·5 inch, 21⅓ feet; main deck, 5·5 inch aft, 11⅔ feet. Ammunition carried: 100 for each 12 in., 275 for each 5·5 inch, 300 for each 3 pdr. Westinghouse refrigerators in magazines. 77°F.

**Torpedo Notes.*—8 searchlights (36 inch), also 2—30 inch. Carries 12 torpedoes and 30 blockade mines.

**Engineering Notes.*—Pressure: 256 lbs. outer shafts: H.P. turbines; inner, L.P. Condensers (2): 32,076 sq. feet cooling surface. Turbines: 300 r.p.m. Belleville oil fuel system.

Name	*Builder*	*Machinery*	*Laid down*	*Completed*	*Trials Full power*	*Boilers*	*Best recent speed*
J. Bart	Brest		Nov., '10	June '13	=22·01	Belleville	22·6
Courbet	Lorient		Sept., '10	Sept. '13	=20·74	Niclausse	
Paris	La Seyne		Nov., '11	Aug. '14	35,610=21·6	Belleville	
France	St. Nazaire		Nov., '11	July '14	...	Belleville	

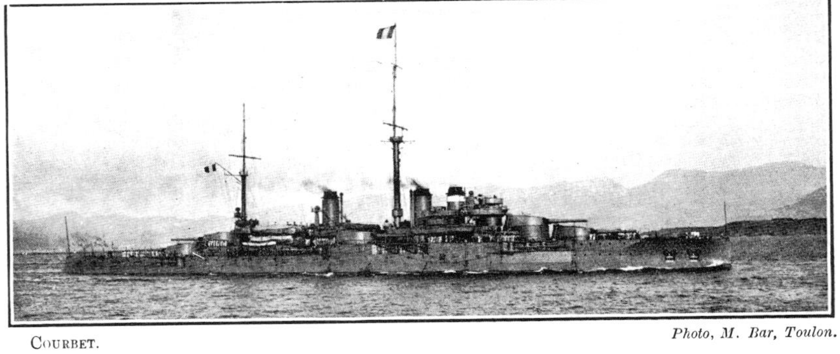

Courbet. *Photo, M. Bar, Toulon.*

Note:—Rig reported altered 1918-1919 as shown by Silhouettes, viz: *J. Bart* and *Courbet*, topgallant masts added to mainmast; mainmast of *Paris* and *France* cut down to stump.

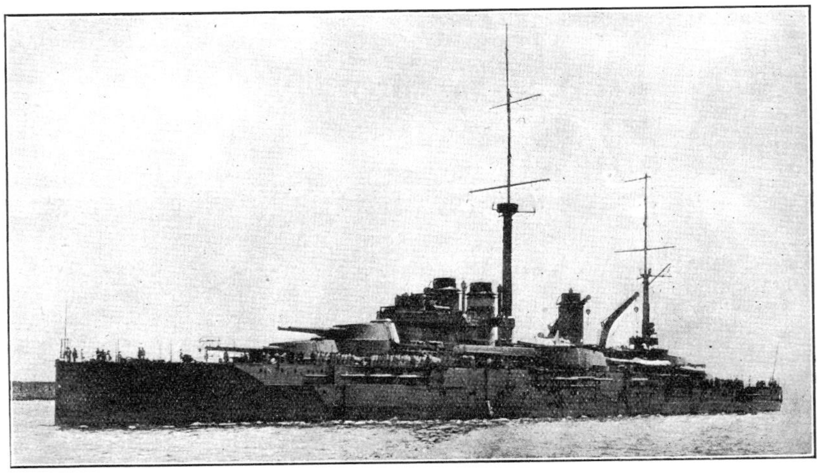

Jean Bart. This ship only has "goose-neck" cranes in place of derricks. *Photo, Geiser, Algiers.*

General Notes—Designed by M. Lyasse. Construction very fine and highly finished in details. Average cost about £2,175,000. The heavy weight of deep 7" belt at ends makes them pitch in a head sea. On the other hand, *J. Bart* was twice torpedoed in the bows by an Austrian submarine and her heavy bow belt contributed largely to her survival.

* Unofficial.

1907 FRENCH BATTLESHIPS ("SEMI-DREADNOUGHTS") (*Cuirassés d'Escadre*) (19 knot).

(Danton Class—6 Ships).

DANTON, MIRABEAU, DIDEROT, CONDORCET, VERGNIAUD & VOLTAIRE (Jan., 1909).
Normal displacement, 18,400 tons. Complement, 681 (as flagship 753).
Length (*waterline*), 475¾ feet. Beam, 84¾ feet. *Maximum* draught, 27½ feet. Length *over all*, 480 feet.

Guns (M '06)
4—12 inch, 50 cal. (*AAAAAA*).
12—9·4 inch, 50 cal. (*AAA*).
16—12 pdr., S.A.
10—3 pdr., S.A.
Torpedo tubes (M '04, 18 inch).
2 *submerged*.

Armour:
10" Belt (amidships)...........*aaa*
6" Belt (ends) ....*b*
3" Deck (flat on upper belt) ...
3" Deck (below belt) ....
Protection to vitals ......=*aaaa*
9"—6" Lower deck side......*aa-b*
2½" Upper belt (bow) ....*ϵ*
12½" Turrets (big guns) (N.C) *aaa*
11" Turret bases (N.C) ....*aa*
8¾" Secondary turrets (6) (N.C) *aa*
12" Conning tower (N.C) ...*aaa*
Total weight about 4800 tons.

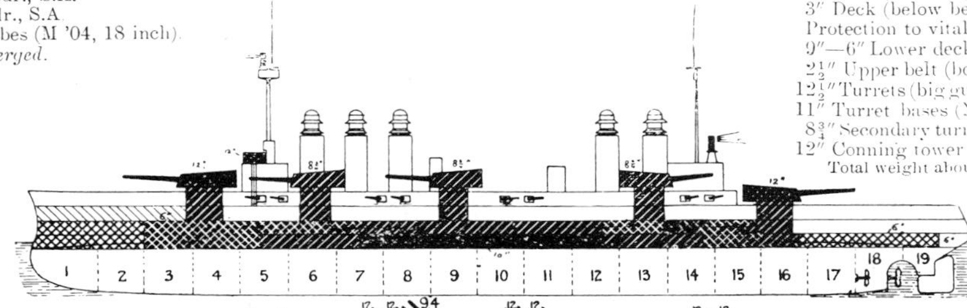

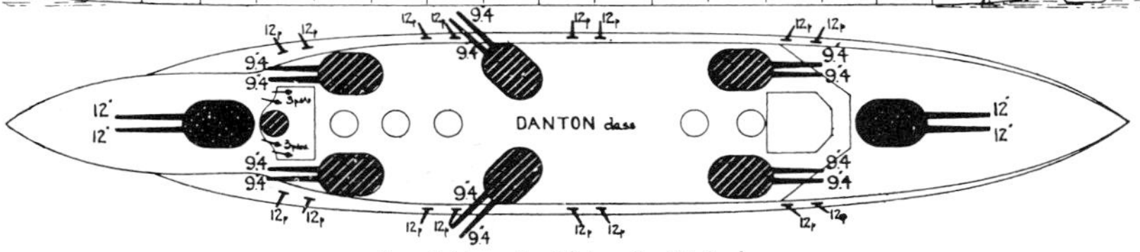

Ahead:
2—12 in.
4—9·4 in.

Astern:
2—12 in.
4—9·4 in.

Broadside: 4—12 in., 6—9·4 inch.

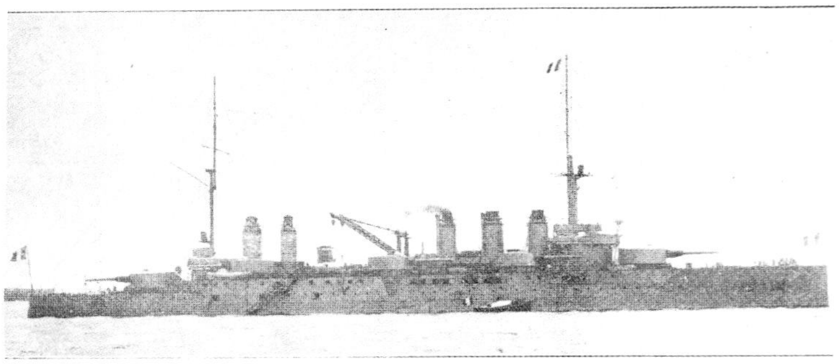

Danton.

Machinery: Parsons turbine. 4 screws. Boilers: Belleville and Niclausse. Designed H.P. 22,500=19·4 kts. Coal: *normal* 925 tons: *maximum* 2100 tons. *Nominal radius* 13,800 at 10 kts., 2000 at full power.

Armour Notes.—Main belt is about 6½ feet wide, about 2½ feet of it below waterline. Lower edge is 3" thick. There is a deck on top of the main belt as well as below it, also lateral armoured bulkheads extend from the lower armoured deck to the bilge keels.

Gunnery Notes.—Arcs of fire: Big guns, 260°. Secondary guns about 140° or more. Rounds carried: 12 in., 74 per gun; 9·4 in., 100 per gun; 12 pdrs., 500 per gun.

Engineering Notes.—Bellevilles of these ships have 332 elements and 8852 tubes. Niclausse 339 elements and 8814 tubes.

General Notes.—These ships belong to the 1906-7 programme. Designer, M. L'Homme.

Name.	*Builder*	*Machinery.*	*Laid down*	*Completed.*	*Trials. 24 hrs.*	*10 hrs.*	*3 hrs.*	*Boilers*	*Best recent speed.*
Danton	Brest Yard	F. & Ch., Medit.	Feb., '08	Mar., '11	=18·16	=19·44	=20·18	Belleville	20·66
Mirabeau	Lorient Yard	St. Nazaire	May, '08	July '11	=18·27	=19·73	=20·18	Belleville	
Diderot	St. Nazaire	St. Nazaire	1907	June '11	=18·4	=19·48	=19·9	Niclausse	
Condorcet	St. Nazaire	St. Nazaire	1907	June '11	=18·02	=19·31	=19·7	Niclausse	
Vergniaud	Bordeaux	F. & Ch., Medit.	July, '08	Sept., '11	=17·74	=19·20	=19·63	Niclausse	19·25
Voltaire	La Seyne	F. & Ch., Medit.	June, '07	June '11	=18·60	=19·78	=20·66	Belleville	

Average cost, £2,190,000 each.

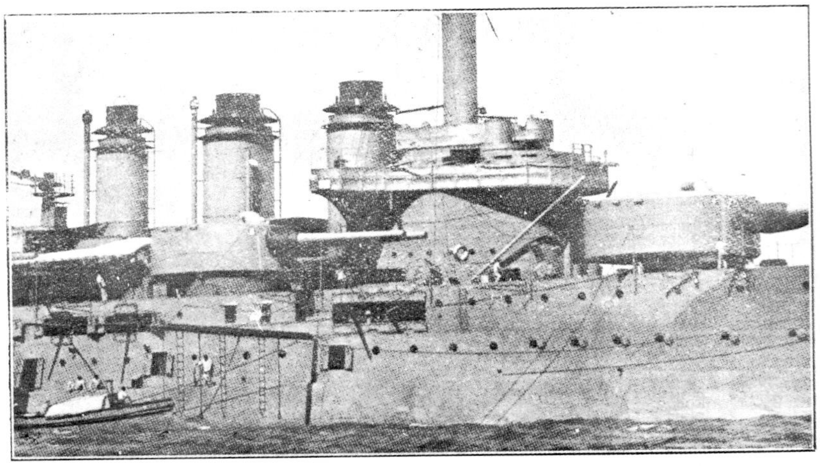

1907 FRENCH BATTLESHIPS ("SEMI-DREADNOUGHTS") (*Cuirassés de 1er rang*)

(Danton Class—4 Ships).

DIDEROT (April, 1909), **CONDORCET** (April, 1909), **VERGNIAUD** (April, 1910), and **VOLTAIRE** (Jan., 1909).

Normal displacement, 18,890 tons. Complement, 923.

Length (*waterline*), 475¾ feet. Beam, 84⅔ feet. { *Mean* draught, 27 feet. / *Max.* ,, 28⅔ ,, } Length *over all*, 481 feet.

Guns (M '02-'06):
4—12 inch, 45 cal. (A^5).
12—9·4 inch, 50 cal. (A^3).
16 or 14—3 in. (14 pdr.), 65 cal.
(2 —3 pdr., S.A.)
4—3 pdr. (AA.)
2—3 pdr. (landing).
2—1 pdr.

Torpedo tubes (M'04, 18 inch):
2 *submerged* (broadside).

Armour:
10½" Belt (amidships) ......
6" Belt (ends) ....
3" Deck (flat on upper belt)
3" Deck (below belt) ...
9"-6" Lower deck side
2½" Upper belt (bow) ......
12½" Turrets (big guns) (N.C)
11" Turret bases (N.C)......
8¾" Secondary turrets (6) (N.C.) ....
12" Conning tower (N.C.)...
Total weight about 4800 tons.

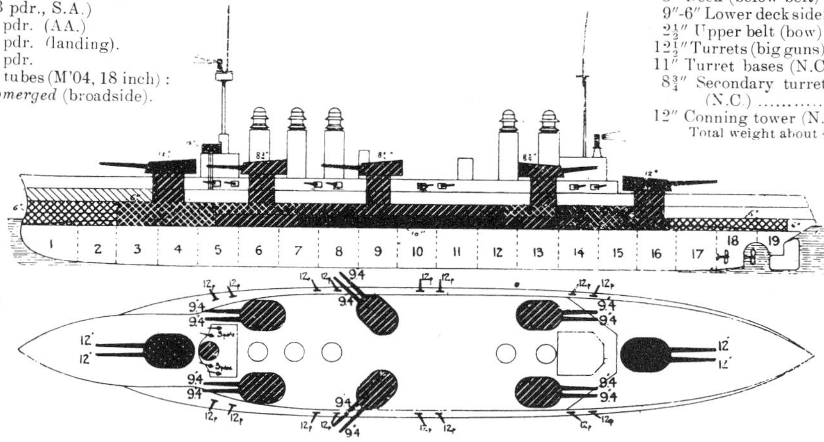

Ahead:
2—12 in.
4—9·4 in.

Astern:
2—12 in.
4—9·4 in.

Broadside: 4—12 in., 6—9·4 in.

Machinery: Parsons turbine. 4 screws. Boilers: 26 Belleville or Niclausse. Designed H.P. 22,500 = 19·25 kts. Coal: *normal* 965 tons: *maximum* 2100 tons. Endurance: 3750 miles at 10 kts., 2300 at 18½ kts.

Armour Notes.—Main belt is about 6½ feet wide, about 2½ feet of it below waterline. Lower edge is 3" thick. There is a deck on top of the main belt as well as below it. Fore bulkhead 7", aft ditto, 8"–7".

Gunnery Notes (unofficial).—Arcs of fire: Big guns, 260°. Secondary guns about 140° or more. Rounds carried: 12 in., 74 per gun; 9·4 in., 100 per gun; 12 pdrs., 500 per gun. The 14 pdr. guns are a Schneider Canet model. Some 14 pdr. and 3 pdr. removed during the War; may not be remounted. 14 pdr. positions on plans not correct.

Engineering Notes.—Bellevilles of these ships have 332 elements and 8852 tubes. Niclausse 339 elements and 8814 tubes. Both types equipped for burning oil fuel.

Name.	*Builder*	*Machinery.*	*Laid down*	*Completed.*	*Trials.* 24 hrs.	10 hrs.	3 hrs	*Boilers*	*Best recent speed*
Diderot	St. Nazaire	St. Nazaire	Oct. '07	Sept.,'11	=18·4	=19·48	=19·9	Niclausse	
Condorcet	St. Nazaire	St. Nazaire	Aug. '07	June '11	=18·02	=19·31	=19·7	Niclausse	
Vergniaud	Bordeaux	F. & Ch., Medit.	Nov. '07	Dec. '11	=17·74	=19·20	=19·63	Niclausse	
Voltaire	La Seyne	F. & Ch., Medit	July, '07	Aug. '11	=18·60	=19·78	=20·66	Belleville	19·25

General Notes.—Average cost, £2,190,000 each. They are not very successful ships, and consume quantities of coal at cruising speed. Some of these have lateral anti-torpedo "caissons" along hull below waterline; others have not. *Danton* of this class lost during War. *Voltaire* twice torpedoed by U-boat 1918 and repaired.

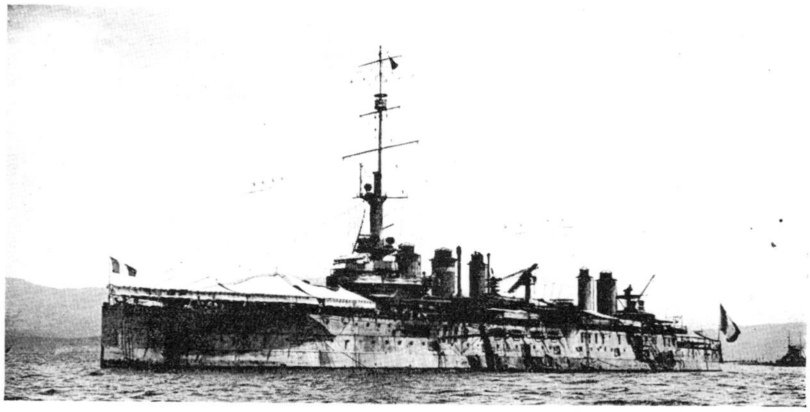

Condorcet.

Danton torpedoed by U-boat off Sardinia 19 March 1917.

Vergniaud has had her mainmast cut down to height of funnels; no photo available of this ship.

Mirabeau of this class stranded on Crimean Coast, Feb., 1919. Salved April, 1919, after removal of forward 12 inch barbette and side armour. Will be used as a Target Ship.

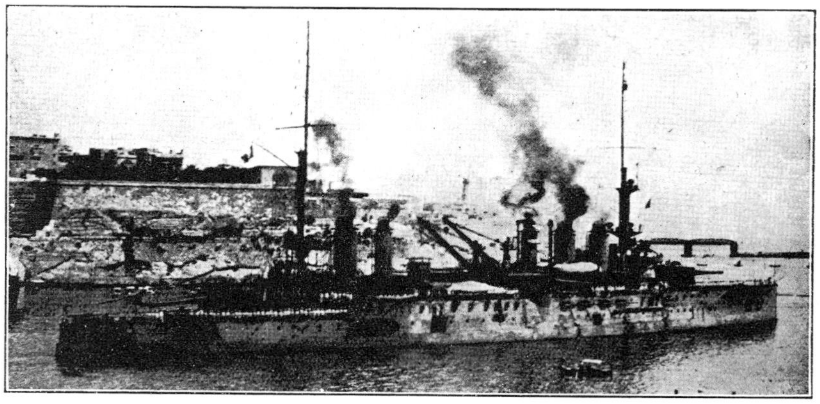

Diderot (and Voltaire).

1903-1 FRENCH BATTLESHIPS (*Cuirassés de 2e rang*) (18 knot).

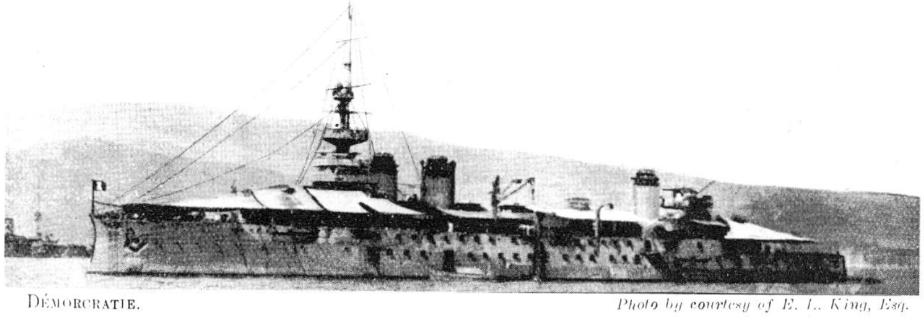

Démocratie. *Photo by courtesy of E. L. King, Esq.*

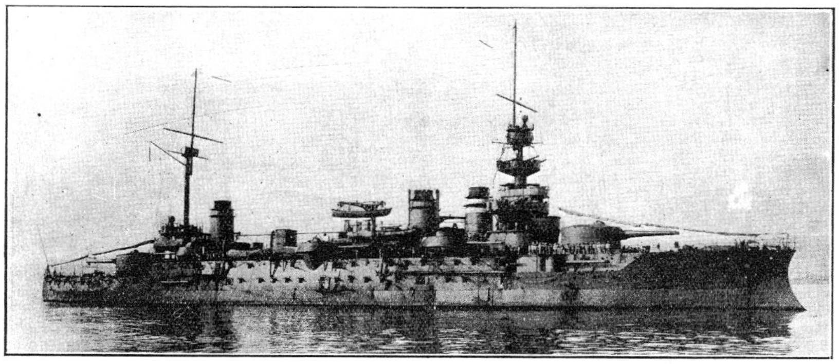

Justice (Verité stump topmast to mainmast). *Photo, Geiser, Algiers.*

DÉMOCRATIE (April, 1904), **JUSTICE** (September, 1904), **VERITÉ** (May, 1907). *Normal* displacement, 14,868 tons. Complement, 762. Length (*waterline*), 439 feet. Beam, 79½ feet. *Maximum* draught 28 feet. Length *over all*, 443¾ feet. **Guns**: 4—12 inch, 45 cal. (A^5), 10—7·6 inch, 50 cal. (*A*)., 12 or 13—9 pdr., 4—3 pdr., 4—3 pdr (AA.), 2—3 pdr. (landing), 2—1 pdr. Torpedo tubes (1904 pattern): 2 *submerged*. Armour: 11¾" Belt (amidships), 9" Belt (forward), 7" Belt (aft), 2¾" Deck, 10" Upper belt (amidships), 5½" Upper belt (ends), 3" Top of belt (forward) (N.C.), 12½" Main turrets (N.C.), 11" Turret bases (N.C.), 5½" Casemates (4) (N.C.), 5½" Secondary turrets (6) (N.C.), 11" Conning tower (N.C.) Machinery: 3 sets vertical inverted triple expansion, 4-cylinder. 3 screws. Boilers: 22 Belleville or 24 Niclausse. Designed H.P. 18,000 = 18 kts. Coal: *normal* 900 tons; *maximum* 1285 tons. *Nominal* radius: 6000 at 10 kts.

Notes.—*Justice* built at La Seyne 1903-7, *Democratie* at Brest, 1903-7, both engined by F. & C. de La Med. *Verité* built at Bordeaux, 1903-8, and engined by Indret. Made 19¼–19½ kts. on trials and all still steam well.

Notes (unofficial).

All ships listed on this page will probably be relegated to reserve or used as Training Ships. *Verité* and *Republique* will probably become Gunnery Training Ships; their after 12 inch turrets may be removed and replaced by smaller guns for instructional purposes. *Patrie* may be modified for service as a Torpedo Training Ship.

During the war, some of the lighter guns in *Démocratie*, *Justice*, and *Verité* were removed and may not be remounted.

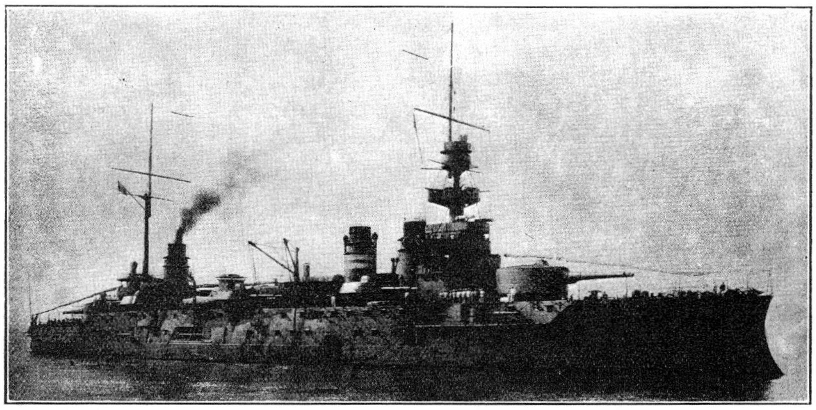

Republique. *Photo, Geiser, Algiers.*

REPUBLIQUE (Sept., 1902) & **PATRIE** (Dec., 1903). Displacement: 14,865 tons. Complement: 789. Length (*waterline*), 439 feet. Beam, 79½ feet. *Maximum* draught, 27½ feet. Length *over all*, 443¾ feet. Guns—(M '93-'96): 4—12 inch, 45 cal. (A^4), 18—6·4 inch, 50 cal., 25—3 pdr., 2—1 pdr. Torpedo tubes (18 in.): 2 *submerged*. Armour: 11¾" Belt (amidships), 7" Belt (ends), 3" Deck (flat below belt), 10"–5" Upper belt, 3" Upper Belt (forward), 12½" Turrets, 11" Turret (bases), 5½" Casemates, 5½" Small turrets, 4" Bases to these, 13" Conning tower. Machinery: 3 sets vertical inverted triple expansion. 3 screws. Boilers: 24 Niclausse. Designed H.P. 18,000 = 18 kts. Coal: *normal* 905 tons; *maximum* 1825 tons. *Nominal* radius 6,000 at 10 kts.

Notes.—*Republique* built at Brest, 1901-6, machinery by Indret; *Patrie* built at La Seyne, 1902-6, machinery by F. & C. de la Med. Both made 19 kts. on trials

1899 FRENCH BATTLESHIP (18 knot).

SUFFREN (July, 1899).

Displacement, 12,750 tons. Complement, 730.

Length (*waterline*), 410 feet. Beam, 70 feet. *Maximum* draught, $28\frac{1}{4}$ feet. Length *over all*, $422\frac{1}{2}$ feet.

Guns—(M. '96):
4—12 inch, 45 cal. (*AAAA*).
10—6·4 inch, 45 cal.
8—4 inch
22—3 pdr.
Torpedo tubes (18 inch)
2 *submerged.*
2 *above water* (section 4).

Armour:
12″ Belt (amidships) .... *aaa*
9″ Belt (ends) .... *aa*
3″ Deck (flat below belt) ...
$1\frac{2}{3}$″ Deck on top of main belt
Protection to vitals...... = *aaaaa*
13″ Turrets (N.C.) nearly... *aaaa*
10″ Turret bases .... *aa*
8″ Turret hoists .... *a*
$5\frac{1}{4}$″—$3\frac{1}{2}$″ Lower deck (side) *b-e*
$5\frac{1}{4}$″ Battery (redoubt, N.C.) *c*
$5\frac{1}{4}$″ Small turrets (N.C.) ... *c*
12″—10″ Conning tower ... *aaa*
6″ Tube to it................ *b*
(Total weight *about* 4100 tons)

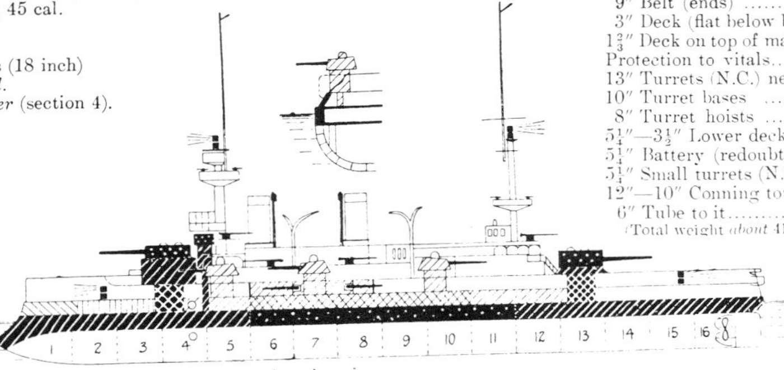

Ahead:
2—12 in.
6—6·4 in.
4—4 in.

Astern:
2—12 in.
6—6·4 in
4—4 in.

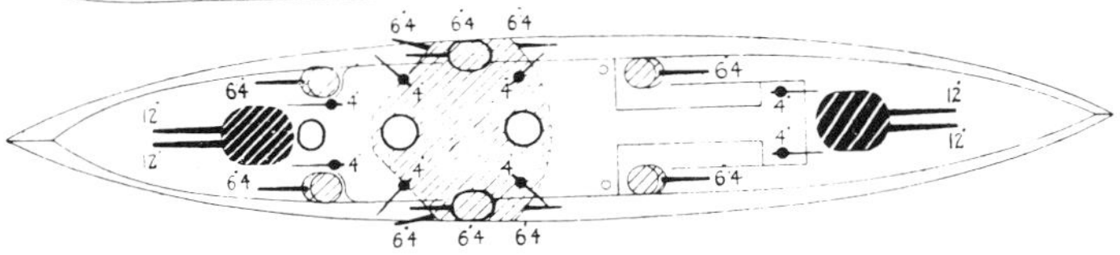

Broadside 4—12 in., 5—6·4 in., 4—4 in.

Machinery: 3 sets vertical triple expansion. 3 screws. Boilers: Niclausse. Designed H.P. 16,200 = 18 kts.
Coal: *normal* 820 tons; *Maximum* 1150 tons; also 60 tons of oil.
Armour Notes.—Belt is $8\frac{1}{4}$ feet wide, 5 feet of it below waterline; lower edge averages 6″ thick.
Gunnery Notes.—Loading positions, big guns: all round. Balanced turrets. Hoists, electric for all guns. Big guns manœuvred electrically and hydraulic. Secondary turrets, electrically.
Arcs of fire: big guns 260°; midship secondary turrets 180°; other 6·4 in. guns 135° from axial line.
Ammunition carried: 12 in., 90 rounds per gun; 6·4 in., 150 rounds per gun.
Height of guns above water: bow turret 30 feet.
Engineering Notes.—Coal consumption about $10\frac{1}{2}$ tons an hour at 12,000 H.P., and about $14\frac{1}{2}$ tons at 16,000 H.P.—18 kts.
General Notes.—Cost, *complete*, £1,200,000. Conning tower in two compartments.

Torpedoed by U-boat off Lisbon 26 November 1916.

Name	*Builder*	*Machinery*	*Laid down*	*Completed*	*Refit*	*Trials*	*Boilers*	*Best recent speed*
Suffren	Brest Yard	Indret	Jan.'99	1903	1908	16,715 = 18	Niclausse	16

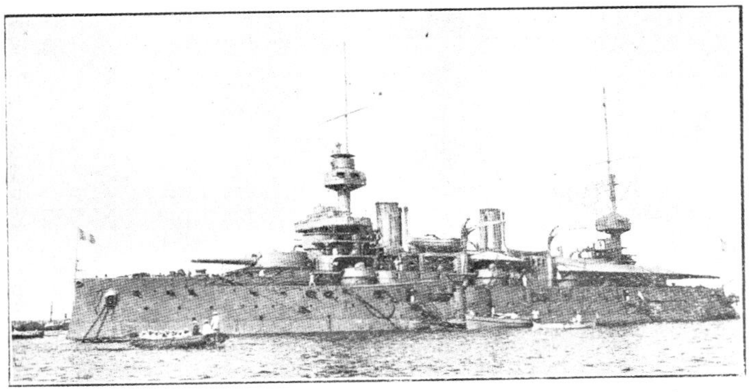

SUFFREN. *Photo by favour of M. Gautrieu.*

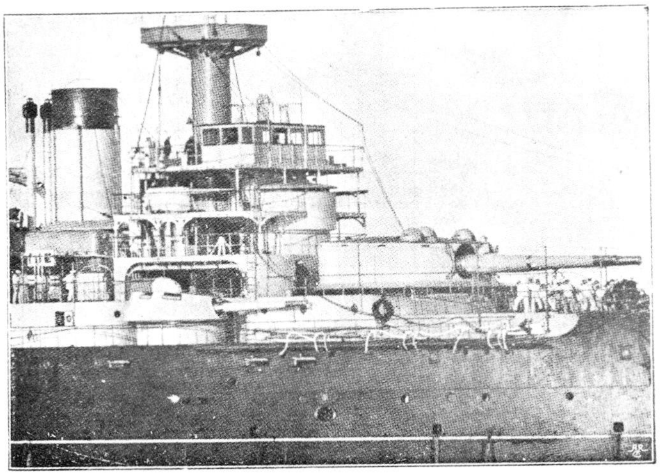

Details of conning tower, etc. Starboard side.

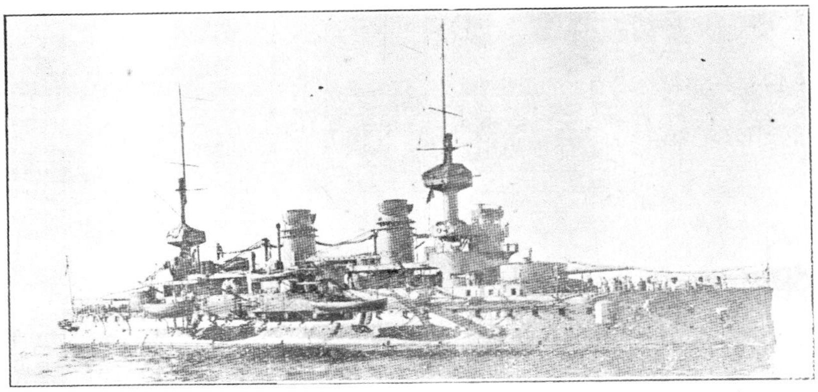

Photo, Geiser.

CHARLEMAGNE (October, 1895), ST. LOUIS (September, 1896), GAULOIS (October, 1896).

Displacement, 11,260 tons. Complement, 631.

Length (*waterline*), $380\frac{3}{4}$ feet. Beam, $67\frac{1}{2}$ feet. *Maximum* draught, 28 feet. Length *over all*, $387\frac{1}{2}$ feet.

Guns (M. '93):
4—12 inch (*AAA*).
10—5·5 inch
8—4 inch
20—3 pdr.
Torpedo tubes (18 inch):
4 *submerged.*

Armour (Harvey):
16″ Belt (amidships) ...*aaaa*
10″ Belt (ends) (chrome) ...*a*
$2\frac{3}{4}$″ Armour deck (flat on belt).
$1\frac{1}{2}$″ Deck (flat below belt). ...
Protection to vitals... = *aaaaa*
9″ Fore turret ....*a*
11″ After turret ....*aa*
8″ Turret hoists ....*b*
3″ Battery ....*e*
5″ Battery bulkheads ......*d*
12″ Conning tower.........*aaa*
(Total weight, *about* 4,000 tons.)

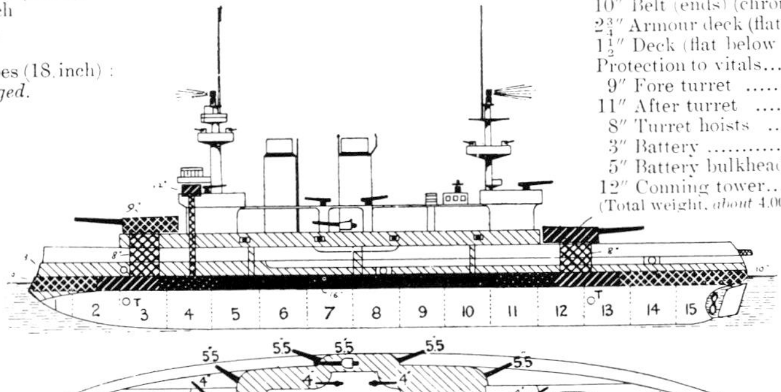

Ahead:
2—12 in.
6—5·5

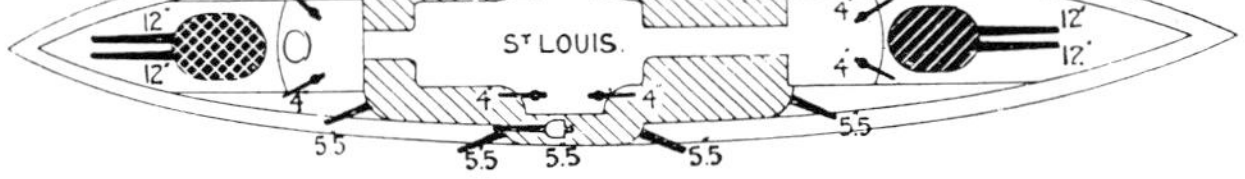

Astern:
2—12 in.
6—5·5

Broadside: 4—12 in., 5—5·5 in.

Machinery: 3 sets 4 cylinder triple expansion. 2 screws. Boilers: 20 Belleville. Designed H.P. 14,500 = 18 kts. Coal: *normal* 680 tons; *maximum* 1100 tons, also 200 tons oil.

Name	*Builder*	*Machinery*	*Laid down*	*Completed*	*Refit*	*Trials: 24 hrs. at 4 hrs. full power*	*Boilers*	*Present best speed*
Charlemagne	Brest		July,'94	1899	1908	9123 = 16·15 15,294 = 18·1	Belleville	...
St. Louis	Lorient		Mar.,'95	1900	1908	= 16·2 = 18·3,	Belleville	...
Gaulois	Brest	Ch. de la Loire	Jan.,'96	1899	1907	13,400 = 17·7 14,963 = 18·2	Belleville	...

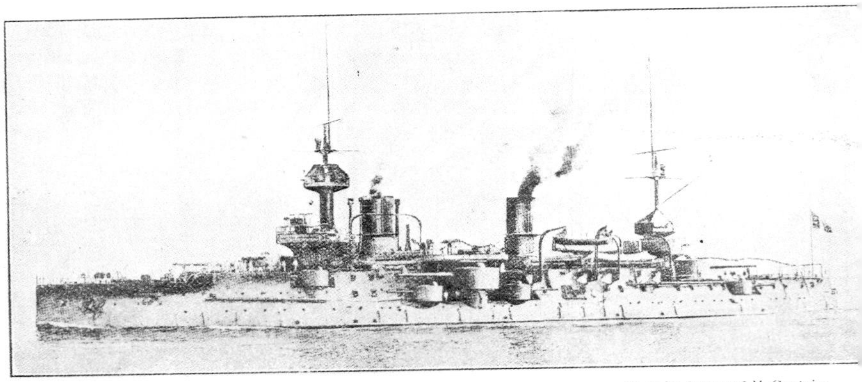

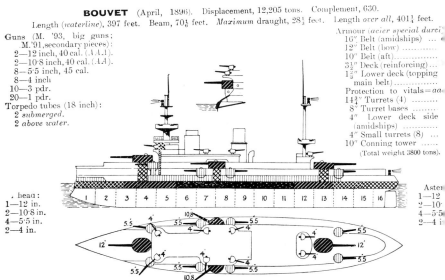

Photo by favour of M. Gautrieu.

BOUVET (April, 1896). Displacement, 12,205 tons. Complement, 630.

Length (*waterline*), 397 feet. Beam, $70\frac{1}{6}$ feet. *Maximum* draught, $28\frac{1}{3}$ feet. Length *over all*, $401\frac{1}{4}$ feet.

Guns (M. '93, big guns; M.'91, secondary pieces):
2—12 inch, 40 cal. (*AAA*).
2—10·8 inch, 40 cal. (*AA*).
8—5·5 inch, 45 cal.
8—4 inch
10—3 pdr.
20—1 pdr.
Torpedo tubes (18 inch):
2 *submerged.*
2 *above water.*

Armour (*acier special durci*)
16″ Belt (amidships) ...
12″ Belt (bow) ....
10″ Belt (aft)...............
$3\frac{1}{2}$″ Deck (reinforcing)...
$1\frac{2}{3}$″ Lower deck (topping main belt)...............
Protection to vitals = *aa*
$14\frac{3}{4}$″ Turrets (4) ....
8″ Turret bases ....
4″ Lower deck side (amidships) ....
4″ Small turrets (8) ...
10″ Conning tower ......
(Total weight 3800 tons).

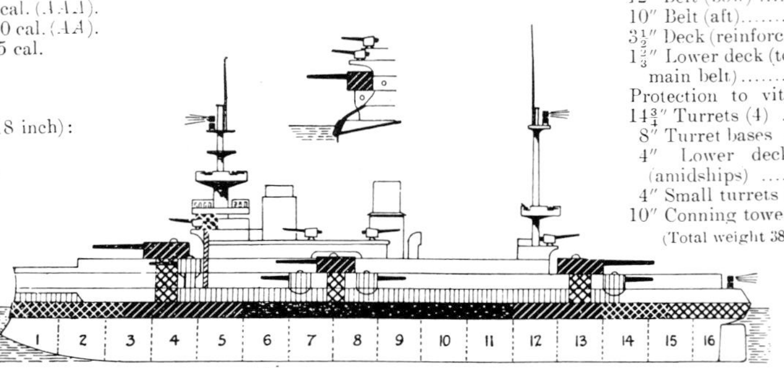

Ahead:
1—12 in.
2—10·8 in.
4—5·5 in.
2—4 in.

Astern:
1—12
2—10·
4—5·5
2—4 i

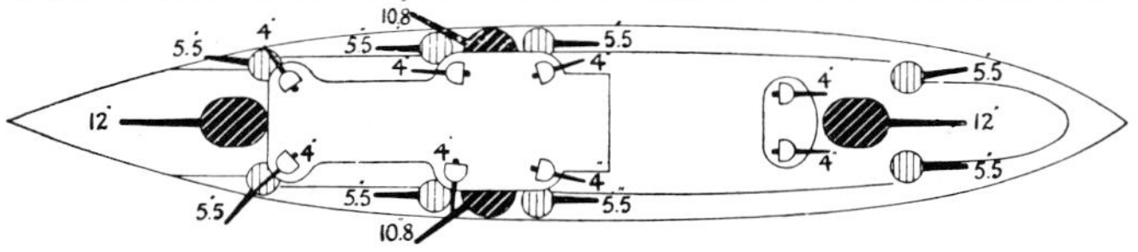

Broadside: 2—12 in., 1—10·8 in., 4—5·5 in., 4—4 in.

Machinery: 3 sets vertical triple expansion 3 cylinder. 3 screws. Boilers: 24 Belleville (1894 m in 3 groups. Designed H.P. 14,000 = 17 kts. Coal: *normal* 620 tons; *maximum* 800 tons.
Armour Notes.—Belt is about $7\frac{1}{4}$ feet wide; 4 feet of it below waterline; lower edge is 8″ and 5″ aft.
Height of guns above water: Bow turret, about 28 feet; other big turrets about 21 feet.
General Notes.—Laid down at Lorient, January, 1893. Completed 1898. Cost about £1,200,000.
Sunk in Darduelles 18 March 1915.

Charlemagne paid off 1918. *Gaulois* sunk by U-boat in Agean 27 December 1916.

Coast Defence Ships

Photo, Geiser.

HENRI QUATRE (Aug., 1899). Displacement, 8807 tons. Complement, 457. Length (*waterline*), 354½ feet. Beam, 72¾ feet. *Maximum* draught, 23 feet. Guns—(M. '93–'96): 2—10·8 inch, 40 cal. (A³), 7—5·5 inch, 45 cal., 12—3 pdr., 2—1 pdr. Torpedo tubes (18 inch): 2 *submerged* (20° before beam). Armour (Harvey-nickel): 11¾″ Belt (amidships), 8″ Belt (ends), 5″–3″ Armour deck, flat, 10″ Turrets, 11½″ Turret bases, 4½″ Lower deck side, 4½″ Battery (redoubt), 4½″ Small turret (aft), 8″ Conning tower. Machinery: 3 sets vertical triple expansion. 3 screws. Boilers: 12 Niclausse. Designed H.P. 11,500 = 17·2 knots. Coal: *normal* 735 tons; *maximum* 1100 tons. Built at Cherbourg D.Y. 1897-1902.

REQUIN (1885, re-constructed 1901-3). 7214 tons. Complement, 332. Length, (*w.l.*) 324·4 feet. Beam, 73 feet. *Mean* draught, 23 feet. Guns: 2—10·8 inch (40 cal.), 8—3·9 inch, 12 smaller Armour (compound): 19½″ belt (amidships), 12½″ belt (ends), 3—4″ deck, flat on belt, turrets (Harvey Nickel) 9½″ with 8½″ bases, 11¾″ conning tower. Machinery: 2 sets compound. Niclausse boilers. Designed H.P. 11,200 = 15·5 kts. Coal: *normal* 400 tons, *maximum* 800 tons.

1891 OLD FRENCH BATTLESHIPS. (*Cuirassés d'escadre.*)

Photo by favour of M. Gautrieu.

CARNOT (1894). 12,150 tons. Complement 621. Dimensions: 380½ (*w.l.*) × 70½ × 28 (*max.*) feet. Guns: 2—12 inch, 45 cal. (M. '91), 2—10·8, 45 cal. (M. '91), 8—5·5, 4—9 pdr., 18—3 pdr. Tubes (18 inch): 2 sub. Armour (steel): 17¾″—10″ belt, 13¾″ big guns, 4″ secondary, 6″ C.T. Designed H.P. 15,000 = 18 kts. Coal: *max.* 700 tons. D'Allest boilers.

JAURÉGUIBERRY (1893). 11,900 tons. Comp. 607. Dimensions: 364 (*w.l.*) × 72½ × 29 (*max.*) feet. Guns: 2—12 inch (M. '91), 2—10·8 (M. '87), 8—5·5, 16—3 pdr. Tubes: 2—18 inch (sub.) Armour (steel): 17¾″—9¾″ belt; 14½″ turrets, 4″ small guns, 9″ C.T. Designed H.P. 14,300 = 17·8 kts. Coal: *max.* 1,100 tons, including oil. D'Allest boilers.

CHARLES MARTEL (1893). 11,882 tons. Dimensions: 390 (*w.l.*) × 70½ × 27¾ feet (*max.*). Guns: 2—12 inch (M. '87), 2—10·8 (M. '87), 8—5·5, 4—9 pdr., 20—3 pdr. Tubes (18 inch): 2 sub. Armour (steel): 17¾″—11″ belt, 14¾″ big guns, 4″ secondary guns. Designed H.P. 14,500 = 18 kts. Coal: *max.* 1000 tons (including oil). D'Allest boilers.

1905 FRENCH ARMOURED CRUISERS (*Croiseurs Cuirassés*) (23 knots).

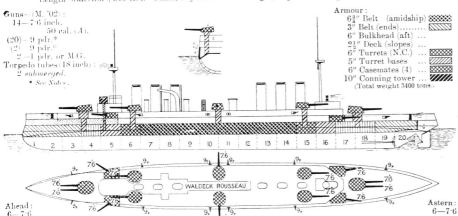

WALDECK-ROUSSEAU. (WALDECK ROUSSEAU CLASS—2 SHIPS). *Photo, Geiser, Algiers.*

EDGAR QUINET (Sept., 1907), **WALDECK ROUSSEAU** (March, 1908).

Normal displacement, 14,100 tons. Complement, 892.

Length (*waterline*), 515 feet. Beam, 70⅔ feet. *Max.* draught, 27½ feet. Length *over all*, 521⅓ feet.

Guns—(M. '02):
14—7·6 inch, 50 cal. (*A*).
(20)—9 pdr.*
(2) 9 pdr.*
2—1 pdr. or M.G.
Torpedo tubes (18 inch):
2 *submerged.*
* *See Notes.*

Armour:
6¾" Belt (amidship)
3" Belt (ends).........
6" Bulkhead (aft) ...
2½" Deck (slopes) ...
6" Turrets (N.C.) ...
5" Turret bases ...
6" Casemates (4) ...
10" Conning tower ...
(Total weight 3400 tons).

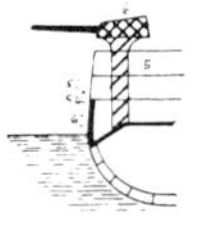

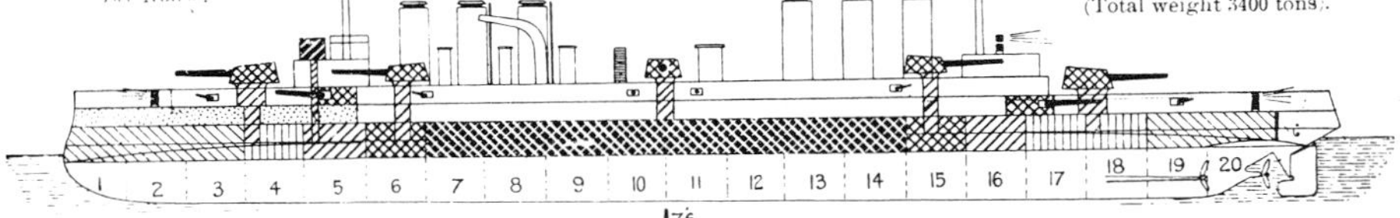

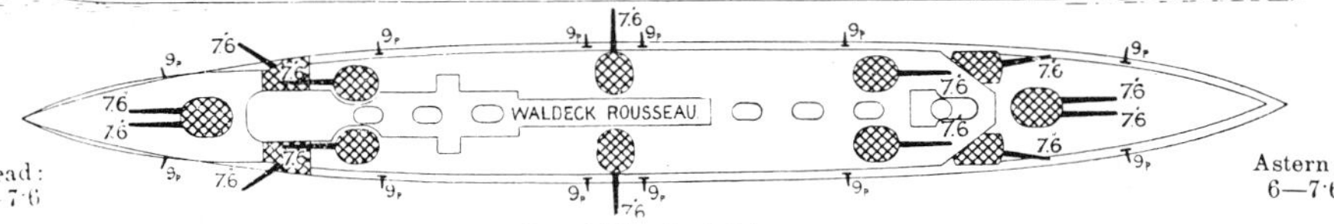

Ahead: 6—7·6

Astern: 6—7·6

Broadside: 9—7·6 in.

Machinery: 3 sets vertical triple expansion. 3 screws. Boilers: *See Notes.* Designed H.P. 36,000 = 23 kts. Coal: *normal* 1,242 tons; *maximum* 2,300 tons. *Nominal endurance:* 6560 miles at 10 kts.

Gunnery Notes.—9 pdr. positions on plans not correct. Reported in 1919 that *W. Rousseau* had only 12—9 pdr., 2—9 pdr. AA., and perhaps, 4—3 pdr. AA.

Name	*Builder*	*Machinery*	*Laid down*	*Com-pleted*	*Trials:* 30 boilers 10 hours	*Trials:* Full power 3 hours	*Boilers*	*Best recent speed*
E. Quinet	Brest Yard		Nov., '05	1911	36,828 = 23·8	40,294 = 23·9	40 Belleville	
W. Rousseau	Lorient Yard		June, '06	1911		35,286 = 23·1	42 Niclausse	

ERNEST RENAN (March, 1906),

Normal displacement 13,640 tons. Complement 824.

Length (*waterline*), 515 feet (*o.a.* 521⅔ feet). Beam, 70 feet. *Max.* draught, 27½ feet.

Guns:
4—7·6 inch, 50 cal. (*A*)
12—6·5 inch, 45 cal.
16—9 pdr.
2—9 pdr.
8—3 pdr.
2—1 pdr.
Torpedo tubes (18 inch):
2 *submerged.*
(1904 Model torpedoes)

Armour:
6¾" Belt (amidships)
3½" Belt (ends) ......
6" Bulkhead (aft) ...
2½" Deck (slopes) ...
6" Main turrets (N.C.)
4"--5" Turret bases
4" Casemates (4)(N.C)
4" Secondary turrets (8)
5" Bases to these ...
8" Conningtower (N.C)
(Total weight about 3400 ton

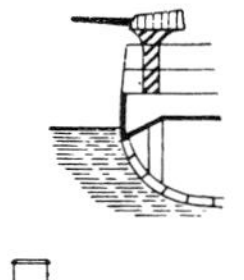

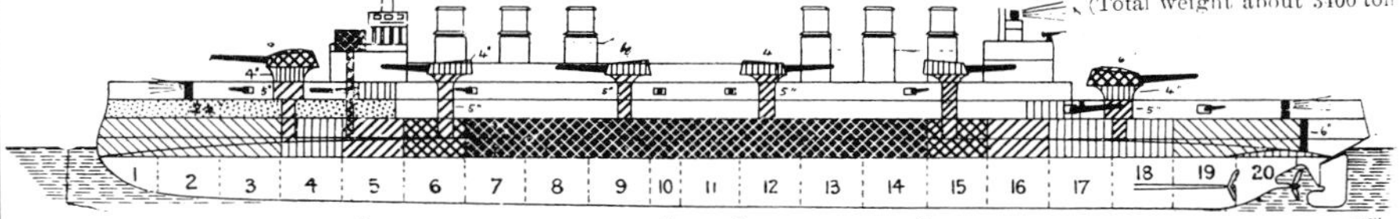

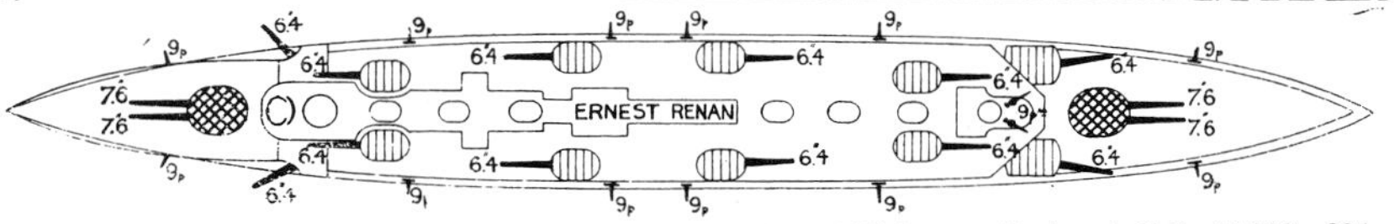

Machinery: 3 sets vertical triple expansion. 3 screws. Boilers: 42 Niclausse. Designed H.P. 36,000 = 23 kts. Coal: *normal* 1354 tons; *maximum* 2300 tons, *Nominal endurance*: 6700 miles at 10 kts.

Armour Notes.—Belt is 12¼ feet wide, 4¾ feet of it below waterline. Upper edge 5" thick; bottom 3½".

**Gunnery Notes.*—Loading positions, big guns: all round. Hoists: electric to all guns. All guns manœuvre electrically and hand. Arcs of fire: Big turrets 240°; secondary turrets 150°; casemates, 110°. Height of guns above water: Bow and secondary turrets, 29½ feet; after turret, 22 feet. Forward casemates 20 feet; after casemates, 12 feet.

General Notes.—Laid down at St. Nazaire, Aug., 1904; completed, 1909. Made 24·24 kts. on first trial with 37,685 H.P. Mainmast removed 1918.

* Gunnery Notes unofficial.

1904-1 FRENCH ARMOURED CRUISERS (22-21 knot). 1899-97.

Photo, Geiser.

JULES MICHELET (Aug., 1905). Displacement 13,370 tons. Complement 770. Length (*waterline*), 489 feet. Beam, 70¼ feet. *Max.* draught, 27⅔ feet. Guns: 4—7·6 inch, 50 cal. (*A*), 12—6·5 inch, 45 cal., 2—9 pdr., 24—3 pdr., 2 M.G. Torpedo tubes (18 inch): 2 *submerged.* Armour: 6¾" Belt (amidship), 3" Belt (ends), 6" Bulkhead (aft), 2½" Deck (slopes), 6" Turrets, 5" Turret bases, 4" Casemates (4), 4" Small turrets (8), 5" Bases to these, 8" Conning tower. Machinery: 3 sets vertical triple expansion. 3 screws. Boilers: 28 Du Temple-Guyot. Designed H.P. 29,000 = 22 kts. (Trials, 30,438 = 22·9.) Coal: *normal* 1330 tons; *maximum* 2100 tons. Begun at Lorient D.Y. 1904, completed 1908.

JULES FERRY. *Photo, Geiser, Algiers.*

JULES FERRY (August, 1903), & **VICTOR HUGO** (March, 1904). *Average* displacement 12,518 tons. Complements, 737—731. Length (*o.a.*), *J.F.* 486⅔ feet., *V. H.* 489 feet. Beam, 70¼ feet. *Mean* draught, 26½ feet. Guns (M. '96): 4—7·6 inch, 45 cal., 16—6·5 inch, 45 cal., 24—3 pdr., 2—9 pdr., 2 M.G. Torpedo tubes (18 in.): 2 *submerged.* Armour: 6¾" Belt (amidships), 3" Belt (ends), 5" Bulkhead (aft), 2¼" Deck (slopes), 8" Turrets, 8" Turret bases, 5½" Casemates (4), 5½" Small turrets, 8" Conning tower. Machinery: 3 sets vertical 4 cylinder triple expansion. 3 screws. Boilers: 28 Guyot in *J. Ferry*; 28 Belleville in *V. Hugo.* Designed H.P. 27,500 = 22 kts. Coal: *normal* 1330 tons; *maximum* 2100 tons. Endurance at 10 kts., 6630; at 20 kts., 2600 miles.

Notes.—*J. Ferry* built at Cherbourg, 1901-5; *V. Hugo* at Lorient, 1903-7. Both engined by Indret, and made about 23 kts. on trials. *Leon Gambetta* of this class lost during the war.

GLOIRE. *Photo, Geiser, Algiers.*

GLOIRE (June, 1900), **MARSEILLAISE** (July, 1900), **CONDE** (March, 1902), and **AMIRAL AUBE** (May, 1902). *Average* displacement 10,376 tons. Complement, 630. Length (*waterline*), 452¾ feet. Beam, 66¼ feet. *Maximum* draught, 25½ feet. Length *over all*, 458⅔ feet. Guns (M.'96): 2—7·6 inch, 45 cal. (*A*), 8—6·5 inch, 45 cal., 6—3·9 inch, 2—9 pdr., 18—3 pdr. Torpedo tubes (18 in.) 2 *submerged*). Armour: 6¾"—4" Belt, 2½" Deck (slopes), 8" Turrets (N.C.), 4" Hoists, 5" Lower deck side, 2¼" Bow, 4¾" Casemates (4), 4¾" Small turrets (4), 3¾" Bases to these, 8" Conning tower. Machinery: 3 sets vertical triple expansion. 3 screws. Boilers: 28 Belleville or Niclausse. Designed H.P. 20,500 = 21 knots. Coal: *normal* 970 tons; *maximum* 1700 tons.

Notes.—*Gloire* and *Condé* built at Lorient, 1899-1904; *Marseillaise* at Brest, 1900-03; *A. Aube* at St. Nazaire, 1900-04. Made 21·5, 21·3, 21·6, and 22·8 kts. on trials respectively.

DUPLEIX (April, 1900), & **DESAIX** (March, 1901). Displacement 7552 tons. Complement 520. Length (*waterline*), 433 feet. Beam, 58½ feet. *Mean* draught, 24¼ feet. Guns—(M. '96): 8—6·4 inch, 45 cal., 4—3·9 inch, 2—9 pdr., 10—3 pdr., 4 M.G. Torpedo tubes (18 in.): 2 *submerged.* Armour: 4" Belt (amidships), 3¼" Belt (bow), 2¾" Armour deck, 4" Turrets, 4" Turret bases, 6" Conning tower. Machinery: 3 sets 3 cylinder vertical triple expansion. 3 screws. Boilers: 24 Belleville. Designed H.P. 17,100 = 21 kts. Coal: *normal* 880 tons; *maximum* 1200 tons. Begun at Rochefort and St. Nazaire, 1897-8, and completed 1903-4. *Kleber* of this class lost during the war.

1898-6 FRENCH ARMOURED CRUISERS. 1893-'90

GUEYDON (September, 1899), **MONTCALM** (March, 1900). Displacement 9102 tons. Complement 600. Length (*waterline*), 452¾ feet. Beam, 63⅔ feet. *Max.* draught, 25 feet. Length *over all*, 459 feet. Guns (M. '93 & '96): 2—7·6 inch, M. '93, 8—6·5 inch, M. '93-'96, 2—9 pdr., 20—3 pdr. Torpedo tubes (18 inch): 2 *submerged*. Armour (Harvey Nickel): 6¾″ Belt (amidships), 4″ Belt (ends), 3″ Forecastle, 2″ Deck (on slopes), 3″-2¼″ Lower deck side, 8″ Turrets, 5″ Turret bases, 4″ Casemates (8), 6″ Conning tower. Machinery: 3 sets vertical triple expansion. 3 screws. Boilers: 20 Niclausse or Normand. Designed H.P. 19,600 = 21 kts. Coal: *normal* 1030 tons; *maximum* 1,650 tons. Begun at Lorient and La Seyne, 1898: completed, 1902.

Dupetit Thouars sunk by U-boat 7 August 1918.

BRUIX. (L. TREVILLE same, but no topmast to mainmast.)

BRUIX (Rochefort, 1894). 4810 tons. Complement, 375. Guns (M '87): 2—7·6 inch (45 cal.), 6—5·5 inch, 4—9 pdr., 1—3 pdr. 4—18 inch tubes *above water* (*probably removed*). Armour: 3⅝″ Belt and 4″ Turrets (steel). Designed H.P. 8700 (*f.d.*) = 18·5 kts. Boilers: 16 Belleville. Coal: 540 tons.

War loss: *Amiral Charner* (1893) Torpedoed by U-boat off Syria 8 February 1916.

LATOUCHE-TREVILLE (Havre, 1892). 4760 tons. Complement 368. Designed H.P. 8000 (*f.d.*). Coal: 530 tons. Appearance and other details as *Bruix* above. Both these old cruisers have rendered excellent service during the war, *Latouche-Treville* specially distinguishing herself on numerous occasions.

(*Cadets' Training Ship.*)

JEANNE D'ARC (June, 1899). Displacement 11,300 tons. Complement 657. Length (*waterline*), 475⅔ feet. Beam, 63⅔ feet. *Maximum* draught, 26½ feet. Guns—(M. '93): 2—7·6 inch, 40 cal. (*B*), 14—5·5 inch, 45 cal., 16—3 pdr., 8—1 pdr. Torpedo tubes (18 inch): 2 *submerged*. Armour (Harvey): 6″ Belt (amidships), 4″ Belt (bow), 3″ Belt (aft), 2¼″ Deck (on slopes), 7¾″ Turrets, 4″ Turret bases, 3″ Lower deck, 5″ Casemates (8), 6″ Conning tower. Machinery: 3 sets vertical inverted triple expansion. 3 screws. Boilers: 48 Du Temple (small tube). Designed H.P. 33,000 = 23 kts. (Best actual: 29,690 I.H.P. = 21·7). Coal: *normal* 1400 tons; *maximum* 1900 tons. Laid down at Toulon, October, 1896. Completed 1902.

Mainmast reported removed. (*Gunnery School Ship.*) *Photo, Geiser.*

POTHUAU (1895). Displacement 5,460 tons. Complement 424. Length (*waterline*), 371 feet. Beam, 50½ feet. *Maximum* draught, 22½ feet. Guns—(M '93): 2—7·6 inch, 40 cal., 10—5·5 inch, 45 cal., 12—3 pdr., 8 M.G. Torpedo tubes: 4 *above water*. Armour: 3⅓″ Belt (amidships), 1¼″ Belt (ends), 3⅜″ Deck (reinforcing belt), 7″ Turrets, 3″ Hoists to these, 2″ Casemates, 2″ Hoists to these, 9½″ Conning tower. Machinery: 2 sets horizontal triple expansion. 2 screws. Boilers: 18 Belleville. H.P. 10,400 = 19 kts. Coal: *normal* 538 tons; *maximum* 790 tons.

Copyright photo, M. Bar, Toulon.

JURIEN DE LA GRAVIÈRE (July, 1899). Displacement, 5690 tons (sheathed and coppered). Complement 469. Length (*waterline*). 449½ feet. Beam, 49¼ feet. *Mean* draught, 23 feet. Guns: 8—6·5 inch, 2—9 pdr., 45 cal., 10—3 pdr., 6 M.G. Torpedo tubes (18 inch): 2 *submerged*. Armour (Harvey Nickel): 3″ Deck (cellulose belt), 6½″ Conning tower, 2″ Chrome shields, 1¾″ Casemates. Machinery: 2 sets vertical triple expansion. 3 screws. Boilers: 24 Guyot. H.P. *full power*, 18,400 = 22·9 kts. Present speed is poor. Coal: *normal* 560 tons; *maximum* 1100 tons. Laid down at Lorient, Nov. 1897. Completed 1903.

Copyright photo, M. Bar, Toulon.

D'ESTRÉES (Rochefort, Oct., 1899). Displacement 2460 tons (sheathed and coppered). Complement 250. Length (*waterline*), 311⅔ feet. Beam, 39⅓ feet. *Mean* draught, 17½ feet. Guns—(M'93 & '91): 2—5·5 in., 45 cal., 5—3·9 in., 45 cal., 1—9 pdr., 8—3 pdr. Torpedo tubes: (*removed*). Armour (hard steel): 1½″ Deck (cellulose belt). Machinery: 2 sets triple expansion. 2 screws. Boilers: 8 Normand. Designed H.P. 8500 = 20 to 21 kts. Coal: *normal* 350 tons; *maximum* 550 tons. Begun, 1897; completed 1899.

GUICHEN (May, 1897). Displacement, 8,280 tons (sheathed). Complement, 560. Length (*waterline*), 436⅓ feet. Beam, 54¾ feet. *Maximum* draught, 24½ feet. Guns—(M. '91): 2—6·5 inch, 45 cal., 6—5·5 inch, 45 cal., 12—3 pdr., 5—1 pdr. Torpedo tubes: (*removed*). Armour (Harveyed): 2½″ Deck (cellulose belt), 1½″ Casemates, 2″ Gun shields, 6¼″ Conning tower (fore). Machinery: 3 sets 4 cylinder triple expansion. 3 screws. Boilers: 28 Lagrafel d'Allest. Designed H.P. 24,000 (*f.d.*) = 23 kts. Coal: *normal* 1,460 tons; *maximum* 2,030 tons. Laid down at St. Nazaire, 1895; completed, 1899.

D'ENTRECASTEAUX (June, 1896). Displacement, 8,123 tons (sheathed and coppered). Complement 521. Length (*waterline*), 393½ feet. Beam, 58½ feet. *Maximum* draught, 26 feet. Guns—(M. '93): 2—9·4 inch, 40 cal. (*may have been removed*), 12—5·5 inch, 45 cal., 12—3 pdr., 4 Maxims. Torpedo tubes (18 inch): 2 *submerged*. Armour (Harvey): 3¼″ Armour deck, 9″ Turrets, 4″ Turret bases, 2⅔″ Casemates (8, all chrome steel), 10″ Conning tower. Machinery: 2 sets triple expansion. 2 screws. Boilers: Cylindrical (5 double-ended). Designed H.P. 14,500 = 19·5 kts. (*never made*); present speed 18 kts. or *less*. Coal: *normal*, 650 tons; *maximum*, 950 tons. Laid down at La Seyne, 1894, completed 1899.

1895-1886 OLD FRENCH PROTECTED CRUISERS.

This Old Cruiser is rated as an "Aviso" or Sloop.

Now has short mainmast.

LAVOISIER (1897). 2,320 tons. Complement 248. Armament (M. '91): 4—5·5 inch, 45 cal., 2—3·9 inch, 10—3 pdr. 2—18 inch tubes *above water*. Armour: 1½″ Deck, 2″ Main deck sponsons. H.P. *about* 7,000=21·5 kts. Coal: *maximum* 380 tons. Boilers: 16 Belleville.

DESCARTES (1894). Displacement, *about* 4030 tons. Complement, 378. Guns: 4—6·5 inch, 45 cal., 10—3·9 inch, 8—3 pdr., 4—1 pdr. Torpedo tubes: 2—18 inch, *above water*. Armour: 2″ Deck, 2″ Casemates to 6·5 guns on main deck. Designed H.P. 8500=19 kts. Coal: *maximum* 680 tons. Boilers: 16 Bellevilles (*without* economisers).

CASSARD (1896), **DU CHAYLA** (1895). Old Cruisers of about 3,950 tons. Complement, 374. Length (*waterline*), 324¾ feet. Beam, 45 feet. *Maximum* draught, 22 feet. Guns—(M. '87): 6—6·5 inch, 45 cal., 4—3·9 inch, 8—3 pdr., 2—14 inch tubes *above water*. Armour: 3″ Deck, 2″ Sponsons to the four main deck 6·4 inch guns. H.P. 10,000=19·8 kts. Coal: *maximum,* 624 tons. Boilers: Lagrafel d'Allest. *Friant* of this class now Repair Ship.

COSMAO.

SURCOUF.

COSMAO (1889), **SURCOUF** (1889). Old Cruisers of about 2000 tons. Armament: 4—old 5·5 inch, 7 or 5—3 pdr., 4 machine. Designed H.P. 6000=20 kts. Coal: 260 to 300 tons.

FRENCH "AVISOS"—SLOOPS OR DESPATCH VESSELS, CONVOY TYPE.

SCARPE. (*Suippe* same, but with straight stem.)

Note that the two 3·9 inch guns, fore and aft, are disguised as derrick booms, while the 9 pdr. guns amidships, on each beam, are hidden behind lowering bulwarks.

ANCRE.

AILETTE (Brest D.Y., 1918).   **SCARPE** (—— 1918).
ANCRE (Lorient D.Y., 1918).   **SUIPPE** (Lorient D.Y., 1918).
ESCAUT (Brest D.Y., 1918).

Despatch Vessels of 650 tons. Dimensions: 256 feet 2 inches × 26 feet 5 inches × 8 feet 10 inches. Guns: 4—3·9 inch, 2—9 pdr. A.A., one or two M.G. Designed H.P. 5000=21 kts. Machinery: reciprocating. Boilers: two (type unknown). 2 screws. Oil fuel: 135 tons =4000 miles at 10 kts. Complement, 65.

Note.—Modifications of *Aisne, Marne, Meuse,* &c., described on a later page. Externally they are disguised by varying appearances as mercantile vessels, like convoy sloop *Ville D'Ys* below. Built under 1917 War Programme.

(See Silhouette for appearance.)

VILLE D'YS (ex-*Andromède,* Swan Hunter, Wigham Richardson & Co., Wallsend-on-Tyne, June, 1917. Convoy sloop of 1490 tons. Dimensions: 255 feet 3 inches (*p.p.*) 276 feet (*o.a.*) × 35 feet × 12 feet 3 inches. Guns: 2—5·5 inch, 3—14 or 9 pdr. Designed I.H.P. 2500=17 kts. Machinery: 1 set 4-cyl. triple-exp. Boilers: 2-cyl. 1 Screw. Coal: 270 tons = 2400 miles at 12 kts. Complement, 108 (war, probably inclusive of "panic" parties), about 90 (peace).

Note.—Generally same build as British convoy sloops. Built under 1916 War Programme. Reported to have been begun for British Navy as *Andromeda* and turned over to French Navy.

FRENCH "AVISOS"—SLOOPS OR DESPATCH VESSELS

ALDEBARAN.

ALTAIR.

(Builders' Photo, by courtesy of Messrs. Wm. Hamilton & Co).

("ETOILE" or "STAR" Class—7 Ships.)

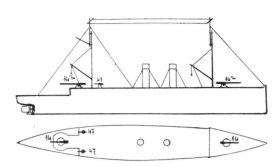

(Plans by courtesy of Ministry of Marine).

ALDEBARAN ⎫ (Barclay, Curle, Whiteinch,   **BELLATRIX** (Henderson, Glasgow, 1916).
ALGOL ⎬   N.B., 1916).   **CASSIOPÉE** ⎫ (Barclay, Curle, Whiteinch, N.B.,
ALTAIR ⎫ (Wm. Hamilton, Port   **REGULUS** ⎬   1917).
ANTARÈS ⎬   Glasgow, N.B., 1916).

Sloops, displacing 1250, 1420 and 1470 tons. Dimensions : $225\frac{1}{4} \times 33\frac{1}{2} \times 11$-$12\frac{1}{4}$ feet. Guns : 2—5.5 inch, 2—6 pdr. A.A. Are fitted as Fleet Sweeping Vessels. Designed I.H.P. 2500 = 17 kts. (All made 17.2-17.6 kts. on trials.) Machinery : 1 set. 4 cyl. triple expansion. Boilers : Not known. 1 screw. Coal : 260 tons = 2400 miles at 12 kts. Complement, 92.

Notes.—These sloops are practically replicas of the British "Flower Class" Sloops, being built in pairs by British shipyards. *Rigel*, the companion boat to *Bellatrix* by Messrs. Henderson, lost during the War. All built under 1916 War Programme.

FRENCH "AVISOS"—DESPATCH VESSELS OR SLOOPS.

OISE (& SOMME ?).

YSER (& MEUSE ?).

Note.

Though the design of these Despatch Vessels is uniform, the latitude allowed to the building yards has resulted in differing appearances. Classification by appearance has not been positively established, but it is believed that the vessels built by same yard have the same appearance.

AISNE (Lorient D.Y., 1916).   **SOMME** (Brest D.Y., 1917).
MARNE (Lorient D.Y., 1916).   **OISE** (Brest D.Y., 1917).
MEUSE (Rochefort D.Y. 1918).,   **YSER** (Rochefort D.Y., 1917).

MARNE (& AISNE ?).

Despatch Vessels displacing 650-680 tons. Dimensions : $256\frac{1}{6} \times 26\frac{5}{12} \times 8\frac{5}{8}$ feet. Armament : 4—3.9 inch, 3—9 pdr. A.A., 2—6 pdr. Designed I.H.P. 4000 = 20.5-21 kts. Machinery : Reciprocating. Boilers : 2 (types unknown). 2 screws. Oil fuel : 135-145 tons = 4000 miles at 10 kts. Complement, 97. All built under 1916 War Programme.

FRENCH GUNBOATS—*Continued.*

"Avisos"—Despatch Vessels or Sloops *(Continued)*

Gunboats

> Clipper bow, 1 funnel, 2 pole masts.

CHAMOIS (Port de Bouc, 1905). Despatch Vessel of 431 tons. Dimensions : $168\frac{2}{3} \times 25\frac{1}{3} \times 9\frac{1}{2}$ feet. Guns (*not known*). H.P. 600 = 12 kts. Boilers : du-T. Guyot. Coal : 70 tons. Was Training Ship for Navigation before the War.

CONQUERANTE.

VAILLANTE type :—2 Diesel-engined boats.

CONQUERANTE (1917), **VAILLANTE** (1917). Builders unknown. 457 tons. Dimensions : *about* 211 $\times$ 22$\frac{7}{12}$ $\times$ 8$\frac{1}{6}$ feet. Guns : 2—3·9 inch. Carry D.C. B.H.P. 1800 = 17 kts. Machinery : 2 sets of 900 B.H.P. Sulzer-Diesel engines. Oil fuel : 30 tons. Complement, 65.

Notes.—Are a modified *Friponne* design, for which see below. Both built under 1917 War Programme.

Despatch Vessel **FLAMANT**, built 1915-18, has been assigned to Fisheries Protection Duty, and is listed with Miscellaneous French Ships on a later page.

Sloop—Present existence doubtful.

KERSAINT (1897). 1296 tons (sheathed). Dimensions : $225\frac{1}{4} \times 34\frac{1}{2} \times 15$ feet. Guns : 1—5·5 inch, 5—3·9 inch, 7 small. No torpedoes. Designed H.P. 2400 = 15 kts. 1 screw. Coal : 200 tons = 2000 miles at 12 kts.

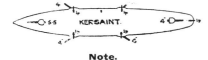

Note.

This Sloop reported to have been stranded on a coral reef near Tahiti (Pacific), during March, 1919, but her total loss has not yet been officially announced. Considering her age, it is not likely that salvage will be attempted.

IMPATIENTE.

FRIPONNE type :—7 Diesel-engined boats.

BOUFONNE (Lorient D.Y., 1916).
CHIFFONNE (———. 1917).
DILIGENTE (Brest D.Y., 1916).
FRIPONNE (Lorient D.Y., 1916).
IMPATIENTE (Brest D.Y., 1916).
MIGNONNE (Brest D.Y., 1917).
SURVEILLANTE (Brest D.Y., 1916).

Displacement : 355 tons. Dimensions : 199$\frac{2}{3}$ $\times$ 22$\frac{7}{12}$ $\times$ 8$\frac{1}{6}$ feet. Guns : 2—3.9 inch. Carry D.C. and may also be equipped as Mine Sweepers. B.H.P. 900 = 15 kts. Machinery : 2 sets 450 B.H.P. Sulzer-Diesel engines. Oil : 30 tons = 3000 miles at 10 kts., 1600 miles at 15 kts. Complement, 50.

Notes.—Generally the same design as the 27 *Ardent* type (steam-driven) Gunboats on next page, but above seven Gunboats have Diesel engines and no funnels. *Mignonne*, 1917 War Programme, others all 1916 War Programme.

(ARDENT type—27 Steam-engined boats.)

ARDENT.

DEDAIGNEUSE.   *Copyright Photo, M. Bar, Toulon.*

AGILE (Brest D.Y., 1916).	**ETOURDI** (Lorient D.Y., 1916).
ALERTE (Rochefort D.Y., 1916).	**EVEILLE** (La Seyne, 1917).
ARDENT (Brest D.Y., 1916).	**GRACIEUSE** (Lorient D.Y.. 1916).
AUDACIEUSE (Port de Bouc. 1917).	**IMPETUEUSE** (———, 1917).
BATAILLEUSE (Port de Bouc. 1917).	**INCONSTANT** (Brest D.Y., 1916).
BELLIQUEUSE (Bordeaux, 1917).	**LURONNE** (———, 1917).
BOUDEUSE (La Seyne, 1916).	**MALICIEUSE** (Chantiers de Provence, Port de Bouc, 1916).
CAPRICIEUSE (Nantes. 1916).	
COURAGEUSE (Rochefort D.Y., 1916).	**MOQUEUSE** (Lorient D.Y., 1916).
CURIEUSE (Lorient D.Y., 1916).	**RAILLEUSE** (Chantiers de Provence, Port de Bouc, 1917).
DEDAIGNEUSE (Bordeaux, 1916).	
EMPORTÉ (———, 1916).	**SANS SOUCI** (Lorient D.Y., 1916).
ENGAGEANTE (Brest D.Y., 1917).	**TAPAGEUSE** (Port de Bouc, 1916).
ESPIÈGLE (Rochefort D.Y., 1916).	

Displacement : 350 tons. Dimensions : 197$\frac{1}{3}$ $\times$ 22$\frac{7}{12}$ $\times$ 8$\frac{1}{6}$ feet. Guns : 2—3.9 inch. Carry D.C. Designed I.H.P. 1800-1200 = 17-15 kts. Machinery : Reciprocating. Boilers : Various water-tube types. Fuel : 85 tons coal = 3000 miles at 10 kts., 1600 miles at full speed. Complement, 55.

Notes.—Built as Anti-Submarine Gunboats or "Cannonieres Contre-Sousmarins." At the end of the War, many of these boats were reported to have been converted for Mine Sweeping Service. Some have been engined with machinery stripped from old Coastal Torpedo Boats ("Torpilleurs de Defence Mobile"). They vary a little in build, but the illustrations given are believed to be typical of these boats. Note that masts are stepped well to starboard of the centre-line. *Audacieuse, Batailleuse, Impetueuse* and *Luronne*, 1917 War Programme ; all others, 1916 War Programme.

BOUDEUSE.   *Copyright Photo, M. Bar, Toulon.*

FRENCH GUNBOATS (*Continued*).

Old Torpedo Gunboats (*Contre-Torpilleurs*).

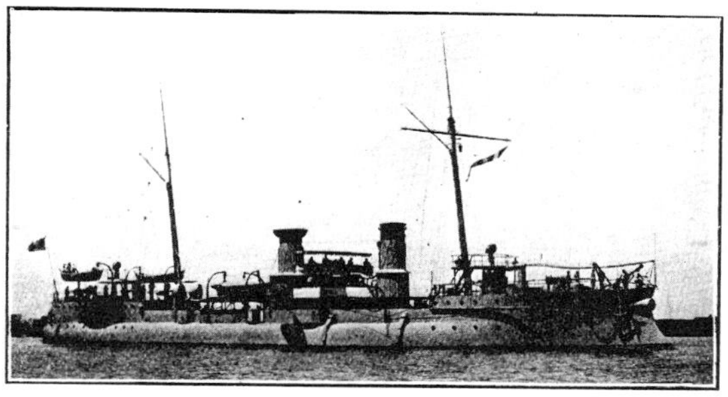

Now has small pole mainmast.

D'IBERVILLE (1893). Displacement, 967 tons. Complement, 140. Length, 262½ feet. Beam, 26⅝ feet. *Maximum* draught, 13 feet. Guns: 1—3·9 inch (bow), 3—9 pdr., 6—3 pdr. Designed H.P. 5000 = 21·5 kts. Coal: *maximum* 145 tons. Cylindrical boilers.

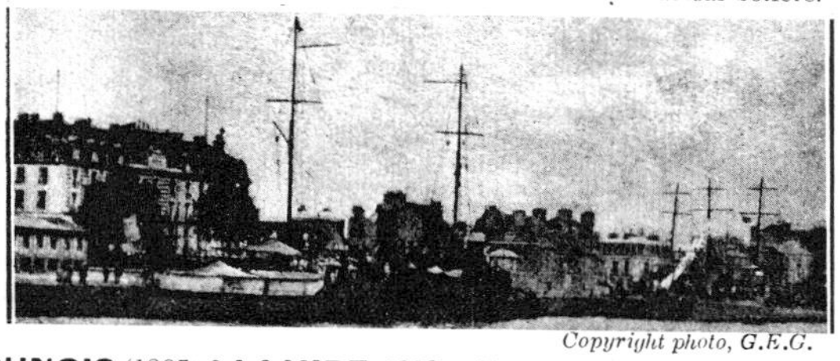

Copyright photo, G.E.G.

DUNOIS (1897) & **LA HIRE** (1898). Torpedo Gunboats. Displacement, 900 tons. Complement, 148. Length, 254½ feet. Beam, 27⅝ feet. *Maximum* draught, 12¾ feet. Guns: in *Dunois* 6—9 pdr., in *La Hire* 12—3 pdr. No tubes. Designed H.P. 6400 = 23 kts. (never made), now 19-20 kts. Coal: 160 tons. Boilers: Normand.

Gunboats.

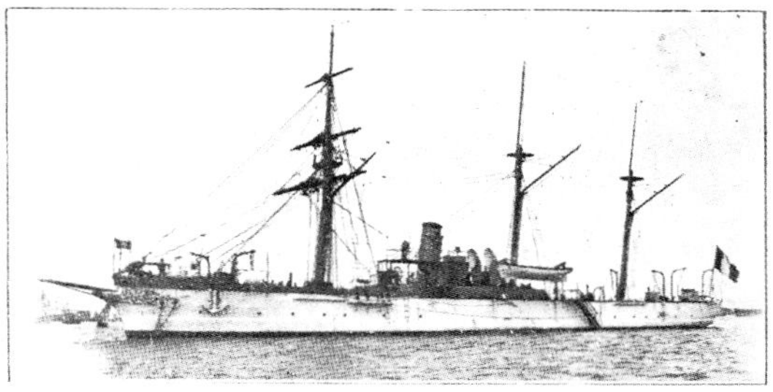

SURPRISE (1896), **DÉCIDEE** (1899), **ZÉLÉE** (1900). 680 tons. Armament: 2—4 inch, 4—9 pdr., 4—1 pdr. No torpedoes. Complement, 93. Designed H.P. 900 = 13·4 kts. 2 screws. Coal: 73 tons. *Décidée* and *Zélée* have Niclausse boilers.

Note:— All lost in war.

River Gunboats (*Cannonières Fluviales*).

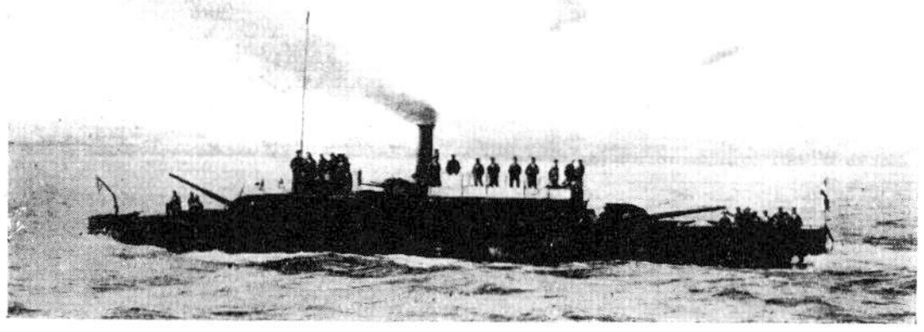

E and F.

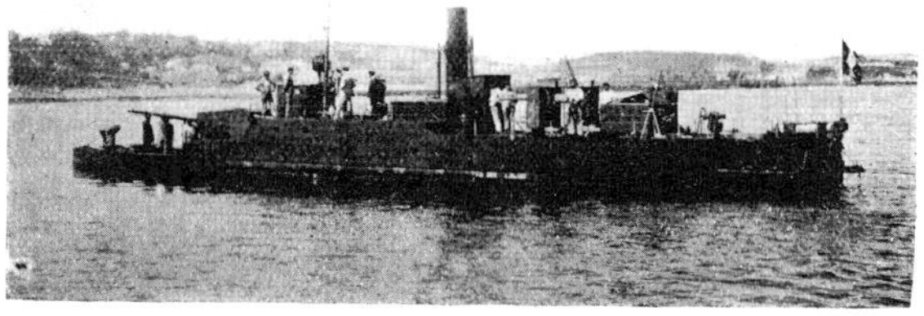

C and D.

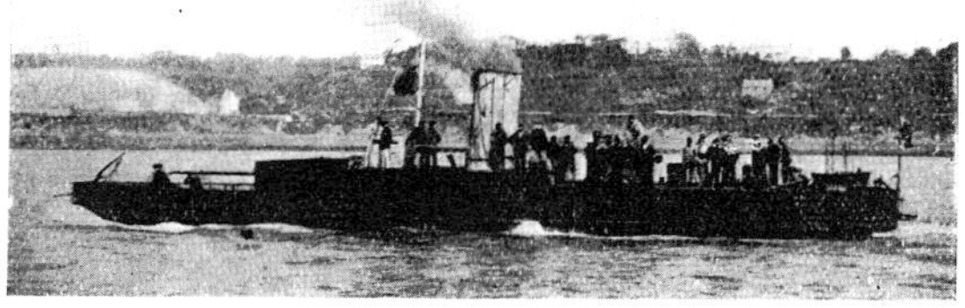

A and B.

A—L. (Brest and Lorient N.Y., 1915). —— tons. 91·8 × 16·4 × 5 feet. Are variously armed as follows:—(*a*) 1—5·5 inch, 2 or 1—6 pdr. AA., 2 M.G., (*b*) 2—3·9 inch, 1—14 pdr. AA., 2 M.G. Speed: 10 kts. These boats were built during the War for service on the rivers Marne, Meuse and Yser. The French Rhine Flotilla consists of 4 of the above gunboats, 3 Submarine Chasers and 20 M.L.

River Gunboats (*Continued*).

Note: All boats in this column built for service abroad.

Has 1 mast forward with 1 fighting top, 2 funnels and a small pole mast aft.)

BALNY (1914). Built by Chantiers de Bretagne, Nantes. 213 tons. Dimensions: 171½ × 22 × 3¾ feet. H.P., 800 = 14 kts. Guns: 6—1 pdr., 2 machine. Fouché w.t. boilers. Coal: 27 tons.

DOUDART DE LA GRÉE (1909). 230 tons 167¼ × 22 × 3¼ feet. Guns: 6—1 pdr. H.P. 920 = 14 kts. Coal: 50 tons. Complement, 57 Built by Chantiers de Bretagne, Nantes.

PEI-HO (1901). 123 tons. Speed, 10 kts. Guns: 3—1 pdr.

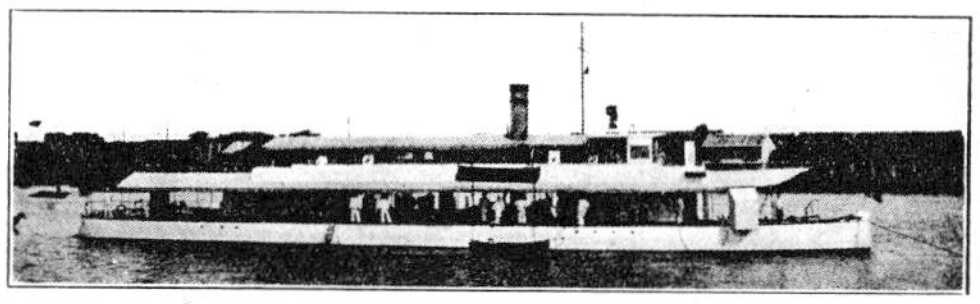

ARGUS and **VIGILANTE** (1900). Both built by Thornycroft. 130 tons. Speed, 13 kts. Guns: 2—3·5 inch, 4—1 pdr. (In China.)

FRENCH DESTROYERS. (*Destroyers*).

90 + *1* Destroyers.*

Totals.	Class.	First Begun.	Last Completed	*Normal* Displacement.	I.H.P.	*Max.* Speed.	*Max.* Coal or Oil	Complement.	*Max.* Draught.	Tubes.
				tons.		kts.	tons.		feet.	
2	*Tribal* class	1917	1917	690	10000	29	100+120	87	9⅚	4
4	*Temeraire* class	1910	1914	950	18000	32 *t*	240+92	102	10¼	4
1	*E. Gabolde* class	1913	†	905	20000	31 *t*	200	...	10	6
12	*Bory* class	1910	1915	880-780	17000-13500	31-30 *t*	200-140	83	10	4
3	*Casque* class	1908	1912	820-790	14400-13000	31 *t*	140	83	10	4
11	*Huzzard* class	1906	1912	514-407	8600-7200	28 *t* & *tr*	100-110	77-69	10	3
21	*Claymore* class	1903	1911	415-340	6400	30½-28	80	71	11½	2
18	*Mousquet* class	1900	1904	370-310	7300-6000	30¾-28	75	71	10½	2
4	*Flamberge* class	1900	1902	310	5600-4800	27-26	70	71	10½	2
3	*Durandal* class	1899	1901	305					8½	2
2	*Pique* class	1900	1902	310	5700	26	70	71	8¾	2

t = turbines. *tr* = turbines and reciprocating.

* Ex-Russian boats not included in this total.

† *E. Gabolde* not yet finished.

3 Russian T.B.D.*

The following Russian Destroyers have been taken over temporarily by the French navy. At present, they are under the French flag and manned by French crews.

1 boat: ***Quentin Roosevelt*** (Russian *Boiki*). For details see Russian (Baltic) Section.

2 boats: ***R1*** and ***R2*** (Russian *Bespokoini* and *Kapitan Saken*). For details see Russian (Black Sea) Section.

* These boats are not included in Table in preceding column.

12 Tribal Boats. (1917 War Programme.)

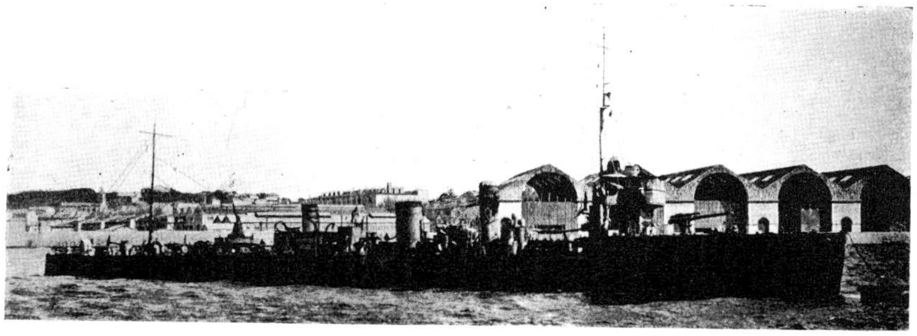

KABYLE *Copyright Photo, M. Bar, Toulon.*

12 built by Japanese Yards: ***Algerien, Annamite, Arabe, Bambara, Hova, Kabyle, Marocain, Sakalave, Senegalais, Somali, Tonkinois, Touareg.*** Built by Kawasaki Co., Mitsu Bishi Co., and other Japanese Yards. All begun March, 1917, launched May and July, 1917, and completed July and September, 1917. Average time of construction 5 months. 690 tons. Dimensions: 260 (*p.p.*), 271¾ (*o.a.*) × 27¼ × 7¾ feet. *Normal* draught, 9⅚ feet: *load* draught, Armament: 1—4·7 inch, 4—12 pdr. (one 12 pdr. is AA.) and 4—18 inch torpedo tubes in two twin deck mountings. Designed H.P. 10,000 = 29 kts.; made about 30 on trials. turbines and boilers. Fuel: 100 tons coal + 120 tons oil = 3000 miles at 15 kts. and 950 miles at full speed. Complement, 87.

Note.—These boats are practically replicas of the Japanese *Kaba* class T.B.D.

FRENCH DESTROYERS.

4 Temeraire type:—Purchased Boats.

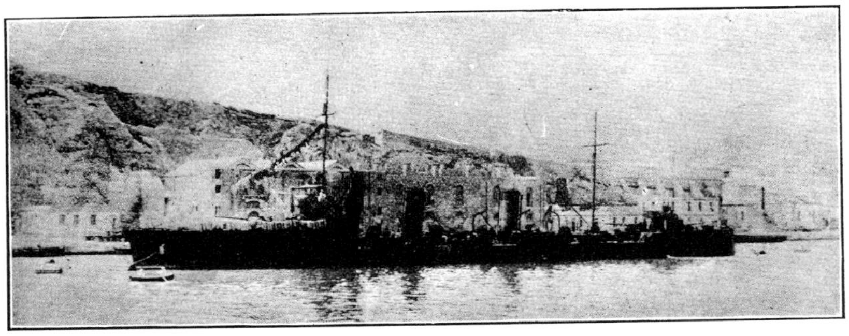

TEMERAIRE.

4 *Chantiers de Bretagne* (*Nantes*): **Aventurier** (ex-*Salta*), **Intrépide** (ex-*Rioja*). **Opiniâtre** (ex-*San Juan*), and **Temeraire** (ex-*Mendoza*) (all 1911). *Normal* displacement: 950 tons; *full load*, 1180 tons. Dimensions: $284\frac{1}{2} \times 28\frac{1}{4} \times 8\frac{5}{6}$ feet *normal* draught. *Full load* draught, $10\frac{1}{4}$ feet. Armament (Bethlehem): 4—4 inch, 4—18 inch tubes. Designed H.P. 18,000=32 kts. Machinery: Curtis turbines + 5 White-Forster boilers. Fuel capacity: 240 tons coal + 92 oil. Radii of action: 3,000 miles at 15 kts.

Note.—Built for Argentina and purchased by France immediately before outbreak of war.

1 Special Boat. (1913 Programme).

(Building or Completing).

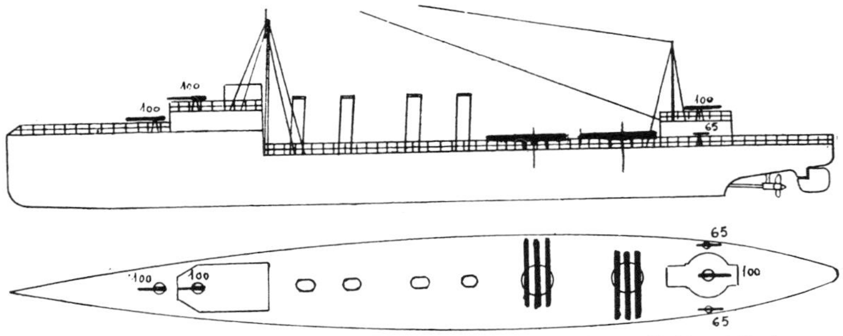

Plans by courtesy of French Ministry of Marine.

1 *Normand. Havre*: **Enseigne Gabolde** (——). 905 tons. Dimensions: 269 × 26·9 × 10 feet. Armament: 3—3·9 inch. 2—9 pdr., 6—18 inch torpedo tubes in two triple deck mountings. Designed H.P. 20,000=31 knots. Parsons geared turbines. Normand boilers. Fuel: 200 tons.

Note.—On plans 100=3·9 inch and 65=9 pdr. guns. Work on this T.B.D. was suspended during the War. Began in Dec., 1913; launch not yet reported.

12 Bory Type.

General Note.—All these boats are armed with 2—3·9 inch, 4—9 pdr., 4—18 inch tubes in pairs. All adapted for mine sweeping and carry D.C. Endurance: about 1,500 miles at 15 kts. and 400—500 at full speed. Complement, 83. They differ according to builders in appearance, dimensions, H.P., turbines, &c. Tubes are in echelon, and not on centre line as shown in plan.

War Losses: Boutefeu, Dague, Faulx, Fourche, Renaudin.

(1913 Programme).

81 + *3* Destroyers. (1914)

Totals.	Class.	First Begun	Last Completed.	*Normal* Displacement.	I.H.P.	*Max.* Speed.	*Max.* Coal.	Complement.	*Max.* Draught.
				tons.		kts.	tons.		feet.
3		1912	1914		...	...	...	...	...
6	*Bisson*	1911	1913		14300	30	140	87	10
2	*Henry*	1909	1913	450	8600	28	80	80	...
12	*Bouclier*	1908	1912	714	14000	31	120 (oil)	80	$10\frac{3}{4}$
5		1907	1910						
3	*Spahi*	1906	1909	428	7200	28	80	80	$9\frac{3}{4}$
3		1906	1909						
2	*Branlebas*	1906	1908	328	6800	25	80	62	10
6	*Gabion*	1905	1907	335	6800	28	75	62	$10\frac{1}{2}$
13	*Coutelas*	1903	1906						
14	*Arc*	1902	1904	303	6300	28	75	62	$10\frac{1}{2}$
9	*Arbélète*	1900	1902						
3	*Yatagan*	1900	1902	310	6300	26	75	62	10
3	*Durandal*	1899	1901	310	5000	28	84	62	10

Completing.

1 *Ch. de Bretagne* (*Nantes*). **Magon** (1913), 791 tons. Dimensions: $257\frac{1}{2} \times 25\frac{3}{4} \times 9\frac{3}{4}$ feet. Designed H.P. 15,000=30 kts. Rateau turbines.

Completing.

1 *Schneider & Cie* (*Creusot*), **Mangini** (1913), 791 tons. Dimensions: $257\frac{1}{2} \times 25\frac{3}{4} \times 9\frac{3}{4}$ feet. Designed H.P. 15,000=30 kts. Zoelly turbines. Du Temple-Guyot boilers.

Bisson class.

Note.—The *Bisson* class all carry 2—4 inch, 4—9 pdr., 4—18 inch tubes in pairs. Nominal radius 1170 at 14 kts., 2300 at 10 kts.

Completing.

Dockyard built (*at Rochefort*). **Protet** (1913) (*at Toulon*). **Commandant Lucas** (1912). 791 tons. Dimensions: $257\frac{1}{2} \times 25\frac{3}{4} \times 9\frac{3}{4}$ feet. Designed H.P. 15,000=30 kts. Also (*at Toulon*), **Bisson** (1912) and **Renaudin** (1913). 756 tons. Dimensions: $256 \times 26 \times 9\frac{3}{4}$ feet. Designed H.P. 14,300=30 kts. Trials: *Renaudin* 32·2 kts.
The three later boats are **Enseigne Roux, Mech. Prin. Lestin,** and **N.** 850 tons.

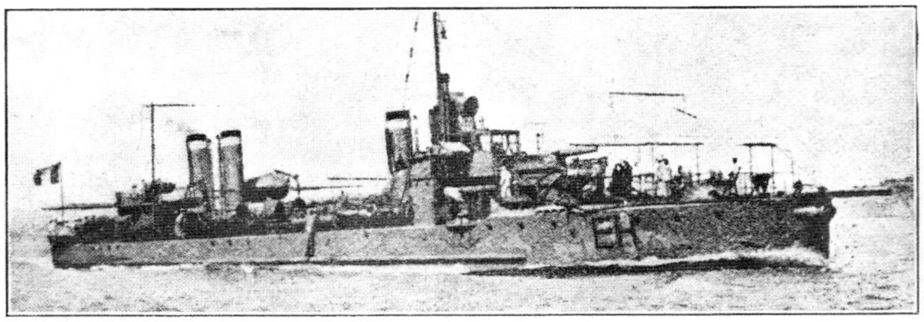

2 *Henry* class:—**Enseigne Henry, Aspirant Herbert** (*Rochefort*). Armament: 6—9 pdr., 3—18 inch tubes. Nominal radius 1170 at 14 kts. Dimensions: $216 \times 21\frac{1}{3} \times 7\frac{1}{4}$ feet. 3 screws. Designed H.P. 8600=28 kts. Trials: *E. Henry* 28·3 kts., *A. Herbert* 28·5 kts.

Note.—These boats have *four* funnels in pairs, the foremost funnel being close up against the chart house.

1910 type FRENCH DESTROYERS.

Note.—All these boats have armament : 2—4 inch, 4—9 pdr., 4—18 inch tubes (in pairs). *Nominal* radius of all : 1170 at 14 kts., or 2300 at 10 kts. Oil fuel only, 120 tons. All have the same deck plan, but they differ according to builders in appearance, dimensions, horse power, turbines, &c.

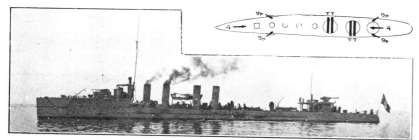

2 *Ch. de la Bretagne (Nantes).* **Fourché** (1910), and **Faulx** (1911). 734 tons. Dimensions: 246×25×9¼ feet. Designed H.P. 12,330=31 kts. Rateau turbines. Du T-Guyot boilers. Trials: *Fourché*, 33·8; *Faulx*, 32·2.

2 *Ch de la Gironde (Bordeaux).* **Cimeterre** (1910). **Dague** (1911). 720 tons. Dimensions: 256×26×9¼ feet. Designed H.P. 13,315=31 kts. Breguet turbines. Du Temple Guyot boilers. Trials: *Cimeterre*, 32·75; *Dague*, 33·2.

Same appearance as above.

2 *Ch. de St. Nazaire (St. Nazaire).* **Dehorter** (1911), **Mehl** (1911). 756 tons. Dimensions: 256×25¾×10 feet. Designed H.P. 13,810=31 kts. Turbines: Parsons. Boilers: Normand.

2 *Normand (Havre).* **Bouclier** (1910). 692 tons. Dimensions: 233×25×10 feet. Designed H.P. 12,000=32 kts. *Also* **Garnier** (1911). 732 tons. Dimensions: 246×25¾×10¼ feet. Designed H.P. 13,810=31 kts. Turbines: Parsons. Boilers: Normand. Trials: *Bouclier*, 12,825=35·4; *Garnier*.

11 Hussard type.

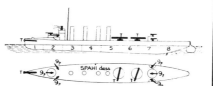

Differ in design according to builders, but all armed with 6—9 pdr. guns and 3—18 in. tubes (2 deck and 1 bow). Designed H.P. ranges from 8600 S.H.P. down to 7200 I.H.P. for speed of 28 kts., but *Voltigeur, Cavalier, Chasseur* and *Mameluk* made over 30 kts. on trials. Radius of action, about 1000 miles at 15 kts., but *Cavalier* and *Janissaire* (oil fuel in both) about 1300 miles at 15 kts. Complements, 77 to 79. *Maximum* fuel in all, about 100 tons. Plans opposite for all five boats on this page; remaining seven on next page as plans for *Hussard.*

MAMELUK (and other boats). *Copyright photo, M. Bar, Toulon.*

2 *Ch. de la Loire (Nantes):* **Hussard** (1908), 409 tons, and **Mameluk** (1909) 407 tons. Dimensions: 216½×22½×9¼ feet. 1 *Dyle & Bacalan (Bordeaux):* **Lansquenet** (1909), 542 tons. Dimensions: 221×20·8×10 feet. 1 *F. & C. de la Med. (Havre):* **Spahi** (1908), 455 tons. Dimensions: 224×21¼×9¼ feet. Machinery of all, reciprocating. Boilers: *Spahi,* Normand; others, Du Temple-Guyot. Coal: 100 tons in all. Trials: *Hussard,* 30·4; *Mameluk,* 30·6; *Spahi,* 28·7; *Carabinier* lost during the War.

3 *Dyle & Bacalan (Bordeaux).* **Boutefeu** (1911). 703 tons. Dimensions: 252½×25×9¼ feet. Designed H.P. 13,810=31 kts. Turbines: Zoelly (Schneider). Boilers: Du Temple-Guyot. *Also* **Riviere** (1911), **Bory** (1911). 716 tons. Dimensions: 252½×26×9¼ feet. Designed H.P. 13,300=31 kts. Trials: *Riviere* 32·27 kts.

1 *Forges et Ch. de la Mediterranée (La Seyne).* **Casque** (1910). 732 tons. Dimensions: 252½×25×10 feet. Designed H.P. 14,000=32 kts. Parsons turbines. Normand boilers. Trials: 14,205=35·6 kts.

CAVALIER. (Other boats may also have raised fore funnels.) *Copyright photo, M. Bar, Toulon.*

1 *Ch. de la Bretagne (Nantes):* **Voltigeur** (1909), 445 tons. Dimensions: 215×22½×9¼ feet. 2 *Normand (Havre):* **Cavalier** (1910), 527 tons, and **Chasseur** (1909), 492 tons. Dimensions: 222×22×10 feet. Turbines: *Voltigeur,* Rateau with reciprocating; *Chasseur, Cavalier.* Parsons. Boilers: Normand; oil-burning in *Cavalier.* Fuel: *Voltigeur* and *Chasseur,* 100 tons coal. *Cavalier,* 110 tons oil only. Trials: *Voltigeur,* 31·5; *Chasseur,* 30·4; *Cavalier,* 31·1.

War loss: *Fantassin.*

Copyright photo, M. Bar, Toulon.

1 *Ch. de la Gironde (Bordeaux).* **Tirailleur** (1908). 479 tons. Dimensions: 207×22·8×9¼ feet. Breguet turbines and reciprocating engines. Du Temple-Guyot boilers. Coal: 100 tons. Trials: 28·82.

Copyright photo, M. Bar, Toulon.

1 *Ch. de Normandie (Rouen).* **Janissaire** (1910). 514 tons. Dimensions: 223×21·9×10·3 feet. Parsons turbines. White-Forster boilers. Oil 100 tons. On trial made 28·5 kts.

1906 design. FRENCH DESTROYERS.—*Spahi* class.

Note.—These boats have all an armament of 6—9 pdr. and 3—18 inch tubes, of which one is in the bow. All have a maximum nominal radius of 1700 at 14 and 2300 at 10 kts. The fuel carried by all is *maximum* capacity 100 tons; the *normal* varies. The boats differ considerably in appearance, there is also variety in their deck plans, dimensions, machinery, etc., according to the builders. All are designed for H.P. 7200 = 28 kts.

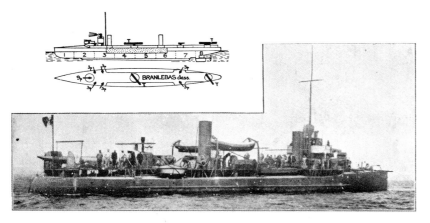

1 *Dyle & Bacalan (Bordeaux).* **Lansquenet** (1909), 417 tons. Dimensions: 210×21¼×9¾ feet. Machinery reciprocating. *Normal* coal, 37 tons.

1 *Ch. de la Loire (Nantes).* **Hussard** (1908), **Mameluk** (1909), 403 tons. Dimensions: 216½×21¾×9¾ feet. *Normal* coal 37 tons.
1 *Normand (Havre).* **Spahi** (1908), 421 tons. Dimensions: 213×21¾×9¾ feet. *Normal* coal 38 tons.
1 (?) **Carabinier** (1908), 409 tons. Dimensions: 210×21×9¾ feet. *Normal* coal 30 tons.
Machinery of all, reciprocating. Boilers: Spahi, Normand; others, Du Temple-Guyot. Trials: Hussard, 30·4; Mameluk, 30·6; Spahi, 28·7; Carabinier, 27·5.

2 *Branlebas* class. **Branlebas, Fanfare.** These are armoured. ¾" belts amidships. Armament: 1—9 pdr., 6—3 pdr., 2—18 in. tubes (M '04 torpedoes). Boilers: Guyot. *Maximum* radius: 2300 miles at 10 kts.

Photo, Bissonier.

6 *Gabion* class. **Etandard, Fanion, Gabion, Oriflamme, Sape, Sabretache.**
13 *Coutelas* class. **Cognee, Coutelas, Carquois, Claymore, Fleuret, Glaive, Mortier, Obusier, Pierrier, Poignard, Stylet, Tromblon, Trident.**
Armament: 1—9 pdr., 4—6 pdr., 2—18 in. tubes. Normand boilers. *Maximum* radius, 2300 at 10 kts.
13 *Arc* class. **Arc, Belier, Bombarde, Catapulte, Dard, Francisque, Fronde, Harpon, Mousqueton, Pistolet, Sabre, Javeline, Mousquet.**
(*Hache, Massue,* and *Baliste* of above type are now mine layers).

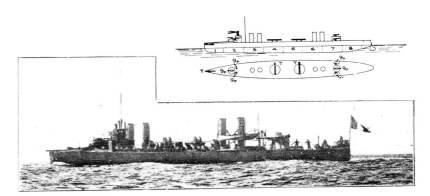

ARC, ARBALETE, YATAGAN, and DURANDAL class.

3 *Yatagan* class. **Épée, Pique, Yatagan** (4 funnels).
Armament: 1—9 pdr., 6—3 pdr., 2—15 in. tubes. Normand boilers. *Max.* radius, 2000 at 10 kts.

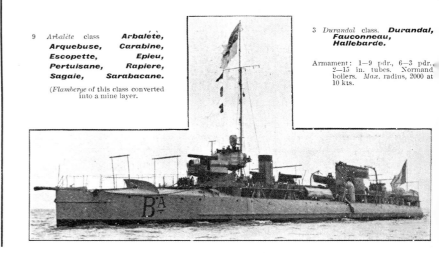

9 *Arbalète* class **Arbalète, Arquebuse, Carabine, Escopette, Epieu, Pertuisane, Rapiere, Sagaie, Sarabacane.**

(*Flamberge* of this class converted into a mine layer.)

3 *Durandal* class. **Durandal, Fauconneau, Hallebarde.**

Armament: 1—9 pdr., 6—3 pdr. 2—15 in. tubes. Normand boilers. *Max.* radius, 2000 at 10 kts.

War losses: *Etendard, Branlebas, Mousquet, Carabine, Catapulte, Yatagan.*

FRENCH TORPEDO BOATS.

Sea-going Torpedo Boats—*(continued)*.

1 *F. & C. de la Méditerranée, Granville:* **Grondeur** (1892). 2—1 pdr. 2 torpedo tubes.

63 (*or less*) *Normand* type Nos. **369—295**, of 96 to 101 tons. *Nominal* full speed radius 200 miles. At 10 kts., 1800 mile.

Notes.—A large number of these Torpedo Boats were modified during the War for service as Coastal Patrol Boats, Guardships over Net Barrages, Boom Defences, &c., and for short-distance convoy work. The two amidships 15 inch torpedo tubes were removed and replaced by either a 14 pdr. gun (75 mm. field gun on naval mounting) or by a 9 pdr. gun or 2—3 pdr. guns. The stem 15 inch tube was retained, although it was of little use at full speed or in any seaway.

103 *(or less)* Torpilleurs de Defence Mobile.

Totals.	Numbers.	First Begun	Last Completed	Displacement	I.H.P.	Max. Speed	Coal	Complement	Tubes	Max. Draught
				tons		kts.	tons			
63	369—295	'03	'07	96-101	2000	26	11	23	3—1	8¾
39	292—208	1899	1904	86-94	1500-2000	25	11	22	2	9
1	193	1894	1899	80	1100	21	10	16	2	8½

Notes on Torpilleurs de Defence Mobile.

Uncertain how many of these boats are now in service. Reported during 1919 that majority were being surveyed, with a view to breaking-up ; only those numbered above 300 may be kept for further service.

Following boats have double numbers or number and name :—*292* (*21S*), *291* (*20S*), *286* (*19S*), *285* (*18S*), *284* (*17S*), *255* (*16S*), *242* (*6S*), *222* (*Rouable*), *215* (*Foyer*), *208* (*Marteau*), *193* (*Moulouya*).

All boats are *Normand* types. Several exceeded 27 kts. on original trials, but few can exceed 25 kts. now.

All originally armed with 2—1 pdr. guns and 2 or 3—15 inch tubes, but these have been removed from some boats—see *Notes* below.

War losses: *251, 300, 317, 319, 325, 331, 333, 347, 348.*

39 (*or less*) *Normand* type : **292—208** and **193,** of 86-94 and 80 tons. From *No. 202* and upwards, two funnels—appearance more or less as 369-295 above.

Notes.—Many of these old boats have been disarmed and dismantled, to provide engines for new gunboats.

FRENCH SC-BOATS, MINE LAYERS AND SUBMARINES.

Submarine Chasers (*Chasseurs de Sousmarins*).

Same appearance as U.S. SC-boats.

97—100 foot type: **C1, C4—C51** and **C52—100.** Built by U.S. Navy Yards and smaller shipbuilding firms, 1917-18. *Designed* displacement, 54 tons; *actual* displacement, 77 tons. Dimensions: 105 ft. (*p.p.*), 110 ft. (*o.a.*) × 14 ft. 8⅞ in. × 5 ft. 5⅛ in. (*mean* hull draught). Machinery: 3 sets of 220 B.H.P. Standard petrol motors, totalling 660 B.H P = 17 kts. Petrol : 2400 gallons = 900 miles at 10 kts. Armament : *C1—C50* were sent across the Atlantic with 2—6 pdrs. only and may still retain these guns : *C51—C100* have 1—3 inch (23 cal.) gun. M.G. may have been added by French Navy. Carry depth charges. Complement, 26.

Notes.—Begun for U.S. Navy as follows : *SC 5, SC 7—16, SC 28—33, SC 65—67, SC 75—76, SC 140—142, SC 146, SC 160—163, SC 170—176, SC 243, SC 249, SC 313—319, SC 347—348, SC 350* (all boats of first U.S. contract). *SC 357—404, SC 406* (second U.S.) contract for French Government). The U.S. *SC 177,* being in European waters, was transferred to the French Navy in place of *SC 405* under second contract. Were renumbered as *C1—49* and *C50—99* of French Navy, out of which *C2, C3* and another boat (*C 100?*) have been lost.

* For builders under SC-numbers see Submarine Chaser Section of U.S. Navy. Details taken from article by Com. J. A. Furer, Construction Corps. U.S.N., published in "Journal, U.S. Naval Institute."

M. L. (*Vedettes*).

French Official War Photo.

70—85 foot type : **V1—20, V22, V24—26, V28—61** (built in England 1917) and **V62—73** (built in Canada 1917-18). About 30—35 tons. Complement, 8—10. Length, 80—85 feet. Beam, 12—13 feet. Draught, 4-5 feet. Armament : 1—75 mm. field gun converted to naval mounting. 2 D.C. Machinery : 2 sets petrol motors—20—22 kts. *nominal.* 19 kts. about best *maximum* at sea for any length of time. Radius of action : about 500 miles at full speed and 1000 miles at 12-15 kts. *or less.* Fuel : about 2000 galls. petrol. *V21, V23* and *V27* lost during the War.

12 "SEA-GOING TORPEDO BOATS."

(Torpilleurs de haute mer.)

2 screws. 15 inch torpedoes. Boilers : Normand, Thornycroft, and Du Temple Guyot.

Copyright photo, G. E. G.

11 *Normand* type : **Bourrasque, Cyclone, Mistral,* Rafale, Siroco*** (Normand, Havre); **Simoun,* Typhon*** (F. & C. de la Med., Granville); **Audacieux,* Trombe*** (F. & C. de la Bretagne, Nantes); **Borée, Tramontane** (Dyle & Bacalan, Bordeaux). All launched 1900-01. 2—3 pdr. guns and 3 tubes. Radius of action ; 2500 miles at 10 kts. * These boats have ⅜" armour amidships.
Aquilon, Filibustier, Grenadier All built 1892-99.

2 *Normand* type: **Forban** (1895). **Chevalier** (1895). 2—3 pdr., 2 tubes. Radius of action: 2000 miles at 12 kts.

FRENCH SUBMARINES—OCEAN-GOING BOATS.

Surrendered German Submarines.

The following German Submarines were assigned to the French Navy during 1919. No attempt is made to describe these boats, because, after being examined, they are to be dismantled and broken up.* These boats are not to be incorporated in the French Navy. Those who desire particulars are referred to the German Submarine Section of 1918 "Fighting Ships."

1 Cruiser : *U139* boat.

3 Converted Mercantiles : *U151*, *U153*, *U157*.

16 Ocean-going boats : *U166*, *U160*, *U129*, *U113*, *U108*, *U105*, *U94*, *U91*, *U81*, *U57*, *U55*, *UB142*, *UB126*, *UB94 UB84*, *UB73*.

8 Mine-Laying boats : *U79*, *UC104*, *UC103*, *UC100*, *UC74*, *UC58*, *UC27*, *UC23*.

5 Coastal boats : *UB24*, *UB14*, *UB8*, *UB6*, *UB1*.

Several of the above boats foundered or were wrecked when being navigated from British to French ports.

* The French Submarine *Roland Morillot*, ex-German *UB26*, is a prize of war and outside the terms of this agreement between the Allied Navies.

---

2 Joessel Class (Ocean-going—*Diesel*.)

2 *Simonet* type : **Fulton** (1919) and **Joessel** (1917). Both built at Cherbourg D.Y. Displacements : 900 tons *on surface*, 1250 tons *submerged*. Dimensions : × × feet. Machinery : *on surface*, 2 sets Schneider Diesel engines, 2700 B.H.P. = 16½ kts. Endurance *on surface* and *submerged* about the same as *Lagrange* class in next column. Armament : 1 or 2—14 pdr. guns and 8 or 10 tubes, and/or torpedoes carried in external cradle gears. Complement, 40.

---

2 Gustave Zédé Class.

(Ocean-going : one boat *Diesel*, one boat *steam*.)

Note.—These two Submarines are usually rated together as a class. They have the same dimensions, displacement, and armament, but for comparative purposes, they were built with different systems of surface propulsion.

1 *Simonet* type : **Néreide** (Cherbourg D.Y., 1914). Displacements, dimensions, armament and complement, as *Gustave Zédé* below. Machinery : 2 sets 2 cycle 8 cyl. 1200 B.H.P. Schneider-Carels Diesel engines, 2400 H.P. = 20 kts. *on surface*. Electric motors + batteries 1700 H.P. = 10 kts. *submerged*. Radius of action : *about 3500 miles at 12 kts. on surface.*

1 *Simonet* type : **Gustave Zédé** (Cherbourg D.Y., 1913). Displacements : 787 tons *on surface*, 1000 tons *submerged*. Dimensions : 243 × 19½ × 12¾ feet. Machinery : 2 sets geared turbines + 4 Normand-Du Temple oil-burning boilers, 4000 H.P. = 19 kts. *on surface*. Electric motors + batteries, 1700 H.P. = 10 kts. *submerged*. Radii of action : 2300 miles at 10 kts. and 1800 miles at 14 kts. *on surface*. Armament : 1—14 pdr. and 1—3 pdr. Q.F. guns. Torpedo tubes : 2—18 inch tubes + 6—18 inch torpedoes carried in external dropping gears. Complement, 40.

---

3 Lieut. O'Byrne Class (Sea-going—*Diesel*).

Building or completing.

3 *Laubeuf* type : **Lieutenant O'Byrne, Dupetit-Thouars,** and **Henri Fournier,** building or completing by Schneider, Chalon-sur-Saone. Displacements : *about* 350 tons *on surface*, 500 tons *submerged*. Dimensions : *about* 173.9 × 15.4 × feet. Machinery : 2 sets Schneider-Carels Diesel engines, 1000 B.H.P. = 14 kts. *on surface*. *Submerged* speed : 8½ kts. Armament : 1 small Q.F. gun and 4 torpedo tubes. Complement, 24.

---

4 Lagrange Class (Ocean-going—*Diesel*).

4 *Hutter* type : **Lagrange** (1917), **Laplace** (——),* **Regnault** (1919),† and **Romazotti** (1917). All launched at Toulon D.Y., 1917. Displacements : 840 tons *on surface*, 1130 tons *submerged*. Dimensions : 246⅔ × 21 × 13 feet. Machinery : *on surface*, 2 sets 1300 B.H.P. Sulzer-Diesel engines, totalling 2600 B.H.P. for 16½ kts. *Submerged* speed : 11 kts. Endurance : *on surface*, 2500 miles at 14 kts., 4200 miles at 10 kts. When *submerged*, 115 miles at 5 kts. Armament : either (a) 1—3·9 inch gun and 1—14 pdr. gun, or (b) 2—14 pdr. guns. 10—18 inch tubes or torpedoes carried in external cradle gears. Complement, 40.

* *Laplace* also reported as built at Rochefort D.Y.
† *Regnault* not yet finished : is being modified to obviate defects developed by *Lagrange* on trials.

---

2 Dupuy de Lôme Class (Ocean-going—*Steam*).

SANÉ. *Copyright photo, M. Bar, Toulon.*

2 *Hutter* type : **Dupuy de Lôme** (1915) and **Sané** (1916). Both built at Toulon D.Y. Displacements : 833 tons *on surface*, 1100 tons *submerged*. Dimensions : 246⅔ × 21 × 13 feet. Machinery : *on surface*, 2 sets of turbines and oil-fired boilers : I.H.P. 4000 = 18 kts. *Submerged* speed : 11 to 12 kts. Endurance : 1350 miles at 14 kts. *on surface*, 150 miles at 5 kts. *submerged*. Armament : 2—14 pdr. guns and 8—18 inch torpedo tubes and/or external cradle gears. Complement, 40.

(Ocean-going Types continued on next page.)

---

3 Armide Class (Sea-going—*Diesel*).

3 *Laubeuf* type " De " : **Amazone,** (1916), **Antigone** (1916), and **Armide** (ex-Japanese No. 14, 1915). Built by Schneider et Cie, Chalon-sur-Saone. Displacements : 460 tons *on surface*, 665 tons *submerged*. Dimensions : 184⅔ × 17 × 10½ feet. Machinery : 2 sets, Schneider-Carels Diesel engines, 2200 H.P. = 17½ kts. *on surface*, *Submerged* speed : 11 kts. Armament : 1—1 pdr. Q.F. gun. Torpedo tubes : 2 internal + 4 torpedoes carried in external dropping gears.

Note.—*Amazone* and *Antigone* begun for Greek Navy : *Armide* for Japanese Navy. All three taken over for French Navy during War. Reported that *Amazone* and *Antigone* have been converted to Mine-Layers.

---

1 Daphné Class (Sea-going—*Diesel*).

1 *Hutter* type : **Daphné** (Toulon D.Y., 1915). Displacements : 640 tons *on surface*, 945 tons *submerged*. Dimensions : 223 × 18½ × 12½ feet. Machinery : 2 sets 800 B.H.P. Sulzer Diesel engines, 1600 H.P. = 15 kts. *on surface*. *Submerged* speed : 11 kts. Endurance : *on surface* (a) 2300 miles at 14 kts., (b) 4000 miles at 11-12 kts., 100 miles at 5 kts. when *submerged*. Armament : 1—14 pdr. gun, 10—18 inch torpedo tubes or torpedoes carried in external dropping gears. Complement, 35. Is an enlarged *Archimède* design. *Diane* of this type lost during the War.

---

4 Experimental Boats.

Building.

1 *Bourdelle* type : **Amiral Bourgois.** $\frac{555}{735}$ tons. Dimensions : 181 × 26¼ × 12 feet. Oil surface motor, 1560 h.p. = 15 kts. 7—18 inch tubes (m. 1901).

1 *Maurice* type : **Charles Brun.** $\frac{355}{450}$ tons. Dimensions : 144½ × 16½ × 12 feet. Surface motor, steam, 1300 = 15·8 kts. 6—18 inch tubes (1901 model).

1 *Radiguet* type : **Mariotte.** $\frac{530}{630}$ tons. Dimensions : 213 × 14 × 12½ feet. Petrol surface motor, 1440 = 15 kts. 7—18 inch tubes (1904 m.)

Note.—Sunk in Dardanelles 26 July 1915.

FRENCH SUBMARINES—SEA-GOING TYPES. (*Continued*).

3 Bellone class (Sea-going—*Diesel*).

2 *Radiguet* type: **Clorinde** (Rochefort D.Y., 1913), **Cornelie** (Rochefort, 1913). Displacements: 410 tons *on surface*; 570 tons *submerged*. Electric motors + batteries of 410 H.P. All other details as the *Amarante* class above.

1 Special boat (Sea-going—*Steam*).

1 *Hutter* type: **Archimede** (Cherbourg D.Y., 1909). $\frac{577}{810}$ tons. Dimensions: $199\frac{3}{4} \times 18\frac{1}{4} \times 13\frac{1}{2}$ feet. Machinery: 2 sets triple expansion steam engines, 1700 H.P. = 15 kts. *on surface*. *Submerged* speed, 10–11 kts. Endurance: 2500 miles at 10 kts. *on surface*; *submerged*, 100 miles at 5 kts. Armament: 1—3 pdr. gun; 6—18 inch (M'04) torpedoes carried in external dropping gears + 1 bow tube. Complement, 31. Has proved very successful in service.

33 Laubeuf Boats.

(The 33 boats in this group are all of one general *Laubeuf* type, differing only in minor details.)

11 *Cherbourg Laubeufs*: **Brumaire, Floreal, Frimaire, Fructidor, Germinal, Messidor, Nivose, Pluviose, Prairial, Thermidor, Ventose.** Also **Euler, Foucault, Franklin** (of which all except *Brumaire, Frimaire,* and *Nivose* (petrol) are steam driven on the surface (*see below*.)

10 *Rochefort Laubeufs*: **Berthelot, Cugnot, Faraday, Fresnel, Giffard, Montgolfier, Newton, Papin, Volta, Watt** (of which *Cugnot, Giffard* and *Watt* are steam, all the rest oil motors.) (*see next page.*)

9 *Toulon Laubeufs*: **Ampere, Arago, Bernouilli, Colomb, Curie, Gay-Lussac, Joule, Leverrier, Monge** (of which all are oil motors on surface).

The whole of the above 33 boats are of $\frac{398}{550}$ tons. Dimensions: 168 x 16½ x 10 feet. H.P., 700 = 12 kts, surface speed, with maximum radius 2000 miles. Submerged speed, 7¾ kts. Torpedoes, 7—18 inch (m. 1901), except in Toulon boats (6 only).

War losses: *Foucault, Floreal, Prairial, Freshnel, Bernouilli, Joule* and *Monge*.

FRENCH SUBMARINES—MINE-LAYING AND COASTAL BOATS.

2 Paul Chailly class (Mine Laying).

Building or Completing.

2 boats, *type unknown*: **Paul Chailley,** begun at Havre, 1917, **Pierre Callot,** begun at Bordeaux, 1917. No details known, beyond the fact that both are large Mine-Layers. Will probably be completed during 1920.

1 Captured German boat (Coastal—*Diesel*).

Photo by courtesy of Señor Pascual Rey, Corunna.

Above view of German *UB 23* is generally correct for appearance of ROLAND MORILLOT.

1 *ex-German* boat: **Roland Morillot** (ex-German *UB 26*, launched by Weser Co., Bremen, 1916, captured during 1916). Displacements: 263 tons *on surface*, 324 tons *submerged*. Dimensions: $118\frac{1}{2} \times 14\frac{1}{4} \times 12$ feet. Machinery: 2 sets, 140 H.P. 6-cylinder oil motors = 8¼ kts. *on surface*; *submerged* speed, 5¾ to 6 kts. Endurance: 4500 miles at 5 kts. *on surface*; 70 miles at 3 kts. *submerged*. Armament: 1—3 pdr., 1 M.G., 2 (bow) 18 inch torpedo tubes. Carries 4 torpedoes. Oil: 22·28 tons. Complement, 21.

6 Emeraude class (Coastal—*Diesel*).

4 *Maugas* type: **Emeraude** (1906), **Opale** (1906), **Rubis** (1907), and **Topaze** (1908). Dimensions: *about* 149 × 12.8 × 12.3 feet. *Surface* displacement, about 390 tons; *submerged*, 447 tons. Speeds: 11-12 kts, *on surface*; 8 kts. *submerged*. 1—9 pdr. gun and 4—18 inch torpedo tubes. Complement, 25. *Saphir* of this class lost during the War.

Note:—The fifth boat, *Turquoise*, captured by Turks during the War. Was repaired and commissioned for service in the Turkish Navy as the *Mustedieh Ombashi*. Has been recovered by the French Navy, but its is doubtful if she will be assigned to any active form of service. *Saphir* wrecked in Dardanelles.

5 boats, various.

Early small edition of Brumaire, etc.

2 *Laubeuf*: **Circe, Calypso.** $\frac{351}{450}$ tons. Dimensions; 154 × 16½ × 10 feet. 6—18 inch torpedoes.

Note—*Circe* sunk 20 September 1918.

2 *Laubeuf:* **Algrette** and **Cignone.** $\frac{172}{351}$ tons. Enlarged *Tritons.* Dimensions: 118 × 13 × 13 feet. 4—18 torpedo launching tubes. H.P. 200 = 10.5 kts. Maximum surface radius, 600 miles at 8 kts.

5 boats, various.

1 *Mangas:* **Follet** (*ex Farfadet*). $\frac{185}{200}$ tons. Dimensions: 135 × 10 × 10 feet. Electric power only. Speed above, 12 kts., submerged, 8 kts. Nominal radius, 50 above, 30 below. 4—18 inch torpedoes (old type launching gear).

1 *Berlin:* **Argonaute** (*ex Omega*). $\frac{168}{301}$ tons. Dimensions: 154½ × 14 × 9½ feet. Surface motor Diesel. H.P. 200 = 11 kts. Submerged speed, 8 kts.

4 *Laubeuf:* **Triton, Silure, Espadon, Sirene.** $\frac{106}{200}$ tons. Dimensions: 111½ × 12¼ × 13 feet. Steam on surface H.P. 250 = 11 kts. or so. *Maximum* surface radius, 600 at 8 kts. Armament, 4—18 inch launching gears.
Surface motor is a triple expansion steam engine, fired with heavy petroleum. Flash boiler, Fulmen accumulators. Can nominally do 70 miles submerged at 5 kts. but cannot really keep under so long. Boats built like torpedo boats with a double skin and submerged by the admission of water into the space between the skins.

FRENCH DEPOT SHIPS, MINE LAYERS & SWEEPERS.

Submarine Depot Ship.

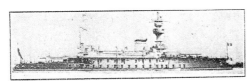

TREHOUART (1893). 6535 tons. Dimensions *about* 293 × 58½ × 24½ feet. Armament (M '87): 2—12 inch, 45 cal. (specially fitted for high angle fire), 8—4 inch, 4—3 pdr., 2—18 inch tubes *above water.* Armour: 17¾″ belt, 14½″ turrets. Designed H.P. 8400 = 17 kts. Boilers: Belleville (without economisers). Coal: *maximum* 337 tons.

An old armoured ship, **TOURVILLE** (ex *Gironde*, 1878), is used as a Harbour Depot Ship, also Sloop *Satellite.* Destroyers are also employed as Tenders to Submarines.

T.B. **No. 273** and Repair Ship **Friant** (next page) attached to Submarine Flotillas.

Note: Also *Kanguroo* sunk off Funchal By U.38 3 December 1916.

Aircraft Carriers.

(*Portes-Avions.*)

Photo, M. Bar, Toulon.

CAMPINAS (ex-liner of Chargeurs Reunis, built ———, and taken over during war). 3319 tons. Dimensions: 357.6 × 42.7 × 23.2 feet. Guns: not known. I.H.P. 1460 = 11.8 kts. on trials; present best speed, 10 kts. 1 set triple-exp. engines. 2 Boilers. Coal: 988 tons. Two hangars for 6-10 machines and K.B. gear.

(*Also Aviation School Ship.*)

FOUDRE (October, 1895). Displacement 6100 tons. Complement 328. Length, 380½ feet. Beam, 51¼ feet. *Maximum draught,* 23½ feet. Guns: 8—3.9 in., 4—9 pdr., 2—3 pdr. Armour: Deck 3½″, 4″ casemates. Designed H.P. 11,500 = 19 kts. *Trials* (1897): I.H.P. 11,930 = 19.57 kts.

Note.—Russian (Black Sea) seaplane carrier **ALMAZ** is temporarily in French navy. Carries 4 seaplanes.

324

Mine Layers (*Mouilleurs de Mines.*)

CHATEAURENAULT (1898) 8018 tons. Dimensions: 457 × 56 × 22½ feet. Armament: 2—6.4, 6—5.5, 10—3 pdr. Armour: 3″ deck. Designed H.P. 23,000 = 23 kts. Boilers: Normand-Sigaudy. Coal: *maximum* 2100 tons. Made 24.5 kts. on first trials.

Note—Lost in Ionian Sea 14 December.

PLUTON. *Photo by courtesy of Messrs. A. Normand.*

PLUTON (1913), 660 tons, & **CERBERE** (1912). Both built by Messrs. Augustin Normand, Havre. 566 tons. Dimensions: 193½ × 27½ × 10¾ feet. Guns: 2—3.9 inch and 1—3 pdr AA. Designed H.P. 6000 = 20 kts. Coal: 150 tons. Carry 120 mines.

Destroyers (*used for Mine-Laying.*)

Carquois (1907), **Hache** (1906), **Massue** (1906), **Baliste** (1904), **Sarbacane** of *Arbalete* class and **Flamberge** —all described on preceding pages.

Submarine Mine Layers.

Paul Chailly and *Pierre Callot* listed on an earlier page. Two submarines of *Amarante* class have been adapted for mine laying; names and number of mines carried not known. Also in use in 1914 *Casabianca* and *Cassini.*

Mine Sweepers (*Dragueurs de Mines*).

Note.—All destroyers of the *Bouclier* class, and nearly all gunboats of the *Diligente, Fripomne* and *Vaillante* types are fitted as mine sweepers, also various Torpedo Boats and Submarine Chasers.

Photo wanted.

CHARRUE (1914), **HERSE** (1914), **PIOCHE** (1914), **RATEAU** (1914). 255 tons. Guns: 2—3 pdr. Designed H.P. 600 = 12 kts. Coal: 35 tons.

FRENCH MISCELLANEOUS

Mine Sweepers—(continued).

ORIENT (1908), 380 tons. **IROISE** (1907), 240 tons.
LORIENTAIS (1901), 430 tons. **DAMIER** (1897), 155 tons.
ALCYON I (——), 300 tons. Speeds: 8-10 kts. Above ships
are Trawlers purchased into Navy 1910-12. Further Mine-
Sweeping Trawlers, which may not be permanently retained for
naval service, are listed on next page.

Oil Tankers (Petroliers.)

Same appearance as "Rhône" below.

—————— (ex-*Meuse*, 1915, present name not known). 7500 tons.
Speed, 13 kts. Carries 6400 tons of oil as cargo.

See Silhouettes for appearance.

GARONNE (1911). Oil Tanker. 10,800 tons. H.P. 2600=13 kts.
Carries 7000 tons oil as cargo.

Photo, M. Bar, Toulon.

RHÔNE (1910). Oil Tanker. 7830 tons. H.P. 2100=11 kts.
Carries 4500 tons oil as cargo.

Special Service.

CHAMOIS (1906). 425 tons. Guns: 4—3 pdr. Designed H.P.
40=15 kts. Boilers: Du Temple. (*Pilotage School*).

Salvage Ship.

For appearance, see Silhouettes.

VULCAIN (1909). 330 tons. Speed: 13 kts.

Repair Ship. (Navire-Atelier.)

FRIANT (1893). Old Cruiser of 3944 tons, converted for service as
Repair Ship. Present H.P., speed and armament, not known.

Transports.

No Photos available.
For "Seine," see Silhouette.

SEINE (1913). 3160 tons. Designed H.P. 1950=13 kts. Guns:
2 -3·9 inch, 1—9 pdr. Coal: 295 tons.
LOIRET (ex-S.S. *Paris*, purchased 1900). 2200 tons. Guns: 1—9 pdr.
H.P. 1060=11 kts.
Also *Aneturus, Evangéline, Gâvres, Marguerite VI* and *Prado.*

DROME (1887). 2200 tons. 2 small guns. Speed, 11 kts.
Photo, N.D.
Sunk by mine Jan 1918.

Hospital Ships. (Navires-hôpital.)

VINH-LONG (1881), **BIEN HOA** (1880). 5500 tons. Speed:
nominal 13 kts. Draughts: about 22 feet.
DUGUAY-TROUIN (ex-*Tonquin*, 1878). 5445 tons. Designed
H.P. 2700=14 kts.

FRENCH MISCELLANEOUS.

Navy Trawlers.

Following Trawlers built during the War to the order of the
Ministry of Marine, for service as Patrol Boats, Mine Sweepers,
&c. Some may be sold out to private owners now.

"Bird" Class :—

*Canard, Colombe, Coq, Faisan, Gelinotte, Héron, Paon, Perdreau,
Pigeon, Pingouin, Pintade, Pluvier, Ramier, Tourterelle,
Vanneau,* all 677 tons.

*Alouette, Becfigu, Bergeronnette, Caille, Canari, Chardonneret,
Colibri, Corneille, Engoulevant, Etourneau, Fauvette, Grive,
Linotte, Loriot, Martinet, Martin-Pêcheur, Mauviette, Merle,
Moineau, Ortolan, Passereau, Perruche, Pie, Pierrot, Pinson,
Picvet, Roitelet, Rossignol, Rouge-Gorge, Sansonnet,* all of 460
tons.

"Fish" Class :—

Equille, Gardon, Goujon, Lamproie, Murène, all 669 tons; *Ablette,
Anguille, Barbeau, Brême, Brochet, Carpe,* all 460 tons;
Perche, Tanche, Truite. 410 tons.

"Insect" Class :—

Cigale, Coccinelle, Criquet, Libellule, all 430 tons.

"Flower" Class :—

*Campanule, Clematite, Jacynthe, Jonquille, Lavande, Marjolaine,
Paquerette, Perce-Niege, Renoncle, Sauge, Tulipe, Violette.*
Have Diesel engines and no funnels.

"Tree" Class :—

Cedre, Chêne, Erable, Frêne, Hêtre, Orme, Platane, Peuplier, all
360 tons.

"Rock" Class :—

Albâtre, Basalte, Gypse, Meulière, Pyrite, Silex, Quartz, all 380
tons.

Miscellaneous :—

Autruche, Caribou, Eole, Onagre, all 471 tons; *Mathurin* and
Troupier, with Sulzer Diesel engines, *Coetlogon, Nemerica,
Thuga, Victoire, Yucca,* &c., &c.

Tugs. (Remorqueurs.)

Two large sea-going boats, **CENTAUR** (1915) & **TRAVAILLEUR.**
Following Tugs of 360 tons built during the War :—
Clameur, Fracas, Tapage, Tintamare, Tumulte, Vacarme.
Crabe, Calmar, Homard, Tourteau.
Also many other smaller tugs and tanks.

Training Ships. (Navires-Ecole.)

At the time these pages were prepared, the allocation of French
Warships for Training Duties had not been definitely decided
on. It is proposed that the majority of French Armoured
Cruisers shall be employed on Training Duties.

For Gunnery :—

Battleships **VERITÉ, REPUBLIQUE,** Coast Defence Ship
REQUIN, Old Cruisers **POTHUAU** and **LATOUCHE-
TRÉVILLE**—all described on preceding pages.

HAVRE. Gunboat. No details known, but reported to be an
old Cross-Channel Steamer purchased into the Navy during
War.

For Torpedoes :—

Battleship **PATRIE** and Armoured Cruiser **VICTOR HUGO,**
both described on preceding pages. Also 6 Torpedo Craft,
names unknown.

For Hydrophone Experiments :—

5 Submarines and Torpedo Boats. Names not known.

For Training Personnel for Submarines :—

Some old Submarines may be retained for this service. Names
not yet known.

For Engineers :—

For Cadets :—

Cruiser **JEANNE D'ARC** used for this Duty up to 1914.
She has reverted to same service now. Is described on an
earlier page.

Surveying Ships.

Photo, N.D.

MANCHE (1890), **VAUCLUSE** (1891). About 1600 tons.
Armament: *Manche* has 1—9 pdr. and 2—3 pdr.; *Vaucluse* has
2 -3 pdr. Speed about 10-11 kts.
UTILE (1894). 400 tons. Speed: 13 kts. Guns: 1—3 pdr.
Also *Sonde* (1911) of 51 tons. 10 kts. speed.

Yacht.

JEANNE BLANCHE (1894, rebuilt 1913). 420 tons. Guns: 4—
1 pdr. H.P. 820=12 kts. Complement, 37.

IBIS (1883). 254 tons. Draught, 8 feet. Guns: 2—9 pdrs.
H.P. 424=12 kts. 1 screw. (*Coastguard Service*)

Fishery Protection.

FLAMANT (Dec., 1916). Despatch Vessel of 610 tons. 154×28×
13 feet. Guns: 1—14 pdr., 1—1 pdr. I.H.P. 1100=13 kts.
Coal: 100 tons.
T.B.D. **Rafale** (described on an earlier page).
Trawlers *Sentinelle* and *Sajou.*

MOROCCO.

(French Protectorate.)

SIDI-EL-TURKI.

SIDI-EL-TURKI (1898). 450 tons. 154 × 23 × 13 feet.
Guns: 2—12 pdr. *Maximum* speed: 12.5 kts.

1 funnel, 3 masts.

EL HASSANEH (1882). 1164 tons. 240¾ × 34 × feet.
Guns: 1 old 6 inch, 4 machine. *Nominal* speed: 10 kts.
Coal: 100 tons.

NOOR-EL-BAHR (1898) and two Coastguard Ships, built in
Germany about 1906, also reported to exist.

(ROYAL) ITALIAN NAVY.

Revised 1919, from **Official List**, "Regia Marina Italiana, Maggio 1919," and other information furnished by courtesy of H.E. The Minister of Marine.

Correction to above Map: *delete* AUSTRIA.

Principal Mercantile Ports.

Genoa (*Genova*), Naples (*Napoli*), Leghorn (*Livorno*), Palermo, Venice (*Venezia*), Catania (Sicily).

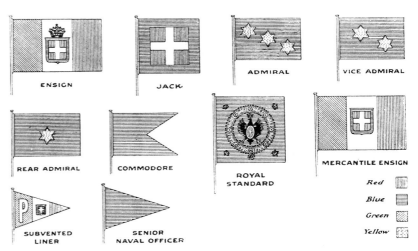

ENSIGN · JACK · ADMIRAL · VICE ADMIRAL

REAR ADMIRAL · COMMODORE · ROYAL STANDARD · MERCANTILE ENSIGN

SUBVENTED LINER · SENIOR NAVAL OFFICER

Red · Blue · Green · Yellow

Private Docks.

GENOA : Three graving docks. Bacino di Darsena, $267\frac{1}{2} \times 78\frac{3}{4} \times 22$ feet ; No. 1, $571 \times 81\frac{3}{4} \times 30\frac{1}{4}$ feet ; No. 2, $702 \times 60\frac{1}{4} \times 28$ feet. Floating dock, $257 \times 46 \times 17$ feet, 2900 tons lift.
LEGHORN ; Orlando Bros., $451 \times 71\frac{3}{4} \times 23$ feet. 2 patent slips for 1500 tons.
NAPLES : Municipal No 1, $659\frac{1}{4} \times 95 \times 33\frac{1}{4}$; No. 2, $348\frac{3}{4} \times 60 \times 23$ feet.
PALERMO (Sicily) : Dock, $565 \times 85\frac{3}{4} \times 27\frac{3}{4}$ feet. Patent slip, 1500 tons.

Colonies : Eritrea, Italian Somaliland, Tripoli and Cyrenaica (Libia Italiana).
Minister of Marine : Contr' Ammiraglio Sechi (June, 1919).
Personnel : About 40,000 *active* personnel *before war.*

Mercantile Marine (*1916*).

684 steamers of 1,035,815 tons *net.*
517 sea-going sailing ships of 210,814 tons *net.*

Coinage.

Lira (100 centesimi) = 10*d.* British, about 20 cents. U.S.A. Value varies.

ITALIAN NAVAL PORTS (**ADRIATIC**) & UNIFORMS.

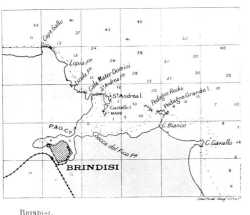

BRINDISI.

BRINDISI. No docks known to exist Admiralty Chart No. 1492.

VALONA. Fleet Anchorage used by Italian Navy. Admiralty Chart No. 1589.

Charts to Uniform Scale, divided into 2,000-yard squares.   Soundings in fathoms.   Heights in feet.

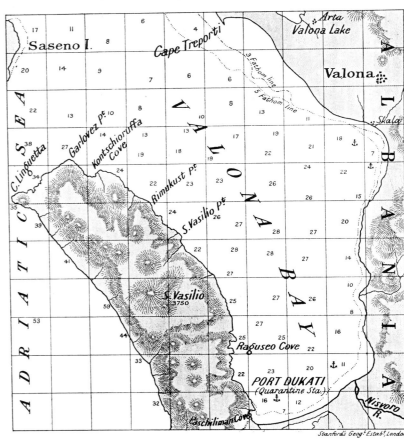

VALONA.

Uniforms.

(*Note.*—A five pointed silver star is worn on lapel of coat.)

INSIGNIA OF RANK ON SLEEVES.   *NOTE.*—STAFF OFFICERS HAVE NO CURL.

| Ammiraglio *Admiral.* | Vice-Ammiraglio. *V.-Admiral.* | Contr'-Ammiraglio. *R.-Admiral.* | Capitano di Vascello. *Captain (senior).* | Capitano di Fregata. *Captain (junior).* | Capitano di Corvetta. *Commander.* | Tenente di Vascello. *Lieut.* | Sottotentete di Vascello. *Sub-Lieut.* | Guardia-marina. *Midshipman.* |

(*) Sotto-Ammiraglio: New rank reported introduced, equivalent to British Commodore, and intermediate between Contr' Ammiraglio and Capitano di Vascello.

Lesser rank Allievo di marina (*Naval Cadet*).

Note.—Primo tenento has a gold band on shoulder strap for 12 years seniority. All lieutenants have stars on their shoulder straps corresponding to their stripes.

Other branches : Ingeguere (*Constructor*). Macchinista (*Engineers*). Medico (*Doctor*), Commissario (*Paymaster*)—with relative rank with the executives, without curl.

Colours : *Constructors*, dark purple ; *Engineers*, black ; *Doctors*, blue ; *Paymasters*, red.

Note.—All officers under arms on duty wear a blue sash over right shoulder, ending in a blue knot at left hip ; worn with belt. Officers on staff duty wear it on opposite shoulder, and without belt. Undress tunic has insignia of rank on shoulder straps, with stars as stripes. Senior lieutenants wear a piece of gold under the stars of shoulder strap.

ITALIAN NAVY.
OFFICIAL TABLE OF NAVAL ORDNANCE.

Official Designation:— Calibre mm/length cal. Mark A=Armstrong, V=Vickers S=. Date of introduction.	381/40 A. V. e S. 1914	305/46 A. e V. 1909	305/40 A. 1900-04	254/45 A. 1907	254/45 V. 1906	254/40 A. 1899-93	203/45 A. 1897	190/45 A. e V. 1908-1906	152/50 A. 1918-1913	152/45 S. 1911	152/40 A. 1899-1916	120/50 A. e V. 1909	120/45 A. 1913-18	102/45 S.-A. 1917	102/35 S. 1914-15	76/50 A. e V. 1909	76/45 S. 1911	76/17 S. 1912
Designation by Calibre, c/m.	38.1	30.479	30.479	25.4	25.4	25.4	20.32	19.05	15.24	15.24	15.24	12	12	10.2	10.2	7.62	7.62	7.62
Calibre, in inches	15	12	12	10	10	10	8	7.5	6	6	6	4.75	4.75	4	4	3	3	3
Lengths — Total, in feet	51.67	47.77	41.707	39.07	38.715	34.699	31.126	29.22	25.94	23.42	20.77	20.38	18.38	15.715	12.247	13.271	11.722	4.593
Lengths — Rifled Bore, in inches	511.7	477.9	383.42	358.4	370.5	341.1	308.9	281.7	256.6	21.92	199.8	204.64	174.64	150.74	114.29	126	107.2	44.88
Lengths — Powder Chamber, in inches	81.5	97.7	92.12	74.91	74.91	55.19	47.4	51.65	44.6	44.6	37.7	28.64	35.03	27.16	23.50	22	25.4	—
Lengths — Bore, in calibres	34.11	37.3	31.95	35.84	37.05	34.11	38.61	37.5	42.77	36.54	33.31	43.31	36.96	37.53	28.46	42	35.73	14.96
No. of Grooves	120	72	48	60	70	42	32	44	36	56	28	36	36	40	32	28	25	24
Twist of Rifling, in calibres	44.927	30	00—600 600—30	30	00—30	30	00—30	00—30	33	36	30	30	30	—	—	20	35.9	22
Total Weight, in tons	83.56	62.99	51.77	34.49	35.339	30.511	19.586	14.478	8.100	7.025	6.503	3.662	4—035	2.327	1.200	1.122	0.698	0.104
Firing Charge — Armour-piercing projectile, lb		346	194	185	185	90.38	51.807	70.987			18.077							
Firing Charge — Common Shell H.E., lb.	326.27	279.9	194	185	185	90.38	51.807	70.987	32.79	30.64	13.077	14.66	9.589	9.479	6.50	3.02	3.571	0.529
Weight — Armour-piercing projectile, lb.	—	997.2	942.7	494	494	494	269	200.39			107.07							
Weight — Shell H.E., lb.	1929	884.4	881.74	489.8	489.8	189.8	256.23	498.5	110.22	103.61	102.38	48.74	48.74	30.31	30.31	14.05	14.05	11.68
Weight — Shrapnel, lb.												55.33	55.33	33.28	33.28	15.08	15.08	11.68
Bursting Charge — Armour-piercing projectile, lb.		16.63	9.79	4.37	4.37	4.37	2.003	2.332			1.014							
Bursting Charge — Shell H.E., lb.	84.85	53.13	53.13	29.86	29.86	29.86	14.704	11.706	5.996	7.528	6.90	2.711	2.711	2.866	2.866	1.102	1.102	0.782
Bursting Charge — Shrapnel, lbs.												0.65	0.65	0.474	0.474	0.236	0.236	0.165
Muzzle Velocity, in ft. secs.	2296.6	2755.9	2346.8	2788.77	2788.77	2411.46	2.559	2788.77	2854	2723	2280	2788	2460	2788	2460	2460	2460	1230
Muzzle Energy —Total tons per sq. inch	20	18.63	15.75	17.71	17.71	15.09	16	17.98	18.37	16.86	13.73	18.37	15.75	18.37	18.37	18.37	15.75	12.47

15" 40 cal. in *Caracciolo* and *Faa' di Bruno*.
12" 46 „ *Duilio* class (2 ships), *G. Cesare* class (2 ships), and *D. Alighieri*.
12" 40 „ *V. Emanuele* class (4 ships).
10" 45 „ *S. Marco* class (2 ships) and *Pisa*.
10" 40 „ *A. di St. Bon* class (2).
8" 45 „ *V. Emanuele* class (4 ships).
7.5" 45 „ *San Marco* class (2), and *Pisa*.
6" 50 „ *Caracciolo, Duilio* class (2 ships).
4.7" 50 „ *Dante Alighieri, Marsala* class (2), *Quarto*, and *Libia*.

Note.—Above list of guns mounted in various classes is unofficial. 12 inch and 7.5 inch guns of unknown types reported to be mounted in "Mobile Batteries."

Torpedoes, Mines, D.C., Air Bombs, &c.

No reliable details available. Torpedoes manufactured by State Arsenals and Whitehead & C., Societa Italiana, Naples.

Colour of Ships.

Battleships, Cruisers, Light Cruisers, Destroyers, are all very light grey. Destroyers have identity letters, taken from their names, painted on bows, *e.g.*, AC = *G. Acerbi*, AU = *Audace*, BR = *P. Bronzetti*, IV = *Impavido*, PL = *R. Pilo*, OR = *V. Orsini*, MT = *A. Mosto*, etc.

Official Classification of Ships.   (C)=for Colonial Service.

"Navi di Battaglio."
1st Class: *Caracciolo*, A. Doria, C. Duilio, C. di Cavour, G. Cesare, Dante Alighieri
2nd Class: V. Emanuele, R. Elena, Roma, Napoli, San Giorgio, San Marco, Pisa
3rd Class: A. di St. Bon, E. Filiberto, Dandolo

Esploratori.—
N. Bixio, Marsala, Quarto, *Leone*, *Tigre*, *Pantera*, *Lince*, *Aquila*, *Nibbio*, *Falco*, *Sparviero*, C. Mirabello, C. A. Racchia, A. Riboty, A. Poerio, G. Pepe, Agordat, Coatit

"Navi Sussidiarie."
1st Class: Sardegna, Sicilia, Re Umberto, Zenson, Cortellazzo, Bronte, Trinacria, Eritrea, Europa
2nd Class: Campania (C), Basilicata (C), Libia, Etruria (C), Lombardia (C), Piemonte (C), Etna, Vulcano, G. Bausan, Bengasi, F. Gioia, A. Vespucci
3rd Class: Faa' di Bruno, A. Magnaghi, Acheronte, Flegetonte, Cocito, Lete, Stige, Eridano, Anteo

4th Class.
S. Caboto (C), E. Carlotto (C), Goito, Tripoli, Minerva, Iride, Montebello
Archimede, Guiliana, Cunfida, Misurata, Tobruk, C. Verri, Ciclope, Atalante
Ercole], Tevere, Garigliano, Verde, Pagano, Miseno, Palinuro

Note.—Destroyers, "Sea-Going Torpedo Boats," Coastal T.B. and Submarines are as listed on subsequent Ship Pages. Above Table merely shows how Official Classification departs from order of Classification adopted for "Fighting Ships." On Ship Pages, tonnages and fuel capacities are stated in *metric* tons.

ITALIAN DOCKYARDS.
Private Yards.
(All undertake Naval Construction).

GIO. ANSALDO & C. (Genoa & Sestri Ponente, also at Cornigliano & Sampierdarena, &c., consists of 28 establishments in various parts of Italy.) Build, engine, and completely equip warships and mercantile vessels of all types. Slips: 3 large and 8 smaller at Sestri Ponente, also three slips at Genoa Harbour, also other slips at Cantiere Savoia, Corrigliano. Area of works: hectares. Number of Employees, 60,000. (Also see Ansaldo-San Giorgio Co.)

FRATELLI ORLANDO & C. (Leghorn). Build and engine warships and mercantile vessels of all types. Are affiliated to Acciaierie di Terni (Armour Plate and Shell Foundry) and Vickers-Terni (Ordnance Works). No. of slips: Docks, one, 451 feet (o.a.)×71½ feet×23 feet. Area of works: hectares. Number of employees:

ODERO & C. (Sestri Ponente, near Genoa). Build and engine warships of all classes. No. of slips: Area of works: . Number of employees: . (Build battleships at Foce, near Genoa). (Above are the three greatest Italian warship-building firms).

ANSALDO-SAN GIORGIO, LTD. (Muggiano, Spezia). Build warships and mercantile vessels. Specialise in construction of Laurenti type submersibles and Diesel engines.
C. & T. T. PATTISON (Naples). Build destroyers, torpedo boats, mine sweepers, &c., also boilers, turbines, &c.
CANTIERE NAVALE FRANCO TOSI (Leghorn & Taranto). Build destroyers, torpedo boats, submarines and mine layers or sweepers. Also boilers, turbines ("Tosi" type), and Diesel engines.
CANTIERE NAVALE RIUNITI (Spezia & Palermo). Build torpedo craft and submarines.

OFFICINE MECCANICHE (Milan & Naples). Build Belluzo turbines and other machinery.
OFFICINE INSUBRI (Milan). Construct large Diesel engines for naval purposes.

S. A. V. I. N. E. M. (Societa Anonima Veneziana Industrie Navale e Meccaniche), Giudeca, Venice. Build boilers, machinery, &c.

ITALIAN WARSHIPS : RECOGNITION SILHOUETTES.

Scale : 1 inch = 160 feet.

ONE FUNNEL.

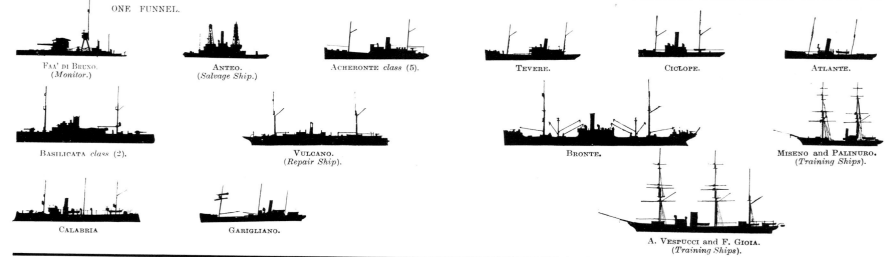

Faa' di Bruno. (Monitor.) — Anteo. (Salvage Ship.) — Acheronte class (5). — Tevere. — Ciclope. — Atlante.
Basilicata class (2). — Vulcano. (Repair Ship). — Bronte. — Miseno and Palinuro. (Training Ships).
Calabria. — Garigliano. — A. Vespucci and F. Gioia. (Training Ships).

Scale : 1 inch = 160 feet.   ITALIAN WARSHIPS : RECOGNITION SILHOUETTES

TWO FUNNELS.

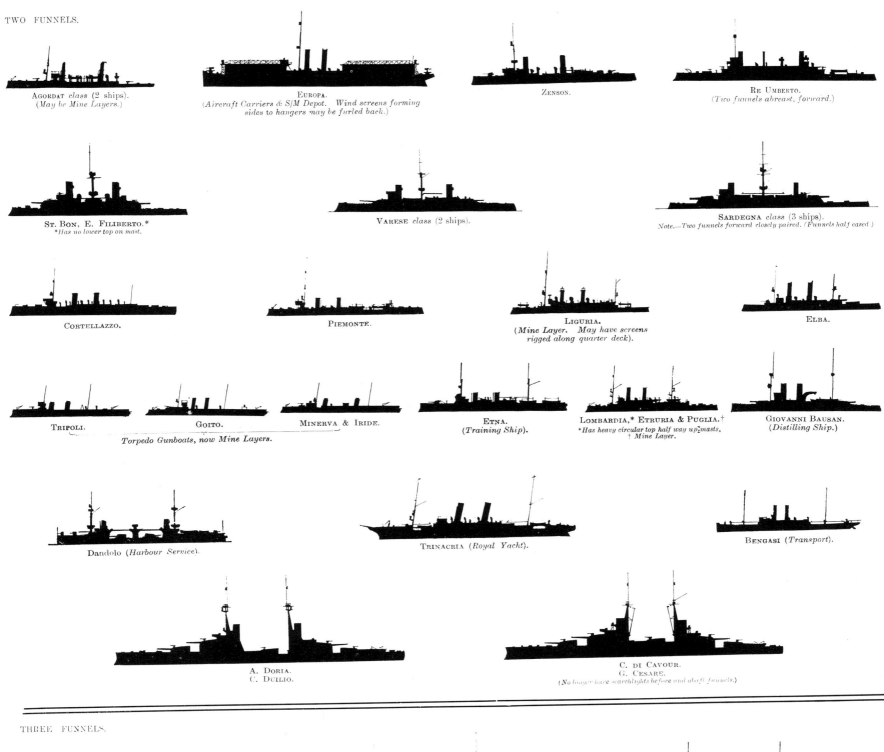

AGORDAT *class* (2 ships).
(*May be Mine Layers.*)

EUROPA.
(*Aircraft Carriers & S/M Depot. Wind screens forming sides to hangers may be furled back.*)

ZENSON.

RE UMBERTO.
(*Two funnels abreast, forward.*)

ST. BON, E. FILIBERTO.*
*Has no lower top on mast.

VARESE *class* (2 ships).

SARDEGNA *class* (3 ships).
Note.—*Two funnels forward closely paired. (Funnels half cased.)*

CORTELLAZZO.

PIEMONTE.

LIGURIA.
(*Mine Layer. May have screens rigged along quarter deck*).

ELBA.

TRIPOLI.   GOITO.   MINERVA & IRIDE.
Torpedo Gunboats, now Mine Layers.

ETNA.
(*Training Ship*).

LOMBARDIA,* ETRURIA & PUGLIA.†
*Has heavy circular top half way up masts.
† Mine Layer.

GIOVANNI BAUSAN.
(*Distilling Ship*.)

DANDOLO (*Harbour Service*).

TRINACRIA (*Royal Yacht*).

BENGASI (*Transport*).

A. DORIA.
C. DUILIO.

C. DI CAVOUR.
G. CESARE.
(*No longer have searchlights before and abaft funnels.*)

THREE FUNNELS.

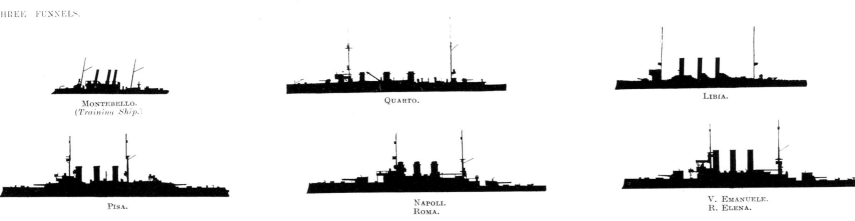

MONTEBELLO.
(*Training Ship.*)

QUARTO.

LIBIA.

PISA.

NAPOLI.
ROMA.

V. EMANUELE.
R. ELENA.

ITALIAN WARSHIPS—RECOGNITION SILHOUETTES

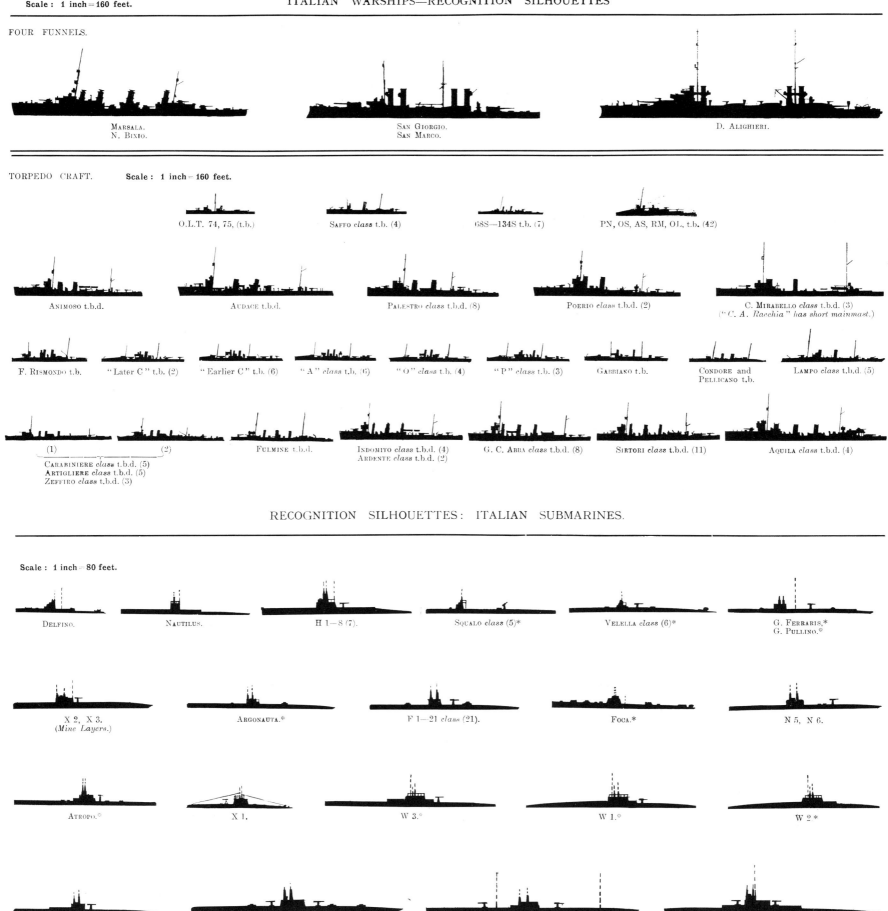

Scale : 1 inch = 160 feet.

FOUR FUNNELS.

MARSALA.
N. BIXIO.

SAN GIORGIO.
SAN MARCO.

D. ALIGHIERI.

TORPEDO CRAFT.   Scale : 1 inch = 160 feet.

O.L.T. 74, 75, (t.b.)

SAFFO class t.b. (4)

688—1348 t.b. (7)

PN, OS, AS, RM, OL, t.b. (42)

ANIMOSO t.b.d.

AUDACE t.b.d.

PALESTRO class t.b.d. (8)

POERIO class t.b.d. (2)

C. MIRABELLO class t.b.d. (3)
("C. A. Racchia" has short mainmast.)

F. RISMONDO t.b.

"Later C" t.b. (2)

"Earlier C" t.b. (6)

"A" class t.b. (6)

"O" class t.b. (4)

"P" class t.b. (3)

GABBIANO t.b.

CONDORE and
PELLICANO t.b.

LAMPO class t.b.d. (5)

(1)   (2)
CARABINIERE class t.b.d. (5)
ARTIGLIERE class t.b.d. (5)
ZEFFIRO class t.b.d. (3)

FULMINE t.b.d.

INDOMITO class t.b.d. (4)
ARDENTE class t.b.d. (2)

G. C. ABBA class t.b.d. (8)

SIRTORI class t.b.d. (11)

AQUILA class t.b.d. (4)

RECOGNITION SILHOUETTES: ITALIAN SUBMARINES.

Scale : 1 inch = 80 feet.

DELFINO.

NAUTILUS.

H 1—8 (7).

SQUALO class (5)*

VELELLA class (6)*

G. FERRARIS,*
G. PULLINO.⊕

X 2, X 3.
(Mine Layers.)

ARGONAUTA.*

F 1—21 class (21).

FOCA.*

N 5, N 6.

ATROPO.⊕

X 1.

W 3.⊕

W 1.⊕

W 2 *

N 1—4 class (4).

A. BARBARIGO class (4).

G. PACINOTTI.

P. MICCA class (6).

* These boats may be
    (a) Out of commission or for training duties ;
    (b) Awaiting disposal ;
    (c) Under survey for sale ;
    (d) Condemned for sale.

1912 ITALIAN DREADNOUGHTS.

(DUILIO CLASS— 2 SHIPS).
CAIO DUILIO (April, 1913) and ANDREA DORIA (March, 1913).
Normal displacement, 24,500 tons. Complement, 1074.

Length (*p.p.*) 554·3 feet. Beam, 91·8 feet. *Mean* draught, 30·7 feet. Length *over all*, 575 feet, 9ins.

Guns (Armstrong or Vickers) :
13—12 in., 46 cal. (A⁵).
16—6 inch (50 cal.)
13—14 pdr.*
6—14 pdr. (A.A.)
2 M.G.
4 landing.
Torpedo tubes (18 inch) :
2 broadside (*submerged*).
1 stern (*submerged*).
*3—14 pdr. temporarily
  removed during war.

Armour (Terni) :
9¾"–8" Belt (amidships) ▦
5" Belt (ends)..............
1¾" and 1 ¾" Decks .....
6¾" Lower deck side ......
9½" Barbettes .... ▦
11 Turrets to these ...... ▦
6¾" Battery.................
11" Conning tower (fore) . ▦
6¼" Conning tower (aft) . ▦

ANDREA DORIA.

Note.

To distinguish from *C. di Cavour* class, note that *both* tripod masts are before funnels. Funnels are also *equal* in height. Amidships triple barbette is on same level as *quarter-deck* triple—compare *Cavour* class where it is on level with forecastle triple. General appearance much lighter than *Cavours*.

Ahead :
5—12 in.
4—6 in.

Astern :
5—12 in.
4—6 in.

Broadside : 13—12 in., 8—6 in.

Machinery : Parsons turbine. 4 screws. Boilers : 20 Yarrow. Designed S. H.P. 24,000 = 22 kts., but actually need 33,000–35,000 S.H.P. for this speed. Coal : *normal* 1000 tons ; *maximum* 1200 tons and 800 tons oil fuel = about 4000 miles at 10 kts. and 2600 miles at 19 kts.

†*Gunnery Notes* : (As *C. di Cavour* class on next page. Range-finders mounted to the rear of roof of each barbette
†*Torpedo Notes* : (shield in armoured hoods and over each C.T. 3 inch (14 pdrs.) are 50 cal. Armstrong or 60 cal. Vickers. 8 searchlights. †All details unofficial.

Name	Builder	Machinery	Laid down	Completed	Trials H.P.=kts.	Boilers	Best recent speed
Caio Duilio	Castellamare D.Y.	Ansaldo	Apr.'12	1915	35,000 = 22.	Yarrow	
Andrea Doria	Spezia	Ansaldo	Mar.'12	May '15	32,000 = 21.5.	Yarrow	

General Notes.—Are improved type of *C. di Cavour* design, 16—6 inch being substituted for 18—4·7 inch. Otherwise—and excepting altered appearance—there is very little difference between the classes. Designed by Engineer–Gen. Masdea. These ships exceed their designed displacement of 22,500 tons in the same manner as *Cavour* and *Cesare* and require to develop 10,000 S.H.P. in excess of designed S.H.P., to reach their designed speed.

CAIO DUILIO. Has had a circular F.C. or R.F. top added to fore tripod mast. In summer of 1918 had no fore topmast.

1910 ITALIAN DREADNOUGHTS. Nos. 4, 3, 2

CONTE DI CAVOUR (Aug., 1911), GIULIO CESARE (Oct., 1911)
LEONARDO DA VINCI (Nov., 1911).

Normal displacement, 22,000 tons. Complement, 957.

Length (*waterline*), 575½ feet. Beam, 91¾ feet. *Mean* draught, 27¾ feet. Length *over all*, 577 feet.

Guns (see *Notes*) :
13—12 in., 46 cal. (·1⁵).
18—4·7 inch.
14—3 inch.
Torpedo tubes (18 inch) :
2 broadside (*submerged*).
1 stern (*above water*).

Armour (see *Notes*) :
9¾" Belt (amidships) ... aaa
4" Belt (ends) .... d
1¾" Deck ....
Protection to vitals ... aaaa
8¾" Lower deck redoubt aa
9½" Barbettes .... aa
9½" Turrets to these ... aa
5" Battery c
11" Conning tower ...... aaa

GIULIO - CESARE.

Ahead :
—12 in.

Astern :
5—12 in.

Broadside : 13—12. in.

Machinery : Parsons Turbine. 4 screws. Boilers : *see Notes*. Designed H.P. 24,000 = 22·5 knots.
Coal : *normal* 1000 tons ; *maximum* 2500 tons.

Gunnery Notes.—L. da V., Vickers ; others, Elswick.
Armour Notes.—C. di C., Terni ; G.C., Bethlehem ; L. da V., Midvale.
Torpedo Notes.—Bullivant Net defence to all.

LEONARDO DA VINCI

Note.

Third ship in this class, **LEONARDO DA VINCI**, was sunk by explosion at Taranto in August 1916. She was refloated 18 August, 1919.

Name	Builder	Machinery	Laid down	Completed	Trials	Boilers	Best recent speed
C. di Cavour	Spezia	Orlando	Aug. 10	'15		Blechynden	
G. Cesare	Odero	Odero	1910	'14		Babcock	
L. da Vinci	Ansaldo	Ansaldo	1911	'14		Blechynden	

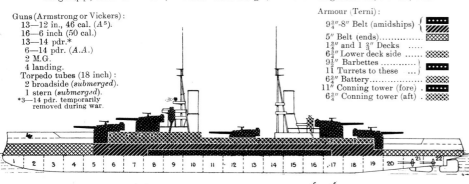

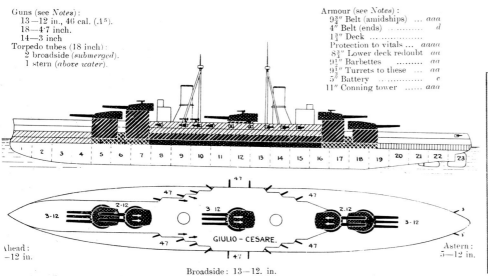

1909 ITALIAN DREADNOUGHT.

DANTE ALIGHIERI (August, 1910).*

Normal displacement, 20,500 tons. Complement, 991.

Length (p.p.) 519·7 feet. Beam, 87·4 feet. *Mean* draught, 30·1 feet. Length *over all*, 549·5 feet.

* Official Italian List gives 20 Oct., 1910, as launching date.

Guns (Elswick) :
12—12 in., 46 cal. (A⁵)
20—4·7 inch, 50 cal.
12—14 pdr., 50 cal.⊙
6—14 pdr.. AA.
2 M.G.
4 landing.
Torpedo tubes (18 inch.) :
2 broadside (*submerged*).
1 stern (*submerged*).

⊙ 3—14 pdr. temporarily removed during war.

Armour (Terni) :
9⅞″ Belt (amidships)
6″ Belt (forward)
4¾″ Belt (aft)
1¼″ & 1⅛″ Decks
8¾″ Lower deck redoubt
9″ Barbettes
11″ Turrets to these
4″ Secondary Turrets (4)
4″ Batteries
11″ Conning tower
8″ C.T. (aft)

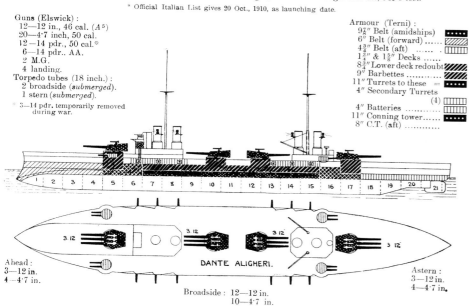

Ahead :
3—12 in.
4—4·7 in.

DANTE ALIGHERI.

Astern :
3—12 in.
4—4·7 in.

Broadside : 12—12 in.
10—4·7 in.

Machinery : Parsons turbine. 4 screws. Boilers : 23 Blechynden. Designed S.H.P. 24,000 = 23 kts, but actually requires about 31,000 H.P. for this speed. Coal : *normal* 1000 tons ; *maximum* 2200 tons, + 300 tons oil fuel = 4520 miles at 10 kts. and about 3000 miles at 19 kts.

⊙ *Gunnery Notes.*—Triple turrets are to Armstrong design, hydraulic power with special Ansaldo electric gear as reserve. 4·7 inch reported to have been fitted with improved breech mechanism in 1913-14 to give faster rate of fire.

* Not from any official source.

Name	Builder	Machinery	Laid down	Com-pleted	Trials H.P = kts.	Boilers.	Best recent speed
D. Alighieri	Castellamare	Ansaldo	June '09	Sep. '12	31,980 = 23·8	Blechynden	

General Notes.—Designed by Engineer-Gen. Masdea. Was originally designed for 19,500 tons displacement, with a draught of 28¼ feet *mean*, but alterations made during construction resulted in an addition of 1000 tons to displacement and about 2½ feet to draught. Consequently, she only attains her designed speed with difficulty. Triple steering gear, steam, special Ansaldo electric gear and manual power.

Detail view of amidships triple barbette.   *Photo by courtesy of "Daily Mirror"*

1901-03 ITALIAN BATTLESHIPS.

(V. Emanuele Class—4 Ships.)
VITTORIO EMANUELE (Oct., 1904), REGINA ELENA (June, 1904), NAPOLI (Sept., 1905), ROMA (April, 1907).

Displacement, 12660 tons. Complement, 743.

Length (p.p.), 435 feet. Beam, 73⅓ feet. { Maximum draught, 27⅓ feet. } Length *over all*, 475 feet 5″.
{ Mean ,, 25⅓ ,, }

Guns :
2—12 inch, 40 cal.
12—8 inch, 45 cal.
16—14 pdr., 40 cal.
4—14 pdr., A.A.
2—3 pdr.
2 Maxims.
2 landing.
Torpedo tubes (18 in.) :
2 *submerged* (broadside).

Armour (Terni) :
9·8″ Belt
4″ Belt (ends)
2·4″ Deck (reinforcing)
8″ Bulkheads
8″ Barbettes (N.C.)
8″ Turrets
8″ Lower deck (side)
2″ Lower deck (bow)
6″ Secondary turrets (6)
3¼″ Tertiary battery
10″ Conning tower (N.C.)

V. Emanuele.   Note crows' nests high on each mast.

Note.

R. Elena as V. Emanuele, but differs thus : (a) No crows' nests high up on masts. (b) Forward. S.L. platforms rather higher up foremast. (c) Flying bridge over C.T. as shown on Silhouettes for V. Emanuele and R. Elena.

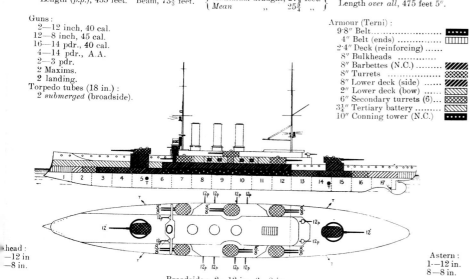

Ahead :
—12 in
—8 in.

Astern :
1.—12 in.
8—8 in.

Broadside : 2—12 in., 6—8 in.

Machinery : 2 sets 4 cylinder vertical inverted triple expansion. Designed H.P. 19,000 = 21·5 kts. 2 screws. Boilers : *V. Emanuele* and *R. Elena*, 28 Belleville ; *Napoli*, 22 Babcock & Wilcox, and *Roma*, 18 Babcock & Wilcox. Coal : *normal* 1000 tons ; *maximum* 2000 tons.

Aircraft and Gunnery Notes.—14 pdr. A.A. are mounted singly on crowns of 12-inch turrets and central 8-inch turrets, but *Roma* has no A.A. guns or crown of fore 12-inch turret. R.F. positions over fore C.T. and behind each central 8-inch turret, 2—14 pdr. on each 8 in. turret, the 14 pdr. battery ports being plated up now. 4 large S.L. in 2 tops on each mast and small S.L. at after end of boat deck.

ROMA (*Napoli* same appearance).   Note different shape of funnels. Foremast is *against* fore funnel, and has F.C. top. "Starfish" low on mainmast.

Name	Builder	Machinery	Laid down	Com-pleted	Last Refit	First Trials : 24 hours	6 hours	Boilers	Best recent speed
V. Emanuele	Castellamare	Orlando	Sept.'01	Sept.'07		16,000 = 21	19,424 = 21·5	Belleville	
R. Elena	Spezia	Odero	Sept.'01	May,'07		15,473 = 20·33	19,298 = 22·7	Belleville	21·9
Napoli	Castellamare	Hawthorn Gup.	Oct.'03	Nov.'08		15,400 = 20·3	20,400 = 22·1	Babcock	
Roma	Spezia	Ansaldo	Sept.'03	Dec.'08		16,000 = 20·5	21,900 = 22	Babcock	22

General Notes.— Designed by the late General Cuniberti. Average cost per ship, £1,000,000. The *Napoli* and *Roma* have less superstructure and are somewhat lighter, but have the same horse power (not fitted as flagships).

AMMIRAGLIO DI ST. BON (April, 1897), & **EMANUELE FILIBERTO** (Sept., 1897).
Displacement, 9800 tons. Complement, 541. 344½ (p.p.) × 69¼ × 24¾ feet (max. draught.) Guns:
4—10 inch, 40 cal., 8—6 inch, 40 cal. (removed temporarily), 8—4·7 inch (removed temporarily)
in A. di St. Bon, 4—14 pdr. AA., 8—6 pdr., 2—1 pdr.; in E.F. 6—14 pdr., 4—14 pdr., AA.,
2—1 pdr. In both, 1 M.G., 1 landing, and 4—18 inch tubes above water. Armour (Harvey
nickel) : 9¾″ Belt (amidships), 4″ Belt (ends), 3″ Deck, 6″ Bulkheads, 6″ Lower deck side, 7″
Barbettes, 6″ Hoods to these (fronts), 6″ Battery, 6″ Conning tower. 2 screws. Boilers : 12 cylindrical.
Designed H.P. 13,500 = 18 kts. Coal : 1000 tons.

Re Umberto after 1916-17 reconstruction.   (Photo by courtesy of the Ministry of Marine).

SICILIA (1891). 13,298 tons. **SARDEGNA** (1890). 13,822 tons.   **RE UMBERTO** (1887,
rebuilt 1916-17). 13,251 tons. Complement about 730. Guns (Armstrong) : 4—old 13·5 inch (40
cal.), *4—14 pdr. AA. Torpedo tubes : 5 above water. Armour (steel) : 4″ Belt with 4½″-2″ Deck
+ 2¾″ Bulkheads, 14¼″ Barbettes, 11¾″ Conning tower.   I.H.P. 15,000 = 20 kts.   Boilers : 16-18
cylindrical. Coal : about 1400 tons.   * Removed from Re Umberto.

(BRIN CLASS—2 SHIPS).
BENEDETTO BRIN (Nov., 1901), & **REGINA MARGHERITA** (May, 1901).
Displacement 13,427 tons. Complement 720.
Length (p.p.), 426½ feet. Beam, 78 feet. Mean draught, 27¼ feet.   Length over all, 455 feet.

Guns :
4—12 in., 40 cal. (A.A.A.A.).
4—8 inch (A).
12—6 inch
20—12 pdr.
2—1 pdr.
2 Maxims.
Torpedo tubes (18 inch) :
4 submerged.
(With ammunition 1473 tons.)

Armour (Terni) :
6″ Belt .... a
2″ Belt (at ends) .... f
3″ Armour deck (reinforcing)
 Protection to vitals ...... = aa
8″ Barbettes and bulk-
 head (N.C.) .... a
8″ Hoods to big guns (N.C.) = aa
6″ Casemates (N.C.) ...... b
6″ Battery (N.C.) .... b
12″ Conning tower (N.C.) ... aaa
(Total 3155 tons.)

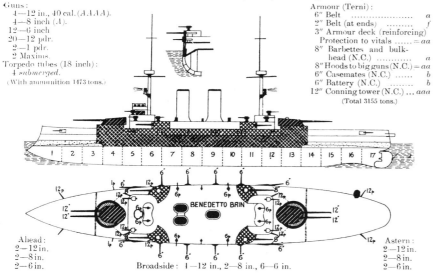

Ahead :
2—12 in.
2—8 in.
2—6 in.
Astern :
2—12 in.
2—8 in.
2—6 in.
Broadside : 1—12 in., 2—8 in., 6—6 in.

Machinery : About 1,600 tons. 2 sets 4 cylinder triple expansion. 2 screws. Boilers : (26) Brin,
Belleville ; Margherita, Niclausse. Designed H.P. natural draught 15,500 = 18 kts. ; forced 19,000 = 20
kts Coal : normal 1,000 ; maximum 2,000 tons.   Nominal radius 10,000 at 10 kts.
Gunnery Notes.—Big guns : central pivot mountings, load at any elevation.
 Arcs of fire : Big guns 240°, 8 in. and end 6 in. 135° from axial line ; other 6 in. 125°.
Armour Notes.—The main belt is 10½ feet wide. Armoured main deck 1¾″ extends whole length of
ship.
Engineering Notes.—Machinery and boilers weigh 1603 tons.

Name	Builder	Machinery	Laid down	Com-pleted	Last Refit	First Trials		Boilers	Best recent speed
B. Brin	Castellamare	Hawthorn Gup.	Feb. '99	1904		15,600 = 18	20,478 = 20·4	Belleville	
R. Margherita	Spezia	Ansaldo	Nov. '98	1901		17,600 = 18·5	19,822 = 20·2	Niclausse	

General Notes.—Freeboard, 21 feet forward. Weight of hull, 6195 tons. Forward funnels paired
abreast. Average cost per ship, complete, £1,150,000.

Benedetto Brin destroyed by internal explosion at Brindisi 27 September 1915.
Regina Margherita mined and sunk off Valona 11 December 1916.

SARDEGNA   SICILIA
(Funnels of the *Re Umberto*, as photo.)

RE UMBERTO before 1916-17 reconstruction.   No photo available of *Sardegna* and *Sicilia* ; they are as
above photo but have half-cased funnels as sketched.   For description v. preceding column.

DANDOLO (1878) (reconstructed 1897). 12,262 tons. Complement, 281. Guns : 4—10 in., 40 cal.,
7—6 in. (3 of these temporarily removed), 5—4·7 in. (all these temporarily removed), 11—14 pdr.
AA., 16—6 pdr., 2—1pdr. Tubes : 4—18 inch above water. Armour (steel) : Belt amidships,
21½″, Turrets (Harvey), 10″.   H.P. 7400 = 15·5 kts.   4 return flame boilers.   2 screws.   720
tons coal.

Torpedo Schoolship. **ITALIA** (1880).   Displacement 15,654 tons.   Complement 675.

Length (waterline), 400¼ feet. Beam, 75½ feet. Maximum draught, 33 feet.

 Guns : 4—old 100 ton, 8—old 6 in., 4—old 4·7, 32 small guns. Armour : No belt, 3″ deck and 19″
steel redoubt on upper deck for big guns.   Original speed between 17 and 18 kts. Coal about 3000 tons
maximum.
Note—No longer in commission 1919.

BENEDETTO BRIN.   *Photo by favour of C. de Grave Sells, Esq.*

REGINA MARGHERITA.   *Photo, Bougault, Toulon.*
Difference—Brin has much shorter funnels than *Margherita.*

1905-07 ITALIAN ARMOURED CRUISERS.

(SAN GIORGIO CLASS—2 SHIPS.)

SAN GIORGIO (July, 1908), **SAN MARCO** (December, 1908).

Displacement $\begin{cases} \textit{San Giorgio, } 10,200 \text{ tons} \\ \textit{San Marco, } 11,000 \text{ tons} \end{cases}$ Complement $\begin{cases} \textit{S.G. } 689 \\ \textit{S.M. } 691 \end{cases}$

Length (*p.p.*). 429 feet 11 in. Beam, 69 feet. $\begin{cases} \textit{S.G. mean} \text{ draught: } 24 \text{ feet, } \textit{max. } 26\frac{1}{4} \text{ feet.} \\ \textit{S.M. mean} \quad ,, \quad 25\frac{1}{2} \text{ feet, } \textit{max. } 27 \text{ feet.} \end{cases}$

Length *over all*, $462\frac{1}{4}$ feet.

SAN MARCO.

Guns :
4—10 inch, 45 cal.
8—7·5 inch, 45 cal.
10—14 pdr.
6—14 pdr. AA.
2—3 pdr.
2 machine.
2 landing.
Torpedo tubes (18 inch) :
2 *submerged* (broadside).
1 *submerged* (stern).

Note to Plans.

Now rigged with *two* masts.

Armour (*S.M.*, Midvale ;
S.G., Terni).
8″ Belt (amidships) ...
$2\frac{1}{4}$″ Belt (ends)
$1\frac{3}{4}$″ & $1\frac{1}{2}$″ Decks.........
7″ Lower deck redoubt
8″ Main barbettes ...
$5\frac{1}{4}$″ Turrets to these...
7″ Citadel ....
$6\frac{1}{4}$″ Secondary turrets
$9\frac{3}{4}$″ Conning towers (4)

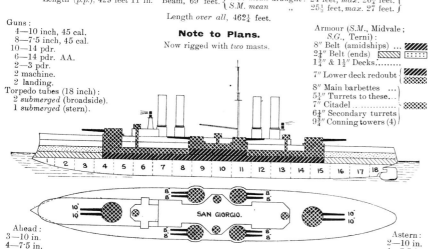

SAN GIORGIO.

Ahead :
3—10 in.
4—7·5 in.

Astern :
2—10 in.
4—7·5 in.

Broadside : 4—10 in., 4—7·5 in.

Machinery : *S. Marco*, Parsons turbine ; 4 screws. *S. Giorgio*, 2 sets 4 cylinder inverted triple expansion ; 2 screws. Boilers : various. See *Notes*. Designed H.P., *S. Giorgio*, 18,000 I.H.P.=22·5 kts. ; *S. Marco*, 20,000 S.H.P.=23 kts. Coal : *normal* 700 tons ; *maximum* 1570 tons. Endurance : at 10 kts., 6270 miles for *San Giorgio*, 4800 miles for *San Marco* ; 2640 miles at 20 kts. for *San Giorgio*, about 2500 miles at $21\frac{1}{4}$ kts. for *San Marco*.

Gunnery Notes.—All guns electrically controlled. Central pivot mountings. Fore 10 inch, 31 feet above waterline ; after 10 inch, 22 feet ; 8 inch guns 22 feet above water. Armoured fire-control towers between 7·5 inch barbettes. (These details are *not* official.)

SAN GIORGIO.

Name.	Builder.	Machinery.	Laid down.	Completed.	Trials full power		Boilers.	Best recent speed
					H.P.	Kts.		
S. Giorgio	Castellamare D.Y.	Ansaldo	May,'05	June'10	19,595	= 23	14 Blechynden	
S. Marco	Castellamare D.Y.	Ansaldo	Jan.,'07	July'10	23,030	= 23·75	14 Babcock	

General Notes.—Designed by Engineer Lieut-Gen. Masdea. In 1913, *S. Giorgio* grounded badly off C. Posillipo (Bay of Naples), but was salved and repaired. She was again badly damaged by stranding in Straits of Messina early in 1914.

To distinguish between these two ships note the following differences :

SAN GIORGIO.
Side built up under fore bridges into superstructure.
FOREMAST : has small top with wide yard under same. Topmast is *abaft*. Both yards wide and far apart. This mast is rather shorter than main mast.
Searchlights on bridge between foremast and 1st funnel.
1ST FUNNEL : has no searchlight platforms.
2ND FUNNEL : searchlights *low* on *after* side.
MAINMAST : has box top.
3RD FUNNEL : bridge across fore side.
4TH FUNNEL : searchlights *low* (on after side).
ALL FUNNELS : *half-cased* for about quarter of height.

SAN MARCO.
Side not built up under fore bridges.
FOREMAST : has no top. Two narrow yards` close together and high up on topmast. Topmast is *before* mast. Mast is equal in height to mainmast.
1ST FUNNEL : Searchlights built off fore side.
2ND FUNNEL : searchlights *high* on *fore* side.
MAINMAST : has no top.
3RD FUNNEL : no bridge.
4TH FUNNEL : searchlights *high* (on after side).
ALL FUNNELS : *plain* with low berthings.

1905. ITALIAN ARMOURED CRUISER.

PISA (Sept., 1907).

Displacement, 10,600 tons. Complement, 685.

Length (*p.p.*), $426\frac{1}{2}$ feet. Beam, 68 feet 11 ins. *Mean* draught $24\frac{1}{2}$ feet. *Maximum* draught, $25\frac{1}{2}$ feet.

Length *over all*, 460 feet 11 ins.

Corrections to Plans.

Now has foremast with R.F. top and searchlight bridge across fore side of first funnel.

Guns (Vickers) :
4—10 inch, 45 cal.
8—7·5 inch, 45 cal.
14—14 pdr., 50 cal.
6—14 pdr. (AA)
2—3 pdr.
2 M.G.
2 landing.
Torpedo tubes (18 inch) :
2 *submerged* (broadside)
1 *submerged* (stern)

Armour (Vickers) :
8″ Belt (amidships) ......
$3\frac{1}{2}$″ Belt (ends) ...
$1\frac{3}{4}$″ & $1\frac{1}{2}$″ Decks ....
7″ Lower deck redoubt

$6\frac{1}{2}$″ Main barbettes ...
8″ Turrets to these......
7″ Citadel ....
7″ Secondary turrets ..
7″ Conning tower ......

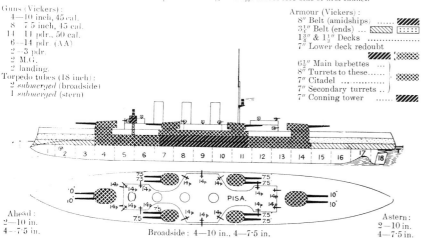

PISA.

Ahead :
2—10 in.
4—7·5 in.

Broadside : 4—10 in., 4—7·5 in.

Astern :
2—10 in.
4—7·5 in.

Machinery : 2 sets 4 cylinder inverted triple expansion. 2 screws. Boilers : 22 Belleville. Designed H.P. 20,000=23 kts. Coal : *normal* 680 tons ; *maximum* 1570 tons. Endurance : 6,270 miles at 10 kts., 2,300 miles at $21\frac{1}{4}$ kts.

Gunnery Notes.—All guns electrically controlled. Central pivot mountings. Guns 22 feet above water.

Name.	Builder.	Machinery.	Laid down.	Completed.	Trials		Boilers.	Best recent speed
Pisa	Orlando, Leghorn	Orlando	July,'05	Dec.,'01	24 hrs.	=21·4 kts.	Belleville	
					6 hrs. 20,528	=23·3 ,,		

general Notes.— Designed by Engineer-General Orlando. The *San Giorgio* class (v. preceding page) is a slightly enlarged *Pisa*. A sister-ship, *Amalfi*, lost in the war, torpedoed by Austrian submarine 17 July 1915.

Note.

The addition of a foremast to this Armoured Cruiser, during the War, has considerably changed her appearance. It is possible for her to be mistaken now for one of the two Battleships, *Victor Emanuele* and *Regina Elena*. *Pisa* can easily be picked out by these features : (*a*) flush-decked hull from end to end ; (*b*) hull not recessed for end-on fire of beam turrets ; (*c*) main barbettes close to central superstructure ; (*d*) only two small turrets slightly sponsoned, on each beam ; (*e*) foremast well away from fore funnel ; (*f*) searchlight bridge across fore funnel ; (*g*) funnels thicker and not so high as those in *V. Emanuele* class ; (*h*) small space between mainmast and third funnel ; (*i*) superstructure abaft mainmast very long ; (*j*) sloping stern with sternwalk.

F. FERRUCCIO.   *Photo, Civicchioni.*

VARESE (Aug., 1899), **FRANCESCO FERRUCCIO** (April, 1902). Displacement, 7350 tons. Complement 552. Length (*p.p.*), 344 feet. Beam, 59¾ feet. *Maximum draught, about* 24 feet. Guns: 1—10 inch, 45 cal., 2—8 inch, 45 cal., 14—6 inch, 40 cal. (12 temporarily removed during war), 6—14 pdr., 5—14 pdr. AA., 1 machine, 2—3 pdr., 1 lar.ding. Torpedo tubes (18 inch): 4 *above water*, in 6 inch casemates. Armour (Terni): 6″ Belt (amidships), 3″ Belt ends, 1½″ Deck, 6″ Lower deck (redoubt), 6″ Barbettes (N.C.), 6″ Hoods to these (N.C.), 6″ Battery (N.C.), 5″ Battery bulkheads, 6″ Conning tower (N.C.). Machinery: 2 sets triple expansion. 2 screws. Boilers (24): *Varese*, 24 Belleville; *F. Ferruccio*, 24 Niclausse. Designed H.P. 13,500 = 20 kts. Coal: *normal* 650 tons; *maximum* 1215 tons.

General Notes:—Varese built by Orlando, 1898—1901. *F. Ferruccio* at Venice, 1899—1904. Made about 20 kts. on trials, but present speed about 17 kts. *G. Garibaldi* of this class lost during the war. Torpedoed by Austrian submarine 18 July 1915.

Old Cruiser (Non-effective).

No mainmast now.)

VETTOR PISANI (1895). Old Cruiser of 7250 tons. Complement, 400. Guns: Removed. Armour (Harvey): 6″–4½″ Belt, 1½″ Deck, 6″ Lower deck side and Battery, 6″ Conning tower; vertical plating may have been stripped from hull. H.P. 13,000 = 18·6 kts. now. 8 cylindrical boilers. Fuel: Oil only.

Note.—Sister ship *Zenson* (ex-*Carlo Alberto*) now Transport; as also is another old Cruiser, *Cortellazzo* (ex-*Marco Polo*), of a different type. Both these converted Cruisers are listed as Miscellaneous Ships on later pages,

---

ITALIAN NAVY.   **1913** Italian (Colonial) Cruisers.

BASILICATA.   *Photo by courtesy of the Minister of Marine.*

BASILICATA (July, 1914) *and* **CAMPANIA** (July, 1914). Displacement, 2480 tons (sheathed and coppered). Complement, 240. Length (*p.p.*) 249·4 feet. Beam, 41⅓ feet. *Max. draught,* 16¾ feet. Length *over all,* 272·3 feet.

Guns:
6—6 inch, 45 cal.*
2 - 14 pdr.*
3—14 pdr. AA.
Torpedo tubes:
2 *above water.*
* *These guns temporarily removed during war. May not yet be remounted.*

Armour:
1″ Deck ...
2″ Conning tower......

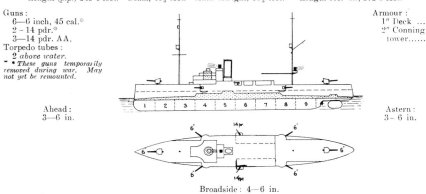

Ahead:
3—6 in.

Astern:
3– 6 in.

Broadside: 4—6 in.

Machinery: 2 sets vertical triple expansion. 2 screws. 4 cylindrical boilers. Designed H.P. 5000 = 16·5 kts. (*not attained on trials*). Coal: *normal* 200 tons, *full load* 500 tons = 4300 miles at 10 kts. and about 2000 miles at 15 kts.

Name	Builder	Machinery	Laid down	Completed	Trials	Boilers	Best recent speed
Basilicata	Castellamare D.Y.		Aug. '13	Aug. '17	About 5000 H.P. = 15·7 kts. {	Cyl.	
Campania	Castellamare D.Y.		Aug. '13	Sept. '16		Cyl.	

General Notes.—Were built for Colonial Service. Both were built in tandem on one slip, and successively launched on the same day. Are an improved *Calabria* type. *Basilicata* destroyed internal explosion at Port Said 13 August 1919.

1911 ITALIAN (SCOUT) CRUISERS. (Mine Layers.)

Note.—These two Ships and "Quarto" (v. next page) are officially rated as "Esploratori" (Scouts) with the Destroyers (or Flotilla Leaders) of over 1000 tons.

(NINO BIXIO CLASS—2 SHIPS).

MARSALA (March, 1912), **NINO BIXIO** (Dec., 1911).

Displacement, 3,500 tons. Complement, 298.

Length (*p.p.*), 429·8 feet. Beam, 42·8 feet. *Mean* draught, 13·4 feet. Length *over all,* 460 feet

Guns:
6—4·7 inch (50 cal.)
6—3 inch (14 pdr.)
2—2 pdr. AA.
Torpedo tubes (18 inch):
2 *above water.*
Also mine-laying gear.)

Armour:
1½″ Deck (amidships)
¾″ Deck (ends) ......

MARSALA. To distinguish, note (a) only *one* top on foremast; (b) only one yard, high up on fore topmast; (c) main topmast removed, leaving old top standing as truck of mainmast *over* yard; (d) Searchlights to port and starboard of *fourth* funnel.

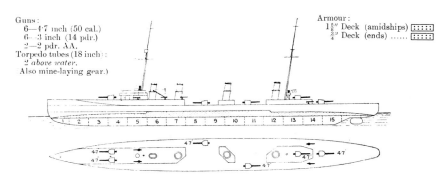

Machinery: Curtis turbine. 3 screws. Boilers: 14 Blechynden (12 oil-burning, 2 coal-burning). Designed S.H.P. 22,500 = 28 kts. Fuel capacity: 130 tons coal + 520 tons oil = 3000 miles at 10 kts.

Name	Builder	Machinery	Laid down	Completed	Trials kts.	Boilers	Best recent speed
Marsala	Castellamare D.Y.	Off. Mecc, Naples	Feb. '11	Sept. '14	= 27·3	Blechynden	
Nino Bixio	Castellamare D.Y.		Feb. '11	May '14		Blechynden	

General Notes.—Carry 200 blockade mines. Designed by Engineer-General Rota.

NINO BIXIO. To distinguish note the following: (a) *three* tops on foremast (lowest with searchlights) and yard under upper top; (b) pole mainmast shorter than that in *Marsala* with short yard and top under yard; (d) searchlights to port and starboard of *third* funnel.

1909 ITALIAN SCOUT CRUISER (**Mine Layer**).

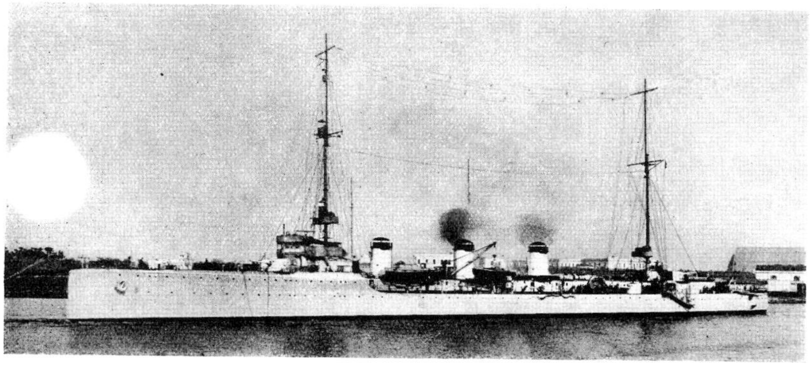

QUARTO (Aug., 1911).

Displacement, 3,280 tons. Complement, 253.

Length (*p.p.*), 413·4 feet. Beam, 42·1 feet. *Mean* draught, 13 feet. Length *over all*, 431¾ feet.

Guns:
6—4·7 inch (50 cal.)
6—3 inch (14 pdr.)
2—2 pdr. AA.
Torpedo tubes (18 inch):
2 *above water*.
(Also mine-laying gear.)

Armour:
1⅛″ Deck (amidships)
¾″ Deck (ends)

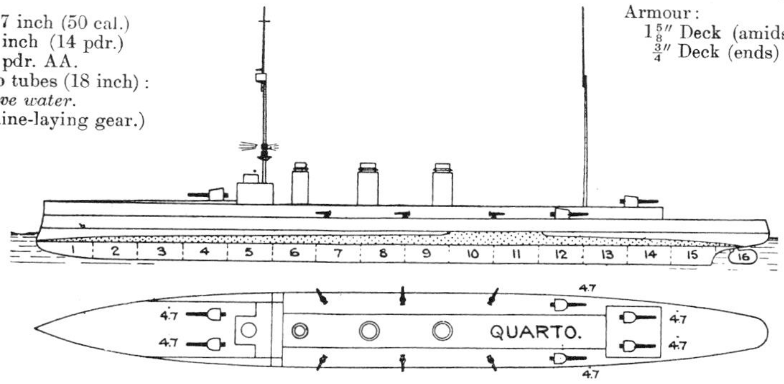

Machinery: Parsons turbine. 4 screws. Boilers: 10 Blechynden (8 oil-burning, 2 coal-burning). Designed S.H.P. 25,000 = 28 kts. Fuel capacity: *maximum*, 50 tons coal + 490 tons oil = 3270 miles at 10 kts., or 1220 miles at 25·7 kts.

Name	*Builder*	*Machinery*	*Laid down*	*Com-pleted*	*Trials* *H.P.*		*kts.*	*Boilers*	*Best recent speed*
Quarto	Venice Y.	Odero	Oct.'09	Sep.'12	28,400	=	28·6	Blechynden	29·5

General Notes.—Carries 200 blockade mines. Designed by Engineer-Col. Truccone.

1907 ITALIAN CRUISER.

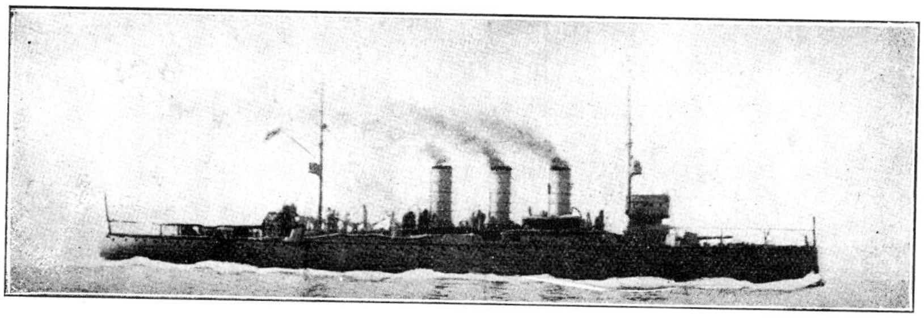

LIBIA (ex Turkish *Drama*, Nov., 1912). 4500 tons. Complement, 317. Dimensions: 340 (*o.a.*) × 47½ × 16 feet. Armament: 2—6 inch, 45 cal., 8—4·7 inch, 50 cal., 2—14 pdr. AA., 6—1 pdr. 2—18 inch tubes (*above water*). Deck, 4″. Designed H.P. 12,500 = 22 kts. 16 Niclausse boilers. Coal: *normal* 275 tons, *maximum* 640 tons. Endurance: 4500 miles at 10 kts. Built and engined by Ansaldo. Was begun by Ansaldo for Turkish Navy in 1911 and appropriated by Italy on outbreak of Turko-Italian War. Not completed until 1913.

OLD ITALIAN COLONIAL CRUISER.

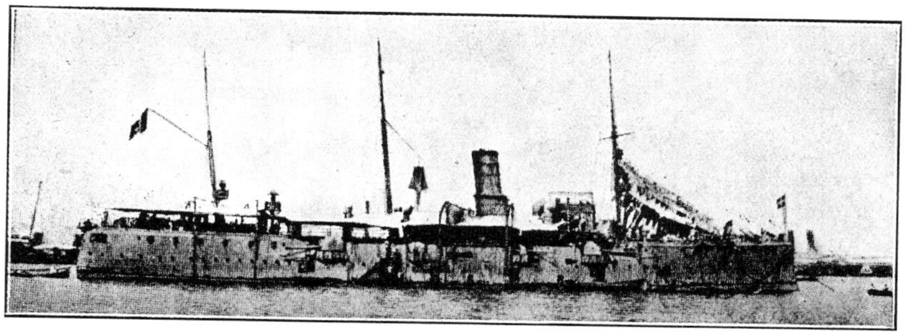

CALABRIA (1894). 2492 tons. Sheathed and zinced. Complement, 208. Dimensions: 265¾ (*o.a.*) × 41⅔ × 17¼ feet (*max.*) Armament: 4—6 inch, 6—6 pdrs., 2—1 pdr., 2 Machine, 2—18 inch tubes (*above water*). 2″ Deck. Designed H.P. 4000 = 16 kts. Boilers: 4 Cylindrical. Coal: *maximum* 500 tons. Built at Spezia.

OLD ITALIAN CRUISERS.

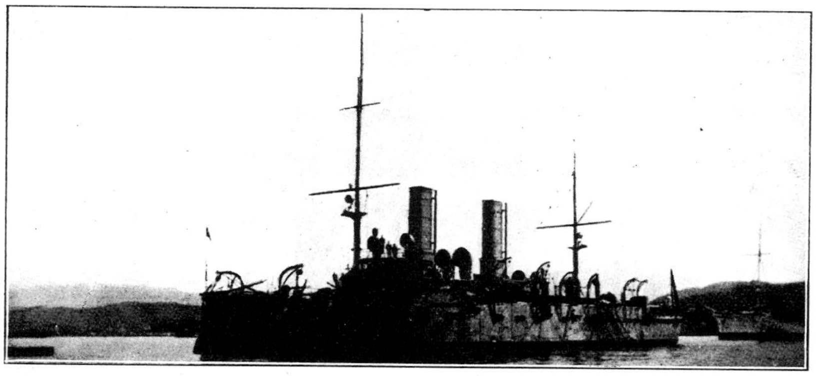

Elba. (Flagship, C-in-C.)

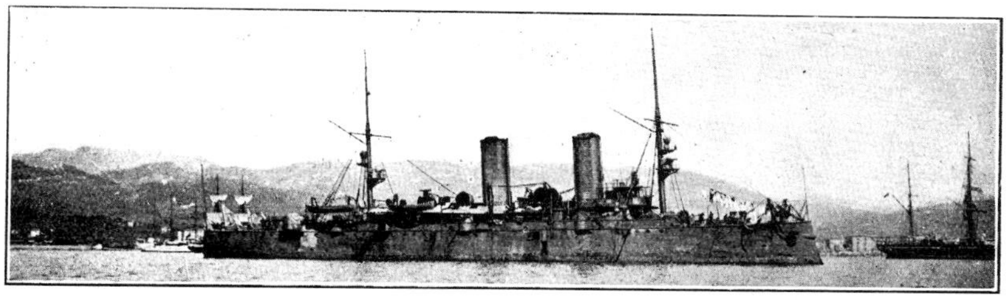

Puglia

Lombardia similar, but has only one big circular fighting top round each mast, just above ensign gaffs. Present appearance of Etruria not known.

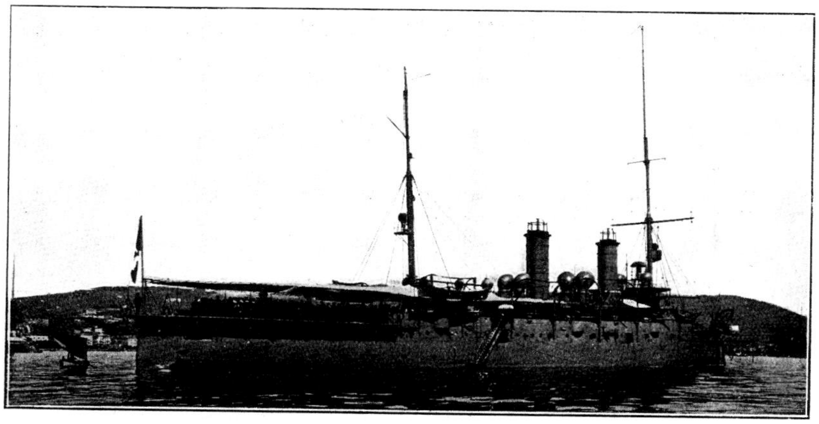

Liguria

	PUGLIA	**ELBA**	**LIGURIA**	**LOMBARDIA**	**ETRURIA**
Launched ..	1898	1893	1893	1893 (rebuilt '07)	1889
Displ. (tons) ..	3100	2730	2460	2280	2280
Length (ft. *o.a.*)	289⅓	289⅓	289⅓	278½	278¼
Beam (ft.) ..	40⅓	41⅓	40⅔	39½	39½
Max. draught (ft.)	19¼	17½	19¼	16⅔	16⅔
Guns	7—14 pdr. A.A.	6—4.7 inch*	4—14 pdr. A.A.	4—4.7 inch*	6—4.7 inch*
Torpedo Tubes (*above water*)	2—18 inch	2—18 inch*	———	2—18 inch*	2—18 inch*
Designed I.H.P.†	7500	7500	7500	7500	7500
Speed (knots) ..	19.5	19.5	19.5	19.5	19.5
Coal (tons) ..	480	500	500	430	430
Complement ..	164	204	154	191	152

* Reported to be disarmed; guns and tubes removed. † All have four cylindrical boilers.

Note.

PUGLIA } **LIGURIA** } **Both Mine Layers. Each carries and lays 60 mines.**

LOMBARDIA served during War as Submarine Depot Ship; may be so employed still.

ETRURIA sunk by internal explosion at Livorno 13 August, 1918. Has been raised and is being repaired.

OLD ITALIAN CRUISERS—*Continued.*

PIEMONTE (Elswick, 1888). 2640 tons. Complement, 264. Dimensions (*p.p.*), 305 × 38 × 16⅜ feet (*maximum*). Armament: 10—4·7 inch, 1—14 pdr. AA., 6—6 pdr., 2—1 pdr., 1 Maxim. 2—18 inch tubes (*above water*). Deck, 3″. Conning tower, 3″. H.P. 12,197 = 22·3 kts. *on trials.* 4 Cylindrical boilers. Coal: *normal* 200 tons, *maximum* 560 tons.

(*Training Ship for Cadets.*)   *Photo, Abrahams, Devonport.*

ETNA (1885). 3740 tons. Complement, 239. Dimensions: 283½ × 43½ × 20 feet (*maximum*). Armament: 2—6 inch*, 1—14 pdr.*, 2—6 pdr.* Deck, 2″. Designed H.P. 6400 = 17 kts. 4 cyl. boilers. Coal: 630 tons.

* Disarmed during later stages of the War and served as a Harbour Flagship. May have resumed old duty as Cadets' Training Ship. Guns given as officially listed by Ministry of Marine.

GIOVANNI BAUSAN (Elswick, 1883). 3330 tons. Dimensions: 278 × 42 × 19 feet. Armament: 2—old 10 inch, 4—6 inch, 4—6 pdr., 2—1 pdr., 2 M. 3—14 inch tubes (*above water*). Deck 1½″. Conning tower 2″. Designed H.P. 6550 = 17·5 kts. Coal 600 tons.

No longer in commission in 1919.

ITALIAN FLOTILLA LEADERS

4 Aquila class.

(All three alike.)   *Photo by courtesy of the Ministry of Marine.*

4 *Pattison* type: **Falco*** (1919), **Nibbio*** (1918), **Sparviero*** (1917), **Aquila*** (1916). 1600 tons. Dimensions: 308·5 (*p.p.*) × 31 × 10·7 feet (*mean*). Guns: (*a*) *Falco*, 6—4·7 inch, 40 cal., 2—14 pdr., 40 cal., 2—2 pdr. AA.; (*b*) *Nibbio, Sparviero, Aquila,* 3—6 inch, 40 cal., 4—14 pdr. 40 cal., AA., 2—2 pdr. AA. Tubes: 4—18 inch, in two twin deck mountings. Designed S.H.P. 44,000 = 34 kts. 2 Tosi turbines. 4 Thornycroft oil-burning boilers. 2 screws. Endurance: 1700 miles (15 kts.), 380 miles (full speed).

Note.—These four destroyers were to have been built for the Rumanian Navy. Were originally named *Vifor, Viscol, Vartez* and *Vijelie.* Appropriated for Italian Navy on outbreak of war with Austria-Hungary.
*All four are Mine Layers, carrying 50 mines each.

C. MIRABELLO. *High* mainmast. Bridge abaft of fore-funnel. Funnel caps strongly conical in shape.
3 *Ansaldo* type: **Carlo Mirabello*** (1914), **Carlo Alberto Racchia** (1916), ▼**Augusto Riboty*** (1915). 1540 tons. Dimensions: 331·4 (*p.p.*) × 32 × 10·6 feet (*mean*). Guns: in *C. A. Racchia*, 6—4 inch, 35 cal., 2—2 pdr. AA. Tubes: 6—... inch in three twin deck mountings; *C. Mirabello* and *A. Riboty*, 8—4 inch, 1 or 2—2 pdr. AA. and 4 tubes in two twin deck mountings. Made 33·75 kts. on trials. 4 Yarrow oil-burning boilers. 2 Parsons turbines. 2 screws. Endurance: 2840 miles (15 kts.), 500 miles (full speed).
*These two boats are Mine Layers, each carrying 100 mines.

3 Mirabello class.

C. A. RACCHIA. *Short* mainmast, no bridge athwartship abaft of first funnel. Funnel caps are slightly conical.
(For description, see next column.)

2 Poerio class.

G. PEPE.
2 *Ansaldo* type: **Alessandro Poerio** (1914), **Guglielmo Pepe** (1914). 1030 tons. Dimensions: 272·6 (*p.p.*) × 26·3 × 9·3 feet. Armament: 4 inch, 5 in *Poerio*, 6 in *Pepe*, 2—2 pdr. AA. 4—18 inch torpedo tubes in two twin-deck mountings. H.P. 20,000 = 30 kts. 3 Yarrow oil-burning boilers. 2-shaft Parsons turbines. Endurance: 2930 miles (15 kts.), 745 miles (full speed).

Cesare Rossarol mined near Pola 18 November 1918.

ITALIAN DESTROYERS (*Cacciatorpediniere*).

11 Sirtori class.

V. ORSINI.

11 *Odero* type: **Agostino Bertani,* Giacomo Medici,* Giuseppe la Farina,*** and **Nicola Fabrizi*** (all 1917); **Angelo Bassini,* Francesco Stocco, Giacinto Carini,* Giovanni Acerbi, Giuseppe la Masa,* Giuseppe Sirtori,** and **Vicenzo Orsini** (all 1916). 810 tons. Dimensions: 238 (*p.p.*) × 24 × 9.2 feet (*mean*). Guns: (a) *A. Bertani, G. Medici, G. la Farina,* 6—4 inch, 2—14 pdr. (b) *N. Fabrizi, A. Bassini, G. Carini, G. la Masa,* 4—4 inch, 2—12 pdr. (c) *F. Stocco, G. Acerbi, V. Orsini,* 6—4 inch, 2—2 pdr. A.A. Tubes (in all): 4—18 inch, in two twin-deck mountings. Made about 34·1 kts. on trials. 2 Tosi turbines. 4 Thornycroft oil-burning boilers. 2 screws. Endurance: 1700 miles (15 kts.), 470 miles (full speed). ▪ *Benedetto Cairoli,* of this class, lost during War.

* These 7 boats are Mine Layers, each carrying 10 mines.

8 Palestro class.

PALESTRO.   *Photo by courtesy of Flli. Orlando.*

8 *Orlando* type: **Calatafimi, Castelfidardo, Confienza, Curtatone. Monzambano, Palestro, San Martino, Solferino.** Launched 1918-19. 880 tons.* Dimensions: 256.6 (*p.p.*)* × 24.9 × 8.7 feet (*mean*). Guns: 4—4 inch, 45 cal., 2—14 pdr., 30 cal. A.A., 2—2 pdr. A.A. Tubes: 4 in two twin-deck mountings. Designed S.H.P. 24,009 = 32 kts. 2 Zoelly turbines. 4 Thornycroft oil-burning boilers. 2 screws.

* In *Calatafimi, Castelfidardo, Curtatone* and *Monzambano*, length *p.p.* is about 262.5 feet, and displacement is about 950 tons.

1 Special Boat.

1 *Yarrow* type: **Audace** (ex-Japanese *Kawakaze*, Scotstoun, N.B., 1915). 955 tons. Dimensions: 275 (*p.p.*) × 27½ × 9½ feet (*mar.*). Guns: 7—4 inch, 2—2 pdr. A.A. Tubes: 4—18 inch, in two twin mountings. Made 34.5 kts. on trials. 2-shaft Parsons turbines and 3 Yarrow large-tube, oil-burning boilers. Endurance: 2180 miles (15 kts.), 560 miles (full speed).

Note.—This boat must not be confused with *Audace* built in 1912-13 by Orlando, as a sister boat to *Animoso* (v. next page). The Orlando *Audace* was sunk during the War, and the Japanese *Kawakaze* (closely resembling the lost *Audace*) was purchased by Italy and re-named *Audace*.

(see *Animoso* for loss of previous *Audace*.)

8 Abba class.

G. C. ABBA.

2 *Pattison* boats: **Francesco Nullo, Antonio Mosto,** (both 1914).
6 *Odero* boats: **Rosolino Pilo, Giuseppe Carlo Abba, Ippolito Nievo, Simone Schiaffino, Pilado Bronzetti** (all 1914), **Giuseppe Missori** (1915). 770 tons. Dimensions: 236.2 (*p.p.*) × 24 × 8.8 feet (*mean*). Guns: 5—4 inch, 2—2 pdr. A.A. Tubes: 4 single 18 inch. Made about 31.8 kts. on trials. 2 Tosi turbines and 4 Thornycroft oil-burning boilers. 2 screws. Endurance: 1700 miles (15 kts.), 440 miles (full speed).

1 Special boat.

1 *Orlando* type: **Animoso** (1913). 700 tons. Dimensions: 245.4 (*p.p.*) × 24.6 × 8.4 feet (*mean*). Guns: 5—4 inch, 2—2 pdr. A.A. Tubes: 4 single 18 inch. On trials made 36.1 kts. with (about) 18,000 S.H.P. 2-shaft Zoelly turbines and 4 White-Forster oil-burning boilers. 2 screws. Endurance: 1650 miles (15 kts.), 410 miles (full speed). Her sister boat, *Audace*, was lost during the War.

4 Indomito class.

INDOMITO.

4 *Pattison* type (Thornycroft design): **Indomito** (1912), **Impavido, Insidioso, Irrequieto** (1913). 690 tons. Dimensions: 238 (*p.p.*) × 24 × 8.4 feet. Guns: 5—4 inch, 2—2 pdr. A.A. Tubes: 2—18 in.-h, but *Indomito* only has 4 single 18 inch. On trials 18,200 S.H.P. = 35.8 kts. 2 Tosi turbines and 4 oil-burning Thornycroft boilers. 2 screws. Endurance: 1520 miles (15 kts.), 360 miles (full speed). *Impetuoso* and *Intrepido* of this class lost in the War.

Impetuoso torpedoed by Austrian submarine 10 July 1916. *Intrepido* mined off Kolonas 4 December 1915.

2 Ardente class.

ARDITO.

2 *Orlando* type: **Ardito** (1912), **Ardente** (1912). 686 tons. Dimensions: 238 (*p.p.*) × 24 × 8.4 feet (*mean*). Guns: 5—4 inch, 2—2 pdr. A.A. Tubes: 2 single 18 inch. On trials, 15,150 S.H.P. = 23.4 kts. 2-shaft Parsons turbines and 4 oil-burning Thornycroft boilers. 2 screws. Endurance: 1520 miles (15 kts.), 360 miles (full speed).

ITALIAN DESTROYERS.—(Continued.)

10 Carabiniere/Artigliere class.

ASCARO. Some boats rigged like this.

GARIBALDINO. Has been lost, but some of the boats detailed below are rigged like this, with very short pole mast right at stern.

10 Ansaldo (Improved *Nembo*) type :—

5 *Carabiniere* class : **Ascaro** (1912), **Pontiere** (1910, reconstructed 1913), **Alpino, Carabiniere, Fuciliere** (1909). *Ascaro* 398 tons, others 420 tons. Dimensions, H.P., speed as *Artigliere* class below, except *Ascaro*, with 2—14 pdr. and 4—6 pdr. Carry 90 tons oil fuel, except *Ascaro*, with 50 tons coal+33 tons oil. Endurance : 915 miles for *Ascaro*, 1250 miles for others, all at 15 kts. *Garibaldino* lost during War.

5 *Artigliere* class : **Corazziere** (1909), **Lanciere, Artigliere** (1906), **Bersagliere, Granatiere** (1906). 390 tons. Dimensions : 211¼ (*p.p.*) × 20 × 6⅝ to 7 feet (*mean*). Guns : 4—14 pdr. Tubes : 3 single 18 inch. On trials, 6500 I.H.P. = 29·1 kts. 3 Thornycroft boilers and 2 screws. 80 tons coal. Endurance : 1000 miles at 15 kts. Note: *Caribaldino* sunk in collision 16 July 1918.

3 Zeffiro class.

ZEFFIRO.

Espero, Zeffiro 3 funnels as above. *Aquilone* 2 funnels as silhouettes, *q.v.*

3 *Nembo* class (Thornycroft pattern) : **Aquilone** (1902), **Espero, Zeffiro** (both 1904). Built by Pattison, Naples. 380 tons. Dimensions : 208 (*p.p.*) × 19½ × 7½ feet. Armament : 4—14 pdr., 4—18 inch tubes. Boilers : 3 Thornycroft, oil-burning in *Aquilone* and *Espero* (80 tons coal), coal-burning in *Zeffiro* (60 tons oil). On trials, 5350 I.H.P. = 30·3 kts. *Turbine* and *Nembo* and *Borea* of this class have been lost during the War. Endurance : 1000 miles at 15 kts.

5 Lampo class.

5 *Schichau* type : **Dardo, Euro, Lampo, Strale, Ostro** (1899-1901). 320 tons. Dimensions : 196¾ × 21¼ × 8¼ feet. Armament : 4—14 pdr., 2—18 inch tubes. All have Schulz boilers. 31·2 kts. on trials. Endurance : 1100 miles at 15 kts.

1 Old Boat.

1 *Odero* type : **Fulmine** (1898). 340 tons. Dimensions : 200 × 21 × 8¾ feet. Armament : 4—6 pdr., 2—18 inch tubes. 4 Blechynden boilers. Designed for 28 kts. but never exceeded 26 kts. Endurance : 820 miles at 15 kts.

ITALIAN TORPEDO BOATS.

28 Sea-going Boats (*Torpediniere di alto mare*).

No.	Class.	Date.	Displacement.	H.P.	Max. Speed.	Fuel.	Complement.	Tubes.	Max. Draught
			tons.		kts.	tons.			feet.
2	"*Later C*" (PN)	1908-9	216	3000	25	30 tons oil	33	3	7⅓
6	"*Earlier C*" (PN)*	1906-7	216	3000	25	40 tons coal	35	3	7½
6	"*A*" (OS)*	1906-7	216	3000	25	40 tons coal / 30 tons oil	35 / 33	3	7½
1	*Gabbiano* (SY)	1907	162	2000	25	18 tons oil	27	2 or 3	7½
4	"*O*" (OS)*	1905-7	210	3000	25	40 tons coal	35	3	7¼
3	"*P*" (PN)*	1905-6	210	3000	25	30 tons coal	32	3	7¼
4	"*S*" (S)	1905-6	210	3000	25	40 tons coal	35	2	..
1	*Pellicano* (OS)	1899	154	2700	26	38 tons coal	28	2	7¾
1	*Condore* (AS)	1898	169	2300	26	26 tons oil	26	2	7

(PN)=Pattison, Naples. (OS)=Odero, Sestri-Ponente. (S)=Schichau. (SY)=Spezia D.Y.

*Note.—All belong to a common design and are armed with 2—14 pdr., 3—18 inch tubes, arranged as *Pegaso* plan. The 3—3 pdr. guns, shown on plans, were replaced during war by 2—14 pdr. guns.

PEGASO

(For appearance, see Silhouettes.)

(For appearance, see Silhouettes.)

6 "*Earlier C*" class : **Canopo, Centauro** (both 1907), **Cassiopea, Calliope, Cigno, Clio** (all 1906). Built by Pattison, Naples. 216 tons. Dimensions : 164·3 × 17·4 × 5·7 feet (*mean*). Guns : 2—14 pdr. AA. Tubes : 3 single 18 inch. On trials, 3260 I.H.P. = 27·2 kts. 2 coal-burning Thornycroft boilers and 2 screws.

Mainmast removed from some boats.

6 "*A*" class : **Airone, Ardea, Albatros, Astore, Arpia** (all 1907), **Alcione** (1906). Built by Odero, Sestri-Ponente. 216 tons. Dimensions : 164·3 × 17·4 × 5·7 feet (*mean*). Guns : 2—14 pdr. AA. Torpedo tubes : 3 single 18 inch. On trials, 3260 I.H.P. = 25·8 kts. 2 Thornycroft coal-burning boilers, except *Airone* with 2 Thornycroft oil-burning boilers and 30 tons oil instead of 40 tons coal. 2 screws in all.

2 "*Later C*" class : **Calipso, Climene** (Pattison, Naples, 1908). 216 tons. Dimensions : 164·3 × 17·4 × 5·7 feet (*mean*). Guns : 1—14 pdr., 1—14 pdr. AA. Tubes : 3 single 18 inch. On trials, 3183 I.H.P. = 26 kts. 2 oil-burning Thornycroft boilers and 2 screws.

ITALIAN TORPEDO BOATS.

Sea-going Torpedo Boats (*continued.*)

3 "*P*" class : **Pegaso, Procione, Pallade** (all 1905). Built by Pattison, Naples. 210 tons. Dimensions : 164.3 × 17.4 × 5.7 feet. Guns : 2—14 pdr. AA. Tubes : 3 single 18 inch. On trials, 3160 I.H.P. = 26.6 kts. 2 Thornycroft coal-burning boilers and 2 screws. *Perseo* sunk during the war.

Photo, Ciricchioni.

4 "*S*" class : **Saffo, Sagittario, Sirlo, Spica** (Schichau, 1905). 210 tons. Dimensions : 164 × 19.7 × 5.2 feet (*mean*). Guns : 2—14 pdr. AA. 2 single 18 inch tubes. On trials, I.H.P. 3120 = 26 kts. ▲ 2 Schulz-Thornycroft coal-burning boilers and 2 screws. *Serpente* and *Scorpione* sunk during the war.

PELLICANO. (*Condore* has funnels more apart.)

1 *Odero* boat : **Pellicano** (1899). 154 tons. Guns : 2—3 pdr. Tubes : 2—14 inch. Speed : 23 kts. 2 Blechynden boilers.

1 *Ansaldo* boat : **Condore** (1898). 170 tons. Guns : 1—14 pdr., 2—3 pdr. Tubes : 2—14 inch. Speed : about 20 kts. (25.7 trials). 2 Normand boilers.

Photo by courtesy of Flli. Orlando.

2 *Orlando* boats : **74 O.L.T., 75 O.L.T.,** Built at Leghorn. Begun 1917. Launched Oct., 1917–Jan., 1918., finished June–Sept., 1918. 200 tons. Guns : 1 or 2—14 pdr. AA. Torpedo tubes : 2—18 inch. S.H.P. 4500 = 29 kts. 2-shaft turbines and 2 water-tube boilers.

4 *Cantiere Navale Riuniti* boats : **70 C.P.-73 C.P.** Built at Palermo. Begun 1917, launched 1918. finished 1919. Details as 12 Pattison boats in next column, except that these boats are (*a*) 169 tons displacement, and have (*b*) two 14 pdr. AA. and (*c*) 2—18 inch torpedo tubes in *two single* deck mountings, (*d*) Speed : 28 to 31 kts.

Photo by courtesy of Flli. Orlando.

6 *Orlando* boats : **58 O.L-63 O.L.** Built at Leghorn. Begun 1915-16, launched April–Sept., 1916. Completed May–Oct., 1916. Details generally as 12 Pattison boats in next column. But I.H.P. 3700 = 28.1 kts.

Now rigged with 2 pole masts.

1 *Navy* type : **Gabbiano** (Spezia D.Y., 1907). 162 tons. Dimensions : 159 × 17.5 × 5.5 feet. Guns : 2—3 pdr. Tubes : 2 or 3 single. On trials 2200 I.H.P. = 26 kts. 2 coal-burning Normand boilers and 2 screws.

4 "*O*" class : **Orfeo** (1907), **Olimpia, Orsa** (both 1906), **Orione** (1905). Built by Odero, Sestri-Ponente. 210 tons. Dimensions : 167.3 × 19.7 × 5 feet (*mean*). Guns : 1—14 pdr., 1—14 pdr. AA. Tubes : 3 single 18 inch. On trials, 3300 I.H.P. = 25.4 kts. 2 coal-burning Blechynden boilers and 2 screws. Both deleted during the war.

Photo, Ciricchioni.

2 Boats. *Aquila* class (Schichau type). **Avvoltoio, Sparviero.** Armament : 2—1 pdr., 2—18 inch tubes.

(1 funnel. 1 mast.)

6 *Ansaldo* boats : **52 A.S.-57 A.S.** Built 1915-16 at Sestri-Ponente. Details as 12 Pattison boats below.

6 *Odero* boats : **46 O.S.-51 O.S.** Built 1915-16 at Sestri-Ponente. Details as 12 Pattison boats below.

12 *Pattison* boats : **40 P.N.-45 P.N.** (begun 1915, launched and completed 1916), **64 P.N.-69 P.N.** (begun 1916 and completed 1917-18). All built at Naples. About 160-165 tons. Dimensions - 139½ × 15 × — feet. Guns : 1—14 pdr. AA. Tubes : 2—18 inch in one twin mounting. I.H.P. 3500 = 28 to 29 kts. Machinery - 2 sets recipro. triple expansion. Boilers : Thornycroft.

ITALIAN TORPEDO BOATS AND SUBMARINES.

Coastal Torpedo Boats *(Continued.)*

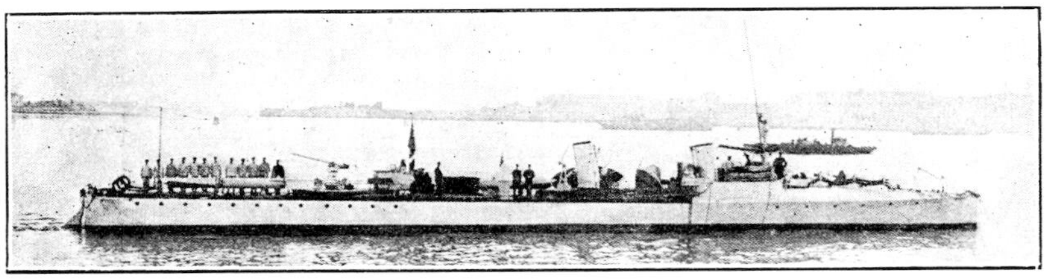

Appearance of all boats as above. *Official photo.*

1 *Navy Yard* boat: **39 R.M.** (Spezia Navy Yard).
16 *Pattison* boats: **33 P.N.—38 P.N.**, **6 P.N.—12 P.N.**, **1 P.N.—4 P.N.**
11 *Odero* boats: **18 O.S.—24 O S.**, **13 O.S.—16 O.S.**
8 *Ansaldo* boats: **25 A.S.—32 A.S.**

36 boats in all. Launched 1911-13. Completed 1911-1 Average 125 tons. Dimensions: 139½ × 15 × 5 fee Guns: 1—6 pdr. Tubes: 2—18 inch. I/S.H.P. 270 3200 = 27·5-31·5 kts. Oil: 15 tons.

Boilers: 2 Thornycroft oil-burning, except *39 R.M.* with special type. Machinery: 2 sets triple expansion, excep (*a*) *39 R.M.* with 3 sets triple expansion and 1 B.P. turbine to 3 screws; (*b*) *31 A.S.* with 3-shaft Parsons turbine: (*c*) *32 A.S.* with 2-shaft Bergmann turbines. *5 P.N.*, *17 O.S. 36 P.N.*, lost in War.

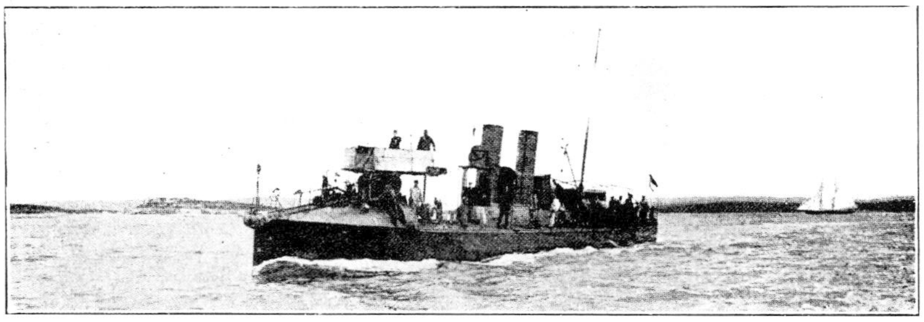

Now has pole mast just abaft fore bridge.

1 *ex-Austrian* boat: **Francesco Rismondo** (ex-Austrian *No. 11*). Armed with 2—3 pdr. and 2—17·7 inch tubes Oil fuel only. White-Forster boilers. Deserted to Italian Navy, October, 1917.

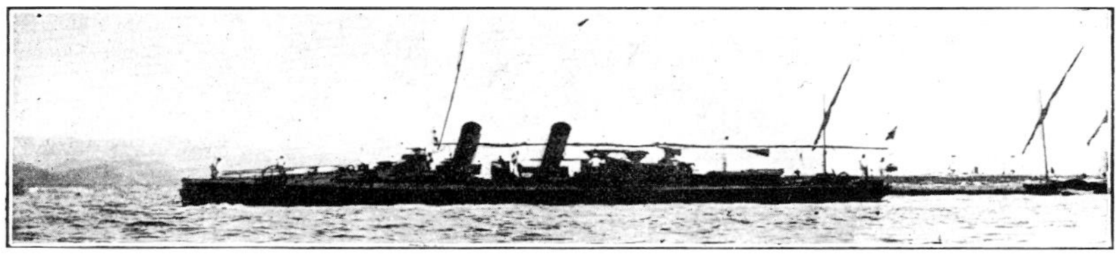

(*All relegated to Harbour Duties.*)

7 *Schichau* type: **134 S, 128 S, 115 S, 114 S, 113 S, 102 S, 68 S.** 80-85 tons. Speed: 17-19 kts. Armament: 2—1 pdr., 2—14 inch tubes. (*Several have been re-boilered.*)

(M. A. S. Boats with torpedo tubes described on a later page.)

Note: Following deleted during the war – *82S, 88S, 98S, 101S, 104S, 105S*. In addition 6 Thornycroft Type, *29, 31, 38, 39, 43* and *56* deleted.

11 Ocean-going Boats — *(Sommergibili d'alto mare).*

(*See Silhouettes for appearance*).

6 *Cavallini* type: ***Angelo Emo,* Lorenzo Marcello,* Lazarro Mocenigo,* Galvani, Pietro Micca, Torricelli*** (Spezia Navy Yard). Dimensions: 206¾ × 19⅔ × 14 feet. Guns: 2—14 pdr. (40 cal.) AA. 6—17·7 inch torpedo tubes. Machinery: In first three, 2 Tosi Diesel motors *on surface* and 2 Savigliano electric motors *when submerged*; last three have 2 Ansaldo Diesel and 2 Ansaldo electric motors. Carry 60 tons oil fuel. Other details as Table. Completed 1917-1919.

*These 3 boats begun at Venice D.Y., Aug., 1914. They were dismantled and taken to Spezia in the summer of 1915 and laid down for a second time.

4 *Fiat-Laurenti* type: ***Agostino Barbarigo,*** (1914), ***Andrea Provana*** (—), ***Sebastiano Veneiro*** (—), ***Giacomo Nani*** (Fiat-San Giorgio Co., Spezia). Dimensions: 213¼ × 19¾ × 13¼ feet. Guns: 2—14 pdr. AA. 6—17·7 inch torpedo tubes. Machinery as *G. Pacinotti* below. Carry 60 tons oil. Completed between Dec., 1917 and Dec., 1918. Other details as Table.

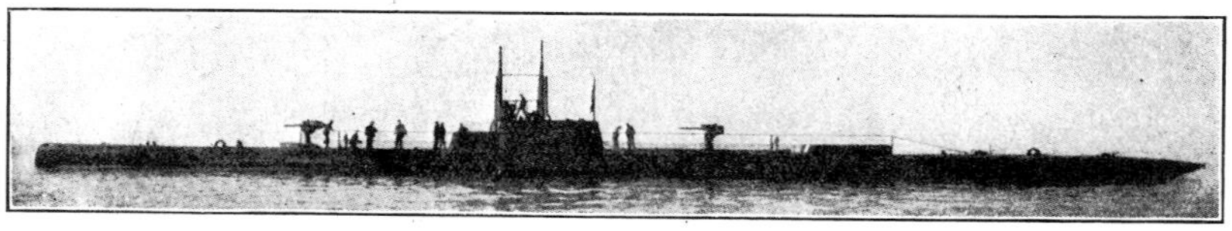

Photo, Ansaldo-San Giorgio Co.

1 *Fiat-Laurenti* type: ***G Pacinotti*** (Spezia, 1915 or 1916). Dimensions: x x feet. Guns: 2—14 pdr. (40 cal) A.A. 5—17.7 inch torpedo tubes (3 bow, 2 stern). Machinery: 2 Fiat Diesel engines *on surface*, 2 Savigliano electric motors *when submerged*. A sister boat, *Alberto Guglielmotti*, was mistaken for a German U-boat by a British Auxiliary and destroyed 10 March 1917. Another boat, *Balilla*, possibly of this class was sunk 14 July 1916.

A.—Summary of Submarines *(Sommergibili).*

Note.—This Table only includes boats given in the Official List furnished by the Ministry of Marine. Other Submarines, not mentioned in Official List, but believed to be in existence are relegated to a second Table B.

No.	Type.	First begun.	Completed.	Displacement	B.H.P. / Kw.	Speed. kts.	Endurance.	Tubes.	Complement	Max. draug't
										feet
*	*Ocean-going:*			*	*	*		*		
6	*P. Micca* (C)	1914	'17-'19	810 / 1241	2600 / 900	17 / 10	...	6	32	14
4	*A. Barbarigo* (FL)	1913	'17-'18	747 / 925	2600 / 900	17·5 / 10	3000 at 12 kts. / ..	6	32	13¼
1	*G. Pacinotti* (FL)	1913	1916	700 / 870	2600 / 900	18 / 10	3000 at 12 kts. / ...	5	32	..
	Coastal:—									
2	*N5 N6* (B)	1917	'18-'19	276 / 357	620 / 330	13·6 / 8	...	2	21	10
4	*N1—N4* (B)	1915	'17-'18							
7	*H1—H8* (H)	1916	1917	361 / 141	480 / 500	12·6 / 11	2000 at 13 kts. / 30 at 6 kts.	4	22	12⅓
(21)	*F1—F21* (FL)	1915	'16-'17	260 / 318	700 / 238	13 / 8	1600 at 8·5 kts. / 80 at 4 kts.	2	21	10¼
1	*Nautilus* (B)	1912	1913	225 / 303	600 / 260	13·2 / 8	...	3	19	9¼
	Mine-Laying									
2	*X2, X3* (B)	1916	1917	403 / 468	660 / 235	9·2 / 6·3	1200 at 12 kts. / ...	(†) 6 *or* 9	..	13
1	*X1* (ex-German)	1915	1915	182 / 210	80 / 100	6·8 / 5·2	1100 at 4 kts. / 50 at 2·5 kts.	6	14	9⅔

(C) = Cavallini design; (FL) = Fiat-Laurenti design; (B) = Bernardis design; (H) = "Holland" (Electric Boat Co.) design.

* Details in these columns are all official, with the reservation that the Ministry of Marine gives a total of *six* boats for "F" class. Since *F 13, 15, 17* have been built by F'lli Orlando, the official total is probably a mistake.

† Total of mine-discharge chutes; figures are *not* official.

(*Description by classes on following pages.*)

37 Coastal Boats— *(Sommergibili Costieri)*

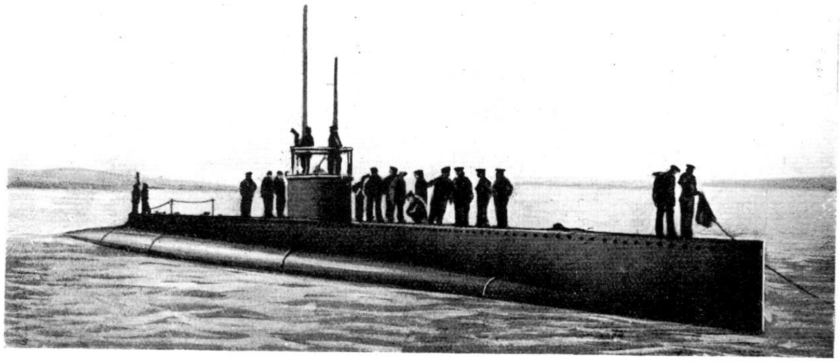

N 5. *Photo by courtesy of the Ministry of Marine.*

2 *Bernardis* type: ***N 5*** (1917), ***N 6*** (1918). Both built by Tosi, Taranto. Dimensions: 152½ × 14¾ × 10 feet. Machinery: 2 Tosi Diesel engines *on surface*. Guns, tubes and electric motors as *N 1—4* below. Other details as Table.

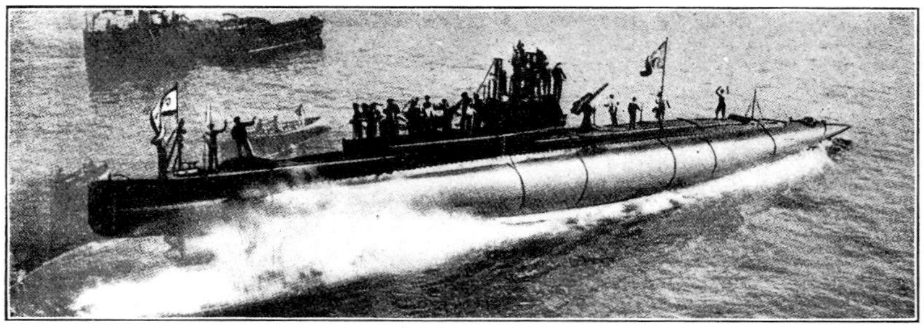

N 1—4. *Photo, Ansaldo-San Giorgio Co.*

4 *Bernardis* type: ***N1—4*** (Ansaldo-San Giorgio Co., Spezia, 1916-17). Dimensions: 150½ × 14¾ × 10 feet. Guns: 1—14 pdr. (30 cal.) AA. 2 bow 18 inch tubes. Machinery: 2 Sulzer-Ansaldo Diesel engines *on surface*; 2 Tecnomasio Italiano electric motors *when submerged*. Oil: 9-10 tons. Are an "Improved *Nautilus*" class. Other details as Table.

ITALIAN SUBMARINES.

Coastal Boats (Continued).

H 2.

7 *Holland* type: **H1, H2** (1916) **H3** - **H8** (1917). All built by Canadian Vickers Co., Montreal. Dimensions: 150½ × 15¼ × 12½ feet. Guns: 1—14 pdr. (30 cal.) A.A. 4—18 inch bow tubes. Machinery: 2 Nlseco Diesel engines *on surface*; 2 Dynamic Electric Co. motors *when submerged*. Oil: 14 tons. Other details as Table.

H5 accidently sunk by British submarine 16 April 1918.

F 7.

21 (or less) *Fiat Laurenti* type: **F1, F2, F3, F5, F7**-12, **F14, F16. Fl8—21**, built by Fiat-San Giorgio Co., Spezia and Odero, Sestri-Ponente: **F4, F6, F13, F15, F17**, built by Orlando, Leghorn. Launched and completed 1916-17. Dimensions: 149½ × 13¼ × 10½ feet. Guns: 1—14 pdr. (30 cal.) A.A. 2—17.7 inch bow tubes. Machinery: 2 Fiat Diesel *on surface*; 2 Savigliano electric motors *when submerged*. Oil: 12 tons. Are an "Improved *Medusa*" type.

1 *Bernardis* type: **Nautilus** (Venice Navy Yard, 1913). Dimensions: 134½ × 14 × 9½ feet. 2—18 inch bow tubes and 1 revolving 18 inch deck tube. Machinery: 2 Sulzer-Diesel engines *on surface*; 2 Ansaldo electric motors *when submerged*. Carries 6 tons oil. A sister-boat, *Nereide*, Torpedoed by Austrian submarine 5 August 1915.

9 Small Coastal Boats.

Note.—Considering the small size and feeble radius of these boats, they are hardly worth maintaining in effective condition. They will probably be scrapped very soon—if they have not already been broken up.

3 boats (*type unknown*): **B1—3** (Spezia D.Y., 1916). Dimensions: about 50 × 7½ × 8 feet. Endurance :1 200 miles *on surface* at a low speed. 2—17.7 inch bow tubes. *B 4, B5* were begun, but work on them was stopped. They were never finished.

6 boats (*type unknown*): **A 1** (1915), 30 tons, **A2—4, A5, A6** (all 1916) 50 tons. Electric motors only for surface and submerged propulsion. Endurance: 25 miles at 5 kts. *on surface*. One torpedo tube. Were placed out of commission in 1918. Although they had a complement of 5, they were often referred to as "one man" submarines.

7 Coastal Boats.

W 3.

W 2.

2 *Armstrong Laubeuf* type: **W2** (1915. **W3** (1915), both built by Armstrongs at Selby, Yorks., for British Navy. Ceded to Italy about 1916. Dimensions: 149½ × 17 × 9½ feet. Diesel engines of about 750 H.P. Otherwise as *W 1* below. *W 1* lost during War (8 August 1917).

3 Mine Laying Boats (Sommeergibi—Affondamine)

2 *Bernardis* type: **X2, X3** (Ansaldo, Spezia, 1916). Dimensions about 140 × 18 × 13 feet. Guns: 1—14 pdr. (30 cal.) A.A. Carry 18 mines in 6 or 9 discharge chutes. Machinery: 2 Ansaldo Diesel *on surface*; 2 Ansaldo electric *submerged*. Carry 14½ tons of fuel. (Other details as Table.)

X 1, AS REPAIRED FOR ITALIAN NAVY.

1 (*type unknown*): **X1** (ex-German *UC 12*, ex-Austrian *XVI*). Launched by Weser Co., Bremen, May, 1915. Ceded to Austria by Germany, transported in sections by rail to Pola, June, 1915, and there assembled in four days. Engaged in mine-laying operations in the Adriatic 1915-16, and in December, 1915, she transported rifles and munitions from Cattaro to rebel Arab tribes in Northern Africa. Destroyed during 1916 off Taranto, raised in two parts from 100 feet depth, placed on slip, re-built and re-commissioned for service in Italian Navy. Dimensions: 110½ (o.a.) × 10½ × 9¾ feet. Machinery: 1—4 cyl. Benz motor *on surface*; 1 Siemens-Schukert electric motor *submerged*. One M.G. Carries 12 mines in 6 discharge chutes.

7 Coastal Boats (Continued).

> *No Photo available—See Silhouette.*
> Resembles Greek "*Delfin*" class but has large C.T.

1 *Armstrong-Laubeuf* type: **W 1** (1914), built by Armstrongs for British Navy, and ceded to Italy about 1916. Dimensions: 171½ × 15½ × 9 feet. 1—3 A.A. gun. 2—18 inch bow tubes. Surface Diesel engines of about 700 H.P. Endurance: 2500 miles at 8 kts. *on surface*, 65 miles at 5 kts. *submerged*.

1 *Fiat-Laurenti* type: **Argonauta** (ex-Russian ———?; Spezia, 1914). Dimensions: 147⅜ × 13¾ × 8½ feet. 1 Q.F. gun. 2—18 inch torpedo tubes. Fiat-Diesel engines. Radii of action: 950 miles at 12 kts. *on surface*; 57 miles *submerged*.

S 1

3 *Scott-Laurenti* type: **S1** (1914) **S2, S3** (1915), all built by Scotts S. B. & E. Co., Greenock, N.B., for British Navy as *S 2, 3, 4*, ceded to Italy about 1916. Dimensions: 148 × 13¾ × 9½ feet. 1 Q.F. gun. 2—18 inch bow tubes. Fiat type Diesel engines. Endurance: 1600 miles at 8½ kts. *on surface*; 75 miles at 5 kts. *submerged*.

16 ITALIAN COASTAL SUBMARINES—(Non-effective).

Note.

None of the Submarines, listed on this page are included in the Official List furnished by the Ministry of Marine. At the end of the War, all the boats given in column on right were out of commission. Some may have been broken up, while the remainder will probably be sold and broken up in the near future.

1 *Carallini* type: **Galileo Ferraris** (Spezia, 1913). Dimensions: 137·8 × 13¼ × 12 feet. 1—14 pdr. AA. gun. 6—18 inch tubes.

Also

1 *Carallini* type: **Giacinto Pullino,** sister to *G. Ferraris* above. Captured Aug., 1916 and became Austro-Hungarian *XVIII*. Recovered by Italian Navy, Nov., 1916. Will probably not be re-commissioned for Italian Navy.

1 *Krupp-Germania* type: **Atropo** (Kiel, 1912). Dimensions: 146 × 14½ × 8⅝ feet. 2—18 in. tubes in bows. 2 sets 300-350 H.P. Krupp-Diesel engines. Radii of action: 1300 miles at 12¼ kts. *on surface*; 40 miles at 8 kts. *submerged.*

VELELLA. *Official War Photo.*

6 *Laurenti* type: **Argo** (1912), **Velella** (1911), by Fiat Co., **Jantina** (1913), **Salpa** (1912), by Cantiere Riuniti, Spezia, **Fisalia** (1912), **Zoea** (1912), by Orlando, Leghorn. Dimensions: 147½ × 13¼ × 9⅝ feet. 1 small Q.F. or dismountable M.G. 2—18 inch tubes in bows. Fiat Diesel engines. 2 Siemens-Schuckert electric motors. Radii of action: 650—800 miles at 12—13¼ kts. *on surface*; *about* 45—50 miles *submerged* at 6 kts. Some made 14·7 kts. on surface during first trials. *Julea* mined 10 August 1916 and *Medusa* torpedoed by Austrian submarine 9 June 1915.

1 *Fiat-Laurenti* type, **Foca** (Spezia, 1908). Dimensions: 140 × 14 × 8¼ feet. 2—18 inch tubes in bows. Fiat petrol motors. Radii of action: 875 miles *on surface*; 40 miles *submerged.*

5 *Fiat-Laurenti* type: **Glauco** (1905), **Squalo** (1906), **Narvalo** (1907), **Otaria** (1908), **Tricheco** (1908). All built at Venice Navy Yard. Dimensions: 120¼ × 14¼ × 8¼ feet. 1 dismountable M.G. 2—18 inch tubes. First three have 680 H.P. Thornycroft petrol motors, and displace 150 tons *on surface*, 175 tons *submerged*. Last two have 700 H.P. Fiat heavy oil motors, and displace 175 tons *on surface*, 200 tons *submerged*. Radii of action: 900 miles at 8 kts. *on surface*; 40 miles at 5 kts. *submerged.* *Also*

1 old *Pullino* type **Delfino** (1894). Electric Motor only of 150 H.P. 1 tube.

ITALIAN "MOBILE BATTERIES." (*Batteria semovente.*)

Not completed by June, 1919.

THREE "MOBILE BATTERIES," building or completing. 630 tons. Guns: 1—15 inch 40 cal. and some smaller AA. guns. No other details communicated by Ministry of Marine.

Photo by courtesy of the Ministry of Marine.

FAA' DI BRUNO (Venice D.Y., 1916-17). 2,500 tons. Dimensions: 220 (o.a.) × 65½ × 6 feet. Complement, —. Guns: 2—15 inch, 40 cal., 2—14 pdr. AA., 2—1½ pdr. AA. Armour: —" Barbette. —" Deck. H.P. 100 = 4 kts. Has only a small engine and 1 screw to raise enough speed to move ship. Hull is box-shaped, without bow or stern.

CARSO, CUCCO, MONFALCONE and VODICE. Some (or all) built at Venice D.Y. about 1916-17. Displacement, dimensions, H.P., not known, but design similar to *Faa' di Bruno.* Speed: 6 kts. Guns: in *Carso* only, 2—7.5 inch; in *Cucco, Monfalcone* and *Vodice*, 1—12 inch in each.

ITALIAN GUNBOATS.

Lagoon Gunboats (*Cannoniere lacunari*).

APE, VESPE. Built at Venice D.Y. 1918. About 50 tons. Dimensions: 60 × 10 × 2¼ feet. Guns: 1—14 pdr. and 10 machine. H.P. and speed unknown.

(*For Venetian Lagoons.—Have served as Mine Layers.*)

BRONDOLO (1909), **MARGHERA** (1909). 120 tons. Dimensions: 125 × 11 × 2¼ feet. Guns: 1—14 pdr. During War, each fitted to carry and lay 60 mines. Designed H.P., 450 = 13 kts. Coal: 12 tons. Complement, 17.

There are also about 62 small ships under 200 tons *gross* for service in Venetian Lagoons.

Colonial and River Gunboats.

SEBASTIANO CABOTO (Palermo, 1913). Colonial gunboat (*Cannoniera per Servizio Coloniale*). 1050 tons. Complement, 111. Dimensions: 196.8 × 31.8 × 9.2 feet. Guns: 6—14 pdr., 4 machine. Designed H.P., 1200 = 13 kts. 2 screws. 2 cyl. (direct flame) boilers. Coal: 100 tons. Was built for S. American Station.

(*For service on Chinese Rivers.*)

ERMANNO CARLOTTO (Shanghai, 1914). Shallow-draught river gunboat (*Cannoniera fluviale per la Cina*). 220 tons. Dimensions: 140 × 24½ × 3 feet. Guns: 2—14 pdr., 4 machine. Designed H.P., 1100 = 14 kts. 2 Yarrow boilers. Complement, 73.

Note: *Curtatone* and *Volturno* of 1156 tons listed in 1914. Disposal unknown.

ITALIAN MISCELLANEOUS.

M. A. S. 1—434 (Motobarche Armate).

Note.—Correspond to British C.M.B. and M.L. types. May carry Depth Charges, Hydrophones, Smoke Boxes, etc.

Photo, Messrs. Ansaldo & Co.

"TIPO VELOCISSIME." 12 BUILT (1917-19) + 4 ON TRIALS. 18 tons. Length : 59 feet. Motors (Isotta Fraschini) : 1600 B.H.P. = 35 kts. Guns : 3 M.G. Torpedo tubes : 2.

"TIPO VELOCI." 14 BUILT (1917-19) + 1 ON TRIALS. 30 tons. Length : 72.2 feet. Motors (Isotta Fraschini) : 1900 B.H.P.=30 to 33 kts. Guns : 1—14 pdr., 30 cal., 1 M.G. Torpedo tubes : 2—18 inch in some.

Same appearance as British M.L.

TYPE C : 127 BUILT (1916-19) + 35 *BUILDING.* 40 tons. Length : 80 feet. Motors (Standard) : 450 B.H.P. =19 kts. Guns : 1—14 pdr., 40 cal. (*A.A.*) and 1 M.G. Are much the same as British *ML 1—151.*

TYPE B : 46 BUILT (1916-19) + 8 *BUILDING.* 19 tons. Length : 59 feet. Motors (Isotta-Fraschini) : 500 B.H.P. = 18 kts. Guns : 1—14 pdr., 30 cal. and one or two M.G.

Mine Layers (*Navi Affondamine*).

Note.—All vessels in section A—F are fully described and illustrated on preceding pages.

A :—Light Cruisers.

NINO BIXIO, MARSALA, QUARTO. } Carry 200 mines each.

B :—Old Cruisers.

LIGURIA, PUGLIA. Carry 60 mines each.

C :—Flotilla Leaders.

4 *Aquila* class : **Aquila, Falco, Nibbio, Sparviero.** Carry 50 mines each.
2 *Mirabello* class : **Augusto, Riboty, Carlo Mirabello.** Carry 100 mines each.

D :—Destroyers.

7 boats of *G. Sirtori* class, viz : **Angelo Bassini, Agostino Bertani, Giacinto Carini, Giacomo Medici, Giuseppe la Farina, Giuseppe la Masa, Nicola Fabrizi.** Each carries 10 mines.

X1, X2, X3, described in Submarine Section, 18 mines each.

F :—Lagoon Gunboats.

BRONDOLO, MARGHERA. 60 mines each.

G :—Old Torpedo Gunboats.

(May no longer be Mine Layers).

AGORDAT (1899) & **COATIT** (1899). 1313 tons. Complement, 175. Dimensions : 287½ × 30½ × 12 feet. Armament : 2—4·7 inch, 4—14 pdr. A.A., 2—14 inch tubes (*above water*). Deck, ¾". Designed H.P., 8000 = 23 kts. 8 Blechynden boilers. Coal : *normal* 180 tons ; *maximum* 300 tons.

VOLTA (1883). 2480 tons. Armament : 5—6 pdrs. Designed H.P. 2500 = 14 kts. Coal : 460 tons.

M. A. S. (*Continued*).

M.A.S. 91—102, 218—232 (built by Orlando).

With two torpedoes.

TYPE A : 175 BUILT (1916-19) + 11 *BUILDING.* 12 tons. Length : 52½ feet. Motors (Isotta-Fraschini or Sterling, or F.I.A.T.) : 400 to 500 B.H.P. = 24 to 26 kts. Guns : (*a*) 1—3 pdr., 40 cal. and 1 M.G., or (*b*) 1—6 pdr., 43 cal. and 1 M.G. Several have 2 torpedo tubes or dropping gears.

"Grillo" Boats.

TOTAL NUMBER NOT KNOWN. About 20 tons. Dimensions : 36 × 6 × — feet. 1—15 H.P. electric motor and tunnel screw = 5 kts. 1—20 H.P. electric motor driving endless climbing chains for surmounting booms. 2—18 inch torpedoes carried in dropping gears. Complement, 3. Designed by Gen. Prunieri.

Has mainmast now. (*May not be Mine Layer now.*)

Photo, Spartiali.

IRIDE (1891). 946 tons. Complement, 115. Guns : 6—14 pdr. AA. Tubes : 2. I.H.P., 4240 = 20·7 kts. 2 screws. 4 loco boilers. Coal : 130 tons.

Mine Layers (*Old Torpedo Gunboats*)—continued.

No photo available.
Almost same in appearance as Iride in preceding column.

MINERVA (1892). 940 tons. Complement, 83. Length : 246 feet. Beam : 27 feet. *Max.* draught : 12½ feet. Guns : 3—14 pdr., 1—14 pdr. AA. 2—1 pdr. AA. Carries 60 mines. Armour : 1½" deck. Designed H.P., 4000 = 19 kts. 4 Blechynden boilers. Oil fuel : 80 tons.

Sister ship *Partenope* was deleted during the war as was *Montebello* of 860 tons.

GOITO (1887, rebuilt 1906). 857 tons. Complement, 83. Guns : Removed during War. Deck 1½". Designed H.P., 2600 = 18 kts. 3 screws. 6 loco. boilers. Oil fuel : 72 tons.

TRIPOLI (1886, rebuilt 1906) (1898). 860 tons. Complement, 83. Guns : 1—14 pdr., 1—14 pdr. AA. Carries 60 mines. Designed H.P., 2400 = 18 kts. 3 screws. 6 loco. boilers. Oil fuel : 72 tons.

"Subsidiary Ship" (*Nave Sussidiaria*).

Not completed by June, 1919.)

NAME AND TYPE UNKNOWN. Is building at Riva Trigosa. 10,500 tons. Dimensions : 328.1 × — × — feet. Estimated speed : 10 kts. Has special underwater protection.

Seaplane Carrier & Submarine Depot Ships.
(*Nave per trasporto idrovolanti e appoggio Sommergibili.*)

EUROPA (ex-liner of La Veloce Nav. Italiana) (1907). 8800 tons. Dimensions : 454.7 × 53.4 × 20.5 feet. Speed : 15 kts. 1 screw. 2 cyl. boilers. Guns : 2 or more small Q.F. For Seaplanes and Kite Balloons.

Note.—Old Cruiser *LOMBARDIA* (described on an earlier page) served during War as a Submarine Depot Ship. Uncertain if she is still so employed.

Submarine Salvage Ship.
(*Pontone per ricupero Sommergibili.*)

ANTEO (Smulders, Schiedam, 1914). Special Salvage Ship for Submarines. 2100 tons. Dimensions : 164 × 73¾ × — feet. I.H.P., 750 = 8 kts. 2 screws. 2 cyl. boilers. 2 cranes, each lifting 200 tons.

Fuel Ships (*Navi rifornimento carbone e naftetine*).
Oil Tankers (*Cisterne per nafta*).

Not completed, May, 1919.

SIX OIL TANKERS building or completing. of "Improved Acheronte" class. No details available.

ACHERONTE, COCITO, FLEGETONTE, LETE, STIGE (all 1914-15). Oil tankers. 1204 tons. Armament : ? H.P., 400. Fiat Diesel engines = kts. Cargo : 760 tons oil fuel.

GIOVE* (——). **NETTUNO*** (——). Oil tankers. 10,310 tons. Dimensions : 416½ × 50¾ × 24 feet. Armament : 6—14 pdr. H.P. and speed not known. Cargo : 6000 tons oil fuel.

*These two Ships are not mentioned in Official List furnished by the Ministry of Marine, Rome. They may have been (*a*) sunk during the War, or (*b*) transferred to Mercantile Marine.

ITALIAN MISCELLANEOUS.

Fuel Ships (Continued.)

BRONTE (1904). Fleet Collier, Oil Tanker and Transport. 9460 tons. Complement, 79. Guns : 4—6 pdr. With full cargo, 3700 I.H.P. = 11·5 kts. ; with reduced cargo, 4300 I.H.P. = 14·5 kts. 2 screws. 4 cyl. boiler. Carries 6,000 tons coal or 4000 tons oil + 2000 tons coal. Own coal : 550 tons. *Sterope* (sister ship) lost during War.

Note.—*Garigliano* (see third column) can also carry a small cargo of oil fuel.

Repair Ship (*Nave Officina*).

VULCANO (ex *Savoia*, 1885). 3260 tons. Complement, 199. Guns : 4—6 pdr. I.H.P., 3340 = 15·2 kts. 1 screw. 8 loco. boilers. Coal : 600 tons.

Note.—*Bronte* (see above) is rated as a Transport.

Tugs (*Rimorchiatori*), Tankers (*Cisterna*), Distilling Ships (*Navi Distillatrice*)

TITANO (1913). High Sea Tug. 970 tons. Guns : 2—6 pdr. H.P., 1970 = 15 kts. 2 screws. 2 Gennardini boilers. Coal : 160 tons.

ERIDANO (1911). Tanker 1260 tons. Guns: 2—3 pdr. Designed H.P., 1200 = 12.7 kts. 2 screws. 2 Yarrow boilers. Coal: 120 tons. Carries 400 tons water.

Official photo.

CICLOPE (1903). High Sea Tug. 850 tons. Dimensions : 177 × 29½ × 12 feet. Armament : 2—6 pdr. H.P., 1900 =13.6 kts. 2 screws. 4 Thornycroft boilers. Coal : 195 tons.

TEVERE (1897). Tanker 960 tons. Guns: 2—1 pdr. H.P., 620 = 11 kts. 1 screw. 2 Thornycroft boilers. Coal: 150 tons. Carries 320 tons water.

Transports (Continued.)

ERITREA (ex *Kaiseri*, captured from Turkey, 1911). 4350 tons. Guns : 6—6 pdr. I.H.P., 1000 = kts. 1 screw. 2 cyl. boilers. Can carry 1700 tons cargo.

(See Silhouettes.)

ZENSON (ex-cruiser *Carlo Alberto*, 1896). 7200 tons. Disarmed during War. I.H.P., 13,000* = 20 kts.* 2 screws. 6 cyl. boilers. Coal : 1000 tons.*

*These figures probably reduced on conversion to Naval Transport.

Official photo.

CORTELLAZZO (ex-cruiser *Marco Polo*, 1892). 4900 tons. Guns : Not known. Armour removed during War. I.H.P., 10,650* = 17·8 kts. 2 screws. 4 cyl. boilers. Coal : 720* tons.

*These figures probably reduced on conversion to Naval Transport.

Armed Tugs, Tanks, &c.

ATLANTE (1892). 776 tons, and **ERCOLE** (1892). High Sea Tugs. 853 tons. Armament : 2—6 pdr. Designed H.P., 1830 and 1700 = 13 kts. 2 screws. 4 cyl. boilers. Coal : 150 tons.

GIOVANNI BAUSAN (1883). Distilling Ship, late Cruiser. 3500 tons. Complement, 152. No guns. I.H.P., 6470 = 17.4 kts. 2 screws. 4 cyl. boilers. Has 4 Spampani distillers for 200 tons water per 24 hours. Coal : 590 tons.

VERDE & PAGANO (1877). Tankers. 390 tons. Armament: 2—1 pdr. Original speed: 9 kts. Coal: 35 tons. Carry 105 tons water. Also 232 other Tugs, 33 Harbour Tankers. 12 Lagoon Tugs are *building.*

Transports (Continued.)

BENGASI (ex-*Derna*, captured from Turkey, 1911). Built 1890. 3560 tons. Complement, 64. Guns : 2—6 pdr., 4—3 pdr. I.H.P., 2000 = 13.6 kts. 1 screw. 4 cyl. boilers. Can carry 1050 tons as cargo.

(Also Oil Tanker.)

GARIGLIANO (1887). 1300 tons. Complement, 42. Armament : 2—12 pdr. H.P., 537 = 11 kts. 1 screw. 1 cyl. boiler. 120 tons coal. Can carry 200 tons cargo and 85 tons oil (as cargo).

Small Mine-Sweeping Tugs.

Appearance much as "Tevere"

RD 1—RD 29 (builders unknown, 1916-18). **RD 30—RD 44** (builders unknown, 1918-19). **RD 45—49** (Pattison, Naples, 1918-19). No details known of these vessels.

Royal Yacht.

Photo, Seward, Weymouth.

TRINACRIA (ex *America*), 1884. 9200 tons. Complement, 180. Dimensions : 441⅜ × 51¼ × 27 feet. Armament : 4—6 pdr., 2—1 pdr. Designed H.P., 6000 = 15 kts. 1 screw. 6 cyl. boilers. Coal : 1500 tons.

Despatch Vessels.

CICLOPE (1903). 844 tons. 177 × 29¼ × 12 feet. Armament: 2—6 pdr., 2—1 pdr. H.P. 2298 = 15 kts. Coal : 170 tons.

GALILEO (1887). 970 tons. Armament: 4—4.7 in., 2—6 pdr., 2 machine. H.P. 1100 = 15 kts. Coal: 220 tons.

ITALIAN MISCELLANEOUS.

Armed Yachts (*Yacht Armato*).

TOBRUK (1897). 700 tons. Complement, 38. Dimensions: 184 × 25 × 15½ feet (*mean*). Guns: 2—14 pdr. (*A.A*). I.H.P., 560 = 11.5 kts. 1 screw. 1 cyl. boiler. Coal: 170 tons.

MISURATA (1894). 700 tons. Complement, 33. Dimensions 191⅓ × 25½ × 14 feet (*mean*). Guns: 2—14 pdr. (*AA*) I.H.P., 780 = 12.5 kts. 1 screw. 1 cyl. boiler. Coal 120 tons.

GIULIANA (1893). 1100 tons. Complement, 46. Dimensions 22½ × 28 × 15 feet (*mean*). Guns: 4—6 pdr. I.H.P. 700 = 11.9 kts. 1 screw. 1 cyl. boiler. Coal: 180 tons.

CUNFIDA (ex-*Shipka*, 1892, captured during Turko-Italian War). 560 tons. Complement, 36. Dimensions: 151½ × 22½ × — feet. Guns: 1—14 pdr., 1—14 pdr. (AA). I.H.P. 700 = 12·9 kts. 1 screw. 2 cyl. boilers.

ARCHIMEDE (——). 815 tons. Guns: 4—6 pdr. I.H.P. —— = 13 kts. 1 screw. 1 cyl. boiler.

Note—Captured by Germans at Odessa, June, 1918. Re-captured December, 1918.

CAPITANO VERRI (ex-*Thetis*, captured during Turko-Italian War). 640 tons. Guns: 3—6 pdr. I.H.P., 355 = 10.5 kts. 1 screw. 1 cyl. boiler.

Surveying Ships. (*Servizio Idrografico*).

AMMIRAGLIO MAGNAGHI (Ansaldo, —/8/14). 2050 tons. Complement, 137. Dimensions: 229½ × 37½ × 12½ feet. Guns: 4—14 pdr. I.H.P., 2000 = 14 kts. Machinery: 2 sets vertical triple expansion. Boilers: 4 cylindrical.

STAFFETTA listed in 1914 of 1800 tons.

Cable Ship.

CITTA DI MILANO (1886). 2123 tons. Armament: 2—6 pdr., 2—1 pdr. Original speed: 9 kts.
Wrecked June 1919.

Caprera (1904). Armed Merchant Cruiser. 5040 tons (gross). Torpedoed by an enemy Submarine, 5th February, 1918.
Prometeo (1906). Armed Merchant Cruiser. 4450 tons (gross). Torpedoed by an enemy Submarine, 18th March, 1918.
Citta di Messina (1910). Armed Merchant Cruiser. 3495 tons (gross). Torpedoed by an Austrian Submarine, in the Straits of Otranto, 23rd June, 1916.
Citta di Palermo (1910). Armed Merchant Cruiser. 3415 tons (gross). Mined, in the Lower Adriatic, 8th January, 1916.
Verbano (1908). Armed Boarding Steamer. 2700 tons displacement. Guns: 4—6 pdr. Mined, 13th November, 1918.
Citta di Sassari (1910). Armed Boarding Steamer. 2167 tons (gross). Torpedoed by an enemy Submarine, 2nd December, 1917.

Training Ships (*Navi Scuola*).

For Cadets :
Cruiser **ETNA,** described on a previous page.

Also

AMERIGO VESPUCCI (1882). 2660 tons. Complement, 279. Armament : 4—4·7 inch.* Armour : 1½″ deck amidships. H.P., 3340 = 14 kts. 1 screw. 8 locomotive boilers. Coal : 500 tons.

*Removed during War.

FLAVIO GIOIA (1881). 3016 tons. H.P., 4156 = 15·kts. All other details as *Amerigo Vespucci*.

Training Ships (*continued*).

(*Stokers' Training-Ship*).   *Official photo.*
MONTEBELLO (1887). Late Torpedo Gunboat of 820 tons. Complement, 108. Guns : 4—6 pdr.* Armour : 1½″ deck. I.H.P. 4240 = 20·7 kts. (*trials*). Machinery : 2 sets vertical triple expansion. Boilers : For training duties, (*a*) 6 water-tube types, and (*b*) 3 of mixed types. Coal : 100 tons.
*Removed during War.

(*Boys' Training Ships*).
MISENO (1886). **PALINURO** (1886). 552 tons. Armament : 2—14 pdr. (Anti-aircraft). I.H.P., 430 = 10 kts. 1 screw. 1 cylindrical boiler. Coal : 52 tons.

AUSTRIAN NAVY.

Modern Naval Guns.

Notation.	Bore.		Official Designation.		Weight.	Weight, A.P. Shot.	Initial Velocity.	Maximum penetration A.P. capped against K.C. a´r at impact.	
		Bore.	Length/ Calibres	Model.				11,000 yds.	5000 yds.
	in.	c/m.			tons.	lbs.	ft. secs.	in.	in.
A^5	12	30·5	L/45		52	992	2625	10·6	19·6
AA	9·4	24	L/45		26·2	474	2625	4·2	10·9
A	9·4	24	L/40	S	27.5	474	2312	...	10·7
A	9·4	24	L/40	K.K/'97	30·2	474	2378	...	...
A	9·4	24	L/40	K.K/'94	27·8	474	2264	...	...
A	7·5	19	L/42		12·1	214	2625	3·5	7·1
	5·9	15	L/50	K/'13	...	100	...	...	...
	5·9	15	L/50		5·8	100	2887	...	4·3
	5.9	15	L/40	S	4·3	100	2264	...	...
	5·9	15	L/40	K	4·4	100	2264	...	...
	4·7	12	L/45		..	...	...	...	...
	4·7	12	L/40		2·1	52	2264	...	...
	3·9	10	L/50	K/'10	...	...	...	...	...
	3·9	10	L/50	K/'07	1·9	30	2954	...	...

In Model column S=Skoda ; K=Krupp. In addition to the above there are 24 other models of older, smaller and Howitzer guns officially listed. Also new anti-aircraft guns, of which no particulars can be secured.

Torpedoes and tubes used : Whitehead-Fiume types (20·8, 17·7, and 14-inch).

Scale : 1 inch = 160 feet.

Ships whose names are not in capitals are for harbour and subsidiary service.

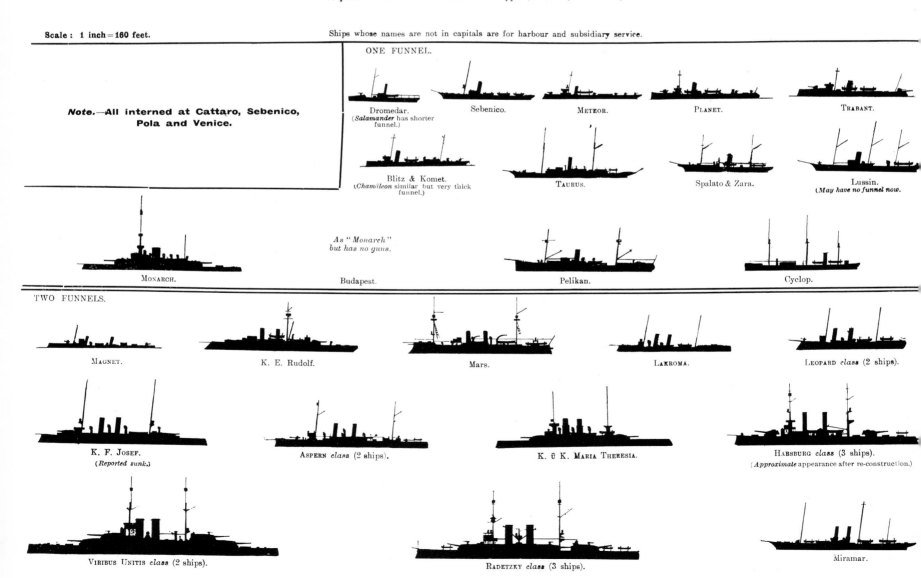

Note.—All interned at Cattaro, Sebenico, Pola and Venice.

ONE FUNNEL.

Dromedar.
(*Salamander* has shorter funnel.)

Sebenico.

METEOR.

PLANET.

TRABANT.

Blitz & Komet.
(*Chamӕleon* similar but very thick funnel.)

TAURUS.

Spalato & Zara.

Lussin.
(*May have no funnel now.*)

MONARCH.

As "Monarch" but has no guns.

Budapest.

Pelikan.

Cyclop.

TWO FUNNELS.

MAGNET.

K. E. Rudolf.

Mars.

LAKROMA.

LEOPARD class (2 ships).

K. F. JOSEF.
(*Reported sunk.*)

ASPERN class (2 ships).

K. ü K. MARIA THERESIA.

HABSBURG class (3 ships).
(*Approximate* appearance after re-construction.)

VIRIBUS UNITIS class (2 ships).

RADETZKY class (3 ships).

Miramar.

Scale : 1 inch = 160 feet.   AUSTRO-HUNGARIAN RECOGNITION SILHOUETTES.

THREE FUNNELS.

Note :-

All interned at Cattaro, Sebenico, Pola and Venice.

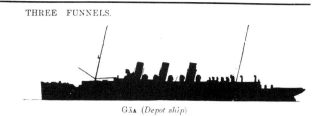

Gäa (*Depot ship*).

Satellit.

Kaiser Karl VI.

Erzherzog Karl *class* (3 ships).

Sankt Georg.

TORPEDO CRAFT.   Scale : 1 inch = 160 feet.   FOUR FUNNELS.

Old t.b.
(*Used for subsidiary
duties.*)

Nos. 20–49 *class* t.b.
(*Reconstructed
Schichau type.*)

Nos. 13–18 *class* t.b.

Nos. 1–12 *class* t.b.

Nos. 50–73 & 74–100 *classes* t.b.

Admiral Spaun and Saida *classes*.

Tatra *class* t.b.d. (9 or 10).

Huszar *class* t.b.d. (10), also Varasdinier.
(*Heights of funnels vary*).

SUBMARINES.   Scale : 1 inch = 80 feet.

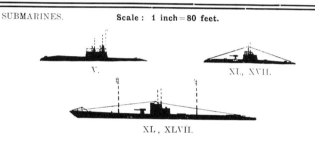

V.   XI, XVII.

XVII—XXXII.   XXI, XXII.   XL, XLVII.

1910 AUSTRIAN DREADNOUGHTS.

(V. Unitis Class—2 Ships).
PRINZ EUGEN (November, 1912), **TEGETTHOF** (March, 1912).

Displacement, 20,000 tons. *Full load*, 21,370 tons. Complement, 1,050.

Length (*w.l.*), 495¾ feet. Beam, 89½ feet. { Mean draught, 26¾ feet. } Length *over all*, 530 feet.
{ *Max.* draught, 28 feet. }

Guns (Skoda) :
12—12 inch, 45 cal. (A⁵)
12—5·9 inch, 50 cal.
4—11 pdr. (anti-aircraft)
2—3 pdr.
(2—9 pdr. landing)
4 machine
Torpedo tubes (20·8 inch) :
4 submerged

Armour (special chrome nickel)
11″ Belt (amidships) ......
4¾″ Belt (ends) ..
7¼″ Upper Belt(amidships)
1¾″ Deck ....
6¾″ Battery ....
11″—7″ Turrets ....
11″ Barbettes ....
11¾″ Conning tower (forward)

9¾″ Conning tower (aft)
6½″ Range-finding position

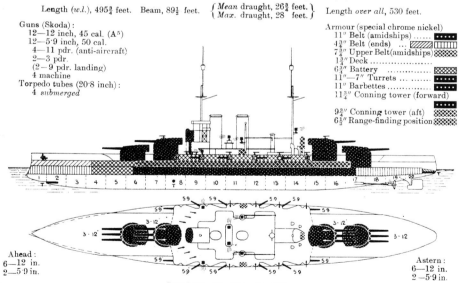

Viribus Unitis (now sunk, but *Tegetthof* and *Prinz Eugen* same).   *Photo Alfieri.*

Ahead :
6—12 in.
2—5·9 in.

Astern :
6—12 in.
2—5·9 in.

Broadside : 12—12 in., 6—5·9 in.

Machinery : Turbine, see *Notes.* 4 screws. Boilers : Yarrow. Designed H.P. 25,000=20 kts.
Coal : *normal* 900 tons; *maximum* 1700 tons (+ oil : 200 tons).

Gunnery Notes—12-inch same model as in *Radetzky* class. Heights of guns above w.l. 29¼ feet for end triples, 45 feet for super-firing triples. 5·9-inch battery about 20 feet above w.l. Arcs of fire 300° for end triples ; 320° for super-firing 12-inch. End 5·9 inch about 135°, others about 120°. 120 rounds per 12-inch and 200 per 5·9-inch gun carried. Magazine cooling controlled from central station. Range-finding positions are in upper parts of each C.T., and 2 amidships above 5·9-inch battery. Goerz R.F.

Torpedo Notes—Tubes are 2 broadside, 1 bow, 1 stern. Bullivant net defence right up to stern. 5 or 7—42½″ searchlights.

Armour Notes—Main and upper belts 15—16 feet deep. Usual internal protection against torpedoes by lateral bulkheads in way of magazine and machinery spaces, but it is not of much practical value. Austrian plans show armoured upper-works and funnel bases, but this is doubtful.

Note.

TEGETTHOF interned at Venice. Reported refitting for service in
Italian Navy.

PRINZ EUGEN interned at Cattaro. (1919)
VIRIBUS UNITIS sunk by torpedo from Italian CMB night of 1
November 1918.
SZENTISTVAN torpedoed by Italian MTBs off Premuda Is. 10 June
1918.

Name	Builder	Machinery	Laid down	Completed	Trials	Turbines	Boilers	Best recent speed
P. Eugen	Stab. Tecnico	Stab. Tecnico	Jan., '12	May, '14	=20·81	Parsons	12 Yarrow	
Tegetthof	Stab. Tecnico	Stab. Tecnico	Sep., '10	July, '13	≈19·75	Parsons	12 Yarrow	

General Notes.—These ships are very well designed, all details being carefully planned, but they are said to be
unstable. Arcs of fire for all guns are large. Reports of first trials with the triple turrets are very contradictory,
but they do not seem to have come up to expectation.

1907   AUSTRIAN BATTLESHIPS (*Schlachtschiffe*) — 20 knot.

(RADETZKY CLASS—3 SHIPS).

ERZHERZOG FRANZ FERDINAND (Sept., 1908), **ZRINYI** (April, 1910),
and **RADETZKY** (July, 1909).

Displacement, 14,500 metric tons. Complement, 876.

Length (*waterline*), 448 feet. Beam, 80⅓ feet. *Mean* draught, 26½ feet. Length *over all*, 456 feet (*p.p.* 429¾).

Guns (Skoda) :
4—12 inch, 45 cal. (A^5)
8—9·4 inch, 45 cal. (A^3)
20—3·9 inch, 50 cal.
6—11 pdr., 45 cal.
2—3 pdr.
(2—9 pdr. landing)
3 machine
Torpedo tubes (17·7 inch) :
2 *submerged* (broadside)
1 *submerged* (stern)

Armour (Krupp) :
9″ Belt (amidships) ....
4″ Belt (ends) ....
2″ Deck on slopes, 1¾″ flat ...
6″ Upper belt ....
3″ Upper belt (bow) ....
9¾″ Big gun turrets (N.C.) =
9¾″ Bases to these (N.C.)
8″ Secondary turrets (N.C.) =
4¾″ Battery ....
10″ Conning tower (N.C.) ...
(Total weight 3150 tons.)

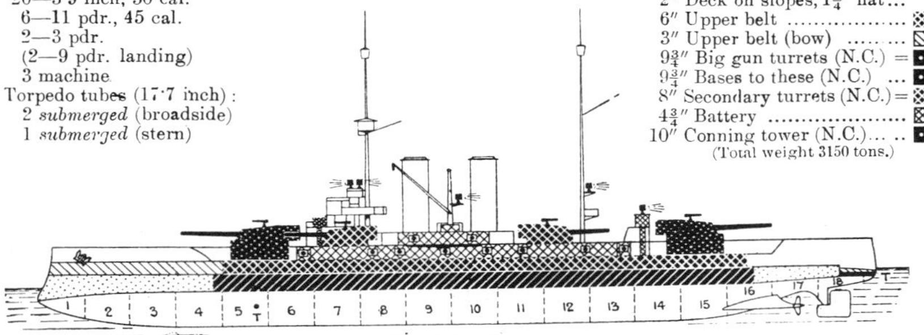

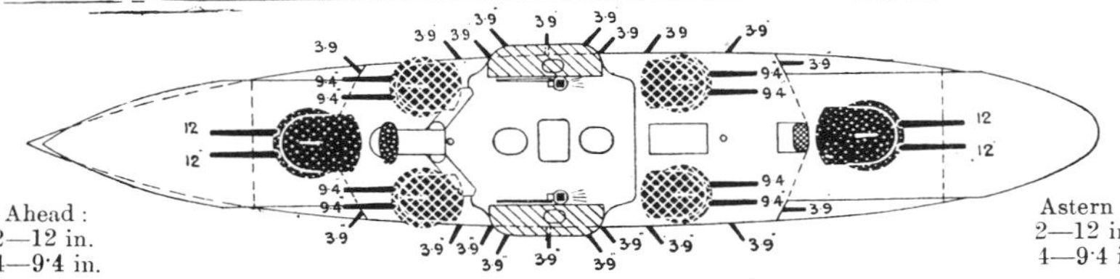

Ahead :
2—12 in.
4—9·4 in.

Astern :
2—12 in.
4—9·4 in.

Broadside : 4—12 in., 4—9·4 in.

Machinery : 2 sets 4 cylinder vertical triple expansion. 2 screws. Boilers : 12 Yarrow. Designed H.P. 20,000=20 kts. Coal : *normal* 750 tons ; *maximum* 1580 tons + 166 tons oil fuel.

Armour Notes.—Main belt is 285½ feet long by 7½ feet deep, 5 feet of it below water. 6″ bulkheads. Upper belt same length. Battery, etc., 180 feet long.

Gunnery Notes.— Big guns have arcs of fire 290°. Bow ones 29½ feet above normal waterline, after, 26 feet. Manœuvred electrically. 9·4 average 24½ feet above water. Battery guns 16 feet above water. These have arcs of fire 130°—100°. The 12 inch are extremely powerful guns, but the 9·4's are not a new model. Two range and fire control towers amidships above upper 3·9 inch battery guns.

Torpedo Notes.—Net defence fitted (Bullivant). There is also special internal protection against mines and torpedoes, consisting of internal fore and aft bulkheads, built up by two layers of high-tensile steel.

Name	Built and engined at	Laid down	Completed	Trials	Boilers	Best recent speed
Ers. F. Ferdinand	All at	Sept., '07	1910	20,600=20·68	Yarrow	
Zrinyi	Stabilimento	Oct., '08	1911	=20·5	in all	
Radetzky	Tecnico	Dec., '07	1911	=20·5		

E. F. FERDINAND.   *Photo, Spartali.*

Note.

E. F. FERDINAND interned at Venice. Reported that, after examination, it has been decided that she is not worth repairing for service in Italian Navy. RADETZKY and ZRINYI both interned at Spalato.

FULL BROADSIDE DETAIL VIEW OF RADETZKY.   *Photo, Alfieri.*

1901   AUSTRIAN BATTLESHIPS (20 knot).

(E. KARL CLASS—3 SHIPS).

ERZHERZOG KARL (Oct., 1903), **ERZHERZOG FRIEDRICH** (April, 1904), and
ERZHERZOG FERDINAND MAX (May, 1905).

Displacement, 10,600 metric tons. Complement, 748.

Length (*waterline*), 408 feet. Beam, 71¾ feet. *Mean* draught, 24⅔ feet. Length (*p.p.*), 390½ feet.

Guns (Skoda) :
4—9·4 inch, 40 cal.
12—7·5 inch, 42 cal.
12—11 pdr., 45 cal.
(Some anti-aircraft)
(2—9 pdr., landing)
8—3 pdr.
3 machine
Torpedo tubes (17.7 inch) :
2 *submerged*

Armour (Krupp) :
8¼″—6″ Belt (amidships)
9″ Bulkheads ....
2″ Belt (bow) ....
3″ Deck (flat on belt) ...
2¾″ Deck (at ends) ....
9½″ Barbettes............
9½″ Turrets ....
9½″ Turret bases ......
5″ Lower deck (side) .....
6¾″ ,, ,, (bulkhead)
6″ Battery (N.C.) ......
6″ Small Turrets (N.C.)
8½″ Conning tower ......
(Total weight 2922 tons.)

Ahead:
2—9·4 in
4—7·5 in

Astern :
2—9·4 in.
4—7·5 in.

ERZHERZOG KARL

Broadside: 4—9·4 in., 6—7·5 in.

Machinery : 2 sets 4 cylinder triple expansion. 2 screws. Boilers : 12 Yarrow. Designed H.P. 18,000=19 kts. Coal : *normal* 550 tons ; *maximum* 1315 tons. (E. F. Max also carries a small amount of oil fuel, about 35 tons.)

Armour Notes.—Belt is 8¼ feet wide by 225 feet long ; 3½ feet of it below waterline ; lower edge is about 6″ thick.

Gunnery Notes.—Loading positions, big guns : all round. Hoists, electric. Big guns manœuvred electrically, secondary guns electrically. Big guns with 20° elevation have a range of 17,000 yards. Arcs of fire : Big guns, 260°.
Height of guns above water : Bow turret, 20½ feet. After turret, 20 feet. Main deck battery, 13 feet.

Torpedo Notes.—6 searchlights.

Engineering Notes.—On the average 126 revs. = 19 kts. ; 128 = 19·5 kts. ; 138 = 20·5 kts.

General Notes.—The double bottom extends 240 feet amidships only. Average cost per ship £912,500.

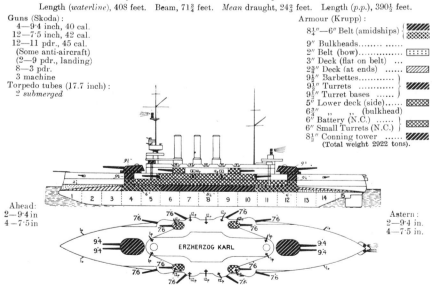

ERZHERZOG KARL.

Note :—All interned at Cattaro.

Small fire controls now fitted high up on foremast of all ships as E. Karl above.

Name	Builder	Machinery	Laid down	Completed	Last Refit	Trials		Boilers	Recent best speed
						n.d.	f.d.		
E. Karl	Triest	All by	1901	Feb.,'05		13,180=19·16	17,926=20·36	Yarrow	
E. Friedrich	Triest	Stabilimento	1902	Oct.,'06		14,100=19·01	18,130=20·57	in	
E. Ferdinand Max	Triest	Tecnico	1903	Apr.,'07		14,390=19·57	18,600=20·76	all	

AUSTRIAN SECOND CLASS BATTLESHIPS.

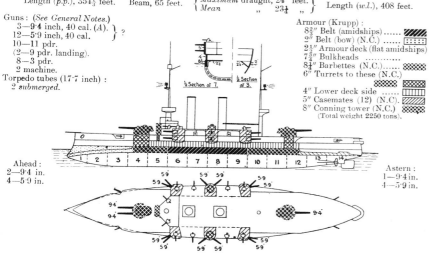

Note.—Appearance after reconstruction is shown *approximately* by plans below.

HABSBURG (Sept., 1900), **ARPAD** (Sept., 1901), **BABENBERG** (Oct., 1902).

Displacement, 8300 metric tons.   Complement, 623.

Length (*p.p.*), 354⅓ feet.   Beam, 65 feet. { Maximum draught, 24 feet. } { Mean „ 23¼ „ } Length (*w.l.*), 408 feet.

Guns: (*See General Notes.*)
3—9·4 inch, 40 cal. (A). }
12—5·9 inch, 40 cal. } ?
10—11 pdr.
(2—9 pdr. landing).
8—3 pdr.
2 machine.
Torpedo tubes (17·7 inch):
2 submerged.

Armour (Krupp):
8⅔″ Belt (amidships) ......
2″ Belt (bow) (N.C.) ......
2½″ Armour deck (flat amidships)
7¾″ Bulkheads
8¼″ Barbettes (N.C.) ......
6″ Turrets to these (N.C.)

4″ Lower deck side ......
5″ Casemates (12) (N.C.)
8″ Conning tower (N.C.)
(Total weight 2250 tons).

Ahead:
2—9·4 in.
4—5·9 in.

Astern:
1—9·4 in.
4—5·9 in.

Broadside: 3—9·4 in., 6—5·9 in.

Machinery: 2 sets triple expansion, 4 cylinder.   2 screws.   Boilers: 16 Belleville (model, 1900).
Designed H.P. 15000 = 18·5 kts.   Coal: *normal* 500 tons, *maximum* 840 tons.

General Notes.—First two built at Triest, last at Pola.   Machinery by Stab. Tecnico, in all.   Made 19·6 kts. on first trials.   *Habsburg* reconstructed and partly reboiled 1911.   *Arpad* reconstructed in 1912 and *Babenberg* in 1913. Superstructures were greatly reduced, funnels shortened, fore bridges and charthouse rebuilt are of fore-turret enlarged.   About 70-80 tons removed from each ship.   May now have 20·8 tubes.   9·4 inch guns Skoda in *Babenberg*, Krupp in other ships.

(To distinguish from *K. K. VI* note *cranes, no ventilators* and position of searchlight on foremast).

SANKT GEORG (December, 1903).

Displacement, 7300 metric tons.   Complement, 628.
Length (*waterline*), 383⅝ feet.   Beam, 61½ feet.   *Max.* draught, 21⅓ feet.

Guns (Skoda) (M. '01):
2—9·4 inch, 40 cal.
5—7·5 inch, 42 cal.
4—5·9 inch, 40 cal.
9—11 pdr.
(2—7 pdr. landing).
10—3 pdr.
2 machine.
Torpedo tubes (17·7 inch):
2 submerged.

Armour (Krupp):
8¼″ Belt (amidships) ...
2″ Belt (forward) ......
2½″ Armour deck...
7½″ Bulkheads .. ..
8¼″ Lower deck side...
8″ Barbette...............
5″ Turret (aft).........
5″ Double casemates (4)

Ahead:
2—9·4 in.
2—7·5 in.
2—5·9 in.

Astern:
3—7·5 in.
2—5·9 in.

Broadside: 2—9·4 in., 3—7·5 in., 2—5·9 in.

Machinery: 2 sets triple expansion.   2 screws.   Boilers: 16 Yarrow.   Designed H.P. *natural* draught, 12,300 = 21 knots; *forced*, 14,000 = 21.   Coal: *normal* 600 tons; *maximum* 1000 tons.
Gunnery Notes.—Loading positions, big guns all round.   Hoists: electric and hand.   Big guns manœuvred electrically; 7·5 in. guns, electric; 6 in. guns, hand.   Arcs of fire: Big guns 240°.

Name	Builder	Machinery	Laid down	Completed	Trials	Boilers	Best recent speed
S. Georg	Pola	Stab. Tecnico	1903	1906	13,095 = 21·3 15,270 = 22	Yarrow	22·3

General Notes.—Cost £581,583.   Ventilators shown in above elevation by error.

Note.—HABSBURG, ARPAD, BABENBERG and BUDAPEST
interned at Pola.   MONARCH interned at Cattaro.

Photo, Laroux.

MONARCH (May, 1895).   Displacement, 5600 metric tons.   Complement, 433.   Length (*waterline*), 318 feet.   Beam, 55¾ feet.   *Mean* draught, 21 feet.   Length *over all*, 323 feet.   Guns (Krupp M. '86): 4—9·4 inch, 40 cal.; 6—5·9 inch, 40 cal.; (2—9 pdr. landing), 12—3 pdr., 2 machine.   Torpedo tubes (17·7 inch): 2 submerged.   Armour (Harvey): 10½″ Belt (amidships), 4¾″ Belt (bow), 2½″ Armour deck (aft), 2½″ Deck flat on belt, 9¾″ Bulkhead (aft), 10½″ Barbettes, 8″—5″ Hoods to these, 3″ Lower deck redoubt, 3″ Battery redoubt, 8″ Conning tower, 4″ Conning tower (aft).   Machinery: 2 sets vertical triple expansion.   2 screws.   Boilers: 8 cylindrical.   Designed H.P. 8500 = 17 kts.   Coal: *normal* 300 tons; *maximum* 500 tons.

BUDAPEST, sometimes referred to as *OFENPEST,* launched April, 1896.   Sister ship to *Monarch* described above, but has 16 Belleville boilers without economisers.   *Wien,* the third unit of the class, was sunk in Triest Harbour by Captain Rizzo of the Italian Navy 9/10 November 1917.   *Budapest* was also torpedoed on this occasion.   She did not sink, but was so heavily damaged, it appears she was deemed unfit for full repairs.   According to report, all her guns were removed, she was roughly repaired and is now only used as a floating Barracks or Harbour Depot Ship.

There are also two other old battleships, *Kronprinz Erherzog Rudolf* and *Mars.*   The former is Port Defence Ship at Cattaro; the latter is now a Training Ship.   Both are described with other Miscellaneous Ships on a later page.

KAISER KARL VI (Oct., 1898).   Displacement, 6300 metric tons.   Complement, 546.   Length (*waterline*), 390½ feet.   Beam, 56½ feet.   *Mean* draught, 20½ feet.   Guns (Krupp and Skoda): 2—9·4 inch, 40 cal. (A), 8—5·9 inch, 40 cal. (2—7 pdr. landing), 16—3 pdr., 2 machine guns; torpedo tubes, 17·7 inch, (2 *above water* behind 3″ armour).   Armour (Harvey-nickel): 8¾″ Belt (amidships); 8″ Fore bulkhead; 7″ After bulkhead; 4″ Engine hatches; 2½″ Armour deck (ends); 1½″ Armour deck (amidships); 8″ Barbettes; 3½″ Lower deck redoubt; 3″ Double casemates (4).   Machinery: 2 sets 4-cylinder triple expansion.   2 screws. Boilers: 18. Belleville.   Designed H.P. 12,000 = 20 kts.   Coal: *normal* 500 tons; *maximum* 820 tons. Laid down by Stab. Tecnico, Triest, 1896; completed 1899.   Trials: H.P. 12,900 = 20·83 kts.

Note.

SANKT GEORG interned at Cattaro.

KAISER KARL VI interned at Sebenico.

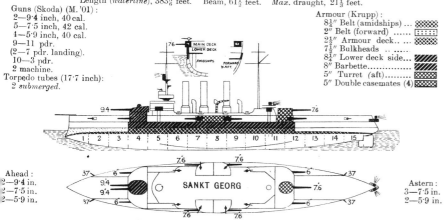

1911 AUSTRIAN LIGHT CRUISERS (*Kleine Kreuzer*). **1908**

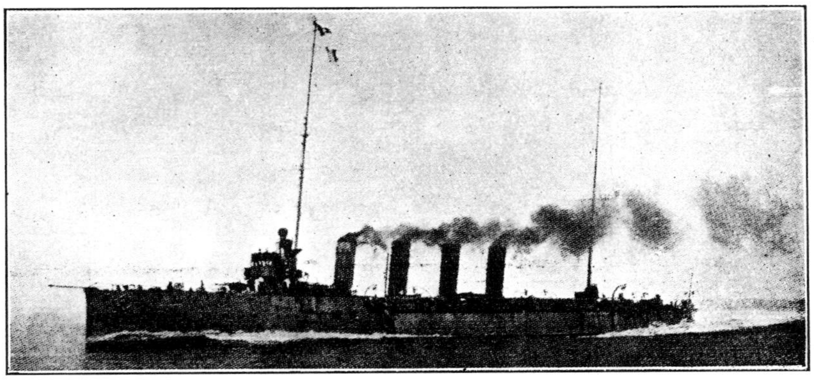

All now have small crow's nest high on foremast, and short mainmast.

SAIDA. (IMPROVED SPAUN CLASS). *Official Photo.*

SAIDA (Oct., 1912), **HELGOLAND** (Nov., 1912), **NOVARA** (Feb., 1913).

Normal displacement, 3500 metric tons. Complement, 318.

Length (*w.l.*), 410¾ feet. Beam, 42 feet. *Mean* draught, 15 feet. Length *over all*, 428½ feet.

Guns:
Saida {
9—4·1 inch.
1—3 inch (anti-aircraft).
1 machine.
1 landing.

Torpedo tubes (in all) 6—17·7 inch: 3 pairs *above water*.

Guns:
Other 2 {
8—3·9 inch (50 cal. semi-auto).
1 machine.
1 landing.

Armour (steel):
2½" Belt (amidships).........
2" Bulkheads ....
¾" Deck............................

Machinery: Turbine (*see Notes*). 4 screws. Boilers: 16 Yarrow. Designed H.P. 25,000=27 kts. Coal: *normal*, 450 tons; *maximum*, 750 tons. Radius of action as *Ad. Spaun*.

Name	*Builder*	*Machinery*	*Laid down*	*Completed*	*Trials*	*Turbines*	*Boilers*	*Best recent speed*
Saida	Monfalcone	Prager Masch.	Sep.'11	May, '14		Pfenniger	Yarrow	29·2
Helgoland	Fiume	Danubius	Oct.'11	Oct., '14		A.E.G.	Yarrow	
Novara	Fiume	Danubius	Feb.'12	Oct., '14		A.E.G.	Yarrow	

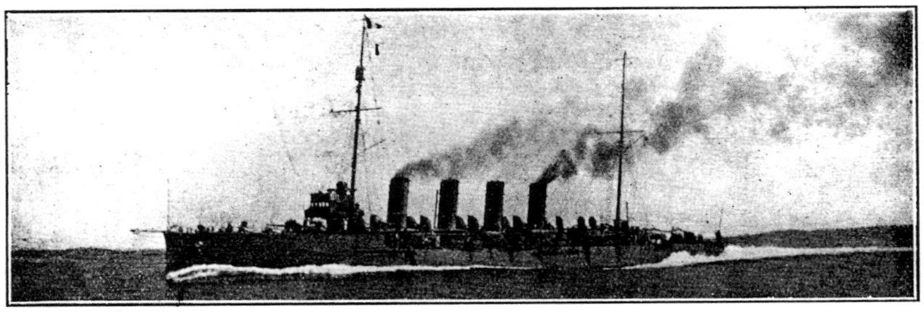

Now has short mainmast.

ADMIRAL SPAUN (October, 1909).

Normal displacement, 3500 metric tons. Complement, 320.

Length (*w.l.*), 410¾ feet. Beam 42 feet. *Mean* draught, 15 feet. Length *over all*, 428½ feet.

Guns:
7—3·9 inch (50 cal., semi-auto.)
1 Machine.
Torpedo tubes (17·7 inch): 8 *above water*, in 4 pairs.

Armour:
2⅓" Belt ......
2" Bulkheads
¾" Deck .. ...

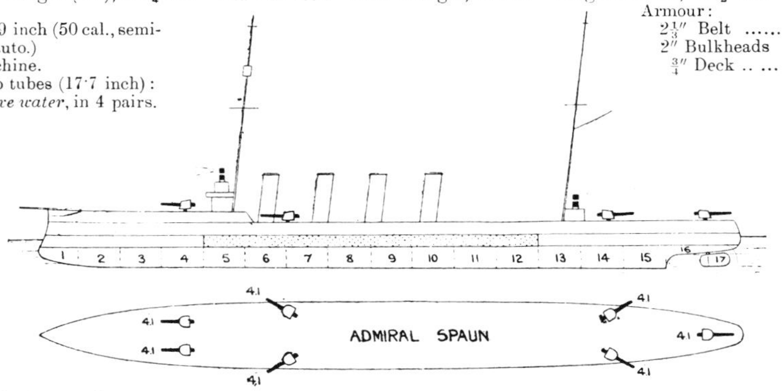

Machinery: Parsons turbine. 4 screws. Boilers: 16 Yarrow. Designed H.P. 20,000=26 kts. Coal: *normal* 450, *maximum* 780 (with oil fuel). Radii of action: 860 miles at *full power* (27 kts.), 1600 miles at 24 kts.

Name	*Builder*	*Machinery*	*Laid down*	*Completed*	*First Trials*	*Boilers*	*Present best speed*
A. Spaun?	Pola	Stab Tecnico	Jan.'08	1910	25,000=27·02	Yarrow	29

Note.—SAIDA and ADMIRAL SPAUN interned at Venice, both reported refitting for service in Italian Navy. HELGOLAND and NOVARA interned at Cattaro.

AUSTRIAN CRUISERS.

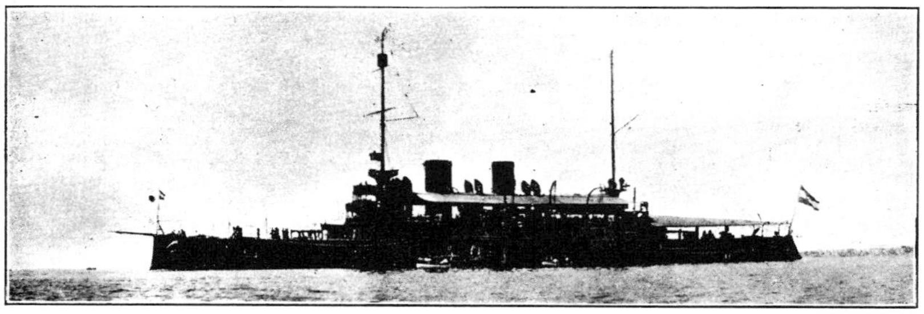

Photo, Spartali.

Interned at Pola.

KAISERIN-UND-KÖNIGIN-MARIA-THERESIA (1893, rebuilt 1909). 5200 metric tons. Complement, 468. Length (*p.p.*), 351 feet. Beam, 52½ feet. *Mean* draught, 21½ feet. Length *over all*, 374 feet. Guns: 2—7·5 inch, 42 cal.; 8—5·9 inch, 35 cal.; (2—7 pdr. landing), 16—3 pdr., 1 Machine. Torpedo tubes (17·7 inch): 4 *above water*. Armour (steel): 4" Belt (amidships); 2¼ "Armour deck, 4" Lower deck (redoubt); 4" Barbettes; 4" Sponsons; 4" Conning tower; 4" Bulkheads; 4" Hoods to barbettes; 4" Shields to upper deck guns. Machinery: 2 sets horizontal triple expansion. 2 screws. Boilers: 10 cylindrical. Designed H.P. *natural* 5880=17 kts.; *forced* 9500=19 kts. Coal: *normal* 600 tons; *maximum* 740 tons.

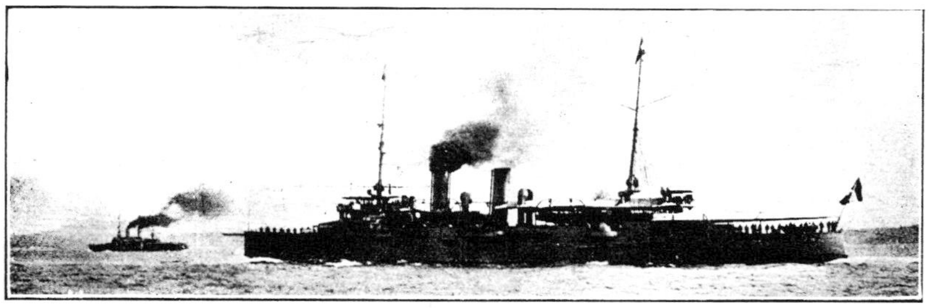

Interned at Cattaro.

***KAISER-FRANZ-JOSEF** (1889, rebuilt 1905). 4000 metric tons. Complement, 441. Length (*waterline*), 321½ feet. Beam, 48¼ feet. *Mean* draught, 19 feet. Guns (re-armed 1905-06): 2—5·9 inch, 40 cal.; and 6—5·9 inch, 35 cal.; (2—7 pdr. landing), 16—3 pdr., 1 Machine. Torpedo tubes (14 inch): 3 *above water*. Armour (steel): 2¼" Armour deck; 3½" Barbettes, 3½" Hoods to these; 4" Conning tower. Machinery: 2 sets horizontal triple expansion. 2 screws. Boilers: 4 cylindrical, double-ended. Designed H.P.: *natural* 6400=18 kts.; *forced* 8000=19 kts. Coal: *normal* 400 tons; *maximum* 720 tons.

***Reported, October 1919, to have foundered at Cattaro.**

Note: *Kaiserin Elisabeth*, sister ship sunk off Chiposan Kiao-Chau Bay 3 November 1914.

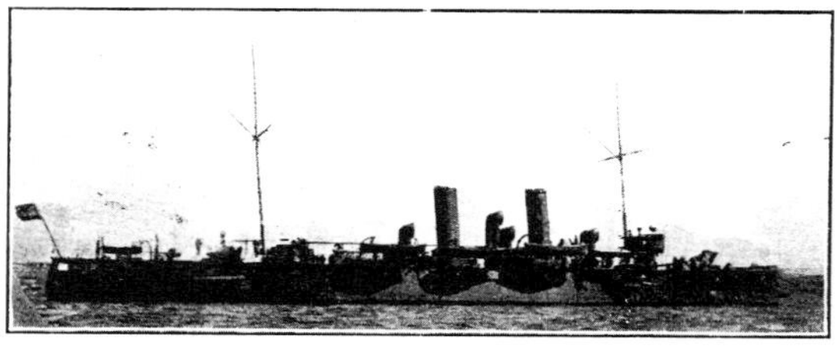

Both interned at Pola.

Now carry a small crow's nest high on the foremast.

ASPERN (May, 1898), 2400 tons. **SZIGETVAR** (October, 1900), 2300 tons. Complement, 305. Length (*w.l.*), 315¾ feet. Beam 39⅓ feet. *Maximum* draught, 17 feet (varies a little). Guns: 8—4·7 inch (40 cal.(, 10—3 pdr., 1 machine. Torpedo tubes (17·7 inch) (2 *submerged*). Armour: 2" deck amidships. Machinery: 2 sets triple expansion, by Stab. Tecnico. 2 screws. Boilers: 8 Yarrow. Designed H.P. 7800=20 kts. Coal: *normal* 300 tons; *maximum* 480 tons. Both built at Pola.
Zenta of this class lost in the war – Sunk by French squadron off Antivari 16 August 1914.

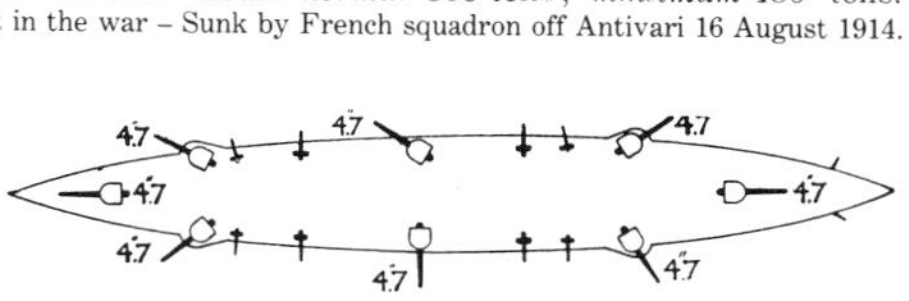

Old "Torpedo Cruisers."

See silhouettes and "Lakroma" (on Miscellaneous page) which they resemble.

LEOPARD (Elswick, 1885), **PANTER** (Elswick, 1885). 1530 tons. Complement, 202 *average*. Dimensions: 226⅓ (*w.l.*) × 32¾ × 14 feet (*mean* draught). Guns (new): 4—9 pdr., 10—3 pdr. Torpedo tubes: 4—14 inch (*submerged*). Armour: 2" deck over engines. Machinery: Vertical inverted triple expansion. 2 screws. Boilers were cylindrical but may have been replaced by new Yarrow. Designed H.P. 6000=18 kts. Coal: *normal* 200 tons; *maximum* 300 tons.

Note.

These two old ships have been reconstructed at an unknown date. They are still officially classed with the Austro-Hungarian "Active Fleet," but may only be used now for subsidiary service. A later ship of this type, *Lakroma* (ex-*Tiger*) was converted to an Admiralty yacht. Her photo and details will be found among Miscellaneous Ships at end of this section. Disposal of these ships, 1919, not known.

AUSTRIAN TORPEDO GUNBOATS. (Interned at Pola.)

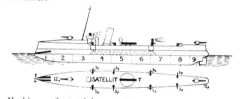

MAGNET.

MAGNET (Schichau, 1896). 510 tons.
Complement, 80.

Guns :
6—3 pdr.
1 machine.
Torpedo tubes (T) :
3 above water.

Armour :
¾" over engines.

Machinery : 2 sets triple expansion. 2 screws. Boilers : Thornycroft. Designed H.P. 6000 = 23 kts. Coal : 105 tons.

Has three funnels now. See Silhouettes.

SATELLIT (Schichau, 1892). 540 tons. Complement, 84.

Guns :
1—9 pdr.
8—3 pdr.
1 machine.
Torpedo tubes :
2 above water.

Armour :
¾" over engines.

Machinery : 2 sets triple expansion. 2 screws. Boilers : 2 Yarrow. Designed H.P. 4000 = 23 kts. (trial in bad weather 4600 = 21·87 kts).

Note.

The torpedo-gunboats described on page preceding this, are listed in the *Austro-Hungarian "Almanach für die K. und K. Kriegsmarine"* as (and with) destroyers.

TRABANT (Triest, 1890). 540 tons. Complement, 84. Guns : 2—9 pdr., 8—3 pdr., 1 machine. Torpedo tubes (T) : 2 above water. Armour : ¾" over engines. Machinery : 2 sets triple expansion. 2 screws. Boilers : 4 locomotive. Designed H.P. 3500 = 20 kts. Coal : 150 tons.

PLANET (1889, Jarrow). 480 tons. Complement, 84. Guns : 2—9 pdr., 8—3 pdr., 1 machine. Torpedo tubes (T) : 3 above water. Armour : ¾" over engines. Machinery : 2 sets triple expansion. 2 screws. Boilers : locomotive. Designed H.P. 3500 = 20 kts.

AUSTRIAN DESTROYERS (*Torpedofahrzeuge*).

BLITZ (Schichau, 1888), KOMET (Schichau, 1888). 360 tons.
Complement, 61.

Guns :
8—3 pdr.
Torpedo tubes :
3 above water.

Armour :
¾" over engines.

BLITZ AND KOMET.

Machinery : 1 set triple expansion. 1 screw. Boilers : *Blitz*, locomotive ; *Komet*, Yarrow (new in 1912). Designed H.P., 2600 = 21 kts. Coal capacity : 120 tons.

No photo available. See Silhouettes.

METEOR (Schichau, 1887). 350 tons. Complement, 61.

Guns :
8—3 pdr.
1 machine.
Torpedo tubes :
3 above water.

Armour :
¾" over engines.

METEOR.

Machinery : 1 set triple expansion. 1 screw. Boilers : locomotive. Designed H.P. 2600 = 21 kts. Coal : 120 tons.

(20 + 1) Destroyers

No.	Type	Date	Displacement tons	H.P.	Max. speed kts.	Fuel tons	Complement	T. Tubes	Max draug't
1	Honved	Bldg.	386	17,000 (t)	32·5	95 coal & oil	102	4	...
5	Dukla	'14-'17							
1	Varasdinier	'12-'15	400	6000 (t)	28	80 coal	...	4	...
4	Tatra type	'11-'13	850	17,000 (t)	32·5	95 coal & oil	102	2	9
6	Huszar type (Y)	'07-'10	400	6000	28	90 coal	65	2	8
2		'07-'09							
1		'06-'08							
1		'05-'07							

(**Y**) = Yarrow type.   (t) = Turbines.

Disposal of Destroyers, 1919.

At Cattaro : *Dukla, Lika,* Triglav,* Uszok, Reka, Pandur.*

At Pola : *Balaton, Csepel, Orjen, Tatra, Varasdinier, Dinara, Huszar, Velebit, Csikos, Turul, Scharfschütze, Ulan, Uskoke.*

At Porto Ré (near Fiume) : *Honved* (unfinished).

* Not to be confused with T.B.D. of same name and type, sunk during the War.

Varasdinier (ex-Chinese *Lung Tuan*, 1913). 400 tons. Dimensions : 219·8 × 20·3 × 8 feet. Yarrow boilers. Armament : 6—11 pdr. (2 of 45 calibre length and remainder 30 calibre length), 4— 17·7 inch tubes in two twin deck mountings.

(8 + 1) Tatra Class.

ORJEN.

9 *Tatra* class, named **Honved** (not finished), **Dukla, Lika, Triglav, Uszok** (built 1914-17), and **Tatra, Balaton, Csepel** (1912), **Orjen** (1913). All built by Danubius Co., Fiume. Armament : 2—3·9 inch, 4—11 pdr., 2—11 pdr. AA, 1 machine, 4—20·8 inch tubes. A.E.G. turbines. 5 Yarrow boilers. Dimensions : 274×25½×8¼ feet. Oil fuel, also coal. All made 32·5 to 33 kts. on trials. Tenth boat of class, *Locuen*, reported not begun.

Lika mined and **Triglav** sunk by French gunfire off Durazzo 29 December 1915.

---

(10) Huszar Class.

Later Six Huszars.

Photo, Spartiali.

Earlier Five Huszars.

Photo, Spartiali.

10 *Huszar* class named : **Huszar** (1905), **Ulan** (1906), **Uskoke, Scharfschütze** (1907), **Pandur, Turul** (1908), **Csikos, Dinara, Reka, Velebit** (1909). Yarrow type. 400 tons. Dimensions : 219·8×20·3×6 feet. Armament : 6—11 pdr., 1 machine, 2—17·7 inch tubes. Designed H.P. 6000 = 28 kts. 4 Yarrow boilers. Coal : 90 tons. *Huszar* built by Yarrow ; rest by Stab. Tecnico.

Wildfang mined June 1917. **Streiter** sunk by British aircraft at Durazzo 27 May 1918. **Dinara** sunk at Durazzo by Italian MAS craft and **Scharfschütze** sunk off Durazzo by British destroyers both on 2 October 1918.

AUSTRIAN TORPEDO BOATS. (*Torpedoboote.*) Interned at Cattaro, Pola and Sebenico.

50 Sea-going. **34** Coastal (= total of **84**) **Torpedo Boats.**

Coastal Torpedo Boats.

Short mast now stepped before forebridge

9 boats: Nos. **1—10** and **12** (1909-10). Armament: 2—3 pdr., 2—17·7 inch tubes. Oil fuel only. First six, Yarrow boilers. Last six, White Forster boilers. *No. 11* now in service in Italian Navy as *Francesco Rismondo*.
Note.—Nos. 3 and 7 captured by French, 1918.

74 T—81 T, 98 M—100 M, one funnel, one mast aft, high bridges.
82 F—97 F, 2 funnels (fore raised) and one mast aft of funnels.

27 "*Standard design*" boats, Nos. **74 T—81 T** (Trieste), **82 F—97 F**, (Fiume), **98 M—100 M** (Monfalcone) 250 tons. Oil fuel and coal-burning Yarrow boilers. Armament: 2—11 pdr. (one of these AA.), 1 machine, 4—17·7 inch torpedo tubes in 2 twin deck mountings. Dimensions: 178·3×18·7×4·9 feet.
87F sunk off Durazzo by Italian MAs craft 2 October 1918.

Nos. 13—16 have short mast stepped against fore funnel.

6 *Yarrow*: Nos. **13—18** (1898-99). Guns: 2—3 pdr. 2 or 3—17·7 inch tubes. All Yarrow boilers, except No. 18, Schulz-Thornycroft.

23 boats (ex *Kaiman* class), No. **50 E** (Yarrow, Poplar, 1905), Nos. **52 T—63 T** (Trieste, 1906-7), **64 F—73 F** (Fiume, 1908-9). 200 tons. Guns: 4—3 pdr., 1 machine. 3 tubes. Dimensions: 180×18—4½ feet. 51 T lost during the war.

51E may have been sunk.

14—40, 45, Armament: 2—1 pdr., 2—14 inch tubes. (All reconstructed as above photo). Yarrow boilers. Nos. 22 and 26 War Losses. Several deleted during the war.

AUSTRIAN SUBMARINES.

See Silhouettes.

4 boats: **XL, XLI, XLIII, XLVII.** Built 1917-18. Details of first two uncertain, but XLIII and XLVII believed to be ex-German *UB 43* and *UB 47*, sold to Austria. Probably all four boats are alike. Dimensions: 142 × 19 × 12 feet. Periscope depth: 42 feet. Armament: 1—4·1 inch or 22 pdr., 5—19·7 inch tubes (4 bow, 1 stern). Diesel engines: 2 sets M.A.N. 4-cycle. 2 screws. Oil: *normal,* 35 tons; *maximum,* 71 tons. Lubricating oil: 7 tons. Diving depth: 245 feet limit. Dive to 30 feet in 40 secs. Complement, *about* 35.

5 boats: **XXVII, XXVIII, XXIX, XXXI** and **XXXII.** Details not certain; but from view of XXVIII at Venice, it appears that these boats are of the German *UB 1—17* type, re-erected or built by Whiteheads, of Fiume. Dimensions: 118 × 14½ × 11¾ feet. Armament: 1—11 pdr. AA., 2 (bow)—19·7 or 20·8 inch tubes. Machinery: 2—140 B.H.P. Diesel motors. 2 screws. Oil: *normal,* 22 tons; *maximum,* 28 tons. 3 tons lubricating oil. *Maximum* diving depth: 163 feet. Dive to 30 feet in 40 secs. Complement, *about* 21.

Similar to Danish *Ægir* Class,
but with steel bridge screen.

2 boats: **XXI, XXII.** Built by Whitehead, Fiume, 1916-17. From view of XXI at Venice, these boats are much the same type as the Hay-Whitehead boats *Ægir, Galathea, Neptune,* &c., built for Danish Navy. Armed with 1—11 pdr. AA. and 2 bow tubes.

Note.

Disposal of boats as follows :—

Interned at Cattaro :—*XXII. XXIX. XXI. XLI. XLIII. XLVII.*

Interned at Pola :—*I. II. XI. XV. XVII. XXVII. XXXII.*

Interned at Venice :—*V. XXI. XXVIII. XL.* These boats may be taken over for Italian Navy.

Interned at Fiume :—*IV.*

Incomplete Boats.

At Pola :—5 boats.

At Fiume :—5 boats (2 nearly ready).

At Monfalcone :—3 boats.

Above may have been dismantled or broken up under Allied supervision. Not included in Table.

AUSTRIAN SUBMARINES.

2 boats : **XVII** (built by Weser Co., and erected at Pola, 1915), **XI** (built by Krupp, Germania 1914—15, and re-erected at Pola). Dimensions : 92 × 10·3 × 9¼ feet. Armament : 1—11 pdr. AA. and 2 (bow)—17·7 inch tubes. One 60 B.H.P. heavy oil engine. Can make 8·5 kts. for short periods *on surface* by using oil and electric motors together, but only 6·5 with oil motor. Oil : 3·5 tons and 5 tons lubricating oil. Diving depth : 163 feet. Submerge to 30 feet in 30 secs. Complement, 16.
Details are same as German *UB 1—17* class.

2 *Krupp-Germaia* type: **III** (1908) **IV** (1908). Dimensions: 141¾ x 12.3 x 9¾ feet. 2 sets of 300 H.P. Körting motors. Armed with 1—11 pdr. A.A. gun and 3—17.7 inch tubes. Cost *about* £62,500. This boat is badly over-engined and suffers from excessive vibration. The *maximum* surface speed cannot be kept up fo any length of time. Both sunk – *III* by gunfire 12 August 1915 and *IV* off Cattaro, October 1914.

Appearance unknown.

1 boat : **XV** (built 1913-14). No details known.

2 *Lake* type : **II, I** (1908). Built at Pola. Dimensions : 100 × 11¼ × feet. 3—17·7 inch tubes : 2 in bow and 1 in stern. Can make 10½ knots awash. Dive in 2½ minutes. Cost, £60,320 each. Are badly over-engined and cannot make designed speed on surface without excessive vibration.

Note: The situation of the Austrian submarines is unclear. The following numbered boats were sunk, *XVI, XX, XXIII, XXX* and *XXXI. XII* was torpedoed, salved and taken over by Italy. At least six other submarines (unidentified) were sunk – total of losses may have been as high as 20.

1 *Whitehead-Holland* type: **V.** and **VI.** Built at Fiume in 1909. Dimensions: 105 x 13¾ x ⅝ feet. Dive in 3/¾4 minutes. Can make 10¼ kts awash. 3—17.7 inch tubes. *U 6* has been sunk during the war. Practically identical with the U.S. "C" class submarines. *VI* sunk by gunfire of British drifters *Dulcie Doris* and *Evening Star II* in Adriatic 13 May 1916.

Subsidiary Local Defence.

(At Cattaro.)

KRONPRINZ ERZHERZOG RUDOLF (1887). 6900 tons. Guns : 3 old 12 inch, 6—4·7 inch, 12—11 pdr. (old). 16 smaller. Probably disarmed now and only a hulk. Belt, 12 inch steel amidships. Original speed, 16 kts. Complement 454.

MARS (*ex Tegetthoff*) (1878). 7390 tons. Guns : 6—old 9·4 inch Krupp, 5—old 6 inch. Belt, 14½″ iron. Original speed (re-engined 1892), 16 kts.

Repair Ship.

VULKAN (1910). 950 tons. Guns : *nil.* Diesel motors. 1200 h.p. Speed, 15 kts.

Submarine Depot Ships.
(Vorattsschiffe für Unterseeboote.)

GAA (1891), *ex Moskva* (Russian), *ex Furst Bismark* (German liner), 13,000 tons. Armament, 4—4·7 inch, 4—11 pdr. H.P. 16,000 = 19 kts. Complement 331.

LUSSIN (1883, 1914). 1000 tons. Guns : 4—3 pdr. Machinery : (1914), 1800 h.p. Diesel motors = 14 kts. Complement 154.

PELIKAN (1891). 2430 tons. Guns : 2—9 pdr., 8—3 pdr., and carries 30 torpedoes. H.P. 4000 = 14 kts. Coal : 400 tons. Complement 196.

(A special salvage ship, Herkules, is described on the next page.)

GIGANT (1889). 260 tons. H.P. 400—11 kts.

Mine Layers (*Minenleger*)

CHAMÄLEON (1913). 1100 tons. Dimensions : 288½ × 30 × 9 feet. Guns : 4—14 pdr. (2 are AA). Designed H.P. 5500 = 21 kts. Yarrow boilers. Carries 300 mines.

BASILISK (1902). 314 tons. Armament : 2—3 pdr., 4 machine. Speed 11 kts. Complement 40. Carries about 150 mines.

CARNIOL (No. V.) of Austrian Lloyd line. 2812 tons gross. About 200 mines carried.

SALAMANDER (1891). 268 tons. Armament : 2—3 pdr. Speed, 10 kts. Complement 20. Carries about 90 mines.

DROMEDAR (1891). 175 tons. Guns : 3—3 pdr. Speed, 10 kts. Complement 20. Carries about 50 mines.
There are two other old ships **Delta** and **Aurora** (1871-3). 1340 tons. 11 knots *nominal* speed, used as mine depot ships. They are practically non-effective. Also **Gastein** (No. IV.) of Austrian Lloyd line, 3815 tons gross. Depot for about 700 mines.

Mine Sweepers.

10 Old Torpedo boats, *Nos. 27, 29, 30, 33—38 & 40,* all about 80 tons displacement, were fitted as mine-sweepers before the war. There are also a large number of requisitioned craft used for this service.

Fuel Ships (*Kohlendampfer*)

POLA (1914), **TEODO** (1915). Colliers. 13,200 tons. Dimensions : 429¾ × 57 × 25¼ feet. Designed H.P., 6200 = 14 kts. Yarrow boilers. Guns : not known. Carry 7000 tons coal as cargo.

AUSTRIAN MISCELLANEOUS.

Fuel Ships (continued).

Photo wanted.

VESTA (1892). Oil tanker. 2130 tons. Designed H.P., 1200 = 10 kts.

Repair Ship (Werkstättenschiff).

For appearance, v. Silhouettes.

CYCLOP (1871). 2150 tons. Designed H.P., 850 = 11 kts. Guns: 2—11 pdr. Complement. 93.

Salvage Ship (Bergungsdampfer).

Photo wanted.

HERKULES (1910). 1500 tons. Dimensions: 210 × 33¾ × 13 feet. Designed H.P., 2500 = 10 kts. Yarrow boilers. Complement. 81.

Subsidiary Service Vessels.

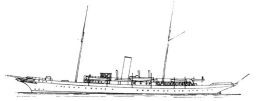

Elevation by courtesy of Messrs. G. L. Watson & Co., Glasgow.

TAURUS (ex-*Nirvana*, 1904). 1300 tons. Dimensions: 220 × 30 × 13 feet. Designed H.P., 2000 = 15 kts. Guns: 2—3 pdr., 2—1 pdr. Coal, 230 tons.

(Interned at Constantinople.)

Subsidiary Service Vessels (continued).

LAKROMA (ex-*Tiger*, 1887). Old "Torpedo Cruiser" used as Admiralty Yacht. 1680 tons. Designed H.P., 6000 = 18 kts. Guns: 6—3 pdr. Complement, 177.

(For appearance, v. Silhouettes.)

MIRAMAR (1872). Used as Imperial Yacht. 1830 tons. Designed H.P., 2000 = 17 kts. (Paddle-wheel steamer). Guns: 2—3 pdr., 2—1 pdr. Complement, 159.

also

Dalmat (1896). Yacht. 260 tons. Designed H.P., 325 = 12 kts. Guns: one or two small Q.F. and machine.

Training Ships.

Old battleship **MONARCH** used for this duty before the war; she is described on a previous page.

MARS (ex *Tegetthof*) (1878, 1893). 7500 tons. Guns: 6 old 9·4 inch Krupp, 5—old 5·9 inch, 2—old 11 pdr., 15 smaller. Belt, 14½" iron. Original speed (re-engined 1892), 16 kts. Complement 574.

Training Ships (continued).

(**Note.**—The following three gunboats were used before the war as seagoing Gunnery Training Ships—hence their mixed armaments. They have been kept in good repair, re-boilered, and are said to be capable of still making their designed speeds).

SEBENICO (Pola, 1882). 890 tons. H.P., 800 = 14 kts. Coal: 200 tons. Guns: 1—5·9 inch, 1—4·7 inch, 1—11 pdr, 8—3 pdr., 2—1 pdr., 2 machine. 2 *submerged* 14 inch tubes.

SPALATO (Triest, 1879). **ZARA** (Pola, 1879). 840 tons. H.P., 800 = 14 kts. Guns: *Spalato*, 2—4·7 inch, 1—3·9 inch, 1—7 pdr., 8—3 pdr., 1—1 pdr., 1 machine; 1 *submerged* 14 inch tube. *Zara*: 2—3·4 inch (14 pdr.), 1—7 pdr., 4—3 pdr., 3 machine; 2 *submerged* 14 inch tubes.

Training ship *Beethoven* and Auxiliary *Bathori* sunk in 1914.

(Tenders to "Mars.")

Albatros and **Nautilus.** Each was built in 1873, displaces 570 tons, and is armed with 1—11 pdr. and 2—3 pdr. guns H.P., 400 = kts. speed.

Note: information for this section was very difficult to obtain. As a result there are certain gaps and inconsistencies which still cannot be resolved (1989).

FLAGS (1919)— Not known. A new National Ensign is reported to have been adopted, with the Russian words, "The Soviets of the federal Republics," on a red ground.

UNIFORMS (1919)—Shoulder markings abolished, and rank is now indicated by stripes on cuff, as in British navy. *All* ranks now have gold buttons. Officers' caps have an anchor badge, on a red ground and encircled by a wreath, much the same as in the British Navy. Ranks are distinguished thus:—

Admiral : ¾-inch top stripe with curl and three stars round curl; two 1-inch lower stripes.

Vice-Admiral : Same as Admiral but only *two* stars.

Kontre-Admiral : Same as Admiral but only *one* star, above curl.

Kapitan (*I Ranga*) : Same as Admiral but *no* stars.

Kapitan (*II Ranga*) : Two 1-inch gold stripes, top with curl.

Starchi Leitenant : One 1-inch or ¾-inch top stripe with curl, and *three* ½-inch gold stripes below.

Lietenant : Same as above but only *two* ½-inch gold stripes below.

Mitchman : Same as above but only *one* ½-inch gold stripe below.

Pra'porchi : This is a temporary rank, about equivalent to Sub-Lieut., R.N.R. in British Navy. One ½-inch gold stripe *without* curl.

Note.—The above particulars relate to changes introduced by the Kerensky Government. Under the Bolshevist Administration it is said that all marks of rank in the Fleet and Army have been abolished.

Modern Naval Guns (Obukhoff).

Notation.	Designation.	Length in Calibres.	Weight of Guns.	Weight of A.P. Shot.	Initial Velocity (approximate).	Maximum Penetration with A.P. Capped Shell against K.C. Armour.			Danger Space against average warship at			Usual Rounds per minute.
						8000 yds.	5000 yds.	3000 yds.	10,000 yards.	5000 yards.	3000 yards.	
	inch.	calibres.	tons.	lbs.	t.s.	in.	in.	in.	yards.	yards.	yards.	
A⁷	14	45	82·6	1486	2525	...	...	22½	...	...	...	...
A⁶	12	50	48·2	714	3000	...	14½	20	...	...	...	...
A⁴	12	40	43·5	714	2600	6½	14	18	150	460	750	0·30
A A	12	35	56	714	2200	4½	8	11	120	380	580	0·25
A³	10(V)	50	35	497	3000	6	12¾	15½	...	...	...	...
A³	10	45	32	490	2500	5	10½	13	130	450	700	0·45
A	8(V)	50	17	216	3300	...	7½	10½	...	...	...	...
A	8	45	15½	188	2800	...	6	9½	105	430	625	1
D*	6	45	7½	89	2900	...	4½	6	60	250	485	3
E*	6	45	7	89	2600	...	3¼	5	50	200	430	3
F*	5·1	55	...	...	...	...	...	...	...	...	...	...
F*	4·7	45	2¼	46	2600	...	...	...	...	...	...	about 4
F*	3	60	14 cwt.	13½	2700	...	...	...	...	...	...	...
F*	3	35	12	13¼	2600	...	...	...	...	...	...	...

⃰ = Brass cartridge cases.   V = Vickers.   *Maximum rates of 10 inch and 8 inch are 3 and 6 rounds per minute. These guns are in the Rurik.*

Officially revised by order of the Minister of Marine. 1913, *not in 1914.*   **(Certain 1914 corrections have been omitted).**

Guns.

Baltic Ships.

14"45 in *Kinburn* class (4 ships) not yet completed.

12"50 in *Gangoot* class (4 ships).

12"40 in *Respublika* class (2 ships), *Slava*.

12"35 in *Tchesma*.

10"50 in *Rurik*.

8"50 in *Respublika* class (2 ships), *Petr Veliki* and *Rurik*.

8"45 in *Bayan* class (2 ships), *Saria Svobodi*, *Gromoboi* and *Rossiya*.

6"45 in *Slava*, *Grajdanin*, *Petr Veliki*, *Bayan*, and all cruisers.

5·1"55 in *Kinburn* class (4 ships) and *Admiral Butakoff* class (4 ships).

Black Sea Ships.

12"50 in *Volia*.

12"40 in *Evstafi* class (2 ships) and *Boretz za Svobodu*.

10"45 in *Rostislav*.

8"50 in *Evstafi* class (2 ships).

6"45 in *Evstafi* class (2 ships), *Boretz za Svobodu*, *Rostislav*, *Tri Sviatitelia*.

5·1"55 in *Admiral Nakhimov* class (4 ships) and *Gen. Korniloff*.

Note.—A considerable number of guns have been dismounted from Russian warships for service on various land fronts.

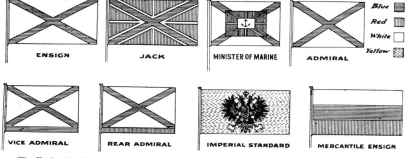

ENSIGN   JACK   MINISTER OF MARINE   ADMIRAL

Blue   Red   White   Yellow

VICE ADMIRAL   REAR ADMIRAL

IMPERIAL STANDARD   MERCANTILE ENSIGN

The *Ensign* is white, with a blue St. Andrew's cross; the *Jack* red, with a blue St. Andrew's cross.
Admiral's Flag: ensign made square; Vice-Admiral ditto, with a blue line at bottom; Rear-Admiral the same, with a red line. Port Admirals have a central rectangle in flag, with blue crossed anchors.
Mercantile Ensign : white, blue and red, in lines.
Imperial Standard : yellow, with black two-headed eagle, &c., in centre.

SEVASTOPOL   to   miles.

Batum	...	...	...	400
Biserta	...	...	...	1300
Constantinople	...	...	298
Gibraltar	...	...	2000
Kertch	...	...	175
Malta	...	...	1000
Nikolaieff	...	...	200
Novorossisk	...	...	200
Odessa	...	...	165
Piræus	...	...	660
Salonika	...	...	643
Toulon	...	...	1654

LIBAU   to   miles.

Brest	...	...	1430
Cherbourg	...	...	1220
Copenhagen	...	...	465
Danzig	...	...	360
Gibraltar	...	...	2330
Kiel	...	...	550
Memel	...	...	230
Revel	...	...	50
Rosyth	...	...	1010
Vladivostock	...	12,405
Windau	...	...	50

KRONSTADT   to   miles.

Abo	...	...	250
Bornholm	...	...	627
Brest	...	...	1680
Cherbourg	...	...	1470
Copenhagen	...	...	715
Danzig	...	...	558
Gibraltar	...	...	2580
Helsingfors	...	...	150
Kiel	...	...	800
Libau	...	...	250
Memel	...	...	480
Revel	...	...	150
Rosyth	...	...	1345
St. Petersburg (By sea canal)	...	21
Vladivostock	...	12,655
Windau	...	...	200

VLADIVOSTOCK   to   miles.

Hong Kong	...	...	1740
Kiao-chau	...	...	1150
Maitsuru	...	...	470
Manila	...	...	2080
Matsumai	...	...	380
Nagasaki	...	...	620
Port Arthur	...	...	1170
Sassebo	...	...	600
Wei-hai-wei	...	...	950

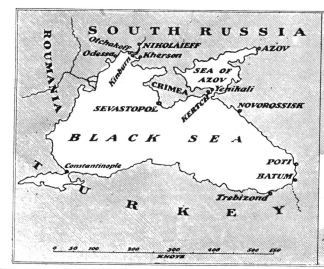

Scale : 1 inch = 160 feet.

RUSSIAN WARSHIPS (1 and 2 Funnels), RECOGNITION SILHOUETTES.

ONE AND TWO FUNNELS.   (For Two Funnel Battleship types, see next page).

MINREP class.
(2 may be Finnish now)
(Mine sweepers.)

KHRABRI.   GROZIASTCHI.

BUG.

Gunboats ; appearance may be altered now.

NAROVA & ONEGA (Minelayers).

PETSHORA.

VOLGA (Mine layer).
KHABAROVSK similar).

ANADYR

BAKAN.
(May be Finnish now).

BORGA & LAKHTA.
(*May be Finnish now).

EVROPA.

RIGA

AFRICA.

MANDJUR (Vladivostock).

VOIN (Training Ship).

NIKOLAIEFF.

ERMAK (Ice breaker).

KHIVINETZ.

AMUR (Mine layer).

PETR VELIKI (Ice Breaker).

SARIA SVOBODI (Reported Sunk).

TCHESMA (White Sea).

GRAJDANIN.

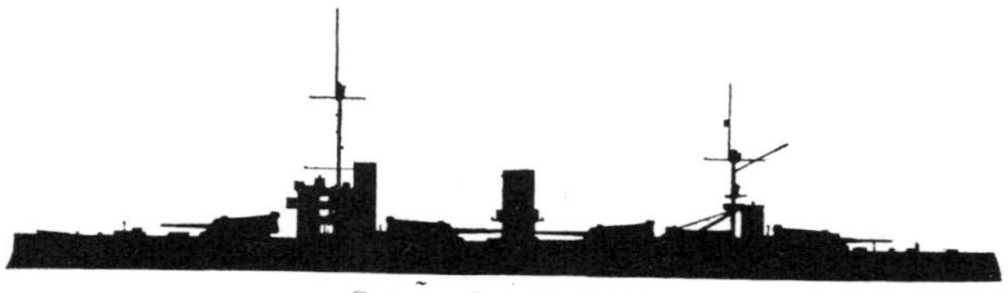

GANGUT class (4 ships).

RESPUBLIKA class (2 ships).

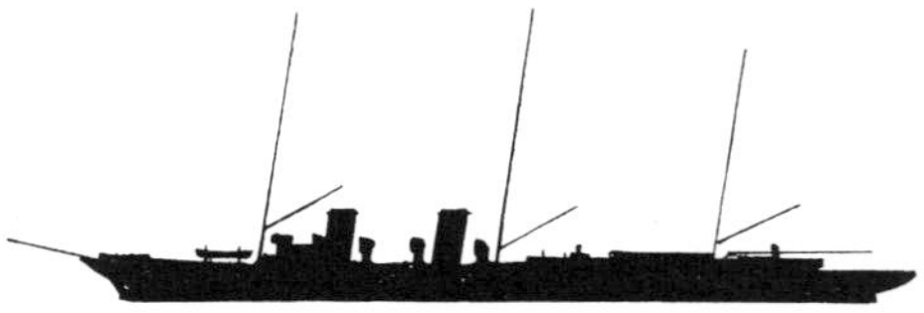

Ex-Shtandart and Kretchet.
(Yachts).

THREE FUNNELS.

BOGATYR (Reported Sunk).

AVRORA class (2 ships, Scuttled as Block Ships?).

OKEAN (Training Ship).

FOUR FUNNELS.

RURIK.

ANGARA (Repair or Depot Ship).

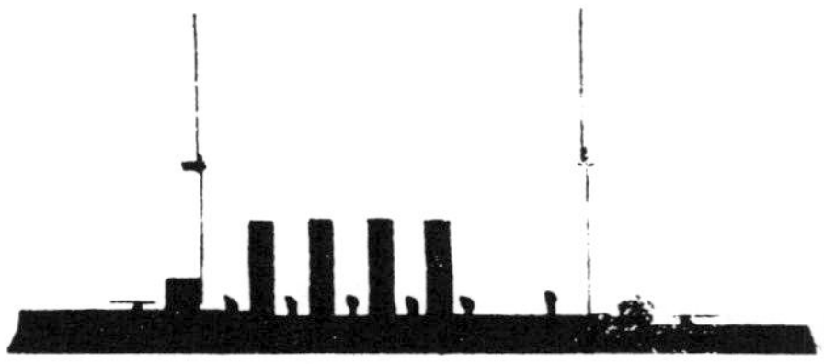

VARIAG (White Sea).

FIVE FUNNELS.

British GLORY IV (Russian ASKOLD) Laid up in the Clyde.

ROSSIA & GROMOBOI.

BAYAN class (2 ships).

RECOGNITION SILHOUETTES—RUSSIAN TORPEDO CRAFT.

Scale : 1 inch = 160 feet.

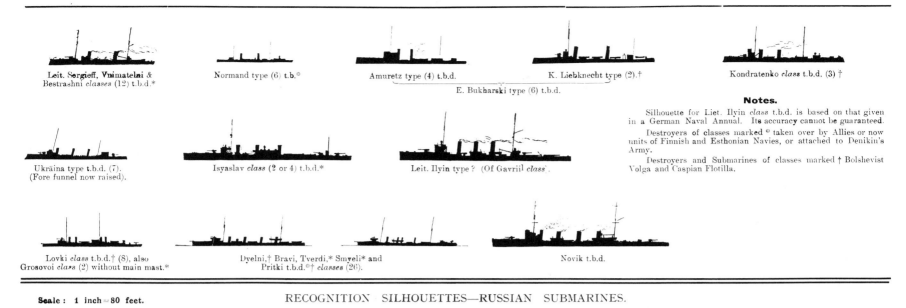

Leit. Sergieff, Vnimatelni & Bestrashni *classes* (12) t.b.d.*

Normand type (6) t.b.*

Amuretz type (4) t.b.d.
E. Bukharski type (6) t.b.d.

K. Liebknecht type (2).†

Kondratenko *class* t.b.d. (3) †

Ukräina type t.b.d. (7). (Fore funnel now raised).

Isyaslav *class* (2 or 4) t.b.d.*

Leit. Ilyin type ? (Of Gavriil *class*).

Notes.

Silhouette for Liet. Ilyin *class* t.b.d. is based on that given in a German Naval Annual. Its accuracy cannot be guaranteed.

Destroyers of classes marked ⊕ taken over by Allies or now units of Finnish and Esthonian Navies, or attached to Denikin's Army.

Destroyers and Submarines of classes marked † Bolshevist Volga and Caspian Flotilla.

Lovki *class* t.b.d.† (8), also Grosovoi *class* (2) without main mast.*

Dyelni,† Bravi, Tverdi,* Smyeli* and Pritki t.b.d.⊕† *classes* (26).

Novik t.b.d.

RECOGNITION SILHOUETTES—RUSSIAN SUBMARINES.

Scale : 1 inch = 80 feet.

Byeluga *class* (4 ?)

Alligator *class* (4)

Believed captured by Germans, 19.8.

All Bubnov type ; appearance not known.

Kataska *class* (2). Makrel *class* (2).* Minoga.*

Volga & Caspian.

Sviatoi Georg.

(*White Sea.*)

"Improved Bubnov" type.

(Silhouette only approximate ; may be boats of Edinorog, Tigr and Volk *classes*).

RUSSIAN BLACK SEA SILHOUETTES.

Scale : 1inch = 1 foot.

DESTROYERS.

Kap. Saken. (France).

Bespokoini (France).
Derski (British).
Bistri (engines destroyed).
Pospyeshni }
Puilki } Denikin.

Zavidni }
Zavetni } Engines
Jeevoi } destroyed.
Jootki }
Jarki (Denikin).
Zvonki (Greek).
Zorki (Italy).

Svirepi }
Strogi } Denikin.

Scale : 1″ = 80 feet.

AG 2—6 (Submarines) (*If completed*).

SEVASTOPOL. Two slips. Two large docks (487 × 85 × 32 and 445 × 85 × 28). One basin. Admiralty Chart No. 963.

NIKOLAIEFF. Building yard only. Floating dock, 558 × 136 × 30 feet (30,000 tons), *building.* Strongly fortified approaches. Too shallow water for use as a base, channel only navigable for ships of 25 feet *maximum* draught. A private yard exists here.

NOVORISSISK. Used as Base by General Denikin's Warships.

Other fortified Black Sea bases without yards or docks ; Batûm, Kinburn, Otchakoff, Azov, Kertch, Yenakali, Poti (all well fortified).

Commercial harbours at Odessa, Batûm.

SEVASTOPOL.

BLACK SEA PORT.

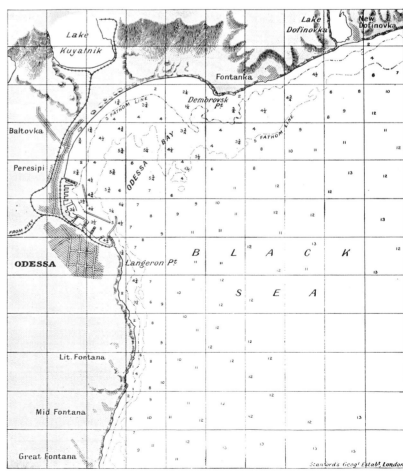

ODESSA. One Private Floating Dock (Russian Steam Navigation and Trading Co.) 381 × 63 (clear between sides) × 19½ feet (on blocks). Patent slip for vessels up to 1000 tons. Admiralty Chart No. 603.

RUSSIAN NAVY.

BALTIC SECTION

(INCLUSIVE OF SHIPS IN THE WHITE SEA, AT VLADIVOSTOK AND ON AMUR RIVER).

The Baltic Fleet is completely disorganised. Owing to desertion of *personnel*, executions of naval officers, looting and mishandling of ships, very few ships can now be deemed effective. During 1919, the Bolshevist Active Fleet was reported to consist of **PETROPAVLOVSK, ANDREI PERVOSVANNI, OLEG,** the Destroyers *Gavriil, Azard, Konstantin, Svoboda* (First Flotilla), *Vsadnik, Gaidamak, Amuretz, Ussurietz* (Second Flotilla), and three or seven Submarines. First two ships named are out of action and **OLEG** is sunk.

As regards ships listed as building and completing: all work ceased in June, 1917, and practically nothing further has been done to advance construction during the past two years.

It is not worth while dividing the Russian Navy pages into Bolshevist and Anti-Bolshevist sections, a list is given of ships in the White Sea and at Vladivostok—that is, *not* under Bolshevist control. Vessels named in heavy type are listed on following pages; those in small type cannot be described for lack of details. Ships not included in the White Sea, Vladivostok or Amur River lists may be taken as under Bolshevist control.

It must be added that details of the White Sea ships refer to conditions before the Allied evacuation of Northern Russia. It is probable that many vessels were brought to Allied Ports in the autumn of 1919, while those left in the White Sea or Dvina River may have been scuttled or disabled.

Various ex-Russian Baltic Warships have been transferred to the Esthonian and Finnish Navy Sections (*q.v.*).

RUSSIAN (NON-BOLSHEVIST) WARSHIPS, FLEET AUXILIARIES, &c.

WHITE SEA (Summer, 1919).		VLADIVOSTOCK.	AMUR RIVER FLOTILLA.
Old Battleship :— **TCHESMA**	*Ice Breakers :—* **KANADA** (reported returned to Canada, listed in Canadian Section as *Earl Grey*).	*Destroyers :—* **Besposhtchadni** **Bravi**	**GROSA** **SHKWAL** **SHTORM**
Cruisers :— **VARYAG** **GLORY VI.** (British. *alias* Russian *Askold*)*	**SVIATOGOR** (paid off at Devonport, Sept., 1919. Is listed in British Navy Section). *Ilya Mourometz*	**Boiki*** **Bodri** **Grosni** **Leit. Maleieff**	**SMERTCH** **TYFUN** **URAGAN** **VIKHR**
Destroyers :— **Leit. Sergieff** **Kapt. Yurassovski** **Bestrashni** **Beshumni** **Grosovoi** **Vlastni**	*Mikula Salianinovich* (Both above with French Personnel.) *Kniaz Pojarski* *Kozma Minin* *Tugs and Ice Breakers :—* About 10.	**Insh. Mech. Anastassoff** **Tverdi** **Totchni** **Trevoshni** **Smyell** **Serditi** **Statni** **Skori**	**VYUGA** **OROKANIN** **MONGOL** **BURIAT** **VOGUL** **SIBIRIAK** **KOREL** **KIRGIZ**
Submarines :— **Sviatoi Georg** **Delfin**	*Motor Patrol Boats :—* About 8 or 10.	*Gunboat :—* **MANDJUR** (Minelayer)	**KALMUIK** **SIRIANIN**
Trawlers :— About 30-40 (about 15 of *Axe* class with British crews).	*Dvina Flotilla :—* *Advokat* } Gunboats. *Gorodoff* } *Razlyff* (may be Armed Yacht *Rasviet*). Various Armed Barges.	*Mine Layers :—* **DIOMID** **PATROKL** **ULIS** **MONGUGAI**	**VOTYAK** *Kopya* *Palash* *Pika*
Yachts :— *Alvina* *Josephine* (Above reported to have U.S. crews now.) *Yaroslavni*		*Miscellaneous :—* *Aleut* *Kamchadal* *Okhtosk* *Orel*	*Pistolet* *Pulya* *Shtik*
Auxiliaries :— **TAIMYR** **VAIGATCH** **BAKAN** *Ludmilla* *Kolquieff*		**SHILKA** **TOBOL**† *Takut*	
Miscellaneous :— **PAHKTUSOV** **XENIA** *Advance* *Antony* *Cheviot* *Inei* *Kingfisher* *Koupava* *Olen* *Orlik* *Sniedzhinka* *Strepet*		* Destroyer *Boiki* now in Mediterranean as French Destroyer *Quentin Roosevelt*. † Said to have been sunk 1916, as a Mercantile Vessel.	
* *Glory IV* now laid up in the Gareloch, Firth of Clyde.			

1912 RUSSIAN BATTLE-CRUISERS. Nos. 8, 7, 6, 5.

BORODINO (1917?) **ISMAIL** (June, 1915), **KINBURN** (Oct., 1915), **NAVARIN** (1917?).

Normal displacement, *about* 32,500 tons. Complement,

Length, *about* 728¼ feet. Beam, 98 feet. Draught, 28¾ feet.

Guns :
  12—14 inch, 45 cal. (A⁷)
  24—5·1 inch, 55 cal.
  4—4 inch (anti-aircraft)
  4 machine
Torpedo tubes :
  6 *submerged*.

Armour :
  12″ Belt ....
  ″ Belt (bow) ....
  ″ Belt (aft) ....
  ″ Deck ....
  ″ Turrets ....
  ″ Battery ....

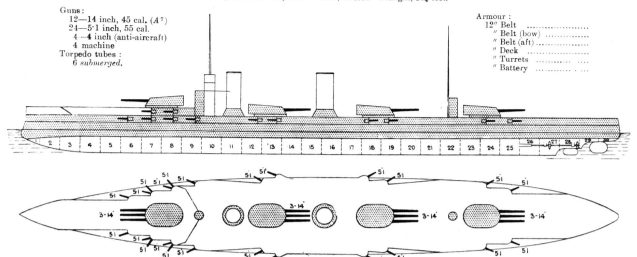

Notes.

Owing to lack of materials and labour, work was stopped on these ships in 1917. It is very doubtful if they will ever be completed now.

Plans are based on information and sketches furnished **by** the Naval Attache of the Russian Embassy, 1917.

Machinery : Parsons turbines. screws. Boilers : 25 Yarrow. Designed H.P. = 68,000 = 26½ kts.
Coal : *normal*   tons ; *maximum* 1,950 tons + 1575 tons oil fuel.

Name	Builder	Machinery	Laid down	Completed	Trials	Turbines	Boilers	Best recent speed
Borodino	Galernii	(All by	Dec.'12				(	
Ismail	Baltic Works	Franco-	Dec.'12	?			All	
Kinburn	Baltic Works	Russian Co.)	Dec.'12				Yarrow	
Navarin	Galernii		Dec.'12				)	

1909 RUSSIAN BATTLE-CRUISERS (23 knot). Nos. 4, 3, 2, 1

GANGŪT (Oct., 1911), **POLTAVA** (July, 1911), **PETROPAVLOVSK** (Sept., 1911), **SEVASTOPOL** (June, 1911).

Normal displacement, 23,370 metric tons. Complement, 1125.

Length *over all*, 594 feet. Beam, 87 feet. *Mean* draught, 27½ feet.

Guns
  12—12 inch, 50 cal. (A⁶).
  16—4·7 inch, 50 cal.
  2—9 pdr. (anti-aircraft).*
  1—3 pdr.
  8 Machine.
Torpedo tubes (18 inch) :
  4 *submerged*.
  °2—11 pdr. AA.
  in *Poltava*

Armour (Krupp) :
  8¾″ Belt (amidships) ...
  5″-2″ Belt (ends)
  3″-4″ Internal belt (*see notes*)
  3″ Deck..............
  12″-10″ Turrets..
  8″ Turret bases........
  6″ Battery ....
  10″ Conning tower......

POLTAVA.

Note: *PETROPAVLOVSK*, after being torpedoed by British C.M.B. on 18 August 1919 sank in shallow water and on an even keel at Kronstadt. She can easily be raised and is therefore not deleted. *POLTAVA* aground. *GANGUT* laid up at Petrograd. Condition of *SEVASTOPOL* unknown.

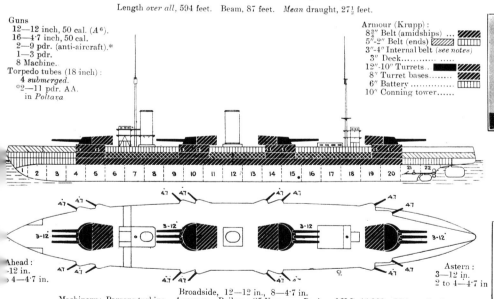

Ahead :
  —12 in.
  4—4·7 in.

Astern :
  3—12 in.
  2 to 4—4·7 in

Broadside, 12—12 in., 8—4·7 in.

Machinery : Parsons turbine. 4 screws. Boilers : 25 Yarrow. Designed H.P. 42,000 = 23 kts. Coal : *normal*, 1000 tons ; *maximum*, 3000 tons. Also 1170 tons oil.

Gunnery Notes.—The port plate above each gun is in the form of a hinged flap, allowing each 12-inch gun to elevate to 30—40° *maximum*. Arcs of fire : End triple 12-inch barbettes, 310° ; central barbettes, 130° *each beam* ; aft group of 4—4·7 inch, 90° ; other 4·7 inch, 85°.

Armour Notes.—Belt is about 15 feet wide, 5 feet of it below water, uniform thickness. There is a *secondary* 3′-4″ internal belt 11 feet inboard above protective deck, extending between the end barbettes. The space between main belt and internal belts is divided up into w.t. compartments.

Name	Builder	Machinery	Laid down	Completed	Trials : Full power		Boilers	Best recent speed
Gangūt	Galernii I.	Franco-Rus. Wks.	June,'09	Jan.'14		= 23	Yarrow	
Poltava	Galernii I.	Franco-Rus. Wks.	June,'09	Jan.'15	About	= 23	Yarrow	
Petropavlorsk	Baltic Works	Baltic Works	June,'09	Jan.'14	50,000	= 23	Yarrow	
Sevastopol	Baltic Works	Baltic Works	June,'09	Jan.'15		= 23·4	Yarrow	

General Notes.—The late Gen. Vittorio Cuniberti prepared the original designs for this class—compare general resemblance to his Italian *Dante Alighieri*. The Ministry of Marine afterwards altered the plans to include Russian ideas of armouring, ice-breaking bows and other special features. The design of these ships has been very severely criticised, but, although abnormal in many details, they may have proved quite successful in service.

GANGUT.

1903 RUSSIAN BATTLESHIPS (*Lineiny Korably*). (18 kts.)

(Respublika Class—2 Ships.)

RESPUBLIKA (ex-*Imperator Parel Perri*, Sept., 1907) & **ANDREI PERVOSVANNI** (Oct., 1906).
Normal displacement, 17,680 metric tons. Complement, 933.
Length (*waterline*), 454 feet. Beam, 80 feet. *Mean draught*, 27 feet. Length *over all*, 460 feet.

Guns :
4—12 inch, 40 cal. (A⁴).
14—8 inch, 50 cal. (A).
12—4·7 inch, 50 cal.
2—3 pdr.
8 Machine.
Torpedo tubes (18 inch) :
2 *submerged* (broadside).

*Docked, Aug. 1919, after being torpedoed by British CMB.

Armour (Krupp) :
8½″ Belt (amidships) ....
5″ Belt (bow) ....
4″ Belt (aft) ....
3″ Deck ....
2″ Splinter deck ....
10″ Big turrets (N.C.) ....
5″ Turret bases (*see notes*) ...
7″ Small turrets ....
4″ Bases (*see notes*) ....
5″—3″ Main deck side ....
5″ Battery (N.C.) ....
3″ Q.F. Battery (amidships)...
8″ Conning tower (N.C.) ....
6″ After C.T. (N.C.) ....
(Total weight 4100 tons).

Ahead :
2—12 in.
6—8 in.

Astern :
2—12 in.
6—8 in.

Broadside: 4—12 in., 7—8 in.

Machinery : 2 sets triple expansion. 2 screws. Boilers : 25 Belleville. Designed H.P. 17,600 = 18 kts. (c.f. trials). Coal : *normal* — tons ; *maximum*, Respublika 1,325 tons, A.P. 1,500 tons.
Armour Notes.—Belt is 7½ feet wide, 5 feet of it below waterline ; lower edge is 3″ thick. Turret bases 5″—4″ according to the side armour forming additional protection to them. 3″ floor to batteries. 2″ lateral "anti-torpedo" bulkheads.
Gunnery Notes.—Loading positions, big guns : all round. Hoists : electric. Big guns manœuvred electrically ; secondary turrets, electrically. Arcs of fire : Big guns, 270° ; secondary guns, 150°.
Torpedo Notes—6 searchlights.

Name	Builder	Machinery	Laid down	Completed	Last refit	Trials	Boilers	Best recent speed
A. Pervosvanni	Galernii Island	Baltic Works	Jan., '03	Aug.,'10		18,596 = 17	Belleville	
Respublika	Baltic Works	Baltic Works	Sept.,'03	Sept.'10		17,775 = 17·7	Belleville	11

°Full speed, 1918.

General Notes.—Design altered during construction in order to embody Japanese war lessons : armour thinned and extended to cover hull, Q.F. battery increased, etc., etc. Hulls unpierced ; all ventilation through decks.

A. PERVOSVANNI. (Note derricks.) *Photo, Seward, Weymouth.*

Note.—Both ships now rigged as Silhouette.

RESPUBLIKA. (Note cranes.)

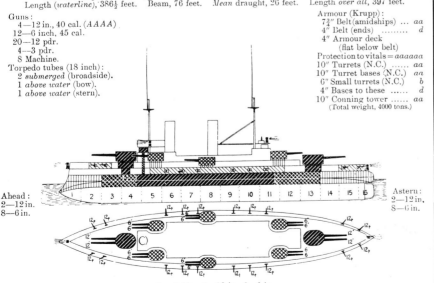

SLAVA (August, 1903).

Nominal displacement, 13,566 tons ; actual *normal* about 15,000 tons. Complement, 750.
Length (*waterline*), 386½ feet. Beam, 76 feet. *Mean draught*, 26 feet. Length *over all*, 397 feet.

Guns :
4—12 in., 40 cal. (AAAA).
12—6 inch, 45 cal.
20—12 pdr.
4—3 pdr.
8 Machine.
Torpedo tubes (18 inch) :
2 *submerged* (broadside).
1 *above water* (bow).
1 *above water* (stern).

Armour (Krupp) :
7¾″ Belt (amidships) ... aa
4″ Belt (ends) .... d
4″ Armour deck
(flat below belt)
Protection to vitals = aaaaaa
10″ Turrets (N.C.) ..... aa
10″ Turret bases (N.C.) ... an
6″ Small turrets (N.C.) ... b
4″ Bases to these ...... d
10″ Conning tower ...... aa
(Total weight, 4000 tons.)

Ahead :
2—12 in.
8—6 in.

Astern :
2—12 in.
8—6 in.

Broadside: 4—12 in., 6—6 in.

Machinery : 2 sets vertical 4 cylinder triple expansion. 2 screws. Boilers : 20 Belleville.
Designed I.H.P. 16,000 = 18 kts. Coal : *normal* 750 tons ; *maximum* 1250 tons.
Armour Notes.—Belt is 6¾ feet wide, 5 feet of it below waterline ; lower edge is 7″ thick amidships ; upper belt is 5¾ feet wide.

Sunk in Gulf of Riga by German gunfire 17 October 1917.

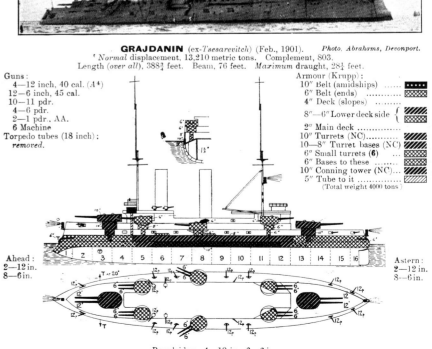

GRAJDANIN (ex-*Tsesarevitch*) (Feb., 1901). *Photo. Abrahams, Devonport.*

Normal displacement, 13,210 metric tons. Complement, 803.
Length (*over all*), 388¾ feet. Beam, 76 feet. *Maximum draught*, 28¼ feet.

Guns :
4—12 inch, 40 cal. (A⁴).
12—6 inch, 45 cal.
10—11 pdr.
4—6 pdr.
2—1 pdr. AA.
6 Machine.
Torpedo tubes (18 inch) :
removed.

Armour (Krupp) :
10″ Belt (amidships) ......
6″ Belt (ends) ....
4″ Deck (slopes) ....
8″—6″ Lower deck side {
2″ Main deck ....
10″ Turrets (NC) ....
10″—8″ Turret bases (NC)
6″ Small turrets (6) ...
6″ Bases to these ....
10″ Conning tower (NC)...
5″ Tube to it ....
(Total weight 4000 tons)

Ahead :
2—12 in.
8—6 in.

Astern :
2—12 in.
8—6 in.

Broadside :—4—12 in., 6—6 in.

Machinery : 2 sets triple expansion. 2 screws. Boilers : 20 Belleville, without economisers.
Designed H.P. 16,300 = 18 kts. Coal : *normal* 800 tons ; *maximum* 1350 tons. Laid down at La Seyne, Toulon, 1899, completed 1903.

(In White Sea).

TCHESMA (ex-*Tango*, ex-*Poltava*) (Nov., 1894). Displacement 10,960 tons. Complement, 700. Length, 369 feet. Beam, 72½ feet. *Maximum* draught, 27 feet. Guns (Obukhoff): 4—12 inch, 40 cal. (*AA*), 12—6 inch, 45 cal., and 8—12 pdr. Armour (compound): Belt 15″ (partial). Turrets (steel) 10″, small turrets 5″. Designed H.P. 11,000=17 kts. Boilers: 16 Miyabara. Coal: *maximum* 1050 tons. Sunk at Port Arthur in the Russo-Japanese War 1904; salved in 1905 by the Japanese and re-named *Tango*. Retroceded to Russia by Japan, March, 1916.

PERESVIET (1898). 13,500 tons. Guns: 4—10 in., 45 cal.; 10—6 in., 45 cal.; 16—12 pdr., This ship was sold to Russia in March 1916. Stranded and refloated then on passage to White Sea via Indian Ocean and Suez canal. When 10 miles off Port Said she struck two U-boat laid mines, caught fire and sank on 4 January 1917.

(Officially rated as "Cruisers.")   *Photo, Abrahams, Devonport.*

ADMIRAL MAKAROV (May 1906, re-fitted 1916). **BAYAN** (August, 1907).
Displacement, 7900 metric tons. Complement, 568—593.
Length (o.a.), 449⅔ feet. Beam, 57·5 feet. *Mean* draught, 21·3 feet.

Guns:
3—8 inch, 45 cal. (*A*).
12—6 inch, 45 cal.
2—11 pdr. (*A.M*).
1—1 pdr., AA. (*Bayan*.)
2—3 pdr.
Torpedo tubes (18 inch):
2 submerged.

Armour (Krupp):
8″ Belt (amidships)
4″ Belt (forward)
2″ Armour deck...
2½″ deck (aft) .....
6″ bulkhead (aft)...
3¼″-2½″ Upper belt
6″ Turrets ″ ....
″ Turret bases ...
2½″ Battery.........
5½″ Conning tower

Note.

Re-armed during War. Extra 8 inch mounted without shield between 4th funnel and mainmast. 4—6 inch added—positions unknown.

Machinery : 2 sets vertical triple expansion. 2 screws. Boilers: 26 Belleville. Designed H.P. 16,500= 21 kts. Coal: *normal* 750 tons; *maximum Bayan* 950 tons, A.M. 1050 tons.

Notes.—*Bayan* laid down at New Admiralty Yard, Petrograd, 1905, and completed 1910. Machinery by Franco-Russian Co. *Admiral Makarov* begun by La Seyne, Co., Toulon, 1905, completed 1908. Machinery by builders. *Pallada* sunk by U 26, in Finnish Gulf, October 1914.

Has F.C. top on foremast now.   *Photo, Abrahams, Devonport.*

Disabled, but may be repaired and in commission.
RURIK (Nov., 1906).
Normal displacement, 15,190 tons. Complement, 899.
Length *over all*, 529 feet. Beam, 75 feet. *Mean* draught, 26 feet. Length (*p.p.*), 490 feet.

Guns (Vickers) :
4—10 inch, 50 cal. (*A* ³)
8—8 inch, 50 cal. (*A*)
20—4·7 inch, 50 cal.
2—3 pdr.
2—1 pdr., AA.
2 machine.
Torpedo tubes (18 inch) :
2 submerged (broadside).

Armour (Krupp):
6″ Belt (amid.) (K.C.)
4″ Belt (bow) (N.C.)
3″ Belt (stern) (N.C.) ...
1½″ Armour deck ....
8″ Turrets (K.C.) ....
6″ Turret bases ....
7″ Secondary turrets .....
3″ Redoubt (N.C.) ... ...
3″ Battery (N.C. ....
8″ Conning tower (N.C.)

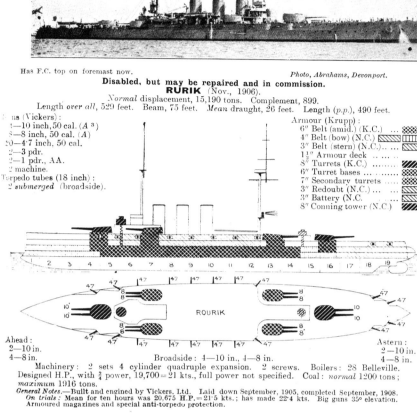

Ahead :
2—10 in.
4—8 in.

Astern :
2—10 in.
4—8 in.

Broadside : 4—10 in., 4—8 in.

Machinery : 2 sets 4 cylinder quadruple expansion. 2 screws. Boilers : 28 Belleville. Designed H.P., with ¾ power, 19,700=21 kts., full power not specified. Coal : *normal* 1200 tons; *maximum* 1916 tons.

General Notes.—Built and engined by Vickers, Ltd. Laid down September, 1905, completed September, 1908. On trials : Mean for ten hours was 20,675 H.P.=21·5 kts.; has made 22·4 kts. Big guns 35° elevation. Armoured magazines and special anti-torpedo protection.

Тромобой. **GROMOBOI** (May, 1899).   *Photo, Abraham & Sons, Devonport.*

Displacement, 13,430 metric tons. Sheathed and coppered. Complement, 868.
Length (*waterline*), 472½ feet. Beam, 68½ feet. *Mean* draught, 27¾ feet.

Guns (as re-armed) :
6—8 inch, 45 cal. (*A*).
20—6 inch, 45 cal.
2—9 pdr. AA.
2—3 pdr.
Torpedo tubes :
2 submerged.
(broadside).

Armour (Harvey-nickel) :
6″ Belt ....
2″ Deck ....
6″ Bulkheads ....
4″ Lower deck (amidships)
6″ Casemates (14) ......
2″ Hoists........ ....
10″ Conning tower ....
(Total *about* 2100 tons.)

Note.

Re-armed during war.
Present gun positions not known.

Machinery : 3 sets triple expansion. 3 screws Boilers :——— Designed H.P. 14,500=19 kts. Coal : *normal* 800 tons; *maximum* 2300 tons.

Armour Notes.—Belt is 7 feet wide by about 330 feet long.

General Notes.—Laid down at Baltic Works, 1898; completed 1901; re-fitted 1907, when 2 above water tubes were removed, and upper deck guns casemated in. Made 20·1 kts. on first trials, with 15,499 H.P., but best recent speed known of is 18·5 kts.

Россія **ROSSIYA** (May, 1896).

Displacement, 12,195 tons (sheathed and coppered). Complement, 833.

Length (over all), 480 feet. Beam, 68½ feet. Mean draught, 26 feet.

Guns (as re-armed):
4—8 in., 45 cal. (A)
14—6 in., 45 cal.
2—3 pdr.
2—M.G.
Torpedo tubes:
removed

Armour (Harvey):
8"–5" Belt
4" Belt (aft) ....
2½" Deck ....
[Deck flat on belt].
6" Bulkheads ......
4" Lower deck
(amidships)
6" Battery bulkh'ds
2" Casements to 8")
2" Screens in battery

Note.

8—6 inch removed during war.
Present best speed 17—17½ kts.

Machinery: 3 sets vertical triple expansion. 3 screws. Boilers (fitted 1907): 32 Belleville in 4 groups.
Designed H.P.: 14,500 = 19 kts. Coal: normal 1000 tons; maximum 2500 tons.

Armour Notes.—Belt is carried right aft, but incomplete forward. It is about 7 feet wide. 4" armour in wake of engines. 6" bulkheads protect battery from raking fire.

General Notes.—Laid down at Baltic Works, 1893; completed 1898; re-fitted 1907, when all torpedo tubes were removed. Made 20·25 kts. on first trials, with 18,446 H.P.

RUSSIAN CRUISERS (**NON-EFFECTIVE**).

Laid up in the Gareloch, Firth of Clyde, 1919.

British **GLORY IV**, alias Russian **ASKOLD** (April, 1900). 6000 metric tons. Complement, 600. Dimensions: 430¼ (o.a.) × 55½ × 20¾ feet (mean draught). Armament: 12—6 inch, 45 cal.; 10—11 pdr., 2—3 pdr. AA., 2 M.G. Torpedo tubes (18 inch): 2 submerged (broadside), 2 above water. Fitted for Minelaying. Armour: 3" Deck, 4" Funnel bases, 6" C.T. Machinery: 3 sets triple expansion. 3 screws. Boilers: 18 Schulz-Thornycroft. Designed H.P. 19,500 = 23 kts. Coal: normal, 720 tons; maximum, 1050 tons. Was in Far East, 1914, and served with Allied Fleets during the War.

(White Sea—dismantled at Liverpool, 1917.)

VARIAG (ex Soya, ex Variag) (Oct., 1899). 6600 tons. Complement, ——. Dimensions: 416 (w.l.) × 52 × 21 feet (max. draught). Armament: 2—12 pdr. Armour: 3" Deck, 6" C.T. Machinery: 2 sets 4-cylinder inverted triple expansion. Designed H.P. 20,000 = 23 kts. Coal: normal, 770 tons; maximum, 1300 tons. Sunk at Chemulpo (Korea), Feb., 1904, during Russo-Japanese War. Salved, Aug., 1905, repaired by Japanese and re-named Soya. Retroceded to Russia by Japan, March, 1916.

1913 RUSSIAN LIGHT CRUISERS.

Note.

Plans given below are based on those published in an Enemy Naval Annual. Their accuracy cannot be guaranteed.

ADMIRAL BUTAKOFF (not launched). **ADMIRAL GREIG** (Dec. 1916), *ADMIRAL SPIRIDOFF* (not launched), and **SVIETLANA** (June, 1915).
Displacement, 6800 metric tons. Complement,
Length, 507¾ feet. Beam, 50⅓ feet. Draught, 18⅓ feet.

Guns:
15—5·1 inch, 55 cal.
4—4 in. (anti-aircraft)
4—3 in.
4 machine
Torpedo Tubes:
2 submerged
Carry 100 mines

Armour:
3" Belt......
1" Deck ....
3" Gun shields ......
" Conning tower ......

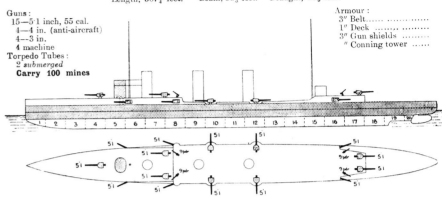

Machinery: Brown Curtis or Parsons turbines. Boilers: 25 Yarrow. H.P. 50,000 = 29·5 kts. Coal: normal, tons; maximum, 1170 (with oil fuel).

Name	Builder and Machinery.	Laid down	Completed	Trials	Turbines.	Best recent speed.
Ad. Butakoff	Putilov Yard, Petrograd	Nov. '13				
Ad. Greig	Baltic Works, Reval*	Dec. '13	?			
Ad. Spiridoff	Putilov Yard, Petrograd	Nov. '13				
Svietlana	Baltic Works, Reval *	Dec. '13				

General Notes.—Built under 1912 Naval Programme. Are equipped for carrying seaplanes. Ad. Butakoff and Ad. Spiridoff were originally intended for Siberian Fleet in Pacific. Four sister ships of the Admiral Nakhimoff class building in Black Sea.
* Towed to Petrograd, 1918.

Present existence of these 3 Cruisers very doubtful.

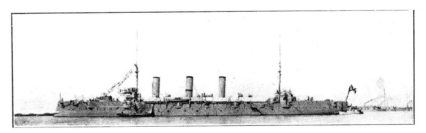

Reported sunk at Kronstadt by British C.M.B., August, 1919.

BOGATYR (January, 1901). 6650 tons. Complement, 565. Dimensions: 433 (w.l.) × 54½ × 20¼ feet (max. draught). Length over all, 440 feet. Armament: 16—5.1 inch, 55 cal., 4 M.G. Torpedo tubes (18 inch): 2 submerged (broadside). Armour: 3" Deck, 3" Turrets, 3" Casemates (4). Machinery: 2 screws. Boilers: Normand-Sigaudy. Designed H.P. 19,500 = 23 kts. Coal: normal, 900 tons; maximum, 1270 tons. Fitted for Minelaying. Oleg sunk by British C.M.B., June, 1919.

(Діана: Аврора.) **DIANA** (October, 1899) & **AVRORA** (May, 1900). 6830 metric tons. Complement, 573. Dimensions: 410 (w.l.) × 55 × 21¼ feet (mean draught). Armament: Avrora, 10—6 inch, 45 cal., 5—6 pdr. AA., 2 M.G.; Diana, 10—5.1 inch, 4—6 pdr., 4—6 pdr. AA. Carries 125 mines. Torpedo tubes (18 inch), no tubes in Diana: 2 submerged (broadside) in Avrora. She is also fitted for Minelaying. Machinery: 3 sets horizontal 3-cylinder. Designed H.P. 11,600 = 20 kts. 3 screws. Boilers: 24 Belleville. Coal: normal, 960 tons; maximum, 970 tons. Looted by Bolshevist crews, 1917, and abandoned in the Neva, 1918; said to have been scuttled there as Blockships.

1901 RUSSIAN CRUISERS. 1899

Photo, Lieut. O'Brien, R.N.

JEMTCHUG (Aug., 1903). 3050 tons. Complement, 334. Dimensions: 345 × 49 × *Mean* draught, 16 feet. Guns: 6—4·7 inch., 45 cal., 6—3 pdr., 2—1 pdr. Torpedo tubes (14 inch) *above water*: 4 broadside, 1 stern. Armour: 2″ Deck. Machinery: 2 sets 4 cylinder triple expansion. 2 screws. Boilers: 16 Yarrow. Designed H.P. 19,000 = 24 kts. Coal: 500 tons; *maximum* 600 tons.

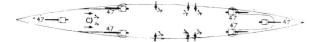

RUSSIAN GUNBOATS AND DESPATCH VESSELS.

For Amur River Monitors of the *Grosa* type, and the Caspian Sea gunboats *Ardahan* and *Kars*, see later pages.

Armoured Gunboat.

KHRABRI (1895). 1740 tons. Complement, 197. Guns: 1—6 inch, 45 cal.; 5—5.1 inch, 55 cal.; 2—1 pdr., 1—1 pdr. AA., 2 M.G. Armour: 5″ Harvey, waterline belt amidships, 3″ ditto aft. Designed H.P. 2000 = 14 kts. Niclausse boilers. Coal: *maximum*, 160 tons.

Note.—Re-fitted and re-armed, 1916. Appearance may be altered.

Gunboats.

(Disarmed, April, 1919.)

KHIVINETZ (1905). Displacement, 1340 tons. Complement, 161. Guns: 4—4.7 inch, 2—3 pdr. AA. Machinery: Triple expansion. 2 screws. Boilers: 8 Belleville. Designed H.P. 1400 = 13½ kts. Coal: *normal*, 100 tons; *maximum*, 190 tons.

Gunboats (Mine Layers).

Photo, Capt. Alan Burgoyne, M.P.
(Disarmed.)

GROZIASTCHI (1890). 1640 tons. Complement, 176. Guns: 4—6 inch, 2—11 pdr. Armour: 5″ Belt amidships, 3″ Aft, with 3¾″ Bulkhead forward. Designed H.P. 2000 = 14 kts. Coal: 150 tons. Belleville boilers. Carries 20-30 mines.

Note.—Re-fitted and re-armed, 1916. May now be of different appearance.

(At Vladivostok.)

MANDJUR (1886). 1440 tons. Guns (old): 2—8 inch, 1—6 inch, 4—9 pdr. Torpedo tubes: 1—14 inch (in bow). Designed speed: 13 kts. Coal: 250 tons. Complement, 160.

Fitted as Minelayer. Carries *about* 50 mines.

River Gunboats—Location unknown.

8 *Gunboats*: (Names or Numbers unknown, built 1915-17). —— tons. Dimensions: 66 × 19 × 2½ feet. Guns: 2—3 inch (mountain type), 2 M.G. Speed: 12½ kts.

GROSA, SCHKWAL, SCHTORM, SMERTCH, TIFUN, URAGAN, WICHR, WYUGA (——1910). Displacement, 950 tons. Complement, . Length (*waterline*), 233 feet. Beam, 42⅓ feet. Draught, . Guns: 2—6 inch (one forward, one aft), 4—12 pdr. in pairs in midship turrets. Armour: 4½″ turrets. Machinery: Diesel motors. 1000 h.p. = 11 kts. Fate unknown.

GILIAK (Oct., 1906), **KORIETZ** (1907), **SIVOUTCH** (1907), **BOBR** (1908). Displacement, 960 tons. Complement, 170. Guns: 2—4·7 inch, 4—12 pdr., 3 machine. Machinery: Triple expansion. 2 screws. Boilers: 4 Belleville. Designed H.P. 800 = 12 kts. Coal: 60 tons.

Sivoutch sunk 1915. *Bobr* captured by Germans April 1918 and transferred to Estonia as *Lembrit*.

Despatch Vessels.

Lastotchka (Yarrow, 1904). 120 tons. Speed 18 kts. Turbine engines.

Razvyedchik and *Dozorni* (both 1904). 100 tons. Complement 23. Guns: 1—1 pdr., 1 machine. Speed, 16 kts. Both re-fitted 1915-1916.

(May be in Finnish Navy.)

BAKAN (1896). 883 tons. Guns: 2—11 pdr., 4—3 pdr. H.P. 800 = 11 kts. Coal: 130 tons. Complement, 98.

Note.—Re-fitted and re-armed, 1916. Appearance may be changed.

Also :—

Porashayustchi (ex-Destroyer of *Pritki* type).

Petrol T. B. No. 1.

Abrek, Berkut, Harpun, Kitobol, Kondor, Konvoir, Namet, Nived, Ozilya, Periskop, Rognieda, Sputnik, Yakor.

RUSSIAN DESTROYERS (*Eskadrenny Minonossetz* if over 400 tons, *Minonossetz* if under).

No.	Type	Date	Displacement	H.P.	*Max.* speed	Coal or *Oil*	Complement	Tubes / *Mines*	*Max.* Draught
4	"Hogland type"	1916–?	1550	34,000	32*t*	tons *300*	..	12/*80*	11
3	*Zabiaka*	1912–15	1610	32,000	35*t*	*400*	110	12/*80*	9¼
4	*Isyaslav*	1912–?	1350	32,700	35*t*	*150*	110	12/*80*	9⅜
27	*Gavryil*	1912–?	1260	30,000	35*t*	*150*	110	12/*80*	9¾
1	*Novik*	1910–12	1200	33,000	32*t*	400	140	8/*80*	10½
3	*Kondratenko* class (K)	1904–06	625	7300	25	190	98	3/*50*	9½
6	*E. Bukharski* class (K)	1904–07	580	6500	25	150–200	94	3/*25*	8½
7	*Ukräina* class	1903–07	500	6200	25	130	85	3/*16*	8
2	*Leit. Sergieff* (S)	1903–05	350	6000	29	95	64	3	7½
10	*Vnimatelni* (S) / *Bestrashni* (S)	1904–07 / 1899–01	355	6000	27	125	64	3/*16*	6
8	*Lovki* class (N)	1904–05	330	5700	27	60	65	2/*15*	7
2	*Grosovoi* class (N)*	1899–01	310	5700	26	80	59	2/*6*	8
10	*Dyelni* class (Y)	1904–06	350	5700	26	100	64	2/*14*	6
4	*Bravi* class (Y)	1902–06							
5	*Tverdi* class (Y)*	1905–06	300	3800	25	60	59	2	6
4	*Smyeli* class (Y)*	1899–03	380	3800	26½	70	52	1/*18*	6½
3	*Pritki* class (Y)*	1895–01	220	3800	27	60	52	1/*18*	7½

*These are officially rated with torpedo boats.

Types:—(K) = Krupp. (S) = Schichau. (N) = Normand. (Y) = Yarrow.

4 Hogland type (Mine Layers).

4 *boats* (not named), begun 1916, by Petrograd Metal Works. 1550 tons. Dimensions: 324⅜ × 31⅙ × 11 feet. Guns: 5—4 inch, 2—9 pdr. AA., 4 M.G. Torpedo tubes (18 inch): 12 in 4 triples. To carry 80 mines each. S.H.P. 34,000 = 32 kts. Turbines. Oil: *about* 300 tons.

3 Zabiaka type (Mine Layers).

3 *Petrograd Metal Works:* ***Orphei, Pobieditel, Zabiaka*** (all 1914). 1610 tons. Dimensions: 321½ × 30½ × 9¼ feet. Guns: 4—4 inch, 1—2 pdr. AA. pom-pom, 2 M.G. Torpedo tubes (18 inch): 12 in 4 triples. Carry 80 mines. Designed S.H.P. 32,000 = 35 kts. Oil: 400 tons. Complement, 110.

RUSSIAN DESTROYERS.

2 (+ 2) Isyaslav type (Mine Layers).

4 *Reval Shipbuilding Co.:* ***Briatshislav, Feodor Stratilat, Isyaslav, Priamislav,*** 1350 tons. Dimensions: 344½ × 31¼ × 9⅜ feet. Designed H.P. 32,700 = 35 kts. Parsons turbines and Normand boilers. Armament: 4—4 inch, 1—9 pdr. AA., 2 M.G. Torpedo tubes (18 inch): 12, in 4 triple deck mountings. Oil: 150 tons. Builders are sometimes referred to as Lange & Becker, Böcker & Co., or Chantiers de Nord-Ouest.

Note.—Azard captured by British, now Esthonian *Lennuk*. *Feodor-Stratilat* towed to Petrograd 1918, not yet finished. *Briatshislav* not finished.

12 (+ 15 ?) Gavryil type (Mine Layers.)

4 *Petrograd Metal Works:* ***Azard, Desna*** (*Desna* reported sunk at Petrograd, July, 1919), ***Lieutun, Samsūn.***

7 *Putilov Works, Petrograd:* ***Kapitan 2r. Isyimettiev, Kapitan 2r. Kern°, Kapitan 2r. Konon Zotov,* Kapitan 2r. Kroun°, Kapitan-Leit. Belli,* Leit. Dubassov,° Leit. Ilyin.***

7 *Russo-Baltic S. B. Co. (Reval):* ***Gavryil,§ Konstantin, Mietshislav, Mikhail,*† Sokol,*† Svoboda, Vladimir*†.***

9 *Ziese Yard, Riga:* ***Hogland,*‡ Grengamn,*‡ Khios,*‡ Kulm,*‡ Patras,*‡ Rymnik,*‡ Smolensk,*‡ Stirsuden,*‡ Tenedos*‡.***

* Not finished, 1919. Towed from Reval (†) or Riga (‡) to Petrograd, February, 1918. § Reported sunk 1919 but not deleted from totals.

Displacement: 1260 tons. Dimensions: 314¾ × 30½ × 9¾ feet. Designed H.P. 30,000 = 35 kts. All have turbines and oil fuel only. Armament: 4—4 inch, 1—2 pdr. AA., 2 M.G. Torpedo tubes (18 inch): 12, in 4 triple deck mountings. Carry 80 mines. Complement, 110. Oil: 150 tons.

Note.—Bolshevist *Spartak*, ex Kerensky *Mikula Maklej*, ex Czarist *Kapitan Kingsbergen*, captured by British and now Esthonian *Wambola*.

Following sunk in war: **Grom** and **Gavryil** plus one unidentified.

1911 Special Boat (Mine Layer.)

1 *Putilov-Vulkan* boat: ***Novik*** (Putilov Yard, Petrograd, 1911). 1200 tons. Dimensions: 336 × 31.2 × 9.8 feet. Designed H.P. 33,000 = 32 kts. A. E. G.-Curtis turbines and 400 tons oil fuel only. Complement, 112 (60 now). *Trials:* 42,800 = 36.3 kts. Armament: 4—4 inch, 1—2 pdr. AA., 4 M.G., 8—18 inch tubes in 4 twin deck mountings. Carries 80 mines.

Note.—Built at the expense of the Putilov Co., as an experiment, and taken over for the Russian Navy.

3 Gen. Kondratenko type (Mine Layers.)

3 "*Kondratenko*" *class*, named ***Gen. Kondratenko, Sibirski-Strelok*** (Helsingfors, 1906), ***Pogranitchnik***, (Crichton Yard, Abö, 1905). 625 tons. Dimensions: 246.7 × 26.9 × 8.5 feet. Designed H.P. 7300 = 25 kts. Coal: 215 tons. Complement, 101–98. All armed with 3—4 inch, 2—3 pdr., 3 M.G., and 3—18″ deck tubes, in one twin and one single mounting. Carry 50 mines.

Notes.—Much the same build as *Amuretz* class, (next page), but have a raised poop. *Okhotnik* lost during the war.

RUSSIAN DESTROYERS—*Continued.*

Emir Bukharski type (Mine Layers).

4 Later boats, named **Gaidamak, Vsadnik,** (Krupp-Germania Yard, Kiel, 1905), **Amuretz,** (Riga, 1905), **Ussurietz** (Helsingfors, 1907), the last two being built from materials supplied by Krupps. 570 tons. Dimensions: *Gaidamak* and *Vsadnik*, 233×24.2×7.5 feet. *Amuretz* and *Ussurietz*, 233×23.6×7.8 feet. Designed H.P. 6500 in first two, 6200 in second two=25 kts. Coal: 205 tons. Complement, 97–94. All armed with 2—4 inch, 1—3 pdr., 1—1 pdr. AA., 4 M.G., and 3—18 inch deck tubes. Carry 25 mines.

(With Bolshevist Volga Flotilla.)

2 Earlier boats, named **Yakob Sverdlov** (ex *Emir Bukharski*), **Karl Liebknecht** (ex *Finn*), (Helsingfors, 1905-4.) 580 tons. Dimensions: 237.8×26.9×7.7 feet. Designed H.P. 6200=25 kts. Machinery of *Y. Sverdlov* by Schichau. Coal: 150 tons. Complement: 97–94. Armament: 2—4 inch, 2 or 1—1 pdr., 4 M.G., and 3 deck torpedo tubes. Carry 25 mines. *Moskvityanin* sunk in Caspian Sea, 1919.
Dobrovolets sunk in Gulf of Riga 21 August 1916.

7 Ukräina type (Mine Layers).

Fore funnel now raised.

7 *"Ukräina" class,* named **Donskoi-Kasack** (1907), **Stereguchi Strashni** (all 1905), **Turkmenetz-Stavropolski,*** **Ukräina, Voiskovoi** (all 1904), **Zabaikaletz** (1907.) All built by Lange's Yard, Riga. 500 tons. Dimensions: 240 × 23¾ × 7½ feet. Designed H.P. 6200=25 kts. Boilers: 4 Normand. Coal: 50 tons *normal,* 135 tons *full load.* Complement, 88–85. Armament: 3—4 inch, 1—1 pdr., 2 M.G., and 2 torpedo tubes (18″). Carry 16 mines. *Bolshevist Volga Flotilla.
Kasanetz sunk 28 October 1918.

2 Leit. Sergieff type.
10 Vnimatelni type (Mine Layers).

2 *Schichau, Danzig.* **Leit. Sergieff,*** **Kapitan Yurassovski*** (both launched 1905). 350 tons. Dimensions: 202½ × 22½ × 7½ feet. Designed H.P. 6000 = 29 kts. 4 Thornycroft boilers. Coal: 95 tons. Complement, 64. All armed with 2—11 pdr., 5—3 pdr., and 3 tubes.

3 *Schichau, Elbing.* **Bestrashni,*** **Besposhtchadni,†** **Beshumni*** (all launched 1899).

Also :—

7 *Schichau, Danzig.* **Boyevoi, Burni, Insh. Mech. Svereff, Insh. Mech. Dmitrieff, Vnimatelni, Vnushitelni, Vuinoslivi.** (All built by Schichau, Danzig, and launched 1905–6). 355 tons. Dimensions: 208½×23×6 feet. Designed H.P. 6000=27 kts. 4 Schichau Boilers. Coal: 125 tons. Complement, 64. All armed with 2—11 pdr., 6 M.G., and 3—18″ tubes. Carry 16 mines.
Bditelni sank 27 November 1917. *In White Sea. †At Vladivostok.

RUSSIAN DESTROYERS—*Continued.*

8 Lovki type (Mine Layers).

8 *"Lorki" class,* named **Lovki, Likoi,** (Normand Le Havre, 1905), **Legki, Iskusni, Krepki** (La Seyne, 1905), **Metki,°** **Molodetski, Mostchni** (F. & C. de la Med. Havre, 1905). 330 tons. Dimensions: 185⅛ × 21 ×5¾ feet. Designed H.P. 5700=27 kts. Boilers: 4 Normand. Coal: 100—110 tons. Complement, 65. All armed with 2—11 pdr., 2 M.G., and 2 deck tubes (18″). Carry 15 mines.
*Bolshevist Volga Flotilla.
Following sunk in war: **ispolnitelni, Letutchi, Lieut Burakpov.**

2 Grosovoi type (1 boat Mine Layer).

(Are officially rated as Torpedo Boats. Both in White Sea.)

2 *"Grosovoi" class,* named **Grosovoi, Vlastni.** (F. et C. de la Med., Le Havre, 1900). 310 tons. Dimensions: 185⅞ × 19½ × 6½ feet. Designed H.P. 5700=26 kts. Boilers: 4 Normand. Coal: 60 tons. Complement, 59. Both armed with 2—11 pdr., 1 M.G., and 2 deck tubes (18″). *Vlastni* carries 6 mines.

26 Yarrow or Modified Yarrow type (1907-1894.)

10 *"Dyelni" class,* named **Dyelni,*** **Dostoini,*** **Dieyatelni,*** **Rastoropni,*** **Razyastchi, Silni, Stroini,*** **Storoshevoi,*** (launched 1906-5.) **Gremyastchi, Vidni** (1905-4.) Re-armed with 2—4 in., 2 M.G. Tubes: 2—18″. Carry 14 mines.

Bolshevist Volga Flotilla

4 *"Bravi" class,* named **Bravi,†** **Boiki,§** **Bodri,†** **Grosni†** launched 1905-2.) No mainmast.
†At Vladivostok, disarmed. §*Boiki* now in Mediterranean as French T.B.D. *Quentin Roosevelt.*

Above T.B.D. all built by Nevski Works, Petrograd, and displace 350 tons. Dimensions: 210×21×6½ feet. Designed H.P. 5,700=26 kts. Boilers: 4 Normand in *Dyelni* class, 4 Yarrow in *Bravi* class. Coal: 80 tons. Complement, 64. *Bravi* class armed with 1—11 pdr., 5—3 pdr., and 2 deck torpedo tubes, but *Bravi, Boiki, Bodri* have stem tube.

As above photo but *Smyeli* class no mainmast and straight stems, and *Pritki* class straight stems with mainmast.

Following Boats officially rated as Torpedo Boats :—

5 *"Tverdi" class,* named **Leit.†** **Maleieff,†** **Insh. Mech. Anastassoff,†** **Tverdi,†** **Totchni,†** **Trevoshni†** (Okhta Works, Petrograd, 1906; re-erected at Vladivostok.

7 *"Smyeli" class,* named **Smyeli,†** **Serditi,†** **Statni,†** **Skori,†** (Nevski Works, Petrograd, 1901, re-erected at Port Arthur). **Riasvi, Riany, Prosorlivy.**

"Pritki" class, named **Pritki*** (ex *Sokol*, Yarrow. Poplar. 1895). **Protchni** (Izhora Works, Petrograd, 1900–1899). **Retivi*** (Nevski Works Petrograd, 1901). **Podvishny, Poraschamschtshy, Posluschny**

Above T.B.D. displace 350—220 tons (see Summary Table). Dimensions: *about* 190×18½×5½–6 feet. H.P. 3800 =27–25 kts. (4000 = 29 kts in *Pritki*.) Boilers: 4 locomotive in *Tverdi* class, 4 Yarrow in others. Coal: 65 tons. Complement, 59–52. All armed with 2—11 pdr., 2 M.G., 2—18″ tubes in *Tverdi* class: others 1—15″ tube and 18 mines.

*Bolshevist Volga Flotilla. †At Vladivostok, disarmed.

RUSSIAN TORPEDO BOATS AND SUBMARINES.

RUSSIAN (BALTIC) TORPEDO BOATS.

No.	Type	Date	Dis-place-ment	H.P.	Max. speed	Fuel	Comple-ment	T. Tubes	Max. draug't
6	Nos 220, 222, 219, 217, 216, 214 (N)	1902–04	150	5700	29	30	25	2	5
1	Nos. 212, 213 (N)	1902	190	3800	24	60	26	2	5
3	Nos. 142, 140, 134, 129, 128	1894–98	120	2000	21	20	20	3	6¾
1	Petrol T.B. No. 1	1904	..	..	..	..	..	..	..

(N) = Normand type.

5 *Norman* type. **Nos. 214, 216, 217, 219, 220, 222** (1902-4.). Guns: 2–3 pdr., and 2-15 in. tubes, (double mounted).
Other and older t.b. have 2—1 pdr. and 3 tubes.

2 pole masts.
No funnel.

1 ———— type. **Petrol T.B. No. 1.** 3 small guns. 1 tube. Used now as a despatch vessel.

RUSSIAN SUBMARINES.

10 ? Holland Type (Mine-layers).

Doubtful if ever begun.

10 *Holland* boats: *G 1—10*, ordered from Nobel & Lessner, 1916. 262×22¼×14 feet. Guns: 2–12 or 11 pdr., 2 M.G.
Tubes: 10. Dropping gears: 6. Mines: 10. Other details as Table.

10 ? Bubnov Type (Mine-layers).

Doubtful if ever begun.

10 *Bubnov* boats: *B 1—4* (Baltic Works, Petrograd), *B 5—10* (Russo-Baltic Works, Reval). 261×23×11 feet. Guns,
tubes, dropping gears, mines, as *G 1—10* above. Other details as table.

1 Laurenti Boat.

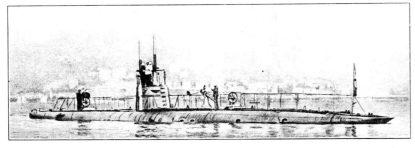

Photo by courtesy of Messrs. Ansaldo-San Giorgio.
(In White Sea.)

1 *Laurenti-Ansaldo* type : **Sviatoi Georg** (Ansaldo-San Giorgio, Spezia, 1916 or 1917). Dimensions : *about* 150 ×
14 × 10 feet. Machinery : 2 sets of 350 H.P., 6-cyl. 2-cycle Fiat Diesel engines *on surface.* Radius of action :
about 1500 miles at cruising speed *on surface,* 70 or 80 miles at a low speed *submerged.* Armament : 1 small Q.F. and
2 bow 18-inch torpedo tubes. Is generally similar to Spanish *Monturiol* and Brazilian *F* classes. Arrived at
Archangel, Sept., 1917.

(Inclusive of Baltic and Siberian flotillas.)

No.	Type	Date	Dis-place-ment.	H.P.	Max. speed kts.	Fuel tons	Tubes and Gear.	Comple-ment	Max. draug't
10	*G 1—10* (H)	?	960/1260	2200/700	16/9	60	16*	..	14
10	*B 1—10* (B)	?	970/1265	3150/700	17/9	58	16*	..	13
1	*Sviatoi Georg* (LA)	1916–17	250/370	700/500	13/8·5	For 1500 miles / For 70-80 miles	2	..	..
1	*Forel* (B)	1912–17	650/784	840/900	11/9	40	4*	..	12½
2	*Edinorog* (B)	1912–17	Do.	2640/900	16/9	40	12	..	12½
2	*Volk* (B)	1912–16	Do.	500/840	10/9	40	12	52	12½
7	*Tigr* (B)	1912–17	Do.	500/900	10/9	40	8	..	12⅔
4	*Alligator* (L)	1908	450/500	400/400	8/7	15	4	23	16
1	*Moinga* (B)	1908	117/177	480/140	11/5·5	5	2	20	9
2	*Makrel* (B)	1907	150/200	120/100	7·5/5	2¾	4	16	9½
4	*Byeluga* (H)	1904	110/120	160/60	8·5/6	2	1	16	10
2	*Kataska* (B)	1904	150/200	120/100	9/7	3	4	20	9½
1	*Delfin* (B)	1903	115	..	10/8	..	2	12	..

(B) = Bubnov type. (LA) = Laurenti-Ansaldo type. (L) = Lake type. (H) = Holland type.
* Mine Layers.

12 "Improved Bubnov" Type (1 boat Mine-layer).

1 *Special* boat: **Forel,** (Baltic Works, Petrograd, 1912—17) Mine-layer. Different H.P. and speeds to other boats,—
see Table. Guns: 1– 6 pdr., 1—1 pdr., AA, 1 M.G. 4 Tubes. Carries 40—50 Mines.

2 *Edinorog* type: **Smaya, Yasy,** (Nobel & Lessner, Reval, 1912—17). Guns: 2 or 1—6 pdr., 1—1 pdr. AA., 1 M.G.
Tubes: 1. Dropping Gears: 8.

2 *Volk* type: **Vyepr, Volk** (Baltic Works, Petrograd, 1912—16). Guns: 2—6 pdr., 1—1 pdr. AA. Tubes: 4.
Dropping Gears: 8. Have Diesel engines removed from Amur River Gunboats.

7 *Tigr* type: **Kuguar, Leopard, Pantera, Ryss, Tigr, Tur, Yaguar** (Nobel & Lessner, Reval, 1912-17).
Guns: 2—6 pdr., 1—1 pdr. AA., 1 M.G. Tubes: 4. Dropping Gears: 8.

General Notes: All launched 1915-16. Dimensions: 223×11½×12⅔ feet. Other details as Table. *Bars, Gepard, Lvitsa,
Ugor* and *Edinorog* war losses. Mine-layer *Ersh* sunk by H.M. ships *Valorous* and *Vancouver,* 1919.

RUSSIAN SUBMARINES—*Continued.*

4 Lake Type.

Photo, Lieut.-Col. Alan H. Burgoyne, M.P.

All reported to have been captured by the Germans, 1918.

4 *Lake* type: **Alligator, Drakon, Kaiman, Krokodil** (1908). Dimensions: 133×14×16 feet. Naptha (or light oil) motors for surface. Armament: 1—3 pdr., 1 machine, 4—18 inch tubes, 2 dropping gears for 18 inch torpedoes.
Also listed in 1914, fate unknown: *Ossetyr, Bytschok, Kefal Paltus* and *Plotva*.

1 Bubnov Type.

No photo available.

Bolshevist Volga Flotilla.

1 *Bubnov* type: **Minoga** (1908, re-built 1915). Dimensions: 197×18⅝×8 feet. Diesel engines. 1—1 pdr. gun. Two 18 inch tubes.

4 Old Holland Type.

Reported that all were captured by Germans, in 1918.
5 early *Holland* type: **Byeluga, Piskar, Sterliard, Tchuka, Som.** (1904). 1—1 pdr., gun. 1-15 inch dropping gear.

2 Old Bubnov Type.

Bolshevist Volga Flotilla.

3 early *Bubnov* type: **Ugor** (ex *Graf Sheremetier*), **Kasatka,** (Built about 1914-15). **Skat** similar to *Makrel* and *Okua*, but have 1-1 pdr, and 1 M.G.

3 Old Bubnov Type.

Illustrated in
"Fighting Ships" up to
1915-16.

In White Sea.

1 old *Bubnov* boat **Delfin** (1903). Used to be armed with 2—15 inch dropping gears. Present value almost *nil.*
Following lost during war: *Akula* November 1915, AG 11, 12, 13, 14, 15 (all of 350 tons, class unknown).

2 Bubnov Type.

No photo Available.

Bolshevist Volga Flotilla.

2 early *Bubnov* type: **Makrel, Okun** (1907). Displacement, 150/200 tons. 4—18 inch dropping gears.

RUSSIAN DEPOT SHIPS AND MINE LAYERS.

Motor Patrol Boats.

Total number unknown. Some in the Baltic; others in the White and Black Seas. Builders: chiefly U.S. firms, 1915-16. —— tons. Dimensions: 60 × 10 × 2⅝ feet, but others may be 80-85 feet long. Machinery: Twin or triple sets of petrol motors (12-cyl., Standard, Dusenberg, Van Blerck, &c). H.P. 500-600 = 25-26 kts. designed speed. Some made 30.1 kts. on trials in smooth water, but best sea speed is only about 20 kts. for short periods. Fuel: 4000 galls. petrol = 600 miles at cruising speed. Guns: One (11 pdr., 6 or 3 pdr. ?), and perhaps M.G. Depth charges may also be carried. Crew, about 8-10.

Coast Patrol Boats :—

Barsuk	*Mesen*	*Stvol*
Dulo	*Palash*	*Tumba*
Gornostai	*Pistolet*	*Tzapfa*
Griff	*Pulra*	*Vladimir*
*Kobchik**	*Ruslan*	*Voron*
Korsun	*Shaska*	*Vuidra*
Kunitsa	*Sobol*	*Yastreb*

** May be in Finnish Navy now.*

Destroyer Depot Ships.

Repair Ships, **ANGARA** and **KAMA** attached to T.B.D. Flotillas.

Submarine Depot Ships.

Cruiser **DIANA** : for details, see preceding pages with other cruisers.

No photo available.
(Resembles German "Vulkan.")

VOLKHOV (Putilov, 1913). 2400 tons. Dimensions : 315 × 69 × 11¾ feet. Diesel engines. H.P. 1200 = 10 kts. Radius 3600 miles. Can raise 1000 tons.

Note.—Carries all essential stores for submarines (oil fuel, reserve accumulators, &c.), and has compressed air, distilling and charging plant, workshops, &c.

(At Vladivostok ?)
TOBOL (1899). 5500 tons. H.P. 2500 = 8 kts. Not certain if this ship, or another of same name, was sunk in 1916. Reported to be Transport at Vladivostok, 1919.

KHABAROVSK (1895). 2800 tons. H.P. 1800 = 12·5 kts. Guns: 2—11 pdr.. 2—3 pdr., 2 M.G. Coal: 390 tons. Complement, 132.

EVROPA (1878). 3200 tons. H.P. 12,000 = 13 kts. Guns: 4—3 pdr.; tubes: 2 *above water,* 1 *submerged.* Coal: 390 tons.

Seaplane Carrier.

ORLITZA (——). 3000 tons. 10 kts. speed. Guns : 8—11 pdr., 2 M.G. Carries 4 seaplanes.

Mine Layers.

(At Vladivostok).
DIOMID, PATROKL, ULIS (1913-14). 600 tons. Complement, 41. Dimensions : 160×26½× feet, Guns : *Not known.* H.P. —— = 12 kts. speed.

AMŪR (1907). 3608 tons. Complement, 318. Dimensions : 320× 46×14½ feet. Armament : 9—4·7 inch, 4 M.G. H.P. 4700 = 17 kts. Boilers : 12 Belleville. Coal : 670 tons. Carries 320 mines. *Yenessei* of this type lost in the war.
VASSILI VELIKI Lost in White Sea April 1916.

RUSSIAN AUXILIARIES

Mine Layers (continued).

LADFOGA (ex-*Minin*) Torpedoed by U-boat 15 August 1915.

VOLGA (1905): 1711 tons. Complement, 266. H.P. 1600 = 13 kts. Babcock boilers. Armament : 4—3 pdr. Carries 236 mines. Coal : 160 tons.

USSURI (1901). 3200 tons. Complement, 210. Dimensions : 236 × 36 × 15 feet. Guns : 3—11 pdr., 4—3 pdr., 2 M.G. H.P. 1056 = 10 kts. Carries 500 mines.

(Transport, at Vladivostok.)

SHILKA (Elswick, 1896). 3500 tons. Complement, 205. Dimensions : 278 × 39.4 × 17 feet. Guns : 4—4.7 inch, 8—11 pdr., 4 M.G. H.P. 1650 = 11 kts.

(At Vladivostok.)

MONGUGAI (Flensburg, 1891). 2500 tons. Complement, 193. Dimensions : 202 × 30 × 18 feet. Guns : 7—3 pdr. H.P. 6000 = 9 kts.

Repair Ships—(continued).

ANADYR (1896). 12,000 tons. Speed : 13 kts.

ANGARA (Clydebank, 1898, ex *Anegawa Maru*, ex *Angara*). 5920 tons. H.P. 3000 = 13 kts. (less at present). Belleville boilers. Coal : 800 tons. Captured in the Russo-Japanese War. In 1911, presented to Russia by the Emperor of Japan.

Salvage Ships.

Assistans	*Meteor*	*Silach*
Hero	*Nordmir*	*Solid*
Karin	*Protektor*	

Transports.

32 ships laid up in Baltic. Auxiliary Cruiser *Orel* and 3 or 4 Transports at Vladivostok.

Mine Layers (continued).

ONEGA (ex *Gertzog Edinburgski*, 1875). 4840 tons ; and **NAROVA** (ex *General Admiral*, 1872). 5030 tons. Speed : 12-13 kts. Guns : 4—11 pdr., 4 M.G. Complete 6″ iron belt. Carry 600 mines.

Also :—
Ilmen, * *Lena, Lovat, Luga, Msta,* * *Svir,* * *Ural.*
*May be in Finnish Navy now.

Mine Sweepers.

ISKRA, PLAMYA, PATRON (Middlesborough, 1913-14). 500 tons. Dimensions : 146 × 24½ × 10 feet. Guns : 2—11 pdr. H.P. 650 = 11 kts.

MINREP. (Now has a main mast.)

FUGAS, MINREP, * **PROVODNIK, SAPAL,** * **VZRUIV** (1911). 150 tons. Guns : 2—3 pdr. Speed : 10 kts.
*May be in Finnish Navy now. |
Also about 14 other small craft and about 5 Torpedo Boats fitted as Sweepers.

RUSSIAN MISCELLANEOUS.

Transports—(continued).

BORGÅ (1882), 4700 tons, and **LAKHTA** (1889), 5000 tons. Speed : 10 kts.

SAMOYED (1895). 1300 tons. Speed : 12 kts.

PAKHTUSOV (——). 1100 tons. Speed : 9 kts. In White Sea.

TAIMYR (1908), **VAIGATCH** (1908). In White Sea. 1290 tons. Speed : 10 kts. *(Surveying Ships.)*

MURMAN (1912, for White Sea). 500 tons.
(Also other ships, chartered or requisitioned for period of war.)

Hospital Ships.

14 laid up in Baltic.

Oil Tankers.

Aramis	*Olga*	*Tamara*
Elena	*Spinoza*	*Tatiana*
Nina		

Ice Breakers.

Ilya Mourometz, Kniaz Pojarski, Kozma Minin, Mikula Salianinovich, were in White Sea, 1919, under control of Allies.

Gorod Revel and *Herkules* are in the Baltic.

Repair Ships.

OKA (1914), **KAMA** (1911). 2000 tons. Speed : 10 kts.

PETSHORA (1910). **SUCHON, MESEN.** 2000 tons. Speed: 10 kts. Coal: 170 tons.
Note: Fate of *Suchon* and *Mesen* unknown.

(In White Sea.)

XENIA (ex *Cayo Soto*, 1900). 5900 tons. Speed : 11 kts. Guns : 2—11 pdr., 2—3 pdr., 2 M.G. Coal : 400 tons.

Ice Breakers (continued).

TSAR MIKHAIL FEODOROVITCH (Vulkan, Stettin, 1914). 1391 tons *gross*. Dimensions : 244 × 57 × 27½ feet. H.P. = 10 kts. speed.

(In the Baltic.)

ERMAK (Elswick, 1898). 8000 tons. Dimensions : 305 × 71 × 25 feet. 1¼″ Steel belt. H.P. 10,000 = 16 kts. Coal : 3000 tons.

(In the Baltic.)

PETR VELIKI (1872, re-constructed 1905). Displacement, 966_ tons. Armament (new in 1905) :* 4—8 inch (50 cal.), 12— inch (45 cal.), 12—12 pdr., 4—6 pdr., 8—3 pdr., 2 M.G. H.P. 8260 = 13 kts. Coal : 1200 tons. Present speed : 11 kts.
* All guns probably removed now.

Armed Yachts.

Ex-**SHTANDART** (1895). 5557 tons. Guns: 8—3 pdr. H.P. 10,600 = 21 kts. Belleville boilers.

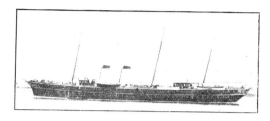

(Flagship, Bolshevist C-in-C. Baltic).

KRETCHET (ex-*Polarnaya-Sviedza*, 1890). 3640 tons. Guns: 6—12 pdr. H.P. 5600 = 18·8 kts. Cylindrical boilers.

Ex-**ALEXANDRIA** (1903). 500 tons. 14·5 kts. Paddle-wheel Yacht. There are also 9 small Yachts of from 800—180 tons.

Gunnery School Ships.

Reported sunk at Kronstadt.

SARIA SVOBODI (ex-*Imperator Aleksandr II*, 1887, re-constructed 1905). Displacement 9390 metric tons. Complement, 648. Armament: 2—12 inch (30 cal.); 6—6 inch (45 cal.); 4—4·7 inch, 2—3 pdr., 1 machine, 2—3 inch AA. Armour (Compound): Belt 14″ 6″, Barbette 12″. Designed H.P. 8500 = 15 kts. Coal: 1080 tons.

Sunk at Kronstadt August 1919. Possibly torpedoed by British CMBs.

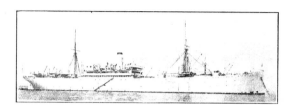

(And Transport.)   *Photo, Seward, Weymouth.*

RIGA (ex *Belgravia*), (Blohm & Voss, 1899). 14,500 tons. Complement, 273. Guns: 2—6 inch, 8—4·7 inch, 8—12 pdr., 4—6 pdr., 4—3 pdr., 18 machine. H.P. 4000 = 12 kts. An Enemy Naval Annual refers to a sister ship, *Argun*, of which nothing is known in this country. Also *Vyemi*.

Diving School.

Old *Afrika* (1877), 2600 tons.

Engineers' Training Ships.

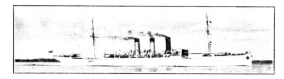

(And Transport.)

OKEAN (Howaldt, 1902). 11,900 tons. H.P. 11,000 = 18 kts. Coal: 1600 tons. Boilers: 6 Belleville, 6 Niclausse, 3 Yarrow, 2 Thornycroft. Complement, 700.

Also Despatch vessels *Lastotchka*, *Petrel T.B. No. 1*., Auxiliaries *Nicolai Pogolski Buksir*, *Byelomor*, *Kotka*, *Samoyed*.

Mine and Torpedo School Ships.

NIKOLAIEFF (ex-*Palatia*) (1894). 13,500 tons. Complement, 272. H.P. 4200 = 13 kts. Guns: 2—11 pdr., 4—3 pdr. Tubes: 4 above water.

Also *Aziya*, *Osvoboditelni*, *Khoper*,° *Terek*, ° Motor boat *No. 5*.
 °*Mine-layer.*

DVINA (ex-*Parniat Azova*). Torpedoed by British CMBs at Kronstadt 18 August 1918.

Old Training Ship.

VOIN (1893). 1280 tons. Guns: 4—12 pdr. Speed, 9 kts.

WIERNY deleted during war.

FLOTILLAS ON DVINA AND AMUR RIVERS.

AMUR RIVER FLOTILLA.

Scale: 1 inch = 160 feet.

NO FUNNELS.

GROSA *class* (8 ships).

River Monitors & Gunboats.

Photo: "Motor Ship & Motor Boat."

GROSA, SHKWAL, SHTORM, SMERTCH, TYFUN, URAGAN, VIKHR, VYUGA (———1910). Displacement, 950 tons. Complement, . Length (*waterline*), 233 feet. Beam, 42⅔ feet. Draught, 4½ feet. Guns: 2—6 inch (one forward, one aft), 4—4·7 inch in pairs in midship turrets, 4 machine. Armour: 4½″ turrets. Machinery: Nobel-Lessner Diesel motors. 1000 h.p. = 11 kts.

Note.—The machinery has been removed from all of the above ships to provide engines for new Submarines built during the War. Their 6-inch guns have been removed for shore service.

River Monitors & Gunboats *(continued)*.

OROKANIN, MONGOL, BURIAT, VOGUL, SIBIRIAK, KOREL and **KIRGIZ, KALMUIK, SIRIANIN, VOTYAK** (1909). 190 tons. Complement, 40. Dimensions: 164 × 27 × 2 feet. Guns: 2—11 pdr.,* 2 machine,° but last four have 1—4·7 inch* and 1 machine gun.* Designed H.P., 500 = 11 kts. Coal: 145 tons.

 * The Bolshevists removed all guns from these ships.

Kopyo, Palash, Pika, Pistolet, Pulya, Shtik.

These are motor patrol-boats (1908) of 24 tons, 16 kts. speed, each armed with 1—3 inch mountain gun and a M.G.

Note.—*Kinjal, Rapira, Sablya, Shashka*, transported to Black Sea and Danube during the War.

DVINA RIVER FLOTILLA.

Gunboats.

ADVOKAT.

GORODOFF.

RAZLYFF.

Note.—Above three gunboats were under the White Ensign during the British operations in Northern Russia.

Supposed that there is the usual extemporised Fleet of River Steamers and Armed Barges, &c., used by the Allies and Bolshevists in Northern Russia. British Aircraft have attacked Bolshevist Craft of this kind on various occasions. But no details are available of these ships.

RUSSIAN NAVY.

BLACK SEA SECTION

(INCLUSIVE OF CASPIAN SEA AND VOLGA RIVER FLOTILLAS.)

The Russian Black Sea Fleet no longer exists. The following account gives a summary of this Fleet's dissolution.

When the Austro-German Armies were advancing, in 1918, on the Crimean Naval Ports, the Destroyer *Gnievni* was blown up at Sebastopol. When the fall of Sebastopol was imminent, the two Dreadnoughts **SVOBODNAYA ROSSIA** and **VOLYA** proceeded to Novorossisk in company with Destroyers and various Auxiliaries. Other ships took refuge in the Sea of Azov. **SVOBODNAYA ROSSIA** was torpedoed and sunk by the Russian Destroyer *Kertch*. The Destroyers *Feodnissi, Gadjibey, Kaliaklya, Kertch, Pronsitelni, Gromki, Leit. Shestakov, Kap. Leit. Baranoff, Smietlivi* and *Stremitelni* were partially destroyed and scuttled in 1918.

When the Allied Fleet entered the Black Sea, the Dreadnought **VOLYA** was taken over by the British. Destroyers were divided thus : *Derski* (British), *Schastlivi* (British, wrecked at Mudros), *Bespokoini, Kapitan Saken* (France), **ZORKI** (Italy), *Zvonki* (Greece). Seaplane Carrier, **ALMAZ,** taken over by France.

In April, 1919, Bolshevist Armies were advancing on Odessa and Sebastopol, and it became necessary to scuttle or disable Russian Warships at those ports. The Submarines *AG 1, Gagara, Orlan, Morsh, Kashalot, Kit, Narval, Krab* (minelayer), *Karp, Karas* were scuttled and other Submarines removed. The machinery of the following ships was completely destroyed by explosives : **EVSTAFI, IOANN ZLATOUST, BORETZ ZA SVOBODU, ROSTISLAV, TRIA SVIATITELIA, SINOP, PAMIAT MERKURIYA,** *Buistri, Jeevoi, Jootki, Zavidni,* **ZAVETNI, BERESAN.**

The "Denikin Volunteer Fleet" consists of **GENERAL KORNILOFF,** *Pospyeschni, Puilki, Jarki, Strogi, Svirepi, Burevestnik, Utka, Lebed, Pelikan, Nerpa, Tyulen,* **DONETZ, KUBANETZ, TERETZ** and various Armed River Barges, Auxiliaries, etc.

Scale : 1 inch = 160 feet.

RUSSIAN BLACK SEA FLEET.—RECOGNITION SILHOUETTES.

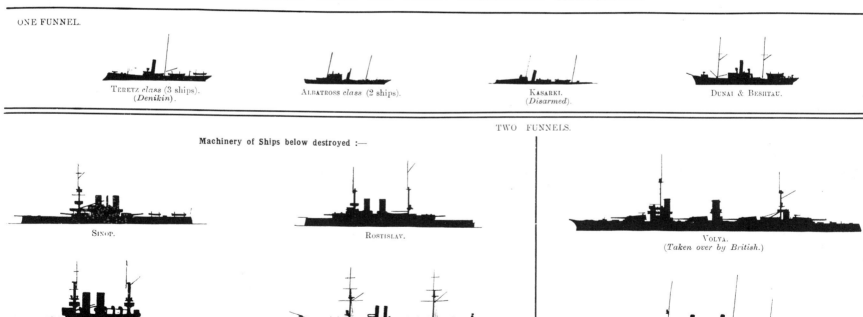

ONE FUNNEL.

TERETZ *class* (3 ships). (Denikin).

ALBATROSS *class* (2 ships).

KASARKI. (Disarmed).

DUNAI & BESHTAU.

TWO FUNNELS.

Machinery of Ships below destroyed :—

SINOP.

ROSTISLAV.

VOLYA. (Taken over by British.)

TRI SVIATITELIA. (Has been reconstructed. Present appearance probably differs from above).

BEREZAN.

ALMAZ. (Seaplane Carrier taken over by France.)

Machinery of all destroyed.

THREE FUNNELS.

EVSTAFI *class* (2 ships).

BORETZ ZA SVOBODU.

GEN. KORNILOFF (Denikin.)
P. MERKURIA (**Machinery destroyed**).
(Turrets now removed and replaced by guns in shields.)

1914-11 BLACK SEA DREADNOUGHTS.

VOLYA (April, 1914), and **DEMOKRATIYA** (18th Oct., 1916).

	Length. (o.a.)	Beam.	Draught.	Displacement.
Volya	551 feet 2 inches	× 89 feet 8 inches	× 27 feet 4 inches	(*max.*) = 22,600 tons
Demokratiya	597 feet 1 inch	× 95 feet 1 inch	× 29 feet 5 inches	= 27,300 tons

Complement.—1252 (*Volya*).

Corrections to Plans: Fore funnel should be close to foremast, mainmast should be much further aft with C.T. abaft same. Also have overhanging or "yacht" stems. Two foremost 5·1 inch removed from *Volya*.

Guns: (*Volya*).
12—12 inch, 50 cal. (A⁶)
18—5·1 inch, 55 cal.⁶
8—11 pdr.⁶
4—9 pdr. (anti-aircraft)⁶
4—3 pdr.⁶
4 machine⁶
Torpedo tubes (18.)
  4 submerged.
Demokratiya.
20—5·1 inch.
4—4 inch AA.
4—M.G.

Armour:
12″–8″ Belt (amidships)
5″–4″ Belt (bow)
4″ Belt (stern)
3″ Deck
9″–8″ Upper Belt
12″ Turrets and Bases
5″ Battery
12″ Conning tower (fore)
8″ Conning tower (aft)

SVOBODNAYA ROSSIYA (has been sunk).

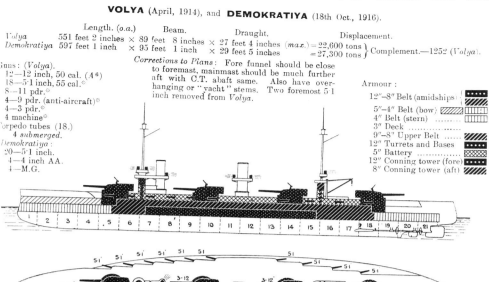

VOLYA.

Machinery: Parsons or Brown-Curtis. 4 screws. Boilers: 20 Yarrow. Designed H.P., *Volya*, 26,500; H.P. *Demokratiya* 27,900. Speed of both, 21 kts. *Volya*, 2,300 tons *maximum*. Oil 720 tons. (Fuel for *Demokratiya* unknown).

Name.	Builder.	Machinery.	Laid down.	Completed.	Trials.	Turbines.	Boilers.	Best recent speed.
Volya	Nikolaieff (B)		Aug.'11	June,'17	29040 = 21·1		Yarrow	
Demokratiya	Nikolaieff (B)		July'11	?			Yarrow	

B = Bunge & Ivanoff—Brown (Clydebank)

General Notes.—Design generally resembles *Gangut* class. Original names were *Imperator Aleksandr Treti* (now *Volya*), and *Imperator Nikolai Vtoroi* (now *Demokratiya*). Completion of first two ships *Imp. Maria* and *Imp. Ekaterina Vtoroi* (latter re-named *Svobodnaya Rossia*), was accelerated after the beginning of the war. *Imp. Maria*, the first ship of this class, destroyed by explosion at Sebastopol during the war.
Svobodnaya Rossia was destroyed at Novorossisk to avoid internmment 18 June 1918.

Notes.

VOLYA taken over by British.
DEMOKRATIYA not finished. All work stopped on her two years ago.
Imperatritza Maria salved 1919. Funnels, masts, barbettes, C.T., &c., removed. She has been docked *upside down* at Nicolaieff.

1903 DISABLED RUSSIAN BLACK SEA BATTLESHIPS. 1898

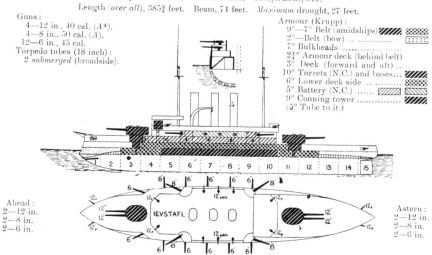

IOANN ZLATOUST (AND EVSTAFI).

Photo by favour of Kapitan Ketlinsky.

EVSTAFI CLASS—(2 SHIPS).
EVSTAFI (Nov., 1906) & **IOANN ZLATOUST** (May, 1906).

Displacement, 13,000 metric tons. Complement, 879.
Length (*over all*), 385¾ feet. Beam, 74 feet. *Maximum* draught, 27 feet.

Guns:
4—12 in., 40 cal. (A⁴).
4—8 in., 50 cal. (A).
12—6 in., 45 cal.
Torpedo tubes (18 inch):
  2 submerged (broadside).

Armour (Krupp):
9″–7″ Belt (amidships)
2″–Belt (bow)
7″ Bulkheads
2½″ Armour deck (behind belt)
3″ Deck (forward and aft)
10″ Turrets (N.C.) and bases
6″ Lower deck side
5″ Battery (N.C.)
9″ Conning tower
(5″ Tube to it.)

Ahead:
2—12 in.
2—8 in.
2—6 in.

Astern:
2—12 in.
2—8 in.
2—6 in.

Machinery: **Destroyed** 25/4/19. Coal: *normal* 670 tons, *maximum* 1000 tons. *Erstafi* built at Nikolaieff, *I. Zlatoust* at Sevastopol. Both laid down 1903. Completed 1910.

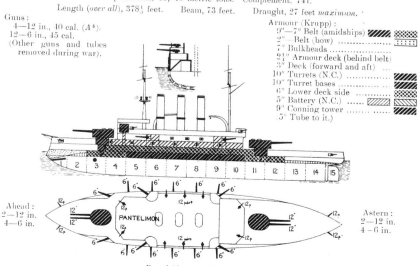

BORETZ ZA SVOBODU (*ex Pantelimon*, *ex Kniaz. P. Tavritcheski*) (Oct., 1900).
Displacement, 12,840 metric tons. Complement, 741.
Length (*over all*), 378½ feet. Beam, 73 feet. Draught, 27 feet *maximum*.

Guns:
4—12 in., 40 cal. (A⁴).
12—6 in., 45 cal.
(Other guns and tubes removed during war).

Armour (Krupp):
9″–7″ Belt (amidships)
2″–Belt (bow)
7″ Bulkheads
2½″ Armour deck (behind belt)
3″ Deck (forward and aft)
10″ Turrets (N.C.)
10″ Turret bases
6″ Lower deck side
5″ Battery (N.C.)
9″ Conning tower
5″ Tube to it.

Ahead:
2—12 in.
4—6 in.

Astern:
2—12 in.
4—6 in.

Broadside: 4—12 in., 8—6 in.
Machinery: **Destroyed** 25/4/19. Coal: *normal* 670 tons, *maximum* 1100 tons. Laid down at Nikolaieff 1898, completed 1903.

RUSSIAN OLD BATTLESHIPS. (BLACK SEA.) All Disabled.

Ростиславъ ROSTISLAV (Sept. 1896).
Displacement, 9020 metric tons. Complement, 641.

Length (*waterline*), 341 feet. Beam, 69 feet. Mean draught, 25 feet. Length *over all*, 348 feet.

Guns (Obukhoff) :
4—10 inch, 45 cal. (A³)
8—6 inch, 45 cal.
18—11 pdr.
6—9 pdr. AA.
3 machine

Armour (Harvey)
15″—8″ Belt (amidships) ▪▪▪▪ ▨
3″ Deck (flat on belt) ....
12″ Fore turret .... ▨
9″ After turret .... ▨
6″ Turret bases ....
6″ Lower deck redoubt...... ▨
6″ Small turrets ... ... ▨
6″ Small turret bases ......
10″ Conning tower.............. ▨
(Total weight 2400 tons.)

Ahead :
2—10 in.
4—6 in.

Astern :
2—10 in.
4—6 in.

Machinery : **Destroyed** 25/4/19. Coal : *normal* 500 tons ; *maximum* 800 tons. Liquid fuel also carried.
General Notes.—Laid down at Nikolaieff, 1895, and completed for sea, 1898. Cost about £850,000.

(Before reconstruction). *Photo by favour of H.I.H. Grand Duke Alexander.*

TRI SVIATITELIA. (Nov., 1893, reconstructed, 1912). 13,530 tons. Complement, 744.
Guns : 4—12 inch (40 cal.) ; 14—6 inch, 2—6 pdr. AA., 2—1 pdr., 3 M.G. Tubes : 2—18 inch *submerged*. Armour (Creusot special) : 16″ Belt (incomplete) with 12″ bulkheads and 3″ deck flat on top edge of belt. 16″ lower deck redoubt and 5″ battery redoubt over. 16″ turrets with 12″ bases. 12″ (fore) C.T. Machinery : **Destroyed** 25/4/19. Coal : *normal* 750 tons ; *maximum* 900 tons.

SINOP (1887, re-constructed, 1910). 11,230 tons. Complement, 656. Dimensions : 339×69×29 feet. Armament : 4—8 inch, 12—6 inch, 2—3 pdr., 4 M.G. Armour (compound) : 16″—10″ Belt, 12″ Redoubt. Machinery : **Destroyed** 24/5/19. Coal : *max.* 850 tons.

Note.—Another old battleship, Georgi Pobiedonosetz, sister to above, is in service still. Only a Port Guardship, and is disarmed.

(1916-15 RUSSIAN BLACK SEA CRUISERS. 1903-2

Note.

The Plans given below are based on those published in an Enemy Naval Annual. Their accuracy cannot be guaranteed in any way. Last two ships may never be completed.

ADMIRAL NAKHIMOFF (Oct., 1915),* **ADMIRAL LAZAREFF** (June 1916),
ADMIRAL KORNILOFF (not launched). *ADMIRAL ISTOMIN* (not launched).
* Almost finished, May 1918.
Displacement, 6750 metric tons. Complement

Length (*waterline*), 507 feet. Beam, 49⅝ feet. Draught, 18½ feet. Length (*over all*), 519¾ feet.

Guns :
15—5·1 inch (55 cal.)
4—9 pdr. (anti-aero)
4 machine
Torpedo tubes (18″)
2 *submerged*.
Carry 100 mines.

Armour :
3″ Belt ....
1″ Deck ....
3″ Gun Shields ....

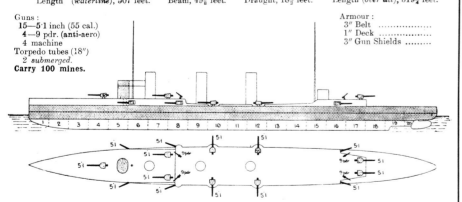

Machinery : Curtis turbine. Boilers : 13 Yarrow. Designed H.P. 55,000 = 29·75 kts. Coal (or oil *only*) : normal tons ; maximum tons.

Name	Builders	Machinery	Laid down	Completed	Trials	Boilers	Best recent speed
Ad. Nakhimoff	Nikolaieff†		Nov. '13			Yarrow	
Ad. Lazareff	Nikolaieff†		Nov. '13			Yarrow	
Ad. Korniloff	Nikolaieff†		Sept. '14	?			
Ad. Istomin	Nikolaieff†		Sept. '14	?			

General Notes.—Sister ships to Admiral Butakoff class, described on a previous page in Baltic Section. Are equipped for carrying seaplanes.
† Begun by Russian S.B. Co., Nicolaieff, to be completed by Nicolaieff S.B. & Engineering Co.

Protected Cruisers.

GENERAL KORNILOFF (*October*, 1902), **PAMIAT MERKURIA** (*ex Kagul*), (June, 1903).
6750 tons. Complement, 573. Dimensions : 436×54×20½ feet. Armament : *Gen. Korniloff* 16—5·1 inch, *P. Merkuria* 16—6 inch, 2—11 pdr. Tubes (18 inch) : 2 torpedo tubes *submerged*. Armour : 3″ Deck, Turrets and Casemates (4). Machinery : 2 sets 4 cylinder triple expansion. 2 screws. Boilers : 16 Normand. Designed H.P. 19500 = 23 kts.* Coal : *normal* 700 tons ; *maximum* 1100 tons.
* Machinery of *P. Merkuria* destroyed 25/4/19.

Notes : *Gen. Korniloff* with Gen. Denikin's Naval forces. Turrets fore and aft shown in above photo now removed and replaced by 5·1 inch in shields. This ship has borne the names of *Kagul* and *Otchakoff* five times since 1902, viz.:—*Kagul* (1902), *Otchakoff* (1902-6), *Kagul* 1906-17, *Otchakoff* (1917-18), *Kagul* (1918-19).

RUSSIAN BLACK SEA DESTROYERS.

Black Sea Destroyers.

Completing at Nicolaieff.

1 boats : *Cerigo, Korfu, Levkos, Zante :* 1325 tons. Dimensions : 303½ × 29½ × 9 feet. Armament : 4—4 inch, 1—2 pdr. (anti-aircraft), 12 tubes in 4 triple deck mountings. Turbine engines. Oil fuel only : 390 tons.

Following destroyed in June 1918: *Feodonissi, Gadjibsey, Kaliakrya* and *Kerch.*

No Photo available.

2 boats *Bespokoini, Derski* ᵇ (1914). 1088 tons. 307½ × 29½ × 9 feet. Armed as *Bistri* type below but carry no mines. S.H.P. 25,500 = 34 kts. Oil. 255—280 tons.

ᵃ Taken over by French.
ᵇ Taken over by British.

Following lost in war: *Gniveni, Shastlivy, Pronsitelny.*

No photo available — see Silhouettes.
2 masts, 3 funnels.

3 boats (1913-14), named: *Bistri,* Pospyeshni,† Pulki,†* 1110 tons. Dimensions : 324½ × 30 × 9 feet. Armament : 4—4 inch, 2—3 pdr. (anti-aircraft), 5-twin 18 inch tubes. Carry 80 mines. H.P. 25,500 = 34 kts. Parsons turbine. 5 boilers. Oil fuel only. 351 tons.

* Engines destroyed, April 27th, 1919.
† Attached to Gen. Denikin's Army

1 boat (1907): *Kapitan Saken* * (ex *Pushkin*). 800 tons. Dimensions : 242⅞ × 27½ × 8 feet. H.P. 6500 = 26 kts. Armament : 2—4.7 inch (30 cal.), 2—3 pdr. AA., 3 M.G., 3—18 inch tubes. Carries 80 mines. Normand Boilers. Coal : 200 tons.

*Taken over by French.
Following lost in War: *Lieut. Zatzarrenny, Lieut. Shestakov, Kap-Lieut Baranov.*

7 boats (*Laird* type) *Zavidni,* Zavetni,* Jeevoi,* Jootki,* Jarki,‡ Zvonki,‡ Zorki∥* (1905). 350 tons. Dimensions : 210 × 21 × 6½ feet (*normal* draught). *Maximum* draught : 7½ feet. H.P. 5700 = 26 kts. Boilers : 4 Yarrow. Carry 90 tons coal or coal = oil. Armament : 2—11 pdr., 2 M.G. 2—18 inch tubes. 18 mines.
*Engines destroyed. *Denikin's Army. ‡To Greece. ∥To Italy.

Following lost in war: *Zhivuchi* and *Lieut. Pushtchin.*

2 boats (early *Yarrow* type): *Strogi,* Svirepi** (1901). 376 tons. Dimensions : 190 × 18½ × 5 feet. H.P. 3800 = 26 kts. Boilers : Yarrow. Carry 70 tons, coal. Armament : 2—11 pdr., 2 M.G., 2—15 inch tubes. 12 mines. *Maximum* draught : 6½ feet.
Following lost in war: *Stremitelny, Smetlivy.* *Denikin's Army.

RUSSIAN (BLACK SEA) SUBMARINES.

5 *Holland* type : *AG 4—6* (were still in packing cases, at Nicolaieff, March, 1918). *AG 2, AG 3* (almost finished, March, 1918). Dimensions : 150½ × 15¼ × 12½ feet. 4—18 inch bow tubes. Nlseco Diesel engines. Same type as Chilean *H* Submarines. Other details as Table.

4 *Improved Bubnov* type : *Burevestnik,* Utka,* Lebed** (1916), *Pelikan** (1917). Dimensions : 223 × 14⅜ × 12⅞ feet. Guns : *Burevestnik, Lebed,* 1—11 pdr. : *Utka,* 2—11 pdr., 1—1 pdr., 1 M.G. ; *Pelikan,* 1—11 pdr., 1—1 pdr., 1 M.G. Have 4 tubes and 4 dropping gears (8 gears in *Utka*). B.H.P. and speeds vary, see Table. Have Diesel engines taken from Amur River Gunboats. Other details as Table.

*Gen. Denikin's Army.

2 *Improved Bubnov* type (*Volk* class) : *Nerpa,* Tyulen** (1913), built at Nikolaieff. Dimensions : 220 × 14½ × 12⅞ feet. Guns : 1—11 pdr., 1—6 pdr. Tubes : 4. Dropping gears : 8. Have Diesel engines taken from Amur River Gunboats. *Are faster submerged than on surface.* Other details as Table.

*Gen. Denikin's Army.

Note: The following boats were scuttled in 1919: *Gagara, Orian, Morsh, Kaschalot, Kit, Marval, Krab, Karp* and *Karas.*

(RUSSIA ?) BLACK SEA MISCELLANEOUS.

Gunboats.

Fore and mizzen masts now removed.

TERETZ (1887), **DONETZ** (1887), **URALETZ.** 1280-1295 tons. Complement, 135. Guns (new in 1904-06): 2—6 inch (45 cal.); 1—4.7 inch (45 cal.); (2—11 pdr. in *Donetz*), 4—3 pdr., 2—1 pdr. H.P. *Donetz* 2000 = 12 kts.,* *Teretz* 1500 = 11 kts., *Kubanetz* 1500 = 13.5 kts. Boilers (new in 1904-06): Belleville. Coal: 220-237 tons.

Note:— All three attached to gen. Deniken's Army. *Kubanetz scuttled in 1914.*

Patrol Boats.

ALBATROSS, BAKLAN (1909). 100 tons. Guns: 6—1 pdr. Speed: 9½ kts. Identical with *Minrep* class in Baltic Section.

Chaika (1910). 25 tons. 1—1 pdr.

Also: *Ledorez, Lidia, Pantikopela.*

Anti-Submarine Patrols.

16 Motor Launches.

Danube Motor Patrol Boats.

Kinjal, Shaska, Sablya, Rapira (1910). 24 tons. 1—3 inch mountain gun, 1 M.G. B.H.P. 200=16 kts. Transported from Amur River during War.

BOLSHEVIST
VOLGA FLOTILLA.

These ships have access to the Caspian Sea, provided that there is free passage to the delta of the Volga. The Bolshevist Naval Base at Stato Terechnaya on the Caspian Sea, was destroyed during British naval operations in the summer of 1919.

Destroyers :—

    Karl Liebknecht
    Yakob Sverdlov
    Turkhmenetz-Stavropolski
    Dostoini
    Rastoropni
    Dyatelni
    Dyelni
    Storoshevoi
    Mietki
    Prytki
    Proschni
    Retyvi

Submarines :—

    Yaguar
    Minoga
    Makrel
    Okun
    Kataska

Armed Barges.

K 12, K 15. Guns : 2—6 inch.
K 1, 3, 5, 7, 10, 11, 17. Guns : 1—6 inch.
K 2, 4, 6, 8, 14, 16, 19. Guns : 2—3 inch.
K 9. Guns : 1—3 inch.

Note.—In Sea of Azov and Don River, in support of General Denikin's Armies.

Submarine Depot Ships.

BERESAN (1870). 3050 tons. Guns : 6—3 pdr. or 2—1 pdr. Machinery destroyed, April 28th, 1919.

Also : *Dneprovetz* and *Voz.*

Seaplane Carrier.

ALMAZ* (1903). 3300 tons. Complement, 294. Dimensions : 363 × 43½ × 17½ feet. Guns : 7—4.7 inch. Armour : 3″ Deck over machinery. Designed H.P. 7500 = 19 kts. Belleville boilers. Coal : 650 tons. Carries 4 seaplanes.

*Taken over by France.

Scale : 1 inch = 160 feet.

KARS & ARDAGAN.

Gunboats.

Photo: "Motor Ship & Motor Boat."

ARDAGAN (1909) & **KARS** (1909). 630 tons. Armament : 1—4.7 inch, 2—4 inch, 1—3 inch. Machinery : Nobel-Lessner Diesel motors. 1000 H.P. = 14 kts.

Despatch Vessels.

ASTRABAD (1900). 325 tons. Guns : 5—3 pdr. Speed : 11 kts.

Mine Layers.

BESHTAU, DUNAI (1891). 1620 tons. Complement, 234. Guns : 2—6 pdr., 4—3 pdr., 2 M.G. Speed : 13½ kts. Coal 130 tons. Carry 350 mines.

PROOT (ex *Moscwa*, of the Volunteer Fleet). 5500 tons. Armament : 8—3 pdr., 2—1 pdr. Speed : 12 kts.

Scuttled 29 October 1914 to avoided capture.

Despatch Vessel.

(*Disarmed.*)

KASARSKI (1889, ex Torpedo Gunboat). 400 tons. Complement, 64. Armament : 2—11 pdr., 2 M.G. Designed H.P. 3500 = 21 kts. Coal : 55 tons.

Salvage Ship.

Chernomor.

Repair and Depot Ship.

KRONSTADT. Repair ship for Black Sea Fleet. 16,000 tons. 13 kts.

CASPIAN SEA FLOTILLA.
Taken over by British Government, March—Autumn, 1919.

Despatch Vessels—*continued.*

GEOK TEPE (1883). 1010 tons. Guns : 4—4 pdr., 4 M.G. Speed : 11 kts.

Surveying Ship.

ARAKS (1900). 745 tons. Guns : 4—3 pdr. Designed H.P. 800 = 12½ kts.

Hospital Ship.

Skobelev.

Miscellaneous.

Asia	*Kruger*	*Venture*
*Caspia**	*Sergie*	*Windsor Castle*
Emile Nobel	*Slava*	*Zoraster*
*Leila**		

*Reported captured from Bolshevists. Above Armed Vessels (under White Ensign) in action with Bolshevist warships, May 21st, 1919, when Ammunition Carrier, *Caspia*, and the *Lelia* were captured. No details known of these ships.

BULGARIAN NAVY.

Note that the red of the flag is crimson.

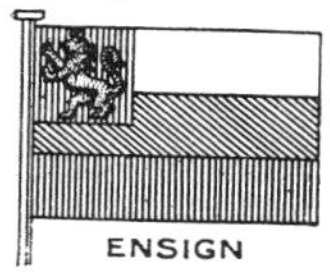

ENSIGN

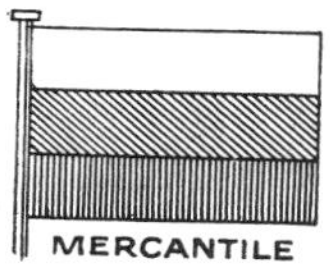

MERCANTILE

RECOGNITION SILHOUETTES.

Scale : 1 inch = 160 feet.

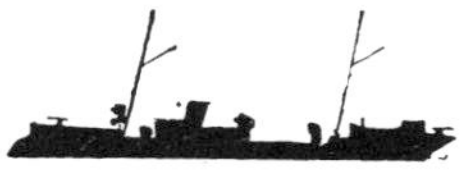

NADEZHDA.

Torpedo boats.

Scale : 1 inch = 80 feet.

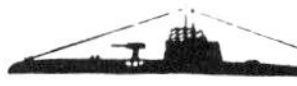

XVIII. (Submarine).

Torpedo Gunboat.

(*Used as a Royal Yacht and Training Ship.*)

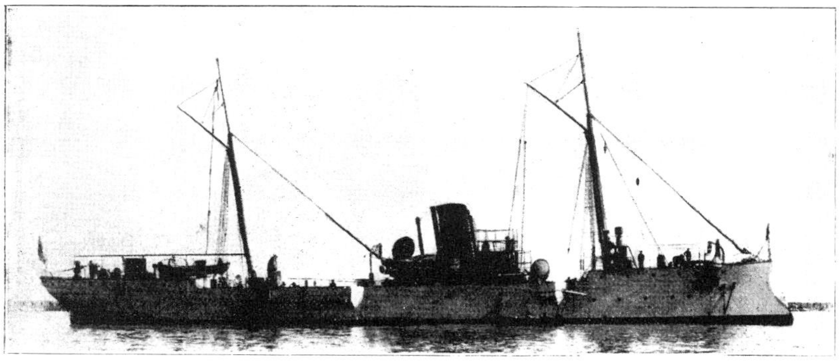

Photo, Geiser.

Internal at Sevastopol.

NADEZHDA (Bordeaux, 1898). 715 tons. Dimensions: 220 × 27¼ × 10 feet. Guns (Creusot): 2—3·9 in., 2—9 pdr., 2—3 pdr. Torpedo tubes: 2 *above water*. Armour: *Nil.* Designed H.P. 2600 = 17 kts. (18·85 trial.) Boilers: Lagrafel d'Allest. Complement 97.

Miscellaneous Ships, interned at Varna.

SIMEON VELIKI. 600 tons. Guns: 2—12 pdr., 4—3 pdr. 70 H.P. **ASJEN.** 400 tons. Guns: 4—3 pdr. 70 H.P. **ALEXANDER I.** No details known.

KROUM, KATATCHIA, KALIAVRA, STRIELA also listed.

4 Torpedo Boats.

All taken over by Allies.

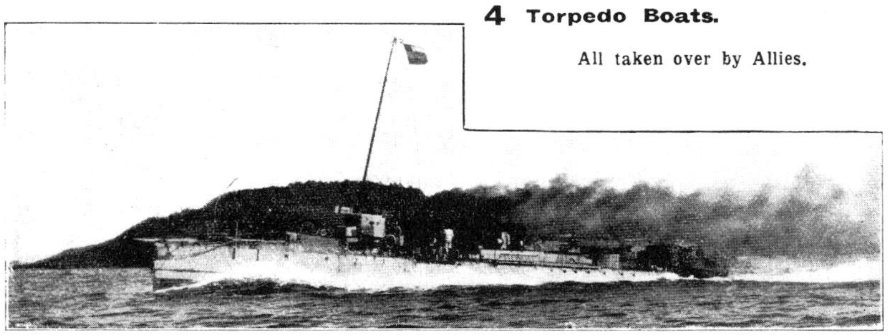

5 *Creusot* boats: ***Smyeli, Khrabry, Deraki, Strogi, Schumni*** (built in sections in France; reassembled at Varna, 1907-8). 100 ton. Dimensions: 126½x13¼x8¾ feet. Armament: 3—3 pdr., 3—18 inch tubes. Designed H.P. 2000=26 kts. 1 screw. Du temple boilers. Complement 23. ***Letyastchi*** lost in 1918.

Vedette Boats.

Botef, Levski. Small craft of 12 tons, armed with spar torpedoes. Interned at Varna. *Boris, Liuben Karavelor, Raina, Rakovski, Voivode, Stefan Karajo, Hadji Lemeter*, all small motor Vedette boats. Six taken over by Allies, disposal of other boat not known.

Submarine.

Probably Austrian "XVIII" ceded to Bulgaria.

Same appearance as Austrian *XVII* and *XI* on a preceding page.

Taken over by French Navy.

1 boat: ***XVIII*** (1916). 127/166 tons. Dimensions: 92 × 10¾ × 9¾ feet. Armament: 1—1 pdr. or M.G., 2—17·7 inch torpedo tubes. H.P. 60 = 6·5 *on surface* with oil engine only (8·4 with electric motors for short periods). 120 H.P. = 5½ kts. *submerged*. Endurance: 1600 miles at 5 kts. *on surface*, 50 miles at 2½ kts. *submerged*. Complement, 16. Oil: 3·5 tons.

HUNGARIAN DANUBE FLOTILLA.

Note.

All ships transferred to the Hungarian Government from the late Austro-Hungarian Navy in October, 1918.

Flags.

Minister of Defence :—

Personnel :—

During the regime of the Bela Kun Government at Buda-Pest, a Danube Monitor was re-named **POSZONY.** Identity of this ship not known.

RECOGNITION SILHOUETTES.

Scale: 1 inch = 160 feet.

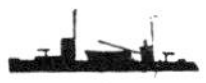

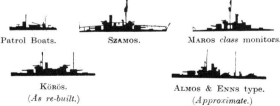

Patrol Boats.

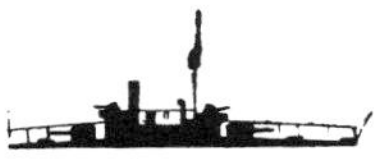

SZAMOS.

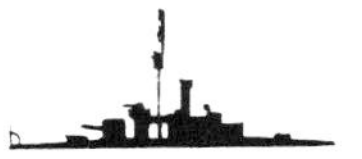

MAROS *class* monitors.

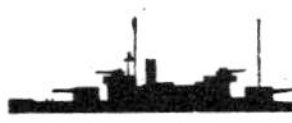

KÖRÖS.
(*As re-built.*)

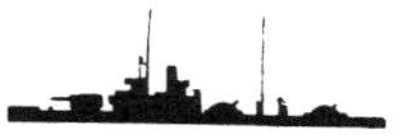

ALMOS & ENNS type.
(*Approximate.*)

Monitors.

For *Temes*, see next page. Has been so largely reconstructed, she might be regarded as a new Monitor, launched in 1915.

ALMOS (1915), **SAVA** (1915), **BOSNIA** (1915), **RAGUSA** (1915). All completed 1916. Reported to be identical with *Enns* and *Inn* below. *Bosnia* and *Sava* built under 1914-15 Austro-Hungarian Naval Programme. All surrendered. *Bosnia* and *Sava* taken over by British and Serbs.

ENNS* (1913), **INN*** (1913). 528 tons. Dimensions: 190 × 33¾ × 4¼ feet. Designed H.P. 1500 = 13 kts. Boilers: Yarrow. Armament: 2—4.7 inch + 3—4.7 inch howitzers, 2—11 pdr., 6 M.G. Armour: 1½" Belt and Bulkheads, 1" Deck, 2" C.T. and Turrets (2). Complement, 86. Fuel: Oil only. Belong to 1912 Austro-Hungarian Naval Programme.

* *Inn* mined and sunk in the Danube River, Sept. 22nd, 1917. Subsequently salved, repaired and returned to active service. *Enns* taken over by British and Serbs.

TEMES. Originally sister to *Bodrog*,* and launched 1904. Sunk, October, 1914; raised, June, 1916. Has been so largely rebuilt, she is now practically a new Monitor. Present armament said to be: 2—4.7 inch, 4—11 pdr., 6 M.G. Other details not known.

* *Bodrog*, Serbian prize.

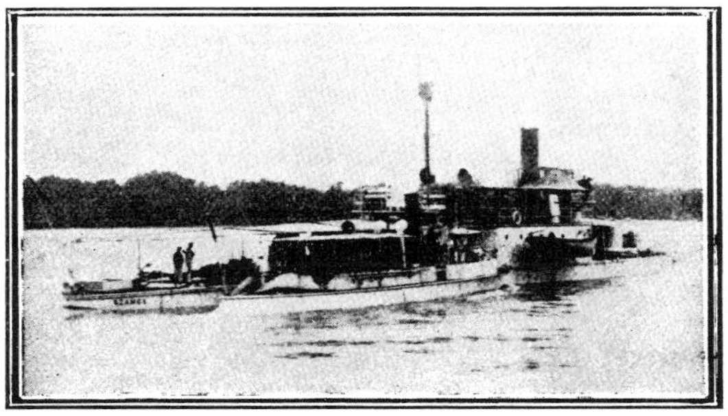

***KÖRÖS** (1892), ***SZAMOS** (1892). 440 tons. Dimensions: 177⅙ × 29½ × 4 feet. Designed H.P. 1200 = 10 kts. Boilers: Yarrow. Guns: 2—4.7 inch (35 cal.), 2—9 pdr., 2 M.G. Armour: 2" Belt, ¾" Deck, 3" Turret, 2" C.T. Complement, 79-80. Coal: 80 tons.

**Körös* sunk, April 1915, but subsequently raised, repaired, and returned to active service.

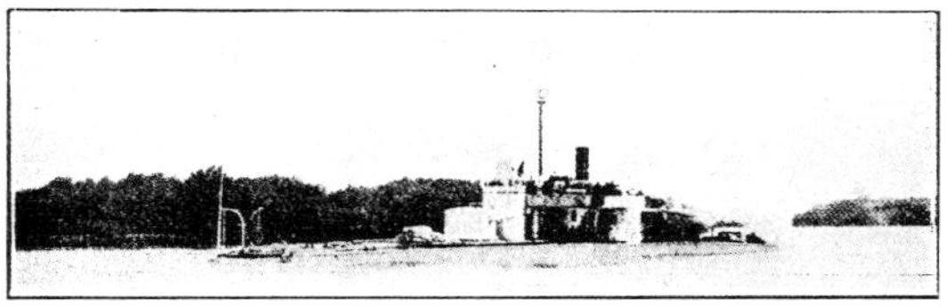

***LEITHA** (1871), ***MAROS** (1871). Both reconstructed, 1894. 305 tons. Dimensions: 164 × 20¾ × 3½ feet. H.P. 700 = 8 kts. Guns: 1—4.7 inch (35 cal.), 2 or 3—11pdr., 3 M.G. Armour: 1¾" Belt, 1" Deck, 2" Turret. Complement, 57. Coal: 20 tons.

*Taken over by British and Serbs.

Torpedo Vessel.

VEKSEL. (——) No details known, but said to be armed with 1—3.9 inch. 1 M.G. and 2 torpedo tubes.

Mining Craft.

MINELAYER (NAME UNKNOWN). No exact details available, but said to be armed with 2—11 pdr. and 2—3 pdr. guns and to carry 30 mines.

TULIN. Barge, propelled by motor engines and carrying 140 mines.

Scouts.

Barsch,* Borsto, Fogos,* Isuka,* Kompo, Vels,* Visa. Guns: 1 or 2—3 pdr.

* Taken over by British and Serbs.

Patrol Boats.

2 *boats* (numbers not known), **g, h** (1909), 18 tons, 22 kts., 1 M.G.: **f** (1907), 12 tons, 22 kts., 1 M.G.: **b, d** (1906-9), 40 tons, 14 kts. Guns: 1 or 2 small. Complement 13.

Also several motor launches.

Miscellaneous.

Elina, *Samarna* } Armed Steamers, each having 2—11 pdrs.
Val. 594 tons *gross* }
Hebe. Armed Yacht.
Bayo, *Boski* } Armed Trawlers.

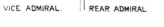

RED ▨ WHITE ☐

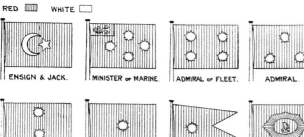

ENSIGN & JACK.	MINISTER of MARINE.	ADMIRAL of FLEET.	ADMIRAL.

VICE ADMIRAL.	REAR ADMIRAL.	COMMODORE.	IMPERIAL STANDARD.

Note:

All ships interned at the Golden Horn, in the Bosphorous and Gulf of Ismid, under Allied supervision.

Uniforms.

| ADMIRAL OF FLEET. | ADMIRAL. | VICE ADMIRAL. | REAR ADMIRAL. | COMMODORE. | CAPTAIN. | LIEUT. CAPTAIN. |

| COMMANDER. | LIEUT COMMANDER. | LIEUTENANT. | SUB-LIEUTENANT. |

INSIGNIA OF RANK, AUTHORISED 1910.

Other branches.—Without the curl.
Doctors.—Crimson.
Engineers.—Scarlet.
Constructors.—Blue.
Paymasters.—White.

Scale : 1 inch = 160 feet.

BRITISH OR U.S.A.		TURKEY.
Admiral of the Fleet	=	Buyuk Amiral.
Admiral	=	Amiral.
Vice-Ad.	=	Vice-Amiral.
Rear-Ad.	=	Liva-Amiral.
Commodore	=	Commodore.
Captain	=	Galion Capitani.
Commander	=	Fregate Capitani.
"	=	Corvette Capitani.
Lieut. Commander	=	Birindji Yuzbachi.
Lieutenant	=	Yuzbachi.
Sub-Lieut.	=	Mulazim.
Midshipman	=	Mehendis.

Arsenal : Constantinople (*see next page*).

Mercantile Marine : Latest available totals are, 95 steamers of 74,396 tons *gross*, and 963 sailing ships of 205,029 tons *gross*. Many of these, however, have been lost in convoys destroyed by the Russian Black Sea Fleet and through the operations of Allied submarines in the Sea of Marmora. Captured vessels were probably been recovered, on occupation of Sebastopol, Odessa, Batum and other Black Sea Ports.

Minister of Marine :

Colour of ships : Large ships, light grey ; ships smaller than (and including) *Muin-i-Zaffer*, khaki ; destroyers, black.

Principal Ports : Trebizond, Sinope, Samsoun, Smyrna, Alexandretta ;* Beyrût,* Basrah,† Jaffa,† Hodieda,† Djeddah.

*Occupied by Allied Forces. †Occupied by Anglo-Indian Expeditionary Force.

Coinage : Lira (Medjidie) of 100 piastres = 18s. British, $4·28 U.S.A. One piastre (4 cents U.S.A.) = about 2d. British. These are *nominal* values. Rate of exchange has depreciated owing to the war.

Personnel : about 6000-8000 all ranks.

Tables of Distances.

(A) CONSTANTINOPLE to (*Mediterranean Ports.*)

		miles.
Alexandria	... ...	722
Alexandretta	... ...	810
Beyrout	... ...	810
Brindisi	... ...	786
Cattaro ...	... ...	880
Corfu ...	... ...	682
Gibraltar	... ...	1800
Malta ...	... ...	830
Mudros Bay ...	... ...	190
Piraeus	... ...	344
Pola (*a*)	... ...	996
" (*b*)	... ...	1098
Port Said	... ...	786
Salonika	... ...	333
Smyrna	... ...	273
Toulon ...	... ...	1343
Triest (*a*)	... ...	1050
" (*b*)	... ...	1152
Wilhelmshaven (*c*)	... ...	3355
" (*d*)	... ...	3803
Zeebrugge (*c*)	... ...	3089
" (*d*)	... ...	3905

a) By Canal of Corinth.
(*b*) By Cape Matapan.
(*c*) By English Channel.
(*d*) By north of Scotland & west of Ireland.

(B) CONSTANTINOPLE to (*Black Sea Ports.*)

		miles.
Batoum	... ...	586
Burgas ...	... ...	126
Nicolaieff	... ...	394
Odessa ...	... ...	342
Sulina (mouth of Danube River.)	...	254
Trebizond	... ...	496
Varna...	... ...	146

SMYRNA to

		miles.
Alexandretta	... ...	623
Beyrout	... ...	623
Corfu ...	... ...	529
Cattaro ...	... ...	727
Gibraltar	... ...	1641
Malta ...	... ...	677
Mudros Bay ...	... ...	133
Piraeus ...	... ...	196
Pola (*a*)	... ...	848
" (*b*)	... ...	945
Salonika	... ...	254

(*a*) By Canal of Corinth.
(*b*) By Cape Matapan.

TURKISH RECOGNITION SILHOUETTES. (*Strictly copyright.*)

ONE FUNNEL.

MUIN-I-ZAFFER.

MALATIA (Gunboat.)

KEMAL REIS class (3) (Gunboats).

AIDAN REIS class (4) (Gunboats).

RESCHID PACHA. (Transport).

TIRI-MUJGHIAN. (Training Ship).

TWO FUNNELS.

BERC-I-SATVET class (2) (Torpedo Gunboats).

TOORGOOD REIS.

SULTAN SELIM.

THREE FUNNELS.

ERTOGRUL. (Royal Yacht.)

MEDJIDIEH (*is dismantled*).

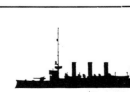
HAMIDIEH.

TORPEDO CRAFT.

Drach class (2) t.b.

Muvanet-i-Milet class (2) t.b.d.

Sivri-Hissar class (2) t.b.

Samsoun class (2) t.b.d.

Ack Hissar class (2) t.b.

1908 TURKISH BATTLE-CRUISER.

SULTAN SELIM (ex German *Goeben*, March, 1911).

Displacement, 22,640 tons. Complement, 1013.
Length (*w.l.*), 610¼ feet. Beam, 96 ft. 10 in. Draught (*max. load*), 26 ft. 11 in.

Guns (see Notes):
10—11 in. 50 cal.
12—5·9 in. 45 cal.
12—3·4 in. 22 pdr.
2 M.G.
1 landing

Torpedo tubes (19·7 in.):
1 bow
2 broadside ⎱ all
1 stern ⎰ *submerged*

19·7 in. T.T.

Dir. Con.

Anti-Torp. Pro.:—
2″—1″ deep H.T. Steel B.H., between extreme barbettes : Minute internal subdivision.

Armour (Krupp):
11″ Belt (amidships) ......
5″—4″ Belt (bow) ....
4″ Belt (stern) ....
9″—8″ Barbettes ....
10″—8″ Gunhouses ....
5″ Battery ....
10″ Fore C.T. ....
8″—3″ Double Com. Tube
8″ After C.T. ....
6″—3″ Com. Tube ....
3″—″ R.F. Towers ......
3¾″—1″ Decks ....
″ Roofs to Gunhouses...
3″ Roof, Fore C.T.

MOLTKE

Head:
—11 in.
—5·9 in.
19·7 in. T.T.

Astern:
6—11 in.
2—5·9 in.
1—19·7 in. T.T.

Broadside: 10—11 in., 6—5·9 in., 2—19·7 in. T.T. (angling 30° before to 30° abaft beam).

Photo, Topical.

Note.—In above illustration, the fourth 5·9 inch gun from bows does not appear to be mounted ; it may have been destroyed when this ship was mined in 1914, and never replaced. Figures and positions on plan opposite for 5·9 inch guns are those originally mounted.

Machinery: Parsons turbine, 4 shaft, direct drive. Boilers: 24 Schulz-Thornycroft = German "Marine Type." Designed H.P. nominally 52,000 for 25 kts., but when new she could develop 70,000 H.P.=27 kts. Coal: *normal* about 1000 tons ; *maximum* 3050 tons. Oil fuel: 200 tons.

Gunnery Notes.—All guns German Navy Models, with German Navy type of fire-controls, R.F., &c. 11-inch have large degree of elevation, and range is only limited by maximum visibility. 5·9 inch range up to 16,500 yards. Two R.F. towers are sunk into the deck, near amidships (echelon) barbettes.

Torpedo Notes.—Torpedoes and torpedo tubes, German Navy type. Torpedoes probably German G VII*** (23-ft. steam heater) type with 430 lbs. charge and *max.* ranges of (*a*) 11,700 yards at 28 kts., (*b*) 5,500 yards at 35 kts. Stern *submerged* torpedo tube is on starboard quarter. 8—60″ controlled S.L. Torpedo nets removed during War.

Armour and Protection Notes.—Like all other German Battle Cruisers, this ship is heavily armoured and minutely subdivided. Main belt between extreme barbettes is *about* 350 feet long, 11″ at w.l. tapering to about 8″ on upper edge, and 6″ on lower edge. Barbette bases only 1″ where covered by belt.

Engineering Notes.—Endurance is (*a*) 5,350 miles at 10 kts., (*b*) 2,370 miles at a continuous *max.* sea-going speed of 23 kts.

Name	Builder	Machinery	Ordered Begun	Began Trials	Trials (mean) H.P. kts.	Completed
Sultan Selim	Blohm & Voss, Hamburg	Blohm & Voss, Hamburg	Dec. 7, '08 April, 1909	May, 1912	71,275 = 27.2*	July, 7 '12‡

*Stated to have developed 85,661 H.P. + 27.9 kts. on trials, but this must be *max.* H.P. and best run on mile.
‡Extra trials run up to Oct., 1912.

General Notes.—Built under 1909 German Navy Programme as "H." as a sister to German *Moltke*. Proceeded to Mediterranean about 1913, with Cruiser *Breslau*, it being intended that these two ships should operate from Austro-Hungarian naval bases. With *Breslau*, this Battle Cruiser escaped from Messina to Constantinople in the first days of War, and was nominally transferred to the Turkish Navy as the *Sultan Selim*, the *Breslau* (now sunk) was also becoming the pseudo-Turkish *Midilli*. On November 18th, 1914, *Goeben* fought an indecisive action with the three Russian pre-Dreadnoughts of the *Evstafi* type. During this action, or shortly afterwards, *Goeben* was heavily injured by a double mine explosion. The first mine struck the starboard bows over the provision store rooms, shattering the hull from the belt to the docking keel ; the second mine exploded on the port side over a coal bunker, disabling the third barbette. It took three months to effect repairs at Constantinople by means of cofferdams. *Goeben* appears to have been again mined on another date during 1915 or 1916. During 1917 she was again injured by bombs dropped from a British Handley-Page aeroplane during a raid on Constantinople. In January, 1918, *Goeben* and *Breslau* sank the British Monitors *Raglan* and *M 's* at Imbros, but both ships were mined. *Breslau* sank and *Goeben* was beached near Nagara Point, where she was repeatedly attacked by bombing 'planes. An unsuccessful attempt was also made by submarine against her. She was towed off, and after the capture of Sebastopol she was taken there to be docked, re-fitted, overhauled, and to have her boilers re-tubed. *Goeben* has probably had more narrow escapes from destruction than any other Dreadnought or Battle Cruiser in existence ; she certainly is a remarkable testimonial to the thorough under-water protection of German Dreadnoughts and Battle Cruisers. She is also known to the Turkish Navy by the unofficial name of *Yavouz*. Interned in Gulf of Ismid with other Turkish warships at end of War.

TURKISH BATTLESHIPS. (*Haty-harb-Zirchlissi.*)

Both photos taken 1913.

TURGUT REIS (1891, rebuilt 1903).

9901 tons. Complement, 579. Dimensions: 379⅔ × 64 × 24⅞ feet (*maximum* draught). Guns: 4—11 inch, 40 cal. + 2—11 inch, 35 cal. (all probably removed), 8—4.1 inch, 35 cal. : 8—3.4 inch (15 pdr.), 2 landing, 2 AA. guns, 4 M.G. Torpedo tubes (18 inch) : 2 submerged (broadside). Armour (compound) : 15¾″ Belt amidships, 12″ Belt at ends, 2½″ Deck, flat on belt, 11¾″ Barbettes, with 5″ shields, 3″ Battery. 12″ C.T. Machinery : 2 sets vertical triple expansion. Boilers : 12 cylindrical return flame (new in 1909). Designed H.P. 9000=17 kts. ; present speed much less. Coal : *normal*, 600 tons ; *maximum*, 812 tons + 98 tons oil. Endurance : 5300 miles at 10 kts., 2600 miles at 15¼ kts. Originally was German battleship *Weissenburg*. Purchased 1910. Reported to be practically worn out.

Sister ship *Hairedin Barbarossa* (ex-*Kurfürst Frederich Wilhellm*) torpedoed by British submarine E11 off Constantinople 8th August 1915.

MESSUDIYEH (1874).

Reconstructed at Genoa, 1902.

Displacement, *circa* 10,000 tons. Complement, 600 (as flagship 640).

Length, 331 feet. Beam, 59 feet. *Maximum* draught, 27 feet.

Guns (Vickers) :
2—9·2 inch, 40 cal. (*A*).
12—6 inch, 45 cal.
14—12 pdr.
10—6 pdr.
2—3 pdr.
2 Field (14 pdr.)

Armour (iron) :
12″ Belt ....
1½″ Deck (flat on belt) ...
Protection to vitals is ......
12″ Battery ....
3″ Barbettes (Terni) ......

MESS'OUDIYEH

Machinery: 2 sets inverted triple expansion, 4 cylinder. 2 screws. Boilers : 16 Niclausse in 4 compartments. Designed H.P. 11,000=16 kts. Coal : 600 tons.

Note.—The old armour remains, except for the barbettes and the special protection to steering gear, &c., aft. Torpedoed by British submarine B11 off Chanak 13 December 1914.

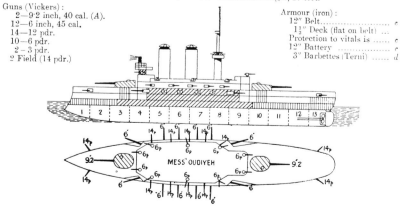

MUIN-I-ZAFFER (1869).

Rebuilt by Ansaldo, 1904-7. 2362 tons. Complement, 220. Guns (Krupp, M. '06) : 4—5.9 inch, 40 cal. ; 6—3 inch (12 pdr.), 2—3 pdr. Torpedo tubes (14 inch) : 1. Armour (old, iron) : 6″—3″ Battery, 6″ Bulkheads, 5″ compound. 1 screw. Boilers (new in 1906) : cylindrical. Designed H.P. 6500 = 15.5 kts. Coal (*max.*) : 220 tons.

Note.—Old *Idjlalieh* still exists but is utterly useless.

(Training Ship.)

(Dismantled ; only 1 mast and 1 funnel now.)

HAMIDIEH (ex *Abdul Hamid*, Elswick, Spet., 1903). 3830 tons. Complement, 302. Dimensions : 368 × 47½ × 16 feet (*mean* draught). Guns : 2—5.9 inch, 45 cal. Torpedo tubes (18 inch) : 2 *above water*. Armour : 4″ Deck. Machinery : 2 sets 4-cylinder triple expansion. 2 screws. Boilers : cylindrical. Designed H.P. 12,000 = 22 kts. (*forced draught*). Coal : *normal*, 275 tons ; *maximum*, 750 tons. Endurance : 5550 miles at 10 kts.

MEDJIDIEH (ex Russian *Prut*, ex Turkish *Medjidieh*, launched 1903). Mined and sunk in Black Sea, 1915. Salved, repaired and re-fitted at Nikolaev for Russian Navy, 1915-16. Seized by Austro-German Armies at Sebastopol, 1918, and returned to Turkish Navy. 3300 tons. Complement, 365. Dimensions : 225 × 40 × 17½ feet. Guns (as re-armed for Russian Navy) : 4—5.1 inch (Vickers 1914), 4 M.G. Deck 1″. H.P. 12,000 = 22 kts. Niclausse boilers, but may have another type now. Coal : 600 tons. Endurance : 4700 miles at 10 kts. Built by Cramps, Philadelphia.

As *Breslau* escaped British forces with *Goeben* (later *Sultan Selini* then *Yavuz*) in August 1914 and entered Constantinople. After actions with Russian ships in Black Sea left Darduelles with *Goeben* to attack Mudros January 1918. Sunk British monitors *Raglan* and *M28* then struck a mine and eventually sank 20 January 1918.

TURKISH SLOOP, GUNBOATS AND TORPEDO GUNBOATS.

Old Sloop.

ZUHAF (Germania, 1894). 632 tons. Dimensions : 190 × 24 × 11½ feet. Guns : 4—6 pdr., 2—1 pdr. Torpedo tubes (14 inch) : 2 *above water*. Designed H.P. 650 = 11 kts. Coal : 120 tons. Complement, 82.
Note.—Reported to have been fitted out as a Mine Layer.

Gunboats (*Ganbot*).

4 *St. Nazaire* type : **AIDAN REIS** (June, 1912), **BURACK REIS** (May, 1912), **SAKIZ** (Feb., 1912), and **PREVESAH** (Jan., 1912). 502 tons. Dimensions : 178½ × 27⅞ × 8 feet. H.P. 1025 = 14 kts. Guns : 2—3.9 inch (50 cal.), 2—6 pdr., 4 M.G.
GIASSIA REIS (?) scuttled to avoid capture at Çesme.

3 *La Seyne* type : **KEMAL REIS** (ex *Durack Reis*, Feb., 1912), **HIZIR REIS** (Feb., 1912) and **ISSA REIS** (Dec., 1911). 413 tons. Dimensions : 154½ × 25¾ / 4½ feet. Guns : 3—3 inch (12 pdr.), 2—3 pdr., 2 M.G. H.P. 850 = 14 kts.

Gunboats—*Continued*.

1 *Creusot* type : **MALATIA** (1907). 210 tons. Dimensions : 154¼ × 19⅝ × 6⅜ feet. Guns : 2—3 pdr. Torpedo tubes : 1 *above water*. H.P. 350 = 12½ kts. Coal : 44 tons. Complement, 30.
Note.—This class originally consisted of eight vessels, viz., *Aintab, Baffra, Malatia, Ordu, Gudjedag, Refadie, Tachkeupru, Nev Shihir.* Five of the class (including *Refadie*) were sunk in the Turco-Italian War, 1912. The others were destroyed in the late war.

MARMARIS (1907). 500 tons. Guns : 4—9 pdr., 2—1 pdr., H.P. 950 = 14 kts. Built by Schneider-Canet, at Creusot.

Sunk by British sloop *Odin* in River Tigris 2 June 1915.

BARIK - I - ZAFFER (Constantinople, 1908). 198 tons. Dimensions : 121½ × 18 × 5½ feet. Guns : 4—12 pdr., 2 M.G. Torpedo tubes (14 inch) : 2 *above water*.
Note.—Various sister ships of *Barik-i-Zaffer* believed to have been destroyed during the War, but their names cannot be ascertained exactly.

NUREL BAHR (1903) of 200 tons. Torpedoed by British submarine E14 in Sea of Mareuara 1 May 1914.

YOZGAD (1906) **KASTAMUNI** (1906) of 185 tons. *Kastamuni* sunk by gunfire of three Russian destroyers in Black Sea 10 December 1915. *Yozgad* paid off 1919.

Gunboat—Existence Doubtful

Timsah of 120 Tons reported to have been seen at Constantinople in June 1919. *Timsah* mined and injured beyond repair. *Kilid-el-Bahr, Sedd-el-Bahr* and *Reshanieh* probably sunk during the war.

Torpedo Gunboats (*Torpedo Muhribi*).

BERK-I-SATVET (Dec., 1906) and **PEIK-I-SHEVKET** (Nov., 1906). Both built at Krupps' Germania Yard, Keil. 1014 tons. Dimensions : 262½ x 27⅔ x 9½ feet. Guns : 2—3.9 inch, 4—6 pdr., 2—1 pdr., 2 M.G. Torpedo tubes : 3. Designed H.P. 5100 = 22 kts. Coal : 240 tons.

Note—*Berk-i-Satbet* torpedoed by British Submarine E 2, and *Peik-i-Shevket* by E 14, both during 1915. Either boat (or both boats) beached and salved. They have not been sunk, as was believed during the War.

PELENÇ-I-DERIA (1890) of 880 tons. Sunk by British submarine E11 off Seraglio Point, Constantinople on 22 May 1915.

TURKISH WARSHIPS

TURKISH DESTROYERS.

Note.

6 New Destroyers were reported to have been begun in 1917 at Constantinople, to German designs, £T1,190,000 being voted for their construction. No report has been received of their launching. If begun, it is very doubtful if they will ever be finished now.

2 *Schichau* boats: **Muvanet-i-Milet** and **Noumoune-i-Hamiyet.** Both 1909. 607 tons. Dimensions: 233½ × 27⅔ × 10½ feet. Armament: 2—3·4 in. (22 pdr.), 2 machine, 3—18 in. tubes. Schulz-Thornycroft boilers and Schichau (Melms and Pfenninger) turbines. On trials from 36·2 to 34·5 kts., but can only make about 27 now. Endurance: 1200 miles at 15 kts. Were originally built for the German Navy as S 165—S 168, and sold to Turkey in 1910. *Yadighiar-i-Milet* and another boat (called *Mahabet-i-Milet* or *Gairet-i-Vatanié*), both sunk during the War.

Destroyers—*(continued)*.

3 *French type* boats: **Samsoun, Bassra,** both launched at Bordeaux (1907), and **Tasnoz** launched by Creusot, Chalons, (1907). 290 tons. Dimensions: 185×21×9½ feet. Armament: 1—12 pdr., 6—3 pdr., 2—18 inch tubes. Endurance: 975 miles at 15 kts. Are practically the same as French *Durandal* class:

Yar Hisar torpedoed by British submarine EII in Sea of Moruiara 3 December 1915.

1 *Krupp* boat: **Berk-Efsan** (1891). 270 tons. Dimensions: 187×21¼×8 feet. Armament: 6—6 pdr., 2—14 in. tubes.

TURKISH TORPEDO BOATS AND SUBMARINES.

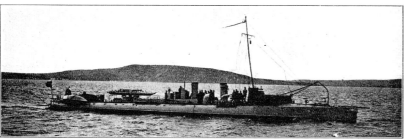

2 *Creusot* boats: **Sultan-Hisar, Sivri-Hisar** (1906) Dimensions: 124x14x1½ feet. Armament: 2—1 pdr., 3-18 inch tubes. (1 bow, 2 deck). For other details v. Table. *Timur Hisar* driven ashore in Khios 17 April 1915, and *Hamid-Abad* sunk in Black Sea 20 October 1914.

Torpedo Boats—*(continued)*.

2 *Ansaldo* boats: **Ak-Hisar** (1904) and **Younous** (1902) Dimensions: 165x18½x5½ feet, Armament: 2—1 pdr., 2-18 inch tubes. Endurance: 2000 miles at 14 kts. For other details v. table.

Note: Several more of this type were sunk during the war.

During the War, the Germans and Turks attempted to refit and overhaul two old derelict Nordenfeldt Submarines, built about 1889. One of these boats, ex-*Abdul Hamid*, was re-named with the Turkish equivalent of "Porpoise." It is believed that the re-construction of these curiosities proved an absolute failure.

2 *Ansaldo* boats: **Drach** (1905) and **Moussoul** (1905). Dimensions: 167×18×4½ feet. Armament: 2—1 pdr., 2—14 in. tubes. For other details v. Table. *Kutaya* and *Urfa* of this class lost during the war. *Anatolia* of this class, captured during Balkan war, now Greek *Nikopolis*. *Alpagot* (or *Eliagot*), *Tocad* and *Angora* were sunk during the Balkan and Italian Wars, 1911-12.

TURKISH MISCELLANEOUS.

9 Motor Launches.

4 boats of 15 kts. speed, built about 1912-13. No other details known.

Photo, Messrs. J. I. Thornycroft & Co.

5 boats: *Names or numbers not known.* Are Thornycroft type motor patrol boats, built 1911, for customs, police and coast-guard duties. Dimensions: × × 2½ feet. Guns: 2 M.G. or 1 small Q.F. 140 H.P. Thornycroft petrol motor = 11 kts. Bullet-proof steel over conning position and engines.

Note.—Originally 20 of these boats were built. Two were captured during the Turco-Italian War. One captured during the war on the Tigris river and served for a time as H.M.S. *Flycatcher*, but was transferred later to British Army.

Depot Ships

ALI PASA (ex-*Port Royal*) Purchased 1911.

NEJDMI SHEVKET. No details known.

Transports.

RESCHID PASHA (ex *Port Antonio*). 4458 tons.

OURLA. No details known.

Bezzmi-Alem exists still. Was seen at Constantinople, June, 1919, but has probably gone on Mercantile Service.

GUL DJENIAD (ex-*Ottawa*, ex-*Cerunanic*)
KARA DENIZ (ex-*Darmstadt*)
AK DENIZ (ex-*Oldenburg*)
BAHR AHMED (ex-*Roland*)
All purchased 1911.

Mine-Layers.

NUSRAT (Germania, 1912). 364 tons. Dimensions: 131¼ × 24½ × 8¼ feet. Guns: 2 M.G. H.P. 1200 = 15 kts. Carries 25 mines.

KIRESUND (1877). 3056 tons *gross*. 10 kts.

INTIBAH. No details known.

Mine Sweepers.

CASTOR, POLLUX. No details known.

Yachts.

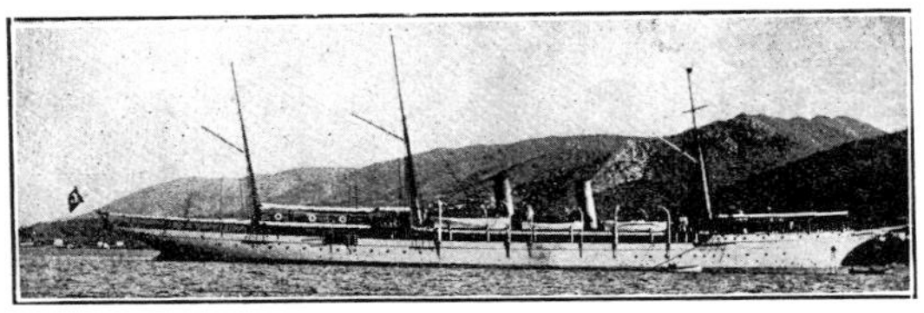

(*Royal Yacht.*)

ERTOGRUL (Elswick, 1903). 900 tons. Dimensions: 260 (*p.p.*) × 27⅘ × 11½ feet. Guns: 8—3 pdr. H.P. 2500 = 21 kts. Machinery: Hawthorn Leslie. Boilers: Cylindrical.

(There is also another small Royal Yacht, **Senguedlu** built at Elswick in 1903, of 180 tons, and 14 kts. speed.)

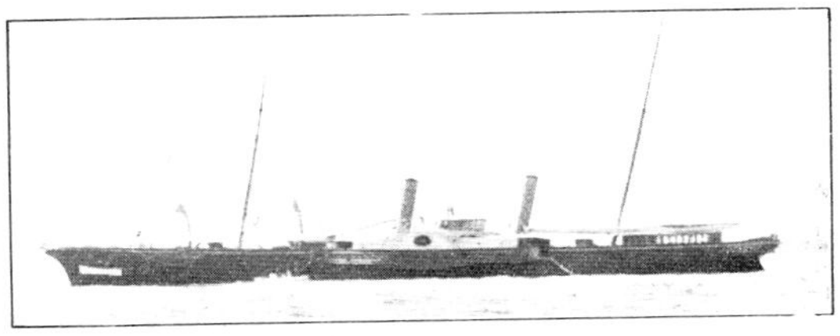

IZZEDIN, ISMAIL, THALIA (1865) 1075 tons. Guns: 2—3.5 inch, 2 M.G. H.P. 350 = 12 kts.

STAMBOUL (——, 1865, 1888). 910 tons. Guns: 2—4.7 inch, 2 M.G. H.P. 350 = 17 kts. *nominal.* Real speed much less now.

GALATA }
SUGUTLI } No details known.

Another small yacht, *Aintab*, exists.

Training Ships.

Cruiser **HAMIDIEH** described on an earlier page.

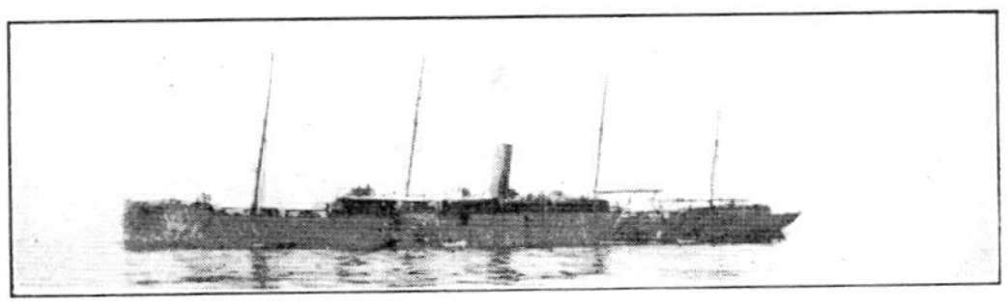

TIRI-MUJGHIAN (ex *Pembroke Castle*, 1883). 4052 tons. Dimensions: 400¼ × 42½ × 21⅓ feet. Guns: 8—3 pdr. Speed: 14 kts.

Hospital Ship **MIDHAT PAŞA** (ex-*Port Ontario*) 4455 Tons. Sunk in 1915.

(ROYAL) SWEDISH NAVY.

Revised from the 1919 Edition of the Official Handbook "Svenska Marinens Rulla."

Illustrated from photos taken or collected by S. Anderson, Esq.

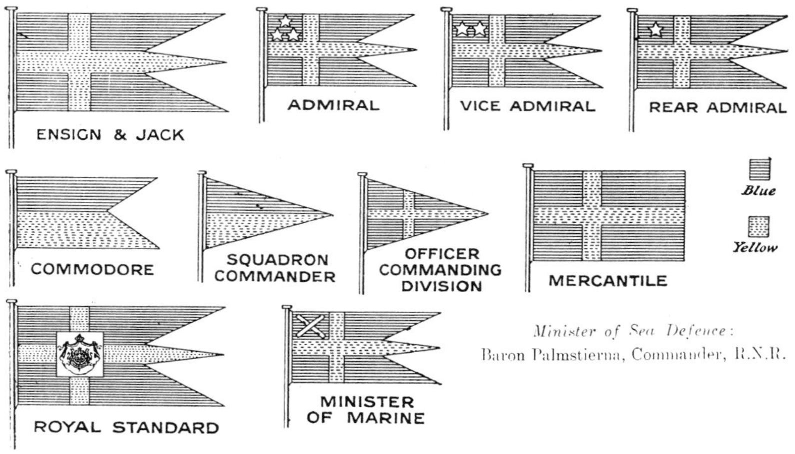
ENSIGN & JACK
ADMIRAL
VICE ADMIRAL
REAR ADMIRAL
COMMODORE
SQUADRON COMMANDER
OFFICER COMMANDING DIVISION
MERCANTILE
Blue
Yellow
ROYAL STANDARD
MINISTER OF MARINE

Minister of Sea Defence: Baron Palmstierna, Commander, R.N.R.

Modern Swedish Guns (Bofors).

(*All details are unofficial*).

Notation	Designation (c/m)	Designation (inches)	Length in calibres	Model	Weight of Gun	Weight of A.P. shot	Initial velocity	*Max.* penetration firing A.P. capped at K.C.: 8000 yds.	5000 yds.	3000 yds.	Danger Space against average warship, at: 10,000 yards	5000 yards	3000 yards	*Nom.* per minute
	c/m	inches			tons	lbs.	ft.secs.	in.	in.	in.				
A5	28	11	45	'11	41	760½	2576†	10½	15	18	..	..	..	1·2
AA	25.4	10	42	'94	29	450	2362	..	8	11	125	340	675	1
A	21	8.3	44	'98	17	275½	2460†	..	7	9½	100	425	600	2
C	15.2	6	50	'03	7¼	100	2789†	..	..	7	75	230	460	6
E	15.2	6	45	'98	6	100	2460	..	..	6	60	200	410	6
	12	4.7	50	'11	3¾	46½	2822	..	..	..	..	..	..	8
F	12	4.7	45	'94	2	46½	2430	..	..	3½	..	..	..	8

Guns marked † in the velocity column fire Bofors special nitro-compound.

Torpedo.

Whiteheads. *Submerged* tubes (Elswick pattern), except in *Oden & Svea* class. Torpedoes, 18 in., 15 in. and 14 in. Since 1911 torpedoes have all been manufactured at Karlskrona.

Wireless. Marconi.

INSIGNIA OF RANK ON SLEEVES.

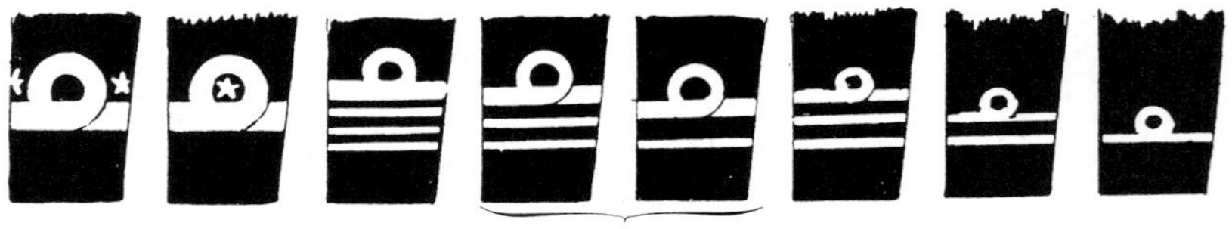

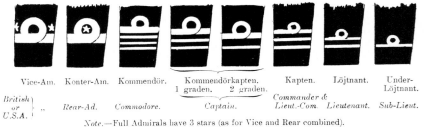

	Vice-Am.	Konter-Am.	Kommendör.	Kommendörkapten. 1 graden.	Kommendörkapten. 2 graden.	Kapten.	Löjtnant.	Under-Löjtnant.
British or U.S.A.	,,	*Rear-Ad.*	*Commodore.*	*Captain.*		*Commander & Lieut.-Com.*	*Lieutenant.*	*Sub-Lieut.*

Note.—Full Admirals have 3 stars (as for Vice and Rear combined).

Reserve officers have *blue* above the stripes. All civilian officers have stripes without the curl, and colour between stripes as follows:—Constructors and Engineers, *violet blue*; Doctors, *red*; Paymasters, *white*.

Swedish Arsenals.

KARLSKRONA. One t.b. slip. Dry docks: (Oscar II.), 410×69×24¾; (No. 1), 203×50×19¾; (No. 2), 265×50×19¾; (No. 3), 209×50×19¾; (No. 4), 236×50×19¾; (No. 5), 212×50×19¾; (No. 6), 233×50×19. Submarine Station. Is fortified.

STOCKHOLM. One t.b. slip. One dry dock, 410×58½×22¾ feet. There are also two private docks (Beckholmen), at Stockholm. (No. 1), 328×55×18 feet; (No. 2), 321½ × 35½ × 11½ feet. Mining and Torpedo Craft Station. Is fortified.

Swedish Private Yards

(that build warships).

LINDHOLMEN (Lindholmens Mekaniska Verkstad och Varf) Gothenburg. Two slips, 220 and 187 feet long. One dry dock, 402×58½×20 feet. One 60-ton crane. Electric and pneumatic plant. Total employees 900.

GÖTAVERKEN. Gothenburg. One or two slips (up to 8000 tons), and two slips (2500 and 1200 tons). No docks. Employees 700. 12,000-ton Floating Dock at this port.

BERGSUND (Bergsunds Mekaniska Verkstad och Varf) Stockholm. One slip, 151 feet long. No docks. One 40-ton crane. Employees 600.

FINNBODA (same firm as above) Stockholm. One slip, 226 feet long. 60-ton crane. Employees 700. One large floating dock, one small.

KOCKUM (Kockums Mekaniska Verkstads Aktiebolag) Malmö. One slip, 400 feet or over, and another, 275 feet long. Two dry docks (Harbour Commissioners) 502×66×23¾ feet and 236×34×12½ feet. 45-ton crane. Electric, pneumatic, and hydraulic power throughout yard. Employees 1000. One large dry dock building or completed.

At ORESUND (Landskrona) there is a dock suitable for ships up to 15,000 tons.

Mercantile Marine.

—— steamers of 917,000 tons *gross*.
1174 sailing of 175,891 tons *gross*.

Principal Trade Ports.

Gothenburg, Stockholm, Malmö, Norrköping, Helsingborg, Gefle and Sundervall.

Coinage.

1 krona = about 1s. 1¼d. British, 25 cents U.S.A. (18 kronor = £1).

General Notes.—Personnel: About 4,000. *Colour of Ships*: Grey.

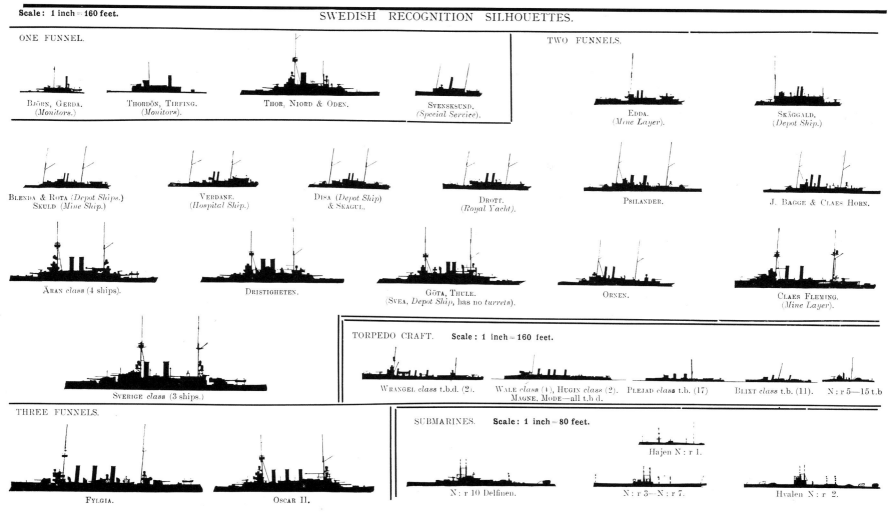

Scale: 1 inch = 160 feet.

SWEDISH RECOGNITION SILHOUETTES.

ONE FUNNEL.

BJÖRN, GERDA. (*Monitors.*)   THORDÖN, TIRFING. (*Monitors*).   THOR, NIORD & ODEN.   SVENSKSUND. (*Special Service*).

TWO FUNNELS.

EDDA. (*Mine Layer*).   SKÄGGALD. (*Depot Ship*).

BLENDA & ROTA (*Depot Ships.*) SKULD (*Mine Ship.*)   VERDANE. (*Hospital Ship.*)   DISA (*Depot Ship*) & SKAGUL.   DROTT. (*Royal Yacht*).   PSILANDER.   J. BAGGE & CLAES HORN.

ÄRAN *class* (4 ships).   DRISTIGHETEN.   GÖTA, THULE. (SVEA, *Depot Ship*, has no *turrets*).   ORNEN.   CLAES FLEMING. (*Mine Layer*).

SVERIGE *class* (3 ships.)

TORPEDO CRAFT.   **Scale : 1 inch = 160 feet.**

WRANGEL *class* t.b.d. (2).   WALE *class* (1), HUGIN *class* (2). MAGNE, MODE—all t.b d.   PLEJAD *class* t.b. (17)   BLIXT *class* t.b. (11).   N : r 5—15 t.b

THREE FUNNELS.

FYLGIA.   OSCAR II.

SUBMARINES.   **Scale : 1 inch = 80 feet.**

Hajen N : r 1.

N : r 10 Delfinen.   N : r 3—N : r 7.   Hvalen N : r 2.

SWEDISH COAST DEFENCE BATTLESHIPS (*Kustpansarfartyg*)

From *Sverige* class, down to and including *Svea* class, officially rated as *1 kl. Pansarbåtar.*

(SVERIGE CLASS—3 Ships.)

SVERIGE (May, 1915), **DROTTNING VICTORIA** (Sept., 1917) and **GUSTAV DEN FEMTA** (Feb., 1918).

Displacement : *Sverige*, 7185 tons ; *D. Victoria* and *Gustav V* about 7,400 tons. Complement, 408.

Length (*w.l.*) { *Sverige*, 392·8 feet ; *D.V. & G.V*, 396·6 feet } Beam, 61 feet. *Max.* draught, 21 feet.

Guns (Bofors) :
4—11 inch 45 cal. (A⁵)
8—6 inch, 50 cal.
6—14 pdr.
2—6 pdr.
2 machine.
Torpedo tubes (18 inch) :
2 *submerged* (broadside).

Armour : (Carnegie).
8″ Belt (amidships)......
6″ Belt (ends).........
13″ Deck (slopes) ... ..
4″ Redoubt..............
8″ Big gun turrets .....
5″—3″ Small turrets
8″ Conning tower .. ..

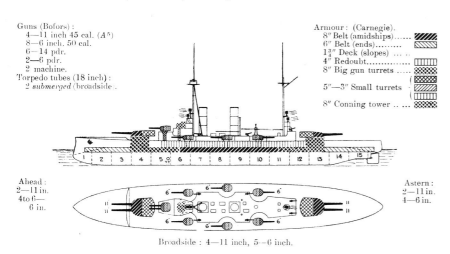

Ahead :
2—11 in.
4 to 6—6 in.

Astern :
2—11 in.
4—6 in.

Broadside : 4—11 inch, 5—6 inch.

Machinery : In *Sverige*, Curtis turbines by Bergsund Co., 4 screws ; in *Gustav V* and *Drottning Victoria*, Westinghouse geared turbines by the Motala Company, 2 screws. Boilers : 12 Yarrow. Designed S.H.P. 20,000 in *Sverige*, 22,000 in *D. Victoria* and *Gustav V* = 22·5 kts. Coal : *Normal* 350 tons ; *maximum* 700 tons + 100 tons oil.

Engineering Notes.— In *D. Victoria* and *Gustav V*, Westinghouse turbines consist of 2 sets on each shaft, each containing two turbines of the " divided-flow " type, driving propellers through double-pinion reduction gears (total weight of turbines and reduction gears about 120 tons) :

Shaft H.P.	22,000	15,000	3,150
R.P.M. (turbines)........	3,600	3,186	2,070
R.P.M. (propellers)........	200	177	115
Speed (knots)	22·5	20	12·5

General Notes.—*Sverige* was sanctioned 1911 ; but upon a change of Government was cancelled by the Liberals. The nation then voluntarily subscribed a sum which at the end of April, 1912, amounted to nearly £970,000 for the building of this ship, which was estimated to cost £670,000 ; the balance was devoted towards commencement of *D. Victoria* and *Gustav V* under the 1915-19 Naval Programme.

Photos by courtesy of S. Anderson, Esq.

Name.	Builder.	Machinery.	Laid down.	Completed.	Trials.	Boilers.	Best recent speed.
Sverige	Götaverken, Gothenburg	Bergsund Co.	Feb., '13	May, '17		Yarrow in all	
D. Victoria		Motala Co.	?	'18-'19			
Gustav V	Kokum Co., Malmö	Motala Co.	Dec., '14	'18-'19			

SWEDISH COAST DEFENCE BATTLESHIPS. (*Kustpansarfartyg*).

Oscar II : Present appearance.

OSCAR DEN ANDRA (1906).

Displacement, 4660 tons. Complement, 329.
Length (*w.l.*) 316⅓ feet. Beam, 50½ feet. *Maximum* draught, 18 feet.

Guns :
  2—8·3 inch, 45 cal. (*A*).
  8—6 inch, 50 cal.
  10—6 pdr.
  1—1 pdr.
Torpedo tubes (18 inch) :
  2 *submerged* (Elswick).

Armour (Krupp) :
  6″—4″ Belt (amidships)
  2″ Deck (slopes)
  6″ Bulkheads
  4′ Lower deck redoubt
  7½″—5″ Big gun
    turrets (N.C.)
  7′ Hoists to these
  5″—3″ Small tur-
    rets (N.C.)
  7″ Conning tower

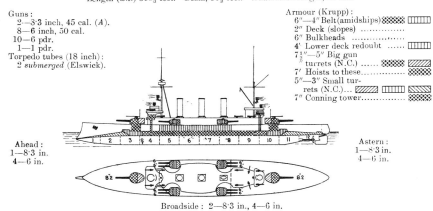

Ahead :
  1—8·3 in.
  4—6 in.

Astern :
  1—8·3 in.
  4—6 in.

Broadside : 2—8·3 in., 4—6 in.

Machinery : 2 sets triple expansion. 2 screws. Boilers : 12 Yarrow. Designed H.P. 9000 = 18·3 kts. Coal : *normal* 350 tons ; *maximum* 500 tons = 2950 miles at 10 kts.

Notes.— Four searchlights carried—one on each chart-house, and one on each mast. Built by Lindholmen Co. On *trial* : 9400 = 18·96 kts.

Photo, Karlsson, Karlskrona.

DRISTIGHETEN (1900).

Displacement, 3620 tons. Complement, 262.

Length (*w.l.*), 285 feet. Beam, 48¼ feet. *Maximum* draught, 17 feet.

Guns :
  2—8·3 inch, 45 cal. (*A*).
  6—6 inch, 45 cal.
  10—6 pdr.
  1—1 pdr.
Torpedo tubes (18 inch) :
  2 *submerged* (Elswick).

Armour (Krupp) :
  8″ Belt (amidships)
  2″ Deck (flat on belt)
  8″ Turrets
  8″ Turret supports
  3¾″ Battery
  3¾″ Hoists
  8″ Conning tower

Ahead :
  1—8·3 in.
  2—6 in.

Astern :
  1—8·3 in.
  2—6 in.

Broadside : 2—8·3 in., 3—6 in.

Machinery : 2 sets triple expansion. Designed H.P. 5000 = 16 kts. *natural* draught. 2 screws.
Boilers : 8 Yarrow. Coal : *normal* 280 tons ; *maximum* 310 tons = 2040 miles at 10 kts.
First trials : I.H.P. 5557 = 16·8 kts.
  Built by Lindholmen Co. 4 searchlights. Fire control and tripod fore-mast, fitted 1911-12.

TAPPERHETEN.

(ÅRAN Class—4 Ships).

Photo, Karlsson, Karlskrona.

Note.—Appearance now as plans below and silhouettes. Ventilators removed and searchlights now on masts.
ÅRAN (1902), **VASA** (Dec., 1901), **TAPPERHETEN** (1902) & **MANLIGHETEN** (Dec., 1903).

Displacements : *Aran*, 3650 tons ; *Vasa*, 3745 tons ; *Tapperheten* and *Manligheten*, 3840 tons.
Length, (*w.l.*) 287 feet. Beam, 49¼ feet. *Maximum* draught, 16¾ to 17½ feet.
Complement, 301. (*Manligheten* 285).

Guns :
  2—8·3 inch, 45 cal. (*A*).
  6—6 inch, 45 cal.
  10—6 pdr.
  1—1 pdr.
Torpedo tubes (18 inch) :
  2 *submerged* (Elswick).

*Tapperheten and Manligheten have only 8—6 pdr.

Armour (Krupp) :
  7″ Belt (amidships)
  2″ Deck (flat on belt)
  7″ Bulkheads
  7½″—5″ Turrets
  8″ Supports
  5½″—2½″ Small turrets (N.C.)
  Hoists, etc.
  8″ Conning tower

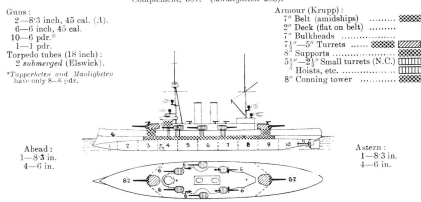

Ahead :
  1—8·3 in.
  4—6 in.

Astern :
  1—8·3 in.
  4—6 in.

Broadside : 1—8·3 in., 3—6 in.

Machinery : 2 sets triple expansion. 2 screws. Boilers : 8 Yarrow. Designed H.P. 7400 for *Manligheten*, 6500 for others = 17 kts. Coal : *maximum*, 300 tons. Endurance : 2000 at 10 kts.
Notes.—Where built : *Aran*, Lindholmen ; *Vasa*, Bergsund ; *Tapperheten* and *Manligheten*, Kockum. These ships carry 4 searchlights.

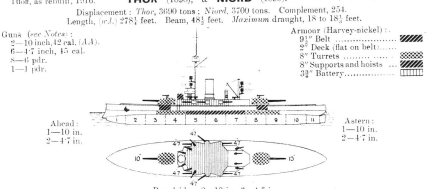

THOR, as rebuilt, 1916.   **THOR** (1898), & **NIORD** (1898).   Photo, Karlsson, Karlskrona.

Displacement : *Thor*, 3690 tons ; *Niord*, 3700 tons. Complement, 254.
Length, (*w.l.*) 278½ feet. Beam, 48½ feet. *Maximum* draught, 18 to 18½ feet.

Guns (*see Notes*) :
  2—10 inch, 42 cal. (*A*).
  6—4·7 inch, 45 cal.
  8—6 pdr.
  1—1 pdr.

Armour (Harvey-nickel) :
  9½″ Belt
  2″ Deck (flat on belt)
  8″ Turrets
  8″ Supports and hoists
  3¾″ Battery

Ahead :
  1—10 in.
  2—4·7 in.

Astern :
  1—10 in.
  2—4·7 in.

Broadside : 2—10 in., 3—4·7 in.

Machinery : 2 sets, vertical triple expansion. 2 screws. Boilers : 6 Cylindrical. Designed H.P. 5000 = 16 kts. Coal : *normal*, 280 tons ; *maximum*, 300 tons = 2530 miles at 10 kts.

Name	Builder	Machinery	Laid down	Completed	Last refit	First trials (*f.d.*) :—	Boilers	Best recent speed
Thor	Bergsund	} By builders	1896	1899	1916	= 16·7	Cylindrical	
Niord	Lindholmen		1896	1900	1917	= 16·5	Cylindrical	

Notes.—The big guns of *Thor* are Canet, those of *Niord* are Bofors. 4 searchlights. *Thor* was rebuilt in 1916 and *Niord* in 1917, their appearance being greatly altered. As originally built, they had two masts and two funnels, like *Svea* class, on next page. Now they are almost identical with the re-built *Oden*, also given on next page.

Photo, Karlsson, Karlskrona.

ODEN as re-built 1915. Appearance is now almost the same as that of *Thor* and *Niord* on preceding page, but note that there is no ventilator abeam of the conning tower; chart house is slightly deeper fore and aft, and small topmast to stump of old mainmast is much higher. As will be seen by comparing photos and plans the 4·7 inch guns are differently arranged. Has plain top on tripod mast. *Thor* and *Niord* have a ringed top.

ODEN (March, 1896).

Normal displacement, 3715 tons. Complement, 243.

Length (*w.l.*), 278¼ feet. Beam, 48½ feet. *Maximum* draught, 18¼ feet.

Guns (Canet and Bofors):
2—10 inch, 42 cal. (A.A.) Canet.
6—4·7 inch, 45 cal. Bofors.
8—3 pdr.
1—1 pdr.

Armour (Harvey-nickel):
10″ Belt (amidships)......
2″ Deck (flat on belt)
10″ Turrets ....
10″ Supports and hoists
3¾″ Battery.............
9¾″ Conning tower ......

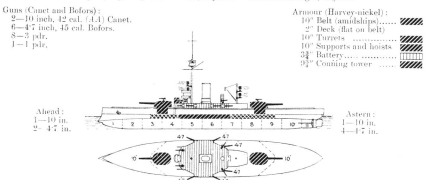

Ahead:
1—10 in.
2—4·7 in.

Astern:
1—10 in.
4—4·7 in.

Machinery: 2 screws. Boilers: 6 cylindrical. Designed H.P. 5000 = 16 kts. Coal: *normal* 275 tons; *maximum*, 300 tons. Endurance: 2530 miles at 10 kts.

Laid down by Bergsund Co., 1894. Completed 1898. 4 searchlights. Re-constructed 1915, when appearance was greatly changed. Appearance was originally like *Svea* class in next column.

SWEDISH MONITORS.

THORDÖN AND TIRFING.

THORDÖN, 1505 tons, & **TIRFING**, 1524 tons, (launched 1866—67, and reconstructed 1903—1905). Complement 91.

Guns: *Thordön*. 2—4·7 inch, 8—3 pdr.   Armour (iron), 4½″ belt, 18″ turret
　　　Tirfing. 2—4·7 inch, 8—6 pdr.. 　　 ,, 　　 4½″ ,, 10¾″ ,,

Both have a 9½″ conning tower. 1 screw. H.P. 380 = 6—7 kts. Coal: 115—120 tons.

John Ericsson deleted during war.

Official Illustration.

BJÖRN & **GERDA** (built 1873—74, and reconstructed 1909—1910). 459 tons. Complement 48.
Guns: 1—4·7 inch, 3—6 pdr., Armour (iron), 2¼″ belt. 16½″ casemate. H.P., 155 = 8 kts., but *Gerda* only, 133 H.P. for 7 kts. 2 screws. Coal: *maximum* 25 tons.

Berserk, Folke, Hildur, Silve and *Ulf* deleted during the war.

THULE.
Forebridges run to tripod legs; no funnel caps.
(*Old Gunboat with raking masts and funnels.*)

(SVEA).

Photo by courtesy of S. Anderson, Esq.
GÖTA
still has derricks just before fore funnel.

SVEA* CLASS—2 SHIPS.

GÖTA (1889), & THULE (1893).

	Length (w.l.) (feet)		Beam (feet)		Draught (feet)		Displacement.
Göta...	258·5	×	47·9	×	17	=	3393 tons.
Thule	260·8	×	47·9	×	18·4	=	3305 tons.

Complement 265 and 269.

Guns:
1—8·3 inch, 45 cal. (A.)
7—6 inch, 45 cal.
9—6 pdr.
1—1 pdr.
Torpedo tubes: (15 inch):
1 submerged (bow), but
Thule has none.

Armour (Creusot):
11¾″—8″ Belt........
2″ Deck (flat on belt) ...
2″ Deck (at ends) ....
10½″ Conning tower ...
Armour (Krupp):
7½″ fore turret (N.C.) ...
5″ Hoist to this (N.C.) ...
5″ Secondary turrets (7)
4″ Hoists to these ....

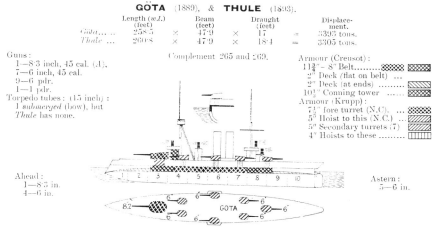

Ahead:
1—8·3 in.
4—6 in.

Astern:
5—6 in.

Broadside: 1—8·3 in., 4—6 in.

Machinery: 2 sets horizontal triple expansion. 2 screws. Boilers: 6 cylindrical. Designed I.H.P. 4650 = 15 kts. Coal: *normal* 200 tons; *maximum* 288 to 300 tons.

Notes.—Completely reconstructed, 1901—04. *Göta* built by Lindholmen Co., *Thule* by Bergsund Co. *Göta* has square funnels, *Thule* round ones. 4 searchlights. Tripods fitted 1911-12.
Svea of this class transferred to Depot Ships.

SWEDISH ARMOURED CRUISER (*Pansarkryssare*.) 22 KT.

FYLGIA (Dec., 1905).

Displacement, 4810 tons. Complement, 362.

Length (w.l.), 377⅔ feet. Beam, 48½ feet. *Max.* draught, 19¾ feet.

Guns (M. '00):
8—6 inch, 45 cal.
14—6 pdr.
2—1 pdr.
Torpedo tubes (18 inch):
2 submerged.

Armour (Krupp):
4″ Belt ....
2″ Deck (slopes) ......
5″—2″ Turrets
4″ Hoists and supports
4″ Conning tower......

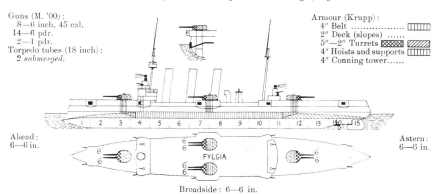

Ahead:
6—6 in.

Astern:
6—6 in.

Broadside: 6—6 in.

Machinery: 2 sets triple expansion. 2 Screws. Boilers: 12 Yarrow. Designed H.P. 12,000 = 21·5 kts. Coal: *normal* 350 tons; *maximum* 900 tons = 5770 miles at 10 kts.

General Notes: Laid down by Bergsund Co. at Finnboda in 1903 and completed 1907. Trials: 12,440 H.P. = 22·7 kts. Machinery by builders. (There are no sponsons under beam 6-inch turrets, as incorrectly shown on elevation, plan and section above.)

SWEDISH DESTROYERS (*Jagare*).

10 Destroyers.

4 *Wale* class:—**Wale** ('06), **Ragnar** ('07) **Sigurd** ('07), **Vidar** ('09). 460 to 462 tons. Dimensions : 216×20¼×8¾ feet. Armament : *Wale*, 2—14 pdr., 4—6 pdr., 2 machine ; other boats, 4—14 pdr., 2 machine ; 2—18 inch tubes in all. 4 Yarrow boilers. Hull on Thornycroft lines. All built in Sweden. Coal : 80 tons. Radius of action : 920 miles at 15 kts.

1 *Thornycroft*: **Magne** (1905). Dimensions : 215¾ × 20¼ × 9 feet. Armament: 6—6 pdr., 2 machine, 2 single 18 inch tubes aft. 4 Thornycroft boilers. Endurance : 920 miles at 15 kts.

WRANGEL AND WACHTMEISTER completing.   *Photo, S. Anderson, Esq.*

2 *Wrangel* class : **Wrangel** and **Wachtmeister** (Lindholmen Co., Gothenburg, both launched 1917.) Dimensions : 236¼×21½×9¼ feet. Armament : 4—14 pdr., 2 machine guns, 2 or 4 torpedo tubes (size unknown.) Designed S.H.P., 11,000 (*n.d.*), 13,000 (*f.d.*)=26-27 kts. Have de Laval turbines. Completed, early 1918.

No photo available.

Appearance same as *Wale* class in next column.

1 *Yarrow*: **Mode** (1902). Dimensions : 220 × 20¼ × 8¼ feet. 4 Yarrow boilers. Armament : 6—6 pdr., 2 machine. Tubes : 2 single, aft. (18 inch). Endurance : 980 miles at 15 kts.

2 *Hugin* class : **Hugin** (1911), **Munin** (1912). 460 tons. Dimensions : 216¾ × 21¼ × 8½ feet. Guns : 2—14 pdr., 2 machine. Torpedo tubes : 2—18 inch. 4 Yarrow boilers. Curtis turbines. S.H.P., 8,000 = 30 kts. Fuel : 80 tons coal + 3 tons oil. Endurance : 800 miles at 15 kts. *Hugin* built by Goteborg Co., and *Munin* by Kockum Co., Malmö.

SWEDISH TORPEDO BOATS (*Torpedobatar.*)

FIRST CLASS (*continued*):—

BLIXT.   *Photo. S. Anderson, Esq.*

11 *Blixt* class : **Blixt** '93, **Bris** ('00), **Kapella** ('04), **Meteor** ('99), **Mira** ('02), **Orion** ('03), **Orkan** ('00), **Stjerna** ('99), **Sirius** ('03), **Virgo** ('02), **Vind** ('00). Guns : 2—1 pdr. Torpedo tubes : 2—15 inch. All built in Sweden.

Comet, Gondul and *Guder* deleted before 1919.

SECOND CLASS : —

FIRST CLASS :—

Castor doing 28·3 kts.

17 *Plejad* class : **Astrea** ('07), **Castor** ('07), **Iris**, **Plejad** ('05), **Pollux** ('07), **Thetis** ('07), **Spica** ('07), **Vega** ('07), **Vesta**, **Argo**, **Antares**, **Arcturus**, **Altair**, **Polaris**, **Perseus**, **Regulus**, **Rigel** ('09-'10). Armament : (except for *Plejad*, *Castor* and *Pollux*, which have 2—3 pdr., 2—6 pdr., 2—18 inch tubes. Except *Plejad* (by Normand, Le Havre), all built in Sweden.

No. 11.

10 second class boats : **N:r 5—15** (No. 13 vacant) Armament : 1—1 pdr., 2—18 inch tubes.

(Vedette Boats of 23-85 tons are listed on a later page, with Swedish Miscellaneous Ships).

12 of this class deleted before 1919.

SWEDISH SUBMARINES (*Undervattensbatar*, but officially listed as *Undervattenstorpedfartyg*).

1st Class Submarines.

2nd Class Submarines.

Uncertain how many of these boats have been completed.

6 *Laurenti* type : **N:r 11 Aborren** (1917), **N:r 12 Gäddan** (1918), **N:r 13 Laxen** (1918), **N:r 17 Otter** (——), **N:r 18 Sälen** (——), all built by Kockum Co., Malmö ; **N:r 14 Bavfer** (——), **N:r 15 Hvalrossen** (——). **N:r 16 Iller** (——), all built by Karlskrona D.Y. No details yet known. The conjunction of numbers and names given above is more or less conjectural and open to future correction.

Navy type : **N:r 3, N:r 4**, both built by Stockholm D.Y., **N:r 5, N:r 6**, Kockum Co., **N:r 7**, Bergsund Co., all built 1910-11. Dimensions : 139½×14⅞×9⅞ feet. 2—18 inch tubes. These are improved *Hajens*. Radius of action at full speed (15 kts.), 475 miles.

Photo, Karlsson, Karlskrona.

1 *Navy* type : **N:r 10 Delfinen** (Bergsund Co., Stockholm, 1915). Armament : 1 machine gun, and 2—18 inch bow tubes.

2 *Laurenti* type : **N:r 9 Svärdfisken, N:r 8 Tumlaren** (Kockum Co., Malmö, 1914). 2—18 inch bow tubes.

SWEDISH MISCELLANEOUS.

Gunboat (*Kanonbat*).

1 *Laurenti-Fiat* type : **Hvalen N:r 2** (Spezia, 1909). Dimensions : 139×14×9½ feet. 2—18 inch bow tubes. 3 sets of 8-cyl. Fiat petrol engines. 3 screws.

Photo, S. Anderson, Esq.

SKAGUL (1878). 589 tons. Guns : 2—4·7 inch, 4—6 pdr Speed : 13 kts. Coal : 94 tons.

Note.—Present employment of above ship not known.

When running on surface may have two masts raised, one right in bow and other right at stern.
1 *Holland* type : **Hajen N:r 1** (Stockholm D.Y., 1904). Dimensions : 65×12×9½ feet. 1—18 inch bow tube. 3 torpedoes carried. Petrol motor. 1 screw.

Torpedo Gunboats (*Torpedkryssare*).

Depot Ships (*Depotfartyg*).

Note :—Gunboat *Rota*, given on next page as a "Mine Ship" is officially rated as a "Depot Ship." Other old Vessels used as Parent Ships are *Stockholm* (for T.B. at Karlskrona), *Saga* (for Submarine at Karlskrona) and *Freja* (for Torpedo Craft at Stockholm).

Depot Ships—*continued*.

Is included in Illustration of "Gota" and "Thule" on a preceding page.

PSILANDER.

SVEA. Old Coast Defence Battleship, built by Lindholmen Co., 1886, rebuilt 1904. 3273 tons. Dimensions : 248·4×48·5×17·4 feet. Guns : 4—4·7 inch, 2—6 pdr. Armour : 11¾″—8″ Belt, 2″ Decks, 10¼″ C.T. 2 screws. 6 cyl. boilers. I.H.P. 4650=15 kts. Coal : 290 tons.

Photo, S. Anderson, Esq.

DISA (1877, rebuilt 1908). 512 tons. Guns : 1—5·9 inch, 1—4·7 inch, 2—6 pdr., 2 machine. Speed : 11 kts. Coal : 98 tons.

JAKOB BAGGE and CLAS HORN.

ORNEN.

PSILANDER (1900), **CLAS UGGLA** (1898), 814 tons, **JAKOB BAGGE**, 835 tons, **CLAS HORN** (1898), 846 tons, **ORNEN** (1896), 844 tons. Designed H.P. 4000=20 kts., *natural draught*. Coal, 100 tons. Armament : 2—4·7 inch, 4—6 pdr., 1—15 inch *submerged bow tube*.

General Notes : To distinguish between these ships compare relative positions of foremast, bridges, and fore funnel. In 1917, some (or all) of these four ships had extremely high top-gallant masts for W/T, and appeared to have a single stiffening strut to foremast, giving the appearance of a fore tripod mast when seen full broadside.

As rebuilt. (*Submarine Depot Ship.*) *Photo, Karlsson, Karlskrona.*
SKAGGALD (1879, rebuilt 1913). 670 tons. Guns : 4—14 pdr. Speed : 13 kts. Coal : 94 tons.

Photo, S. Anderson, Esq.

BLENDA (1874, re-built 1908). 464 tons. Guns : 2—6 pdr. Speed : 11 kts. Coal : *about* 95 tons.

SWEDISH MISCELLANEOUS.

Balloon Ship (Ballongfartyget).

No Photo available.
No funnels; no masts.

N : r 1 (1902). 264 tons. Assigned to Coastal Defence.

Mine Ships (Minfartyg).

Official photo.

CLAES FLEMING (1914). 1,748 tons. Dimensions: 262 × 32·8 × 13·7 feet. Guns: 4—4·7 inch (50 cal.), 6 machine. Speed: 20 kts. Parsons turbines.

EDDA (1885) (1907). 662 tons. Guns: 4—6 pdr. Speed: 13·5 kts. Coal: 80 tons.

These are the only two Swedish warships officially rated as "Mine Ships." *Skuld* and *Rota* are not so rated officially.

Mine Ships—Continued.

Photo, Karlsson, Karlskrona.

SKULD (1879). Old Gunboat, 604 tons. Guns: 1—6 pdr. Speed: 13½ kts. Coal, 94 tons.

Note.—In 1919, the 2nd Mining Division consisted of *Skuld* (above), *Svensksund* (*v.* next page), and Vedette Boats N : r 23, 24, 25 (see N : r 26—23 on next page).

Photo, S. Anderson, Esq.
(Is also rated as a "Depot Ship.")

ROTA (1878). 540 tons. Guns: 2—6 pdr. Speed: 13 kts. Coal: about 95 tons.

Note.—In 1919, the 1st Mining Division consisted of *Rota* (above) and Vedette Boats *Sökaren*, N : r 20, 21, 22 (all listed on next page).

Hospital Ship (Lasarettsfartyg).

VERDANDE (1879). 514 tons. Speed: 13½ kts. Coal: 94 tons.

Royal Yacht.

(Is officially rated as "Chefsfartyg" or "Flagship.")

DROTT (1877). 633 tons. Guns: 4—3 pdr. Designed H.P., 960 = 13 kts. Coal: 100 tons.

Surveying Ships (Sjökarteverkets fartyg).

SVENSKUND (see next page) is occasionally used as a Surveying Ship.

Five small vessels are employed on this service, viz.:—*Ejdern* (1916), 93 tons; *Tarnan* (1889, rebuilt 1909), 54 tons; *Falken* (1888), 157 tons; *Svalan* (1881), 127 tons, and *Ran* (1857) of 199 tons.

Pilot Vessels (Lotsverketsfartyg),

There are ten of these vessels, the largest and most modern being:—*Vega* (1901), of 285 tons; *Malmö* (1897), of 138 tons; *Göteborg* (1894), of 132 tons; and *Gäfle* (1892), of 110 tons. The remaining six, built 1885—1866, are under 100 tons.

(Continued on next page.)
2 B 2

SWEDISH MISCELLANEOUS.

Patrol or Coastguard Ships (and Mine Sweepers?).

Building or Completing.

SÖKAREN, SVEPAREN, SPRÄNGAREN (1918, Motala Co.). 227 tons. Dimensions: 85·3 × 23 × 9·8 feet. Guns: 1—6 pdr.

Note.—These ships may be fitted out as Mine Sweepers. *Sprängaren* is officially rated as a "Vedette Boat."

Vedette Boats (Vedettbåtar).

No photo available.

N : r 19 (1918). 67 tons. No guns. Speed unknown. Officially rated as "Lysmaskinbåt." ("Searchlight Boat.")

Photo, S. Anderson, Esq.
N : r 26—23 (ex-T.B. *79, 81, 83, 85,* 1903). 62—55 tons. Speed, 20 kts. Guns: 1—1 pdr. May still have 2—15 inch tubes.

No photo available.

N : r 20 (ex-T.B. *Komet,* 1896). 104 tons. Speed, 23 kts. Guns: 1—1 pdr. May still have 2—15 inch tubes.

Vedette Boats—Continued.

No photo available.

N : r 22 (ex-T.B. *Gudur,* 1894). 73 tons. **N : r 21** (ex-T.B. *Gondul,* 1894). 83 tons. Speeds, 19½ kts. Guns: 2—1 pdr. May still each have 2—15 inch torpedo tubes.

Photo, Karlsson, Karlskrona.

N : r 18—N : r 15 (1887-4), 86—72 tons; **N : r 14—N : r 9** (1891-1886), 55—51 tons; **N : r 8—N : r 5** (1885-1880), 49—43 tons; **N : r 5—N : r 1** (1880-1879), 23 tons. Speeds, 19 to 17 kts. All armed with 1—1 pdr. gun. N : r 5—N : r 1 for Coastal Defence. N : r 14—9 and N : r 8—5 are ex-Torpedo Boats 77—61 (alternate numbers); N : r 18—15 are ex-T.B. *4, 3, 2* and *1.*

For Various Special Services.

SVENSKSUND (1891). 394 tons. Guns: 2—6 pdr. Speed: 12½ kts. Coal: 50 tons.

Note.—This ship is employed as (*a*) a Mine Layer, (*b*) a Surveying Ship, (*c*) a Fisheries Protection Vessel, (*d*) an Ice Breaker, and (*e*) a Repair Ship, according to season of the year and when necessity arises for her use on any of these duties.

Training Ships (Ovningsfartyg).

JARRAMAS. *Official illustration.*
JARRAMAS (1900). 337 tons. Speed, 11 kts.
NAJADEN (1897). 355 tons. Speed, 11 kts.

GLADAN. *Photo, S. Anderson, Esq.*
GLADAN (1857). 327 tons. Speed, 10 kts.
FALKEN (1877). 138 tons. Speed, 8½ kts.

The old Corvette *Saga* (1878), of 1,777 tons, is also officially listed as a Training Ship, and is attached to the Karlsrona Submarine Station.

Lastly, there are five very old "Accommodation and other vessels" (*Logements—och andra fartyg*), all probably being useless for fighting purposes.

DANISH WARSHIPS

(ROYAL) DANISH NAVY.

(Officially revised, 1918, by courtesy of H.E. the Minister of Marine. Corrected, 1919, from the Official List "Danmarks og Islands Skibsliste.")

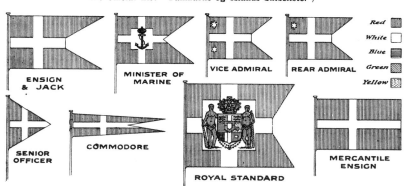

ENSIGN & JACK — MINISTER OF MARINE — VICE ADMIRAL — REAR ADMIRAL

Red, White, Blue, Green, Yellow

SENIOR OFFICER — COMMODORE — ROYAL STANDARD — MERCANTILE ENSIGN

Note.—Division flag pennant, otherwise as commodore.

INSIGNIA OF RANK ON SLEEVES.

1 2 3 4 5 6 7 8 9
Admiral. Vice-Admiral. Kontre-Admiral. Kommandör. Kaptejn. Premier-löjtnant. Löjtnant. Second-löjtnant. Kadet.
Admiral. Vice-Admiral. Rear-Admiral. Captain. Commander. Lieut-Commander. Lieutenant. Sub-Lieut. Midshipman.

and between stripes:— | Branches (with, but after Executive.)
Crimson ... Ingeniör (Engineer). Officers of the Technical Department have rafters (?) in the stripes.
Blue ... Intendant (Paymaster ?)
Ponceau Red ... Læge (Surgeons).

Without curl, but with Corps emblem.

The broad stripes in ranks 1—3 are 2·7 cm. wide.
The narrow " 7 & 9 are 0·7
The other stripes are 1·4 cm. wide. Distance between stripes is 0·7 cm.

Personnel: About 4000, all ranks.
Mercantile Marine: —— steamers of 631,000 tons *gross.* 783 sailing of 109,258 tons *net.* Sea trade chiefly with England, Sweden and Norway.
Oversea Possessions: Iceland, Greenland, Faroes Islands.
Coinage: Krone (100 ore) = about 1s. 1d. British ; 50 cents U.S.A.
Minister of Marine: M. Peter Munch.

Naval Guns. (All details unofficial.)

Bore: ins.	cm.	Length in Calibres.	Make and Date of Model.		Weight of Gun metric tons.	Weight of Projectile. lbs.	Muzzle Velocity. ft.-secs.	Mounted in:
9·4	24	43	Bofors	M. '06	24·5	352	2806	P. Skram
9·4	24	43	Bofors	M. '01	24·3	353	2477	O. Fisher
9·4	24	40	Canet	M. '96	22·9	353	2362	H. Trolle
9·4	24	40	Krupp	M. '93	25·4	353	2362	Skjold
5·9	15	50	Bofors	——	7·5	112	2690	P. Skram (& Valkyrien ?)
5·9	15	43	Bofors	M '96/'01	5·5	112	2296	O. Fisher, H. Trolle
4·7	12	40	Krupp		2·3	44	2362	Skjold, Hejmdal, Gejser

Arsenal.

COPENHAGEN. One slip. One dock (lengthened, 1912), 316½ × 59½ × 20½ feet. Floating docks: No. 1, 157½ × 28½ × 12¾ feet. No. 2, 113 × 31 × 11¾ feet. Coast Defence Battleships, Torpedo Boats, and Submarines built here.

Private Establishments.

COPENHAGEN. (BURMEISTER & WAIN). Several large building slips. Dry dock, 469 × 66 × 23 feet, and three patent slips. Floating dock : 492 × 77 × 25 feet. Construct submarines and specialise in the building of large Diesel-engined mercantile ships. (*Note :* These details refer to conditions before the war. The shipbuilding establishment is believed to have been greatly enlarged in 1915-17.)
GAMLE. One slip. One dry dock, 232 × 52 × 15½ feet.
COPENHAGEN FLOATING DOCK CO. One dry dock (Gamle), 246 × 52 × 15½ feet. Floating docks : No. 1, 296 × 50 × 16½ feet. No. 2, 130 × 45 × 12 feet. No. 3, 310 × 55½ × 16 feet. There are also at Copenhagen two small patent slips.
ELSINOR. Dry docks (a) 379 × 57 × 18 feet (New Dock);
(b) 335 × 43 × 14 feet (Elsinor Dry dock);
Also a patent slip.
AARHUS. Patent slip, able to take a small torpedo boat.
Other private shipbuilding companies are : Elsinore Co., Elsinore ; Copenhagen Co., at Copenhagen and Elsinore ; Stuhr, at Aalborg and the Frederikshavn Co., Frederikshavn.

Note.

All displacements given in metric tons. Where measurement of length is not stated, it can be taken as between perpendiculars (*p.p.*) All draughts *max. load aft.* unless otherwise stated.

DANISH WARSHIPS : RECOGNITION SILHOUETTES.

Scale : 1 inch = 80 feet.

* These Silhouettes are from drawings furnished by courtesy of the Ministry of Defence.

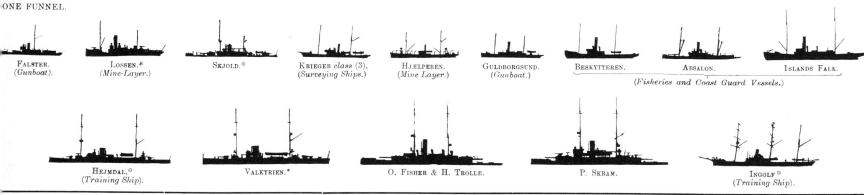

ONE FUNNEL.

FALSTER. (Gunboat). — LOSSEN.* (Mine-Layer.) — SKJOLD.☉ — KRIEGER *class* (3). (Surveying Ships.) — HJÆLPEREN. (Mine Layer.) — GULDBORGSUND. (Gunboat.) — BESKYTTEREN. — ABSALON. — ISLANDS FALK.
(Fisheries and Coast Guard Vessels.)

HEJMDAL.☉ (Training Ship). — VALKYRIEN.* — O. FISHER & H. TROLLE. — P. SKRAM. — INGOLF☉ (Training Ship).

TWO FUNNELS.

(Yacht bow, 2 masts raking. two bell-topped funnels raking, paddle wheels.)
DANNEBROG (Royal Yacht). — GEJSER.*

TORPEDO CRAFT. Scale ; 1 inch = 160 feet.

—mleren *class* t.b.☉ (3).
—os. 4 & 5 t.b. (2).
Ormen t.b.☉

Hvalrossen *class* t.b. (3). Fore funnels now raised.
Havörnen *class* t.b. (3).
Söridderen *class* t.b.☉ (3)

SUBMARINES. Scale : 1 inch = 80 feet.

Aegir *class* (5 or 6).
Havfruen *class* (6).

DANISH COAST SERVICE BATTLESHIP. (Kyst forsvarsskib.)

Note.
This ship was laid down in February, 1914, and was only launched in 1918. Very little work is being done on her at present, and it is impossible to state when she will be finished.

NIELS JUEL (July, 1918.)
Displacement, 3,900 tons. Complement,
Length (o.a.), 295·1 feet. Beam, 53·5 feet. Draught (full load, aft), 15·8 feet. Length (p.p.), 285·4 feet.

Guns (Krupp) :
2—12 inch, 45 cal. (A⁵.)
8 or 10—4·7 inch, 45 cal.
2—12 pdr., 55 cal. (anti-aircraft)
Torpedo tubes :
2 *submerged* (broadside).
1 " bow).
1 " (stern).

Armour (Krupp):
7″ Belt (amidships) ...
4″ Belt (ends)............
7″ Turrets ....
6″ Casemates (KNC)....
7″ Bulkhead ....
7″ Conning Tower......

(No plans available, but similar to "Pedr Skram.")

Machinery : 2 screws. Boilers : Thornycroft. Designed H.P. 5500 = 16 kts. Coal : tons.
Notes.—Laid down at Copenhagen Royal Yard in Feb., 1914.

P. SKRAM, O. FISHER, H. TROLLE.

For Tabulated details see next page.

Armour (*see Notes*) :
7″ Belt (amidships) ...
4″ Belt (aft) ...
3″ Deck (forward) ...
[Deck flat on belt.]
7″ Turrets ...
6″ Casemates (KNC)...
7″ Bulkhead
7″ Conning tower ...

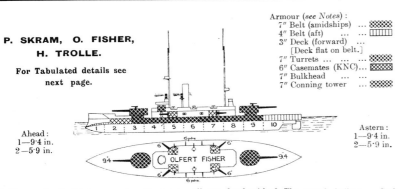

Ahead :
1—9·4 in.
2—5·9 in.

Astern :
1—9·4 in.
2—5·9 in.

Machinery : 2 sets, triple expansion, 2 screws. All are fitted with 6 Thornycroft boilers. Coal (*maximum*) : 255 tons in *O. Fisher* and *P. Skram* ; 245 tons in *H. Trolle*.

Gunnery Notes.—Bofors 1896 models in *P. Skram* ; Bofors 1896-1901 models in *O. Fisher*. In *H. Trolle* 9·4 inch are Canet 1896 model, and 5·9 inch are Bofors 1896 model.

Armour Notes.—Krupp armour in *P. Skram*, Creusot in other ships. Belt is 7 feet deep, 3½ feet above, and 3½ feet below water-line.

Torpedo Notes.—All tubes 18 inch and submerged : 1 bow, 1 stern, 2 broadside in *P. Skram*, 1 bow and 2 broadside in *O. Fisher* and *H. Trolle*.

Engineering Notes.—Trial : H.P. and speeds given in Table on next page as *O. Fisher* and *H. Trolle* did not reach designed speed of 16 kts. with 4200 I.H.P. on trials. Endurance is about 2000 miles at 10 kts. and 1050 miles at 14¾ kts.

General Notes.—All built at Copenhagen Dockyard. In plan above for *O. Fisher*, 6 pdrs. amidships are now 12 pdr. In all 2—12 or 6 pdr. anti-aircraft guns mounted on crowns of 9·4 inch barbettes.

Photo, Ebessen, Aarhus.

PEDER SKRAM. *No ventilators and no yard on mainmast. Funnel rather shorter and thicker than in other 2 ships. Three searchlights round foot of foremast. Also note 12 pdr. guns on roof of 9·4 inch barbettes (are anti-aircraft type now).*

(HERLUF TROLLE CLASS—3 SHIPS—)

The three differ in dimensions and armament as follows :

		PEDER SKRAM.	**OLFERT FISHER.**	**HERLUF TROLLE.**
Launched	...	May, 1908	1903	1899
Displacement (tons)	...	3735	3650	3595
Complement	...	257	255	255
Length (ft.)	...	275¾ (*p.p.*)	271¾ (*p.p.*)	271¾ (*p.p.*)
Beam (ft.)	...	51¾	50¼	49½
Max. draught (ft.)	...	16½	16¼	16½
Armament	...	2—9·4 inch, 43 cal. 4—5·9 in., 50 cal. 6—14 pdr.* 2—6 pdr.⊙ 2—1 pdr. 2 Machine	2—9·4 inch, 43 cal. 4—5·9 inch, 43 cal. 6—12 pdr. 2—6 pdr.⊙ 2—1 pdr. 2 machine	2—9·4 inch, 40 cal. 4—5·9 inch, 43 cal. 12—6 pdr.⊙ 2 machine
All 18 inch tubes.		4 tubes (*submerged*)	3 tubes (*submerged*)	3 tubes (*submerged*)
H.P.	Trials	5400	4600	4400
Speed		15·9	15·8	15·6

* 2 of these guns anti-aircraft type. **(For plans and illustrations, v. preceding page.)**

DANISH COAST SERVICE SHIP
(*Kystforsvarsskibe*).

1918 Photo.

SKJOLD (1896). Laid down at Copenhagen 1893, and completed 1899. Displacement, 2200 tons. Complement, 137. Dimensions : 227½ × 38 × 13¾ feet. Guns (Krupp) : 1—9·4 in., 40 cal., 3—4·7 in., 40 cal., 4—6 pdr., 1 Machine. Armour (Harvey) : 10″ Belt, 3″ Belt (aft), 2″ Deck (bow), [Deck flat on belt amidships.], 8″ Big turret, 5″ Small turrets, 7″ Bulkhead, 8″ Conning tower. Machinery : I.H.P. 2400 = 13·4 kts. Boilers : 4 Thornycroft. Coal capacity : 110 tons (*maximum*).

Deleted by 1919.

Photo, Ebessen, Aarhus.

OLFERT FISHER. *Fore chart house aft of bridges, also chart house at foot of mainmast. Searchlights on towers between foremast and funnel. Ventilators before funnel high.*

Photo, Ebessen, Aarhus.

HERLUF TROLLE. *Has only two searchlights at feet of masts. Ventilators before funnel low.*

DANISH CRUISERS

VALKYRIEN, *as re-constructed.* *Photo, Ebessen, Aarhus.*

VALKYRIEN (1888 re-built, 1913). 3020 tons. Complement, 282. Dimensions : 265¾ *p.p.* × 43¼ × 18 feet (*maximum* draught). Guns : 2—5·9 inch (Bofors, 50 cal.), 2—12 pdr. (Danish), 2—6 pdr. AA., 2 machine, 3—15 inch *above water* tubes (2 bow, 1 stern). 2½ inch deck. Designed H.P. 5300 = 17·4 kts. Coal : 496 tons. Now used as a Training Ship.

Deleted by 1919.

DANISH CRUISERS—(continued).

GEJSER.   HEJMDAL.   *Photo, Ebessen, Aarhus.*

GEJSER (1892, rebuilt 1907). 1282 tons. Complement, 156. Dimensions : 231¾ (p.p.) × 34 × 11¼ feet. Guns (Krupp) : 2—4·7 inch, 4—20 pdr., 4—6 pdr.* 2 machine. 2 torpedo tubes (1—18 inch, 1—15 inch) *above water*. 1¼″ deck amidships. 6″ engine hatches. H.P. 3100 = 17·1 kts. Coal : 150 tons. Boilers, 8 Thornycroft (first ship to be so fitted). Training Ship for Boys.

* 1—6 pdr. converted to AA.

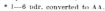

HEJMDAL.   *Photo, Ebessen, Aarhus.*

HEJMDAL (1894, rebuilt 1909). 1313 tons. Complement, 156. Dimensions : 231¾ (p.p.) × 34 × 11¾ feet. Guns (Krupp) : 2—4·7 inch, 4—20 pdr., 4—6 pdr. (1 converted to AA.), 2 machine, 2 torpedo tubes. (1—18 inch, 1—15 inch). 1¼″ deck amidships. 6″ engine hatches. H.P. 3100 = 17 kts. Thornycroft boilers. Coal : 150 tons.

Torpedo Boats

(Plan as *Söridderen* class

VINHUNDEN.   *Photo, Ebessen, Aarhus.*

3 *Schichau* type : **Tumleren, Vindhunden, Spœkhuggeren** (all 1911). First by Schichau, others by Copenhagen Dockyard. Dimensions : 185 × 19 × 7·3 feet. Armament : 2—11 pdr., 5—18 inch tubes, 1 in bows *above water*, other 4 on deck. Turbine engines and Normand boilers in all. Radius of action : 1400 miles at 14 kts.

ORMEN.   *Photo, Ebessen, Aarhus.*

1 *Normand* type : **Ormen** (Copenhagen D.Y. 1907). 121·7 × 14 × 8·5 feet. Armament : 2—1 pdr., 1—18 inch tube (bow, *submerged*), 2—18 inch amidships.

DANISH TORPEDO BOATS

10 *Söhunden* class : **Havhesten, Makrelen, Narvhalen, Nordkaperen, Söhunden** (all launched 1917), **Söloven, Springeren, Stören,** (launched 1916), and *two others* (names not known) *building*. All by Copenhagen D.Y. Dimensions : 126·3 (o.a.) × 13·9 × 8·8 feet *normal draught* (9 feet *full load* draught.) Armament : 2—6 pdr., 30 cal. (anti-aircraft) ; 2—18 inch tubes.

Now have raised fore funnels.   *Photo, Ebessen, Aarhus.*

3 *Hvalrossen* type : **Delfinen, Hvalrossen, Svaerdfisken** (all 1913), built at Copenhagen Dockyard. Dimensions : 148¼ × 17 × 7 feet. Armament : 1—14 pdr. (aft), 4—18 inch tubes in 2 twin-deck mountings amidships.

FLYVEFISKEN.   *Photo, Ebessen, Aarhus.*

3 *Yarrow* type : **Söridderen, Soulven, Flyvefisken** (all 1911). First built by Yarrow, others by Burmeister & Wain, Copenhagen. Dimensions : 181¼ × 18 × 6¼ feet. Armament : 2—14 pdr., 5—18 inch tubes. There are 10 w.t. compartments. On trial did 5300 I.H.P. = 28·2 *max*. Curtis turbines in *Söridderen*. Yarrow boilers in all.

Old Torpedo Boats.

HAJEN.   *Photo, Ebessen, Aarhus.*

3 *Havörnen* class named **Havörnen** (1897, rebuilt 1902). **Hajen** (1896, rebuilt 1908). **Söbjörnen** (1898, rebuilt 1908.) All built at Copenhagen D.Y. Armament : 1—3 pdr., 1 M.G., 4 tubes (all 18 inch in *Havörnen* and *Söbjörnen*; 2—18 inch + 2—15 inch in *Hajen*).

2 *Makrelen* class : **T6** (ex-*Makrelen*), **T7** (ex-*Nordkaperen*), built at Copenhagen, D.Y., 1893. Guns : 2 machine, 4 tubes (2—18 inch, 2—15 inch).

Following five T.B. all used for Subsidiary Service.

Photo wanted.

1 *Navy* type : **No. 1** (ex *Springeren*), built at Copenhagen D.Y., 1891, rebuilt 1902. Armament : 2 machine guns and 2—18 inch torpedo tubes.

No. 4.   *Photo, Ebessen, Aarhus.*

2 *Thornycroft* type : **No. 4** (ex *Havhesten*, 1888, rebuilt 1904-5), **No. 5** (ex *Narchalen*, 1888, rebuilt 1897). Armament : 2 machine guns. Originally had 4 tubes, but now have only 1 or 2—15 inch tubes.

2 *Thornycroft* type : **No. 2** (ex *Söloven*), **No. 3** (ex *Stören*, both 1887, and rebuilt 1897). Armament and tubes as Nos. 4 and 5 above.

(Patrol Boats listed on next page.)

DANISH SUBMARINES & PATROL BOATS.

HAVFRUEN.   *Photo, Ebessen Aarhus.*

6 *Navy* type: **Bellona** (1918), **Flora** (1918), and **Rota** (1917), and *three others,* (names not known.) All built at Copenhagen D.Y. Burmeister & Wain 6-cylinder, 4-cycle Diesel engines. Dimensions: 155.7 × 14.4 × 8.8 feet. Armament: 1—6 pdr. anti-aircraft gun; 4—18 inch torpedo tubes.

6 *Hay-Whitehead* type:—**Havmanden** (1911) and **Havfruen** (1912), **Thetis** (1912), built by Whitehead & Co., Fiume, and **Najaden** (1913), **Nymfen** (1914), **Den Andra April** (1913), built at Copenhagen D.Y. 1 set 6-cyl. Diesel engines. Dimensions: 118¼ × 11.9 × 8 feet. 2—18 inch torpedo tubes. Radius of action: *on surface* (additional to that given in table) 1400 miles at 10 kts; *submerged* 2 hrs. 50 mins. continuous running at 8 kts.

Dykkeren (1909) Apparently deleted before 1919.

RAN: (now has an anti-aircraft gun, probably before C.T.)   *Photo, Ebessen, Aarhus.*

5 *Hay-Whitehead* type:—**Aegir** (1914), **Galathea** (1914), **Neptun** (1914), **Ran** (1915). **Triton** (1914), all built at Copenhagen D.Y. Diesel motors. Dimensions: 133¼ × 12 × 8 feet. Armament: 1—1 pdr. anti-aircraft, and 3-18 inch torpedo tubes. These boats are an enlarged and slightly improved *Havmanden* design.

Patrol Boats.

No.	Date	Tons.	H.P.	Kts.	Guns.	T.T.
9, 8 ...	'94—'95	47	330 =	13	1—3 pdr., 1 M.G.	1—14 inch.
7, 6, 5, 4 ...	'89—'90	22	180 =	12	2 M.G.	2 Spar.
13, 12 ...	1889	25	350 =	17		
10, 11 ...	1888	17	180 =	15	All have	2—14 inch.
15, 14 ...	1886	16	170 =	13	1—1 pdr.	2—14 inch.
3, 2 ...	1884	16	150 =	15		
1 ...	1879	39	350 =	20	1—1 pdr.	1—14 inch.

DANISH MISCELLANEOUS.

Mine Ships—(*Mineskibe*).

TWO SMALL MINELAYERS of 200 tons, building or completing.

LOSSEN (1910). 628 tons. Complement, 53. 149.3 (*p.p.*) × 28 × 9.5 feet. Guns: 2—14 pdrs. I.H.P. 900 = 13 kts. Coal: 20 tons. Carries about 150—180 mines

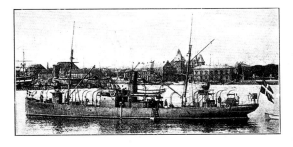

HJÆLPEREN (1890). 283 tons. Complement, 40. 125.6 (*p.p.*) × 22.2 × 7.5 feet. 3 M.G. I.H.P. 330 = 11 kts.

Gunboats (*Kanonbaade*).

(*Employed on Special Service.*)

GULDBORGSUND (1884, re-built 1903). 270 tons. Complement, 46. 119 × 20 × 8.1 feet. Guns: 2—3 pdr., 4 M.G. H.P. 400 = 11.6 kts.

No photo available.

LILLE BELT (1875, re-built 1894). 250 tons. Complement, 30. 85.6 (*p.p.*) × 26.2 × 7.3 feet (*mean* draught). Guns: 2—3 pdr., 4 machine. H.P. 200 = 7.6 kts.

(*Training Ship for Engineers.*)

FALSTER (1873, re-built 1906). 380 tons. Complement, 50. 112.5 (*p.p.*) × 29 × 8.7 feet. Guns: 2—3 pdr., 4 machine. H.P. 500 = 9.8 kts.

Torpedo Transport (*Torpedo Transportbaad*).

SLEIPNER (——) 80 tons. 73 × 14.8 × 5.9 feet (*mean* draught). Guns: not known. I.H.P. 110 = kts.

Repair Ship (*Vaerkstedsskib*).

GRÖNSUND (1883, re-built 1905-6). Old gunboat of 260 tons. Complement, 49. 119 × 20 × 8.1 feet. Guns: 2 M.G. (B?)* H.P. 260 = 11.6 kts.

*Not certain if this ship has been re-built with Diesel engines, or not.

Surveying Ships (*Opmaalingsskibe*).

KRIEGER, MARSTRAND, 170 tons, **WILLIMOËS,** 160 tons. 114 × 17.5 × 6.4 feet (*mean* draught). All launched 1861. Complements, 28 to 39. I.H.P. 240 to 260 = 13 kts., now 11 kts. (*or less*). Guns: 2 machine.

(*Continued on next page.*)

2 c 2

DANISH MISCELLANEOUS.

Fishery Cruiser (*Fiskeriinspektionskib*).

ISLANDS FALK (1906). 760 tons. Complement. 52. 170·6 (*p.p.*) × 29·3 × 14·7 feet. Guns : 2—3 pdr. I.H.P. 1100 = 13 kts.

Coastguard Vessels (*Inspektionsskibe*).

BESKYTTEREN (1900). 447 tons. Comp. 36. 134 × 24·5 × 11·5 feet. Guns : 2 –3 pdr. I.H.P. 620 = 11 kts.

Coastguard Vessels—(*Continued*).

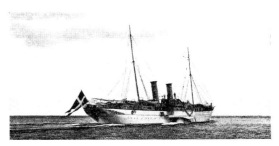

Photo, S. Anderson, Esq.

ABSALON (1877). 292 tons. Complement, 26. 125 (*p.p.*) × 20·1 × 8·8 feet. Guns : 2—3 pdr. H.P. 390 = 10 kts.

DIANA (Holland, 1916). 260 tons. 116·5 (*p.p.*) × 21·6 × 8·8 feet. Guns : 2—3 pdr. I.H.P. 400 = 10·5 kts. Complement, 27.

FENRIS (Holland, 1915). 190 tons. 86·4 (*p.p.*) × 20·7 × 9·2 feet. Guns : 2—3 pdr. I.H.P. 420 = 12 kts. Complement, 18.

SALTHOLM (Copenhagen, 1882). 300 tons. 135·6 (*p p.*) × 22·4 × 8·4 feet. Guns : 2—3 pdr. I.H.P. 380 = kts.

Training Ship for Boys (*Skoleskib*).

INGOLF (1876) 1000 tons. Complement, 125. 193·6 (*p.p.*) × 28 × 13·6 feet. Guns : 3 machine. I.H.P. 600 = 10·5 kts.

Cruiser **VALKYRIEN** (described on a previous page) is also used as a Training Ship for cadets, and gunboat **FALSTER** (*v.* preceding page) as a Training Ship for engineers. Cruiser **GEJSER** to replace *Ingolf* as Training Ship for boys. Also three Cutters, *Bacchus*, *Svanen* and *Thyra*.

Royal Yacht (*Dampskib til Hs. Majestæt Kongens Brug*).

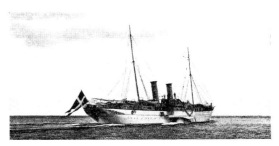

Photo, Ebessen, Aarhus.

DANNEBROG (1879). 1190 tons. 235 (*p.p.*) × 26·8 × 10·4 feet. Guns : 2 small. I.H.P. 940 = 13 kts.

Also *C. F. Grove*, *Kattegat*, *Nordsöen* and *Lerenörn*, all small unarmed vessels of 400-470 tons, used as Light and Beacon Inspection Ships, &c.

ESTHONIAN FLEET.

Compiled, 1919, from details supplied by courtesy of the Naval Staff, Reval.

Commander-in-chief of the Navy and Naval Defences : Captain Johann Pitka.

Mercantile Marine consists of (*a*) 80 steamers, total gross registered tonnage 30,000 tons ; and (*b*) Sailing ships 177, total gross registered tonnage 20,000 tons.

Coinage : Marks and pennies (Finnish system). Present rate of exchange, 45 marks = £1. (Normal rate of exchange, 25 marks = £1.)

Naval Officers and Men : 2,100.

	PALE BLUE.
	BLACK.
	WHITE.

NAVAL & MERCANTILE ENSIGN.

Note—The top bar of Ensign is *pale* blue.

RECOGNITION SILHOUETTES.

Scale : 1 inch = 160 feet.

LEMBIT (*Gunboat*).

WAMBOLA (*T.B.D.*)

LENNUK (*T.B.D.*)

Naval Base, Ports, Harbours, etc.

ROHUKULA (*Naval Base*). (About 3 miles to the S.W. of Hapsal.) Extended and built in 1914-16. Entrance to harbour, 18-20 feet. Depth in harbour, up to about 18 feet. Railway running on quays. Capable of accommodating at present 6 steamers, when completed and repaired, 15 to 20 steamers. Good anchorage in the roadstead. Warehouses, Ship Repairing Shops. Was partly destroyed by fire and bombardment when the Russian Army retired, but now being rebuilt and repaired by Esthonians.

REVAL. (A late Naval Base of the Russian Navy, dredged to take Dreadnoughts.)

A : HARBOUR. Depth at the entrance of the port, up to 35 feet. Depth in the port, 30 feet. There is room to berth in the harbour, under present conditions, 30 large steamers and 10 smaller steamers, besides sailing coasters. Good anchorage in the roads, no tides. The new modern mole in the place of the old wooden jetty, is in the course of completion, but owing to the disturbances which Esthonia has experienced, this work has been temporarily stopped. The Esthonian Government proposes to finish this work on the first possible opportunity, and contemplates making the Port of Reval a modern free port, with all the up-to-date appliances, to accommodate the enormous amount of shipping which will have to pass over Reval (being the nearest point to the Russian Moscow district and Siberia) will be used as a transit port for Russian trade. Large cold storage buildings are in the course of construction. Port of Reval has 8 large grain elevators with capacity for 750,000 poods (about 12,000 tons) and one small elevator. Also three floating cranes to lift from 40 to 60 tons, and one wooden crane. Besides this, 4 floating dry docks, capable of lifting 2,000, 1,250 and 3,000 tons are available. The cranes and floating docks belong to the Esthonian Government, while the elevator, to the town. *Navigation School*. Floating Ships' Repairing Workshops. Also Salvage Steamers belonging to the Esthonian Baltic Salvage Association. Three extensive Shipbuilding Yards (belonging to the Baltic Shipbuilding Co., Ltd., Bekker & Co., Ltd., and the Peter Wharf (late Noble & Lessner) at Telliskoppel). The Telliskoppel Bay being an excellent site for a harbour, the Esthonian Government has decided to build an extensive harbour there.

B : NEW HARBOUR or MINE HARBOUR (MIINI Sadam). This harbour, being situated a short distance from the Harbour of Reval (approximately one mile), is also under construction, and can already accommodate several small coasting vessels. There is a slipway here.

PERNAU. The normal depth on the bar and thence up to 2 miles above floating Bridge, owing to not being dredged during the War, is about 15 feet. This depth can easily be increased by dredging up to 20 feet, that is, level with the roadstead. Accommodation for 6 steamers in the harbour. Three berths, with electric cranes, at the Waldhof Works, situated on the left side of the river. There is also a private quay on the right side of the river.

BALTIC PORT. Depth at entrance to port, 16 to 20 feet. Depth in port, 16 to 20 feet. There is room for two steamers alongside the quay, but as many as four have been accommodated at one time. No tides. Difference in depth caused by the winds. The entrance to port is narrow and difficult. The best anchorage is under the Island of Rogor. *Navigation School*.

NARWA. Average depth on the bar : in spring, 12 feet ; in summer, 18-21 feet. Draft : for entering harbour, 18-21 feet ; for coming to the town, 9-10 feet. Length : of private quays, 2,850 feet ; of public quays, 1,600 feet ; of quays at the mouth of river, 1,100 feet. Anchorage in the roads outside the bar. Four Mooring Buoys. Esthonian Government proposes to improve the harbour arrangements in Narwa, especially for the timber trade, as much as possible. *Navigation School*.

(Continued on next page.)

ESTHONIAN NAVY—PORTS (continued).

HAPSAL. Depth at entrance to port (average), 10 feet. No docks. One wooden jetty, about 250 feet long, with the same depth alongside.

PORT LOKSA. Open coast port, protected by breakwater. Slipway capable of lifting 6–700 tons, also at the same time two or three 400 ton vessels. Depth at entrance, 20 feet. Inside breakwater, 17–18 feet. Alongside quay, 14 feet. Length of quayside, about 500 feet. Capable of accommodating 3 coasting steamers and at the same time small sailing craft. Good anchorage in the roads.

HEINAST (Hainasch). Port protected by breakwater. Draft, 14 feet. Railway. Open port all year round practically. Proposed to be extended to cope with future traffic of Esthonia. *Navigation School.*

KURESAAR (Arensburg). On Island Esel (Oesel). Draft, 12 feet. Quay about 1 mile long. Good anchorage on roads. Protected by Isle Abroka. About 1½ miles from town is a small harbour for small coasting vessels. This will be rebuilt and extended to accommodate larger ships. *Navigation School.*

KERDLA (Kertel). Draft, 12–14 feet. Situated on the Isle of Dago in Bay. Good natural harbour. Capable of accommodating alongside quay 2 or 3 coasting steamers.

PORT KUNDA. Natural harbour in Bay. Good anchorage. Depth, 10–30 feet. Alongside quay, up to 10 feet.

WIRTS (Werder). On the N.W. Coast of Isle Wirts (Schildau). Quay for coasting passenger steamers, also for small sailing craft.

KIHELKOND. Very good natural site for a Naval Base and Wireless Station. Open practically all year round. There is a small harbour for local vessels, also the harbour especially built by the Russians to accommodate torpedo boats.

SPITHAM. A harbour of refuge under construction.

KAESMU (Kaspepwik). Good anchorage. *Navigation School.*

ASSERIN. Quay for small coasting steamers and sailing vessels.

ESTHONIAN DESTROYERS. (*Miini istlejad.*)

1 *Isyaslav* type: **Lennuk** (ex-Russian *Avtroil*, launched by Reval S.B. Co., 1915, completed 1917). 1800 tons. Dimensions : 344½ × 31¼ × 9⅝ feet. Guns : 5—4 inch, 1—9 pdr. anti-aircraft, 2 machine. Torpedo tubes : 9 —18 inch, in 4 triple-deck mountings.* Also designed to carry and lay 80 mines. Designed S.H.P. 32,700 = 32 kts. A.E.G.-Curtis turbines. Oil fuel : 400 tons = 2400 miles at 15 kts. Complement, about 100-110. Captured (with *Wambola* from Bolshevists by British Light Cruisers and Destroyers in the Baltic, 1919, and transferred to Esthonian Navy.

* Tubes reported removed, October, 1919.

1 *Gavril* type : **Wambola** (ex-Bolshevist *Spartak*, ex-Kerensky *Mikula Maklej*, ex-Czarist *Kapitan 2r Kingsbergen*) Launched by Putilov Works, Petrograd, 1915 and completed 1918. 1585 tons. Dimensions : 314½ × 30½ × 9⅝ feet. Guns : 4—4 inch (1—2 pdr. anti-aircraft ? 2 M.G. ?) Torpedo tubes : 9—18 inch, in 3 triple-deck mountings. Also designed to carry and lay 80 mines. Designed S.H.P. 30,000 = 29 kts. A.E.G. Curtis turbines. Oil fuel : about 150 tons. Captured by British Light Cruisers and Destroyers in the Baltic, 1919 (with *Lennuk*) and transferred to Esthonian Navy.

Gunboats.

Note.—Mainmast has been removed.

LEMBIT (ex-German ————, ex Russian *Bobr*, 1907). 875 tons. Dimensions : 218¼ (*o.a.*) × 36 × 8 feet (*max.* draught). Guns : 2—4·7 inch, 4—11 pdr. Used to carry about 50-60 mines. I.H.P. 900 = 12 kts. (trials, 1029 = 11·5 kts.) Coal : 130 tons.

Note.—Above Gunboat was captured by Germans at Helsingfors in 1918 and served for a short time in German Navy.

LAINE (————). About 400 tons. Guns : 2—3 pdr. and some machine. Speed : 12 kts.

Mine Layers.

KALEW, OLEW (ex-Russian Motorships *No. 2* and *No. 8*). 50 tons *gross*. Guns : 1—3 pdr. Speed : 9 kts. Have motor engines.

Mine Sweepers.

| ALICE. | KAETHE. | All four are |
| EDITH. | UNA. | Converted Tugs. |

Also 10 small Mine Sweepers with motor engines.

Transport.

KALEWI POEG (ex-*Aleksei*). 800 tons *gross*. Gun : 1—3 pdr. Speed : 12 kts.

Ice Breaker.

HERCULES (————). 900 tons. Guns : 1—5·1 inch, 1—11 pdr. Speed : 12 kts.

Peipus Lake Flotilla.

Gunboats.

| TAARA. | UKU. |
| TARTU. | WANEMUINE. |

All above ships converted from Passenger Steamers during the War by the Russian Navy. Displacement : 100-200 tons. Speeds : 12·9 kts. Guns : *Taara*, 3—11 pdr. ; *Tartu*, 2—1 pdr. machine ; *Uku*, 1—11 pdr. ; *Wanemuine*, 2—11 pdr.

*Lake Peipus is referred to in Bolshevist Naval Staff reports as Lake Chudak, Tchudskoye, &c.

Transport (on Lake Peipus).

KAJAK (ex-*Severnaja Komuna*, ex-*Gagara*, captured from Bolshevists). 5,100 tons *d.w.c.* Speed : 9 kts.

Also various tugs, small launches and motor-engined craft ; some Lake Peipus.

FINNISH FLEET.

RECOGNITION SILHOUETTES.

Scale : 1 inch = 160 feet.

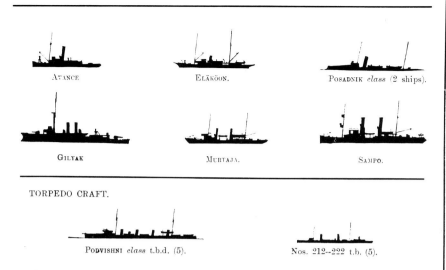

AVANCE   ELÄKÖÖN.   POSADNIK *class* (2 ships).

GILYAK   MURTAJA.   SAMPO.

TORPEDO CRAFT.

PODVISHNI *class* t.b.d. (5).   Nos. 212–222 t.b. (5).

Ports.—Abö, Hango, Helsingfors (last with dock 314 × 56 × 18½ feet).

5 Destroyers.

5 *Yarrow* type : **Podvishni, Poslushni, Prosorlivi** (Izhora Works, Petrograd, 1899–1900). **Ryezvi, Ryani** (Nevski Works, Petrograd, 1901). 220 tons. 190 × 18½ × 7½ feet. Guns : 2—11 pdr., 2 machine. Tubes : 1—15 inch. Carry 14 mines. I.H.P. 3800=27 kts. Boilers : 4 Yarrow. Coal : 60 tons. Complement, 52. Captured from Russia, 1918.

5 Torpedo Boats.

5 *Normand* type : **Nos. 212, 215, 216, 218, 222** (1902–4). 150 tons. 147½ × 16 × 4½ feet. Guns : 2—3 pdr., 1 M.G. Tubes : 2—15 inch in twin mounting. I.H.P. 3700=29 kts. Coal : 30 tons. Complement, 28. Captured from Russia, 1918. Fitted as Minesweepers.

FINNISH NAVY.

Gunboats.

Note:—Mainmast has been removed.

GILYAK (ex-Russian *Gilyak*, 1907). 875 tons. Dimensions : 218½ (*o.a.*) × 36 × 8 feet (*max.* draught). Guns : 2—4·7 inch, 4—11 pdr. Used to carry about 50-60 mines. I.H.P. 900=12 kts. Coal : 135 tons. Captured, 1918, from Russia.

POSADNIK (1892) and **VOEVODA** (1893), 400 tons. Armament : 2 or 3—11 pdr., 2 M.G. Designed H.P. 3500=21 kts. (about 17 now). Coal : 80 tons. Captured from Russia, 1918.

Ice Breakers.

SAMPO (Armstrong, Elswick, 1898). 1339 tons *gross*. Dimensions : 201·8 × 42·9 × 15 feet. *Nominal* H.P. 357=(10 ?) kts.

Ice Breakers (*continued*).

AVANCE (Howaldt, Kiel, 1899). 568 tons *gross*. Dimensions : 136 (*o.a.*) × 35·5 × 13½ feet. *Nominal* H.P. 239=(10 ?) kts.

MURTAJA (Stockholm, 1890). —— tons. Dimensions : 155·8 × 36 × 18 feet. I.H.P. 1126=(9 ?) kts.

Mine Sweepers.

During 1919, estimates were prepared for the construction of a Mine Sweeping Flotilla at a cost of £320,000. The Finnish Government has offered to buy three Swedish vessels, building in Finnish Yards, for use as Mine Sweepers.

Revenue and Coastguard Cruiser.

ELÄKÖÖN (Stockholm, 1886). —— tons. Dimensions ; 155 × 19½ × 9¼ feet. I.H.P. 670= kts. Guns : Used to have 1—14 pdr.

Service Unknown.

KARJALA (ordered by Russian Government, 1916, completed at Crichton's Yard, Abö, 1918, and taken over by Finnish Government). 350 tons. Speed, 14 kts.

Note.—The following Russian Fleet Auxiliaries were abandoned on the evacuation of Abö and Helsingfors, 1918. Not certain if they have been taken over for Finnish Navy :—*Lakhta, Merkuri, Mitava, Pallada, Tovarisch, Zhula* (all Hospital Ships); *Ilmen, Msta, Svir* (Minelayers) : *Zapal, Minrep* (Minesweepers) ; *Kobchik* (Patrol Boat).

Lake Ladoga Flotilla.

Various armed vessels are in service on Lake Ladoga, of which the Bolshevits claim to have sunk "one armed ship" by gunfire early in May, 1919. During July, 1918, small German Submarines appeared on Lake Ladoga, flying the Finnish flag. It is doubtful if these boats are now in service.

POLISH NAVY.

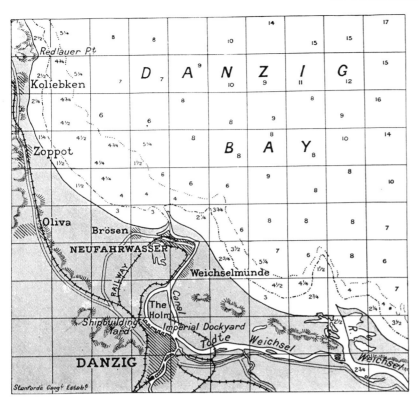

All details relate to status as German Naval Base.

GDANSK (DANZIG). Three small floating docks and three patent slips. Salvage dock, to raise 1200 tons. All for torpedo craft. One building slip (328 feet). Base and Training School for Seaplanes and Navy Airships, Kite Balloons, &c., at Putzig, near Danzig. Men employed: 4000 before war. Machinery: 13 of 1355 H.P., before war.

NEUFAHRWASSER (which was also a minor German Naval Station) and DANZIG, trade about 850,000 tons of shipping cleared annually—over a million tons or more now.

Admiralty Chart No. 3503

Shipyard.

(Late) SCHICHAU (DANZIG). Eight *Slips* (some 885 × 115 feet, three about 500 feet, two smaller). *Docks*: Four floating. *Employees*: About 5000. *Machinery*: About 2000 H.P.

At present the Polish Fleet is only a project, providing for an Establishment of

4 Armoured Cruisers,
12 Large Destroyers,

and a *personnel* of 3500 officers and men.

Personnel, in 1919, reported to be 1500 ex-officers and bluejackets from the late Austrian and Russian Navies.

Vistula Flotilla.

There is a heterogeneous flotilla on the Vistula, composed of armed steamers, launches, &c. No details are available of these craft.

NORWEGIAN FLEET.

(Revised, 1918, from information supplied by courtesy of H. E. the Minister of Defence.)

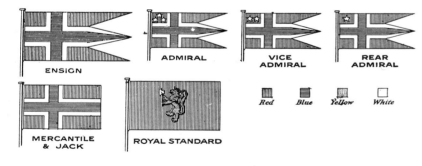

Arsenal.

HORTEN. One dry dock, 346 × 60 × 20½ feet.

Principal Private Yards.

FREDRIKSSTAD: Fredriksstad Mek. Verksted. Docks: 1 small floating.
KRISTIANIA: (*a*) Nylands Verksted. Docks: 1 floating (320 × 61 × 19 feet), 2 smaller floating.
　　　　　(*b*) Akers Mek. Verksted. Docks: 1 dry, 1 floating (both small).
SANDEFJORD: Framnes Mek. Verksted. Docks: 1 floating (360 × 65 × 21 feet), 2 smaller floating.
KRISTIANSAND: Kristiansands Mek. Vervsted. Docks: 1 dry, 330½ × $\frac{36}{52\frac{1}{4}}$ × 18 feet. 3 small slips.
BERGEN: (*a*) Laxevaags Dokkompagni. Docks: 1 dry, 365 × 68 × 18 feet.
　　　　(*b*) Bergens Mek. Verksted. Docks: 1 small dry.
　　　　(*c*) Bergens Dokkompagni. Docks: 1 small dry.
　　　　(*d*) Laxevaags Maskin-og Jernskibsbyggeri. Docks: *none*.
　　　　(*e*) Mjellem & Karlsen Mek. og Patentslipper. Two slips. Docks: *none*.
TRONDHJEM: Trondhjems Mek. Verksted. Docks: 2 small dry.
STAVANGER: Stavanger Stöberi og Dok. Docks: 2 small dry.
PORSGRUND. Porsgrund Mek. Verksted. One small floating dock. One slip.

Mercantile Marine.

—— steamers of 1,597,000 tons *gross*.
987 sailing of 556,057 tons *gross*.

Principal Trade Ports.

Kristiania, Bergen, Trondhjem.

Coinage.

Same as Swedish.

Modern Guns (Elswick).
(All details are *unofficial*)

Nota-tion.	Designation		Length in calibres	Model.	Weight of Gun.	Weight of A.P. shot.	Initial velocity	Max. penetration firing A capped at K.C.		Danger Space against average warship, at			Nom. Rounds per minute.
								5000 yards.	3000 yards.	10,000 yards.	5000 yards.	3000 yards.	
	c/m.	inches.			tons.	lbs.	ft. secs.						
B	20·9	8·2	45	...	18½	309	2300	6½	9¼	100	405	594	...
E	15	6	45	...	7	100	2625	3	4½	67	215	440	8
F	12	4·7	44	...	2¾	44	2570	...	...	...	...	...	10
F	10	4	...	...	...	...	...	...	...	...	...	...	...
F	7·6	3	40	...	⅜	12	2210	...	...	...	...	...	...

Minister of Defence.—C. T. Holtfodt.

Colour of Ships: Coast Defence Ships, Destroyers, Torpedo Boats, Gunboats, &c., all light grey.

INSIGNIA OF RANK ON SLEEVES.

| Admiral. | Vice-Am. | Kontre-Am. | Komman-dör. | Kommandör-Kaptein. | Kaptein. | Premier-Löitnant. | Sekond-Löitnant. |

British or U.S.A. 　,,　　*Vice-Ad.*　*Rear-Ad.*　*Commodore.*　*Captain.*　*Commander.*　*Lieutenant.*　*Sub-Lieut.*

In relative rank Engineers have the same *without curl.*
　,,　　,,　Doctors　,,　,,　,,　and a *red* passepoil above upper stripe.
　,,　　,,　Paymasters　,,　,,　,,　*blue* 　,,　,,　,,
General Notes.—*Personnel*: About 1400 permanent, 1000 yearly conscripts, all seafaring men in reserve.

NORWEGIAN RECOGNITION SILHOUETTES.

Scale : 1 inch = 160 feet.

ONE FUNNEL.

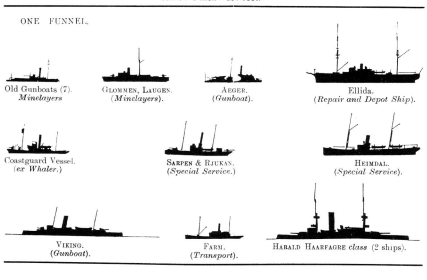

Old Gunboats (7). *Minelayers* — GLOMMEN, LAUGEN. *(Minelayers).* — AEGER. *(Gunboat).* — Ellida. *(Repair and Depot Ship).*

Coastguard Vessel. *(ex Whaler.)* — SARPEN & RJUKAN. *(Special Service.)* — HEIMDAL. *(Special Service).*

VIKING. *(Gunboat).* — FARM. *(Transport).* — HARALD HAARFAGRE *class* (2 ships).

TWO AND THREE FUNNELS.

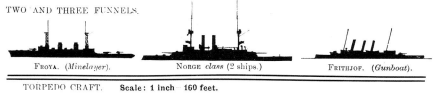

FROYA. *(Minelayer).* — NORGE *class* (2 ships). — FRITHJOF. *(Gunboat).*

TORPEDO CRAFT. **Scale : 1 inch = 160 feet.**

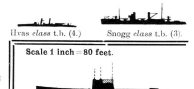

Myg t.b. — Delfin *class* t.b. (9.) — Orn *class* t.b. (5) — Hvas *class* t.b. (4.) — Snogg *class* t.b. (3.)

Scale 1 inch = 80 feet.

Valkyrjen. — Draug *class* t.b.d. (3.) — A 1 *(Submarine.)*

NORWEGIAN SHIPS.

NORWEGIAN COAST DEFENCE BATTLESHIPS. *(Panserskibe.)*

Photo, Wilse, Christiania.

NORGE (March, 1900), EIDSVOLD (June, 1900).

Displacement, 4166 tons. Complement, 270.

Length *(p.p.)*, 290 feet. Length *(over all)*, 301¼ feet. Beam, 50½ feet. *Max.* draught, 17¾ feet.

Guns :
2—8·2 inch, 45 cal. (A).
6—5·9 inch, 45 cal.
8—12 pdr.
6—3 pdr.
Torpedo tubes (18 inch) :
2 submerged.

Armour (Krupp) :
6″ Belt
2″ Deck slopes
8″ Turrets
6″ Bases
5″ Casemates (NC)
6″ Conning tower

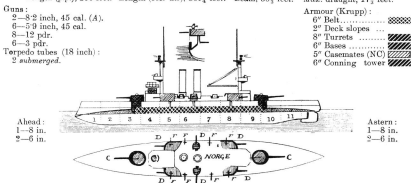

Ahead :
1—8 in.
2—6 in.

Astern :
1—8 in.
2—6 in.

Machinery : 2 screws. Boilers : 6 Yarrow. Designed H.P. 4500 = 16·5 kts. Coal : *normal* 440 tons ; *maximum* 550 tons.

Notes.—Built at Elswick. Completed 1900–1901. Machinery by Hawthorn, Leslie & Co. Excellent seaboats.

Coast Service Battleships *(Panserskibe).*

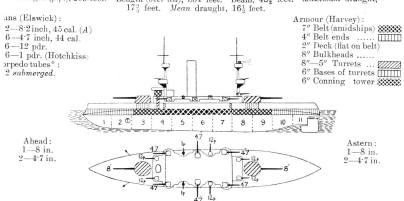

TORDENSKJOLD.   (Both exactly alike.)

HARALD HAARFAGRE (Jan. 1897), TORDENSKJOLD (March, 1897).

Displacement, 3858 tons. Complement, 249.

Length *(p.p.)*, 279 feet. Length *(over all)*, 204 feet. Beam, 48½ feet. *Maximum* draught, 17¾ feet. *Mean* draught, 16½ feet.

Guns (Elswick) :
2—8·2 inch, 45 cal. (A)
6—4·7 inch, 44 cal.
6—12 pdr.
6—1 pdr. (Hotchkiss)
Torpedo tubes* :
2 submerged.

Armour (Harvey) :
7″ Belt (amidships)
4″ Belt ends
2″ Deck (flat on belt)
8″ Bulkheads
8″—5″ Turrets
6″ Bases of turrets
6″ Conning tower

Ahead :
1—8 in.
2—4·7 in.

Astern :
1—8 in.
2—4·7 in.

Machinery : Boilers : 3 cylindrical. 2 screws. Designed H.P. 4500 = 16·9 kts. (made 17·2 on trial, 1897-8.) Coal : *normal* 400 tons ; *maximum* 540 tons.

Notes.—Built at Elswick, and completed 1897-8. Engines by Hawthorn, Leslie & Co. Belt is 174 feet long by 6½ feet deep. Excellent seaboats.

* Tubes are 18 inch in *H. Haafagre* and 17·7 inch in *Tordenskjold.*

---

4 Destroyers *(Torpedobaatsjagare).*

No.	Type	Date	Displacement tons	H.P.	Max. speed kts.	Coal or Oil tons	Complement	T. tubes	Max. draug't feet
3	*Draug*	'08-'14	540	7500	27	95 coal	71	3	9½
1	*Valkyrjen* (S)	1896	410	3300	23	90 coal	59	2	8½

(S) = Schichau.

* *Valkyrjen* is not officially listed with Destroyers, but separately as a " Torpedodivisionsbaat " or Torpedo Division Boat.

Garm (1913), **Draug** (1908), and **Troll** (1910). All built at Horten. 540 tons. Dimensions : 227 × 23½ × 8½ feet. Armament : 6—12 pdr., 3—18 in. tubes. H.P. 7500 (8000 in *Garm*) = 27 kts. Reciprocating engines in last two, turbines in *Garm*. Coal : 95 tons. Complement 71.

Photo, Wilse, Christiania.

1 *Schichau* type : **Valkyrjen** (1896). 410 tons. Dimensions : 150 × 24½ × 8½ feet. Complement 59. Guns : 4—12 pdr., 2 torpedo tubes (18 in.) 2 screws. Boilers : Thornycroft. Designed H.P. 3300 = 23 kts. Coal : 90 tons.

NORWEGIAN TORPEDO BOATS. *(Torpedobaater.)*

2nd Class Torpedo Boats.

GRIB, JO, LOM, ORN, RAVN, as above photo. *Photo, Wilse, Christiania.*
Appearance of KJELL, SKARV, TEIST, not known.

8 {
Kjell (1912), 94 tons; **Skarv, Teist** (1907-08). 92 tons. All 2—3 pdr. guns. Speed of all 3 boats, 25 kts. Complements, 18.
Grib, Jo, Lom (1906) and **Orn, Ravn** (1904). All 70 tons, and about 22—23 kts. Guns: 2—1 pdr., but *Lom* has 2—3 pdr. Complements, 16.
}

Note.—All above 8 boats have 2 tubes, viz., 1 bow and 1 deck.

"Large Torpedo Boats" *(Större Torpedobaater).*

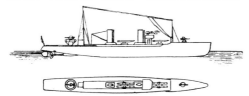

3 new boats: **Snögg, Stegg, Trygg** (1916-17). 220 tons. Dimensions: 173·9 × 18 × 5·2 feet. Guns: 2—12 pdr. Tubes: four (size not known). Designed H.P. 3500 = 25 kts. Fuel capacity: 30 tons coal *and* oil. Complement, 32.

1st Class Torpedo Boats.

Photo, Wilse, Christiania.

1 boats: **Hauk, Falk** (1903), 63 tons; **Hvas, Kjœk** (1900). 64 tons. All have 2—1 pdr. and 2 tubes (1 bow and 1 deck). First two 20 kts., others 19 kts. Complements, 14.

(Same appearance as above but shorter funnels).

8 boats: **Djerv, Dristig, Kvik** (1897-98). 67 tons. Guns: 2—1 pdr. **Blink, Glimt, Lyn** (1896). 45 tons. Guns: 2—1 pdr. **Raket, Varg** (1894). 45 tons. Guns: 1—1 pdr. All 19 kts. speed, and 2 tubes (1 bow, 1 deck). Complements: 14 for all, except last two with 12.

Appearance uncertain. Some may have two funnels abreast with mast between.

9 boats: **Laks, Sild, Sœi Skrei,** (1900). 90 tons and 21 kts. *Photo, Wilse, Christiania.*
Brand, Storm, Trods (1899). 20 kts. } 79 tons.
Delfin, Hval (1896). 19 kts. }
All armed with 2—1 pdr. guns and 2 tubes on deck. Complement, 19. Last two built by Schichau, Elbing.

Hai deleted by 1919.

7 {
Orm, Oter (1888). 41 tons.
Snar (1887), 39 tons; **Pil, Rask** (1886), 34 tons.
Springer, Od (1882-3). 36 tons.
}

Notes.—All 1—1 pdr. All have 2 tubes, except *Od*, with only one. All 19 kts., except *Springer* and *Od*, 18 kts. Complements: 12 for first two, and 11 for last five boats.

NORWEGIAN TORPEDO BOAT AND SUBMARINES.

3rd Class Torpedo Boat.

Myg (1899). Armed with 1—1 pdr. and 1 deck torpedo tube.

4 + ? Submarines *(Undervandsbaater).*

Note.—The only information officially published concerning Norwegian Submarines is: the *A* class, built between 1909 and 1914, and the *B* and *C* classes, not yet completed. No details are publicly communicated. The details given in following table and description of classes are *not* from any official data.

Submarines—*Continued.*

Building ?

2 *Type unknown*: B2, B1, assigned to Kaldnaes Yard, Tonsberg, for construction. No details known.

Note.—Four further boats of this class, B6, B5, B4, B3, reported to be projected. It is doubtful if any of these six boats have yet been begun.

No Photo available—generally similar to A1 below.

3 *Krupp-Germania* type: **A4-A2** (all 1913). Dimensions: 152½ × 16½ × 9½ feet. Surface engines: Krupp-Diesel. 3—18 inch tubes. 4 torpedoes carried.

Note:—*A5* of this class completing at Kiel, was appropriated by Germany on outbreak of war.

Building ?

2 *Holland* type: C2, C1, ordered from Electric Boat Co., U.S.A., about 1915. Dimensions: about 160 × 17 × 10 feet. Armament: 1—12 pdr., 1—18 inch tubes.

Note.—Doubtful if either of the above boats has ever been commenced. The contract may have been cancelled.

1 *Krupp-Germania* type: **A1** (ex-*Kobben*) (1909). 205 tons / 255 tons. Speed: 11·7 kts. / 9 kts. 3—18 inch tubes. 4 torpedoes carried. Körting paraffin engines. Dimensions: 129 × 12 × 9¼ feet.

NORWEGIAN MISCELLANEOUS.

Patrol Boats (*Patruljebaater*).

FIVE NEW BOATS (names or numbers not known, completed 1917). Are 39¼ feet long. 135 H.P. Van Blerck petrol engines = 17 kts. No other details known.

Note.—Above details are not from any official source.

Nos. **1** and **2** (1893). 25 tons. Guns : 2—1 pdr. Speed, 12 kts.

Monitors.

THOR, THRUDVANG, (Built 1869-72, and reconstructed 1895-97). 2000 to 1500 tons. Guns : 2—4·7, 40 cal., 2—9 pdr., 3 machine. Armour (iron) : 7″ belt, 14″ barbette (b), 1″ deck. H.P. 500 = 8 to 8½ kts. Deleted by 1919.

1st Class Gunboats (*Kanonbaater av I. Kl.*).

Photo, Wilse, Christiania.

FRITHJOF (1895). 1382 tons. Complement 166. Dimensions : 222⅔×32¾×13¼ feet. Guns : 2—4·7 inch, 4—12 pdr., 4 M.G. Tube (18 inch), 1 *sub.* (bow). Designed H.P. 2800 = 15 kts. Coal : 160 tons.

Photo, Wilse, Christiania.

VIKING (1891, rebuilt 1903). 1123 tons. Complement 153. Dimensions : 206×30½×12 feet. Armament : 1—4·7 inch forward, 1—5·9 inch aft., 4—12 pdr., 4 M.G. Torpedo tube (18 inch), 1 *sub.* (bow). Designed H.P. 2200 = 15 kts. Coal : 140 tons.

2nd Class Gunboat (*Kanonbaat av 2 Kl.*).

Photo, Wilse, Christiania.

AEGER (1893). 383 tons. Complement 43. Guns : 1—8·2 inch, 1—10 pdr., 2—4 pdr. H.P. 370 = 9·8 kts. Coal : 25 tons. *Max.* draught : 7¼ feet.

Gunboats.
(*Class not known.*)

SLEIPNER (1877). 581 tons. Guns : 1—6 inch, 2—12 pdr., 2—9 pdr., 2—1 pdr. H.P. 450 = 12 kts. Coal : 81 tons. *Max.* draught : 11 feet. Deleted by 1919.

ORKLA (1917), **RAUMA** (1917). 270 tons. Complement — Dimensions : 124·7×23×5·8 feet. Guns : 2—4·7 inch. Designed H.P. 360 = 10 kts. Oil : — tons.

Mine Layers (*Mineutlæggere*).

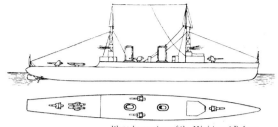

Plans by courtesy of the Ministry of Defence.

FRÖYA (1916). 755 tons. Complement, 79. Dimensions : 248·7 × 27×8·2 feet. Guns : 4—4 inch q.f. Designed H.P. 7000 = 22 kts. Coal : 95 tons, + 60 tons oil. Carries about 200 mines.

Plans by courtesy of the Ministry of Defence.

GLOMMEN (1917), **LAUGEN** (1917). Both built at Kaldnaes Yard, Tonsberg. 335 tons. Complement 35. Dimensions : 137·8 × 27·9 × 6·2 feet. Guns : 2—14 pdr. Designed H.P. 170 = 9·5 kts. Coal : 21 tons. Each carries about 50 mines.

Mine Layers—(*continued*).

VALE (as Minelayer) on right.   *Photo, S. Anderson, Esq.*

Name.	Date.	Tons.	Crew.	Guns.	Speed kts.
Tyr	1888	281	44	1—10·2 in., 1—6,+2—1 pdr.	10·5
Gor	1885	276	44	1—10·2 in. 3—1 pdr.	10·5
Vidar	1881	254	41	1—4·7 in. 3—1 pdr.	9·5
Brage	1876				8·5
Nor	1878	254	38	1—6 in. 3—1 pdr.	8·5
Vale	1878	233	41	1—4·7 in. 3—1 pdr.	8
Uller	1874				

(All fitted as Minelayers).

For Special Service.

Photo, Wilse, Christiania.

HEIMDAL (1892). 640 tons. Complement 62. Guns : 4—9 pdr., 2—1 pdr. H.P. 625 = 12 kts. Coal : 92 tons.

Photo, Wilse, Christiania.

SARPEN (1860), **RJUKAN** (1861). 187 tons. Complement : 48. Guns : 2—9 pdr., 2—1 pdr. H.P. 220 = 10 kts. Coal : 26 tons.

Coastguard Vessels.

Photo, S. Anderson, Esq.

—————— (name not known.) Is an armed whaler used for patrolling and watching Norwegian territorial waters, during the war.

Patrol Boat : *Morelos.*

Armed Auxiliaries : *Brim, Michael Sars, Ranen, Sivert Nielsen.*

Auxiliaries : *Harris, Sir Samuel Scott.*

Armed Trawlers : Three.

Fuel Ships.

—————— (name not known, launched 1916). Oil Tanker. No particulars available.

—————— and —————— (names not known, built 1911). Are Oil Tankers, each carrying 300 tons oil as cargo. Have internal-combustion motors. No other details known.

Transport (*Transportskib.*)

Photo, Wilse, Christiania.

FARM (1900). 300 tons. Complement : 32. Guns : 2—9 pdr., 2—1 pdr. Speed : 10 kts.

Workshop and Mother Ship.
(*Jerksteds-og-Moderskib.*)

Photo, S. Anderson, Esq.

ELLIDA (1880). 1,045 tons. Guns : 4—9 pdr., 2—1 pdr. Speed 10·5 kts.

(ROYAL) NETHERLANDS NAVY.

Revised from the 1919 Edition of the Official Year Book "Koninklijke Marine."

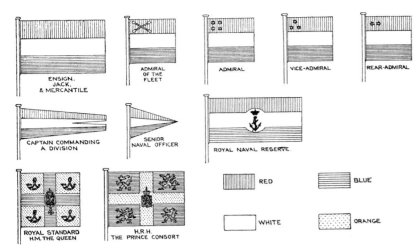

ENSIGN. JACK. & MERCANTILE.

ADMIRAL OF THE FLEET

ADMIRAL

VICE-ADMIRAL

REAR-ADMIRAL

CAPTAIN COMMANDING A DIVISION

SENIOR NAVAL OFFICER

ROYAL NAVAL RESERVE.

ROYAL STANDARD H.M. THE QUEEN

H.R.H. THE PRINCE CONSORT

RED — BLUE — WHITE — ORANGE

Netherlands Uniforms.

1	2	3	4	5	6	7	8	9
Admiraal	Luitenant-Admiraal	Vice-Admiraal	Schout-by-nacht	Kapitein ter Zee	Kapitein Luitenant ter Zee	Luitenant ter Zee 1e Kl.	Luitenant ter Zee 2e Kl.	Luitenant ter Zee 3e Kl.
Corresponding British or U.S. { Admiral of the Fleet	Admiral	Vice-Admiral	Rear-Admiral	Captain	Commander	Lieut. (over 11 years)	Lieut. (under 11 years)	Sub. Lieut.

In relative ranks—

Doctors have insignia 4 to 8 without the curl.
Paymasters „ 5 to 9 „ in silver.
Engineers „ 5 to 8 with the curl with blue velvet between stripes.

The broad stripes in ranks 1—4 are 2 inches wide (5 c/m); 5—8, ⅖ inch (1 c/m); No. 9, ⅕ inch. Distance between stripes is ⅕ inch (5 m/m).

Naval Construction.

None of the Royal Naval Yards in Holland appear to have built any warships for some years past. Warship construction is carried out by three firms : (1) Koninklijke Maatschaapij "de Schelde" (the Royal Company "de Schelde") at Flushing ; (2) Maatschaapij "Fijenoord" Rotterdam, and (3) Nederlandsche Scheepsbouw Maatschaapij, Amsterdam. All these firms built warships of all types, except the last named, which does not build submarines. Werf Gusto (A. F. Smulders), Schiedam, and the Conrad Co., Haarlem, have also built special Submarine Depot Ships for foreign Navies. In the Dutch East Indies, some small auxiliaries have been built at Surabaya, Batavia, &c.

Notes.

For Arsenals, Docks, Slips, &c., in Holland and Dutch East Indies, a revised and extended list is given on the next page but one.

All displacements are given in metric tons. Regarding the two sets of figures given for complements on later pages, (H) denotes complement when serving in home or European waters ; (A) denotes complement when serving in Dutch East Indies or abroad.

Personnel : About 11,000 all ranks, navy and marine infantry (enlisted men).
Mercantile Marine : —— steamers of 1,574,000 tons gross ; 468 sailing of 60,364 tons gross.
Principal Trade Ports : Rotterdam, Amsterdam, Flushing.
Coinage : Guilder (or florin) (100 cents) = 1s. 8d. British, or 40 cents U.S.A.
Oversea Possessions : Dutch East Indies (Sumatra, Java, Borneo, etc.) ; Dutch Guiana (Surinam) Curaçoa.
Minister of Marine :
Colour of Ships : Grey Ships serving in East Indies are white. Submarines have national colours (red, white, blue) painted in vertical stripes over bows.

Naval Guns (Krupp Models). All details unofficial.

Notation	Calibre.		Official Mark.	Long.	Weight of Gun.	Weight A. P. Shell.	Initial Velocity.	Max penetration with A. P. capped against K. C.		
	in.	c/m.		cals.	tons.	lbs.	ft. secs.	8000 in.	·5000 in.	3000 in.
A³	11	28	…	42½	31	595	2920	8	13	15½
A	9·4	24	"No. 2"	40	24½	375	2788	3½	7½	10¾
AA	9·4	24	"No. 1"	40	24½	375	2690	4	8½	10¾
E	8·2	21	"A"	35	16	308½	1740	—	—	3½
F	5·9	15	"No. 6"	50	5⅔	101½	3084	—	—	—
F	5·9	15	…	50	5½	101½	3084	—	—	—
F	5·9	15	"No. 5"	40	5	90⅓	2788	—	—	—
F	5·9	15	"No. 4"	40	4¾	90⅓	2444	—	—	—
F	5·9	15	"No. 2"	40	4¼	100	2231	—	—	—
F	4·7	12	{ "No. 2" { "No 1" }	40	2	52½	2231	—	—	—
F	4·1	10·5	"A"	50	…	40	2897	—	—	—

Velocities of 40-calibre guns are not service ones. In addition, there are 40 and 55 calibre (semi-automatic and anti-aircraft) models of 7·5 c/m. (3 inch, 13 pdr.) guns, a 9 pdr. (7·6 c/m.) Mark "A" mortar, a 5 c/m. 4 pdr., 3·7 c/m. 1 pdr., and various old types.

*"No. 3" model of the 5·9 inch/15 cm. is the same as the "No. 2" model.

Scale : 1 inch = 160 feet.   NETHERLANDS RECOGNITION SILHOUETTES.   (E. I. denotes ships now serving on Dutch East Indies Station.)

ONE FUNNEL.

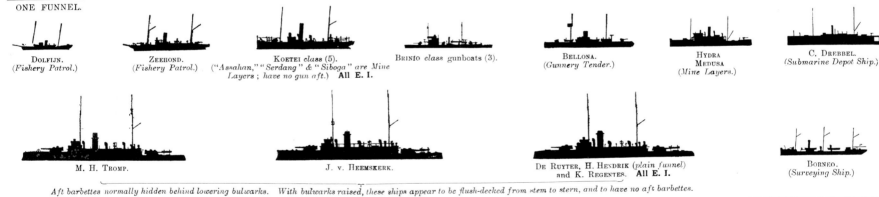

DOLFIJN. (Fishery Patrol.)

ZEEHOND. (Fishery Patrol.)

KOETEI class (5). ("Assahan," "Serdang" & "Siboga" are Mine Layers ; have no gun aft.) All E. I.

BRINIO class gunboats (3).

BELLONA. (Gunnery Tender.)

HYDRA MEDUSA. (Mine Layers.)

C. DREBBEL. (Submarine Depot Ship.)

M. H. TROMP.

J. V. HEEMSKERK.

DE RUYTER, H. HENDRIK (plain funnel) and K. REGENTES. All E. I.

BORNEO. (Surveying Ship.)

Aft barbettes normally hidden behind lowering bulwarks. With bulwarks raised, these ships appear to be flush-decked from stem to stern, and to have no aft barbettes.

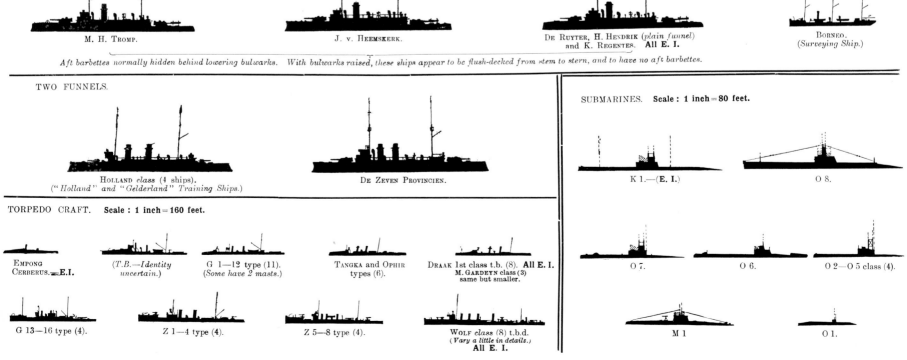

TWO FUNNELS.

HOLLAND class (4 ships). ("Holland" and "Gelderland" Training Ships.)

DE ZEVEN PROVINCIEN.

TORPEDO CRAFT. Scale : 1 inch = 160 feet.

EMPONG CERBERUS. E.I.

(T.B.—Identity uncertain.)

G 1—12 type (11). (Some have 2 masts.)

TANGKA and OPHIR types (6).

DRAAK 1st class t.b. (8). All E. I. M. GARDEYN class (3) same but smaller.

G 13—16 type (4).

Z 1—4 type (4).

Z 5—8 type (4).

WOLF class (8) t.b.d. (Vary a little in details.) All E. I.

SUBMARINES. Scale : 1 inch = 80 feet.

K 1.—(E. I.)

O 8.

O 7.

O 6.

O 2—O 5 class (4).

M 1.

O 1.

DOCKS.

Note.—All the following particulars have been communicated to "Fighting Ships" by courtesy of Koninklijke Nederlandsche Vereeniging, "Onze Vloot" (Royal Netherlands Association, "Our Fleet") during 1918.

Arsenals.

VILLEMSOORD (Nieuwediep).—No slips. Dry dock No. 1: $360\frac{3}{4} \times 68\frac{3}{4} \times 19\frac{1}{2}$ ft. No. 2: $262\frac{1}{4} \times 65\frac{1}{2} \times 15$ ft. Floating dock: $131\frac{1}{2} \times 23 \times 7\frac{3}{4}$ ft.

ELLEVOETSLUIS.—One slip. Dry dock No. 1: $239\frac{1}{2} \times 51\frac{3}{4} \times 14$ ft. No. 2: $231\frac{1}{2} \times 51\frac{3}{4} \times 7\frac{1}{2}$ ft.

Private Establishments.

MSTERDAM:—

Amsterdam Dry Dock Co.—Juliana-dock: Length, 615 ft.; breadth, $118\frac{1}{2}$ ft. For ships with a draught of 20 ft. Carrying capacity, 16,500 tons. Wilhelmina-dock: Length, $424\frac{1}{2}$ ft.; breadth, 96 ft. For ships with a draught of $18\frac{3}{4}$ ft. Carrying capacity, 7500 tons. Koninginne-dock: Length, 400 ft.; breadth, 92 ft. For ships with a draught of 17 ft. Carrying capacity, 4000 tons. Konings-dock: Length, 400 ft; breadth, 72 ft. For ships with a draught of 15 ft. Carrying capacity, 3000 tons.

Floating Dry Dock Co., Ltd.—No. 1: $213\frac{1}{4} \times 62\frac{1}{2} \times 20\frac{1}{2}$ ft. No. 2: $200 \times 62\frac{1}{2} \times 20\frac{1}{2}$ ft. No. 3: $164 \times 62\frac{1}{2} \times 18\frac{1}{4}$ ft.

IDDELBURG:—

The Royal Co.: "De Schelde" (Koninklijke Maatschaapij de Schelde).—Dry dock, $413\frac{1}{2} \times 65\frac{1}{2} \times 13$—15 feet.

TTERDAM:

Municipal Floating Docks.—No. 1: *Length, $157\frac{1}{2}$ ft.; breadth, 69 ft. Carrying capacity, 2000 tons. No. 2: Length, $295\frac{1}{2}$ ft.; breadth, 69 ft. Carrying capacity, 4000 tons. For ships with a draught of $18\frac{3}{4}$ ft. No. 3: Length, 361 ft.; breadth, 69 ft. Carrying capacity, 6000 tons. No. 4: Length, $567\frac{1}{2}$ ft.; breadth, 95 ft. Carrying capacity, 15,000 tons.

* Dock No. 1 can be coupled to dock No. 2.

Ships of $229\frac{1}{2}$ ft. length can be taken into dock No 1, ships of $377\frac{1}{4}$ ft. length into dock No. 2, ships of 459 ft. length into dock No. 3, and ships of 656 ft. length into dock No. 4.

ROTTERDAM (*continued*):—

Rotterdam Dry Dock Co.—Prins Hendrikdock No. 1: Length, $439\frac{3}{4}$ ft.; breadth, 95 ft. For ships with a draught of $19\frac{3}{4}$ ft. Carrying capacity, 7500 tons. Prins Hendrikdock No. 2: Length, 300 ft.; breadth, $70\frac{1}{2}$ ft. For ships with a draught of $18\frac{1}{4}$ ft. Carrying capacity, 3000 tons.

Shipbuilding Co.: "New Waterway."—Dock-harbour: $1312 \times 656 \times 29\frac{1}{2}$ ft. Slips—No 1: Length, $406\frac{1}{2}$ ft.; breadth, $19\frac{3}{4}$ ft. For ships up to 8000 tons. No 2: Length, 400 ft.; breadth, $19\frac{3}{4}$ ft. For ships up to 8000 tons. No. 3: Length, $406\frac{1}{2}$ ft.; breadth, 23 ft. For ships up to 12,000 tons. No. 4: Length, 400 ft.; breadth, 23 ft. For ships up to 12,000 tons. No. 5: Length, 886 ft.; breadth, $39\frac{1}{2}$ ft. For ships up to 18,000 tons.

Wilton's Engine Works & Shipbuilding Yard, Ltd.—Docks—No. 1: Length, $426\frac{1}{2}$ ft.: breadth, 70 ft. For ships up to a length of 492 ft. Carrying capacity, 8500 tons. No. 2: Length, $367\frac{1}{2}$ ft.; breadth, 58 ft. For ships up to a length of $426\frac{1}{2}$ ft. Carrying capacity, 4500 tons. Side slip: $347\frac{3}{4}$ ft. long, for ships to 3000 tons. Wilhelmina-dock: Length, 510 ft.; breadth, 81 ft. For ships up to a length of 574 ft. Carrying capacity, 14,000 tons.

VLISSINGEN (Flushing):—

The Royal Co.: "De Schelde" (K. M. de Schelde.)—Dry dock: $243 \times 52\frac{1}{2} \times 11$ ft.

DUTCH EAST INDIES.

Arsenals.

SOERABAIA or SURABAYA (Java).—Two floating docks: $328 \times 62 \times 22\frac{3}{4}$ ft. and $197 \times 59 \times 17\frac{1}{4}$ ft.

BATAVIA (Java).—Floating dock: $324 \times 67 \times 22$ ft.

SABANG (Sumatra).—Dry dock: $295\frac{1}{4} \times 78\frac{3}{4} \times 34\frac{1}{2}$ ft.

Private Establishments.

Floating dock: $460 \times 82 \times 24\frac{1}{2}$ ft. (property of the Netherlands Government) and another $320 \times 57\frac{1}{2}$ ft. (1400 tons).

NETHERLANDS BATTLESHIP (16 knot)—*Panterschip.*

Photo, Fotopersbureau "Holland," Amsterdam.

DE ZEVEN PROVINCIEN (March, 1909).

Displacement, 6530 tons. Complement, 447 (A), 407 (H).

Length (*o.a.*), 333 feet. Beam, 56·1 feet. *Maximum* draught, 20·2 feet.

Guns (Krupp):
2—11 inch, $42\frac{1}{2}$ cal. (A[3])
4—5·9 inch, 40 cal. "No. 5."
10—13 pdrs., 55 cal. S.A. "No. 1"
1—9 pdr. mortar.
4—1 pdr.
2 machine.
Torpedo tubes:
None.

Armour (Krupp):
6" Belt (amidships)
4" Belt (ends)
2" Deck (on slopes)
$9\frac{3}{4}$" Main Barbettes (N.C.)
$9\frac{3}{4}$" Shields
4" Small Barbettes
$9\frac{3}{4}$" Conning Tower (N.C.)

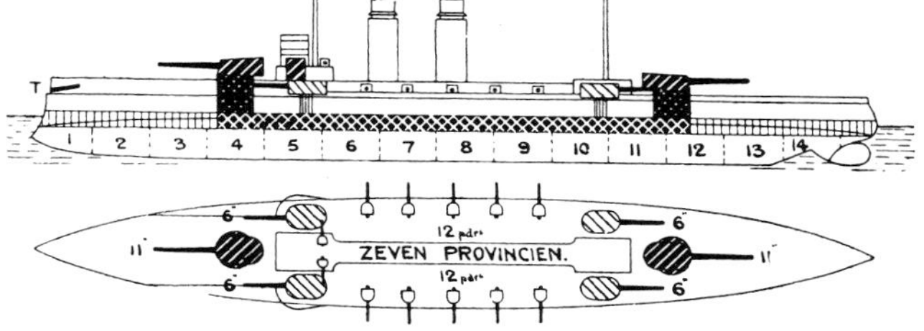

Machinery: 2 sets triple expansion. 2 screws. Boilers: 8 Yarrow. Designed H.P. 8000 = 16 kts. (Trials: 8516 = 16·3 kts.) Coal: *normal*, 700 tons; *maximum*, 1030 tons. Radius of action, 2100 miles at 15·3 kts.; 5100 miles at 8 kts.

Notes.—Main belt is 7 feet wide. Laid down Feb., 1908, at Amsterdam D.Y.

NETHERLANDS BATTLESHIPS (16 knot).—*Panterschepen.*

Note.—Aft barbette is hidden behind lowering bulwarks. *Photo, Fotopersbureau "Holland," Amsterdam.*

JACOB VAN HEEMSKERCK (September, 1906).

Displacement, 5000 tons. Complement, 351.

Length (*o.a.*), $321\frac{1}{2}$ feet. Beam, 49·9 feet; Beam outside sponsons 55·4 feet. *Max.* draught, $18\frac{3}{4}$ feet.

Guns (Krupp):
2—9·4 in., 45 cal. (*AA*). 'No. 2.'
6—5·9 in., 40 cal. 'No. 5.'
6—13 pdrs.
1—9 pdr. mortar.
4—1 pdr.
2 machine.
Torpedo tubes (18 inch):
1 *submerged* (bow).
1 *submerged* (stern).

Armour (Krupp):
6" Belt (amidships)
4" Belt (ends)
2" Deck (reinforcing belt)
$7\frac{3}{4}$" Main Barbettes
4" Hoods to these
6" Small Barbettes
8" Conning tower (K.C.)

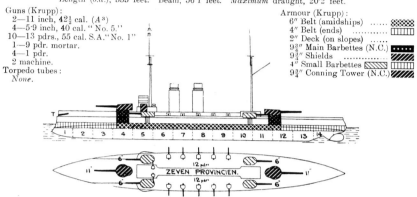

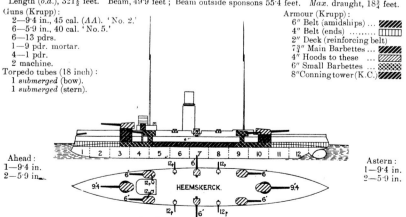

Ahead:
1—9·4 in.
2—5·9 in.

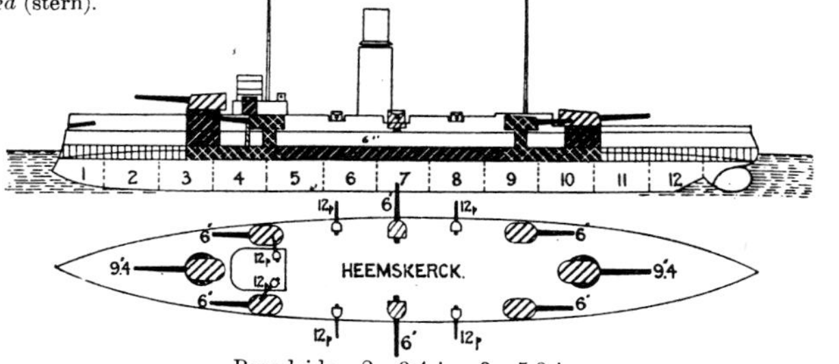

Astern:
1—9·4 in.
2—5·9 in.

Broadside: 2—9·4 in., 3—5·9 in.

Machinery: 2 sets triple expansion. 2 screws. Boilers: 6 Yarrow. Designed H.P. 6400 = 16·5 kts. Coal: *normal* — tons; *maximum* 610 tons.

Notes.—Main belt is 6 feet wide and about 220 feet long. Begun at Amsterdam D.Y., 1905, and completed, May, 1908. *Trials*: I.H.P. 6600 = 16·7 kts. Radius of action: 3300 miles at 10 kts

Note.—Aft barbette is hidden behind lowering bulwarks. *Photo, Geiser.*

MARTEN HARPERTZOON TROMP (1904).

Displacement, 5300 tons. Complement, 349 (H), 377 (A).

Length (*o.a.*), 330·7 feet. Beam, 49·8 feet. *Maximum* draught, 18·7 feet.

Guns—(M. '01):
2—9·4 inch, 40 cal. (*AA*). 'No. 2.'
4—5·9 inch, 40 cal. 'No. 5.'
8—13 pdr. "No. 3"
1—9 pdr. mortar
4—1 pdr.
2 machine.
Torpedo tubes (18 in.):
3 *above water.*

Armour (Krupp):
6" Belt (amidships)
4" Belt (ends)
2" Deck (reinforcing belt)
$7\frac{3}{4}$" Barbettes (N.C.)
4" Hoods to these
3" Small turrets
$7\frac{3}{4}$" Conning tower

Ahead:
1—9·4 in.
2—5·9 in.

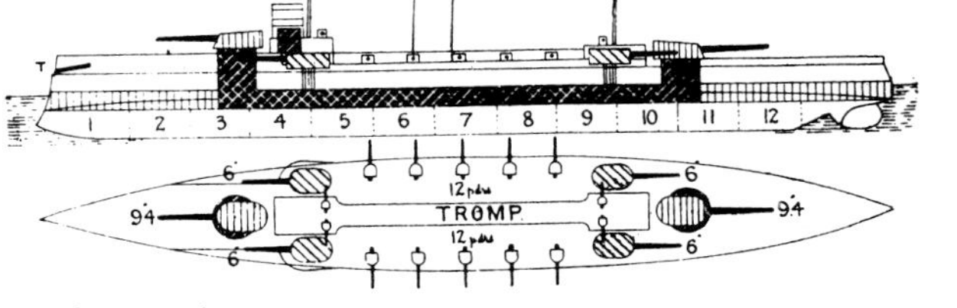

Astern:
1—9·4 in.
2—5·9 in.

Machinery: 2 sets triple expansion. 2 screws. Boilers: 6 Yarrow. Designed H.P. 6400 = 16 kts. Coal: *normal* 680 tons; *maximum* 830 tons. Radius of action: 1600 miles at $14\frac{1}{2}$ kts., 4100 miles at $9\frac{1}{4}$ kts. *Trials* ('06).—6,405 I.H.P. = 16·7 kts. Begun at Amsterdam D.Y., 1903, and completed 1906.

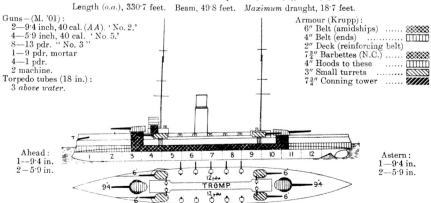

NETHERLANDS BATTLESHIPS. (16 knot).—*Panterschepen*.

All on East Indies Station.

KONINGIN REGENTES (1900), **DE RUYTER** (1901), & **HERTOG HENDRIK** (1902).

Length (o.a.), 316·9 feet. Beam, 49·8 feet. *Maximum draught,* 19 feet.

Displacement, 5080 tons. Complement, 375 (A), 342 (H).

Guns—(M. '99) :
2—9·4 inch, 40 cal. (A). 'No. 1.'
4—5·9 inch, 40 cal. 'No. 4.'*
8—13 pdr.†
1—9 pdr. mortar.
2—1 pdr.
2—1 pdr. (anti-aircraft).
2 machine.
Torpedo tubes (18 in.) :
2 *above water.*‡
1 *submerged* (bow).‡

Armour (Krupp) :
6″ Belt (amidships) ......
4″ Belt (ends)................
2″ Deck (reinforcing belt)
9¾″ Barbettes................
4″ Hoods to these ....
9¾″ Conning tower (fore)

Ahead :
1—9·4 in.
2—5·9 in.

Astern :
1—9·4 in.
2—5·9 in.

Broadside : 2—9·4 in., 2—5·9 in.

Gunnery Notes.— } * Number of 5·9 inch guns may be increased to *six*.
† Number of 13 pdrs. may be reduced to *four*.

‡ *Torpedo Notes.*—In H Hendrik all three tubes are *above water.*

Armour Notes.—The belt is 5¼ feet wide and four feet of it is below the waterline.

Machinery : 2 sets triple expansion. 2 screws. Boilers : 6 Yarrow. Designed H.P. 6300 (6400 in K. R.) = 16 kts. Coal : *normal* 680 tons ; *maximum* 830 tons. Same radius of action as *M. H. Tromp.* K. Regentes begun 1898 and H. Hendrik, 1900, both at Amsterdam D.Y. : De Ruyter begun 1900, by Fijenoord Co., Rotterdam.

DE RUYTER.   Photo, Fotopersbureau "Holland,"

Note.—H. Hendrik has plain funnel. In these ships after barbette may be hidden behind lowering bulwarks.

DUTCH BATTLESHIPS.

Photo, Spartiali.

EVERTSEN (1894), **PIET HEIN** (1894), **KORTENAAR** (1894).

Displacement 3520 tons. Complement 260.
Length, 284 feet. Beam 47 feet. *Maximum draught,* 19 feet.

Guns :
3—8·2 inch, 35 cal. (E).
2—6 inch.
6—12 pdr.
6—1 pdr.
Torpedo tubes :
2 *above water.*

Armour (Harvey) :
6″ Belt (amidships) c
4″ Belt (ends) ....d
2¼″ Deck (flat on belt)......
Protection to vitals ......=c
9½″ Barbette (1) ....a
6″ Hood to this..............c
6″—8″ Shield c
3″—6″ Sponsons ....e
9½″ Conning tower (fore) ...a

Ahead :
2—8·2 in.
2—6 in.

Astern :
1—8·2 in.
2—6 in.

Broadside : 3—8·2 in., 1—6 in.

Machinery : 2 sets triple expansion. 2 screws. Boilers : cylindrical. Designed I.H.P. *forced* 4800 = 16 kts. Coal : *normal,* 250 tons ; *maximum,* 330 tons.
Notes.—The belt is 5¾ feet wide.

Deleted by 1919.

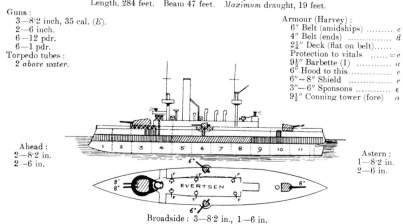

GELDERLAND (See next page.)   Photo, Fotopersbureau "Holland," Amsterdam.

NOORDBRABANT. (See next page.)   Photo, Fotopersbureau "Holland," Amsterdam.

NETHERLANDS NAVY.

Old Protected Cruisers. *(Pantserdekschepen.)*

For Illustrations, see preceding page.

Gelderland has top on foremast *low*. The upper portions of funnels have steam-pipes run inside and are slightly thicker than lower portions. Ventilators between funnels rather prominent.

Noordbrabant has top on foremost fairly high. Compare her funnels with those of *Gelderland*.

(HOLLAND CLASS.)

GELDERLAND (1898), & **NOORDBRABANT** (1899). Displacement 4030 tons. Complement 381 (A), 325 (H). Length, (o.a.) 310·7 feet. Beam, 48½ feet. *Maximum* draught, 17¾ feet.

also

HOLLAND (1896) & **ZEELAND** (1897). Displacement 3900 tons. Complement 381 (A), 325 (H). Length, (o.a.) 306·1 feet. Beam, 48½ feet. *Maximum* draught, 17¾ feet.

Armour (Harvey and steel): 2″ Deck (steel). 4″ Engine hatches, 6″ Gun shields, 4″ Conning tower.

Guns: Re-armed during 1914-15 as follows :—

Gelderland.	*Noordbrabant.*	*Holland.*	*Zeeland.*
4—5·9 inch "No. 3."	10—4·7 inch (viz.:	10—4·7 inch "No. 2."	2—5·9 inch "No. 2."
8—13 pdr. "No. 2."	2—4·7 inch	2—13 pdr. "No. 1."	8—4·7 inch "No. 1."
	"No. 3" + 8—4·7		2—13 pdr. "No. 1."
	inch "No. 2.")		
	2—13 pdr. "No. 1."		

and in all, 1—9 pdr. mortar 4—1 pdr., 2 machine. Torpedo tubes : 1 *submerged* in *Gelderland* and *Noordbrabant* only.

Machinery : 2 sets 3 cylinder triple expansion. 2 screws. Boilers : *Gelderland* class, 12 Yarrow ; *Holland* class, 8 Yarrow and 2 cylindrical. Designed H.P. (*n.d.*) 6400＝17 kts. in *Holland* ; 8400＝ 18·5 kts. in other three ships ; (*f.d.*) about 10,000＝20 kts. Coal : *normal* 470 tons, *maximum* 930 tons in *Gelderland* and *Noordbrabant* ; 1000 tons in *Holland* and *Zeeland*. Radius of action : 2100 miles at 16 kts., 4500 miles at 9·7 kts.

Name	Builder	Machinery	Laid down	Completed	First Trials :	Boilers	Best recent speed
Holland	Amsterdam	...	'95	'98	10,836＝19·75	Yarrow, + 2 cyl.	
Zeeland	Flushing	De Schelde	'95	'98	9818＝19·5		
Gelderland	Rotterdam	Fijenord	Feb.'97	'00	9867＝20	12 Yarrow	
Noordbrabant	Flushing	De Schelde	Mar.'97	'99	10,070＝20·1		

Notes.—*Holland* now serves as a Gunnery Training Ship, and *Gelderland* is employed as a Training Ship for Midshipmen and Cadets. *Zeeland* was to have proceeded to Dutch East Indies during the summer of 1919.

HERMELIJN.   *Photo, Fotopersbureau " Holland," Amsterdam.*
(ALL ON EAST INDIES STATION.)

8 *Yarrow* type: **Fret** (1910), **Wolf** (1910), **Jakhals** (1911), **Bulhond** (1911), **Hermelijn** (1913), **Lynx** (1913), all built by K. M. " de Schelde," Flushing, **Panter** (1913), **Vos** (1913), both built by Fijenoord Co., Rotterdam. 510 tons. Dimensions : 230 (o.a.)×22×6¾ feet *normal* draught, *max.* draught 9½ feet. Armament : 4—13 pdr. (55 cal., semi-auto.) "No. 2," 4 machine. 2—18 inch tubes. Designed H.P. 8000 to 8500＝30 kts, (30 to 30·3 on trials). 4 Yarrow boilers. Radius of action : 2360 miles at 8½ kts. Last four carry 12½ tons oil fuel.

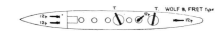

NETHERLANDS TORPEDO BOATS.

Photo wanted.

(Appearance much the same as *Z5—Z8* in preceding column but have only *two* funnels.)

4 *322 ton* boats, **Z 4—Z 1** (Ned. Scheepsb. Mij., Amsterdam, 1916-18.). 322 tons. Dimensions : 201×20¼×6 feet. Guns : 2—13 pdr., 2 machine. Torpedo ·tubes : 4—17·7 inch (one twin deck mounting+2 single ditto). Curtis type turbines. Boilers fitted to burn coal or oil. Carry 46 tons coal+7 tons oil. Radius of action : 425 miles at 20 kts.

Note.—The original boats, *Z 4—Z 1*, building by the German Vulkan Co. in 1914, were appropriated by the German Navy, and are now the German Destroyers *V108—105*. These four " replace " boats were begun by the Nederlandsche Scheepsbouw Maatschappij, Amsterdam, in 1914, but owing to lack of materials they were not finished until 1919, or *after* the *Z8—Z5* boats listed above.

Z 8.   *Photo, Fotopersbureau " Holland," Amsterdam.*

4 *310 ton* boats, **Z 8, Z 7** (K. M. de Schelde, Flushing, 1915), **Z6, Z5** (Fijenoord Co., Rotterdam, 1915). 310 tons. Dimensions : 193×19¾×5½ feet. Guns : 2—13 pdr., 2 machine. Torpedo tubes : 4—17·7 inch (one twin deck mounting+2 single ditto). Designed H.P. 5700 to 5500＝27 kts. (made about 27·4 on trials). Machinery : Reciprocating. Boilers fitted to burn coal or oil. Carry 45 tons coals+7 tons oil. Radius of action : 425 miles at 20 kts. Completed 1916.

G 13.   *Photo, Fotopersbureau, " Holland." Amsterdam.*

4 *180 ton* boats ('12-'14): **G16, G15** (Fijenoord Co., Rotterdam, 1914), **G14, G13** (K. M. de Schelde, Flushing, 1913). 180 tons. Dimensions : 162·4×17×4·6 feet. Armament : 2—13 pdr. "No.4," 3—17·7 inch deck tubes. Designed H.P. 2600＝25 kts. (26 kts. on trials.) Fuel : 44 tons. Boilers burn coal or oil fuel.

NETHERLANDS TORPEDO BOATS.—(Continued.)

G5 (2 masts).   Photo, Fotopersbureau "Holland" Amsterdam.
G6 (1 mast).

(IN EAST INDIES).

3 ('07-'09 boats) :—**G 9, 10 & 12.**
4 ('05-'08 boats) :—**G 8—5.**
4 ('03-'06 boats) :—**G 4—1.**
Armament : 2—4 pdr., 3—17·7 inch deck tubes (98·5 1 bow *submerged*, 2 deck tubes).
Radius : 1230 miles at 8 kts.

Note.—Names of **G8—G1** are *Cornelius Janssen de Haan*, (G 8,) *Jacob Cleydijck*, (G 7,) *Pieter Constant* (G 6), *Roemer Vlacq* (G 5), *Willem Willemsze* (G 4), *Meijndert Jentjes* (G 3), *Jan Danielzoon van de Rijn* (G 2), and *Johan van Brakel* (G 1). They still bear these names, G8—G1 only being their identification marks. G 11 mined and sunk off Vlieland, March, 1918. G 2 mined Feb., 1918 and salved in sections May be rebuilt.

Identity of above T.B. not exactly known, but she is believed to be one of the six boats given below, reconstructed at an unknown date.   Photo, Alfieri.

3 *Draak* class:—**Draak, Krokodil, Zeeslang.** (1906-7).
3 *Sphinx* class:—**Minotaurus, Python, Sphinx.** (1902-3).
2 *Hydra* class:—**Hydra, Scylla.** (1900).
Armament : 2—1 pdr., 3—17·7 inch deck tubes. (3 *Draak* Class ; 1 bow submerged, 1 deck tube).

(*Nominal* radius of all these class boats about 1500 at 8½ kts.)
Note.—All these 8 belong exclusively to the East Indies Marine.

1 *Empong* class: **Empong** (1888). 86 tons.
1 *Ardjoeno* class: **Cerberus** (1888), 84 tons*
Armament : 2—1 pdr., *Empong*, no tubes. 2—17·7 inch deck tubes
+ 1 *submerged* bow in *Cerberus*.
* *Cerberus* belongs to East Indies Marine.

7 *Empong* class: **Empong** (1889). **Foka, Goentor, Habang, Idjen, Ardjoeno, Cyclop.** 86 tons.
All but *Empong* and *Cerberus* deleted by 1919.

Also listed: Lamogan, Makjan, Nobo, Jacob Hobien, Jan Haringh, Jasper Lijnsen. All deleted by 1919.

These are just like *Draak* class but much smaller.

3 ('02-'04 boats) named :—**Tangka, Smeroe, Wajang.**
3 ('00-'02 boats) named :—**Ophir, Pangrango, Rindjani.**
Armament : 2—4 pdr., 3—17·7 inch deck tubes.
Radius : 1630 miles at 8 kts.

3 *M. Gardeyn* class : **Michel Gardeyn (K1), Christiaan Cornelis (K2), Willem Warmont (K3).**
Armament : 2—1 pdr., 2/1 M.G. Tubes removed. Radius : 5100 miles at 9 kts.

NETHERLANDS SUBMARINES (*Onderzeebooten*).

Tabulated Details.

Owing to shortage of materials caused by the war, the completion and commencement of many submarines has been (and will be) much delayed. The total number of completed boats is uncertain. About 10 or 11 boats are finished, or nearly ready ; 8 or 9 boats are building or not yet launched, and 6 or 9 are projected or ordered but not begun. The following details are not derived from any official source, but are based on very reliable details, specially furnished to "Fighting Ships."

All boats with letter *K* (*K 13* to *K 1*) are for Colonial Service in East Indies. (H) submarines are "Holland" type, and all boats of this design are built by the Koninklijke Maatschappij de Schelde, to plans by Electric Boat Co., U.S.A. (HD) submarines are of the Hay-Denny type, all now being built by the Maatschappij Fijenoord, Rotterdam, to plans by Marley F. Hay and Messrs. Denny & Co., Dumbarton. (HW) submarines are of the Hay-Whitehead type, built by the K. M. de Schelde, to plans by Marley F. Hay, and Messrs. Whitehead & Co., Fiume, Austria ; no further boats of this type are now being built.

(*Projected*.)

O 14, O 13 and O 12
K 13, K 12 and K 11
Types not yet settled.
Provided for by 1918 Naval Programme. Will have 20·8 inch torpedo tubes.

Note.—According to the 1918 edition of an enemy Naval Annual, 3 further Colonial submarines, provided for by the 1917 Naval Programme, were begun by an American private company, but the U.S. Government stopped their construction.

Building or Projected.

3 boats,' *type unknown* : O 11, O 10 and O 9, provided for by 1917 Naval Programme. No details known.

O 8.   Photo, Fotopersbureau "Holland."

1 *Holland* type : **O8** (ex-British submarine *H 6*), built by Canadian Vickers Co., Montreal, 1915, wrecked on Schiermonnikoog Island, Jan., 1916, salved Feb., 1916, interned at Nieuwediep, and subsequently purchased by Dutch Government. Displacements : 441 tons on *surface*, about 510 tons *submerged*. Dimensions : 150½ × 15¾ × 12¼ feet. Armament : 4—17·7 inch torpedo tubes. Machinery : 2 sets 6 cyl. Niseco Diesel engines = 12 kts. on *surface*. Max. *submerged* speed 10 kts. Endurance : 1350 miles at 12 kts. on *surface* (16 tons oil carried).

Building.

3 *Holland* type : **K 10, K 9** and *K 8*, building by K. M. de Schelde. No details known, but are practically the same as *K 4* and *K 3*, described below. Provided for by the 1916 Naval Programme.

Completing or building.

2 *Holland* type : **K 4** and **K 3** (K. M. de Schelde, Flushing). Displacement : about 550 tons on *surface*, 825-836 tons *submerged*. Dimensions : 211½ × 18¼ × 11¾ feet. Armament : 1 gun (calibre unknown, but probably a 13 pdr.) and 6—17·7 inch torpedo tubes. Have Diesel engines. *K 4* was to have been completed in 1918 and *K3* by the end of 1917, but both have been greatly delayed owing to shortage of building materials.

M 1. Appearance generally as above.   Photo, Alfieri.

1 ———type : **M 1** (ex-German mine-laying submarine *UC 8*, Vulkan, Hamburg, 1915, stranded on Terschelling Island, Nov., 1915, salved, interned and purchased by Dutch Government, 1917). Displacements : 180 tons *surface*, 191 tons *submerged*. Dimensions : 111½ × 10½ × 9 feet. Guns : 1 machine. No torpedo tubes but carries 12 mines in 6 mine-laying tubes before conning tower. Machinery : 1—4 cyl. oil engine = 6 kts. (7·5 kts. for short periods with electric motors), on *surface* ; max. *submerged* speed : 5 kts. (1 hour). Endurance : 900 miles at 4 kts. on *surface* ; 50 miles at 2½ kts. *submerged*.

NETHERLANDS SUBMARINES.—*Continued.*

Building or Completing.

4 *Hay-Denny* type: *K 7, K 6, K 5* (*building*) and **K 2** (launched 1917.) All by M. Fijenoord, Rotterdam. Displacements: 550 tons *on surface*, 800 tons *submerged*. Dimensions: $177 \times 16\frac{1}{4} \times$ feet. Armament: 1—13 pdr. (anti-aircraft) and 6—17·7 inch torpedo tubes, of which two are *broadside* tubes. Machinery: 2 sets, 8-cyl. Diesel engines = 16 kts. *on surface*. *Max. submerged* speed $8\frac{1}{2}$ kts. Endurance: 3500 miles (*normal*), 5500 miles (*extreme*), at 11 kts. *on surface*; 3 hours continuous running at $8\frac{1}{2}$ kts. *submerged*.

K 7, K 6, and *K 5* are an improved *K 2* type.

Photo, Fotopersbureau "Holland."

1 *Hay-Denny* type: **O 7** (M. Fijenoord, Rotterdam, 1916). Displacements: 176 tons *on surface*, 230 tons *submerged*. Dimensions: $105 \times 12 \times 9\frac{1}{4}$ feet. 3—17·7 inch torpedo tubes (2 bow, 1 stern). Machinery: 1 set 6-cyl. Diesel engines = $11\frac{1}{2}$ kts. *on surface*. *Max. submerged* speed $8\frac{1}{2}$ kts. Endurance: 750 miles at 10 kts. *on surface*; 3 hours continuous running *submerged* at $8\frac{1}{2}$ kts.

Photo, Fotopersbureau "Holland."

1 *Holland* type: **O 6** (K. M. de Schelde, Flushing, 1916). Displacements: about 170 tons *on surface*; 208 tons *submerged*. Dimensions: $112\frac{1}{4} \times 12 \times 9\frac{1}{4}$ feet. 3—17·7 inch torpedc tubes. 1 set of 6-cyl. Diesel engines = 11·5 kts. *on surface*; max. *submerged* speed, $8\frac{1}{2}$ kts.

(On East Indies Station.) *Photo by courtesy of Marley F. Hay, Esq.*

1 *Hay-Whitehead* type: **K 1** (K. M. de Schelde, Flushing, 1913). Displacements: 330 tons *on surface*, 390 tons *submerged*. Dimensions: $148·3 \times 14·2 \times 9\frac{2}{3}$ feet. 3—17·7 inch torpedo tubes (2 bow, 1 stern). Machinery: 2 sets 8-cyl. Diesel engines = 17 kts. *on surface*. *Max. submerged* speed 9 kts. Endurance: 1700 miles (*normal*), 2250 miles *extreme*), at 11 kts. *on surface*; $3\frac{3}{4}$ hours continuous running at 8·9 kts. *submerged*.

4 *Hay-Whitehead* type: Nos. **O 2** (1911), **O 3** (1912), **O 4** and **O 5** both 1913.) All built by K. M. de Schelde, Flushing, Displacements: 133 tons *on surface*, 150 tons *submerged*. Dimensions: $98·4 \times 9\frac{1}{4} \times 9$ feet. Armament: 2—17·7 inch tubes (a spare torpedo carried for each). Machinery: 1 set 6-cyl. Diesel engines = 11 kts. *on surface*. *Max. submerged* speed $8\frac{2}{3}$ kts. Endurance: 760 miles at 10 kts. *on surface*; 3 hours continuous running at $8\frac{2}{3}$ kts. *submerged*.

No Photo available of "O 1"—see Silhouettes.

1 *Holland* type: **O 1** (ex *Luctor et Emergo*, K. M. de Schelde, Flushing, 1905). Dimensions: $67 \times 13\frac{1}{2} \times 9\frac{1}{4}$ feet. 1—17·7 inch bow torpedo tube. Designed speed was 9 kts. *on surface* and 7 kts. *submerged*, but on trials she only made 7·2 kts. *on surface* and 5·5 kts. *submerged*. Is of little practical worth now.

NETHERLANDS "ARMOURED" GUNBOATS. (*Pantersbooten.*)

(All these photographs by Fotopersbureau "Holland," Amsterdam.)

BRINIO. Ventilators used as stanchions to forebridge. After bridge stands *abaft* mainmast. Small uncapped funnel.

FRISO. Thin and tall funnel.

GRUNO. Capped funnel and ensign gaff to mainmast.

BRINIO (1912), **FRISO** (1912), **GRUNO** (1913). All built by Amsterdam D.Y. 540 tons. Complement 52. Dimensions: 172·2 (*o.a.*) × 27·9 × 9·1 feet *max.* draught. Armament: 4—4·1 inch semi-automatic, 2 machine. Armour: 2″ Belt, $\frac{2}{3}$″ Deck, 2″ Conning tower. Machinery: 2 sets of Diesel engines (Kromhout, M.A.N., or Werkspoor types). B.H.P. 1200 = 14 kts. Oil, 25 tons.

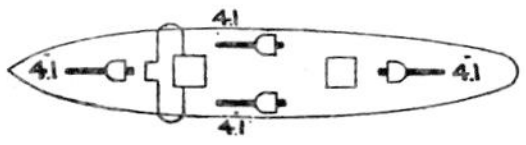

Gunboats (*Kanonerbooten*).

REINIER-CLAESZEN (1891). 2490 tons. Complement, 160. Dimensions: $229\frac{1}{2} \times 44\frac{1}{4} \times 14\frac{1}{2}$ feet (*mean*). Armament: 1—old 8·2 inch, 35 cal.; 1—6·7 inch, 35 cal.; 4—6 pdr.; 3—1 pdr.; 2—14 inch tubes (*above water*). Armour (compound): $4\frac{3}{4}$″—4″ Belt, 3″ Deck, 11″ Bow turret, 11″ Conning tower. H.P. 2000 = 12·5 kts. Coal: *maximum* 160 tons.

Deleted by 1919.

(All on East Indies Station.)

ASSAHAN* (1900), **KOETEI** (1898), **SIBOGA*** (1898), **SERDANG*** (1897), **MATARAM** (1896). **EDI** (1896). About 810 tons *average*. Armament: 2—4.1 inch (in *,ataram* and *Koetei* only) 1—4.1 inch in others, 1—9 pdr. mortar, 4—1 pdr. H.P. 1350—1400 = 13 kts. Coal: 130—150 tons. Complement, 55. *Max* draught, 12 ft.

***Note.**—*Assahan*, *Serdang* and *Siboga* are mine-layers. Other two ships officially rated as "Flottielje-vaartuigen" or "Flotilla Vessels."

Edi deleted by 1919.

BRAGA, HEFRING, NJORD, THOR, TYR, WODAN. Are old iron twin-screw Gunboats, built 1876-79. 280 tons (*Hefring* and *Njord* = 270 tons). Complements, 34–30. Dimensions: 91·5 to 91·8 (*o.a.*) × 26·9 × 7·8 to 8·1 feet (*max.* draught). Guns: In *Braga*, *Hefring*, *Wodan*, 1—4·7 inch "No. 3" or "No 1," 2—1 pdr., 1 machine; in *Njord* and *Tyr*, 1—5·9 inch "No. 2," 3—1 pdr.; in *Thor*, 1—13 pdr. "No. 1," 3—1 pdr, 1 M,G., but is to be re-armed as *Njord* and *Tyr*. H.P. 100 to 170 = $7\frac{1}{2}$ to $8\frac{1}{3}$ kts. Coal: 30 tons.

Mine Layers (*Minjenleggers*).

TWO NEW MINE LAYERS; first begun under 1917 Naval Programme and the second begun under 1918 Naval Programme. Both laid down by Werf Gusto, Schiedam, 1918. 748 tons. Dimensions: 179·8 × 28·5 × 10·4 feet. Guns: 3—13 pdr. semi-auto. "No. 3." Twin screws. No other details known.

Will be of the same type as *Hydra* and *Medusa* (see next page), but will be faster and carry more mines.

(Mine Layers continued on next page).

NETHERLANDS MISCELLANEOUS.

Mine Layers—*continued.*

Photo, Fotopersbureau " Holland."

HYDRA (1911) & **MEDUSA** (1911). Both built at Amsterdam D.Y. 670 tons. Complement 60. Dimensions : 163×29·5×9 feet. Guns : 3—13 pdr. S.A. " No. 2 " 1—1 pdr., 1 M.G. Designed H.P. 800= 11·5 kts. Coal : 72 tons. Radius of action : 1440 miles at 6 kts. Each carries double laying gears for 80 mines.
Note.—There is also a T.B. named *Hydra*, but she is on the East Indies Station.

Photo wanted.

TRITON (N. Shields, 1906). Ex-trawler of 277 tons. Complement 34. 120·5×21·5×11·6 feet. Guns : 2—1 pdr., 1 M.G. Coal : 120 tons. Double mine-laying gear.

Photo wanted.

VULCANUS (Grimsby, 1902). Ex-steam trawler, 410 tons. Complement, 34. 123·7×21·6×10·5 feet. Guns : 2—1 pdr., 1 M.G. Double laying gear for mines.

Surveying Ships (*Opnemingsvaartuigen*).

NEW SURVEYING SHIP, building, under 1915 Naval Programme, to replace old *Raaf* and *Geep.*

Building or completing.

ELLERTS DE HAAN, building by Fijenoord Co., at Rotterdam, to replace old gunboats *Raaf* and *Gup.* No details known.

(On East Indies Station.)
TYDEMAN (1916). No details known.

HYDROGRAAF (1911). 300 tons. Draught 6¼ feet. Speed, 9 kts.

(In East Indies.)
VAN DOORN (1901) **VAN GOGH** (1898). Composite and zinced. 700 tons. Complements, 57 (A), 26 (H). H.P. 390 to 370=10 to 9 kts. Coal : 100—110 tons.

BORNEO (Clydebank, 1892). Composite and coppered. 800 tons. Complement, 57 (A), 26 (H). Speed : 13¼ kts. Coal : 160 tons.

NETHERLANDS MISCELLANEOUS.

Mine Layers—*Continued.*

BALDER (1878), **VIDAR** and **HADDA** (1879), ex-gunboats of 270 tons. Complement 36. Carry 19 mines each (double mine-laying gear). Guns : 2—4 pdr. (semi-auto.) in *Balder* and *Hadda*, 2—1 pdr. in *Vidar.* ; 1 M.G. in all three. Speed : 7 kts. Coal : 30 tons.

DAS (1873), **HAVIK** (1875). Ex-gunboats of 210 tons. Guns : 2—1 pdr., 1 M.G. Speeds : About 6½—7 kts. Complement, 32.
Notes.—For *Serdang* and *Siboga,* gunboats used as mine layers in East Indies, see first column on preceding page.

Mine Sweepers. (*Mijnenvegers.*)

I (v.d. Kuyck en van Ree, Rotterdam), II (Koopman, Dordrecht), III, IV (v.d. Schuigt, Papendrecht). Completed and taken over in 1918. —— tons. Steel. Dimensions : (I) 92·5×20·6× feet ; (II) 100·7×20·5× feet ; (III & IV) 90·2×20× feet. Guns : 1 machine. Complement, 16. No more details available.

Surveying Ships.—*continued.*

No photo.

" Sumbawa." (*In East Indies.*)

LOMBOK, SUMBAWA (1891). 600 tons. Complement, 57 (A), 26 (H). Speed : 12½ kts Coal : 90—120 tons.
Old Gunboats *Raaf* (1889) and *Geep* (1875) are employed as Surveying Ships in the East Indies, but are to be replaced by new Surveying Ship, *Ellerts de Haan,* as noted in preceding column. Both 200 tons and 7 kts. speed.

Gunnery Tender.

BELLONA (1892). Gunnery tender. 930 tons. For Training duty. carries 1—4·7 inch, 4—13 pdr., 2—4 pdr., 8—1 pdr., 2 M.G., of various models. Speed : 8 kts.

Fishery Patrols.

(Mainmast now removed.)
ZEEHOND (1892). 720 tons. Complement, 72. Armament : 2— 1 pdr. Speed : 11 kts. Coal : 78 tons.

Submarine Depot Ships (*Depotschepen*).

Photo, Fotopersbureau, " Holland."

CORNELIS DREBBEL (1915). 800 tons. Guns : 1—1 pdr. Complement 73. Has Diesel engines.

VALI (1878). 840 tons. Guns : 1—1 pdr. Speed : 9 kts.

Fuel Ship. (*Brandstvfvoorraadschip.*)

ULFR. No details known.

Fishery Patrols—*continued.*

DOLFIJN (1889). 290 tons. Complement, 42. Armament : 2— 1 pdr. Speed : 10·7 kts. Coal : 29 tons.

Miscellaneous.

About 20 obsolete old vessels, used as harbour training ships, store hulks, barracks, transports, &c. All are practically worthless for military purposes.

Dutch East Indies Marine.

Consists of the 4 gunboats of *Assahan* class, 8 torpedo boats of the *Draak* class (and old torpedo boat *Cerberus*), surveying ships, *van Doorn, van Gogh, Borneo, Lombok* and *Sumbawa.*
All these ships described on this and preceding pages.

Miscellaneous Vessels belonging to the East Indies Government.

No photographs are available of any of the following ships. It is not definitely known which are armed and which are not.

DENEB (1914), **BELLATRIX** (1913), **CANOPUS** (1913), **ALDEBAREN** (1912), **ALBATROS** (1910), **ZWALUW** (1910), **SPEURDER** (1908).

KWARTEL (1901). Old Gunboat. 355 tons. May have 4—6 pdr. and 4—1 pdr. guns. Armour : 1″ deck. H.P. 550=12 kts. Coal : 23 tons.

SPITS (1899), **TELEGRAAF** (1899), **BRAK** (1898), **DOG** (1898) **HAZENWIND** (1898), **EDI** (1896), **NIAS** (1894), **ARGUS** (1892), **CYCLOOP** (1892).

GLATIK (1894), **FLAMINGO** (1891), **PELIKAAN** (1891), **ZWAAN** (1891). All old Gunboats. 400 tons. Guns : probably a few 13 and 1 pdr. H.P. 480=11·3 kts. Coal : 45 tons.

ZEEDUIF (1890). Old Gunboat. 420 tons. Guns : may have 2— 13 pdr. and 2—4 or 1 pdr. Speed : 10½ kts. Coal : 40 tons.

REIGER (1887). Old composite-built Gunboat. 390 tons. Guns : may have 2—13 pdr. and 2 machine. Speed : 10 kts. Coal : 43 tons.

CERAM (1886), **JAVA** (1885), **WACHTER** (——).

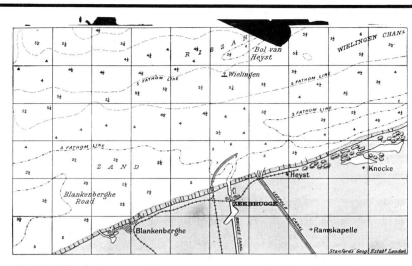

ZEEBRUGGE.—Small port on Belgian coast, occupied and fortified by Germany during the war. Connected to Bruges by canal (6¼ miles) 230 feet wide at water level, 72¼ feet wide at bottom × 26¼ feet deep. 515¼ feet of quayage. Lock 840 feet between gates × 65⅔ feet at entrance × 18 feet depth at low tides. Oil tanks situated in Inner Port. Mole 1970 yards long, where the Germans established batteries and depôts for torpedo craft, submarines, and seaplanes. Coast was heavily fortified by Germans, batteries including naval guns of 15 inch calibre and downwards, the largest guns ranging up to 25,000 yards. Port works, &c., wrecked by Germans on evacuation. Small wet dock at Blankenberghe (14 feet depth of water). Admiralty Chart No. 120.

OSTEND. Is connected by canal with Bruges. During German occupation coast was heavily fortified. Bomb proof Submarine shelters, also slips for building and repairing small submarines, repair workshops, &c. German Destroyer and Submarine basin lay between the Old and New Bassins de Chasse. Old Bassin de Chasse said to be partly filled in by Germans for use as an Aerodrome. One or two floating docks existed to take 1 large T.B.D. or two small Submarines, and perhaps one or two small graving docks were built. All port works &c. were wrecked by the Germans on evacuation. The Tirpitz battery at Hamilton Farm, near Mariakerke consisted of 4—11·2 inch guns and could range up to 30,000 yards *extreme*.

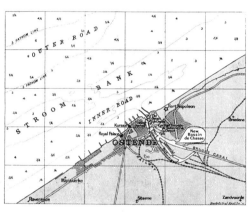

Flags.

Uniforms.

Minister of Defence:

Personnel: officers and men, active list. officers and men, reserve list.

Mercantile Marine: steamers of tons gross, tons gross, also about trawlers and fishing craft. sailing vessels of

Colonies:

Coinage: ≈ s. d. British currency.

BELGIAN NAVY.

Following Ports within Belgium are connected with sea :—

ANTWERP. Eight Dry Docks. Municipal: No. 1, 506 × 81¼ × 23 feet ; No. 2, 248 × 39¼ × 14 feet ; Nos. 4, 5, & 6, 440½ × 49¼ × 16 feet. J. Cockerill : 400 × 41 × 17½ feet. Also 2 others 330 × 42 × 14 and 300 × 36 × 13 feet. About 12 wet docks, coaling basin, and 11 quays, all well equipped, with fixed and moveable cranes, and lit by arc lamps.

BRUGES. Connected to Ostend and Zeebrugge by canals. 5 wet docks. Was extensively used by Germans as a naval base during the war. Various bomb-proof shelters for Submarines were built here.

GHENT. Two dry docks, No. 1, 446 × 42⅔ × 18 feet. No. 2, 255 × 36 × 15 feet. 7 wet docks. Carels Works located here.

Shipbuilders.

Messrs. JOHN COCKERILL & CO., Hoboken, near Antwerp. Works looted or destroyed by Germans.

3 Torpedo Boats.

3 boats : **A1** (ex-German A14), **A2** (ex-German A12) and **A3** (ex-German A4) Built 1915. Displace about 80 tons. Dimensions 140 × 19½ × 8 feet. Guns : 1—4 pdr. (aft.), 1 M.G. Torpedo tubes : 1 or 2 deck 17·7 inch. Speed about 15 knots. Complement about 30.

Note : Above three boats abandoned by Germans on evacuation of Flanders and captured. A fourth Torpedo boat of above type salved and used as Patrol and Police Boat by Port Authorities at Antwerp.

RECOGNITION SILHOUETTES : TORPEDO BOATS.

Scale : 1 inch 160 = feet.

A1—A3.

Belgian Congo.

(On Lake Tanganyika).

NETTA (launched December, 1915). Torpedo Boat. No details known.

(Both on Lake Kivu).

PAUL RENKIN, Gunboat, launched during the War. No details available.

One Motor Patrol Boat (name unknown), launched during the War. No details known.

(ROYAL) SPANISH NAVY.

(Corrected, 1919, from the "Lista Official de los Buques de Guerra y de los Mercantes," issued by the Ministry of Marine. Illustrations and other information furnished by the courtesy of Alferez de Nairo M. Mille).

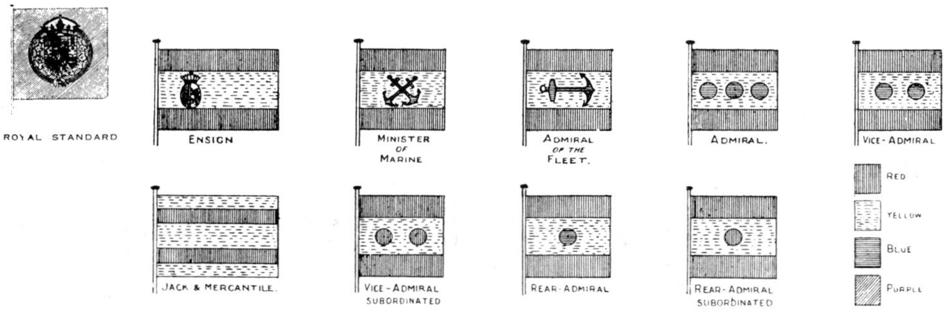

ROYAL STANDARD
ENSIGN
MINISTER OF MARINE
ADMIRAL OF THE FLEET.
ADMIRAL.
VICE-ADMIRAL
JACK & MERCANTILE.
VICE-ADMIRAL SUBORDINATED
REAR-ADMIRAL
REAR-ADMIRAL SUBORDINATED
RED
YELLOW
BLUE
PURPLE

Uniform Insignia.

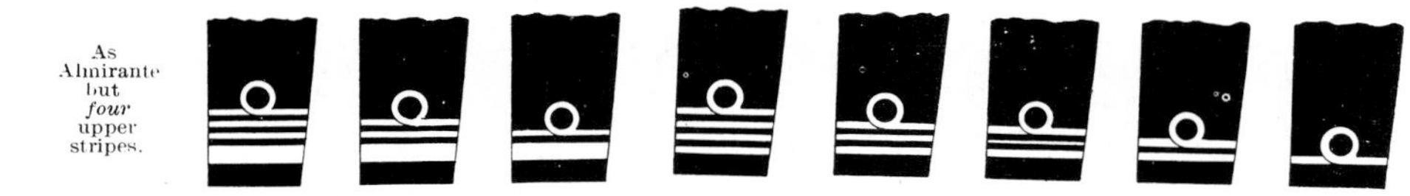

As Almirante but *four* upper stripes.

Capitan-General de la Armada. *Admiral of the Fleet* | Almirante. *Admiral.* | Vice-Almirante. *Vice-Admiral* | Contra Almirante. *Rear-Admiral.* | Capitan de Navio. *Captain.* | Capitán de Fragata. *Commander* | Capitán de Corbeta. *Lieutenant-Commander.* | Teniente de Navio. *Lieutenant.* | Alferez de Navio. *Sub-Lieutenant.*

Other branches, *without the curl*, have distinguishing colours as follows:—

Engineers ...	*green.*	Astronomical ...	*green brown.*
Constructors ...	*blue.*	Pharmaciens ...	*yellow.*
Doctors ...	*red.*	Chaplains ...	*violet.*
Paymasters ...	*white.*		

Personnel: about 11,000 officers and men, 5000 marines—16000 in all. *Minister of Marine*: Admiral Lobaton (May, 1919).

Colour of Ships: Light grey.

General.

Naval School is at Cadiz on land. At Ferrol, the old frigate *Villa de Bilbao* (1843, 1313 tons, is a school for quartermasters, (*Escuela de Marineria*): also corvette, *Nautilus* (*Escuela de cabos de mar*), built 1868. 1700 tons. Guns: 1—6 inch, 6—5 pdr. Complement 221. The battleship *Pelayo* is training ship for gunnery, and cruisers *Reina Regente* and *Carlos V* are training ships for midshipmen and cadets. *Carlos V* is Flagship of the Training Squadron.

(*All details unofficial*).

Principal Naval Guns in Service.

Notation.	Nominal Calibre.		Model.	Length in calibres	Weight of Gun.	Weight of A.P. shell.	Initial velocity	*Max.* penetration A.P. capped direct impact at K.C. at		Danger Space against average ship, at			Rounds per minute.
								5000 yards.	3000 yards.	10,000 yards.	5000 yards.	3000 yards.	
	c/m.	inches.			tons.	lbs.	ft. secs.	inches.	inches.				
*A*5	30·5	12	V'09	50	66	850	3010	17	20	...	...	...	2
AA	*32*	12·5	...	35	47½	1036	2034	8	11	...	...	...	...
B	*28*	11	...	35	32½	837	2034	5½	8	...	...	...	...
AA	*28*	10·8	...	40	30	507	2625	8½	11¾	110	420	720	0·5
A	*24*	9·4	...	40	17	318	2625	7¼	9½	110	350	620	1
D	*24*	9·4	...	35	21	439	2034	4	6¼	60	250	500	0·5
D	*15*	6	V.	50	7¾	100	3100	...	8¾	...	...	...	10
F	*15*	5·9	...	45	4½	88	2625	...	3	25	200	430	5–6

V = Vickers.

Naval Yards, &c.

FERROL. Dry docks. (1) "Victoria Eugenia," 573 × 82 × 37 feet (completed 1913), (2) "San Julian," 437½ × 72¼ × 29 feet. Ferrol is the big shipyard. It has a large coal depôt, good bay, well fortified.

CARTAGENA. One dry dock, 492 × 82 × 31½ feet. One floating, 6000 tons. Cruisers, gunboats and torpedo craft building yard. Very strongly fortified.

LA CARRACA (CADIZ). Dry docks. (1) 238½ × 55½ × 23¼ feet, (2) 328 × 70½ × 23½ feet, (3) 192½ × 57 × 18½ feet, (4) 925 × 85 × 34 feet (in two lengths). No slips. Only used as base for Morocco coast gun boats. S.E.C.N. ordnance and munitions factory located here.

MAHON. Very small yard.

Private Establishments.

Warship building is carried out in the Naval Yards by the "Sociedad Española de Construcion Naval," (S. E. C. N.), an Anglo-Spanish shipbuilding syndicate in which the British firms of Sir W. G. Armstrong-Whitworth, Ltd., Vickers, Ltd., and John Brown & Co. have a large interest. In carrying out Naval Programmes these three firms supply materials, ordnance, armour, etc., and skilled supervision of work. The S. E. C. N. has built large Ordnance factories for the production of guns, gun-mountings, shells, &c., at the Arsenal of La Carraca (Cadiz), and in Reinosa. S.E.C.N. Shipbuilding Yards have been created at Ferrol, Cartagena, Matagorda, and Sestao (Bilbao). A new yard at Cadiz is projected by the Asociacion Hispano-Britanica.

Private Docks.

BARCELONA (Los Astilleros de Euskalduna) Floating dock, 367 × 68 × 20 feet.
CADIZ. Compania Trans-Atlantica dock, 512 × 64 × 23 feet.
BILBAO. Compania Euskalduna dock, 605 × 60 × 25 feet. Two smaller.
SANTANDER. Gamazo dock, 445 × 57 × 23½ feet.
GIJON. Cifuentes Co. dock, 288 × 46 × 12 feet.

Mercantile Marine: —— steamers of 709,000 tons *gross*; 270 sailing vessels of 35,942 tons *gross*. About 400,000 tons is said to be building.

Coinage: Peseta (100 centimes) = 9½d. Ps. 29 = £1.

Colonial Possessions, &c.: Rio de Oro, Adrar, Rio Muni (or Spanish Guinea), Annobon, Fernando Po, Corisco Islands, Great and Little Elobey; all on Atlantic Coast of Africa. Canary Islands (Atlantic), *Ceuta (Straits of Gibraltar), and Spanish Morocco. There is a Protectorate in the north and west of Morocco, with controlled Ports at Ceuta, Melilla, Alhucemas, Gomera, and Chafarina.

* Administered as a province.

Scale: 1 inch = 160 inch.

SPANISH RECOGNITION SILHOUETTES. (*Re-arranged 1919*).

ONE FUNNEL.

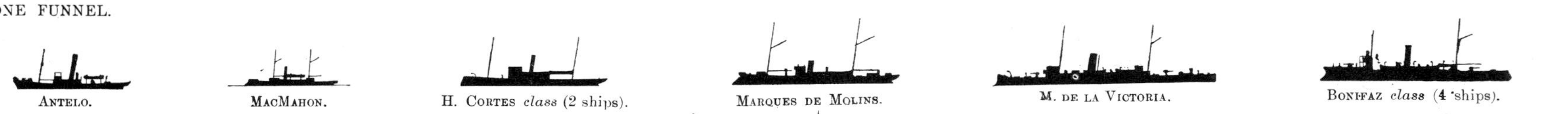

ANTELO. MACMAHON. H. CORTES *class* (2 ships). MARQUES DE MOLINS. M. DE LA VICTORIA. BONIFAZ *class* (4 ships).

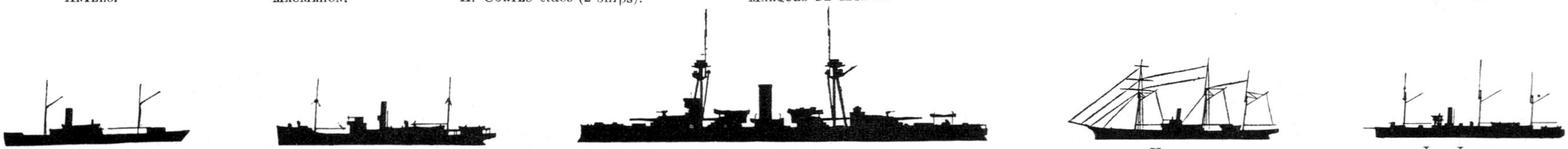

DELFIN *class* (3 ships). ALMIRANTE LOBO. *Now has W/T top gallant masts.* ESPANA *class* (3 ships). URANIA (*Surveying Ship*). INF. ISABEL.

TWO FUNNELS.

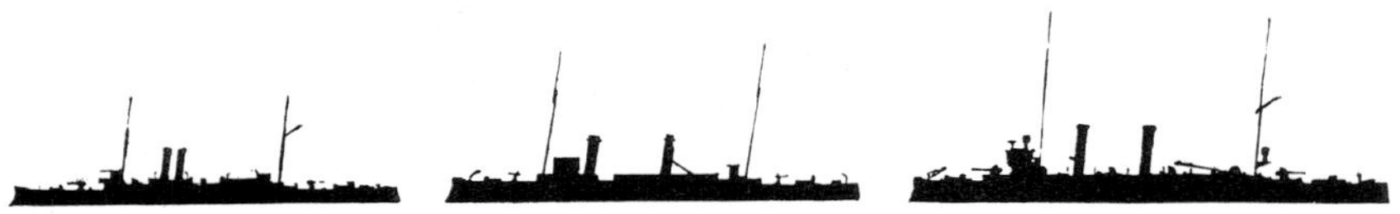

D. M. DE MOLINA. D. A. DE BAZAN. EXTREMADURA.

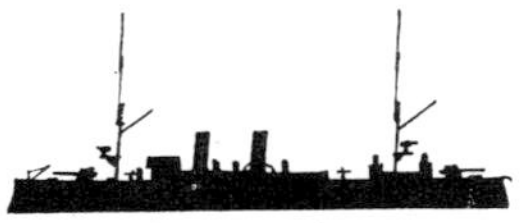

RIO DE LA PLATA (*Mine Layer*).

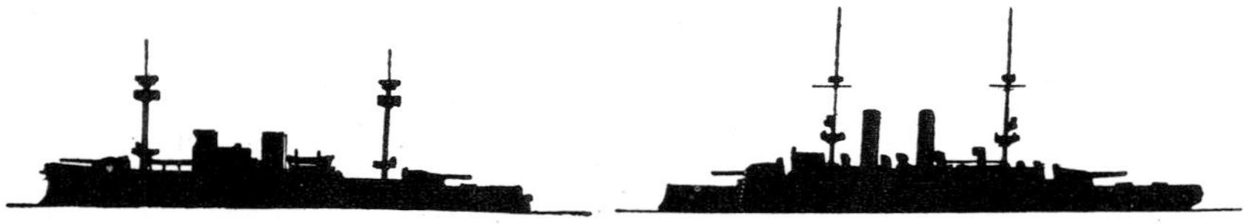

PELAYO (*Training Ship*). CATALUNA *class* (2 ships).

THREE FUNNELS.

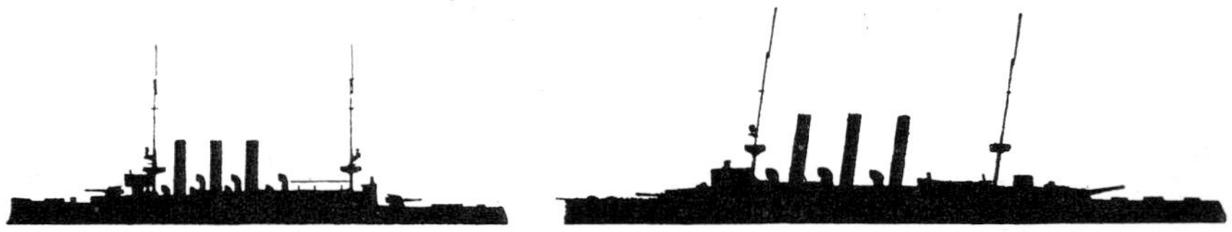

REINA REGENTE. (*Training Ship*). CARLOS V. (*Flagship, Training Squadron*).

TORPEDO CRAFT. **Scale: 1 inch = 160 feet.**

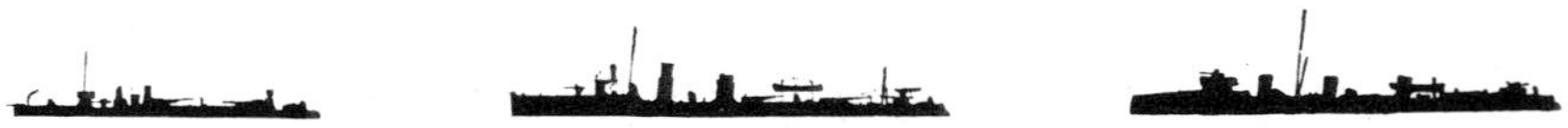

No. 1—24 (t.b.) (*Some have no tubes.*) Bustamante *class* t.b.d. (3) AUDAZ *class* (4). "*Terror*" *has mainmast.* (*Mine Layers*).

SUBMARINES. **Scale: 1 inch = 30 feet.**

"A" OR MONTURIOL *class* (3). (*Have 1—3 pdr. gun.*) ISAAC PERAL. (*Has a 3 inch gun just before C.T.*)

1909 SPANISH DREADNOUGHTS (19·5 kts.) No. **3, 2, 1.** (*Acorazados*).

ESPAÑA (Feb., 1912), **ALFONSO TRECE** (May, 1913), & **JAIME PRIMERO** (Sept., 1914).

Normal displacement, 15,452 tons. Complement, 735.

Length (*waterline*), 435 feet. Beam, 78¾ feet. *Max.* draught, 25½ feet. Length (*over all*), 459⅙ feet.

Guns (Vickers) :
8—12 inch, 50 cal. (A⁶).
20—4 inch. 50 cal.
2—3 pdr.
2 Maxims.
(2 landing).
Torpedo tubes :
none.

Armour (Krupp) :
8″ Belt (amidships) ......
3″ Belt (bow) ....
4″ Belt (aft) ....
1½″ Deck ....
6″ Lower deck side ......
8″ Turrets (N.C.) ......
10″ Turret bases (N.C.) ...
3″ Battery (N.C.) ......
10″ Conning tower ....
6″ After C.T. (Hadfield)

Ahead :
6—12 in.
4—4 in.

ESPANA.

Astern :
6—12 in.
4—4 in.

Broadside : 8—12 in., 10—4 in.

Machinery : Parsons turbine. 4 screws. Boilers : 12 Yarrow. Designed H.P. 15,500 = 19·5 kts. Coal : *normal* 900 tons ; *maximum* 1850 tons + 20 tons oil fuel = nominal radius of 5000 miles at 10 kts.. and 3100 miles at 16¾ kts.

Gunnery Notes.—12 inch manœuvred by hydraulic power ; all-round loading at any angle of elevation. Magazine capacity is 80 rounds per 12 inch gun, but there is ample storage for more than this. Arcs of fire : end, 12 inch. *about* 270° ; echelon, 12 inch. 180° own beam (*nominal*) and about 80° far beam. Heights of guns over normal waterline : 12 inch, 24½ feet ; 4 inch, 13½ feet. Total weight *about* 2550 tons. (These notes are not from any official source).

Armour Notes.—Main belt is 6 feet 7 inches deep, 4 feet 7 inches of this being below waterline and 2 feet above. On plans 8 inch belt amidships should extend to bases of end barbettes. Hull without armour = 5600 tons.

Machinery Notes.—Engines = 1320 tons.

Torpedo Notes.—Bullivant net defence. No torpedo tubes installed.

Name	Builder	Machinery	Laid down	Completed	Trials (Full Power)	Boilers	Best recent speed
España			Dec. '09	1914	21,582 = 20·2		
Alfonso XIII	Ferrol Yard	S.E.C.N.	Feb. '10	1915	= 20·36	Yarrow in all.	
Jaime I			Feb. '12	1919⁶			

⁶ By April, 1919, only 5—12 inch guns had not been delivered for *Jaime I*. She was still short of various other special fittings, but was otherwise complete.

ESPAÑA.

Photo (1919), A. de N. M. Mille.

ALFONSO XIII.

Photo (1919), A. de N. M. Mille.

SPANISH NAVY.

2nd Class Battleship.

(*Acorazado de 2ᵃ Clas.*)

(*Gunnery Training Ship.*)

Photo (1918), Casau, Cartagena.

PELAYO (1887) (1897) (1910).

Length (*o.a.*) 341⅚ feet. Beam, 65¼ feet. *Maximum* draught, 25⁵⁄₁₂ feet.
Displacement, 9733 tons. Complement, 621.

Guns :
2—12·6 inch, 35 cal.
2—11 inch, 35 cal.
9—5·5 inch, 35 cal.
12—6 pdr.
9 or 5—1 pdr.
2 landing.
Torpedo tubes :
removed.

Armour (steel) :
16″ Belt (amidships) ...
12″ Belt (ends) ....
3½″ Deck (flat below belt).
16″ Barbettes............
2″ Hoods to these ......
3″ Battery (Harvey)...

PELAYO.

Machinery : 2 sets vertical compound. 2 screws. Boilers : 16 Niclausse (in 4 groups). Designed H.P. 6800 = 15 kts. Coal : *normal* 500 tons ; *maximum* 676 tons. Built at La Seyne. Reconstructed there in 1897. Was partially rebuilt in 1910.

(1st Class Cruisers.)

Cruçeros de 1ᵃ Clas.

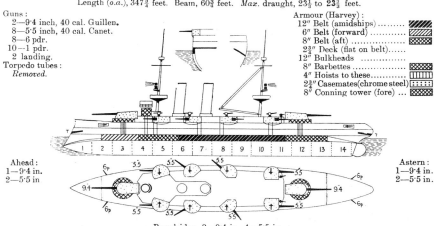

(CATALUNA CLASS—2 Ships.)

Photo, Casau, Cartagena.

PRINCESA DE ASTURIAS (1896) & **CATALUNA** (1900)

Displacement, *P. de A.* 7427 tons, *C.* 7405 tons. Complement, 546.
Length (*o.a.*), 347¾ feet. Beam, 60¾ feet. *Max.* draught, 23¼ to 23¾ feet.

Guns :
2—9·4 inch, 40 cal. Guillen.
8—5·5 inch, 40 cal. Canet.
8—6 pdr.
10—1 pdr.
2 landing.
Torpedo tubes :
Removed.

Armour (Harvey) :
12″ Belt (amidships) ....
6″ Belt (forward) ....
8″ Belt (aft) ....
2¾″ Deck (flat on belt)......
12″ Bulkheads ....
8″ Barbettes ....
4″ Hoists to these..........
2¾″ Casemates (chrome steel)
8″ Conning tower (fore) ...

Ahead :
1—9·4 in.
2—5·5 in.

Astern :
1—9·4 in.
2—5·5 in.

Broadside : 2—9·4 in., 4—5·5 in.

Machinery : 2 sets horizontal triple expansion. 2 screws. Boilers : 6 cylindrical. Designed H.P. *natural* 10,500 = 18 kts. Coal : *maximum* 1178 tons in *C.* and 1007 in *P. de A.*

SPANISH NAVY.

1st Class Cruiser (*Crucero de 1a Clas*).

CARLOS CINCO (1895). 9903 tons. Comp., 583. Dimensions: 404¾ (*o.a.*) × 67 × 27⅓ feet, *max.* draught ; *mean* draught, 25 feet. Armament (Hontoria, 35 cal.): 2—11 inch, 8—5·5 inch, 4—4·1 inch, 10—6 pdr., 8—1 pdr., 2 Machine. Torpedo tubes (14 inch): 2 *above water*. Armour: 2½″ Deck, 10″ Barbettes with 4″ Hoods and 8″ Hoists, 2″ over Battery, 12″ C.T. Boilers: 12 cyl. Designed H.P. 15,000, made 19 kts. on trial. Coal : *max* 2008 tons.

2nd Class Cruiser (*Crucero de 2a Clas*).

(1919 Photo, A. de N. M. Mille.)

REINA REGENTE (Sept., 1906) 5778 tons. Complement, 452. Dimensions : 337 × 52½ × 16½ feet. Guns : 10—5·9 inch, (45 cal.), 12—6 pdr., 8—1 pdr., 2—3 inch Field. Armour : 3½″ Deck and C.T., 3″ Gun Shields. Machinery : Reciprocating. 2 screws. Boilers : Belleville. Designed H.P. 11,000 = 19·5 kts. Coal : 1178 tons.

3rd Class Cruisers (*Cruceros de 3a Clas*).

Photo (1918), A. de N. M. Mille.

EXTREMADURA (Cadiz, 1900). 2100 tons. Complement, 266. Dimensions : 288⅔ × 36½ × 16½ feet. Guns : 8—4 inch (50 cal. Vickers), 4—6 pdr., 4—1 pdr., no tubes. Armour : 1½″ Deck. Machinery : 2 screws. Boilers : Thornycroft. H.P. 7000 = 19 kts. Coal : *max.* 425 tons.

(Is now equipped as a Mine Layer).　　　*Photo (1919), A. de N. M. Mille.*

RIO DE LA PLATA (Havre, 1898). 1920 tons. Comp., 213. Dimensions : 250½ × 35½ × 15½ feet, *maximum* draught ; *mean* draught, 14¼ feet. Guns : 2—5·5 inch, 35 cal., 4—4·1 inch, 6—9 pdr., 4—1 pdr. No tubes. Armour : 1½″ Deck. Machinery : Reciprocating. 2 screws. Boilers : Normand-Sigaudy. H.P. 7000 = 19 kts. Coal : *max.* 370 tons.

SPANISH DESTROYERS.

3 New Boats.

Building ?

3 *New* Ocean-going Destroyers (names not known) 3 building at Cartagena by S.E.C.N. Displacement : 1145 tons, (*normal*) 1325 tons (*full load*). Dimensions : 275 × 27 × 10½ feet. Designed H.P. 33,000 = 34 kts. Will have Parsons turbines and 4 Yarrow boilers. Guns : 3—4 inch (40 cal.), 2—2 pdr. anti-aircraft. Torpedo tubes : 4—21 inch in 2 twin deck mountings. Full 265 tons oil only. To be finished in 1920-21.

3 *Bustamante* Class.

BUSTAMANTE.　　　*Photo, Casau, Cartagena.*

3 *Bustamante* class : named **Bustamante** (1913), **Villaamil** (1913), **Cadarso** (ex *Requesens*, 1911). All built at Cartagena D.Y., 364 tons. Dimensions : 221½ × 22 × 5½ feet. Armament : 5—6 pdr. S.H.P. 6250 = 28 kts. Tubes : 2—18 inch in first two and 2—15 inch in *Cadarso* only. Yarrow or Normand boilers. Parsons turbine. 3 screws. Coal : 79 tons = 900 miles at 15 kts. Complement 70.

4 *Audaz* Class.

AUDAZ.

OSADO (PROSERPINA, rebuilt 1916, appearance may be changed.)

1st, 2nd, and 3rd boats of the *Audaz* class :—**Audaz, Osado**, and **Proserpina**, Clydebank, 1897, *Proserpina* rebuilt 1916). 457 tons. 229 × 22½ × 9 feet. I.H.P. 7200 (7950 in *Osado*) = 29·3 to 31 kts. on trials. Guns : 2—11 inch, 2—6 pdr., 2—1 pdr. Torpedo tubes : 2—15 inch. Coal : 93 tons = 1020 miles at 15 kts. Complement 74.

Photo (1919), A. de N. M. Mille.

4th boat of *Audaz* Class : **Terror** (Clydebank, 1895). 450 tons. 221 × 22 × 9½ feet. I.H.P. 6000 = 29.5 kts. Guns : 2—6 pdr., 2—2½ pdr. Torpedo tubes : 2—15 inch. Coal : 104 tons = 1100 miles at 15 kts. Complement 73.

(All above 4 boats fitted for Mine Laying).

SPANISH TORPEDO BOATS AND SUBMARINES.

18 (+ 4) 1st Class Torpedo Boats (Torpederos de 1ª Clas).

Photo (1919), A. de N. M. Mille.

22 Vickers-Normand. **2** (1911). **1, 3, 5, 6** (1912), **4** 1912, rebuilt 1916), **7, 8, 13** (1914), **9, 11, 12, 14** (1915), **10, 15, 16** (1916), **17, 18, 19,** *20* (1918), **21,** *22* (1919). 177 tons. Dimensions: 164×16½×4⁵⁄₆ feet (*max.* draught). Armament: 3—3 pdr., 3—18 in. tubes, twin amidships and single aft. (Nos. *1, 4, 5, 17, 18* no tubes; *15* and *16* only 2 tubes.) H.P. 3750=26 kts. Parsons turbines and Normand boilers. Coal: 23 tons. 3 screws (Nos. 1—7). 2 screws (Nos. 8—22). Complement 31. Nos. *23* and *24* abandoned 1919.

Note.—Following three old T.B. may still exist: *1—1st Class* boat, **Halcon** (**No. 41**), built 1887, rebuilt 1905. 235 tons. I.H.P. 1650=20 kts. Armament: 2—2½ pdr., 2 tubes. Coal: 25 tons. *2—2nd Class* boats: **Habana** (**No. 45**), built 1886. 61 tons. I.H.P. 780=19 kts. Armament: 1 M.G. and 2 tubes. Coal: 25 tons; **Orion** (**No. 42**), built 1885. 89 tons. I.H.P. 1000=21 kts. Armament: 2—1 pdr., 2 tubes. Coal: 18 tons.

Also listed: *Acevedo, Julian Ordonez* deleted by 1919.   finished.

Submarines (continued.)

Building.

6 *Holland* type: Names and numbers not known. Began at Cartagena, July, 1916. Are an improved and enlarged *Isaac Peral* type. Displacements: 610 tons *on surface*, 740 tons *submerged*. Dimensions about 210 × 18½ × 11¼ feet. Machinery: *on surface*, 2 sets Diesel engines, totalling 1400 B.H.P.=16 kts.; *when submerged*, electric motors and batteries of 850 H.P.=10—10½ kts. Guns: 2 (calibre unknown, but one is *AA.* type). Torpedo tubes: 4 or 6 (size uncertain).

Photo (1919), A. de M. N. Mille.

MONTURIOL (A1). These boats have a tall telescopic mast for W/T. abeam of after periscope on port side of C.T. also 1—3 pdr. gun mounted, now shown in above view.

Laurenti-Fiat type: **Narciso Monturiol** (**A1**), **Cosmo Garcia** (**A2**) and **A3,** (all built by Fiat San Giorgio Co., Spezia. 1915-17). Displacements: 260 tons *on surface*, 382 tons *submerged*. Dimensions: 149·6 × 13·8 × 10·2 feet. Machinery: *on surface*, 2 sets of 350 H.P., 6-cylinder, 2-cycle Fiat Diesel engines= 700 H.P.; *when submerged*, 2 electric motors of 250 H.P.+batteries=500 H.P. Maximum speeds: 13 kts. *on surface* and 8¼ kts. *submerged*. Radii of action: *on surface*, 650 miles at full speed and 1600 miles at 8¼ kts.; *when submerged*, 18 miles at 8 kts. and 85 miles at 4 kts. Guns: 1—3 pdr. Torpedo tubes: 2—18 inch in bows. Complement 17.

Note: Each boat is internally sub-divided into 8 w.t.c. Maximum diving depth 130 feet (about 22 fathoms). Detachable lead keel, weighs 9¼ tons. Fitted with telephone buoy, Fessenden submarine signalling and receiving apparatus, and Marconi W/T. For rescue and salvage work there are 6 lifting rings outside hull, and 3 escape hatches within hull, for crew. 2 Periscopes about 3½ inches diameter.

SPANISH SUBMARINES AND GUNBOATS.

Submarines—(Continued).

Photo (1919), A. de N. M. Mille.

ISAAC PERAL: Has a tall folding mast for W/T. just before conning tower; two ventilators on top of C.T. may also be raised, when on surface. These details are not shown in above illustration.

1 *Holland* type: **Isaac Peral** (Fore River Co., U.S.A., July, '16). Displacement: 488 tons *on surface*, 750 tons *submerged*. Complement 32. Dimensions: 197 × 19 × 11 feet. Machinery: *on surface*, 2 sets of 600 H.P. Niseco Diesel engines=1200 H.P. for 15 kts. speed (made 15·36 on trials); *submerged*, electric motors + batteries of 680 H.P.=10 kts. speed. Radii of action: 3700 miles *on surface*, at cruising speed of about 11 kts.; 100 miles *submerged*, at 5 kts. Armament: 1—3 in. Q.F. (anti-aircraft and disappearing mounting), 4 torpedo tubes in bows.

1st Class Gunboats (Cañoneros de 1ª Clas).

Projected.

"A," "B" and "C," building by S.E.C.N., at Cartagena. Displacement, 1500 tons. Speed, 18 kts. Provided for by 1915 Naval Programme. No other details known.

1st Class Gunboats—(Continued).

RECALDE.   *Photo (1919), A. de N. M. Mille.*

BONIFAZ (1911), **LAURIA** (1912), **LAYA** (1910), **RECALDE** (1910). 787 tons. Complement, 121. Dimensions: 213¾×30×9½ feet (*max*) draught. Guns: 4—14 pdr. 2 machine. Designed H.P. 1100=14 kts. Made 14·5 kts. on trial. Yarrow boilers. Coal: 148 tons. Radius, 3000 at 10 kts.

Photo (1919), A. de N. M. Mille.

DON ALVARO DE BAZAN (1897). 810 tons. 236×27×11½ feet. Guns: 6—6 pdr., 2—2½ pdr., 2 M.G. I.H.P. 3500=19 kts. Coal: 168 tons. Complement 121.

(Continued on next page).

First Class Gunboats.—*Continued.*

MARQUES DE LA VICTORIA (1897, reconstructed 1917-18), 810 tons. $233 \times 27 \times 10\frac{3}{4}$ feet. Guns: 8—6 pdr., 2 M.G. I.H.P. 3500 = 19 kts. Coal: 168 tons. Complement, 121.

Photo (1918), Alferez de Navio, M. Mille.

Photo (1916), Alferez de Navio, M. Mille.

DOÑA MARIA DE MOLINA (1896) 810 tons. $236 \times 27 \times 11\frac{1}{4}$ feet. Guns: 8—6 pdr., 2 M.G. H.P. 3500 = 19 kts. Coal: 183 tons. Complement, 121.

Photo (1914), Alferez de Navio, M. Mille.

INFANTA ISABEL (1885, reconstructed 1911). 1136 tons. $221\frac{1}{2} \times 32 \times 15$ feet. Guns: 1—9 pdr., 10—6 pdr. I.H.P. 1500 = 12 kts. 1 screw. Coal: 194 tons. Complement, 194.

Second Class Gunboats. (*Cañoneros de 2a clas.*)

VASCO NUNEZ DE BALBOA (1895) & **HERNAN CORTES** (1895). 295 tons. $155 \times 21\frac{1}{2} \times 7$ feet. Guns: 2—3 pdr., 2—1 pdr. or Maxims. I.H.P. 500 = 10 kts. 1 screw. Coal: 61 tons. Complement, 54.

As re-boilered with one funnel. (*1919 photo, A. de N., M. Mille.*)

MARQUES DE MOLINS (1893). 560 tons. $177\frac{1}{2} \times 23 \times 10\frac{1}{2}$ feet. Guns: 4—6 pdr., 3—machine. Speed, 13 kts. Coal: 134 tons. Complement, 93.

Third Class Gunboat. (*Cañonero de 3a clas.*)

Photo (1916) Alferez de Navio, M. Mille.

MACMAHON (1887). 114 tons. $91\frac{1}{2} \times 16 \times 5$ feet. Guns: 2—2½ pdr., 1—1 pdr. I.H.P. 150 = 7 kts. Coal: 10½ tons.

River Gunboats. (*Lanchas-Cañoneras.*)

1919 Photo, Alferez de Navio, M. Mille.

CARTAGENERA (1908). 27 tons. Complement, 12. $53.5 \times 11.8 \times 3.9$ feet. Guns: 1 pom-pom. I.H.P. 120 = 12 kts.

No photo available.

Also listed in 1914: *Nueva España, Ternerario, Pouce de Leon, General Concha.* All deleted by 1919.

PERLA (1887). 42 tons. 7 kts. 1 machine gun.

Submarine Salvage Vessel.

(*Buque para salvamento de submerinos.*)

(Photograph wanted.)

KANGARU (1917). Double hulled type, with interior docking space. Built by Werf Conrad, Haarlem, Holland. About 3000 tons. Length, 275.4 feet; beam, 65.4 feet; draught (with submarine docked), 13 feet. Can dock submarine up to 151 feet long. Salvage power: Can raise 650 tons, from $27\frac{1}{8}$ fathoms. H.P. 1000 = 10 kts.

SPANISH MISCELLANEOUS.

Mining Vessels.

Mine Layers.

Old Cruiser **RIO DE LA PLATA** and old Destroyers of the *Audaz* class have been equipped for this duty. Also some (or all) of the 15 Coastguard and Fisheries Vessels of the *Esmeralda* type (see third column of this page) can be used as Mine Layers.

Auxiliaries.

Hercules (Repair Ship), *Bermea, Donestierra, Guipozcoa, Mariano, Primero de Meiro,* and three others.

Royal Yacht **GIRALDA**.

Gunnery Ship **NUMANCIA** 7500 tons.

Transport. (*Transporte.*)

Photo (1919), A. de N. M. Mille.

ALMIRANTE LOBO (1909). 2545 tons. Guns: 2—5 pdr. Designed H.P. 4300 = 12 kts. *Nominal* radius, 4540 at 10 kts.

Photo (1919), A. de N. M. Mille.

ANTELO (1903). Ocean-going Tug, Mine Layer, Mine Sweeper and Training Ship for Mining Service. 342 tons. $131.2 \times 21.6 \times 6.8$ feet. I.H.P. 650 = 11 kts. Coal: 32 tons. Carries 40 mines.

Surveying Ship. (*Comisión Hidrografica.*)

URANIA (1895). 801 tons. $195 \times 26 \times 10\frac{1}{2}$ feet. Guns: 2—6 pdr. 2 screws. I.H.P. 350 = 10 kts. Coal: 200 tons. *Nominal* radius, 6400 at 8 kts.

Coastguard and Fisheries Vessels. (*Guardapescas.*)

ESMERALDA, INTREPIDA, PRONTA (Malaga) (————), **LIEBRE, SANTA MARIA** (Cadiz) (————), **SERPIENTE** (Algeciras) (————), **CUERVO** (Alicante) (————), **CEDIDA** (Valencia) (————), **RADIANTE** (Barcelona) (————), **FLECHA, GARZA, PEZ** (Balearic Islands) (————), and *3 others building,* provided for under new Naval Programme. All equipped for mine-laying and sweeping in war-time. 300 tons. Dimensions: $114.8 \times 19.7 \times$ feet. Speed, 16 kts. Machinery: 2 sets Diesel engines. Complement, 70.

Note.—Ports given are *not* building yards but stations to which these ships will be assigned, when completed.

"Delfin"

Photo, Alferez de Navio, M. Mille.

DELFIN, DORADO, GAVIOTA (1910-11). 158 tons. Guns: 1—5 pdr. Speed, 11 kts.

Scale:—1″ = 160 feet.

BODROG.

Danube Monitor.

Official Photo, L.N.A.

Note.

Reported that various Austrian Warships interned at Cattaro and Sebenico will be assigned to the Serbs, Croats and Slovenes.

Various Hungarian Monitors and River Craft have surrendered to the British and Serbs, and are interned at Belgrade. These ships are listed in Hungarian Danube Flotilla Section, but their names are :

Danube Monitors :—Bosnia, Enns, Köros, Leitha, Maros, Sara, Temes.

Scouts :—Barsch, Fogos, Isuka, Vels.

All the above will probably be transferred to the Navy of the Serbs, Croats and Slovenes.

BODROG (1904). 433 tons. Dimensions : $183\frac{3}{4} \times 31\frac{1}{4} \times 4$ feet. Designed H.P. 1400 = 13 kts. Boilers : Yarrow. Armament : 2—4·7 inch (45 cal.) + 1—4·7 inch howitzer, 2—3 pdr., 1 or 3 machine. Armour : $1\frac{1}{2}''$ Belt and Bulkheads, 1″ Deck, $3''$—$1\frac{1}{2}''$ Turrets and Conning tower. Complement, 79. Coal : 62 tons.

SERBIA. (Purchased 1916.) Under 100 tons. Speed : 12 kts. Is unarmed. National colours painted on funnel. Mainmast now removed.

PORTUGUESE FLEET.

Portuguese Navy.—Re-illustrated 1919, from photographs furnished by courtesy of Captain Ernest Vasconcellos, and A. W. Paterson, Esq., of Lisbon.

Revised 1919, from Official " Lista dos Navios da Marinha de Guerra e da Marinha Colonial." Also corrected from information furnished by courtesy of the Portuguese Naval Attache, and Lieut. H. Reuterdahl, U.S.N./R.F. All armaments list are not from any official data. Ships marked with asterisk (*) form part of the Colonial Navy. All displacements in English tons unless otherwise stated.

Naval Bases.

LISBON. Some small slips. Government dry dock : $258 \times 56\frac{3}{4} \times 12$ feet. Harbour Board dry docks : No. 1, $549 \times 82 \times 32\frac{1}{4}$ feet ; No. 2, $328 \times 49 \times 27$ feet. Private dock, H. Parry & Sons (Cacilhas) : No. 1, $225 \times 37 \times 9$ feet. There are also two smaller docks (H. Parry & Son).

S. PAULO DE LOANDA (ANGOLA). There is a small floating dock here of 1,100 tons capacity, capable of taking any of the gunboats employed on this station.

Note.— During war, batteries and other defences were erected at Porto Delgada in the Azores, while the port was used by U.S. troopships, &c. If these new defences are turned over to Portuguese Navy, Porto Delgada can serve as a defended anchorage and coaling base for War Vessels.

Scale: 1 inch = 160 feet. RECOGNITION SILHOUETTES.

ONE FUNNEL.

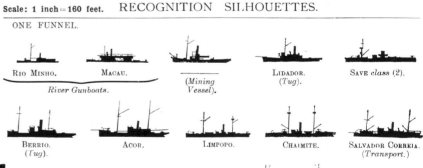

RIO MINHO. MACAU. *(Mining Vessel).* LIDADOR. *(Tug).* SAVE class (2).

River Gunboats.

BERRIO. *(Tug).* ACOR. LIMPOPO. CHAIMITE. SALVADOR CORREIA. *(Transport.)*

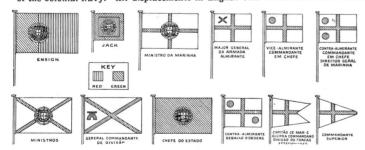

VULCANO *(Mine Layer).*

BEIRA class (5).

SAÕ GABRIEL.

SADO (2). *(Mine Layer.)*

PEDRO NUNEZ. *(Auxiliary Cruiser).*

SADO (1). *(Gunboat).*

ZAMBEZE.

For :—
Two Funnel Types ;
Torpedo Craft ;
Submarines ;

See next page.

Naval Uniforms.

Britush or U.S. rank.

Almirante.* / Admiral.

Vice-Almirante.† / Vice-Admiral.

Contra-Almirante. / Rear-Admiral.

Capitão de Mar e Guerra. / Captain.

Capitão de Fregata. / Commander.

Capitão Tenente. / Lieut-Commander.

Primeiro Tenente. / Lieut.

Segundo Tenente. / Sub-Lieut.

Guarda Marinha. / Midshipman

* Admiral has four *gold* stars. † Vice-Admiral has four *silver* stars.

Staff officers same but *without* executive curl. Colour between stripes—*Surgeons*: red ; *Engineers*: violet ; *Paymasters*: blue ; *Constructors*: purple red. On visor of cap, *Admirals*: 2 oak leaves ; *Captains*: 1 oak leaf ; *Commanders*: 1 narrow stripe. Uniforms like British Navy. Chin strap of gold cord, but officers of lieutenant's rank and below have black chin straps.

Personnel :

Mercantile Marine : 162 steamers of 319,954 tons *gross*, 219 sailing of 49,547 tons *gross*.

Trade Ports: Lisbon and Oporto.

Oversea Possessions : Cape Verde Islands, Madeira and Azores, Guinea (Senegambia), St. Thomas and Prince Islands (Gulf of Guinea), Timor (East Indies), Goa, Damao and Diu (India), Macao (China), Angola (Congo), Portuguese East Africa.

Coinage : Escudo (1000 reis) = 4s. 5d. British, $1.06 U.S.A. ; 4500 reis = £1 English.

Colour of Ships : Dark grey.

PORTUGUESE FLEET.

RECOGNITION SILHOUETTES—*Continued.*

Scale : 1 inch = 160 feet.

Old Battleship (*Cruzador*).

TWO FUNNELS.

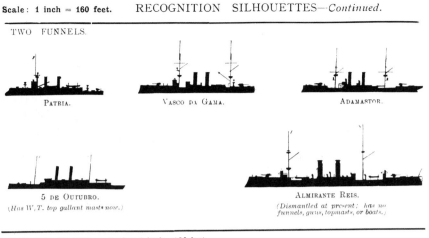

PATRIA.   VASCO DA GAMA.   ADAMASTOR.

5 DE OUTUBRO.
(*Has W.T. top gallant masts now.*)

ALMIRANTE REIS.
(*Dismantled at present; has no funnels, guns, topmasts, or boats.*)

TORPEDO CRAFT.   **Scale : 1 inch = 160 feet.**

No. 2, No. 3 (t.b.)   TEJO t.b.d.
(*as reconstructed*).   DOURO class t.b.d. (2).

SUBMARINES.   Scale : 1 inch = 80 feet.

FOCA class (3).   ESPADARTE.

VASCO DA GAMA (Blackwall, 1876, reconstructed and lengthened by Orlando 1902). 2982 tons. Comp., 259. Dimensions: 232·9 × 40¼ × 18¼ feet. Guns (new in 1902): 2—8 inch, 1—6 inch, 1—12 pdr., 8—3 pdr. No torpedo tubes. Armour (iron): 9″—7″ Belt, 7¾″ (Terni) Barbettes. Machinery: 2 sets triple expansion. 2 screws. Designed H.P. (new): 6000 = 15·5 kts. Boilers: Cylindrical. Coal : 300 tons.

Protected Cruisers (*Cruzadores*).

Photo by favour of Major Maunsell, R.A.

ALMIRANTE REIS (ex *Dom Carlos I.*, Elswick, 1896). 4186 tons. Comp., 418. Dimensions : 360·8 × 46½ × 17·5 feet. Guns (Elswick): 4—6 inch, 45 cal., 8—4·7 inch, 45 cal., 14—3 pdr., 2—1 pdr., 3 Machine. Torpedo tubes (14 inch): 2 *above water*. Deck, 4½″. Machinery : 2 sets triple expansion. 2 screws. Boilers: 12 Yarrow. H.P. 12,000 = 19·5 kts. Coal: 820 tons.

Note.—Dismantled 1918 for re-construction and long refit.

Protected Cruisers—(*Continued*).

PORTUGUESE FLEET.

Photo, Abrahams & Sons.

SAŌ GABRIEL (F. & C. de la Med., 1898). 1809 tons. Comp., 242. Dimensions : 246 × 35·5 × 14·3 feet. Guns (Canet): 2—5·9 inch, 4—4·7 inch, 8—3 pdr., 2—1 pdr., 3 machine. Torpedo tubes: 1—18 inch (bow) *above water*. 1″ Deck, 2½″ C.T. Machinery : 2 sets triple expansion. 2 screws. H.P. 3000 = 15 kts. Coal: 289 tons. Boilers : 4 Normand-Sigaudy.

REPUBLICA (*ex R. D. Amelia*) (1899). 1683 tons. Comp., 263. Dimensions : 246 × 36 × 14⅔ feet. Guns: 4—6 inch, 45 cal., 2—4 inch, 45 cal., 4—3 pdr., 2—1 pdr. 2—18 inch tubes (*above water*). 1½″ Deck, 2″ C.T. Boilers : Normand Sigaudy. Designed H.P. 5400 = 18 kts. Coal : 322 tons.

Deleted by 1919.

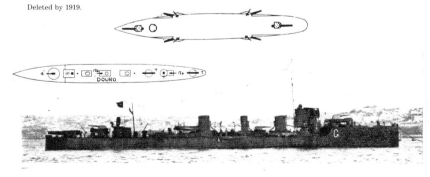

4 *Yarrow* type. *Vouga* and *Tamega* (both building at Lisbon D.Y.), **Douro** (1913) and **Guadiana** (1911). 660 tons. Dimensions: 240 × 23½ × 7⅞ feet, *max.* draught. Armament: 1—4 inch, 2—12 pdr., 2 tubes. Parsons turbines; 3 Yarrow boilers. Coal: 146 tons = 1600 miles at 15 kts. Built by Yarrow and assembled at Lisbon. On trials, *Douro* made 30·3 kts., good for 27 now.

ADAMASTOR (Orlando, 1896). 1729 tons. Comp., 206. Dimensions: 242·1 × 35·1 × 15·3 feet. Guns (Krupp): 2—old 5·9 inch, 4—4·1 inch, 4—9 pdr., 2—1 pdr., 3 machine. Torpedo tubes (14 inch): 3 *above water* (bow and broadside). Armour : 1¼″ Deck, 2¾″ C.T. Machinery : 2 sets triple expansion. 2 screws. Boilers : 8 cylindrical. H.P. *forced* 4000 = 18·19 kts. Coal: 420 tons.

1 *Navy* type. **Tejo** (Lisbon D.Y. 1901, rebuilt 1917). 526 tons. Dimensions: 229⅔ × 23 × 8·2 feet. Armament: 1—3·9 inch (aft), 1—3 inch (forward). 2—14 inch tubes. Machinery : 2 sets triple expansion. 2 screws. Boilers: White-Forster. H.P. 7000 = 27 kts. (estimated). Wrecked in 1910, salved, but reconstruction not finished till 1917.

PORTUGUESE TORPEDO BOATS—SUBMARINES—MISCELLANEOUS.

Torpedo Boats. (Torpedeiros).
(For appearance see Silhouettes.)

2 old *Yarrow* type. **No. 1, No. 2** and **No. 3, No. 4** (Poplar, 1886). 66 metric tons. Dimensions: $119\frac{2}{3}$ x $12\frac{2}{3}$ x 3.4 feet. Armament: 2 M.G. and 2 tubes. Designed H.P. 700=19 kts. (much less now). 1 screw. Coal: about 18 tons. Complement, 22. Nos 1 and 4 deleted by 1919.

Resemble Spanish *Monturiol* type.

Laurenti-Fiat type: **Foca, Golfinho,** and **Hidra** (all built at Spezia, 1916–1917). Dimensions : $117\frac{1}{4} \times 13\cdot8 \times 10\frac{1}{4}$ feet. Armament : 2—18 inch bow torpedo tubes. 4 torpedoes. Machinery : 2 sets of 300 H.P. 6-cylinder Fiat-Diesel engines *on surface*; electric motors + batteries *submerged*. Maximum speeds : 15 kts. *on surface* and 8½ kts. *submerged*. Radius of action : about 650 miles at full speed, and 1500 miles at 7–8 kts. *on surface* : about 15–20 miles at 9½ kts. and 80–85 at 4 kts. *submerged*.

1 *Laurenti-Fiat* type : **Espadarte** (Spezia, 1912). Displacement, $\frac{245}{300}$ tons. Dimensions : $148 \times 13\frac{1}{4} \times 9\cdot7$ feet. Torpedo tubes : 2—18 inch (bow). 4 torpedoes carried (4000 yds at kts.). Machinery : 2 sets 300 H.P. 6-cyl. Fiat-Diesel engines *on surface*; electric batteries + motors *submerged*. Maximum speeds, 13½ kts. *above* and 8 kts. *below* water. Radius of action : About same as for *Foca* class above.

Auxiliary Cruiser (*Cruzador auxiliar*).

PEDRO NUNEZ (ex-s.s. *Melange* of Empraza Naçional, Lisbon. 1889). 5574 metric tons. 356× × feet. Guns : several 4·7 inch and smaller Q.F. I.H.P 2300 = about 16 kts. 1 screw. Complement 209.

"Aviso," or Despatch Vessel.

CINCO DE OUTUBRO (ex *Amelia*, ex *Banshee* ; Ramage & Ferguson, Leith, 1900). 1343 tons. 226·9 × 28·9 × 14 feet. Guns : 2—3 pdr., 4—1 pdr. H.P. 1800 = 15 kts. 2 screws. Cylindrical boilers. Coal : 230 tons. Complement, 225.

Gunboats (*Canhoneiras*).

Photo, R. E. Forrest, Esq.

BENGO (1917), **MANDOVI** (1917), **QUANZA** (1918), **BEIRA** (1910) and **IBO** (1910). All built at Lisbon D.Y. 463 tons. Dimensions : $147\frac{3}{5} \times 27\frac{1}{4} \times 6\cdot8$ feet. Guns : in *Bengo, Mandovi*, and *Quanza*, 4—3 pdr. : in *Beira* and *Ibo*, 2—3 pdr., 2 M.G. 2 field. H.P. 700 = 13 kts. Coal : 85 tons. Radius : 3200 miles at 9 kts. Boilers : Cylindrical. 2 screws. Complement 71.

Gunboats (*continued*).

SAVE (1908) and **LURIO** (1907). Both built at Lisbon D.Y. 305 tons. Dimensions : 140·4 × 23·6 × 5·9 feet. Guns : 2—3 pdr., 1 machine. H.P. 500 = 12½ kts. Boilers : Cylindrical. 2 screws. Coal : 61 tons. Complement 51.

ZAMBEZE (Lisbon, 1886). Wood. 606 tons. $146 \times 26\frac{1}{4} \times 11$ feet. Guns : 3—3·9 inch (old), 1—1 pdr., 1 M.G. H.P. 460 = 10 kts. Cylindrical boilers. Coal : 90 tons. Complement, 65.

Mine Layers. (*Vapores lanca minas.*)

VULCANO (1910). Built by Thornycroft. 151 tons. $110 \times 19\frac{1}{2} \times 4\frac{1}{2}$ feet. 2 dropping gears forward. H.P. 412 = 12 kts. 2 screws. Cylindrical boiler. Complement, 24.

For appearance, see Silhouettes.

RIO SADO (2) (1905). 2558 metric tons. 229.6 x 36 x 14.8 feet. Guns : 1 M.G. aft. H.P. 500 = 11 kts. 1 screw. Cylindrical boilers. Coal : 100 tons. Complement 69.

Photo, Sub-Lieut. Poyntz, R.I.M.

SADO (1) (Birkenhead, 1875). 635 tons. $149\frac{1}{2} \times 28\frac{1}{4} \times 10\frac{3}{4}$ feet. Guns : 2—4·1 inch, 2—9 pdr., 1—1 pdr., 1 machine. H.P. 500 = 11 kts. Cylindrical boilers. Coal : 84 tons. Complement, 30.

*PATRIA (Lisbon D.Y., 1903). 626 tons. Dimensions : 196·8 × 27·5 × 8·4 feet. Guns : 4—3·9 inch, 6—3 pdr., 1 machine. ½″ waterline belt. H.P. 1890 = 16·7 kts. Cylindrical boilers. 2 screws. Complement 88.

No Photo available.

CHAIMITE (Parry & Sons, Lisbon, 1898, rebuilt 1913). 335 tons. $134 \times 26\frac{1}{4} \times 6\cdot6$ feet. Guns : 2—3 pdr., 2 machine. H.P. 480 = 11 kts. Cylindrical boilers. Coal : 120 tons. Complement, 25.

LIMPOPO (Poplar, 1890). 288 tons. $124 \times 21 \times 6\frac{1}{2}$ feet. Guns : 2—3 pdr., 1 machine. H.P. 523 = 11·3 kts. Complement, 54.

MINING VESSEL (name and details not known).

ACOR (ex-s.s. *Gomes VII*, 1874). 330 tons. 136·1 × 19 × 9 feet. Guns : 1—3 pdr. I.H.P. 360 = 9 kts. ; could make 11 with sail out. Complement 53. Has been employed on fisheries and surveying duties. Will probably be condemned soon.

PORTUGUESE MISCELLANEOUS.

Small River Gunboats. *(Lancha Canonheiras.)*

No photo available of *Tete.*

TETE (Yarrow, Scotstoun. Begun Feb., 1918, completed Mar., 1919). Stern wheel type for Zambese River. 70 ton. 89 (*o.a.*) × 20 × 4 feet. Guns: 2—1 pdr. Hotchkiss, 2 M.G. I.H.P. 80 = 9 kts. Boiler: locomotive. Fuel: wood. Destroyed by boiler explosion up the Zambezi R. February 1917.

*MACAU (Yarrow, 1909). 133 tons. 119⅜ × 19·8 × 2 feet. Guns: 2—6 pdr., 3 machine. H.P. 250 = 11·8 kts. Boilers: Yarrow. Complement, 24.

°**FLECHA,** is also given in Official Navy List as **FLEXA** (1909). tons. 68·8 × 13·1 × 2·2 feet. Guns: 1 or 2 small. 1 screw. Speed 10 kts. Complement 7.

Note.—There is also a Flotilla of 7 launches for River Service in Portuguese India, with civilian crews. They are under the command of the "Captain of Ports."

°**RIO MINHO** (Lisbon D.Y., 1904). 38 tons. Paddle wheel. 80·7 × 13·1 × 1·9 feet. H.P. 64 = 7½ kts. Guns: 2—1 pdr. Complement 68, are nominally borne on her books, the majority of these ranks and ratings being actually at various shore stations on the Portugese bank of the river Minho, for fisheries, customs duties, &c.

PORTUGUESE MISCELLANEOUS.

Tugs. *(Reborcadores.)*

Transports *(continued.)*

SALVADOR CORREIA (Birkenhead, 1895). 300 metric tons. 140 × 21 × 7 feet. Guns: 2 M.G. H.P. 450 = 11 kts. 1 screw. Cylindrical boilers. Coal: 80 tons. Complement, 19.

Also

°*Bissau* (1913). 300 metric tons.

°*Massabi* (1886). 266 metric tons.

**Vilhena.*

Above three vessels serve as Transports in the Colonies of Guinea and Angola; they have mixed complements of naval officers and civilians.

BERRIO (1898). 498 metric tons. 132·9 × 22·5 × 10·5 feet. Guns: 1 M.G. in bows. H.P. 1070 = 12·27 kts. 2 screws. Complement 44.

Auxiliaries.

Capitanio, Salvation, for Colonial Service.

DIU (1889) of 740 tons.
ZAIRE (1884) of 558 tons.
Both above deleted by 1919.

LIDADOR (1884). 252 metric tons. Iron. 113·8 × 20 × 6·9 feet. H.P. 400 = 11 kts. 2 screws. Complement, 41.

Naval Transports. *(Transportes.)*

***CHINDE** (1911). tons. 240 (*p.p.*) × 33·5 × feet. I.H.P. 950 = kts. 1 screw.

Naval Transports *(continued).*

°***PÈBANE.** 148 H.P. 1 screw. Complement 37. No other details known.

***PUNGUÉ** (1895). tons. 232 (*p.p.*) × 24·1 × feet. I.H.P. 424 = kts. 1 screw.

Salvage Vessel. *Vapor de Salvação.*

PATRÃO LOPEZ (——). 1109 metric tons. 157·5 (*p.p.*) × 26·2 × 14·6 feet. Complement, 53.

For Fisheries Protection.

CARREGADO (1912). 107 metric tons. 80 (*p.p.*) × 18 × feet. Guns: not known. I.H.P. 300 = kts. 1 screw. Is stationed at Algarve.

Note.—Gunboat *Acor* and River Gunboat *Rio Minho* may be employed on this service, from time to time.

For Various Duties.

°**DILLY** (is also referred to in Official Navy List as **DILI**). 500 metric tons. 140 (*p.p*) × 25 × 10·3 feet. I.H.P. 500 = 11 kts. 1 screw. Complement 12.

LINCE (1911). 78 metric tons. 88·5 (*p.p.*) × 14 × 5·5 feet. I.H.P. 300 = kts. 2 screws. Complement (nominally) 53.

Trawlers, Patrol Vessels and Armed Launches.

The following Vessels were in Naval Service in May, 1919, but were probably only requisitioned for the duration of the war. They are not included in Official Navy List. *Manuel Azevedo* and *H. Capello* may be permanently retained by the Navy; the other vessels will probably revert to private use.

Trawlers:—

A. de Castilhos.	*Manuel Azevedo.*
A. P. de Arcos.	*M. Victoria.*
C. Sores.	*P. Lopez.*
H. Capello.	

Patrol Vessels:—

Galco.	*T Andres.*
Republica.	*Tresirmos.*

Armed Launches:—

Guarda Marinha Janeira.	*Tenente Roby.*

Also the old wooden sailing frigate *Dom Fernando* (1842), of 1849 tons; is totally non-effective for fighting purposes. Used as Gunnery Training Ship.

ROYAL HELLENIC NAVY.
(GREEK FLEET.)

Officially Revised, 1919, by courtesy of H.E. The Minister of Marine.

VICE ADMIRAL.

Note to Flags.—Royal Standard and Admirals' flags were altered about two years ago, but their present design cannot be ascertained.

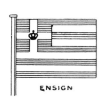

ENSIGN

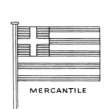

MERCANTILE

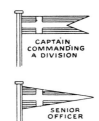

CAPTAIN COMMANDING A DIVISION

SENIOR OFFICER

Blue

White

Red

Nauarkos. *Admiral.* Antinauarkos. *Vice-Admiral.* Yponauarkos. *Rear-Admiral.* Ploiarkos. *Captain.* Antipliarkos. *Commander. 1st class*

Plotarkis. *Comdr.* Ypoploiarkos. *Lieutenant-Commander.* Anti-poploiarkos. *Lieutenant.* Simaiophoros. *Sub-Lieut.*

Other branches, without the curl :—
Surgeons : *purple velvet.*
Apothecaries : *green velvet.*
Constructors : *black velvet.*
Engineers : *violet velvet.*
Paymasters : *scarlet cloth.*

For details of Docks, Canal of Corinth, Fleet Anchorages, &c., See next page.

SALONIKA. Port has the shape of square wet dock and is very safe, with good anchorage. Ample quayage, which may have been further enlarged during the Allied use of this port. Was netted, mined and patrolled during War, and aircraft stations established here. No dry docks. Admiralty Chart No. 2070.

Scale : 1 inch = 160 feet.

GREEK NAVY: RECOGNITION SILHOUETTES.

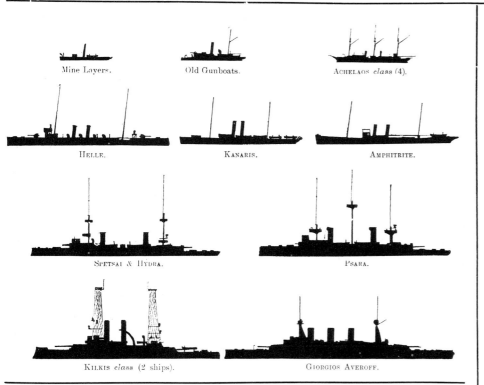

Mine Layers.   Old Gunboats.   ACHELAOS *class* (4).

HELLE.   KANARIS.   AMPHITRITE.

SPETSAI & HYDRA.   PSARA.

KILKIS *class* (2 ships).   GIORGIOS AVEROFF.

TORPEDO CRAFT.   Scale : 1 inch = 160 feet.

NIKOPOLIS t.b.   V 12, 14, 15, 16, t.b.   AIGLI *class* t.b. (6).   KERAVNOS *class* t.b.d. (2).

THYELLA *class* t.b.d. (4).   NIKE *class* t.b.d. (3).   LEON t.b.d.

Scale : 1 inch = 80 feet.

DELFIN *class* submarines (2).   AETOS *class* t.b.d. (3).

Fleet Anchorages.

During the War, the Allied Fleets made extensive use of Greek Harbours and Anchorages. **MUDROS BAY** (Lemnos) became the chief base of the British Eastern Mediterranean Fleet and Allied Squadrons during the War, being netted, mined and patrolled   A R.N. Airship Station was established at Mudros for anti-submarine service, with an outlying station at Kassandra. R.A.F. Stations were also created at Bessonreau, Imbros, Romanos, Syros, Stavros, Skyros, Syra, Thasos, Talikna, and Thermi-Mitylene (all under C.-in-C. Mediterranean & R.A. Aegean). **IMBROS** and **SUDA BAY** (latter with R.A.F. Station) were also used as Fleet Anchorages. **CORFU** became the principal base of the French Fleet, being netted, mined and patrolled by British R.N. Trawlers from N.E. of Corfu to Sasseno Island near Valona. Milo, Salomina and the Gulf of Patros were also netted. It is possible that some of the permanent works at these bases and stations may become the property of the Greek Government, and be used by the Greek Navy in the future.

Canal of Corinth.

Length : 6 kilometres = 3¾ miles *approx.*   Breadth : (*a*) at surface 24·6 metres = 80·7 feet, (*b*) at bottom 21 metres = 68·9 feet.   Depth : 8 metres = 26¼ feet.   Not navigable by Dreadnoughts and Battle Cruisers.

Docks. *(For Salonika, see preceding page.)*

SALAMIS (Arsenal). Government floating, 311 × 59 × 23 feet (3,000 tons).
Private Docks : There are two dry docks at Piræus (Harbour Trust), viz., "Vasilefs Giorgios," 460 × 69 × 29½ feet ; "Vasilissa Olga," 320 × 51 × 26 feet.
Mercantile Marine : 334 steamers of 695,105 tons *gross*, 585 sailing of 108,685 tons *gross*.
Chief Ports : Piræus, Syra, Volo, and Salonika.
Oversea trade chiefly with England, Russia, and Austria.
Coinage : Drachma (100 lepta) = about 9½d. British, 18 cents U.S.A.
Personnel : About 4000 (conscript 2 years or enlistment).
Minister of Marine : Admiral Condouriotis.

GREEK NAVY.

(1904) Battleships.

LEMNOS.

KILKIS (*ex Idaho*) (December, 1905), & **LEMNOS** (*ex Mississippi*) (September, 1905). *Normal* displacement, 13,000 tons. *Full load* displacement, 14,465 tons. Complement, 802. Length (*waterline*), 375 feet. Beam, 77 feet. *Max load draught*, 24¾ feet. Length *over all*, 382 feet. Guns: 4—12 inch, 45 cal. (A⁵), 8—8 inch, 45 cal., 8—7 inch, 45 cal., 12—3 inch, 13 pdr., 4—6 pdr. (saluting), 2—6 pdr. (anti-aircraft), 4—1 pdr., 8 M.G. (landing). Torpedo tubes (21 inch): 2 *submerged*. Armour (Midvale): 9″ Belt (amidships), 4″ Belt (ends), 3″ Armour deck, 12″—8″ Turrets, 10″—7½″ turret bases (N.C.), 6½″-6″ Secondary turrets (N.C.), 7″ Lower deck (redoubt), 7″ Battery (redoubt), 9″ Conning tower. Machinery: 2 sets vertical 4 cylinder triple expansion. 2 screws. Boilers: 8 Babcock. Designed H.P. 10,000=17 kts. (can only make 12 kts. now). Coal: *normal*, 750 tons; *maximum*, 1824 tons=6920 miles at 10 kts. Authorised 1903 for U.S. Navy; laid down at Cramp's, Philadelphia, May, 1904, and completed early in 1908. Sold to Greece early in 1914.

Spetsai. Re-fitting, 1919.

Psara. Stokers' Training Ship.

PSARA (1890, rebuilt 1897), **SPETSAI** (1889, rebuilt 1900), **HYDRA** (1889, rebuilt 1900). Displacement, 4808 tons. Complement, 440. Length (*o.a.*) 344½ feet. Beam, 51⅙ feet. *Mean draught*, 18 feet. Guns (Canet): 2—10·6 inch, 36 cals., 1—10·6 inch, 30 cals., 3—5·9 inch, 45 cals., 1—3·9 inch, 50 cals., 8—9 pdr., 4—3 pdr., 8 to 6—1 pdr. Torpedo tubes: 1—15 inch, 2—14 inch (all *above water*). Armour (Creusot steel): 12″—4¾″ Belt (lower), 3″ Belt (upper), 2¼″ Deck (flat), 13¾″ Battery redoubt. 12″ Barbette (aft), 6″ Hood, 6″ Hoists (main guns), 12″ Conning tower. Machinery: 2 sets vertical triple expansion. 2 screws. Boilers: Belleville (1914-15). H.P. 6700 =17 kts. Coal: *normal* 400 tons; *maximum*: others, 690 tons. Built by F. & C. de la Med., 1887–1892. All three are now fitted with flying topmasts, as *Hydra*. Appearance of *Spetsai* and *Psara* has been slightly changed by removal of the thin "auxiliary funnel" before fore funnel.

(1887-8) Coast Defence Ships.

SPETSAI. *Photo, Mons. C. B. Rontiri.*

PSARA. *Photo, Mons. C. B. Rontiri.*

HYDRA.

(1907) Armoured Cruiser.

Photo by favour of M. C. B. Rontiri.

GIORGIOS AVEROFF (March, 1910).

Normal displacement, { 9,960 tons. / 10,118 metric tons. } Complement, 550.

Length (*over all*), 462 feet. Beam, 69 feet. *Maximum* draught, 24¾ feet. Length (*p.p.*), 426 feet.

Guns (Elswick):
4—9·2 inch, 45 cal. (A³).
8—7·5 inch, 45 cal. (A).
16—14 pdr.
1—12 pdr. (anti-aircraft)
4—3 pdr.
2 M.G.
Torpedo tubes (18 inch):
2 *submerged* (broadside).
1 ,, (stern).

Armour (Terni):
8″ Belt (amidships) ....
3½″ Belt (ends) ....
2″ Deck ....
7″—6″ Upper belt ....
4″ Upper belt (ends) ....
8″ Main barbettes (N.C.) ...
6½″ Turrets to these (N.C.)
7″ Citadel ....
7″ Secondary turrets (N.C.)
7″ Conning towers (4) ......

Ahead:
2—9·2 in.
4—7·5 in.

Broadside: 4—9·2 in., 4—7·5 in.

Astern:
2—9·2 in.
4—7·5 in.

Machinery: 2 sets 4 cylinder triple expansion. 2 screws. Boilers: 22 Belleville Designed H.P. 19,000=22·5 kts. Trials: 21,500=23·9. Coal: *normal* 660 tons; *maximum* 1500 tons = 7125 miles at 10 kts.; 2489 miles at 17¾ kts. Built by Orlando, 1905-11.
Gunnery Notes—All big guns electrically controlled. 12 pdr. anti-aircraft gun mounted on after superstructure.
General Notes.—Cost £950,750. Sister to Italian *Pisa* with certain modifications as to armament and rig. This is the Italian ship formerly known as "X." Under the will of a deceased Greek millionaire, M Giorgios Averoff, about £300,000 was left for increasing the Navy. This sum was devoted towards the part purchase of the above vessel, the balance of her cost being defrayed by the State. Still has shell holes in funnels from Balkan war.

(1912) Light Cruiser.

HELLE.

HELLE (May, 1912).

Normal displacement, 2600 tons. Complement, 232.

Length (*over all*), 322 feet. Beam, 39 feet. Draught, 14 feet.

Guns (Armstrong):
2—6 inch.
4—4 inch.
2—14 pdr., 3 inch.
1—6 pdr. anti-aircraft.
2—3 pdr.
2—1 pdr.
Torpedo tubes (18 inch):
2 *above water*.

Armour (steel):
2″ Deck on slopes ...
1″ Deck on flat ....

Machinery: Parsons turbine. 3 screws. Boilers: Thornycroft. Designed H.P. 6000=20 kts. Coal: *normal*, 400 tons; *maximum*, 600 tons + 100 tons of oil fuel.=5250 miles at 10 kts.; 3320 miles at 17¾ kts.

Name	Builder	Machinery	Laid down	Completed	Trials: 4 hours.	Trials: Full Power.	Boilers	Best recent speed
Helle	N.Y. Shipblg.	N.Y. Shipblg.	1910	Nov.,'13	7500=20·3	8650=21	Thornycroft	

General Notes.—Built as the *Fei-Hung* for China. Purchased 1914.

GREEK DESTROYERS.

Note:—All boats reported to have been re-armed by French Navy during War. Armaments may now be different to those given below.

Now have high foremast for W. T. rig.

2 *Vulkan* type: **Keravnos, Nea Genea** (ex-German V5, V6, (both launched 1912, re-built 1918). 562 tons. Dimensions: 233 × 25 × 10 feet. Armament: 4—3·4 inch (15 pdr.), 2—18 inch tubes. A.E.G.-Curtis turbines. S.H.P. 16,500 = 32·5 kts. (about 26 now). Schulz boilers. Fuel: 137 tons coal + 80 tons oil. 2000 miles at 15 kts.

Now have short pole mainmast at stern.

4 *Thyella* class. Yarrow type: **Thyella, Sphendoni, Navkratousa** and **Lonkhi** (1906-07). 350 tons. Dimensions: 220½ × 20½ × 6 feet, *mean* draught; *max.* draught, 9 feet. Armament: 2—11 pdr., 4—6 pdr. 2 tubes (18 inch). Speed: 30 kts. (about 28 *max.* now). Coal: 80 tons. Endurance: 1110 to 1250 miles at 15 kts. Complement 70.

3 *Nike* class. Vulkan Stettin type: **Aspis** (1906), **Niki** (1905), and **Velos** (1906). 350 tons. Dimensions: 220½ × 20½ × 6 feet, *mean* draught; *max.* draught, 9 feet. H.P. 6700 = 30 kts. (about 28 now). Armament: 2—12 pdr. 4—6 pdr. 2 tubes (18 inch). Coal: 90 tons. Complement 70. Endurance: 1140 to 1250 miles at 15 kts.

Doxa of this class was lost during the War. Torpedoed by U-boat 27 June 1917.

Has *three* funnels.

LEON only of the *Aetos* class.

4 boats: **Kriti, Lesvos, Chios, Samos** (——1915).

Notes to Plans.—*Aetos, Jerax,* & *Panther* have 5 funnels, being set to port and starboard of centre line. *Leon* has *three* funnels. In all boats the 6 pdr. AA. gun mounted on "bandstand" abaft last funnel.

AETOS, JERAX, & PANTHER as above view.

4 *Cammell-Laird* type: **Aetos, Jerax, Leon, Panther** (all launched 1911). 980 tons *normal*, 1175 *full load*. Dimensions: 293 × 27½ × 8¼ feet, *normal* draught; *full load* draught, 10 feet. Armament: 4—4 inch Bethlehem, 1—6 pdr. AA. 4—18 inch tubes. 4 spare torpedoes in carriers on upper deck. 2 searchlights. S.H.P. 19,750 = 32 kts. (30 about *max.* now). Combined Parsons and Curtis turbines. 5 White-Forster boilers. Coal: 213 tons + 84 tons oil = 3000 miles at 15 miles. These were 4 boats, *San Luis, Santa Fé, Tucuman,* and *Santiago,* built for the Argentine. Purchased by Greece, Oct., 1912.

GREEK TORPEDO CRAFT.

6 *Vulkan* type: **Aigli, Alkyone, Arethousa, Dafni, Doris, Thetis** (all launched 1913). 120 tons. Dimensions: 147½ × 9½ × 4 feet. Armament: 2—6 pdr. Bethlehem, 3—18 inch tubes. S.H.P. 2100 = 25 kts. Trials: *Aigli* 26·2, *Doris* 25·7.

4 *Ansaldo* type: **Nikopolis** (ex-Turkish *Anatolia,* 1905). 160 tons. Dimensions: 167 × 18 × 6 feet (*mean* draught). Armament: 2—1 pdr. Bethlehem (1915). 1—18 inch tube. H.P. 2700 = 24 kts. Coal: 60 tons. Complement 20. Captured, 1912.

4 *Vulkan* type: **V16, V15, V14, V12** and **V11** (1885) (re-engined, etc., 1905). 85 tons. Dimensions: 128 × 15¼ × 6½ feet. Guns: 1—1 pdrs., 1 M.G. 2—14 inch bow tubes. H.P. 1000 = 18 kts. Coal 22 tons. Complement 20. V11 deleted before 1919.

2 Submarines.

2 *Laubeuf-Schneider* type: **Delphin** (8/11) and **Xiphias** (6/12). Dimensions: 164 × × feet. 1—18 inch bow tube and 4 torpedoes, carried in dropping gear on beam. Carry 6 torpedoes. Machinery: 2 sets, Schneider-Carels Diesel engines *on surface*; electric motors and batteries *submerged.* Cost of both boats defrayed by a national and voluntary subscription. For other details see Table.

GREEK MISCELLANEOUS.

Torpedo Depot Ship.

KANARIS (1870). 1083 tons. Dimension: $298\frac{1}{2} \times 20\frac{5}{8} \times 10\frac{1}{4}$ feet. Guns: 1—4 inch, 2—14 pdr., 2—6 pdr., 2 machine. H.P., 1200 = 14 kts. Coal: 200 tons. Complement 190.

Hospital Ship.

AMPHITRITE (Birkenhead, 1864, 1885). 1950 tons. Dimensions: $298\frac{1}{2} \times 26 \times$ feet. Guns: 4—1 pdr. H.P., 1200 = 14 kts. (Funnels have been lengthened since this photo was taken.)
— Previously the Royal Yacht.

Mine Layers.

MONEMBASIA, AIGIALIA, NAUPLIA (1881). 290 tons. Dimensions: $75\frac{1}{2} \times 13\frac{1}{4} \times 8\frac{1}{2}$ feet. H.P. 60 = 9 kts. Coal : 60 tons. Carry about 20 mines each.

Old Gunboats.

ACHELAOS, ALPHIOS (Blackwall, 1884), **PENEIOS, EUROTAS** (Dumbarton, 1884). All rebuilt 1895-7. 404 tons. Dimensions: $131\frac{1}{4}$ (p.p.) $\times 24\frac{1}{2} \times 11$ feet. Guns: 2 old 3·7 in., in first three (+4 M.G. in *Eurotas*.) *Peneios* has only 4 M.G. H.P. 400 = 11 kts. Complement 60.

AKTION. *French official War Photo.*

AKTION & AMBRAKIA (Blackwall 1881, re-built 1910). 433 tons. Dimensions: 128 (p.p.) $\times 25 \times 9\frac{1}{2}$ feet. Guns: 1—old 10·2 inch, 2—14 pdr. (in *Aktion* only), 1—1 pdr. H.P. 380 = 11 kts. Complement 70.

Note.—Foremast in one or both ships now removed.

Old Gunboats *(continued.)*

SALAMINIA (1858), and **SYROS** (1858). 374–300 tons. Guns: not known. *Nominal* speeds: 10 kts. Coal: 62–42 tons. Complement 55–42.

Used only for transferring crews and officers from the Naval Arsenal.

Submarine Depot Ship.

1 funnel, schooner-rigged.

SPHAKTERIA (1885). 1000 tons. H.P., 2400 = 16 kts. Guns: 2—1 pdr.

Oil Tanker.

PROMETHEUS. No details known. Can carry up to 4125 tons of oil fuel.

Salvage Tug.

(1 funnel, 2 masts, schooner-rigged, swan bow.)
TENEDOS (——). 100 tons.

Gunnery Training Ship.

1 funnel, barque-rigged, ram bow.

NAUARKOS MIAULIS (La Seyne, 1879). 1770 tons. Guns: various, from 12 pdr. downwards, and including 6 pdr. anti-aircraft for training purposes.

RUMANIAN NAVY.

RECOGNITION SILHOUETTES.

Scale : 1 inch = 160 feet.

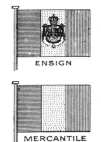

ENSIGN

MERCANTILE

I. BRATIANU *class.*

ELISABETA.

SIRETUL *class.*

NALUCA t.b.

MIRCEA.

ALEXANDRU CEL BUN.

Personnel : ?

Mercantile Marine : In 1916-17, 41 steamers of 75,174 tons *gross*. Some of these may have been destroyed during war.

Docks : At Galatz, on the Danube River, there used to be a floating dock in two sections, $264 \times 56 \times 16\frac{1}{2}$ feet (2400 tons). May have been destroyed during war.

Addenda.

Following additional Rumanian Warships reported just before going to Press:—

Patrol Boats. **ARGESUL, FROTUGUL, GRANICERUL, ILEANA, PANDURUL, PORUMBITSA, POTERAZUL, RANDUNICA, SENTINELA, SILISTRIA, SRUTUL, SVIMULET, TROTUS, TELERMAN, VEDEA, VEGHETORUL.**

Six Motor Boats, lettered *A* to *F*.

Training Ship. **STEFAN CEL MARE.**

Hospital Ship. **PRINCEPO MIRCEA** (and 10 Hospital Barges).

Cruiser.

ELISABETA (Elswick, 1887, rebuilt 1905). 1380 tons. Complement 150. Length, $239\frac{1}{2}$ feet. Beam, $33\frac{1}{2}$ feet. *Mean* draught, $12\frac{1}{4}$ feet. Guns: (4—4·7 inch have been landed for service ashore during war and may not be re-mounted), 4—12 pdr. (modified for anti-aircraft fire), 4 machine, 2 S.L. Torpedo tubes (14 inch): 4 *above water.* Armour (Steel): $3\frac{1}{2}''$ Deck (amidships), $1\frac{3}{4}''$ Deck (ends). Designed H.P. 4700 = 17·3 kts. Coal : 300 tons.

Danube Monitors.

ION BRATIANU (1907), **MIHAIL COGALNICEANU** (1908), **ALEXANDRU LAHOVARI** (1908), and **LASCAR CATARGIU** (1907). Displacement 670 tons. Complement, 110. Dimensions: $208\frac{1}{4} \times 33\frac{1}{3} \times 5\frac{1}{4}$ feet. Guns: 3—4·7 inch, 2—3 pdr. anti-aircraft, 2 machine, 2—14 inch S.L. Armour: 3″ Belt, 3″ Deck, 3″—2″ Turrets. H.P., 1800 = 13 kts. Coal: 60 tons. Built by Stabilimento Tecnico, Trieste.

RUMANIAN MISCELLANEOUS.

Coastguard Cruisers.

BISTRITSA.

BISTRITSA, OLTUL, SIRETUL (Blackwall, 1888). 96 tons. Dimensions : 100×13½×5¾ feet. Guns : 1—6 pdr., 1—1 pdr. H.P., 380=12 kts. Coal : 12 tons. Complement, 30.

1 funnel.

GRIVITZA (1880). 104 tons. Dimensions : 198½×17×5⅝ feet. Armament : 2—6 pdr., 2—1 pdr., 2 machine. H.P., 180= 9 kts. Coal : 18 tons. Complement, 30.

FULGERUL (1873). 85 tons. Dimensions : 82×15⅔×4¼ feet. Guns : 1—6 pdr., 1—1 pdr. H.P., 100=7½ kts. Coal : 10 tons. Complement, 18.

Mine Layer.

(v. Silhouette).

ALEXANDRU CEL BUN (1882). 104 tons. Dimensions : 75½×15×5¾ feet. Guns : 2—1 pdr., 2 machine. H.P. 100=9 kts. Coal : 12 tons. Complement, 20. Previously training ship.

Training Ship.

MIRCEA (1882). 360 tons. Guns : 4 machine. Speed : about 6 kts.

Patrol Boats.
(All armed with 2 machine guns).

Opanez, Rahova, Smardan (1882). 45 tons. 1—1 pdr. Speed : 9 kts.
Romania (1883). 111 tons. Speed : 9 kts.
Prutul (1893). 31 tons. Speed : 8 kts.

11 Torpedo Boats.

2 funnels abreast.

2 *Naluca* class. **Naluca, Sborul** (1888, reconstructed, 1907). Dimensions : 120½×11½×6⅝ feet. Armament : 1 machine gun. 2 tubes. 1 spar torpedo. *Smecel* lost in Black Sea 17 May 1917.

8 *Major Sontu* class : **Capt. Nicolae Lascar Bogdan, Capt. Romano Mihail, Capt. Valter Maracineau, Lieut. Demetre Calinescu, Major Constantine Ene, Major Demetre Giurescu, Major Nicolae Ivan, Major Giurge Sontzu** (Thames Iron Works, 1906). Dimensions : 190×13×2¾ feet. Armament : 1—3 pdr., 1 machine, 2 sets of dropping gears and 2—14 inch spar torpedoes. 1—20 inch S.L. For other details, see Table.

ARGENTINE FLEET.

Note.—The Ensign, Jack and Mercantile blue is *sky blue*, not ordinary flag blue.

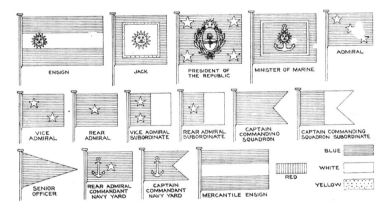

Sub-Lieutenant.

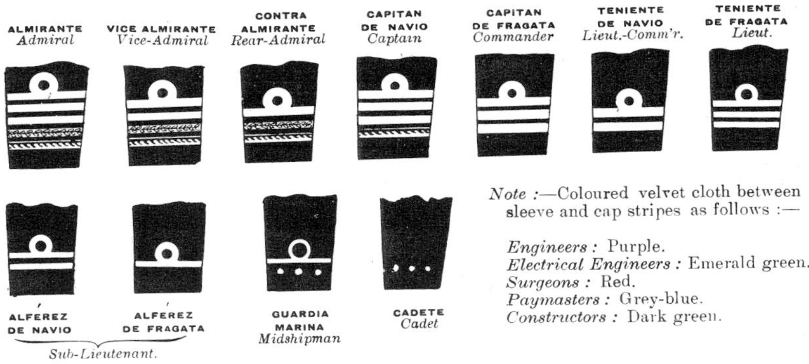

Note :—Coloured velvet cloth between sleeve and cap stripes as follows :—

Engineers : Purple.
Electrical Engineers : Emerald green.
Surgeons : Red.
Paymasters : Grey-blue.
Constructors : Dark green.

Arsenals.

(1) **BUENOS AIRES.** Dry docks : (Eastern) 590½ × 65½ × 25 feet, and (Western) 492 × 65½ × 25 feet.

(2) **PUERTO BELGRANO** (Bahia Blanca). Dry docks : (1) 683×84×32½ feet, (2) 683×114×43.

(3) **RIO SANTIAGO.** New dock, 672 × 114 × 36 feet. Two floating docks, (1) 1500 tons lift (2) 300 tons lift.

General Notes.

Mercantile Marine : 317 steamers of 222,533 tons *gross*, including sailing vessels and ships over 100 tons

Personnel : about 9500 all ranks. *Reserve :* about 8000 *Special reserve :* 10,000.

Minister of Marine :

Notation.	Nominal Calibre.		Maker.	Length in Calibres.	Muzzle Velocity.	Weight A.P. Projectile.	Max.penetration against K.C. with capped A.P. at		Danger Space against average warship, at			Service Rounds per minute.
							5000 yards.	3000 yards.	10,000 yards.	5000 yards.	3000 yards.	
	inches	c/m.		calibres.	ft. secs.	lbs.	inches.	inches.				
A⁶	12	30·5	B	50	2900	870	19	23				2
A	10	25·4	E	40	2207	500	7	9½				·6
C	9·4	24	K	35	{2300} {2133}	352	4½	6				·4
A	8	20·3	E	45	2660	210	6½	9				1
B	8	21	E	40	2286	210	4	6				
E	8	20	K	35	2120	200	3	5				
D	6	15	B	50	2600	105		8¼				
D	6	15	C	50	2625	88	4	6	74	240	465	5
E⁕	6	15		45	2500	100	3	4½	66	210	435	
F⁕	6	15		40	2200	100	3	3¾	37	150	360	
F⁕	4·7	12	C	50	2600	46·3	...	3½				
F⁕	4·7	12	E	45	2570	45	...	2¾				
F⁕	4·7	12	E	40	2230	45	...					

⁕ = Brass cartridge case used.

In the Maker's column B = Bethlehem. E = Elswick ; K = Krupp ; C = Canet ; V = Vickers.

The above details of Argentine Naval Ordnance are not taken from any official source and must be regarded as merely approximate.

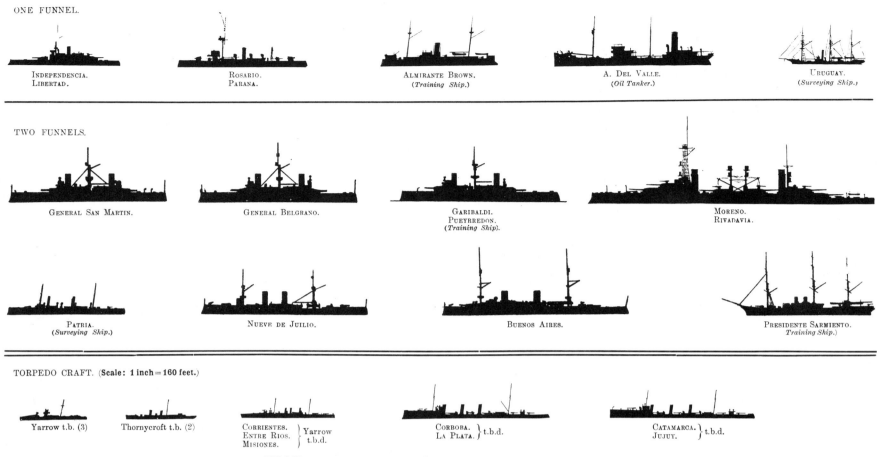

Scale: 1 inch = 160 feet.

ARGENTINE RECOGNITION SILHOUETTES.

ONE FUNNEL.

INDEPENDENCIA. LIBERTAD.

ROSARIO. PARANA.

ALMIRANTE BROWN. (Training Ship.)

A. DEL VALLE. (Oil Tanker.)

URUGUAY. (Surveying Ship.)

TWO FUNNELS.

GENERAL SAN MARTIN.

GENERAL BELGRANO.

GARIBALDI. PUEYRREDON. (Training Ship).

MORENO. RIVADAVIA.

PATRIA. (Surveying Ship.)

NUEVE DE JUILIO.

BUENOS AIRES.

PRESIDENTE SARMIENTO. Training Ship.)

TORPEDO CRAFT. (Scale: 1 inch = 160 feet.)

Yarrow t.b. (3)

Thornycroft t.b. (2)

CORRIENTES. ENTRE RIOS. MISIONES. } Yarrow t.b.d.

CORBOBA. LA PLATA. } t.b.d.

CATAMARCA. JUJUY. } t.b.d.

(1910) ARGENTINE DREADNOUGHTS (Nos. **1** & **2**).

RIVADAVIA (26 Aug., 1911) & MORENO (23 Sept., 1911).

Normal displacement, 27,940 tons. *Full load,* 30,600 tons. Complement, 1215.

Length *(w.l.),* 577½ feet. Beam, 95 feet. *Max load draught,* 28 feet. Length *over all,* 585 feet.

Guns (Bethlehem):
12—12 inch, 50 cal. *Dir. Con. ?*
12—6 inch, 50 cal.
16—4 inch, 50 cal.
4—3 pdr.
6 M.G.
(4 landing).
Torpedo tubes (21 inch):
2 *submerged*
(broadside).

Armour (Krupp):
11"—8" Belt (amidships)
5" Belt (bow) N.C.
4" Belt (stern) N.C.
3" Deck (slopes)
9"—8" Side above belt
12"—9" Big gun turrets
6" Secondary battery (N.C.)
12" Conning Tower (forward)
9" Do. (aft.)
Total weight: 7600 tons.

RIVADAVIA. *Photo by courtesy of the Ministry of Marine.*

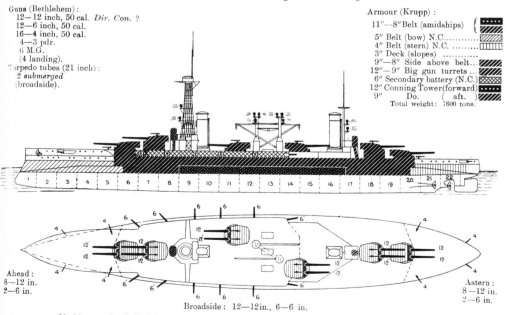

Ahead:
8—12 in.
2—6 in.

Astern:
8—12 in.
2—6 in.

Broadside: 12—12 in., 6—6 in.

General Notes.—Built under 1908 Programme. Gave considerable trouble on trials, as steam consumption exceeded contract rate. Turbines were re-bladed completely before these ships got through their trials. They are said to have so heavy a coal consumption, plans are being prepared for conversion to "all oil fuel." On a voyage, Buenos Ayres—New York—Buenos Ayres, in 1918, one of these ships consumed 15,000 tons of coal, or 4000 tons more than the estimated normal cruising consumption with auxiliaries running.

Machinery: Curtis Turbines. 3 screws. Designed S.H.P. 39,500 = 22·5 kts. Boilers: 18 Babcock. Coal capacity: *normal,* 1600 tons; *maximum,* 4000 tons. Oil: 660 tons. *Nominal radius:* 3930 miles at full speed, 7740 miles at 10 kts. (see *General Notes*).

Gunnery Notes.—Heights of barbettes over normal draught w.l.: No. 1, 29¼ feet; No. 2, 37½ feet; Nos. 3 and 4 (echelon), and No. 5, 29 feet; No. 6, 20 feet; 6 inch guns, 19½ feet above w.l. Arcs of fire: end barbettes, Nos. 1 and 6, 270°; Nos. 2 and 5 (super-firing), 300°; Nos. 3 and 4 (echelon) 180° own beam and 100° far beam. R.F. on heads of derrick posts.

Armour Notes.—Main belt is 8 feet deep, 4¾ feet above water-line and 3¼ feet below same at normal draught. It is 240 feet long, but 11" section is only 2 feet deep from top edge of belt, and then tapers to 5" on lower (under-water) edge. Belt under end barbettes is 10" tapering to 5" as main belt. Upper belt 400 feet long, 9" lower edge, 8" top edge, 6" battery above this. Funnel bases, 1½" nickel steel for 15 feet above deck. Protective decks, 1½" upper, 3" lower. Two Director stations behind upper belt at bases of C.T. communication tubes. Barbettes: bases are 9" where exposed. Shields to these: 12" port-plate, 9" sides, 11" back, 3" roof.

Anti-Torpedo Defence—3" longitudinal wing bulkheads in way of machinery and magazine spaces. ¾" nickel steel flats under magazines, boilers, and engine rooms. Total weight, 680 tons (included in 7,600 tons total weight of armour given above). 12 searchlights.

RIVADAVIA.

Torpedo Notes.—Bullivant net defence. 12—38 inch searchlights. Electric installation at 115 volts.

Name	Builder	Machinery	Laid down	Completed	Trials	Boilers	Best recent speed
Rivadavia	Fore River Co. N.Y. Ship-building	Fore River Co.	May, '10	Dec., 1914	39,750 = 22·5	Babcock	
Moreno			July, '10	Mar. 1915		Babcock	

ARGENTINE ARMOURED SHIPS.

GEN. BELGRANO: Searchlight on mast now on tower abaft 2nd funnel. Small Q.F. in fighting top on mast removed.

GEN. SAN MARTIN: One fighting top has been removed from mast. This ship is now almost of same appearance as Belgrano.

Photo by courtesy of the Ministry of Marine, (LIBERTAD).

GARIBALDI.   *Photo by courtesy of Ministry of Marine.*

GENERAL BELGRANO (July, 1897), **GENERAL SAN MARTIN** (1896), both by Orlando, Leghorn, **GARIBALDI** (1895), by Ansaldo, Sestri, Ponente. All 6840 tons. Length (*o.a.*), 328 ft. Beam, 59,⁷₂ feet. *Max.* draught, 23¼ feet. Complements, (*G.B.*) 425, (*G.S.M.*) 431, (*G.*) 414. Armament: *Belgrano* 2—10 inch, 14—6 inch, 4-—12 pdr., 4—6 pdr., 4—18 inch tubes *above water*. *San Martin*: 4—8 inch, 10—6 inch, 6—4·7 inch. 2—12 pdr., 4—18 inch tubes *above water*. *Garibaldi*: 2—10 inch, 10—6 inch, 6—4·7 inch, 2.—12 pdr., 4—6 pdr. Armour: (Krupp in *G.B.*, Harvey Nickel in *G.S.M.*, Harvey in *G.*), 6″ Belt with 3″ at ends and 1½″–2″ deck, 6″ Lower deck side, 6″ Battery, 6″ Barbettes, 6″ Bulkheads, 3″ Gunhouses, 6″ C.T. Machinery: 2 sets triple expansion. Boilers: 8 cylindrical, single-ended. H.P. 13000=20 kts. Coal: *normal*, about 400 tons; *maximum* (*G.B.*) 1150 tons, (*G.S.M.* & *G.*) 1137 tons. Endurance: about 6000 miles at 10 kts.

·**Note.**— A fourth ship of this type, **PUEYRREDON,** now employed as a Training Ship

ARGENTINE COAST DEFENCE BATTLESHIPS.

INDEPENDENCIA.   *Photo by courtesy of the Ministry of Marine.*

INDEPENDENCIA (1891), & **LIBERTAD** (ex-*Nueve de Julio*) (1890). Both built at Laird's, Birkenhead. Displacement 2300 tons. Complement 196. Length (*p.p*) 240 feet. Beam, 43 feet. *Max.* draught, 13 feet. Guns: 2—9·4 inch, 35 cal. (Krupp), 4—4·7 inch, 40 cal. (Elswick), 6—3 pdr. Armour (compound): 8″ Belt (amidships), 2″ Deck (flat on belt,) 8″ Bulkhead (forward), 6″ Bulkhead (aft), 8″ Barbettes and bases, 5″ Shields to big guns (fronts), 4″ Conning tower. Machinery: Compound vertical. 2 screws. Boilers: 4 double cylindrical. Designed H.P. 3000=14 kts. Coal: *normal* 230 tons; *maximum* 356 tons. Endurance: 3000 miles at 10 kts.

Old Protected Cruisers. ARGENTINE NAVY.

Photo, Abrahams & Son, Devonport.

BUENOS AIRES (Elswick, 1895). Displacement 4780 tons. Sheathed and coppered. Complement 375. Length (*o.a.*), 403½ feet. Beam, 47¾ feet. *Maximum* draught, 19 feet. Guns (Elswick): 2—8 inch, 45 cal. (*A*), 4—6 inch, 45 cal., 6—4·7 inch, 45 cal., 12—3 pdr. Torpedo tubes: 5 *above water*. Armour (steel): 5″ Deck (amidships), 5″ Engine hatches, 4½″ Gun shields, 3″ Hoists to guns, 6″ Conning tower (Harvey). Machinery: 2 sets vertical 4-cylinder (2 low-pressure cylinders). 2 screws. Boilers: 4 double-ended and 4 single-ended. Designed H.P. 13,000=23 kts.; 17,000=24 kts. Coal: *normal* 400 tons; *maximum* 1000 tons. Endurance: 6400 miles at 10 kts.

Training Ships.

Now has W.T. aerials from truck of mast to bow and stern, as *Garibaldi* on preceding page.

PUEYRREDON (Ansaldo, 1897). Armoured ship. *Normal* displacement, 6840 tons. Complement, 427. Guns (Elswick): 2—10 inch, 40 cal. (*A*), 10—6 inch, 40 cal., 6—4·7 inch, 40 cal., 2—12 pdr. 4—6 pdr., Torpedo tubes (18 inch): 4 *above water* (behind armour). All other details as *General Belgrano*, described on a preceding page, except :—(*a*) Armour (Terni); (*b*) 16 Belleville boilers. (*c*) *maximum* coal capacity 1000 tons=4800 miles at 10 kts. Laid down 1896, completed 1901. Made 19·94 kts. on first trials. Machinery:—Ansaldo-Maudslay.

Photo by courtesy of the Ministry of Marine.

NUEVE DE JULIO (Elswick 1892) Displacement 3540. Complement 315 Length, (*o.a.*) 354¾ feet. Beam, 44 feet. *Maximum* draught, 19¼ feet. Guns (Elswick): 4—6 inch, 40 cal., 8—4·7 inch, 40 cal.,10—3 pdr. Torpedo tubes: 3 *above water*. Armour (steel): 4½″ Deck, 5″ Glacis to engines, Cofferdam amidships. Machinery: 2 sets vertical 4 cylinder (2 low-pressure cylinders). 2 screws. Boilers: 8—single-ended. Designed H.P. (forced) 14,500=22·5 kts. Coal: *normal* 300 tons; *maximum* 770 tons. Endurance: 5500 miles at 10 kts.

(Gunnery Training Ship.)

ALMIRANTE BROWN (Samuda, Poplar, 1880, reconstructed at La Seyne, 1907). Old Coast Defence Battleship. 4200 tons. Dimensions: 240 (*p.p.*) × 50 × 20½ feet. Complement, 290. Guns: 10—6 inch (50 cal.), 4—4·7 inch (50 cal.), 8—6 pdr. Torpedo tubes: 2—18 inch *above water*. Armour (compound): 9″ Belt with 7″ Bulkheads and 1½″ Flat Deck, 8″ Central battery. Designed H.P. 4500=14 kts. (present speed, 11 kts.) Boilers: Cylindrical. Coal: 622 tons.

Training Ships *continued.*

PRESIDENTE SARMIENTO (1898). Built at Birkenhead. 2850 tons. Complement 294. Dimensions: $251\frac{5}{12} \times 43\frac{1}{4} \times 23\frac{1}{4}$. Guns: 2—4·7 inch, 50 cal., 2—4 inch, 2—6 pdr., 2—3 pdr. Torpedo tubes: 3 *above water.* Designed H.P. 2800 = 15 kts. Coal: 330 tons. Boilers: 1 Niclausse, 1 Yarrow, 2 cylindrical single-ended.

Armoured River Gunboats.

Official photo, 1918.

PARANA (April, 1908) & **ROSARIO** (July, 1908). Both built at Elswick. Displacement, 1055 tons. Complement, 142. Length, $329\frac{2}{3}$ feet. Beam, $32\frac{2}{3}$ feet. Draught, $7\frac{4}{12}$ feet. Guns: 2—6 inch Howitzers, 6—12 pdr., 8 Machine, 2 landing. Armour: 3″ Belt (amidships), $1\frac{1}{2}$″—1″ Deck, 3″ Conning tower. H.P. 1600 = 15 kts. 2 Yarrow boilers. Coal: 120 tons. *Nominal* radius, 2400 miles at $10\frac{1}{2}$ kts.

ROSARIO

ARGENTINE MISCELLANEOUS.
Surveying Ships.

ALFEREZ MACKINLAY (1914). 783 tons. H.P., 520 = 10 kts.

(Gunboat.)

PATRIA (Birkenhead, 1893). Displacement, 1070 tons. Dimensions: $251\frac{5}{12} \times 30\frac{2}{3} \times 11\frac{1}{4}$ feet. Complement, 156. Guns: 2—4·7 inch, 40 cal., 4—6 pdr., 2—3 pdr. Machinery: 2 sets triple expansion. 2 screws. Boilers: 4 double-ended Yarrow. Designed H.P. 4500 = 20·5 kts. Coal: 260 tons. Endurance: 3200 miles at 10 kts.

PATRIA

See Silhouettes.

URUGUAY (Birkenhead, 1874). 550 tons (sheathed). Original speed: 11 kts. Coal: 90 tons. Is an old iron Gunboat. Loaned 1918 to a Meteorological Surveying Expedition.

Oil-Tankers.

INGENERIO LUIS A. HUERGO (1917). 7378 tons. Dimensions: × × 22·5 feet. Designed H.P. 1600 = 10 kts.

Torpedo Gunboats.

ESPORA (1890). (Reconstructed 1905). Displacement, 550 tons. Complement, 124. Guns: 2—3 inch, 14 pdr., 5—3 pdr. Torpedo tubes: 1 *above water* (bow). Armour: *Nil.* Machinery: 2 sets triple expansion. 2 screws. Boilers: 6 Yarrow. Designed H.P. *forced* 3000 = 19·5 kts. Coal: *normal* 100 tons; *maximum* 130 tons. Built at Laird's, Birkenhead. Reconstructed 1905. Deleted by 1919.

Oil-Tankers—*continued.*

Official photo.

ARISTÓBULO DEL VALLE (1917). 5,400 tons. Dimensions: × × 21·6 feet. Designed H.P. 1400 = 9·5 kts.

MINISTRO EZCURRA (1914). 2600 tons. H.P., 1243 = $10\frac{1}{2}$ kts.

Transports, &c.

VICENTE-FIDEL-LOPEZ (1906). 725 tons. H.P., 480 = 9·3 kts.
GUARDIA-NACIONAL (1890). 6500 tons. H.P., 1850 = 14 kts.
PIEDRABUENA (1874). Old iron Gunboat, sister to *Uruguay* in preceding column. Guns: 1 machine.

Also *Azopardo* and *Ingenerio Iribas*, both detached on Surveying Service, *Chaco*, *Guarda-Nacional*, *Pampa*, *Primero de Mayo*.

Tugs.

ONA (1913), **QUERANDI** (1914). Both built by Thornycrofts. These are large sea-going vessels and powerful salvage craft of 615 tons, 1200 H.P. and 11 kts. speed. During war, they performed more patrol work than any other ships of the fleet. In 1914, the Admiralty wished to take them over, but the Argentine Government insisted on delivery.

There are 7 other Tugs, built about 1900, the largest being **TECHUELCHE** and **FUEGUINO** of 310 tons and $11\frac{1}{2}$ kts. speed. Also *Fulton*.

Old Monitors.
(On Subsidiary Service).

EL PLATA, LOS ANDES (1874). 1535 tons. H.P., 750 = 9 kts. *nominal.* Guns: 2—8 inch, 1—4·7 inch, 1—12 pdr., 4 or 2—6 and 3 pdr.

ARGENTINE TORPEDO CRAFT.

CORRIENTES

7 Destroyers. *(Cazatorpederos.)*

No.	Type	Date	Displacement	H.P.	Max. speed	Fuel	Complement	T. tubes	Max. draug't
			tons		kts.	tons			feet
2	*Cordoba* (S)	'10-'12	950	20,000	32	290 coal + 50 oil	99	4	8
2	*Catamarca* (K)	'10-'12	950	18,000	32	250 coal + 100 oil	99	4	$8\frac{1}{2}$
3	*Corrientes* (Y)	'96-'98	340	4000	26	80 coal	66	3	$8\frac{1}{4}$

K = Krupp.   S = Schichau.   Y = Yarrow.

Photo by courtesy of the Ministry of Marine.

4 *Ch. de Bretagne.* **Mendoza, Rioja, Salta, San Juan** (—, 1911). 950 tons. $289\frac{1}{2} \times 28\frac{1}{4} \times 10\frac{1}{4}$ feet. Armament: 4—4 inch (Beth.), 4—21 inch tubes. 2 searchlights. Rateau turbines. H.P. 18,000 = 32 kts. Coal: 256 tons. Oil: 80 tons. On trial *Mendoza* did 32·98 (average). Apparently deleted by 1919, but no evidence as to their disposal.

Photo by courtesy of the Ministry of Marine.

2 (German) type: **Cordoba** (Schichau, Nov., 1910), **La Plata** (Germania, Jan., 1911). 950 tons. $295 \times 29\frac{1}{2} \times 7\frac{3}{4}$ feet. Armament: 4—4 inch (Beth.), 4—21 inch tubes. Curtis (A.E.G.) turbines. Boilers: 5 Schulz-Thornycroft. Designed S.H.P. 20,000 = 32 kts. Coal: 290 tons. Oil: 50 tons. Endurance: 2700 miles at 15 kts., 715 miles at full Speed Trials (max.): *Cordoba*, 34·2; *La Plata*, 34·7.

2 (German) type: **Catamarca** (Schichau, Jan., 1911), **Jujuy** (Germania, March, 1911). 950 tons. $288\frac{3}{4} \times 27 \times 8\frac{1}{4}$ feet. Armament: 4—4 inch (Beth.), 4—21 inch tubes. Curtis (A.E.G.) turbines. Boilers: Schulz-Thornycroft. Designed S.H.P. 18,000 = 32 kts. Coal: 250 tons. Oil: 110 tons. Endurance: 3000 miles at 15 kts. 800 miles at full speed.

3 *Yarrow* type: **Corrientes, Entre Rios, Misiones** (—1896). Dimensions: $190 \times 19\frac{1}{2} \times 8\frac{1}{4}$ feet. 1″ armour protection amidships. Armament: 1—14 pdr., 3—6 pdr., 2—1 pdr., 3 tubes (18 inch). 6 Yarrow boilers. Coal: 80 tons. Endurance: 900 miles at 15 kts. Other details as table.

5 Torpedo Boats. *(Torpederos).*

No.	Type	Date	Displacement	H.P.	Max. speed	Fuel	Complement	T. tubes	Max. draug't
			tons		kts.	tons			feet
2	*Comodoro Py* (T)	'90-'91	110	1700	24·5	24	43	3	$3\frac{1}{2}$
3	*Buchardo* (Y)	'90-'91	85	1200	23	22	28	2	6

T = Thornycroft.   Y = Yarrow.

2 Thornycroft type: **Comodoro Py** (1891) and **Murature** (1890). Dimensions: $150 \times 11\frac{1}{2} \times 3\frac{1}{4}$ feet. Armament: 2—3 pdr., 1 M.G., 3—18 inch tubes. Thornycroft boilers. Endurance: 1200 miles at 15 kts. Other details as Table above.

4 Yarrow type: **Bathurst, Buchardo, Jorge, Thorne** (all 1890.) Dimensions: 130 x 14 x 6 feet. Armament: 2—3 pdr., 1 M.G., 3-18 inch tubes. Endurance: 1200 miles at 15 kts. *King* and *Pinedo* of this class deleted by 1919.

BRAZILIAN FLEET.

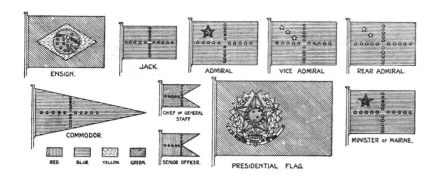

ENSIGN.   JACK.   ADMIRAL.   VICE ADMIRAL.   REAR ADMIRAL.

COMMODOR.   CHIEF OF GENERAL STAFF   PRESIDENTIAL FLAG.   MINISTER OF MARINE.

RED.   BLUE.   YELLOW.   GREEN.   SENIOR OFFICER.

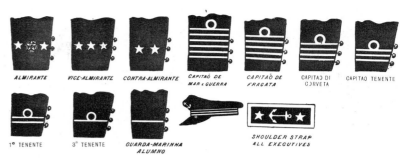

ALMIRANTE   VICE-ALMIRANTE   CONTRA-ALMIRANTE   CAPITAŌ DE MAR E GUERRA   CAPITAŌ DE FRAGATA   CAPITAŌ DI CORVETA   CAPITAŌ TENENTE

1° TENENTE   3° TENENTE   GUARDA-MARINHA ALUMNO   SHOULDER STRAP ALL EXECUTIVES

Mercantile Marine.

283 steamers, 266,605 tons *gross.*
79 sailing, 14,068 „ „
49 German steamers, of 253,795 tons, have been seized and placed into service, two of which have been sunk.

Guns in Service.°

Nota-tion.	Calibre.		Length in calibres	Weight of A.P. shell.	Muzzle Velocity.	Max. penetration A.P. capped at K.C. at		Danger Space against average ships at			Service rounds per minute
						5000 yards.	3000 yards.	10,000 yards.	5000 yards.	3000 yards.	
	inch.	c/m.	cals.	lbs.	ft. secs.	inch.	inch.				
HEAVY	12	30·5	45	850	2800	...	...	...	...	...	2
MEDIUM	9·2	23	45	380	2700	9	11½	...	...	...	·8
LIGHT {	6	15	40	100	2500	4 4½	5	65	200	420	6
	6	15	50	100	2640		5½	72	240	460	6
	4·7	12	40	45	2150	..	..	..	..	..	8
	4·7	12	50	45	2630	...	..	..	..	..	8

° **Note.** = These particulars of the Brazilian Naval Ordnance are not derived from any official source and must be regarded as only approximate.

Scale : 1 inch = 160 feet.

Almirante is only a war appointment : *Vice-Almirante* is the highest place rank.

Capitao di Corveta is equivalent to a British Lieut-Commander. *Capitao tenente* a lieutenant. *1° tenente* = sub-lieutenant. Civilian ranks have the same stripes *without* the curl, and plus colours above top stripe and below bottom one as under :

Constructors.—No colour, but a ball above the stripes.
Engineers (Machinista).—Green.
Doctors (Cirurgiao).—Red.
Paymasters (Commissario).—White.

Shoulder straps for engineers carry a screw propeller, for doctors a stethoscope, for paymasters two quill pens crossed. These devices are also worn on the collar of tunic.

Caps.—Admirals have a broad gold band with oak leaf device, the other commissioned ranks narrow gold bands as on sleeves.

Warrant officers and men carry white distinctive sleeve badges, as follows :—*Torpedo*, torpedoes ; *gunnery*, two crossed guns ; *navigation*, two crossed anchors ; *signal*, two crossed flags ; *quartermasters*, a wheel ; *engine room complements*, a screw propeller.

Marine Infantry—Scarlet tunics with black insignia : five stripes for first sargento, four for second ditto, two for cabo. White helmets as the British. No commissioned officers.

Brazilian sailors enter as boys at about twelve years. They do three years in a school, then ten months special instruction, then serve twelve years with the fleet. Volunteers three to twenty years. There are nineteen schools for boys.

Arsenals.

RIO DE JANEIRO. 6 Docks. Government are "Guanabara" (Cobras Island). 423×70×20 feet ; "Santa Cruz," 258½×54⅔×18 feet. Government Floating Dock, "Affonso Penna," lengthened in 1912 to 715¾×102×36 feet (30,000 tons), requires 54 feet depth of water to dock ship of 30 feet draught. A seventh Floating Dock, 350 (o.a) × 136 feet (to lift 6000 tons), completing by Messrs. Vickers Ltd., 1919. This dock was taken over for British Navy during war, but released in 1919. 3 Private Docks, Mocangué No. 1, 400×60×16 feet ; Mocangué No. 2, 370×50×16 feet. Lage Bros, "Cruziero" (Vianna Island), 400×58×18 feet.

PARA. 2 Floating Docks, "Affonso Penna" and "Lauro Müller," each 235×45×12 feet (1700 tons).

LADARIO River.

Personnel.—About 10,000 of all ranks and ratings.

Minister of Marine—Senhor Raul Soares (July, 1919).

BRAZILIAN RECOGNITION SILHOUETTES.

ONE FUNNEL.

PERNAMBUCO.   ACRE *class*   OYAPOCK.   *1 funnel, 1 mast, Clipper bow.* J. BONIFACIO. (*Yacht.*)   AMAPÁ.   M. HERMES.   JAGUARAYO.*   M. DO. CONTO.°

River Craft.   *Tugs and Despatch Vessels.*
Mining Vessels.

REPUBLICA.   C. COMEZ. (*Mine Layer*).   DEODORO *class* (2 ships).   CEARA (S/M. Depôt Ship). (*Double hulls at stern.*)   TIRADENTES.   BENJ. CONSTANT. (*Training Ship.*)

TWO FUNNELS.

BAHIA *class* (2 ships).

MINAS GERAES *class* (2 ships).

TORPEDO CRAFT.   Scale : 1 inch = 160 feet.

GOYAZ t.b.   Yarrow type, t.b.d (10 Para *class*.)

SUBMARINES.

Scale : 1 inch = 80 feet.

F *class* (3).
(*May have one or two folding masts*).

TYMBIRA.   BARROSO.

(1907) BRAZILIAN DREADNOUGHTS Nos. 2 & 1.

(MINAS GERAES CLASS—2 SHIPS).

MINAS GERAES (Sept., 1908), **SAO PAULO** (April, 1909).

Normal displacement 19,200 tons. *Full load* 21,200 tons. Complement 850.

Length (*waterline*) 530 feet; (*p.p.*), 500 feet. Beam 83 feet. *Max.* load draught, 25 feet. Length *over all*, 543 feet

Guns (Elswick):
12—12 inch, 45 cal.
22—4·7 inch, 50 cal.
8—3 pdr.
4 M.G.
Torpedo tubes:
Dropping gear for boats and carry torpedoes for this purpose.

Armour (Krupp):
9″ Belt
6″—4″ Belt (bow) N.C.
6″—4″ Belt (aft) N.C.
$2\frac{1}{4}$″ Deck (slopes)
9″—6″ Upper belt
9″ Bulkheads
9″ Battery (main deck)
12″—8″ Turrets (K.C.)
12″ Conning tower (fore)
9″ Conning tower (aft)

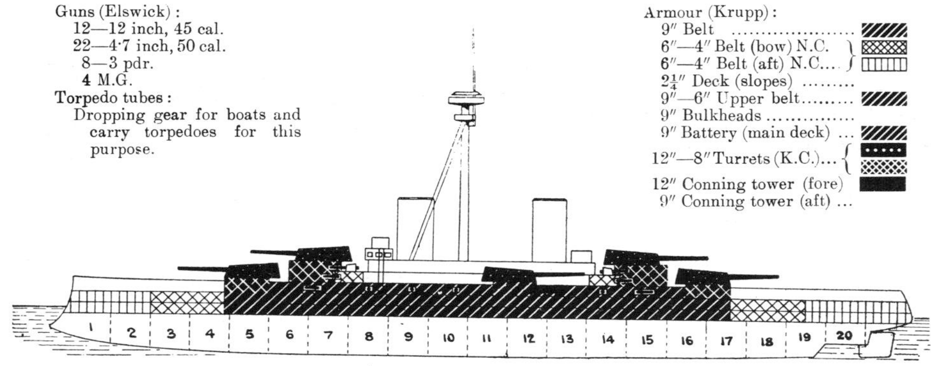

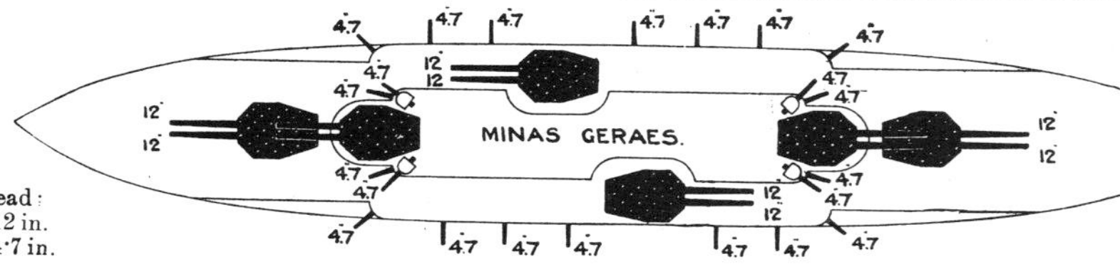

Ahead:
8—12 in.
6—4·7 in.

Astern:
8—12 in.
6—4·7 in.

Broadside: 10—12 in., 11—4·7 in.

Machinery: 2 sets triple expansion. 2 screws. Designed S.H.P. 23,500 = 21 kts. *f.d.* Boilers: 18 Babcock. Coal: *normal* 800 tons; *maximum* 2360 tons+350 tons oil. Endurance: about 3600 miles at 19 kts., and about 8000 miles at 10 kts.

Gunnery Notes.—Arcs of fire: Centre-line 12-inch guns 270-280°; beam 12-inch 180° *nominal*. Main deck, 4·7 inch 100°; 4·7 inch in superstructure casemates, 90°. 3 pdr. guns can be transferred to landing mountings.

Torpedo Notes.—$\frac{4}{5}$ net defence (Bullivant). S.L. not controlled.

Engineering Notes.—66 revs. = about 10 kts; 126 = 20 kts.; 148 about 21·5 kts. Heating surface, 55,370 sq. ft. Grate area, 1868 sq. ft.

Armour Notes.—Main belt $22\frac{1}{2}$ ft. deep, 5 ft. of this being below waterline. Belt does not run up to stern.

Name.	*Builder.*	*Machinery.*	*Laid down.*	*Completed.*	*Trials.* 30 hour at $\frac{3}{4}$	*Trials.* Full power	*Boilers.*	*Best recent speed.*
M. Geraes	Elswick	Vickers	1907	Jan.'10	16,177 = 19·13	25,519 = 21·2	Babcock	
S. Paulo	Vickers	Vickers	1907	July '10	16,067 = 19·85	25,517 = 21·2	Babcock	

General Notes.—Both ships were somewhat over normal displacement on trials. Have been in poor condition for several years past and cannot raise anything like full designed speed until machinery is fully overhauled.

* Not from any official source.

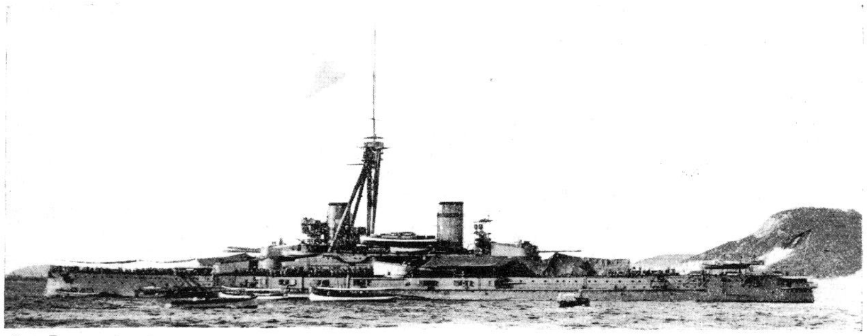

SAO PAULO.

Notes added in 1919.—In view of experiences gained by the war, the following remarks are added: (*a*) armouring is generally inadequate to give protection against the latest types of A.P. and H.E. shells; (*b*) main deck 4·7 inch are not much use in any seaway; (*c*) these ships lack any director systems of control for 12 inch or 4·7 inch guns but may have a few small-base R.F.; (*d*) searchlights are uncontrolled and inadequate in number.

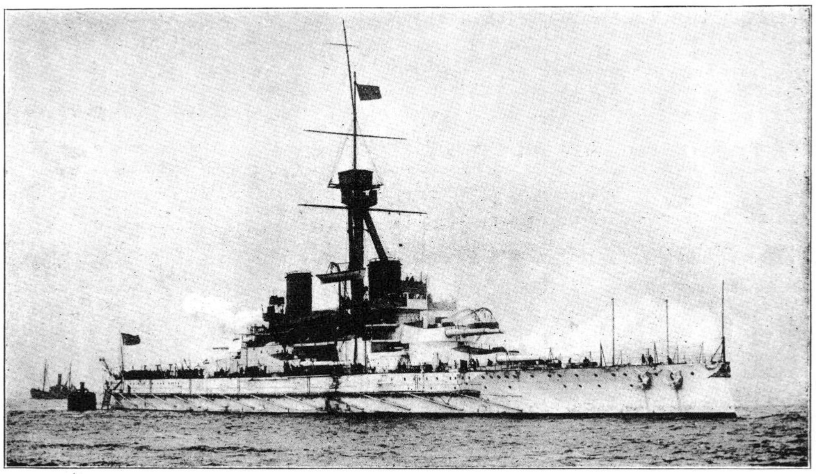

M. GERAES.

(1908) Light Cruisers (*Cruzadores*).

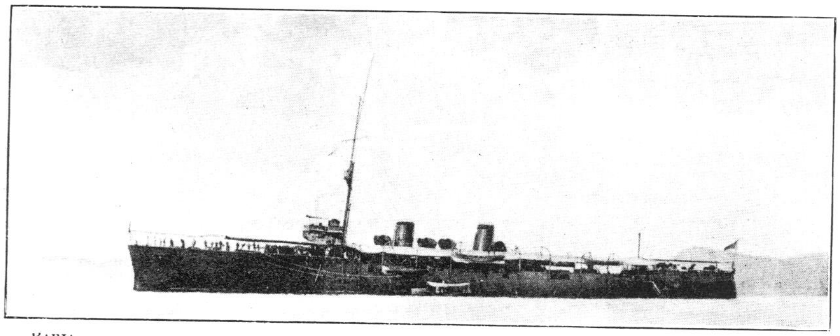

BAHIA.

BAHIA (Jan., 1909) & **RIO GRANDE DO SUL** (April, 1909).

Normal displacement 3000 tons. Complement 320.

Length { (*p.p.*), 380 feet. (*o.a.*), $401\frac{1}{2}$,, } Beam, 39 feet. *Max.* draught, 13 feet. 5 ins.

Guns (Elswick):
10—4·7 inch, 50 cal.
6—3 pdr.
Torpedo tubes (18 inch):
2 *above water*

Armour:
$1\frac{1}{2}$″ Deck
3″ Conning tower

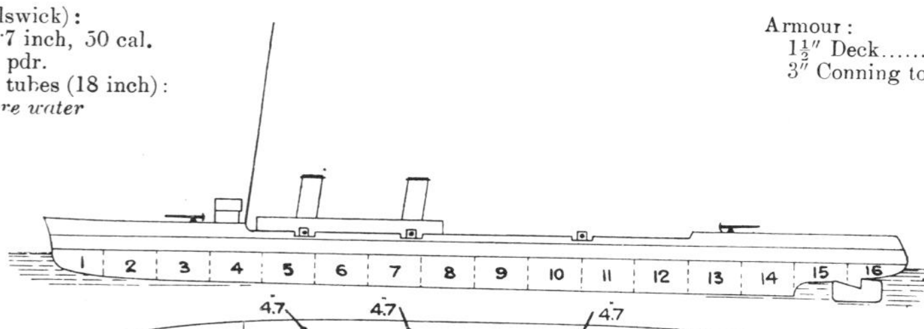

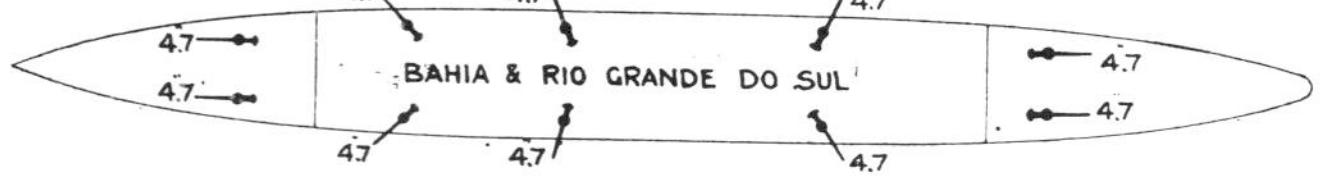

Ahead:
2—4·7 in.

Astern:
2—4·7 in.

Broadside: 5—4·7 inch.

Machinery: Parsons turbine. 3 screws. Boilers: 10 Yarrow. Designed S.H.P. 18,000 = 25 kts. Coal: *normal* 150 tons, *maximum* 650 tons. Endurance: about 1400 miles at $23\frac{1}{2}$ kts., 3500 miles at 10 kts.

Name	*Builder*	*Machinery*	*Laid down*	*Completed*	*Trials* 6 hours $\frac{3}{4}$.	*Trials* Full power.	*Boilers*	*Best recent speed*
Bahia	Elswick	Vickers	1908	1910	= 24	20,101 = 27·02	Yarrow	
Rio G. do Sul	Elswick	Vickers	1908	1910	= 24	20,600 = 27·41	Yarrow	

General Notes.—Reported to be in poor condition up to 1917 and not capable of raising more than 18 kts. But, during 1918, they may have been repaired and put in effective condition.

(1896) Coast Defence Vessels (*Encouraçados*).

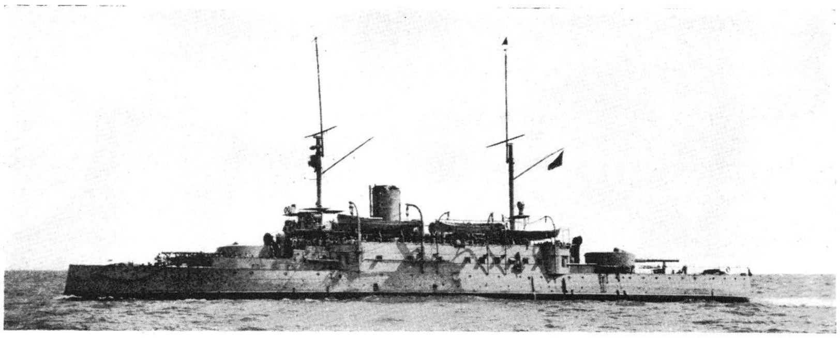

DEODORO (ex-*Ypiranga*, 1898) & **FLORIANO** (1899). Both built at La Seyne. Displacement 3162 tons. Complement 200. Length (*p.p.*), $267\frac{1}{2}$ feet. Beam, 48 feet. *Max.* draught, $13\frac{1}{4}$ feet. Guns: 2—9·4 in., 45 cal.; 4—4·7 in., 50 cal.; 4—6 pdr., 2 M.G. (2 field). Armour (Harvey-nickel): $13\frac{3}{4}$″ Belt (amidships), 4″ Belt (ends), $1\frac{1}{2}$″ Deck (reinforcing belt), 8″ Turrets, 3″ Casemates, 5″ Conning tower. Machinery: 2 sets triple expansion. 2 screws. Boilers: (1912), Babcock. Designed H.P. 3400 = 15 kts. Coal: 246 tons. Radius of action: 2500 miles at 10 kts. Reported to be in very bad condition.

(1895) Protected Cruiser.

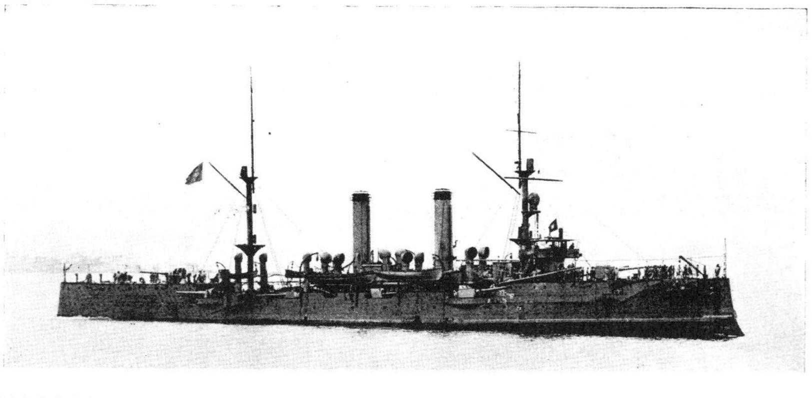

BARROSO (Elswick, 1896). 3450 tons (sheathed and coppered). Comp. 375. Dimensions (*p.p.*): $330 \times 43\frac{3}{4} \times 16\frac{5}{6}$ feet. Guns (Elswick): 6—6 in., 50 cal.; 4—4·7 in., 50 cal.; 10—6 pdr., 4—1 pdr., 4 Maxims, (2 field.) Armour: $3\frac{1}{2}$″ Deck (amidships). Machinery: 2 sets 3-cyl. triple expansion. 2 screws. Boilers: cylindrical. Designed H.P. *forced* 7500 = 20.5 kts. Coal: *normal* 450 tons; *maximum* about 850 tons. Endurance: 6500 miles at 10 kts. Refitted 1916-17. Two sister-ships, *Abreu* and *Amazonas*, were purchased by the U.S. for the Spanish-American War, and are now the U.S. *Albany* and *New Orleans*.

Gunboat.

REPUBLICA (Elswick, 1892). 1300 tons. Comp. 132. Dimensions: 210½ (p.p.) × 35 × 15 feet. Guns (Elswick): 6—4·7 inch, 4—6 pdr. 6 M.G. Torpedo tubes (18 inch), 4 above w. Armour: 2½″ deck. Designed H.P. 3800 = 16 kts. Cyl. boilers. Coal: 170 tons.

Note.—It is doubtful if the following two Ships are still in Service; they may have been scrapped during 1918-19.

Torpedo Gunboat.

TYMBRIA (ex-Caramura, 1986), **TOPY, TAMOYO** 1030 tons. Complement 110. Dimensions: 259 x 30 x 10¼ feet. Armament (Krupp): 2—4.7 inch, or 4.1 inch, 50 cal. 6—6 pdr., 2—1 pdr., 3—14 inch tubes. Armour: 1″ Deck. Designed H.P. 7000 = 23 kts. Coal: 260 tons. Built by Krupp. Last Pair deleted by 1919.

GUSTAVO SAMPAIO (Elswick, 1896). 500 tons. Complement 95. Guns: 2—3·5 inch (Krupp), 4—3 pdr. 3—14 inch tubes. Designed H.P. 2300 = 18 kts. Coal: 150 tons.

Deleted by 1919.

Armed Merchantile Cruiser and Fleet Collier.

BELMONTE (ex-German S.S. *Valesia*, Rostock, 1912.) 5227 tons *gross*. Dimensions: 364¾ × 51 × feet. Guns: 4—4·7 inch. 6—6 pdr. H.P. 2700 = 12 kts. Can take about 6500 tons coal as cargo.

Note.—Above ship seized in Brazilian port, 1917, after declaration of war against Germany.

Tugs.

(Officially rated as Despatch Vessels).

AMAPÁ (ex-Tug *Cayapo*). **GOYTACAZ.** No details known.
LAURINDO PITTA (1910). 304 tons.

MARECHAL HERMES. Sea-going Tug. No details known.

JAGUARAYO. Sea-going Tug. No details known. Attached to Mining Flotilla; may be Mine-Layer and/or Mine-Sweeper.

MARIA DO CONTO. Sea-going Tug. No details known. Attached to Mining Flotilla; may be Mine-Layer and/or Mine-Sweeper.

BRAZILIAN MISCELLANEOUS.

Gunboat.

TIRADENTES (Elswick, 1892). 800 tons. Dimensions: 170½ × 29½ × 12 feet. Complement 100. Guns: 4—4·7 inch, 2—6 pdr., 5 Nordenfelts. Tubes: 2—14 inch. Designed H.P. 1200 = 14·7 kts. Coal: 140 tons.

River Craft.

JAVARY, MADEIRA, SOLIMOES (— Vickers, 1913). 1200 tons. Dimensions: 265 × 49 × 8½ feet. Armament: 2—6 inch (forward), 2—4·7 inch Howitzers (aft), 4—3 pdr. Armour: 2″ sides. Designed H.P. = 11½ kts. Nominal radius, 4000 miles Machinery: Triple expan. Boilers: 2 Yarrow. Coal and oil fuel.

PERNAMBUCO (1909-10) River Monitor, built at Rio.) **MARANHAO** 470 tons. Dimensions: 146 x 24 x 5¼ feet. H.P. 800 = 11 kts. Coal: 45 tons. Guns: 3—4.7 inch, 10 machine. Armour: 6.6″-4″ belt, 4″ deck, 3½★ conning tower, 6″ turret. Took 20 years to build.
Maranhao deleted by 1919.

Training Ship.

Photo, Abrahams, Devonport.

BENJAMIN CONSTANT (La Seyne, 1892, reconstructed 1911). 2750 tons. Comp. 380. Guns (Elswick): 8—4·7 inch, 45 cal. 2—12 pdr., 2—1 pdr. Torpedo tubes (14 inch), 1 above w. Armour: 2″ deck. Designed H.P. 4000 f.d. = 15 kts. Cyl. boilers. Coal: 260 tons.

Also Brigs *Caravellas, Cidade de Manaos* and *Recife*.

Yachts.

Appearance:—clipper bow, 1 mast, 1 funnel.

JOSÉ BONIFACIO. Ex-U.S. Yacht *Nourmaha* (?), 768 tons, 8½ knts. speed. No other details known.

TENENTE ROSA, TENENTE RIBEIRO (1911). 152 tons. Speed: 12½ kts. One or two small guns.

SILVA-JARDIM. No details known.

River Craft—*continued.*

ACRE, MISSOES (Yarrow, 1904) **AMAPA, JURUA** 200 tons. Dimensions: 120 x 20 x 2 feet. Armament: 1—3.4 inch (15 pdr) howitzer, 1—6 pdr., 4 maxims. H.P., 300 = 11 kts. Complement, 30.
Last two deleted by 1919.

JUTAHY, TEFFE (1890-92, refitted 1917). River Gunboats of 33 tons. Dimensions: 90 (p.p.) × 15 × 5 feet. Guns: 1—3 pdr., 2 M.G. H.P. = 11 kts. Coal: 7 tons.

Note :—These two Ships have also—but very doubtfully—been reported as vessels of "180 tons and 9 kts. speed, of much the same appearance as *Acre* and *Missoes*." Probably have been confused with Commercial River Steamers bearing same names.

OYAPOCK (—). Despatch Vessel of 195 tons, 14 kts. speed.

For Service with Seaplane.

The Brazilian Navy possess about ten Seaplanes of Curtiss and other types. It is not known if any Ship has been fitted out as a Seaplane carrier or as Tender to Seaplanes.

ANDRADA (ex *America*, ex *Britannia*) (1890). 2600 tons. Guns: 2—4·7 inch, 2—14 pdr. Original speed: 17 kts.

Mine Layers.

CARLOS GOMEZ (ex-*Itaipu*, 1892). 1800 tons. Complement 100. Dimensions: 301 × 39 × 10 feet. Designed H.P. 4000 = 16 kts. (*less now*). Guns: *not known*. Coal: 400 tons. Can carry up to 550 mines *maximum*.

Mine Sweepers.

Tugs *Jaguarayo* and *Maria do Conto* (both listed on next page) are probably fitted out for this service.

BRAZILIAN TORPEDO CRAFT, SUBMARINE AND SUBMARINE TENDER.

10 Destroyers.

10 *Yarrow* type: **Amazonas, Matto Grosso, Piauhy, Para** (all launched 1908), **Rio Grande do Norte, Parahyba, Alagoas, Santa Catharina** (all launched 1909), **Parana, Sergipe** (both launched 1910). Displacement 560 tons. Dimensions: 240 × 23½ × (*Mean* draught) 7⅝ feet. Armament: 2—4 inch, 4—3 pdrs., 2—18 in. tubes. Designed H.P. 8000 = 27 kts. Machinery: 2 sets triple expansion reciprocating. 2 double-ended Yarrow boilers. Majority of these boats retubed 1917-18. Coal: 140 tons. Nominal radius: 1600 miles at 15 kts. On acceptance trials with 6563 to 8877 H.P. they made 27·1 to 28·7 kts. Hulls of several are said to be in bad condition.

Note:—The numbers on after funnel are thus : 1, *Amazonas*; 2, *Para*: 3, *Piauhy*; 4, *R. G. do Norte*; 5, *Parahyba*; 6, *Alagoas*; 7, *Sergipe*; 8, *Parana*; 9, *S. Catherina*; 10, *Matto Grosso*.

1 Torpedo Boat.

1 *Yarrow* type: **Goyaz** (1907) 150 tons. Dimensions: 152 × 15¼ × 4¾ feet. Guns: 2—3 pdr. Torpedo tubes: 2 single 18-inch. Turbine and reciprocating engines. Designed speed, 26½ kts. Yarrow boilers. Worn out and practically unfit for futher service.

3 *Silvado* type. **Silvado, Pedro-Ivo, Pedro-Affonso.** Armament: 2—1 pdr., 3—14 inch tubes. Deleted by 1919.

3 Submarines.

Photo by favour of Ansaldo San Giorgio Co.

3 *Laurenti-Fiat* type: **F 5, F 3, F 1** (Spezia, 1913-14). Built by Fiat-San Giorgio Co. Dimensions : 150 × 13·8 × 9·8 to 12 feet draught. Displacement : 250 tons *on surface*; 305 tons *submerged*. Machinery : 2 sets 350 H.P. 6-cylinder, 2-cycle Fiat Diesel engines *on surface*=700 H.P. 2 sets 250 H.P. electric motors + batteries = 500 H.P. *submerged.* Speeds : (maximum) 13½ kts. *on surface*, 8 to 8½ kts. *submerged.* Radii of action : *on surface* about 800 miles at full speed, 1600 miles at 8½ kts.; when *submerged*, 18 miles at full speed, or 100 miles at 4 kts. Torpedo tubes : 2—18 inch in bows. Complement about 20.

Submarine Carrier, Depot, Docking and Salvage Ship.

(Also serves as Training Ship for submarine service.)

Photo by courtesy of the Fiat San Giorgio Co.

CEARA (Spezia, 1915). Length (*p.p.*) 328 feet. Beam, 52 feet. Draught and displacement (with all stores) vary thus : (*a*) with dock empty and dock-gate closed 4100 tons at 14 feet draught ; (*b*) with dock-gate open and dock flooded to float submarine in, 4130 tons at 17½ feet ; (*c*) with gate closed and submarine docked, 4560 tons at 15 feet ; (*d*) with gate closed and submarine under hydraulic pressure test in dock, 6160 tons at 20¼ feet ; (*e*) with dock empty and gate closed, and when raising submarines by double cranes at stern, 4615 tons at 15 feet. tons for submarines (sufficient fuel carried to fill tanks of six submarines four times). Radius of action : Machinery : 2 sets 6-cylinder, 2-cycle Fiat-Diesel engines. 4100 B.H.P. = 14 kts. Fuel : 400 tons (own bunkers) + 4000 miles at 10 kts. Guns : 4—4 inch, 2 smaller. Built by Fiat-San Giorgio Co. Completed 1916.

Note.—This ship has been specially designed and completely equipped to serve as a depot ship, salvage ship, and floating dock for a flotilla of 6 submarines. There is a central, circular caisson dock 216½ feet long (to dock submarines up to 198 feet length and 25½ feet beam) between the double hulls, and two salvage cranes at stern for raising 400 tons deadweight. Equipment for service to submarines includes two 150 Kw. charging dynamos, two electric-driven and one steam-driven 75-150 atmos. air compressors, refrigerating plant, workshops, powerful pumps to empty dock in 2 hours, &c. ; carries spare batteries, torpedoes, stores, &c., for 6 submarines.

CHILEAN FLEET.

Revised and Re-Illustrated, 1919.

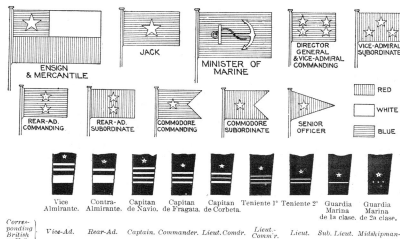

ENSIGN & MERCANTILE	JACK	MINISTER OF MARINE	DIRECTOR GENERAL & VICE-ADMIRAL COMMANDING	VICE-ADMIRAL SUBORDINATE
REAR-AD. COMMANDING	REAR-AD. SUBORDINATE	COMMODORE COMMANDING	COMMODORE SUBORDINATE	SENIOR OFFICER

RED / WHITE / BLUE

Vice Almirante.	Contra-Almirante.	Capitan de Navio.	Capitan de Fragata.	Capitan de Corbeta.	Teniente 1°	Teniente 2°	Guardia Marina de la clase.	Guardia Marina de 2a clase.

Corresponding British or U.S. : Vice-Ad. Rear-Ad. Captain. Commander. Lieut.-Comdr. Lieut.-Comm'r. Lieut. Sub. Lieut. Midshipman.

Other Branches the same without the star, and colours as follows :—Engineers (blue), Paymasters (white), Doctors (red).

Minister of War and Marine :

Personnel : About 7500, of whom about 1000 are conscripts, the rest volunteers.

Mercantile Marine : 87 steamers, of 89,515 tons *gross* ; 33 sailing vessels, 26,178 tons *gross.*

Bases : Talcahuano. One dry dock, 614 × 87 × 30½ feet. New dock *building*, 856 × 117 × 36 feet. One small floating dock, 216 × 42 × 15 feet.

Valparaiso. One small wooden floating dock, and two large *projected* in the Harbour Works.

TORPEDO CRAFT.

Scale : 1 inch = 160 feet.

I. Hyatt *class* t.b. (5)
Tomé *class* t.g.b. (2 ships).
Thompson t.b.d.

Orella *class* t.b.d. (4
(*Also with higher funnels*).
O'Brien *class* t.b.d. (2)

Alm.-Lynch *class* t.b.d (2)
(*Fore funnel in each now raised.*)

Scale: 1 inch = 160 feet. RECOGNITION SILHOUETTES. (Revised 1919.)

Alm. Cochrane.
(*Torpedo School*)
P. Errazuriz.
General Baquedano.
(*Training Ship.*)

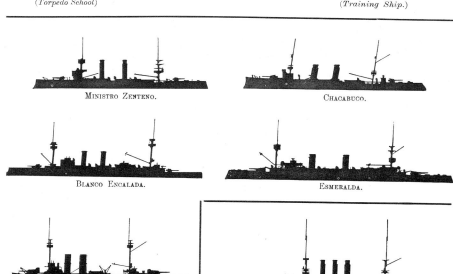

Ministro Zenteno.
Chacabuco.
Blanco Encalada.
Esmeralda.

Capitan Prat.
General O'Higgins.

SUBMARINES.   Scale : 1 inch = 80 feet.

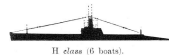

H *class* (6 boats).

(1888) Battleship.

Copyright photo, G. Allan, Valparaiso.

CAPITAN PRAT (La Seyne, 1890). *Reconstructed* 1909. 6902 tons. Complement 500. Length (*p.p.*) 328 feet. Beam, 60¾ feet. *Maximum* draught, 22⅜ feet. Guns (Canet): 4—9·4 inch, 35 cal. (*A*). 8—4·7 inch, 45 cal., 10—6 pdr., 4—3 pdr., 10—1 pdr., 1 Maxim. Torpedo tubes (18 inch): 2 *above water*. Armour (Creusot): 12″ Belt (amidships), 3″ Deck (flat on belt), 10½″ Barbettes, 2″ Barbette hoods, 4″ Redoubt (amidships), 2″ Small turrets. Machinery: 2 sets horizontal triple expansion. 2 screws. Boilers: new in 1909, 12 Babcock. H.P. 12,000 = 18 kts. (about 16 kts. now). Coal: *normal* 400 tons; *maximum* 775 tons = circa 4650 miles at 10 kts.

(1895) Armoured Cruiser.

Copyright photo, G. Allan, Valparaiso.

ESMERALDA (Elswick, 1896, re-fitted 1910). 7050 tons. Sheathed and coppered. Complement 500. Length (*p.p.*), 436 feet. Beam, 53 feet, 2 ins. Draught (*mean*), 20¼ feet. Guns (Elswick): 2—8 inch, 40 cal. (*B*), 12—6 inch, 40 cal., 12—12 pdr. (2 field). Torpedo tubes (18 inch): 2 *submerged*. Armour (Harvey): 6″ Belt, 2″ Deck, 6″ Bulkheads, 4½″ Shields to guns, 4½″ Hoists. Machinery: 2 sets 4 cylinder triple expansion. 2 screws. Boilers: 2-ended cylindrical. H.P. 18,000 = 22·25 kts. (still steams well and can do 21 kts. now). Coal: *normal* 550 tons; *maximum* 1350 tons. Endurance: (*a*) 2400 miles at 24 kts., (*b*) 7680 miles at 10 kts.

1896. Protected Cruisers (*continued.*)

Copyright photo, G. Allan, Valparaiso.

MINISTRO ZENTENO (Elswick, 1896.) 3420 tons. Complement, 350. Length, (*p.p.*) 330¼ feet. Beam, 43¾ feet. *Max.* draught, 16⅜ feet. Armament: 8—6 in., 10—6 pdr., 4—1 pdr., 4 Maxims. Armour: 3½″ Deck, 4″ Conning tower. Designed H.P. 7500 = 20 kts. (16 kts. now.) Cylindrical boilers. Coal: *maximum* 850 tons. Endurance: 6450 miles at 10 kts.

1893.

Copyright photo, G. Allan, Valparaiso.

BLANCO ENCALADA (Elswick, 1893). 4420 tons. Sheathed and coppered. Complement 427. Length (*p.p.*), 370 feet. Beam, 46½ feet. *Maximum* draught, 19½ feet. Armament: 2—8 inch, 40 cal., 8—6 inch, 40 cal., 2—4·7 inch. 4—12 pdr., 8—3 pdr., 4—1 pdr. Armour: 4″ Deck, 6″ Shields to 8″ guns, 6″ Conning tower. Boilers: cylindrical (retubed 1908-9). Designed H.P. *forced* 14,500 = 22·75 kts. (about 21·5 kts. now.) Coal: *maximum* 850 tons. Endurance: 5000 miles at 10 kts.

(1896) Armoured Cruiser.

Copyright photo, G. Allan, Valparaiso.

GENERAL O'HIGGINS (Elswick, 1897). 8500 tons. Sheathed and coppered. Complement 500. Length (*p.p.*), 412 feet. Beam, 62¾ feet. *Max.* draught, 22 feet. Guns (Elswick): 4—8 inch, 45 cal. (*A*), 10—6 inch, 40 cal., 8 or 10—12 pdr., 10—6 pdr., 4 M.G. Torpedo tubes (18 inch): 2 *submerged*. Armour (Harvey-nickel): 7″-5″ Belt (amidships), 2″ Deck (slopes), 7½″ Port plates to 8 inch gun turrets and front, 6″ Hoists to these, 6″ Gun houses, 6in. guns, 9″ Conning tower. Machinery: 2 sets triple expansion. 2 screws. Boilers: 30 Belleville (in 3 groups). Designed H.P. *natural* 10,000 = 19 kts.; *forced* 16,000 = 21·5 kts. (still steams very well and can do 21 kts. now). Coal: *normal* 700 tons; *maximum* 1200 tons. Endurance: (*a*) 2250 miles at 20 kts., (*b*) 6000 miles at 10 kts.

(1897) Protected Cruiser.

Copyright photo, G. Allan, Valparaiso.

CHACABUCO (Elswick, 1898, (purchased 1902). 4500 tons. Complement 400. Length (*p.p.*), 360 feet. Beam, 46½ feet. *Maximum* draught, 17 feet. Guns (Elswick): 2—8 inch, 45 cal. 10—4·7 inch, 40 cal., 12—12 pdr., 6—3 pdr. Armour (Harvey nickel): 4½″ Deck (amidships), 1¾″ Deck (ends), 4½″ Fronts 8 in. gun shields, 2½″ Sides 8in. gun shields, 2½″ Shields 4·7 in. guns, 5″ Conning tower. Machinery: Boilers, cylindrical. I.H.P. 15,500 = 24 kts. *forced*. Still steams well, and can do 23 kts. now) 2 screws. Coal: *normal* 300 tons; *maximum* 1028 tons. Electric training and elevating gear to 8 inch guns. Laid down at Elswick, 1897, as a speculation. Completed 1902, and purchased by Chile.

1890. Protected Cruiser.

Copyright photo, G. Allan, Valparaiso.

PRESIDENTE ERRAZURIZ (La Seyne, 1890, refitted 1908). 2080 tons. Complement, 170. Dimensions: 268½ *p.p.* × 35¾ × 14½ feet. Guns (new in 1908): 2—6 inch, 4—5·9 inch, 4—6 pdr., 4—1 pdr. Armour: 2¼″ Deck, 3″ shields to guns. Machinery: 2 sets horizontal triple expansion. 2 screws. Boilers: Belleville (1908). Designed H.P. 5400 = 19 kts. (12·5 kts. now). Coal: 280 tons. Endurance: 2900 miles at 10 kts.

Sloop and Training Ship.

Copyright photo, G. Allan, Valparaiso.

GENERAL BAQUEDANO (1898). 2500 tons, sheathed and coppered. Armed with 4—4·7 inch guns, 2—12 pdr., and 2—6 pdr., I.H.P. 1500 = 13·75 kts. Belleville boilers. Coal: 300 tons. Built by Elswick. Best recent speed: 12 kts.

Torpedo Gunboats.

TOMÉ (ex *Almirante Lynch*, 1890) & **TALCAHUANO** (ex *Almirante Condell*, 1890). Displacement, 720 tons. Length, 240 feet (*o.a.*). Beam, 27½ feet. *Maximum* draught, 11 feet. Complement, 87. Guns: *Tomé*, 3—12 pdr., 2 M.G.; *Talcahuano*, 1—4·7 inch (aft), 2—12 pdr., 2 M.G. Torpedo tubes *in both*: 5—14 inch, viz., 1 bow, 4 broadside, all *above water*. Armour: Double skin (amidships), 1″ Bulkheads. Machinery: 2 sets triple expansion. 2 screws. Boilers: Belleville, *without* economisers. Designed I.H.P. 4500=20 kts. (exceeded on *trial*). Coal: 220 tons. Endurance: 3100 miles.

Laid down at Birkenhead, 1889. Completed 1892. Reconstructed 1900.

Destroyers.

No.	Type	Date	Displacement	H.P.	Max. speed	Fuel	Complement	T. tubes	Max. draug't
			tons.		kts.	tons			feet
2	*Lynch* (W)	'11–'14	1430	30,000	31t	427 coal, 80 oil	·160	3	11
1	*Capitan Thompson* (E)	'98–'00	350	6500	30	120 coal	65	2	5½
2	*C. O'Brien* (L)	'00–'02	311	6000	30	90	65	2	8½
4	*C. Orella* (L)	1896	300	6000	30	90	65	3	8½

(E)=Elswick. (L)=Laird. (W)=White. (t)=Turbines.

ALM. CONDELL (centre), AL. LYNCH (behind). (Fore funnels now raised.) *Copyright photo, G. Allan, Valparaiso.*

2 *White*: **Almirante Lynch** (1912), **Al. Condell** (1913). Dimensions: 320×32½×11 feet. *Normal* displacement: 1430 tons. *Full load*: 1850 tons. Armament: 6—4 inch, 4 M.G., 3—18 inch tubes. Designed H.P. 30,000=31 kts. Turbines: Parsons. Boilers: White-Forster. 3 screws. Fuel: 427 tons coal + 80 tons oil = 2750 miles at 15 kts. Trials: *Al. Lynch*, 31·8 kts. (6 hours); *Al. Condell*, 34 kts. Complement 160.

Note.—See British Navy Section for three other boats of this class, now H.M. ships *Botha*, *Broke* and *Faulknor*.

Submarines.

H 2. *Copyright photo, G. Allan, Valparaiso.*

6 Holland: **H1, H2, H4, H5, H6** (Fore River Co., U.S.A., 1915–17). Displacements: 355 tons. Dimensions: 105′ × 15⅞′ × 12½ feet. H.P. 480/620 = 13/5 kts. Machinery: *for surface* 2 sets 210 H.P. Nlseco Diesel engines When *submerged* electric motors and batteries can develop 610 H.P.=11 kts. for one hour only. Endurance: 2800 miles at 11 kts. *on surface*; 30 miles at 5 kts. *submerged*. Oil: 17½ tons. Torpedo tubes: 1—18 inch (bow). Complement 22.

Notes.—These boats are believed to be units of the British H 11—20 group of submarines, built by the Fore River Co., U.S.A., during 1915. The Admiralty intended to take them over and equip them with torpedo tubes at the Canadian Vickers Co., Yard at Montreal—provided that these boats could legally be delivered in an unarmed state. The U.S. Government decided the submarines could not leave any U.S. port, so long as the United States remained neutral, and all the boats were interned at Boston. They were released on the U.S. declaration of war, 1917. With the approval of the U.S. authorities, the above six boats were ceded to Chile by Great Britain, in part payment for the Chilian warships building in British yards in August, 1914, and appropriated for the British Navy.

Antofagasta, *Iquique*.

Other Ships.

A large armed transport *Angamos* was in service up to about 1918. She may have been sold out recently for Mercantile Service. No details are known of this ship.

Contramastor Ortiz and *Galvez* (1909), *Valparaiso* (1897). Tugs.

Meteoro, 800 tons, 14 kts.; *Porvenir*, 350 tons, 12 kts., and *Yelcho*, 300 tons, 14 kts., are used as Lighthouse Supply Ships.

Condor Toro and *Huemel* (1889), 11 kts. speed, and about 12 other very old ships are used for Harbour Duty and Subsidiary Service.

Transports *Rancagua* (8000 Tons), *Maipo* (6000 Tons), *Casma* (300 Tons).

Destroyers

1 *Elswick*. **Capitan Thompson** (1899). 350 tons. Dimensions: 213 (*p.p.*) × 21½ × 5½ feet. Armament: 1—12 pdr., 5—6 pdr., 2—18 inch tubes. Designed H.P. 6500=30 kts. Coal: 120 tons = 1150 miles at 15 kts. [*Photo, Abrahams.*]

CAPITAN O'BRIEN. *Copyright photo, G. Allen, Valparaiso.*

2 *Laird*: **Capitan O'Brien** & **Capitan Merino Jarpa** (both 1901). Armament: 1—12 pdr., 5—6 pdr., 2—18 inch tubes, one amidships, one aft. Boilers: Laird-Normand. Other details as Laird boat below. *And as O'Brien except that the funnels are shorter:—*

4 *Laird*: **Capitan Orella, Capitan Munoz Gamero, Teniente Serrano,** & **Guardia Marina Riquelme** (all 1896). 311 tons. Dimensions: 213 (*p.p.*) × 21½ × 8½ feet. Armament: 1—12 pdr., 5—6 pdr., 3—18 inch tubes. Boilers: Normand. Designed H.P. 6500=30 kts., but some can only do 23 now. Coal: 90 tons. *Nominal* radius 900 miles at 15 kts. All reboilered and refitted 1909. Complement 65. (*Torpedo Boats on next page.*)

CHILEAN TORPEDO BOATS, SUBMARINES
AND MISCELLANEOUS VESSELS
Torpedo Boats.

3 or 5 *Yarrow* type: **Injeniero Hyatt, Cirujano Videla** (Yarrow, Poplar, 1896). **Injeniero Mutilla,*** **Guardia Marina Contreras** and **Teniente Rodriguez*** (Balcachuamo, 1896–1901). 128 tons. Dimensions: 152½ × 15½ × 7½ feet. Armament: 3—6 pdr., 3—14 inch torpedo tubes. Designed H.P. 2000=25 to 27·5 kts. Yarrow boilers. Coal: 40 tons. Complement 28 and 32.

Injeniero Mutilla and *Rodriguez* may have been scrapped in 1918.

Gunnery and Torpedo School Ship.

Photo, Allen, Valparaiso.

ALMIRANTE COCHRANE (1874, reconstructed 1896). 3500 tons. Dimensions 210 (*p.p.*) × 45¾ × 20½ feet. Guns: 4—4·7 inch, 2—12 pdr., 4—3 pdr., 2 M.G. Armour (iron): 9″—4½″ Belt, 8″ Battery. H.P. 4300=12 kts. (not over 8 kts. now). Cylindrical boilers. Coal: 350 tons. Complement 306.

Submarine Depot Ship.

Photo, Grimm, Valparaiso.

HUASCAR (1865, captured from Peru, 1870). Old Turret Ship of 1870 tons. Speed: 10 kts. *nominal*. Guns: 2—10 inch.

COLOMBIA.

ENSIGN   **MERCANTILE**

Gunboat.

ALMIRANTE LEZO (*ex* Carthagena, *ex* El Baschir), (1892). Displacement 1200 tons. Complement . Length, 229½ feet. Beam, 32¾ feet. Draught, 8½ feet. Guns: 2—4·7 inch, 4—4 inch, 4—14 inch tubes. Designed H.P. 2300=16 kts. Built by Orlando, for Morocco. Purchased 1902. Deleted by 1919.

BOLIVAR (*ex* Libertador, *ex* Ban Righ). 981 tons gross. Guns: 2—3 pdr. Deleted by 1919.

CHÉRCINTO (1896). 643 tons. Dimensions: 185 (*p.p.*)×31× 12 feet. Guns: not known. Designed H.P. 400=about 12 kts.

GENERAL PINZON (1881). 740 tons. Deleted by 1919.

River Gunboats.

ESPERANZA (1897), **GENERAL NERINO** (1895), both built at Perth Amboy, U.S.A. Stern-wheelers of 400 tons. Dimensions: 140 (*p.p.*)×9×3 feet. Guns: 3 M.G. Designed H.P. 430=15 kts. No other details known.

M. L. (*Motor Launches*).

Cauca (1913). 50 tons. Dimensions: 110×17×4 feet. Guns: none at present.* Speed, 12 kts.

Guarda Costas 1, 2, 3, 4 (Yarrow, 1913). 20 tons. Dimensions: 80×12½×3½ feet. Guns: No. 3 has 1—1 pdr., no guns in others yet.* H.P. 160=12 kts. Fuel: 1800 galls. petrol=2400 miles at 10 kts.

*Guns detained in Great Britain during the war.

Old Transport *Bogota* is still in service.

Gunboats.

DIEZ DE OCTUBRE (Cramp, 1911), **VEINTE Y CUATRO DE FEBRERO** (Cramp 1911). 218 tons. Dimensions: 110 ×20×8 feet. Guns: 1—3 pdr., 2—1 pdr. Speed, 12 kts. Coal, 50 tons.

Photo by courtesy of the Ministry of War.

BAIRE (Schichau, 1906). 500 tons. Dimensions: 196×23×9 feet. Guns: 2—6 pdr., 2—3 pdr., 1 machine. H.P. 1200=14 kts. Babcock boilers. Coal, 120 tons.

Note.—Refitted in a U.S. Navy Yard, 1917; may now have a new armament.

Transport.

KYDONIA (ex-German ship). No details known.

COSTA RICA.

1 Yarrow torpedo boat (1892). Speed, 15 kts.

CUBA.

RED.   SKY BLUE.

Mercantile Marine: 35 steamers of 29,286 tons *gross*; 146 sailing vessels of 15,132 tons *gross*; also 6 German steamers of 19,464 tons, seized on declaration of war, 1917.

A Government dockyard is projected in Havana Bay, near the Morro Castle. To have a 4000 ton Floating Dock. Naval Academy at Mariel to be transferred to vicinity of Dockyard.

RECOGNITION SILHOUETTES.

Scale : 1 inch = 160 feet.

E. VILLUENDAS.   HATUEY.

Revenue Cutters.

DIEZ DE OCTUBRE *class.*   BAIRE.

CUBA.   PATRIA. (*Training Ship.*)

CUBA—*Continued.*

Submarine Chasers.

4—*110 foot* boats, late U.S. *SC274, SC302, SC312, SC314.* For illustration and all details see U.S. Navy Section.

Note : 6 further boats reported ceded to Cuba; numbers not known.

Revenue Cutters.

MATANZAS (1912), **VILLAS** (1912). Details as *Habana* and *Pinar del Rio.*

HATUEY (ex U.S. *Pentooset*, 1903, bought 1907) 538 tons. 212×27 ×15 feet. Guns: 2—6 pdr., 2—3 pdr., 2—1 pdr. I.H.P. 1350 =13 kts. Coal, 150 tons.

Photo by courtesy of the Ministry of War.

ENRIQUE VILLUENDAS (1899). 178 tons. 132+20×9 feet. Guns: 2—3 pdr., 1 M.G. I.H.P. 600=16 kts. Coal, 55 tons.

Light Cruisers.

CUBA (Cramp, 1911). 2055 tons. Dimensions: (*p.p.*) 260×39×14 feet. Armament:* 2—4 inch, 4—6 pdr., 4—3 pdr., 4—1 pdr., 2 machine. H.P. 6000=18 kts. Babcock boilers. Coal, 250 tons.

*Note.—Was re-fitted in U S A during 1918, when her armament was altered. Present guns carried not known; armament given above is that mounted during 1911-18.

PATRIA (Cramp, 1911). 1100 tons. Dimensions: (*p.p.*) 200×36×13 feet. Guns: 2—12 pdr.

(*Training Ship*).

HABANA (1912), **PINAR DEL RIO** (1912). Both wooden vessels of 80 tons, built at Havana. Dimensions: 100 × 18 × 6 feet. Guns: 1—1 pdr. I.H.P. 200=12 kts. 1 screw. Coal: 20 tons.

Revenue Cutters.—*Continued.*

MARTI (1898). 50 tons. Guns: 1—1 pdr. Speed 15 kts. Coal: 15 tons.

CESPEDES (ex-Spanish gunboat, 1896). 40 tons. Guns: 1—1 pdr. Speed, 12 kts. Coal: 110 tons.

MACEO (ex-Spanish gunboat, 1896). 35 tons. Guns: 1—1 pdr. Speed, 10 kts. Coal, 8 tons.

AGRAMONTE (ex-Spanish gunboat, 1895). 45 tons. Guns: 1—1 pdr. Speed, 11 kts. Coal, 10 tons.

VEINTE DE MAYO (Glasgow, 1895). 203 tons. 141×18·5×10·5 feet. Guns: 2—3 pdr., 2—1 pdr. I.H.P. 500=12 kts. Coal, 50 tons.

YARA (Glasgow, 1895). 449 tons. 155×26×13 feet. Guns: 2—6 pdr., 2—1 pdr. I.H.P. 600=12 kts. Coal, 150 tons.

ALFREDO (——) 40 tons. Guns: 1—1 pdr. Speed, 11 kts.

GUAIMARO. No details known.

ORIENTE (——). 210 tons. 160×21×13 feet. Guns: 2—6 pdr., 2—1 pdr. I.H.P. 700=12 kts. Coal, 80 tons.

ECUADOR.

ENSIGN

MERCANTILE

Minister of War and Marine: Sr. R. Pino y Roca.

Mercantile Marine: 7 steamers of 1942 tons *gross*; 4 sailing vessels of 1882 tons *gross*.

Silhouette Scale : 1 inch = 160 feet.

(Silhouettes revised, 1918.)

COTOPAXI.

PATRIA.

L. BOLIVAR.

Flag Notes.—To distinguish from Colombian flag, note that centre bar is *sky-blue*. Mercantile flag also has no badge, compared with Colombia.

Note :—The following three photographs have kindly been collected for " Fighting Ships " by Mr. George Chambers, Captain of the Port of Guayaquil.

Torpedo-Gunboat.

LIBERTADOR BOLIVAR (ex *A. Simpson*, 1896, purchased from Chile, 1907). Displacement 750 tons. Length, 240 feet. Beam, 27½ feet. *Maximum* draught, 10½ feet. Guns (Elswick): 4—3 pdr., 2 Maxims. Torpedo tubes (18 inch) : 3 *above water*. Armour (Harvey): 1″ Belt, 4½″ Gun shields, 1″ Hood to steering gear, 1″ Bulkheads. Machinery : 2 sets triple expansion. 2 screws. Boilers : 4 Normand. Designed I.H.P. *forced* 4500 = 21·5 kts. Coal : 100 tons. Built by Laird. *Apparently deleted before 1918.*

Ex **PAPIN** (1886, French navy). 811 tons. Guns : two old 5·5 inch, 1—4 inch, five small. Designed H.P. 860 = 12 kts. Single screw, composite. *Apparently deleted before 1918.*

Gunboat.

COTOPAXI (1884). 300 tons. 135 *(p.p.)* × 21 × 9 feet. Guns : 2 small Q.F. I.H.P. 175. *Max.* speed, 10½ kts. In 1917, is on commercial charter and may possibly have been outright.

Coastguard Vessel.

PATRIA (ex-Yacht *Cavalier*, bought from G. & Q. Railway). 300 tons. Guns : 4 machine. No other details known.

These two ships may no longer be Naval vessels.

HAYTI.

ENSIGN

MERCANTILE

RED

BLUE

YELLOW   GREEN

According to information received from Port-au-Prince, March, 1919, all Haytian Warships were sold out of service during 1915. This Republic now only maintains two unarmed Auxiliary Schooners for Coastguard Duties.

HONDURAS.

RECOGNITION SILHOUETTE.

Scale : 1 inch = 80 feet.

LIBERIA.

Gunboats.

TATUMBLA (——). 200 tons. Dimensions : not known. Complement, 44. Guns : 2 small. H.P. —— = 12 kts. Coal : 100 (?) to

By courtesy of "Motor Ship

LIBERIA (ex Liberian *Mesurado*, Blandy Bros., Las Palmas, 1914). 24 tons. Dimensions : 85 × 12 × 4½ feet. Guns: Nordenfelt, 1 M.G. H.P. 120 (2—60 H.P. Parsons paraffin engines) = 12–14 kts. Fuel : 500 galls. paraffin. 1 small searchlight. Built for Liberian Government as a Revenue Cutter, but never delivered. Purchased by Honduras.

Torpedo Boat (and Minelayer).

1 *boat, type unknown :* **Tarqui** (——). 20 tons. Carries 1 torpedo tube and fitted as Minelayer. No other details known.

MEXICAN NAVY.

ENSIGN   MERCANTILE

Minister of Marine: Sr. Augustin Castro.

Mercantile Marine : 31 steamers of 33,975 tons *gross*; 16 sailing vessels of 2,630 tons *gross.*

RECOGNITION SILHOUETTES.

Silhouette Scale : 1 inch = 160 feet.

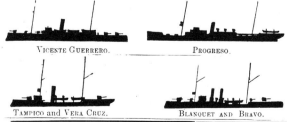

VICENTE GUERRERO.   PROGRESO.

TAMPICO and VERA CRUZ.   BLANQUET and BRAVO.

Old Cruiser.

Photo, Oscar Parkes, Esq.

ZARAGOZA (Granville, 1891) (refit 1910). 1200 tons. Comp. 270. Dimensions : 213¼ × 33 × 16 feet. Guns (Schneider-Canet) : 6—4·7 inch, 40 cal., 2—6 pdr., 2—1 pdr. Designed H.P. 1300 = 15·5 kts. Cylindrical boilers. 1 screw. Coal : 200 tons. *Deleted by 1919.*

Torpedo Gunboat.

Photo, J. Romanez, Esq.

BLANQUET (ex *Morelos*) and **BRAVO** (Odero, 1903). 1210 tons. Comp. 130. Dimensions : 240 *(p.p.)* × 32⅝ × 10 *(mean)* feet. Armament (Bethlehem) : 2—4 inch, 4—6 pdr., 1—14 inch tube (bow) *above water*. Designed H.P. 2500 = 17 kts. Blechynden boilers 2 screws. Coal : 280 tons.

TAMPICO (1902) **VERA CRUZ** (1902). Both built at Elizabeth Port, N.J. 984 tons. Comp. 164 (*Vera Cruz*), 110 (*Tampica*). Dimensions : 200 × 33 × 11 feet. Armament : in *Tampica*, 2—4 inch, 4—6 pdr.; in *Vera Cruz*, 4—4 inch, 6—6 pdr. In both ships 1—14 inch tube (bow) *above water*. Designed H.P. 2400 = 15 kts. Mosher boilers. 2 screws. Coal : 200 tons.

Gunboats.

GENERAL JESUS CARRANZA. No details known.

Transports.

VICENTE GUERRERO (Vickers, 1908). 1850 tons. Dimensions : 245 × 35 × 17 feet. Guns : 6—4 inch, 2—3 pdr. Designed H.P. 1200 = 12 kts.

OAXACO. Transport.

There are possibly 4 other steamers in existence, unarmed or nearly so.

PROGRESO (Odero, 1907). 1560 tons. Complement 69. Dimensions : 230 × 34 × 10 feet. Guns : 4—6 pdr., 2 M.G. Designed H.P. 1400 = 13 kts. Sunk by insurgents in 1914 or 1915, but since salved and repaired.

PLAN DE GUADALUPE (ex *Dolphin*, Wilmington, 1892). 824 tons. Dimensions : 213 *(o.a.)* × 32 × 15 feet. Guns : not known. Designed H.P. —— = 14 kts.

Also *Oaxaco, Bonita* and *Sonora,* subventioned merchantmen.

Armed Tugs.

PACIFICO. No details known.

Also two Revenue Cutters, names unknown.

NICARAGUA.

Gunboat.

MOMOTOMBO (——) 400 tons. Guns : 2—12 pdr., 1—6 pdr.
No other details known.

Also Auxiliaries **OMOTEPE** and **MAXIMO JERAZ** (ex s.s.
Venus). No details known.

PANAMA.

PADILLA (ex *Cuscatlan*), (1890). 75 tons. Armament : 1—1 pdr. Speed, 10 kts.

DARIAN (1895) and **GATAN** (1897). Stern wheel gunboats of 400 tons. Armament : 3—1 pdr.
¼″ armour to engines. Designed speed 15 kts. (ex *Esperanza* and *Gen. Nerino*).

CHERCUITO (1896). 643 tons. Armament : 2—1 pdr. Designed speed 12 kts.

PERU.

(Revised, 1916, from particulars supplied by favour of H. E., The Minister of War and Marine.)

PERU ENSIGN — PERUVIAN VICE-ADMIRAL — PERUVIAN CAPTAIN

Mercantile flag the same but without centre device.

Rear Admiral has one sun.

Colour of Ships : Brown grey.

Mercantile Marine : 12 steamers of 26,590 tons *gross* ; 40 sailing vessels of 10,950 tons *gross*.

Minister of War & Marine : Col. C. A. de la Fuente.

Light Cruisers.

CORONEL BOLOGNESI. The *A. Grau* is identical *except* that she has a poop.

.("*A Grau*" *Submarine Depot Ship*).

ALMIRANTE GRAU (March, 1906) & **CORONEL BOLOGNESI** (Nov., 1906).

Displacements : 3,200 tons. Complement, 315.

Length (*p.p.*) : 370 feet. Beam, 40½ feet. *Maximum* draught, 14¼ feet.

Guns (Vickers) :
2—6 inch, 50 cal.
8—14 pdr.
8—1 pdr.
Torpedo tubes (18 inch) :
2 *submerged*.

Armour :
1½″ Deck (amidships) =
3″ Conning tower ..
3″ Gun Shields ...

Ahead :
1—6 in.

Astern :
1—6 in.

Broadside : 2—6 in.

Machinery : 4 cylinder vertical triple expansion. 2 screws. Boilers : 10 Yarrow. Designed H.P.
14,000 = 24 kts. (not above 20 now, unless re-boilered. Coal : *normal*,   tons ; *maximum*, 550 tons.
Endurance : 3,700 miles at 10 kts.

General Notes.—Built and engined by Messrs. Yarrow, Ltd., about 1905-7.

COMMANDANTE AGUIRRE (Ex *Dupuy de Lôme*). (Brest, 1890). (Purchased 1911.)
Displacement, 6400 tons. Complement, 521.
Length (*waterline*) 374 feet. Beam, 51½ feet. *Maximum* draught, 26⅙ feet. Deleted by 1919.

PERUVIAN RECOGNITION SILHOUETTES.

Scale : 1 inch = 160 feet.

C. BOLOGNESI.

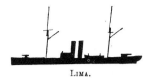
LIMA.

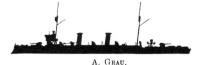
A. GRAU.

T. RODRIGUEZ t.b.d.

Scale : 1 inch = 80 feet.

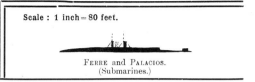
FERRE and PALACIOS.
(Submarines.)

Uniforms.

Vice-Almirante.	Contra-Almirante.	Capitan de Navio.	Capitan de Fragata.	Capitan de Corbeta.	Teniente 1°.	Teniente 2°.	Alferez de Fragata.
		Captain.	*Commander.*		*Lieut. Comm'r.*	*Lieut. Junior.*	*Sub. Lieutenant.*

Engineers the same without the sun.

Other branches have the same stripes without the sun, and in addition colours as follows :—

Torpedo, *light blue* ; Constructor, *green* ; Electricians, *light green* ; Doctors, *red* ; Paymasters, *blue*.

LIMA (Ex *S. S. Socrates*, Kiel, 1880). 1790 tons.
H.P., 2000 = 10 kts. Coal : 300 tons =
Guns : 4—4 inch, 8—3 pdr. Complement,
131. Deleted by 1919.

Gunboat.

AMERICA (1904). 100 tons. Guns : 2—3
pdr. No other details known.

CONSTITUCION IQUITOS CHALAIO
Deleted by 1919.

Destroyer.

Photo by courtesy of Messrs. Schneider et Cie.

1 *Schneider-Creusot* :—**Teniente Rodriguez** (1909, ex-*Actée*). 490 tons Dimensions : 212×21·5×14½ feet. H.P.
8,600 = 28 kts. (much less now). Schneider-Zoelly turbines, du Temple boilers Coal : 100 tons = 1200 miles at
10 kts. Armament : 6—9 pdr., 3—18 inch tubes, (2″ deck amidships and 1 bow tube above water). Complement 60.

Submarines.

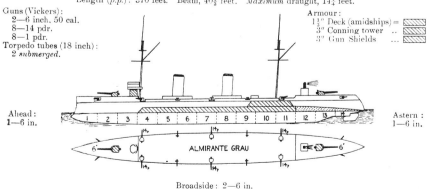

2 *Laubeuf* type : **Ferre** (1912), and **Palacios** (1913). Built by Schneider-Creusot. $\frac{300}{400}$ tons. Complement : 19.
Schneider-Carels Diesel motors. H.P. $\frac{400}{200} = \frac{14}{9}$ kts. (present speed about 12·9 kts *on surface*, 7·5 kts. *submerged.*)
Endurance : 2000 miles at 10 kts. 1 bow torpedo tube, 4 external dropping gears for torpedoes.

URUGUAYAN NAVY.

RECOGNITION SILHOUETTES.

Scale: 1 inch = 160 feet.

Vanguardia *class.* Corsario *class.* B. de R. Branco. 18 de Julio.

Uruguay.

*Minister of War and Marine :—*Dr. Arturo Gaze.

Monte Video.

Personnel :—

*Mercantile Marine :—*27 steamers of 20,298 tons *gross ;* 48 sailing vessels of 24,537 tons *gross.*

Coinage : Gold Peso of 100 Centesimos = 4s. 3d.

Ports, Yards, &c.

MONTE VIDEO.—The National Dock (Dique Naçional) is operated by the Naval Authorities. Length, 459 feet. Breadth, 55 feet. Can take ships drawing up to 19 feet. Steam and electric pumps can empty dock in eight hours. This dock is said to be in need of repairs. Dique Maria (at Montes) 280 × 51 × 12 feet 4 inch to 15 feet 2 inch. Has 2 steam pumps and lifting engine of 30 tons, also fixed and moving cranes The firm Varadero del Cerro have a yard, well equipped for repairs, with a small slipway. The National Port Administration has bought the Varadero Lussich, a repairing yard with a small slipway.

Torpedo Gunboat & Training Ship.

URUGUAY (Vulkan, Stettin, 1910). 1150 tons. Complement, 125. Dimensions : 278$\frac{3}{4}$ (*p.p.*) × 30$\frac{5}{6}$ × 12 feet (*max.* draught). Guns (Skoda) : 2—4·7 inch, 45 cal., 4—12 pdr., 6—1 pdr. (Vickers). 4 M.G. Torpedo tubes : 2—18 inch *above water.* Armour : $\frac{2}{3}$" nickel steel over boilers and engines. 4 Normand boilers. H.P. 8,000 = 23 kts. Coal : 210 tons = 3,000 miles at 10 kts.

Note.—Is fitted for service as Training Ship for midshipmen. Old Gunboat, *Gen. Suarez*, is a Harbour Training Ship.

Harbour Service Vessels.

Vanguardia class. *Photo, A. J. Carbone.*

Corsario class. *Photo, A. J. Carbone.*

Old Cruiser.

MONTE VIDEO (ex-*24 de Agosto*, ex-*Dogali*, ex-*Salamina*, Elswick, 1890, purchased from Italy, 1908). 2050 tons. Complement, 250. Dimensions : 250 (*p.p.*) × 37 × 16$\frac{1}{4}$ feet (*max.* draught). Guns : 6—6 inch, 9—6 pdr., 6 M.G. Torpedo tubes : 4 *above water.* Armour : 2"—1" deck, 4$\frac{1}{2}$" gun shields, 2" conning tower. Machinery : 2 sets horizontal and 4 double-ended boilers. H.P. 7500 = 17 kts. Coal : 480 tons.

Photo, A. J. Carbone.

Torpedo Boat.

1 boat, type unknown : **Oriental** (launched 1907, builder not known). 80 tons. Dimensions : 107 (*p.p.*) × 12 × 7 feet. Guns and tubes not known. Speed : 18 kts. Coal : 8 tons.

INGENERIO, LA VALLEJA, OYARVIDE. These are three armed tugs for Naval Harbour Services, built about 1908, displace about 60 tons each. Guns : 3 pdr. or M.G. Speed, 13 kts. *Chapicuy, Corsario, Tangarupa, Yaguary,* also exist, but are believed to be Government and not Naval Vessels. No information has been supplied to assist in determining which of the seven ships named above belong to *Vanguardia* class or which to *Corsario* class.

Yacht.

DIEZ Y OCHO DE JULIO. 678 tons. Complement, 85. 4 small guns and 2 machine guns. Speed, 12 kts. Presidential Yacht.

Note. —May have been sold out for commercial service.

VENEZUELAN NAVY.

(Revised in Venezuela, 1918.)

ENSIGN MERCANTILE

Personnel :

Minister of War and Marine : General C. Jiménez Rebolledo.

Warship-Port : Puerto Cabello. Steel floating dock here (3000 tons capacity) built in four sections on self-docking system, and worked by electricity.

Mercantile Marine : 11 steamers of 5,298 tons *gross,* 8 sailing vessels of 1,097 tons *gross.*

RECOGNITION SILHOUETTES.

Scale 1 inch = 160 feet.

Miranda.

J. F. Ribas.

General Salom.

M. Sucre.

Surveying Ship.

Photo, A. J. Carbone.

BARON DE RIO BRANCO (ex-*Maldonado*). Old paddle-wheel gunboat, transferred to Ministry of Interior, 1912, for Surveying Duties. 300 tons. Carries 4 small Q.F. and 2 M.G. Speed, 12 kts.

Gunboats.

BOLIVAR (*ex* Spanish). 571 tons. Dimensions : 190 × 32 × 13 feet Guns : 6—6 pdr. 2—14 inch tubes. Speed : 10 kts. Deleted by 1919.

23 de MAYO. 130 tons. Guns : 1 machine. Deleted by 1919.

ZAMORA. 740 tons. Guns : 2 machine. Deleted by 1919.

Gunboats—*Continued.*

Photo by courtesy of T. Ivor. Rees, Esq.

MARISCAL SUCRE (ex-Spanish *Isla de Cuba*, 1886, captured by U.S., 1898, and sold to Venezuela, 1912). 1125 tons. Dimensions: 192 × 30 × 12¼ feet. Guns: 2—4 inch, 2—6 pdr., 6—3 pdr., 2—1 pdr. H.P. 2000 = 13 kts. Coal: 200 tons. Endurance: 2640 miles at 10 kts. Complement 92.

MIRANDA (Clydebank, 1895; purchased from Spain, 1898). 200 tons. Dimensions: 135 × 19 × 8 feet. Guns: 4—6 pdr. H.P. 315 = 12 kts. Coal: 36 tons. Endurance: 850 miles at 8 kts. Complement 45.

VENEZUELA continued

GENERAL SALOM (ex-*Restaurador*, purchased 1900; built as U.S. private yacht *Atlanta*, 1884). 750 tons. Dimensions: 243 × 26 × 13 feet. Guns: 1—12 pdr., 4—6 pdr., 1 machine. H.P. 1900 = 14 kts. Coal: 200 tons. Endurance: 2200 miles at 10 kts. Complement 63.

Armed Tug.

Photo by favour of Ellis Greu & Co., N.Y.

JOSÉ FELIX RIBAS (ex-*Zumbador*, built 1894). 300 tons. Dimensions: 127 × 23 × 12 feet. Guns: 2—6 pdr. Speed, 10 kts. Coal: 78 tons. Endurance: 1440 miles at 10 kts. Complement 44.

Transports.

SALIAS (ex-S.S. *Julia*, transferred from Ministry of Hacienda to Navy, 1914). Only details known: H.P. 150. Complement, 18.

Brigantine **Antonio Diaz**, used as Naval Coal transport. 300 tons. Dimensions: 109 × 26 × 12 feet. Complement 16. Is armed to some extent.

CHINESE FLEET.
(Revised 1919.)

Note on Spelling of Chinese Warship Names.

The transliteration of Chinese names depends first upon the dialect in which the characters happen to be spelt, and secondly, on the system used by the foreigner to represent that dialect. The official dialect in Pekingese and a widely adopted system of representing it is that known as "Wade's Spelling." In this Edition of "Fighting Ships," it has been thought advisable to adopt some standard form of spelling Chinese Warship Names. Accordingly, "Wade's Spelling" has been introduced, all aspirates, accents and tonic marks being omitted.

NATIONAL FLAG.	ENSIGN.	MINISTER OF THE NAVY	VICE MINISTER OF THE NAVY
ADMIRAL.	VICE ADMIRAL.	REAR ADMIRAL	COMMODORE
SENIOR NAVAL OFFICER.	GUARD SHIP		

RED.   BLUE.   YELLOW.   WHITE.   BLACK.

Uniforms.

Admiral. | Vice-Admiral. | Rear-Admiral. | Captain. | Commander. | Lieut.-Comm'r. | Lieut. | Sub-Lieut. 1st Class. | Sub-Lieut. 2nd Class.

Personnel: *Minister of Marine*—Lin Kueng Shung.

Mercantile Marine: (Exclusive of German and Austrian vessels seized during 1917):—72 steamers of 95,560 tons *gross*; 7 sea-going sailing vessels of 865 tons *gross*. Also a large and unknown number of sailing craft (junks, etc.), for coastal trade and the larger rivers.

Shanghai is the principal port, about 4¼ million tons entering and being cleared per annum.

Docks.

FU-CHAU-FU. *Arsenal.* (See next page.)

TAKU. *Arsenal.* Government Dock: 340 × 39 × 14 feet. Private Docks: No. 1, 335 × 36 × 10 feet. No. 2, 315 × 36 × 11 feet. No. 3, 300 × 28 × 11 feet. No. 4, 300 × 40 × 11 feet.

KIANGNAN (Shanghai). *Arsenal.* Government Dock, 390 × 70 × 19 feet. Private Docks (Kiangnan Dock & Engineering Co., Ltd.), New Dock, 473 × 74 × 21¼ feet; Cosmopolitan, 560 × 77¼ × 24 feet; Old Dock, 400 × 53 × 16 feet; Tunkado, 362 × 67 × 16 feet.

WHAMPOA. *Arsenal.* No Government Docks, but 2 Private: Cooper, 430 × 65 × 16 feet; Locksun, 450 × 75 × 18 feet

AMOY. Private Dock, 360 × 60 × 16½ feet.

Private Yards.

Small gunboats are built by the Kiangnan Dock & Engineering Co., Shanghai (12 building slips), and the Yangtse Works, Hankow.

CHINESE IDENTIFICATION AND SIGNAL SILHOUETTES
Scale: 1 inch = 160 feet.

RIVER GUNBOATS.

CHIEN CHUNG *class* (3).   LI CHIEH.   CHIANG HSI *class* (2)   LI SUI.

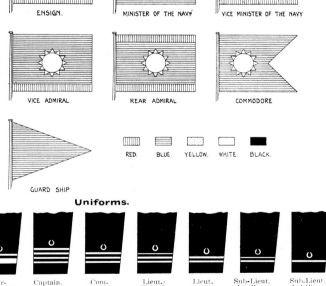

LIEN CHING.   CHIANG HENG *class* (4 ships).   CHU TAI *class* (6 ships).

YING JUI *class* (2 ships).   CHIEN WEI *class* (2 ships).

HAI YUNG *class* (3 ships).

TORPEDO CRAFT.

HU PENG *class*, or Nos. 7—10 (t.b.)

HAI CHI.   FEI YING.

1910   CHINESE PROTECTED CRUISERS.   1897-0

Chao-Ho.

YING JUI (July, 1911) & CHAO HO (Oct., 1911).

Normal displacement { Ying Jui: 2,750 tons. / Chao Ho: 2,600 tons. } Complement, 279.

Ying Jui: Length (p.p.) 330 feet. Beam, 42 feet. Max. load draught, 14 feet 11 inches.
Chao Ho: "   320   "   39   "   "   14   "

Guns (see Notes):
2—6 inch, 50 cal.
4—4 inch, 50 cal.
2—14 pdr., 50 cal.
6—3 pdr.
2—1 pdr.
Torpedo tubes (18 inch):
2 above water.

Armour:
3″ Deck (amidships)
1½″ Deck (ends) ...
3″ Conning tower
″ Gun shields......

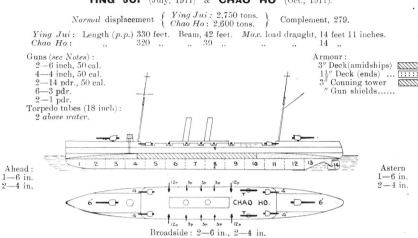

Ahead:
1—6 in.
2—4 in.

Astern
1—6 in.
2—4 in.

Broadside: 2—6 in., 2—4 in.

Machinery: Parsons turbine. Boilers: see notes. 4 screws. Designed H.P. (6000 S.H.P.= 20 kts.) 8000 = 22 kts. Coal: normal: 220 tons; maximum: 550 tons. Oil: 50 tons in Ying Jui, 100 tons in Chao Ho. Endurance: about 4500—5000 miles at 10 kts., and about 2900 miles at 18 kts.

Gunnery Notes.—Vickers models in Ying Jui; Elswick in Chao Ho.

Name	Builder	Machinery	Laid down	Completed	Trials $\frac{4}{5}$ths	Full power	Boilers
Ying Jui	Vickers	Vickers	1910	1912	5391=20·7	8797 = 22·23	White-F. + cyl.
Chao Ho	Elswick	Hawthorn	1910	1912	...	8622 = 22·12	6 Yarrow

HAI YUNG (1897), HAI CHOU (1897) and HAI CHEN (1898).
Displacement, 2950 metric tons. Complement 295. Length (p.p.) 314 feet. Beam, 40¾ feet. Maximum draught, 19 feet. Guns (Krupp): 3—5·9 inch, 40 cal., 8—4·1 inch, 40 cal., 6—1 pdr., and 6 machine. Torpedo tubes (14 inch): 1 bow (submerged). Armour: 2¾″ Deck (amidships), 1½″ deck (ends), 2″ gun shields, 1½″ conning tower. Designed H.P. 7,500 = 19·5 kts. 8 cylindrical boilers. Coal: normal 200-220 tons; maximum 500-580 tons. All three ships built by Vulkan Co., Stettin.

Photo, Symonds & Co

HAI CHI (Elswick, 1898).
Displacement, 4,300 tons. Complement, 431. Length (p.p.) 424 feet. Beam, 46⅝ feet. Mean draught, 16¾ feet; max. 19 feet. Guns (Elswick): 2—8 inch, 45 cal., 10—4·7 inch, 45 cal., 12—3 pdr., 4—1 pdr., 6 machine. Torpedo tubes (18 inch): 5 above water. Armour (Harvey): 5″ Deck (amidships), 1½″ deck (ends), 4½″ gun shields, 4″ ammunition hoists, 6″ conning tower. Designed H.P.: 17,000 (f.d.) = 24 kts. Boilers: 12 cylindrical. Coal: normal 400 tons, maximum 990 tons.

CHINESE GUNBOATS & RIVER GUNBOATS.

Gunboats.

YUNG PENG, YUNG HSIANG (Kawasaki Co., Kobe, Japan, 1912—13). 830 tons. Dimensions: 205 (p.p.) × 29¼ × 8 feet. Guns: 1—4·1 inch, 1—12 pdr., 4—3 pdr., 2—1 pdr. H.P. 1350 = 13·5 kts. Coal: 190 tons. Complement 105.

River Gunboats.

YUNG CHIEN, YUNG CHI. Begun 1915, by Kiangnan Dock Co., Shanghai. 900 tons. Dimensions: 215½ × 29¼ × 10 feet. Guns: 1—4 inch, 1—12 pdr., 4—3 pdr., 2—1 pdr. Designed H.P. 1400 = 13·5 kts. Coal: 150 tons.

CHIEN CHUNG (6/15).   **YUNG AN** (1915).
KUNG CHEN (1915).

All built by Yangtse Works, Hankow. 90 tons. Dimensions: 110 × 18½ × 3 feet. H.P. 450 = 11 kts., but Chien-Chung made 13 kts. on trials in 1915. Guns: 1—3·4 inch howitzer. 4 M.G. Complement, 42.

CHIANG HSI (Krupp, 1911). **CHIANG KUN** (Vulkan, 1912).
Dimensions: 146 (p.p.) × 24 × 3 feet. Displacement: 140 tons. H.P. 500 = 12 kts. Boilers: 2 Schulz. Coal: 30 tons. Guns: 1—3·4 (22 pdr.) howitzer, 4 machine. Complement, 42.

Note.—The three River Gunboats Chiang Ku, Chiang Kung and Chiang Ta, supposed to have been built at Hankow about 1908, are now reported as never having been commenced.

River Gunboats—Continued.

LI SUI (ex-German Otter, Tecklenborg, 1909. Interned in China, 1914, and taken over for Chinese Navy about 1917). 256 tons. Dimensions: 173·9×28·5×2·6 feet. Guns: 2—6 pdr., 3 M.G. Armour: 2″ on waterline, 2″ C.T. I.H.P. 1300 = 14 kts. Boilers: 4 Schulz. Coal: 79 tons. Complement (was 47).

LI CHIEH (ex-German Vaterland, Elbing, 1903. Interned at Nankin, August, 1914, and taken over for Chinese Navy, 1917). 217 tons. Dimensions: 157·5×26·2×2·6 feet. Guns: 1—3·4 inch (22 pdr.) howitzer, 1—4 pdr., 2 M.G. I.H.P. 1400 =13 kts. Boilers: 2 Schulz. Coal: 79 tons. Complement (was 47).

CHU CHIEN.   CHU TAI.⁰   CHU YU (1).
CHU KUAN.   CHU TUNG.   CHU YU (2).

All built by Kawasaki Yard, Kobe, 1906-07. 745 tons. Complement, 91. Dimensions: 200 × 29½ × 8 feet. Armament: 2—4·7 inch, 2—12 pdr., 4 machine. Machinery: 2 sets vertical triple expansion. 2 screws. Boilers: Water-tube. Designed H.P. 1350 = 13 kts. Coal: 150 tons.

Sodo of this class apparently deleted by 1919.

River Gunboats—Continued.

CHIANG CHEN.   CHIANG LI.
CHIANG HENG.   CHIANG YUAN.

All built by Kawasaki Yard, Kobe, 1906-07. 550 tons. Complement, 91. Dimensions: 180 × 28 × 7 feet. Armament: 1—4·7 inch (bow), 1—12 pdr. (aft), 4—3 pdr., 4 Maxims. Machinery: 2 sets vertical triple expansion. 2 screws. Boilers: water-tube. Designed H.P. 950 = 13 kts. Coal: 113 tons.

Torpedo Gunboats.

KIEN WEI

CHIEN WEI (1902) and **CHIEN AN** (1900). Displacement, 850 tons. Complement, 139. Guns: 1—4·1 inch, 3—9 pdr., 6—1 pdr. Torpedo tubes: 2 above water. Armour: 1″ belt and deck (amidships). Designed H.P.: 6500 = 23 kts. (about 18 now). Coal: 180 tons. Built at Fu-Chau-Fu.

FEI YING (July, 1895). Displacement, 850 tons. Complement, 145. Guns (Krupp): 2—4·1 inch, 6—3 pdr., 4 M.G., 3 tubes (above water). Designed H.P. 5500 = 22 kts. Boilers: 8 Yarrow. Coal: 170 tons. Built at Stettin.

Destroyers.

3 *Schichau* type : **Chien Kang, Tung An, Yu Chang** (—1912), 390 tons. Dimensions : 198 × 21·3 × 6 feet. Armament : 2—12 pdr., 2—3 pdr., 2—18 inch tubes. Designed H.P. 6000 = 30 kts. Coal, 80 tons. Complement, 66.

First called *Fu Po, Fei Hung* and *Chang Feng* but names were altered by Yuan Shih Kai.

Also **Lung Tuan** built by Stabilimento Tecnico.

CHINESE MISCELLANEOUS.

Despatch Vessels.

WU FENG (Tsingtao, 1912). 200 tons. Dimensions : 124 × 20 × 7 feet. H.P. 300 = 10 kts. Guns : 4—3 pdr. Complement, 46.

LIEN CHING (Shanghai, 1910). Dimensions : 150 (*p.p.*) × 24 × 9½ feet (*mean*). 500 tons. I.H.P. 900 = 13·5 kts. Cylindrical boilers fitted with Howden's f.d. Coal : 95 tons. Guns : 4—6 pdr. Complement 61.

Training Ship.

TUNG CHI (1895). Steel. 1700 tons. Guns : 2—5·9 inch, 5—4 inch. 5—1 pdr., 2 M.G. Speed : 11·2 kts. 1 Screw. No other details known.

Transport.

FU AN. No details known.

Torpedo Boats.

4 *Kawasaki-Normand* type : **Hu Peng** or **No. 7, Hu E** or **No. 8, Hu Ying** or **No. 9, Hu Chun** or **No. 10** (Kobe, Japan, 1907-8). 97 tons. Dimensions : 135 × 15½ × 7¾ feet. Armament : 2—3 pdr., 3 M.G., 3—18 inch tubes (1 bow *above water* and 2 deck). Designed H.P. 1200 = 23 kts. Coal, 28 tons *normal*. Complement : 34.

2 *Vulcan* type : **Su*** or **No. 4, Chen*** or **No. 2** (1895). 90 tons. 144 × 17 × 7 feet. Armament : 4 M.G., 3 torpedo tubes. Complement 38.

2 *Schichau* type : **Lieh*** or **No. 3, Chang*** or **No. 1** (1895). 62 tons. 130 × 15 × 5 feet. Armament : 6 M.G., 3 torpedo tubes. H.P. 600 = 16 kts. Complement 36.

* These four T.B. sometimes have suffix *Ting* (Boat) or *Tzu* (meaningless) added to their names.

CHINESE PROVINCIAL GOVERNMENT VESSELS.

Note.—These Ships do not belong to the Chinese Navy, but to the Water Police of the Provinces named. They might, however, be used for National Defence in the event of War.

Gunboats.

(All belong to Water Police of Kwang Tung Province.)

KUANG YU (1891). Wooden vessel of 600 tons displacement. Dimensions : 156 × 24 × 10 feet. Guns : 9 machine. Designed H.P. 400 = 11 kts. (never attained). Coal : 110 tons. Complement 72.

KUANG CHEN.   **KUANG LI.**
KUANG HENG.   **KUANG YUAN.**

Built 1886. Steel. 300 tons. Dimensions : 110 × 18 × 7 feet. Guns : one old Krupp, 4½ tons (5·9 inch), 1 old 3·5 inch. I.H.P. 78 = 7 kts.

KUANG CHIN (China, 1885—7). Wooden vessel of 560 tons. Dimensions : 250 × 34 × 10 feet. Guns : 2—4·1 inch, 1—12 pdr., 2—2 pdr. H.P. 312 = 9 kts. 1 screw. Coal : 110 tons. Complement 71.

KUANG KENG (China, 1883). Composite vessel of 560 tons. Guns : 1—4·7 inch, 1—12 pdr. H.P. 400 = 11 kts.

River Gunboats.

(Both belonging to Water Police of Chechiang Province.)

CHE CHING *class* (2).

(*Scale* : 1 inch = 160 *feet*).

CHE CHING, CHE TING (Kiangnan Dock Co., Shanghai, 1914). Dimensions : 146 × 24 × 2 feet. 144 tons. H.P. 750 (*f.d.*) = 13 kts. Boilers : Yarrow. Guns : 1—3·4 inch howitzer, 2—3 pdr., 8 machine. Complement, 41.

Old Torpedo Boats.

(All belong to Water Police of Kwang Tung Province.)

5 *Schichau* type :

Lei Chung	**Lei Kan** (1)	**Lei Tui**
Lei Li	**Lei Kan** (2)	

All built in Germany, 1884-5. 26 tons. Armament : 1 or 2 M.G., 1 torpedo tube. H.P. 420 = 19 kts. (much less now).

4 type unknown :

Lei Chen	**Lei Ken**
Lei Kun	**Lei Sun**

All built 1884-5. No details known.

ROYAL SIAMESE NAVY.

(Revised, 1919.)

Flags (1919).

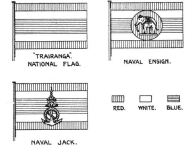

"TRAIRANGA". NATIONAL FLAG.   NAVAL ENSIGN.

RED.   WHITE.   BLUE.

NAVAL JACK.

Arsenal.

BANGKOK.—Dry dock : 474 feet (over blocks), 513 feet (over all) × 45 feet (at entrance) × 15 to 16 feet H.W.O.S. Sheer legs with lift of 40 tons and travelling crane with lift of 10 tons. Workshops and plant are modern and capable of effecting repairs for the whole fleet.

Private Docks. (Bangkok.)

Dry Dock Co., No. 1 ; 300 × 45 × 11½ feet. Samsen Dry Dock, 215 × 33 × 13 feet.

Personnel : 5000. Reserve : 20,000. Royal Naval Academy for Navigation and Engineering at Phra Rajwangderm, with accommodation for 120 cadets. There are about six Provincial Training Establishments, so that men recruited locally can receive preliminary training before being drafted to ships of the Royal Navy.

Naval W/T Stations : At Bangkok and Singora, with radius of 310 miles by day and 600 miles at night.

RECOGNITION SILHOUETTES.

Scale : 1 inch = 160 feet.

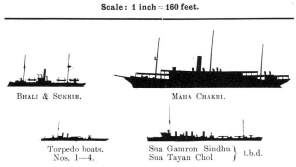

BHALI & SUKRIB.   MAHA CHAKRI.

Torpedo boats. Nos. 1—4.

Sua Gamron Sindhu } t.b.d.
Sua Tayan Chol }

Royal Yacht.

Photo, G. E. Bailey, Esq.

MAHA CHAKRI (Kawasaki Co., Kobé, Japan, 1918). About 2,400 tons *gross*. Complement, Length, 298 feet (*w.l.*), 335 feet (*o.a.*). Beam, 40 feet. Draught, feet. Guns : Not known. Machinery (*see Notes*) : 2 sets triple exp. Boilers : 4 (type unknown) coal and oil burning. I.H.P. about 2000 = 15 kts. Oil fuel : 200 tons = 2000 miles endurance.

Notes.—The hull of the old Royal Yacht *Maha Chakri* was sold to the Kawasaki Co. in 1917, but the engines and other fittings were removed, overhauled and renovated for installation in the new *Maha Chakri* described above.

Gunboats.

BHALI. Tops on *both* masts and yard on mainmast.

SUKRIB. Top on mainmast *only*.

BHALI (1901), **SUKRIB** (1901). 580 tons. 162 × 23 × 10 feet. Guns : 1—4·7 inch, 5—6 pdr., 4—1 pdr. Designed H.P. 500 = 11·4 kts. Complement, 83.

> *No photograph available.*
> 1 funnel, 2 masts, with one military top.

MURATHA (1898). 530 tons. 145 × 23 × 10 feet. Guns : 1—4·7 inch, 4—6 pdr., 3—1 pdr. Designed H.P. 500 = 11·4 kts.

MAHUT RAJAKUMAR (*ex Filipinas*) (1887). 700 tons. Guns : 2—old 4·7 inch, 4—6 pdr., 3—1 pdr. 1 tube. Original speed : 14 kts. (11·5). Possibly deleted by 1919.

SIAMESE NAVY—*Continued*
Transport.

VIDU (   ). 850 tons. 176 × 27⅙ × 13½ feet. Speed, 10 kts.

Also 10 other steamships serving as Despatch Vessels for Coastal and River Duties. No detailed information can be secured of these craft. There are 50 to 60 steamers and launches from 100 tons downwards for River Service.

Custom Cruisers.

SRIYA MONTHON (Thornycroft, 1908). Guns: 1—6 pdr.
Designed H.P. 700 = 14·5 kts. Deleted by 1919.

2 Destroyers.

Sua-Tayan-Chol. *Photo, G. E. Bailey, Esq.*

Sua-Gamron-Sindhu (1912), 585 tons, and **Sua-Tayan-Chol** (1908), 375 tons. Both built by Kawasaki Co., Kobé, Japan. Dimensions: 227 (*p.p.*) × 21¼ × 6 feet. H.P. 6000 = 27 kts. Coal: 100 tons = 1000 miles at 10 kts. Armament: 1—12 pdr., 5—6 pdr., 2 M.G.; 2—18 inch tubes. Complement: 75.

4 Torpedo Boats.

No. 2. *Photo, G. E. Bailey, Esq.*

4 *Kawasaki* boats:—No. **1, 2** and **3** (1908), and No. **4** (1913), 120 tons. 131·6 × 16·2 × 3·6 feet. H.P. 1200 = 22 kts. Armament: 1—6 pdr., 1—3 pdr., 2—18 inch tubes. Complement: 29.

PERSIA.

ENSIGN

MERCANTILE

Silhouette Scale: 1 inch = 160 feet.

PERSEPOLIS.

Gunboat.

Photo, Lieut. Frewin, R.N.

PERSEPOLIS (1885). Dimensions: 207 × 32¾ × 19¼ feet. 1200 tons. H.P. 450 = 10 kts. Guns: 4 old 2·7 in., 2 machine.

Note: Gunboat *Mozaffir* served with and in H.M. Navy during the War. It is not known what has become of this ship.

Imperial Yacht.

SELIKA (1902). 400 tons

SARAWAK.

ALINE (1875). Gunboat of 175 tons. 2 small guns.
ADEN (1884). Steamer of 300 tons. Armed with 1 gun.
LORNA DOONE (1881). Steamer of 118 tons. 2 small guns.

SHIPS LOST IN THE WAR.

Compiled by F. E. McMurtrie.

BRITISH.

13 BATTLESHIPS.

AUDACIOUS (1912). 23,000 tons. Guns: 10—13.5 in., 16—4 in. Mined off North coast of Ireland, 27th October, 1914.

VANGUARD (1909.) 19,250 tons. Guns: 10—12 in., 50 cal.; 18—4 in. Destroyed by internal explosion, at Scapa Flow, 9th July, 1917. For appearance, see photo of ST. VINCENT.

KING EDWARD VII (1903). 16,350 tons. Guns: 4—12 in. IX, 40 cal.: 4—9.2 in. X, 45 cal.; 10—6 in. VIII, 45 cal.; 12—12 pdr., etc. Mined off N. Scottish coast, lat. 58.43 N., long. 4 12 W., 6th January, 1916.

BRITANNIA (1904). Sister to KING EDWARD VII, above. Torpedoed by a German Submarine off Cape Trafalgar, 9th November, 1918.

BULWARK (1899). 15,000 tons. Guns: 4—12 in. IX, 40 cal.; 12—6 in. VII, 45 cal.; 18—12 pdr., etc. Destroyed by internal explosion at Sheerness, 26th November, 1914.

FORMIDABLE (1898). Sister to BULWARK, above. Torpedoed by German Submarine U 24, off Portland Bill, 1st January, 1915.

IRRESISTIBLE (1898). Sister to BULWARK, above. Sunk by torpedo from White Cliffs, in the Dardanelles, 18th March, 1915.

OCEAN (1898). 12,950 tons. Guns: 4—12 in. VIII, 35 cal.; 12—6 in., 40 cal.; 12—12 pdr., etc. Sunk by torpedo, from White Cliffs, in the Dardanelles, 18th March, 1915.

GOLIATH (1898). Sister to OCEAN, above. Torpedoed by Turkish Destroyer MUAVENET-I-MILET, off De Tott's Battery, in the Dardanelles, 13th May, 1915.

TRIUMPH (1903). 11,985 tons. Guns: 4—10 in., 45 cal.; 14—7.5 in. II, 50 cal.; 14—14 pdr., etc. Torpedoed by German Submarine U 51 off Gaba Tepe, Gallipoli peninsula, 25th May, 1915.

RUSSELL (1901). 14,000 tons. Guns: 4—12 in. IX, 40 cal.; 12—6 in. VII, 45 cal.; 12—12 pdr., etc. Mined off Malta, 27th April, 1916.

CORNWALLIS (1901). Sister to RUSSELL, above. Torpedoed by German Submarine, 60 miles S.E. of Malta, 9th January, 1917.

MAJESTIC (1895). 14,900 tons. Guns: 4—12 in. VIII, 35 cal.; 12—6 in., 40 cal.; 16—12 pdr., etc. Torpedoed by German Submarine U 23, off W. beach, Gallipoli peninsula, 27th May, 1915.

3 BATTLE CRUISERS.

QUEEN MARY (1912). 27,000 tons. Guns: 8—13.5 in., 16—4 in. Blown up by gunfire of German Battle-Cruisers during Battle of Jutland, 31st May, 1916. For appearance, see photo of PRINCESS ROYAL.

INDEFATIGABLE (1909). 18,750 tons. Guns: 8—12 in., 50 cal.; 16—4 in. Blown up by gunfire of German Battle-Cruisers, during Battle of Jutland, 31st May, 1916. For appearance, see photo of NEW ZEALAND

INVINCIBLE (1907). 17,250 tons. Guns: 8—12 in. XI, 45 cal.; 16—4 in. Blown up by gunfire of German Battle-Cruisers during Battle of Jutland, 31st May, 1916. For appearance, see photo of INFLEXIBLE.

15 CRUISERS.

DEFENCE (1907). 14,600 tons. Guns: 4—9.2 in. XI, 50 cal.; 10—7.5 in., II, 50 cal.; 16—12 pdr., etc. Blown up by gunfire of German Battle Fleet during Battle of Jutland, 31st May, 1916.

NATAL (1905). 13,550 tons. Guns: 6—9.2 in. X, 45 cal.; 4—7.5 in. II, 50 cal., etc. Blown up by explosion in after magazine, in Cromarty Firth, 30th December, 1915.

COCHRANE (1905). Sister to NATAL, above. Wrecked in estuary of the Mersey, 14th November, 1918.

WARRIOR (1905). Sister to NATAL, above. Foundered after being disabled by gunfire in the Battle of Jutland, 1st June, 1916.

BLACK PRINCE (1904). 13,550 tons. Guns: 6—9.2 in. X, 45 cal.; 10—6 in. XI, 50 cal., etc. Sunk by gunfire of a German Battleship during Battle of Jutland, 31st May, 1916.

MONMOUTH (1901). 9,800 tons. Guns: 14—6 in. VII, 45 cal.; 9—12 pdr., etc. Sunk by gunfire of German Cruisers, SCHARNHORST and GNEISENAU, off Coronel, Chile, 1st November, 1914.

ABOUKIR (1900). **HOGUE** (1900). **CRESSY** (1899). 12,000 tons. Guns: 2—9.2 in. VIII, 40 cal.; 12—6 in. VII, 45 cal.; 13—12 pdr., etc. All three torpedoed by German Submarine U 9, in North Sea, lat. 52.18 N., long. 3.41 E., 22nd September, 1914.

ARGYLL (1904). 10,850 tons. Guns: 4—7.5 in. I, 45 cal.; 6—6 in. VII, 45 cal., etc. Wrecked on Bell Rock, East Coast of Scotland, 28th October, 1915.

HAMPSHIRE (1903). Sister to ARGYLL, above. Mined 1½ miles W. of the Orkneys, 5th June, 1916.

GOOD HOPE (1901). 14,100 tons. Guns: 2—9.2 in. IX, 45 cal.; 16—6 in. VII, 45 cal.; 12—12 pdr., etc. Sunk by gunfire of German Cruisers, SCHARNHORST and GNEISENAU, off Coronel, Chile, 1st November, 1914.

DRAKE (1901). Sister to GOOD HOPE, above. Torpedoed by German Submarine, in Rathlin Sound, off North Coast of Ireland, 2nd October, 1917.

ARIADNE (1898). 11,000 tons. Guns: 16—6 in., 40 cal., etc. 13—12 pdr. etc. Torpedoed by German Submarine, off Beachy Head, 26th July, 1917. (This vessel was employed as a Minelayer.)

HAWKE (1891). 7,350 tons. Guns: 2—9.2 in., 30 cal.; 10—6 in., etc. Torpedoed by German Submarine U 9, off East Coast of Scotland, 15th October, 1914.

14 LIGHT CRUISERS.

CASSANDRA (1916). 4,120 tons. Guns: 5—6 in., 2—3 in. AA. Mined in the Baltic, night of 4-5th December, 1918. For appearance, see photo of C type Light Cruiser.

ARETHUSA (1913). 3,520 tons. Guns: 2—6 in., 6—4 in. Mined off Felixstowe, 11th February, 1916. For appearance, see photo of UNDAUNTED.

NOTTINGHAM (1913). 5,440 tons. Guns: 9—6 in., etc. Torpedoed by German Submarine in North Sea, lat. 55.34 N., long. 0.12 E., 19th August, 1916. For appearance, see photo of LOWESTOFT.

AMPHION (1911). 3,440 tons. Guns: 10—4 in., etc. Mined off Thames estuary, 6th August, 1914. For appearance, see photo of ACTIVE.

FALMOUTH (1910). 5,250 tons. Guns: 8—6 in., etc. Foundered in North Sea, lat. 54 N., long 0.2 W., 20th August, 1916, after being torpedoed four times by German Submarines. For appearance, see photo of YARMOUTH.

PATHFINDER (1904). 2,940 tons. Guns: 9—4 in. Torpedoed by German Submarine U 21, off St. Abb's Head, East Coast of Scotland, 5th September, 1914.

The following six obsolete Light Cruisers were blown up and sunk as blockships.

VINDICTIVE (1897). 5,750 tons, at Ostend. 10th May. 1918.

BRILLIANT (1891) and **SIRIUS** (1890). 3,600 tons, at Ostend. 23rd April, 1918.

INTREPID and **IPHIGENIA** (1891), 3600 tons. **THETIS** (1890). 3,400 tons. all three at Zeebrugge, 23rd April, 1918.

LIGHT CRUISERS—*continued*.

HERMES (1898). 5600 tons. Guns: 11—6 in., 40 cal.; 9—12 pdr., etc. Torpedoed by German Submarine U 27, in Straits of Dover, 31st October, 1914, while employed as a Seaplane Carrier.

PEGASUS (1897). 2,135 tons. Guns: 8—4 in., etc. Sunk by gunfire of German Cruiser KÖNIGSBERG, at Zanzibar, 20th September, 1914.

SHIPS LOST IN THE WAR.—BRITISH *continued.*

8 MONITORS.

Raglan (1915). 6,150 tons. Guns: 2—14 in., 2—6 in., 2—12 pdr., etc. Sunk by gunfire of German Battle-Cruiser Goeben, in action off Imbros, 20th January, 1918. For appearance, see photo of Abercrombie class.
Glatton (1914). 5,700 tons. Guns: 2—9.2 in., 4—6 in., etc. Caught fire in Dover Harbour, and torpedoed to avoid magazine explosion, 16th September, 1918. For appearance, see photo of Gorgon, on page 90. (This vessel was officially classed as a Coast Defence Ship.)
M 30 (1915). 535 tons. Guns: 2—6 in., etc. Sunk by fire of Turkish batteries in Gulf of Smyrna, 13th May, 1916. For appearance, see photo of M 29.
M 28 (1915). 570 tons. Guns: 1—9.2 in., 1—12 pdr., etc. Sunk by gunfire of German Battle-Cruiser Goeben, in action off Imbros, 20th January, 1918. For appearance, see photo of M 26.
M 27 and **M 25** (1915). Sisters to M 28, above. Both lost during operations in the Dvina River, North Russia, 17th September, 1919.
M 21 (1915). 540 tons. Armament as M 28. Mined off Ostend, 20th October, 1918.
M 15 (1915). Sister to M 21, above. Torpedoed by a German Submarine, off Gaza, 11th November, 1917.

20 SLOOPS.

Anchusa (1917). 1290 tons. Guns: 2—4 in., etc. Torpedoed by a German Submarine, off the North Coast of Ireland, 16th July, 1918. For appearance, see photo of Polyanthus.
Arbutus (1917). Sister to Anchusa, above, but employed as a Special Service Ship. Foundered in St. George's Channel, during very heavy weather, after being torpedoed by a German Submarine, 16th December, 1917.
Bergamot (1917). Sister to Anchusa, above, but employed as a Special Service Ship. Torpedoed by a German Submarine, in the Atlantic, 13th August, 1917.
Candytuft (1917). Sister to Anchusa, above, but employed as a Special Service Ship. Torpedoed by a German Submarine, off Bougie, 18th November, 1917.
Cowslip (1917). Sister to Anchusa, above. Torpedoed by a German Submarine, off Cape Spartel, 25th April, 1918.
Gaillardia (1917). Sister to Anchusa, above. Mined off the Orkneys, night of 22nd-23rd March, 1918.
Rhododendron (1917). Sister to Anchusa, above. Torpedoed by a German Submarine, in the North Sea, 5th May, 1918.
Alyssum (1915). 1250 tons. Armament as Anchusa. Mined off S.W. Coast of Ireland, 18th March, 1917.
Arabis (1915). Sister to Alyssum, above. Torpedoed by German Destroyers, off Dogger Bank, night of 10-11th February, 1916.
Genista (1916). Sister to Alyssum, above. Torpedoed by a German Submarine, off West Coast of Ireland, 23rd October, 1916.
Gentian and **Myrtle** (1915). Sisters to Alyssum, above. Both mined in the Gulf of Finland, 16th July, 1919.
Mignonette (1916). Sister to Alyssum, above. Mined off S. W. Coast of Ireland, 17th March, 1917.
Nasturtium (1915). Sister to Alyssum, above. Mined in the Mediterranean, 27th April, 1916.
Primula (1915). Sister to Alyssum, above. Torpedoed by German Submarine U 35 in Eastern Mediterranean, 1st March, 1916.
Salvia (1916). Sister to Alyssum, above, but employed as a Special Service Ship. Torpedoed by a German Submarine off West Coast of Ireland, 20th June, 1917.
Tulip (1916). Sister to Alyssum, above, but employed as a Special Service Ship. Torpedoed by a German Submarine in the Atlantic, 30th April, 1917.
Aster (1915). 1200 tons. Armament as Anchusa. Mined in the Mediterranean, 4th July, 1917.
Lavender (1915). Sister to Aster, above. Torpedoed by a German Submarine in the English Channel, 5th May, 1917.
Begonia (1915). Sister to Aster, above, but employed as a Special Service Ship. Missing, believed torpedoed by a German Submarine in the Atlantic, October, 1917.

Note.—For appearance of above vessels, see photo of "Flower" class Sloop.

26 MINESWEEPERS.

(**Note.**—P. = Paddle; S. = Screw; T. = Tunnel.)

Roedean (ex Roebuck) (1897). S. 1094 tons (gross). Sunk at Longhope, 13th January, 1915.
St. Seiriol (1914). P. 928 tons (gross). Mined off the Shipwash Light Vessel, 25th April, 1918.
Newmarket (1907). S. 833 tons (gross). Missing, Eastern Mediterranean; last reported 16th July, 1917.
Clacton (1904). S. 820 tons (gross). Torpedoed by a German Submarine at Chai Aghizi, in the Levant, 3rd August, 1916.
Ascot (1916). P. 810 tons displacement. Guns: 2—12 pdr., etc. Torpedoed by a German Submarine, off Farn Islands, 10th November, 1918.
Ludlow (1916). Sister to Ascot, above. Mined off the Shipwash, 29th December, 1916.
Plumpton (1916). Sister to Ascot, above. Mined off Ostend, 19th October, 1918.
Redcar (1916) and **Kempton** (1916). Sisters to Ascot, above. Both mined off Spindle Buoy, to north of Gravelines, 24th June, 1917.
Cupar (1918). S. 800 tons displacement. Guns: 2—12 pdr., etc. Mined off the Tyne, 5th May, 1919.
Kinross (1918). Sister to Cupar, above. Mined in the Ægean, 16th June, 1919.
Penarth (1918). Sister to Cupar, above. Mined off the Yorkshire Coast, 4th February, 1919.
Blackmorevale (1916). S. 750 tons displacement. Guns: 1—12 pdr., etc. Mined off Montrose, 1st May, 1918.
Erin's Isle (1912). P. 633 tons (gross). Mined off the Nore, 7th February, 1919.
Queen of the North (1895). P. 590 tons (gross). Mined off Orfordness, 20th July, 1917.
Brighton Queen (1897). P. 553 tons (gross). Mined off Nieuport, 6th October, 1915.
Duchess of Hamilton (1890). P. 553 tons (gross). Mined off the Longsand, 29th November, 1915.
Hythe (1905). P. 509 tons (gross). Lost by collision with Armed Boarding Steamer Sarnia, off Cape Helles, night of 28-29th October, 1915.
Lady Ismay (1911). P. 495 tons (gross). Mined near the Galloper, 21st December, 1917.
Fair Maid (1915). P. 432 tons (gross). Mined near Cross Sand Buoy, 9th November, 1916.
Nepaulin. (1892). P. 378 tons (gross). Mined near Dyck Light Vessel, 20th April, 1917.
Princess Mary II (1911). P. 326 tons (gross). Mined in the Ægean, 2nd August, 1919.
Duchess of Montrose (1902). P. 322 tons (gross). Mined off Dunkirk, 18th March, 1917.
Marsa (1902). P. 317 tons (gross). Lost by collision at entrance to Harwich Harbour, 18th November, 1917.
Fandango (1918). T. 280 tons displacement. Mined in the Dvina River, North Russia, 3rd July, 1919.
Sword Dance (1918). Sister to Fandango, above. Mined in the Dvina River, North Russia, 24th June, 1919.

Note.—For appearance of certain of the above vessels, reference should be made to the illustrations of various types of Minesweepers.

5 TORPEDO GUNBOATS.

Hazard (1894). 1070 tons. Guns: 2—4.7 in. Lost by collision off Portland Bill, 28th January, 1918, while employed as a Submarine Depot Vessel.

Speedy (1893). 810 tons. Guns: 2—4.7 in. Mined in North Sea, 30 miles off the Humber, 3rd September, 1914.

Jason (1892). Similar to Speedy, above. Employed as a Minesweeper. Mined near Coll Island, West Coast of Scotland, 7th April, 1917.
Niger (1892). Sister to Jason, above. Torpedoed by German Submarine, in the Downs, 11th November, 1914.
Seagull (1889). 735 tons. Guns: 2—4.7 in. Lost by collision with a Merchant Vessel, in the Firth of Clyde, 30th September, 1918.

69 FLOTILLA LEADERS and DESTROYERS.

(**a**) *3 Flotilla Leaders.* For appearance, see photos of "Scott," "Broke," and "Kempenfelt" types.
Scott (1917). 1800 tons. Guns: 5—4.7 in., 1—3 in. AA., etc. Tubes: 6—21 in. Torpedoed by a German Submarine, off the Dutch Coast, 15th August, 1918.
Tipperary (1913). 1737 tons. Guns: 6—4 in., etc. Tubes: 4—21 in. Sunk by gunfire during Battle of Jutland, 1st June, 1916.
Hoste (1916). 1666 tons. Guns: 4—4 in., etc. Tubes: 4—21 in. Foundered after collision with Negro, during very bad weather, in the North Sea, 21st December, 1916.

(**b**) *66 Destroyers.*
Vehement (1917). 1367 tons. Guns: 4—4 in., 1—3 in. AA., etc. Tubes: 4—21 in. Mined in the North Sea, 2nd August, 1918.
Verulam (1917). Sister to Vehement, above. Mined off Seskaer Island, Gulf of Finland, night of 3rd-4th September, 1919.
Vittoria (1917). Sister to Vehement, above. Torpedoed by a Russian (Bolshevik) Submarine in the Gulf of Finland, 1st September, 1919.
Ulysses (1917). 1090 tons. Guns: 3—4 in., etc. Tubes: 4—21 in. Lost by collision with a merchantman in the Firth of Clyde, 29th October, 1918.
Tornado (1917). 1091 tons. Similar to Ulysses, above. Torpedoed by German Submarine, off the Maas Lightship, night of 22nd-23rd December, 1917.
Torrent (1916). 1069 tons. Similar to Ulysses, above. Torpedoed by German Submarine, off the Maas Lightship, night of 22nd-23rd December, 1917.
Simoom (1916). 1072 tons. Similar to Ulysses, above. Blown up by gunfire of German Destroyers, during action off Schouwen Bank, 23rd January, 1917.
Setter (1916). 1040 tons. Similar to Ulysses, above. Lost by collision with Sylph, during foggy weather, off Harwich, 17th May, 1917.
Recruit (new) (1916). 1075 tons. Similar to Ulysses, above. Mined in the North Sea, 9th August, 1917.
Ulleswater (1917). 923 tons. Armament as Ulysses, above. Torpedoed by a German Submarine, off the Dutch Coast, 15th August, 1918.
Strongbow (1916). 898 tons. Armament as Ulysses, above. Sunk by gunfire of three German Light Cruisers, in convoy action, off Norwegian Coast, 17th October, 1917.
Surprise (1916). 910 tons. Armament as Ulysses, above. Torpedoed by a German Submarine, off the Maas Lightship, night of 22nd-23rd December, 1917.
Pheasant (1916). 1025 tons. Armament as Ulysses, above. Mined off the Orkneys, 1st March, 1917.
Partridge (1916). 1016 tons. Sister to Pheasant, above. Sunk by gunfire of four German Destroyers, in convoy action, off Norwegian Coast, 12th December, 1917.
Narbrough (1916), 1010 tons. **Opal** (1915), 1000 tons. Sisters to Pheasant, above. Both wrecked outside Scapa Flow, during a violent gale and snowstorm, 12th January, 1918.
Negro (1916). 1025 tons. Sister to Pheasant, above. Lost by collision with Hoste, during very bad weather, in the North Sea, 21st December, 1916.
North Star (1916). 1042 tons. Sister to Pheasant, above. Sunk by fire of German batteries, at Zeebrugge, 23rd April, 1918.
Nomad (1916) and **Nestor** (1915). 1025 tons. Sisters to Pheasant, above. Sunk by gunfire of German Battle Fleet, in Battle of Jutland, 31st May, 1916.
Nessus (1915). 1022 tons. Sister to Pheasant, above. Lost by collision with Amphitrite, during foggy weather, in the North Sea, 8th September, 1918.
Marmion (1915). 1029 tons. Sister to Pheasant, above. Lost by collision in the North Sea, 21st October, 1917.
Mary Rose (1915). 1017 tons. Sister to Pheasant, above. Sunk by gunfire of three German Light Cruisers, in convoy action, off the Norwegian Coast, 17th October, 1917.
Turbulent (1916). 1080 tons. Guns: 5—4 in. Tubes: 4—21 in. Rammed by a large German warship, in the Battle of Jutland, 1st June, 1916.
Medusa (1915). 1007 tons. Guns: 3—4 in., etc. Tubes: 4—21 in. Foundered, after collision with Laverock, off Schleswig Coast, 25th March, 1916.
Lassoo (1915). 1010 tons. Armament as Medusa, above. Torpedoed by a German Submarine, off the Maas Lightship, 13th August, 1916.
Laforey (1913). 995 tons. Sister to Lassoo, above. Mined in the English Channel, 23rd March, 1917.
Louis (1913). 965 tons. Sister to Lassoo, above. Wrecked in Suvla Bay, 31st October, 1915.
Fortuno (1913). 1000 tons. Similar to Lassoo, above. Sunk by gunfire of German Battle Fleet, in Battle of Jutland, about midnight, 31st May-1st June, 1916.
Ardent (1913). 981 tons. Armament as Medusa. Sunk by gunfire of German Battle Fleet, in Battle of Jutland, 1st June, 1916.
Contest (1913). 957 tons. Similar to Ardent, above. Torpedoed by a German Submarine, in the approaches to the English Channel, 18th September, 1917.
Lynx (1913). 935 tons. Sister to Contest, above. Mined off Moray Firth, 9th August, 1915.
Paragon (1913). 917 tons. Sister to Contest, above. Torpedoed in action with German Destroyers, in the Straits of Dover, 18th March, 1917.
Shark (1912). 935 tons. Sister to Contest, above. Disabled by gunfire of German Light Cruisers, and subsequently torpedoed, in Battle of Jutland, 31st May, 1916.
Sparrowhawk (1912). 935 tons. Sister to Contest, above. Disabled by collision with Broke, in Battle of Jutland, and sunk by Marksman, to avoid falling into enemy hands, 1st June, 1916.
Arno (1914). 550 tons. Guns: 4—12 pdr. Tubes: 3—18 in. Lost by collision, off the Dardanelles, 23rd March, 1918.
Ariel (1911). 763 tons. Guns: 2—4 in., 2—12 pdr. Tubes: 2—21 in. Mined in the North Sea, 2nd August, 1918.
Attack (1911). 785 tons. Sister to Ariel, above. Torpedoed by a German Submarine, 11 miles off Alexandria, 30th December, 1917.
Phœnix (1911). 765 tons. Sister to Ariel, above. Torpedoed by an enemy Submarine, in the Adriatic, 14th May, 1918.
Comet (1910). 747 tons. Guns: 2—4 in., 2—12 pdr. Tubes: 2—21 in. Torpedoed by an enemy Submarine, in the Mediterranean, 6th August, 1918.
Goldfinch (1910). Sister to Comet, above. Wrecked on Start Point, Sanday Island, Orkneys, during a fog, night of 18-19th February, 1915.
Maori (1909). 1035 tons. Guns: 2—4 in. Tubes: 2—18 in. Mined 2 miles N.W. of Weilingen Lightship, near Zeebrugge, 7th May, 1915.
Staunch (1910). Sister to Comet, above. Torpedoed by a German Submarine, off Gaza, 11th November, 1917.
Pincher (1910). 975 tons. Guns: 1—4 in., 3—12 pdr. Tubes: 2—21 in. Wrecked on the Seven Stones, 24th July, 1918.
Racoon (1910). 913 tons. Sister to Pincher, above. Wrecked on the North Coast of Ireland, in a snowstorm, 9th January, 1918.
Wolverine (1910). 986 tons. Sister to Pincher, above. Lost by collision off North West Coast of Ireland, 12th December, 1917.
Nubian (1909). 1062 tons. Torpedoed by German Destroyers, in action off Folkestone, 27th October, 1916.
Zulu (1909). 1027 tons. Armament as Maori, above. Mined in action, in Dover area, 27th October, 1916.
N.B.—The undamaged portions of Nubian and Zulu were united to form one Destroyer, named Zubian, and the casualty resulting is therefore counted as the loss of one unit

SHIPS LOST IN THE WAR—BRITISH *continued.*

DESTROYERS—*continued.*

Ghurka (1907). 880 tons. Guns: 5—12 pdr. Tubes: 2—18 in. Mined 4 miles S.E. of Dungeness buoy, 8th February, 1917.

Velox (1902). 420 tons. Guns: 1—12 pdr., 5—6 pdr. Tubes: 2—18 in. Mined off the Nab Light Vessel, 25th October, 1915.

Success (1901). 385 tons. Armament as VELOX, above. Wrecked off Fife Ness, 27th December, 1914.

Myrmidon (1900). 370 tons. Similar to SUCCESS, above. Lost by collision with s.s. HAMBOURNE, in the English Channel, 26th March, 1917.

Coquette (1897). 355 tons. Armament as VELOX, above. Mined off the East Coast, 7th March, 1916.

Derwent (1903). 555 tons. Guns: 1—12 pdr. (12 cwt.), 3—12 pdr. (8 cwt.). Tubes: 2—18 in. Mined off Havre, 2nd May, 1917.

Kale (1904). 545 tons. Sister to DERWENT, above. Mined in the North Sea, 27th March, 1918.

Eden (1903). 540 tons. Sister to DERWENT, above. Lost by collision in the English Channel, 17th June, 1916.

Foyle (1903). 550 tons. Armament as DERWENT, above. Mined in the Straits of Dover, 15th March, 1917.

Itchen (1903). Sister to FOYLE, above. Torpedoed by a German Submarine, in the North Sea, 6th July, 1917.

Erne (1903). 550 tons. Armament as DERWENT, above. Wrecked off Rattray Head, Aberdeen Coast, 6th February, 1915.

Falcon (1899). 408 tons. Armament as VELOX. Lost by collision in the North Sea, 1st April, 1918.

Fairy (1897). 380 tons. Similar to FALCON, above. Sunk through damage sustained in ramming German Submarine UC 75, in the North Sea, 31st May, 1918.

Cheerful (1897). 370 tons. Armament as VELOX. Mined off the Shetlands, 30th June, 1917.

Bittern (1897). 360 tons. Similar to CHEERFUL, above. Lost by collision with s.s. KENILWORTH, off Portland Bill, 4th April, 1918.

Flirt (1897). 380 tons. Armament as VELOX. Torpedoed by German Destroyers, in the Straits of Dover, 27th October, 1916.

Recruit (1896). 385 tons. Armament as Velox. Torpedoed by a German Submarine, near the Galloper Lightship, 1st May, 1915.

Lightning (1895). 320 tons. Armament as VELOX. Mined off the East Coast, 30th June, 1915.

Boxer (1894). 280 tons. Guns: 1—12 pdr., 5—6 pdr. Tube: 1—18 in. Lost by collision, in the English Channel, 8th February, 1918.

2 PATROL BOATS.

P 26 (1915). 613 tons. Guns: 1—4 in., etc. Mined off Havre, 10th April, 1917. For appearance, see photo of P boat on page 115.

P 12 (1915). Sister to P 26, above. Lost by collision, in English Channel, 4th November, 1918.

11 TORPEDO BOATS.

No. 24 (1908). 319 tons. Guns: 2—12 pdr. Tubes: 3—18 in. Wrecked off Dover breakwater, 28th January, 1917. For appearance, see photo of No. 36, on page 115.

No. 13 (1907). 270 tons. Armament as No. 24. Lost by collision in the North Sea, 26th January, 1916.

No. 12 (1907). 263 tons. Armament as No. 24, above. Torpedoed by a German Submarine in the North Sea, 10th June, 1915.

No. 11 (1907). Sister to No. 12, above. Mined off the East Coast, 7th March, 1916.

No. 10 (1907). 245 tons. Armament as No. 24, above. Torpedoed by a German Submarine in the North Sea, 10th June, 1915.

No. 9 (1907). Sister to No. 10, above. Lost by collision in the North Sea, 26th July, 1916.

No. 117 (1904). 197 tons. Guns: 3—3 pdr. Tubes: 3—14 in. Lost by collision in the English Channel, 10th June, 1917.

No. 96 (1894). 130 tons. Armament as No. 117, above. Lost by collision with a Mercantile Fleet Auxiliary in the Straits of Gibraltar, 1st November, 1915.

No. 90 (1895). Sister to No. 96, above. Capsized during heavy weather, in the Straits of Gibraltar, 25th April, 1918.

No. 064 (1886). 87 tons. Guns: 2—1 in. Nordenfelt. Tubes: 5—14 in. Wrecked in the Ægean Sea, 21st March, 1915.

No. 046 (1886). 79 tons. Similar to No. 064 above, but only 4 tubes. Foundered during heavy weather in the Eastern Mediterranean, 27th December, 1915.

58 SUBMARINES.

L 55 (1918). 1070 tons. Guns: 1—4 in. Tubes: 6—18 in. Sunk by gunfire of Bolshevik Destroyers in the Gulf of Finland, 4th June, 1919. For appearance, see photo of L type Submarine.

L 10 (1918). Sister to L 22, above. Sunk in action with German Destroyer S 33, off Texel, night of 3rd-4th October, 1918.

K 17 (1917). 2650 tons. Guns: 1—4 in., 1—3 in. AA. Tubes: 8—18in. Rammed by FEARLESS during tactical exercises in the North Sea, 31st January, 1918. For appearance, see photo of K type Submarine.

K 4 (1916). Sister to K 17, above. Rammed by INFLEXIBLE, during tactical exercises in the North Sea, 31st January, 1918.

K 1 (1916). Sister to K 17, above. Lost by collision with K 4 in the North Sea, 18th November, 1917.

J 6 (1915). 1900 tons. Guns: 1—4 in. Tubes: 6—18 in. Sunk by gunfire of a Special Service Ship in mistake for an enemy Submarine, 15th October, 1918.

H 10 (1915). 434 tons. Tubes: 4—21 in. Lost in the North Sea, 19th January, 1918.

H 6 (1915). Sister to H 10, above. Stranded on Schiermonnikoog, 18th January, 1916, and acquired by Dutch Navy (now Dutch O 8).

H 5 (1915). Sister to H 10, above. Lost by collision in the Irish Sea, 6th March, 1918.

H 3 (1915). Sister to H 10, above. Sunk in the Adriatic, 15th July, 1916.

G 11 (1916). 975 tons. Guns: 1—12 pdr., etc. Tubes: 1—21 in., 4—18 in. Wrecked off Howick, 22nd November, 1918. For appearance, see photo of G type Submarine.

G 9 (1916). 965 tons. Otherwise as G 11. Sunk by PETARD, off Norwegian Coast, in mistake for an enemy Submarine, 16th September, 1917.

G 8 (1916). Sister to G 9, above. Lost in the North Sea, 14th January, 1918.

G 7 (1916). Sister to G 9, above. Lost in the North Sea, 1st November, 1918.

E 50 (1916). 807 tons. Guns: 1—12 pdr. Tubes: 5—18 in. Lost in the North Sea, 31st January, 1918. For appearance, see photo of E type Submarine.

E 49 (1916). Sister to E 50, above. Mined off the Shetlands, 12th March, 1917.

E 47 (1916). Sister to E 50, above. Lost in the North Sea, 20th August, 1917.

E 37 (1915). Sister to E 50, above. Lost in the North Sea, 1st December, 1916.

E 36 (1916). Sister to E 50, above. Lost in the North Sea, 19th January, 1917.

E 34 (1917). Sister to E 50, above. Mined in Heligoland Bight, 20th July, 1918.

E 30 (1915). Sister to E 50, above. Lost in the North Sea, 22nd November, 1916.

E 28 (1915). Sister to E 50, above. Lost, date and details unknown.

E 26 (1915). Sister to E 50, above. Lost in the North Sea, 6th July, 1916.

E 24 (1915). Sister to E 50, above. Mined in Heligoland Bight, 24th March, 1916.

E 22 (1915). Sister to E 50, above. Sunk by a German Submarine in the Southern part of the North Sea, 25th April, 1916.

E 20 (1915). Sister to E 50, above. Sunk by the enemy in the Dardanelles, 6th November, 1915.

E 19 (1915). Sister to E 50. Blown up in Helsingfors Bay to avoid capture by the enemy, 3rd April, 1918.

E 18 (1915). 805 tons. Similar to E 50. Lost in the Baltic, 24th May, 1916.

E 17 (1915). Sister to E 18, above. Wrecked off Texel, 6th January, 1916.

E 16 (1914). Sister to E 18, above. Mined in Heligoland Bight, 22nd August, 1916.

E 15 (1914). Sister to E 18, above. Stranded on Kephez Point, in the Dardanelles, and torpedoed by picket boats of H.M.S. TRIUMPH and MAJESTIC, to prevent the enemy salving her, 18th April, 1915.

E 14 (1914). 795 tons. Similar to E 18, above. Sunk by enemy gunfire, off Kum Kale, Dardanelles, 28th January, 1918.

E 13 (1914). 791 tons. Similar to E 18, above. Damaged by gunfire of German Destroyers while stranded on Island of Saltholm, 18th August, 1915; interned at Copenhagen, 3rd September, 1915; sold to Danish shipbreakers in March, 1919.

E 10 (1913). 805 tons. Sister to E 18, above. Lost in the North Sea, 18th January, 1915.

E 9 (1913). 807 tons. Similar to E 18, above. Blown up in Helsingfors Bay, to avoid capture by the enemy, 3rd April, 1918.

E 8 (1913). 795 tons. Sister to E 14, above. Blown up in Helsingfors Bay, to avoid capture by the enemy, 4th April, 1918.

E 7 (1913). 791 tons. Sister to E 13, above. Sunk by the enemy, in the Dardanelles, 4th September, 1915.

E 6 (1912). Sister to E 7, above. Mined in the North Sea, 26th December, 1915.

E 5 (1912). Sister to E 7, above. Lost in the North Sea, 7th March, 1916.

E 3 (1912). Sister to E 7, above. Sunk by German Cruiser STRASSBURG, in Heligoland Bight, 18th October, 1914.

E 1 (1912). 795 tons. Similar to E 3, above. Blown up in Helsingfors Bay, to avoid capture by the enemy, 3rd April, 1918.

AE 2 (1913). 791 tons. Similar to E 7, above. Sunk by gunfire of Turkish vessels, in the Sea of Marmora, 30th April, 1915.

AE 1 (1913). Sister to AE 2, above. Foundered off the Bismarck Archipelago, Pacific, 14th September, 1914.

D 6 (1911). 620 tons. Guns: 2—12 pdr. Tubes: 3—18 in. Sunk by a German Submarine, off the North Coast of Ireland, 28th June, 1918.

D 5 (1911). Sister to D 6, above. Mined off Great Yarmouth, 3rd November, 1914.

D 3 (1910). Sister to D 6, above. Sunk by a French airship, in the English Channel, in mistake for an enemy Submarine, 15th March, 1918.

D 2 (1910). 600 tons. Similar to D 6, above. Lost in the North Sea, 1st December, 1914.

C 35 (1909). 321 tons. Tubes: 2—18 in. Blown up in Helsingfors Bay, to avoid capture by the enemy, 5th April, 1918.

C 34 (1910). Sister to C 35, above. Sunk by a German Submarine, off the Shetlands, 21st July, 1917.

C 33 (1910). Sister to C 35, above. Lost in the North Sea, 4th August, 1915.

C 32 (1909). Sister to C 35, above. Ran ashore and blown up, in the Gulf of Riga, 17th October, 1917.

C 31 (1909). Sister to C 35, above. Lost off the Belgian Coast, 4th January, 1915.

C 29 (1909). Sister to C 35, above. Mined in the North Sea, 29th August, 1915.

C 27 (1909). Sister to C 35, above. Blown up in Helsingfors Bay, to avoid capture by the enemy, 5th April, 1918.

C 26 (1909). Sister to C 35, above. Blown up in Helsingfors Bay, to avoid capture by the enemy, 4th April, 1918.

C 16 (1908). 316 tons. Similar to C 35, above. Accidentally rammed by a Destroyer of MEDEA type, subsequently salved, but found too badly damaged to be worth repairing.

C 3 (1906). Sister to C 16, above. Blown up at Zeebrugge Mole, 23rd April, 1918.

B 10 (1906). 316 tons. Tubes: 2—18 in. Destroyed by bombs from an Austrian Aeroplane, while under repair, at Venice, 9th August, 1916.

81 AUXILIARIES.

(a) **17 Armed Merchant Cruisers** (Gross tonnage in each case).

Calgarian (1914). 17,515 tons. Torpedoed by a German Submarine, off North Coast of Ireland, 1st March, 1918.

Oceanic (1899). 17,274 tons. Wrecked on Foula Island, Shetlands, 8th September, 1914.

Alcantara (1913). 15,300 tons. Torpedoed in action with German Armed Merchant Cruiser GREIF, in the North Sea, lat. 61.48 N., long. 1.40 E., 29th February, 1916.

Avenger (1915). 15,000 tons. Torpedoed by a German Submarine, in the North Atlantic, 14th June, 1917.

Laurentic (1908). 14,892 tons. Torpedoed by a German Submarine, off the North West Coast of Ireland, 23rd January, 1917.

Orama (1911). 12,927 tons. Torpedoed by a German Submarine, in the Atlantic, 19th October, 1917.

Otranto (1909). 12,124 tons. Stranded on Island of Islay, in heavy weather, after being severely damaged by collision with s.s. KASHMIR, 6th October, 1918.

Otway (1909). 12,077 tons. Torpedoed by a German Submarine, in the North Atlantic, 23rd July, 1917.

Marmora (1903). 10,509 tons. Torpedoed by a German Submarine, off the South Coast of Ireland, 23rd July, 1918.

Moldavia (1903). 9500 tons. Torpedoed by a German Submarine, in the English Channel, 23rd May, 1918.

India (1896). 7940 tons. Torpedoed by a German Submarine, off Bodo, West Fjord, 8th August, 1915.

Hilary (1908). 6329 tons. Torpedoed by a German Submarine, in the Atlantic, 25th May, 1917.

Patia (1913). 6103 tons. Torpedoed by a German Submarine, in the Bristol Channel, 13th June, 1918.

Bayano (1913). 5948 tons. Torpedoed by a German Submarine, off Corsewall Point, Galloway, 11th March, 1915.

Viknor (1888). 5386 tons. Mined off the North Coast of Ireland, 13th January, 1915.

Champagne (1895). 5360 tons. Torpedoed by a German Submarine, in the Atlantic, 9th October, 1917.

Clan MacNaughton (1911). 4985 tons. Foundered in a heavy gale, off the North Coast of Ireland, 3rd February, 1915.

(b) **3 Commissioned Escort Ships** (Gross tonnage in each case).

Mechanician (1900). 9044 tons. Torpedoed by a German Submarine, 8 miles West of St. Catherine's Point, 20th January, 1918.

Quernmore (1898). 7302 tons. Torpedoed by a German Submarine, 160 miles W. by N. ¾N. from Tory Island, 31st July, 1917.

Bostonian (1915). 5736 tons. Torpedoed by a German Submarine, 34 miles S. by E. ½E. from Start Point, 10th October, 1917.

(c) **12 Armed Boarding Steamers** (Gross tonnage in each case).

Tithonus (ex TITANIA, 1908). 3463 tons. Torpedoed by a German Submarine, in the North Sea, 28th March, 1918.

Fauvette (1912). 2644 tons. Mined off the East Coast, 9th March, 1916.

Dundee (1911). 2187 tons. Torpedoed by a German Submarine, in the approaches to the English Channel, 3rd September, 1917.

SHIPS LOST IN THE WAR—BRITISH *continued*.

Grive (1905). 2037 tons. Foundered in bad weather, off the Shetlands, 24th December, 1917, after being torpedoed by a German Submarine.

Duke of Albany (1907). 1997 tons. Torpedoed by a German Submarine, 20 miles East of Pentland Skerries, 25th August, 1916.

Tara (ex HIBERNIA, 1900). 1862 tons. Torpedoed by German Submarine U 35, in Solum Bay, Western Egypt, 5th November, 1915.

Louvain (1897). 1830 tons. Torpedoed by a German Submarine, in the Eastern Mediterranean, 20th January, 1918.

Stephen Furness (1910). 1712 tons. Torpedoed by a German Submarine, in the Irish Sea, 13th December, 1917.

Fiona (1905). 1611 tons. Wrecked off Pentland Skerries, 6th September, 1917.

Sarnia (1910). 1498 tons. Torpedoed by a German Submarine, in the Mediterranean, 12th September, 1918.

Ramsey (1895). 1443 tons. Torpedoed by German Auxiliary Minelayer METEOR, in the North Sea, to South East of Pentland Firth, 8th August, 1915.

Snaefell (1910). 1368 tons. Torpedoed by a German Submarine, in the Mediterranean, 5th June, 1918.

(d) **16 Special Service Ships (" Q Boats ")**. (Gross tonnage in each case.)

Perugia (1901). 4348 tons. Torpedoed by a German Submarine, in the Gulf of Genoa, 3rd December, 1916.

Bradford City (1910). 3683 tons. Torpedoed by a German Submarine, in the Straits of Messina, 16th August, 1917.

Remembrance (1910). 3660 tons. Torpedoed by a German Submarine, in the Mediterranean, 14th August, 1916.

Willow Branch (1892). 3314 tons. Torpedoed by a German Submarine, off the West Coast of Africa, to East of Cape Verde Islands, 25th April, 1918.

Dunraven (1910). 3117 tons. Foundered at entrance to English Channel, 10th August, 1917, after being torpedoed by a German Submarine.

Zylpha (1894). 2917 tons. Torpedoed by a German Submarine, to the South West of Ireland, 15th June, 1917.

Bracondale (1903). 2095 tons. Torpedoed by a German Submarine, in the Atlantic, 7th August, 1917.

Glenfoyle (1913). 1680 tons. Torpedoed by a German Submarine, in the Atlantic, 18th September, 1917.

Westphalia (1913). 1467 tons. Torpedoed by a German Submarine, in the Irish Sea, 11th February, 1918.

Peveril (1904). 1459 tons. Torpedoed by a German Submarine, outside the Straits of Gibraltar, 6th November, 1917.

Lady Patricia (1916). 1372 tons. Torpedoed by a German Submarine, in the Atlantic, 20th May, 1917.

Warner (1911). 1273 tons. Torpedoed by a German Submarine, off West Coast of Ireland, 13th March, 1917.

Penshurst (1906). 1191 tons. Torpedoed by a German Submarine, off the Bristol Channel, 25th December, 1917.

Vala (1894). 1016 tons. Believed to have been torpedoed by a German Submarine ; last reported in lat. 47 N., long. 9.32 W., 21st August, 1917.

Lady Olive (1913). 701 tons. Torpedoed by a German Submarine, in the English Channel, 19th February, 1917.

Stock Force (1917). 732 tons. Torpedoed by a German Submarine, in the English Channel, 30th July, 1918.

Note.—More than a dozen other Special Service Vessels, of under 500 tons gross, were also lost.

(e) **5 Fleet Messengers** (Gross tonnage in each case).

Osmanieh (1906). 4041 tons. Mined in the Eastern Mediterranean, 31st December, 1917.

Ermine (1912). 1777 tons. Torpedoed by a German Submarine, in the Ægean, 2nd August, 1917.

Princess Alberta (1905). 1586 tons. Mined between Stavros and Mudros, 21st February, 1917.

Redbreast (1908). 1313 tons. Torpedoed by a German Submarine, in the Mediterranean, 15th July, 1917.

Chesterfield (1913). 1013 tons. Torpedoed by a German Submarine, 42 miles N.E. by E. ½E. from Malta, 18th May, 1918.

Note.—Four Fleet Messengers, of under 500 tons gross, were also lost.

(f) **17 Armed Yachts.** (Tonnage by yacht measurement in each case.)

Ægusa (ex ERIN, 1896). 1242 tons. Mined near Malta, 28th April, 1916.

Goissa (1893). 1023 tons. Mined in the Dardanelles, 15th November, 1915.

Resource II (ex ENCHANTRESS). 1000 tons. Destroyed by fire, in Southampton Harbour, 12th November, 1915.

Iolaire (1902). 999 tons. Wrecked off Stornoway, 1st January, 1919.

Mekong (1906). 899 tons. Wrecked on Christthorpe Cliff, 12th March, 1916.

Clementina (1887). 625 tons. Beached after collision, off Tor Cor Point, 5th August, 1915.

Kethailes (1903). 611 tons. Lost by collision, off Blackwater Lightship, 11th October, 1917.

Conqueror II (1889). 526 tons. Torpedoed by a German Submarine, in Fair Island Channel, 26th September, 1916.

Irene (1890). 543 tons. Mined off North Foreland, lat. 51.29 N., long. 1.27 E., 9th November, 1915.

Hersilia (1895). 454 tons. Wrecked on Eilean Chuai, Hebrides, 6th January, 1916.

Verona (1890). 437 tons. Mined off Portmahomack, 24th February, 1917.

Sanda (1906). 351 tons. Sunk by fire of German batteries, off Belgian Coast, 25th September, 1915.

Zaida (1900). 350 tons. Sunk by a German Submarine, in the Gulf of Alexandretta, 17th August, 1916.

Zarefah (1905). 279 tons. Mined off Mull Head, Deer Ness, 8th May, 1917.

Aries (1880). 268 tons. Mined off Leathercoat, 31st October, 1915.

Rhiannon (1914). 138 tons. Mined off Longsand, 20th July, 1915.

Marcella (1887). 127 tons. Lost by collision in the Downs, 24th March, 1916.

(g) **11 Miscellaneous Auxiliaries.**

Campania (1893). 18,000 tons displacement. Guns : 6—4.7 in., 1—3 in. AA. Aircraft Carrier. Lost by collision with GLORIOUS, during a gale, in the Firth of Forth, 5th November, 1918.

Princess Irene (1914). 5934 tons gross. Minelayer. Destroyed by internal explosion, at Sheerness, 27th May, 1915.

Fisgard II (1869). 6010 tons displacement. Repair Ship. Foundered in bad weather, off Portland Bill, 17th September, 1914.

Lowtyne (1892). 3231 tons gross. Not classified. Torpedoed by a German Submarine, 3½ miles E.S.E. from Whitby, 10th June, 1918.

Ben-My-Chree (1908). 3888 tons displacement. Aircraft Carrier. Sunk by fire of Turkish batteries, in Kastelorizo Harbour, 11th January, 1917.

White Head (1880). 1172 tons gross. Not classified. Torpedoed by a German Submarine, 40 miles N.N.E. of Suda Bay, 15th October, 1917.

Dalkeith (ex DALHOUSIE, 1889). 741 tons gross. Salvage Vessel. Sunk by a German Submarine, during salvage operations, at San Pietro Island, Sardinia, 29th March, 1917.

Thrush (1889). 805 tons displacement. Salvage Vessel. Wrecked near Glenarm, County Antrim, 11th April, 1917.

Majestic II (1901). 408 tons gross. Patrol Paddler. Foundered, near Oran, 28th July, 1916.

Duchess of Richmond (1910). 354 tons gross. Patrol Paddler. Mined, 28th June, 1919.

Stirling Castle (1899). 271 tons gross. Patrol Paddler. Blown up, from unknown cause, off West Coast of Malta, 26th September, 1916.

General Note.—The following small craft were lost during the War, but space does not permit of particulars being given :—

29 Motor Launches (M.L. 566, 561, 541, 540, 534, 474, 431, 424, 421, 403, 356, 278, 255, 254, 253, 247, 230, 197, 191, 149, 121, 110, 64, 62, 55, 52, 40, 19, 18).

17 Coastal Motor Boats (Nos. 79 A, 71 A, 67 A, 62 BD, 50, 47, 42, 40, 39 B, 33 A, 18 A, 11, 10, 8, 2, 1).

AMERICAN.

ARMOURED CRUISER.

SAN DIEGO (1904). 13,680 tons. Guns : 4—8 in., 45 cal. ; 14—6 in., 50 cal. ; 20—3 in., etc. Mined, 10 miles off Fire Island, N.Y., 19th July, 1918. For appearance, see photo of HUNTINGTON.

2 DESTROYERS.

Jacob Jones (1915). 1150 tons. Guns : 4—4 in., 50 cal. Tubes : 8—21 in. Torpedoed by German Submarine, off the Scillies, 6th December, 1917. No photo available.

Chauncey (1901). 420 tons. Guns : 2—3 in., etc. Tubes : 2—18 in. Lost by collision with U.S.S. CAYA, in the Straits of Gibraltar, 19th November, 1917. For appearance, see photo of STEWART.

2 SUBMARINES.

G 2 (1914). 700 tons. Guns : 1—3 in. AA. Tubes : 5—21 in. Foundered in Long Island Sound, off New London, 27th July, 1919. For appearance, see photo of G 1, on page 223.

F 1 (1911). 350 tons. Tubes : 4—21 in. Lost by collision with F 3 during a fog, in American waters, 17th December, 1917. No photo available.

7 AUXILIARIES.

Cyclops (1910). 19,360 tons. Fleet Collier. Missing, supposed foundered in bad weather in the Western Atlantic, end of March, 1918. For appearance, see photo of JUPITER, on page 230.

McCulloch (1898). 1280 tons. Coastguard Cruising Cutter. Lost by collision, in the Pacific, October, 1917.

Tampa (1912). 1181 tons. Coastguard Cruising Cutter. Torpedoed by German Submarine, while employed on convoy duty in English Channel, 26th September, 1918. No photo available.

Alcedo (1895). 981 tons gross. Armed Yacht. Torpedoed by German Submarine, in Bay of Biscay, 15th November, 1917.

Mohawk (1902). 980 tons. Coastguard Cruising Cutter. Lost by collision, off New York, 1st October, 1917.

Wakiva II (1907). 852 tons gross. Armed Yacht. Lost by collision, in the Bay of Biscay, 22nd May, 1918.

Guinevere (1908). 499 tons gross. Armed Yacht. Wrecked on French Atlantic Coast, 25th January, 1918.

Note.—The Sloop SCHURZ (lost by collision, 21st June, 1918) is not listed here, as she already appears in the German Losses as the GEIER.

JAPANESE.

BATTLESHIP.

KAWACHI (1910). 21,420 tons. Guns : 12—12 in., 45 and 50 cal. ; 10—6 in., 50 cal. ; 8—4.7 in. ; 12—12 pdr. Destroyed by internal explosion, in Tokuyama Bay, 12th July, 1918.

BATTLE CRUISER.

TSUKUBA (1905). 13,750 tons. Guns : 4—12 in., 45 cal. ; 12—6 in., 45 cal. ; 12—4.7 in. ; 2—14 pdr., etc. Destroyed by internal explosion, at Yokosuka, 14th January, 1917.

2 LIGHT CRUISERS.

OTOWA (1903). 3000 tons. Guns : 2—6 in., 50 cal. ; 6—4.7 in. ; 4—12 pdr. Wrecked near Damio Point, Shima Prefecture, 1st August, 1917.

KASAGI (1898). 4760 tons. Guns : 2—8 in., 10—4.7 in., 12—12 pdr., etc. Wrecked in Tsugaru Straits, July, 1916. For appearance, see photo of CHITOSE.

COAST DEFENCE SHIP.

TAKACHIHO (1885). Old Cruiser, of 3700 tons, re-employed as a Minelayer. Guns : 8—6 in. Torpedoed by German Destroyer S 90, 60 miles south of Kiao Chau Bay, night of 17th-18th October, 1914.

DESTROYER.

Shirotaye (1906). 380 tons. Guns : 6—12 pdr. Tubes : 2—18 in. Wrecked during engagement with German Gunboat JAGUAR, in Kiao-Chau Bay, 4th September, 1914. For appearance, see photo of ARARE type, on page 272. (This vessel was subsequently raised, but found to be beyond repair.)

TORPEDO BOAT.

No. 33 (1901). 84 tons. Guns : 2—3 pdr. Tubes : 3—18 in. Mined at entrance to Kiao-Chau Bay, 11th November, 1914.

AUXILIARY.

Shijiki (1916). Fleet oiler. 5300 tons. Lost in a typhoon off Tanegashima, 15th August, 1919.

FRENCH.

4 BATTLESHIPS.

DANTON (1909). 18,400 tons. Guns: 4—12 in., 50 cal.; 12—9.4 in.; 16—12 dpr., etc. Torpedoed by German Submarine U 64, 20 miles from Coast of Sardinia, 19th March, 1917. For appearance, see DANTON class

SUFFREN (1899). 12,750 tons. Guns: 4—12 in., 45 cal.; 10—6.4 in.; 8—3.9 in., etc. Torpedoed by German Submarine, 50 miles N.W. of Lisbon, 26th November, 1916.

BOUVET (1896). 12,000 tons. Guns: 2—12 in., 2—10.8 in., 8—5.5 in., 8—3.9 in., etc. Sunk by torpedo from White Cliffs, in the Dardanelles, 18th March, 1915.

GAULOIS (1896). 11,260 tons. Guns: 4—12 in., 10—5.5 in., 8—3.9 in., etc. Torpedoed by German Submarine, in the Ægean Sea, 27th December, 1916. For appearance, see photo of ST. LOUIS.

5 CRUISERS.

LEON GAMBETTA (1901). 12,300 tons. Guns: 4—7.6 in., 16—6.4 in., etc. Torpedoed by Austrian Submarine U5, in Straits of Otranto, 20 miles off Cape Leuca, night of 26-27th April, 1915.

DUPETIT-THOUARS (1901). 9500 tons. Guns: 2—7.6 in., 8—6.4 in., 4—3.9 in., etc. Torpedoed by German Submarine, while on convoy duty in North Atlantic, 7th August, 1918. For appearance, see photo of MONTCALM.

KLÉBER (1902). 7700 tons. Guns: 8—6.4 in., 4—3.9 in., etc. Mined, off Cap St. Mathieu, Brest, 27th June, 1917. For appearance, see photo of DESAIX.

CHATEAURENAULT (1898). 8000 tons. Guns: 2—6.4 in., 6—5.5 in., etc. Torpedoed by enemy Submarine, in the Ionian Sea, 14th December, 1917.

AMIRAL CHARNER (1893). 4750 tons. Guns: 2—7.6 in., 6—5.5 in., etc. Torpedoed by German Submarine, off Syrian Coast, 8th February, 1916. For appearance, see photo of BRUIX

2 SLOOPS.

Rigel (1915). 1200 tons. Guns: 2—5.5 in., etc. Torpedoed by German Submarine U 35, off Algiers, 2nd October, 1916. For appearance, see ETOILE type Sloop.

2 MINELAYING GUNBOATS.

Casabianca (1895). 1000 tons. Guns: 1—3.9 in., etc. Lost, by explosion of own mines, near Smyrna, night of 3rd-4th June, 1915.
Cassini (1894). Sister to CASABIANCA, above, but without mainmast. Torpedoed by enemy Submarine, in Mediterranean, 28th February, 1917.

3 GUNBOATS.

Zelee (1899). ▼ 650 tons. Guns: 2—3.9 in., etc. (Disarmed at time of loss.) Sunk by gunfire of German Cruisers, SCHARNHORST and GNEISENAU, at Papeete, Tahiti, 22nd September, 1914.

Decidee (1899). Sister to ZELEE. Lost during 1919, details not advised.
Surprise (1895). Similar to ZELEE. Torpedoed by German Submarine U 38, at Funchal, 3rd December, 1916.

13 DESTROYERS.

Renaudin (1913). 756 tons. Guns: 2—3.9 in., 4—9 pdr. Tubes: 4—18 in. Torpedoed by Austrian Submarine U6, off Durazzo, 18th March, 1916. For appearance, see photo of BISSON.

Faulx (1911). 745 tons. Armament as RENAUDIN. Lost by collision in Straits of Otranto, 10th March, 1918.
Fourché (1910). Sister to FAULX, above. Torpedoed by Austrian Submarine U 15, in Straits of Otranto, 23rd June, 1916.
Dague (1910). Sister to FAULX, above. Mined, off Antivari, 24th February, 1915.
Boutefeu (1911). 700 tons. Armament as RENAUDIN. Mined in the Straits of Otranto, 15th May, 1917. For appearance, see photo of COMMANDANT BORY.
Fantassin (1909). 450 tons. Guns: 6—9 pdr. Tubes: 3—18 in. Lost by collision with MAMELUK, near Corfu, 5th June, 1916.
Carabinier (1908). 416 tons. Armament as FANTASSIN. Wrecked on Syrian Coast, 13th November, 1918. For appearance, see photo of MAMELUK.
Etendard (1908). 335 tons. Guns: 1—9 pdr., etc. Tubes: 2—18 in. Torpedoed by German Destroyers, off Dunkirk, 25th April, 1917. For appearance, see photo of CLAYMORE, on page 315.
Branlebas (1907). 330 tons. Guns: 1—9 pdr., etc. Tubes: 2—18 in. Mined, off Dunkirk, 9th November, 1915. For appearance, see photo of FANFARE, on page 315.
Mousquet (1902). 300 tons. Guns: 1—9 pdr., etc. Tubes: 2—15 in. Sunk by gunfire of German Cruiser EMDEN, at Penang, 28th October, 1914. For appearance, see photo of MOUSQUETON, on page 316.
Carabine (1903). Sister to MOUSQUET, above. Lost by accident, date not advised.
Catapulte (1902). Sister to MOUSQUET, above. Lost by collision, near Bizerta, 18th May, 1918.
Yatagan (1900). 300 tons. Guns: 1—9 pdr., etc. Tubes: 2—15 in. Lost by collision with s.s. TEVIOT, off Dieppe, 3rd December, 1916.

9 TORPEDO BOATS.

Nos. 348 and **347** (1906). 97 tons. Guns: 2—1 pdr. Tubes: 3—18 in. Lost by collision, off Toulon, 9th October, 1914. For appearance, see photo of No. 361, page 317.
No. 333 (1906). Sister to No. 348, above. Lost by collision in the Western Mediterranean, 12th March, 1918.
No. 331 (1906). Sister to No. 348, above. Lost by collision, off Cape Barfleur, 17th June, 1915.
No. 325 (1906). Sister to No. 348, above. Mined, off the Coast of Tunis, 22nd January, 1919.
No. 319 (1905). Sister to No. 348, above. Mined, off Nieuport, 15th January, 1915.
No. 317 (1905). Sister to No. 348, above. Mined, off Calais, night of 28th-29th December, 1916.
No. 300 (1905). Similar to No. 348, above, but with 14 in. tubes. Mined, off Havre, 1st February, 1916.
No. 251 (1901). 88 tons. Guns: 2—1 pdr. Tubes: 2—14 in. Lost by collision, in the English Channel, date not reported. For appearance, see photo of No. 176.

12 SUBMARINES.

Diane (1914). 630 tons. Tubes, etc.: 10. Lost in English Channel, about 10th March, 1918. No photo available.

Mariotte (1911). 530 tons. Tubes: 7—18 in. Sunk, by German Submarine, in the Dardanelles, 26th July, 1915.
Ariane (1914). 410 tons. Tubes: 8—18 in. Torpedoed by German Submarine, off entrance to Gulf of Bizerta, 19th June, 1917. No photo available.
Foucault (1910). 392 tons. Tubes: 6—18 in. Sunk by bombs from Austrian Seaplane, in Lower Adriatic, 15th September, 1916. For appearance, see photo of COULOMB, on page 321.
Floreal (1908). Sister to FOUCAULT, above. Lost by collision, off Salonika, 2nd August, 1918.
Prairial (1908). Sister to FOUCAULT, above. Lost by collision with merchantman, off Havre, night of April 28th-29th, 1918.
Fresnel (1908). Similar to FOUCAULT, above. Stranded on Albanian Coast, in a fog, and destroyed by gunfire of Austrian Destroyer VARASDINIER, 5th December, 1915.
Bernouilli (1911). Similar to FOUCAULT, above. Sunk by Austrian Submarine, in the Adriatic, about 13th February, 1918.
Joule (1910). Sister to BERNOUILLI, above. Mined in Sea of Marmora, 1st May, 1915.
Monge (1909). Sister to BERNOUILLI, above. Rammed and sunk by Austrian Cruiser HELGOLAND, off Cattaro, 29th December, 1915.
Saphir (1908). 390 tons. Tubes: 2—18 in. Wrecked in avoiding minefield in the Dardanelles, 17th January, 1915. For appearance, see photo of EMERAUDE, on page 322.
Circe (1907). 350 tons. Torpedoed by Austrian Submarine, off Cattaro, 20th September, 1918.
The two following losses are not counted in the total given above:—
Curie (1910). Similar to FOUCAULT, above. Sunk by fire of Austrian batteries, at Pola, 23rd December, 1914. Subsequently salved, and now Austrian U 14. Restored to France, November, 1918.
Turquoise (1908). Sister to SAPHIR, above. Sunk by gunfire of Turkish vessels, in the Sea of Marmora, 31st October, 1915. Salved on 3rd November, and re-named MUSTEDIEH-OMBASHI by Turks. Restored to France, December, 1918.

12 AUXILIARIES.

Gallia (1913). 14,966 tons (gross). Armed Cruiser. Torpedoed by German Submarine U 35, to South of Sardinia, 4th October, 1916.
Provence II (1914). 13,753 tons (gross). Armed Cruiser. Torpedoed by German Submarine U 35, in the Mediterranean, 26th February, 1916.
Burdigala (1897). 12,009 tons (gross). Armed Cruiser. Torpedoed by German Submarine, in the Mediterranean, 14th November, 1916.
Sant'Anna (1910). 9350 tons (gross). Armed Cruiser. Torpedoed by German Submarine, in the Mediterranean, 10th May, 1918.
Himalaya (1902). 9000 tons (gross). Armed Cruiser. Torpedoed by German Submarine, off Algerian Coast, 22nd June, 1917.
Carthage (1910). 5601 tons (gross). Armed Cruiser. Torpedoed by German Submarine, off Cape Helles, Gallipoli, 4th July, 1915.
France IV (1896). 4025 tons (gross). Armed Cruiser. Torpedoed by German Submarine, in Western Mediterranean, November, 1915.
Kanguroo (1912). 2493 tons (gross). Submarine Depot Vessel. Torpedoed by German Submarine U 38, at Funchal, 3rd December, 1916.
Drome (1887). 2200 tons displacement. Fleet Auxiliary. Mined in Gulf of Lions, January, 1918.
Golo II (1905). 1380 tons (gross). Armed Boarding Steamer. Torpedoed by German Submarine, near Corfu, 22nd August, 1917.
Italia (1904). 1305 tons (gross) } Armed Boarding Steamers. Lost through enemy action,
Corse (No particulars available) } date not reported.

ITALIAN.

4 BATTLESHIPS.

LEONARDO DA VINCI (1911). 22,380 tons. Guns: 13—12 in., 46 cal.; 18—4.7 in.; 14—14 pdr., etc. Sunk by fire and explosion, at Taranto, 2nd August, 1916; since salved, but believed to be beyond repair. For appearance, see photos of CONTE DI CAVOUR and GIULIO CESARE.

AMALFI (1908). 10,000 tons. Guns: 4—10 in., 45 cal.; 8—7.5 in., 45 cal.; 16—14 pdr., etc. Torpedoed by Austrian Submarine, in Upper Adriatic, 7th July, 1915. For appearance, see photo of PISA.

BENEDETTO BRIN (1901). 13,215 tons. Guns: 4—12 in., 40 cal.; 4—8 in.; 12—6 in.; 20—14 pdr., etc. Destroyed by internal explosion, at Brindisi, 27th September, 1915.
REGINA MARGHERITA (1901). Sister to B. BRIN, above, but armed with 4 extra 6 inch in place of 8 inch guns. Mined off Valona, 11th December, 1916.

ARMOURED CRUISER.

GIUSEPPE GARIBALDI (1899). 7234 tons. Guns: 1—10 in., 45 cal.; 2—8 in., 45 cal.; 14—6 in.; 10—14 pdr., etc. Torpedoed by Austrian Submarine, off Cattaro, 18th July, 1915.

2 LIGHT CRUISERS.

BASILICATA (1914). 2560 tons. Guns: 6—4.7 in., 6—14 pdr., etc. Sunk by an internal explosion, at Port Said, 13th August, 1919. No photo available.
ETRURIA (1891). 2280 tons. Guns: 6—4.7 in., etc. Blown up in Leghorn Harbour, 13th August, 1918. For appearance, see photo of PUGLIA.

MONITOR.

Alfriedo Capellini (1916). Guns: 2—15 in., 40 cal.; 2—14 pdr. Capsized off Ancona, 14th November, 1918.

MINELAYING GUNBOAT.

Partenope (1889). 900 tons. Guns: 2—14 pdr., etc. Torpedoed by enemy Submarine, off Bizerta, 24th March, 1918. For appearance, see photo of MINERVA, on page 366.

9 DESTROYERS.

Cesare Rossarol (1915). 1030 tons. Guns: 6—4 in. Tubes: 4—21 in. Mined near Pola, 18th November, 1918. For appearance, see photo of A. POERIO.
Benedetto Cairoli (1917). 770 tons. Guns: 4—4 in., 2—14 pdr. Tubes: 4—18 in. Lost by collision, 10th April, 1918. No photo available.
Impetuoso (1913). 680 tons. Guns: 1—4.7 in., 4—14 pdr., etc. Tubes: 2—18 in. Torpedoed by Austrian Submarine U 17, in Straits of Otranto, 10th July, 1916. For appearance, see photo of INDOMITO.
Intrepido (1912). Sister to IMPETUOSO, above. Mined off Valona, 4th December, 1915.
Audace (1912). Similar to IMPETUOSO, above. Lost by collision, off Cape Colonna, 29th August, 1916.

Garibaldino (1910). 388 tons. Guns: 4—14 pdr. Tubes: 3—18 in. Lost by collision, 16th July, 1918.

Turbine (1901). 320 tons. Guns: 1—14 pdr., etc. Tubes: 4—18 in. Sunk by gunfire of Austrian Destroyers Csepel, Lika and Tatra, off Barletta, 24th May, 1915. For appearance, see photo of Aquilone type, on page 354.

Nembo (1901). Sister to Turbine, above. Torpedoed by Austrian Submarine, in Adriatic, 17th October, 1916.

Borea (1901). Sister to Turbine, above. Sunk by an Austrian Light Cruiser, 15th May, 1917.

6 TORPEDO BOATS.

Perseo (1905). 210 tons. Guns: 3—3 pdr. Tubes: 3—18 in. Lost by collision, March, 1917. For appearance, see photo of " P " type Torpedo Boat, on page 356.

Scorpione (1905). Similar to Perseo, above, but armament disposed differently. Lost by collision, 15th May, 1917. For appearance, see photo of " S " class Torpedo Boat, on page 356.

Serpente (1905). Sister to Scorpione, above. Mined in the Adriatic, June, 1916.

No. 36 PN (1913) 120 tons. Guns: 1—6 pdr. Tubes: 2—18 in. Mined in the Adriatic, 10th November, 1918.

No. 17 OS (1912). Sister to No. 36 PN, above. Mined in the Upper Adriatic, 2nd July, 1915.

No. 5 PN (1911). Similar to No. 17 OS, above. Torpedoed by an Austrian Submarine, in the Upper Adriatic, 26th June, 1915.

7 SUBMARINES.

Balilla (1914). 680 tons. Guns: 2—14 pdr., AA. Tubes: 5—18 in. Sunk in Cattaro Bay, night of 14th-15th July, 1916.

Alberto Guglielmotti (1914). Similar to Balilla, above. Accidentally sunk by a British Destroyer, in Sardinian waters, 10th March, 1917. For appearance, see photo of Angelo Emo, on page 359.

H 5 (1916). 356 tons. Tubes: 4—18 in. Accidentally sunk by a British Submarine, 16th April, 1918. For appearance, see photo of " H " type Submarine, on page 360.

W 4 (1914). 320 tons. Tubes, etc.: 5—18 in. Lost in the Adriatic, about 8th August, 1917. For appearance, see photo of " W " type Submarine, on page 362.

Jalea (1913). 245 tons. Tubes: 2—18 in. Mined, in the Gulf of Trieste, 10th August, 1916. For appearance, see photo of Argo, on page 363.

Medusa (1911). Sister to Jalea, above. Torpedoed by an Austrian Submarine, in the Adriatic, 9th June, 1915.

Nereide (1912). 225 tons. Tubes: 2—18 in. Torpedoed by an Austrian Submarine, off Pelagosa, 5th August, 1915. For appearance, see photo of Nautilus.

Note.—The loss of the Submarine Giacinto Pullino, captured by the Austrians, in August, 1916, is not counted here, as she is understood to have been restored to Italian hands.

RUSSIAN.

(B.S. = BLACK SEA.)

6 BATTLESHIPS.

(B.S.) **SVOBODNAYA ROSSIYA** (1914). 24,000 tons. Guns: 10—12 in., 50 cal.; 20—5.1 in., etc. Destroyed at Novorossisk, to avoid internment, 18th June, 1918. For appearance, see photo.

(B.S.) **IMPERATRITSA MARIA** (1913). 22,435 tons. Similar to Svobodnaya Rossia, above. Sunk by fire and explosion, at Sevastopol, 20th October, 1916; since salved, but doubtful if worth repairing.

PETROPAVLOVSK (1911). 23,000 tons. Guns: 12—12 in., 50 cal.; 16—4.7 in., etc. Torpedoed by British C.M.Bs., at Kronstadt, 18th August, 1919. For appearance, see photo of Poltava.

SLAVA (1903). 15,000 tons. Guns: 4—12 in., 40 cal.; 12—6 in., 45 cal.; 20—12 pdr., etc. Sunk by gunfire of German Squadron, in Gulf of Riga, 17th October, 1917.

PERESVIET (1898). 13,500 tons. Guns: 4—10 in., 45 cal.; 10—6 in., 45 cal.; 16—12 pdr., etc., Mined near Port Said, 4th January, 1917.

5 CRUISERS.

PALLADA (1906). 7775 tons. Guns: 2—8 in., 45 cal.; 8—6 in., 45 cal.; 22—12 pdr., etc. Torpedoed by German Submarine U 26, in Gulf of Finland, 11th October, 1914. For appearance, see photo of Bayan.

OLEG (1903). 6770 tons. Guns: 12—6 in., 45 cal.; 8—11 pdr., etc. Torpedoed by a British C.M.B., in the Gulf of Finland, 17th June, 1919.

BOGATYR (1901). Similar to Oleg, above. Torpedoed by British C.M.Bs., at Kronstadt, 18th August, 1919.

AVRORA (1900) and **DIANA** (1899). 6700 tons. Guns: 10—6 in., 45 cal.; 20—11 pdr., etc. Both scuttled by Bolsheviki, for use as blockships, in Gulf of Finland, 1919.

24 DESTROYERS.

(B.S.) **Feodonissi, Gadjibey, Kaliakrya, Kertch** (1914-15). 1325 tons. Guns: 3—4 in., 1—9 pdr. Tubes: 15—17.7 in. All irreparably damaged, to avoid falling into enemy hands, at Novorossisk, 18th June, 1918. No photo available.

Desna (1915). Similar to Feodonissi, etc., above. Sunk in Neva, 17th July, 1919.

Grom (1915). Similar to Feodonissi, etc., above. Sunk by gunfire of German Squadron, near Oesel Island, Gulf of Riga, 14th October, 1917.

Gavryil (1915), and another, unidentified. Similar to Grom, above. Sunk in action with British Destroyers, in Kuporia Bay, Gulf of Finland, 21st October, 1919. at Sevastopol, May, 1918. No photo available.

(B.S.) **Gnievni** (1913). 1100 tons. Guns: 3—4 in., 1—9 pdr. Tubes: 5—17.7 in. Blown up, (B.S.) **Shastlivi** (1913). Sister to Gnievni, above. Foundered, off Mudros, 1919.

(B.S.) **Pronsitelni** (1913). Sister to Gnievni, above. Irreparably damaged, to avoid falling into enemy hands, at Novorossisk, 18th June, 1918.

Okhotnik (1906). 600 tons. Guns: 2—4.7 in., etc. Tubes: 3—17.7 in. Mined, near Oesel Island, Gulf of Riga, 26th September, 1917. For appearance, see photo of Kondratenko, on page 565.

(B.S.) **Leitenant Zatzarennyi** (1907). 615 tons. Guns: 1—4.7 in., 5—11 pdr. Tubes: 3—17.7 in. Mined, off Sulina, 1st July, 1917. For appearance, see photo of Kapitan Saken.

(B.S.) **Leitenant Shestakoff** and **Kapitan-Leitenant Baranoff** (1907). Sisters to Leit. Zatzarennyi, above. Both irreparably damaged, to avoid falling into enemy hands, at Novorossisk, 18th June, 1918.

Dobrovoletz (1905). 570 tons. Guns: 2—4 in. Tubes: 3—17.7 in. Mined, at Swalferort, Gulf of Riga, 21st August, 1916. For appearance, see photo of Emir Bukharski, on page 566.

Kasanetz (1905). 500 tons. Armament as Dobrovoletz. Torpedoed by a German Submarine, off Odensholm, 28th October, 1916. For appearance, see photo of Strashni type, on page 566.

Bditelni (1906). 355 tons. Guns: 2—11 pdr. Tubes: 3—17.7 in. Mined, off Mantyluoto, Finnish Coast, 27th November, 1917. For appearance, see photo of Destroyer of this type, on page 566.

(B.S.) **Zhivuchi** (1905). 350 tons. Guns: 1—11 pdr. Tubes: 2—17.7 in. Mined, off Sevastopol, 28th April, 1916. For appearance, see photo of Zavidni type, on page 583.

(B.S.) **Leitenant Pushtchin** (1904). Sister to Zhivuchi, above. Torpedoed by an enemy Submarine, off Varna, 9th March, 1916.

Leitenant Burakoff (1904). 330 tons. Guns: 2—11 pdr. Tubes: 2—17.7 in. Mined, off Mariehamn, Aland Islands, 13th August, 1917. For appearance, see photo of Lovki type, on page 567.

Ispolnitelni (1905) and **Letutchi** (1905). Sisters to Leit. Burakoff, above. Foundered in the Gulf of Finland, 16th December, 1914.

(B.S.) **Stremitelni** (1901). 240 tons. Guns: 1—11 pdr., etc. Tubes: 2—14 in. Irreparably damaged, to avoid falling into enemy hands, at Novorossisk, 18th June, 1918.

29 SUBMARINES.

Bars (1915). 650 tons. Tubes: 6—17.7 in. Sunk by the enemy, in the Baltic, 21st May, 1917; reported to have been salved, by Germans, but ultimate fate uncertain. No photo available.

Ersh (1915). Sister to Bars, above. Sunk by British Destroyers, Valorous and Vancouver, in Gulf of Finland, 7th August, 1919.

Livitza (1915). Sister to Bars, above. Lost in the Baltic, July, 1917.

Gepard (1915). Sister to Bars, above. Lost in the Baltic, October, 1917.

Edinorog (1915). Similar to Bars, above. Scuttled, to avoid falling into enemy hands, at Reval, February, 1918.

Igor (1915). Similar to Bars, above. Lost in the ice, off Reval, February, 1918.

(B.S.) **Gagara** and **Orlan** (1916). Similar to Bars, above. Scuttled, to avoid falling into Bolshevik hands, April, 1919.

(B.S.) **Morsh** (1913). 460 tons. Tubes, etc.: 8—17.7 in. Lost in the Black Sea, June, 1917 (also reported to have been scuttled, to avoid falling into Bolshevik hands, in April, 1919). No photo available.

(B.S.) **Kashalot, Kit. Narval** (1913). Sisters to Morsh, above. All three scuttled to avoid falling into Bolshevik hands, April, 1919.

AG 14 (1916). 350 tons. Tubes: 4—18 in. Lost in the Baltic, September, 1917. No photo available.

AG 15, 13, 12, 11 (1916). Sisters to AG 14, above. Blown up or scuttled, to avoid falling into enemy hands, at Hango, April, 1918.

Alligator, Drakon, Kaiman, Krokodil (1908). 450 tons. Tubes: 4—18 in. Believed to have been captured by the Germans, at Reval, in March, 1918; ultimate fate uncertain.

(B.S.) **Krab** (1912). 500 tons. Tubes: 2—17.7 in. Scuttled, to avoid falling into Bolshevik hands, April, 1919. No photo available.

(B.S.) **Karp** and **Karas** (1907). 200 tons. Tubes: 1—17.7 in. Scuttled, to avoid falling into Bolshevik hands, April, 1919.

Byeluga, Piskar, Sterliad (1904). 110 tons. Tubes: 1—17.7 in. Believed to have been captured by the Germans, at Reval, in March, 1918; ultimate fate uncertain. No photo available.

Tchuka (1904). 105 tons. Otherwise as Byeluga, etc., above. Believed to have been captured by Germans, at Reval, March, 1918; ultimate fate uncertain.

GERMAN.

11 BATTLESHIPS.

BAYERN (1915). 28,000 tons. Guns: 8—15 in.; 16—5.9 in., 50 cal.; 4—3.4 in. AA. For appearance, see photo of Baden, on page 515.

KRONPRINZ WILHELM (1914), **MARKGRAF** (1913), **GROSSER KURFÜRST** (1913,) and **KÖNIG** (1913). 25,390 tons. Guns: 10—12 in., 50 cal.; 14—5.9 in., 50 cal.; 4—3.4 in. AA.

KÖNIG ALBERT (1912), **PRINZREGENT LUITPOLD** (1912), **KAISERIN** (1911), **FRIEDRICH DER GROSSE** (1911), and **KAISER**. 24,700 tons. Guns: 10—12 in., 50 cal.; 14—5.9 in., 50 cal.; 2—3.4 in.

The above ten Battleships were scuttled by their crews at Scapa Flow, on 21st June, 1919, to avoid surrender under the Peace Terms.

POMMERN (1905). 13,200 tons Guns: 4—11 in., 40 cal.; 14—6.7 in., 40 cal.; 20—22 pdr. Torpedoed by British Destroyers in Battle of Jutland, about midnight, 31st May-1st June, 1916. For appearance, see photo of Deutschland type.

6 BATTLE CRUISERS.

HINDENBURG (1915). 26,600 tons. Guns: 8—12 in., 50 cal.; 16—5.9 in., 50 cal.; 8—3.4 in. AA.

DERFFLINGER (1913). 26,300 tons. Guns: 8—12 in., 50 cal.; 14—5.9 in., 50 cal.; 8—3.4 in. AA.

Both above ships scuttled by their crews at Scapa Flow, 21st June, 1919.

LÜTZOW (1913). Generally similar to Derfflinger, above. Sunk by gunfire of British Battle Cruisers, during Battle of Jutland, 31st May, 1916.

SEYDLITZ (1912). 25,000 tons. Guns: 10—11 in., 50 cal.; 12—5.9 in., 45 cal.; 2—3.4 in. Scuttled by her crew at Scapa Flow, 21st June, 1919.

MOLTKE (1910). 23,000 tons. Guns: 10—11 in., 50 cal.; 12—5.9 in., 45 cal.; 2—3.4 in. Scuttled by her crew at Scapa Flow, 21st June, 1919.

VON DER TANN (1909). 19,400 tons. Guns: 8—11 in., 50 cal.; 10—5.9 in., 45 cal.; 4—3.4 in. Scuttled by her crew at Scapa Flow, 21st June, 1919.

102 DESTROYERS.

(For appearance of most of these vessels, see photos of corresponding types, pages 531 & 537.)

H 145 (1917). Details uncertain; probably enlarged edition of B 112, below. Scuttled at Scapa Flow, 21st June, 1919.

S 138, S 136, S 131 (1917). Probably similar to H 145, above. Scuttled at Scapa Flow, 21st June, 1919.

V 129 (1917). Probably similar to H 145, above. Scuttled at Scapa Flow, 21st June, 1919.

B 112, B 111, B 110, B 109 (1917). 1300 tons. Guns: 4—4.1 in. Tubes: 6. Scuttled at Scapa Flow, 21st June, 1919.

V 107 (1914). 320 tons. Guns: 2—13 pdr. (?). Tubes: 4. Lost, date and circumstances unknown.

G 104, G 103, G 101 (1916). 1250 tons. Guns: 4—4.1 in. Tubes: 6. Scuttled at Scapa Flow, 21st June, 1919.
V 99 (1914). 1300 tons. Armament as G 104, etc., above. Sunk by gunfire of Russian Gunboat SIVUCH, in Gulf of Riga, 19th August, 1915.
G 96 (1915). 1000 tons. Guns: 3—4.1 in. Tubes: 6. Mined off Ostend, 26th June, 1917.
G 94, G 93, G 87 (1915). Sisters to G 96, above. Sunk at the mouth of the Jade, 30th March, 1918.
G 92, G 91, G 89, G 86 (1915). Sisters to G 96, above. Scuttled at Scapa Flow, 21st June, 1919.
G 90 (1915). Sister to G 96, above. Sunk in the Baltic, 11th November, 1916.
G 88 (1915). Torpedoed by a British C.M.B., off Zeebrugge, night of 7th-8th April, 1917.
G 85 (1915). Sister to G 96, above. Torpedoed by British Destroyer BROKE, off Goodwin Sands, 21st April, 1917.
V 84 (1915). Similar to G 96, above. Sunk, off the mouth of the Ems, previous to June, 1917.
V 83, V 82, V 78, V 70 (1915). Sisters to V 84, above. Scuttled at Scapa Flow, 21st June, 1919.
V 77, V 67 (1915). Sisters to V 84, above. Sunk in Flanders, 7th July, 1918.
V 76, V 75 (1915). Sisters to V 84, above. Mined in the Gulf of Finland, 16th November, 1916.
V 74 (1915). Sister to V 84, above. Blown up at Bruges during evacuation of Flanders, October, 1918.
V 72 (1915). Sister to V 84, above. Sunk in the Baltic, 11th November, 1916.
V 68 (1915). Sister to V 84, above. Sunk in the North Sea, 6th August, 1918.
S 66, S 62 (1915). Similar to G 96, above. Mined off the West Coast of Jutland, July, 1918.
S 65, S 56, S 55, S 53, S 52, S 50, S 49 (1914-15). Sisters to S 66, above. Scuttled at Scapa Flow, 21st June, 1919.
S 64 (1915). Sister to S 66, above. Mined in the Southern portion of the Sound, October, 1917.
S 61 (1915). Sister to S 66, above. Sunk in Flanders, 7th July, 1918.
S 59 (1915). Sister to S 66, above. Sunk in the North Sea, 11th November, 1916.
S 58, S 57 (1915). Sisters to S 66, above. Mined in the Gulf of Finland, 16th November, 1916.
V 48 (1915). 900 tons. Guns: 2—4.1 in., 1—3.4 in. Tubes: 6—19.7 in. Sunk, during Battle of Jutland, 31st May, 1916. (It is believed this was the Destroyer sunk by H.M.S. OBEDIENT, MARVEL, MINDFUL and ONSLAUGHT.)
V 47 (1915). Sister to V 48, above. Sunk in Flanders, 7th July, 1918.
V 45 (1915). Sister to V 48, above. Scuttled at Scapa Flow, 21st June, 1919.
G 42 (1914). Similar to V 48, above. Rammed and sunk by British Flotilla Leader SWIFT, off Goodwin Sands, 21st April, 1917.
G 41 (1914). Sister to G 42, above. Blown up at Bruges, during evacuation of Flanders, October, 1918.
G 40, G 39, G 38 (1914). Sisters to G 42, above. Scuttled at Scapa Flow, 21st June, 1919.
G 37 (1914). Sister to G 42, above. Mined off Walcheren, November, 1917.
S 36, S 32 (1914). Similar to V 48, above. Scuttled at Scapa Flow, 21st June, 1919.
S 35 (1914). Sister to S 36, above. Sunk during Battle of Jutland, 31st May, 1916 (probably by Light Cruisers SOUTHAMPTON and DUBLIN).
S 34 (1914). Sister to S 36, above. Sunk in the North Sea, 3rd October, 1918.
S 33 (1914). Sister to S 36, above. Torpedoed in action with British Submarine L 10, in Heligoland Bight, 3rd October, 1918.

S 31 (1914). Sister to S 36, above. Driven ashore by gunfire of Russian Destroyer NOVIK, in Gulf of Riga, 19th August, 1915.
V 30 (1914). Similar to V 48, above. Mined on voyage from Germany to surrender, 20th November, 1918.
V 29, V 27 (1914). Sisters to V 30, above. Sunk by gunfire of British Battleships, during Battle of Jutland, 31st May, 1916.
V 25 (1914). Sister to V 30, above. Lost during February, 1915.
S 22 (1913). 570 tons. Guns: 2—3.4 in. Tubes: 4—19.7 in. Sunk 25th March, 1916.
S 21 (1913). Sister to S 22, above. Lost early in the War, date uncertain.
S 20 (1913). Sister to S 22, above. Sunk by gunfire of British Light Cruiser CENTAUR, off Belgian Coast, 5th June, 1917.
S 17 (1913). Sister to S 22, above. Mined during May, 1917.
S 16 (1913). Sister to S 22, above. Sunk in the North Sea, January, 1918.
S 15 (1913). Sister to S 22, above. Laid up after being badly damaged in action of 5th June, 1917, and abandoned on evacuation of Bruges, October, 1918.
S 14 (1913). Sister to S 22, above. Lost during February, 1915.
S 13 (1913). Sister to S 22, above Lost during January, 1916.
G 12 (1912). Similar to S 22, above. Sunk in the North Sea, 8th September, 1915.
V 4 (1911). Similar to S 22, above. Sunk (probably by British Destroyers) during Battle of Jutland, 31st May, 1916.
G 194 (1911). 648 tons. Guns: 2—3.4 in. Tubes: 4—17.7 in. Rammed and sunk by British Light Cruiser CLEOPATRA, near Sylt, 25th March, 1916.
Another (unidentified) of G 194 type. Torpedoed by British Submarine E 9, between Windau and Gothland, 4th June, 1915.
V 191 (1910). 656 tons., otherwise similar to G 194, above. Torpedoed by British Submarine E9, in the Baltic, 17th December, 1915.
V 188 (1910). Sister to V 191, above. Torpedoed by British Submarine E 16, in the North Sea, near the German Coast, 26th July, 1915.
V 187 (1910). Sister to V 191, above. Sunk by gunfire of British Destroyer DEFENDER, during action in Heligoland Bight, 28th August, 1914.
S 177 (1909). 636 tons. Guns: 2—3.4 in. Tubes: 4—17.7 in. Mined off Libau, latter part of 1915.
T 172 (1909). 636 tons. Guns: 2—3.4 in. Tubes: 3—17.7 in. Sunk in the North Sea, 7th July, 1918.
V 162 (1908). 613 tons. otherwise similar to T 172, above. Lost about August, 1916.
V 150 (1907). 554 tons. Guns: 2—3.4 in. Tubes: 3—17.7 in. Lost by collision, in May, 1915.
T 138 (1906). 530 tons. Guns: 1—3.4 in., 3—4 pdr. Tubes: 3—17.7 in. Sunk in the North Sea, 7th July, 1918.
T 129 (1905). 485 tons. Guns: 4—3 pdr. Tubes: 3—17.7 in. Sunk off mouth of Elbe, 1st May, 1917.
T 124 (1904). 470 tons, otherwise similar to T 129, above. Lost by collision with Danish s.s. ANGLO-DANE, at entrance to the Sound, 23rd November, 1914.
T 123 (1904). Sister to T 124, above. Sunk in the North Sea, 1st May, 1917.
T 122 (1904). Sister to T 124, above. Mined near Heligoland, October, 1918.
T 119, T 118, T 117, T 115 (1903). 420 tons, otherwise similar to T 124, above. Sunk by gunfire of British Light Cruiser UNDAUNTED and Destroyers LANCE, LEGION, LENNOX and LOYAL, off Dutch Coast, 17th October, 1914.
T 116 (1903). Sister to T 119, etc., above. Torpedoed by British Submarine E 9, off the mouth of the Ems, 6th October, 1914.
T 100 (1900). 400 tons. Guns: 3—4 pdr. Tubes: 3—17.7 in. Sunk in the Baltic, 15th October, 1918.
T 90 (1899). Sister to T 100, above Wrecked in course of attack on Japanese Cruiser TAKACHIHO, 60 miles South of Kiao-Chau Bay, night of 17th-18th October, 1914.

203 SUBMARINES.

(For convenience of reference, boats surrendered or otherwise disposed of are noted below, though not included in above total.)
(**U 1, U 2, U 4**, all broken up in Germany; **U 3** surrendered.)
U 5. Sunk in the North Sea, December, 1914.
U 6. Destroyed by Submarine E 16, in the North Sea, 15th September, 1915.
U 7. Sunk in the North Sea, January, 1915.
U 8. Sunk by Destroyers MAORI and GHURKA, in Straits of Dover, 4th March, 1915.
(**U 9.** Surrendered.)
U 10. Sunk in the North Sea, May, 1916.
U 11. Sunk in the North Sea, December, 1914.
U 12. Rammed by Destroyer ARIEL, off Aberdeen Coast, 10th March, 1915.
U 13. Sunk in the North Sea, 12th September, 1914.
U 14. Rammed by Trawler HAWK, after being disabled by gunfire, off Peterhead (lat. 57.15 N., long. 0.32 E.), 5th June, 1915.
U 15. Rammed by Light Cruiser BIRMINGHAM, off the Orkneys, 9th August, 1914.
U 16. Foundered, in the Elbe, on voyage to England to surrender, 22nd February, 1919.
(**U 17.** Broken up in Germany.)
U 18. Rammed by Minesweeping Trawler 96, one mile off Hoxa entrance to Scapa Flow, 24th November, 1914.
(**U 19.** Surrendered.)
U 20. Stranded at Harbooere, West Coast of Jutland, 4th November, 1916, and blown up by her crew the following day.
U 21. Sunk in the North Sea, on voyage to England to surrender, 22nd February, 1919.
(**U 22.** Surrendered.)
U 23. Torpedoed by Submarine C 27, working in conjunction with Trawler PRINCESS LOUISE, in the North Sea, 20th July, 1915.
(**U 24, U 25**, both surrendered.)
U 26. Lost in the Baltic, August, 1915.
U 27. Sunk off the South of Ireland, 19th August, 1915.
U 28. Destroyed in the White Sea, 2nd September, 1917.
U 29. Rammed by Battleship DREADNOUGHT, about lat. 58.21 N., long. 1.12 E., 18th March, 1915.
(**U 30.** Surrendered.)
U 31. Destroyed, January, 1915.
U 32. Destroyed in the Mediterranean, 8th May, 1918.
(**U 33.** Surrendered.)
U 34. Sunk in the Mediterranean, 9th November, 1918.
(**U 35.** Interned at Ferrol, and surrendered to the French in 1919.)
U 36. Sunk by gunfire of Special Service Vessel PRINCE CHARLES, near North Rona, 24th July, 1915
U 37. Lost in the North Sea, about June, 1915.
(**U 38**, surrendered; **U 39**, interned at Cartagena, 18th May, 1918, and surrendered to the French, 17th March, 1919.)
U 40. Sunk by Submarine C 24, working in conjunction with a Trawler, 50 miles S.E. by S. of Girdle Ness, 23rd June, 1915.
U 41. Sunk by Armed Merchant Cruiser BARALONG, off South of Ireland, 24th September, 1915.
(**U 42** was to have been number of a Submarine ordered in Italy before the War; this vessel was completed for the Italian Navy under the name of BALILLA—vide Italian losses.)
(**U 43.** Surrendered.)
U 44. Destroyed in the North Sea, 12th August, 1917.
U 45. Torpedoed by Submarine D 7, off North of Ireland, 12th September, 1917.
(**U 46.** Surrendered.)
U 47. Blown up at Pola or Cattaro, end of October, 1918.
U 48. Destroyed by gunfire of Destroyer GIPSY and five Drifters, while stranded on Goodwins, 24th November, 1917.
U 49. Rammed by P 61, in the Atlantic, 11th September, 1917.
U 50. Lost in the North Sea, between 1st and 11th October, 1917.
U 51. Torpedoed by Submarine H 5, in Heligoland Bight, 14th July, 1916.
(**U 52, U 53, U 54, U 55.** All surrendered.)
U 56. Destroyed in the Arctic Sea, 2nd November, 1916.
(**U 57.** Surrendered.)
U 58. Sunk by U.S. Destroyers FANNING and NICHOLSON, off South of Ireland, 17th November, 1917.
U 59. Destroyed in the North Sea, 14th May, 1917.
(**U 60.** Surrendered and subsequently foundered 9 miles S.E. of Berry Head, 12th June, 1919.)
U 61. Sunk in St. George's Channel, 26th March, 1918.
(**U 62, U 63.** Both surrendered.)
U 64. Destroyed in the Mediterranean, 17th June, 1918.
U 65. Blown up at Pola or Cattaro, end of October, 1918.
U 66. Lost in the North Sea, between 1st and 11th October, 1917.
(**U 67.** Surrendered.)
U 68. Sunk off the South of Ireland, 22nd March, 1916.
U 69. Sunk by Destroyer PATRIOT, in the North Sea, 12th July, 1917.
(**U 70, U 71.** Both surrendered.)
U 72. Blown up at Pola or Cattaro, end of October, 1918.
U 73. Blown up at Pola or Cattaro, end of October, 1918.
U 74. Sunk in the North Sea, 27th May, 1916.
U 75. Sunk in the North Sea, 13th December, 1917.
U 76. Sunk in the Arctic Sea, 26th January, 1917.
U 77. Lost in the North Sea, 7th July, 1916.
U 78. Destroyed by Submarine G 2, in the North Sea, 28th October, 1918.
(**U 79, U 80, U 82.** All surrendered.)
U 81. Destroyed in the Atlantic, 1st May, 1917.
U 83. Sunk off S.W. of Ireland, 17th February, 1917.
U 84. Sunk in St. George's Channel, 26th January, 1918.
U 85. Sunk in English Channel, 12th March, 1917.
(**U 86.** Surrendered.)
U 87. Sunk in the Irish Sea, 25th December, 1917.
U 88. Sunk in the Atlantic, 17th September, 1917.
U 89. Rammed by Cruiser ROXBURGH, off N.E. of Ireland, 12th February, 1918.
(**U 90, U 91.** Both surrendered.)
U 92. Sunk in the North Sea, 9th September, 1918.
U 93. Sunk by Special Service Vessel PRIZE, in English Channel, 7th January, 1918.
(**U 94.** Surrendered to the French.)
U 95. Lost about January, 1918.
(**U 96, U 98.** Both surrendered.)
U 97. Foundered on voyage to England to surrender, 21st November, 1918.
U 99. Sunk off the West of Ireland, 20th June, 1917.
(**U 100, U 101.** Both surrendered.)
U 102. Lost, probably in the North Sea, September, 1918.
U 103. Rammed by s.s. OLYMPIC, in English Channel, 12th May, 1918.
U 104. Sunk by Sloop JESSAMINE, off South of Ireland, lat. 51·59 N., long. 6.26 W., 25th April, 1918.
(**U 105.** Surrendered to the French.)
U 106. Lost in the North Sea, between 5th and 9th October, 1917.
(**U 107, U 108.** Both surrendered, latter to the French.)
U 109. Destroyed in Dover area, 26th January, 1918.
U 110. Sunk off North of Ireland, 15th March, 1918.
(**U 111, U 112, U 113, U 114.** All surrendered.)
(**U 115, U 116.** Both unfinished, and destroyed on stocks, at Schichau Yard, Elbing.)
(**U 117, U 118, U 119, U 120, U 121, U 122, U 123, U 124, U 125, U 126.** All surrendered.)
(**U 127** to **U 134**, inclusive, were never completed.)
(**U 135, U 136**, both surrendered; **U 137, U 138**, were not built; **U 139, U 140, U 141**, all surrendered.)
(**U 142** to **U 150**, inclusive, were never completed.)
(**U 151, U 152, U 153.** All surrendered.)
U 154. Torpedoed by Submarine E 35, in the Atlantic, in latitude of Cape St. Vincent, 11th May, 1918.
(**U 155.** Surrendered.)
U 156. Sunk in the North Sea, 25th September, 1918.
(**U 157.** Interned 11th November, 1918, and subsequently surrendered.)
(**U 158, U 159.** Were not built.)
(**U 160, U 161, U 162, U 163, U 164.** All surrendered.)
(**U 165** was never completed; **U 166, U 167**, both surrendered.)
(**UA** was surrendered.)
UB 1. Lost in the Mediterranean, about August, 1915.
(**UB 2.** Broken up in Germany.)
UB 3. Sunk in the North Sea, 24th April, 1916.
UB 4. Sunk in the North Sea, 11th August, 1915.

(UB 5. Broken up in Germany.)
(UB 6. Stranded on Voorne Island, off Hellevoetsluis, 13th March, 1917, interned by Dutch Government, and surrendered at Harwich, 25th February, 1919.)
UB 7. Destroyed by Russians, in Black Sea, October, 1916.
(UB 8. Surrendered. UB 9, broken up in Germany.)
UB 10. Destroyed on evacuation of Flanders, October, 1918.
(UB 11. Broken up in Germany.)
UB 12. Lost in the North Sea, about August, 1918.
UB 13. Lost, March, 1916.
(UB 14. Surrendered.)
UB 15. Lost in the Mediterranean, about May, 1916.
UB 16. Sunk by Submarine E 34, in the North Sea, 10th May. 1918.
UB 17. Sunk in English Channel, 25th February, 1918.
UB 18. Sunk in English Channel, 17th November, 1917.
UB 19. Sunk by Special Service Ship PENSHURST, in English Channel, lat. 50 N., long. 2.48 W., 30th November, 1916.
UB 20. Destroyed by seaplanes 8676 and 8862, in the North Sea, 29th July, 1917.
(UB 21. Surrendered.)
UB 22. Sunk in the North Sea, 19th January, 1918.
(UB 23. Interned at Coruna, 29th July, 1917, and surrendered to the French after Armistice.)
(UB 24, UB 25. Both surrendered to the French.)
UB 26. Sunk in the English Channel, 5th April, 1916; subsequently salved by the French, and commissioned as ROLAND MOULLOT.
UB 27. Sunk in the North Sea, 29th July, 1917.
(UB 28. Surrendered.)
UB 29. Sunk by Destroyer ARIEL 12 miles S.W. of Bishop Rock Lighthouse, 6th December, 1916.
UB 30. Sunk in the North Sea, 13th August, 1918.
UB 31. Destroyed in Dover area, 2nd May, 1918.
UB 32. Destroyed by Seaplane 9860, 27 miles North of Cape Barfleur, 18th August, 1917.
UB 33. Mined in Dover area, 11th April, 1918.
UB 35. Destroyed in Dover area, 26th January, 1918.
UB 36. Lost in June, 1917.
UB 37. Sunk by Special Service Ship PENSHURST, in English Channel, 14th January, 1917.
UB 38. Destroyed in Dover area, 8th February, 1918.
UB 39. Sunk in English Channel, 17th May, 1917.
UB 40. Destroyed on evacuation of Flanders, October, 1918.
UB 41. Sunk in the North Sea, 5th October, 1917.
(UB 42. Surrendered.)
(UB 43. Sold to Austria.)
UB 44. Destroyed in the Mediterranean, 30th July, 1916.
UB 45. Sunk in the Black Sea, 30th October, 1916.
UB 46. Sunk in the Dardanelles, 16th December, 1916.
(UB 47. Sold to Austria.)
UB 48. Blown up at Pola or Cattaro, end of October, 1918.
(UB 49, UB 50, UB 51. All surrendered.)
UB 52. Torpedoed by Submarine H 4, in the Adriatic, lat. 41.46 N., long. 18.35 E., 23rd May, 1918.
UB 53. Sunk in the Adriatic, 3rd August, 1918.
UB 54. Sunk in the North Sea, 11th March, 1918.
UB 55. Sunk in Dover area, 22nd April, 1918.
UB 56. Sunk in Dover area, 19th December, 1917.
UB 57. Sunk in the North Sea, 14th August, 1918.
UB 58. Sunk in Dover area, 10th March, 1918.
UB 59. Found scuttled at Bruges, October, 1918.
(UB 60, UB 62, UB 64. All surrendered.)
UB 61. Sunk in the North Sea, 29th November, 1917.
UB 63. Sunk in the North Sea, 28th January, 1918.
UB 65. Destroyed by explosion of own torpedo, in action with U.S. Submarine L2, off S.W. of Ireland, 10th July, 1918.
UB 66. Sunk in the Mediterranean, 18th January, 1918.
(UB 67. Surrendered.)
UB 68. Sunk by own crew, after being disabled by gunfire of Sloop SNAPDRAGON and Trawler CRADOSIN, 60 miles N.E. of Malta, 4th October, 1918.
UB 69. Sunk in the Mediterranean, 8th January, 1918.
UB 70. Sunk in the Mediterranean, by British Destroyer BASILISK and U.S.S. SYDONIA, 8th May, 1918.
UB 71. Sunk in Straits of Gibraltar, 21st April, 1918.
UB 72. Torpedoed in English Channel, 12th May, 1918.
(UB 73. Surrendered to the French.)
UB 74. Rammed and depth charged, by Armed Yacht LORNA, off Portland Bill, 26th May, 1918.
UB 75. Sunk in the North Sea, 10th December, 1917.
(UB 76, UB 77, UB 79, UB 80. All surrendered.)
UB 78. Sunk in English Channel, 9th May, 1918.
UB 81. Sunk in English Channel, 2nd December, 1917.
UB 82. Sunk off North of Ireland, 17th April, 1918.
UB 83. Sunk in the North Sea, 10th September, 1918.
(UB 84. Surrendered to the French.)
UB 85. Sunk in the Irish Sea, 30th April, 1918.
(UB 86, UB 87, UB 88. All surrendered.)
UB 89. Foundered, on voyage to England to surrender.
UB 90. Sunk in action with Submarine L 12, off Norwegian Coast, 16th October, 1918.
(UB 91, UB 92, UB 93, UB 94, UB 95, UB 96, UB 97, UB 98, UB 99, UB 100, UB 101, UB 102. All surrendered.)
UB 103. Destroyed in Dover area, 16th September, 1918.
UB 104. Sunk in the North Sea, 19th September, 1918.
(UB 105, UB 106. Both surrendered.)
UB 107. Sunk in the North Sea, 27th July, 1918.
UB 108. Lost about July, 1918.
UB 109. Destroyed in Dover area, 29th August, 1918.
UB 110. Rammed by Destroyer GARRY, off Roker, lat. 54.39 N., long. 0.55 W., 19th July, 1918, and subsequently raised by British.
(UB 111, UB 112, UB 114. All surrendered.)
UB 113. Lost, probably in the North Sea, September, 1918.
UB 115. Sunk in the North Sea, 29th September, 1918.
UB 116. Sunk in the North Sea, 28th October, 1918.
(UB 117, UB 118. Both surrendered.)
UB 119. Lost about May, 1918.
(UB 120, UB 121, UB 122. All surrendered.)
UB 123. Sunk in the North Sea, 19th October, 1918.
UB 124. Sunk off North of Ireland, 20th July, 1918.
(UB 125, UB 126, UB 128. All surrendered.)
UB 127. Lost, probably in the North Sea, September, 1918.
UB 129. Blown up at Pola or Cattaro, end of October, 1918.
(UB 130, UB 131, UB 132, UB 133 all surrendered; UB 134, UB 135, never completed; UB 136, surrendered; UB 137 to UB 141, inclusive, never completed; UB 142, UB 143, UB 144, UB 145, all surrendered; UB 146, UB 147, never completed; UB 148, UB 149, UB 150, all surrendered; UB 151, UB 152, UB 153, never completed; UB 154, UB 155, both surrendered.)
UC 1. Sunk in the North Sea, 24th July, 1917.
UC 2. Sunk in the North Sea, 2nd July, 1915.
UC 3. Sunk in the North Sea, 23rd April, 1916.
UC 4. Destroyed on evacuation of Flanders, October, 1918.
UC 5. Captured while stranded on Shipwash Shoal, 27th April, 1916.
UC 6. Sunk in the North Sea, 28th September, 1917.
UC 7. Sunk in the North Sea, 21st August, 1916.
UC 8. Stranded on Terschelling, 6th November, 1915, and acquired by Dutch Navy as M 1.
UC 9. Sunk in the North Sea, about October, 1915.

UC 10. Sunk in the North Sea, 6th July, 1916.
UC 11. Sunk in the North Sea, 26th June, 1918.
UC 12. Sunk in the Mediterranean, 17th March, 1916; subsequently salved by Italians.
UC 13. Sunk by Russians, in Black Sea, about November, 1916.
UC 14. Sunk in the North Sea, about October, 1917.
UC 15. Sunk in the Black Sea, November, 1916.
UC 16. Destroyed by paravanes and depth charges of Destroyer MELAMPUS, off Selsea Bill, 23rd October, 1917.
(UC 17. Surrendered.)
UC 18. Sunk in the North Sea, 12th March, 1917.
UC 19. Destroyed by depth charges of Destroyer LLEWELLYN, in Straits of Dover, 4th December, 1916.
(UC 20, UC 22, UC 23. All surrendered.)
UC 21. Sunk in the North Sea, 27th September, 1917.
UC 24. Sunk off Cattaro, 24th May, 1917.
UC 25. Blown up at Cattaro or Pola, end of October, 1918.
UC 26. Rammed by Destroyer MILNE, off mouth of Thames, lat. 51.4 N., long. 1.40 E., 9th May, 1917.
(UC 27, UC 28, UC 31. All surrendered.)
UC 29. Sunk off S.W. of Ireland, 7th June, 1917.
UC 30. Sunk in the North Sea, 19th April, 1917.
UC 32. Sunk in the North Sea, 23rd February, 1917.
UC 33. Sunk in the Irish Sea, 26th September, 1917.
UC 34. Blown up at Pola or Cattaro, end of October, 1918.
UC 35. Sunk by French Patrol Vessel AILLY, off Sardinian Coast, 16th May, 1918.
UC 36. Destroyed by bombs of Seaplane 8663, 20 miles E.N.E. of Noord Hinder Lightship, 20th May, 1917.
(UC 37. Surrendered.)
UC 38. Sunk in the Mediterranean, 14th December, 1917.
UC 39. Sunk in the North Sea, 8th February, 1917.
UC 40. Foundered on voyage to England to surrender, 21st February, 1919.
UC 41. Sunk in the North Sea, 21st August, 1917.
UC 42. Sunk off South of Ireland, 10th September, 1917.
UC 43. Torpedoed by Submarine G 13, about 9 miles N.W. of Muckle Flugga Lighthouse, 10th March, 1917.
UC 44. Mined off South of Ireland, 4th August, 1917.
(UC 45. Surrendered.)
UC 46. Rammed by Destroyer LIBERTY, in Straits of Dover, 8th February, 1917.
UC 47. Rammed and depth charged, by P 57, in the North Sea, 18th November, 1917.
UC 48. Interned at Ferrol, 23rd March, 1918, and scuttled by her crew, off Coruna, 15th March, 1919.
UC 49. Sunk in the North Sea, 31st May, 1918.
UC 50. Destroyed by depth charges of Destroyer ZUBIAN, in English Channel, Dover area, 4th February, 1918.
UC 51. Sunk by Destroyer FIREDRAKE, in the North Sea, 13th November, 1917.
(UC 52. Surrendered.)
UC 53. Blown up at Pola or Cattaro, end of October, 1918.
UC 54. Blown up at Pola or Cattaro, end of October, 1918.
UC 55. Sunk in the North Sea, 29th September, 1917.
(UC 56. Interned at Santander, 24th May, 1918, and surrendered to French after Armistice.)
UC 57. Lost in the Baltic, between 19th and 22nd November, 1917.
(UC 58, UC 59, UC 60. All surrendered.)
UC 61. Stranded in Dover area, and blown up by crew, 26th July, 1917.
UC 62. Lost in the North Sea, about October, 1917.
UC 63. Sunk by Submarine E 52, near Straits of Dover, 1st November, 1917.
UC 64. Destroyed in Dover area, 20th June, 1918.
UC 65. Torpedoed by Submarine C 15, 3rd November, 1917.
UC 66. Sunk in English Channel, 12th June, 1917.
(UC 67. Surrendered.)
UC 68. Sunk by Submarine C 7, in the North Sea, 5th April, 1917.
UC 69. Sunk in English Channel, 6th December, 1917.
UC 70. Sunk in the North Sea, 28th August, 1918.
UC 71. Sunk off Heligoland, 20th February, 1919.
UC 72. Sunk in the North Sea, 22nd September, 1917.
(UC 73, surrendered; UC 74, interned at Barcelona, 21st November, 1918, and since surrendered.)
UC 75. Rammed by Destroyer FAIRY, in the North Sea, 31st May, 1918.
(UC 76. Surrendered.)
UC 77. Destroyed in Dover area, 10th July, 1918.
UC 78. Destroyed in Dover area, 2nd May, 1918.
UC 79. Sunk by Submarine E 45, in the North Sea, 19th October, 1917.
(UC 80 to UC 85, at the Imperial Yard, Danzig, and UC 86 to UC 89, at the Weser Yard, Bremen, were destroyed on the stocks.)
(UC 90. Surrendered.)
UC 91. Foundered in the North Sea, on voyage to England to surrender, 10th February, 1919.
(UC 92, UC 93, UC 94, UC 95, UC 96, UC 97, UC 98, UC 99, UC 100, UC 101, UC 102, UC 103, UC 104, UC 105, UC 106, UC 107, UC 108, UC 109, UC 110, UC 111, UC 112, UC 113, UC 114. All surrendered.)
(Full details of various types comprised above, will be found under German Navy Surrendered Section.)

33 MINESWEEPERS.

FM 3 (1918). Foundered, 1918 or 1919.
M 95 (1917). Mined, April, 1918.
M 92, M 83 (1917). Mined, 1st August, 1918.
M 91 (1917). Mined, 10th March, 1918.
M 67, M 64 (1917). Sunk in the North Sea, April, 1918.
M 63 (1917). Mined, 28th June, 1917.
M 62 (1917). Mined, July or August, 1918.
M 57 (1916). Reported lost, date uncertain.
M 56 (1916). Mined, off mouth of Ems, previous to July, 1917.
M 55 (1916). Wrecked, 29th October, 1917.
M 49 (1916). Mined, off Schleswig Coast, previous to June, 1917.
M 47 (1916). Sunk, 11th June, 1917.
M 41 (1916). Mined, 6th September, 1918.
M 40, M 36 (1916). Mined in the North Sea, March, 1918.
M 39 (1916). Mined, in the North Sea, April, 1918.
M 38 (1916). Reported lost, date uncertain.
M 31 (1916). Mined, in the Eastern Baltic, 18th June, 1917.
M 27 (1916). Sunk, in the Baltic, March, 1917.
M 26 (1916). Mined, off Schleswig Coast, May, 1917.
M 24 (1916). Mined, off Schleswig Coast, previous to May, 1917.
M 23 (1916). Mined, off mouth of Ems, June, 1917.
M 22 (1916). Mined, 14th October, 1918.
M 18 (1916). Reported lost, date uncertain.
M 16 (1915). Mined, off Schleswig Coast, previous to June, 1917.
M 15, M 14 (1915). Mined, off Schleswig Coast, previous to July, 1917.
M 12 (1915). Mined, about September, 1917.
M 11 (1915). Mined, 29th December, 1917.
M 9 (1915). Mined, off mouth of Ems, previous to July, 1917.
M 6 (1915). Mined, July or August, 1918.